D1326203

# BMW 3-Series
## Service and Repair Manual

Mark Coombs and Steve Rendle

(3210-296)

**Models covered**
BMW 3-Series (E36) models with four-cylinder and six-cylinder petrol engines,
Saloon and Coupe models
**Four-cylinder engines:** 1.6 litre (1596 cc) & 1.8 litre (1796 cc), including 1.8 litre DOHC version
**Six-cylinder engines:** 2.0 litre (1991 cc) & 2.5 litre (2494 cc) - **up to** early 1995 (engine code M50)

*Covers major mechanical features of Cabriolet models*
*Does not cover Touring (Estate), Compact or M3 models*
*Does not cover later six-cylinder engines (code M52) introduced from early 1995, or diesel engines*



ABCDE
FGHIJ
KL

A book in the **Haynes Service and Repair Manual Series**



ISBN **1 85960 210 X**

**British Library Cataloguing in Publication Data**
A catalogue record for this book is available from the British Library.

Printed in the USA

**Haynes Publishing**
Sparkford, Nr Yeovil, Somerset BA22 7JJ, England

**Haynes North America, Inc**
861 Lawrence Drive, Newbury Park, California 91320, USA

**Editions Haynes S.A.**
Tour Aurore - La Défense 2, 18 Place des Reflets,
92975 PARIS LA DEFENSE Cedex, France

**Haynes Publishing Nordiska AB**
Box 1504, 751 45 UPPSALA, Sweden

# Contents

## LIVING WITH YOUR BMW

# Contents

## REPAIRS & OVERHAUL

The new BMW 3 Series was introduced in the Spring of 1991 and was originally available with a choice of 1.6 litre (1596 cc), 1.8 litre (1796 cc), 2.0 litre (1991 cc) and 2.5 litre (2494 cc) engines. At first, models were only available in four-door Saloon form only, but later, a whole range of different body styles was made available.

All engines are derived from the well-proven engines which have appeared in many BMW vehicles. The engine is of four-cylinder (1.6 and 1.8 litre engine) or six-cylinder (2.0 and 2.5 litre engine) overhead camshaft design, mounted longitudinally with the transmission mounted on its rear. Both manual and automatic transmissions were available.

All models have fully-independent front and rear suspension, with suspension struts and trailing arms.

A wide range of standard and optional equipment is available within the BMW 3 Series range to suit most tastes, including central locking, electric windows, an electric sunroof, an anti-lock braking system, and an air bag. An anti-lock braking system and air conditioning system are available as options on certain models.

Provided that regular servicing is carried out in accordance with the manufacturer's recommendations, the BMW should prove reliable and very economical. The engine compartment is well-designed, and most of the items requiring frequent attention are easily accessible.

**BMW 318i Saloon**

**BMW 320i Coupe**

## The BMW 3-Series Team

Haynes manuals are produced by dedicated and enthusiastic people working in close co-operation. The team responsible for the creation of this book included:

| | |
|---|---|
| **Authors** | Mark Coombs<br>Steve Rendle |
| **Sub-editor** | Carole Turk |
| **Editor & Page Make-up** | Bob Jex |
| **Workshop manager** | Paul Buckland |
| **Photo Scans** | John Martin<br>Paul Tanswell |
| **Cover illustration & Line Art** | Roger Healing |
| **Wiring diagrams** | Matthew Marke |

We hope the book will help you to get the maximum enjoyment from your car. By carrying out routine maintenance as described you will ensure your car's reliability and preserve its resale value.

## Your BMW 3 Series manual

The aim of this manual is to help you get the best value from your vehicle. It can do so in several ways. It can help you decide what work must be done (even should you choose to get it done by a garage). It will also provide information on routine maintenance and servicing, and give a logical course of action and diagnosis when random faults occur. However, it is hoped that you will use the manual by tackling the work yourself. On simpler jobs it may even be quicker than booking the car into a garage and going there twice, to leave and collect it. Perhaps most important, a lot of money can be saved by avoiding the costs a garage must charge to cover its labour and overheads.

The manual has drawings and descriptions to show the function of the various components so that their layout can be understood. Tasks are described and photographed in a clear step-by-step sequence.

## Acknowledgements

Thanks are due to Champion Spark Plug, who supplied the illustrations showing spark plug conditions. Thanks are also due to Sykes-Pickavant Limited, who provided some of the workshop tools, and to all those people at Sparkford and Newbury Park who helped in the production of this manual.

**We take great pride in the accuracy of information given in this manual, but vehicle manufacturers make alterations and design changes during the production run of a particular vehicle of which they do not inform us. No liability can be accepted by the authors or publishers for loss, damage or injury caused by any errors in, or omissions from, the information given.**

Working on your car can be dangerous. This page shows just some of the potential risks and hazards, with the aim of creating a safety-conscious attitude.

# General hazards

### Scalding

- Don't remove the radiator or expansion tank cap while the engine is hot.
- Engine oil, automatic transmission fluid or power steering fluid may also be dangerously hot if the engine has recently been running.

### Burning

- Beware of burns from the exhaust system and from any part of the engine. Brake discs and drums can also be extremely hot immediately after use.

### Crushing

- When working under or near a raised vehicle, always supplement the jack with axle stands, or use drive-on ramps. ***Never venture under a car which is only supported by a jack.***

- Take care if loosening or tightening high-torque nuts when the vehicle is on stands. Initial loosening and final tightening should be done with the wheels on the ground.

### Fire

- Fuel is highly flammable; fuel vapour is explosive.
- Don't let fuel spill onto a hot engine.
- Do not smoke or allow naked lights (including pilot lights) anywhere near a vehicle being worked on. Also beware of creating sparks (electrically or by use of tools).
- Fuel vapour is heavier than air, so don't work on the fuel system with the vehicle over an inspection pit.
- Another cause of fire is an electrical overload or short-circuit. Take care when repairing or modifying the vehicle wiring.
- Keep a fire extinguisher handy, of a type suitable for use on fuel and electrical fires.

### Electric shock

- Ignition HT voltage can be dangerous, especially to people with heart problems or a pacemaker. Don't work on or near the ignition system with the engine running or the ignition switched on.

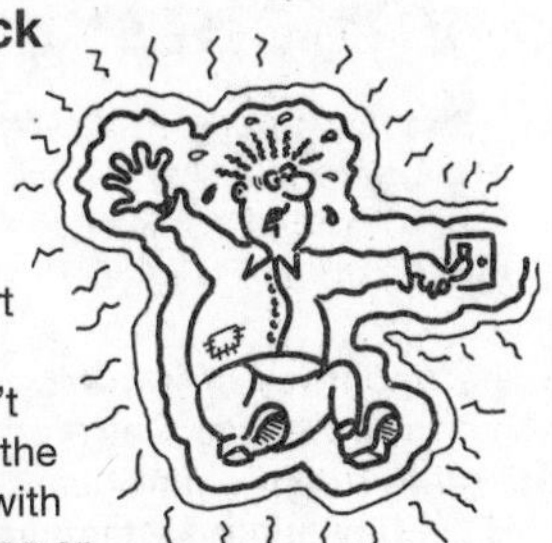

- Mains voltage is also dangerous. Make sure that any mains-operated equipment is correctly earthed. Mains power points should be protected by a residual current device (RCD) circuit breaker.

### Fume or gas intoxication

- Exhaust fumes are poisonous; they often contain carbon monoxide, which is rapidly fatal if inhaled. Never run the engine in a confined space such as a garage with the doors shut.

- Fuel vapour is also poisonous, as are the vapours from some cleaning solvents and paint thinners.

### Poisonous or irritant substances

- Avoid skin contact with battery acid and with any fuel, fluid or lubricant, especially antifreeze, brake hydraulic fluid and Diesel fuel. Don't syphon them by mouth. If such a substance is swallowed or gets into the eyes, seek medical advice.
- Prolonged contact with used engine oil can cause skin cancer. Wear gloves or use a barrier cream if necessary. Change out of oil-soaked clothes and do not keep oily rags in your pocket.
- Air conditioning refrigerant forms a poisonous gas if exposed to a naked flame (including a cigarette). It can also cause skin burns on contact.

### Asbestos

- Asbestos dust can cause cancer if inhaled or swallowed. Asbestos may be found in gaskets and in brake and clutch linings. When dealing with such components it is safest to assume that they contain asbestos.

# Special hazards

### Hydrofluoric acid

- This extremely corrosive acid is formed when certain types of synthetic rubber, found in some O-rings, oil seals, fuel hoses etc, are exposed to temperatures above 400ºC. The rubber changes into a charred or sticky substance containing the acid. *Once formed, the acid remains dangerous for years. If it gets onto the skin, it may be necessary to amputate the limb concerned.*
- When dealing with a vehicle which has suffered a fire, or with components salvaged from such a vehicle, wear protective gloves and discard them after use.

### The battery

- Batteries contain sulphuric acid, which attacks clothing, eyes and skin. Take care when topping-up or carrying the battery.
- The hydrogen gas given off by the battery is highly explosive. Never cause a spark or allow a naked light nearby. Be careful when connecting and disconnecting battery chargers or jump leads.

### Air bags

- Air bags can cause injury if they go off accidentally. Take care when removing the steering wheel and/or facia. Special storage instructions may apply.

### Diesel injection equipment

- Diesel injection pumps supply fuel at very high pressure. Take care when working on the fuel injectors and fuel pipes.

***Warning: Never expose the hands, face or any other part of the body to injector spray; the fuel can penetrate the skin with potentially fatal results.***

# Remember...

### DO

- Do use eye protection when using power tools, and when working under the vehicle.
- Do wear gloves or use barrier cream to protect your hands when necessary.
- Do get someone to check periodically that all is well when working alone on the vehicle.
- Do keep loose clothing and long hair well out of the way of moving mechanical parts.
- Do remove rings, wristwatch etc, before working on the vehicle – especially the electrical system.
- Do ensure that any lifting or jacking equipment has a safe working load rating adequate for the job.

### DON'T

- Don't attempt to lift a heavy component which may be beyond your capability – get assistance.
- Don't rush to finish a job, or take unverified short cuts.
- Don't use ill-fitting tools which may slip and cause injury.
- Don't leave tools or parts lying around where someone can trip over them. Mop up oil and fuel spills at once.
- Don't allow children or pets to play in or near a vehicle being worked on.

The following pages are intended to help in dealing with common roadside emergencies and breakdowns. You will find more detailed fault finding information at the back of the manual, and repair information in the main chapters.

## If your car won't start and the starter motor doesn't turn

- ☐ If it's a model with automatic transmission, make sure the selector is in 'P' or 'N'.
- ☐ Open the bonnet and make sure that the battery terminals are clean and tight.
- ☐ Switch on the headlights and try to start the engine. If the headlights go very dim when you're trying to start, the battery is probably flat. Get out of trouble by jump starting (see next page) using a friend's car.

## If your car won't start even though the starter motor turns as normal

- ☐ Is there fuel in the tank?
- ☐ Is there moisture on electrical components under the bonnet? Switch off the ignition, then wipe off any obvious dampness with a dry cloth. Spray a water-repellent aerosol product (WD-40 or equivalent) on ignition and fuel system electrical connectors like those shown in the photos. Pay special attention to the ignition coil wiring connector and HT leads.

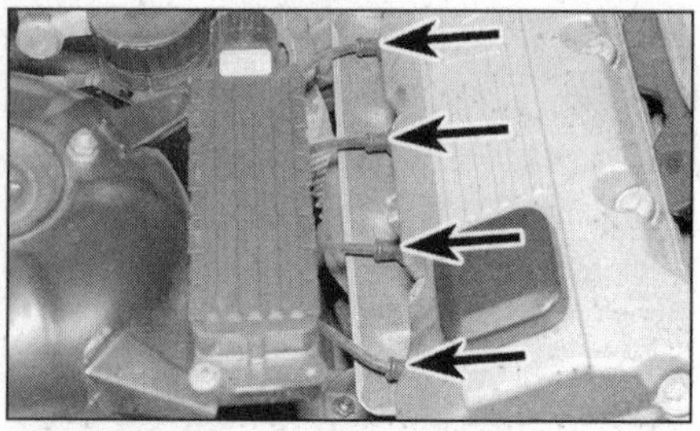

**A** Check that the spark plug HT leads are securely connected by pushing them onto the plugs - 4-cylinder models.

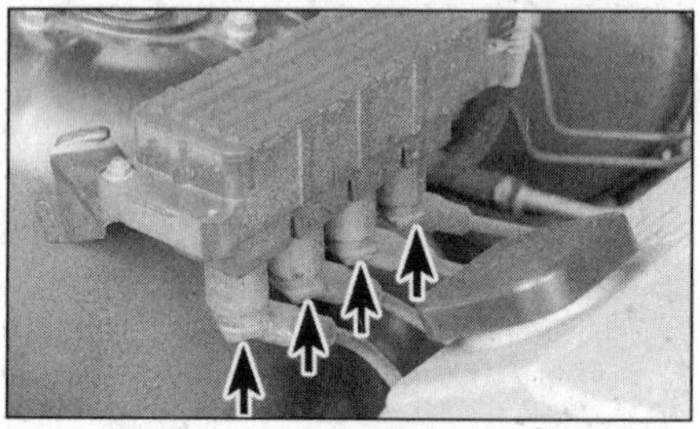

**B** Check that the HT leads are securely connected to the ignition coil - 4-cylinder models.

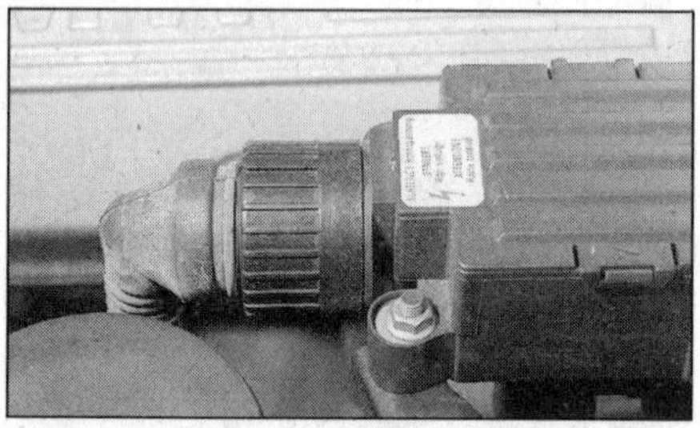

**C** Check that the wiring connector is securely connected to the ignition HT coil - 4-cylinder models.

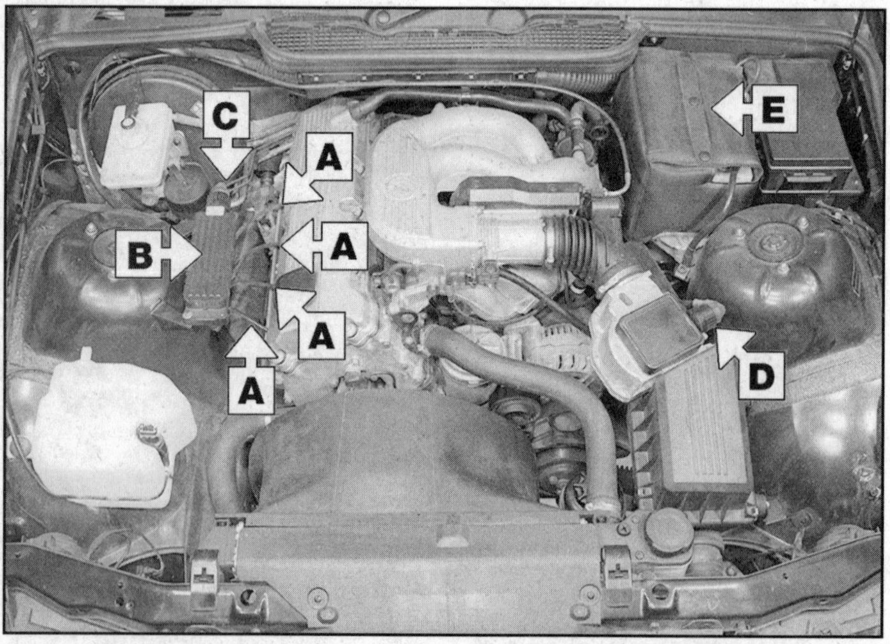


Check that electrical connections are secure (with the ignition switched off) and spray them with a water dispersant spray like WD40 if you suspect a problem due to damp

**D** Check the airflow meter wiring connector (where applicable) with the ignition switched off.

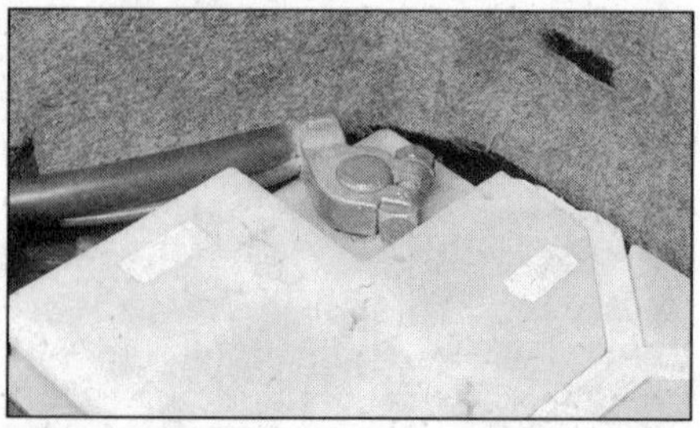

**E** Check the security and condition of the battery terminals - 6 cylinder model shown.

# Jump starting

**HAYNES HiNT** *Jump starting will get you out of trouble, but you must correct whatever made the battery go flat in the first place. There are three possibilities:*

***1** The battery has been drained by repeated attempts to start, or by leaving the lights on.*

***2** The charging system is not working properly (alternator drivebelt slack or broken, alternator wiring fault or alternator itself faulty).*

***3** The battery itself is at fault (electrolyte low, or battery worn out).*

When jump-starting a car using a booster battery, observe the following precautions:

- ✔ Before connecting the booster battery, make sure that the ignition is switched off.
- ✔ Ensure that all electrical equipment (lights, heater, wipers, etc) is switched off.
- ✔ Make sure that the booster battery is the same voltage as the discharged one in the vehicle.
- ✔ If the battery is being jump-started from the battery in another vehicle, the two vehicles MUST NOT TOUCH each other.
- ✔ Make sure that the transmission is in neutral (or PARK, in the case of automatic transmission).

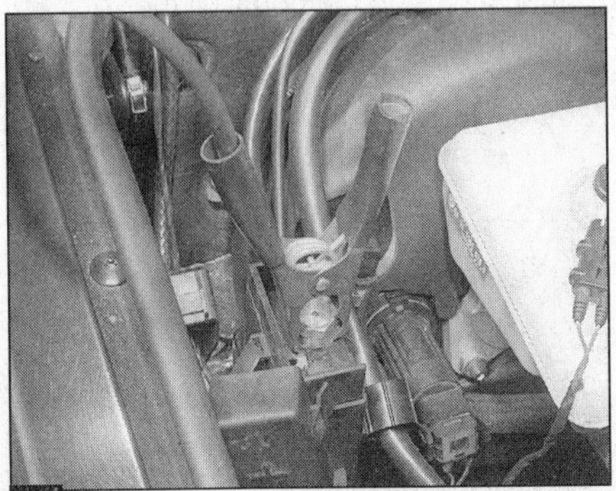

**1** On 4-cylinder models, connect one end of the red jump lead to the positive (+) of the flat battery. On 6-cylinder models, unclip the cover from the terminal on the right-hand side of the engine and connect the red jump lead to the terminal.

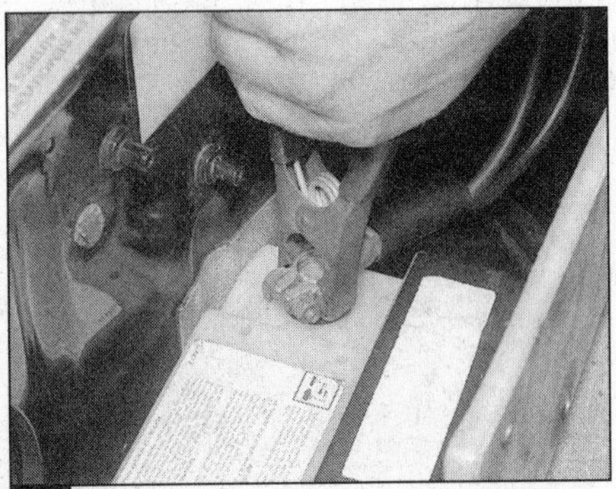

**2** Connect the other end of the red lead to the positive (+) terminal of the booster battery.

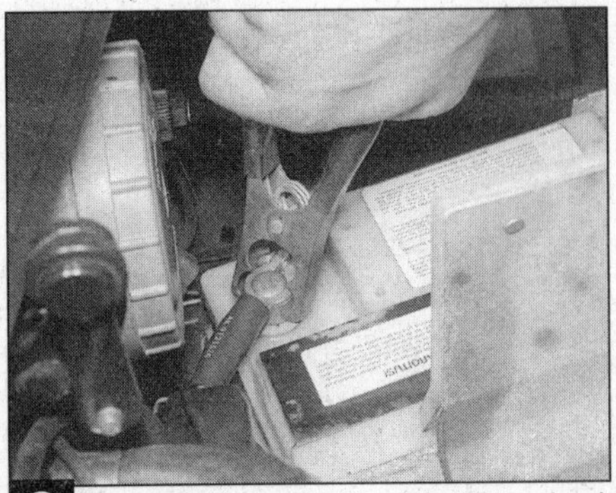

**3** Connect one end of the black jump lead to the negative (-) terminal of the booster battery

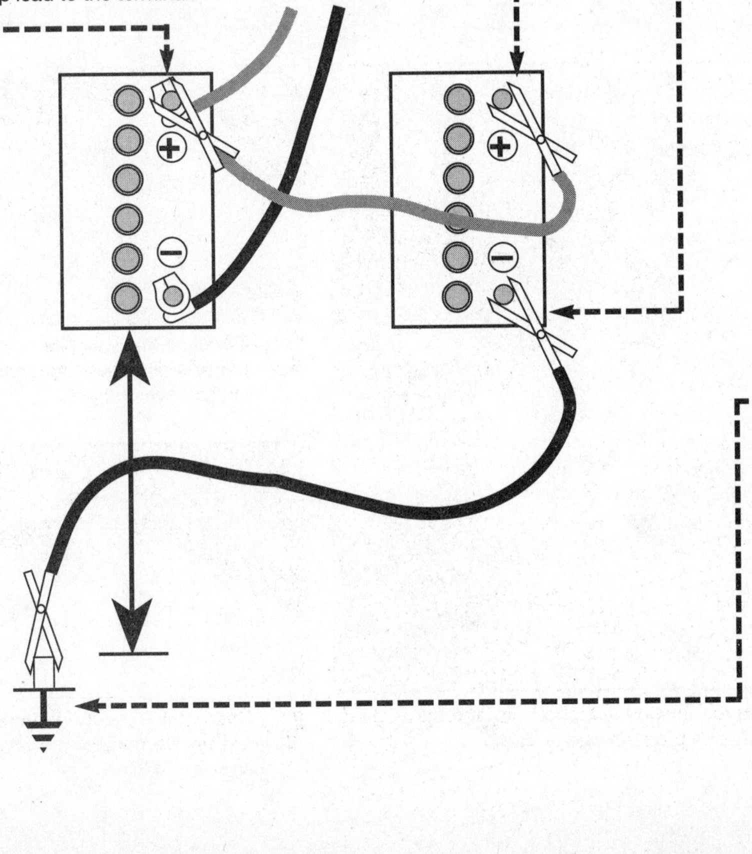

**4** Connect the other end of the black jump lead to a bolt or bracket on the engine block, well away from the battery, on the vehicle to be started.

**5** Make sure that the jump leads will not come into contact with the fan, drive-belts or other moving parts of the engine.

**6** Start the engine using the booster battery, then with the engine running at idle speed, disconnect the jump leads in the reverse order of connection. On 6-cylinder models, securely refit the cover to the engine bay positive (+) terminal.

# Wheel changing

Some of the details shown here will vary according to model. For instance, the location of the spare wheel and jack is not the same on all cars. However, the basic principles apply to all vehicles.

***Warning: Do not change a wheel in a situation where you risk being hit by other traffic. On busy roads, try to stop in a lay-by or a gateway. Be wary of passing traffic while changing the wheel – it is easy to become distracted by the job in hand.***

## Preparation

- ☐ When a puncture occurs, stop as soon as it is safe to do so.
- ☐ Park on firm level ground, if possible, and well out of the way of other traffic.
- ☐ Use hazard warning lights if necessary.
- ☐ If you have one, use a warning triangle to alert other drivers of your presence.
- ☐ Apply the handbrake and engage first or reverse gear (or Park on models with automatic transmission.
- ☐ Chock the wheel diagonally opposite the one being removed – a couple of large stones will do for this.
- ☐ If the ground is soft, use a flat piece of wood to spread the load under the jack.

## Changing the wheel

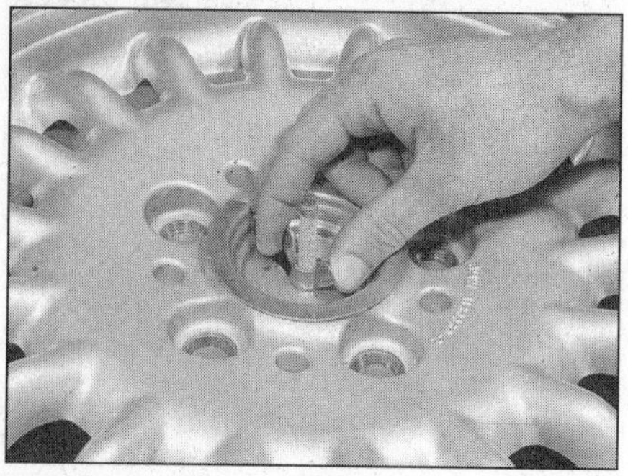

1 The spare wheel and tools are stored in the luggage compartment. Remove the cover then slacken the retaining nut and remove the retaining plate. Lift out the jack and spare wheel from the luggage compartment.

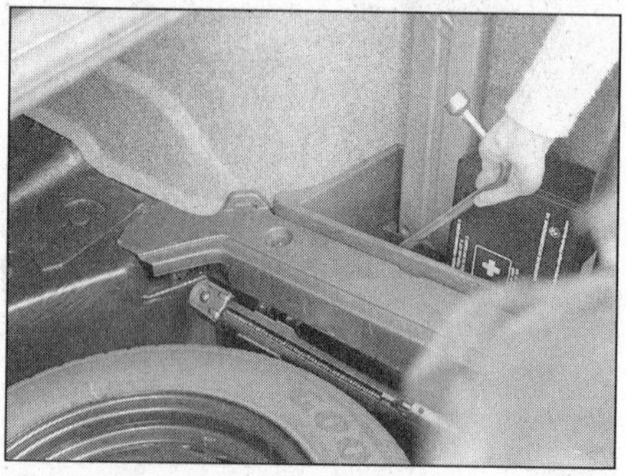

2 Remove the wheelbrace from behind the box on the right-hand side of the luggage compartment.

3 Remove the wheel trim/hub cap (as applicable) then slacken each wheel bolt by a half turn. If anti-theft wheel bolts are fitted, they can be slackened using the adapter supplied in the tool kit attached to the boot lid.

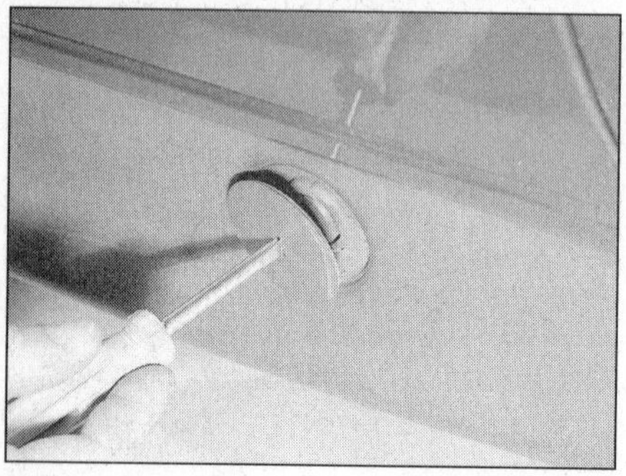

4 Unscrew the relevant access cover from the sill and fully insert the vehicle jack.

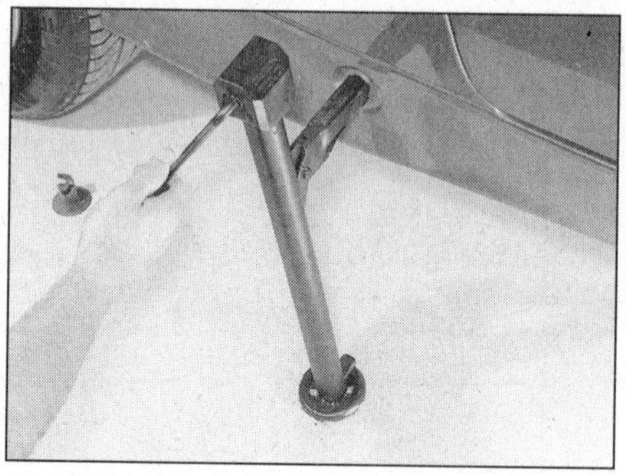

5 Make sure the jack is located on firm ground then turn the jack handle clockwise until the wheel is raised clear of the ground. Unscrew the wheel bolts and remove the wheel. Fit the spare wheel and screw in the bolts. Lightly tighten the bolts with the wheelbrace then lower the vehicle to the ground.

6 Securely tighten the wheel bolts in the sequence shown then refit the wheel trim/hub cap (as applicable). Stow the punctured wheel and tools back in the luggage compartment and secure them in position. Note that the wheel bolts should be slackened and retightened to the specified torque at the earliest possible opportunity.

## Finally...

- ☐ Remove the wheel chocks.
- ☐ Stow the jack and tools in the correct locations in the car.
- ☐ Check the tyre pressure on the wheel just fitted. If it is low, or if you don't have a pressure gauge with you, drive slowly to the nearest garage and inflate the tyre to the right pressure.
- ☐ Have the damaged tyre or wheel repaired as soon as possible.

# Identifying leaks

Puddles on the garage floor or drive, or obvious wetness under the bonnet or underneath the car, suggest a leak that needs investigating. It can sometimes be difficult to decide where the leak is coming from, especially if the engine bay is very dirty already. Leaking oil or fluid can also be blown rearwards by the passage of air under the car, giving a false impression of where the problem lies.

***Warning: Most automotive oils and fluids are poisonous. Wash them off skin, and change out of contaminated clothing, without delay.***

**HAYNES HiNT** *The smell of a fluid leaking from the car may provide a clue to what's leaking. Some fluids are distinctively coloured. It may help to clean the car and to park it over some clean paper as an aid to locating the source of the leak. Remember that some leaks may only occur while the engine is running.*

## Sump oil

Engine oil may leak from the drain plug...

## Oil from filter

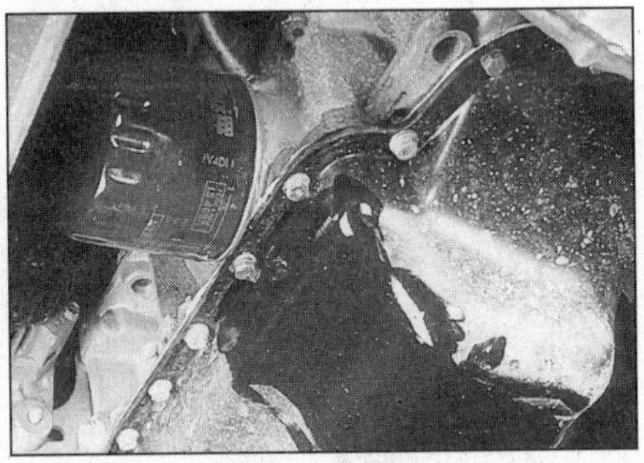

...or from the base of the oil filter.

## Gearbox oil

Gearbox oil can leak from the seals at the inboard ends of the driveshafts.

## Antifreeze

Leaking antifreeze often leaves a crystalline deposit like this.

## Brake fluid

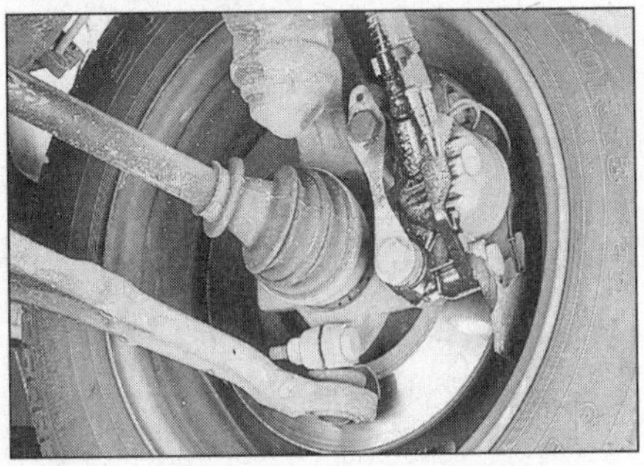

A leak occurring at a wheel is almost certainly brake fluid.

## Power steering fluid

Power steering fluid may leak from the pipe connectors on the steering rack.

# Towing

When all else fails, you may find yourself having to get a tow home – or of course you may be helping somebody else. Long-distance recovery should only be done by a garage or breakdown service. For shorter distances, DIY towing using another car is easy enough, but observe the following points:

☐ Use a proper tow-rope – they are not expensive. The vehicle being towed must display an 'ON TOW' sign in its rear window.

☐ Always turn the ignition key to the 'on' position when the vehicle is being towed, so that the steering lock is released, and that the direction indicator and brake lights will work.

☐ Only attach the tow-rope to the towing eyes provided.

☐ Before being towed, release the handbrake and select neutral on the transmission.

☐ Note that greater-than-usual pedal pressure will be required to operate the brakes, since the vacuum servo unit is only operational with the engine running.

☐ On models with power steering, greater-than-usual steering effort will also be required.

☐ The driver of the car being towed must keep the tow-rope taut at all times to avoid snatching.

☐ Make sure that both drivers know the route before setting off.

☐ Only drive at moderate speeds and keep the distance towed to a minimum. Drive smoothly and allow plenty of time for slowing down at junctions.

☐ On models with automatic transmission, special precautions apply. If in doubt, do not tow, or transmission damage may result.

☐ The towing eye is supplied as part of the tool kit which is fitted to the boot lid. To fit the eye, carefully prise out the access cover from the front/rear bumper (as applicable). Screw the eye into position and tighten it securely.

# Introduction

There are some very simple checks which need only take a few minutes to carry out, but which could save you a lot of inconvenience and expense.

These "Weekly checks" require no great skill or special tools, and the small amount of time they take to perform could prove to be very well spent, for example;

☐ Keeping an eye on tyre condition and pressures, will not only help to stop them wearing out prematurely, but could also save your life.

☐ Many breakdowns are caused by electrical problems. Battery-related faults are particularly common, and a quick check on a regular basis will often prevent the majority of these.

☐ If your car develops a brake fluid leak, the first time you might know about it is when your brakes don't work properly. Checking the level regularly will give advance warning of this kind of problem.

☐ If the oil or coolant levels run low, the cost of repairing any engine damage will be far greater than fixing the leak, for example.

# Underbonnet check points

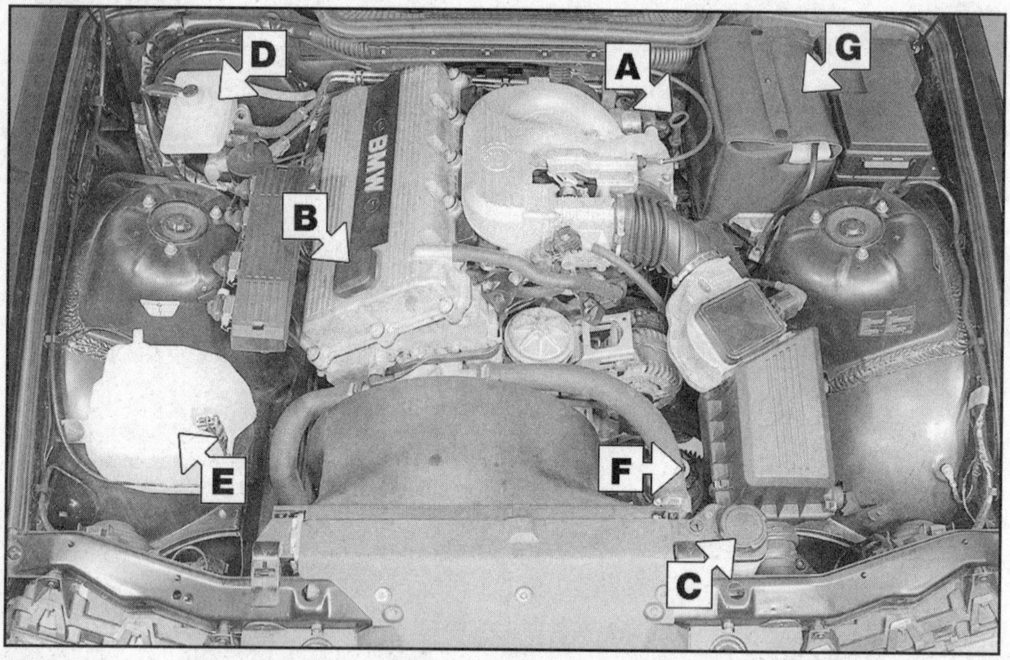


◀ **4-cylinder engine (1.8 litre shown)**

**A** *Engine oil level dipstick*
**B** *Engine oil filler cap*
**C** *Coolant expansion tank*
**D** *Brake and clutch fluid reservoir*
**E** *Screen washer fluid reservoir*
**F** *Battery*
**G** *Power steering fluid reservoir*

◀ **6-cylinder engine (2.0 litre shown)**

**A** *Engine oil level dipstick*
**B** *Engine oil filler cap*
**C** *Coolant expansion tank*
**D** *Brake and clutch fluid reservoir*
**E** *Power steering fluid reservoir*
**F** *Screen washer fluid reservoir*

# Engine oil level

## Before you start

✔ Make sure that your car is on level ground.
✔ Check the oil level before the car is driven, or at least 5 minutes after the engine has been switched off.

> **HAYNES HiNT** ***If the oil is checked immediately after driving the vehicle, some of the oil will remain in the upper engine components, resulting in an inaccurate reading on the dipstick!***

## The correct oil

*Modern engines place great demands on their oil. It is very important that the correct oil for your car is used (See "Lubricants, fluids and tyre pressures").*

## Car Care

● If you have to add oil frequently, you should check whether you have any oil leaks. Place some clean paper under the car overnight, and check for stains in the morning. If there are no leaks, the engine may be burning oil *(see "Fault Finding").*

● Always maintain the level between the upper and lower dipstick marks (see photo 3). If the level is too low severe engine damage may occur. Oil seal failure may result if the engine is overfilled by adding too much oil.

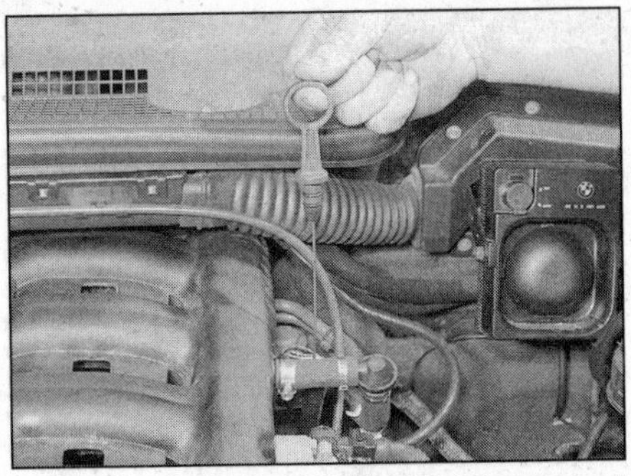

**1** The dipstick top is often brightly coloured for easy identification (see "*Underbonnet check points*" on pages 0•10 and 0•11 for exact location). Withdraw the dipstick.

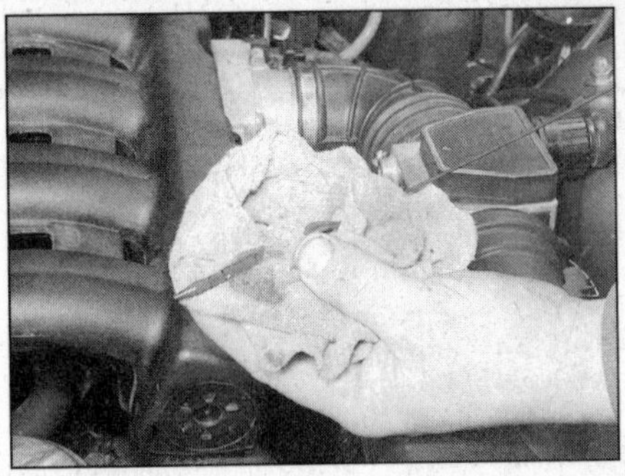

**2** Using a clean rag or paper towel remove all oil from the dipstick. Insert the clean dipstick into the tube as far as it will go, then withdraw it again.

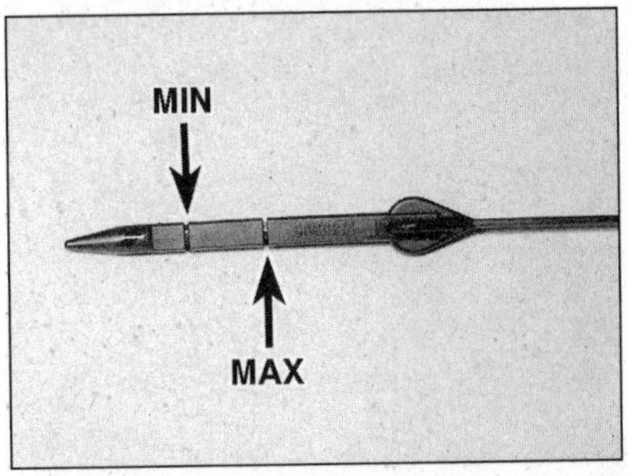


**3** Note the oil level on the end of the dipstick, which should be between the upper ("MAX") mark and lower ("MIN") mark. Approximately 1.0 litre of oil will raise the level from the lower mark to the upper mark.

**4** Oil is added through the filler cap. Unscrew the cap and top-up the level; a funnel may help to reduce spillage. Add the oil slowly, checking the level on the dipstick often. Don't overfill (see "*Car Care" left*).

# Coolant level

> ***Warning: DO NOT attempt to remove the expansion tank pressure cap when the engine is hot, as there is a very great risk of scalding. Do not leave open containers of coolant about, as it is poisonous.***

## Car Care

● With a sealed-type cooling system, adding coolant should not be necessary on a regular basis. If frequent topping-up is required, it is likely there is a leak. Check the radiator, all hoses and joint faces for signs of staining or wetness, and rectify as necessary.

● It is important that antifreeze is used in the cooling system all year round, not just during the winter months. Don't top-up with water alone, as the antifreeze will become too diluted.

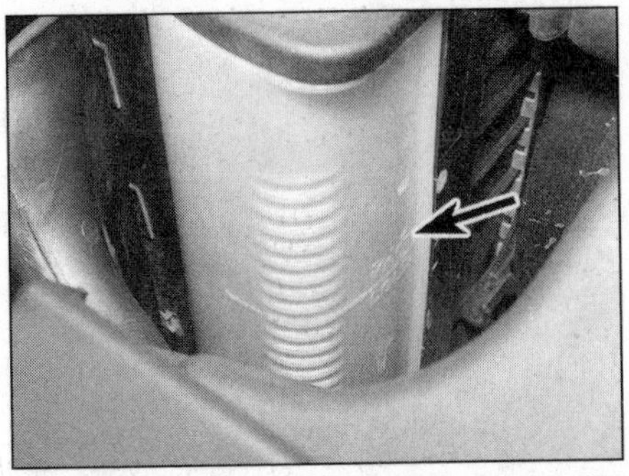

**1** The coolant level varies with the temperature of the engine. When the engine is cold, the coolant level should be between the "KALT/COLD" mark on the expansion tank. When the engine is hot, the level may rise above the "KALT/COLD" mark.

**2** If topping up is necessary, **wait until the engine is cold**. Slowly unscrew the expansion tank cap, to release any pressure present in the cooling system, and remove it.

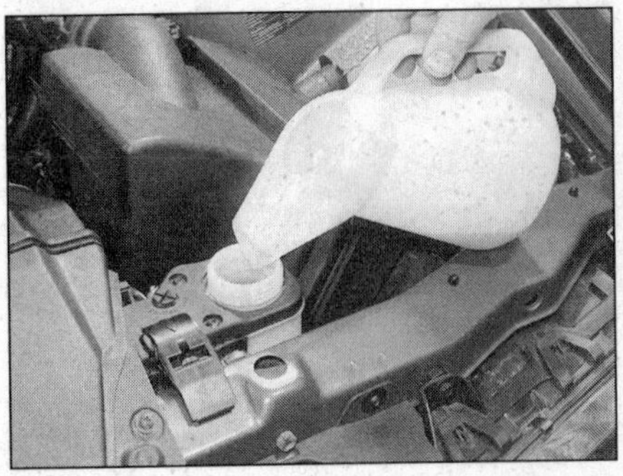

**3** Add a mixture of water and antifreeze to the expansion tank until the coolant level is up to the "KALT/COLD" mark. Refit the cap and tighten it securely.

# Brake and clutch fluid level

***Warning:***
- ***Brake fluid can harm your eyes and damage painted surfaces, so use extreme caution when handling and pouring it.***
- ***Do not use fluid that has been standing open for some time, as it absorbs moisture from the air, which can cause a dangerous loss of braking effectiveness.***

**HAYNES HiNT**
- ***Make sure that your car is on level ground.***
- ***The fluid level in the reservoir will drop slightly as the brake pads wear down, but the fluid level must never be allowed to drop below the "MIN" mark.***

## Safety First!

- If the reservoir requires repeated topping-up this is an indication of a fluid leak somewhere in the system, which should be investigated immediately.

- If a leak is suspected, the car should not be driven until the braking system has been checked. Never take any risks where brakes are concerned.

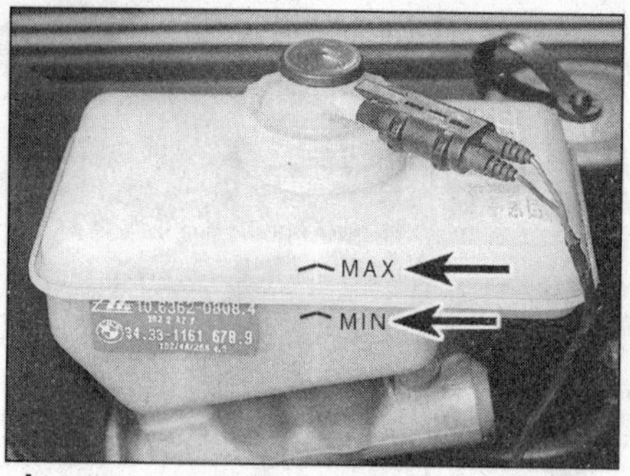


1 The "MAX" and "MIN" marks are indicated on the side of the reservoir. The fluid level must be kept between the marks at all times.

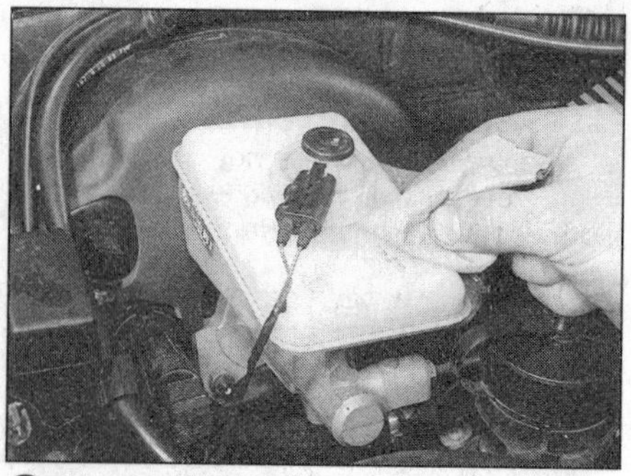

2 If topping-up is necessary, first wipe clean the area around the filler cap to prevent dirt entering the hydraulic system.

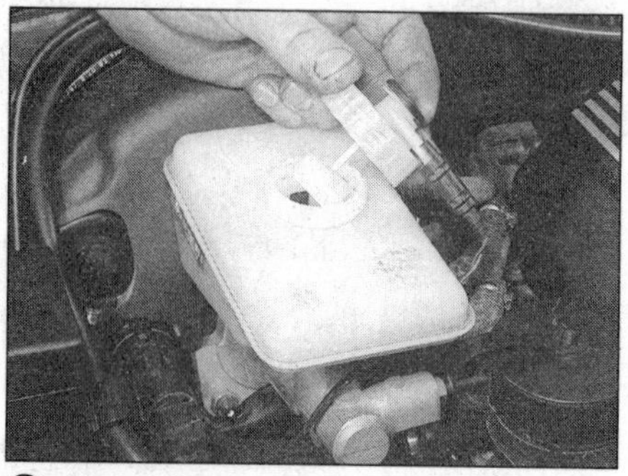

3 Unscrew the reservoir cap and carefully lift it out of position, taking care not to damage the level switch float. Inspect the reservoir, if the fluid is dirty the hydraulic system should be drained and refilled (see Chapter 1).

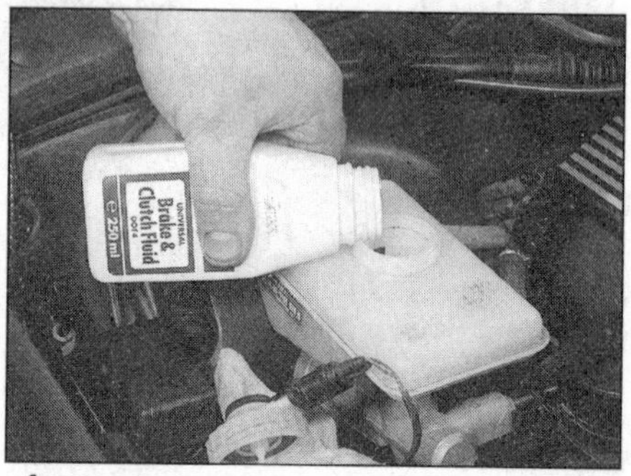

4 Carefully add fluid taking care not to spill it onto the surrounding components. Use only the specified fluid; mixing different types can cause damage to the system. After topping-up to the correct level, securely refit the cap and wipe off any spilt fluid.

# Power steering fluid level

## Before you start:

- ✔ Park the vehicle on level ground.
- ✔ Set the steering wheel straight-ahead.
- ✔ The fluid level should be checked with the engine running at idle speed.

**HAYNES HiNT** ***For the check to be accurate, the steering must not be turned while the level is being checked.***

## Safety First!

- The need for frequent topping-up indicates a leak, which should be investigated immediately.

1 The reservoir is located near the front of the engine compartment. Wipe clean the area around the reservoir filler neck and unscrew the filler cap/dipstick from the reservoir (6-cylinder engine shown).

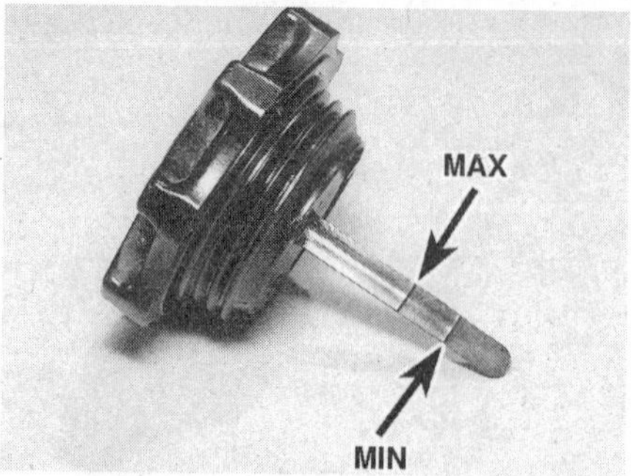


2 Start the engine and dip the fluid with the reservoir cap/dipstick (rest the cap on the filler neck, do not screw it fully into position). The fluid level should be between "MIN" and "MAX". When the engine is stopped the level may rise above the "MAX" mark.

3 When topping-up, use the specified type of fluid and do not overfill the reservoir. When the level is correct, securely refit the cap and switch off the engine.

# Screen washer fluid level*

***On models with a headlight washer system, the screen wash is also used to clean the headlights**

Screenwash additives not only keep the winscreen clean during foul weather, they also prevent the washer system freezing in cold weather - which is when you are likely to need it most. Don't top up using plain water as the screenwash will become too diluted, and will freeze during cold weather. ***On no account use coolant antifreeze in the washer system - this could discolour or damage paintwork.***

1 The screen washer fluid reservoir is located in the front right-hand corner of the engine compartment. The level is visible through the reservoir body, if topping up is necessary, open up the cap.

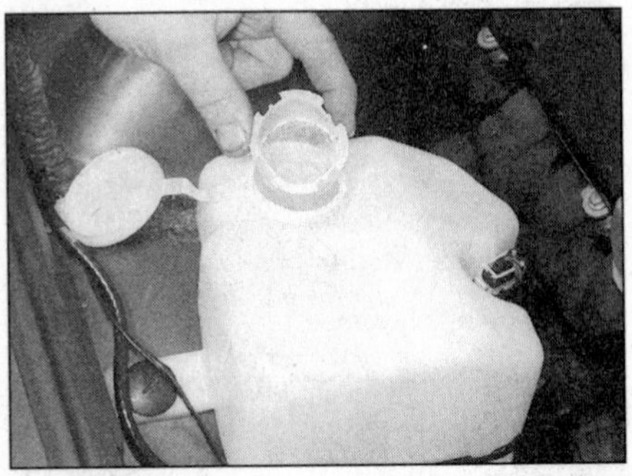

2 Prior to topping up, check that the reservoir filter is clean and free from obstruction.

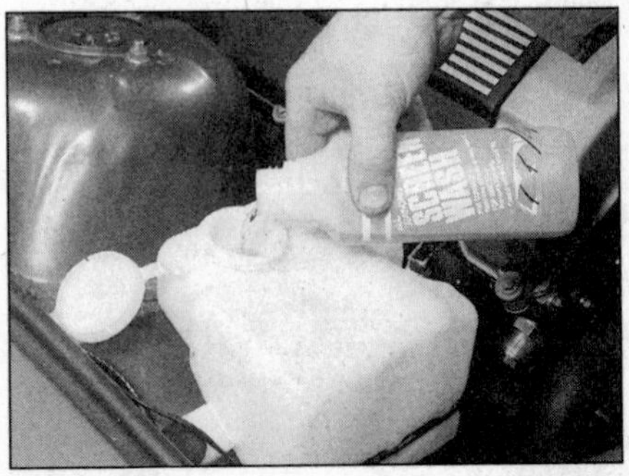

3 When topping-up, add a screenwash additive in the quantities recommended by the manufacturer.

# Wiper blades

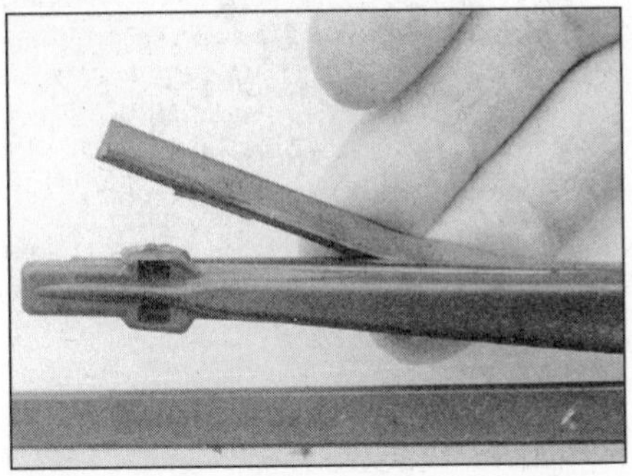

1 Check the condition of the wiper blades; if they are cracked or show any signs of deterioration, or if the glass swept area is smeared, renew them. Wiper blades should be renewed annually.

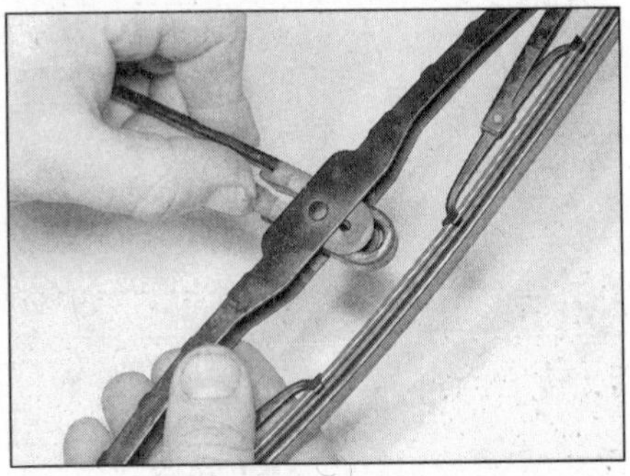

2 To remove a wiper blade, pull the arm fully away from the screen until it locks. Swivel the blade through 90°, press the locking tab with your fingers and slide the blade out of the arm's hooked end.

# Tyre condition and pressure

It is very important that tyres are in good condition, and at the correct pressure - having a tyre failure at any speed is highly dangerous. Tyre wear is influenced by driving style - harsh braking and acceleration, or fast cornering, will all produce more rapid tyre wear. As a general rule, the front tyres wear out faster than the rears. Interchanging the tyres from front to rear ("rotating" the tyres) may result in more even wear. However, if this is completely effective, you may have the expense of replacing all four tyres at once!

Remove any nails or stones embedded in the tread before they penetrate the tyre to cause deflation. If removal of a nail does reveal that the tyre has been punctured, refit the nail so that its point of penetration is marked. Then immediately change the wheel, and have the tyre repaired by a tyre dealer.

Regularly check the tyres for damage in the form of cuts or bulges, especially in the sidewalls. Periodically remove the wheels, and clean any dirt or mud from the inside and outside surfaces. Examine the wheel rims for signs of rusting, corrosion or other damage. Light alloy wheels are easily damaged by "kerbing" whilst parking; steel wheels may also become dented or buckled. A new wheel is very often the only way to overcome severe damage.

New tyres should be balanced when they are fitted, but it may become necessary to re-balance them as they wear, or if the balance weights fitted to the wheel rim should fall off. Unbalanced tyres will wear more quickly, as will the steering and suspension components. Wheel imbalance is normally signified by vibration, particularly at a certain speed (typically around 50 mph). If this vibration is felt only through the steering, then it is likely that just the front wheels need balancing. If, however, the vibration is felt through the whole car, the rear wheels could be out of balance. Wheel balancing should be carried out by a tyre dealer or garage.

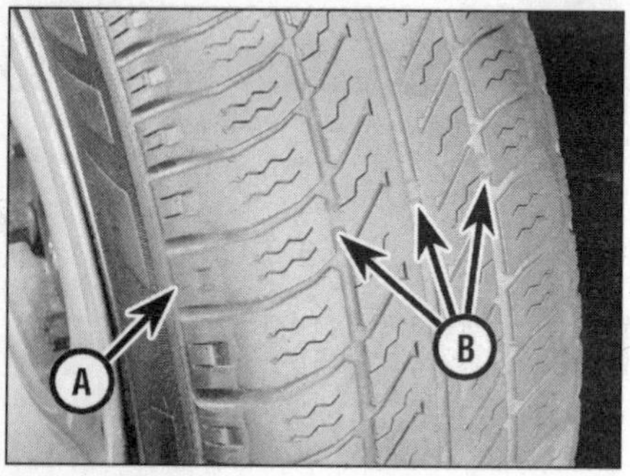


**1 Tread Depth - visual check**

The original tyres have tread wear safety bands (B), which will appear when the tread depth reaches approximately 1.6 mm. The band positions are indicated by a triangular mark on the tyre sidewall (A).

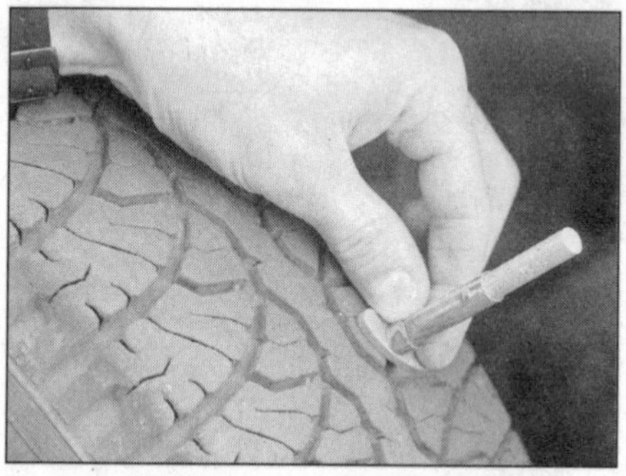

**2 Tread Depth - manual check**

Alternatively, tread wear can be monitored with a simple, inexpensive device known as a tread depth indicator gauge.

**3 Tyre Pressure Check**

Check the tyre pressures regularly with the tyres cold. Do not adjust the tyre pressures immediately after the vehicle has been used, or an inaccurate setting will result.

# Tyre tread wear patterns

### Shoulder Wear

**Underinflation (wear on both sides)**
Under-inflation will cause overheating of the tyre, because the tyre will flex too much, and the tread will not sit correctly on the road surface. This will cause a loss of grip and excessive wear, not to mention the danger of sudden tyre failure due to heat build-up.
*Check and adjust pressures*

**Incorrect wheel camber (wear on one side)**
*Repair or renew suspension parts*

**Hard cornering**
*Reduce speed!*

### Centre Wear

**Overinflation**
Over-inflation will cause rapid wear of the centre part of the tyre tread, coupled with reduced grip, harsher ride, and the danger of shock damage occurring in the tyre casing.
*Check and adjust pressures*

*If you sometimes have to inflate your car's tyres to the higher pressures specified for maximum load or sustained high speed, don't forget to reduce the pressures to normal afterwards.*

### Uneven Wear

Front tyres may wear unevenly as a result of wheel misalignment. Most tyre dealers and garages can check and adjust the wheel alignment (or "tracking") for a modest charge.

**Incorrect camber or castor**
*Repair or renew suspension parts*

**Malfunctioning suspension**
*Repair or renew suspension parts*

**Unbalanced wheel**
*Balance tyres*

**Incorrect toe setting**
*Adjust front wheel alignment*

**Note:** *The feathered edge of the tread which typifies toe wear is best checked by feel.*

# Battery

***Caution:** Before carrying out any work on the vehicle battery, read the precautions given in "Safety first" at the start of this manual.*

✔ Make sure that the battery tray is in good condition, and that the clamp is tight. Corrosion on the tray, retaining clamp and the battery itself can be removed with a solution of water and baking soda. Thoroughly rinse all cleaned areas with water. Any metal parts damaged by corrosion should be covered with a zinc-based primer, then painted.

✔ Periodically (approximately every three months), check the charge condition of the battery as described in Chapter 5A.

✔ If the battery is flat, and you need to jump start your vehicle, see ***Roadside Repairs***.

HAYNES HiNT

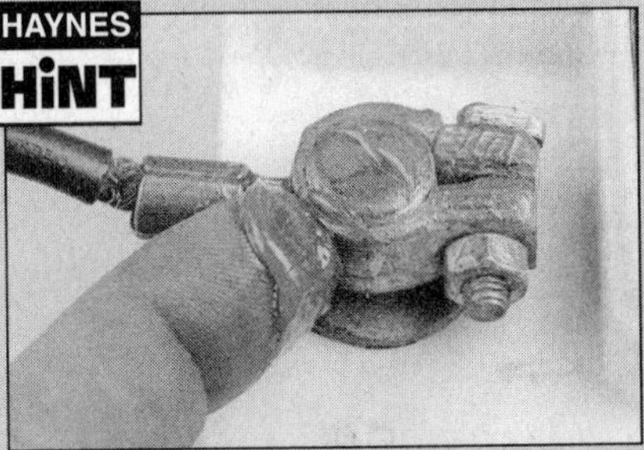

***Battery corrosion can be kept to a minimum by applying a layer of petroleum jelly to the clamps and terminals after they are reconnected.***

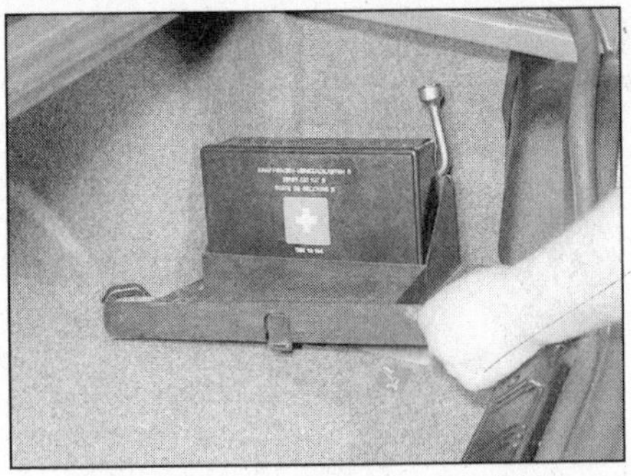

1 The battery is located in the right-hand rear corner of the engine compartment on 4-cylinder models. On 6-cylinder models, lift out the first aid box holder from the luggage compartment to reveal the battery.

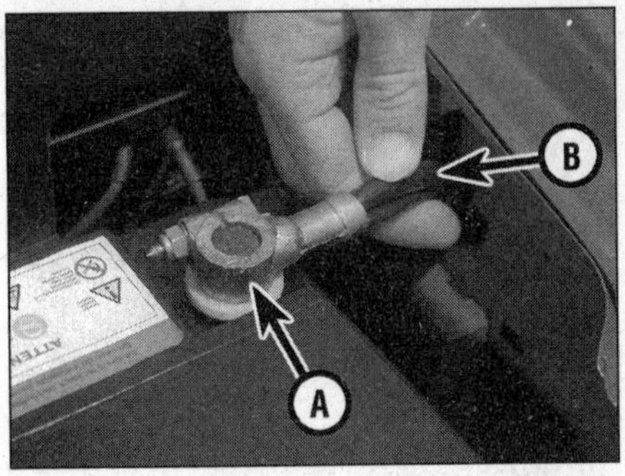


2 Check the tightness of battery clamps (A) to ensure good electrical connections. You should not be able to move them. Also check each cable (B) for cracks and frayed conductors.

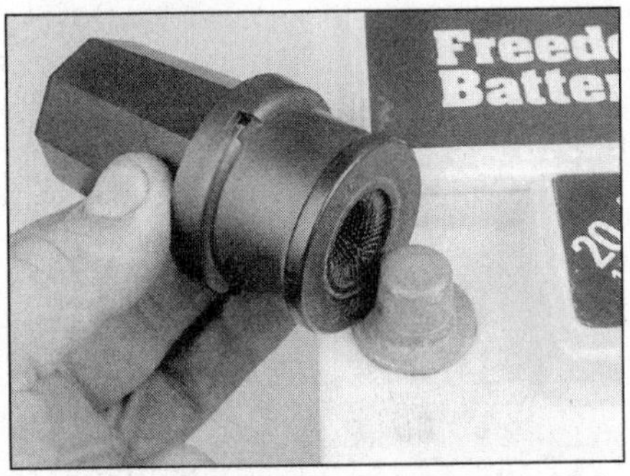

3 If corrosion (white, fluffy deposits) is evident, remove the cables from the battery terminals, clean them with a small wire brush, then refit them. Automotive stores sell a tool for cleaning the battery post . . .

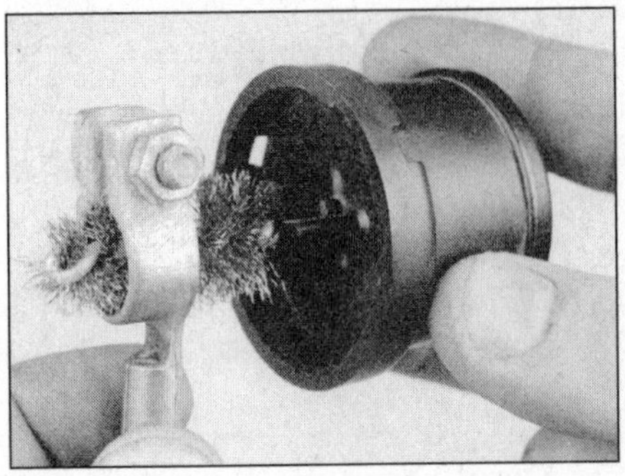

4 . . . as well as the battery cable clamps

# Bulbs and fuses

✔ Check all external lights and the horn. Refer to the appropriate Sections of Chapter 12 for details if any of the circuits are found to be inoperative.

✔ Visually check all accessible wiring connectors, harnesses and retaining clips for security, and for signs of chafing or damage.

HAYNES HiNT ***If you need to check your brake lights and indicators unaided, back up to a wall or garage door and operate the lights. The reflected light should show if they are working properly.***

1 If a single indicator light, stop light or headlight has failed, it is likely that a bulb has blown and will need to be replaced. Refer to Chapter 12 for details. If both stop lights have failed, it is possible that the switch has failed (see Chapter 9).

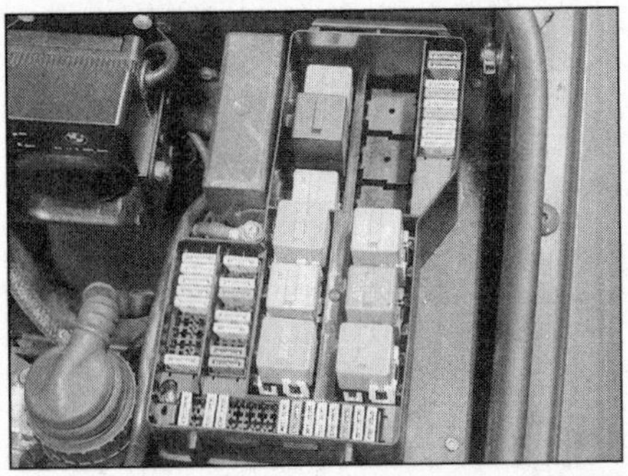

2 If more than one indicator light or tail light has failed it is likely that either a fuse has blown or that there is a fault in the circuit (see Chapter 12). The fuses are located behind in the fusebox in the left-hand rear corner of the engine compartment.

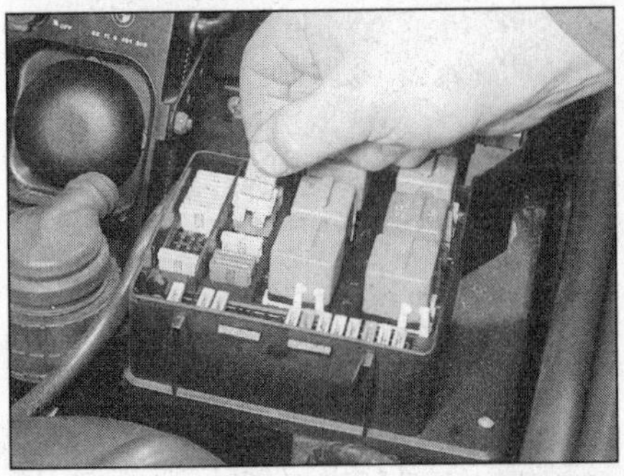

3 To replace a blown fuse, simply pull it out and fit a new fuse of the correct rating (see Chapter 12). If the fuse blows again, it is important that you find out why - a complete checking procedure is given in Chapter 12.

## Lubricants and fluids

| | |
|---|---|
| Engine | Multigrade engine oil, viscosity SAE 10W/40 to 20W/50, to API SG/CD |
| Cooling system | Ethylene glycol based antifreeze |
| Manual transmission | Dexron II type ATF* |
| Automatic transmission | Dexron II type ATF* |
| Final drive unit | Hypoid gear oil* |
| Braking system | Hydraulic fluid to SAE J1703F or DOT 4 |
| Power steering | Dexron II type ATF* |

*Refer to your BMW dealer for brand name and type recommendations*

## Tyre pressures

| 1.6 and 1.8 litre (except 318is) models: | Front | Rear |
|---|---|---|
| Up to four passengers: | | |
| 185/65 R 15 88 Q, T, and H M+S tyres | 2.2 bar (31 psi) | 2.5 bar (36 psi) |
| 185 65 R 15 H and 205/60 R 15 91 Q, T, and H M+S tyres | 2.0 bar (28 psi) | 2.3 bar (33 psi) |
| All other tyres | 1.8 bar (26 psi) | 2.0 bar (28 psi) |
| Full load: | | |
| 185/65 R 15 88 Q, T, and H M+S tyres | 2.5 bar (36 psi) | 3.0 bar (43 psi) |
| 185 65 R 15 H and 205/60 R 15 91 Q, T, and H M+S tyres | 2.3 bar (33 psi) | 2.8 bar (40 psi) |
| All other tyres | 2.0 bar (28 psi) | 2.5 bar (36 psi) |
| **1.8 litre (318is models) and all 2.0 litre models:** | | |
| Up to four passengers: | | |
| 185 65 R 15 H 88 and 205/60 R 15 91 Q, T, and H M+S tyres | 2.2 bar (31 psi) | 2.6 bar (37 psi) |
| All other tyres | 2.0 bar (28 psi) | 2.3 bar (33 psi) |
| Full load: | | |
| 185 65 R 15 H 88 and 205/60 R 15 91 Q, T, and H M+S tyres | 2.6 bar (37 psi) | 3.1 bar (44 psi) |
| All other tyres | 2.2 bar (31 psi) | 2.7 bar (38 psi) |
| **2.5 litre models:** | | |
| Up to four passengers: | | |
| 185 65 R 15 H and 205/60 R 15 91 Q, T, and H M+S tyres | 2.2 bar (31 psi) | 2.6 bar (37 psi) |
| All other tyres | 2.0 bar (28 psi) | 2.4 bar (34 psi) |
| Full load: | | |
| 185 65 R 15 H and 205/60 R 15 91 Q, T, and H M+S tyres | 2.6 bar (37 psi) | 3.1 bar (44 psi) |
| All other tyres | 2.4 bar (34 psi) | 2.9 bar (41 psi) |

**Note:** *Pressures apply only to original equipment tyres and may vary if any other make of tyre is fitted; check with the tyre manufacturer or supplier for correct pressures if necessary. Note that the correct pressures for each individual vehicle are given on a sticker which is attached to the driver's door pillar (note that the information on the sticker may vary slightly from that given above, if this is the case consult your BMW dealer for the latest information).*

# Chapter 1
# Routine maintenance and servicing

1

## Contents



## Degrees of difficulty

| | | | | |
|---|---|---|---|---|
| **Easy,** suitable for novice with little experience | **Fairly easy,** suitable for beginner with some experience | **Fairly difficult,** suitable for competent DIY mechanic | **Difficult,** suitable for experienced DIY mechanic | **Very difficult,** suitable for expert DIY or professional |

## Lubricants and fluids

Refer to *"Weekly checks"*

## Capacities

| | |
|---|---|
| **Engine oil (including filter)** | |
| M40 and M43 4-cylinder engines | 4.0 litres |
| M42 4-cylinder engines | 4.5 litres |
| 6-cylinder engines | 6.5 litres |
| **Cooling system** | |
| M40 and M43 4-cylinder engine models | 6.0 litres |
| M42 4-cylinder engine models | 6.5 litres |
| 6-cylinder models | 10.5 litres |
| **Transmission** | |
| Manual transmission | 1.1 litres |
| Automatic transmission | 3.0 litres |
| **Final drive unit** | |
| All models: | |
| 4-cylinder models | 1.1 litres |
| 6-cylinder models | 1.7 litre |
| **Power-assisted steering** | |
| All models (approximate) | 1.5 litres |
| **Fuel tank** | |
| All models (approximate) | 65 litres |

## Engine

| | |
|---|---|
| Oil filter: | |
| 4-cylinder engines | Champion X120 |
| 6-cylinder engines | Champion X121 |

## Cooling system

| | |
|---|---|
| Antifreeze mixture: | |
| 28% antifreeze | Protection down to -15°C (5°F) |
| 50% antifreeze | Protection down to -30°C (-22°F) |

**Note:** *Refer to antifreeze manufacturer for latest recommendations.*

## Fuel system

| | |
|---|---|
| Air filter element: | |
| 4-cylinder engines | Champion U527 |
| 6-cylinder engines | Champion U607 |
| Fuel filter: | |
| 1.6 litre M40 4-cylinder engine | Champion L226 |
| 1.8 litre M40 4-cylinder engine | Champion L206 |
| M42 4-cylinder engine | Champion L226 |
| M43 4-cylinder engine | No information available |
| 6-cylinder engine | Champion L206 |

## Ignition system

| | |
|---|---|
| Spark plugs: | |
| M40 4-cylinder engine | Champion C9YCC |
| M42 4-cylinder engine | Champion C7YCC |
| M43 4-cylinder engine | No information available |
| 6-cylinder engines | Champion C7YCC |
| Spark plug electrode gap* | 0.8 mm |

**The spark plug gap quoted is that recommended by Champion for their specified plugs listed above. If spark plugs of any other type are to be fitted, refer to their manufacturer's recommendations.*

## Auxiliary drivebelts

| | |
|---|---|
| Air conditioning compressor drivebelt tensioning torque (see Section 7): | |
| Used drivebelt | 7.0 to 8.5 Nm (5.0 to 6.0 lbf ft) |
| New drivebelt | 5.0 to 6.5 Nm (4.0 to 5.0 lbf ft) |

## Brakes

| | |
|---|---|
| Brake pad friction material minimum thickness | 2.0 mm |
| Brake shoe friction material minimum thickness | 1.5 mm |

## Wiper blades

| | |
|---|---|
| Driver's side: | |
| All models except Cabriolet | Champion VX53 or X53 |
| Cabriolet models | Champion VX55 or X55 |
| Passenger's side | Champion VX51 or X51 |

## Torque wrench settings

| | Nm | lbf ft |
|---|---|---|
| Engine sump oil drain plug: | | |
| M12 plug | 35 | 26 |
| M22 plug | 60 | 44 |
| Cylinder block coolant drain plug | 28 | 21 |
| Automatic transmission oil drain plug: | | |
| A4S 310 R 4-speed transmission | 25 | 18 |
| A5S 300 J 5-speed transmission | 35 | 26 |
| Automatic transmission oil filler/level plug: | | |
| A4S 310 R 4-speed transmission | 33 | 24 |
| A5S 300 J 5-speed transmission | 40 | 30 |
| A5S 310 Z 5-speed transmission | 100 | 74 |
| Manual gearbox oil drain plug | 50 | 37 |
| Manual gearbox oil filler/level plug | 50 | 37 |
| Final drive unit filler/level and drain plugs | 70 | 52 |
| Spark plugs | 30 | 22 |
| Roadwheel bolts | 100 | 74 |



## Underbonnet view of a 1.8 litre (M43 engine) model

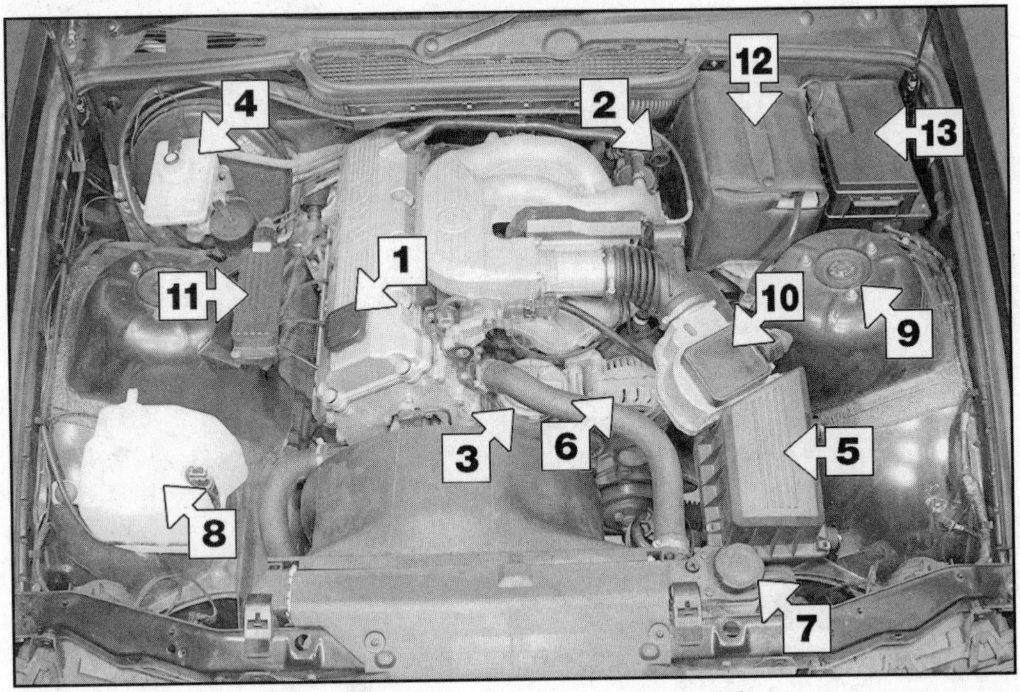


1 Engine oil filler cap
2 Engine oil dipstick
3 Oil filter
4 Brake and clutch fluid reservoir
5 Air cleaner housing
6 Alternator
7 Coolant expansion tank
8 Washer fluid reservoir
9 Suspension strut upper mounting
10 Air flow meter
11 Ignition HT coil
12 Battery
13 Fusebox

## Underbonnet view of a 1.8 litre (M42 engine) model

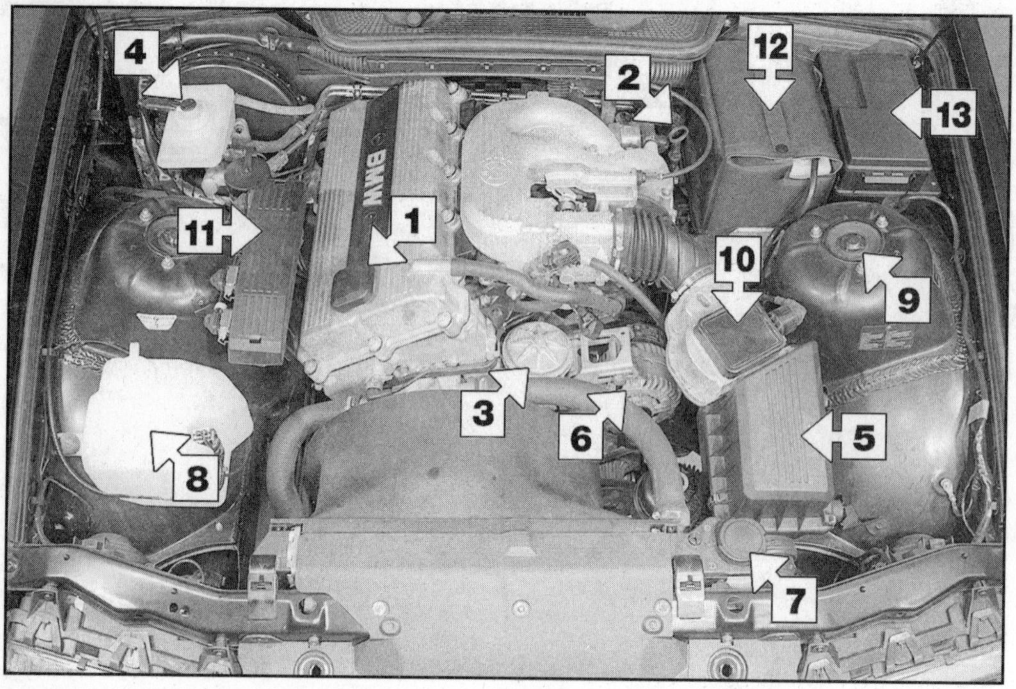


1 Engine oil filler cap
2 Engine oil dipstick
3 Oil filter
4 Brake and clutch fluid reservoir
5 Air cleaner housing
6 Alternator
7 Coolant expansion tank
8 Washer fluid reservoir
9 Suspension strut upper mounting
10 Air flow meter
11 Ignition HT coil
12 Battery
13 Fusebox

## Underbonnet view of a 2.0 litre (M50 engine) model

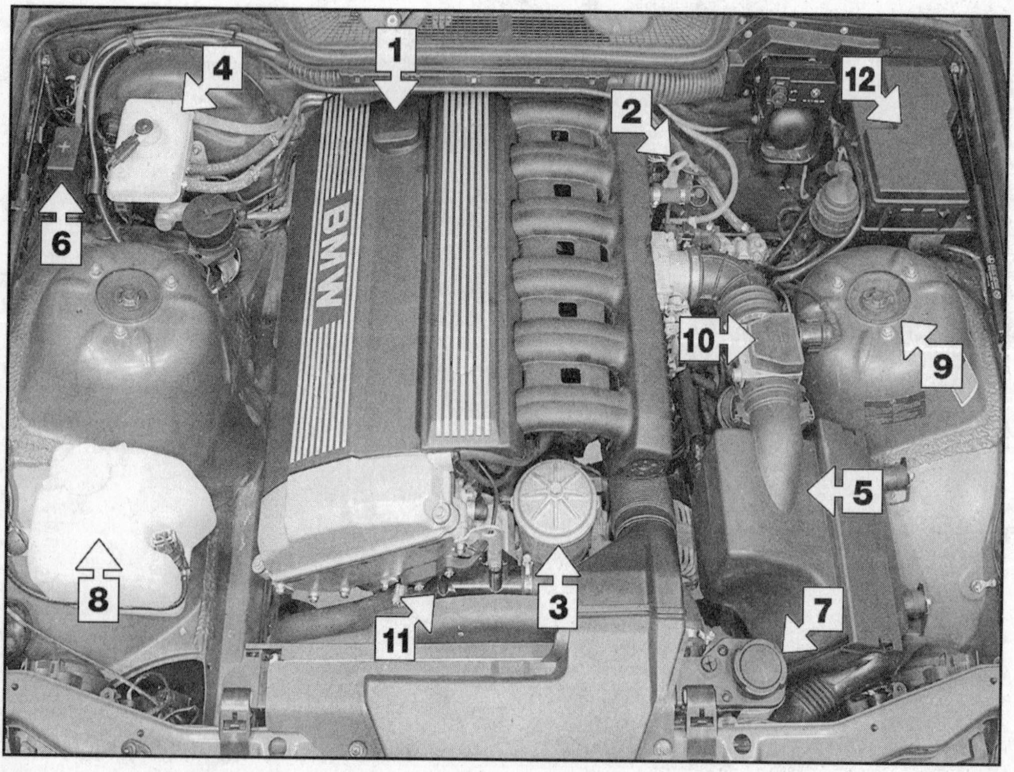


1 Engine oil filler cap
2 Engine oil dipstick
3 Oil filter
4 Brake and clutch fluid reservoir
5 Air cleaner housing
6 Jump starting (+) terminal
7 Coolant expansion tank
8 Washer fluid reservoir
9 Suspension strut upper mounting
10 Air mass meter
11 Thermostat housing
12 Fusebox

## Front underbody view (2.0 litre model shown - other models similar)

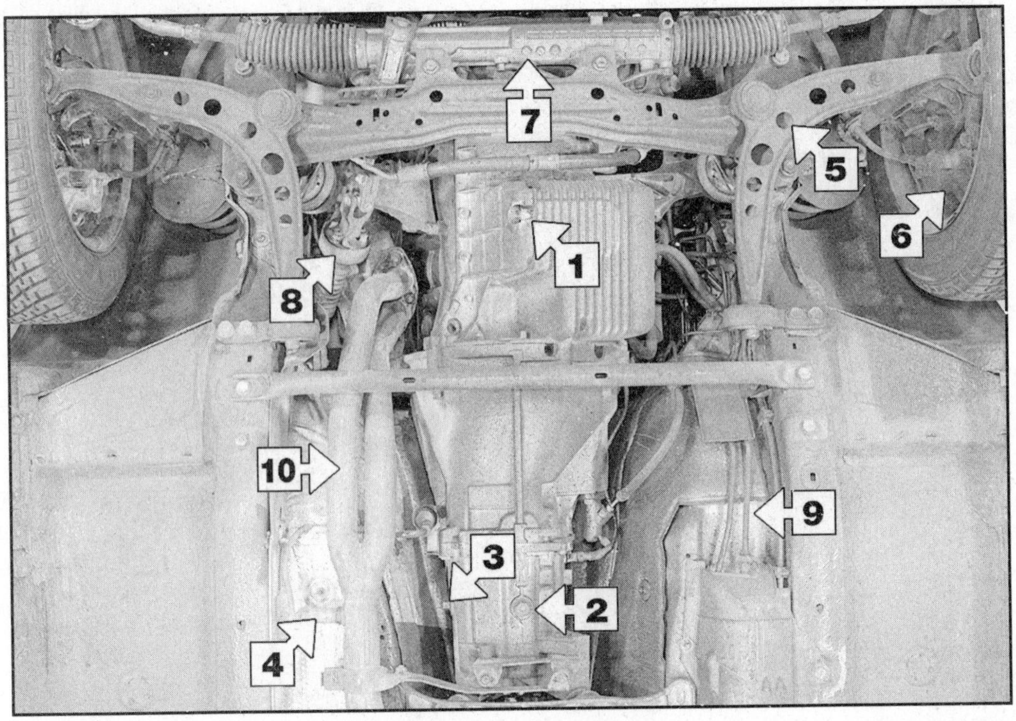


1 *Engine oil (sump) drain plug*
2 *Manual transmission drain plug*
3 *Manual transmission filler/level plug*
4 *Oxygen sensor*
5 *Front suspension lower arm*
6 *Front brake caliper*
7 *Steering gear assembly*
8 *Steering column intermediate shaft*
9 *Fuel lines*
10 *Exhaust front pipe*



## Rear underbody view (2.0 litre model shown - other models similar)

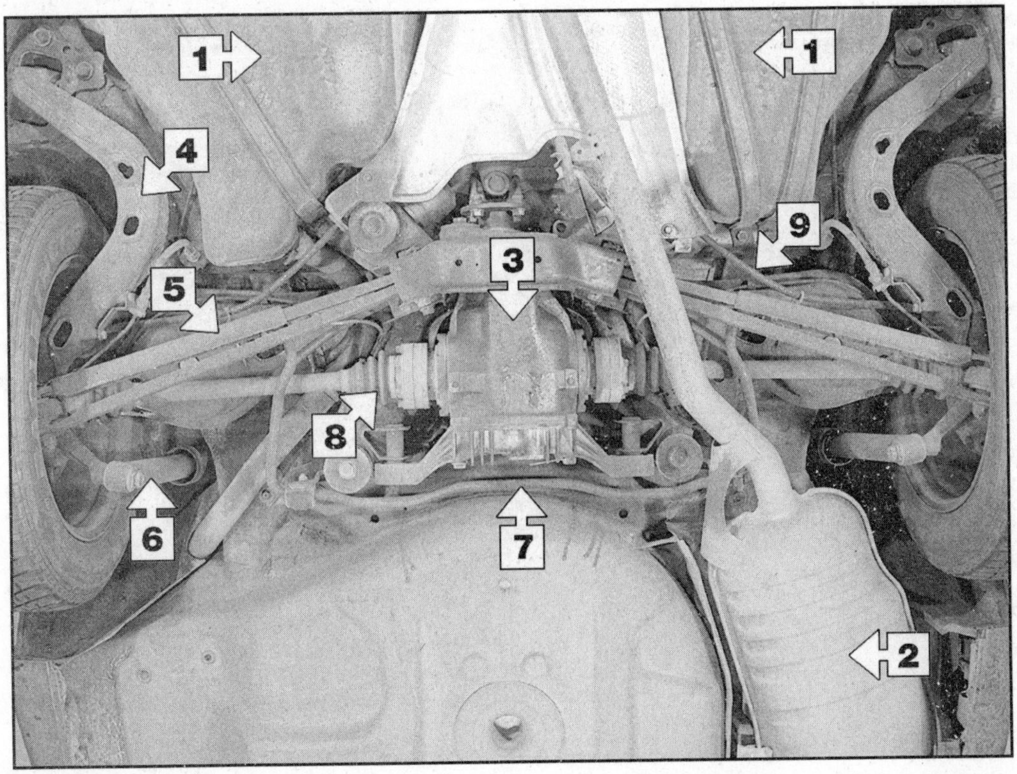


1 *Fuel tank*
2 *Exhaust tailpipe*
3 *Final drive unit*
4 *Rear suspension trailing arm*
5 *Rear suspension lower control arm*
6 *Rear shock absorber*
7 *Rear suspension anti-roll bar*
8 *Driveshaft*
9 *Handbrake cable*

All BMW 3 series models are equipped with a service interval display indicator and a row of LEDs in the instrument panel.

When the ignition is switched on, the panel and LEDs will illuminate for a few seconds and then go out. The green LEDs indicate the amount of time until the next service, the fewer LEDs lit then the nearer the next service interval is. When the yellow LED is lit, a service is due and the display will show whether an oil service or inspection is needed; the clock symbol will be illuminated if the additional annual inspection operations are required. If the red LED is illuminated then the service is overdue.

There are two different inspection services, Inspection I and Inspection II, these should be carried out alternately with some additional items to be included every second Inspection II. If you are unclear as to which inspection schedule was carried out last time start with Inspection II (including the additional items).

To reset the service interval display indicator a BMW service tool is required. Aftermarket alternatives to the BMW tool are produced by several leading tool manufacturers and should be available from larger car accessory shops.

## Every 250 miles (400 km) or weekly

- ☐ Refer to *"Weekly checks"*

## Oil service

- ☐ Renew the engine oil and filter (Section 3)
- ☐ Reset the service interval display (Section 4)

## Inspection I

- ☐ Renew the engine oil and filter (Section 3)
- ☐ Check the automatic transmission fluid level (Section 5)
- ☐ Check all underbonnet components and hoses for fluid leaks (Section 6)
- ☐ Check the condition of the auxiliary drivebelt(s), and adjust/renew if necessary (Section 7)
- ☐ Check the steering and suspension components for condition and security (Section 8)
- ☐ Check the front brake pad thickness (Section 9)
- ☐ Check the rear brake pad thickness - rear disc brake models (Section 10)
- ☐ Check the rear brake shoe lining thickness - rear drum brake models (Section 11)
- ☐ Check the operation of the handbrake (Section 12)
- ☐ Check the exhaust system and mountings (Section 13)
- ☐ Check the condition and operation of the seat belts (Section 14)
- ☐ Lubricate all hinges and locks (Section 15)
- ☐ Renew the pollen filter element (where fitted) (Section 16)
- ☐ Check the headlight beam alignment (Section 17)
- ☐ Check the operation of the windscreen/headlight washer system(s) (as applicable) (Section 18)
- ☐ Check the engine management system (Section 19)
- ☐ Carry out a road test (Section 20)
- ☐ Reset service interval display (Section 4)

## Inspection II

*Carry out all the operations listed under Inspection I, along with the following:*

- ☐ Renew the spark plugs (Section 21)
- ☐ Renew the air filter element (Section 22)
- ☐ Renew the automatic transmission fluid (Section 23)
- ☐ Renew the final drive unit oil (Section 24)
- ☐ Check the condition of the driveshaft gaiters (Section 25)
- ☐ Check the condition of the handbrake shoe linings - rear disc brake models (Section 26)
- ☐ Reset the service interval display (Section 4)

***Additional work to be carried out every second inspection II:***

- ☐ Renew the manual gearbox oil (Section 27)
- ☐ Renew the fuel filter (Section 28)
- ☐ Check the clutch (Section 29)
- ☐ Renew the timing belt - M40 engine (Section 30) - The timing belt should be renewed at this interval or every 4 years (whichever comes sooner)

## Annual service

**Note:** *BMW specify that the following should be carried out whenever the service display clock illuminates or at least every 2 years.*

- ☐ Renew the brake fluid (Section 31)
- ☐ Renew the coolant (Section 32)
- ☐ Reset the service interval display (Section 4)

# Maintenance procedures

## 1 Introduction

### General information

**1** This Chapter is designed to help the home mechanic maintain his/her vehicle for safety, economy, long life and peak performance.

**2** The Chapter contains a master maintenance schedule, followed by Sections dealing specifically with each task in the schedule. Visual checks, adjustments, component renewal and other helpful items are included. Refer to the accompanying illustrations of the engine compartment and the underside of the vehicle for the locations of the various components.

**3** Servicing your vehicle in accordance with the service indicator display and the following Sections will provide a planned maintenance programme, which should result in a long and reliable service life. This is a comprehensive plan, so maintaining some items but not others at the specified service intervals, will not produce the same results.

**4** As you service your vehicle, you will discover that many of the procedures can - and should - be grouped together, because of the particular procedure being performed, or because of the proximity of two otherwise-unrelated components to one another. For example, if the vehicle is raised for any reason, the exhaust can be inspected at the same time as the suspension and steering components.

**5** The first step in this maintenance programme is to prepare yourself before the actual work begins. Read through all the Sections relevant to the work to be carried out, then make a list and gather all the parts and tools required. If a problem is encountered, seek advice from a parts specialist, or a dealer service department.

## 2 Intensive maintenance

**1** If, from the time the vehicle is new, the routine maintenance schedule is followed closely, and frequent checks are made of fluid levels and high-wear items, as suggested throughout this manual, the engine will be kept in relatively good running condition, and the need for additional work will be minimised.

**2** It is possible that there will be times when the engine is running poorly due to the lack of regular maintenance. This is even more likely if a used vehicle, which has not received regular and frequent maintenance checks, is purchased. In such cases, additional work may need to be carried out, outside of the regular maintenance intervals.

**3** If engine wear is suspected, a compression test (refer to the relevant Part of Chapter 2) will provide valuable information regarding the overall performance of the main internal components. Such a test can be used as a basis to decide on the extent of the work to be carried out. If, for example, a compression test indicates serious internal engine wear, conventional maintenance as described in this Chapter will not greatly improve the performance of the engine, and may prove a waste of time and money, unless extensive overhaul work is carried out first.

**4** The following series of operations are those most often required to improve the performance of a generally poor-running engine:

### Primary operations

*a) Clean, inspect and test the battery (See "Weekly checks").*
*b) Check all the engine-related fluids (See "Weekly checks").*
*c) Check the condition and tension of the auxiliary drivebelt (Section 7).*
*d) Renew the spark plugs (Section 21).*
*e) Check the condition of the air filter, and renew if necessary (Section 22).*
*f) Check the fuel filter (Section 28).*
*g) Check the condition of all hoses, and check for fluid leaks (Section 6).*

**5** If the above operations do not prove fully effective, carry out the following secondary operations:

### Secondary operations

All items listed under "Primary operations", plus the following:

*a) Check the charging system (see relevant Part of Chapter 5).*
*b) Check the ignition system (see relevant Part of Chapter 5).*
*c) Check the fuel system (see relevant Part of Chapter 4).*



# Oil service

## 3 Engine oil and filter renewal

**1** Frequent oil and filter changes are the most important preventative maintenance work which can be undertaken by the DIY owner. As engine oil ages, it becomes diluted and contaminated, which leads to premature engine wear.

**2** Before starting this procedure, gather together all the necessary tools and materials. Also make sure you have plenty of clean rags and newspapers handy, to mop up any spills. Ideally, the engine oil should be warm, as it will drain better, and more built-up sludge will be removed with it. Take care, however, not to touch the exhaust or any other hot parts of the engine when working under the car. To avoid any possibility of scalding, and to protect yourself from possible skin irritants and other harmful contaminants in used engine oils, it is advisable to wear gloves. Access to the underside of the car will be improved if it can be raised on a lift, driven onto ramps, or jacked up and supported on axle stands (see *"Jacking and vehicle support"*). Whichever method is chosen, make sure the car remains level, or if it is at an angle, so that the drain plug is at the lowest point. Where necessary remove the splash guard from under the engine.

**3** Working in the engine compartment, locate the oil filter housing on the left-hand side of the engine, in front of the inlet manifold.

**4** Place a wad of rag around the bottom of the housing to absorb any spilt oil.

**5** Unscrew the through-bolt, then slowly remove the cover, and lift the filter cartridge out **(see illustrations)**. Note that some

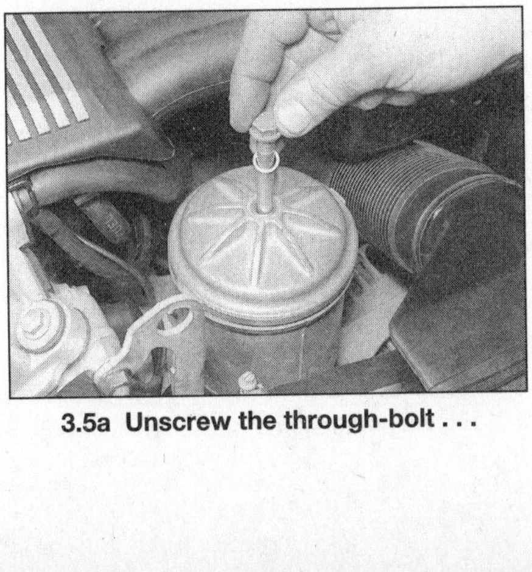

**3.5a Unscrew the through-bolt . . .**

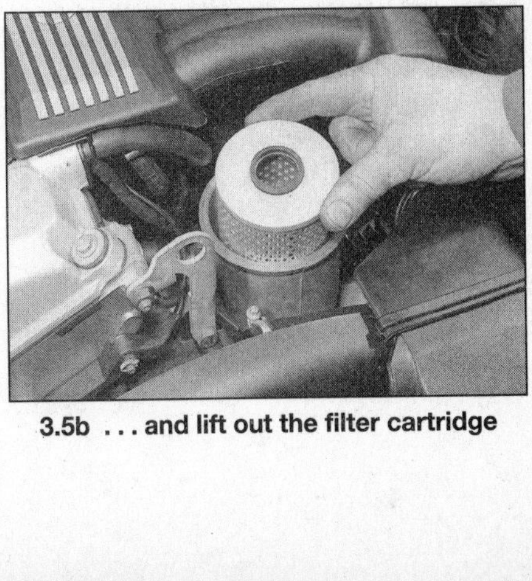

**3.5b . . . and lift out the filter cartridge**

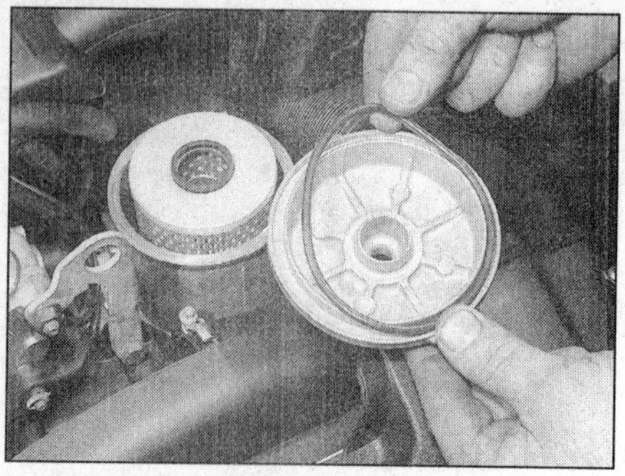

3.8a Fit a new O-ring to the cover . . .

3.8b . . . and to the through-bolt

HAYNES HiNT

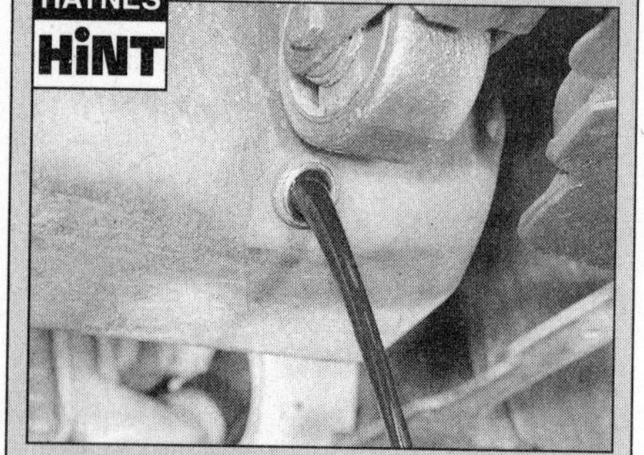

*Keep the drain plug pressed into the sump while unscrewing it by hand last couple of turns. As the plug releases, move it away sharply so the stream of oil issuing from the sump runs into the container, not up your sleeve!*

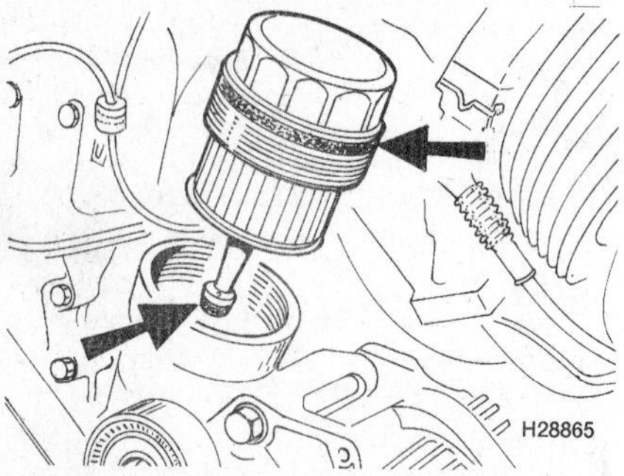


3.8c Fit new O-rings (arrowed) to the cover and through-bolt on M43 engines with a screw-fit cover

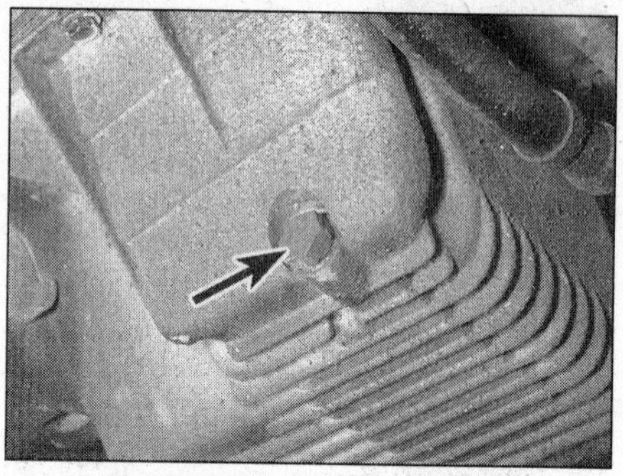

3.11 Sump drain plug (arrowed) - M42 4-cylinder engine shown

OIL CARE
FOLLOW THE CODE
OIL BANK LINE
0800 66 33 66

***Note:** It is antisocial and illegal to dump oil down the drain. To find the location of your local oil recycling bank, call this number free.*

M43 4-cylinder engines may have a screw-fit cover on the oil filter housing instead of a through-bolt. The oil will drain from the housing back into the sump as the cover is removed.

**6** Recover the O-rings from the cover, and from the bottom of the through-bolt.

**7** Using a clean rag, wipe the mating faces of the housing and cover.

**8** Fit new O-rings to the cover and the through-bolt **(see illustrations)**.

**9** Lower the new filter cartridge into the housing.

**10** Smear a little clean engine oil on the O-rings, then refit the cover, and refit and tighten the through-bolt, ensuring that the washer is in place under the bolt head.

**11** Working under the car, slacken the sump drain plug about half a turn **(see illustration)**. Position the draining container under the drain plug, then remove the plug completely. If possible, try to keep the plug pressed into the sump while unscrewing it by hand the last couple of turns.

**12** Recover the drain plug sealing ring.

**13** Allow some time for the old oil to drain, noting that it may be necessary to reposition the container as the oil flow slows to a trickle.

**14** After all the oil has drained, wipe off the drain plug with a clean rag. Check the sealing washer condition, and renew it if necessary. Clean the area around the drain plug opening, then refit and tighten the plug.

**15** Remove the old oil and all tools from under the car, then lower the car to the ground (if applicable).

**16** Remove the dipstick then unscrew the oil filler cap from the cylinder head cover. Fill the engine, using the correct grade and type of oil (see *"Weekly checks"*). An oil can spout or funnel may help to reduce spillage. Pour in half the specified quantity of oil first, then wait a few minutes for the oil to fall to the sump. Continue adding oil a small quantity at a time until the level is up to the lower mark on the dipstick. Finally, bring the level up to the upper mark on the dipstick. Insert the dipstick, and refit the filler cap.

**17** Start the engine and run it for a few minutes; check for leaks around the oil filter seal and the sump drain plug. Note that there may be a delay of a few seconds before the oil pressure warning light goes out when the engine is first started, as the oil circulates through the engine oil galleries and the new oil filter, before the pressure builds up.

**18** Switch off the engine, and wait a few minutes for the oil to settle in the sump once more. With the new oil circulated and the filter completely full, recheck the level on the dipstick, and add more oil as necessary.

**19** Dispose of the used engine oil safely, with reference to *"General repair procedures"* in the *Reference* section of this manual.

## 4 Resetting the service interval display

**Note:** *The following is for use with the special BMW service tool and adapter. If an aftermarket tool is being used, refer to the instructions supplied by its manufacturer.*

**1** Turn the ignition off, then plug BMW service interval resetting tool (No. 62 1 110) and adapter (No. 62 1 140) into the diagnostic socket.

**2** Ensure that all electrical items are switched off then turn on the ignition switch. **Note:** *Do not start the engine.*

**3** Press and hold the red Inspection button; the green (function check) light will illuminate. After about 3 seconds the red lamp should also light, remain on for about 12 seconds, and then go out. Release the Inspection button and the green (function check) light will go out.

**4** If the clock (annual service) symbol was illuminated at the same time as the oil service or inspection indicator, wait 10 seconds then repeat the operation in paragraph 3.

**5** Turn off the ignition switch and disconnect the resetting tool and adapter from the diagnostic connector.

**6** Turn the ignition switch on and check that the all service interval display green LEDs (the yellow and red LEDs may also light) and indicator illuminate and then go out.

# Inspection I

## 5 Automatic transmission fluid level check

### 4-speed transmission

#### Models with dipstick

**1** Since transmission fluid expands as it heats up, the fluid level should only be checked when the transmission is warm (at normal operating temperature). If the car has just been driven at least 20 miles (32 km), the transmission can be considered warm. ***Caution: If the car has just been driven for a long time at high speed or in city traffic, in hot weather, or if it has been used for towing, an accurate fluid level cannot be obtained. Allow the transmission to cool for about 30 minutes.***

**2** Immediately after driving the car, park it on a level surface, apply the handbrake and start the engine. While the engine is idling, depress the brake pedal and move the selector lever through all the gear positions, beginning and ending in "P".

**3** The automatic transmission fluid dipstick is located in the rear left-hand corner of the engine compartment.

**4** With the engine still idling, pull the dipstick out of the tube, wipe it off with a clean, lint-free cloth, push it all the way back into the tube, and withdraw it again, then note the fluid level.

**5** The level should be between the two marks **(see illustration)**. If the level is low, add the specified automatic transmission fluid through the dipstick tube - use a clean funnel, preferably equipped with a fine mesh filter, to prevent spills. ***Caution: Be careful not to introduce dirt into the transmission when topping up.***

**6** Add just enough of the recommended fluid to fill the transmission to the proper level. It takes about half a litre to raise the level from the low mark to the high mark when the fluid is hot, so add the fluid a little at a time, and keep checking the level until it is correct.

**7** On completion, stop the engine.

**8** The condition of the fluid should also be checked along with the level. If the fluid is black or a dark reddish-brown colour, or if it smells burned, it should also be renewed (see Section 23).

#### Models without dipstick

**Note:** *A new filler/level plug sealing ring will be required on refitting.*

**9** The fluid level is checked by removing the filler/level plug from the transmission fluid pan. If desired, jack up the car and support on axle stands (see "*Jacking and vehicle support*") to improve access, but make sure that the car is level.

**10** Proceed as described in paragraphs 1 and 2.

**11** Working under the car, place a container under the transmission fluid pan, then unscrew the filler/level plug **(see illustration)**. Recover the sealing ring.

**12** The fluid level should be up to the lower edge of the filler/level plug hole.

**13** If necessary, top-up the fluid until it overflows from the plug hole.

**14** The condition of the fluid should also be checked along with the level. If the fluid is black or a dark reddish-brown colour, or if it smells burned, it should also be renewed (see Section 23).

**15** Refit the filler/level plug, using a new sealing ring; tighten to the specified torque.

**16** Stop the engine and, where applicable, lower the car to the ground.

### 5-speed transmission

#### Models with dipstick

**17** Proceed as described for the 4-speed transmission in paragraphs 1 to 8.

#### Models without dipstick

**18** On models not fitted with a dipstick, checking of the automatic transmission fluid level should be referred to a BMW dealer.

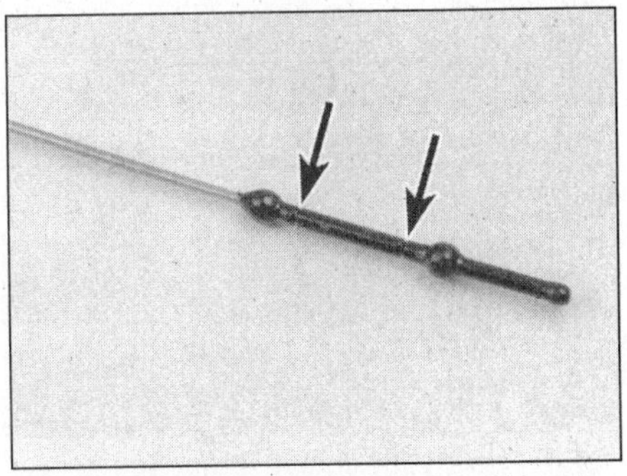

**5.5 Automatic transmission fluid level dipstick markings (arrowed)**

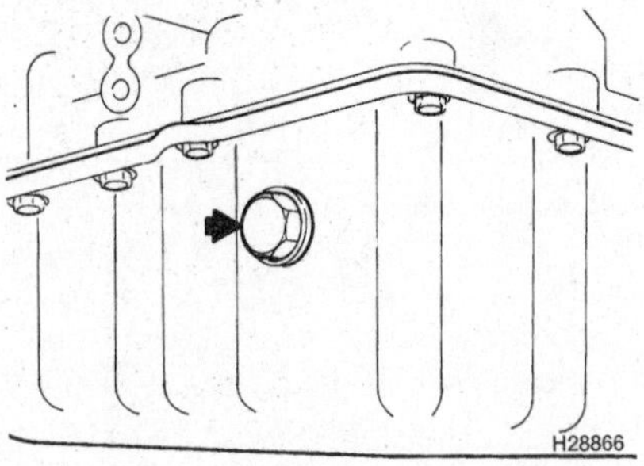


**5.11 Automatic transmission filler/level plug (arrowed)**

## 6 Hose and fluid leak check

**1** Visually inspect the engine joint faces, gaskets and seals for any signs of water or oil leaks. Pay particular attention to the areas around the camshaft cover, cylinder head, oil filter and sump joint faces. Bear in mind that, over a period of time, some very slight seepage from these areas is to be expected - what you are really looking for is any indication of a serious leak **(see Haynes Hint)**. Should a leak be found, renew the offending gasket or oil seal by referring to the appropriate Chapters in this manual.

**2** Also check the security and condition of all the engine-related pipes and hoses. Ensure that all cable-ties or securing clips are in place and in good condition. Clips which are broken or missing can lead to chafing of the hoses, pipes or wiring, which could cause more serious problems in the future.

**3** Carefully check the radiator hoses and heater hoses along their entire length. Renew any hose which is cracked, swollen or deteriorated. Cracks will show up better if the hose is squeezed. Pay close attention to the hose clips that secure the hoses to the cooling system components. Hose clips can pinch and puncture hoses, resulting in cooling system leaks.

**4** Inspect all the cooling system components (hoses, joint faces etc.) for leaks. A leak in the cooling system will usually show up as white- or rust-coloured deposits on the area adjoining the leak. Where any problems of this nature are found on system components, renew the component or gasket with reference to Chapter 3.

**5** Where applicable, inspect the automatic transmission fluid cooler hoses for leaks or deterioration.

**6** With the car raised, inspect the petrol tank and filler neck for punctures, cracks and other

HAYNES HiNT

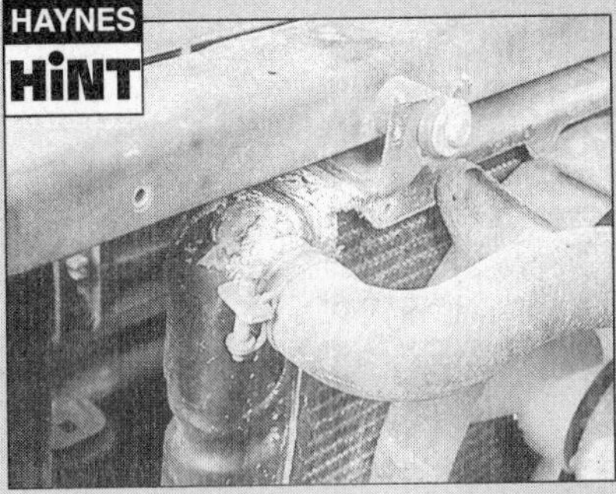

***A leak in the cooling system will usually show up as white - or rust - coloured deposits on the area adjoining the leak***

damage. The connection between the filler neck and tank is especially critical. Sometimes a rubber filler neck or connecting hose will leak due to loose retaining clamps or deteriorated rubber.

**7** Carefully check all rubber hoses and metal fuel lines leading away from the petrol tank. Check for loose connections, deteriorated hoses, crimped lines, and other damage. Pay particular attention to the vent pipes and hoses, which often loop up around the filler neck and can become blocked or crimped. Follow the lines to the front of the car, carefully inspecting them all the way. Renew damaged sections as necessary.

**8** Closely inspect the metal brake pipes which run along the car underbody. If they show signs of excessive corrosion or damage they must be renewed.

**9** From within the engine compartment, check the security of all fuel hose attachments and pipe unions, and inspect the fuel hoses and vacuum hoses for kinks, chafing and deterioration.

**10** Where applicable, check the condition of the power steering fluid hoses and pipes.

## 7 Auxiliary drivebelt(s) check and renewal

### *Drivebelt checking - general*

**1** Due to their function and construction, the belts are prone to failure after a period of time, and should be inspected periodically to prevent problems.

**2** The number of belts used on a particular car depends on the accessories fitted. Drivebelts are used to drive the coolant pump, alternator, power steering pump and air conditioning compressor.

**3** To improve access for belt inspection, if desired, remove the viscous cooling fan and cowl as described in Chapter 3.

**4** With the engine stopped, using your fingers (and a torch if necessary), move along the belts, checking for cracks and separation of the belt plies. Also check for fraying and glazing, which gives the belt a shiny appearance. Both sides of the belts should be inspected, which means the belt will have to be twisted to check the underside. If necessary turn the engine using a spanner or socket on the crankshaft pulley bolt to that the whole of the belt can be inspected.

### *M40 and M42 4-cylinder engines - drivebelt renewal*

#### Air conditioning compressor drivebelt

**5** Access is most easily obtained from under the car. If desired, jack up the front of the car and support securely on axle stands (see *"Jacking and vehicle support"*).

**6** Slacken the tensioner pulley bolt, and slide the drivebelt from the pulleys.

**7** Loosen the tensioner pulley bolt until the tensioner roller rotates smoothly with no friction.

**8** Fit the drivebelt round the pulleys, then engage a hexagon bit and torque wrench with the hexagon cut-out in the tensioner pulley and apply the specified torque (see Specifications) to the pulley. Tighten the tensioner pulley bolt **(see illustration)**.

**9** Where applicable, lower the car to the ground.

#### Power steering pump drivebelt

**10** Access is most easily obtained from under the car. If desired, jack up the front of the car and support securely on axle stands (see *"Jacking and vehicle support"*).

**11** Where applicable, remove the air conditioning compressor drivebelt as described previously in this Section.

**12** Loosen the power steering pump tensioner locknut, then turn the tensioner nut to slacken the drivebelt until it can be slid from the pulleys **(see illustration)**. If necessary, slacken the power steering pump mounting bolts to allow the pump to pivot.

**13** Engage the belt with the pulleys, then turn the tensioner nut to tension the drivebelt. As a guide, it should be possible to push the belt at the centre of the belt run between the power steering pump and crankshaft pulleys to give a deflection of approximately 2.0 mm under moderate finger pressure.

**14** When the drivebelt is correctly tensioned, tighten the tensioner locknut, and where applicable tighten the power steering pump mounting bolts.

**15** Where applicable, lower the car to the ground.

#### Alternator/coolant pump drivebelt

**16** Where applicable, remove the air conditioning compressor and/or power steering pump drivebelt(s), as described previously in this Section.

**17** If the drivebelt is to be re-used, mark the running direction of the belt before removal.

**18** To improve access, remove the viscous cooling fan and shroud as described in Chapter 3.

**19** Make a careful note of the routing of the drivebelt before removal.

**20** Loosen the nut at the rear of the alternator tensioner bolt, then turn the bolt as necessary to slacken the belt **(see illustration)**. If necessary slacken the lower alternator mounting bolt to allow the alternator to pivot.

**21** Slide the drivebelt from the pulleys.

**22** If the original belt is being refitted, observe the running direction mark made before removal.

**23** Engage the belt with the pulleys, ensuring that it is routed as noted before removal.

**24** Lever the tensioner bolt to tension the drivebelt. As a guide, it should be possible to push the belt at the centre of the belt run between the alternator and coolant pump pulleys to give a deflection of approximately 5.0 mm under moderate finger pressure.

**25** When the drivebelt is correctly tensioned, tighten the tensioner nut, and where applicable tighten the lower alternator mounting bolt.

**26** Refit the viscous cooling fan and shroud as described in Chapter 3.

**27** Where applicable, refit the air conditioning compressor and/or power steering pump drivebelt(s), as described previously in this Section.

### *M43 4-cylinder engine - drivebelt renewal*

#### Air conditioning compressor drivebelt

**28** Proceed as described for M40 and M42 engines in paragraphs 5 to 9.

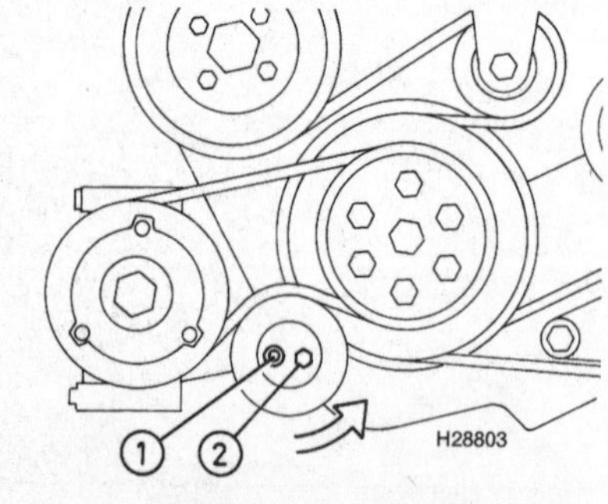


**7.8 Air conditioning compressor drivebelt tensioner - M40 and M42 4-cylinder engines**
*1 Pulley bolt 2 Hexagon cut-out*

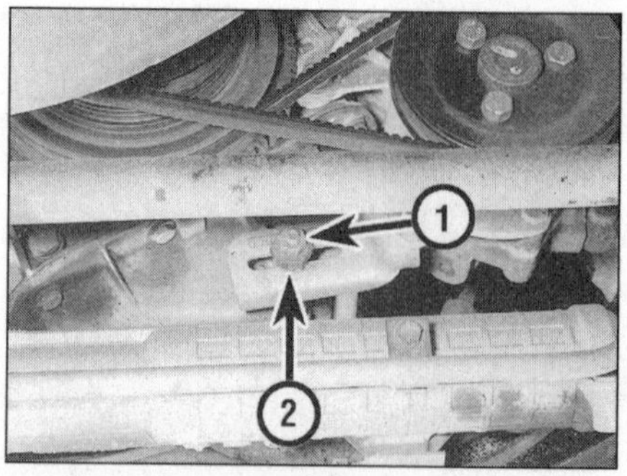


**7.12 Power steering pump drivebelt tensioner locknut (1) and tensioner nut (2) - M42 4-cylinder engine**

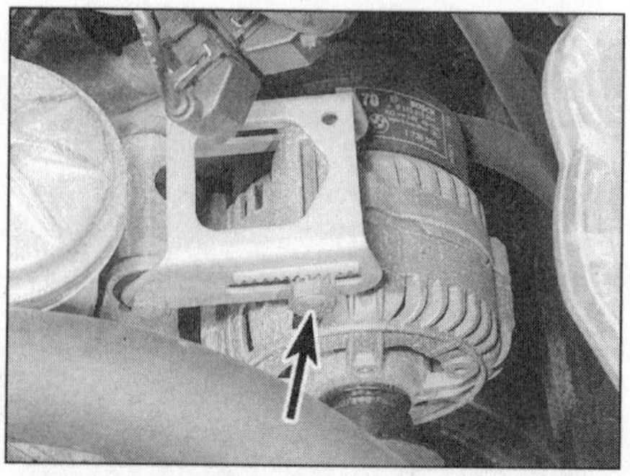

**7.20 Alternator/coolant pump drivebelt tensioner bolt (arrowed) - M42 4-cylinder engine**

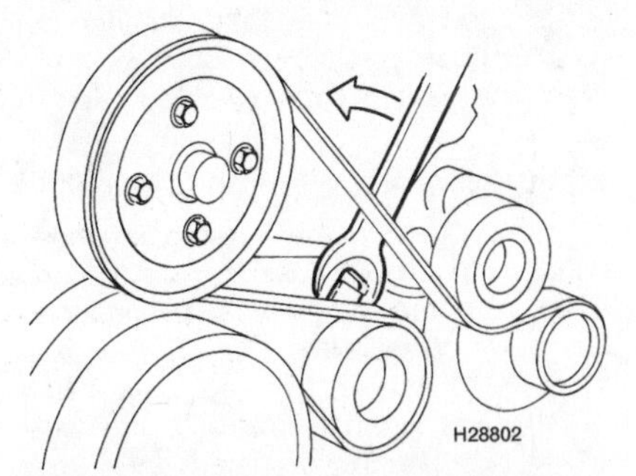


**7.31 Using a spanner engaged with the lug on the tensioner, compress the drivebelt tensioner piston - M43 engine with hydraulic belt tensioner**

### Coolant pump/alternator/ power steering pump drivebelt - models with hydraulic belt tensioner

**29** Where applicable, remove the air conditioning compressor drivebelt as described previously in this Section.
**30** Proceed as described in paragraphs 17 to 19.
**31** Using a spanner engaged with the lug on the tensioner, compress the tensioner piston (anti-clockwise), and slide the drivebelt from the pulleys **(see illustration)**.
**32** Release the tensioner once the drivebelt has been removed.
**33** If the original belt is being refitted, observe the running direction mark made before removal.
**34** Again, compress the tensioner, and engage the belt with the pulleys, ensuring that it is routed as noted before removal. Make sure that the belt engages correctly with the grooves in the pulleys.
**35** Refit the viscous cooling fan and shroud with reference to Chapter 3.
**36** Where applicable, refit the air conditioning compressor drivebelt as described previously in this Section.

### Coolant pump/alternator/power steering pump drivebelt - models with mechanical belt tensioner

**37** Where applicable, remove the air conditioning compressor drivebelt as described previously in this Section.

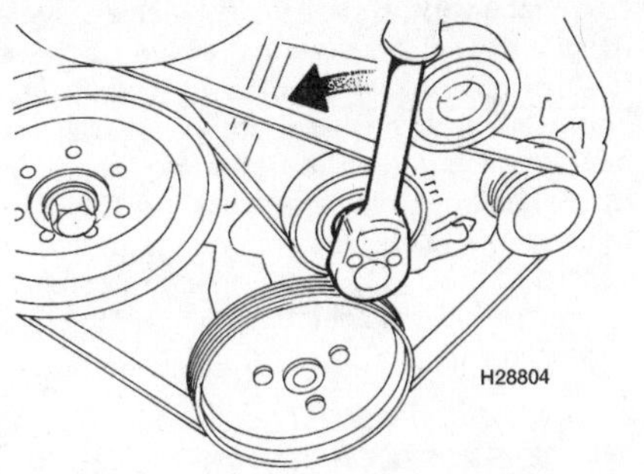


**7.40 Engage a hexagon key with the pulley bolt and lever anti-clockwise to compress the tensioner - M43 engine with mechanical belt tensioner**

**38** Proceed as described in paragraphs 17 to 19.
**39** Prise the cover from the centre of the tensioner pulley.
**40** Engage a hexagon key and extension bar with the pulley bolt, then lever the pulley (anti-clockwise) to compress the tensioner, and slide the drivebelt from the pulleys **(see illustration)**.
**41** If desired, to aid refitting the tensioner can be compressed fully and locked in position using a metal rod engaged with the holes in the tensioner and backplate - note that the tensioner has a powerful spring, so a strong rod will be required **(see illustration)**.
**42** If the original belt is being refitted, observe the running direction mark made before removal.
**43** If the tensioner has not been locked in position, compress the tensioner, and engage the belt with the pulleys, ensuring that it is routed as noted before removal. Make sure that the belt engages correctly with the grooves in the pulleys.
**44** Where applicable, compress the tensioner until the locking rod can be removed, then withdraw the rod and release the tensioner.
**45** Refit the viscous cooling fan and shroud with reference to Chapter 3.
**46** Where applicable, refit the air conditioning compressor drivebelt as described previously in this Section.

## 6-cylinder engine - drivebelt renewal

### Air conditioning compressor drivebelt

**47** Access is most easily obtained from under the car. If desired, jack up the front of the car and support securely on (see *"Jacking and vehicle support"*).
**48** Where applicable, prise the cover from the centre of the tensioner pulley.
**49** Engage a hexagon bit and extension bar with the tensioner bolt, and lever the tensioner clockwise **(see illustration)**. Slide the belt from the pulleys.
**50** Lever the tensioner until the drivebelt can be fitted around the pulleys, then release the tensioner. Ensure that the belt is engaged with the grooves in the pulleys.
**51** Where applicable, refit the pulley cover and lower the car to the ground.

### Coolant pump/alternator/ power steering pump drivebelt

**52** Where applicable, remove the air conditioning compressor drivebelt as described previously in this Section.
**53** Proceed as described in paragraphs 17 to 19.
**54** Prise the cover from the centre of the tensioner pulley.
**55** Engage a hexagon key and extension bar with the pulley bolt, then lever the pulley (anti-clockwise) to compress the tensioner, and slide the drivebelt from the pulleys **(see illustration)**.
**56** If the original belt is being refitted, observe the running direction mark made before removal.
**57** Compress the tensioner, and engage the belt with the pulleys, ensuring that it is routed as noted before removal. Make sure that the belt engages correctly with the grooves in the pulleys.
**58** Refit the viscous cooling fan and shroud with reference to Chapter 3.
**59** Where applicable, refit the air conditioning compressor drivebelt as described previously in this Section.

**7.41 Belt tensioner locked in position using metal rod (arrowed) - M43 engine with mechanical belt tensioner**

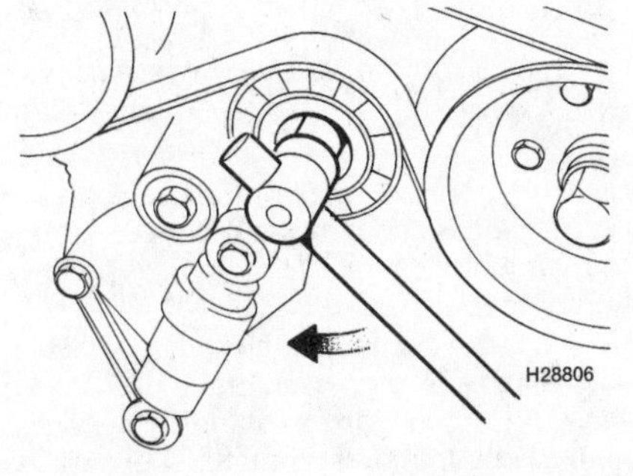


**7.49 Lever the air conditioning drivebelt tensioner clockwise - M50 engine**

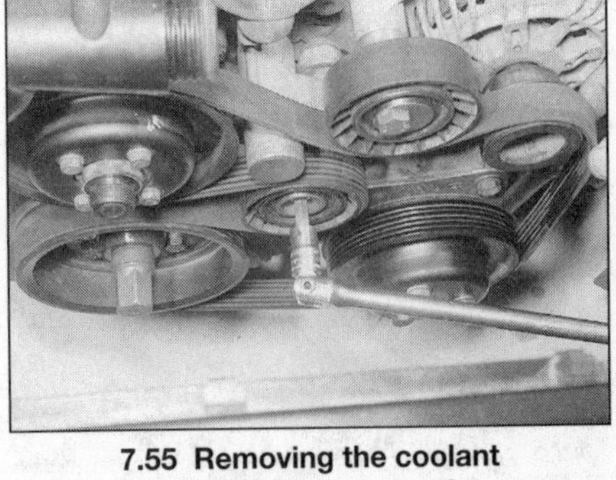

**7.55 Removing the coolant pump/alternator/power steering pump drivebelt - M50 engine**

## 8 Steering and suspension check

### Front suspension and steering check

**1** Raise the front of the car, and securely support it on axle stands (see "*Jacking and vehicle support*").

**2** Visually inspect the balljoint dust covers and the steering rack-and-pinion gaiters for splits, chafing or deterioration. Any wear of these components will cause loss of lubricant, then dirt and water entry, resulting in rapid deterioration of the balljoints or steering gear.

**3** On vehicles with power steering, check the fluid hoses for chafing or deterioration, and the pipe and hose unions for fluid leaks. Also check for signs of fluid leakage under pressure from the steering gear rubber gaiters, which would indicate failed fluid seals within the steering gear.

**4** Grasp the roadwheel at the 12 o'clock and 6 o'clock positions, and try to rock it **(see illustration)**. Very slight free play may be felt, but if the movement is appreciable, further investigation is necessary to determine the source. Continue rocking the wheel while an assistant depresses the footbrake. If the movement is now eliminated or significantly reduced, it is likely that the hub bearings are at fault. If the free play is still evident with the footbrake depressed, then there is wear in the suspension joints or mountings.

**5** Now grasp the wheel at the 9 o'clock and 3 o'clock positions, and try to rock it as before. Any movement felt now may again be caused by wear in the hub bearings or the steering track-rod balljoints. If the inner or outer balljoint is worn, the visual movement will be obvious.

**6** Using a large screwdriver or flat bar, check for wear in the suspension mounting bushes by levering between the relevant suspension component and its attachment point. Some movement is to be expected as the mountings are made of rubber, but excessive wear should be obvious. Also check the condition of any visible rubber bushes, looking for splits, cracks or contamination of the rubber.

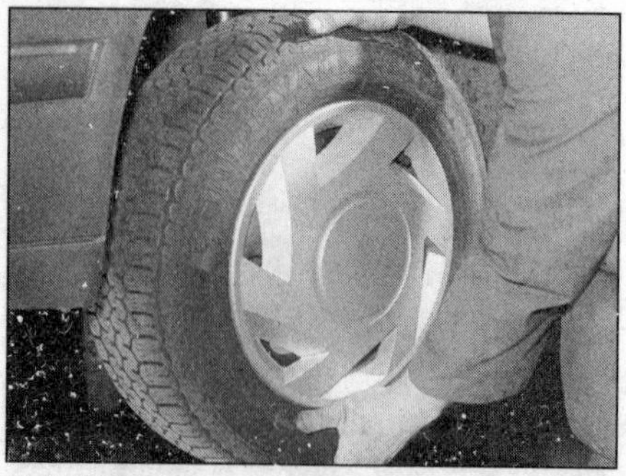

**8.4 Check for wear in the hub bearings by grasping the wheel and trying to rock it**

**7** With the car standing on its wheels, have an assistant turn the steering wheel back and forth about an eighth of a turn each way. There should be very little, if any, lost movement between the steering wheel and roadwheels. If this is not the case, closely observe the joints and mountings previously described, but in addition, check the steering column universal joints for wear, and the rack-and-pinion steering gear itself.

### Suspension strut/ shock absorber check

**8** Check for any signs of fluid leakage around the suspension strut/shock absorber body, or from the rubber gaiter around the piston rod. Should any fluid be noticed, the suspension strut/shock absorber is defective internally, and should be renewed. **Note:** *Suspension struts/shock absorbers should always be renewed in pairs on the same axle.*

**9** The efficiency of the suspension strut/shock absorber may be checked by bouncing the car at each corner. Generally speaking, the body will return to its normal position and stop after being depressed. If it rises and returns on a rebound, the suspension strut/shock absorber is probably suspect. Examine also the suspension strut/shock absorber upper and lower mountings for any signs of wear.

## 9 Front brake pad check

**1** Firmly apply the handbrake, then jack up the front of the car and support it securely on axle stands (see "*Jacking and vehicle support*"). Remove the front roadwheels.

**2** For a comprehensive check, the brake pads should be removed and cleaned. The operation of the caliper can then also be checked, and the condition of the brake disc itself can be fully examined on both sides. Refer to Chapter 9 for further information **(see Haynes Hint)**.

**3** If any pad's friction material is worn to the specified thickness or less, *all four pads must be renewed as a set.*

## 10 Rear brake pad check - models with rear disc brakes

**1** Chock the front wheels, then jack up the rear of the car and support it on axle stands (see "*Jacking and vehicle support*"). Remove the rear roadwheels.

**2** For a quick check, the thickness of friction material remaining on each brake pad can be measured through the top of the caliper body. If any pad's friction material is worn to the specified thickness or less, all four pads must be renewed as a set.

**3** For a comprehensive check, the brake pads should be removed and cleaned. This will permit the operation of the caliper to be checked, and the condition of the brake disc itself to be fully examined on both sides. Refer to Chapter 9 for further information.

HAYNES HiNT

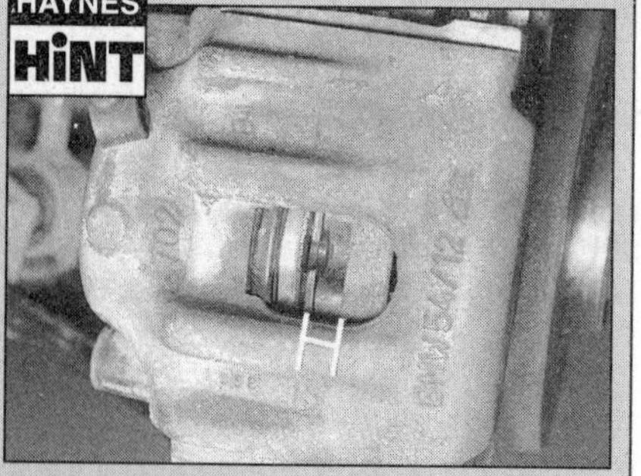

***For a quick check, the thickness of the friction material of the brake pad can be measured through the aperture in the caliper body***

## 11 Rear brake shoe check - models with rear drum brakes

**1** Chock the front wheels, then jack up the rear of the car, and support it securely on axle stands (see "*Jacking and vehicle support*").

**2** For a quick check, the thickness of friction material remaining on one of the brake shoes can be observed through the hole in the brake backplate which is exposed by prising out the sealing grommet **(see illustration)**. If a rod of the same diameter as the specified minimum friction material thickness is placed against the shoe friction material, the amount of wear can be assessed. A torch or inspection light will probably be required. If the friction material on any shoe is worn down to the specified minimum thickness or less, all four shoes must be renewed as a set.

**3** For a comprehensive check, the brake drum should be removed and cleaned. This will allow the wheel cylinders to be checked, and the condition of the brake drum itself to be fully examined (see Chapter 9).

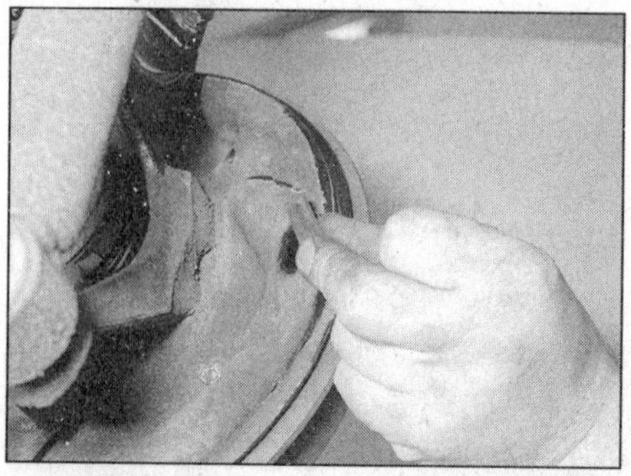

**11.2 Remove the rubber plug and check the brake friction material thickness through the back plate aperture (arrowed)**

## 12 Handbrake check

Check and, if necessary, adjust the handbrake as described in Chapter 9. Check that the handbrake cables are free to move easily and lubricate all exposed linkages/ cable pivots.

## 13 Exhaust system check

**1** With the engine cold (at least an hour after the car has been driven), check the complete exhaust system from the engine to the end of the tailpipe. The exhaust system is most easily checked with the car raised on a hoist, or suitably supported on axle stands, so that the exhaust components are readily visible and accessible.

**2** Check the exhaust pipes and connections for evidence of leaks, severe corrosion and damage. Make sure that all brackets and mountings are in good condition, and that all relevant nuts and bolts are tight **(see illustration)**. Leakage at any of the joints or in other parts of the system will usually show up as a black sooty stain in the vicinity of the leak.

**3** Rattles and other noises can often be traced to the exhaust system, especially the brackets and mountings. Try to move the pipes and silencers. If the components are able to come into contact with the body or suspension parts, secure the system with new mountings. Otherwise separate the joints (if possible) and twist the pipes as necessary to provide additional clearance.

## 14 Seat belt check

**1** Carefully examine the seat belt webbing for cuts or any signs of serious fraying or deterioration. If the seat belt is of the retractable type, pull the belt all the way out, and examine the full extent of the webbing.

**13.2 Check the condition of the exhaust mountings (arrowed)**

**2** Fasten and unfasten the belt, ensuring that the locking mechanism holds securely and releases properly when intended. If the belt is of the retractable type, check also that the retracting mechanism operates correctly when the belt is released.

**3** Check the security of all seat belt mountings and attachments which are accessible, without removing any trim or other components, from inside the car.

## 15 Hinge and lock lubrication

Lubricate the hinges of the bonnet, doors and tailgate with a light general-purpose oil. Similarly, lubricate all latches, locks and lock strikers. At the same time, check the security and operation of all the locks, adjusting them if necessary (see Chapter 11).

Lightly lubricate the bonnet release mechanism and cable with a suitable grease.

## 16 Pollen filter renewal

### *Model without air conditioning*

**1** Working in the engine compartment, remove the rubber seal from the top of the heating/ ventilation system inlet and release the grille from the inlet. On models where the grille is an integral part of the windscreen wiper motor cover panel, to improve access remove the wiper arms and remove the one-piece cover panel (see Chapter 12, Section 16).

**2** Undo the retaining screws and free the wiring harness duct from the inlet duct.

**3** Slacken and remove the retaining screws and retaining plate and remove the inlet from the bulkhead. **Note:** *On 6-cylinder engines it may be necessary to remove the injector and spark plug covers from the engine to enable the inlet to be removed.*

**4** Depress the retaining clips and remove the pollen filter(s) from the side of the blower motor housing.

**5** Clip the new filter(s) onto the housing and refit all disturbed components by reversing the removal procedure.

### *Models with air conditioning*

**6** Remove the heating/ventilation system control unit as described in Chapter 3.

**7** Undo the retaining screws then slide the driver's side lower facia panel to the side, to release its retaining clips, and remove it from the car.

**8** Unclip the air duct from the side of the air distribution housing.

**9** Undo the retaining screws and pivot the control unit mounting bracket forwards to gain access to the pollen filter housing.

**10** Release the retaining clip by rotating it anti-clockwise then remove the cover from the side of the air distribution housing and slide out the pollen filter.

**11** Install the new pollen filter then refit the cover, securing it in position with the retaining clip.

**12** Refit the control unit mounting bracket screws and tighten them securely.

**13** Refit the air duct and lower facia panel.

**14** Install the control unit as described in Chapter 3.

## 17 Headlight beam alignment check

Accurate adjustment of the headlight beam is only possible using optical beam-setting equipment, and this work should therefore be carried out by a BMW dealer or service station with the necessary facilities.

Basic adjustments can be carried out in an emergency, and further details are given in Chapter 12.

## 18 Windscreen/headlight washer system(s) check

Check that each of the washer jet nozzles are clear and that each nozzle provides a strong jet of washer fluid. The headlight jets should be aimed to spray at a point slightly above the centre of the screen/headlight. On the windscreen washer nozzles where there are two jets, aim one of the jets slightly above then centre of the screen and aim the other just below to ensure complete coverage of the screen. If necessary, adjust the jets using a pin.

## 19 Engine management system check

**1** This check is part of the manufacturer's maintenance schedule, and involves testing the engine management system using special dedicated test equipment. Such testing will allow the test equipment to read any fault codes stored in the electronic control unit memory.

**2** Unless a fault is suspected, this test is not essential, although it should be noted that it is recommended by the manufacturers.

**3** If access to suitable test equipment is not possible, make a thorough check of all ignition, fuel and emission control system components, hoses, and wiring, for security and obvious signs of damage. Further details of the fuel system, emission control system and ignition system can be found in Chapters 4 and 5.

## 20 Road test

### Instruments and electrical equipment

**1** Check the operation of all instruments and electrical equipment.

**2** Make sure that all instruments read correctly, and switch on all electrical equipment in turn, to check that it functions properly.

### Steering and suspension

**3** Check for any abnormalities in the steering, suspension, handling or road "feel".

**4** Drive the car, and check that there are no unusual vibrations or noises.

**5** Check that the steering feels positive, with no excessive "sloppiness", or roughness, and check for any suspension noises when cornering and driving over bumps.

### Drivetrain

**6** Check the performance of the engine, clutch (where applicable), gearbox/transmission and driveshafts.

**7** Listen for any unusual noises from the engine, clutch and gearbox/transmission.

**8** Make sure that the engine runs smoothly when idling, and that there is no hesitation when accelerating.

**9** Check that, where applicable, the clutch action is smooth and progressive, that the drive is taken up smoothly, and that the pedal travel is not excessive. Also listen for any noises when the clutch pedal is depressed.

**10** On manual gearbox models, check that all gears can be engaged smoothly without noise, and that the gear lever action is not abnormally vague or "notchy".

**11** On automatic transmission models, make sure that all gearchanges occur smoothly, without snatching, and without an increase in engine speed between changes. Check that all the gear positions can be selected with the car at rest. If any problems are found, they should be referred to a BMW dealer.

### Check the braking system

**12** Make sure that the car does not pull to one side when braking, and that the wheels do not lock prematurely when braking hard.

**13** Check that there is no vibration through the steering when braking.

**14** Check that the handbrake operates correctly without excessive movement of the lever, and that it holds the car stationary on a slope.

**15** Test the operation of the brake servo unit as follows. With the engine off, depress the footbrake four or five times to exhaust the vacuum. Hold the brake pedal depressed, then start the engine. As the engine starts, there should be a noticeable "give" in the brake pedal as vacuum builds up. Allow the engine to run for at least two minutes, and then switch it off. If the brake pedal is depressed now, it should be possible to detect a hiss from the servo as the pedal is depressed. After about four or five applications, no further hissing should be heard, and the pedal should feel much harder.

# Inspection II

## 21 Spark plug renewal

### General

**1** The correct functioning of the spark plugs is vital for the correct running and efficiency of the engine. It is essential that the plugs fitted are appropriate for the engine (the suitable type is specified at the beginning of this Chapter). If this type is used, and the engine is in good condition, the spark plugs should not need attention between scheduled replacement intervals. Spark plug cleaning is rarely necessary, and should not be attempted unless specialised equipment is available, as damage can easily be caused to the firing ends.

### M40 and M43 4-cylinder engines

**2** The spark plugs are located in the right-hand side of the cylinder head.

**3** On M43 engines, to improve access, if desired unbolt the ignition coil from the body, and move it to one side (refer to Chapter 5B if necessary).

**4** If the marks on the original-equipment spark plug (HT) leads cannot be seen, mark the leads 1 to 4, corresponding to the cylinder the lead serves (No 1 cylinder is at the timing belt/chain end of the engine). Pull the leads from the plugs by gripping the end fitting, not the lead, otherwise the lead connection may be fractured.

**5** It is advisable to remove the dirt from the spark plug recesses, using a clean brush, vacuum cleaner or compressed air before removing the plugs, to prevent dirt dropping into the cylinders.

**6** Unscrew the plugs using a spark plug spanner, suitable box spanner, or a deep socket and extension bar **(see illustration)**. Keep the socket aligned with the spark plug - if it is forcibly moved to one side, the ceramic insulator may be broken off. As each plug is removed, examine it as follows.

**7** Examination of the spark plugs will give a good indication of the condition of the engine. If the insulator nose of the spark plug is clean and white, with no deposits, this is indicative of a weak mixture or too hot a plug (a hot plug transfers heat away from the electrode slowly, a cold plug transfers heat away quickly).

**8** If the tip and insulator nose are covered with hard black-looking deposits, then this is indicative that the mixture is too rich. Should the plug be black and oily, then it is likely that the engine is fairly worn, as well as the mixture being too rich.

**9** If the insulator nose is covered with light tan to greyish-brown deposits, then the mixture is correct, and it is likely that the engine is in good condition.

**10** When buying new spark plugs, it is important to obtain the correct plugs for your specific engine (see Specifications).

**11** The spark plug electrode gap is of considerable importance as, if it is too large or too small, the size of the spark and its efficiency will be seriously impaired. The gap should be set to the value given in the Specifications at the beginning of this Chapter **(see illustration)**.

**12** To set the gap, measure it with a feeler blade, then bend the outer plug electrode until the correct gap is achieved **(see illustration)**. The centre electrode should never be bent, as this may crack the insulator and cause plug

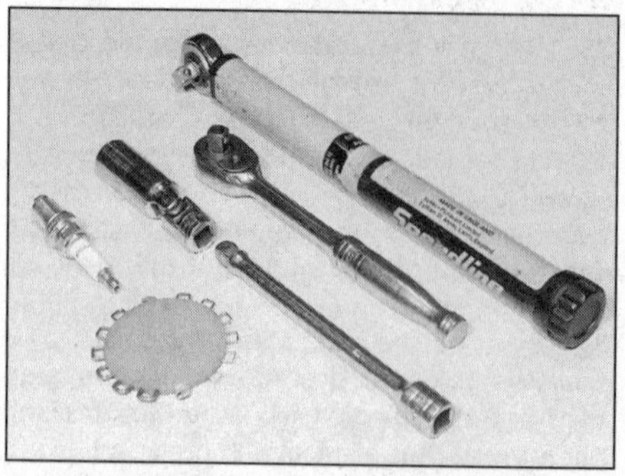

**21.6 Tools required for spark plug removal, gap adjustment and refitting**

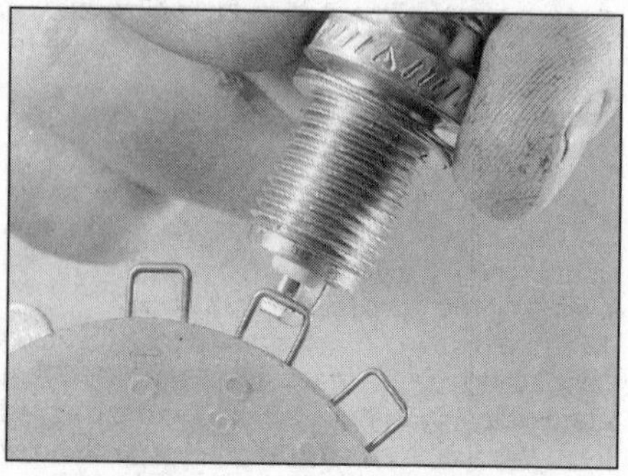

**21.11 Measuring the spark plug gap with a wire gauge**

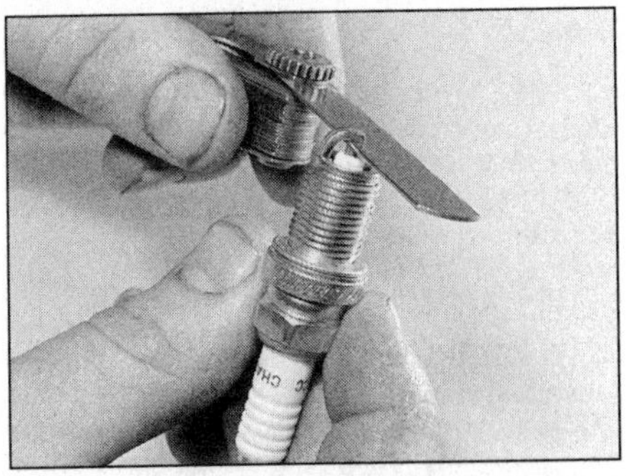

21.12 Measuring the spark plug gap with a feeler blade

21.18 Removing the spark plug cover - M42 engine

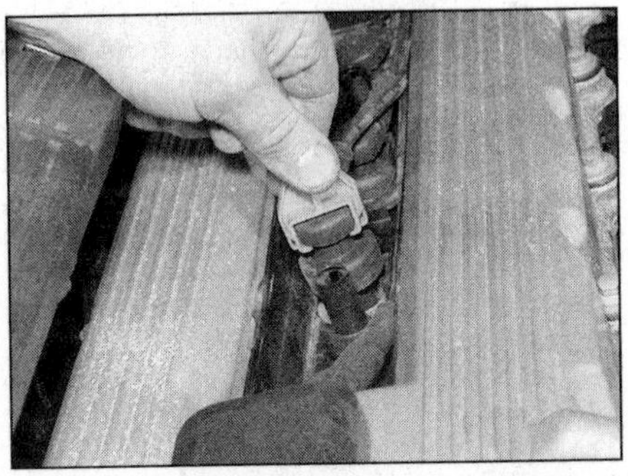

21.19 Pull the HT leads from the spark plugs using the tool provided - M42 engine

21.21 Unscrew the spark plugs using a spark plug spanner - M42 engine

HAYNES HINT

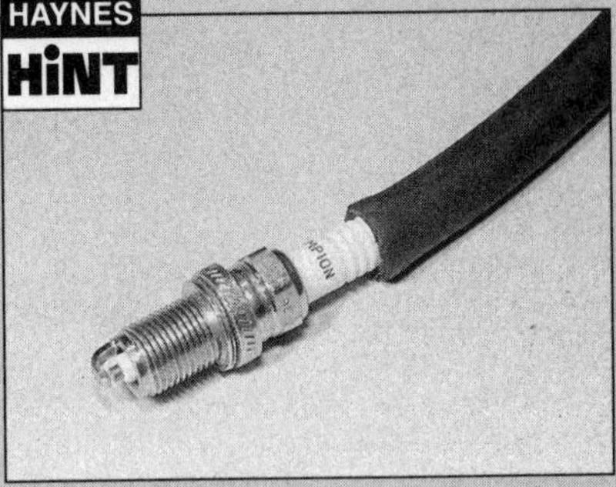

*It is often difficult to insert spark plugs into their holes without cross-threading them. To avoid this possibility, fit a short length of 5/16 inch internal diameter rubber hose over the end of the spark plug. The flexible hose acts as a universal joint to help align the plug with the plug hole. Should the plug begin to cross-thread, the hose will slip on the spark lug, preventing thread damage to the cylinder head.*

failure, if nothing worse. If using feeler blades, the gap is correct when the appropriate-size blade is a firm sliding fit.

**13** Special spark plug electrode gap adjusting tools are available from most motor accessory shops, or from some spark plug manufacturers.

**14** Before fitting the spark plugs, check that the threaded connector sleeves (on top of the plug) are tight, and that the plug exterior surfaces and threads are clean. It is very often difficult to insert spark plugs into their holes without cross-threading them. To avoid this possibility, fit a short length of hose over the end of the spark plug **(see Haynes Hint)**.

**15** Remove the rubber hose (if used), and tighten the plug to the specified torque (see *"Specifications"*) using the spark plug socket and a torque wrench. Refit the remaining plugs in the same way.

**16** Connect the HT leads in the correct order and, where applicable, refit the ignition coil.

## M42 4-cylinder engine

**17** The spark plugs are located under a cover in the centre of the cylinder head.

**18** Working at the top of the cylinder head cover, twist the two fasteners, and remove the spark plug cover from the centre of the cylinder head cover **(see illustration)**.

**19** If the marks on the spark plug (HT) leads cannot be seen, mark the leads 1 to 4, corresponding to the cylinder the lead serves (No 1 cylinder is at the timing belt/chain end of the engine). Using the plastic tool provided (clipped into the end of the HT lead plastic housing), pull the HT leads from the spark plugs **(see illustration)**.

**20** It is advisable to remove any dirt from the spark plug recesses, using a clean brush, vacuum cleaner or compressed air before removing the plugs, to prevent dirt dropping into the cylinders.

**21** Unscrew the plugs using a spark plug spanner, suitable box spanner, or a deep socket and extension bar **(see illustration)**. Keep the socket aligned with the spark plug - if it is forcibly moved to one side, the ceramic insulator may be broken off.

**22** Proceed as described in paragraphs 7 to 15.

**23** Connect the HT leads in their correct order, and clip the lead removal tool into position in its holder.

**24** Fit the spark plug cover, and secure with the fasteners.

## 6-cylinder engine

**25** The spark plugs are fitted under the ignition coils in the centre of the cylinder head.

**26** Remove the ignition coils (Chapter 5B).

**27** It is advisable to remove any dirt from the spark plug recesses, using a clean brush, vacuum cleaner or compressed air before removing the plugs, to prevent dirt dropping into the cylinders.

**28** Unscrew the plugs using a spark plug spanner, suitable box spanner, or a deep socket and extension bar **(see illustration)**. Keep the socket aligned with the spark plug - if it is forcibly moved to one side, the ceramic insulator may be broken off.

**29** Proceed as described in paragraphs 7 to 15.

**30** Refit the ignition coils (see Chapter 5B).

# 22 Air filter element renewal

## 4-cylinder engines

**1** The air cleaner assembly is located at the front left-hand corner of the engine compartment.

**2** Release the four securing clips, and lift off the air cleaner cover **(see illustration)**.

**3** Lift out the filter element **(see illustration)**.

**4** Wipe out the air cleaner housing and the cover.

**5** Lay the new filter element in position, then refit the cover and secure with the clips.

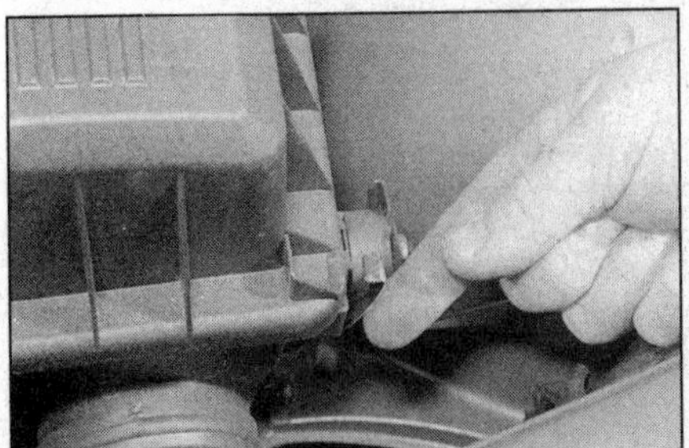

22.2 Releasing an air cleaner cover securing clip - 4-cylinder engine

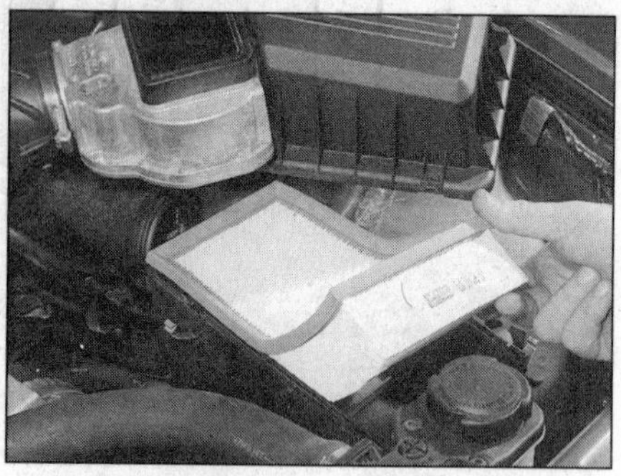

22.3 Lifting out the air filter element - 4-cylinder engine

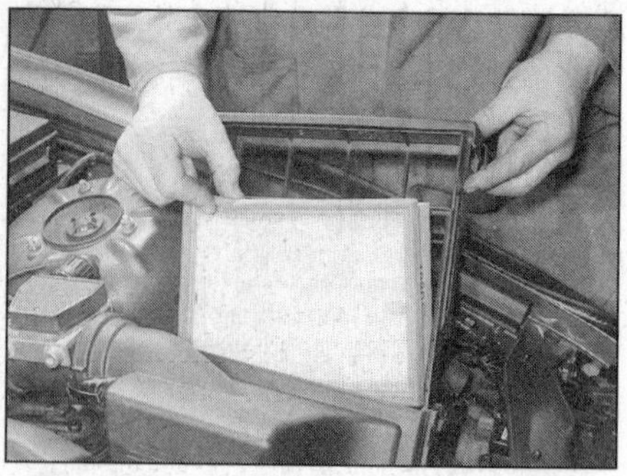

22.8 Lifting out the air cleaner element - 6-cylinder engine

### *6-cylinder engines*

**6** The air cleaner assembly is located at the front left-hand corner of the engine compartment.

**7** Depress the securing clips, and slide the filter element tray up from the housing.

**8** Lift out the filter element **(see illustration)**.

**9** Wipe out the air cleaner housing and the tray.

**10** Lay the new filter element in position, then slide the tray into the housing until it locks in position.

## 23 Automatic transmission fluid renewal

**Note:** *On models fitted with a 5-speed transmission without a dipstick, renewal of the transmission fluid should be entrusted to a BMW dealer, as special equipment is required to check the fluid level on completion.*

**Note:** *A new drain plug sealing ring will be required on refitting.*

**1** The transmission fluid should be drained with the transmission at operating temperature. If the car has just been driven at least 20 miles (32 km), the transmission can be considered warm.

**2** Immediately after driving the car, park it on a level surface, apply the handbrake. If desired, jack up the car and support on axle stands (see *"Jacking and vehicle support"*) to improve access, but make sure that the car is level.

**3** Working under the car, slacken the transmission fluid pan drain plug about half a turn **(see illustrations)**. Position a draining container under the drain plug, then remove the plug completely. If possible, try to keep the plug pressed into the fluid pan while unscrewing it by hand the last couple of turns.

> HAYNES HiNT
>
> ***As the plug releases from the threads, move it away sharply so the stream of fluid issuing from the fluid pan runs into the container, not up your sleeve!***

**4** Recover the sealing ring from the drain plug.

**5** Refit the drain plug, using a new sealing ring, and tighten to the specified torque.

**6** With reference to Section 5, fill the transmission with the specified quantity of the correct type of fluid (see Specifications) - fill the transmission through the dipstick tube or through the filler/level plug hole according to transmission type.

**7** Check the fluid level as described in Section 5, bearing in mind that the new fluid will not yet be at operating temperature.

**8** With the handbrake applied, and the transmission selector lever in position "P", start the engine and run it at idle for a few minutes to warm up the new fluid, then re-check the fluid level as described in Section 5. Note that it may be necessary to drain off a little fluid once the new fluid has reached operating temperature.

## 24 Final drive unit oil renewal

**1** Park the car on level ground.

**2** Locate the filler/level plug in the centre of the final drive unit rear cover. Unscrew the plug and recover the sealing washer.

**3** Place a suitable container beneath the final drive unit, then unscrew the drain plug from the base of the rear cover and allow the oil to drain. Recover the sealing washer.

**4** Inspect the sealing washers for signs of damage and renew if necessary.

**5** When the oil has finished draining, refit the drain plug and sealing washer and tighten it to the specified torque.

**6** Refill the final drive unit through the filler/level plug hole with the exact amount of the specified type of oil; this should bring the oil level up to the base of the filler/level plug hole. If the correct amount was poured into the transmission and a large amount flows out on checking the level, refit the filler/level plug and take the car on a short journey so that the new oil is distributed fully around the final drive components.

**7** On return, park on level ground and allow the car to stand for a few minutes. Unscrew the filler/level plug again. The oil level should reach the lower edge of the filler/level hole. To ensure a true level is established, wait until the initial trickle stops, then add oil as necessary until a trickle of new oil can be seen emerging. The level will be correct when the flow ceases; use only good-quality oil of the specified type.

**8** When the level is correct, refit the filler/level plug and sealing washer and tighten it to the specified torque.

## 25 Driveshaft gaiter check

With the car raised and securely supported on stands, slowly rotate the rear roadwheel. Inspect the condition of the outer constant velocity (CV) joint rubber gaiters, squeezing the gaiters to open out the folds **(see illustration)**. Check for signs of cracking,

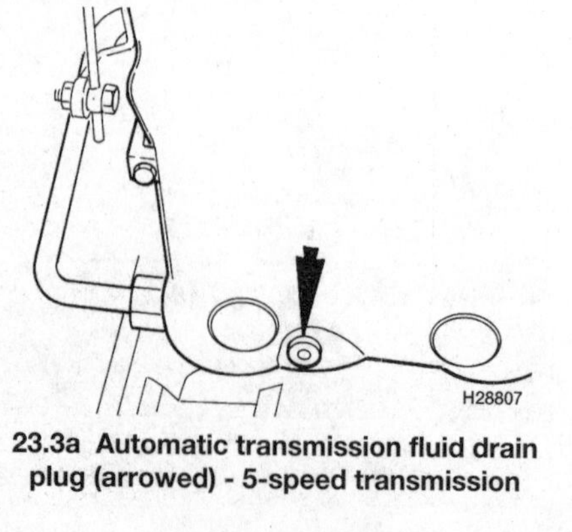


23.3a Automatic transmission fluid drain plug (arrowed) - 5-speed transmission

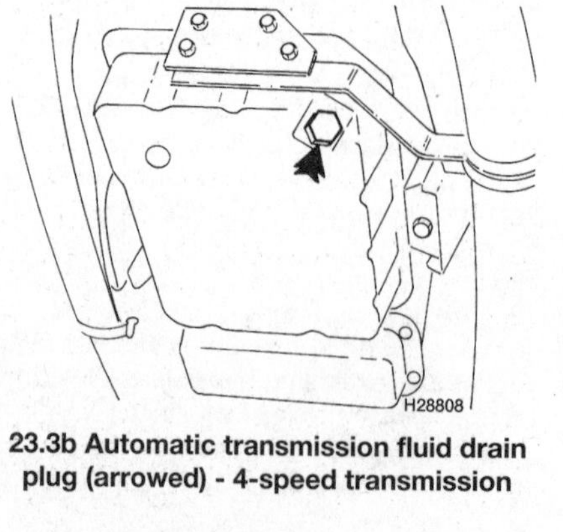


23.3b Automatic transmission fluid drain plug (arrowed) - 4-speed transmission

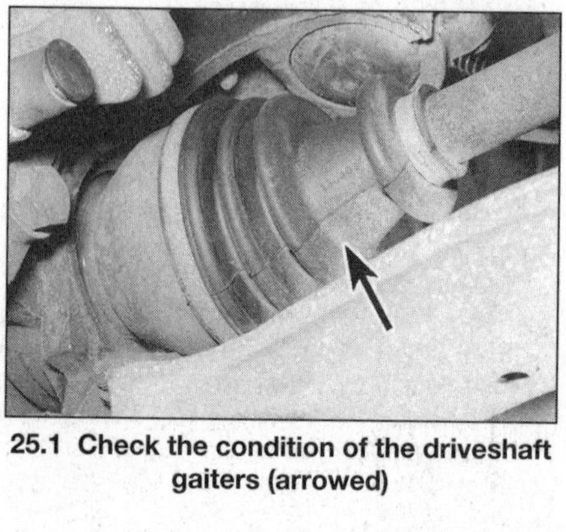

25.1 Check the condition of the driveshaft gaiters (arrowed)

splits or deterioration of the rubber, which may allow the grease to escape, and lead to water and grit entry into the joint. Also check the security and condition of the retaining clips. Repeat these checks on the inner CV joints. If any damage is found, the gaiters should be renewed (see Chapter 8).

At the same time, check the general condition of the CV joints themselves by first holding the driveshaft and attempting to rotate the wheel. Repeat this check by holding the inner joint and attempting to rotate the driveshaft. Any appreciable movement indicates wear in the joints, wear in the driveshaft splines, or a loose driveshaft retaining nut.

### 26 Handbrake shoe check - rear disc brake models

Referring to Chapter 9, remove the rear brake discs and inspect the handbrake shoes for signs of wear or contamination. Renew the shoes if necessary.

# Additional work to be carried out every second Inspection II

### 27 Manual gearbox oil renewal

**Note:** *New gearbox oil drain plug and oil filler/level plug sealing rings may be required on refitting.*

**1** The gearbox oil should be drained with the gearbox at normal operating temperature. If the car has just been driven at least 20 miles (32 km), the gearbox can be considered warm.

**2** Immediately after driving the car, park it on a level surface, apply the handbrake. If desired, jack up the car and support on axle stands (see *"Jacking and vehicle support"*) to improve access, but make sure that the car is level.

**3** Working under the car, slacken the gearbox oil drain plug about half a turn **(see illustration)**. Position a draining container under the drain plug, then remove the plug completely. If possible, try to keep the plug pressed into the gearbox while unscrewing it by hand the last couple of turns.

> **HAYNES HiNT** ***As the plug releases from the threads, move it away sharply so the stream of fluid from the gearbox runs into the container, not up your sleeve!***

**4** Where applicable, recover the sealing ring from the drain plug.

**5** Refit the drain plug, using a new sealing ring where applicable, and tighten to the specified torque.

**6** Unscrew the oil filler/level plug from the side of the gearbox, and recover the sealing ring, where applicable **(see illustration)**.

**7** Fill the gearbox through the filler/level plug hole with the specified quantity and type of oil (see Specifications), until the oil overflows from the filler/level plug hole.

**8** Refit the filler/level plug, using a new sealing ring where applicable, and tighten to the specified torque.

**9** Where applicable, lower the car to the ground.

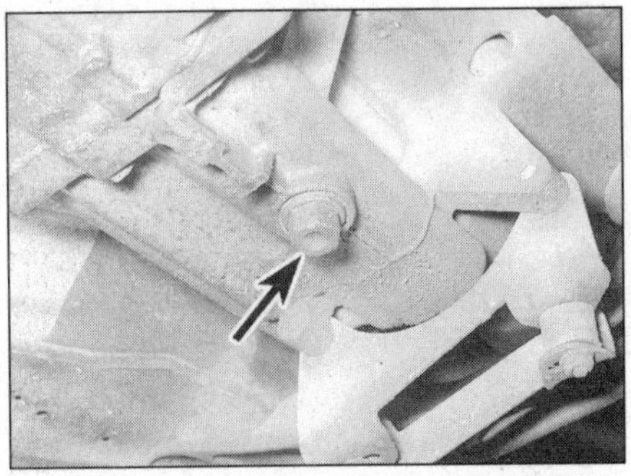

**27.3 Manual gearbox oil drain plug (arrowed)**

**27.6 Manual gearbox oil filler/level plug (arrowed)**

### 28 Fuel filter renewal

#### *4-cylinder engines*

**1** Depressurise the fuel system as described in Chapter 4A.

**2** The fuel filter is located under the car **(see illustration)**.

**3** Jack up the car and support on axle stands (see *"Jacking and vehicle support"*).

**4** Where applicable, remove the securing clips or nuts, and withdraw the fuel filter cover **(see illustration)**.

**5** If possible, clamp the fuel feed and return hoses to minimise fuel loss when the hoses are disconnected.

**6** Place a container under the filter to catch escaping fuel, then slacken the hose clips, and disconnect the fuel hoses from the filter.

**7** Slacken the clamp nut or bolt until the filter can be slid from its mounting clamp **(see illustration)**.

**8** Refitting is a reversal of removal, but make sure that the flow direction arrow on the filter points in the direction of fuel flow (ie, towards the engine), and on completion, pressurise the fuel system with reference to Chapter 4A **(see illustration)**.

1

**28.2 Fuel filter location (arrowed) - M42 4-cylinder engine**

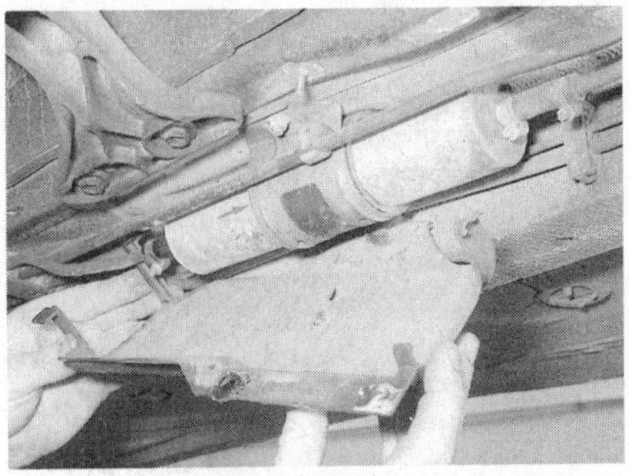

**28.4 Removing the fuel filter cover - M43 4-cylinder engine**

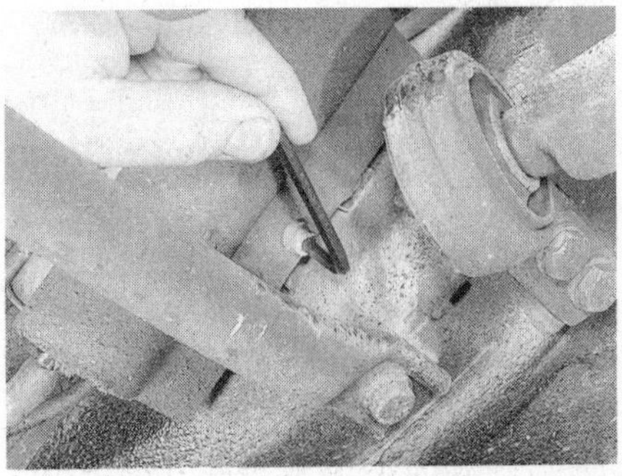

**28.7 Unscrewing the fuel filter clamp bolt - M42 engine**

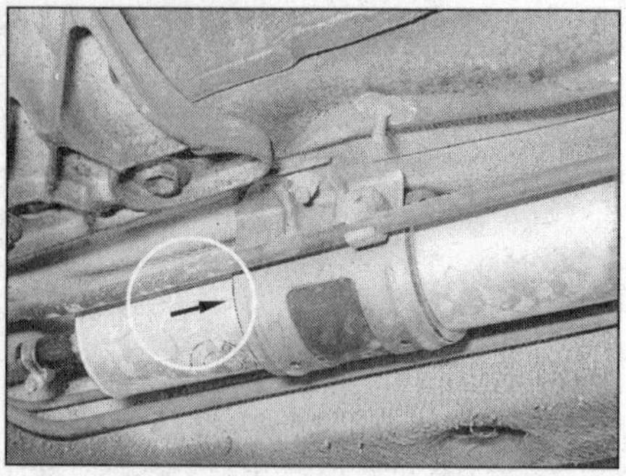

28.8 Ensure the flow arrow points in the direction of fuel flow - M43 engine shown

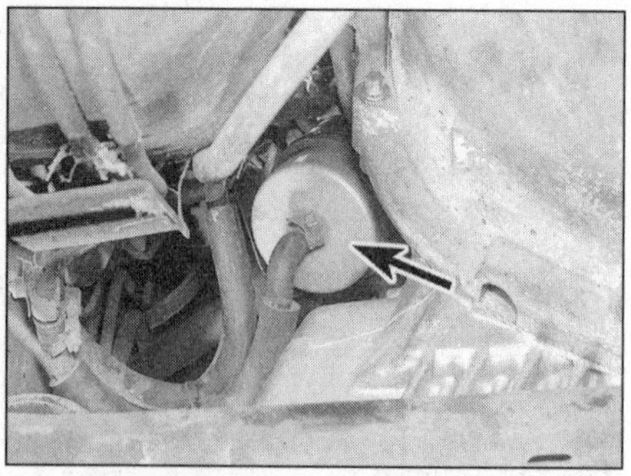

28.10 Fuel filter location (arrowed) seen from underneath - 6-cylinder engine

### *6-cylinder engine*

**9** Depressurise the fuel system (Chapter 4B).
**10** The fuel filter is located on a bracket bolted to the left-hand engine mounting **(see illustration)**.
**11** Working in the engine compartment, to improve access, remove the air trunking connecting the air mass meter to the throttle body, with reference to Chapter 4B if necessary.
**12** Locate the fuel filter outlet hose, which connects to the fuel pipe under the inlet manifold. Clamp the hose to minimise fuel spillage when the hose is disconnected, then slacken the hose clip and disconnect the hose from the pipe.
**13** Jack up the car and support on axle stands (see *"Jacking and vehicle support"*).
**14** Working under the car, locate the fuel filter inlet hose, which connects to the fuel supply pipe under the left-hand side of the car floor. As before, clamp the hose, then disconnect the hose from the pipe.
**15** Again working under the car, slacken the filter clamp bolt or nut, and slide the filter down from under the car.
**16** Disconnect the fuel hoses from the old filter, and fit them to the new filter.
**17** Refitting is a reversal of removal, but make sure that the flow direction arrow on the filter points in the direction of fuel flow (ie, towards the engine), and on completion, pressurise the fuel system with reference to Chapter 4B.

## 29 Clutch check

This check is specified by BMW to check the clutch friction disc for wear. The check involves the use of a special tool, which fits into the clutch slave cylinder aperture in the gearbox bellhousing, once the slave cylinder has been unbolted.

It is unlikely that the clutch wear will be significant unless the car has covered a high mileage, or the clutch has been abused.

If in doubt as to the condition of the clutch friction disc, have the check carried out by a BMW dealer.

## 30 Timing belt renewal - M40 engine

Refer to Chapter 2A.

# Annual service

## 31 Brake fluid renewal

***Warning: Brake hydraulic fluid can harm your eyes and damage painted surfaces, so use extreme caution when handling and pouring it. Do not use fluid that has been standing open for some time, as it absorbs moisture from the air. Excess moisture can cause a dangerous loss of braking effectiveness.***

**1** The procedure is similar to that for the bleeding of the hydraulic system as described in Chapter 9, except that the brake fluid reservoir should be emptied by siphoning, using a clean poultry baster or similar before starting, and allowance should be made for the old fluid to be expelled when bleeding a section of the circuit.
**2** Working as described in Chapter 9, open the first bleed screw in the sequence, and pump the brake pedal gently until nearly all the old fluid has been emptied from the master cylinder reservoir.
**3** Top-up to the "MAX" level with new fluid, and continue pumping until only the new fluid remains in the reservoir, and new fluid can be seen emerging from the bleed screw. Tighten the screw, and top the reservoir level up to the "MAX" level line.
**4** Work through all remaining bleed screws in the sequence until new fluid can be seen at all of them. Be careful to keep the master cylinder reservoir topped-up to above the "MIN" level at all times, or air may enter the system and increase the length of the task.

HAYNES HiNT ***Old hydraulic fluid is usually much darker in colour than the new, making it easy to distinguish the two.***

**5** When the operation is complete, check that all bleed screws are securely tightened, and that their dust caps are refitted. Wash off all traces of spilt fluid, and recheck the master cylinder reservoir fluid level.
**6** Check the operation of the brakes before taking the car on the road.

## 32 Coolant renewal

### *Cooling system draining*

***Warning: Wait until the engine is cold before starting this procedure. Do not allow antifreeze to come in contact with your skin, or with the painted surfaces of the car. Rinse off spills immediately with plenty of water. Never leave antifreeze lying around in an open container, or in a puddle in the driveway or on the garage floor. Children and pets are attracted by its sweet smell, but antifreeze can be fatal if ingested.***

**1** With the engine completely cold, cover the expansion tank cap with a wad of rag, and slowly turn the cap anti-clockwise to relieve the pressure in the cooling system (a hissing sound will normally be heard). Wait until any pressure in the system is released, then continue to turn the cap until it can be removed.
**2** On models where expansion tank is built into the radiator, unscrew the bleed screw from the top of the expansion tank.
**3** Where necessary, undo the retaining screws and remove the undercover from beneath the radiator.
**4** Position a suitable container beneath the drain plug on the base of the radiator. Unscrew the drain plug and allow the coolant to drain into the container.
**5** To fully drain the system, also unscrew the coolant drain plug from the right-hand side of the cylinder block and allow the remainder of the coolant to drain into the container.
**6** If the coolant has been drained for a reason other than renewal, then provided it is clean and less than two years old, it can be re-used, though this is not recommended.
**7** Once all the coolant has drained, refit the bleed screw to the radiator. Fit a new sealing

washer to the block drain plug and tighten it to the specified torque.

## Cooling system flushing

**8** If coolant renewal has been neglected, or if the antifreeze mixture has become diluted, then in time, the cooling system may gradually lose efficiency, as the coolant passages become restricted due to rust, scale deposits, and other sediment. The cooling system efficiency can be restored by flushing the system clean.

**9** The radiator should be flushed independently of the engine, to avoid unnecessary contamination.

### Radiator flushing

**10** To flush the radiator, disconnect the top and bottom hoses and any other relevant hoses from the radiator, with reference to Chapter 3.

**11** Insert a garden hose into the radiator top inlet. Direct a flow of clean water through the radiator, and continue flushing until clean water emerges from the radiator bottom outlet.

**12** If after a reasonable period, the water still does not run clear, the radiator can be flushed with a good proprietary cooling system cleaning agent. It is important that their manufacturer's instructions are followed carefully. If the contamination is particularly bad, insert the hose in the radiator bottom outlet, and reverse-flush the radiator.

### Engine flushing

**13** To flush the engine, remove the thermostat as described in Chapter 3, then temporarily refit the thermostat cover.

**14** With the top and bottom hoses disconnected from the radiator, insert a garden hose into the radiator top hose. Direct a clean flow of water through the engine, and continue flushing until clean water emerges from the radiator bottom hose.

**15** On completion of flushing, refit the thermostat and reconnect the hoses with reference to Chapter 3.

## Cooling system filling

**16** Before attempting to fill the cooling system, make sure that all hoses and clips are in good condition, and that the clips are tight and the radiator and cylinder block drain plugs are securely tightened. Note that an antifreeze mixture must be used all year round, to prevent corrosion of the engine components (see following sub-Section).

**32.17 Where the expansion tank is an integral part of the radiator, unscrew the bleed screw from the top of the tank**

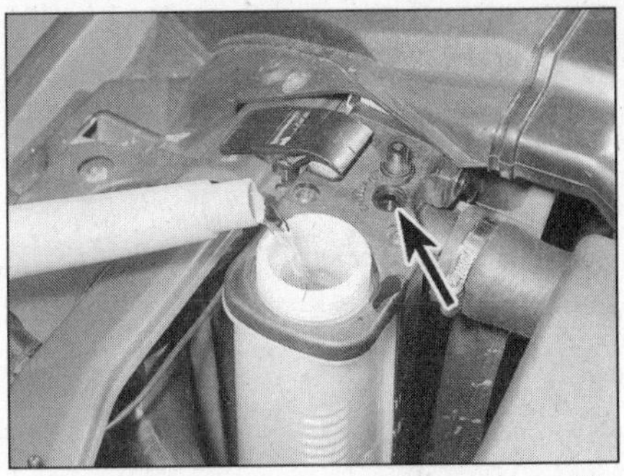

**32.21 Slowly fill the expansion tank until coolant free from air bubbles emerges from the bleed hole (arrowed) then refit the bleed screw**

**17** On models where expansion tank is built into the radiator, unscrew the bleed screw from the top of the expansion tank **(see illustration)**. On 4-cylinder models also slacken the bleed screw which is situated on the top of the thermostat housing.

**18** Remove the expansion tank filler cap and turn the heater temperature control knob to the maximum heat position. Fill the system by slowly pouring the coolant into the expansion tank to prevent airlocks from forming.

**19** If the coolant is being renewed, begin by pouring in a couple of litres of water, followed by the correct quantity of antifreeze, then top-up with more water.

**20** On 4 cylinder models, as soon as coolant free from air bubbles emerges from the thermostat housing screw, tighten the screw securely.

**21** Where the expansion tank is an integral part of the radiator, as coolant free from the air bubbles emerges from the radiator bleed hole, securely tighten the bleed screw **(see illustration)**.

**22** Once the level in the expansion tank starts to rise, squeeze the radiator top and bottom hoses to help expel any trapped air in the system. Once all the air is expelled, top-up the coolant level to the "MAX" mark and refit the expansion tank cap.

**23** Start the engine and run it until it reaches normal operating temperature, then stop the engine and allow it to cool.

**24** Check for leaks, particularly around disturbed components. Check the coolant level in the expansion tank, and top-up if necessary. Note that the system must be cold before an accurate level is indicated in the expansion tank. If the expansion tank cap is removed while the engine is still warm, cover the cap with a thick cloth, and unscrew the cap slowly to gradually relieve the system pressure (a hissing sound will normally be heard). Wait until any pressure remaining in the system is released, then continue to turn the cap until it can be removed.

## Antifreeze mixture

**25** The antifreeze should always be renewed at the specified intervals. This is necessary not only to maintain the antifreeze properties, but also to prevent corrosion which would otherwise occur as the corrosion inhibitors become progressively less effective.

**26** Always use an ethylene-glycol based antifreeze which is suitable for use in mixed-metal cooling systems. The quantity of antifreeze and levels of protection are indicated in the Specifications.

**27** Before adding antifreeze, the cooling system should be completely drained, preferably flushed, and all hoses checked for condition and security.

**28** After filling with antifreeze, a label should be attached to the expansion tank, stating the type and concentration of antifreeze used, and the date installed. Any subsequent topping-up should be made with the same type and concentration of antifreeze.

**29** Do not use engine antifreeze in the windscreen/tailgate washer system, as it will e damage the vehicle paintwork. A screenwash additive should be added to the washer system in the quantities stated on the bottle.

# Chapter 2 Part A:
# 4-cylinder engine in-car repair procedures

## Contents



## Degrees of difficulty

| | | | | |
|---|---|---|---|---|
| **Easy,** suitable for novice with little experience | **Fairly easy,** suitable for beginner with some experience | **Fairly difficult,** suitable for competent DIY mechanic | **Difficult,** suitable for experienced DIY mechanic | **Very difficult,** suitable for expert DIY or professional |



## Specifications

### General

| | |
|---|---|
| Engine code: | |
| 1.6 litre engine up to 1993 model year | M40 B16 |
| 1.6 litre engine from 1994 model year | M43 B16 |
| 1.8 litre single overhead camshaft engine up to 1993 model year | M40 B18 |
| 1.8 litre single overhead camshaft engine from 1994 model year | M43 B18 |
| 1.8 litre double overhead camshaft engine | M42 B18 |
| Displacement: | |
| 1.6 litre engines | 1596 cc |
| 1.8 litre engines | 1796 cc |
| Bore (all engines) | 84.000 mm |
| Stroke: | |
| 1.6 litre engines | 72.000 mm |
| 1.8 litre engines | 81.000 mm |
| Maximum engine power: | |
| 1.6 litre engines | 75 kW at 5500 rpm |
| 1.8 litre engines: | |
| M40 and M43 engines | 85 kW at 5500 rpm |
| M42 engine | 100 kW at 6000 rpm |
| Maximum engine torque: | |
| 1.6 litre engines: | |
| M40 engine | 143 Nm at 4250 rpm |
| M43 engine | 150 Nm at 3900 rpm |
| 1.8 litre engines: | |
| M40 engine | 165 Nm at 4250 rpm |
| M42 engine | 172 Nm at 4600 rpm |
| M43 engine | 168 Nm at 3900 rpm |
| Direction of engine rotation | Clockwise (viewed from front of vehicle) |
| No 1 cylinder location | Timing belt/chain end |
| Firing order | 1-3-4-2 |
| Minimum compression pressure | 10.0 to 11.0 bar |

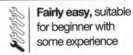

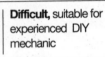

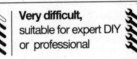

## General (continued)

| | | |
|---|---|---|
| Compression ratio: | | |
| 1.6 litre M40 engine | 9.0 : 1 | |
| 1.6 litre M43 engine and 1.8 litre M43 engine | 9.7 : 1 | |
| 1.8 litre M40 engine | 8.8 : 1 | |
| 1.8 litre M42 engine | 10.0 : 1 | |

## Camshafts

| | |
|---|---|
| Endfloat: | |
| M40 and M43 engines | 0.065 to 0.150 mm |
| M42 engine | 0.150 to 0.330 mm |
| Radial play (freeplay in bearings): | |
| M40 and M43 engines | 0.020 to 0.061 mm |
| M42 engines | 0.020 to 0.054 mm |

## Lubrication system

| | |
|---|---|
| Minimum oil pressure at idle speed: | |
| M40 and M43 engines | 0.5 bar |
| M42 engine | 1.3 to 2.0 bar |
| Oil pressure relief valve spring free-length | 84.1 mm |
| Oil pump rotor clearances: | |
| Outer rotor-to-pump body | 0.120 to 0.196 mm |
| Inner rotor endfloat | 0.020 to 0.065 mm |
| outer rotor endfloat | 0.040 to 0.090 mm |

## Torque wrench settings

| | Nm | lbf ft |
|---|---|---|
| Main bearing cap bolts (all engines): | | |
| Stage 1 | 20 | 15 |
| Stage 2 | Angle-tighten through a further 50° | |
| Cylinder head bolts*: | | |
| Stage 1 | 30 | 22 |
| Stage 2 | Angle-tighten through a further 90° | |
| Stage 3 | Angle-tighten through a further 90° | |
| Cylinder head cover bolts: | | |
| M6 bolts | 10 | 7 |
| M7 bolts | 15 | 11 |
| Sump oil drain plug: | | |
| M12 plug | 35 | 26 |
| M22 plug | 60 | 44 |
| Upper and lower timing chain cover nuts and bolts: | | |
| M6 nuts/bolts | 10 | 7 |
| M8 nuts/bolts | 22 | 16 |
| M10 nuts/bolts | 47 | 35 |
| Timing belt/chain housing bolts: | | |
| M6 bolts | 10 | 7 |
| M8 bolts | 22 | 16 |
| Crankshaft rear oil seal housing bolts: | | |
| M6 bolts | 10 | 7 |
| M8 bolts | 22 | 16 |
| Flywheel bolts* | 120 | 89 |
| Crankshaft vibration damper/pulley-to-hub bolts | 22 | 16 |
| Crankshaft pulley hub/sprocket bolt*: | | |
| M40 engine | 310 | 229 |
| M42 and M43 engines | 330 | 244 |
| Big-end bearing cap bolts*: | | |
| Stage 1 | 20 | 15 |
| Stage 2 | Angle-tighten through a further 70° | |
| Camshaft bearing cap nuts: | | |
| M6 nuts | 10 | 7 |
| M7 nuts | 15 | 11 |
| M8 nuts | 20 | 15 |
| Camshaft sprocket bolt (M40 engine) | 65 | 48 |
| Camshaft sprocket bolts (M42 and M43 engines): | | |
| M6 bolts | 10 | 7 |
| M7 bolts | 15 | 11 |
| Timing chain tensioner cover plug (M42 engine) | 50 | 37 |
| Oil pump cover | 10 | 7 |
| Front subframe bolts* | 105 | 77 |

**Use new bolts*

## 1 General information

### How to use this Chapter

This Part of Chapter 2 describes the repair procedures that can reasonably be carried out on the engine while it remains in the vehicle. If the engine has been removed from the vehicle and is being dismantled as described in Part C, any preliminary dismantling procedures can be ignored.

Note that, while it may be possible physically to overhaul items such as the piston/connecting rod assemblies while the engine is in the car, such tasks are not usually carried out as separate operations. Usually, several additional procedures are required (not to mention the cleaning of components and oilways); for this reason, all such tasks are classed as major overhaul procedures, and are described in Part C of this Chapter.

Part C describes the removal of the engine/transmission from the car, and the full overhaul procedures that can then be carried out.

### Engine description

All 4-cylinder engines are of overhead camshaft design, mounted in-line, with the transmission bolted to the rear end. Three types of 4-cylinder engine have been fitted to the model range. The M40 engine was available in 1.6 and 1.8 litre (single-overhead-camshaft) versions from the introduction of the 3-Series model range until 1993. From the 1994 model year, the M40 engine was superseded by the improved M43 engine. The M42 double-overhead-camshaft 1.8 litre engine is used in the 318iS Coupe models.

On M40 engines, a timing belt drives the single camshaft, and the valves are operated via hydraulic valve lifters and cam followers. The camshaft is supported by bearings machined directly in the cylinder head.

On M42 engines, a double timing chain drives the double overhead camshafts. Hydraulic cam followers are fitted between the camshafts and the valves. Each camshaft is supported by bearings incorporated in bearing castings fitted to the cylinder head.

On M43 engines, a timing chain drives the single camshaft, and the valves are operated via hydraulic valve lifters and cam followers. The camshaft is supported by bearings machined directly in the cylinder head.

The crankshaft is supported in five main bearings of the usual shell-type. Endfloat is controlled by thrust bearing shells on No 4 main bearing.

The pistons are selected to be of matching weight, and incorporate fully-floating gudgeon pins retained by circlips.

The rotor-type oil pump is located at the front of the engine, and is driven directly by the crankshaft.

### Repair operations possible with the engine in the vehicle

The following operations can be carried out without having to remove the engine from the vehicle:

*a) Removal and refitting of the cylinder head.*
*b) Removal and refitting of the timing belt/chain and sprockets.*
*c) Removal and refitting of the camshaft(s).*
*d) Removal and refitting of the sump.*
*e) Removal and refitting of the big-end bearings, connecting rods, and pistons*.*
*f) Removal and refitting of the oil pump.*
*g) Renewal of the engine/transmission mountings.*
*h) Removal and refitting of the flywheel/driveplate.*

** Although it is possible to remove these components with the engine in place, for reasons of access and cleanliness it is recommended that the engine is removed.*

## 2 Compression test - description and interpretation

**1** When engine performance is down, or if misfiring occurs which cannot be attributed to the ignition or fuel systems, a compression test can provide diagnostic clues as to the engine's condition. If the test is performed regularly, it can give warning of trouble before any other symptoms become apparent.

**2** The engine must be fully warmed-up to normal operating temperature, the battery must be fully charged, and all the spark plugs must be removed (Chapter 1). The aid of an assistant will also be required.

**3** Disable the ignition and fuel injection systems by removing the DME master relay, and the fuel pump relay, located in the main fuse box in the engine compartment (see Chapter 12).

**4** Fit a compression tester to the No 1 cylinder spark plug hole - the type of tester which screws into the plug thread is to be preferred.

**5** Have the assistant hold the throttle wide open, and crank the engine on the starter motor. After one or two revolutions, the compression pressure should build up to a maximum figure, and then stabilise. Record the highest reading obtained.

**6** Repeat the test on the remaining cylinders, recording the pressure in each.

**7** All cylinders should produce very similar pressures; a difference of more than 2 bars between any two cylinders indicates a fault. Note that the compression should build up quickly in a healthy engine; low compression on the first stroke, followed by gradually-increasing pressure on successive strokes, indicates worn piston rings. A low compression reading on the first stroke, which does not build up during successive strokes, indicates leaking valves or a blown head gasket (a cracked head could also be the cause). Deposits on the undersides of the valve heads can also cause low compression.

**8** BMW recommended values for compression pressures are given in the Specifications.

**9** If the pressure in any cylinder is low, carry out the following test to isolate the cause. Introduce a teaspoonful of clean oil into that cylinder through its spark plug hole, and repeat the test.

**10** If the addition of oil temporarily improves the compression pressure, this indicates that bore or piston wear is responsible for the pressure loss. No improvement suggests that leaking or burnt valves, or a blown head gasket, may be to blame.

**11** A low reading from two adjacent cylinders is almost certainly due to the head gasket having blown between them; the presence of coolant in the engine oil will confirm this.

**12** If one cylinder is about 20 percent lower than the others and the engine has a slightly rough idle, a worn camshaft lobe could be the cause.

**13** If the compression reading is unusually high, the combustion chambers are probably coated with carbon deposits. If this is the case, the cylinder head should be removed and decarbonised.

**14** On completion of the test, refit the spark plugs (see Chapter 1) and reconnect the fuel pump relay and the DME master relay.



## 3 Top Dead Centre (TDC) for No 1 piston - locating

**Note:** *To lock the engine in the TDC position, and to check the position of the camshafts, special tools will be required. These tools can easily be improvised - see text.*

**1** Top Dead Centre (TDC) is the highest point in the cylinder that each piston reaches as it travels up and down when the crankshaft turns. Each piston reaches TDC at the end of the compression stroke and again at the end of the exhaust stroke, but TDC generally refers to piston position on the compression stroke. No 1 piston is at the timing belt/chain end of the engine.

**2** Positioning No 1 piston at TDC is an essential part of many procedures, such as timing chain removal and camshaft removal.

**3** Proceed as follows according to engine type.

### M40 engine

**4** Remove the cylinder head cover as described in Section 4.

**5** Remove the cover plate to expose the camshaft.

**6** Note the position of the terminal for No 1 HT lead on the distributor cap. If the terminal is not marked, follow the HT lead from the No 1 cylinder spark plug to the cap (No 1

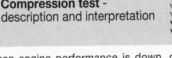

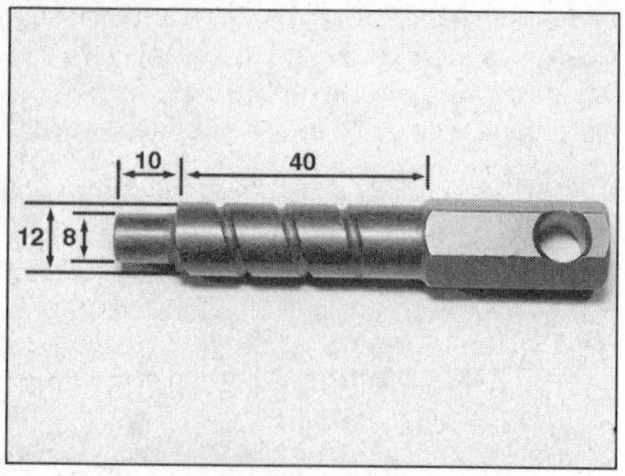


**3.11 Dimensions of flywheel "locking" tool**
*All dimensions in mm*

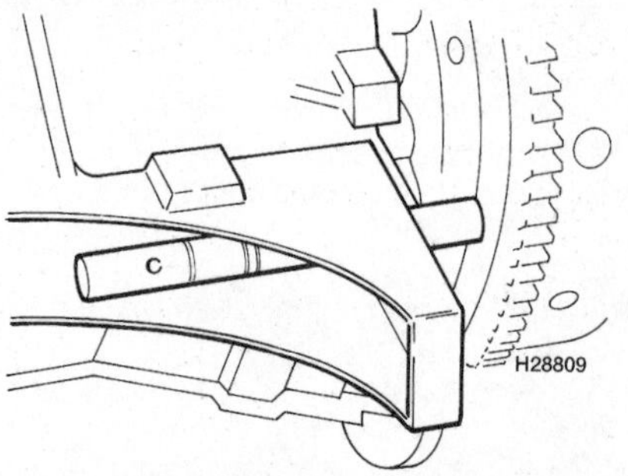


**3.12 Flywheel locking tool engaged with TDC hole in flywheel**

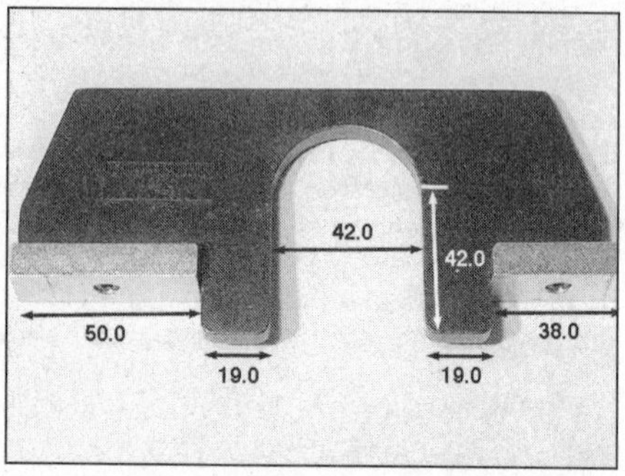


**3.15a Dimensions of camshaft locking template**
*All dimensions in mm*

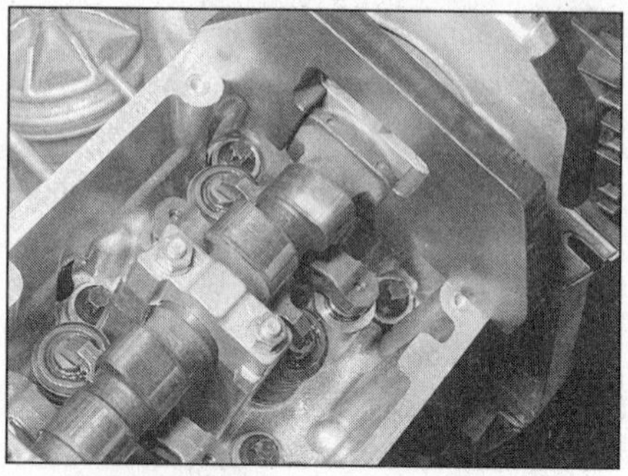

**3.15b Camshaft locking template in position on cylinder head - M40 engine**

cylinder is at the timing belt end of the engine).

**7** Remove the distributor cap with reference to Chapter 5B.

**8** Make a mark on the timing belt cover corresponding to No 1 terminal position in the distributor cap.

**9** Using a spanner or socket on the crankshaft pulley bolt (if desired, remove the viscous cooling fan and cowl, as described in Chapter 3, to improve access), turn the crankshaft clockwise until the rotor arm is approaching the mark made on the timing belt cover.

**10** Pull the blanking plug from the timing hole in the left-hand rear corner flange of the cylinder block.

**11** To "lock" the crankshaft in position, a special tool will now be required. BMW tool No 11 2 300 can be used, but an alternative can be made up by machining a length of steel rod to the dimensions shown **(see illustration)**.

**12** Insert the rod through the timing hole. If necessary, turn the crankshaft slightly until the rod enters the TDC hole in the flywheel **(see illustration)**.

**13** The crankshaft is now "locked" in position with No 1 piston at TDC.

**14** Note that with No 1 piston at TDC, the square flange at the front of the camshaft should be positioned with the sides of the flanges exactly at right-angles to the top surface of the cylinder head (this can be checked using a set-square), and the side of the flange with holes drilled into it uppermost.

**15** For some operations it is necessary to lock the camshaft in position with No 1 piston at TDC. This can be done by making up a template from metal sheet to the dimensions shown - when the camshaft is correctly positioned, the template will fit exactly over the flange at the front of the camshaft, and rest on the upper surface of the cylinder head. Note also that with No 1 piston at TDC, the valves for No 4 cylinder will be "rocking " - ie the valves will be open an equal amount, and therefore the No 4 cylinder cam lobes at the rear of the camshaft will be equally inclined upwards **(see illustrations)**.

**16 Do not** attempt to turn the engine with the flywheel or camshaft locked in position, as engine damage may result. If the engine is to be left in the "locked" state for a long period of time, it is a good idea to place suitable warning notices inside the vehicle, and in the engine compartment. This will reduce the possibility of the engine being cranked on the starter motor.

## *M42 engine*

**17** Remove the cylinder head cover as described in Section 4.

**18** Using a spanner or socket on the crankshaft pulley bolt (if desired, remove the viscous cooling fan and cowl, as described in Chapter 3, to improve access), turn the crankshaft clockwise until the timing arrows on the camshaft sprockets are pointing vertically upwards, and the front cam lobes on the exhaust and inlet camshafts are facing each other **(see illustration)**.

**19** Proceed as described for M40 engines in paragraphs 10 to 13.

**20** Note also that the square flanges on the rear of the camshafts should be positioned with the sides of the flanges exactly at right-angles to the top surface of the cylinder head (this can be checked using a set-square), and the side of the flange with holes drilled into it uppermost.

**21** For some operations it is necessary to lock the camshafts in position with No 1 piston at TDC. This can be done by making up a template from metal sheet to the dimensions shown - when the camshafts are correctly positioned, the template will fit exactly over the flanges at the rear of the camshafts, and rest on the upper surface of the cylinder head **(see illustrations)**.

**22** Refer to paragraph 16.

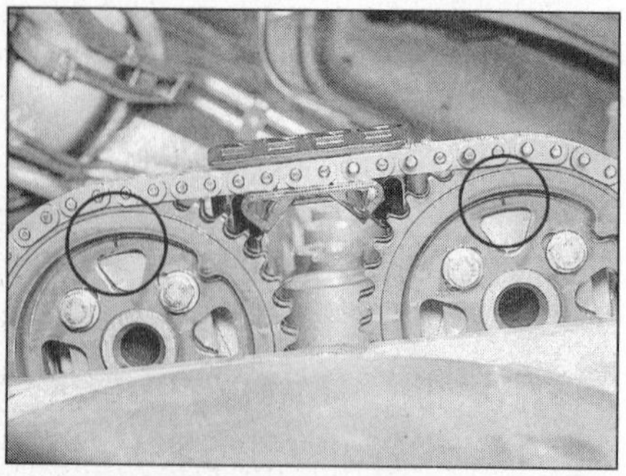

**3.18 Timing arrows on the camshaft sprockets positioned with No 1 piston at TDC - M42 engine**

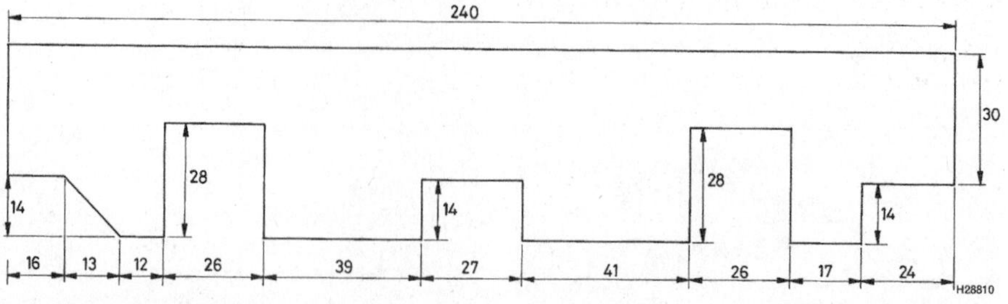


**3.21a Make up a template from metal sheet to the dimensions shown**
*All dimensions in mm*

**3.21b Camshaft locking template in position on cyiinder head - M42 engine**

**3.25 Timing arrow (A) on camshaft sprocket positioned with No 1 piston at TDC, and camshaft locking template (B) in position - M43 engine**

### *M43 engine*

**23** Remove the cylinder head cover (Section 4).

**24** Using a spanner or socket on the crankshaft pulley bolt (if desired, remove the viscous cooling fan and cowl, as described in Chapter 3, to improve access), turn the crankshaft clockwise until the timing arrow on the front of the camshaft sprocket is pointing vertically upwards.

**25** Proceed as described for M40 engines in paragraphs 10 to 16 **(see illustration)**.

## 4 Cylinder head cover - removal and refitting

### *M40 engine*

**Note:** *A new gasket may be needed on refitting.*

#### Removal

**1** Open the bonnet, then raise the bonnet to its fully open position, referring to Chapter 11.

**2** Remove the cover from the distributor cap then, using a screwdriver, carefully prise the HT lead ducting from the cylinder head cover.

**3** Loosen the hose clip, and disconnect the breather hose from the cylinder head cover.

**4** Ensure that all leads and hoses have been moved clear to allow removal of the cover, then unscrew the securing bolts, and lift the cylinder head cover from the engine.

#### Refitting

**5** Thoroughly clean the gasket faces of the cylinder head cover and the engine.

**6** Examine the cover gasket, and renew if necessary, then lay the gasket in position in the cylinder head cover.

**7** Refit the securing bolts and tighten to the specified torque.

**8** Further refitting is a reversal of removal.

### *M42 engines*

**Note:** *New gaskets and/or seals may be required on refitting - see text.*

#### Removal

**9** Open the bonnet, then raise the bonnet to its fully open position, referring to Chapter 11.

**10** Loosen the securing screws and remove the spark plug cover from the centre of the cylinder head cover.

**11** Pull the connectors from the spark plugs.

**12** Slacken the bolts securing the HT lead bracket to the edge of the cylinder head cover and recover the heat shield, then lift the complete HT lead housing/ducting assembly from the cylinder head cover **(see illustrations)**.

**13** Disconnect the breather hose from the cylinder head cover **(see illustration)**.

**14** Unscrew the securing bolts and lift the cylinder head cover from the engine **(see illustration)**. Recover the gaskets (note that there are separate gaskets at the centre of the cover for the spark plug holes).

#### Refitting

**15** Thoroughly clean the gasket faces of the cylinder head cover and the engine.

**16** Check the condition of the sealing rubbers on the cover securing bolts, and renew if necessary. Ensure that the washers and rubber seals are correctly fitted to the securing bolts.

**17** Examine the cover gaskets, and renew if necessary, then lay the gaskets in position on the cylinder head cover **(see illustration)**.

**18** Position the cover on the cylinder head,



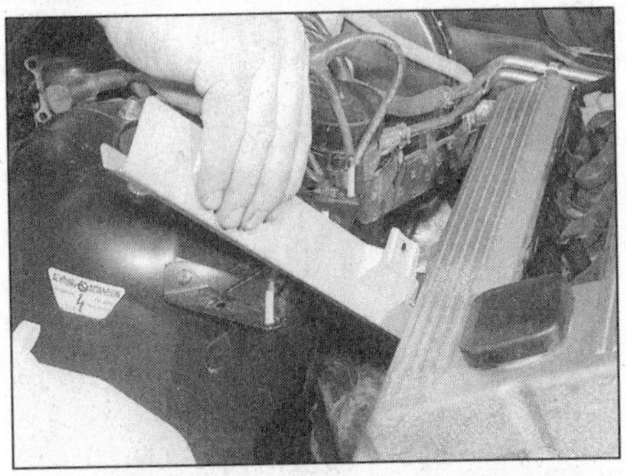

**4.12a Recover heat shield from the edge of the cylinder head cover - M42 engine**

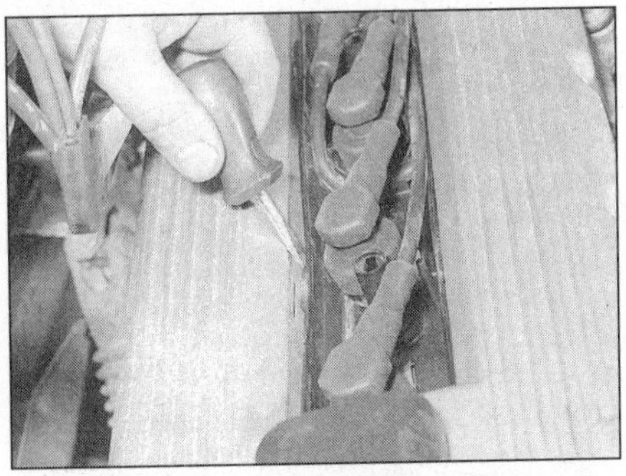

**4.12b Release the securing clips . . .**

**4.12c . . . and lift the complete assembly from the cylinder head cover - M42 engine**

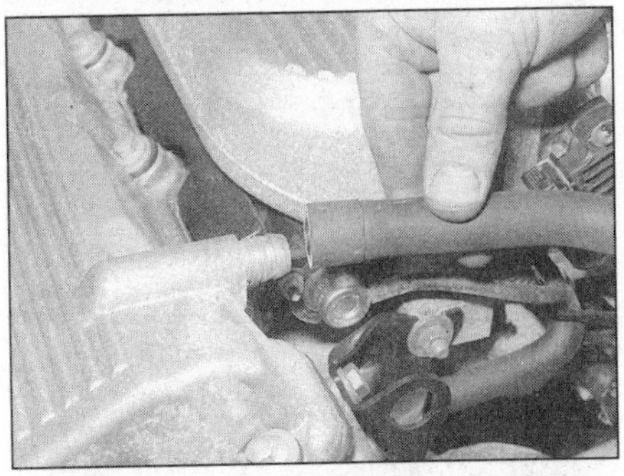

**4.13 Disconnect the breather hose from the cylinder head cover - M42 engine**

**4.14 Lifting off the cylinder head cover - M42 engine**

**4.17 Lay the gaskets in position on the cylinder head cover - M42 engine**

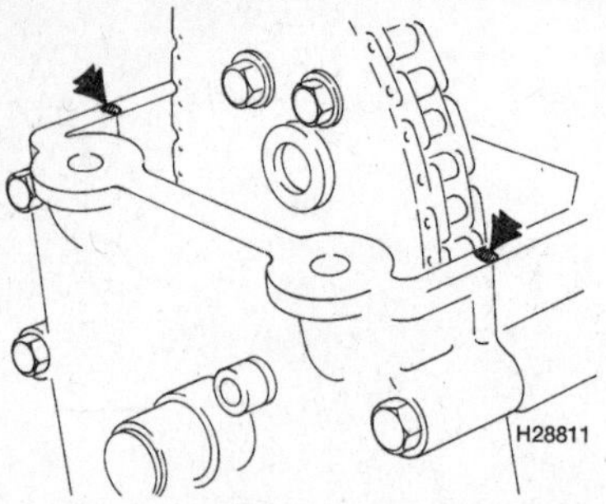


4.26 Apply jointing compound to the joint at the locations arrowed - M43 engine

ensuring that the lugs on the gasket engage with the corresponding cut-outs in the rear of the cylinder head.

**19** Refit the cover securing bolts and tighten to the specified torque.

**20** The remainder of the refitting procedure is a reversal of removal, ensuring that the HT leads are correctly reconnected.

## *M43 engine*

**Note:** *A new gasket and/or seals may be required on refitting - see text.*

### Removal

**21** Open the bonnet, then raise the bonnet to its fully open position, referring to Chapter 11.

**22** Unscrew the securing bolts and lift the cover from the cylinder head. Recover the gasket.

### Refitting

**23** Thoroughly clean the gasket faces of the cylinder head cover and the engine.

**24** Check the condition of the sealing rubbers on the cover securing bolts, and renew if necessary. Ensure that the washers and rubber seals are correctly fitted to the securing bolts.

**25** Examine the cover gasket, and renew if necessary, then lay the gasket in position in the cylinder head cover.

**26** Apply a little jointing compound to the cylinder head cover mating face of the joint between the upper timing chain cover and the cylinder head **(see illustration)**.

**27** Position the cover on the cylinder head, ensuring that the lug on the gasket engages with the corresponding cut-out in the rear of the cylinder head.

**28** Refit the cover securing bolts, and tighten to the specified torque.

# 5 Crankshaft vibration damper/pulley and pulley hub - removal and refitting

## *M40 engine*

### Removal

**1** To improve access, remove the viscous cooling fan and fan cowl assembly as described in Chapter 3.

**2** Remove the auxiliary drivebelt as described in Chapter 1.

**3** Unscrew the securing bolts, and remove the vibration damper/pulley from the hub. If necessary, counterhold the hub using a socket or spanner on the hub securing bolt.

**4** The hub is integral with the crankshaft timing belt sprocket, and removal and refitting are described in Section 8.

### Refitting

**5** Refitting is a reversal of removal, bearing in mind the following points.

a) *Ensure that the locating dowel on the hub/sprocket engages with the corresponding hole in the damper/pulley.*
b) *Tighten the vibration damper/pulley securing bolts to the specified torque.*
c) *Refit the auxiliary drivebelt with reference to Chapter 1.*
d) *Refit the viscous fan and fan cowl assembly as described in Chapter 3.*

## *M42 engine*

### Removal

**Note:** *If the pulley hub is removed, a new securing bolt will be required on refitting, and a torque wrench capable of providing 330 Nm (244 lbf ft) of torque will be required.*

**6** To improve access, remove the viscous cooling fan and fan cowl assembly as described in Chapter 3.

**7** Remove the auxiliary drivebelt as described in Chapter 1.

**8** Unscrew the securing bolts, and remove the vibration damper/pulley from the hub. If necessary, counterhold the hub using a socket or spanner on the hub securing bolt.

**9** To remove the hub, the securing bolt must be unscrewed.

***Warning: The crankshaft pulley hub securing bolt is very tight. A tool will be required to counterhold the hub as the bolt is unscrewed. Do not attempt the job using inferior or poorly-improvised tools, as injury or damage may result.***

**10** Make up a tool to hold the pulley hub. A suitable tool can be fabricated using two lengths of steel bar, joined by a large pivot bolt. Bolt the holding tool to the pulley hub using the pulley-to-hub bolts **(see illustration)**.

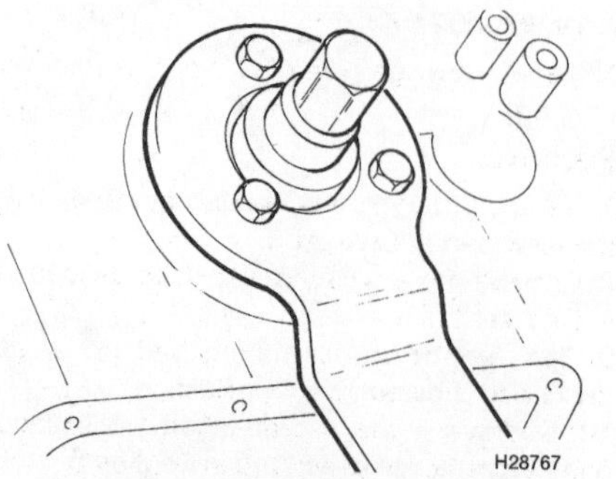


5.10 BMW special tool used to hold crankshaft pulley hub

**11** Using a socket and a long swing-bar, loosen the pulley hub bolt. Note that the bolt is very tight.

**12** Unscrew the pulley hub bolt, and remove the washer. Discard the bolt, a new one must be used on refitting.

**13** Withdraw the hub from the end of the crankshaft. If the hub is tight, use a puller to draw it off.

**14** Recover the Woodruff key from the end of the crankshaft if it is loose.

### Refitting

**15** If the pulley hub has been removed, it is advisable to take the opportunity to renew the oil seal in the lower timing chain cover, with reference to Section 10.

**16** If the pulley hub has been removed, proceed as follows, otherwise proceed to paragraph 20.

**17** Where applicable, refit the Woodruff key to the end of the crankshaft, then align the groove in the pulley hub with the key, and slide the hub onto the end of the crankshaft.

**18** Refit the washer, noting that the shoulder on the washer must face the hub, and fit a **new** hub securing bolt.

**19** Bolt the holding tool to the pulley hub, as during removal, then tighten the hub bolt to the specified torque. Take care to avoid injury and/or damage.

**20** Where applicable, unbolt the holding tool, and refit the vibration damper/pulley, ensuring that the locating dowel on the hub engages with the corresponding hole in the damper/pulley.

**21** Refit the damper/pulley securing bolts, and tighten to the specified torque. Again, counterhold the pulley if necessary when tightening the bolts.

**22** Refit the auxiliary drivebelt as described in Chapter 1.

**23** Refit the viscous cooling fan and cowl as described in Chapter 3.

## *M43 engine*

### Removal

**Note:** *If the pulley hub is removed, a new securing bolt will be required on refitting, and a torque wrench capable of providing 330 Nm (244 lbf ft) of torque will be required.*

**24** To improve access, remove the viscous cooling fan and fan cowl assembly as described in Chapter 3.

**25** Remove the auxiliary drivebelt(s) as described in Chapter 1.

**26** Some engines have a separate vibration damper/pulley which is bolted to a pulley hub, while some engines have a one-piece combined vibration damper/pulley and hub **(see illustration)**.

**27** On models with a separate vibration damper/pulley, unscrew the securing bolts, and remove the vibration damper/pulley from the hub. If necessary, counterhold the hub using a socket or spanner on the hub securing bolt.

**28** On models with a combined vibration

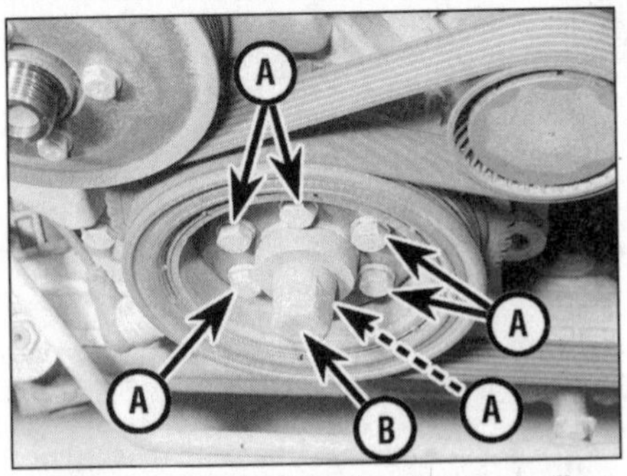


**5.26 Crankshaft vibration damper/pulley bolts (A) and hub bolt (B) - M42 engine with separate vibration damper/pulley and hub**

**6.5 Removing the upper timing belt cover - - M40 engine**

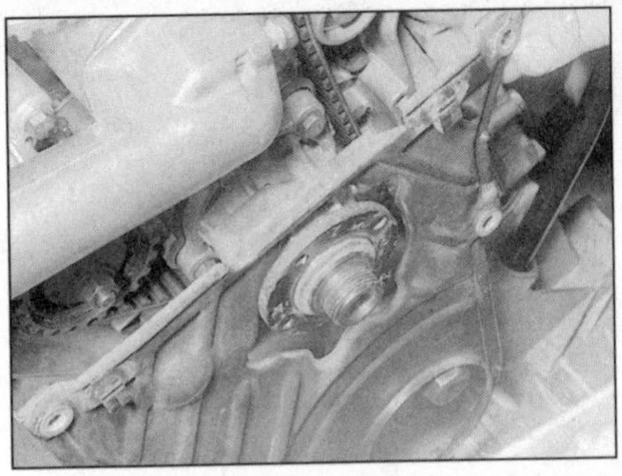

**6.12 Removing the lower timing belt cover - M40 engine**

damper/pulley and hub, or if the pulley hub is to be removed on models with a separate vibration damper/pulley, proceed as described for M42 engines in paragraphs 9 to 14. Note that it will be necessary to obtain suitable bolts to bolt the holding tool to the hub on models with a combined vibration damper/pulley and hub.

### Refitting

**29** On models with a combined vibration damper/pulley and hub, or if the pulley hub has been removed on models with a separate vibration damper/pulley, it is advisable to take the opportunity to renew the oil seal in the lower timing chain cover, with reference to Section 10.

**30** On models with a combined vibration damper/pulley and hub, or if the pulley hub has been removed on models with a separate vibration damper/pulley, proceed as follows, otherwise proceed to paragraph 35.

**31** Where applicable, refit the Woodruff key to the end of the crankshaft, then align the groove in the pulley hub with the key, and slide the hub onto the end of the crankshaft.

**32** Refit the washer, noting that the shoulder on the washer must face the hub, and fit a **new** hub securing bolt.

**33** Bolt the holding tool to the pulley hub, as during removal, then tighten the hub bolt to the specified torque. Take care to avoid injury and/or damage.

**34** On models with a combined vibration damper/pulley and hub, proceed to paragraph 37.

**35** Where applicable, unbolt the holding tool, and refit the vibration damper/pulley, ensuring that the locating dowel on the hub engages with the corresponding hole in the damper/pulley.

**36** Refit the damper/pulley securing bolts, and tighten to the specified torque. Again, counterhold the pulley if necessary when tightening the bolts.

**37** Refit the auxiliary drivebelt as described in Chapter 1.

**38** Refit the viscous cooling fan and cowl as described in Chapter 3.

## 6 Timing belt covers (M40 engine) - removal and refitting

### Upper cover

#### Removal

**1** If desired, to improve access, remove the viscous cooling fan and cowl as described in Chapter 3.

**2** Remove the distributor cap and rotor arm, as described in Chapter 5B.

**3** Unclip the plastic rotor arm housing from the timing belt cover.

**4** Where applicable, release the wiring from the timing belt cover, noting its routing, and move it clear of the working area. If necessary, remove the crankshaft position sensor, as described in Chapter 4A.

**5** Unscrew the securing bolts and remove the timing belt cover **(see illustration)**. Note the locations of the dowel sleeves.

#### Refitting

**6** Refitting is a reversal of removal, bearing in mind the following points

*a) Ensure that the dowel sleeves are in position in the cover as noted before removal.*

*b) Refit the rotor arm and distributor cap with reference to Chapter 5B.*

*c) Where applicable, refit the viscous cooling fan and cowl as described in Chapter 3.*

### Lower cover

**Note:** *A new gasket may be required on refitting.*

#### Removal

**7** Remove the viscous cooling fan and cowl as described in Chapter 3.

**8** Remove the auxiliary drivebelt as described in Chapter 1.

**9** Remove the upper timing belt cover as described previously in this Section.

**10** Remove the crankshaft vibration damper/pulley as described in Section 5.

**11** Where applicable, release the wiring from the timing belt cover, noting its routing, and move it clear of the working area. If necessary, remove the crankshaft position sensor, as described in Chapter 4A.

**12** Unscrew the securing bolts and remove the timing belt cover **(see illustration)**. Recover the gasket.

#### Refitting

**13** Examine the condition of the gasket, and renew if necessary.

**14** Place the gasket in position, then refit the cover and tighten the securing bolts.

**15** Where applicable, refit the crankshaft position sensor, and/or clip the wiring into position.

**16** Refit the crankshaft vibration damper/pulley as described in Section 5.

**17** Refit the upper timing belt cover as described previously in this Section.

**18** Refit the auxiliary drivebelt as described in Chapter 1.

**19** Refit the viscous cooling fan and cowl as described in Chapter 3.

2A

## 7 Timing belt (M40 engine) - removal, refitting and tensioning

**Note:** *BMW recommend that the timing belt is renewed every time that the tensioner roller is slackened. This means that the original belt should never be refitted.*

***Warning: It is essential to ensure that the timing belt is correctly tensioned after fitting, and it is strongly recommended that BMW special tool No 11 2 170 is used for this purpose - see text.***

### Removal

**1** Drain the cooling system as described in Chapter 1.

**2** Remove the upper and lower timing belt covers as described in Section 6.

**3** Position No 1 piston at TDC, and lock the flywheel in position, as described in Section 3.

***Warning: Once the crankshaft has been positioned with No 1 piston at TDC, do not rotate the crankshaft or camshaft until the timing belt has been refitted. If the***

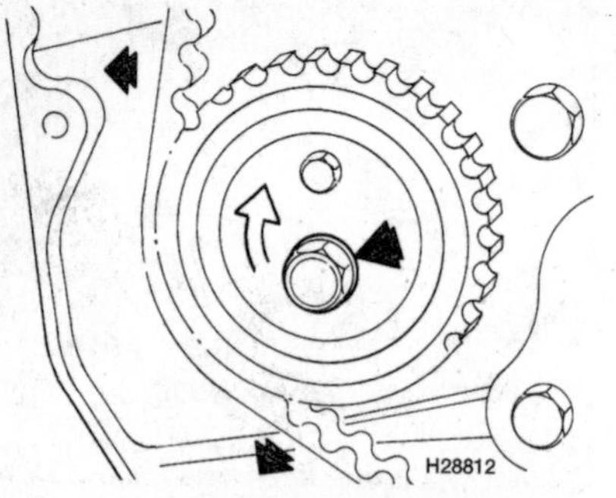


**7.7 Loosen the timing belt tensioner pulley retaining nut (arrowed) - M40 engine**

**7.13 Using the BMW special tool to check the tension of the timing belt - M40 engine**

***crankshaft or camshaft is rotated with the timing belt removed, the valves could hit the pistons causing expensive engine damage.***

**4** With the flywheel locked at TDC, make alignment marks on the camshaft sprocket and the timing belt housing to ensure correct alignment on refitting.

**5** Remove the thermostat as described in Chapter 3.

**6** Loosen the camshaft sprocket bolt. If necessary counterhold the crankshaft sprocket bolt to prevent the engine from turning as the camshaft sprocket bolt is loosened. Note that the camshaft sprocket will slide in the locating groove once the bolt is loosened.

**7** Loosen the tensioner pulley retaining nut, and use an Allen key to rotate the tensioner clockwise **(see illustration)**. This will relieve the tension in the timing belt. Tighten the retaining nut to hold the tensioner in its free position.

**8** Slide the timing belt from the sprockets and tensioner pulley **(see illustration)**.

### *Refitting and tensioning*

**9** Commence refitting by turning the camshaft sprocket as far as possible within its locating groove, then tighten the sprocket bolt to an initial torque of 1 to 3 Nm.

**10** Refit the timing belt over the sprockets and pulleys, starting with the crankshaft sprocket, and finishing with the idler and tensioner pulleys.

**11** Fit the template to lock the camshaft in

**7.8 Sliding the timing belt from the camshaft sprocket - M40 engine**

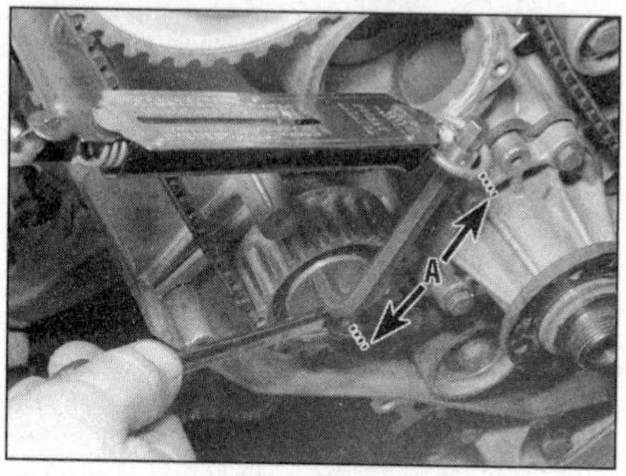


**7.14 Using a spring balance and Allen key to adjust timing belt tension - M40 engine**
*Dimension A = 85.0 mm*

position with No 1 piston at TDC, as described in Section 3.

**12** Loosen the tensioner pulley retaining nut, then use an Allen key to rotate the tensioner anti-clockwise to tension the timing belt.

***Warning: It is important that the timing belt is tensioned correctly. If the belt is over-tightened, it will howl, and there is the possibility of damage to the belt. If the belt is too slack, it may jump on the sprockets, causing expensive engine damage.***

**13** To achieve the correct belt tension, it is strongly recommended that the appropriate BMW tensioning tool No 11 2 170 is obtained. This tool should be used to set the belt tension in conjunction with a temperature gauge - at 20°C, the belt should be tensioned to give a reading on the gauge of 32 ± 2 units. Belt tensioning using the BMW tensioning tool should not be carried out if the engine surface temperature is less than 20°C **(see illustration)**.

**14** A reasonably accurate alternative to the BMW special tool can be improvised using an Allen key and a spring balance **(see illustration)**. Make sure that the spring balance is positioned as shown, since the tensioner pulley is mounted on an eccentric, and different readings will be obtained if the spring balance is moved. The spring balance hook should be positioned 85.0 mm from the end of the Allen key, and a force of 2.0 kg should be applied.

**15** With the belt correctly tensioned, tighten the tensioner pulley retaining nut to the specified torque, then tighten the camshaft sprocket bolt to the specified torque. Prevent the engine from turning using a socket or spanner on the crankshaft sprocket bolt - do not rely solely on the flywheel locking tool.

**16** Remove the tools locking the flywheel and camshaft in position then, using a socket or spanner on the crankshaft sprocket bolt, turn the crankshaft through two complete turns in the normal direction of rotation.

***Warning: It is now necessary to repeat the tensioning procedure. This is necessary to stretch the new belt - if not done, the belt will be too slack, and engine damage may result.***

**17** Refit the flywheel locking tool and the template to lock the camshaft in position, then repeat the tensioning procedure described in paragraphs 12 to 15.

**18** Check that the marks made on the camshaft sprocket and the timing belt housing are still in alignment.

**19** Remove the flywheel locking tool and the template used to lock the camshaft in position.

**20** Refit the thermostat as described in Chapter 3.

**21** Refit the timing belt covers as described in Section 6.

**22** Refill the cooling system as described in Chapter 1.

## 8 Timing belt sprockets and tensioner (M40 engine) - removal and refitting

### *Camshaft sprocket*

#### Removal

**1** Remove the timing belt as described in Section 7.

**2** Fully unscrew the camshaft sprocket bolt, then withdraw the sprocket from the camshaft **(see illustration)**.

**3** Note that the sprocket is not fixed in position on the camshaft using a key. The groove in the end of the camshaft allows the sprocket to move several degrees in either direction. The securing bolt locks the sprocket onto a taper.

**8.2 Removing the camshaft sprocket - M40 engine**

8.10 Removing the crankshaft sprocket bolt - M40 engine

8.11 Removing the crankshaft sprocket - M40 engine

8.17 Removing the timing belt tensioner pulley - M40 engine

### Refitting

4 Position the sprocket on the end of the camshaft, aligning the marks made on the sprocket and the timing belt housing (see Section 7).
5 Refit the sprocket securing bolt, but do not tighten at this stage.
6 Refit and tighten the timing belt as described in Section 7.

## Crankshaft sprocket

### Removal

**Note:** *A new securing bolt will be required on refitting, and a torque wrench capable of providing 310 Nm (229 lbf ft) of torque will be required.*
7 Remove the timing belt (see Section 7).

***Warning: The crankshaft sprocket securing bolt is very tight. A tool will be required to counterhold the sprocket as the bolt is unscrewed. Do not attempt the job using inferior or poorly-improvised tools, as injury or damage may result.***

8 Make up a tool to hold the sprocket. A suitable tool can be fabricated using two lengths of steel bar, joined by a large pivot bolt. Bolt the holding tool to the sprocket using the vibration damper/pulley-to-sprocket bolts **(see illustration 5.10)**.
9 Using a socket and a long swing-bar, loosen the sprocket bolt. Note that the bolt is very tight.
10 Unscrew the sprocket bolt, and remove the washer **(see illustration)**. Discard the bolt, a new one must be used on refitting.
11 Withdraw the sprocket from the end of the crankshaft **(see illustration)**. If the sprocket is tight, use a puller to draw it off.
12 Recover the Woodruff key from the end of the crankshaft if it is loose.

### Refitting

13 Where applicable, refit the Woodruff key to the end of the crankshaft, then align the groove in the sprocket with the key, and slide the sprocket onto the end of the crankshaft.
14 Refit the washer, noting that the shoulder on the washer must face the sprocket, and fit a **new** sprocket securing bolt.
15 Bolt the holding tool to the sprocket, as during removal, then tighten the sprocket bolt to the specified torque. Take care to avoid injury and/or damage.
16 Refit the timing belt (see Section 7).

## Timing belt tensioner and idler pulleys

### Removal

17 Remove the timing belt (Section 7), then simply unbolt the relevant pulley from the engine **(see illustration)**. Recover the washer fitted under the securing nut/bolt.

### Refitting

18 Refitting is a reversal of removal, bearing in mind the following points.

a) *Ensure that the washer is in place under the securing nut/bolt.*
b) *Where applicable, tighten the securing nut/bolt to the specified torque.*
c) *Refit and tension the timing belt as described in Section 7.*

# 9 Timing belt housing (M40 engine) - removal and refitting

## Removal

**Note:** *A new timing belt housing gasket, a new crankshaft front oil seal, and a new crankshaft O-ring will be required on refitting.*
1 Remove the cylinder head (see Section 15).
2 Remove the sump, referring to Section 16.
3 Remove the crankshaft sprocket, and the timing belt tensioner and idler pulleys, with reference to Section 8. If necessary, unscrew the timing belt tensioner mounting stud from the cylinder block.
4 If not already done, remove the Woodruff key from the end of the crankshaft. Hook the key out using a screwdriver if necessary.
5 Withdraw the spacer ring from the front of the crankshaft **(see illustration)**.
6 Unscrew the securing bolts, and withdraw the timing belt housing from the front of the cylinder block **(see illustration)**. Note the locations of the securing bolts, as two different sizes are used.
7 Recover the gasket.
8 With the housing removed, remove the O-ring from the groove in the front of the crankshaft **(see illustration)**.

## Refitting

9 Commence refitting by thoroughly cleaning the mating faces of the timing belt housing and cylinder block.

2A

9.5 Withdrawing the spacer ring from the crankshaft - M40 engine

9.6 Timing belt housing securing bolt locations (arrowed) - M40 engine

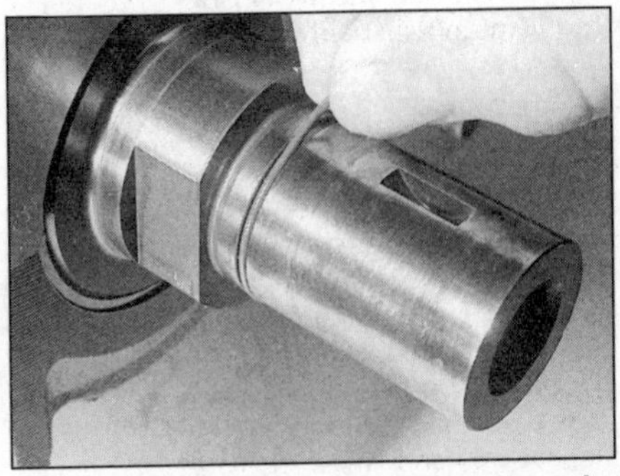

9.8 Remove the O-ring from the groove in the crankshaft - M40 engine

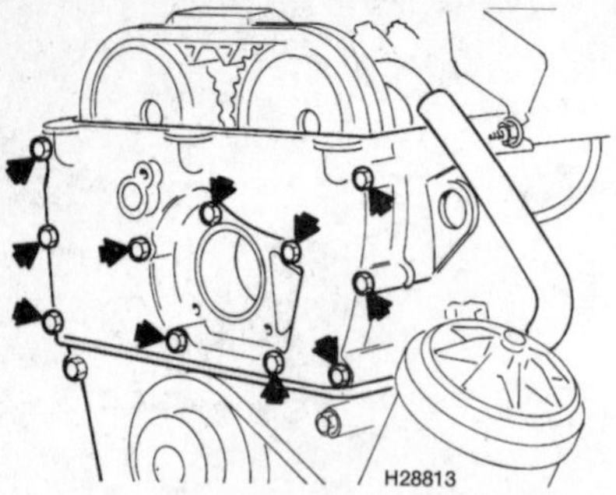


10.6 Upper timing chain cover securing bolt locations (arrowed) - M42 engine

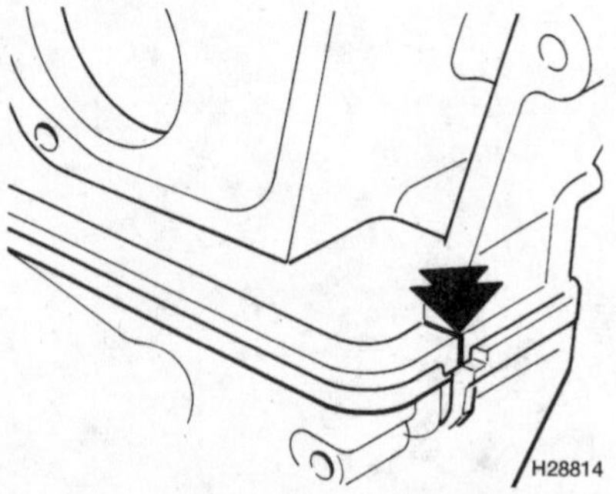


10.9 Apply RTV sealant to joints between the lower gasket, timing chain housing and lower cover (arrowed) - M42 engine

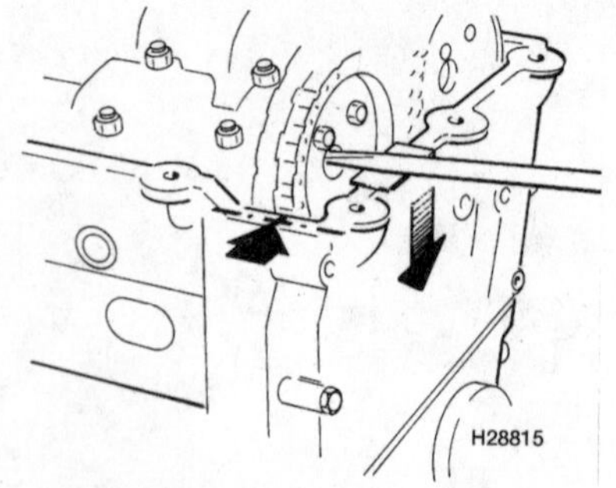


10.11 Press down on the cover using a screwdriver engaged with the camshaft sprocket - M42 engine

**10** Note the fitted depth of the crankshaft front oil seal in the timing belt housing, then lever out the seal.

**11** Clean the oil seal housing, then fit a new oil seal, using a large socket or tube to drive the seal into position to the previously-noted depth.

**12** Fit a new O-ring to the groove in the crankshaft, then position a new gasket on the front of the cylinder block. If necessary, use a little grease to hold the gasket in position.

**13** Offer the timing belt housing into position, ensuring that it engages with the positioning dowels in the cylinder block, then refit the securing bolts in their original locations and tighten to the specified torque. Note that two different sizes of bolt are used, and they have different torque settings.

**14** Fit the spacer ring to the front of the crankshaft, taking care not to damage the oil seal as the spacer is fitted.

**15** Refit the Woodruff key to the crankshaft.

**16** Refit the timing belt tensioner and idler pulleys, and the crankshaft sprocket, as described in Section 8.

**17** Refit the sump as described in Section 16.

**18** Refit the cylinder head as described in Section 15.

## 10 Timing chain covers (M42 and M43 engines) - removal and refitting

### *M42 engine - upper cover*

**Note:** *New gaskets will be required on refitting, and RTV sealant will be required.*

#### Removal

**1** Drain the cooling system (see Chapter 1).

**2** If desired, to improve access, remove the viscous cooling fan and cowl as described in Chapter 3.

**3** Remove the cylinder head cover as described in Section 4.

**4** Remove the camshaft position sensor from the cover, with reference to Chapter 4A if necessary.

**5** Remove the thermostat as described in Chapter 3.

**6** Unscrew the securing bolts, and withdraw the cover from the engine **(see illustration)**. Recover the gaskets.

#### Refitting

**7** Commence refitting by thoroughly cleaning the mating faces of the upper cover, lower cover and timing chain housing.

**8** Position new gaskets on the timing chain housing, and on the top of the lower cover, using a little grease to hold the gaskets in place if necessary.

**9** Apply a little RTV sealant to the joints between the lower gasket, timing chain housing, and lower cover **(see illustration)**.

**10** Offer the upper cover into position, then fit the two middle outer securing bolts - do not tighten the bolts at this stage.

**11** Press down on the upper cover, for example using a screwdriver engaged with the camshaft sprocket **(see illustration)**, until the top surfaces of the upper cover are exactly aligned with the top surface of the cylinder head. Hold the upper cover in this position, then tighten the two securing bolts to the specified torque.

**12** Refit the remaining cover securing bolts, and tighten to the specified torque.

**13** Refit the thermostat as described in Chapter 3.

**14** Refit the camshaft position sensor, with reference to Chapter 4A if necessary.

**15** Refit the camshaft cover as described in Section 4.

**16** Where applicable, refit the viscous cooling fan and cowl as described in Chapter 3.

**17** Refill the cooling system as described in Chapter 1.

### *M42 engine - lower cover*

**Note:** *A new cover gasket and a new crankshaft oil seal will be required on refitting.*

#### Removal

**18** Remove the upper timing chain cover as described previously in this Section.

**19** If not already done, remove the viscous cooling fan and cowl as described in Chapter 3.

**20** Remove the auxiliary drivebelt as described in Chapter 1.

**21** The coolant pump pulley must now be removed. Counterhold the pulley by wrapping an old drivebelt around it and clamping tightly, then unscrew the securing bolts and withdraw the pulley.

**22** Unbolt the crankshaft position sensor from its mounting bracket, and move it to one side, with reference to Chapter 4A. Note that it is preferable to completely remove the sensor to avoid the possibility of damage.

**23** Where applicable, release any wiring/ducting from the cover, and move clear of the working area.

**24** Remove the crankshaft vibration damper/pulley and pulley hub, referring to Section 5.

**25** Unscrew the securing bolts, noting their locations, and remove the lower timing chain cover **(see illustration)**. Recover the gasket.

#### Refitting

**26** Commence refitting by thoroughly cleaning the mating faces of the lower cover, timing chain housing and upper cover.

**27** Note the fitted depth of the crankshaft front oil seal in the cover, then lever out the seal.

**28** Clean the oil seal housing, then fit a new oil seal, using a large socket or tube to drive the seal into position to the previously-noted depth.

**29** Check that the cover positioning dowels are in position in the timing chain housing.

**30** Place a new gasket in position on the timing chain housing, using a little grease to hold the gasket in position if necessary.

**31** Offer the lower cover into position, and refit the securing bolts to their original locations. Tighten the bolts to the specified torque.

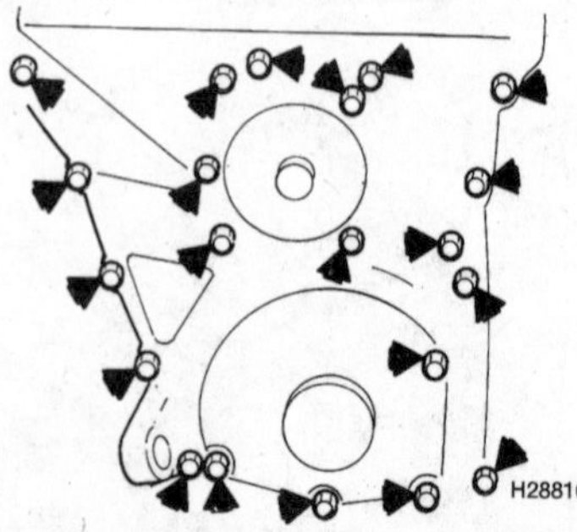


10.25 Lower timing chain cover bolt locations (arrowed) - M42 engine

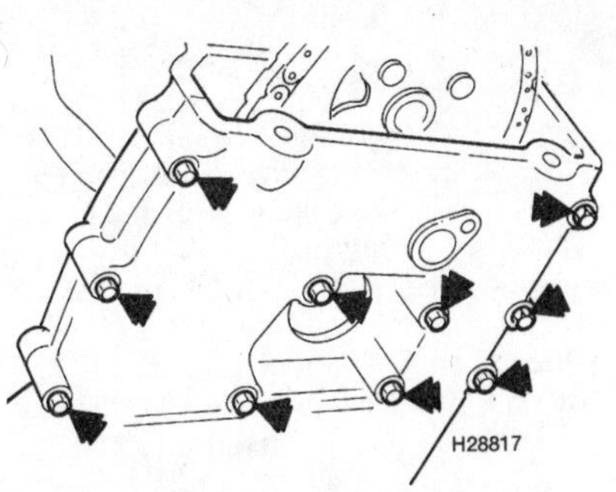


**10.39 Upper timing chain cover bolt locations (arrowed) - M43 engine**

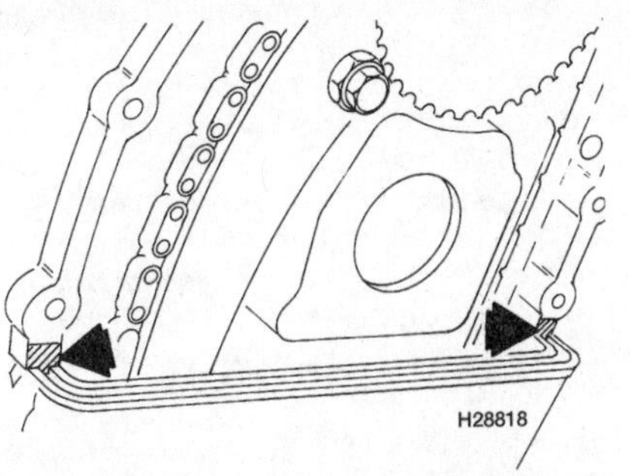


**10.41 Apply sealant to joints (arrowed) between cylinder head, timing chain housing and timing chain covers - M43 engine**

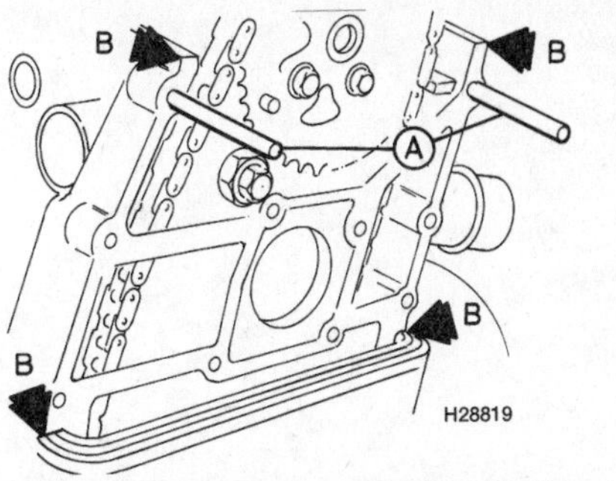


**10.43 Screw two long studs (A) into the upper securing bolts holes, and coat the top and bottom edges of the gasket (B) with sealant - M43 engine**

32 Refit the crankshaft vibration damper/ pulley and pulley hub as described in Section 5.

33 Make sure that any wiring/ducting released during removal is correctly routed and repositioned during refitting.

34 Refit the crankshaft position sensor.

35 Refit the coolant pump pulley and tighten the securing bolts.

36 Refit the auxiliary drivebelt as described in Chapter 1.

37 Refit the upper timing chain cover as described previously in this Section.

38 Refit the viscous cooling fan and cowl as described in Chapter 3.

## *M43 engine - upper cover*

**Note:** *A new gasket, a new rubber seal, and suitable sealant will be required on refitting. To aid refitting, two studs will be required to screw into the cover securing bolt holes, and a thin sheet of metal plate will be required - see text.*

### Removal

39 Proceed as described for M42 engines in paragraphs 1 to 6, noting the following differences **(see illustration)**.

a) *Prise off the securing clips, and withdraw the wiring ducting from the front of the timing chain cover.*

b) *Recover the rubber seal from the top of the lower timing chain cover.*

c) *In production, a one-piece gasket is fitted between the upper and lower timing chain covers and the timing chain housing. If a one-piece gasket is fitted, and the lower timing chain cover is not going to be removed, cut the top section of the gasket level with the top face of the lower timing chain cover, working from the inside outwards. A separate upper gasket is available as a spare part from BMW dealers.*

### Refitting

40 Commence refitting by thoroughly cleaning all gasket faces.

41 Apply sealant to the joints between the cylinder head, timing chain housing and timing chain covers **(see illustration)**.

42 Screw two long studs (or bolts with the heads cut off) into the top timing chain cover securing bolts holes.

43 Place a new upper gasket (see paragraph 39) in position on the timing chain housing. Coat the top and bottom edges of the gasket with sealant **(see illustration)**.

44 Apply sealant sparingly to the ends of the rubber seal grooves in the top of the lower timing chain cover **(see illustration)**.

45 Fit a new rubber seal to the top of the lower timing chain cover, ensuring that it is correctly located in the grooves.

46 To ensure that the rubber seal seats correctly as the upper chain cover is fitted, BMW recommend the use of special tool No 11 2 330. This tool can be improvised using a length of very thin metal sheet (such as printer's litho plate). The sheet must be large enough to cover the whole of the rubber seal.

47 Lightly grease the upper surface of the rubber seal, and the upper and lower surfaces of the metal sheet, then lay the sheet in position on the seal **(see illustration)**.

48 Slide the upper chain cover into position over the positioning studs (see paragraph 42), then insert the four lower outer cover securing screws, and tighten them by hand.

49 Carefully pull the metal sheet from the cover joint.

50 Lay the cylinder head cover in position, without the gasket (between the cylinder head cover and the cylinder head) fitted.

51 Fit two M6 bolts, with large washers under the heads, to the front cylinder head cover bolt locations in the cylinder head (**not** the two front-most bolt locations in the timing chain cover) **(see illustration)**.

52 Tighten the two bolts to push the upper timing chain cover down until the top face of the cover is flush with the top face of the cylinder head.

53 Tighten the previously fitted upper timing chain cover securing screws to the specified torque.

54 Unscrew the positioning studs from the timing chain cover, then refit the remaining cover securing bolts and tighten to the specified torque.

55 Unscrew the two M6 bolts and washers, and lift off the cylinder head cover.

**2A**

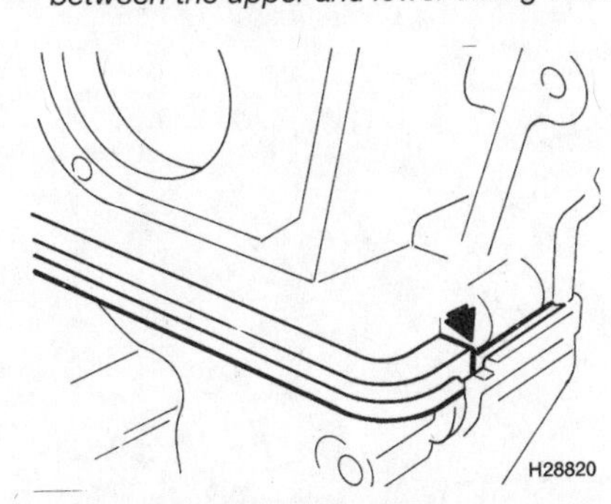


**10.44 Apply sealant to the ends of the rubber seal grooves (arrowed) in the lower timing chain cover - M43 engine**

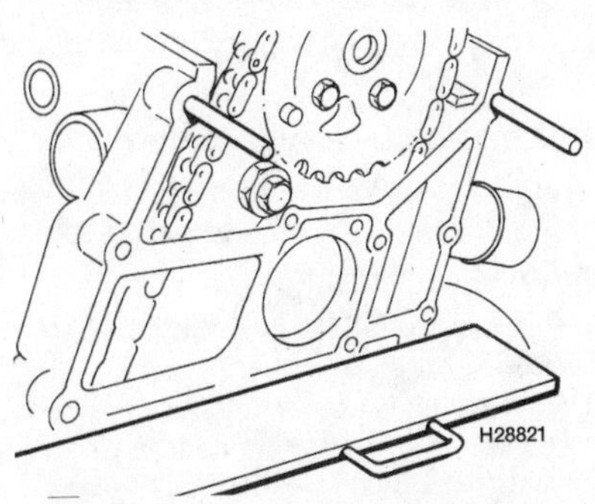


**10.47 Lay the metal sheet in position on the rubber seal - M43 engine**

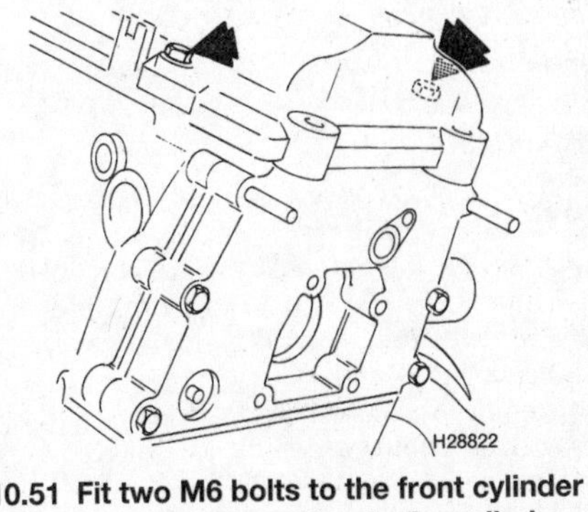


**10.51 Fit two M6 bolts to the front cylinder head cover bolt locations in the cylinder head (arrowed) - M43 engine**

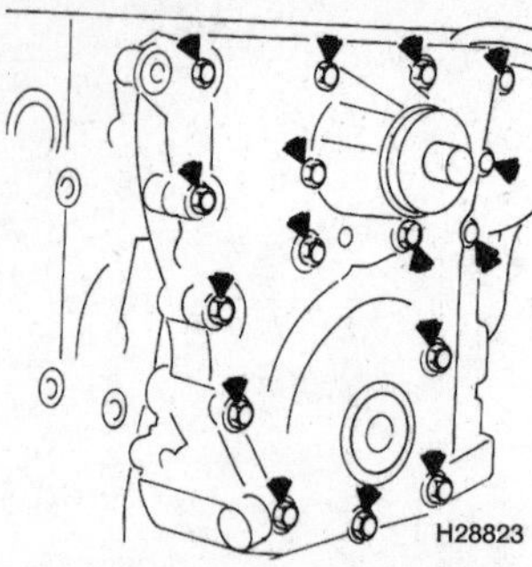


**10.58 Lower timing chain cover bolt locations (arrowed) - M43 engine**

**56** Proceed as described for the M42 engine in paragraphs 13 to 17.

**57** Refit the wiring ducting to the front of the timing chain cover and refit the securing clips.

### *M43 engine - lower cover*

**Note:** *A new gasket and suitable sealant will be required on refitting.*

#### Removal

**58** The procedure is as described for M42 engines in paragraphs 18 to 25, with reference to paragraph 39 **(see illustration)**.

#### Refitting

**59** The procedure is as described for M42 engines in paragraphs 26 to 38, noting the following points.

a) *When refitting, a new one-piece gasket can be fitted between the upper and lower timing chain covers and the timing chain housing. Coat the top edges of the gasket with a little sealant.*

b) *Refit the upper timing chain cover as described previously for the M43 engine in this Section (paragraphs 40 to 57), but if a one-piece gasket is used on refitting, ignore the references to the upper cover gasket. Similarly, if a one-piece gasket is used, there is no need to use the two positioning studs when refitting the upper timing chain cover.*

## 11 Timing chain (M42 and M43 engines) - removal, inspection and refitting

### *M42 engine*

**Note:** *A new timing chain tensioner cover plug seal will be required on refitting.*

#### Removal

**1** Position No 1 piston at TDC, and lock the flywheel in position, as described in Section 3.

**2** Remove the upper and lower timing chain covers, as described in Section 10.

**3** Unscrew the chain tensioner plug from the right-hand side of the engine. Recover the sealing ring **(see illustration)**.

**4** Withdraw the timing chain tensioner assembly from its housing.

**5** Unscrew the securing bolts, and withdraw the upper chain guide from the cylinder head **(see illustration)**.

**6** Unscrew the upper securing bolt from the left-hand chain guide **(see illustration)**.

**7** Unscrew the bolts securing the chain sprockets to the camshafts. Take care not to move the camshafts - if necessary, the camshafts can be counterheld using a 27 mm spanner on the flats provided between Nos 5 and 6 cam lobes **(see illustrations)**.

**8** Withdraw the sprockets from the camshafts, and disengage them from the chain. Note which way round the sprockets are fitted to ensure correct refitting.

**9** Note the routing of the chain in relation to the sprockets, tensioner rail and the chain guides.

**10** Unscrew the securing bolts, and remove the lower chain guide **(see illustration)**.

**11** Manipulate the tensioner rail as necessary to enable the chain to be unhooked from the idler sprocket and crankshaft sprocket and lifted from the engine.

***Warning: Once the timing chain has been removed, do not turn the crankshaft or the camshafts, as there is a danger of the valves hitting the pistons.***

**12** If desired, the tensioner rail can now be removed after removing the clip from the lower pivot.

**13** Similarly, the left-hand chain guide can be removed after unscrewing the remaining bolts.

#### Inspection

**14** The chain should be renewed if the sprockets are worn or if the chain is worn (indicated by excessive lateral play between the links, and excessive noise in operation). It is wise to renew the chain in any case if the

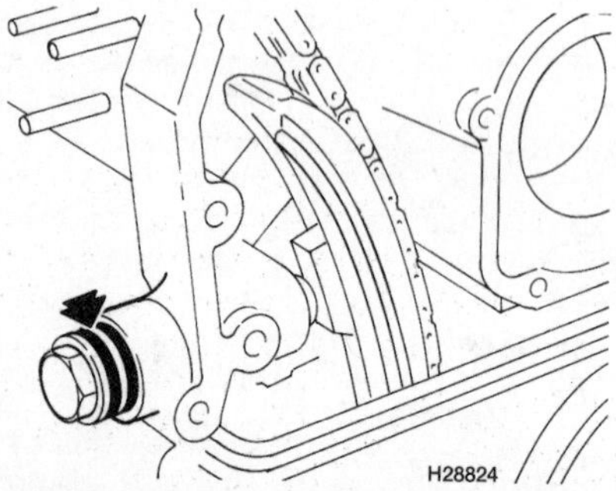


**11.3 Unscrew the chain tensioner plug (arrowed) - M42 engine**

**11.5 Upper chain guide securing bolts (arrowed) - M42 engine**

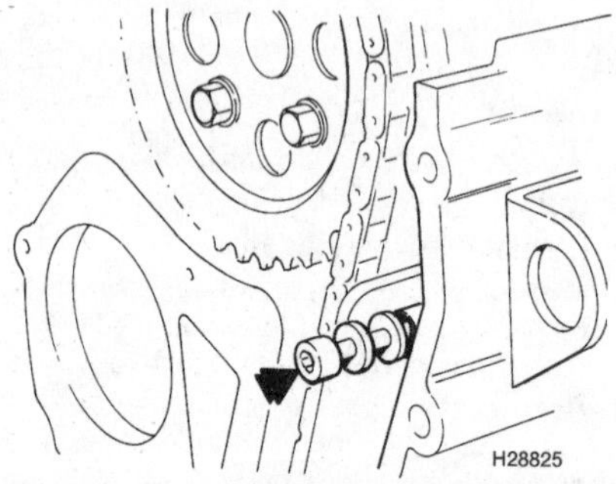


**11.6 Unscrew upper bolt (arrowed) from the left-hand chain guide - M42 engine**

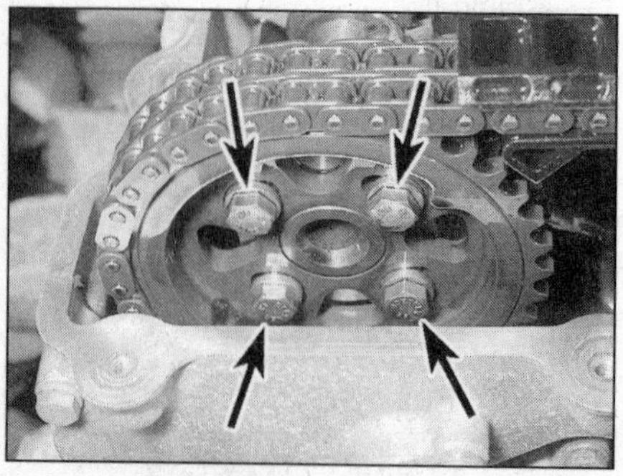

**11.7a Unscrew the camshaft sprocket securing bolts (arrowed) - M42 engine**

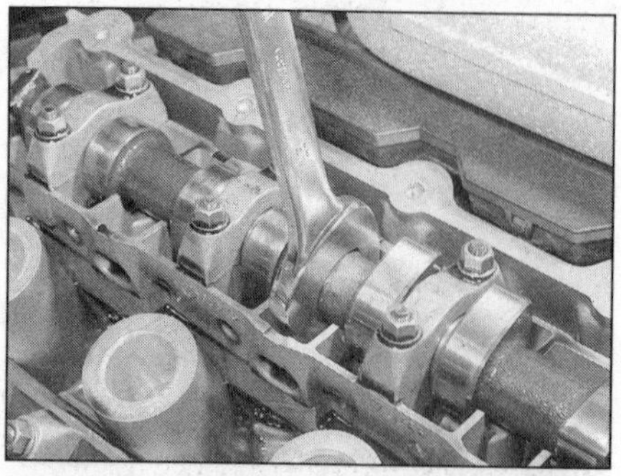

**11.7b Counterhold the camshafts using a spanner on the flats provided - M42 engine**

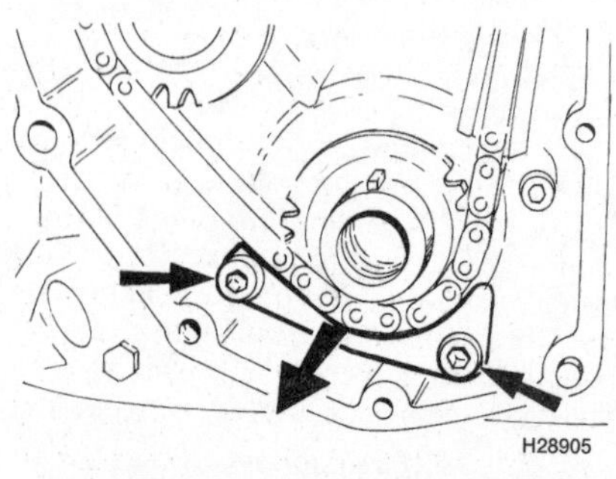


**11.10 Unscrew the bolts (arrowed) and remove the lower chain guide - M42 engine**

engine is dismantled for overhaul. Note that the rollers on a very badly worn chain may be slightly grooved. To avoid future problems, if there is any doubt at all about the condition of the chain, renew it.

**15** Examine the teeth on the sprockets for wear. Each tooth forms an inverted "V". If worn, the side of each tooth under tension will be slightly concave in shape when compared with the other side of the tooth (ie, the teeth will have a hooked appearance). If the teeth appear worn, the sprockets must be renewed. Also check the chain guide and tensioner rail contact surfaces for wear, and renew any worn components as necessary.

### Refitting

**16** Ensure that No 1 piston is still positioned at TDC, with the crankshaft locked in position. Check the position of the camshafts using the template.

**17** Where applicable, refit the tensioner rail and the left-hand chain guide. Refit the two lower chain guide securing bolts, but do not tighten them at this stage. Do not fit the upper securing bolt at this stage.

**18** Engage the chain with the crankshaft sprocket, then refit the lower chain guide and tighten the securing bolts.

**19** Lay the chain in position around the left-hand chain guide and the tensioner rail, ensuring that the chain is routed as noted before removal.

**20** Manipulate the camshaft sprockets until the timing arrows on the sprockets are pointing vertically upwards, then engage the chain with the sprockets.

**21** Fit the sprockets to the camshafts, ensuring that the sprockets are fitted the correct way round as noted before removal, then refit the sprocket securing bolts.

**22** Tighten the sprocket securing bolts to the specified torque - if necessary, the camshafts can be counterheld using a 27 mm spanner on the flats provided between Nos 5 and 6 cam lobes.

**23** Refit the upper securing bolt to the left-hand chain guide, but do not tighten it at this stage.

**24** Refit the upper chain guide and tighten the securing bolts.

**25** The timing chain tensioner must now be fitted, but before fitting, check that the tensioner plunger is retracted as follows. If a new tensioner is being fitted, it should be supplied with the plunger already in the retracted position.

***Warning: It is essential that the following procedure is carried out to ensure that the tensioner plunger is retracted. If the plunger is not fully retracted, it can lock in the extended position, causing the tensioner or timing chain to break, resulting in expensive engine damage.***

a) *Hold the tensioner upright, then knock the bottom end of the tensioner sleeve sharply on a solid surface such as a vice. This should cause the plunger to jump out of the end of the tensioner sleeve. Lift out the plunger and the spring.*
b) *Note the locations of the two circlips on the plunger **(see illustration)**.*
c) *Thoroughly clean the components.*
d) *Ensure that the circlips are correctly located in their respective grooves on the plunger.*
e) *Slide the spring into the sleeve, and engage the plunger with the end of the spring.*
f) *Clamp the assembly in a vice, with the plunger resting in the sleeve so that both circlips are still visible.*
g) *Tighten the vice to compress the plunger into the sleeve, until the first circlip engages with the groove in the sleeve **(see illustration)**.*
h) *Tighten the vice further to compress the plunger into the sleeve until the second circlip is heard to engage positively **(see illustration)**. Do not push the plunger too far into the sleeve, or the circlip will be released, unlocking the plunger.*
i) *Loosen the vice - the plunger should stay retracted in the sleeve.*
j) *If the plunger comes out of the sleeve as the vice is loosened, or if the overall length of the tensioner assembly is greater than specified, then the procedure in paragraphs a) to i) must be repeated **(see illustration)**.*

**26** Refit the tensioner assembly, ensuring that it is fitted with the plunger against the tensioner rail, then refit the tensioner plug using a new sealing ring. Tighten the plug to the specified torque.

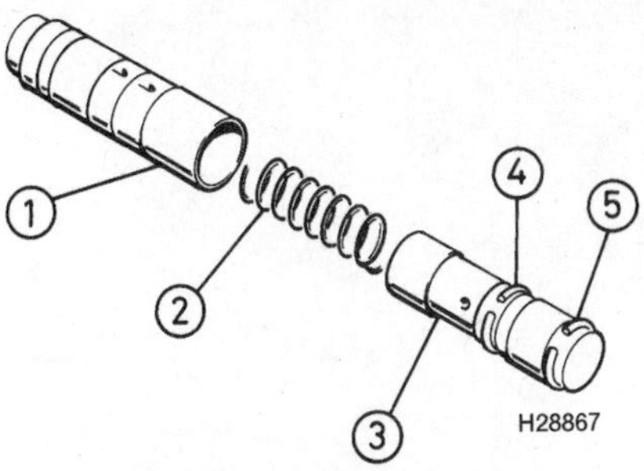


**11.25a Timing chain tensioner components - M42 engine**

*1 Sleeve*
*2 Spring*
*3 Plunger*
*4 Circlip*
*5 Circlip*

**27** Using a screwdriver, lever the timing chain and tensioner rail against the tensioner until the tensioner plunger is released from the sleeve to tension the chain **(see illustration)**.

**28** Once the chain is under tension, the left-hand chain guide securing bolts can be tightened. Using feeler blades, position the guide to give an equal clearance between each side of the guide and the chain, then tighten the securing bolts.

**29** Refit the timing chain covers as described in Section 10.



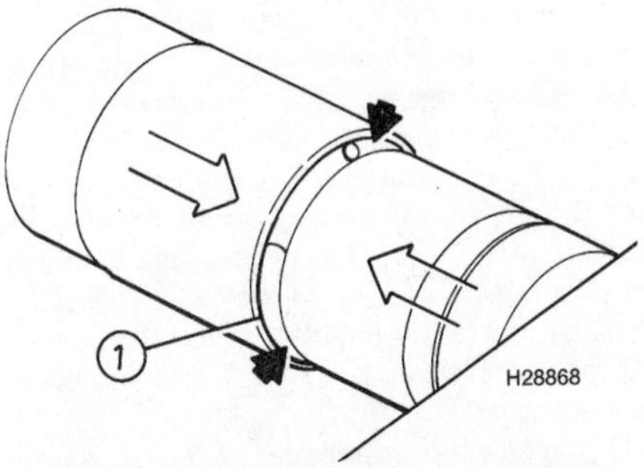


**11.25b Compress the tensioner until the first circlip (1) engages with the groove in the sleeve . . .**

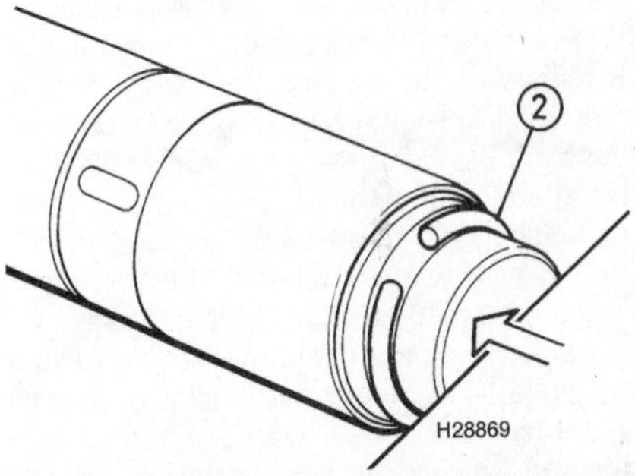


**11.25c . . . then compress the tensioner further until the second circlip (2) is heard to engage positively - M42 engine**

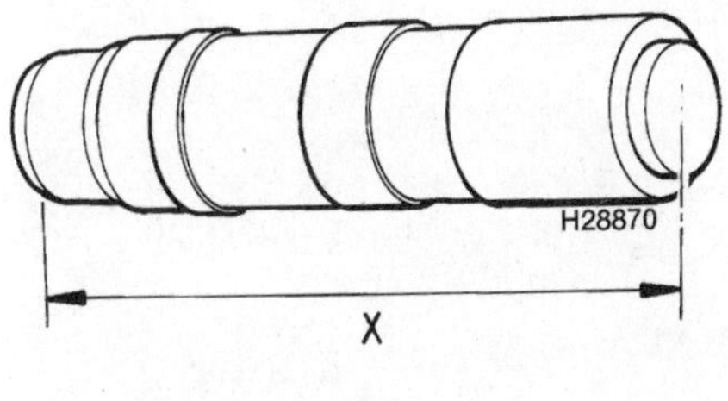


**11.25d Measure the overall length of the tensioner - M42 engine**
*Dimension X = 68.5 mm*

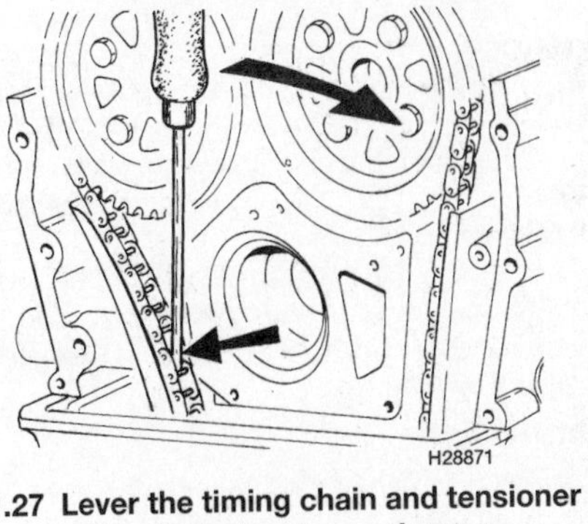


**11.27 Lever the timing chain and tensioner rail until the tensioner plunger is released - M42 engine**

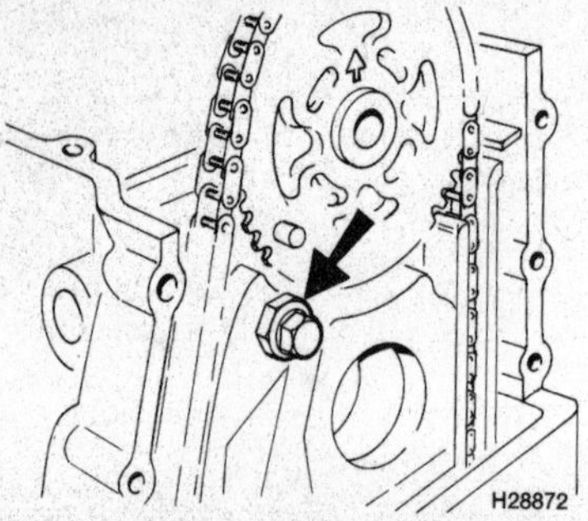


**11.34 Push back on the top of the tensioner rail (arrowed) to relieve the belt tension - M43 engine**

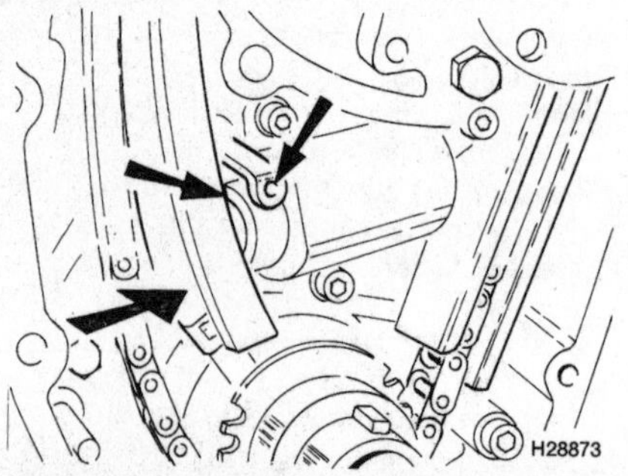


**11.35a Push the end of the tensioner rail to align the tensioner piston groove with the locking pin hole in the tensioner body (arrowed) - M43 engine**

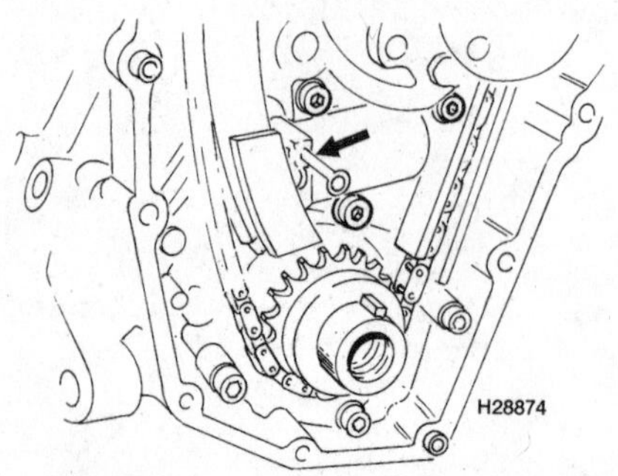


**11.35b Fit a rod or drill (arrowed) to lock the tensioner in position - M43 engine**

**30** Remove the flywheel locking tool and the camshaft positioning template, and refit the cylinder head cover as described in Section 4. ***Caution: When the engine is first started, it must be run at a speed of 3500 rpm for 20 seconds as soon as it starts - this is to ensure that the tensioner is primed with oil. A loud rattling sound will be heard until the tensioner is primed - do not be alarmed by the noise!***

## *M43 engine*

### Removal

**31** Position No 1 piston at TDC, and lock the flywheel in position, as described in Section 3.
**32** Remove the upper and lower timing chain covers, as described in Section 10.
**33** Unscrew the camshaft sprocket bolts.
**34** Push back the top end of the tensioner rail to relieve the tension on the chain until the camshaft sprocket can be removed **(see illustration)**. Withdraw the sprocket from the camshaft, noting which way round it is fitted, then disengage the sprocket from the chain.
**35** Working at the lower end of the tensioner rail, push the end of the rail to retract the hydraulic tensioner piston until the groove in the piston is aligned with the locking pin hole in the tensioner body. Lock the tensioner in position by inserting a metal rod or drill into the locking pin hole to engage with the groove in the piston **(see illustrations)**.
**36** Note the routing of the chain in relation to the chain guide and tensioner rail to aid refitting.
**37** With the tensioner locked in position, slide the chain, complete with the crankshaft sprocket, from the chain housing. Recover the Woodruff key from the end of the crankshaft if it is loose.
**38** If desired, the tensioner rail and the chain guide can be removed from the engine, in which case note their positions to ensure correct refitting.

### Inspection

**39** Refer to paragraphs 14 and 15.

### Refitting

**40** Ensure No 1 piston is still at TDC, with the crankshaft locked in position. Check the position of the camshaft using the template.
**41** Where applicable, refit the chain guide and the tensioner rail, ensuring that they are positioned correctly as noted before removal.
**42** Where applicable, refit the Woodruff key to the end of the crankshaft.
**43** Engage the chain with the crankshaft sprocket, then slide the chain/sprocket assembly into position, ensuring that the sprocket locates on the Woodruff key. Route the chain around the chain guide and tensioner rail as noted before removal.
**44** Remove the locking pin from the chain tensioner to release the tensioner piston.
**45** Push back the top end of the tensioner rail, as during removal, to allow the camshaft sprocket to be fitted. Engage the camshaft sprocket with the chain, ensuring that it is fitted the correct way round as noted before removal, and manipulate the sprocket so that the timing arrow points vertically upwards.
**46** Fit the sprocket to the camshaft, aligning the bolt holes in the camshaft flange with the centres of the elongated holes in the sprocket (the camshaft should be locked in the TDC position using the template - see Section 3). Fit the sprocket securing bolts, and tighten as far as possible by hand.
**47** Release the upper end of the tensioner rail, then tighten the camshaft sprocket bolts to the specified torque.
**48** Remove the flywheel locking tool, and remove the template used to check the camshaft position.
**49** Refit the timing chain covers as described in Section 10.

## 12 Timing chain sprockets and tensioner (M42 and M43 engines) - removal and refitting

## *M42 engine*

### Camshaft sprockets and tensioner

**1** Removal and refitting are described as part of the timing chain removal procedure in Section 11.

### Crankshaft sprocket

**2** Remove the timing chain as described in Section 11.
**3** Slide the sprocket from the crankshaft, and recover the Woodruff key if it is loose.
**4** Refitting is a reversal of removal, but refit the timing chain as described in Section 11.

### Idler sprocket

**5** Remove the timing chain as described in Section 11.
**6** Unbolt the sprocket from the timing chain housing.
**7** Refitting is a reversal of removal, noting the following points.

a) *Ensure that the sprocket is fitted the correct way round - the greater projecting boss on the sprocket should be facing the timing chain housing.*
b) *Ensure that the washer is in place under the securing bolt.*
c) *Refit the timing chain as described in Section 11.*

## *M43 engine*

### Timing chain sprockets

**8** The procedure is described as part of the timing chain removal procedure in Section 11.

### Timing chain tensioner

**9** Position No 1 piston at TDC, and lock the flywheel in position, as described in Section 3.
**10** Remove the upper and lower timing chain covers, as described in Section 10.
**11** Working at the lower end of the tensioner rail, push the end of the rail to retract the hydraulic tensioner piston until the groove in the piston is aligned with the locking pin hole in the tensioner body. Lock the tensioner in position by inserting a metal rod or drill into the locking pin hole to engage with the groove in the piston.
**12** Unscrew the securing bolts and remove the tensioner **(see illustration)**.
**13** **Do not** remove the locking tool from the tensioner until after refitting. **Do not** attempt to dismantle the tensioner - a BMW special tool is required to reassemble the unit.
**14** If a new tensioner is obtained, it will be supplied with a locking device to hold the

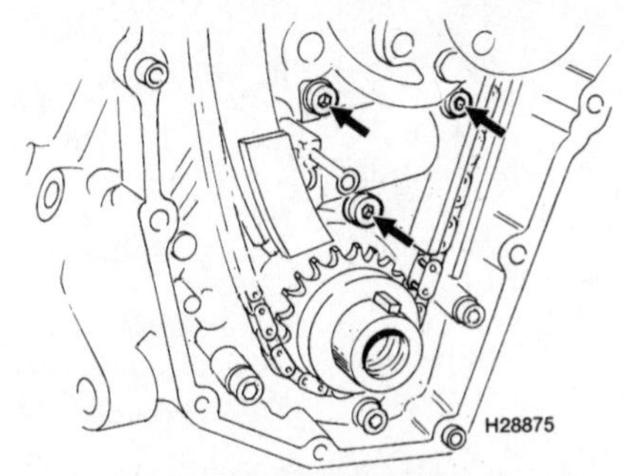


**12.12 Timing chain tensioner securing bolts (arrowed) - M43 engine**

piston in the locked position. In this case, **do not** remove the locking tool until the tensioner has been refitted.

**15** Refitting is a reversal of removal, bearing in mind the following points.

a) *Check the condition of the sealing ring, and renew if necessary.*
b) *Do not remove the locking tool until the tensioner has been refitted.*
c) *Refit the timing chain covers as described in Section 10.*

## 13 Timing chain housing (M42 and M43 engines) - removal and refitting

### *M42 engine*

**Note:** *A new timing chain housing gasket will be required on refitting, and a new oil filter housing gasket and seal may be required.*

#### Removal

**1** Remove the timing chain, tensioner rail and chain guides as described in Section 11.

**2** Remove the timing chain crankshaft and idler sprockets, with reference to Section 12.

**3** Remove the cylinder head as described in Section 15.

**4** Remove the sump, referring to Section 16.

**5** Remove the alternator as described in Chapter 5A.

**6** Disconnect the wiring from the oil pressure warning light switch.

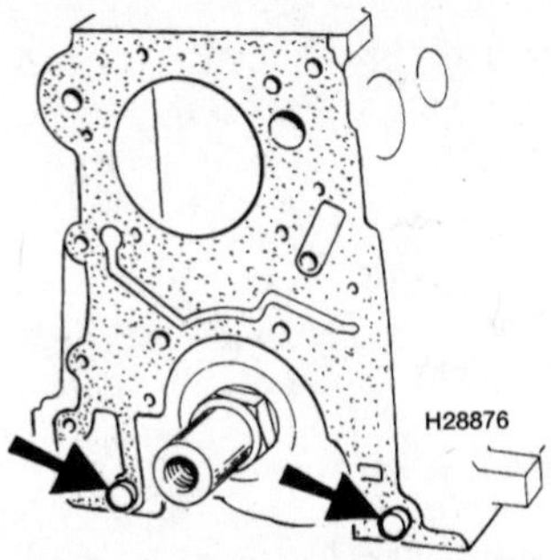


**13.10 Ensure the locating dowels (arrowed) are in place in the block - M42 engine**

**7** If desired, unbolt the oil filter housing from the side of the timing chain housing. Be prepared for oil spillage, and recover the gasket and O-ring.

**8** Unscrew the securing bolts, noting their locations, and withdraw the timing chain housing from the front of the cylinder block. Recover the gasket.

#### Refitting

**9** Thoroughly clean the mating faces of the timing chain housing and the cylinder block.

**10** Ensure the locating dowels are in place in the cylinder block, then lay a new gasket in position on the cylinder block **(see illustration)**.

**11** Refit the timing chain housing, and tighten the securing bolts to the specified torque. Ensure that the socket-head bolts are fitted to their correct locations, and note that the upper right-hand bolt hole is not used. Also ensure that the chain oil spray jet faces the idler sprocket location **(see illustrations)**.

**12** Where applicable, refit the oil filter housing using a new gasket and a new O-ring. Lubricate the O-ring with a little grease before fitting, and tighten the securing bolts.

**13** Reconnect the oil pressure warning light switch wiring.

**14** Refit the alternator (see Chapter 5A).

**15** Refit the sump as described in Section 16.

**16** Refit the cylinder head (see Section 15).

**17** Refit the timing chain crankshaft and idler sprockets, with reference to Section 12.

**18** Refit the chain guides, tensioner rail and timing chain as described in Section 11.

### *M43 engine*

**Note:** *A new gasket, a new rubber seal, and suitable sealant will be required on refitting. To aid refitting, a thin sheet of metal plate will be required - see text.*

#### Removal

**19** Remove the timing chain, sprockets, tensioner rail and chain guide, as described in Section 11.

**20** Remove the timing chain tensioner with reference to Section 12.

**21** Remove the alternator as described in Chapter 5A.

**22** Unbolt the alternator mounting bracket.

**23** Unbolt the oil filter housing from the side of the timing chain housing. Be prepared for oil spillage, and recover the gasket and O-ring.

**24** Remove the sump, referring to Section 16.

**25** Unscrew the securing bolts, noting their locations, and withdraw the timing chain housing from the front of the cylinder block. Recover the gasket.

#### Refitting

**26** Thoroughly clean the mating faces of the timing chain housing, cylinder block and cylinder head.

**27** Check that the timing chain housing locating dowels are in position at the bottom of the cylinder block.

**28** Apply sealant to the upper contact faces on the timing chain housing where the timing chain housing mates with the cylinder head and the timing chain cover, then fit a new rubber seal to the groove in the top of the timing chain housing **(see illustration)**.

**29** Locate a new gasket over the dowels in the cylinder block.

**30** To ensure that the rubber seal seats correctly as the timing chain housing is fitted, BMW recommend the use of special tool No 11 2 330. This tool can be improvised using a length of very thin metal sheet (such as printer's litho plate). The sheet must be large enough to cover the whole of the rubber seal.

**31** Lightly grease the upper surface of the rubber seal, and the upper and lower surfaces of the metal sheet, then lay the sheet in position on the seal.



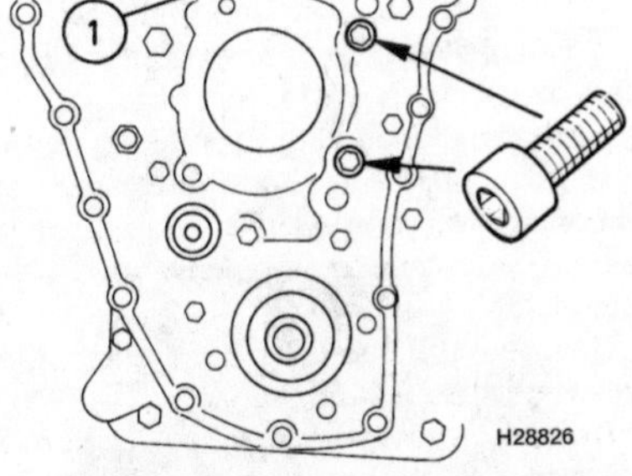


**13.11a Ensure the socket-head bolts are refitted to their correct locations, and note the upper right-hand bolt hole (1) is not used - M42 engine**

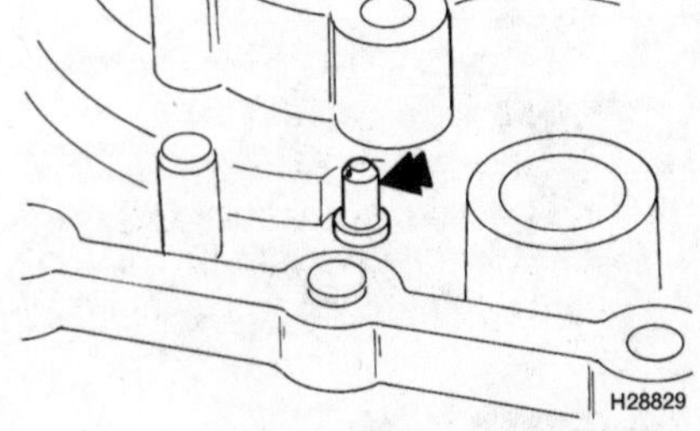


**13.11b Ensure that the oil spray jet (arrowed) faces the idler sprocket location - M42 engine**

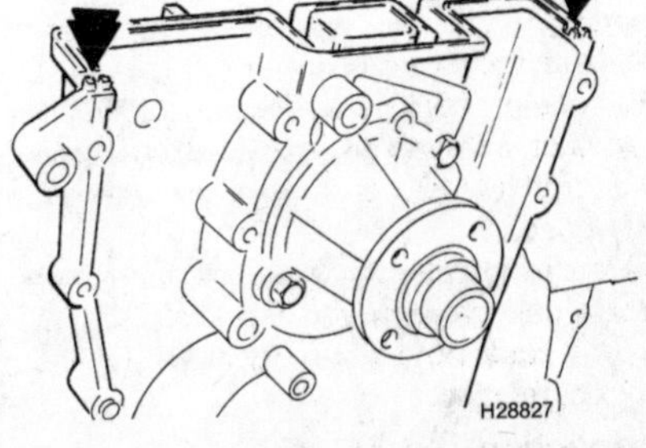


**13.28 Apply sealant to the areas (arrowed) where the timing chain housing mates with the cylinder head and timing chain cover - M43 engine**

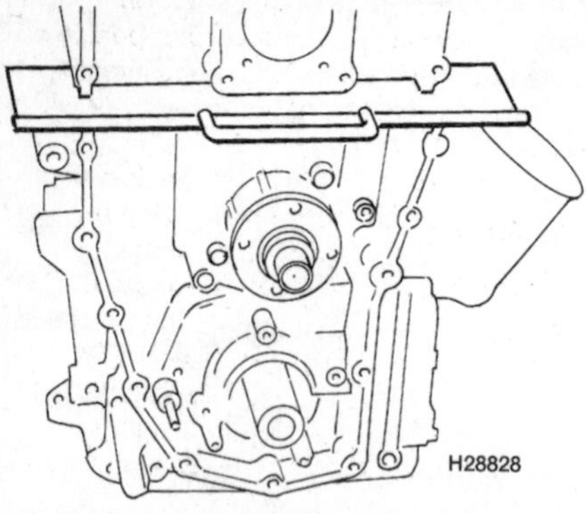


**13.32 Metal sheet in place between timing chain housing and cylinder head - M43 engine**

**32** Slide the timing chain housing into position over the locating dowels, then fit the securing bolts and tighten them to the specified torque **(see illustration)**.
**33** Carefully pull the metal sheet from the joint between the housing and cylinder head.
**34** Refit the sump as described in Section 16.
**35** Refit the oil filter housing, using a new gasket and a new O-ring.
**36** Refit the alternator mounting bracket, then refit the alternator, with reference to Chapter 5A.
**37** Refit the timing chain tensioner with reference to Section 12.
**38** Refit the timing chain guide, tensioner rail, sprockets and timing chain as described in Section 11.

## 14 Camshaft(s) and followers - removal and refitting

### M40 engine

**Note:** *BMW recommend that before removing the camshaft, the valves are depressed using a special tool, and the cam followers are removed. This eliminates the load on the camshaft as the bearing cap nuts are unscrewed. Provided care is taken, and the bearing cap nuts are unscrewed progressively and evenly, the procedure can be carried out without the special tool, as described in the following paragraphs. A new camshaft front oil seal, and new oil spray tube securing bolt seals will be required on refitting.*

#### Removal

**1** Remove the timing belt as described in Section 7.
**2** Unscrew the securing bolts and withdraw the oil spray tube from the camshaft bearing caps. Recover the seals from the securing bolts **(see illustration)**.
**3** Check the camshaft bearing caps for identification marks. The front (timing belt end) cap should be marked "F", and the remaining caps should be marked "2" to "5". Make suitable marks if necessary.
**4** Progressively unscrew and remove the camshaft bearing cap nuts, then remove the bearing caps **(see illustration)**.
**5** Lift the camshaft from the cylinder head, then slide the front oil seal from the camshaft. Take care not to dislodge the cam followers as the camshaft is removed.
**6** Prepare a compartmentalised box, filled with clean engine oil, to store the hydraulic valve lifters so that they are kept in their original fitted order. Note that the cam followers and the thrust pads must also be kept in their original order.
**7** Withdraw the cam followers and the thrust pads, and store them in order so that they can be refitted to their original locations **(see illustrations)**.
**8** Lift the hydraulic valve lifters from the cylinder head, and place them in the oil-filled box **(see illustrations)**.

#### Inspection

**9** Clean all the components, including the bearing surfaces in the bearing castings and bearing caps. Examine the components carefully for wear and damage. In particular, check the bearing and cam lobe surfaces of the camshaft(s) for scoring and pitting. Examine the surfaces of the cam followers for signs wear or damage. Renew components as necessary.

#### Refitting

**10** Lubricate the valve lifter bores in the cylinder head, then fit the valve lifters to their original locations.
**11** Locate the thrust pads and the cam followers on the valves and the valve lifters in their original positions.
**12** Lubricate the bearing surfaces in the cylinder head, then lay the camshaft in position so that the valves of No 1 cylinder are

**14.2 Removing an oil spray tube securing bolt - M40 engine**

**14.4 Removing the camshaft front bearing cap - M40 engine**

**14.7a Withdraw the cam followers . . .**

**14.7b . . . the thrust pads . . .**

**14.8a . . . and the valve lifters - M40 engine**

**14.8b Place the valve lifters in an oil-filled box - M40 engine**

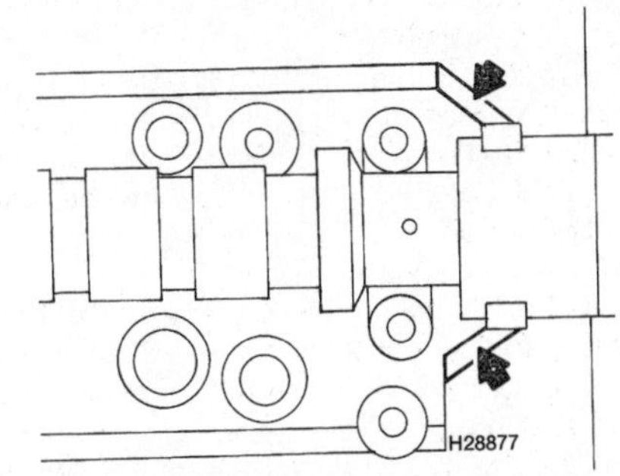


**14.14 Apply sealant to the cylinder head faces where the front bearing cap fits (arrowed) - M40 engine**

both open, and the valves of No 4 cylinder are "rocking" (exhaust closing and inlet opening). Note also that the square flange at the front of the camshaft should be positioned with the side of the flange exactly at right-angles to the top surface of the cylinder head (this can be checked using a set-square), and the side of the flange with holes drilled into it uppermost. The position of the camshaft can be checked by fitting the template described in Section 3.

**13** Lubricate the bearing surfaces in the bearing caps.

**14** Apply a little RTV sealant to the cylinder head faces where the edge of the front bearing cap fits **(see illustration)**.

**15** Fit the bearing caps to their correct locations, as noted before removal, then fit the securing nuts, and tighten progressively to the specified torque.

**16** Wrap a length of adhesive tape around the front of the camshaft to protect the lip of the new oil seal as it is fitted.

**17** Carefully locate the new oil seal in position, then press it in by hand initially so that it enters the bore **(see illustration)**. Drive the seal fully into the housing using a socket or tube of suitable diameter.

**18** Remove the tape from the end of the camshaft.

**19** Fit new seals to the oil spray tube securing bolts, then refit the spray tube and tighten the bolts.

**20** Refit the timing belt as described in Section 7.

**14.17 Wrap tape (arrowed) around the front of the camshaft and fit a new oil seal - M40 engine**

## *M42 engine*

***Warning: BMW tool 11 3 260 will be required for this operation. This tool is extremely difficult to improvise due to its rugged construction and the need for accurate manufacture. Do not attempt to remove and refit the camshafts without the aid of the special tool, as expensive damage to the camshafts and/or bearings may result.***

### Removal

**21** Remove the upper timing chain cover as described in Section 10.

**22** Position No 1 piston at TDC, and lock the flywheel in position, as described in Section 3.

**23** Unscrew the timing chain tensioner plug from the right-hand side of the engine. Recover the sealing ring.

**24** Withdraw the timing chain tensioner assembly from its housing.

**25** Unscrew the securing bolts and withdraw the upper chain guide from the cylinder head.

**26** Unscrew the upper securing bolts from the left-hand chain guide.

**27** Unscrew the bolts securing the chain sprockets to the camshafts. Take care not to move the camshafts - if necessary, the camshafts can be counterheld using a 27 mm spanner on the flats provided between Nos 5 and 6 cam lobes.

**28** Withdraw the sprockets from the camshafts, and disengage them from the chain. Note which way round the sprockets are fitted to ensure correct refitting.

**29** Ensure that tension is kept on the timing chain - tie the chain up or support it using wire, to prevent it from dropping into the lower timing chain cover.

***Warning: To avoid any possibility of piston-to-valve contact when refitting the camshafts, it is necessary to ensure that none of the pistons are at TDC. Before proceeding further, remove the locking rod from the timing hole in the cylinder block, then turn the crankshaft approximately 90° clockwise using a spanner or socket on the crankshaft pulley hub bolt.***

**30** Remove the template from the camshafts.

**31** Unscrew the spark plugs from the cylinder head.

**32** Check the camshaft bearing caps for identification marks. The caps are numbered from the timing chain end of the engine, and the marks can normally be read from the exhaust side of the engine. The exhaust camshaft bearing caps are marked "A1" to "A5", and the inlet camshaft caps are marked "E1" to "E5" **(see illustration)**.

**33** Mount BMW special tool 11 3 260 on the cylinder head by screwing the mounting bolts into the spark plug holes. Position the tool so that the plungers are located over the relevant camshaft bearing caps (ie, inlet or exhaust camshaft) **(see illustration)**.

**34** Apply pressure to the camshaft bearing caps by turning the eccentric shaft on the tools using a spanner **(see illustration)**.

**35** Unscrew the camshaft bearing cap nuts.

***Warning: Do not attempt to unscrew the camshaft bearing cap nuts without the special tools in place, as damage to the camshaft and/or bearings may result.***

**36** Release the pressure on the special tool shaft, then unbolt the tool from the cylinder head.

**37** Lift off the bearing caps, keeping them in order, then lift out the camshaft.

**38** The camshaft bearing casting can now be lifted from the cylinder head. This should be done very slowly, as the cam followers will be released as the casting is lifted off - if the casting is lifted off awkwardly, the cam



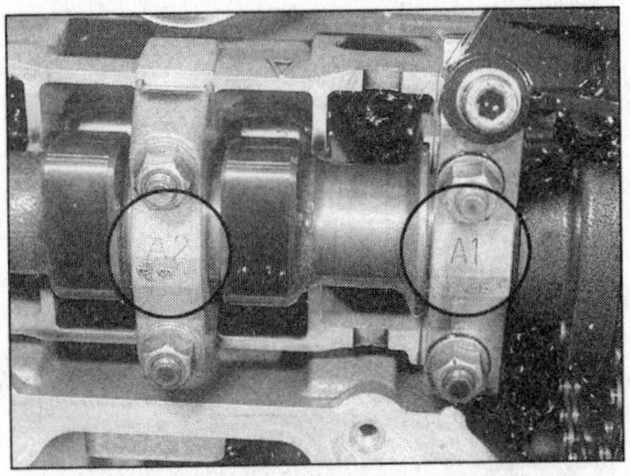


**14.32 Camshaft bearing cap identification marks - M42 engine**

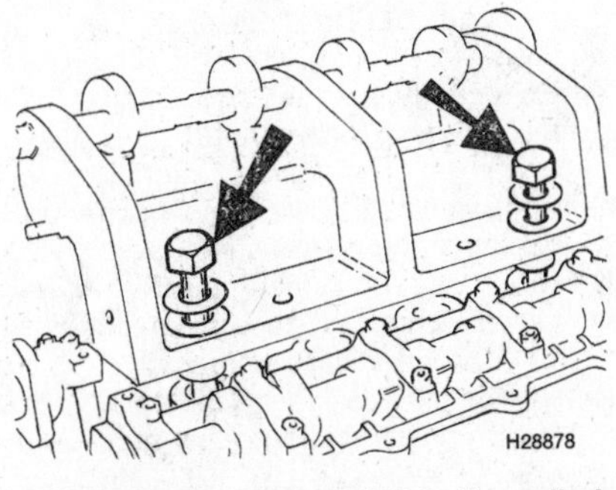


**14.33 Fit BMW tool 11 3 260 to the cylinder head by screwing the bolts (arrowed) into the spark plug holes - M42 engine**

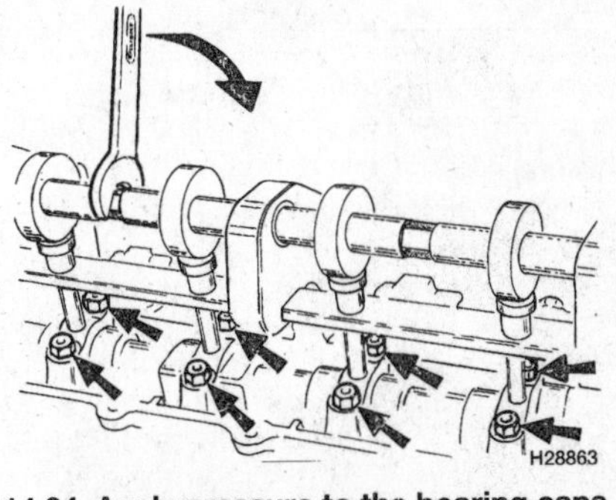


**14.34 Apply pressure to the bearing caps, and unscrew the bearing cap nuts (arrowed) - M42 engine**

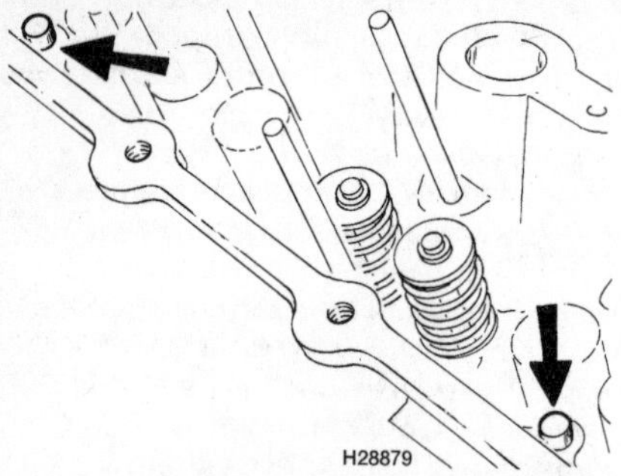


**14.42 Ensure that the bearing casting locating dowels (arrowed) are in position - M42 engine**

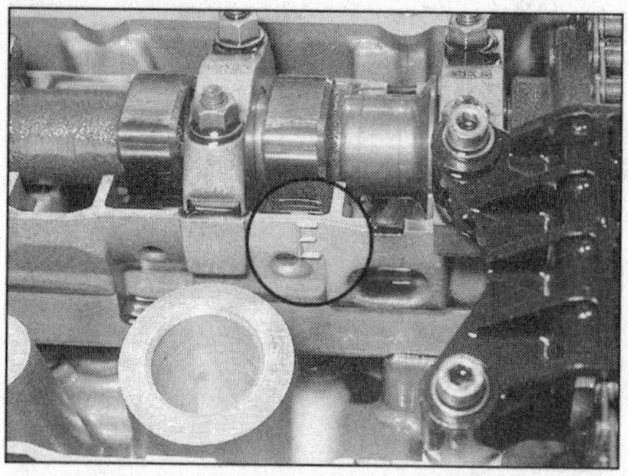

**14.47 Camshaft bearing casting identification mark - M42 engine**

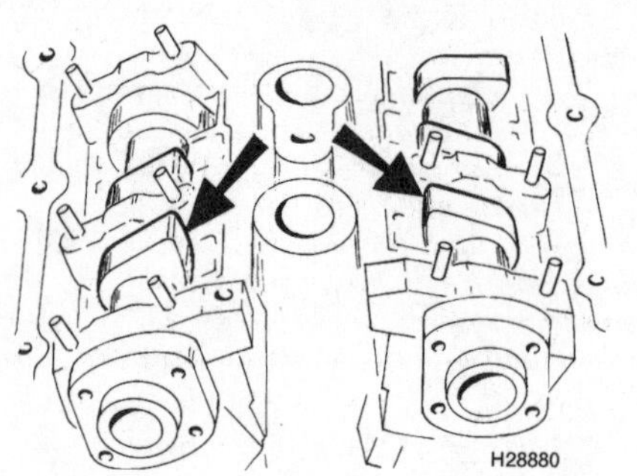


**14.51 Position the camshafts to that the tips of the front cam lobes (arrowed) face one another - M42 engine**

followers may fall out. Do not allow the cam followers to fall out and get mixed up, as they must be fitted to their original locations.

**39** With the bearing casting removed, lift the cam followers from the cylinder head. Identify the followers for location, and store them upright in a container of clean engine oil to prevent the oil from draining from inside the followers. Do not forget to mark the cam followers "Inlet" and "Exhaust".

**HAYNES HiNT** *Store each cam follower in a labelled plastic cup filled with oil.*

**40** Repeat the procedure on the remaining camshaft.

### Inspection

**41** Refer to paragraph 9.

### Refitting

**42** If the camshaft lower bearing castings have been removed, check that the mating faces of the bearing castings and the cylinder head are clean, and check that the bearing casting locating dowels are in position on the studs at Nos 2 and 5 bearing locations **(see illustration)**.

**43** The bearing casting(s) and cam followers must now be refitted.

**44** The simplest method of refitting these components is to retain the cam followers in the bearing casting, and refit the components as an assembly.

**45** Oil the bearing casting contact surfaces of the cam followers (avoid allowing oil onto the top faces of the followers at this stage), then fit each follower to its original location in the bearing casting.

**46** Once all the followers have been fitted, they must be retained in the bearing casting, so that they do not fall out as the assembly is refitted to the cylinder head (see illustrations and Haynes Hints in Chapter 2B, Section 10).

**47** With the cam followers retained in the bearing casting, refit the casting to the cylinder head. Note that the exhaust side casting is marked "A" and the inlet side casting is marked "E". When the castings are refitted, the marks should face each other at the timing chain end of the cylinder head **(see illustration)**.

***Warning: The cam followers expand when not subjected to load by the camshafts, and therefore require some time before they can be compressed. If the camshaft refitting operation is carried out rapidly, there is a possibility that the "closed" valves will be forced open by the expanded cam followers, resulting in piston-to-valve contact. To minimise this possibility, after refitting the camshaft(s) observe the following delays before turning the crankshaft back to the TDC position:***

| Temperature | Delay |
|---|---|
| Room temperature (20°C) | 4 minutes |
| 10°C to 20°C | 11 minutes |
| 0°C to 10°C | 30 minutes |

**48** First identify the camshafts to ensure that they are fitted in the correct locations. The camshafts are stamped in front of the rear square flanges. The exhaust camshaft is marked "A" and the inlet camshaft is marked "E".

**49** Ensure the crankshaft is still positioned at 90° clockwise from the TDC position (see **Warning** at the end of paragraph 29.

**50** Oil the bearing surfaces in the bearing casting.

**51** Position the camshaft on the cylinder head, so that the tips of the front cam lobes on the exhaust and inlet camshafts face one another **(see illustration)**. Note also that the square flanges on the rear of the camshaft should be positioned with the sides of the flanges exactly at right-angles to the top surface of the cylinder head (this can be checked using a set-square), and the side of the flange with holes drilled into it uppermost.

**52** Place the bearing caps in position, noting that the caps carry identification marks. The exhaust camshaft caps are marked "A1" to "A5", and the inlet camshaft caps are marked "E1" to "E5". Place the bearing caps in their original locations as noted before removal.

**53** Re-assemble BMW special tool 11 3 260, and refit it to the cylinder head as during removal.

***Warning: Again, do not attempt to refit the camshafts without the aid of the special tools.***

**54** Apply pressure to the relevant bearing caps by turning the eccentric shaft on the tools using a spanner.

**55** With pressure applied to the bearing caps, refit the bearing cap securing nuts, and tighten them as far as possible by hand.

**56** Tighten the bearing cap nuts to the specified torque, working progressively in a diagonal sequence.

**57** Once the bearing cap nuts have been tightened, unbolt the tools used to apply pressure to the bearing caps.

**58** Repeat the procedure on the remaining camshaft.

**59** Refit the spark plugs.

**60** Refit the template used to check the position of the camshafts. If necessary, turn the camshaft(s) slightly using a spanner on the flats provided until the template can be fitted.

***Warning: Note the warning at the end of paragraph 47 before proceeding.***

**61** Turn the crankshaft back 90° anti-clockwise to the TDC position, then re-engage the locking rod with the flywheel to lock the crankshaft in position.

**62** Manipulate the camshaft sprockets until the timing arrows on the sprockets are pointing vertically upwards, then engage the chain with the sprockets.

**63** Fit the sprockets to the camshafts, ensuring that the sprockets are fitted the correct way round as noted before removal, then refit the sprocket securing bolts.

**64** Tighten the sprocket securing bolts to the specified torque - if necessary, the camshafts can be counterheld using a 27 mm spanner on the flats provided between Nos 5 and 6 cam lobes.

**65** Refit and tighten the left-hand chain guide upper securing bolt.

**66** Refit the upper chain guide and tighten the securing bolts.

**67** The timing chain tensioner must now be fitted, but before fitting, check that the tensioner plunger is retracted as follows **(see illustrations 11.25a to 11.25d in Section 11)**. If a new tensioner is being fitted, it should be supplied with the plunger already in the retracted position.

**Warning: It is essential that the following procedure is carried out to ensure that the tensioner plunger is retracted. If the plunger is not fully retracted, it can lock in the extended position, causing the tensioner or timing chain to break, resulting in expensive engine damage.**

*a) Hold the tensioner upright, then knock the bottom end of the tensioner sleeve sharply on a solid surface such as a vice. This should cause the plunger to jump out of the end of the tensioner sleeve. Lift out the plunger and the spring.*
*b) Note the locations of the two circlips on the plunger.*
*c) Thoroughly clean the components.*
*d) Ensure the circlips are correctly located in their respective grooves on the plunger.*
*e) Slide the spring into the sleeve; engage the plunger with the end of the spring.*
*f) Clamp the assembly in a vice, with the plunger resting in the sleeve so that both circlips are still visible.*
*g) Tighten the vice to compress the plunger into the sleeve, until the first circlip engages with the groove in the sleeve.*
*h) Tighten the vice further to compress the plunger into the sleeve until the second circlip is heard to engage positively. Do not push the plunger too far into the sleeve, or the circlip will be release, unlocking the plunger.*
*i) Loosen the vice - the plunger should stay retracted in the sleeve.*
*j) If the plunger comes out of the sleeve as the vice is loosened, or if the overall length of the tensioner assembly is greater than specified, then procedure in paragraphs a) to i) must be repeated.*

**68** Refit the tensioner assembly, ensuring that it is fitted with the plunger against the tensioner rail, then refit the tensioner plug using a new sealing ring. Tighten the plug to the specified torque.
**69** Using a screwdriver, lever the timing chain and tensioner rail against the tensioner until the tensioner plunger is released from the sleeve to tension the chain.
**70** Remove the template used to lock the camshafts, and remove the locking tool from the flywheel, then refit the upper timing chain cover as described in Section 10.

**Warning: As described in the warning in paragraph 47, the cam followers expand when not subjected to load by the camshafts To minimise the possibility of piston-to-valve contact, after refitting the camshaft(s), observe the following delays before cranking the engine:**

| Temperature | Delay |
|---|---|
| Room temperature (20°C) | 10 minutes |
| 10°C to 20°C | 30 minutes |
| 0°C to 10°C | 75 minutes |

***Caution**: When the engine is first started, it must be run at a speed of 3500 rpm for 20 seconds as soon as it starts - this is to ensure that the tensioner is primed with oil.*

## *M43 engine*

**Note:** *BMW recommend that before removing the camshaft, the valves are depressed using a special tool, and the cam followers are removed. This eliminates the load on the camshaft as the bearing cap nuts are unscrewed. Provided care is taken, and the bearing cap nuts are unscrewed progressively and evenly, the procedure can be carried out without the special tool, as described in the following paragraphs. New oil spray tube securing bolt seals will be required on refitting.*

### Removal

**71** Remove the cylinder head cover as described in Section 4.
**72** Turn the crankshaft to position No 1 piston at TDC, as described in Section 3, but do not fit the tools to lock the crankshaft and camshaft in position.
**73** Turn the crankshaft through one further full revolution clockwise to bring No 4 piston to TDC on the firing stroke, then unscrew the two accessible camshaft sprocket bolts.
**74** Turn the crankshaft again through one further revolution to again position No 1 piston at TDC. Fit the tools to lock the crankshaft and camshaft in position (see Section 3).
**75** Unscrew the remaining two camshaft sprocket bolts which should now be accessible.
**76** Push back the top end of the chain tensioner rail to relieve the tension on the chain until the camshaft sprocket can be removed. Withdraw the sprocket from the camshaft, noting which way round it is fitted, then disengage the sprocket from the chain. Ensure that tension is kept on the chain - tie the chain up or support it using wire, to prevent it from dropping into the timing chain cover.
**77** Unscrew the securing bolts and withdraw the oil spray tube from the camshaft bearing caps **(see illustration)**. Recover the seals from the securing bolts.
**78** Check the camshaft bearing caps for identification marks. The front (timing chain end) bearing cap is not marked, but the remaining caps should be marked "2" to "5" from the timing chain end of the engine **(see illustration)**. Make suitable marks if necessary.
**79** Progressively unscrew and remove the camshaft bearing cap nuts, then remove the bearing caps.
**80** Lift the camshaft from the cylinder head.
**81** Proceed as described for the M40 engine in paragraphs 6 to 8.

### Inspection

**82** Refer to paragraph 9.

### Refitting

**83** Proceed as described for M40 engines in paragraphs 10 to 13.
**84** Fit the bearing caps to their correct locations as noted before removal, then fit the securing nuts, and tighten progressively to the specified torque.
**85** Fit new seals to the oil spray tube securing bolts, then refit the spray tube and tighten the bolts.
**86** Push back the top end of the chain tensioner rail, as during removal, to allow the camshaft sprocket to be fitted. Engage the camshaft sprocket with the chain, ensuring that it is fitted the correct way round as noted before removal, and manipulate the sprocket so that the timing arrow points vertically upwards.
**87** Fit the sprocket to the camshaft, aligning the bolt holes in the camshaft flange with the centres of the elongated holes in the sprocket (the camshaft should be locked in the TDC position using the template - see Section 3). Fit the two upper sprocket securing bolts, and tighten as far as possible by hand.
**88** Release the upper end of the tensioner rail, then tighten the two accessible camshaft sprocket bolts to the specified torque.
**89** Remove the flywheel locking tool, and remove the template used to check the camshaft position.
**90** Turn the crankshaft through one further full revolution clockwise to bring No 4 piston to TDC on the firing stroke, then refit and tighten the remaining two camshaft sprocket bolts.
**91** Refit the cylinder head cover as described in Section 4.

2A

**14.77 Oil spray tube securing bolt (arrowed) - M43 engine**

**14.78 Camshaft bearing cap identification mark - M43 engine**

## 15 Cylinder head - removal and refitting

### M40 engine

***Caution: Keep the cylinder head upright until all of the valve lifters have been removed. If this precaution is not taken, the oil may drain from the valve lifters, rendering them unserviceable.***

**Note:** *New cylinder head bolts and a new cylinder head gasket will be required on refitting.*

#### Removal

**1** Depressurise the fuel system as described in Chapter 4A, then disconnect the battery negative lead.

**2** Drain the cooling system as described in Chapter 1.

**3** Remove the air cleaner assembly and the airflow meter as described in Chapter 4A.

**4** Remove the upper and lower sections of the inlet manifold as described in Chapter 4A.

**5** Disconnect the exhaust front section from the manifold as described in Chapter 4A.

**6** Disconnect the coolant hose from the cylinder head.

**7** Remove the timing belt as described in Section 7.

**8** Unscrew the bolts securing the timing belt housing to the cylinder head.

**9** If not already done, disconnect the wiring plugs from the coolant temperature sensors located in the left-hand side of the cylinder head.

**10** Make a final check to ensure that all relevant hoses and wires have been disconnected to allow cylinder head removal.

**11** Progressively loosen the cylinder head bolts, working in a spiral pattern from the outside of the head inwards.

**12** Remove the cylinder head bolts **(see illustration)**.

**13** Release the cylinder head from the cylinder block and locating dowels by rocking it. Do not prise between the mating faces of the cylinder head and block, as this may damage the gasket faces.

**14** Ideally, an assistant will now be required to help lift the cylinder head from the block - take care as the cylinder head is heavy **(see illustration)**.

**15** Recover the cylinder head gasket.

#### Inspection

**16** Refer to Chapter 2C for details of cylinder head dismantling and reassembly.

**17** The mating faces of the cylinder head and block must be perfectly clean before refitting the head. Use a scraper to remove all traces of gasket and carbon, and also clean the tops of the pistons. Take particular care with the aluminium cylinder head, as the soft metal is easily damaged. Also make sure that debris is not allowed to enter the oil and water

**15.12 Removing a cylinder head bolt - M40 engine**

passages. Using adhesive tape and paper, seal the water, oil and bolt holes in the cylinder block. To prevent carbon entering the gap between the pistons and bores, smear a little grease in the gap. After cleaning each piston, rotate the crankshaft so that the piston moves **down** the bore, then wipe out the grease and carbon with a cloth rag.

**18** Check the block and head for nicks, deep scratches and other damage. If very slight, they may be removed from the cylinder block carefully with a file. More serious damage may be repaired by machining, but this is a specialist job.

**19** If warpage of the cylinder head is suspected, use a straight-edge to check it for distortion, with reference to Chapter 2C.

**20** Clean out the bolt holes in the block using a pipe cleaner or thin rag and a screwdriver. Make sure that all oil and water is removed, otherwise there is a possibility of the block being cracked by hydraulic pressure when the bolts are tightened.

**21** Examine the bolt threads and the threads in the cylinder block for damage. If necessary, use the correct size tap to chase out the threads in the block.

#### Refitting

**22** Ensure that the mating faces of the cylinder block and head are spotlessly clean, that the cylinder head bolt threads are clean and dry, and that they screw in and out of their locations.

**23** Check that the cylinder head locating dowels are correctly positioned in the cylinder block.

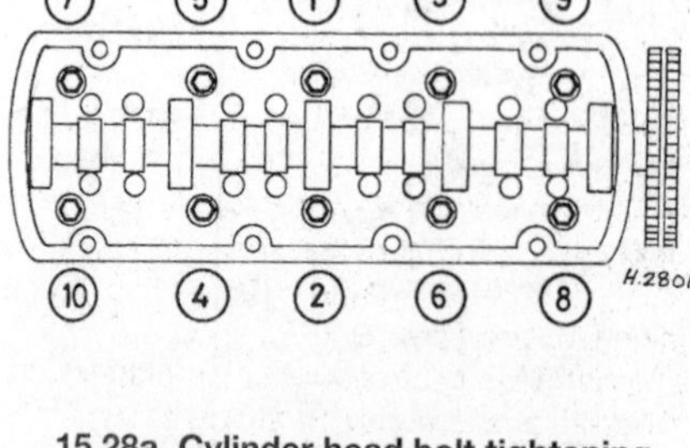


**15.28a Cylinder head bolt tightening sequence - M40 and M43 engines**

**15.14 Lifting off the cylinder head - M40 engine**

**24** Fit a new cylinder head gasket to the block, locating it over the dowels. Make sure that it is the correct way up. Note that 0.3 mm thicker-than-standard gaskets are available for use if the cylinder head has been machined (see Chapter 2C).

**25** If not already done, fit the template to the cylinder head to ensure that the camshaft is correctly positioned (No 1 piston at TDC) - see Section 3, and check that the flywheel is still locked in position.

**26** Lower the cylinder head into position. Ensure that the cylinder head engages with the locating dowels.

**27** Fit the **new** cylinder head bolts, and tighten the bolts as far as possible by hand.

**28** Tighten the bolts in the order shown, and in the stages given in the Specifications - ie, tighten all bolts in sequence to the Stage 1 torque, then tighten all bolts in sequence to the Stage 2 torque, and so on **(see illustrations)**.

**29** Further refitting is a reversal of removal, bearing in mind the following points.

*a) Ensure that all hoses and wires are correctly reconnected and routed as noted before removal.*

*b) Refit the timing belt (see Section 7).*

*c) Reconnect the exhaust front section to the manifold, referring to Chapter 4A.*

*d) Refit the lower and upper sections of the inlet manifold as described in Chapter 4A.*

*e) Refit the air cleaner assembly and the airflow meter, referring to Chapter 4A.*

*f) On completion, refill the cooling system as described in Chapter 1, and prime the fuel system as described in Chapter 4A.*

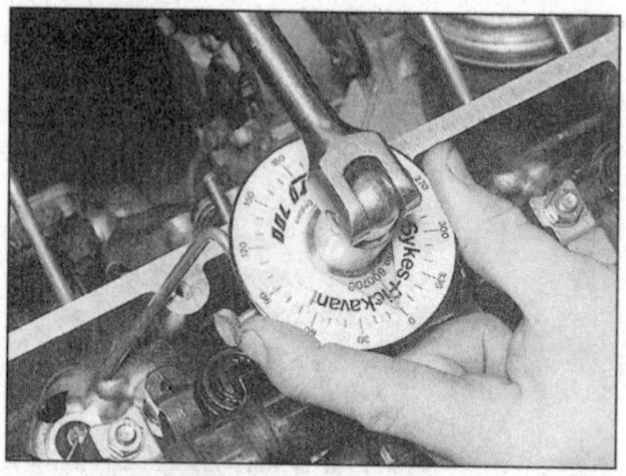

**15.28b Angle-tightening a cylinder head bolt - M40 engine**

*g) When first starting the engine after refitting the cylinder head, if there is a rattling noise from the valve-gear, this is probably due to the hydraulic valve lifters partially draining. If the rattling persists,* ***do not*** *run the engine above 2000 rpm until the rattling stops.*

## *M42 engine*

**Note:** *New cylinder head bolts and a new cylinder head gasket will be required on refitting.*

### Removal

**30** Proceed as described for M40 engines in paragraphs 1 to 4.
**31** Remove the exhaust manifold as described in Chapter 4A.
**32** Disconnect the coolant hose from the cylinder head.
**33** Remove the upper timing chain cover as described in Section 10.
**34** Position No 1 piston at TDC, and lock the flywheel in position, as described in Section 3.
**35** Unscrew the timing chain tensioner plug from the right-hand side of the engine. Recover the sealing ring.
**36** Withdraw the timing chain tensioner assembly from its housing.
**37** Unscrew the securing bolts, and withdraw the upper chain guide from the cylinder head **(see illustration)**.
**38** Unscrew the upper securing bolt from the left-hand chain guide.
**39** Unscrew the bolts securing the chain sprockets to the camshafts. Take care not to move the camshafts - if necessary, the camshafts can be counterheld using a 27 mm spanner on the flats provided between Nos 5 and 6 cam lobes.
**40** Withdraw the sprockets from the camshafts, and disengage them from the chain. Note which way round the sprockets are fitted to ensure correct refitting.
**41** Ensure that tension is kept on the timing chain - tie the chain up or support it using wire, to prevent it from dropping into the lower timing chain cover.
**42** If not already done, disconnect the wiring plugs from the coolant temperature sensors located in the left-hand side of the cylinder head.

**15.37 Unscrewing an upper chain guide securing bolt - M42 engine**

***Warning: To avoid any possibility of piston-to-valve contact when refitting the cylinder head, it is necessary to ensure that none of the pistons are at TDC. Before proceeding, remove the locking rod from the timing hole in the cylinder block, then turn the crankshaft approximately 90° clockwise using a spanner or socket on the crankshaft pulley hub bolt.***

**43** Proceed as described for the M40 engine in paragraphs 10 to 15, but where applicable recover the washers which fit under the cylinder head bolts. Note that the cylinder heads originally fitted in production have captive washers.

### Inspection

**44** Proceed as described for the M40 engine in paragraphs 16 to 21.

### Refitting

***Warning: If the camshafts have been removed from the cylinder head, note the Warnings given in Section 14, regarding expanded cam followers. Additionally, to minimise the possibility of piston-to-valve contact, after refitting the camshaft(s) observe the following delays before refitting the cylinder head.***

| Temperature | Delay |
|---|---|
| Room temperature (20°C) | 4 minutes |
| 10°C to 20°C | 11 minutes |
| 0°C to 10°C | 30 minutes |

**45** Ensure that the mating faces of the cylinder block and head are spotlessly clean, that the cylinder head bolt threads are clean and dry, and that they screw in and out of their locations.
**46** Check that the cylinder head locating dowels are correctly positioned in the cylinder block.

***Warning: To avoid any possibility of piston-to-valve contact when refitting the cylinder head, it is necessary to ensure that none of the pistons are at TDC. Before proceeding further, if not already done, turn the crankshaft to position No 1 piston at TDC (check that the locking rod can be engaged with the flywheel, then remove the locking rod and turn the crankshaft approximately 90° clockwise using a spanner or socket on the crankshaft pulley hub bolt.***

**47** Fit a new cylinder head gasket to the block, locating it over the dowels. Make sure that it is the correct way up. Note that 0.3 mm thicker-than-standard gaskets are available for use if the cylinder head has been machined (see Chapter 2C).
**48** If not already done, fit the template to the cylinder head to ensure that the camshaft is correctly positioned (No 1 piston at TDC) - see Section 3.
**49** Lower the cylinder head into position. Ensure that the cylinder head engages with the locating dowels.
**50** Fit the **new** cylinder head bolts, complete with new washers where necessary, and tighten the bolts as far as possible by hand. Ensure that the washers are correctly seated in their locations in the cylinder head.

**Note:** *Do not fit washers to any bolts which are fitted to locations where there are already captive washers in the cylinder head. If a new cylinder head is fitted (without captive washers), ensure that new washers are fitted to all the bolts.*

**51** Tighten the bolts in the order shown, and in the stages given in the Specifications - ie, tighten all bolts in sequence to the Stage 1 torque, then tighten all bolts in sequence to the Stage 2 torque, and so on **(see illustration)**.
**52** Turn the crankshaft back 90° anti-clockwise to the TDC position, then re-engage the locking rod with the flywheel to lock the crankshaft in position.
**53** Manipulate the camshaft sprockets until the timing arrows on the sprockets are pointing vertically upwards, then engage the chain with the sprockets.
**54** Fit the sprockets to the camshafts, ensuring that the sprockets are fitted the correct way round as noted before removal, then refit the sprocket securing bolts.
**55** Tighten the sprocket securing bolts to the specified torque - if necessary, the camshafts can be counterheld using a 27 mm spanner on the flats provided between Nos 5 and 6 cam lobes.
**56** Refit and tighten the left-hand chain guide upper securing bolt.
**57** Refit the upper chain guide and tighten the securing bolts.
**58** The timing chain tensioner must now be fitted, but before fitting, check that the tensioner plunger is retracted as follows **(see illustrations 11.25a to 11.25d in Section 11)**. If a new tensioner is being fitted, it should be supplied with the plunger already in the retracted position.

***Warning: It is essential that the following procedure is carried out to ensure that the tensioner plunger is retracted. If the plunger is not fully retracted, it can lock in***

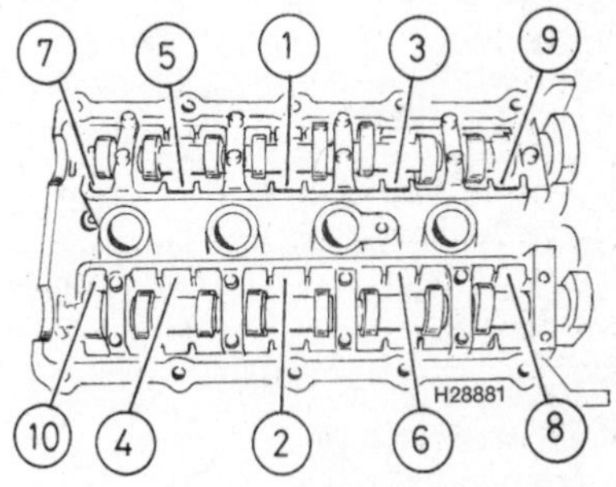


**15.51 Cylinder head bolt tightening sequence - M42 engine**

2A

***the extended position, causing the tensioner or timing chain to break, resulting in expensive engine damage.***

- *a) Hold the tensioner upright, then knock the bottom end of the tensioner sleeve sharply on a solid surface such as a vice. This should cause the plunger to jump out of the end of the tensioner sleeve. Lift out the plunger and the spring.*
- *b) Note the locations of the two circlips on the plunger.*
- *c) Thoroughly clean the components.*
- *d) Ensure the circlips are correctly located in their respective grooves on the plunger.*
- *e) Slide the spring into the sleeve, and engage the plunger with the end of the spring.*
- *f) Clamp the assembly in a vice, with the plunger resting in the sleeve so that both circlips are still visible.*
- *g) Tighten the vice to compress the plunger into the sleeve, until the first circlip engages with the groove in the sleeve.*
- *h) Tighten the vice further to compress the plunger into the sleeve until the second circlip is heard to engage positively. Do not push the plunger too far into the sleeve, or the circlip will be release, unlocking the plunger.*
- *i) Loosen the vice - the plunger should stay retracted in the sleeve.*
- *j) If the plunger comes out of the sleeve as the vice is loosened, or if the overall length of the tensioner assembly is greater than specified, then procedure in paragraphs a) to i) must be repeated.*

**59** Refit the tensioner assembly, ensuring that it is fitted with the plunger against the tensioner rail, then refit the tensioner plug using a new sealing ring. Tighten the plug to the specified torque.

**60** Using a screwdriver, lever the timing chain and tensioner rail against the tensioner until the tensioner plunger is released from the sleeve to tension the chain.

**61** Further refitting is a reversal of removal, bearing in mind the following points.

- *a) Refit the upper timing chain cover as described in Section 10.*
- *b) Refit the exhaust manifold as described in Chapter 4A.*
- *c) Refit the lower and upper sections of the inlet manifold as described in Chapter 4A.*
- *d) Refit the air cleaner assembly and the air mass meter as described in Chapter 4A.*
- *e) On completion, refill the cooling system as described in Chapter 1, and prime the fuel system as described in Chapter 4A.*

***Caution: When the engine is first started, it must be run at 3500 rpm for 20 seconds as soon as it starts - this is to ensure that the tensioner is primed with oil.***

## M43 engine

**Note:** *New cylinder head bolts and a new cylinder head gasket will be required on refitting.*

### Removal

**62** Proceed as described for the M40 engine in paragraphs 1 to 6.

**63** Remove the upper timing chain cover as described in Section 6.

**64** Remove the ignition coils as described in Chapter 5B.

**65** Remove the spark plugs as described in Chapter 1.

**66** If not already done, disconnect the wiring plugs from the coolant temperature sensors located in the left-hand side of the cylinder head.

**67** Disconnect the heater coolant hoses at the bulkhead and heater valve.

**68** Turn the crankshaft to position No 1 piston at TDC, as described in Section 3. Lock the crankshaft and camshaft in position as described.

**69** Unscrew the camshaft sprocket securing bolts.

**70** Push back the top end of the chain tensioner rail to relieve the tension on the chain until the camshaft sprocket can be removed. Withdraw the sprocket from the camshaft, noting which way round it is fitted, then disengage the sprocket from the chain. Ensure that tension is kept on the chain - tie the chain up or support it using wire, to prevent it from dropping into the lower timing chain cover.

**71** Unscrew the bolts securing the chain tensioner rail and the chain guide to the cylinder head.

***Warning: To avoid any possibility of piston-to-valve contact when refitting the cylinder head, it is necessary to ensure that none of the pistons are at TDC. Before proceeding further, remove the locking rod from the timing hole in the cylinder block, then turn the crankshaft approximately 45° anti-clockwise using a spanner or socket on the crankshaft pulley hub bolt.***

**72** Proceed as described for the M40 engine in paragraphs 10 to 13.

**73** Ideally, two assistants will now be required to help remove the cylinder head. Have one assistant hold the timing chain up, clear of the cylinder head, making sure that tension is kept on the chain. With the aid of another assistant, lift the cylinder head from the block - take care, as the cylinder head is heavy. Support the timing chain from the cylinder block using wire.

**74** Recover the cylinder head gasket, and recover the rubber seals from the top of the timing chain housing and the lower timing chain cover.

### Inspection

**75** Proceed as described for the M40 engine in paragraphs 16 to 21.

### Refitting

**76** Ensure that the mating faces of the cylinder block, timing chain housing, and head are spotlessly clean, that the cylinder head bolt threads are clean and dry, and that they screw in and out of their locations.

**77** Check that the cylinder head locating dowels are correctly positioned in the cylinder block.

***Warning: To avoid any possibility of piston-to-valve contact when refitting the cylinder head, it is necessary to ensure that none of the pistons are at TDC. Before proceeding further, if not already done, turn the crankshaft to position No 1 piston at TDC (check that the locking rod can be engaged with the flywheel, then remove the locking rod and turn the crankshaft approximately 45° anti-clockwise using a spanner or socket on the crankshaft pulley hub bolt.***

**78** Fit a new cylinder head gasket to the block, locating it over the dowels. Make sure that it is the correct way up. Note that 0.3 mm thicker-than-standard gaskets are available for use if the cylinder head has been machined (see Chapter 2C).

**79** Fit new rubber seals to the top of the timing chain housing - do not fit the lower timing chain cover rubber seal at this stage.

**80** If not already done, fit the template to the cylinder head to ensure that the camshaft is correctly positioned (No 1 piston at TDC) - see Section 3.

**81** Lower the cylinder head into position. As the cylinder head is lowered, push the timing chain tensioner rail away from the centre of the engine to allow the cylinder head to be lowered onto the block. Ensure that the cylinder head engages with the locating dowels.

**82** Fit the **new** cylinder head bolts, and tighten the bolts as far as possible by hand.

**83** Tighten the bolts in the order shown in **illustration 15.28a**, and in the stages given in the Specifications - ie, tighten all bolts in sequence to the Stage 1 torque, then tighten all bolts in sequence to the Stage 2 torque, and so on.

**84** Refit and tighten the bolts securing the timing chain tensioner rail and the chain guide to the cylinder head.

**85** Turn the crankshaft 45° clockwise, to position No 1 piston at TDC again, then refit the flywheel locking tool refit the template to check the position of the camshaft, as described in Section 3.

**86** Push back the top end of the chain tensioner rail, as during removal, to allow the camshaft sprocket to be fitted. Engage the camshaft sprocket with the chain, ensuring that it is fitted the correct way round as noted before removal, and manipulate the sprocket so that the timing arrow points vertically upwards.

**87** Fit the sprocket to the camshaft, aligning the bolt holes in the camshaft flange with the centres of the elongated holes in the sprocket (the camshaft should be locked in the TDC position using the template - see Section 3). Fit the sprocket securing bolts, and tighten as far as possible by hand.

**88** Release the upper end of the tensioner rail, then tighten the camshaft sprocket bolts to the specified torque.

**89** Remove the flywheel locking tool, and remove the template used to check the camshaft position.

**90** Further refitting is a reversal of removal, bearing in mind the following points.

a) *Ensure that all hoses and wires are correctly reconnected and routed as noted before removal.*
b) *Refit the lower and upper sections of the inlet manifold as described in Chapter 4A.*
c) *Refit the air cleaner assembly and the air mass meter with reference to Chapter 4A.*
d) *Reconnect the exhaust front section to the manifold, referring to Chapter 4A.*
e) *Refit the spark plugs as described in Chapter 1.*
f) *Refit the upper timing chain cover as described in Section 6.*
g) *On completion, refill the cooling system as described in Chapter 1, and prime the fuel system as described in Chapter 4A.*

## 16 Sump - removal and refitting

### *M40 engine*

**Note:** *New gaskets, and RTV sealant will be required on refitting, and a new oil pick-up pipe sealing ring will be required.*

#### Removal

**1** The sump consists of two sections.

**2** Drain the engine oil (see Chapter 1).

**3** Apply the handbrake, then jack up the front of the vehicle and support securely on axle stands (see *"Jacking and vehicle support"*).

**4** Remove the front section of the exhaust system as described in Chapter 4A.

**5** Open the bonnet, then raise the bonnet to its fully open position, referring to Chapter 11.

**6** Remove the air cleaner assembly and airflow meter, as described in Chapter 4A.

**7** Remove the heater/ventilation inlet air ducting from the rear of the engine compartment as follows.

a) *Lift the grille from the top of the ducting (on certain Coupe models, it will be necessary to remove the securing screws and lift off the complete scuttle grille assembly).*
b) *Working through the top of the ducting, remove the screws securing the cable ducting to the air ducting and move the cable ducting clear.*
c) *Unscrew the nuts and/or screw(s) securing the air ducting to the bulkhead (where applicable, bend back the heat shielding for access).*
d) *Remove the air ducting by pulling upwards.*
e) *Move the previously removed cable ducting clear of the cylinder head cover.*

**8** Remove the viscous cooling fan and fan cowl assembly as described in Chapter 3.

**9** Unscrew the dipstick tube bracket securing bolt, and pull the dipstick tube from the sump. Move the dipstick tube/bracket assembly to one side, complete with the idle speed control valve which is attached to the bracket. If necessary, disconnect the hoses and wiring from the valve.

**10** Unbolt the power steering fluid reservoir, and move the reservoir to one side, taking care not to strain the fluid hose.

**11** Where applicable, remove the power steering pump as described in Chapter 10.

**12** Unbolt the earth cable(s) from the engine mounting bracket(s).

**13** Make a final check to ensure that all surrounding components have been moved clear to allow removal of the sump.

**14** Position a hoist and lifting tackle to support the engine both from the lifting eye at the rear left-hand corner of the cylinder block, and from the lifting bracket at the front of the cylinder head. Check that the lifting tackle does not strain against surrounding components, then raise the hoist to just take the weight of the engine.

**15** Unscrew the nuts securing the left- and right-hand engine mounting brackets to the mounting rubbers, then lift the engine as necessary to allow sufficient clearance for sump removal. Make a careful check to ensure that there is no risk of damaging surrounding components in the engine compartment as the engine is lifted.

**16** Working under the vehicle, unscrew the securing bolts, and withdraw the lower section of the sump **(see illustration)**. Recover the gasket.

**17** Unbolt the oil pick-up pipe, and recover the sealing ring.

**18** Unscrew the securing bolts, and remove the main sump **(see illustration)**. Again, recover the gasket.

#### Refitting

**19** Refitting is a reversal of removal, bearing in mind the following points.

a) *Thoroughly clean all gasket faces.*
b) *Apply a little RTV sealant to the sump mating faces on the cylinder block at the points shown **(see illustration)**.*
c) *Use new gaskets, and use a new sealing ring when refitting the oil pick-up pipe.*
d) *Where applicable, refit the power steering pump as described in Chapter 10.*
e) *Refit the viscous fan and cowl assembly with reference to Chapter 3.*
f) *Refit the front section of the exhaust system as described in Chapter 4A.*
g) *Refill the engine with oil as described in Chapter 1.*

### *M42 and M43 engine*

**Note:** *A new gasket and sealant will be required on refitting.*



#### Removal

**20** Drain the engine oil (see Chapter 1).

**21** Apply the handbrake, then jack up the front of the vehicle and support securely on axle stands (see *"Jacking and vehicle support"*).

**22** Open the bonnet, then raise the bonnet to its fully open position, referring to Chapter 11.

**23** Disconnect the vacuum hose from the brake servo.

**24** Unscrew the bolt securing the dipstick tube to the inlet manifold, then pull the lower end of the tube from the sump, and withdraw the dipstick tube assembly.

**25** Position a hoist and lifting tackle over the engine compartment, and connect the lifting tackle to the front engine lifting bracket.

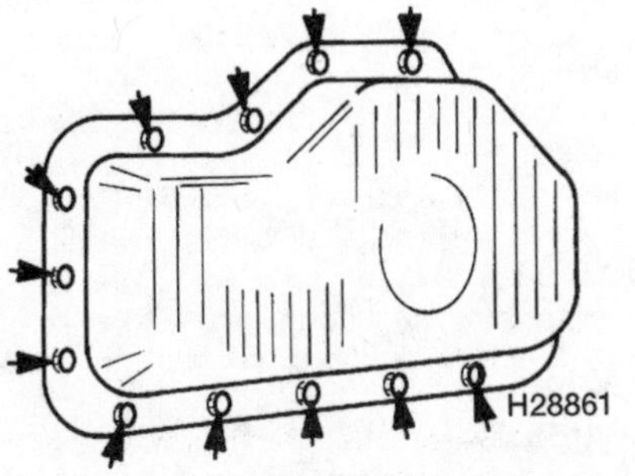


**16.16 Sump lower section securing bolt locations (arrowed) - M40 engine**

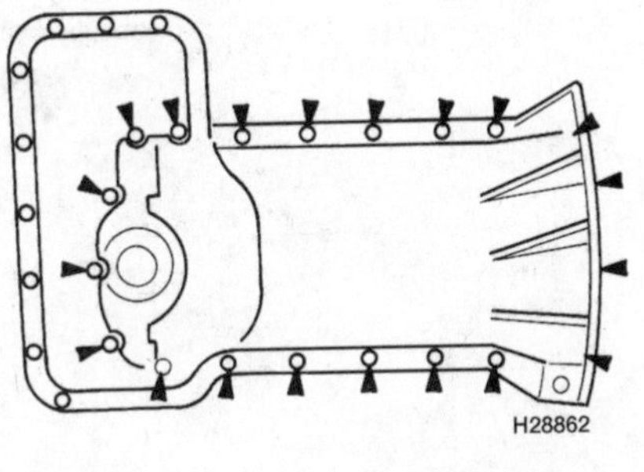


**16.18 Main sump securing bolts (arrowed) - M40 engine**

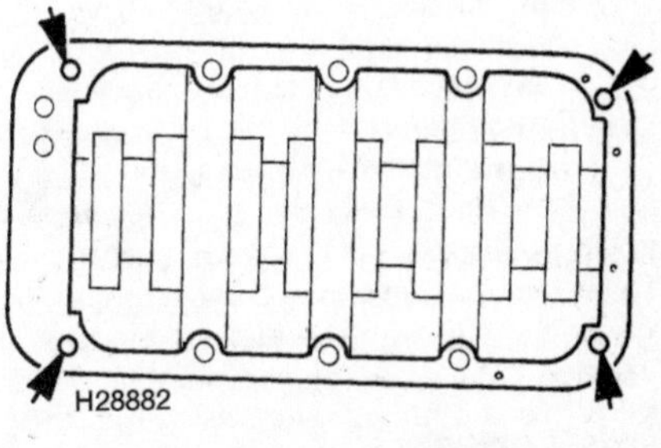


**16.19 Apply sealant to the sump mating faces of the cylinder block at the points arrowed - M40 engine**

16.32a Unscrew the front . . .

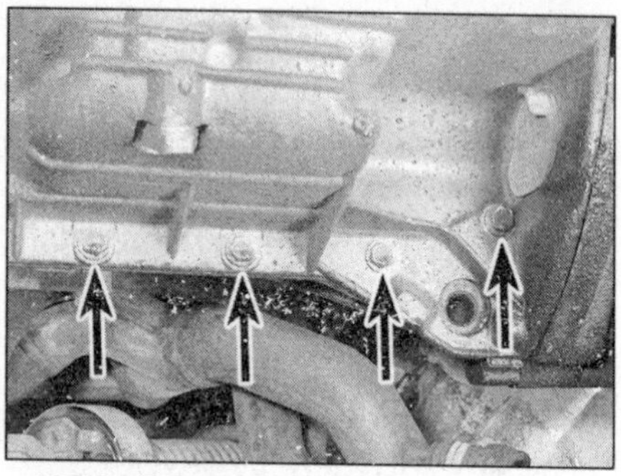

16.34a Four of the sump securing bolts (arrowed) - M42 engine shown

**26** Unbolt the power steering reservoir, and move the reservoir to one side, leaving the fluid lines connected.

**27** Unbolt the earth lead(s) from the engine mounting bracket(s).

**28** Working under the vehicle, unscrew the nuts securing the left- and right-hand engine mountings to the brackets on the subframe.

**29** Raise the lifting tackle to lift the engine approximately 5.0 mm.

**30** Again working under the vehicle, unscrew the bolts securing the suspension lower arms to the body.

**31** Support the centre of the subframe, using a jack and a block of wood.

**32** Unscrew the subframe securing bolts, then lower the subframe slightly using the jack **(see illustrations)**. ***Caution: Do not remove the steering gear from the subframe.***

**33** Where applicable, unclip the fuel pipes and/or the automatic transmission fluid cooler pipes from the brackets on the sump, and move the pipes clear of the working area.

**34** Working under the vehicle, progressively unscrew and remove all the sump securing bolts. The three lower gearbox/transmission-to-engine bolts must be removed, as they screw into the sump **(see illustrations)**.

**35** Lower the sump, and manipulate it out towards the rear of the vehicle. If necessary, lower the subframe further, using the jack, to give sufficient clearance. Similarly, if necessary, unbolt the oil pick-up pipe to ease sump removal.

**36** Recover the sump gasket, and discard it.

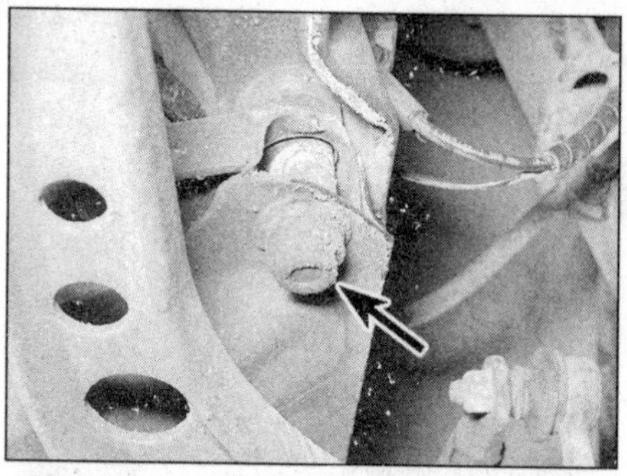

16.32b . . . and rear subframe securing bolts (arrowed) - M42 and M43 engines

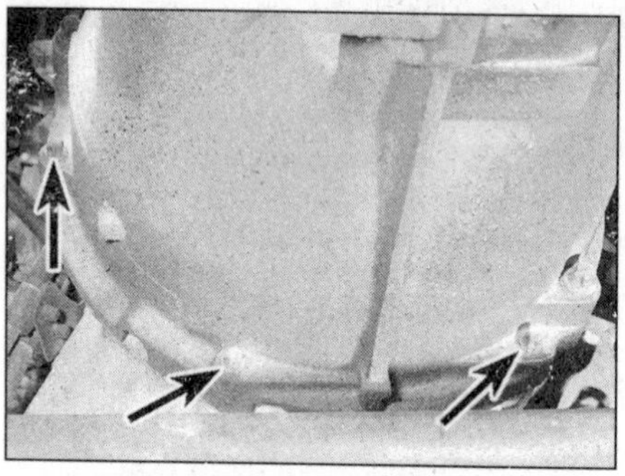

16.34b The three lower gearbox/ transmission-to-engine bolts (arrowed) must be unscrewed to remove the sump - M42 engine shown

### Refitting

**37** Commence refitting by thoroughly cleaning the mating faces of the sump and cylinder block.

**38** Lightly coat the areas where the crankshaft rear oil seal housing and the timing chain housing join the cylinder block with a little gasket sealant.

**39** Place a new gasket in position on the sump flange. If necessary, apply more sealant (sparingly) to hold the gasket in place.

**40** Offer the sump up to the cylinder block, ensuring that the gasket stays in place, and where applicable, refit the oil pick-up pipe using a new gasket.

**41** Refit the sump securing bolts, tightening them finger-tight only at this stage.

**42** Progressively tighten the sump-to-cylinder block bolts to the specified torque.

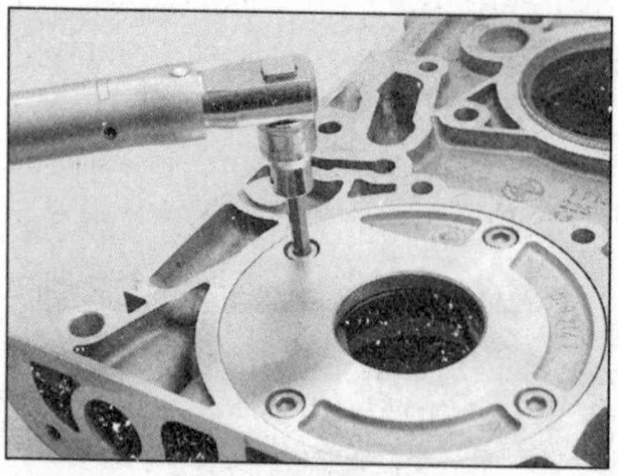

17.4a Unscrew the securing bolts . . .

**43** Tighten the sump-to-gearbox/transmission-to-engine bolts to the specified torque.

**44** Check the condition of the dipstick sealing ring (at the sump end of the tube) and renew if necessary. Refit the dipstick tube and tighten the bracket securing bolt.

**45** On models with automatic transmission, secure the fluid cooler lines to the sump. Similarly, where applicable, clip the fuel pipes into position.

**46** Raise the subframe using the jack, then refit the securing bolts and tighten to the specified torque.

**47** Refit the bolts securing the suspension lower arms to the body, ensuring that the washers are in place, and tighten the bolts to the specified torque.

**48** Lower the engine until the mountings are resting on the subframe, ensuring that the lugs on the engine mountings engage with the corresponding holes in the subframe. Refit the engine mounting nuts and tighten them to the specified torque.

**49** Disconnect and withdraw the engine lifting tackle and hoist.

**50** Further refitting is a reversal of removal, but on completion refill the engine with oil as described in Chapter 1.

## 17 Oil pump - removal, inspection and refitting

### Removal

**1** The oil pump is integral with the timing belt/chain housing.

**2** On M40 engines, remove the timing belt housing as described in Section 9.

**3** On M42 and M43 engines, remove the timing chain housing, referring to Section 13.

### Inspection

**4** Unscrew the oil pump cover from the rear of the timing belt/chain housing to expose the oil pump rotors **(see illustrations)**.

**5** Check the rotors for identification marks, and if necessary mark the rotors to ensure they are refitted in their original positions (mark the top faces of both rotors to ensure they are refitted the correct way up). Remove the rotors from the housing **(see illustrations)**.

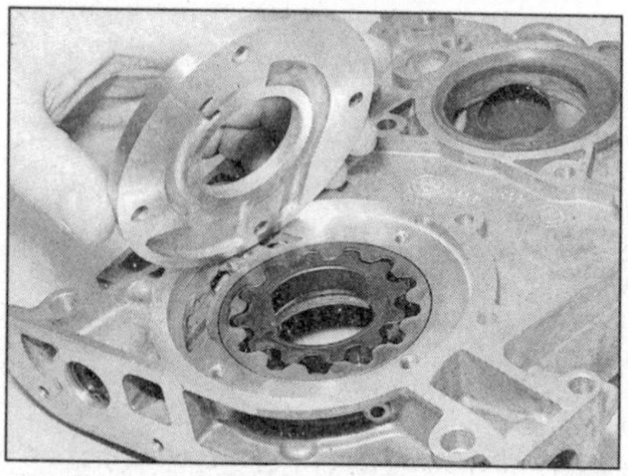

17.4b . . . and remove the oil pump cover - M40 engine shown

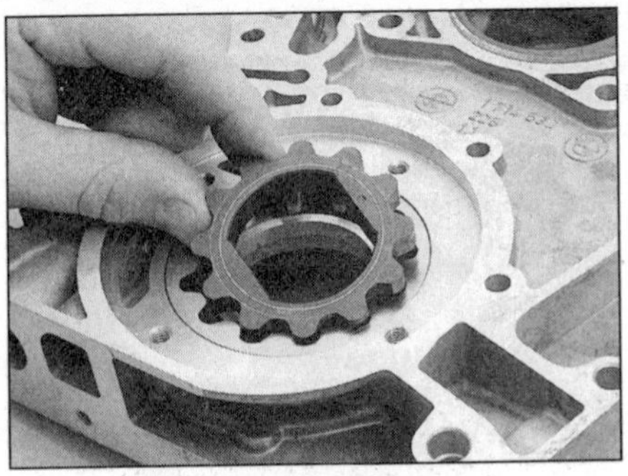

17.5a Remove the inner . . .

17.5b . . . and outer rotors from the oil pump - M40 engine shown

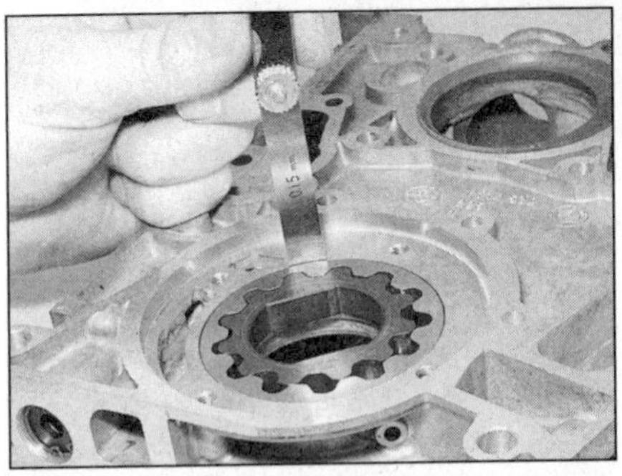

17.7 Measuring the clearance between the oil pump body and the outer rotor - M40 engine shown

17.11a Remove the pressure relief valve circlip . . .

17.11b . . . and remove the sleeve . . .

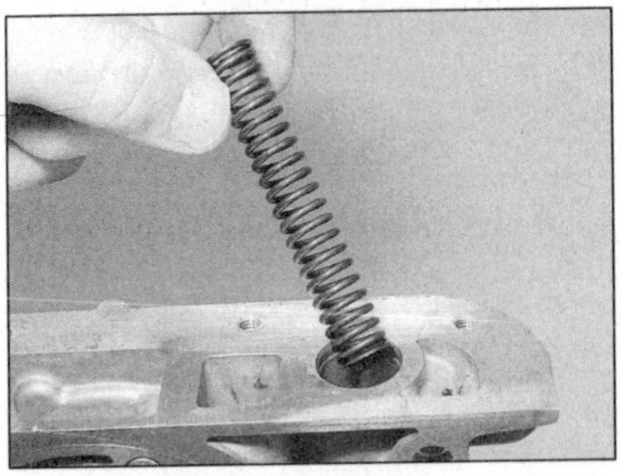

17.11c . . . spring . . .

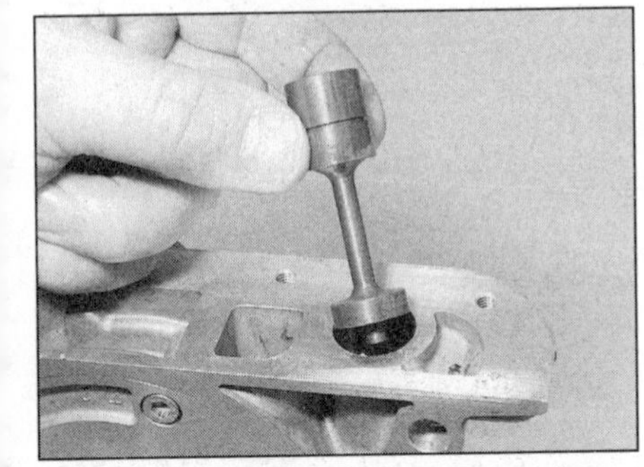

17.11d . . . and piston - M40 engine shown

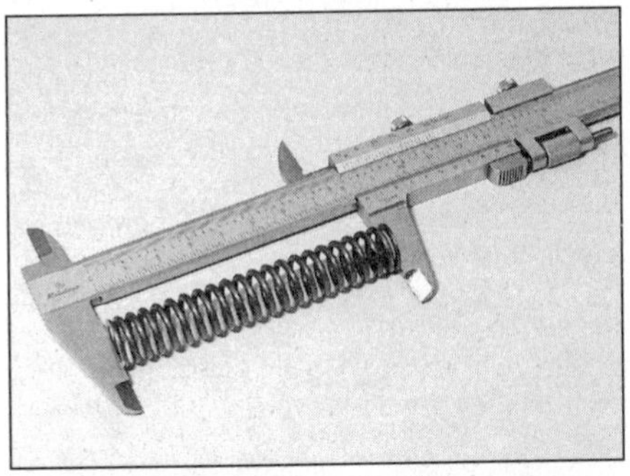

17.11e Check the length of the pressure relief valve spring - M40 engine shown

**6** Clean the housing and the rotors thoroughly, then refit the rotors to the housing, ensuring that they are positioned as noted before removal.

**7** Using feeler blades, measure the clearance between the oil pump body and the outer rotor. Using the feeler blades and a straight edge, measure the clearance (endfloat) between each of the rotors and the oil pump cover mating face **(see illustration)**.

**8** If the clearances are not as given in the Specifications, consult a BMW dealer regarding the availability of spare parts. The rotors should always be renewed as a matched pair. It may be necessary to renew the complete rotor/housing assembly as a unit.

**9** If the clearances are within the tolerances given, remove the rotors, then pour a little engine oil into the housing. Refit the rotors and turn them to lubricate all the contact surfaces.

**10** Refit the oil pump cover plate, and tighten the securing bolts to the specified torque.

**11** To check the oil pressure relief valve, extract the circlip and remove the sleeve, spring and piston. Check that the free-length of the spring is as given in the Specifications **(see illustrations )**.

**12** Reassemble the pressure relief valve using a reversal of the dismantling procedure.

### Refitting

**13** On M40 engines, refit the timing belt housing as described in Section 9.

**14** On M42 and M43 engines, refit the timing chain housing as described in Section 13.

## 18 Oil seals - renewal

2A

### *Crankshaft front oil seal*

#### M40 engine

**1** Remove the crankshaft sprocket (Section 8).

**2** If not already done, remove the Woodruff key from the end of the crankshaft. Hook the key out using a screwdriver if necessary.

**3** Withdraw the spacer ring from the front of the crankshaft.

**4** Measure and note the fitted depth of the oil seal in the housing.

**5** Pull the oil seal from the housing using a hooked instrument. Alternatively, drill a small hole in the oil seal, and use a self-tapping screw and a pair of pliers to remove it.

**6** Clean the oil seal housing and the crankshaft sealing surface.

**7** Dip the new oil seal in clean engine oil, and press it into the housing (open end first) to the previously-noted depth, using a suitable tube or socket.

**8** Fit the spacer ring to the front of the crankshaft, taking care not to damage the oil seal as the spacer is fitted.

**9** Refit the Woodruff key to the crankshaft.

**10** Refit the crankshaft sprocket (Section 8).

#### M42 and M43 engines

**11** Oil seal renewal is described as part of the lower timing chain cover removal and refitting procedure in Section 10.

### Crankshaft rear oil seal

**12** Proceed as described for 6-cylinder engines in Chapter 2B, Section 14.

### Camshaft oil seals

#### M40 engine

**13** A front oil seal is fitted between the front camshaft bearing cap and the cylinder head, but no rear oil seal is fitted (sealing is provided by the cylinder head cover gasket).

**14** To renew the front oil seal, proceed as follows.

**15** Remove the camshaft sprocket as described in Section 8.

**16** Pull the oil seal from the housing using a hooked instrument. Alternatively, drill a small hole in the oil seal, and use a self-tapping screw and a pair of pliers to remove it.

**17** Clean the oil seal housing and the camshaft sealing surface.

**18** Wrap some adhesive tape around the end of the camshaft to protect the new seal as it is fitted.

**19** Dip the new oil seal in clean engine oil, and press it into the housing (open end first) to the previously-noted depth, using a suitable tube or socket.

**20** Remove the adhesive tape from the camshaft.

**21** Refit the camshaft sprocket as described in Section 8.

#### M42 and M43 engines

**22** No camshaft oil seals are fitted. Sealing is provided by the cylinder head cover gasket and the timing chain cover gaskets.

## 19 Flywheel/driveplate - removal and refitting

The procedure is as described for 6-cylinder engines in Chapter 2B, Section 15.

## 20 Crankshaft spigot bearing - renewal

The procedure is as described for 6-cylinder engines in Chapter 2B, Section 16.

## 21 Engine/transmission mountings - inspection and renewal

The procedure is as described for 6-cylinder engines in Chapter 2B, Section 17.

# Chapter 2 Part B:
# 6-cylinder engine in-car repair procedures

## Contents



## Degrees of difficulty

| | | | | |
|---|---|---|---|---|
| **Easy,** suitable for novice with little experience | **Fairly easy,** suitable for beginner with some experience | **Fairly difficult,** suitable for competent DIY mechanic | **Difficult,** suitable for experienced DIY mechanic | **Very difficult,** suitable for expert DIY or professional |

2B

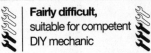

## Specifications

### General

| | |
|---|---|
| Engine code: | |
| 2.0 litre engine | M50 B20 |
| 2.5 litre engine | M50 B25 |
| Displacement: | |
| 2.0 litre engines | 1991 cc |
| 2.5 litre engines | 2494 cc |
| Bore: | |
| 2.0 litre engine | 80.000 mm |
| 2.5 litre engine | 84.000 mm |
| Stroke: | |
| 2.0 litre engine | 66.000 mm |
| 2.5 litre engine | 75.000 mm |
| Maximum engine power: | |
| 2.0 litre engine | 110 kW at 6000 rpm |
| 2.5 litre engine | 141 kW at 6000 rpm |
| Maximum engine torque: | |
| 2.0 litre non-VANOS engine | 190 Nm at 4700 rpm |
| 2.0 litre VANOS engine | 190 Nm at 4200 rpm |
| 2.5 litre non-VANOS engine | 245 Nm at 4700 rpm |
| 2.5 litre VANOS engine | 245 Nm at 4200 rpm |
| Direction of engine rotation | Clockwise (viewed from front of vehicle) |
| No 1 cylinder location | Timing chain end |
| Firing order | 1-5-3-6-2-4 |
| Compression ratio: | |
| 2.0 litre non-VANOS engine | 10.5 : 1 |
| 2.0 litre VANOS engine | 11.0 : 1 |
| 2.5 litre non-VANOS engine | 10.0 : 1 |
| 2.5 litre VANOS engine | 10.5 : 1 |
| Minimum compression pressure | 10.0 to 11.0 bar |

## Camshafts

| | |
|---|---|
| Endfloat | 0.150 to 0.330 mm |
| Radial play (freeplay in bearings) | 0.020 to 0.054 mm |
| Cam height: | |
| Non-VANOS engines: | |
| Inlet | 47.700 ± 0.060 mm |
| Exhaust | 46.800 ± 0.060 mm |
| VANOS engines (inlet and exhaust) | 47.000 ± 0.060 mm |

## Lubrication system

| | |
|---|---|
| Minimum oil pressure at idle speed | 0.5 bar |
| Regulated oil pressure | 4.0 bar |
| Oil pressure relief valve spring free-length | 84.1 mm |
| Oil pump rotor clearances: | |
| Outer rotor-to-pump body | 0.100 to 0.176 mm |
| Inner rotor endfloat | 0.030 to 0.080 mm |
| Outer rotor endfloat | 0.040 to 0.090 mm |

## Torque wrench settings

| | Nm | lbf ft |
|---|---|---|
| Main bearing cap bolts*: | | |
| Stage 1 | 20 | 15 |
| Stage 2 | Angle-tighten through a further 50° | |
| Cylinder head bolts*: | | |
| Stage 1 | 30 | 22 |
| Stage 2 | Angle-tighten through a further 90° | |
| Stage 3 | Angle-tighten through a further 90° | |
| Cylinder head cover bolts: | | |
| M6 bolts | 10 | 7 |
| M7 bolts | 15 | 11 |
| Sump oil drain plug: | | |
| M12 plug | 35 | 26 |
| M22 plug | 60 | 44 |
| Upper and lower timing chain cover nuts and bolts: | | |
| M6 nuts/bolts | 10 | 7 |
| M8 nuts/bolts | 22 | 16 |
| M10 nuts/bolts | 47 | 35 |
| Crankshaft rear oil seal housing bolts: | | |
| M6 bolts | 10 | 7 |
| M8 bolts | 22 | 16 |
| Flywheel bolts* | 105 | 77 |
| Crankshaft vibration damper/pulley-to-hub bolts | 22 | 16 |
| Crankshaft pulley hub bolt* | 410 | 303 |
| Big-end bearing cap bolts*: | | |
| Stage 1 | 20 | 15 |
| Stage 2 | Angle-tighten through a further 70° | |
| Camshaft bearing cap nuts: | | |
| M6 nuts | 10 | 7 |
| M7 nuts | 15 | 11 |
| M8 nuts | 20 | 15 |
| Camshaft sprocket nuts/bolts: | | |
| Stage 1 | 5 | 4 |
| Stage 2 | 22 | 16 |
| Primary timing chain tensioner cover plug | 70 | 52 |
| VANOS solenoid valve | 30 | 22 |
| Oil feed pipe to VANOS adjustment unit | 32 | 24 |
| VANOS oil feed pipe to oil filter housing | 50 | 37 |
| Oil pump bolts: | | |
| M6 bolts | 10 | 7 |
| M8 bolts | 22 | 16 |
| Oil pump cover | 10 | 7 |
| Oil pump sprocket nut | 25 | 18 |
| Oil filter housing-to-cylinder block bolts | 22 | 16 |
| Front subframe bolts* | 105 | 77 |

*Use new bolts*

## 1 General information

### How to use this Chapter

This Part of Chapter 2 describes the repair procedures that can reasonably be carried out on the engine while it remains in the vehicle. If the engine has been removed from the vehicle and is being dismantled as described in Part C, any preliminary dismantling procedures can be ignored.

Note that, while it may be possible physically to overhaul items such as the piston/connecting rod assemblies while the engine is in the car, such tasks are not usually carried out as separate operations. Usually, several additional procedures are required (not to mention the cleaning of components and oilways); for this reason, all such tasks are classed as major overhaul procedures, and are described in Part C of this Chapter.

Part C describes the removal of the engine/transmission from the car, and the full overhaul procedures that can then be carried out.

### Engine description

#### General

The M50 engine is of 6-cylinder double overhead camshaft design, mounted in-line, with the transmission bolted to the rear end.

A timing chain drives the exhaust camshaft, and the inlet camshaft is driven by a second chain from the end of the exhaust camshaft. Hydraulic cam followers are fitted between the camshafts and the valves. Each camshaft is supported by seven bearings incorporated in bearing castings fitted to the cylinder head.

The crankshaft runs in seven main bearings of the usual shell-type. Endfloat is controlled by thrust bearing shells on No 6 main bearing.

The pistons are selected to be of matching weight, and incorporate fully-floating gudgeon pins retained by circlips.

The oil pump is chain-driven from the front of the crankshaft.

#### VANOS variable camshaft timing control system

On models from approximately September 1992, a modified engine was introduced with a variable camshaft timing control system, known as VANOS. The VANOS engines superseded the earlier 6-cylinder engine types across the model range. The VANOS system uses data supplied by the DME engine management system (see Chapter 4B), to adjust the timing of the inlet camshaft via a hydraulic control system (using engine oil as the hydraulic fluid). The camshaft timing is varied according to engine speed, retarding the timing (opening the inlet valves later) at low and high engine speeds to improve low-speed driveability and maximum power respectively. At medium engine speeds, the camshaft timing is advanced (opening the inlet valves earlier) to increase mid-range torque and to improve exhaust emissions.

### Repair operations possible with the engine in the vehicle

The following operations can be carried out without having to remove the engine from the vehicle:

*a) Removal and refitting of the cylinder head.*
*b) Removal and refitting of the timing chain and sprockets.*
*c) Removal and refitting of the camshafts.*
*d) Removal and refitting of the sump.*
*e) Removal and refitting of the big-end bearings, connecting rods, and pistons*.*
*f) Removal and refitting of the oil pump.*
*g) Renewal of the engine/transmission mountings.*
*h) Removal and refitting of the flywheel/driveplate.*

** Although it is possible to remove these components with the engine in place, for reasons of access and cleanliness it is recommended that the engine is removed.*

## 2 Compression test - description and interpretation

**1** When engine performance is down, or if misfiring occurs which cannot be attributed to the ignition or fuel systems, a compression test can provide diagnostic clues as to the engine's condition. If the test is performed regularly, it can give warning of trouble before any other symptoms become apparent.

**2** The engine must be fully warmed-up to normal operating temperature, the battery must be fully charged, and all the spark plugs must be removed (Chapter 1). The aid of an assistant will also be required.

**3** Disable the ignition and fuel injection systems by removing the DME master relay, and the fuel pump relay, located in the main fuse box in the engine compartment (see Chapter 12).

**4** Fit a compression tester to the No 1 cylinder spark plug hole - the type of tester which screws into the plug thread is to be preferred.

**5** Have the assistant hold the throttle wide open, and crank the engine on the starter motor. After one or two revolutions, the compression pressure should build up to a maximum figure, and then stabilise. Record the highest reading obtained.

**6** Repeat the test on the remaining cylinders, recording the pressure in each.

**7** All cylinders should produce very similar pressures; a difference of more than 2 bars between any two cylinders indicates a fault. Note that the compression should build up quickly in a healthy engine; low compression on the first stroke, followed by gradually-increasing pressure on successive strokes, indicates worn piston rings. A low compression reading on the first stroke, which does not build up during successive strokes, indicates leaking valves or a blown head gasket (a cracked head could also be the cause). Deposits on the undersides of the valve heads can also cause low compression.

**8** BMW recommended values for compression pressures are given in the Specifications.

**9** If the pressure in any cylinder is low, carry out the following test to isolate the cause. Introduce a teaspoonful of clean oil into that cylinder through its spark plug hole, and repeat the test.

**10** If the addition of oil temporarily improves the compression pressure, this indicates that bore or piston wear is responsible for the pressure loss. No improvement suggests that leaking or burnt valves, or a blown head gasket, may be to blame.

**11** A low reading from two adjacent cylinders is almost certainly due to the head gasket having blown between them; the presence of coolant in the engine oil will confirm this.

**12** If one cylinder is about 20 percent lower than the others and the engine has a slightly rough idle, a worn camshaft lobe could be the cause.

**13** If the compression reading is unusually high, the combustion chambers are probably coated with carbon deposits. If this is the case, the cylinder head should be removed and decarbonised.

**14** On completion of the test, refit the spark plugs (see Chapter 1) and reconnect the fuel pump relay and the DME master relay.

2B

## 3 Top Dead Centre (TDC) for No 1 piston - locating

**Note:** *To lock the engine in the TDC position, and to check the position of the camshafts, special tools will be required. These tools can easily be improvised - see text.*

**1** Top Dead Centre (TDC) is the highest point in the cylinder that each piston reaches as it travels up and down when the crankshaft turns. Each piston reaches TDC at the end of the compression stroke and again at the end of the exhaust stroke, but TDC generally refers to piston position on the compression stroke. No 1 piston is at the timing chain end of the engine.

**2** Positioning No 1 piston at TDC is an essential part of many procedures, such as timing chain removal and camshaft removal.

**3** Remove the cylinder head cover as described in Section 4.

**4** Unclip the plastic cover from the inlet camshaft **(see illustrations)**.

**5** Using a socket or spanner on the crankshaft pulley bolt, turn the engine clockwise until the tips of the front cam lobes on the exhaust and inlet camshafts face one another. When the

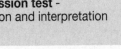

**3.4a Release the securing clips . . .**

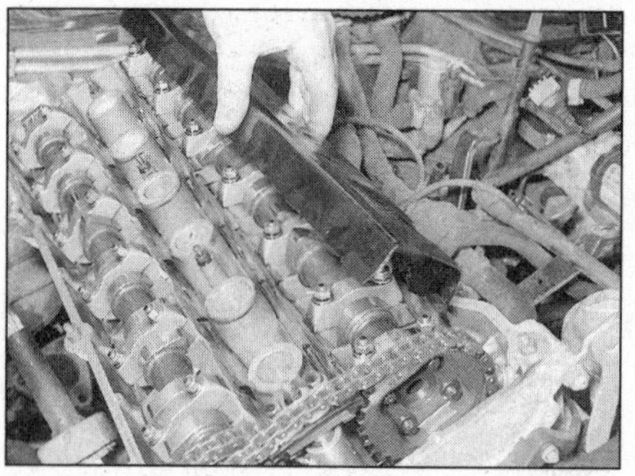

**3.4b . . . and remove the cover from the inlet camshaft**

**3.5a With No 1 piston at TDC, the tips of the front cam lobes face each other . . .**

**3.5b . . . and the arrows on the camshaft sprockets point vertically upwards**

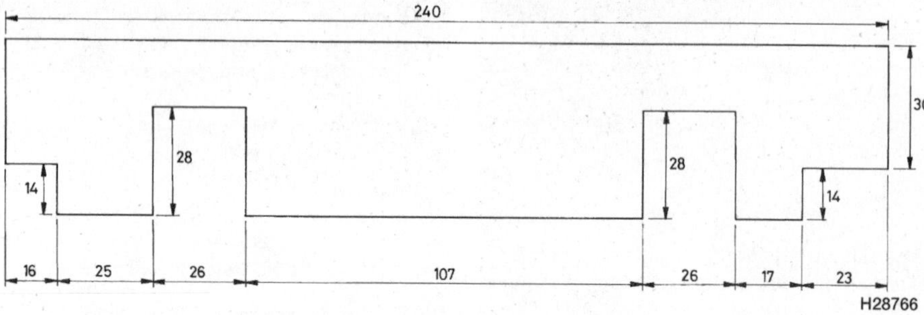


**3.6a Make up a template from metal sheet to the dimensions shown**
*All dimensions in mm*

**3.6b Template in place on upper surface of cylinder head with No 1 piston at TDC**

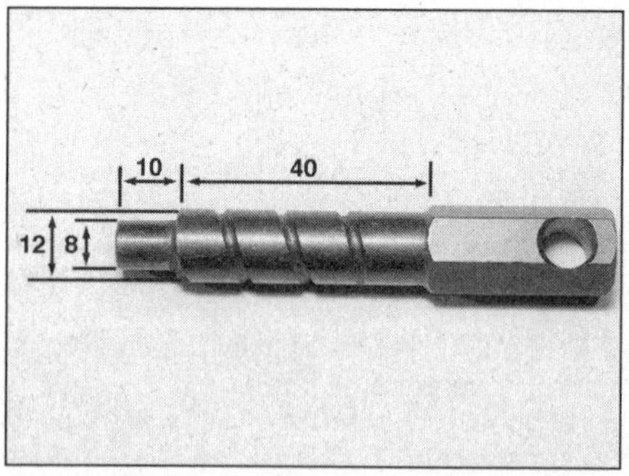


**3.8 Dimensions of flywheel "locking" tool**
*All dimensions in mm*

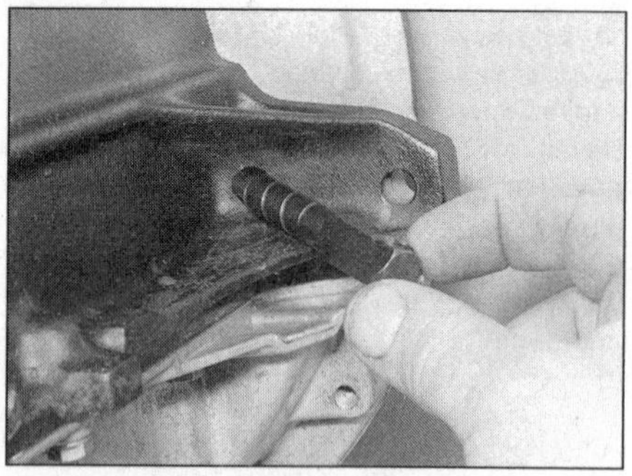

**3.9a Insert the rod through the timing hole . . .**

camshafts are correctly positioned, the arrows on the camshaft sprockets will point vertically upwards (note that there may be arrows at the top and bottom of the sprockets) **(see illustrations)**. Note also that the square flanges on the rear of the camshafts should be positioned with the sides of the flanges exactly at right-angles to the top surface of the cylinder head (this can be checked using a set-square), and the side of the flange with holes drilled into it uppermost.

**6** A more accurate check on the camshaft positions can be made by making up a template from metal sheet to the dimensions shown - when the camshafts are correctly positioned, the template will fit exactly over the camshaft flanges, and rest on the upper surface of the cylinder head **(see illustrations)**. Note that it will be necessary to unbolt the rear camshaft cover studs from the cylinder head to enable the template to be fitted.

**7** Pull the blanking plug from the timing hole in the left-hand rear corner flange of the cylinder block (access is much improved if the starter motor is removed - see Chapter 5A).

**8** To "lock" the crankshaft in position, a special tool will now be required. BMW tool No 11 2 300 can be used, but one can be made up by machining a length of steel rod to the dimensions shown **(see illustration)**.

**9** Insert the rod through the timing hole. If necessary, turn the crankshaft slightly until the rod enters the TDC hole in the flywheel **(see illustrations)**.

**10** The crankshaft is now "locked" in position with No 1 piston at TDC.

***Warning: If, for any reason, it is necessary to turn either or both of the camshafts with No 1 piston positioned at TDC, and either of the timing chain tensioners slackened or removed (or the timing chains removed), the following precaution must be observed. Before turning the camshaft(s), the crankshaft must be turned approximately 30° clockwise away from the TDC position (remove the locking rod from the TDC hole in the flywheel to do this) to prevent the possibility of piston-to-valve contact.***

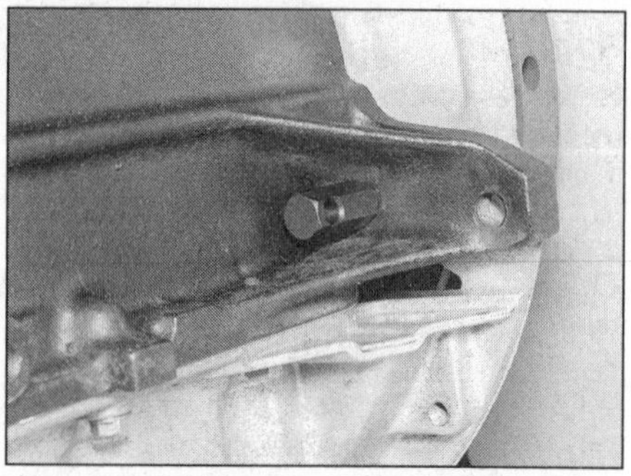

**3.9b . . . until it enters the TDC hole in the flywheel - engine removed for clarity**

**4.4a Prising a securing nut cover plate from the fuel rail cover**

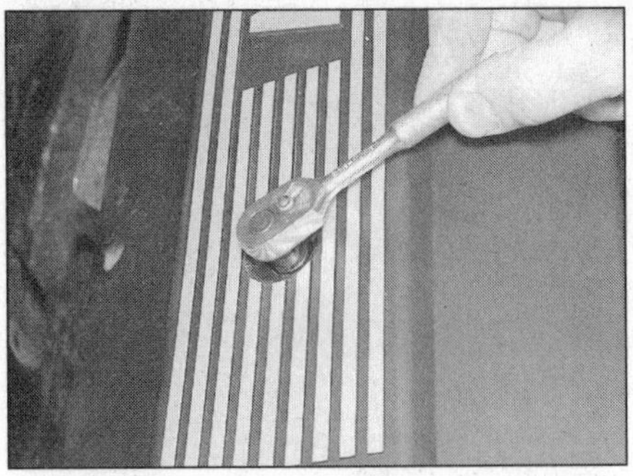

**4.4b Unscrewing a cylinder head plastic cover securing nut**

**4.4c Removing the cylinder head plastic cover**

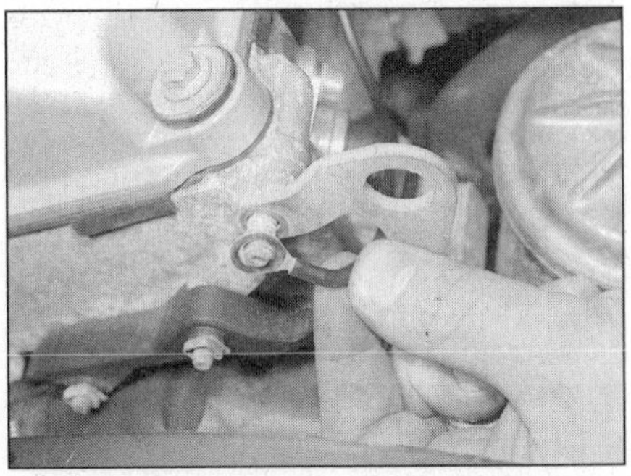

**4.5 Disconnect the earth lead from the upper timing chain cover**

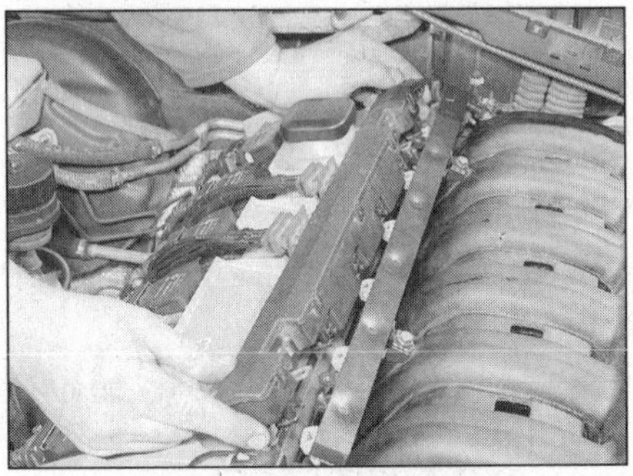

**4.6 Pulling the wiring ducting from the fuel injectors**

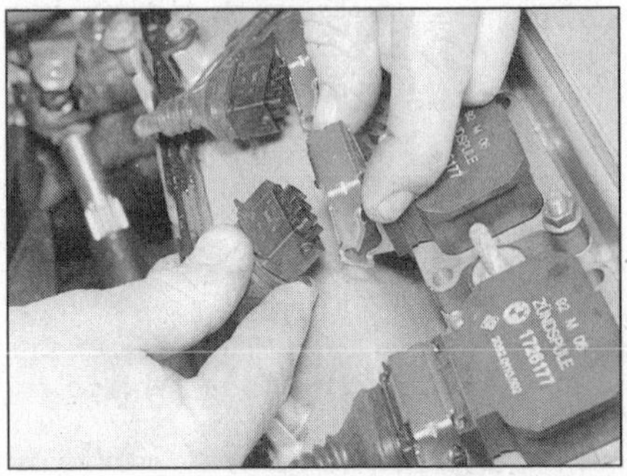

**4.7 Disconnecting a coil wiring plug**

**11 Do not** attempt to turn the engine with the flywheel or camshaft(s) locked in position, as engine damage may result. If the engine is to be left in the "locked" state for a long period of time, it is a good idea to place suitable warning notices inside the vehicle, and in the engine compartment. This will reduce the possibility of the engine being cranked on the starter motor.

## 4 Cylinder head cover - removal and refitting

### *Removal*

**Note:** *New gaskets and/or seals may be required on refitting - see text.*

**1** Open the bonnet, then raise the bonnet to its fully open position, referring to Chapter 11.

**2** Where necessary, to allow sufficient clearance for the cylinder head cover to be removed, remove the heater/ventilation inlet air ducting from the rear of the engine compartment as follows.

*a) Lift the grille from the top of the ducting (on certain Coupe models, it will be necessary to remove the windscreen wiper arms, then remove the plastic securing screws and lift off the complete scuttle grille assembly).*

*b) Working through the top of the ducting, remove the screws securing the cable ducting to the air ducting and move the cable ducting clear.*

*c) Unscrew the nuts and/or screw(s) securing the air ducting to the bulkhead (where applicable, bend back the heat shielding for access).*

*d) Remove the air ducting by pulling upwards.*

*e) Move the previously removed cable ducting clear of the cylinder head cover.*

**3** Remove the engine oil filler cap.

**4** Remove the plastic covers from the fuel rail and the top of the cylinder head cover. To remove the covers, prise out the cover plates and unscrew the two securing nuts. To remove the cover from the cylinder head, lift and pull the cover forwards, then manipulate the cover over the oil filler neck **(see illustrations)**.

**5** Unbolt the earth lead from the left-hand corner of the upper timing chain cover, and where applicable, unbolt the earth strap from the rear of the cylinder head cover **(see illustration)**.

**6** Remove the two nuts securing the engine wiring ducting to the fuel rail, then pull the ducting up to release the wiring plugs from the fuel injectors **(see illustration)**.

**7** Unclip the wiring connectors from the ignition coils. Recover the rubber seals if they are loose **(see illustration)**.

**8** Release the wiring from the clips on the cylinder head cover, then move the complete ducting/wiring assembly to one side, clear of the cylinder head cover.

**9** Unscrew the ignition coil securing nuts, then carefully pull the coils, complete with connectors, from the spark plugs **(see illustration)**. Note the locations of the earth leads and the coil wiring brackets.

**10** Release the securing clip and disconnect the breather hose from the side of the cylinder head cover **(see illustration)**.

**11** Unscrew the securing bolts and the two studs (which also secure the coil earth leads)

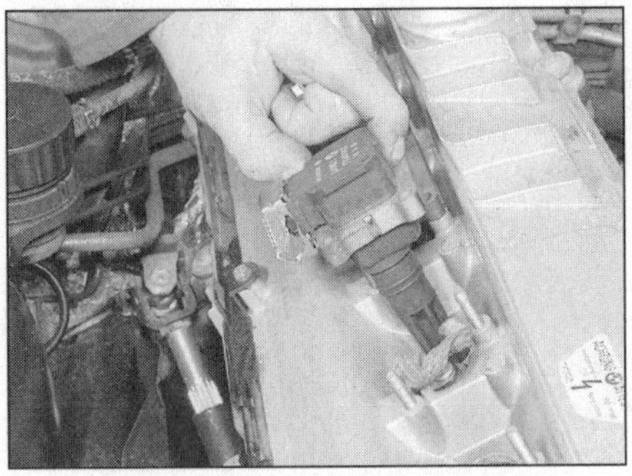

**4.9 Removing an ignition coil**

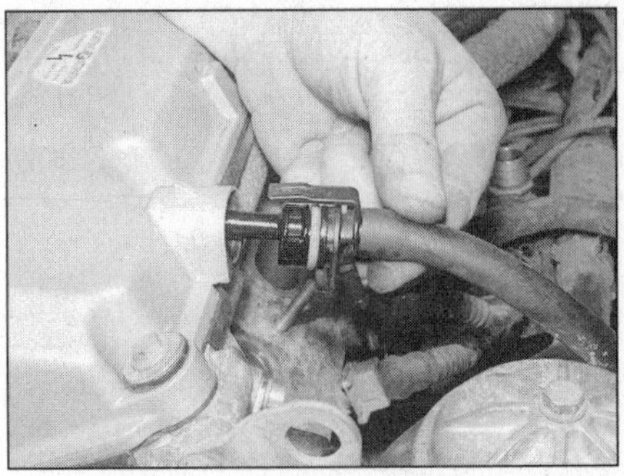

**4.10 Disconnecting the breather hose from the cylinder head cover**

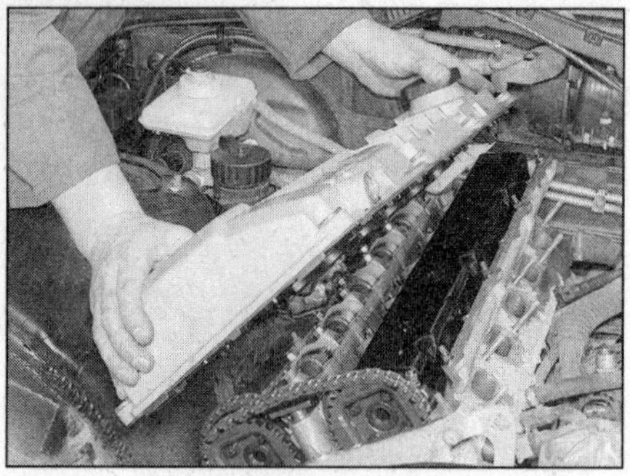

**4.11 Lifting off the cylinder head cover**

and lift off the cylinder head cover. Note the locations of all washers, seals and gaskets, and recover any which are loose **(see illustration)**.

### Refitting

**12** Commence refitting by checking the condition of all seals and gaskets. Renew any which are perished or damaged.

**13** Clean the gasket/sealing faces of the cylinder head and the cylinder head cover, then lay the main (outer) gasket and the two spark plug hole (centre) gaskets in position on the cylinder head **(see illustration)**.

**14** Lay the cylinder head cover in position, taking care not to disturb the gaskets. Check that the tabs on the rear of the main gasket are correctly positioned in the cut-outs in the rear of the cylinder head.

**15** Refit the cylinder head cover bolts and studs, ensuring that the seals are positioned as noted during removal, then tighten the bolts progressively to the specified torque.

**16** Further refitting is a reversal of the removal procedure, bearing in mind the following points.

a) *Check that the ignition coil earth leads are correctly positioned as noted before removal.*
b) *Tighten the coil securing nuts to the specified torque.*
c) *Check that the rubber seals are in place when reconnecting the HT lead plugs to the coils.*

## 5 Crankshaft vibration damper/pulley and pulley hub - removal and refitting

### Removal

**Note:** *If the pulley hub is removed, a new securing bolt will be required on refitting, and a torque wrench capable of providing 410 Nm (303 lbf ft) of torque will be required.*

**1** To improve access, unscrew the securing bolts and/or nuts, and remove the alternator air ducting from the front of the vehicle.

**2** Again to improve access, remove the viscous cooling fan and fan cowl assembly as described in Chapter 3.

**4.13 Lay the gaskets in position on the cylinder head**

**3** Remove the auxiliary drivebelt as described in Chapter 1.

**4** Unscrew the securing bolts, and remove the vibration damper/pulley from the hub **(see illustration)**. If necessary, counterhold the hub using a socket or spanner on the hub securing bolt.

**5** To remove the hub, the securing bolt must be unscrewed.

***Warning: The crankshaft pulley hub securing bolt is very tight. A tool will be required to counterhold the hub as the bolt is unscrewed. Do not attempt the job using inferior or poorly-improvised tools, as injury or damage may result.***

**6** Make up a tool to hold the pulley hub. A suitable tool can be fabricated using two lengths of steel bar, joined by a large pivot bolt. Bolt the holding tool to the pulley hub using the pulley-to-hub bolts **(see illustration)**.

**7** Using a socket and a long swing-bar, loosen the pulley hub bolt. Note that the bolt is very tight.

**8** Unscrew the pulley hub bolt, and remove the washer **(see illustration)**. Discard the bolt, a new one must be used on refitting.

**9** Withdraw the hub from the end of the crankshaft **(see illustration)**. If the hub is tight, use a puller to draw it off.

**10** Recover the Woodruff key from the end of the crankshaft if it is loose.

### Refitting

**11** If the pulley hub has been removed, it is advisable to take the opportunity to renew the oil seal in the lower timing chain cover, with reference to Section 6.

**12** If the pulley hub has been removed, proceed as follows, otherwise proceed to paragraph 16.

**13** Where applicable, refit the Woodruff key to the end of the crankshaft, then align the groove in the pulley hub with the key, and slide the hub onto the end of the crankshaft.

**14** Refit the washer, noting that the shoulder on the washer must face the hub, and fit a **new** hub securing bolt.

**15** Bolt the holding tool to the pulley hub, as during removal, then tighten the hub bolt to the specified torque. Take care to avoid injury and/or damage.

**16** Where applicable, unbolt the holding tool, and refit the vibration damper/pulley, ensuring that the locating dowel on the hub engages with the corresponding hole in the damper/pulley.

**17** Refit the damper/pulley securing bolts,

**5.4 Removing the vibration damper/pulley from the crankshaft**

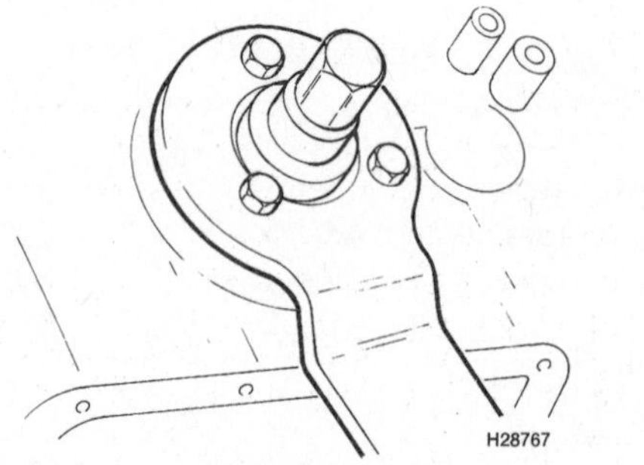


**5.6 BMW special tool used to hold crankshaft pulley hub**

**5.8 Unscrew the pulley hub bolts and remove the washer . . .**

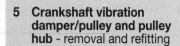

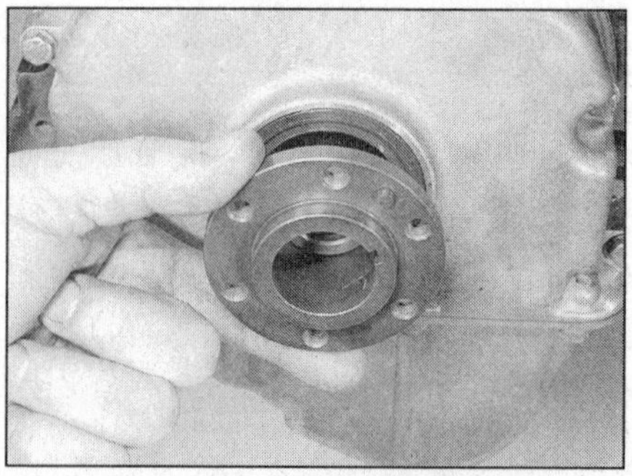

**5.9 . . . then withdraw the hub**

and tighten to the specified torque. Again, counterhold the pulley if necessary when tightening the bolts.

**18** Refit the auxiliary drivebelt as described in Chapter 1.

**19** Refit the viscous cooling fan and cowl as described in Chapter 3.

**20** Refit the alternator air ducting.

## 6 Timing chain covers - removal and refitting

### *Upper cover - engines without VANOS*

**Note:** *A new gasket will be required on refitting.*

#### Removal

**1** Remove the cylinder head cover as described in Section 4.

**2** Release the securing clips, and remove the wiring ducting from the front of the upper timing chain cover **(see illustrations)**.

**3** Unbolt the engine lifting bracket from the front left-hand corner of the cylinder head **(see illustration)**.

**4** Unscrew the securing nuts and remove the upper timing chain cover from the front of the cylinder head **(see illustration)**. Recover the gasket.

#### Refitting

**5** Refitting is a reversal of removal, bearing in mind the following points.

*a) Make sure that the dowel sleeves are in position on the top cover securing studs.*
*b) Use a new cover gasket.*
*c) Refit the cylinder head cover as described in Section 4.*

### *Upper cover - engines with VANOS*

**6** On engines with VANOS, the upper timing chain cover is integral with the VANOS adjustment unit. Removal and refitting of the VANOS adjustment unit is described in Section 9.

### *Lower cover*

**Note:** *New lower timing cover gaskets and a new crankshaft front oil seal will be required on refitting. RTV sealant will be required to coat the cylinder head/cylinder block joint - see text.*

#### Removal

**7** Drain the cooling system as described in Chapter 3.

**8** Remove the sump as described in Section 12.

**9** Remove the cylinder head cover as described in Section 4.

**10** Disconnect the two coolant hoses from the thermostat housing, and disconnect the coolant hose from the rear of the timing chain cover, behind the oil filter assembly.

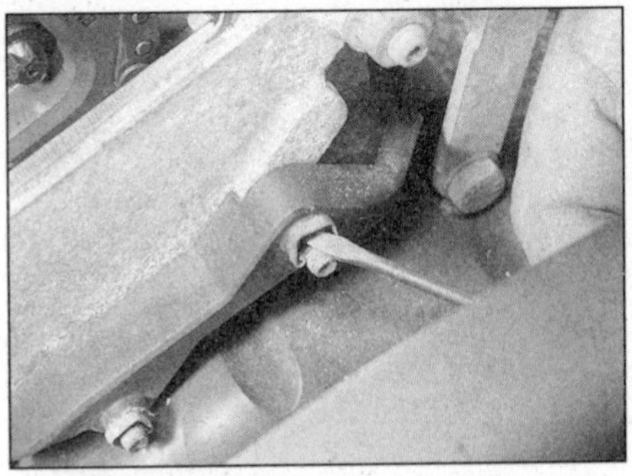

**6.2a Release the securing clips . . .**

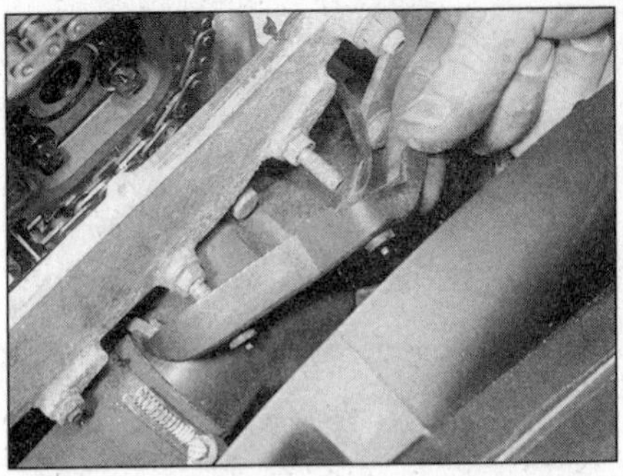

**6.2b . . . and remove the wiring ducting**

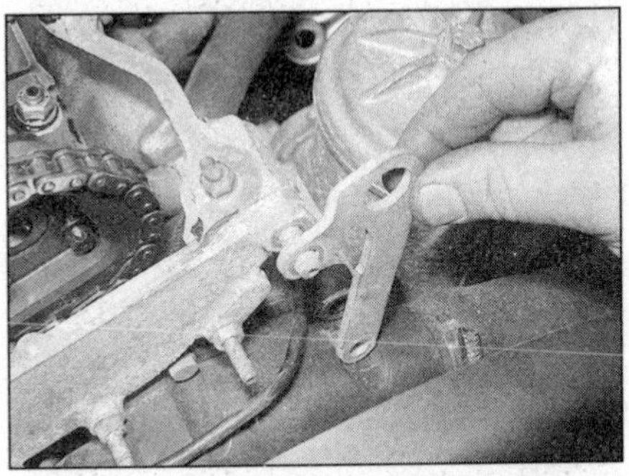

**6.3 Unbolt the engine lifting bracket**

**6.4 Removing the upper timing chain cover**

**11** Unbolt the thermostat housing from the front of the engine, and recover the gasket. Lift out the thermostat.

**12** Unscrew the securing bolt, and withdraw the crankshaft position sensor from the front of the engine. Move the sensor to one side, clear of the working area.

**13** Remove the auxiliary drivebelt tensioner as follows **(see illustrations)**.

*a) Pull the cover from the idler pulley, then unscrew the pulley securing bolt, and remove the pulley.*
*b) Pull the cover from the upper securing bolt, then unscrew the three securing*

**6.13a Pull the cover from the idler pulley (arrowed) . . .**

**6.13b . . . then unscrew the bolt and remove the pulley**

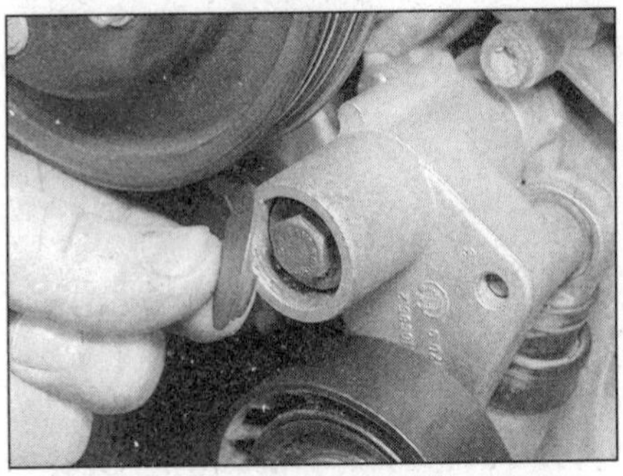

**6.13c Pull the cover from the upper securing bolt**

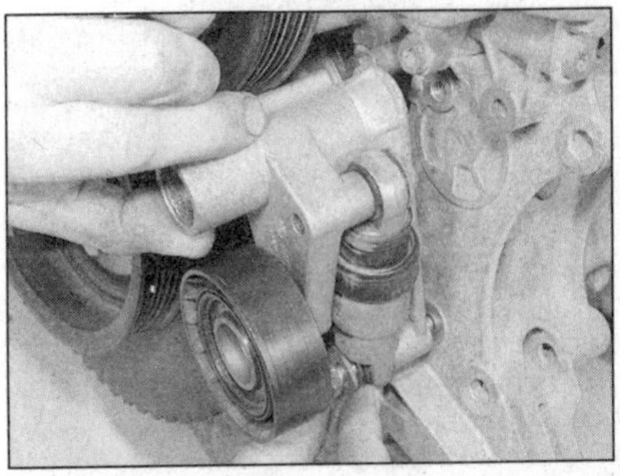

**6.13d Removing the auxiliary drivebelt tensioner**

**6.16 Driving a locating dowel from the lower timing chain cover**

*bolts, and remove the tensioner assembly, complete with the hydraulic tensioner strut. Note that the tensioner strut is filled with oil, and must therefore be stored upright to avoid the oil draining.*

**14** The coolant pump pulley must now be removed. Counterhold the pulley by wrapping an old drivebelt around it and clamping tightly, then unscrew the securing bolts and withdraw the pulley.

**15** Remove the crankshaft damper/pulley and pulley hub as described in Section 5.

**16** Working at the top of the timing chain cover, drive out the two cover dowels. Drive out the dowels towards the rear of the engine, using a pin-punch (less than 5.0 mm diameter) **(see illustration)**.

**17** On models with VANOS, it is now necessary to remove the VANOS adjustment unit (see Section 9), for access to the lower timing chain cover-to-cylinder head bolts.

**18** Unscrew the three lower timing chain cover-to-cylinder head bolts, and lift the bolts from the cylinder head. Note that one of the bolts also secures the secondary timing chain guide **(see illustration)**.

**19** Unscrew the lower timing chain cover-to-cylinder block bolts, then withdraw the cover from the front of the engine **(see illustrations)**. Recover the gaskets.

### Refitting

**20** Commence refitting by levering out the oil seal from the timing chain cover.

**21** Thoroughly clean the mating faces of the cover, cylinder block and cylinder head.

**22** Fit a new oil seal to the timing chain cover, using a large socket or tube, or a block of wood to drive the seal into position **(see illustration)**.

**23** Drive the cover dowels into position in the top of the cover so that they protrude from the rear (cylinder block mating) face of the cover by approximately 2.0 to 3.0 mm.

**24** Position new gaskets on the cover, and hold them in position using a little grease.

**25** Apply a little RTV sealant to the cylinder head/cylinder block joint at the two points where the timing chain cover contacts the cylinder head gasket **(see illustration)**.

**26** Offer the cover into position, ensuring that

**6.18 Remove lower timing chain cover-to-cylinder head bolts. This bolt secures the secondary timing chain guide - secondary timing chain removed for clarity**

the gaskets stay in place. Make sure that the dowels engage with the cylinder block, and fit the cover securing bolts. Tighten the bolts finger-tight only at this stage.

**27** Drive in the cover dowels until they are flush with the outer face of the cover.

**28** Progressively tighten the cover securing bolts to the specified torque (do not forget the three cover-to-cylinder head bolts).

**29** Where applicable, refit the VANOS adjustment unit as described in Section 9.

**30** Refit the crankshaft damper/pulley hub and damper/pulley as described in Section 5.

**31** The remainder of refitting is a reversal of removal, bearing in mind the following points.

*a) Ensure the auxiliary drivebelt hydraulic tensioner strut is fitted correctly. The "TOP/OBEN" arrow must point upwards.*

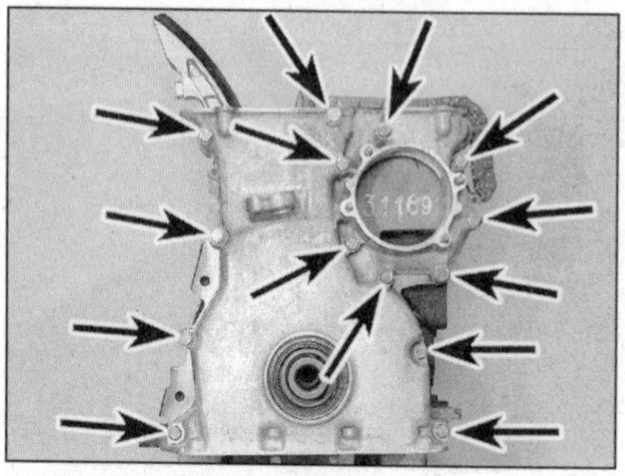

**6.19a Unscrew the securing bolts (arrowed) . . .**

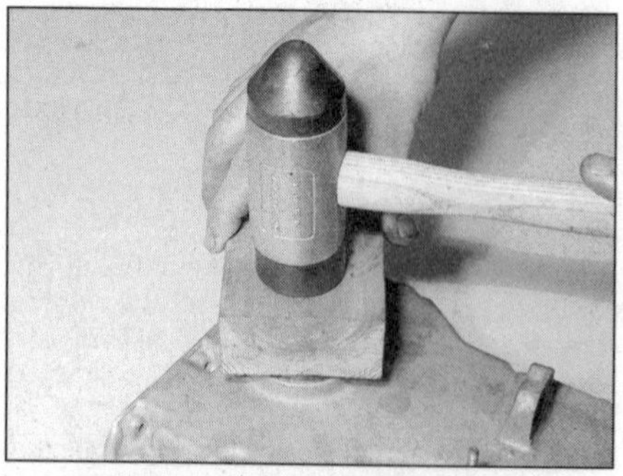

**6.22 Fitting a new oil seal to the lower timing chain cover**

*b) Refit the auxiliary drivebelt with reference to Chapter 1.*

*c) Refit the thermostat and housing with reference to Chapter 3.*

*d) Refit the cylinder head cover (Section 4).*

*e) Refit the sump as described in Section 12.*

*f) On completion, refill the cooling system and check the coolant level, as described in Chapter 1 and "Weekly Checks" respectively.*

## 7 Timing chains - removal, inspection and refitting

### *Secondary (exhaust-to-inlet camshaft) chain - engines without VANOS*

### Removal

**1** Position No 1 piston at TDC, and lock the flywheel in position, as described in Section 3.

**2** Remove the upper timing chain cover, as described in Section 6.

**3** Unscrew the primary timing chain tensioner plunger cover plug from the right-hand side of the engine. Recover the sealing ring **(see illustrations)**.

***Warning: The chain tensioner plunger has a strong spring. Take care when unscrewing the cover plug.***

**4** Recover the spring and withdraw the tensioner plunger.

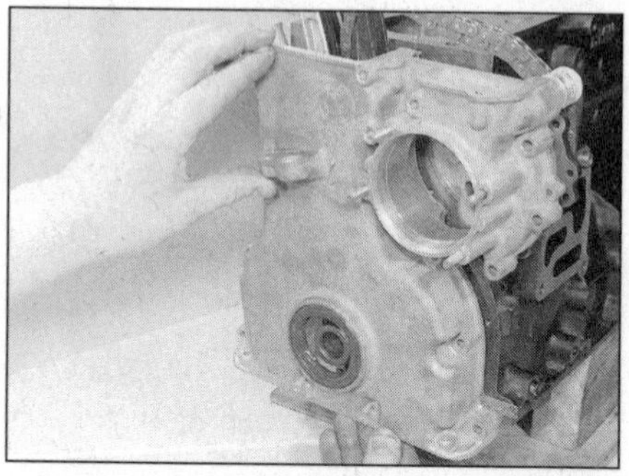

**6.19b . . . and remove the lower timing chain cover - cylinder head removed**

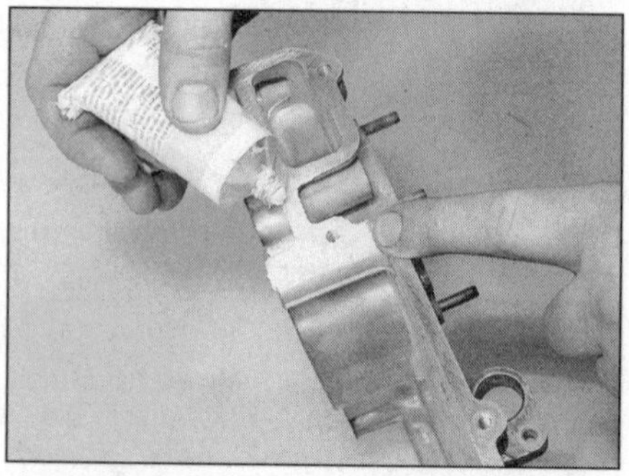

**6.25 Apply a little RTV sealant to the area where the cylinder head gasket contacts the lower timing chain cover**

**7.3a Using a spanner . . .**

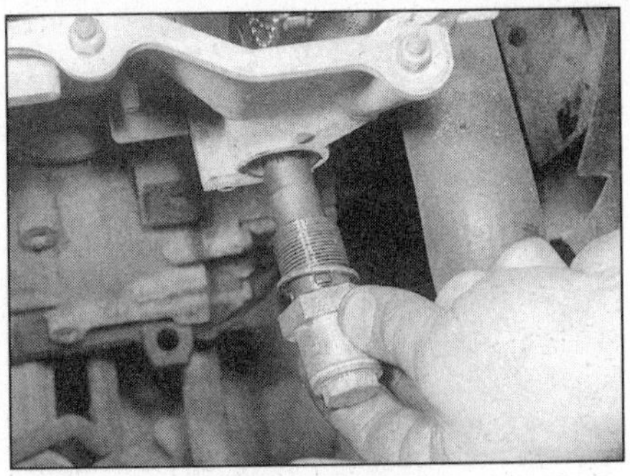

**7.3b . . . unscrew the primary timing chain tensioner assembly**

**7.5 Lock the secondary chain tensioner pad down using a length of rod (arrowed)**

**7.6 Unscrew the bolts securing the secondary chain sprockets to the camshafts**

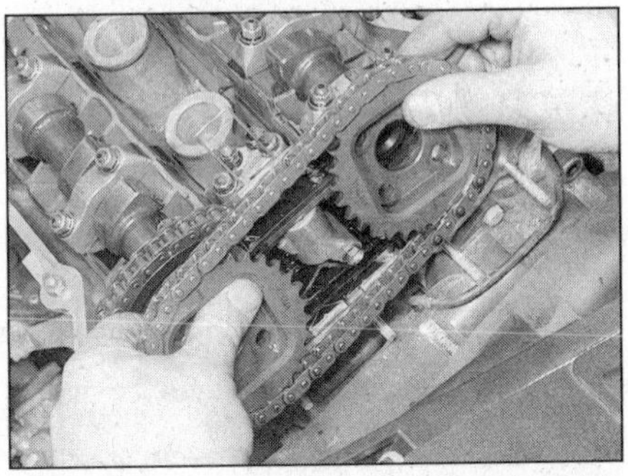

**7.7 Withdraw the sprockets complete with the secondary timing chain**

**7.8 Recover the camshaft position sensor plate from the inlet camshaft**

**5** Press the secondary timing chain tensioner pad down, and lock it in position using a tool made up from a length of welding rod or similar material. Insert the tool through the holes in the top of the tensioner to hold the tensioner plunger down **(see illustration)**.

**6** Unscrew the bolts securing the chain sprockets to the camshafts **(see illustration)**. Take care not to move the camshafts - if necessary, the camshafts can be counterheld using a 24 mm spanner on the flats provided between Nos 10 and 11 cam lobes.

**7** Withdraw the sprockets, complete with the secondary chain, from the front of the camshafts **(see illustration)**.

**8** Recover the camshaft position sensor plate from the front of the inlet camshaft **(see illustration)**.

## Inspection

**9** The chain should be renewed if the sprockets are worn or if the chain is worn (indicated by excessive lateral play between the links, and excessive noise in operation). It is wise to renew the chain in any case if the engine is dismantled for overhaul. Note that the rollers on a very badly worn chain may be slightly grooved. To avoid future problems, if there is any doubt at all about the condition of the chain, renew it.

**10** Examine the teeth on the sprockets for wear. Each tooth forms an inverted "V". If worn, the side of each tooth under tension will be slightly concave in shape when compared with the other side of the tooth (ie, the teeth will have a hooked appearance). If the teeth appear worn, the sprockets must be renewed. Also check the chain guide and tensioner contact surfaces for wear, and renew any worn components as necessary.

## Refitting

**11** Ensure that No 1 piston is still positioned at TDC, with the crankshaft locked in position. Check the position of the camshafts using the template described in Section 3.

**12** Where applicable, fit the camshaft position sensor plate to the inlet camshaft.

**13** Lay the chain over the sprockets, ensuring that the arrows on the front faces of the sprockets are pointing upwards (note that some sprockets have two arrows, which must point vertically up and down), then position the sprockets on the camshafts.

**14** Refit the sprocket securing bolts and tighten them finger-tight only at this stage **(see illustration)**.

**15** Refit the primary timing chain tensioner plunger, ensuring that the guide lugs engage with the tensioner rail.

**16** Fit the tensioner spring, then fit the cover plug, using a new seal, and tighten the plug to the specified torque.

**17** Remove the tool locking the secondary timing chain tensioner in position.

**18** Again, check the position of the camshafts using the template, then tighten the inlet camshaft sprocket securing bolts to the specified torque in the two stages given in the Specifications.

**19** Similarly, tighten the exhaust camshaft sprocket bolts to the specified torque.

**20** Withdraw the flywheel locking rod from the timing hole in the cylinder block, and where applicable remove the template from the camshafts.

**21** Rotate the engine through two complete revolutions clockwise (note that the engine is easier to turn with the spark plugs removed), then refit the locking rod to the timing hole in the cylinder block, ensuring that the tool engages with the flywheel, and check that the template can be refitted to the camshafts without turning the camshafts (the timing arrows on the camshaft sprockets should be pointing vertically upwards). If not, the secondary timing chain and/or sprockets have been incorrectly fitted.

**22** Remove the camshaft template from the cylinder head, and remove the locking rod from the flywheel (refit the blanking plug to the timing hole).

**23** Refit the upper timing chain cover as described in Section 6.

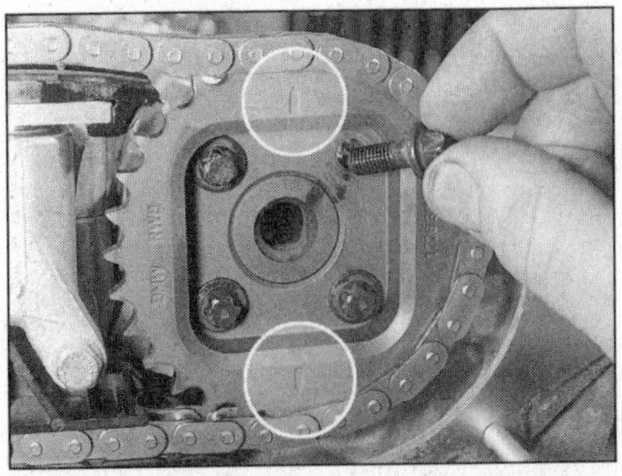

**7.14 Refit the sprocket securing bolts. Note that the arrows on the sprockets must be positioned vertically**

## Secondary (exhaust-to-inlet camshaft) chain - engines with VANOS

### Removal

24 Remove the VANOS adjustment unit as described in Section 9.

25 Remove the exhaust camshaft sprocket securing bolts (the bolts should already have been loosened), and withdraw the thrust plate from the sprocket.

26 Unscrew the inlet camshaft sprocket securing nuts, and withdraw the thrust plate from the front of the sprocket.

27 Withdraw the sprockets, complete with the secondary chain, from the front of the camshafts.

28 If desired, the camshaft position sensor plate can be removed from the front of the inlet camshaft as follows.

*a) Unscrew the three securing studs from the camshaft flange.*

*b) Withdraw the thrust plate.*

*c) Withdraw the sensor plate.*

### Inspection

29 Refer to paragraphs 9 and 10.

### Refitting

30 Ensure that No 1 piston is still positioned at TDC, with the crankshaft locked in position. Check the position of the camshafts using the template.

31 Where applicable, refit the camshaft position sensor plate to the inlet camshaft. Ensure that the thrust plate is refitted, and make sure that the correct studs are used to secure the sensor plate and thrust plate. Tighten the studs to the specified torque. ***Caution: It is possible to mix up the cylinder head cover studs and the camshaft position sensor plate securing studs. The camshaft position sensor plate studs are longer, and have a narrower "hexagon" section (see illustration).***

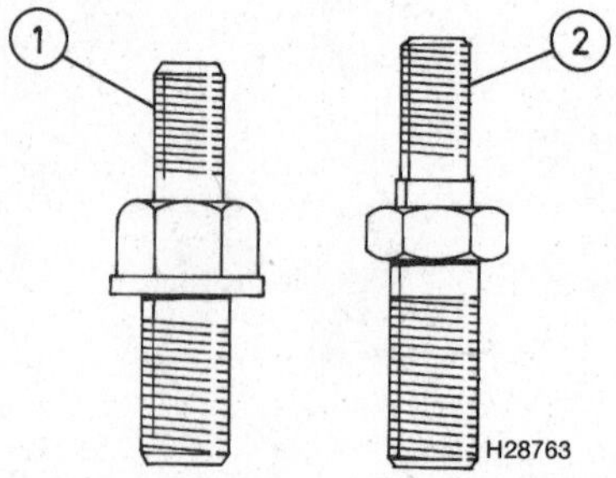


**7.31 Do not mix up the cylinder head cover studs (1) with the camshaft position sensor plate securing studs (2)**

32 Lay the chain over the sprockets, noting that when the sprockets are refitted, the securing bolt holes/studs on the camshafts must be centred in the elongated holes in the sprockets. Note that the inlet camshaft sprocket fits with the flat side facing the VANOS adjustment unit, and the raised collar facing the camshaft.

33 Fit the sprockets to the camshafts, ensuring the securing bolts holes/studs are aligned in the centre of the elongated sprocket holes.

34 Fit the thrust plate to the inlet camshaft sprocket, then fit the sprocket securing nuts, and tighten the nuts to the specified torque.

35 Fit the thrust plate to the exhaust camshaft sprocket, then fit the sprocket securing bolts. Tighten the bolts finger-tight only at this stage.

36 Refit the VANOS adjustment unit as described in Section 9.

## Primary (crankshaft-to-exhaust camshaft) chain - engines without VANOS

### Removal

37 Remove the secondary timing chain as described previously in this Section.

38 Remove the tool locking the secondary timing chain tensioner in position.

39 Remove the lower timing chain cover as described in Section 6.

40 Remove the tool locking the secondary chain tensioner plunger in position, then lift out the plunger and spring, unscrew the securing bolts, and withdraw the secondary chain tensioner from the cylinder head **(see illustrations)**.

41 Unscrew the securing bolts and withdraw the secondary chain guide **(see illustrations)**.

42 Withdraw the primary timing chain sprocket from the exhaust camshaft, complete with the chain **(see illustration)**. Remove the sprocket. Note carefully which way round the sprocket fits, to ensure correct refitting.

43 Note the routing of the chain in relation to the tensioner rail and the chain guide.

**7.40a Lift out the plunger and spring . . .**

**7.40b . . . then unscrew the securing bolts . . .**

**7.40c . . . and withdraw the secondary chain tensioner**

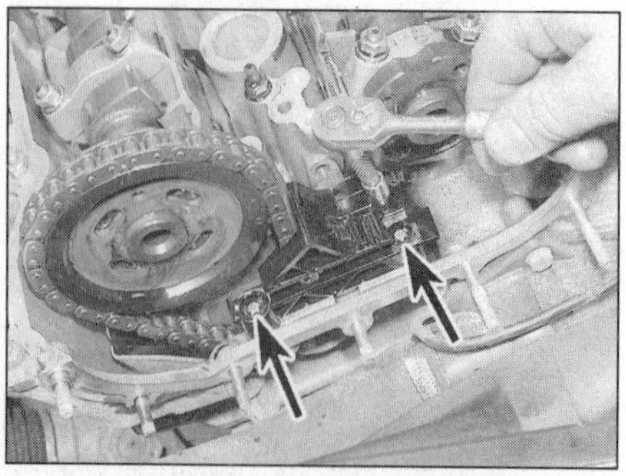

**7.41a Unscrew the securing bolts . . .**

**7.41b . . . and withdraw the secondary chain guide**

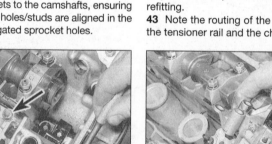

**7.42 Withdraw the primary timing chain sprocket complete with the chain**

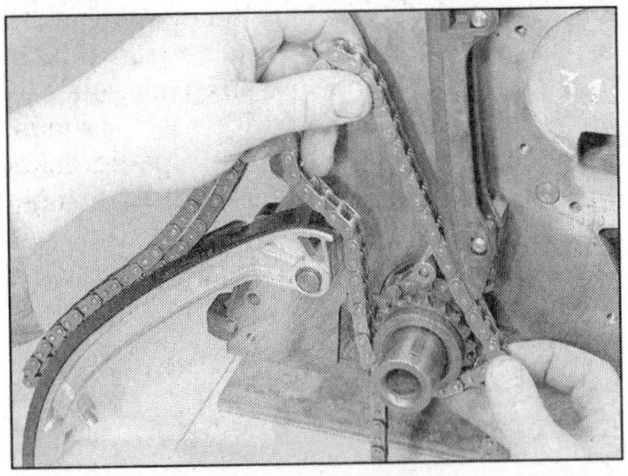

7.44 **Manipulate the tensioner rail and unhook the chain from the crankshaft sprocket - viewed with engine removed**

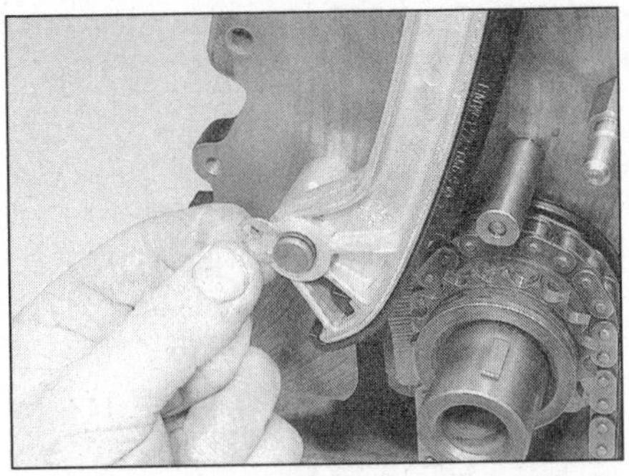

7.45 **Remove the clip from the lower pivot to remove the tensioner rail - viewed with engine removed**

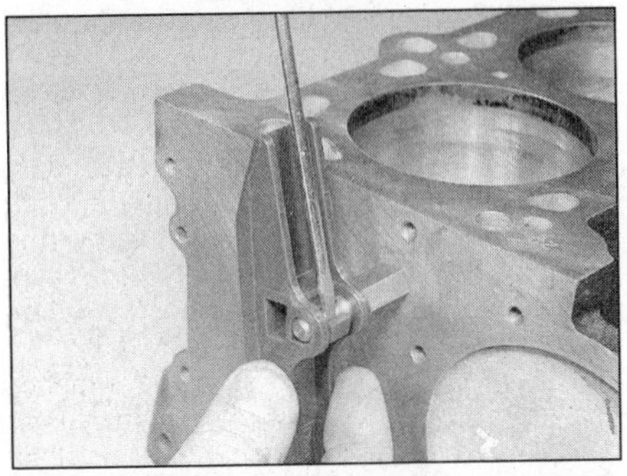

7.46 **Release the retaining clips to remove the chain guide**

7.51 **Tapped holes in the camshaft flange should be positioned at the left-hand ends of the elongated slots in the sprocket**

**44** Manipulate the tensioner rail as necessary to enable the chain to be unhooked from the crankshaft sprocket and lifted from the engine **(see illustration)**.

***Warning: Once the primary timing chain has been removed, do not turn the crankshaft or the camshafts, as there is a danger of the valves hitting the pistons.***

**45** If desired, the tensioner rail can now be removed after removing the clip from the lower pivot **(see illustration)**.

**46** Similarly, the chain guide can be removed after releasing the upper and lower retaining clips. Take care when releasing the retaining clips, as the clips are easily broken **(see illustration)**.

### Inspection

**47** Refer to paragraphs 9 and 10.

### Refitting

**48** Ensure No 1 piston is still at TDC, with the crankshaft locked in position. Check the position of the camshafts using the template.

**49** Commence refitting by engaging the chain with the crankshaft sprocket.

**50** Where applicable, refit the chain guide and the tensioner rail, ensuring that the chain is correctly routed in relation to the guide and tensioner rail, as noted before removal. Take care when refitting the chain guide, as the clips are easily broken.

**51** Manipulate the exhaust camshaft primary chain sprocket until the timing arrow on the sprocket is pointing vertically upwards, then engage the chain with the sprocket. Fit the sprocket to the exhaust camshaft, aligning the sprocket so that the tapped holes in the camshaft flange are positioned at the left-hand ends of the elongated slots in the sprocket **(see illustration)**. Ensure that the sprocket is fitted the correct way round as noted before removal.

**52** Refit the secondary chain guide and the secondary chain tensioner. The tensioner plunger fits with the cut-out in the plunger on the right-hand side of the engine.

**53** Refit the secondary timing chain as described previously in this Section, but do not refit the cylinder head cover until the lower timing chain cover has been refitted.

**54** Refit the lower timing chain cover as described in Section 6.

## *Primary (crankshaft-to-exhaust camshaft) chain - engines with VANOS*

**Note:** *BMW special tool No 11 3 390 or a suitable equivalent will be required to carry out this operation.*

### Removal

**55** Remove the secondary timing chain as described previously in this Section.

**56** Unscrew the timing chain tensioner plunger cover plug from the right-hand side of the engine. Recover the sealing ring.

***Warning: The chain tensioner plunger has a strong spring. Take care when unscrewing the cover plug.***

**57** Recover the spring and withdraw the tensioner plunger.

**58** Proceed as described in paragraphs 38 to 46 of this Section.

### Inspection

**59** Refer to paragraphs 9 and 10.

### Refitting

**60** Proceed as described in paragraphs 48 to 52 of this Section.

**61** Fit special tool No 11 3 390 into the tensioner aperture (see Section 9), then turn the adjuster screw on the tool until the end of the screw just touches the tensioning rail. Note that the exhaust camshaft sprocket should now have moved anti-clockwise so that the tapped holes in the camshaft flange are centred in the elongated holes in the sprocket.

**62** Refit the secondary timing chain as described previously in this Section.

## 8 Timing chain sprockets and tensioners - removal and refitting

## *Camshaft sprockets*

**1** Removal, inspection and refitting of the sprockets is described as part of the secondary timing chain removal and refitting procedure in Section 7.



## *Crankshaft sprocket*

### Removal

**2** The sprocket is combined with the oil pump drive sprocket. On some engines, the sprocket may be a press-fit on the end of the crankshaft.

**3** Remove the primary timing chain as described in Section 7.

**4** Slide the sprocket from the front of the crankshaft. If the sprocket is a press-fit, use a three-legged puller to pull the sprocket from the crankshaft. Protect the threaded bore in the front of the crankshaft by refitting the pulley hub bolt, or by using a metal spacer between the puller and the end of the crankshaft. Note which way round the sprocket is fitted to ensure correct refitting.

**5** Once the sprocket has been removed, recover the Woodruff key from the slot in the crankshaft if it is loose.

### Inspection

**6** Inspection is described with the timing chain inspection procedure in Section 7.

### Refitting

**7** Where applicable, refit the Woodruff key to the slot in the crankshaft.

**8** Slide the sprocket into position on the crankshaft. Ensure that the sprocket is fitted the correct way round as noted before removal. If a press-fit sprocket is to be refitted, before refitting, the sprocket must be heated to a temperature of 150°C. **Do not**

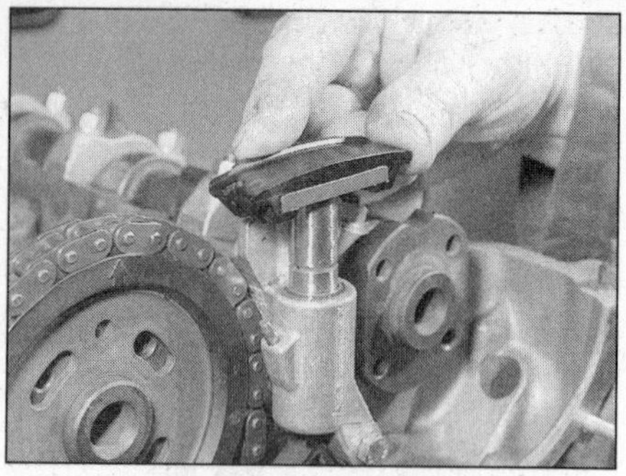

8.12a Withdraw the secondary chain tensioner plunger . . .

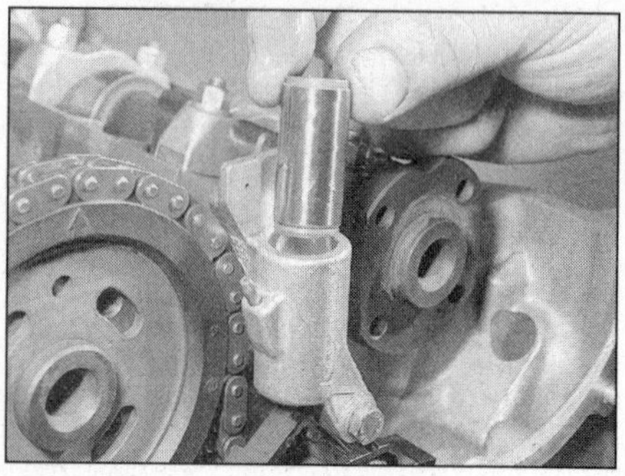

8.12c . . . and plunger housing

exceed this temperature, as damage to the sprocket may result.

**9** Once the sprocket has been heated to the given temperature, align the slot in the sprocket with the Woodruff key, then tap the sprocket into place with a socket or metal tube.

***Warning: When the sprocket is heated, take precautions against burns - the metal will stay hot for some time.***

**10** Refit the primary timing chain as described in Section 7.

## Secondary chain tensioner

### Removal

**11** Remove the secondary timing chain as described in Section 7.

**12** Remove the tool locking the secondary timing chain tensioner in position, then withdraw the plunger, spring and plunger housing **(see illustrations)**.

**13** Unscrew the securing bolts and withdraw the chain tensioner housing from the cylinder head **(see illustration)**.

### Inspection

**14** Inspect the tensioner, and renew if necessary. Check the plunger and the plunger housing for wear and damage. Inspect the chain contact face of the plunger slipper for wear, and check the condition of the spring. Renew any components which are worn or damaged.

**15** When refitting the plunger to the tensioner, note that the cut-out in the plunger should be positioned on the right-hand side of the engine when the assembly is refitted.

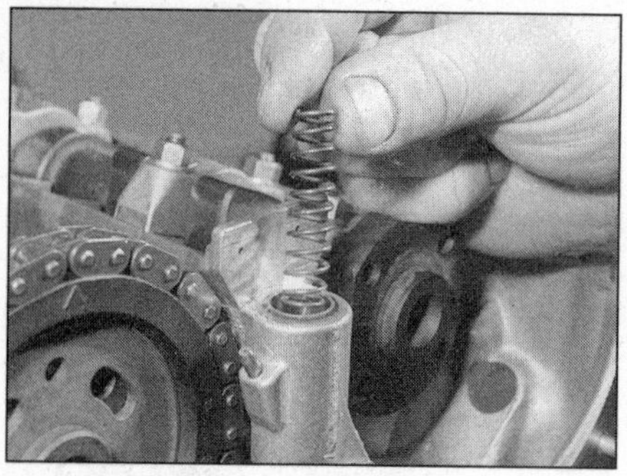

8.12b . . . spring . . .

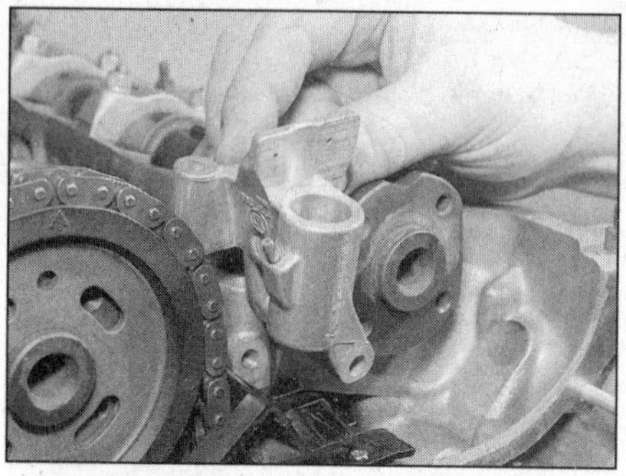

8.13 Withdrawing the secondary timing chain tensioner housing

### Refitting

**16** Refit the chain tensioner and tighten the securing bolts to the specified torque.

**17** Refit the tool to lock the tensioner in position.

**18** Refit the secondary timing chain as described in Section 7.

## Primary chain tensioner

**19** Removal and refitting is described as part of the primary timing chain removal procedure in Section 7.

# 9 Variable valve timing (VANOS) components - removal, inspection and refitting

## VANOS adjustment unit

**Note:** *Before the refitting procedure can be completed, the operation of the VANOS system and the inlet camshaft position adjustment **must** be checked by a BMW dealer. BMW special tool No 11 3 390 or a suitable equivalent will be required to carry out this operation. A new VANOS unit gasket will be required on refitting.*

### Removal

**1** Unscrew the securing bolts and/or nuts, and remove the alternator air ducting from the front of the vehicle.

**2** Remove the viscous cooling fan and fan cowl assembly as described in Chapter 3.

**3** Remove the cylinder head cover as described in Section 4.

**4** Unscrew the union bolt, and disconnect the oil feed pipe from the front of the VANOS adjustment unit **(see illustration)**. Recover the sealing rings.

**5** Disconnect the solenoid valve wiring connector. The connector is clipped to the wiring harness located behind the oil filter housing.

**6** Unscrew the securing nut and bolt, and remove the engine lifting bracket from the front of the engine.

**7** Release the securing clips, and remove the wiring ducting from the front of the VANOS adjustment unit.

**8** Unclip the plastic cover from the inlet camshaft.

**9** Position No 1 piston at TDC, and lock the flywheel in position, and check the position of the camshafts using the template, as described in Section 3.

**10** Unscrew the two cover plugs from the front of the VANOS adjustment unit to expose the lower exhaust camshaft sprocket securing bolts **(see illustration)**. Recover the sealing rings.

**11** Fully loosen the four exhaust camshaft sprocket securing bolts. The two lower bolts are reached through the holes in the front of the VANOS adjustment unit.

**12** Press the secondary timing chain tensioner pad down, and lock it in position using a tool made up from a length of welding rod or similar material. Insert the tool through the holes in the top of the tensioner to hold the tensioner plunger down **(see illustration 7.5)**.

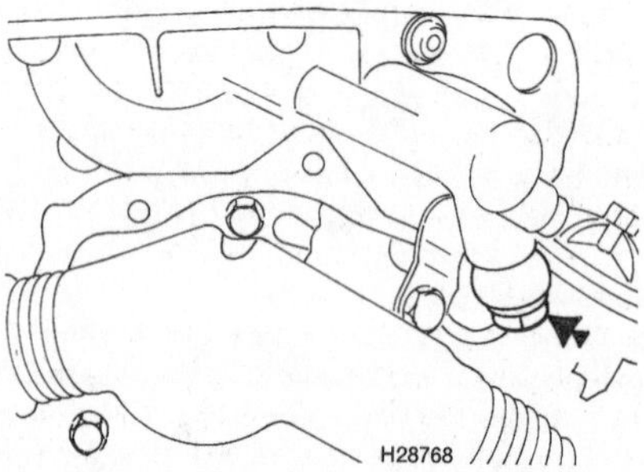


9.4 VANOS adjustment unit oil feed pipe union bolt (arrowed)

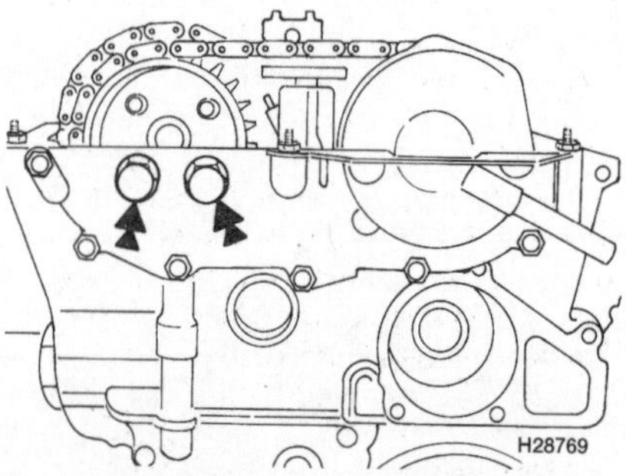


9.10 Unscrew the two cover plugs (arrowed) to expose the camshaft sprocket securing bolts

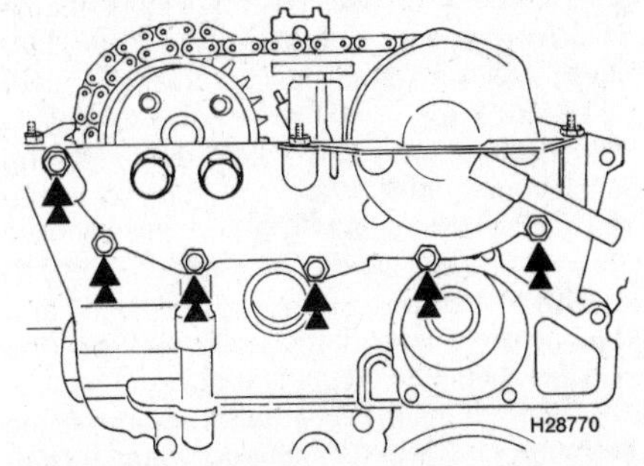


**9.13 Unscrew the securing nuts (arrowed) and remove the VANOS adjustment unit**

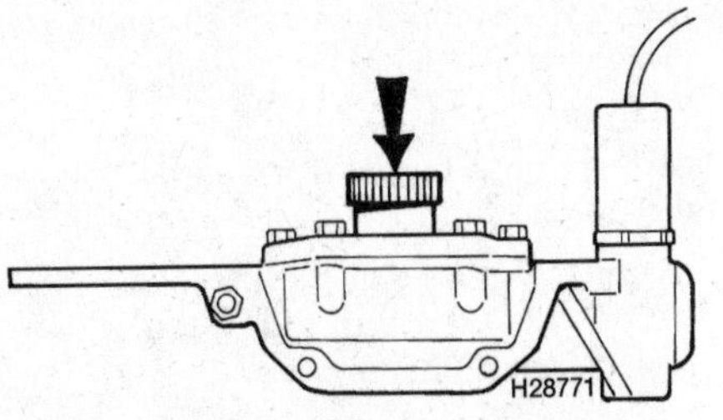


**9.15 Press the splined shaft into the VANOS adjustment unit as far as the stop**

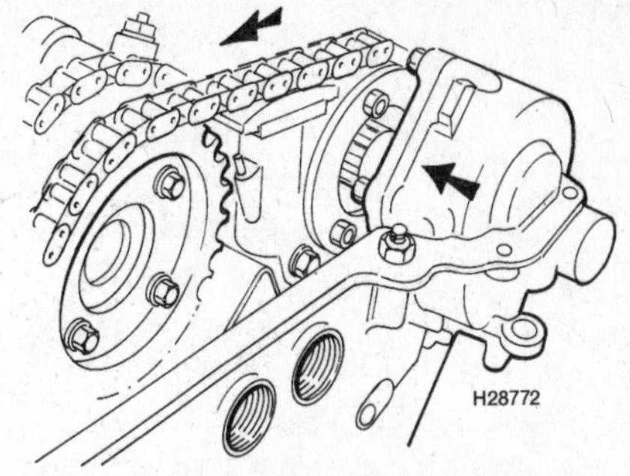


**9.21 The sprockets and chain will turn anti-clockwise as the VANOS unit is fitted**

**13** Unscrew the securing nuts and remove the VANOS adjustment unit from the front of the engine **(see illustration)**. Recover the gasket.

## Inspection

**14** To test the operation of the VANOS adjustment unit, special equipment is required. Testing must therefore be entrusted to a BMW dealer.

## Refitting

**15** Commence refitting by pressing the splined shaft into the VANOS adjustment unit until the shaft reaches the stop in the housing **(see illustration)**.

**16** Make sure that the dowel sleeves are in position on the top VANOS adjustment unit securing studs in the cylinder head.

**17** Fit a new gasket over the studs on the cylinder head, and apply a little sealant to the corners of the joint surfaces between the cylinder head and the VANOS adjustment unit.

**18** Turn the inlet camshaft sprocket clockwise as far as possible by hand (the camshafts should be locked in position by fitting the template described in Section 3, so turn the sprocket until it reaches the clockwise stop).

**19** Offer the VANOS adjustment unit into position and, if necessary, rotate the splined shaft on the VANOS adjustment unit slightly until the internal splines on the VANOS adjustment unit shaft engage with the splines on the camshaft. **Do not** turn the camshaft or the camshaft sprocket.

**20** It is now necessary to engage the VANOS adjustment unit shaft outer splines with the internal splines on the camshaft sprocket. Turn the camshaft sprocket slowly by hand anti-clockwise until the VANOS adjustment unit shaft splines mesh with the sprocket.

***Warning: It is essential to ensure that that the FIRST suitable spline meshes when the sprocket is turned back anti-clockwise from its clockwise stop.***

**21** Push the VANOS adjustment unit fully onto the cylinder head studs, noting that the camshaft sprockets and chain will turn anti-clockwise slightly as the VANOS adjustment unit is pushed into position (this is due to the helical sprocket splines). As the unit is pushed into position, guide the sprockets and chain anti-clockwise as necessary by hand **(see illustration)**.

**22** Refit and tighten the VANOS adjustment unit securing nuts.

**23** Remove the tool locking the secondary timing chain tensioner in position.

**24** Unscrew the primary timing chain tensioner plunger cover plug from the right-hand side of the engine **(see illustrations 7.3a and 7.3b)**. Recover the sealing ring.

***Warning: The chain tensioner plunger has a strong spring. Take care when unscrewing the cover plug.***

**25** Recover the spring and withdraw the tensioner plunger.

**26** Fit special tool No 11 3 390 into the tensioner aperture, then turn the adjuster screw on the tool until the end of the screw just touches the tensioner rail.

**27** Using a torque wrench, apply a torque of 1.3 Nm to the adjusting screw on the special tool **(see illustrations)**.

**28** Tighten the exhaust camshaft sprocket securing bolts to the specified torque.

**29** Remove the template from the camshafts, then withdraw the locking rod from the timing hole in the cylinder block.

**30** Rotate the engine through two complete revolutions clockwise, then refit the locking rod to the timing hole in the cylinder block, ensuring that the tool engages with the flywheel.

**31** Refit the template to check the position of the camshafts. If the template cannot be fitted with the flywheel locked in position, the VANOS adjustment unit has been incorrectly fitted. **2B**

**32** Unscrew the special tool (No 11 3 390) from the tensioner aperture.

**33** Refit the primary timing chain tensioner plunger, ensuring that the guide lugs engage with the tensioner rail.

**34** Fit the tensioner spring, then fit the cover plug, using a new seal, and tighten the plug to the specified torque.

**35** Refit the camshaft sprocket securing bolt cover plugs to the front of the VANOS adjustment unit, using new sealing rings. Tighten the plugs to the specified torque.

**36** It is now necessary to check the operation of the VANOS system and to adjust the inlet camshaft position. Special tools are required to do this, and the operation **must** be entrusted to a BMW dealer.

**37** Once the VANOS system has been checked and adjusted, remove the camshaft template and flywheel locking tool. The remainder of the refitting procedure is a reversal of removal, bearing in mind the following points.

*a) Use new sealing rings when reconnecting the oil feed pipe to the VANOS adjustment unit.*

*b) Refit the cylinder head cover with reference to Section 4.*

*c) Refit the viscous cooling fan and cowl assembly as described in Chapter 3.*

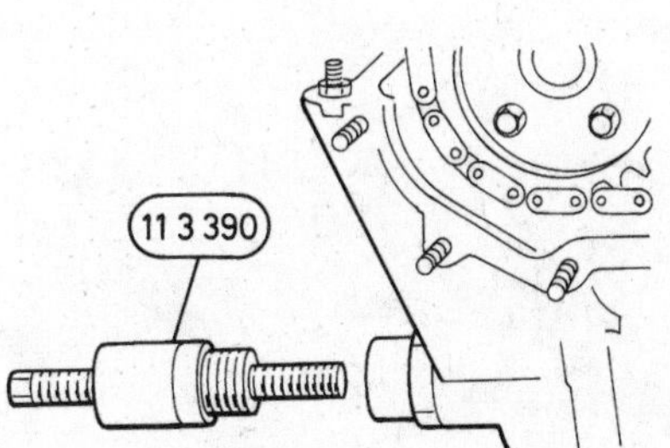


**9.27a Fit BMW special tool No 11 3 390 to the timing chain tensioner aperture . . .**

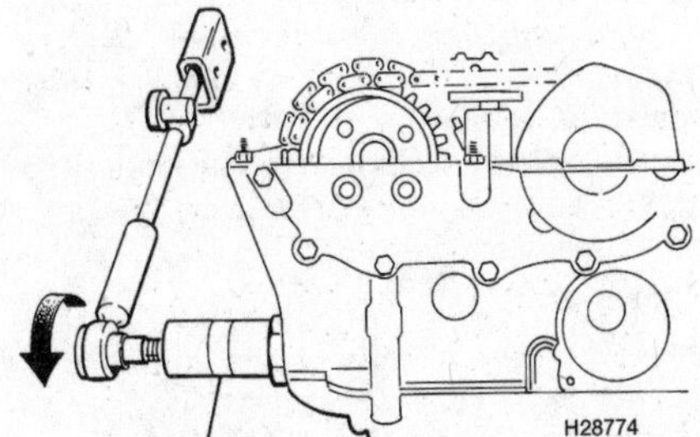


**9.27b . . . then apply the specified torque (see text) to the tool**

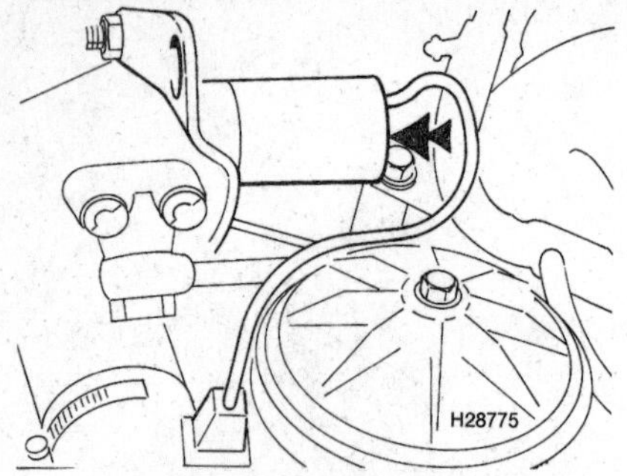


**9.41 VANOS solenoid valve location (arrowed)**

## VANOS solenoid valve

**Note:** *A new sealing ring will be required on refitting.*

### Removal

**38** Ensure that the ignition is switched off.

**39** Unscrew the securing bolts and/or nuts, and remove the alternator air ducting from the front of the vehicle.

**40** Disconnect the solenoid valve wiring connector, which is clipped to the engine wiring harness behind the oil filter assembly.

**41** Using an open-ended spanner, unscrew the solenoid valve and recover the seal **(see illustration)**.

### Inspection

**42** Check that the solenoid plunger can be pulled freely back and forth by hand. If not, the solenoid must be renewed.

**43** Similarly, check that the hydraulic piston in the VANOS adjustment unit can be moved easily. If it is difficult to move the hydraulic piston, the complete VANOS adjustment unit must be renewed.

### Refitting

**44** Refitting is a reversal of removal, but use a new sealing ring.

## 10 Camshafts and followers - removal, inspection and refitting

***Warning: BMW special tools 11 3 260 and 11 3 270 will be required for this operation. These tools are extremely difficult to improvise due to their rugged construction and the need for accurate manufacture. Do not attempt to remove and refit the camshafts without the aid of the special tools, as expensive damage to the camshafts and/or bearings may result.***

## Engines without VANOS

### Removal

**1** Open the bonnet, then raise the bonnet to its fully open position as described in Chapter 11.

**2** Unscrew the securing bolts and/or nuts, and remove the alternator air ducting from the front of the vehicle.

**3** Remove the secondary timing chain as described in Section 7.

**4** Trace the wiring back from the camshaft position sensor, then disconnect the sensor connector. Unscrew the securing bolt, and remove the sensor from the cylinder head **(see illustrations)**.

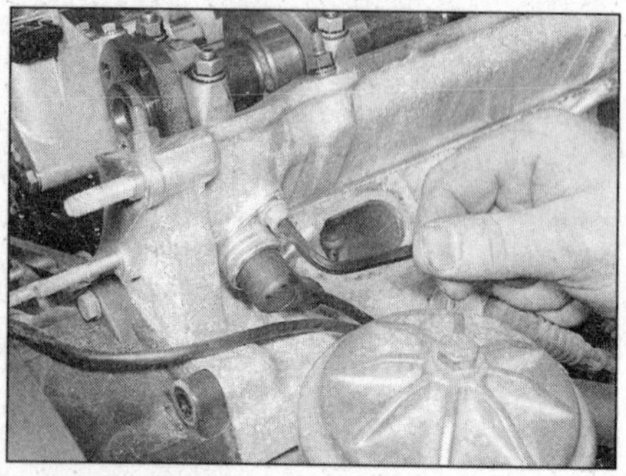

**10.4a Unscrew the securing bolt . . .**

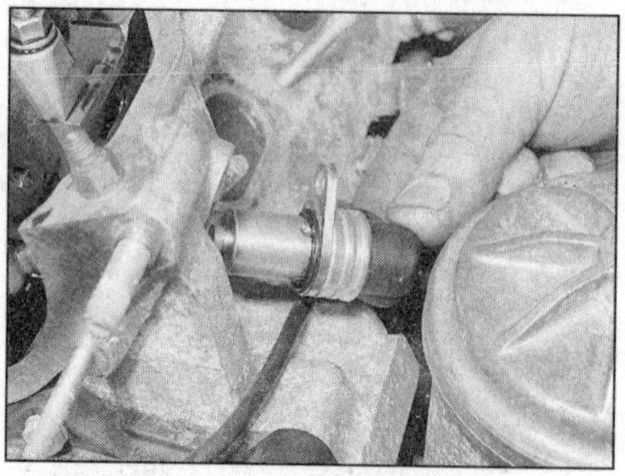

**10.4b . . . and withdraw the camshaft position sensor**

**5** Remove the tool locking the secondary timing chain tensioner in position. Withdraw the plunger and spring.

**6** Unscrew the securing bolts, and withdraw the secondary chain tensioner from the cylinder head.

**7** Unscrew the securing bolts and withdraw the secondary chain guide **(see illustration)**.

**8** Withdraw the primary timing chain sprocket from the exhaust camshaft, complete with the chain. Remove the sprocket.

***Caution: Keep tension on the chain, and tie up the end of the chain using wire or string to prevent it from dropping into the lower timing chain cover and/or disengaging from the crankshaft sprocket.***

***Warning: To avoid any possibility of piston-to-valve contact when refitting the camshaft(s), it is necessary to ensure that none of the pistons are at TDC. Before proceeding further, remove the locking rod from the timing hole in the cylinder block, then turn the crankshaft approximately 30° clockwise using a spanner or socket on the crankshaft pulley hub bolt.***

**9** Remove the template from the camshafts.

**10** Unscrew the spark plugs from the cylinder head.

**11** Check the camshaft bearing caps for identification marks. The caps are numbered from the timing chain end of the engine, and the marks can normally be read from the exhaust side of the engine. The exhaust camshaft bearing caps are marked "A1" to "A7", and the inlet camshaft caps are marked "E1" to "E7".

**12** Unscrew the four camshaft cover securing studs from the centre of the cylinder head **(see illustration)**.

**13** Assemble BMW special tools 11 3 260 and 11 3 270, and mount the tools on the cylinder head by screwing the mounting bolts into the spark plug holes. Position the tools so that the plungers are located over the relevant camshaft bearing caps (ie, inlet or exhaust camshaft) **(see illustration)**.

**14** Apply pressure to the camshaft bearing

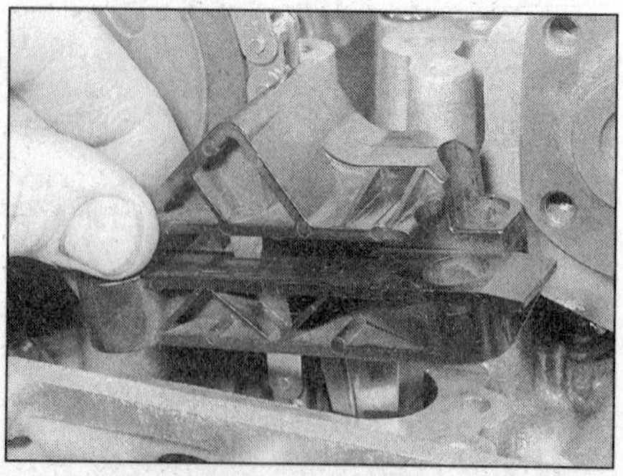

**10.7 Withdraw the secondary chain guide**

**10.12 Unscrew the four camshaft cover securing studs**

**10.13 BMW special tools 11 3 260 and 11 3 270 fitted to cylinder head**

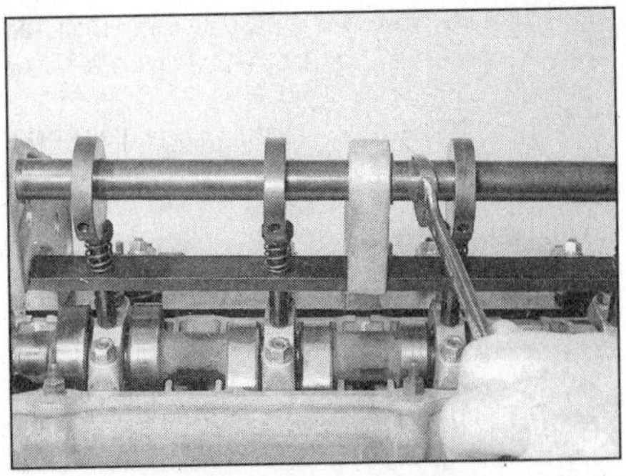

**10.14 Turn eccentric shaft using a spanner to apply pressure to the bearing caps**

HAYNES HiNT

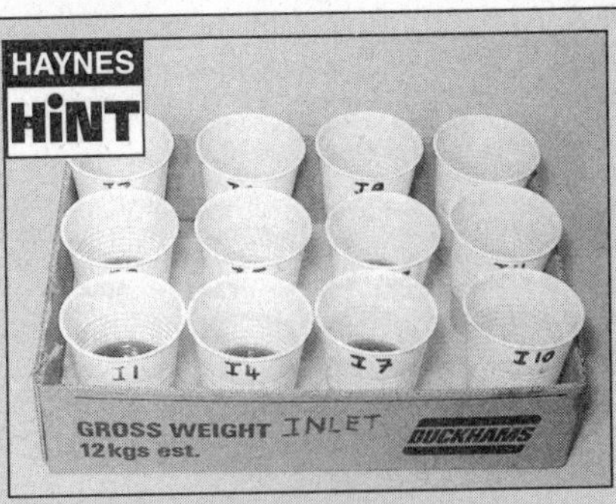


***Store each cam follower in a labelled plastic cup filled with oil***

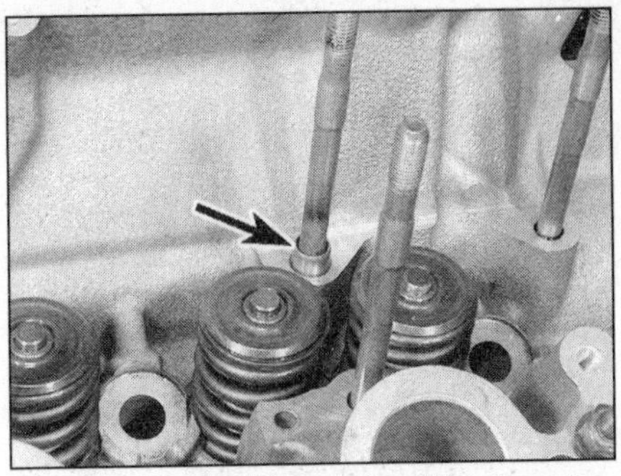

**10.22 Bearing casting locating dowel (arrowed) on cylinder head stud at No 2 bearing location**

caps by turning the eccentric shaft on the tools using a spanner **(see illustration)**.

**15** Unscrew the camshaft bearing cap nuts.

***Warning: Do not attempt to unscrew the camshaft bearing cap nuts without the special tools in place, as damage to the camshaft and/or bearings may result.***

**16** Release the pressure on the special tool shaft, then unbolt the tools from the cylinder head.

**17** Lift off the bearing caps, keeping them in order, then lift out the camshaft.

**18** The camshaft bearing casting can now be lifted from the cylinder head. This should be done very slowly, as the cam followers will be released as the casting is lifted off - if the casting is lifted off awkwardly, the cam followers may fall out. Do not allow the cam followers to fall out and get mixed up, as they must be fitted to their original locations.

**19** With the bearing casting removed, lift the cam followers from the cylinder head. Identify the followers for location, and store them upright in a container of clean engine oil to prevent the oil from draining from inside the followers. Do not forget to mark the cam followers "Inlet" and "Exhaust".

**20** Repeat the procedure on the remaining camshaft.

## Inspection

**21** Clean all the components, including the bearing surfaces in the bearing castings and bearing caps. Examine the components carefully for wear and damage. In particular, check the bearing and cam lobe surfaces of the camshaft(s) for scoring and pitting. Examine the surfaces of the cam followers for signs wear or damage. Renew components as necessary.

## Refitting

**22** If the camshaft lower bearing castings have been removed, check that the mating faces of the bearing castings and the cylinder head are clean, and check that the bearing casting locating dowels are in position on the studs at Nos 2 and 7 bearing locations **(see illustration)**.

**23** The bearing casting(s) and cam followers must now be refitted.

**24** The simplest method of refitting these components is to retain the cam followers in the bearing casting, and refit the components as an assembly.

**25** Oil the bearing casting contact surfaces of the cam followers (avoid allowing oil onto the top faces of the followers at this stage), then fit each follower to its original location in the bearing casting.

**26** Once all the followers have been fitted, they must be retained in the bearing casting, so that they do not fall out as the assembly is refitted to the cylinder head.

**27** With the cam followers retained in the bearing casting, refit the casting to the cylinder head. Note that the exhaust side casting is marked "A" and the inlet side casting is marked "E". When the castings are refitted, the marks should face each other at the timing chain end of the cylinder head.

***Warning: The cam followers expand when not subjected to load by the camshafts, and therefore require some time before they can be compressed. If the camshaft refitting operation is carried out rapidly, there is a possibility that the "closed" valves will be forced open by the expanded cam followers, resulting in piston-to-valve contact. To minimise this possibility, after refitting the camshaft(s) observe the delays listed in the following***

2B

HAYNES HiNT

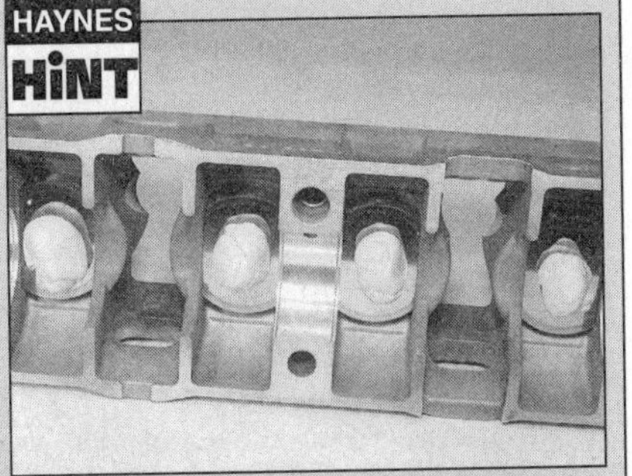

***Stick a small amount of "Blu-Tack" or a similar adhesive compound to the top of each can follower. The adhesive should protrude beyond the lower bearing surface of the casting. Do not use excessive amounts of adhesive, as there is a risk of contaminating the oilways in the bearing castings***

HAYNES HiNT

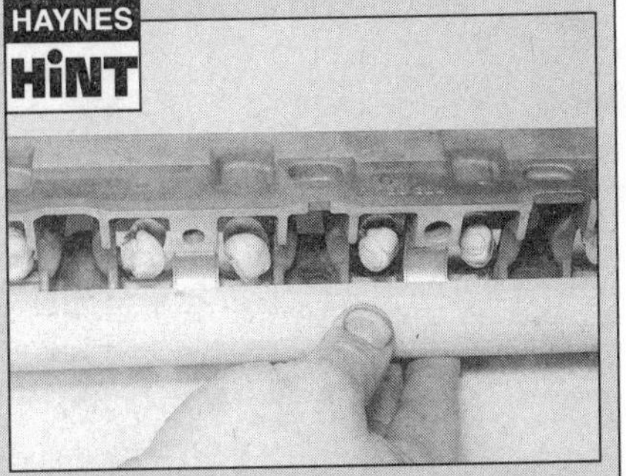

***Press a wooden dowel (such as a length of broom handle) onto the top surface of the adhesive pads so that the pads stick to the dowel, holding the cam followers in the bearing casting. Ensure that no adhesive is pressed out between the surfaces of the cam followers and bearing casting***

HAYNES HiNT

***Leave the pads and dowel in position until the assembly has been refitted to the cylinder head, then remove the dowel, and carefully remove the adhesive from each follower. It is essential that no trace of adhesive is left on the followers or engine components - engine damage could result if the oilways are blocked***

***table before turning the crankshaft back to the TDC position:***

| Temperature | Delay |
|---|---|
| Room temperature (20°C) | 4 minutes |
| 10°C to 20°C | 11 minutes |
| 0°C to 10°C | 30 minutes |

**28** First identify the camshafts to ensure that they are fitted in the correct locations. The inlet camshaft has a small cut-out in the top of the front flange, and the exhaust camshaft has a plain front flange.
**29** Ensure that the crankshaft is still positioned at 30° clockwise from the TDC position (see **Warning** at the end of paragraph 8.
**30** Position the camshaft on the cylinder head, so that the tips of the front cam lobes on the exhaust and inlet camshafts face one another. Note also that the square flanges on the rear of the camshaft should be positioned with the sides of the flanges exactly at right-angles to the top surface of the cylinder head (this can be checked using a set-square), and the side of the flange with holes drilled into it uppermost.
**31** Place the bearing caps in position, noting that the caps carry identification marks. The exhaust camshaft caps are marked "A1" to "A7", and the inlet camshaft caps are marked "E1" to "E7". Place the bearing caps in their original locations as noted before removal.
**32** Re-assemble BMW special tools 11 3 260 and 11 3 270, and refit them to the cylinder head as during removal.

***Warning: Again, do not attempt to refit the camshafts without the aid of the special tools.***

**33** Apply pressure to the relevant bearing caps by turning the eccentric shaft on the tools using a spanner.
**34** With pressure applied to the bearing caps, refit the bearing cap securing nuts, and tighten them as far as possible by hand.
**35** Tighten the bearing cap nuts to the specified torque, working progressively in a diagonal sequence.
**36** Once the bearing cap nuts have been tightened, unbolt the tools used to apply pressure to the bearing caps.
**37** Repeat the procedure on the remaining camshaft.
**38** Refit the spark plugs, and refit the camshaft cover studs to the cylinder head.
**39** Refit the template used to check the position of the camshafts. If necessary, turn the camshaft(s) slightly using a spanner on the flats provided until the template can be fitted.

***Warning: Note the warning at the end of paragraph 27 before proceeding.***

**40** Turn the crankshaft back 30° anti-clockwise to the TDC position, then re-engage the locking rod with the flywheel to lock the crankshaft in position.
**41** Manipulate the exhaust camshaft primary chain sprocket until the timing arrow on the sprocket is pointing vertically upwards, then engage the chain with the sprocket.
**42** Fit the sprocket to the exhaust camshaft, aligning the sprocket so that the tapped holes in the camshaft flange are positioned at the left-hand ends of the elongated slots in the sprocket.
**43** Refit the secondary chain guide and tighten the securing bolts.
**44** Refit the secondary chain tensioner and tighten the securing bolts.
**45** Temporarily refit the tool to lock the secondary chain tensioner in position, then refit the secondary timing chain as described in Section 7.
**46** Refit the camshaft position sensor and reconnect the wiring plug.
**47** Refit the alternator air ducting, then lower the bonnet.

***Warning: As described in the warning in paragraph 27, the cam followers expand when not subjected to load by the camshafts To minimise the possibility of piston-to-valve contact, after refitting the camshaft(s), observe the following delays before cranking the engine:***

| Temperature | Delay |
|---|---|
| Room temperature (20°C) | 10 minutes |
| 10°C to 20°C | 30 minutes |
| 0°C to 10°C | 75 minutes |

## *VANOS engines*

**Note:** *BMW special tool No 11 3 390 or a suitable equivalent will be required to carry out this operation.*

### Removal

**48** Remove the secondary timing chain, and then remove the camshaft position sensor plate, as described in Section 7.
**49** Unscrew the primary timing chain tensioner plunger cover plug from the right-hand side of the engine. Recover the sealing ring.

***Warning: The chain tensioner plunger has a strong spring. Take care when unscrewing the cover plug.***

**50** Recover the spring and withdraw the tensioner plunger.
**51** Proceed as described in paragraphs 5 to 8 of this Section. ***Caution: Keep tension on the primary timing chain, and tie up the end of the chain using wire or string to prevent it from dropping into the lower timing chain cover and/or disengaging from the crankshaft sprocket.***

***Warning: To avoid any possibility of piston-to-valve contact when refitting the camshaft(s), it is necessary to ensure that none of the pistons are at TDC. Before proceeding further, remove the locking rod from the timing hole in the cylinder block, then turn the crankshaft approximately 30° clockwise using a spanner or socket on the crankshaft pulley hub bolt.***

**52** Proceed as described in paragraphs 9 to 13.
**53** Unscrew the securing nuts, and remove the No 1 (timing chain end) inlet camshaft bearing cap. Note that the bearing cap is located on dowels.
**54** Apply pressure to the camshaft bearing caps by turning the eccentric shaft on the special tool.
**55** Proceed as described in paragraphs 15 to 20.

### Inspection

**56** Proceed as described in paragraph 21.
**57** If necessary, the splined VANOS shaft on the front of the inlet camshaft can be renewed. To do this, proceed as follows.

a) *Clamp the camshaft carefully in a soft-jawed vice.*
b) *Unscrew the splined shaft using a hexagon key.*
c) *Fit the new splined shaft and tighten to the specified torque.*

### Refitting

**58** If the camshaft lower bearing castings have been removed, check that the mating faces of the bearing castings and the cylinder head are clean, and check that the bearing casting locating dowels are in position on the studs at Nos 2 and 7 bearing locations.
**59** Proceed as described in paragraphs 23 to 27.
**60** If both camshafts have been removed, first identify the camshafts to ensure that they are fitted in the correct locations. The inlet camshaft has a triangular-shaped front flange, and the splined VANOS shaft screwed into the front (timing chain) end.
**61** Ensure the crankshaft is still positioned at 30° clockwise from the TDC position (see **Warning** at the end of paragraph 51).
**62** Proceed as described in paragraphs 30 to 44.
**63** Fit special tool No 11 3 390 into the primary timing chain tensioner aperture, then turn the adjuster screw on the tool until the end of the screw just touches the tensioning rail **(see illustration 9.27a)**. Note that the exhaust camshaft sprocket should now have moved anti-clockwise so that the tapped holes in the camshaft flange are centred in the elongated holes in the sprocket.
**64** Temporarily refit the tool to lock the secondary chain tensioner in position, then refit the camshaft position sensor plate and the secondary timing chain as described in Section 7.

***Warning: As described in the warning in paragraph 27, the cam followers expand when not subjected to load by the camshafts To minimise the possibility of piston-to-valve contact, after refitting the camshaft(s), observe the following delays before cranking the engine:***

| Temperature | Delay |
|---|---|
| Room temperature (20°C) | 10 minutes |
| 10°C to 20°C | 30 minutes |
| 0°C to 10°C | 75 minutes |

## 11 Cylinder head - removal and refitting

### *Engines without VANOS*

**Note:** *New cylinder head bolts and a new cylinder head gasket will be required on refitting.*

#### Removal

**1** Drain the cooling system as described in Chapter 1.

**2** Remove the inlet and exhaust manifolds as described in Chapter 4B.

**3** Remove the secondary timing chain as described in Section 7.

**4** Trace the wiring back from the camshaft position sensor, then disconnect the sensor connector. Unscrew the securing bolt, and remove the sensor from the cylinder head.

**5** Remove the tool locking the secondary timing chain tensioner in position. Lift out the tensioner pad and spring (note which way round the tensioner pad fits to ensure correct refitting).

**6** Unscrew the securing bolts, and withdraw the secondary chain tensioner from the cylinder head.

**7** Unscrew the securing bolts and withdraw the secondary chain guide.

**8** Withdraw the primary timing chain sprocket from the exhaust camshaft, complete with the chain. Remove the sprocket. Note which way round the sprocket is fitted to ensure correct refitting. ***Caution: Keep tension on the chain, and tie up the end of the chain using wire or string to prevent it from dropping into the lower timing chain cover and/or disengaging from the crankshaft sprocket.***

***Warning: To avoid any possibility of piston-to-valve contact when refitting the cylinder head, it is necessary to ensure that none of the pistons are at TDC. Before proceeding further, remove the locking rod from the timing hole in the cylinder block, then turn the crankshaft approximately 30° clockwise using a spanner or socket on the crankshaft pulley hub bolt.***

**9** Unscrew the bolts securing the lower timing chain cover to the cylinder head (note that one of the bolts also secures the secondary timing chain tensioner).

**10** Disconnect the two coolant hoses from the thermostat cover at the front of the cylinder head **(see illustration)**.

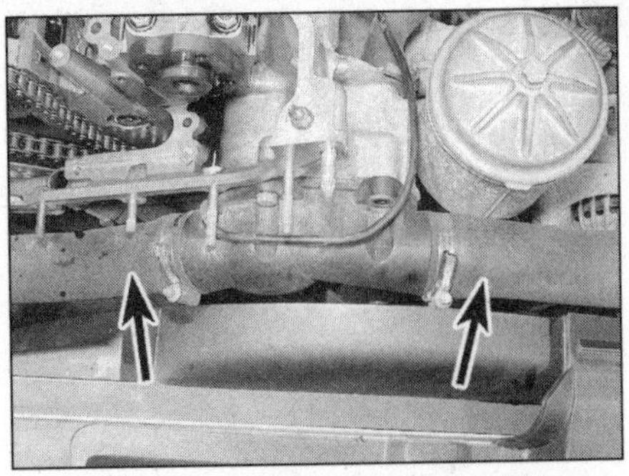

**11.10 Disconnect the two coolant hoses (arrowed) from the thermostat housing**

**11** Disconnect the coolant hose from the rear left-hand corner of cylinder head **(see illustration)**.

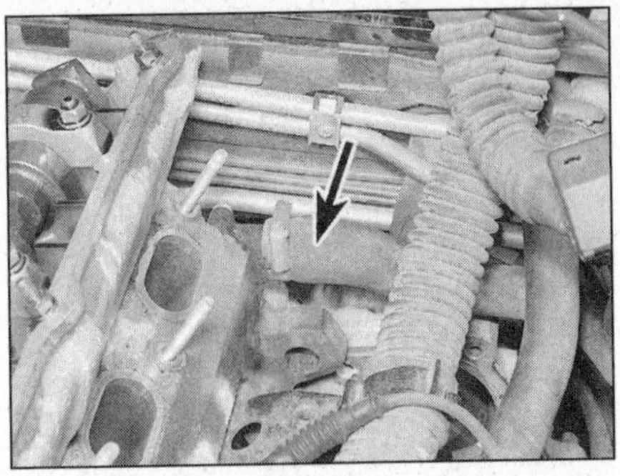

**11.11 Disconnect the coolant hose (arrowed) from the rear left-hand corner of the cylinder head**

**12** Disconnect the remaining small coolant hose from the left-hand side of the cylinder head.

**13** Disconnect wiring plugs from the temperature sensors located in the left-hand side of the cylinder head.

**14** Unscrew the securing bolt and remove the crankshaft position sensor from the front of the engine. Trace the wiring back from the sensor, then disconnect the wiring plug and remove the sensor. ***Caution: Mark the wiring plug for identification, as it is possible to mix up the camshaft sensor and crankshaft sensor wiring plugs.***

**15** Progressively loosen the cylinder head bolts, working in a spiral pattern from the outside of the head inwards **(see illustration)**.

**16** Remove the cylinder head bolts, and recover the washers **(see illustration)**. Note that some of the washers may be captive in the cylinder head, in which case they cannot be withdrawn.

**17** Release the cylinder head from the cylinder block and locating dowels by rocking it. Do not prise between the mating faces of the cylinder head and block, as this may damage the gasket faces.

**18** Ideally, two assistants will now be required to help remove the cylinder head. Have one assistant hold the timing chain up, clear of the cylinder head, making sure that tension is kept on the chain. With the aid of another assistant, lift the cylinder head from the block - take care, as the cylinder head is heavy **(see illustration)**. As the cylinder head is removed, feed the timing chain through the aperture in the front of the cylinder head, and support it from the cylinder block using the wire.

**19** Recover the cylinder head gasket.

#### Inspection

**20** Refer to Chapter 2C for details of cylinder head dismantling and reassembly.

**21** The mating faces of the cylinder head and block must be perfectly clean before refitting the head. Use a scraper to remove all traces of gasket and carbon, and also clean the tops of the pistons. Take particular care with the aluminium cylinder head, as the soft metal is easily damaged. Also make sure that debris is not allowed to enter the oil and water passages. Using adhesive tape and paper, seal the water, oil and bolt holes in the cylinder block. To prevent carbon entering the gap between the pistons and bores, smear a little grease in the gap. After cleaning each piston, rotate the crankshaft so that the piston moves **down** the bore, then wipe out the grease and carbon with a cloth rag.

**22** Check the block and head for nicks, deep scratches and other damage. If very slight, they may be removed from the cylinder block

**11.15 Loosen the cylinder head bolts, working in a spiral pattern . . .**

**11.16 . . . then withdraw the bolts**

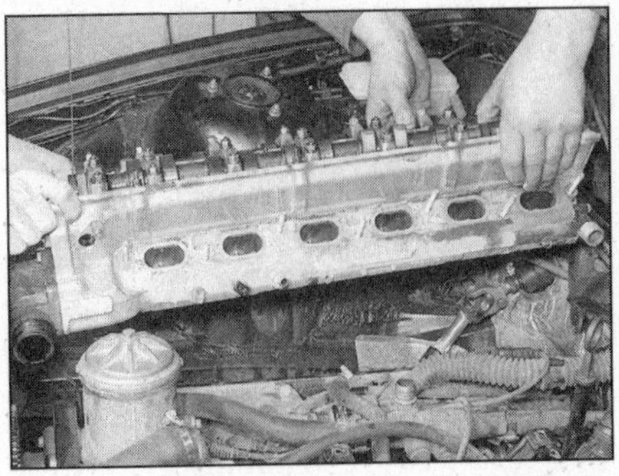

**11.18 Lifting off the cylinder head**

carefully with a file. More serious damage may be repaired by machining, but this is a specialist job.

**23** If warpage of the cylinder head is suspected, use a straight-edge to check it for distortion, with reference to Chapter 2C.

**24** Clean out the bolt holes in the block using a pipe cleaner or thin rag and a screwdriver. Make sure that all oil and water is removed, otherwise there is a possibility of the block being cracked by hydraulic pressure when the bolts are tightened.

**25** Examine the bolt threads and the threads in the cylinder block for damage. If necessary, use the correct size tap to chase out the threads in the block.

## Refitting

***Warning: If the camshafts have been removed from the cylinder head, note the warnings given in Section 10, regarding expanded cam followers. Additionally, to minimise the possibility of piston-to-valve contact, after refitting the camshaft(s) observe the following delays before refitting the cylinder head.***

| Temperature | Delay |
|---|---|
| Room temperature (20°C) | 4 minutes |
| 10°C to 20°C | 11 minutes |
| 0°C to 10°C | 30 minutes |

**26** Ensure that the mating faces of the cylinder block and head are spotlessly clean, that the cylinder head bolt threads are clean and dry, and that they screw in and out of their locations.

**27** Check that the cylinder head locating dowels are correctly positioned in the cylinder block.

***Warning: To avoid any possibility of piston-to-valve contact when refitting the cylinder head, it is necessary to ensure that none of the pistons are at TDC. Before proceeding further, if not already done, turn the crankshaft to position No 1 piston at TDC (check that the locking rod can be engaged with the flywheel, then remove the locking rod and turn the crankshaft approximately 30° clockwise using a spanner or socket on the crankshaft pulley hub bolt.***

**28** Fit a new cylinder head gasket to the block, locating it over the dowels. Make sure that it is the correct way up **(see illustration)**. Note that 0.3 mm thicker-than-standard gaskets are available for use if the cylinder head has been machined (see Chapter 2C).

**29** If not already done, fit the template to the cylinder head to ensure that the camshafts are correctly positioned (No 1 piston at TDC) - see Section 3.

**30** Lower the cylinder head onto the block, engaging it over the dowels.

**31** Fit the **new** cylinder head bolts, complete with new washers where necessary, and tighten the bolts as far as possible by hand. **(see Haynes Hint).** Ensure that the washers are correctly seated in their locations in the cylinder head - fitting is a fiddly operation!

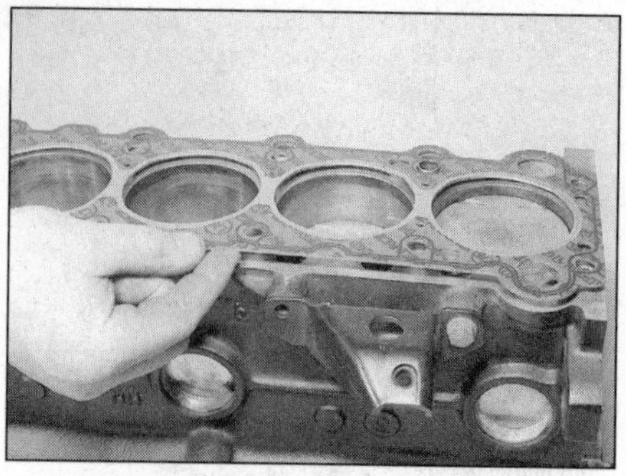

**11.28 Fit a new cylinder head gasket**

**Note:** *Do not fit washers to any bolts which are fitted to locations where there are already captive washers in the cylinder head. If a new cylinder head is fitted (without captive washers), ensure that new washers are fitted to all the bolts.*

**32** Tighten the bolts in the order shown, and in the stages given in the Specifications - ie, tighten all bolts in sequence to the Stage 1 torque, then tighten all bolts in sequence to the Stage 2 torque, and so on **(see illustrations)**.

**33** Refit and tighten the bolts securing the lower timing chain cover to the cylinder head.

**34** Turn the crankshaft back 30° anti-clockwise to the TDC position, then re-engage the locking rod with the flywheel to lock the crankshaft in position.

**35** Manipulate the exhaust camshaft primary chain sprocket until the timing arrow on the sprocket is pointing vertically upwards (note that some sprockets have two arrows opposite each other), then engage the chain with the sprocket.

**36** Fit the sprocket to the exhaust camshaft, aligning the sprocket so that the tapped holes in the camshaft flange are positioned at the left-hand ends of the elongated slots in the sprocket.

**37** Refit the secondary chain guide and tighten the securing bolts.

**38** Refit the secondary chain tensioner and tighten the securing bolts. Refit the spring and tensioner pad, ensuring the pad is fitted the correct way round (as noted before removal).

**HAYNES HiNT**

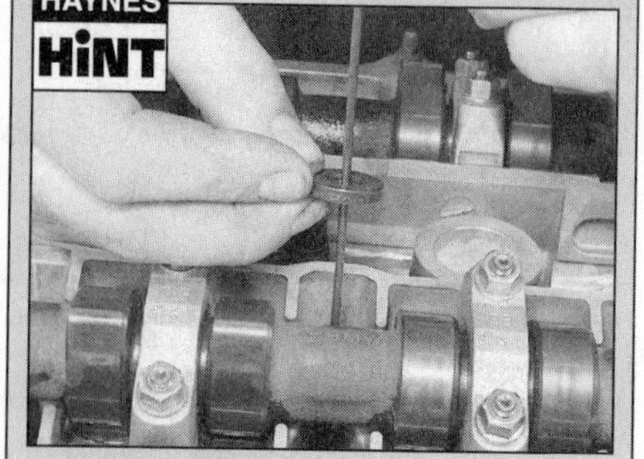

***Fit the washers by guiding them into position using a length of welding rod or stiff wire***

**39** Temporarily refit the tool to lock the secondary chain tensioner in position, then refit the secondary timing chain as described in Section 7.

**40** Further refitting is a reversal of removal, but refit the inlet and exhaust manifolds as described in Chapter 4B, and on completion refill the cooling system as described in Chapter 1.

## *Engines with VANOS*

**Note:** *BMW special tool No 11 3 390 or a suitable equivalent will be required to carry out this operation. New cylinder head bolts and a new cylinder head gasket will be required on refitting.*

### Removal

**41** Proceed as described in paragraphs 1 to 4.

**42** Unscrew the primary timing chain tensioner plunger cover plug from the right-hand side of the engine. Recover the sealing ring.

***Warning: The chain tensioner plunger has a strong spring. Take care when unscrewing the cover plug.***

**43** Recover the spring and withdraw the tensioner plunger.

**44** Proceed as described in paragraphs 5 to 19.

### Inspection

**45** Proceed as described in paragraphs 20 to 25.

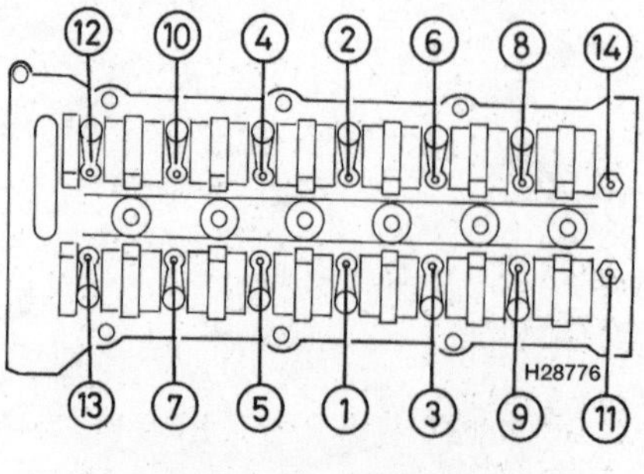


**11.32a Cylinder head bolt tightening sequence - 6-cylinder engines**

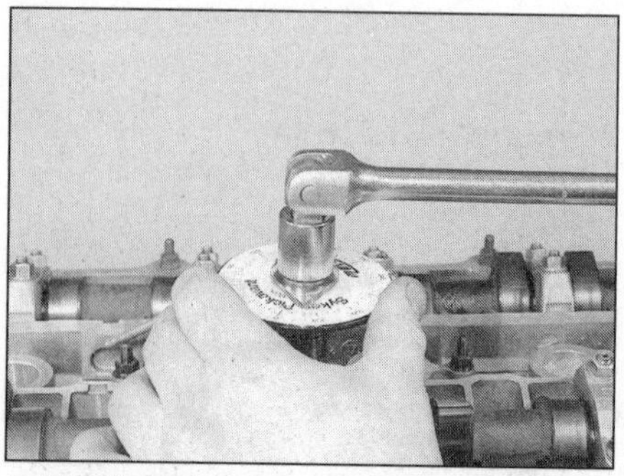

**11.32b Tightening a cylinder head bolt using an angle gauge**

### Refitting

**46** Proceed as described in paragraphs 28 to 38, noting the warning at the beginning of paragraph 28.

**47** Fit special tool No 11 3 390 into the primary timing chain tensioner aperture, then turn the adjuster screw on the tool until the end of the screw just touches the tensioning rail **(see illustration 9.27a)**. Note that the exhaust camshaft sprocket should now have moved anti-clockwise so that the tapped holes in the camshaft flange are centred in the elongated holes in the sprocket.

**48** Proceed as described in paragraphs 39 to 40.

## 12 Sump - removal and refitting

### *Engines without VANOS*

**Note:** *A new sump gasket and/or a new dipstick tube sealing ring may be required on refitting, and suitable gasket sealant will be required.*

### Removal

**1** Drain the engine oil, referring to Chapter 1.

**2** Apply the handbrake, then jack up the front of the vehicle and support securely on axle stands (see *"Jacking, and vehicle support"*).

**3** Remove the exhaust system as described in Chapter 4B.

**4** Open the bonnet, then raise the bonnet to its fully open position as described in Chapter 11.

**5** Unscrew the securing bolts and/or nuts, and remove the alternator air ducting from the front of the vehicle.

**6** Remove the air cleaner assembly and air mass meter, as described in Chapter 4B.

**7** Remove the heater/ventilation inlet air ducting from the rear of the engine compartment as follows.

a) *Lift the grille from the top of the ducting (on certain Coupe models, it will be necessary to remove the securing screws and lift off the complete scuttle grille assembly).*
b) *Working through the top of the ducting, remove the screws securing the cable ducting to the air ducting and move the cable ducting clear.*
c) *Unscrew the nuts and/or screw(s) securing the air ducting to the bulkhead (where applicable, bend back the heat shielding for access).*
d) *Remove the air ducting by pulling upwards.*
e) *Move the previously removed cable ducting clear of the cylinder head cover.*

**8** Remove the viscous cooling fan and fan cowl assembly as described in Chapter 3.

**9** Release the radiator upper securing clips with reference to Chapter 3.

**10** Unscrew the dipstick tube bracket securing bolt, and pull the dipstick tube from the cylinder block.

**11** Unbolt the power steering fluid reservoir from the left-hand engine mounting bracket, and move the reservoir to one side, taking care not to strain the fluid hose.

**12** Remove the auxiliary drivebelt as described in Chapter 1.

**13** Unbolt the power steering pump support bracket from the sump, then unbolt the power steering pump, and move it to one side, clear of the engine, leaving the fluid lines connected. Ensure that the pump is adequately supported, and take care not to strain the fluid lines.

**14** Similarly, on models with air conditioning, unbolt the air conditioning compressor from the engine and suspend it to one side, leaving the refrigerent lines connected.

***Warning: Do not disconnect the refrigerent lines - refer to Chapter 3 for precautions to be taken.***

**15** Unscrew the nuts securing the left- and right-hand engine mounting brackets to the engine mountings. Loosen the nuts approximately four complete turns.

**16** Unbolt the earth cable(s) from the engine mounting bracket(s).

**17** Where applicable, unclip any pipes, hoses and/or wiring from the engine mounting brackets.

**18** Connect an engine hoist and lifting tackle to the engine lifting bracket on the front of the cylinder head, and to the engine mounting brackets. Adjust the lifting tackle so that the engine is equally supported at all three points.

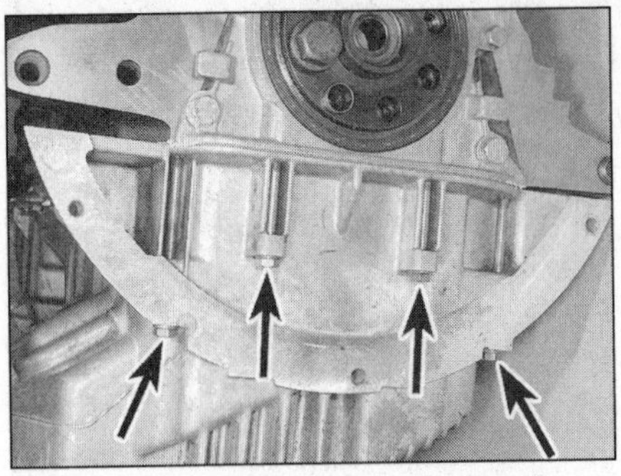

**12.20 The rear sump bolts (arrowed) are accessible through the access slots in the bellhousing - viewed with gearbox and flywheel removed for clarity**

**19** Slowly lift the engine as far as possible, continually checking that no pipes, hoses or wiring is being stretched or trapped.

**20** Working under the vehicle, progressively unscrew and remove all the sump securing bolts. Note that the rear sump securing bolts are accessible through the access slots provided in the gearbox/transmission bellhousing **(see illustration)**. Also note that the three lower gearbox/transmission-to-engine bolts must be removed, as they screw into the sump.

**21** Lower the sump as far as possible (with the engine in the car, the sump cannot be removed until the oil pump and pick-up tube have been removed).

**22** The oil pump drive sprocket securing nut must now be unscrewed - note that the nut has a left-hand thread, ie it must be turned clockwise to loosen it **(see illustration)**. If necessary, prevent the crankshaft from turning as the nut is unscrewed using a spanner or sprocket on the crankshaft sprocket bolt. ***Caution: The oil pump drive sprocket securing nut has a left-hand thread.***

**23** Unbolt the oil pump pick-up tube from its mounting bracket **(see illustration)**.

**24** Unscrew the securing bolts and lower the oil pump into the sump **(see illustration)**.

**25** Slide the sump (with the oil pump) rearwards, and manipulate it out from under the vehicle **(see illustration)**.

**26** Recover the sump gasket.



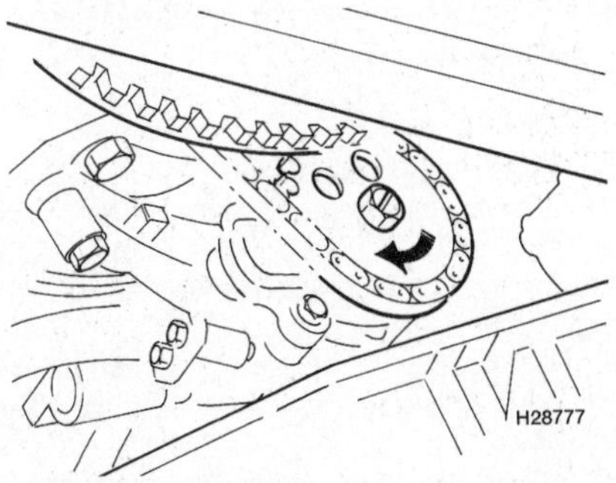


**12.22 Unscrew the oil pump sprocket securing nut - *it has a left-hand thread***

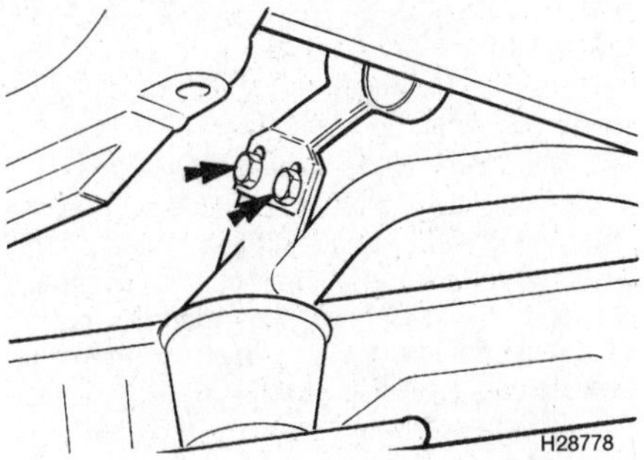


**12.23 Unbolt the oil pick-up pipe from the mounting bracket**

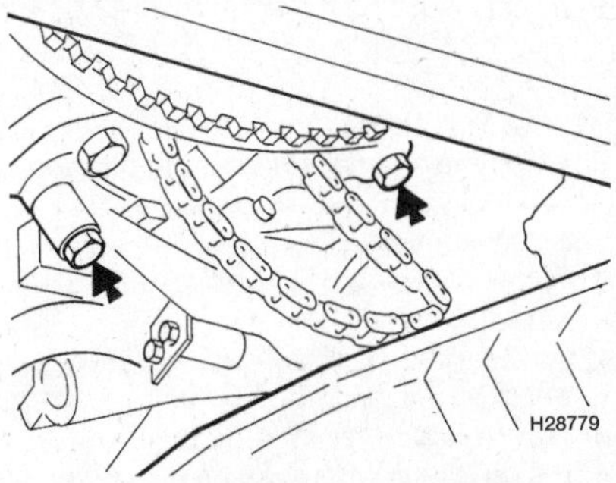


**12.24 Unscrew the oil pump securing bolts (arrowed)**

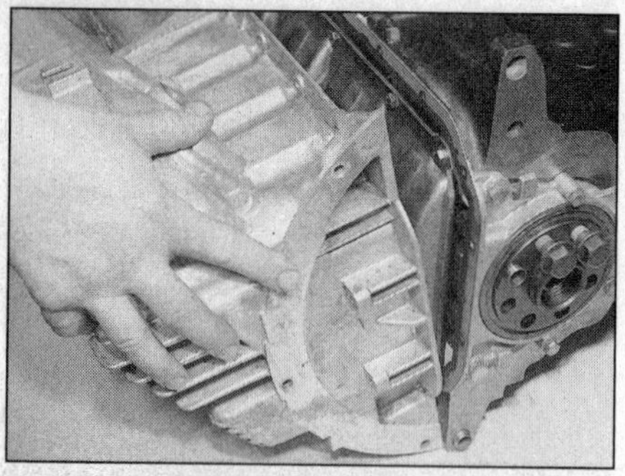

12.25 Removing the sump - viewed with engine removed for clarity

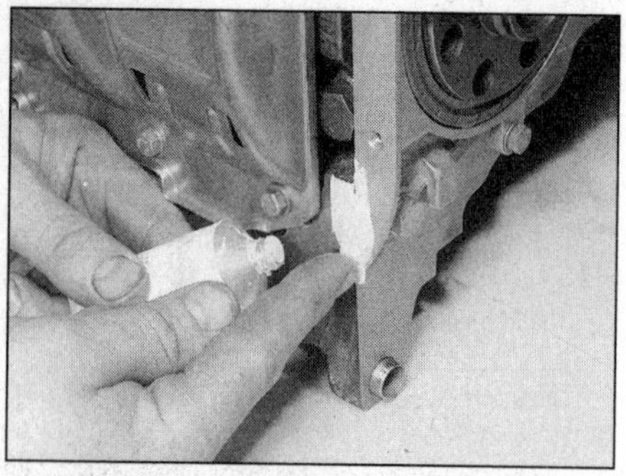

12.28 Applying sealant to the crankshaft rear oil seal housing/cylinder block joint

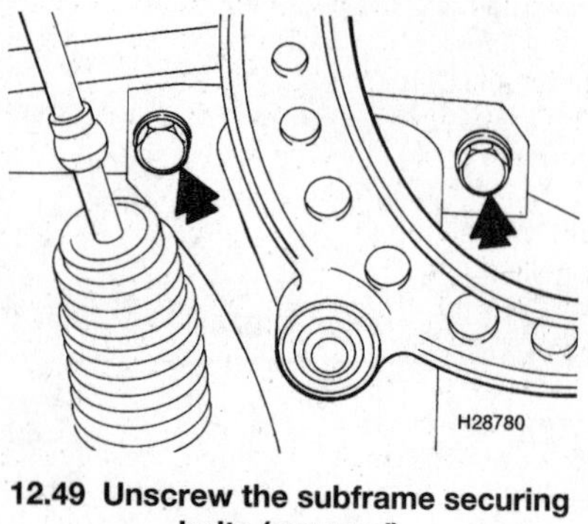


12.49 Unscrew the subframe securing bolts (arrowed)

### Refitting

**27** Commence refitting by thoroughly cleaning the mating faces of the sump and cylinder block. Check the condition of the gasket and renew if necessary.

**28** Lightly coat the areas where the crankshaft rear oil seal housing and front timing chain cover join the cylinder block with a little gasket sealant **(see illustration)**.

**29** Place the gasket in position on the sump flange. If necessary, apply more sealant (sparingly) to hold the gasket in place.

**30** Offer the oil pump into position, ensuring that it locates on the positioning dowels. Refit and tighten the oil pump securing bolts.

**31** Refit and tighten the bolts securing the oil pump pick-up tube to its mounting bracket.

**32** Refit the oil pump drive sprocket, ensuring that it engages with the splines on the oil pump shaft. Make sure that the drive chain is correctly positioned on the crankshaft and oil pump sprockets.

**33** Refit the oil pump drive sprocket securing nut, and tighten it to the specified torque - note that the nut has a left-hand thread, ie it must be turned anti-clockwise to tighten it. If necessary, prevent the crankshaft from turning as during removal. ***Caution: The oil pump drive sprocket securing nut has a left-hand thread.***

**34** Offer the sump up to the cylinder block, ensuring that the gasket stays in place, and refit the sump securing bolts, tightening them finger-tight only at this stage.

**35** Progressively tighten the sump-to-cylinder block bolts to the specified torque.

**36** Tighten the sump-to-gearbox/transmission-to-engine bolts to the specified torque.

**37** Further refitting is a reversal of removal, noting the following points.

*a) When lowering the engine into position, make sure that no pipes, hoses and/or wiring are trapped.*

*b) Tighten the engine mounting nuts to the specified torque.*

*c) Refit and tension the auxiliary drivebelt as described in Chapter 1.*

*d) When refitting the dipstick tube, check the condition of the sealing ring (at the sump end of the tube), and renew if necessary.*

*e) Refit the viscous cooling fan and cowl assembly as described in Chapter 3.*

*f) Refit the exhaust system with reference to Chapter 4B.*

*g) On completion, refill the engine with oil as described in Chapter 1.*

## *VANOS engines*

**Note:** *A new sump gasket and/or a new dipstick tube sealing ring may be required on refitting, and suitable gasket sealant will be required.*

### Removal

**38** On models with VANOS (variable camshaft timing control - see Section 1), the front suspension subframe must be lowered in order to remove the sump. Proceed as follows.

**39** Proceed as described in paragraphs 1 to 6 inclusive.

**40** Set the steering wheel to the straight-ahead position, then loosen the clamp screw, and disconnect the steering intermediate shaft from the steering gear pinion. Refer to *"Steering gear - removal and refitting"* in Chapter 10 for details.

**41** Siphon the power steering fluid from the reservoir, or alternatively, unbolt the reservoir, and drain the fluid into a suitable container. Assuming that the fluid is clean and uncontaminated, save it in a sealed container for re-use.

**42** Working under the vehicle, unscrew the unions and disconnect the power steering fluid lines from the steering gear. Be prepared for fluid spillage.

**43** Where applicable, unclip any pipes, hoses and/or wiring from the engine mounting brackets.

**44** Connect an engine hoist and lifting tackle to the engine lifting bracket on the front of the cylinder head, and to the engine mounting brackets. Adjust the lifting tackle so that the engine is equally supported at all three points. If necessary, remove the air cleaner assembly and air mass meter, as described in Chapter 4B to allow sufficient clearance for the lifting tackle to be connected to the left-hand engine mounting bracket.

**45** Working under the vehicle, unscrew the nuts securing the left- and right-hand engine mountings to the brackets on the subframe.

**46** Raise the lifting tackle to lift the engine approximately 5.0 mm.

**47** Again working under the vehicle, unscrew the bolts securing the suspension lower arms to the body.

**48** Support the centre of the subframe, using a jack and a block of wood.

**49** Unscrew the subframe securing bolts, then lower the subframe slightly using the jack **(see illustration)**. ***Caution: Do not remove the steering gear from the subframe.***

**50** On models with automatic transmission, release the fluid cooler lines from the sump.

**51** Unscrew the dipstick tube bracket securing bolt, and pull the dipstick tube from the sump.

**52** Progressively unscrew and remove all the sump securing bolts. Note that the rear sump securing bolts are accessible through the access slots provided in the gearbox/transmission bellhousing. Also note that the three lower gearbox/transmission to engine bolts must be removed, as they screw into the sump.

**53** Lower the sump from the engine, and manipulate it out from under the vehicle. If necessary, lower the subframe further, using the jack, to give sufficient clearance.

**54** Recover the sump gasket, and discard it.

### Refitting

**55** Commence refitting by thoroughly cleaning the mating faces of the sump and cylinder block. Check the condition of the gasket and renew if necessary.

**56** Lightly coat the areas where the crankshaft rear oil seal housing and front timing chain cover join the cylinder block with a little gasket sealant.

**57** Place a new gasket in position on the sump flange. If necessary, apply more sealant (sparingly) to hold the gasket in place.

**58** Offer the sump up to the cylinder block, ensuring that the gasket stays in place, and refit the sump securing bolts, tightening them finger-tight only at this stage.

**59** Progressively tighten the sump-to-cylinder block securing bolts to the specified torque.

**60** Tighten the sump-to-gearbox bellhousing bolts to the specified torque.

**61** Check the condition of the dipstick

sealing ring (at the sump end of the tube) and renew if necessary. Refit the dipstick tube and tighten the bracket securing bolt.

**62** On models with automatic transmission, secure the fluid cooler lines to the sump.

**63** Raise the subframe using the jack, then refit the securing bolts and tighten to the specified torque.

**64** Refit the bolts securing the suspension lower arms to the body, ensuring that the washers are in place, and tighten the bolts to the specified torque.

**65** Lower the engine until the mountings are resting on the subframe, ensuring that the lugs on the engine mountings engage with the corresponding holes in the subframe. Refit the engine mounting nuts and tighten them to the specified torque.

**66** Disconnect and withdraw the engine lifting tackle and hoist.

**67** Further refitting is a reversal of removal, bearing in mind the following points.

a) *Top-up the fluid level in the power steering fluid reservoir, and bleed the system as described in Chapter 10.*
b) *Reconnect the steering intermediate shaft to the steering gear pinion, with reference to "Steering gear - removal and refitting" in Chapter 10.*
c) *On completion, refill the engine with oil as described in Chapter 1.*

## 13 Oil pump and drive chain - removal, inspection and refitting

### *Oil pump*

#### Removal and refitting

**1** Removal and refitting of the oil pump is described in Section 12 as part of the sump removal and refitting procedure. Note that the oil pick-up pipe must be fitted to the pump before the pump is refitted. With the oil pump removed, it can be inspected as described in the following paragraphs.

#### Inspection

**Note:** *A new pick-up pipe gasket, a new relief valve spring cap O-ring and a new relief valve circlip will be required on refitting.*

**2** Unbolt the pick-up pipe from the pump. Recover the gasket.

**3** Unbolt the cover from the front of the pump **(see illustration)**.

**4** Withdraw the driveshaft/rotor and the outer rotor from the pump body.

**5** Check the pump body, rotors and cover for any signs of scoring, wear or cracks. If any wear or damage is evident, fit new rotors or renew the complete pump, depending on the extent of the damage. Note that it is wise to renew the complete pump as a unit.

**6** Refit the rotors to the pump body, then using feeler blades, measure the clearance between the outer rotor and the pump body.

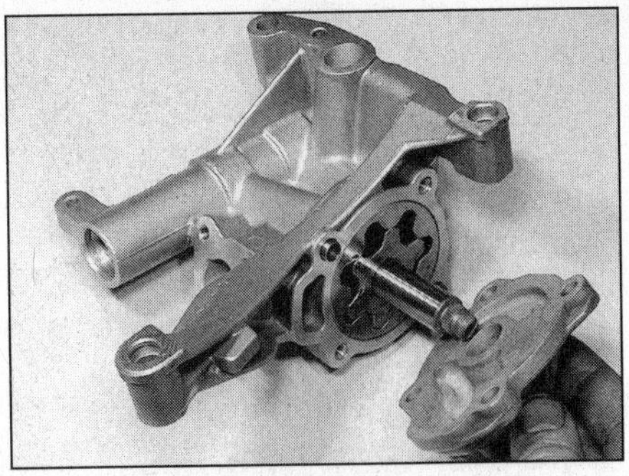

**13.3 Removing the cover from the oil pump**

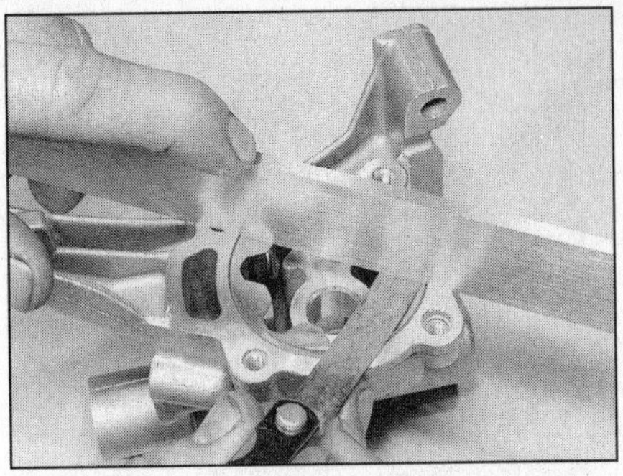

**13.6 Measuring clearance between outer oil pump rotor and pump cover mating face**

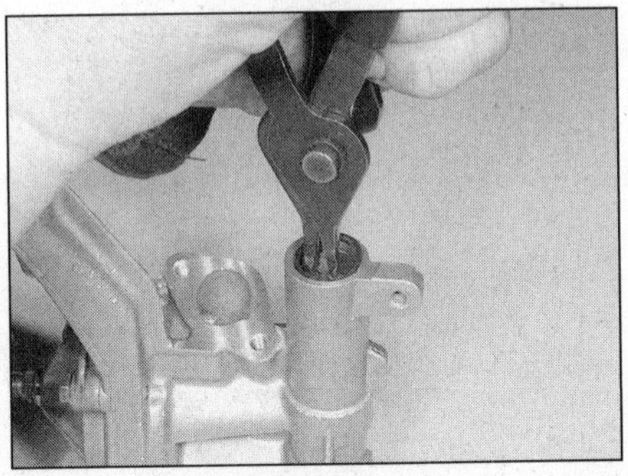

**13.7 Extract the circlip . . .**

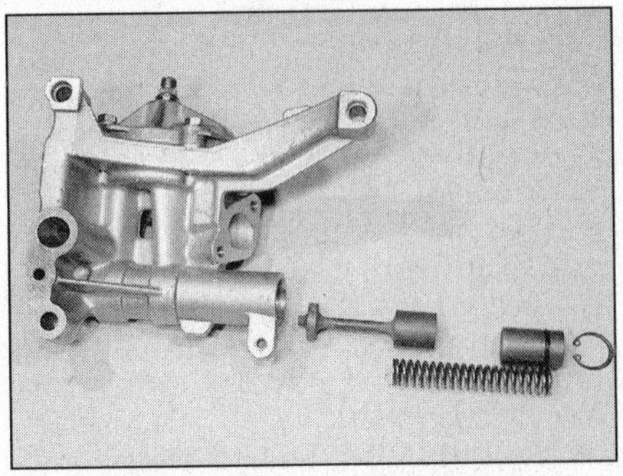

**13.8 . . . and withdraw the oil pressure relief valve components**

Using the feeler blades and a straight edge, measure the clearance (endfloat) between each of the rotors and the oil pump cover mating face **(see illustration)**. Compare the measurements with the values given in the Specifications, and if necessary renew any worn components, or renew the complete pump as a unit.

**7** To remove the pressure relief valve components, press the valve into its housing slightly, using a metal tool, then extract the circlip from the top of the housing using circlip pliers **(see illustration)**.

***Warning: The relief valve has a strong spring. Take care when removing the circlip.***

**8** Withdraw the spring cap, spring and piston from the relief valve housing **(see illustration)**.

**9** Measure the free-length of the relief valve spring, and compare it with the value given in the Specifications. Renew the spring if the free-length is not as specified.

**10** Fit a new O-ring seal to the top of the relief valve spring cap, then refit the components to the housing using a reversal of the removal procedure. Take care not to damage the surface of the spring cap during fitting, and secure the components using a new O-ring.

**11** Refit the rotors to the pump body, then refit the cover to the pump. Ensure that the locating dowels are in position in the pump cover. Refit and tighten the cover bolts.

**12** Thoroughly clean the pick-up pipe strainer, then refit the pick-up pipe to the pump using a new gasket. The tab on the gasket must face the pick-up pipe strainer.

### *Oil pump drive chain*

#### Removal

**13** Remove the primary timing chain as described in Section 7.

**14** Withdraw the chain from the crankshaft sprocket.

#### Inspection

**15** Proceed as described for the secondary timing chain in Section 7.

#### Refitting

**16** Refit the chain to the crankshaft sprocket, then refit the primary timing chain as described in Section 7.

## 14 Oil seals - renewal

### *Crankshaft front oil seal*

**1** The procedure is described as part of the lower timing chain cover removal and refitting procedure in Section 6.

### *Crankshaft rear oil seal*

**Note:** *A new oil seal housing gasket will be required on refitting.*

**2** Remove the flywheel/driveplate, as described in Section 15.

**3** Working at the bottom of the oil seal housing, unscrew the bolts securing the rear of the sump to the housing.

**4** Unscrew the bolts securing the oil seal housing to the cylinder block.

**5** If the housing is stuck to the sump gasket, run a sharp, thin blade between the housing and the sump gasket. Take care not to damage the sump gasket.

**6** Withdraw the housing from the cylinder block. If the housing is stuck, tap it gently using a soft-faced mallet. Do not lever between the housing and the cylinder block, as this may damage the gasket surfaces.

**7** Recover the gasket.

**8** Thoroughly clean all traces of old gasket and sealant from the mating faces of the oil seal housing and the cylinder block. Again, take care not to damage the sump gasket. If the sump gasket has been damaged during removal, it is advisable to fit a new one with reference to Section 12.

**9** Support the oil seal housing on blocks of wood, then drive out the seal from the rear of the housing using a hammer and drift.

**10** Clean the seal mating surfaces in the housing.

**11** Lightly grease the outer edge of the new oil seal, and carefully drive it into position in the housing, using either a large tube of the correct diameter, or a block of wood, to avoid damage to the seal.

**12** Ensure that the locating dowels are in position in the rear of the cylinder block, then locate a new oil seal housing gasket over the dowels.

**13** Lightly grease the inner lips of the oil seal, then carefully offer the housing to the cylinder block, sliding the oil seal over the crankshaft flange. Take care not to damage the oil seal lips.

**14** Refit the housing-to-cylinder block and the sump-to-housing bolts, and tighten them lightly by hand.

**15** Tighten the housing-to-cylinder block bolts to the specified torque, then tighten the sump-to-housing bolts to the specified torque.

**16** Refit the flywheel/driveplate as described in Section 15.

### Camshaft oil seals

**17** No camshaft oil seals are fitted. Sealing is provided by the cylinder head cover gasket and the timing chain cover gaskets.

## 15 Flywheel/driveplate - removal and refitting

### Removal

**Note:** *New flywheel/driveplate securing bolts will be required on refitting, and thread-locking compound may be required.*

**1** Remove the manual gearbox as described in Chapter 7A, or the automatic transmission as described in Chapter 7B, as applicable.

**2** On models with a manual gearbox, remove the clutch as described in Chapter 6.

**3** In order to unscrew the bolts, the flywheel/driveplate must be locked in position. This can be done by bolting a toothed tool (engage the tooth with the starter ring gear) to the cylinder block using one of the engine-to-gearbox bolts **(see illustration)**.

**15.3 Toothed tool used to lock flywheel in position when unscrewing flywheel bolts**

**15.4 Withdrawing the flywheel from the crankshaft**

**15.6 Ensure that the engine/transmission intermediate plate is correctly located**

**15.8 Fitting an encapsulated flywheel bolt**

**4** Progressively unscrew the securing bolts, then withdraw the flywheel/driveplate from the crankshaft **(see illustration)**. Note that the flywheel/driveplate locates on dowels.

> ***Warning: Take care as the flywheel/driveplate is heavy!***

**5** Recover the engine/transmission intermediate plate, noting its orientation.

### Refitting

**6** Refit the engine/transmission intermediate plate, ensuring that it is correctly located on the dowel(s) **(see illustration)**.

**7** Refit the flywheel/driveplate to the end of the crankshaft, ensuring that the locating dowel engages.

**8** Examine the threads of the **new** securing bolts. If the threads are not already coated with thread-locking compound, then apply suitable thread-locking compound to them, then refit the bolts **(see illustration)**.

**9** Tighten the bolts progressively in a diagonal sequence to the specified torque. Counterhold the flywheel/driveplate by reversing the tool used during removal.

**10** Where applicable, refit the clutch as described in Chapter 6.

**11** Refit the manual gearbox or the automatic transmission, as applicable, as described in Chapter 7A or 7B respectively.

## 16 Crankshaft spigot bearing - renewal

**1** On manual gearbox models, a ball bearing assembly is fitted to the end of the crankshaft to support the end of the gearbox input shaft **(see illustration)**.

**2** To renew the bearing, proceed as follows.

**3** Remove the clutch as described in Chapter 6.

**4** Using a slide hammer fitted with a suitable adapter, remove the bearing from the end of the crankshaft.

**5** Thoroughly clean the bearing housing in the end of the crankshaft.

**6** Tap the new bearing into position, up to the stop, using a tube or socket on the bearing outer race.

**7** Refit the clutch as described in Chapter 6.

**16.1 Crankshaft spigot bearing (arrowed)**

## 17 Engine/transmission mountings - inspection and renewal

### Inspection

**1** Two engine mountings are used, one on either side of the engine.

**2** If improved access is required, raise the front of the vehicle and support it securely on axle stands (see "*Jacking and vehicle support*").

**3** Check the mounting rubber to see if it is cracked, hardened or separated from the metal at any point. Renew the mounting if any such damage or deterioration is evident.

**4** Check that all the mounting fasteners are securely tightened.

**5** Using a large screwdriver or a crowbar, check for wear in the mounting by carefully levering against it to check for free play. Where this is not possible, enlist the aid of an assistant to move the engine/transmission back and forth, or from side to side, while you observe the mounting. While some freeplay is to be expected, even from new components, excessive wear should be obvious. If excessive freeplay is found, check first that the fasteners are correctly secured, then renew any worn components as required.

### Renewal

**6** Support the engine, either using a hoist and lifting tackle connected to the engine lifting brackets (refer to *"Engine - removal and refitting"* in Part C of this Chapter), or by positioning a jack and interposed block of wood under the sump. Ensure that the engine is adequately supported before proceeding.

**7** Unbolt the power steering fluid reservoir from the left-hand engine mounting bracket, and disconnect the earth lead(s) from the mounting bracket(s).

**8** Unscrew the nuts securing the left- and right-hand engine mounting brackets to the mounting rubbers, then unbolt the mounting brackets from the cylinder block, and remove the mountings.

**9** Unscrew the nuts securing the mountings to the body, then withdraw the mountings. Recover the metal protector plates from the mountings if they are loose.

**10** Refitting is a reversal of removal, but ensure that the metal protector plates are in position on the mountings, and securely tighten all fixings.

# Chapter 2 Part C:
# General engine overhaul procedures

## Contents



## Degrees of difficulty

| | | | | |
|---|---|---|---|---|
| **Easy,** suitable for novice with little experience | **Fairly easy,** suitable for beginner with some experience | **Fairly difficult,** suitable for competent DIY mechanic | **Difficult,** suitable for experienced DIY mechanic | **Very difficult,** suitable for expert DIY or professional |

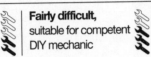

## Specifications

### Cylinder head

| | |
|---|---|
| Maximum gasket face distortion: | |
| All except M43 4-cylinder engines | 0.030 mm |
| M43 4-cylinder engines | 0.050 mm |
| Maximum gasket face machining limit* (all engines) | 0.300 ± 0.050 mm |
| New cylinder head height: | |
| M40 and M43 4-cylinder engines | 141.000 mm |
| M42 4-cylinder engines | 140.000 mm |
| 6-cylinder engines | 140.000 ± 0.050 mm |
| Minimum cylinder head height after machining: | |
| M40 and M43 4-cylinder engines | 140.550 mm |
| M42 4-cylinder engines | 139.550 mm |
| 6-cylinder engines | 139.700 mm |
| Maximum camshaft bearing casting mating face distortion (M42 4-cylinder engines and 6-cylinder engines | 0.050 mm |

**If 0.300 mm of metal or more is removed from the cylinder head gasket face, a 0.300 mm thicker cylinder head gasket must be used when refitting the cylinder head.*

### Valves

| | |
|---|---|
| Valve head diameter: | |
| M40 and M43 4-cylinder engines: | |
| Inlet | 42.000 mm |
| Exhaust | 36.000 mm |
| M42 4-cylinder engines: | |
| Inlet | 33.000 mm |
| Exhaust | 30.500 mm |
| 6-cylinder 2.0 litre engines: | |
| Inlet | 30.000 mm |
| Exhaust | 27.000 mm |
| 6-cylinder 2.5 litre engines: | |
| Inlet | 33.000 mm |
| Exhaust | 30.500 mm |

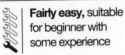

## Valves (continued)

| | | |
|---|---|---|
| Valve stem diameter: | | |
| M40 and M43 4-cylinder engines: | | |
| Inlet: | | |
| Standard | 6.975 | - 0.015 mm |
| 1st oversize | 7.100 | - 0.025 mm<br>- 0.040 mm |
| 2nd oversize | 7.200 | - 0.025 mm<br>- 0.040 mm |
| Exhaust: | | |
| Standard | 6.960 | - 0.015 mm |
| 1st oversize | 7.100 | - 0.040 mm<br>- 0.055 mm |
| 2nd oversize | 7.200 | - 0.040 mm<br>- 0.055 mm |
| M42 4-cylinder engines up to 1992 model year: | | |
| Inlet: | | |
| Standard | 6.975 | - 0.015 mm |
| R1 oversize (head oversize 0.2 mm) | 7.075 | - 0.015 mm |
| R2 oversize (head oversize 0.4 mm) | 7.175 | - 0.015 mm |
| Exhaust: | | |
| Standard | 6.960 | - 0.015 mm |
| R1 oversize (head oversize 0.2 mm) | 7.060 | - 0.015 mm |
| R2 oversize (head oversize 0.4 mm) | 7.160 | - 0.015 mm |
| M42 4-cylinder engines from 1993 model year: | | |
| Inlet: | | |
| Standard | 5.975 | - 0.015 mm |
| R1 oversize (head oversize 0.2 mm) | 6.075 | - 0.015 mm |
| R2 oversize (head oversize 0.4 mm) | 6.175 | - 0.015 mm |
| Exhaust: | | |
| Standard | 5.960 | - 0.015 mm |
| R1 oversize (head oversize 0.2 mm) | 6.060 | - 0.015 mm |
| R2 oversize (head oversize 0.4 mm) | 6.160 | - 0.015 mm |
| 6-cylinder non-VANOS engines: | | |
| Inlet and exhaust: | | |
| Standard | 6.975 mm | |
| 0.1 mm oversize | 7.100 mm | |
| 0.2 mm oversize | 7.200 mm | |
| 6-cylinder VANOS engines: | | |
| Inlet: | | |
| Standard | 5.975 | - 0.015 mm |
| R1 oversize (head oversize 0.2 mm) | 6.075 | - 0.015 mm |
| R2 oversize (head oversize 0.4 mm) | 6.175 | - 0.015 mm |
| Exhaust: | | |
| Standard | 5.960 | - 0.015 mm |
| R1 oversize (head oversize 0.2 mm) | 6.060 | - 0.015 mm |
| R2 oversize (head oversize 0.4 mm) | 6.160 | - 0.015 mm |
| Maximum side-to-side movement of valve in guide (measured at valve head with top of valve stem flush with guide) | 0.500 mm | |

## Cylinder block

| | | |
|---|---|---|
| Cylinder bore diameter: | | |
| All except 6-cylinder 2.0 litre engines: | | |
| Standard | 84.000 | + 0.014 mm |
| Intermediate | 84.080 | + 0.014 mm |
| 1st oversize | 84.250 | + 0.014 mm |
| 2nd oversize | 84.500 | + 0.014 mm |
| 6-cylinder 2.0 litre engines: | | |
| Standard | 80.000 | + 0.014 mm |
| Intermediate | 80.080 | + 0.014 mm |
| 1st oversize | 80.250 | + 0.014 mm |
| 2nd oversize | 80.500 | + 0.014 mm |
| Maximum cylinder bore ovality | 0.010 mm | |
| Maximum cylinder bore taper | 0.010 mm | |

## Pistons

| | |
|---|---|
| Piston diameter: | |
| M40 and M43 4-cylinder engines: | |
| Production standard 0 | 83.985 mm |
| Production standard 00 | 84.065 mm |
| 1st oversize +0.25 | 84.235 mm |
| 2nd oversize +0.5 | 84.485 mm |
| M42 4-cylinder engines and 6-cylinder 2.5 litre engines: | |
| Production standard | 83.980 mm |
| Production intermediate | 84.060 mm |
| Oversize 1 | 84.230 mm |
| Oversize 2 | 84.480 mm |
| 6-cylinder 2.0 litre engines: | |
| Production standard | 79.980 mm |
| Production intermediate | 80.060 mm |
| Oversize 1 | 80.230 mm |
| Oversize 2 | 80.480 mm |
| Piston-to-cylinder bore running clearance | 0.010 to 0.040 mm |
| Maximum play between piston and cylinder wall | 0.150 mm |

## Connecting rods

| | |
|---|---|
| Maximum weight difference between two connecting rods | 4.000 g |

## Crankshaft

| | | |
|---|---|---|
| Endfloat (all engines) | 0.080 to 0.163 mm | |
| Main bearing journal diameter (all engines): | | |
| Standard: | | |
| Yellow | 59.984 to 59.990 mm | |
| Green | 59.977 to 59.963 mm | |
| White | 59.971 to 59.976 mm | |
| 1st undersize (U 0.25): | | |
| Yellow | 59.734 to 59.740 mm | |
| Green | 59.727 to 59.733 mm | |
| White | 59.721 to 59.726 mm | |
| 2nd undersize (U 0.50): | | |
| Yellow | 59.484 to 59.490 mm | |
| Green | 59.477 to 59.483 mm | |
| White | 59.471 to 59.476 mm | |
| Big-end bearing journal diameter: | | |
| M40 and M43 4-cylinder engines, and 6-cylinder VANOS engines: | | |
| Standard | 44.975 | + 0.016 mm |
| 1st undersize | 44.725 | + 0.016 mm |
| 2nd undersize | 44.475 | + 0.016 mm |
| M42 4-cylinder engines and 6-cylinder non-VANOS engines: | | |
| Standard | 45.000 | + 0.009 mm<br>+ 0.025 mm |
| 1st undersize | 44.750 | + 0.009 mm<br>+ 0.025 mm |
| 2nd undersize | 44.500 | + 0.009 mm<br>+ 0.025 mm |
| Maximum run-out of centre main bearing measured at bearings 1 & 5 | 0.150 mm | |
| Main bearing running clearance: | | |
| M40 and M43 4-cylinder engines | 0.020 to 0.046 mm | |
| M42 4-cylinder engines and 6-cylinder engines | 0.020 to 0.058 mm | |
| Big-end bearing running clearance: | | |
| M40 and M43 4-cylinder engines | 0.010 to 0.052 mm | |
| M42 engines and 6-cylinder engines | 0.020 to 0.055 mm | |

## Piston rings

| | |
|---|---|
| End gaps: | |
| M40 and M43 4-cylinder engines except M40 1.6 litre engines: | |
| Top compression ring | 0.200 to 1.000 mm |
| Second compression ring | 0.200 to 1.000 mm |
| Oil control ring | 0.400 to 1.400 mm |
| M40 1.6 litre engines: | |
| Top compression ring | 0.200 to 1.000 mm |
| Second compression ring | 0.200 to 1.000 mm |
| Oil control ring | 0.200 to 1.000 mm |

## Piston rings (continued)

| | |
|---|---|
| End gaps: | |
| M42 4-cylinder engines and non-VANOS 6-cylinder engines: | |
| Top compression ring | 0.200 to 0.400 mm |
| Second compression ring | 0.200 to 0.400 mm |
| Oil control ring | 0.200 to 0.450 mm |
| 6-cylinder VANOS engines: | |
| Top compression ring | 0.200 to 0.400 mm |
| Second compression ring | 0.200 to 0.400 mm |
| Oil control ring | 0.200 to 0.500 mm |
| Ring-to-groove clearance | |
| M40 and M43 4-cylinder engines: | |
| Top compression ring | 0.020 to 0.200 mm |
| Second compression ring | 0.020 to 0.100 mm |
| Oil control ring (M40 1.6 litre engine only) | 0.020 to 0.100 mm |
| M42 4-cylinder engines and non-VANOS 6-cylinder engines: | |
| Top compression ring | 0.020 to 0.052 mm |
| Second compression ring | 0.020 to 0.052 mm |
| Oil control ring | 0.020 to 0.055 mm |
| 6-cylinder VANOS engines: | |
| Top compression ring | 0.020 to 0.055 mm |
| Second compression ring | 0.020 to 0.065 mm |
| Oil control ring | 0.020 to 0.055 mm |

## Torque wrench settings

**4-cylinder engines**

Refer to Chapter 2A Specifications

**6-cylinder engines**

Refer to Chapter 2B Specifications

## 1 General information

Included in this Part of Chapter 2 are details of removing the engine/transmission from the car and general overhaul procedures for the cylinder head, cylinder block/crankcase and all other engine internal components.

The information given ranges from advice concerning preparation for an overhaul and the purchase of replacement parts, to detailed step-by-step procedures covering removal, inspection, renovation and refitting of engine internal components.

After Section 5, all instructions are based on the assumption that the engine has been removed from the car. For information concerning in-car engine repair, as well as the removal and refitting of those external components necessary for full overhaul, refer to Part A or B of this Chapter, as applicable and to Section 5. Ignore any preliminary dismantling operations described in Parts A or B that are no longer relevant once the engine has been removed from the car.

Apart from torque wrench settings, which are given at the beginning of Parts A and B, all specifications relating to engine overhaul are at the beginning of this Part of Chapter 2.

## 2 Engine overhaul - general information

**1** It is not always easy to determine when, or if, an engine should be completely overhauled, as a number of factors must be considered.

**2** High mileage is not necessarily an indication that an overhaul is needed, while low mileage does not preclude the need for an overhaul. Frequency of servicing is probably the most important consideration. An engine which has had regular and frequent oil and filter changes, as well as other required maintenance, should give many thousands of miles of reliable service. Conversely, a neglected engine may require an overhaul very early in its life.

**3** Excessive oil consumption is an indication that piston rings, valve seals and/or valve guides are in need of attention. Make sure that oil leaks are not responsible before deciding that the rings and/or guides are worn. Perform a compression test, as described in Part A or B of this Chapter (as applicable), to determine the likely cause of the problem.

**4** Check the oil pressure with a gauge fitted in place of the oil pressure switch, and compare it with that specified. If it is extremely low, the main and big-end bearings, and/or the oil pump, are probably worn out.

**5** Loss of power, rough running, knocking or metallic engine noises, excessive valve gear noise, and high fuel consumption may also point to the need for an overhaul, especially if they are all present at the same time. If a complete service does not remedy the situation, major mechanical work is the only solution.

**6** A full engine overhaul involves restoring all internal parts to the specification of a new engine. During a complete overhaul, the pistons and the piston rings are renewed, and the cylinder bores are reconditioned. New main and big-end bearings are generally fitted; if necessary, the crankshaft may be reground, to compensate for wear in the journals. The valves are also serviced as well, since they are usually in less-than-perfect condition at this point. Always pay careful attention to the condition of the oil pump when overhauling the engine, and renew it if there is any doubt as to its serviceability. The end result should be an as-new engine that will give many trouble-free miles.

**7** Critical cooling system components such as the hoses, thermostat and water pump should be renewed when an engine is overhauled. The radiator should be checked carefully, to ensure that it is not clogged or leaking. Also, it is a good idea to renew the oil pump whenever the engine is overhauled.

**8** Before beginning the engine overhaul, read through the entire procedure, to familiarise yourself with the scope and requirements of the job. Overhauling an engine is not difficult if you follow carefully all of the instructions, have the necessary tools and equipment, and pay close attention to all specifications. It can, however, be time-consuming. Plan on the car being off the road for a minimum of two weeks, especially if parts must be taken to an engineering works for repair or reconditioning. Check on the availability of parts and make sure that any necessary special tools and equipment are obtained in advance. Most work can be done with typical hand tools, although a number of precision measuring tools are required for inspecting parts to determine if they must be renewed. Often the engineering works will handle the inspection of parts and offer advice concerning reconditioning and renewal.

**9** Always wait until the engine has been completely dismantled, and until all components (especially the cylinder block/crankcase and the crankshaft) have been inspected, before deciding what service and repair operations must be performed by an engineering works. The condition of these components will be the major factor to consider when determining whether to overhaul the original engine, or to buy a reconditioned unit. Do not, therefore, purchase parts or have overhaul work done on other components until they have been thoroughly inspected. As a general rule, time is the primary cost of an overhaul, so it does not pay to fit worn or sub-standard parts.

**10** As a final note, to ensure maximum life and minimum trouble from a reconditioned engine, everything must be assembled with care, in a spotlessly-clean environment.

## 3 Engine removal - methods and precautions

**1** If you have decided that the engine must be removed for overhaul or major repair work, several preliminary steps should be taken.

**2** Locating a suitable place to work is extremely important. Adequate work space, along with storage space for the car, will be needed. If a workshop or garage is not available, at the very least, a flat, level, clean work surface is required.

**3** Cleaning the engine compartment and engine/transmission before beginning the removal procedure will help keep tools clean and organised.

**4** An engine hoist or A-frame will also be necessary. Make sure the equipment is rated in excess of the weight of the engine. Safety is of primary importance, considering the potential hazards involved in lifting the engine/transmission out of the car.

**5** If this is the first time you have removed an engine, an assistant should ideally be available. Advice and aid from someone more experienced would also be helpful. There are many instances when one person cannot simultaneously perform all of the operations required when lifting the engine out of the vehicle.

**6** Plan the operation ahead of time. Before starting work, arrange for the hire of or obtain all of the tools and equipment you will need. Some of the equipment necessary to perform engine/transmission removal and installation safely and with relative ease (in addition to an engine hoist) is as follows: a heavy duty trolley jack, complete sets of spanners and sockets (see *"Tools and Working Facilities"*), wooden blocks, and plenty of rags and cleaning solvent for mopping up spilled oil, coolant and fuel. If the hoist must be hired, make sure that you arrange for it in advance, and perform all of the operations possible without it beforehand. This will save you money and time.

**7** Plan for the car to be out of use for quite a while. An engineering works will be required to perform some of the work which the do-it-yourselfer cannot accomplish without special equipment. These places often have a busy schedule, so it would be a good idea to consult them before removing the engine, in order to accurately estimate the amount of time required to rebuild or repair components that may need work.

**8** Always be extremely careful when removing and refitting the engine/transmission. Serious injury can result from careless actions. Plan ahead and take your time, and a job of this nature, although major, can be accomplished successfully.

**9** On all models, then engine is removed by first removing the gearbox/transmission, then lifting the engine out from above the vehicle.

## 4 Engine - removal and refitting

### *M40 4-cylinder engine*

**Note:** *This is an involved operation. Read through the procedure thoroughly before starting work, and ensure that adequate lifting tackle and/or jacking/support equipment is available. Make notes during dismantling to ensure that all wiring/hoses and brackets are correctly repositioned and routed on refitting.*

### Removal

**1** Depressurise the fuel system as described in Chapter 4A, then disconnect the battery negative lead.

**2** Drain the cooling system as described in Chapter 1.

**3** Drain the engine oil, referring to Chapter 1.

**4** Remove the manual gearbox (Chapter 7A) or the automatic transmission (Chapter 7B), as applicable.

**5** Unless a hoist is available which is capable of lifting the engine out over the front of the vehicle with the vehicle raised, it will now be necessary to remove the axle stands and lower the vehicle to the ground. Ensure that the engine is adequately supported during the lowering procedure.

**6** To improve access and working room, temporarily support the engine from underneath the sump, using a trolley jack and interposed block of wood, then disconnect and withdraw the hoist and lifting tackle used to support the engine during gearbox/transmission removal.

***Warning: Ensure that the engine is securely and safely supported by the jack before disconnecting the lifting tackle.***

**7** Remove the radiator (see Chapter 3).

**8** If not already done, remove the heater/ventilation inlet air ducting from the rear of the engine compartment as follows.

a) *Lift the grille from the top of the ducting (on certain Coupe models, it will be necessary to remove the securing screws and lift off the complete scuttle grille assembly).*
b) *Working through the top of the ducting, remove the screws securing the cable ducting to the air ducting and move the cable ducting clear.*
c) *Unscrew the nuts and/or screw(s) securing the air ducting to the bulkhead (where applicable, bend back the heat shielding for access).*
d) *Remove the air ducting by pulling upwards.*
e) *Move the previously removed cable ducting clear of the cylinder head cover.*

**9** Remove the auxiliary drivebelt with reference to Chapter 1.

**10** Unbolt the power steering pump as described in Chapter 10, and move it to one side, leaving the fluid lines connected.

**11** Similarly, where applicable, unbolt the air conditioning compressor from the engine, and support it clear of the working area, as described in Chapter 3.

***Warning: Do not disconnect the refrigerent lines - refer to Chapter 3 for precautions to be taken.***

**12** Unbolt the power steering reservoir, and move the reservoir to one side, leaving the fluid lines connected.

**13** Unbolt the earth lead(s) from the engine mounting bracket(s).

**14** Remove the air cleaner/airflow meter assembly, and the inlet air trunking as described in Chapter 4A.

**15** Disconnect the heater coolant hoses from the heater pipe and the heater valve on the engine compartment bulkhead, then disconnect the hoses from the engine, and remove the coolant hose assembly. Note the hose routing to aid refitting.

**16** Disconnect the throttle cable from the throttle linkage on the throttle body as described in Chapter 4A.

**17** Disconnect the fuel hoses from the fuel pipes under the inlet manifold, noting their locations to ensure correct refitting **(see illustration)**. Be prepared for fuel spillage and take adequate fire precautions. Clamp or plug the open ends of the hoses and pipes to prevent further fuel loss and dirt ingress.

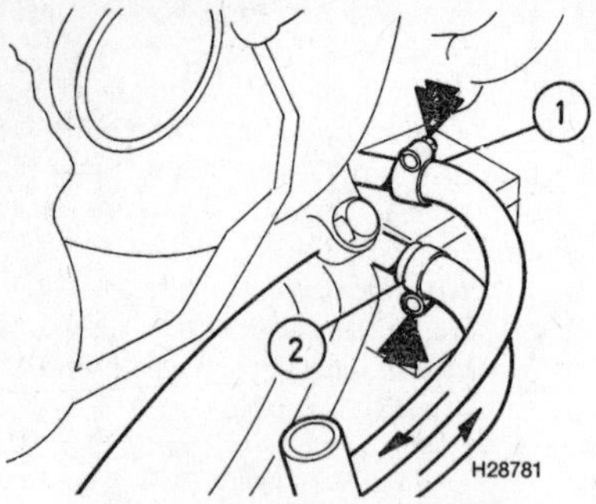


**4.17 Fuel hose connections - M40 4-cylinder engine model**
*1 Fuel return hose 2 Fuel feed hose*

**18** Disconnect the vacuum hose from the brake servo.
**19** Disconnect the HT lead from the ignition coil.
**20** Where applicable, disconnect the battery positive lead.
**21** Disconnect the wiring from the following components **(see illustration)**:

*a) Alternator.*
*b) Camshaft and crankshaft position sensors (mounted on a bracket on the left-hand side of the engine - mark the connectors to avoid confusion on refitting).*
*c) Idle speed control valve.*
*d) Oil pressure warning light switch*
*e) Throttle position sensor.*
*f) Temperature sensors in left-hand side of cylinder head.*
*g) Fuel injector wiring connector at wiring ducting under inlet manifold, near fuel pipes.*
*h) Carbon canister vent valve.*

**22** Pull the idle speed control valve from its rubber mounting.
**23** Unbolt the fuel pipe bracket.
**24** Unscrew the securing nuts and bolts, and remove the inlet manifold support bracket **(see illustrations)**.
**25** Unbolt the wiring ducting from the rear of the engine, and move the ducting/harness assembly to one side, clear of the engine.
**26** Make a final check to ensure that all relevant hoses, pipes and wiring have been disconnected from the engine and moved clear to allow the engine to be lifted out.

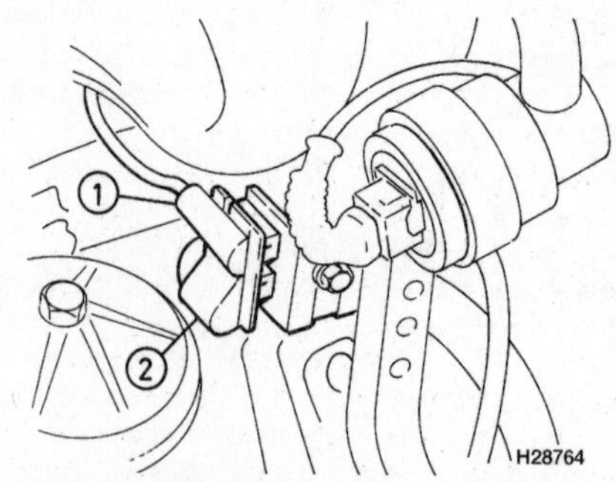


**4.21 Camshaft (1) and crankshaft (2) position sensor wiring connector locations - M40 4-cylinder engine model**

**27** Reposition the lifting tackle and hoist to support the engine both from the lifting eye at the rear left-hand corner of the cylinder block, and from the lifting bracket at the front of the cylinder head **(see illustration)**. Raise the hoist to just take the weight of the engine.
**28** Unscrew the nuts securing the left- and right-hand engine mounting brackets to the mounting rubbers, then unbolt the mounting brackets from the cylinder block, and remove the mountings.
**29** With the aid of an assistant, raise the hoist, and lift the engine from the engine compartment.

### Refitting

**30** Refitting is a reversal of removal, bearing in mind the following points.

*a) Tighten all fixings to the specified torque.*
*b) Ensure that all wiring, hoses and brackets are positioned and routed as noted before removal.*
*c) Reconnect and if necessary adjust the throttle cable with reference to Chapter 4A.*
*d) Refit the auxiliary drivebelt (see Chapter 1).*
*e) Refit the radiator, referring to Chapter 3.*
*f) Refit the manual gearbox or automatic transmission as described in Chapter 7A or 7B respectively.*
*g) On completion, refill the engine with oil, and refill the cooling system as described in Chapter 1.*

## M42 and M43 4-cylinder engines

**Note:** *This is an involved operation. Read through the procedure thoroughly before starting work, and ensure that adequate lifting tackle and/or jacking/support equipment is available. Make notes during dismantling to ensure that all wiring/hoses and brackets are correctly repositioned and routed on refitting.*

### Removal

**31** Proceed as described in paragraphs 1 to 7.
**32** Remove the ignition coil(s) as described in Chapter 5B.
**33** Remove the air cleaner/airflow meter assembly as described in Chapter 4A.
**34** Proceed as described in paragraphs 8 to 13.
**35** Remove the upper and lower sections of the inlet manifold as described in Chapter 4A.
**36** Disconnect the heater coolant hoses from the heater pipe and the heater valve on the engine compartment bulkhead, then disconnect the hoses from the engine, and remove the coolant hose assembly. Note the hose routing to aid refitting.
**37** Disconnect the wiring from the following:

*a) Alternator.*
*b) Temperature sensors in left-hand side of cylinder head.*
*c) Idle speed control valve (mounted on the left-hand side of the engine).*
*d) Oil pressure warning light switch (located in the rear of the oil filter housing).*
*e) Camshaft and crankshaft position sensors and knock sensors, as applicable (the wiring plugs are attached to a bracket on the left-hand side of the engine - make sure that the connectors are marked to ensure correct refitting).*

**38** Check that all relevant wiring has been disconnected from the engine to enable engine removal.
**39** Unscrew the securing bolts, and release any clips (noting their locations) and release the wiring harness/wiring ducting assembly from the engine. Note the routing of all wiring, and note the locations of the brackets to ensure correct refitting (note that the oxygen sensor and reversing light switch wiring also forms part of the engine harness). Move the assembly to one side, clear of the engine.
**40** Make a final check to ensure that all relevant hoses, pipes and wiring have been disconnected from the engine and moved clear to allow the engine to be lifted out.

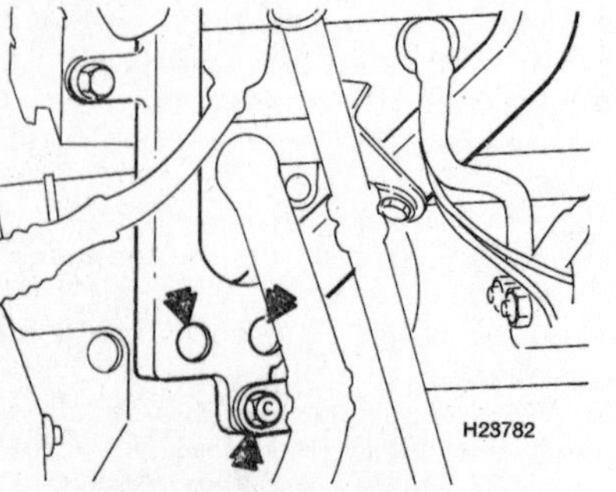


**4.24a Unbolt the inlet manifold support bracket from the engine . . .**

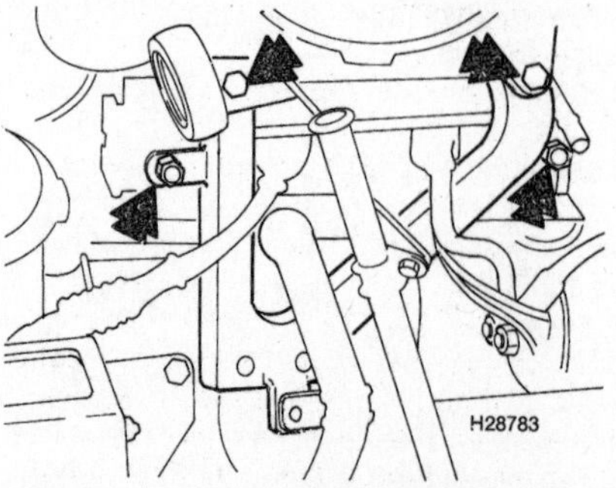


**4.24b . . . and from the manifold and wiring ducting - M40 4-cylinder engine model**

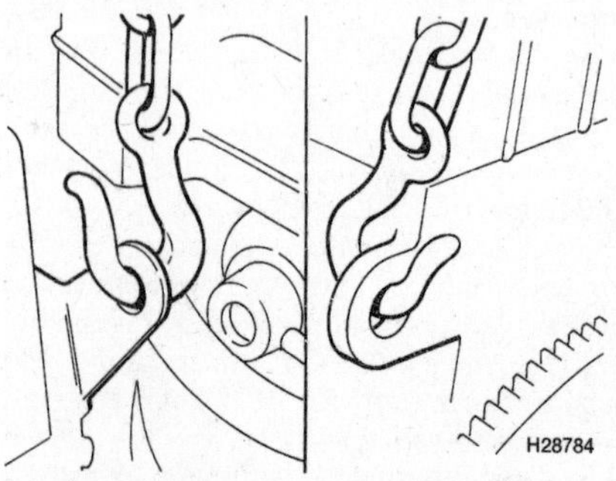


**4.27 Engine lifting eye and lifting bracket locations - M40 4-cylinder engine**

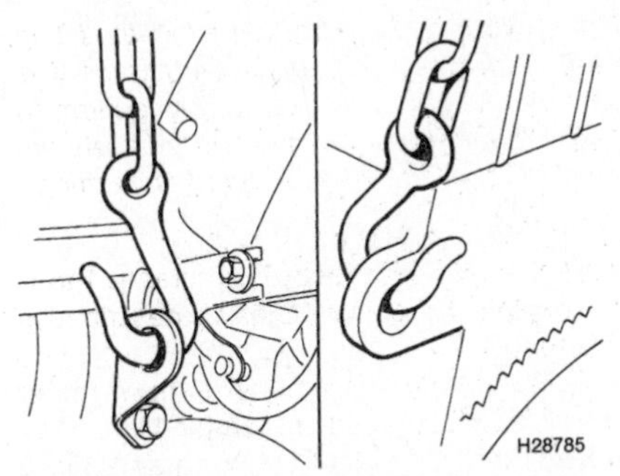


**4.41 Engine lifting eye and lifting bracket locations - M42 and M43 4-cylinder engines**

**41** Refit the front inlet manifold support bracket (which incorporates the engine lifting bracket - the bracket was removed during the manifold removal procedure) to the cylinder head, and tighten the securing bolts **(see illustration)**.

**42** Proceed as described in paragraphs 27 to 29.

### Refitting

**43** Refitting is a reversal of removal, bearing in mind the following points.

*a) Tighten all fixings to the specified torque.*
*b) Ensure that all wiring, hoses and brackets are positioned and routed as noted before removal.*
*c) Refit the auxiliary drivebelt with reference to Chapter 1.*
*d) Refit the lower and upper sections of the inlet manifold as described in Chapter 4A.*
*e) Refit the radiator, referring to Chapter 3.*
*f) Refit the manual gearbox or automatic transmission as described in Chapter 7A or 7B respectively.*
*g) On completion, refill the engine with oil, and refill the cooling system as described in Chapter 1.*

## 6-cylinder engines

**Note:** *This is an involved operation. Read through the procedure thoroughly before starting work, and ensure that adequate lifting tackle and/or jacking/support equipment is available. Make notes during dismantling to ensure that all wiring/hoses and brackets are correctly repositioned and routed on refitting.*

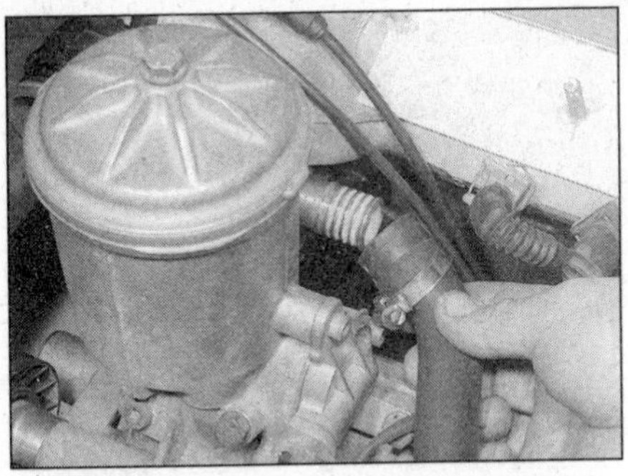

**4.50a Disconnecting coolant hose from coolant pump housing - 6-cylinder engine**

### Removal

**44** Proceed as described in paragraphs 1 to 7.

**45** Remove the engine oil filler cap.

**46** Remove the plastic cover from the top of the cylinder head cover. To remove the cover, prise out the cover plates and unscrew the two securing nuts, then lift and pull the cover forwards. Manipulate the cover over the oil filler neck.

**47** Unbolt the earth lead from the left-hand corner of the upper timing chain cover, and where applicable, unbolt the earth strap from the rear of the cylinder head cover.

**48** Release the locking clips, and disconnect the wiring connectors from the ignition coils. Recover the rubber seals if they are loose.

**49** Release the HT leads from the clips on the cylinder head cover, then move the complete ducting/HT lead assembly to one side, clear of the engine.

**50** Disconnect the coolant hose from the rear of the coolant pump housing, then disconnect the hose from the heater matrix pipe on the engine compartment bulkhead, and remove the coolant hose assembly. Note the hose routing to aid refitting **(see illustrations)**.

**51** Disconnect the wiring from the following components **(see illustration)**:

*a) Alternator.*
*b) Temperature sensors in left-hand side of cylinder head.*
*c) Idle speed control valve (mounted on a bracket on the left-hand side of the engine).*
*d) Oil pressure warning light switch (located in the rear of the oil filter housing).*

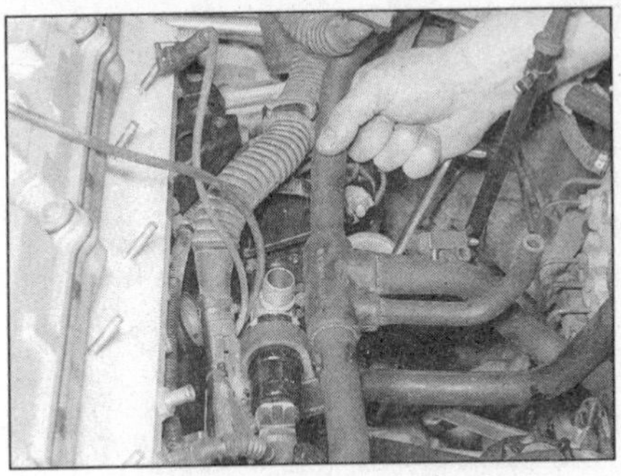

**4.50b Removing the coolant hose assembly - 6-cylinder engine**

*e) Camshaft and crankshaft position sensors and knock sensors, as applicable (the wiring plugs are attached to a bracket on the left-hand side of the engine - make sure that the connectors are marked to ensure correct refitting).*
*f) VANOS solenoid valve (where applicable).*

**52** Check that all relevant wiring has been disconnected from the engine to enable engine removal.

**53** Unscrew the securing bolts, and release any clips (noting their locations) and release the wiring harness/wiring ducting assembly, complete with the idle speed control valve and mounting bracket, from the engine. Note the routing of all wiring, and note the locations of the brackets to ensure correct refitting (note that the oxygen sensor and reversing light switch wiring also forms part of the engine harness). Move the assembly to one side, clear of the engine.

**54** Proceed as described in paragraphs 9 to 13.

**55** Unbolt the inlet manifold support brackets from the engine, noting their locations to ensure correct refitting.

**56** Unbolt the fuel filter bracket/dipstick tube assembly from the engine, then pull the dipstick tube from the cylinder block. Separate the dipstick tube and the fuel filter bracket, then remove the dipstick tube. Move the fuel filter/bracket assembly to one side, clear of the engine **(see illustration)**.

**57** Proceed as described in paragraphs 26 to 29 **(see illustration)**.



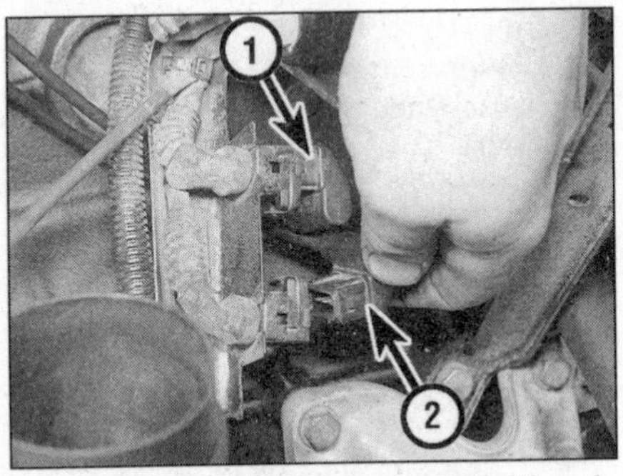


**4.51 Disconnecting the camshaft (1) and crankshaft (2) position sensor wiring plugs - 6-cylinder engine**

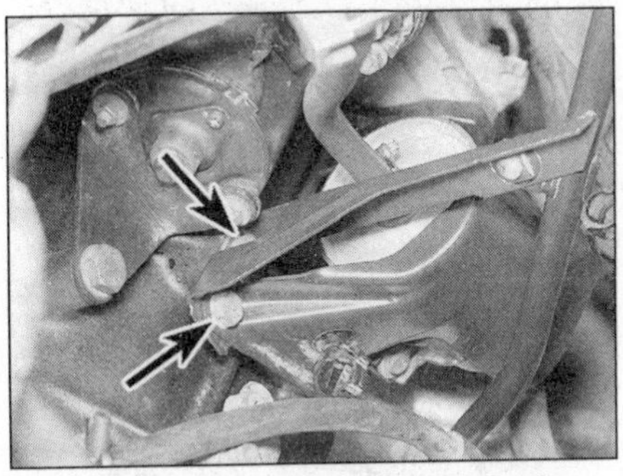

**4.56 Fuel filter bracket/dipstick tube assembly securing bolts (arrowed) - 6-cylinder engine**

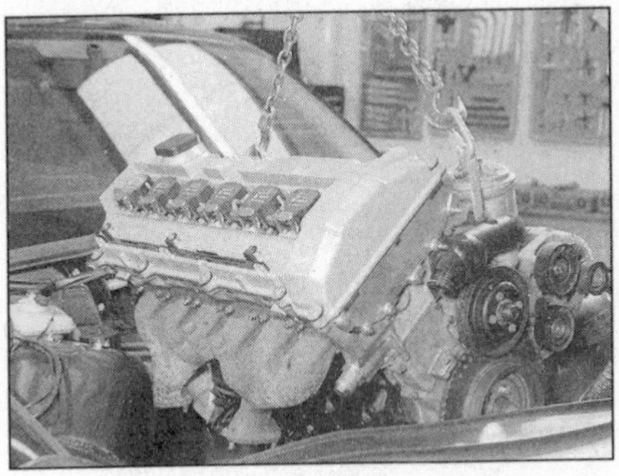

**4.57 Lifting a 6-cylinder engine from the vehicle**

6.3a Compressing the valve springs using a spring compressor tool

6.3b Removing a valve stem oil seal

6.6 Place each valve and its associated components in a labelled polythene bag

### Refitting

58 Refitting is a reversal of removal, bearing in mind the following points.

a) *Tighten all fixings to the specified torque.*
b) *Ensure that all wiring, hoses and brackets are positioned and routed as noted before removal.*
c) *Refit the auxiliary drivebelt (see Chapter 1).*
d) *Refit the radiator, referring to Chapter 3.*
e) *Refit the manual gearbox or automatic transmission as described in Chapter 7A or 7B respectively.*
f) *On completion, refill the engine with oil, and refill the cooling system (Chapter 1).*

## 5 Engine overhaul - dismantling sequence

1 It is much easier to dismantle and work on the engine if it is mounted on a portable engine stand. These stands can often be hired from a tool hire shop. Before the engine is mounted on a stand, the flywheel/driveplate should be removed, so that the stand bolts can be tightened into the end of the cylinder block/crankcase.

2 If a stand is not available, it is possible to dismantle the engine with it blocked up on a sturdy workbench, or on the floor. Be extra-careful not to tip or drop the engine when working without a stand.

3 If you are going to obtain a reconditioned engine, all the external components must be removed first, to be transferred to the replacement engine (just as they will if you are doing a complete engine overhaul yourself). These components include the following:

a) *Ancillary unit mounting brackets (oil filter, starter, alternator, power steering pump, etc.)*
b) *Thermostat and housing (Chapter 3).*
c) *Dipstick tube.*
d) *All electrical switches and sensors.*
e) *Inlet and exhaust manifolds - where applicable (Chapter 4).*
f) *Ignition coils and spark plugs - as applicable (Chapter 4).*
g) *Flywheel/driveplate (Part A or B of this Chapter).*

**Note:** *When removing the external components from the engine, pay close attention to details that may be helpful or important during refitting. Note the fitted position of gaskets, seals, spacers, pins, washers, bolts, and other small items.*

4 If you are obtaining a "short" engine (which consists of the engine cylinder block/crankcase, crankshaft, pistons and connecting rods all assembled), then the cylinder head, sump, oil pump, and timing belt/chain will have to be removed also.

5 If you are planning a complete overhaul, the engine can be dismantled, and the internal components removed, in the order given below, referring to Part A or B of this Chapter unless otherwise stated.

a) *Inlet and exhaust manifolds - where applicable (Chapter 4).*
b) *Timing belt or chains, sprockets and tensioner(s).*
c) *Cylinder head.*
d) *Flywheel/driveplate.*
e) *Sump.*
f) *Oil pump.*
g) *Piston/connecting rod assemblies (Section 9).*
h) *Crankshaft (Section 10).*

6 Before beginning the dismantling and overhaul procedures, make sure that you have all of the correct tools necessary. Refer to *"Tools and working facilities"* for further information.

## 6 Cylinder head - dismantling

**Note:** *New and reconditioned cylinder heads are available from the manufacturer, and from engine overhaul specialists. Be aware that some specialist tools are required for the dismantling and inspection procedures, and new components may not be readily available. It may therefore be more practical and economical for the home mechanic to purchase a reconditioned head, rather than dismantle, inspect and recondition the original head. A valve spring compressor tool will be required for this operation.*

### *M40 and M43 4-cylinder engines*

1 Remove the cylinder head as described in Part A of this Chapter.

2 Remove the camshafts, cam followers and hydraulic valve lifters as described in Part A of this Chapter.

3 Using a valve spring compressor, compress the spring(s) on each valve in turn until the split collets can be removed. Release the compressor, and lift off the spring retainer, springs and spring seats. Using a pair of pliers, carefully extract the valve stem oil seal from the top of the guide **(see illustrations)**.

4 If, when the valve spring compressor is screwed down, the spring retainer refuses to free and expose the split collets, gently tap the top of the tool, directly over the retainer, with a light hammer. This will free the retainer.

5 Withdraw the valve through the combustion chamber.

6 It is essential that each valve is stored together with its collets, retainer, springs, and spring seats. The valves should also be kept in their correct sequence, unless they are so badly worn that they are to be renewed. If they are going to be kept and used again, place each valve assembly in a labelled polythene bag or similar small container **(see illustration)**. Note that No 1 valve is nearest to the timing belt/chain end of the engine.

### *M42 4-cylinder engines*

7 Remove the cylinder head as described in Part A of this Chapter.

8 Remove the camshafts, cam followers and camshaft bearing castings as described in Part A of this Chapter.

9 Proceed as described in paragraphs 3 to 6.

### *6-cylinder engines*

10 Remove the cylinder head as described in Part B of this Chapter.

11 Remove the camshafts, cam followers and camshaft bearing castings as described in Part B of this Chapter.

12 Proceed as described in paragraphs 3 to 6, noting that some engines have single valve springs.

## 7 Cylinder head and valves - cleaning and inspection

1 Thorough cleaning of the cylinder head and valve components, followed by a detailed inspection, will enable you to decide how much valve service work must be carried out during the engine overhaul. **Note:** *If the engine has been severely overheated, it is best to assume that the cylinder head is warped - check carefully for signs of this.*

### *Cleaning*

2 Scrape away all traces of old gasket material from the cylinder head.

3 Scrape away the carbon from the combustion chambers and ports, then wash the cylinder head thoroughly with paraffin or a suitable solvent.

4 Scrape off any heavy carbon deposits that may have formed on the valves, then use a power-operated wire brush to remove deposits from the valve heads and stems.

### *Inspection*

**Note:** *Be sure to perform all the following inspection procedures before concluding that the services of a machine shop or engine overhaul specialist are required. Make a list of all items that require attention.*

#### Cylinder head

5 Inspect the head very carefully for cracks, evidence of coolant leakage, and other damage. If cracks are found, a new cylinder head should be obtained.

6 Use a straight-edge and feeler blade to check that the cylinder head gasket surface is not distorted **(see illustration)**. If it is, it may be possible to have it machined, provided that the cylinder head is not reduced to less than the specified height. **Note:** *If 0.3 mm is machined off the cylinder head, a 0.3 mm thicker cylinder head gasket must be fitted when the engine is reassembled. This is necessary in order to maintain the correct dimensions between the valve heads, valve guides and cylinder head gasket face.*

7 Examine the valve seats in each of the combustion chambers. If they are severely pitted, cracked, or burned, they will need to be renewed or re-cut by an engine overhaul specialist. If they are only slightly pitted, this can be removed by grinding-in the valve heads and seats with fine valve-grinding compound, as described later in this Section.

8 Check the valve guides for wear by inserting the relevant valve, and checking for side-to-side motion of the valve. A very small amount of movement is acceptable. If the movement seems excessive, remove the valve. Measure the valve stem diameter (see later in this Section), and renew the valve if it is worn. If the valve stem is not worn, the wear must be in the valve guide, and the guide must be reamed, and corresponding oversize

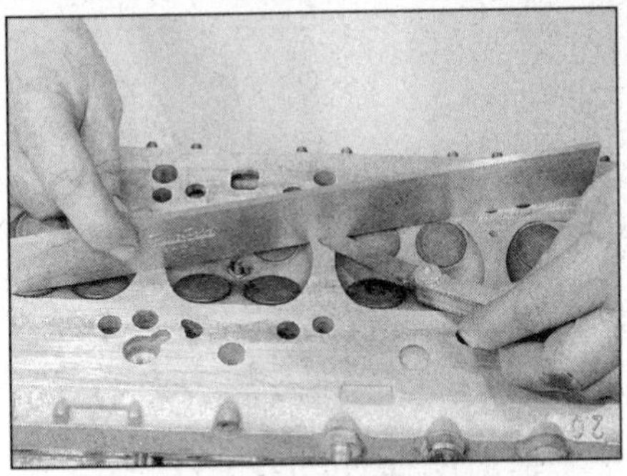

**7.6 Checking the cylinder head gasket face for distortion**

(stem) valves fitted. The reaming of valve guides is best carried out by a BMW dealer or engine overhaul specialist, who will have the necessary tools available.

9 If reaming the valve guides, the valve seats should be re-cut or re-ground only *after* the guides have been reamed.

10 On 6-cylinder engines, unscrew the oil pressure check valve from the bottom of the cylinder head. Check that the valve can be blown through from bottom-to-top, but not from top-to-bottom. Thoroughly clean the valve and fit a new O-ring, then refit the valve to the cylinder head and tighten securely **(see illustration)**.

11 Examine the bearing surfaces in the cylinder head or bearing castings (as applicable) and the bearing caps for signs of wear or damage.

12 On M42 4-cylinder and 6-cylinder engines, check the camshaft bearing casting mating faces on the cylinder head for distortion. Use a straight-edge and feeler blade to check that the cylinder head faces are not distorted. If the distortion is outside the specified limit, the cylinder head and bearing castings must be renewed.

#### Valves

***Warning: The exhaust valves fitted to M40 and M42 4-cylinder engines are filled with sodium to improve their heat transfer. Sodium is a highly reactive metal, which will ignite or explode spontaneously on contact with water (including water vapour in the air). These valves must NOT be disposed of as ordinary scrap. Seek advice***

**7.14 Measuring a valve stem diameter**

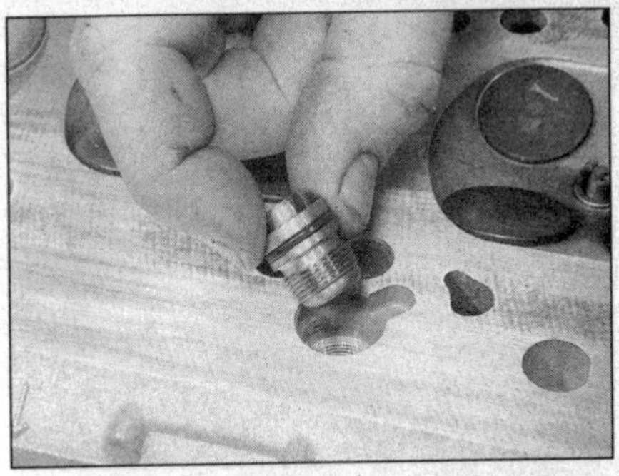

**7.10 Fit a new O-ring (arrowed) to the cylinder head oil pressure check valve**

***from a BMW dealer or your local authority when disposing of the valves.***

13 Examine the head of each valve for pitting, burning, cracks, and general wear. Check the valve stem for scoring and wear ridges. Rotate the valve, and check for any obvious indication that it is bent. Look for pits or excessive wear on the tip of each valve stem. Renew any valve that shows any such signs of wear or damage.

14 If the valve appears satisfactory at this stage, measure the valve stem diameter at several points using a micrometer **(see illustration)**. Any significant difference in the readings obtained indicates wear of the valve stem. Should any of these conditions be apparent, the valve(s) must be renewed.

15 If the valves are in satisfactory condition, they should be ground (lapped) into their respective seats, to ensure a smooth, gas-tight seal. If the seat is only lightly pitted, or if it has been re-cut, fine grinding compound *only* should be used to produce the required finish. Coarse valve-grinding compound should *not* be used, unless a seat is badly burned or deeply pitted. If this is the case, the cylinder head and valves should be inspected by an expert, to decide whether seat re-cutting, or even the renewal of the valve or seat insert (where possible) is required.

16 Valve grinding is carried out as follows. Place the cylinder head upside-down on a bench.

17 Smear a trace of (the appropriate grade of) valve-grinding compound on the seat face, and press a suction grinding tool onto the valve head **(see illustration)**. With a semi-rotary action, grind the valve head to its seat, lifting the

**7.17 Grinding-in a valve**

valve occasionally to redistribute the grinding compound. A light spring placed under the valve head will greatly ease this operation.

**18** If coarse grinding compound is being used, work only until a dull, matt even surface is produced on both the valve seat and the valve, then wipe off the used compound, and repeat the process with fine compound. When a smooth unbroken ring of light grey matt finish is produced on both the valve and seat, the grinding operation is complete. *Do not* grind-in the valves any further than absolutely necessary, or the seat will be prematurely sunk into the cylinder head.

**19** When all the valves have been ground-in, carefully wash off *all* traces of grinding compound using paraffin or a suitable solvent, before reassembling the cylinder head.

### Valve components

**20** Examine the valve springs for signs of damage and discoloration. No minimum free length is specified by BMW, so the only way of judging valve spring wear is by comparison with a new component.

**21** Stand each spring on a flat surface, and check it for squareness. If any of the springs are damaged, distorted or have lost their tension, obtain a complete new set of springs. It is normal to renew the valve springs as a matter of course if a major overhaul is being carried out.

**22** Renew the valve stem oil seals regardless of their apparent condition.

### Cam followers/valve lifters

**23** Examine the contact surfaces for wear or scoring. If excessive wear is evident, the component(s) should be renewed.

## 8 Cylinder head - reassembly

**Note:** *New valve stem oil seals should be fitted, and a valve spring compressor tool will be required for this operation.*

### M40 and M43 4-cylinder engines

**1** Proceed as described in paragraphs 7 to 12.

**2** Refit the hydraulic valve lifters, cam followers and camshafts (see Part A of this Chapter).

**3** Refit the cylinder head as described in Part A of this Chapter.

### M42 4-cylinder engines

**4** Proceed as described in paragraphs 7 to 12.

**5** Refit the camshaft bearing castings, the cam followers and the camshafts as described in Part A of this Chapter.

**6** Refit the cylinder head as described in Part A of this Chapter.

### 6-cylinder engines

**7** Lubricate the stems of the valves, and insert the valves into their original locations **(see illustration)**. If new valves are being fitted, insert them into the locations to which they have been ground.

**8** Working on the first valve, dip the new valve stem seal in fresh engine oil. New seals are normally supplied with protective sleeves which should be fitted to the tops of the valve stems to prevent the collet grooves from damaging the oil seals. If no sleeves are supplied, wind a little thin tape round the top of the valve stems to protect the seals. Carefully locate the seal over the valve and onto the guide. Take care not to damage the seal as it is passed over the valve stem. Use a suitable socket or metal tube to press the seal firmly onto the guide **(see illustrations)**.

**9** Refit the spring seat(s) **(see illustrations)**.

**10** Locate the valve spring(s) on top of the seat(s), then refit the spring retainer **(see illustrations)**.

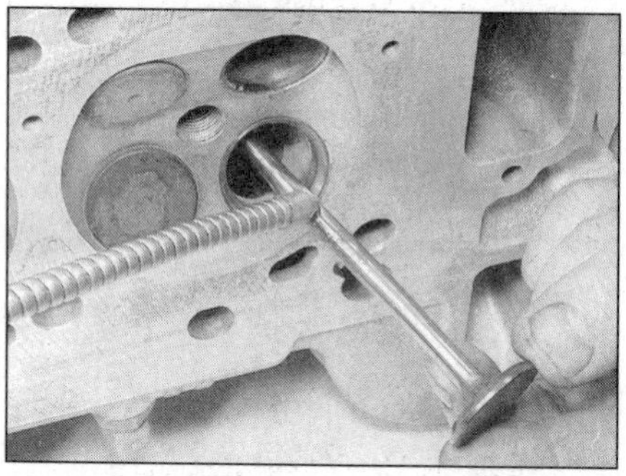

**8.7 Lubricate the valve stem**

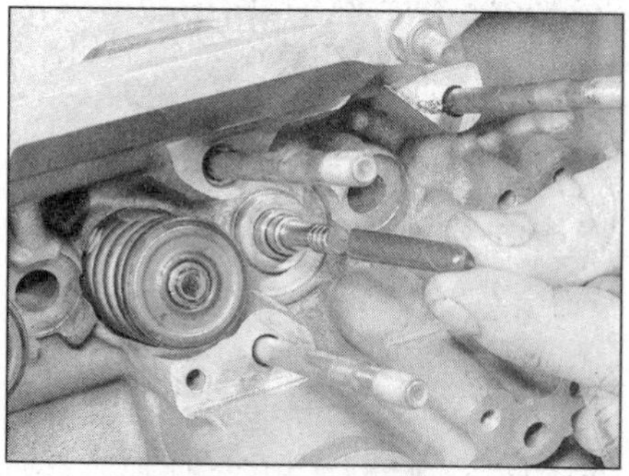

**8.8a Fit the protective sleeve to the valve stem . . .**

**8.8b . . . then fit the oil seal using a socket**

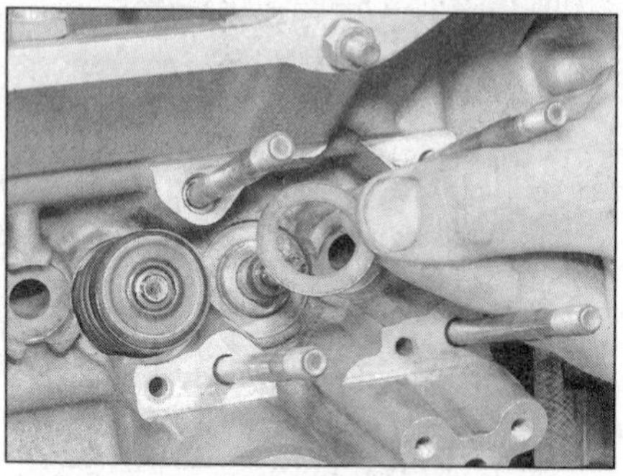

**8.9a Fit the outer . . .**

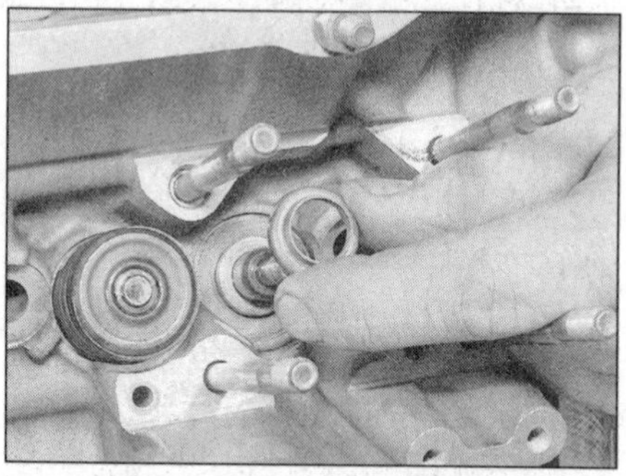

**8.9b . . . and inner spring seats**

**8.10a Fit the inner . . .**

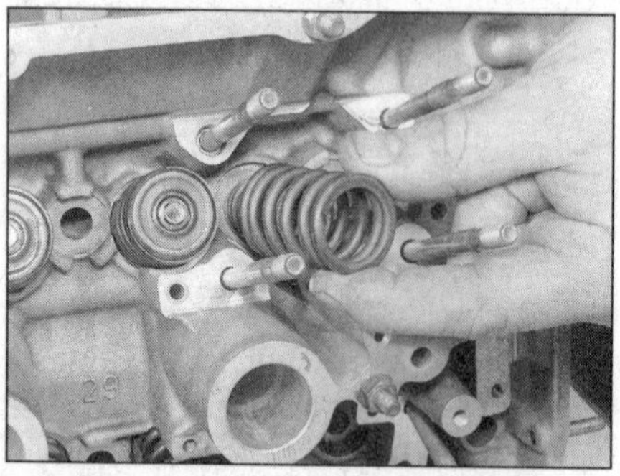

**8.10b . . . and outer valve springs . . .**

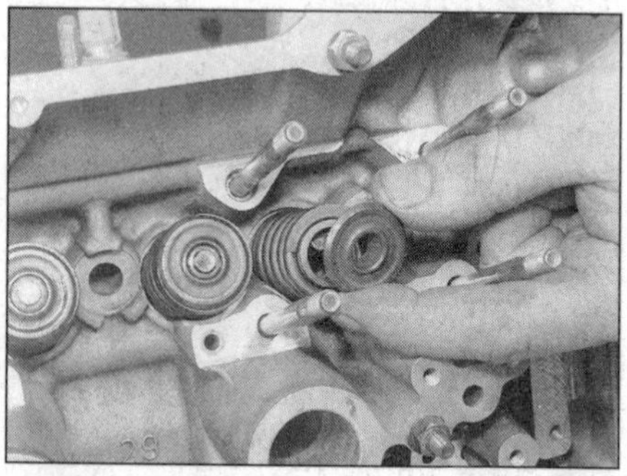

**8.10c . . . followed by the spring retainer**

**HAYNES HiNT**

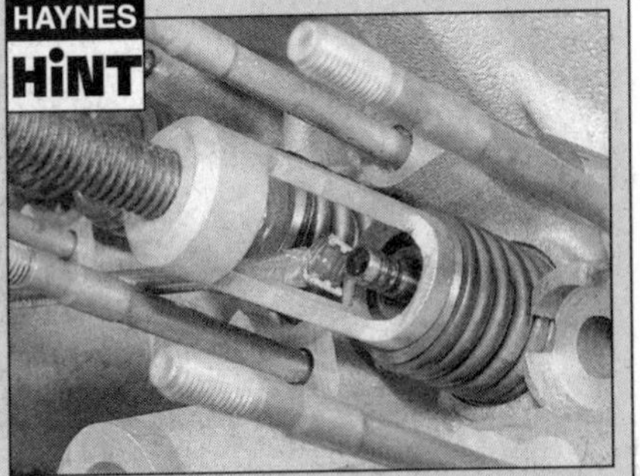

***Use a dab of grease to hold the collets in position on the valve stem while the spring compressor is released***

**11** Compress the valve spring(s), and locate the split collets in the recess in the valve stem. Release the compressor, then repeat the procedure on the remaining valves.

**12** With all the valves installed, support the cylinder head on blocks of wood and, using a hammer and interposed block of wood, tap the end of each valve stem to settle the components.

**13** Refit the camshaft bearing castings, cam followers and camshafts as described in Part B of this Chapter.

**14** Refit the cylinder head as described in Part B of this Chapter.

## 9 Piston/connecting rod assembly - removal

***Warning: On M43 engines with oil spray jets fitted to the cylinder block, take care not to damage the jets as the piston/connecting rod assemblies are removed. BMW recommend that the spray jet alignment is checked using BMW tool No 11 7 320 after removing and refitting the piston/connecting rod assemblies.***

**1** On 4-cylinder engines, remove the cylinder head and sump as described in Part A of this Chapter.

**2** On 6-cylinder engines, remove the cylinder head, sump and oil pump as described in Part B of this Chapter.

**3** Where applicable, unbolt the oil baffle from the bottom of the cylinder block **(see illustration)**.

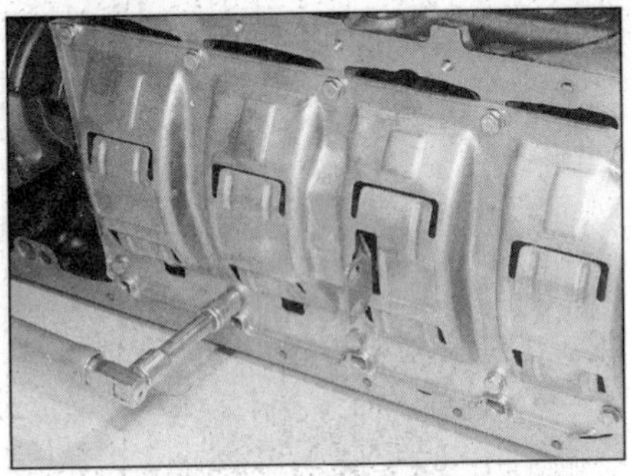

**9.3 Unbolt the oil baffle plate from the cylinder block - 6-cylinder engine**

**4** If there is a pronounced wear ridge at the top of any bore, it may be necessary to remove it with a scraper or ridge reamer, to avoid piston damage during removal. Such a ridge indicates excessive wear of the cylinder bore.

**5** Check the connecting rods and big-end caps for identification marks. Both rods and caps should be marked with the cylinder number on the exhaust manifold side of the engine. Note that No 1 cylinder is at the timing belt/chain end of the engine. If no marks are present, using a hammer and centre-punch, paint or similar, mark each connecting rod and big-end bearing cap with its respective cylinder number on the flat machined surface provided - ensure that the marks are made on the exhaust manifold side of the connecting rods **(see illustration)**.

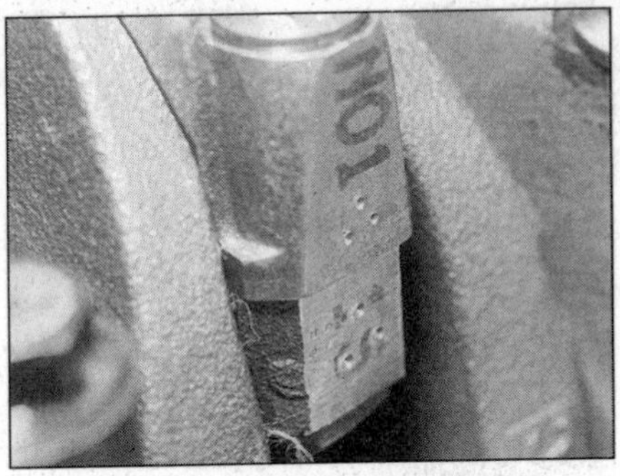

**9.5 Big-end bearing cap marks**

**6** Turn the crankshaft to bring pistons 1 and 4 (4-cylinder engines), or 1 and 6 (6-cylinder engines), as applicable, to BDC (bottom dead centre).

**7** Unscrew the bolts from No 1 piston big-end bearing cap. Take off the cap, and recover the bottom half bearing shell **(see illustration)**. If the bearing shells are to be re-used, tape the cap and the shell together.

**9.7 Removing a big-end bearing cap**

**8** Using a hammer handle, push the piston up through the bore, and remove it from the top of the cylinder block. Recover the bearing shell, and tape it to the connecting rod for safe-keeping.

**9** Loosely refit the big-end cap to the connecting rod, and secure with the bolts - this will help to keep the components in their correct order.

**10** Remove No 4 piston assembly (4-cylinder engines), or No 6 piston assembly (6-cylinder engines), as applicable, in the same way.

**11** Turn the crankshaft as necessary to bring the remaining pistons to BDC, and remove them in the same way.

## 10 Crankshaft - removal

**1** On 4-cylinder engines, remove the sump, the timing belt/chain housing, and the flywheel/driveplate as described in Part A of this Chapter.

**2** On 6-cylinder engines, remove the sump, the primary timing chain, and the flywheel/driveplate, as described in Part B of this Chapter.

**3** Remove the pistons and connecting rods, as described in Section 9. If no work is to be done on the pistons and connecting rods, there is no need to remove the cylinder head, or to push the pistons out of the cylinder bores. The pistons should just be pushed far enough up the bores so that they are positioned clear of the crankshaft journals.

***Warning: If the pistons are pushed up the bores, and the cylinder head is still fitted, take care not to force the pistons into the open valves.***

**4** Check the crankshaft endfloat as described in Section 13, then proceed as follows.

**5** Slacken and remove the retaining bolts, and remove the oil seal carrier from the rear (flywheel/driveplate) end of the cylinder block, along with its gasket **(see illustration)**.

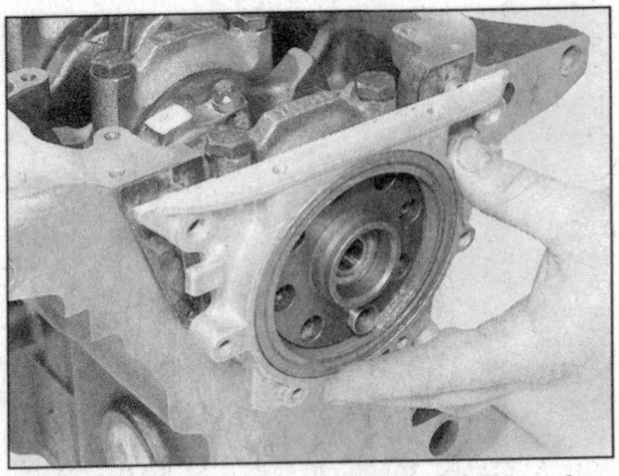

**10.5 Remove the oil seal carrier from the rear of the cylinder block**

**6** On 6-cylinder engines, if not already done, remove the oil pump drive chain and, if necessary, remove the crankshaft sprocket with reference to Part B of this Chapter.

**7** On 4-cylinder engines, the main bearing caps should be numbered 1 to 5 from the timing belt/chain end of the engine. Caps 1 to 3 are numbered, cap No 4 has shoulders

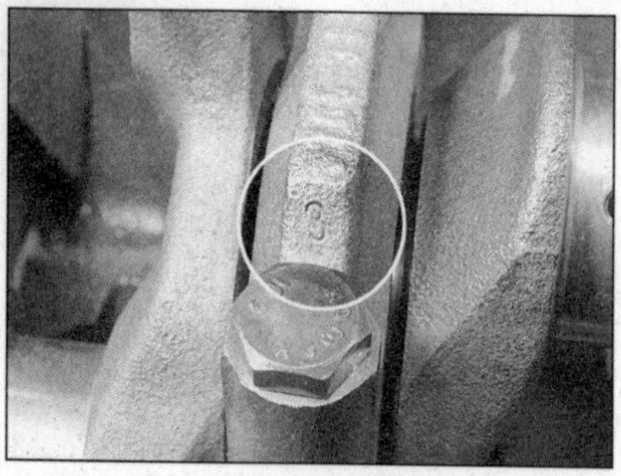

**10.8 Main bearing cap identification number - 6-cylinder engine**

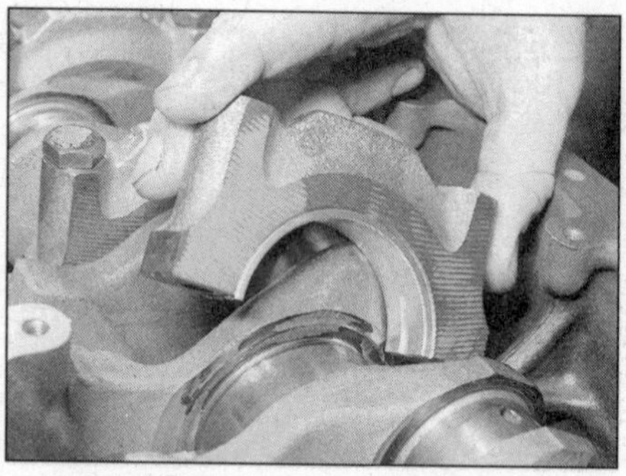

**10.9 Lifting off a main bearing cap**

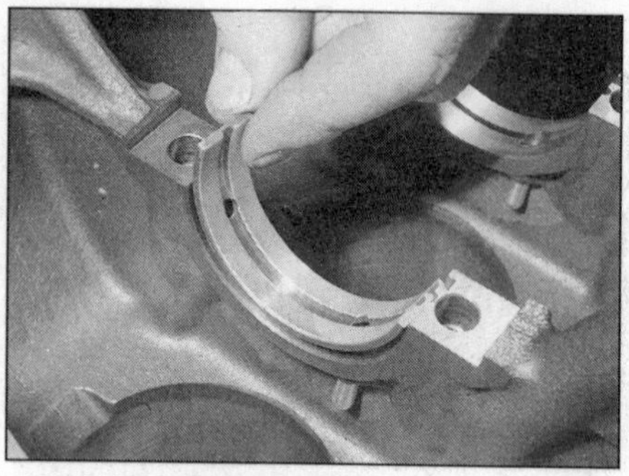

**10.13 Lifting an upper main bearing shell from the cylinder block**

machined into the end faces, and cap No 5 is unmarked. If the bearing caps are not marked, mark them accordingly using a centre-punch.

**8** On 6-cylinder engines, the main bearing caps should be numbered 1 to 7 on the exhaust side of the engine, starting from the timing chain end of the engine **(see illustration)**. If not, mark them accordingly using a centre-punch.

**9** Slacken and remove the main bearing cap retaining bolts, and lift off each bearing cap **(see illustration)**. Recover the lower bearing shells, and tape them to their respective caps for safe-keeping.

**10** On 4-cylinder engines, note that the lower thrust bearing shell, which controls crankshaft endfloat is fitted to No 4 main bearing cap.

**11** On 6-cylinder engines, note that the lower thrust bearing shell, which controls crankshaft endfloat is fitted to No 6 main bearing cap. Also note the oil pick-up tube support bracket, which is secured by the No 5 main bearing cap bolts.

**12** Lift out the crankshaft. Take care as the crankshaft is heavy.

**13** Recover the upper bearing shells from the cylinder block **(see illustration)**, and tape them to their respective caps for safe-keeping. Again, note the location of the upper thrust bearing shell.

## 11 Cylinder block/crankcase - cleaning and inspection

### Cleaning

***Warning: On M43 engines with oil spray jets fitted to the cylinder block between the bearing locations, take care not to damage the jets when working on the cylinder block/crankcase. BMW recommend that the spray jet alignment is checked using BMW tool No 11 7 320 when reassembling the engine.***

**1** Remove all external components and electrical switches/sensors from the block. For complete cleaning, the core plugs should ideally be removed. Drill a small hole in the plugs, then insert a self-tapping screw into the hole. Pull out the plugs by pulling on the screw with a pair of grips, or by using a slide hammer.

**2** Where applicable, pull the piston oil jet spray tubes from the bearing locations in the cylinder block. The tubes are fitted to Nos 2 to 5 bearing locations on 4-cylinder engines, and Nos 2 to 7 bearing locations on 6-cylinder engines **(see illustration)**.

**3** On 4-cylinder engines, where applicable, remove the oil pressure check valve from the top face of the cylinder block. A screw-in type check valve may be fitted, or on later engines, a calibrated jet may be fitted, with a rubber-lined spacer sleeve above **(see illustrations)**.

**4** Scrape all traces of gasket from the cylinder block/crankcase, taking care not to damage the gasket/sealing surfaces.

**5** Remove all oil gallery plugs (where fitted). The plugs are usually very tight - they may have to be drilled out, and the holes re-tapped. Use new plugs when the engine is reassembled.

**6** If any of the castings are extremely dirty, all should be steam-cleaned.

**7** After the castings are returned, clean all oil holes and oil galleries one more time. Flush all internal passages with warm water until the water runs clear. Dry thoroughly, and apply a light film of oil to all mating surfaces, to prevent rusting. Also oil the cylinder bores. If you have access to compressed air, use it to speed up the drying process, and to blow out all the oil holes and galleries.

***Warning: Wear eye protection when using compressed air!***

**8** If the castings are not very dirty, you can do an adequate cleaning job with hot (as hot as you can stand!), soapy water and a stiff brush. Take plenty of time, and do a thorough job. Regardless of the cleaning method used, be sure to clean all oil holes and galleries very thoroughly, and to dry all components well. Protect the cylinder bores as described above, to prevent rusting.

**9** All threaded holes must be clean, to ensure accurate torque readings during reassembly. To clean the threads, run the correct-size tap into each of the holes to remove rust,

**11.2 Remove the piston oil spray jet tubes from the main bearing locations**

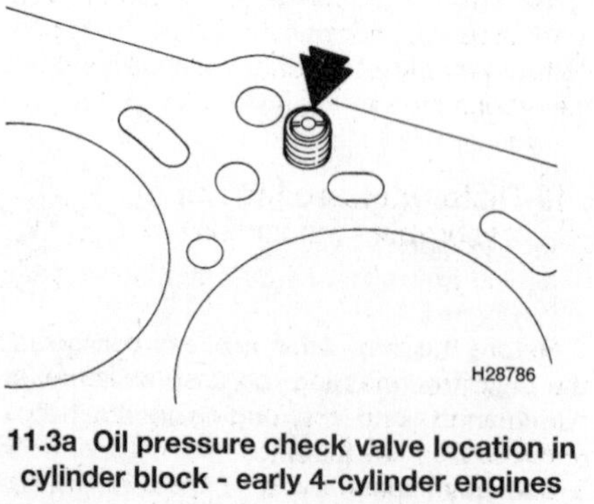


**11.3a Oil pressure check valve location in cylinder block - early 4-cylinder engines**

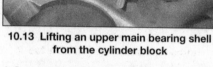

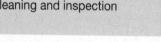

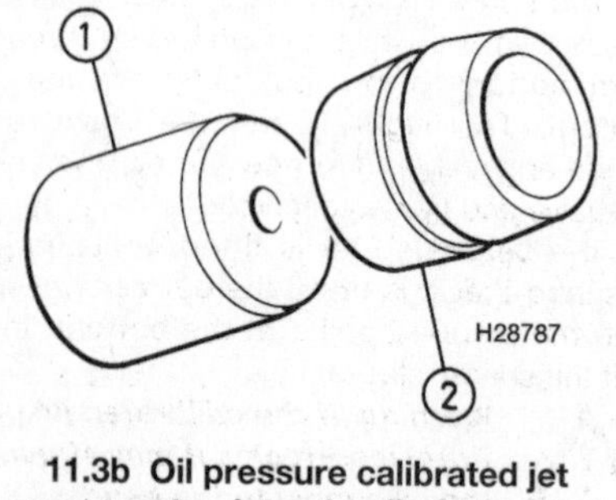


**11.3b Oil pressure calibrated jet components - later 4-cylinder engines**

*1 Jet 2 Spacing sleeve*

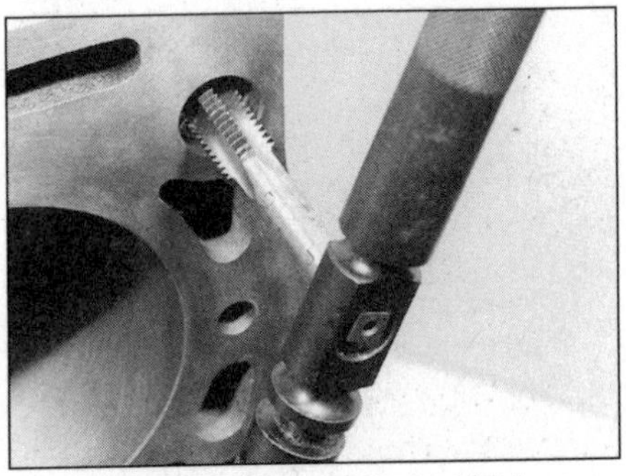

11.9 Cleaning a cylinder block threaded hole using a suitable tap

corrosion, thread sealant or sludge, and to restore damaged threads **(see illustration)**. If possible, use compressed air to clear the holes of debris produced by this operation.

> HAYNES HiNT
> ***A good alternative is to inject aerosol-applied water-dispersant lubricant into each hole, using the long spout usually supplied.***

***Warning: Wear eye protection when cleaning out these holes in this way!***

**10** Ensure that all threaded holes in the cylinder block are dry.

**11** After coating the mating surfaces of the new core plugs with suitable sealant, fit them to the cylinder block. Make sure that they are driven in straight and seated correctly, or leakage could result.

> HAYNES HiNT
> ***A large socket with an outside diameter which will just fit into the core plug can be used to drive core plugs into position.***

**12** Apply suitable sealant to the new oil gallery plugs, and insert them into the holes in the block. Tighten them securely.

**13** Where applicable, thoroughly clean the oil pressure check valve/calibrated jet (see paragraph 3), then refit the components as follows.

**14** If a screw-in type check valve is fitted, check that the valve can be blown through from bottom-to-top, but not from top-to-bottom. Thoroughly clean the valve, and where applicable, fit a new O-ring, then refit the valve and tighten securely.

**15** If a calibrated jet is fitted, refit the jet, ensuring that it is fitted the correct way up, with the stepped collar at the bottom, then refit the spacer sleeve.

***Warning: If the calibrated jet is fitted incorrectly, it may starve the oil supply to the head.***

**16** Where applicable, thoroughly clean the piston oil spray tubes which fit in the bearing

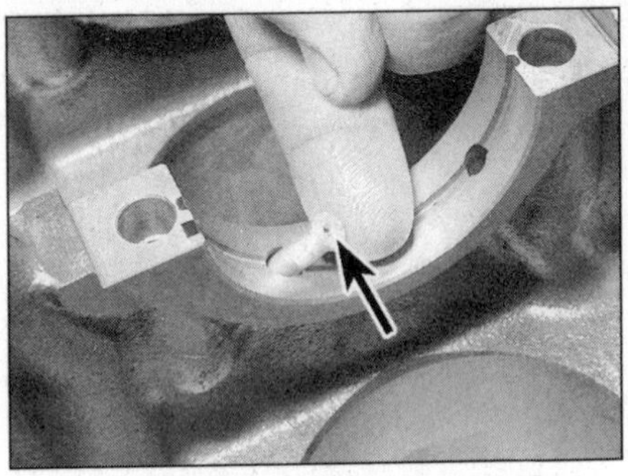

11.16 Clean the holes (arrowed) in the oil spray tubes

locations in the cylinder block, then refit the tubes **(see illustration)**.

**17** If the engine is not going to be reassembled right away, cover it with a large plastic bag to keep it clean; protect all mating surfaces and the cylinder bores as described above, to prevent rusting.

## Inspection

**18** Visually check the castings for cracks and corrosion. Look for stripped threads in the threaded holes. If there has been any history of internal water leakage, it may be worthwhile having an engine overhaul specialist check the cylinder block/crankcase with special equipment. If defects are found, have them repaired if possible, or renew the assembly.

**19** Check each cylinder bore for scuffing and scoring. Check for signs of a wear ridge at the top of the cylinder, indicating that the bore is excessively worn.

**20** If the necessary measuring equipment is available, measure the bore diameter of each cylinder at the top (just under the wear ridge), centre, and bottom of the cylinder bore, parallel to the crankshaft axis.

**21** Next, measure the bore diameter at the same three locations, at right-angles to the crankshaft axis. Compare the results with the figures given in the Specifications. If there is any doubt about the condition of the cylinder bores, seek the advice of a BMW dealer or suitable engine reconditioning specialist.

**22** If the cylinder bore wear exceeds the permitted tolerances, or if the cylinder walls are badly scored or scuffed, then the cylinders will have to be rebored by a suitably-qualified specialist, and new oversize pistons will have to be fitted. A BMW dealer or engineering workshop will normally be able to supply suitable oversize pistons when carrying out the reboring work.

## 12 Piston/connecting rod assembly - inspection

**1** Before the inspection process can begin, the piston/connecting rod assemblies must be cleaned, and the original piston rings removed from the pistons.

**2** Carefully expand the old rings over the top

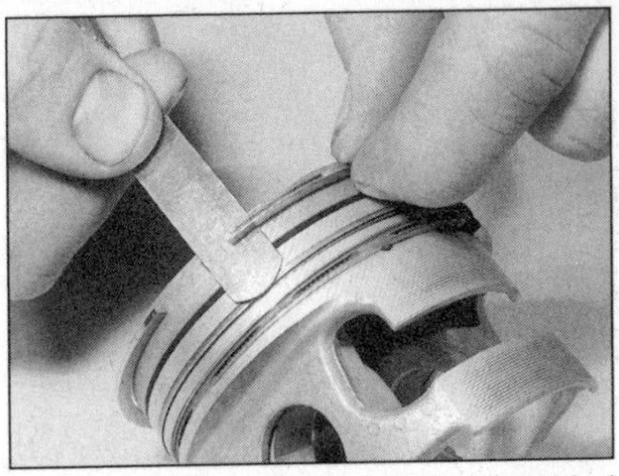

12.2 Removing a piston ring with the aid of a feeler blade

of the pistons. The use of two or three old feeler blades will be helpful in preventing the rings dropping into empty grooves **(see illustration)**. Be careful not to scratch the piston with the ends of the ring. The rings are brittle, and will snap if they are spread too far. They are also very sharp - protect your hands and fingers. Note that the third ring incorporates an expander. Always remove the rings from the top of the piston. Keep each set of rings with its piston if the old rings are to be re-used. Note which way up each ring is fitted.

**3** Scrape away all traces of carbon from the top of the piston. A hand-held wire brush (or a piece of fine emery cloth) can be used, once the majority of the deposits have been scraped away.

**4** Remove the carbon from the ring grooves in the piston, using an old ring. Break the ring in half to do this (be careful not to cut your fingers - piston rings are sharp). Be careful to remove only the carbon deposits - do not remove any metal, and do not nick or scratch the sides of the ring grooves.

**5** Once the deposits have been removed, clean the piston/connecting rod assembly with paraffin or a suitable solvent, and dry thoroughly. Make sure that the oil return holes in the ring grooves are clear.

**6** If the pistons and cylinder bores are not damaged or worn excessively, and if the cylinder block does not need to be rebored, the original pistons can be refitted. Measure the piston diameters, and check that they are within limits for the corresponding bore diameters. If the piston-to-bore clearance is excessive, the block will have to be rebored, and new pistons and rings fitted. Normal piston wear shows up as even vertical wear on the piston thrust surfaces, and slight looseness of the top ring in its groove. New piston rings should always be used when the engine is reassembled.

**7** Carefully inspect each piston for cracks around the skirt, around the gudgeon pin holes, and at the piston ring "lands" (between the ring grooves).

**8** Look for scoring and scuffing on the piston skirt, holes in the piston crown, and burned areas at the edge of the crown. If the skirt is scored or scuffed, the engine may have been

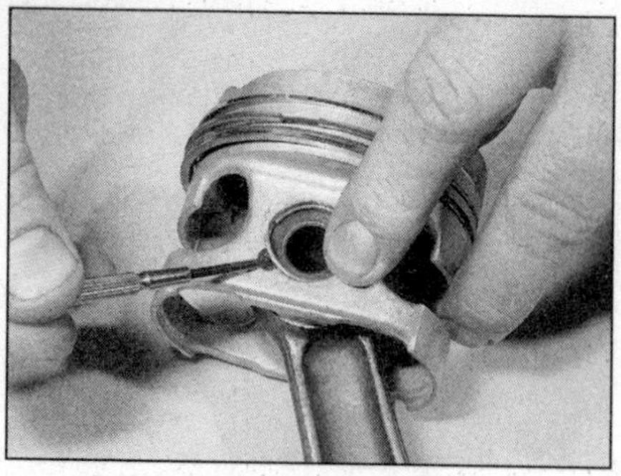

**12.13a Prising out the circlips . . .**

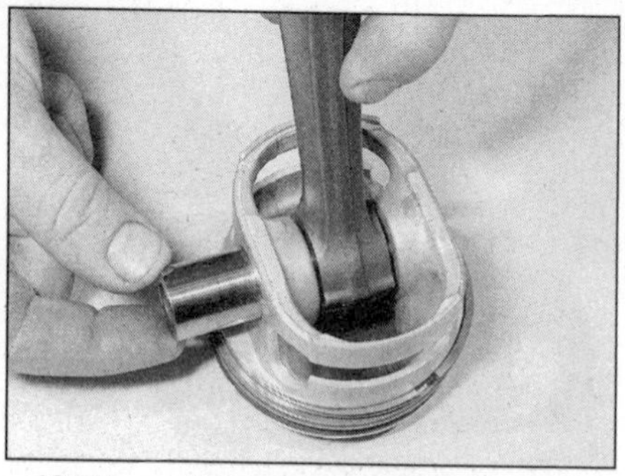

**12.13b . . . to remove the gudgeon pins from the pistons**

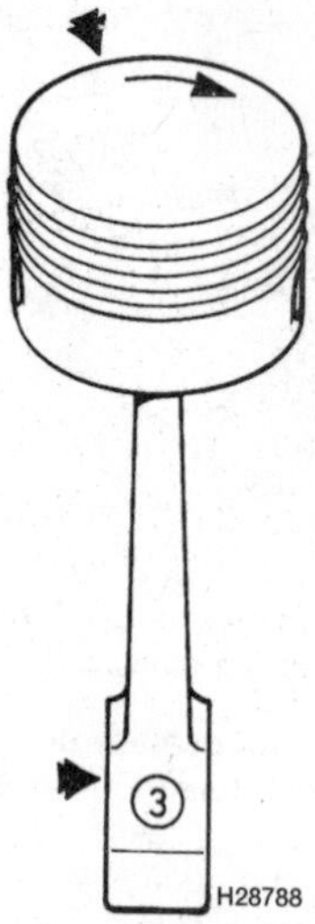


**12.17a The cylinder number markings should be on the exhaust manifold side of the engine, and the arrow on the piston crown should point towards the timing belt/chain end of the engine**

suffering from overheating, and/or abnormal combustion which caused excessively high operating temperatures. The cooling and lubrication systems should be checked thoroughly. Scorch marks on the sides of the pistons show that blow-by has occurred. A hole in the piston crown, or burned areas at the edge of the piston crown, indicates that abnormal combustion (pre-ignition, knocking, or detonation) has been occurring. If any of the above problems exist, the causes must be investigated and corrected, or the damage will occur again. The causes may include incorrect ignition timing, inlet air leaks, or incorrect air/fuel mixture.

**9** Corrosion of the piston, in the form of pitting, indicates that coolant has been leaking into the combustion chamber and/or the crankcase. Again, the cause must be corrected, or the problem may persist in the rebuilt engine.

**10** New pistons can be purchased from a BMW dealer.

**11** Examine each connecting rod carefully for signs of damage, such as cracks around the big-end and small-end bearings. Check that the rod is not bent or distorted. Damage is highly unlikely, unless the engine has been seized or badly overheated. Detailed checking of the connecting rod assembly can only be carried out by a BMW dealer or engine repair specialist with the necessary equipment.

**12** The gudgeon pins are of the floating type, secured in position by two circlips. The pistons and connecting rods can be separated as follows.

**13** Using a small flat-bladed screwdriver, prise out the circlips, and push out the gudgeon pin **(see illustrations)**. Hand pressure should be sufficient to remove the pin. Identify the piston and rod to ensure correct reassembly. Discard the circlips - new ones ***must*** be used on refitting.

**12.17b Installation direction arrow on 6-cylinder engine piston crown**

**14** Examine the gudgeon pin and connecting rod small-end bearing for signs of wear or damage. It should be possible to push the gudgeon pin through the connecting rod bush by hand, without noticeable play. Wear can be cured by renewing both the pin and bush. Bush renewal, however, is a specialist job - press facilities are required, and the new bush must be reamed accurately.

**15** The connecting rods themselves should not be in need of renewal, unless seizure or some other major mechanical failure has occurred. Check the alignment of the connecting rods visually, and if the rods are not straight, take them to an engine overhaul specialist for a more detailed check.

**16** Examine all components, and obtain any new parts from your BMW dealer. If new pistons are purchased, they will be supplied complete with gudgeon pins and circlips. Circlips can also be purchased individually.

**17** Position the piston in relation to the connecting rod, so that when the assembly is refitted to the engine, the identifying cylinder numbers on the connecting rod and big-end cap are positioned on the exhaust manifold side of the engine, and the installation direction arrow on the piston crown points towards the timing belt/chain end of the engine **(see illustrations)**.

**18** Apply a smear of clean engine oil to the gudgeon pin. Slide it into the piston and through the connecting rod small-end. Check that the piston pivots freely on the rod, then secure the gudgeon pin in position with two new circlips. Ensure that each circlip is correctly located in its groove in the piston.

## 13 Crankshaft - inspection

### *Checking crankshaft endfloat*

**1** If the crankshaft endfloat is to be checked, this must be done when the crankshaft is still installed in the cylinder block/crankcase, but is free to move.

**2** Check the endfloat using a dial gauge in contact with the end of the crankshaft. Push the crankshaft fully one way, and then zero the gauge. Push the crankshaft fully the other way, and check the endfloat. The result can be compared with the specified amount, and will give an indication as to whether new thrust bearing shells are required **(see illustration)**.

**3** If a dial gauge is not available, feeler blades can be used. First push the crankshaft fully towards the flywheel end of the engine, then use feeler blades to measure the gap between the web of No 4 crankpin and the thrust bearing shell on 4-cylinder engines, or between No 6 crankpin and the thrust bearing shell on 6-cylinder engines **(see illustration)**.

### Inspection

**5** Clean the crankshaft using paraffin or a suitable solvent, and dry it, preferably with compressed air if available. Be sure to clean the oil holes with a pipe cleaner or similar probe, to ensure that they are not obstructed.

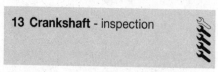

**13.2 Measuring crankshaft endfloat using a dial gauge**

**13.3 Measuring crankshaft endfloat using feeler blades - 6-cylinder engine shown**

***Warning: Wear eye protection when using compressed air!***

**6** Check the main and big-end bearing journals for uneven wear, scoring, pitting and cracking.

**7** Big-end bearing wear is accompanied by distinct metallic knocking when the engine is running (particularly noticeable when the engine is pulling from low speed) and some loss of oil pressure.

**8** Main bearing wear is accompanied by severe engine vibration and rumble - getting progressively worse as engine speed increases - and again by loss of oil pressure.

**9** Check the bearing journal for roughness by running a finger lightly over the bearing surface. Any roughness (which will be accompanied by obvious bearing wear) indicates that the crankshaft requires regrinding (where possible) or renewal.

**10** If the crankshaft has been reground, check for burrs around the crankshaft oil holes (the holes are usually chamfered, so burrs should not be a problem unless regrinding has been carried out carelessly). Remove any burrs with a fine file or scraper, and thoroughly clean the oil holes as described previously.

**11** Using a micrometer, measure the diameter of the main and big-end bearing journals, and compare the results with the Specifications **(see illustration)**. By measuring the diameter at a number of points around each journal's circumference, you will be able to determine whether or not the journal is out-of-round.

**13.11 Measuring a crankshaft main bearing journal**

Take the measurement at each end of the journal, near the webs, to determine if the journal is tapered.

**12** Check the oil seal contact surfaces at each end of the crankshaft for wear and damage. If the seal has worn a deep groove in the surface of the crankshaft, consult an engine overhaul specialist; repair may be possible, but otherwise a new crankshaft will be required.

**13** If the crankshaft journals have not already been reground, it may be possible to have the crankshaft reconditioned, and to fit oversize shells (see Section 17). If no oversize shells are available and the crankshaft has worn beyond the specified limits, it will have to be renewed. Consult your BMW dealer or engine specialist for further information on parts availability.

## 14 Main and big-end bearings - inspection

**1** Even though the main and big-end bearings should be renewed during the engine overhaul, the old bearings should be retained for close examination, as they may reveal valuable information about the condition of the engine. The bearing shells are graded by thickness, the grade of each shell being indicated by the colour code marked on it.

**2** Bearing failure can occur due to lack of lubrication, the presence of dirt or other foreign particles, overloading the engine, or corrosion **(see illustration)**. Regardless of the cause of bearing failure, the cause must be corrected (where applicable) before the engine is reassembled, to prevent it from happening again.

**3** When examining the bearing shells, remove them from the cylinder block/crankcase, the connecting rods and the connecting rod big-end bearing caps. Lay them out on a clean surface in the same general position as their location in the engine. This will enable you to match any bearing problems with the corresponding crankshaft journal. *Do not* touch any shell's bearing surface with your fingers while checking it, or the delicate surface may be scratched.

**4** Dirt and other foreign matter gets into the engine in a variety of ways. It may be left in the engine during assembly, or it may pass through filters or the crankcase ventilation system. It may get into the oil, and from there into the bearings. Metal chips from machining operations and normal engine wear are often present. Abrasives are sometimes left in engine components after reconditioning, especially when parts are not thoroughly cleaned using the proper cleaning methods. Whatever the source, these foreign objects often end up embedded in the soft bearing material, and are easily recognised. Large particles will not embed in the bearing, and will score or gouge the bearing and journal. The best prevention for this cause of bearing failure is to clean all parts thoroughly, and keep everything spotlessly-clean during engine assembly. Frequent and regular engine oil and filter changes are also recommended.

**5** Lack of lubrication (or lubrication breakdown) has a number of interrelated causes. Excessive heat (which thins the oil), overloading (which squeezes the oil from the bearing face) and oil leakage (from excessive bearing clearances, worn oil pump or high engine speeds) all contribute to lubrication breakdown. Blocked oil passages, which usually are the result of misaligned oil holes in a bearing shell, will also oil-starve a bearing, and destroy it. When lack of lubrication is the cause of bearing failure, the bearing material is wiped or extruded from the steel backing of the bearing. Temperatures may increase to the point where the steel backing turns blue from overheating.

**6** Driving habits can have a definite effect on bearing life. Full-throttle, low-speed operation (labouring the engine) puts very high loads on bearings, tending to squeeze out the oil film. These loads cause the bearings to flex, which produces fine cracks in the bearing face (fatigue failure). Eventually, the bearing material will loosen in pieces, and tear away from the steel backing.

**7** Short-distance driving leads to corrosion of bearings, because insufficient engine heat is produced to drive off the condensed water and corrosive gases. These products collect in the engine oil, forming acid and sludge. As the oil is carried to the engine bearings, the acid attacks and corrodes the bearing material.

**8** Incorrect bearing installation during engine assembly will lead to bearing failure as well. Tight-fitting bearings leave insufficient bearing running clearance, and will result in oil starvation. Dirt or foreign particles trapped behind a bearing shell result in high spots on the bearing, which lead to failure.

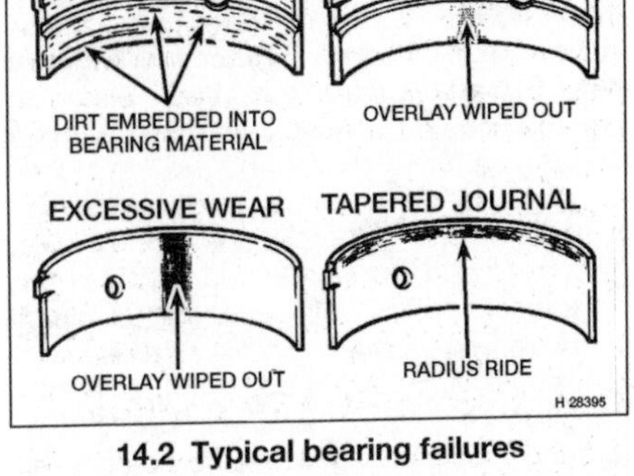

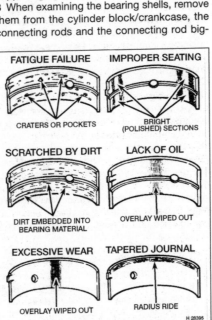

**14.2 Typical bearing failures**

2C

**9** *Do not* touch any shell's bearing surface with your fingers during reassembly; there is a risk of scratching the delicate surface, or of depositing particles of dirt on it.
**10** As mentioned at the beginning of this Section, the bearing shells should be renewed as a matter of course during engine overhaul; to do otherwise is false economy. Refer to Section 17 for details of bearing shell selection.

## 15 Engine overhaul - reassembly sequence

**1** Before reassembly begins, ensure that all new parts have been obtained, and that all necessary tools are available. Read through the entire procedure to familiarise yourself with the work involved, and to ensure that all items necessary for reassembly of the engine are at hand. In addition to all normal tools and materials, thread-locking compound will be needed. A suitable tube of liquid sealant will also be required for the joint faces that are fitted without gaskets.
**2** In order to save time and avoid problems, engine reassembly can be carried out in the following order, referring to Part A or B of this Chapter unless otherwise stated:

*a) Crankshaft (Section 10).*
*b) Piston/connecting rod assemblies (Section 9).*
*c) Oil pump.*
*d) Oil pump and sump.*
*e) Flywheel/driveplate.*
*f) Cylinder head.*
*g) Timing belt/chain, tensioner and sprockets.*
*h) Engine external components.*

**3** At this stage, all engine components should be absolutely clean and dry, with all faults repaired. The components should be laid out (or in individual containers) on a completely clean work surface.

## 16 Piston rings - refitting

**1** Before fitting new piston rings, the ring end gaps must be checked as follows.
**2** Lay out the piston/connecting rod assemblies and the new piston ring sets, so that the ring sets will be matched with the same piston and cylinder during the end gap measurement and subsequent engine reassembly.
**3** Insert the top ring into the first cylinder, and push it down the bore using the top of the piston. This will ensure that the ring remains square with the cylinder walls. Position the ring near the bottom of the cylinder bore, at the lower limit of ring travel. The top and second compression rings are different. The second ring is easily identified by the step on its lower surface, and by the fact that its outer face is tapered.

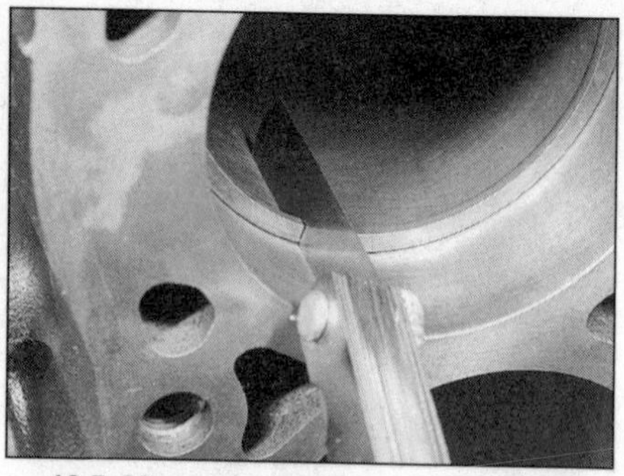

**16.5 Measuring a piston ring end gap**

**4** Measure the end gap using feeler blades.
**5** Repeat the procedure with the ring at the top of the cylinder bore, at the upper limit of its travel **(see illustration)**, and compare the measurements with the figures given in the Specifications.
**6** If the gap is too small (unlikely if genuine BMW parts are used), it must be enlarged, or the ring ends may contact each other during engine operation, causing serious damage. Ideally, new piston rings providing the correct end gap should be fitted. As a last resort, the end gap can be increased by filing the ring ends very carefully with a fine file. Mount the file in a vice equipped with soft jaws, slip the ring over the file with the ends contacting the file face, and slowly move the ring to remove material from the ends. Take care, as piston rings are sharp, and are easily broken.
**7** With new piston rings, it is unlikely that the end gap will be too large. If the gaps are too large, check that you have the correct rings for your engine and for the particular cylinder bore size.
**8** Repeat the checking procedure for each ring in the first cylinder, and then for the rings in the remaining cylinders. Remember to keep rings, pistons and cylinders matched up.
**9** Once the ring end gaps have been checked and if necessary corrected, the rings can be fitted to the pistons.
**10** Fit the piston rings using the same technique as for removal. Fit the bottom (oil control) ring first, and work up. When fitting the oil control ring, where applicable, first insert the expander, then fit the ring with its gap positioned 180° from the expander gap (certain M40 4-cylinder engines have a three-piece steel oil control ring). Ensure that the second compression ring is fitted the correct way up, with its identification mark (either a dot of paint or the word "TOP" stamped on the ring surface) at the top, and the stepped surface at the bottom **(see illustration)**. Arrange the gaps of the top and second compression rings 120° either side of the oil control ring gap, but make sure that none of the rings gaps are positioned over the gudgeon pin hole. **Note:** *Always follow any instructions supplied with the new piston ring sets - different manufacturers may specify different procedures. Do not mix up the top and second compression rings, as they have different cross-sections.*

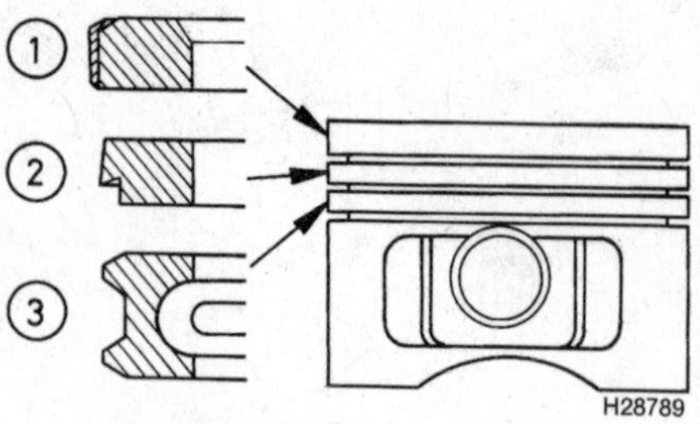


**16.10 Typical piston ring fitting**
*1 Top compression ring*
*2 Second compression ring*
*3 Oil control ring*

## 17 Crankshaft - refitting and main bearing running clearance check

### Selection of new bearing shells

**1** Bearing shells are colour-coded, and the upper and lower bearing shells may be of different thicknesses. BMW recommend that bearing shells matching the colour code on the crankshaft should be fitted to the bearing shell locations in the bearing caps. Bearing shells matching the colour codes on the inside of the crankcase are fitted to the upper bearing shell locations in the crankcase. If the colour code markings in the crankcase have worn off, fit upper bearing shells with the same colour code as the crankshaft. Three different bearing shell thicknesses are available, colour-coded yellow, green and white. Consult a BMW dealer for further details.

### Main bearing running clearance check

**2** The running clearance check can be carried out using the original bearing shells. However, it is preferable to use a new set, since the results obtained will be more conclusive.
**3** Clean the backs of the bearing shells, and the bearing locations in both the cylinder block/crankcase and the main bearing caps.
**4** Press the bearing shells into their locations, ensuring that the tab on each shell engages in the notch in the cylinder block/crankcase or bearing cap. Take care not to touch any shell's bearing surface with your fingers. Note that the upper bearing shells have an oil groove running along the full length of the bearing surface, whereas the lower shells have a short, tapered oil groove at each end. If the original bearing shells are being used for the check, ensure that they are refitted in their original locations. The thrust bearing shells fit

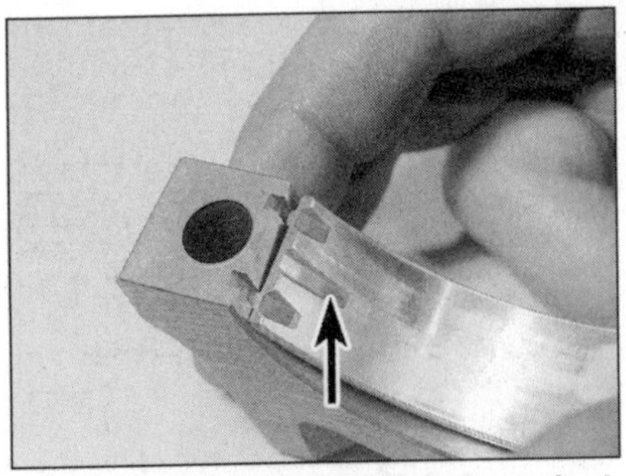

**17.4a The lower bearing shells have short tapered oil grooves (arrowed)**

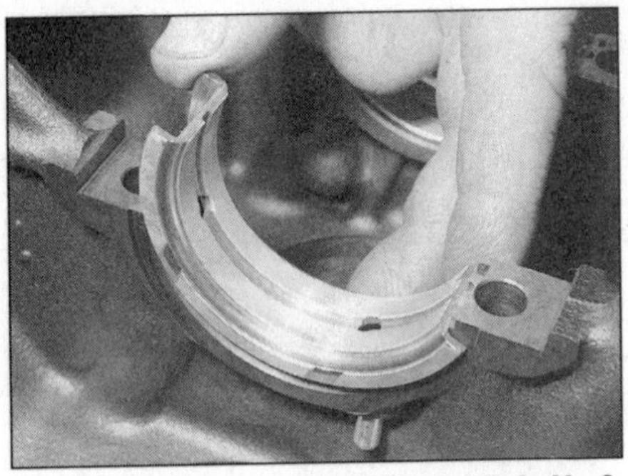

**17.4b The thrust bearing shell s fit in No 6 bearing location on 6-cylinder engines**

in No 4 bearing location on 4-cylinder engines, or No 6 bearing location on 6-cylinder engines **(see illustrations)**.

**5** The clearance can be checked in either of two ways.

**6** One method (which will be difficult to achieve without a range of internal micrometers or internal/external expanding calipers) is to refit the main bearing caps to the cylinder block/crankcase, with bearing shells in place. With the original cap retaining bolts tightened to the specified torque, measure the internal diameter of each assembled pair of bearing shells. If the diameter of each corresponding crankshaft journal is measured and then subtracted from the bearing internal diameter, the result will be the main bearing running clearance.

**7** The second (and more accurate) method is to use an American product known as "Plastigage". This consists of a fine thread of perfectly-round plastic, which is compressed between the bearing shell and the journal. When the shell is removed, the plastic is deformed, and can be measured with a special card gauge supplied with the kit. The running clearance is determined from this gauge. Enquiries at one of the larger specialist motor factors should produce the name of a stockist in your area. The procedure for using Plastigage is as follows.

**8** With the main bearing upper shells in place, carefully lay the crankshaft in position. Do not use any lubricant; the crankshaft journals and bearing shells must be perfectly clean and dry.

**9** Cut several lengths of the appropriate-size Plastigage (they should be slightly shorter than the width of the main bearings), and place one length on each crankshaft journal axis **(see illustration)**.

**10** With the main bearing lower shells in position, refit the main bearing caps. Starting with the centre main bearing and working outwards, tighten the original main bearing cap bolts progressively to their specified torque, in the two stages given in the Specifications.

Take care not to disturb the Plastigage, and *do not* rotate the crankshaft at any time during this operation.

**11** Remove the main bearing cap bolts and carefully lift off the caps, keeping then in order. Again, take great care not to disturb the Plastigage or rotate the crankshaft. If any of the bearing caps are difficult to remove, free them by carefully tapping them with a soft-faced mallet.

**12** Compare the width of the crushed Plastigage on each journal to the scale printed on the Plastigage envelope, to obtain the main bearing running clearance **(see illustration)**. Compare the clearance measured with that given in the Specifications at the start of this Chapter.

**13** If the clearance is significantly different from that expected, the bearing shells may be the wrong size (or excessively worn, if the original shells are being re-used). Before deciding that different-size shells are required, make sure that no dirt or oil was trapped between the bearing shells and the caps or block when the clearance was measured. If the Plastigage was wider at one end than at the other, the crankshaft journal may be tapered.

**14** If the clearance is not as specified, use the reading obtained, along with the shell thicknesses quoted in the Specifications, to calculate the necessary grade of bearing shells required. When calculating the bearing clearance required, bear in mind that it is always better to have the running clearance towards the lower end of the specified range, to allow for wear in use.

**15** Where necessary, obtain the required grades of bearing shell, and repeat the running clearance checking procedure as described above.

**16** On completion, carefully scrape away all traces of the Plastigage material from the crankshaft and bearing shells. Use your fingernail, or a wooden or plastic scraper which is unlikely to score the bearing surfaces.

## Final crankshaft refitting

**Note:** *New main bearing cap bolts must be used when finally refitting the crankshaft.*

**17** Carefully lift the crankshaft out of the cylinder block once more.

**18** Where applicable, ensure that the oil spray jets are fitted to the bearing locations in the cylinder block.

**19** Place the bearing shells in their locations as described earlier. If new shells are being fitted, ensure that all traces of protective grease are cleaned off using paraffin. Wipe dry the shells and connecting rods with a lint-free cloth. Liberally lubricate each bearing shell in the cylinder block/crankcase and cap with clean engine oil **(see illustration)**.

**20** Lower the crankshaft into position so that Nos 1 and 4 cylinder crankpins (4-cylinder engines), or Nos 1 and 6 cylinder crankpins (6-cylinder engines), as applicable, will be at BDC, ready for fitting No 1 piston. Check the crankshaft endfloat as described in Section 13.

**21** Lubricate the lower bearing shells in the main bearing caps with clean engine oil. Make sure that the locating lugs on the shells engage with the corresponding recesses in the caps.

**22** Fit the main bearing caps to their correct locations, ensuring that they are fitted the

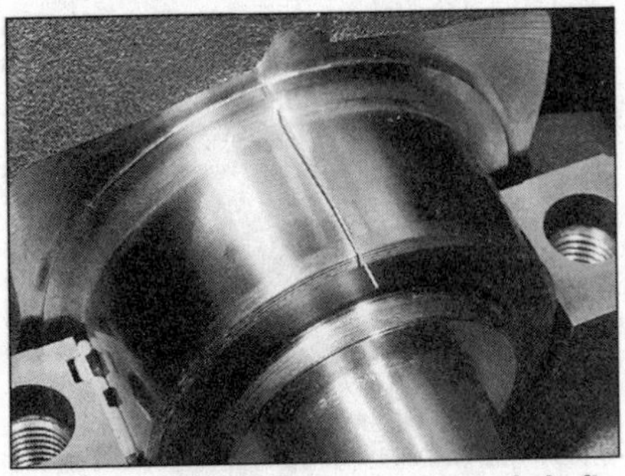

**17.9 Plastigage in place on a crankshaft main bearing journal**

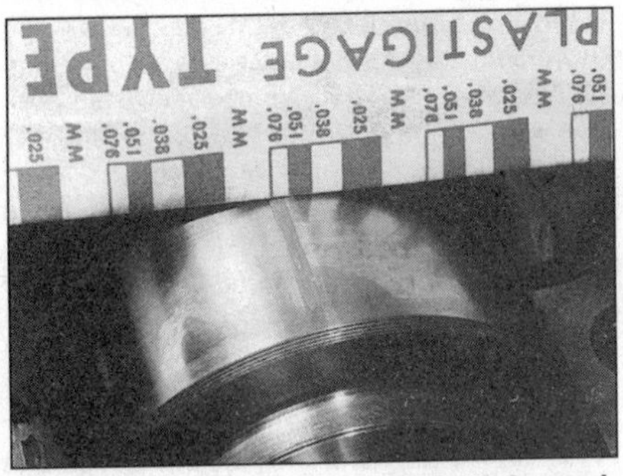


**17.12 Measure the width of the deformed Plastigage using the scale on the card**

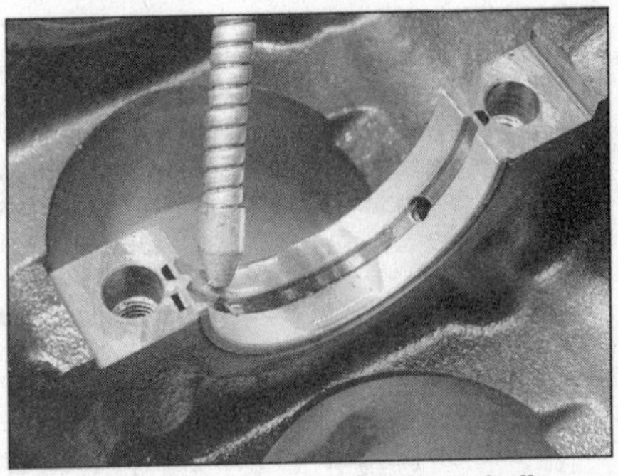

**17.19 Lubricate the bearing shells**

2C

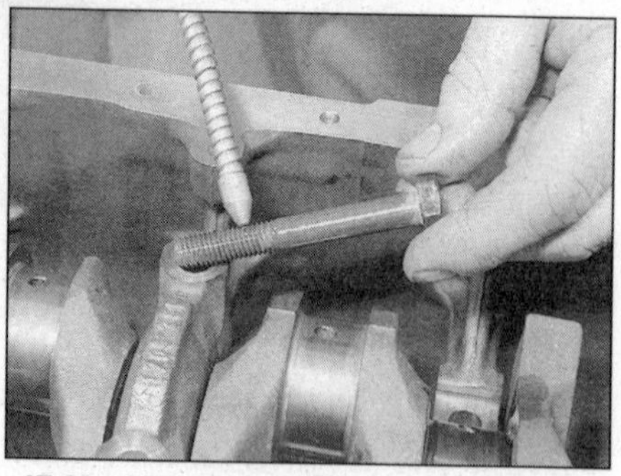

**17.22a Lightly oil the threads of the main bearing cap bolts**

**17.23a Tighten the main bearing cap bolts to the specified torque . . .**

correct way round (the bearing shell tab recesses in the block and caps must be on the same side). Thoroughly clean the **new** main bearing cap bolts, and lightly oil the threads, then insert the bolts, tightening them only loosely at this stage. On 6-cylinder engines, ensure that the oil pick-up tube support bracket is correctly in position on the No 5 main bearing cap bolts **(see illustrations)**.

**23** Tighten the main bearing cap bolts to the specified torque, in the two stages given in the Specifications **(see illustration)**.

**24** Check that the crankshaft rotates freely.

**25** Fit a new crankshaft rear oil seal to the oil seal carrier, then refit the oil seal carrier using a new gasket, as described in Part A or B of this Chapter, as applicable.

**26** Where applicable, on 6-cylinder engines, refit the crankshaft sprocket and the oil pump drive chain, as described in Part B of this Chapter.

**27** Refit the piston/connecting rod assemblies as described in Section 18.

**28** On 4-cylinder engines, refit the flywheel/ driveplate, the timing belt/chain housing, and the sump, as described in Part A of this Chapter.

**29** On 6-cylinder engines, refit the flywheel/ driveplate, the primary timing chain, and the sump, as described in Part B of this Chapter.

**17.22b Ensure that the oil pick-up tube support bracket is in position on No 5 main bearing cap bolts - 6-cylinder engines**

**17.23b . . . then through the specified angle**

## 18 Piston/connecting rod assembly - refitting & big-end bearing clearance check

***Warning: On M43 engines with oil spray jets fitted to the cylinder block, take care not to damage the jets as the piston/connecting rod assemblies are removed. BMW recommend that the spray jet alignment is checked using BMW tool No 11 7 320 after removing and refitting the piston/connecting rod assemblies.***

### Selection of bearing shells

**1** There are a number of sizes of big-end bearing shell produced by BMW; a standard size for use with the standard crankshaft, and oversizes for use once the crankshaft journals have been reground.

**2** Consult your BMW dealer for the latest information on parts availability. To be safe, always quote the diameter of the crankshaft big-end crankpins when ordering bearing shells.

**3** Prior to refitting the piston/connecting rod assemblies, it is recommended that the big-end bearing running clearance is checked as follows.

### Big-end bearing running clearance check

**4** Clean the backs of the bearing shells, and the bearing locations in both the connecting rod and bearing cap.

**5** Press the bearing shells into their locations, ensuring that the tab on each shell engages in the notch in the connecting rod and cap. Take care not to touch any shell's bearing surface with your fingers. If the original bearing shells are being used for the check, ensure that they are refitted in their original locations. The clearance can be checked in either of two ways.

**6** One method is to refit the big-end bearing cap to the connecting rod, using the marks made or noted on removal to ensure that they are fitted the correct way around, with the bearing shells in place. With the original cap retaining bolts correctly tightened, use an internal micrometer or vernier caliper to measure the internal diameter of each assembled pair of bearing shells. If the diameter of each corresponding crankshaft journal is measured and then subtracted from the bearing internal diameter, the result will be the big-end bearing running clearance.

**7** The second, and more accurate method is to use Plastigage (refer to Section 17, paragraph 7).

**8** Ensure that the bearing shells are correctly fitted. Place a strand of Plastigage on each (cleaned) crankpin journal.

**9** Refit the (clean) piston/connecting rod assemblies to the crankshaft, and refit the big-end bearing caps, using the marks made or noted on removal to ensure that they are fitted the correct way around.

**10** Refit the original bearing cap bolts, and tighten the bolts to the specified torque in the two stages given in the Specifications. Take care not to disturb the Plastigage, nor rotate the connecting rod during the tightening sequence.

**11** Dismantle the assemblies without rotating the connecting rods. Use the scale printed on the Plastigage envelope to obtain the big-end bearing running clearance.

**12** If the clearance is significantly different from that expected, the bearing shells may be the wrong size (or excessively worn, if the original shells are being re-used). Make sure that no dirt or oil was trapped between the bearing shells and the caps or block when the clearance was measured. If the Plastigage was wider at one end than at the other, the crankshaft journal may be tapered.

**13** On completion, carefully scrape away all traces of the Plastigage material from the crankshaft and bearing shells. Use your fingernail, or some other object which is unlikely to score the bearing surfaces.

### Final piston/ connecting rod refitting

***Warning: If working on an M43 4-cylinder engine, refer to the warning at the beginning of this Section before proceeding.***

**Note:** *New big-end cap bolts must be used when finally refitting the piston/connecting rod assemblies. A piston ring compressor tool will be required for this operation.*

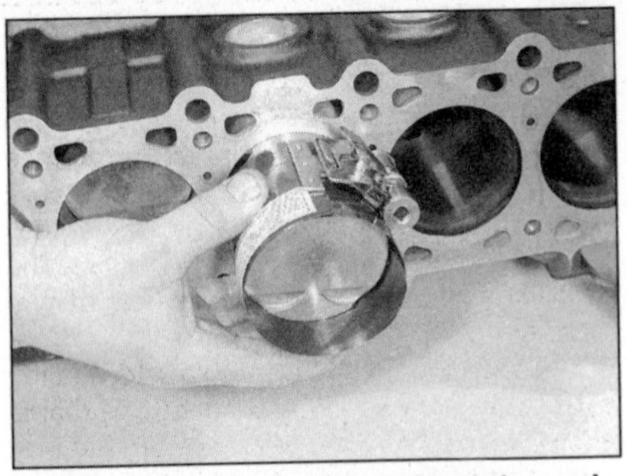

18.18a Insert the piston/connecting rod assembly into the cylinder bore . . .

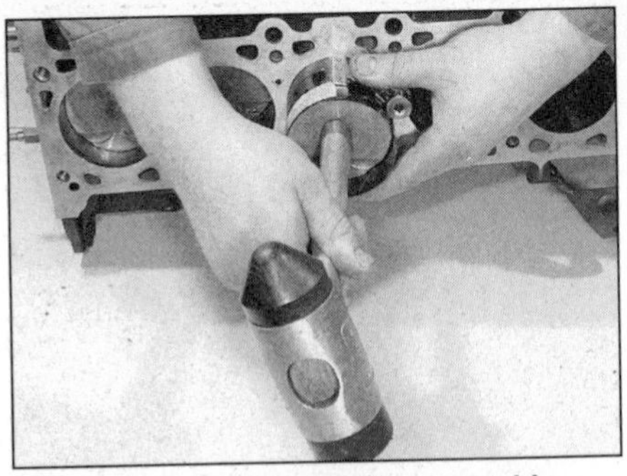

18.18b . . . then tap the assembly into the cylinder

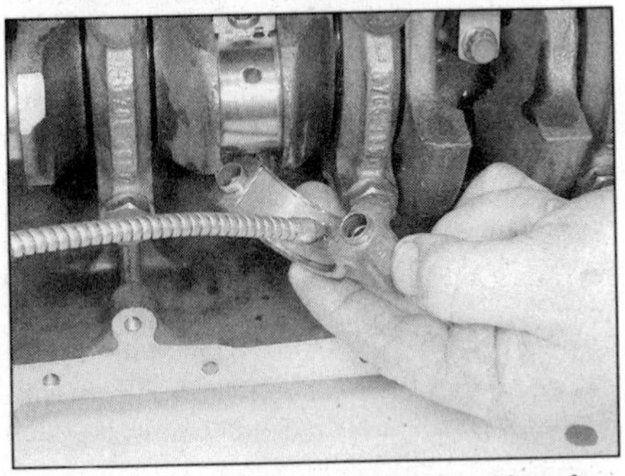

18.19 Lubricate the lower big-end bearing shells before fitting the big-end caps

18.20 Using an angle-measuring gauge to tighten the big-end bearing cap bolts

**14** Note that the following procedure assumes that the main bearing caps are in place (see Section 17).

**15** Ensure that the bearing shells are correctly fitted as described earlier. If new shells are being fitted, ensure that all traces of the protective grease are cleaned off using paraffin. Wipe dry the shells and connecting rods with a lint-free cloth.

**16** Lubricate the cylinder bores, the pistons, and piston rings, then lay out each piston/connecting rod assembly in its respective position.

**17** Start with assembly No 1. Make sure that the piston rings are still spaced as described in Section 16, then clamp them in position with a piston ring compressor.

**18** Insert the piston/connecting rod assembly into the top of cylinder No 1. Ensure that the arrow on the piston crown points towards the timing belt/chain end of the engine, and that the identifying marks on the connecting rods and big-end caps are positioned as noted before removal. Using a block of wood or hammer handle against the piston crown, tap the assembly into the cylinder until the piston crown is flush with the top of the cylinder **(see illustrations)**.

**19** Ensure that the bearing shell is still correctly installed. Liberally lubricate the crankpin and both bearing shells **(see illustration)**. Taking care not to mark the cylinder bores, pull the piston/connecting rod assembly down the bore and onto the crankpin. Refit the big-end bearing cap. Note that the bearing shell locating tabs must abut each other.

**20** Fit **new** bearing cap securing bolts, then tighten the bolts evenly and progressively to the Stage 1 torque setting. Once both bolts have been tightened to the Stage 1 setting, angle-tighten them through the specified Stage 2 angle, using a socket and extension bar. It is recommended that an angle-measuring gauge is used during this stage of the tightening, to ensure accuracy **(see illustration)**. If a gauge is not available, use a dab of white paint to make alignment marks between the bolt and bearing cap prior to tightening; the marks can then be used to check that the bolt has been rotated sufficiently during tightening.

**21** Once the bearing cap bolts have been correctly tightened, rotate the crankshaft. Check that it turns freely; some stiffness is to be expected if new components have been fitted, but there should be no signs of binding or tight spots.

**22** Refit the remaining piston/connecting rod assemblies in the same way.

**23** Where applicable, refit the oil baffle to the bottom of the cylinder block.

**24** On 4-cylinder engines, refit the cylinder head and sump as described in Part A of this Chapter.

**25** On 6-cylinder engines, refit the cylinder head, oil pump and sump as described in Part B of this Chapter.

## 19 Engine - initial start-up after overhaul

***Warning: If the camshafts have been removed on M42 4-cylinder engines or on 6-cylinder engines, observe the recommended delays between refitting the camshafts and starting the engine - refer to the relevant camshaft removal and refitting procedure in Chapter 2A or 2B, as applicable for details.***

**1** With the engine refitted in the vehicle, double-check the engine oil and coolant levels. Make a final check that everything has been reconnected, and that there are no tools or rags left in the engine compartment.

**2** Disable the ignition and fuel injection systems by removing the DME master relay, and the fuel pump relay, located in the main relay box (see Chapter 12), then turn the engine on the starter motor until the oil pressure warning light goes out.

**3** Refit the relays (and ensure that the fuel pump fuse is fitted), and switch on the ignition to prime the fuel system.

**4** Start the engine, noting that this may take a little longer than usual, due to the fuel system components having been disturbed. ***Caution: On M40 engines, when first starting the engine after overhaul, if there is a rattling noise from the valve-gear, this is probably due to the hydraulic valve lifters partially draining. If the rattling persists, do not run the engine above 2000 rpm until the rattling stops. Caution: On M42 engines, if the timing chain tensioner has been removed (see Chapter 2A, Section 11), the engine must be run at 3500 rpm for 20 seconds as soon as it starts - this is to ensure that the tensioner is primed with oil.***

**5** While the engine is idling, check for fuel, water and oil leaks. Don't be alarmed if there are some odd smells and smoke from parts getting hot and burning off oil deposits.

**6** Assuming all is well, keep the engine idling until hot water is felt circulating through the top hose, then switch off the engine.

**7** After a few minutes, recheck the oil and coolant levels as described in Chapter 1, and top-up as necessary.

**8** If new pistons, rings or crankshaft bearings have been fitted, the engine must be treated as new, and run-in for the first 500 miles (800 km). *Do not* operate the engine at full-throttle, or allow it to labour at low engine speeds in any gear. It is recommended that the oil and filter are changed at the end of this period.

# Chapter 3
# Cooling, heating and ventilation systems

## Contents



## Degrees of difficulty

| | | | | |
|---|---|---|---|---|
| **Easy,** suitable for novice with little experience | **Fairly easy,** suitable for beginner with some experience | **Fairly difficult,** suitable for competent DIY mechanic | **Difficult,** suitable for experienced DIY mechanic | **Very difficult,** suitable for expert DIY or professional |

## Specifications

### General

| | |
|---|---|
| Expansion tank cap opening pressure: | |
| 4-cylinder engine | 1.4 ± 0.2 bar |
| 6-cylinder engine | 2.0 ± 0.2 bar |

### Thermostat

| | |
|---|---|
| Opening temperatures: | |
| 4-cylinder engine: | |
| M40 and M42 engine | 88°C |
| M43 engine | 95°C |
| 6-cylinder engine | 80°C |

| Torque wrench settings | Nm | lbf ft |
|---|---|---|
| Thermostat cover bolts | 10 | 7 |
| Cooling fan viscous coupling to coolant pump | 40 | 30 |
| Coolant pump nuts/bolts: | | |
| M6 nuts/bolts | 10 | 7 |
| M8 nuts/bolts | 22 | 16 |

## 1 General information and precautions

### *General information*

The cooling system is of pressurised type, comprising of a pump, an aluminium crossflow radiator, cooling fan, and a thermostat. The system functions as follows. Cold coolant from the radiator passes through the hose to the coolant pump where it is pumped around the cylinder block and head passages. After cooling the cylinder bores, combustion surfaces and valve seats, the coolant reaches the underside of the thermostat, which is initially closed. The coolant passes through the heater and is returned through the cylinder block to the coolant pump.

When the engine is cold the coolant circulates only through the cylinder block, cylinder head, expansion tank and heater. When the coolant reaches a predetermined temperature, the thermostat opens and the coolant passes through to the radiator. As the coolant circulates through the radiator it is cooled by the inrush of air when the car is in forward motion. Airflow is supplemented by the action of the cooling fan. Upon reaching the radiator, the coolant is now cooled and the cycle is repeated.

The cooling fan is driven via a viscous coupling. The viscous coupling varies the fan speed, according to engine temperature. At low temperatures, the coupling provides very little resistance between the fan and pump pulley so only a slight amount of drive is transmitted to the cooling fan. As the temperature of the coupling increases, so does its internal resistance therefore increasing drive to the cooling fan.

Refer to Section 10 for information on the air conditioning system.

### *Precautions*

***Warning: Do not attempt to remove the expansion tank filler cap or disturb any part of the cooling system while the engine is hot, as there is a high risk of scalding. If the expansion tank filler cap must be removed before the engine and radiator have fully cooled (even though this is not recommended) the pressure in the cooling system must first be relieved. Cover the***

***cap with a thick layer of cloth, to avoid scalding, and slowly unscrew the filler cap until a hissing sound can be heard. When the hissing has stopped, indicating that the pressure has reduced, slowly unscrew the filler cap until it can be removed; if more hissing sounds are heard, wait until they have stopped before unscrewing the cap completely. At all times keep well away from the filler cap opening.***

***Do not allow antifreeze to come into contact with skin or painted surfaces of the vehicle. Rinse off spills immediately with plenty of water. Never leave antifreeze lying around in an open container or in a puddle in the driveway or on the garage floor. Children and pets are attracted by its sweet smell. Antifreeze can be fatal if ingested.***

***Refer to Section 10 for precautions to be observed when working on models equipped with air conditioning.***

## 2 Cooling system hoses - disconnection and renewal

**Note:** *Refer to the warnings given in Section 1 of this Chapter before proceeding.*

**1** If the checks described in Chapter 1 reveal a faulty hose, it must be renewed as follows.

**2** First drain the cooling system (see Chapter 1). If the coolant is not due for renewal, it may be re-used if it is collected in a clean container.

**3** To disconnect a hose, release its retaining clips, then move them along the hose, clear of the relevant inlet/outlet union. Carefully work the hose free. While the hoses can be removed with relative ease when new, or when hot, **do not** attempt to disconnect any part of the system while it is still hot.

**4** Note that the radiator inlet and outlet unions are fragile; do not use excessive force when attempting to remove the hoses. If a hose proves to be difficult to remove, try to release it by rotating the hose ends before attempting to free it **(see Haynes Hint)**.

**5** When fitting a hose, first slide the clips onto the hose, then work the hose into position. If clamp type clips were originally fitted, it is a good idea to replace them with screw type clips when refitting the hose. If the hose is stiff, use a little soapy water as a lubricant, or soften the hose by soaking it in hot water.

> HAYNES HiNT ***If all else fails, cut the hose with a sharp knife, then slit it so that it can be peeled off in two pieces. Although this may prove expensive if the hose is otherwise undamaged, it is preferable to buying a new radiator.***

**6** Work the hose into position, checking that it is correctly routed, then slide each clip along the hose until it passes over the flared end of the relevant inlet/outlet union, before securing it in position with the retaining clip.

**7** Refill the cooling system with reference to Chapter 1.

**8** Check thoroughly for leaks as soon as possible after disturbing any part of the cooling system.

## 3 Radiator - removal, inspection and refitting

> HAYNES HiNT ***If leakage is the reason for wanting to remove the radiator, bear in mind that minor leaks can be often be cured using a radiator sealant with the radiator in situ.***

### Removal

**1** Disconnect the battery negative lead.

**2** Drain the cooling system as described in Chapter 1.

**3** Remove the cooling fan shroud as described in paragraphs 1 to 3 of Section 5.

**4** Slacken the retaining clip and disconnect the upper and lower hoses from the radiator.

**5** On models equipped with air conditioning, disconnect the wiring connector from the auxiliary cooling fan temperature switch which is screwed into the end of the radiator.

**6** On models where the expansion tank is incorporated in the radiator, disconnect the wiring connector from the coolant level sensor which is fitted to the base of the expansion tank.

**7** Where necessary, slacken the retaining clip and disconnect the expansion tank hose from the base of the radiator.

**8** On models with automatic transmission where the oil cooler is incorporated into the side on the radiator, slacken the union nuts and disconnect the cooler pipes from the end of the radiator. Be prepared for some fluid loss and plug the pipe ends to minimise fluid loss and prevent entry of dirt into the hydraulic system. Discard the sealing rings fitted to the pipe unions; new ones should be used on refitting.

**9** On all models, using a flat-bladed screwdriver, release the upper retaining clips and lift the radiator upwards and out of position **(see illustrations)**. Recover the mounting rubbers from the front of the body.

### Inspection

**10** If the radiator has been removed due to suspected blockage, reverse flush it as described in Chapter 1. Clean dirt and debris from the radiator fins, using an air line (in which case, wear eye protection) or a soft brush. Be careful, as the fins are easily damaged, and are sharp.

**11** If necessary, a radiator specialist can perform a 'flow test' on the radiator, to establish whether an internal blockage exists.

**12** A leaking radiator must be referred to a specialist for permanent repair. Do not attempt to weld or solder a leaking radiator, as damage may result.

**13** In an emergency, minor leaks from the radiator can be cured by using a radiator sealant in accordance with its manufacturers instructions with the radiator *in situ*.

**14** If the radiator is to be sent for repair or renewed, remove the cooling fan switch/level sensor (where fitted).

**15** Inspect the radiator lower mounting rubbers for signs of damage or deterioration and renew if necessary.

**16** On models where the expansion tank is incorporated into the radiator, if necessary, undo the retaining screws and remove the tank retaining plate from the top of the radiator. Remove the tank and recover its

**3.9a Insert a flat-bladed screwdriver into the upper retaining clip . . .**

**3.9b . . . then release the clip by levering carefully in the direction of the arrow**

**3.9c Lifting the radiator out of position**

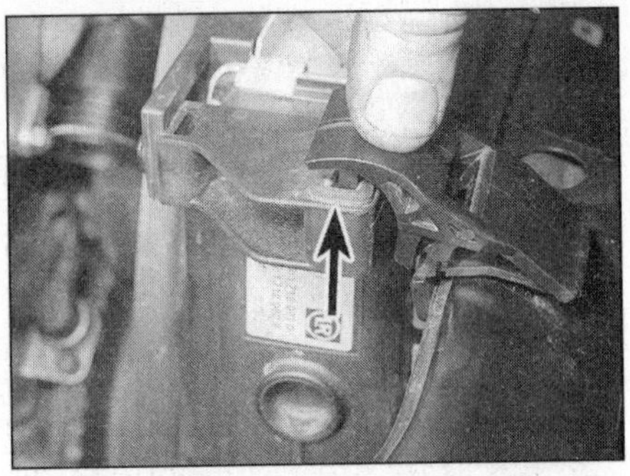

**3.17 On refitting, ensure the retaining clip is correctly engaged with the radiator (arrowed) and clip it in position**

upper and lower sealing rings. Fit new sealing rings to the tank and locate it in the radiator. Refit the retaining plate and tighten its screws.

### Refitting

**17** Refitting is the reverse of removal, noting the following points.

a) *Ensure that the lower mounting rubbers are correctly located in the body then lower the radiator into position, engage it with the mountings and secure it in position with the retaining clips* **(see illustration)**.

b) *On automatic transmission models, fit new sealing rings to the oil cooler pipe unions and securely tighten the union nuts. On completion check the transmission fluid level as described in Chapter 1.*

c) *Ensure that the fan cowl is correctly located with the lugs on the radiator and secure it in position with the clips.*

d) *Reconnect the hoses and securely tighten the retaining clips.*

e) *On completion, reconnect the battery and refill the cooling system (see Chapter 1).*

**4.4 Remove the thermostat housing . . .**

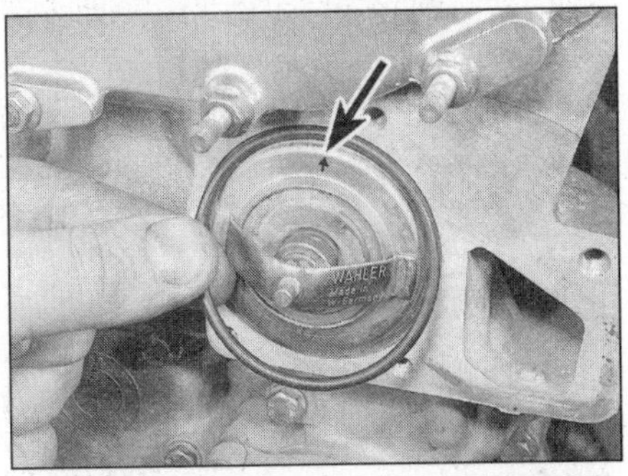



**4.9a Ensure the thermostat is fitted with its bleed hole/arrow marking (arrowed) uppermost and fit the new sealing ring**

## 4 Thermostat - removal, testing and refitting

### Removal

**Note:** *A new thermostat sealing ring and (where fitted) housing gasket/seal will be required on refitting.*

**1** Disconnect the battery negative lead.

**2** Drain the cooling system as described in Chapter 1. To improve access to the thermostat housing, remove the cooling fan and coupling as described in Section 5.

**3** Slacken the retaining clip(s) and disconnect the coolant hose(s) from the thermostat housing on the front of the cylinder head/timing chain cover (as applicable).

**4** Slacken and remove the retaining screws and remove the thermostat housing **(see illustration)**. Recover the housing gasket/seal (where fitted). On 6-cylinder engines, it will be necessary to unbolt the engine lifting bracket to allow the housing to be removed.

**5** Lift the thermostat out from the cylinder head and recover its sealing ring **(see illustration)**.

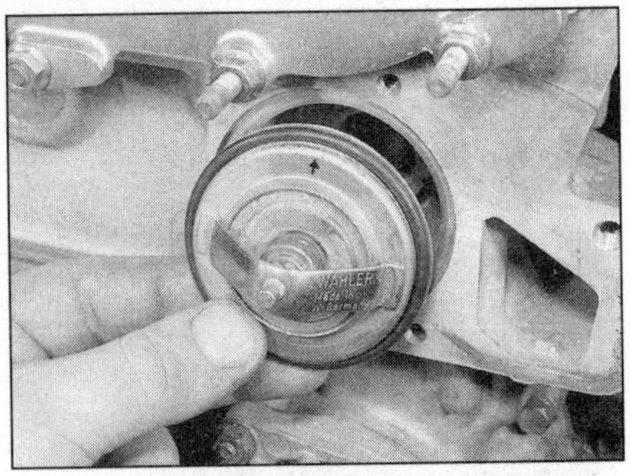



**4.5 . . . and lift out the thermostat and sealing ring**

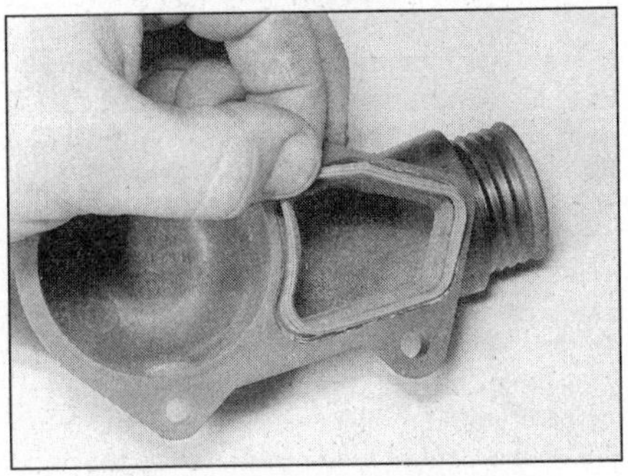

**4.9b Where necessary, fit a new gasket/seal to the thermostat housing**

### Testing

**6** A rough test of the thermostat may be made by suspending it with a piece of string in a container full of water. Heat the water to bring it to the boil - the thermostat must open by the time the water boils. If not, renew it.

**7** If a thermometer is available, the precise opening temperature of the thermostat may be determined, and compared with the figures given in the Specifications. The opening temperature is also marked on the thermostat.

**8** A thermostat which fails to close as the water cools must also be renewed.

### Refitting

**9** Refitting is a reversal of removal, bearing in mind the following points.

a) *Fit the thermostat and new sealing ring to the head/timing cover. Note that the thermostat should be fitted with its bleed hole/arrow marking uppermost* **(see illustration)**.

b) *Fit the new gasket/seal (where necessary) and tighten the thermostat cover bolts to the specified torque* **(see illustration)**.

c) *Where necessary, refit the cooling fan as described in Section 5.*

d) *On completion refill the cooling system as described in Chapter 1.*

## 5 Cooling fan and viscous coupling - removal and refitting

**Note:** *A special 32 mm narrow open-ended spanner will be required to remove the fan and viscous coupling assembly.*

### Removal

**1** Undo the retaining screws and remove the plastic cover from above the radiator.

**2** On 6-cylinder models, disconnect the auxiliary cooling ducts from the shroud and remove them from the engine compartment **(see illustration)**.

**3** Release the fan shroud upper retaining clips by pulling out their centre pins then lift the shroud upwards and out of position. **Note:** *It may be necessary to remove the fan to enable the shroud to be removed.*

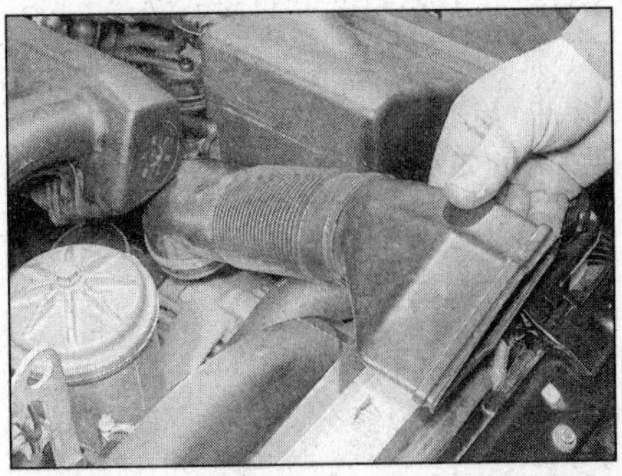

**5.2 On 6-cylinder models unclip the alternator cooling duct and remove it from the engine compartment**

**5.4a Slacken the cooling fan coupling using the special open-ended spanner . . .**

**5.4b . . . and remove the cooling fan**

**4** Using the special open-ended spanner unscrew the viscous coupling from the coolant pump and remove the cooling fan **(see illustrations)**. **Note:** *The viscous coupling has a left-hand thread.*

**5** If necessary, slacken and remove the retaining bolts and separate the cooling fan from the coupling noting which way around the fan is fitted.

### Refitting

**6** Where necessary, refit the fan to the viscous coupling and securely tighten its retaining bolts. Make sure the fan is fitted the correct way around. **Note:** *If the fan is fitted the wrong way around the efficiency of the cooling system will be significantly reduced.*

**7** Refit the fan and shroud. Screw the fan onto the coolant pump and tighten it to the specified torque. Engage the fan shroud with the lugs on the radiator and secure it in position with the retaining clips.

**8** Reconnect the auxiliary cooling ducts (where fitted) to the shroud then refit the plastic cover to the bonnet crossmember and securely tighten its retaining screws.

## 6 Cooling system electrical switches - testing, removal and refitting

### Auxiliary electric cooling fan thermostatic switch - models with air conditioning

#### Testing

**1** Testing of the air conditioning system should be entrusted to a BMW dealer.

#### Removal

**2** The switch is located in the right-hand side of the radiator. The engine and radiator should be cold before removing the switch.

**3** Disconnect the battery negative lead.

**4** Either drain the cooling system to below the level of the switch (as described in Chapter 1), or have ready a suitable plug which can be used to plug the switch aperture in the radiator whilst the switch is removed. If a plug is used, take great care not to damage the radiator, and do not use anything which will allow foreign matter to enter the radiator.

**5** Disconnect the wiring plug from the switch.

**6** Carefully unscrew the switch from the radiator and recover the sealing washer.

#### Refitting

**7** Refitting is a reversal of removal using a new sealing washer. On completion, refill the cooling system as described in Chapter 1 or top-up as described in "Weekly checks".

**8** Start the engine and run it until it reaches normal operating temperature, then continue to run the engine and check that the cooling fan cuts in and functions correctly.

### Coolant temperature gauge sensor

#### Testing

**9** The coolant temperature gauge, mounted in the instrument panel, is fed with a stabilised voltage supply from the instrument panel feed (through the ignition switch and a fuse), and its earth is controlled by the sensor.

**10** The sensor unit is located is screwed into the left-hand side of the cylinder head. There are two sensors screwed into the head; the temperature gauge sensor is the rear sensor of the two, the front one being the fuel injection system temperature sensor. To improve access to the sensor, on 4-cylinder models disconnect the coolant hose and free the cable channel from the manifold (see Chapter 4), and on 6-cylinder engines remove the alternator cooling duct.

**11** The sensor contains a thermistor, which consists of an electronic component whose electrical resistance decreases at a predetermined rate as its temperature rises. When the coolant is cold, the sensor resistance is high, current flow through the gauge is reduced, and the gauge needle points towards the 'cold' end of the scale. If the sensor is faulty, it must be renewed.

**12** If the gauge develops a fault, first check the other instruments; if they do not work at all, check the instrument panel electrical feed. If the readings are erratic, there may be a fault in the instrument panel assembly. If the fault lies in the temperature gauge alone, check it as follows.

**13** If the gauge needle remains at the 'cold' end of the scale, disconnect the wiring connector from the sensor unit, and earth the temperature gauge wire (refer to the Wiring diagrams for details) to the cylinder head. If the needle then deflects when the ignition is switched on, the sensor unit is proved faulty, and should be renewed. If the needle still does not move, remove the instrument panel (Chapter 12) and check the continuity of the wiring between the sensor unit and the gauge, and the feed to the gauge unit. If continuity is shown, and the fault still exists, then the gauge is faulty and should be renewed.

**14** If the gauge needle remains at the "hot" end of the scale, disconnect the sensor wire. If the needle then returns to the 'cold' end of the scale when the ignition is switched on, the sensor unit is proved faulty and should be renewed. If the needle still does not move, check the remainder of the circuit as described previously.

#### Removal

**15** Either partially drain the cooling system to just below the level of the sensor (as described in Chapter 1), or have ready a suitable plug which can be used to plug the sensor aperture whilst it is removed. If a plug is used, take great care not to damage the sensor unit aperture, and do not use anything which will allow foreign matter to enter the cooling system.

**16** Disconnect the battery negative lead.

**17** Disconnect the wiring from the sensor (see paragraph 10).

**18** Unscrew the sensor unit from the cylinder head and recover its sealing washer.

#### Refitting

**19** Fit a new sealing washer to the sensor unit and fit the it to the head, tightening it securely.

**20** Reconnect the wiring connector then refill the cooling system as described in Chapter 1 or top-up as described in "Weekly checks".

### Fuel injection system coolant temperature sensor

#### Testing

**21** The sensor unit is located is screwed into the left-hand side of the cylinder head. There are two sensors screwed into the head; the fuel injection system temperature sensor is the front sensor of the two, the rear one being the temperature gauge sensor. Testing of the should be entrusted to a BMW dealer (see Chapter 4).

#### Removal and refitting

**22** Refer to paragraphs 15 to 20.

## 7 Coolant pump - removal and refitting

**Note:** *A new sealing ring will be required on refitting.*

### Removal

**1** Drain the cooling system as described in Chapter 1.

**7.5 If the coolant pump is a tight fit, draw the pump out of position using two jacking bolts (arrowed)**

**2** Remove the cooling fan and coupling as described in Section 5.

**3** Slacken the coolant pump pulley bolts then remove the auxiliary drivebelt as described in Chapter 1.

**4** Unscrew the retaining bolts and remove the pulley from the pump, noting which way around it is fitted.

**5** Slacken and remove the pump retaining bolts/nuts (as applicable) and withdraw the pump. If the pump is a tight fit, screw two M6 bolts into the jacking holes on either side of the pump and use the bolts to draw the pump out of position **(see illustration)**.

**6** Recover the sealing ring from the rear of the pump **(see illustration)**.

### *Refitting*

**7** Fit the new sealing ring to the rear of the pump and lubricate it with a smear of grease to ease installation.

**8** Locate the pump in position and refit the retaining bolts/nuts. Tighten the bolts/nuts evenly and progressively to the specified torque, making sure the pump is drawn squarely into position.

**9** Refit the pulley to the pump, making sure it is the correct way around, and screw in its retaining bolts.

**10** Refit the auxiliary drivebelt as described in Chapter 1 then securely tighten the pulley bolts.

**11** Refit the cooling fan assembly as described in Section 5.

**12** Refill the cooling system as described in Chapter 1.

## 8 Heating and ventilation system - general information

**1** The heating/ventilation system consists of a four-speed blower motor, face-level vents in the centre and at each end of the facia, and air ducts to the front and rear footwells.

**2** The control unit is located in the facia, and the controls operate flap valves to deflect and mix the air flowing through the various parts of the heating/ventilation system. The flap valves are contained in the air distribution housing,

**7.6 Recover the sealing ring from the rear of the coolant pump**

which acts as a central distribution unit, passing air to the various ducts and vents.

**3** Cold air enters the system through the grille at the rear of the engine compartment. A pollen filter is fitted to the inlet to filter out dust, spores and soot from the incoming air.

**4** The airflow, which can be boosted by the blower, then flows through the various ducts, according to the settings of the controls. Stale air is expelled through ducts at the rear of the vehicle. If warm air is required, the cold air is passed through the heater matrix, which is heated by the engine coolant.

**5** If necessary, the outside air supply can be closed off, allowing the air inside the vehicle to be recirculated. This can be useful to prevent unpleasant odours entering from outside the vehicle, but should only be used briefly, as the recirculated air inside the vehicle will soon deteriorate.

**6** Certain models may be fitted with heated front seats. The heat is produced by electrically-heated mats in the seat and backrest cushions (see Chapter 12). The temperature is regulated automatically by a thermostat, and cannot be adjusted.

## 9 Heater/ventilation components - removal and refitting

### *Models without air conditioning*

#### Heater/ventilation control unit

**1** Disconnect the battery negative lead.

**2** Remove the clock/multi-information display (as applicable) as described in Chapter 12.

**3** Unclip the storage compartment from the front of the centre console and remove it, disconnecting the cigarette lighter wiring.

**4** Pull off the control knobs from each of the heater controls **(see illustration)**.

**5** Slacken and remove the retaining screws and unclip the front panel from the heater control unit **(see illustrations)**.

**6** Free the control unit from the rear of the facia then manoeuvre it downwards and out through the centre console aperture **(see illustration)**.

**7** Disconnect the wiring connector(s) then unclip the control cables and release each cable from the control unit **(see illustration)**. Note each cables correct fitted location and routing; to avoid confusion on refitting label each cable as it is disconnected.

**9.4 Pull off the knobs from each of the heater controls**

**9.5a Undo the retaining screws (arrowed) . . .**

**9.5b . . . and remove the heater control unit front panel**

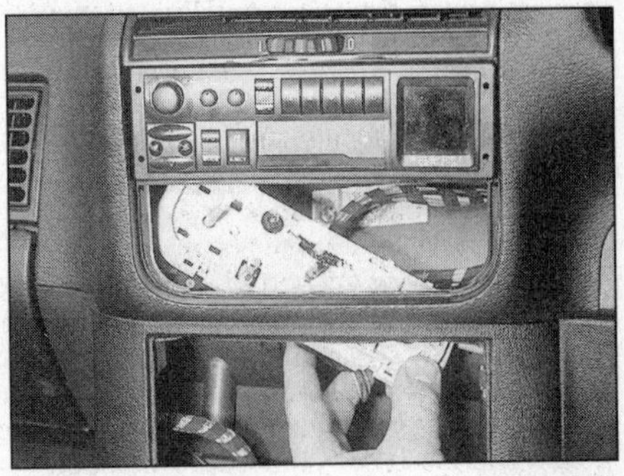

**9.6 Manoeuvre the control unit down and out through the centre console aperture**

**8** Refitting is reversal of removal. Ensure that the control cables are correctly routed and reconnected to the control panel, as noted before removal. Clip the outer cables in position and check the operation of each knob/lever before refitting the storage compartment to the centre console.

### Heater/ventilation control cables

**9** Remove the heater/ventilation control unit from the facia as described above in paragraphs 1 to 6, detaching the relevant cable from the control unit.

**10** On right-hand drive models, undo the retaining screws then unclip the driver's side lower facia panel and remove it from the vehicle. On left-hand drive models, remove the glovebox as described in Chapter 11.

**11** Follow the run of the cable behind the facia, taking note of its routing, and disconnect the cable from the air distribution housing.

**12** Fit the new cable by reversing the removal procedure, ensuring that it is correctly routed and free from kinks and obstructions. Check the operation of the control knob then refit the control unit as described previously in this Section.

### Heater matrix

**13** Working in the engine compartment, remove the rubber seal from the top of the heating/ventilation system inlet and release the grille from the inlet. On models where the grille is an integral part of the windscreen wiper motor cover panel, to improve access remove the wiper arms and remove the one-piece cover panel (see Chapter 12, Section 16).

**14** Undo the retaining screws and free the wiring harness duct from the inlet duct.

**15** Slacken and remove the retaining screws and retaining plate and remove the inlet from the bulkhead. **Note:** *On 6-cylinder engines it may be necessary to remove the injector and spark plug covers from the engine to enable the inlet to be removed.*

**16** Unscrew the expansion tank cap (referring to the Warning note in Section 1) to release any pressure present in the cooling system then securely refit the cap.

**17** Clamp both heater hoses as close to the bulkhead as possible to minimise coolant loss. Alternatively, drain the cooling system as described in Chapter 1.

**18** Unscrew the heater matrix pipe union nut and disconnect the pipe union **(see illustration)**. Be prepared for coolant spillage as the nut is slackened and mop up any coolant.

**19** Recover the sealing rings from the heater pipes and unscrew the nut and washer from the pipe retaining stud **(see illustrations)**.

**20** On right-hand drive models, remove the glovebox as described in Chapter 11. On left-hand drive models, slacken and remove the driver's side lower facia panel retaining screws then unclip the panel and remove it from the vehicle.

**21** Be prepared for coolant spillage and position a suitable container beneath the union on the end of the matrix. To be safe also cover the carpet with rags.

**22** Unclip the wiring from the side of the coolant pipes. Unscrew the bolt securing the coolant pipes to the matrix, and let the coolant drain into the container **(see illustration)**.

**23** Once the flow of coolant stops, remove the pipes from the matrix and recover the sealing rings **(see illustration)**.

**24** Undo the retaining screws and slide the matrix out of position **(see illustrations)**.

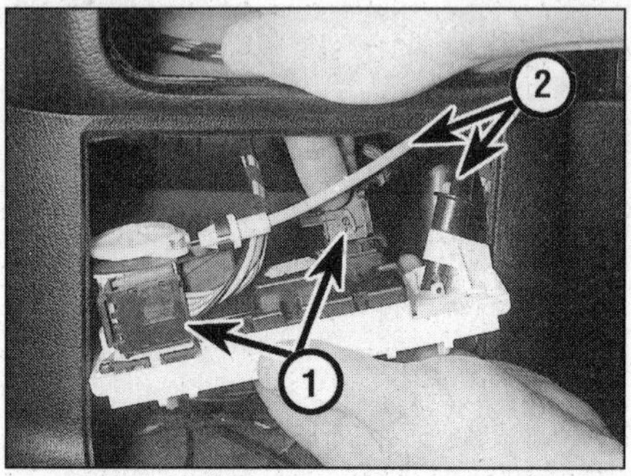


**9.7 Release the clips and disconnect the wiring connectors (1) and cables (2)**

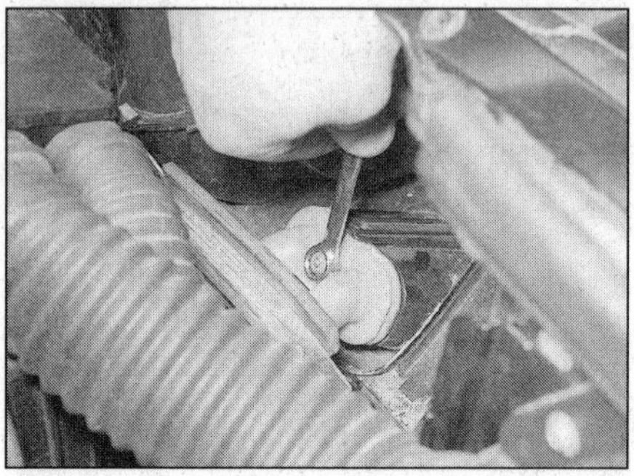

**9.18 Unscrew the heater matrix pipe union retaining nut . . .**

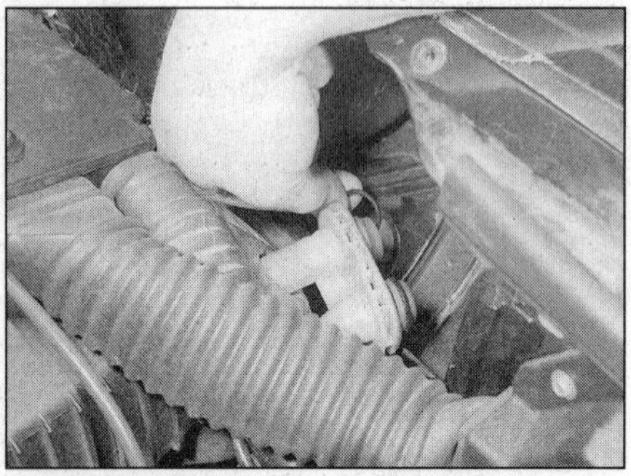

**9.19a . . . then detach the pipes and recover the sealing rings**

**9.19b Slacken and remove the nut and washer (arrowed) from the pipe stud**

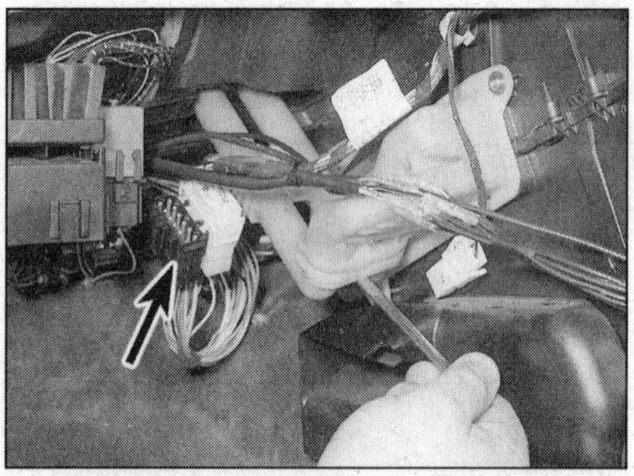

**9.22 Unclip the wiring connectors (arrowed) then undo the retaining bolt . . .**

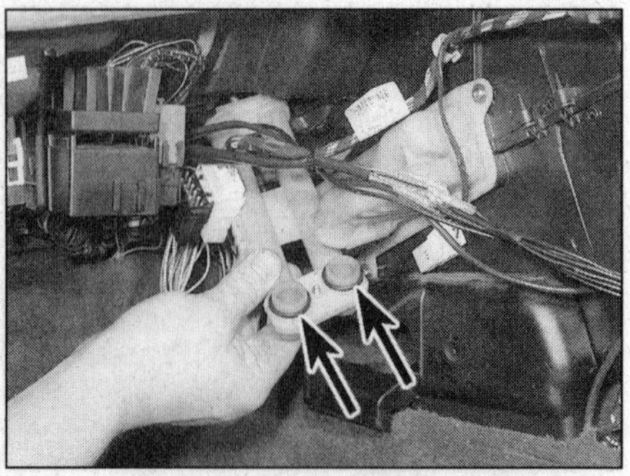

**9.23 . . . and detach the coolant pipes from the matrix. Recover sealing rings (arrowed)**

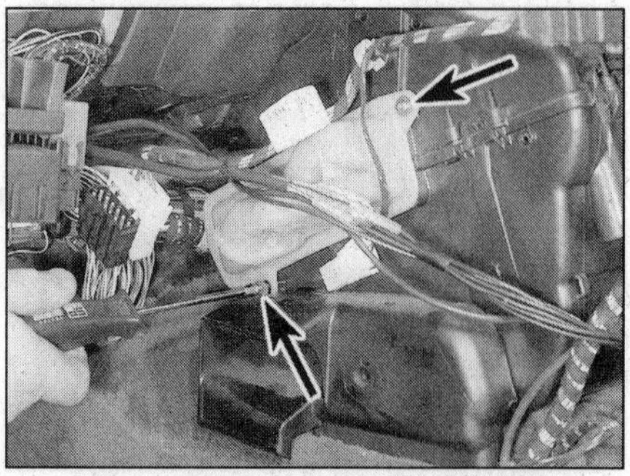

**9.24a Undo the retaining screws (arrowed) . . .**

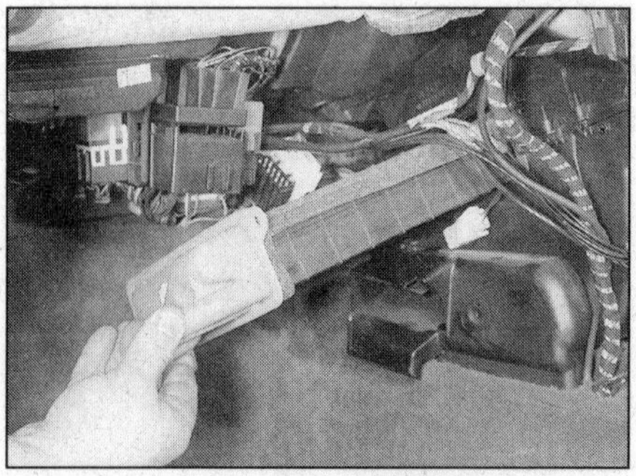

**9.24b . . . and slide the heater matrix out of position**

**9.27 Unclip the end covers and remove them from the motor housing**

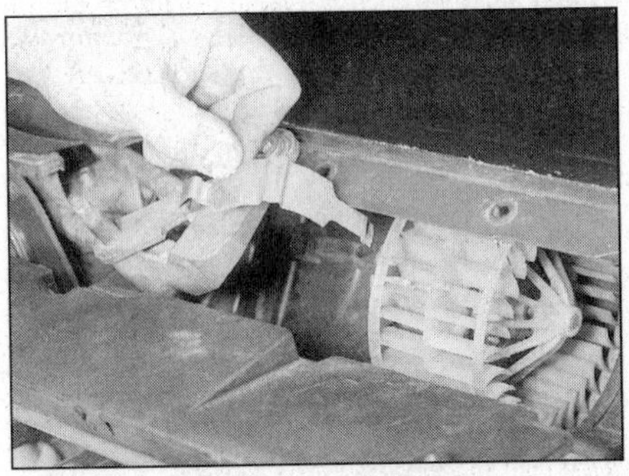

**9.28c Unhook the retaining clip . . .**

**Note:** *Keep the matrix unions uppermost as the matrix is removed to prevent coolant spillage. Mop up any spilt coolant immediately and wipe the affected area with a damp cloth to prevent staining.*

**25** Refitting is the reverse of removal, using new sealing rings. On completion, refill the cooling system as described in Chapter 1.

### Heater blower motor

**26** Disconnect the battery negative terminal. Remove the engine compartment heater inlet as described in paragraphs 13 to 15.

**27** Unclip the blower motor end covers and remove them from the housing **(see illustration)**. Where necessary, also remove the pollen filter.

**28** Release the clips and lift off the blower motor covers. Disconnect the motor wiring then release the motor retaining clip and manoeuvre the motor out of position **(see illustrations)**. **Note:** *On 6-cylinder models, it may be necessary to remove the injector cover from the head to gain the required clearance to remove the motor (see Chapter 4).*

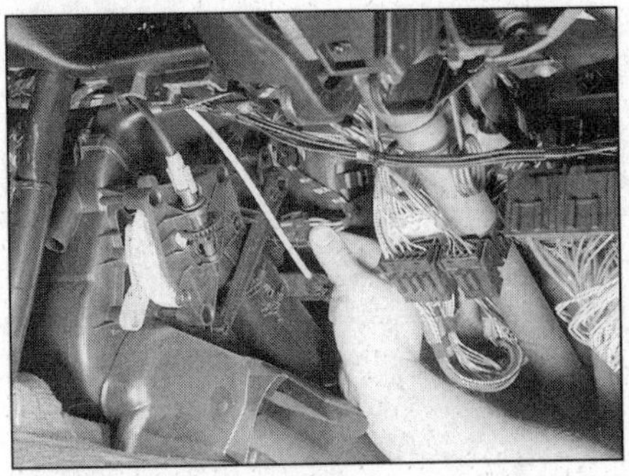

**9.31 Disconnect the wiring connector . . .**

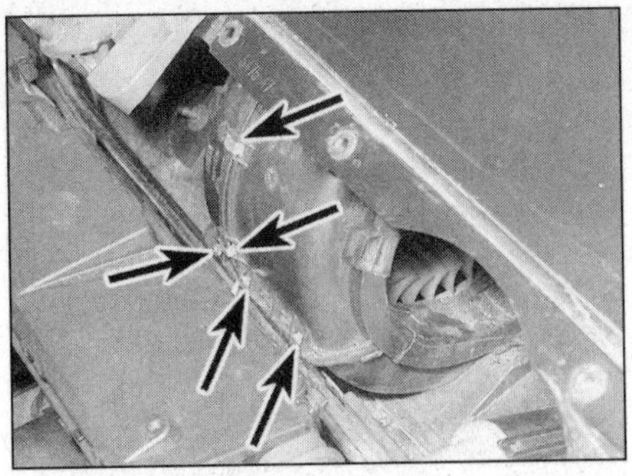

**9.28a Remove the retaining clips (arrowed) . . .**

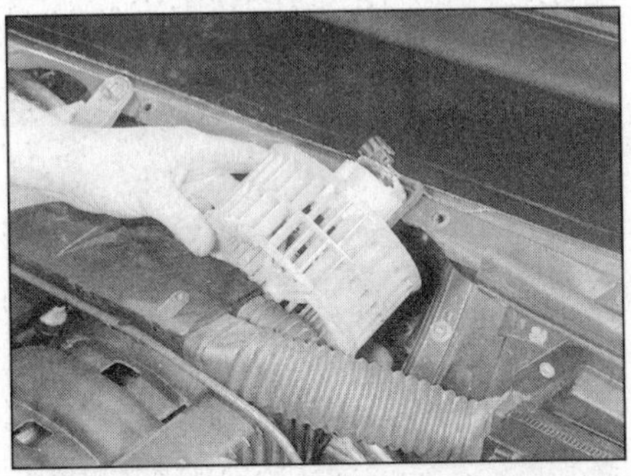

**9.28d . . . then disconnect the wiring and manoeuvre the motor out of position**

**29** Refitting is a reversal of the removal procedure making sure the motor is correctly clipped into the housing and the housing covers are securely refitted.

### Heater blower motor resistor

**30** On right-hand drive models, undo the retaining screws then unclip the driver's side lower facia panel and remove it from the vehicle. On left-hand drive models, remove the glovebox as described in Chapter 11.

**31** Disconnect the wiring connector from the resistor **(see illustration)**.

**32** Release the retaining clips and manoeuvre the resistor out from the front of the air distribution housing **(see illustration)**.

**33** Refitting is the reverse of removal.

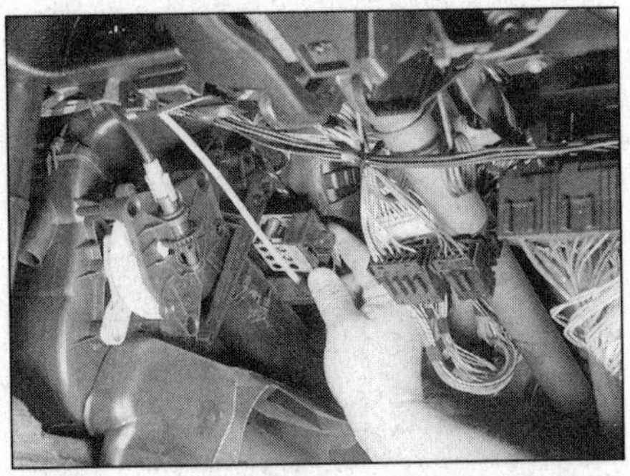

**9.32 . . . then release the clips and remove the blower motor resistor from the housing**

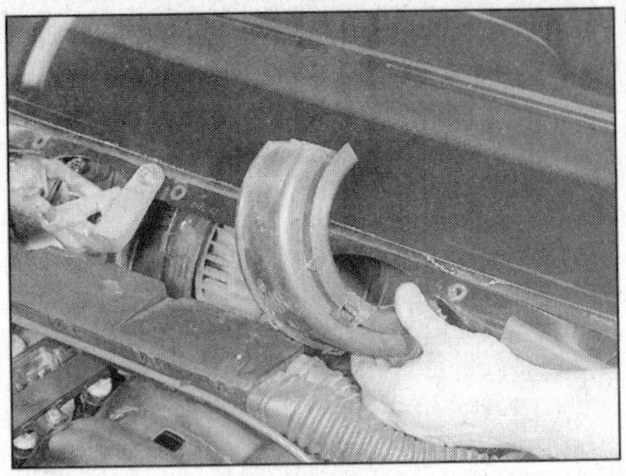

**9.28b . . . and unclip the blower motor covers**

### Heater matrix coolant valve

**34** The coolant valve is mounted onto the engine compartment bulkhead. Unscrew the expansion tank cap (referring to the Warning note in Section 1) to release any pressure present in the cooling system then securely refit the cap.

**35** Clamp both heater hoses as close to the coolant valve as possible to minimise coolant loss.

**36** Disconnect the valve wiring connector(s).

**37** Slacken the retaining clips and disconnect the hoses from the valve then unclip the valve and remove it from the engine compartment.

**38** Refitting is the reverse of removal.

## *Models with air conditioning*

**Note:** *The following information is only applicable to manually controlled air conditioning systems. At the time of writing no information was available on models with the automatic "Climatronic" system.*

3

### Heater control unit - models with manually adjusted controls

**39** Refer to the information given in paragraphs 1 to 8.

### Heater control unit - models automatic air conditioning system

**40** Remove the clock/multi-information display (as applicable) - see Chapter 12.

**41** Reach in behind the control unit and press it out from the facia.

**42** Disconnect the wiring connectors and remove the control unit.

**43** Refitting is the reverse of removal.

### Heater matrix

**44** Remove the centre console as described in Chapter 11.

**45** Remove the heater control unit as described earlier.

**46** Carry out the operations described in paragraphs 13 to 19.

**47** From inside the vehicle, be prepared for coolant spillage and position a suitable container beneath the union on the end of the matrix. To be safe also cover the carpet with rags.

**48** Unscrew the bolts securing the coolant pipes to the matrix and allow the coolant to drain into the container.

**49** Once the flow of coolant stops, disconnect the pipes from the matrix and recover the sealing rings.
**50** Release the air conditioning system control unit from its retaining clips and disconnect its wiring connectors.
**51** Release the wiring harness from its retaining clips and position it clear of the front of the air distribution housing.
**52** Slacken and remove the retaining bolts and remove the cover from the air distribution housing.
**53** Carefully unclip the linkage lever and release the air ducts from the housing then manoeuvre the heater matrix out of position. **Note:** *Keep the matrix unions uppermost as the matrix is removed to prevent coolant spillage. Mop up any spilt coolant immediately and wipe the affected area with a damp cloth to prevent staining.*
**54** Refitting is the reverse of removal, using new sealing rings. On completion, refill the cooling system as described in Chapter 1.

### Heater blower motor

**55** Remove the heating/ventilation inlet as described in paragraphs 13 to 15.
**56** Release the retaining clips and remove the cover from the top of the blower motor.
**57** Disconnect the wiring from the blower motor.
**58** Release the side retaining clips and remove the top section of the blower motor housing.
**59** Release the retaining clips and free the fan from each side of the motor spindle.
**60** Make identification marks on the fans, to ensure that they are correctly positioned on refitting then lift the motor and fans separately out from the housing.
**61** Refitting is the reverse of removal. Install the motor and fans separately, making sure the fans are correctly positioned, and clip the fans onto the motor spindle, aligning the fan cutouts with the spindle locating pins.

### Heater blower motor resistor

**62** Refer to the information given in paragraphs 30 to 33.

### Heater matrix coolant valve

**63** Refer to the information given in paragraphs 34 to 38.

## 10 Air conditioning system - general information and precautions

### General information

**1** An air conditioning system is available on certain models. It enables the temperature of incoming air to be lowered, and dehumidifies the air, which makes for rapid demisting and increased comfort.
**2** The cooling side of the system works in the same way as a domestic refrigerator. Refrigerant gas is drawn into a belt-driven compressor and passes into a condenser mounted in front of the radiator, where it loses heat and becomes liquid. The liquid passes through an expansion valve to an evaporator, where it changes from liquid under high pressure to gas under low pressure. This change is accompanied by a drop in temperature, which cools the evaporator. The refrigerant returns to the compressor and the cycle begins again.
**3** Air blown through the evaporator passes to the air distribution unit, where it is mixed with hot air blown through the heater matrix to achieve the desired temperature in the passenger compartment.
**4** The heating side of the system works in the same way as on models without air conditioning (see Section 8).
**5** The operation of the system is controlled electronically by coolant temperature switch (see Section 6), and pressure switches which are screwed into the compressor high-pressure line. Any problems with the system should be referred to a BMW dealer.

### Precautions

**6** When an air conditioning system is fitted, it is necessary to observe special precautions whenever dealing with any part of the system, its associated components and any items which require disconnection of the system. If for any reason the system must be disconnected, entrust this task to your BMW dealer or a refrigeration engineer.

***Warning: The refrigerant is potentially dangerous and should only be handled by qualified persons. If it is splashed onto the skin it can cause frostbite. It is not itself poisonous, but in the presence of a naked flame (including a cigarette) it forms a poisonous gas. Uncontrolled discharging of the refrigerant is dangerous and potentially damaging to the environment.***

***Warning: Do not operate the air conditioning system if it is known to be short of refrigerant, as this may damage the compressor.***

## 11 Air conditioning system components - removal and refitting

***Warning: Do not attempt to open the refrigerant circuit. Refer to the precautions given in Section 10.***

The only operation which can be carried out easily without discharging the refrigerant is renewal of the compressor drivebelt, which is covered in Chapter 1. All other operations must be referred to a BMW dealer or an air conditioning specialist.

If necessary the compressor can be unbolted and moved aside, without disconnecting its flexible hoses, after removing the drivebelt.

# Chapter 4 Part A:
# 4-cylinder engine fuel and exhaust systems

## Contents



## Degrees of difficulty

| | | | | |
|---|---|---|---|---|
| **Easy,** suitable for novice with little experience | **Fairly easy,** suitable for beginner with some experience | **Fairly difficult,** suitable for competent DIY mechanic | **Difficult,** suitable for experienced DIY mechanic | **Very difficult,** suitable for expert DIY or professional |

## Specifications

### System type

| | |
|---|---|
| All models | Bosch Motronic M1.7 sequential injection |

### Fuel system data

| | |
|---|---|
| Fuel pump type | Electric, immersed in tank |
| Fuel pressure regulator rating | 3.0 ± 0.06 bar |
| Specified idle speed: | |
| M40 engine | 800 ± 40 rpm (not adjustable - controlled by ECU) |
| M42 engine | 850 ± 40 rpm (not adjustable - controlled by ECU) |
| M43 engine | No information available |
| Specified idle mixture CO content: | |
| Models without catalytic converter | 0.7 ± 0.5% |
| Models with catalytic converter | 0.5 to 1.5% (not adjustable - controlled by ECU) |

### Recommended fuel

| | |
|---|---|
| Models without catalytic converter | 95 RON unleaded (UK unleaded premium) or 98 RON leaded (UK 4-star) |
| Models with catalytic converter | 95 RON unleaded (UK unleaded premium). Leaded fuel **must not** be used |

### Torque wrench settings

| | Nm | lbf ft |
|---|---|---|
| Inlet manifold nuts: | | |
| M6 nuts | 10 | 7 |
| M7 nuts | 15 | 11 |
| M8 nuts | 22 | 16 |
| Exhaust manifold nuts: | | |
| M6 nuts | 10 | 7 |
| M7 nuts | 20 | 15 |
| M8 nuts | 22 | 16 |
| Crankshaft position sensor bolt | 7 | 5 |
| Camshaft position sensor bolt | 7 | 5 |
| Fuel rail-to-inlet manifold bolts | 10 | 7 |
| Fuel tank mounting bolts | 23 | 17 |
| Fuel tank retaining strap bolts | 8 | 6 |

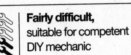

## 1 General information and precautions

### General information

The fuel supply system consists of a fuel tank (which is mounted under the rear of the vehicle, with an electric fuel pump immersed in it), a fuel filter, fuel feed and return lines. The fuel pump supplies fuel to the fuel rail, which acts as a reservoir for the four fuel injectors which inject fuel into the inlet tracts. The fuel filter incorporated in the feed line from the pump to the fuel rail ensures that the fuel supplied to the injectors is clean.

Refer to Section 6 for further information on the operation of the fuel injection system, and to Section 14 for information on the exhaust system.

### Precautions

***Warning: Many of the procedures in this Chapter required the disconnection of fuel lines and connections, which may result in some fuel spillage. Before carrying out any operation on the fuel system, refer to the precautions given in "Safety first!", and follow then implicitly. Petrol is a highly dangerous and volatile liquid, and the precautions necessary when handling it cannot be overstressed.***

***Warning: Residual pressure will remain in the fuel lines long after the vehicle was last used. When disconnecting any fuel line, first depressurise the fuel system as described in Section 7.***

## 2 Air cleaner assembly - removal and refitting

### Removal

**1** Remove the airflow meter and air cleaner cover assembly, as described in Section 12.

**2** Loosen the two nuts securing the air cleaner casing to the mounting bracket, then pull the casing upwards, and unclip the inlet duct from the front body panel **(see illustration)**.

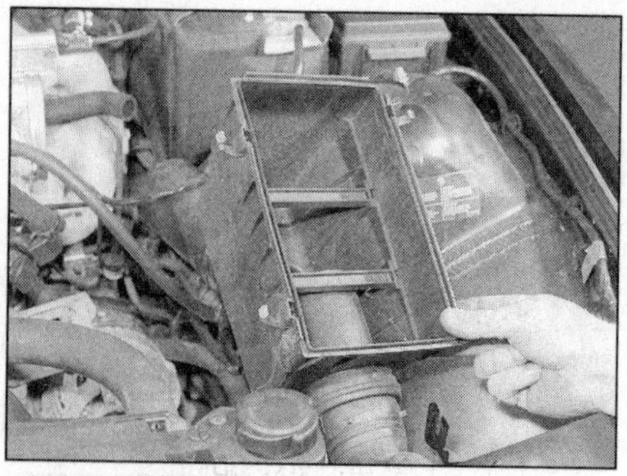

**2.2 Removing the air cleaner assembly - M42 engine model**

### Refitting

**3** Refitting is a reversal of removal, but ensure that the lower mounting engages with the plastic lug on the body, and refit the airflow meter with reference to Section 12.

## 3 Fuel tank - removal and refitting

Refer to Part B of this Chapter.

## 4 Throttle cable - removal, refitting and adjustment

Proceed as described in Part B of this Chapter, but note that it may be necessary to remove the securing screw(s), and fold back or withdraw the cover from the top of the throttle linkage for access to the throttle cable **(see illustrations)**.

## 5 Throttle pedal - removal and refitting

Refer to Part B of this Chapter.

## 6 Fuel injection system - general information

**1** An integrated engine management system known as DME (Digital Motor Electronics) is fitted to all models, and the system controls all fuel injection and ignition system functions using a central ECU (Electronic Control Unit). A Bosch Motronic engine management system is fitted to all models.

**2** On most models, the system incorporates a closed-loop catalytic converter and an evaporative emission control system, and complies with the very latest emission control standards. Refer to Chapter 5B for information on the ignition side of the system; the fuel side of the system operates as follows.

**3** The fuel pump (which is immersed in the fuel tank) supplies fuel from the tank to the fuel rail, via a filter. Fuel supply pressure is controlled by the pressure regulator in the fuel rail. When the optimum operating pressure of the fuel system is exceeded, the regulator allows excess fuel to return to the tank.

**4** The electrical control system consists of the ECU, along with the following sensors:

a) *Airflow meter - informs the ECU of the quantity of air entering the engine.*
b) *Throttle position sensor - informs the ECU of the throttle position, and the rate of throttle opening/closing.*
c) *Coolant temperature sensor - informs the ECU of engine temperature.*
d) *Crankshaft position sensor - informs the ECU of the crankshaft position and speed of rotation.*
e) *Camshaft position sensor - informs the ECU of the inlet camshaft position.*
f) *Oxygen sensor - informs the ECU of the oxygen content of the exhaust gases (explained in greater detail in Part C of this Chapter).*

**5** All the above signals are analysed by the ECU which selects the fuelling response appropriate to those values. The ECU controls the fuel injectors (varying the pulse width - the length of time the injectors are held open - to

**4.1a Withdraw the cover from the throttle linkage . . .**

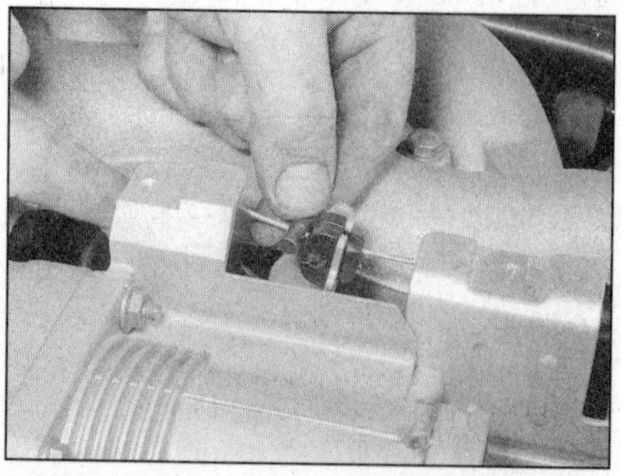

**4.1b . . . for access to the throttle cable**

**4.1c Throttle cable adjuster screw (arrowed)**

provide a richer or weaker mixture, as appropriate). The mixture is constantly varied by the ECU, to provide the best setting for cranking, starting (with a hot or cold engine), warm-up, idle, cruising and acceleration.

**6** The ECU also has full control over the engine idle speed, via an auxiliary air valve which bypasses the throttle valve. When the throttle valve is closed, the ECU controls the opening of the valve, which in turn regulates the amount of air entering the manifold, and so controls the idle speed.

**7** The ECU also controls the exhaust and evaporative emission control systems, which are described in Part C of this Chapter.

**8** The throttle body is coolant heated.

**9** On M42 and M43 engines, a Differential Air Inlet System (DISA) is fitted. Variable length inlet tracts incorporated in the inlet manifold are operated by a butterfly valve according to engine speed and load. This improves engines torque at low and medium engine speeds. The butterfly valve is operated by a vacuum actuator fitted under the manifold.

**10** If there is an abnormality in any of the readings obtained from the sensors, the ECU enters its back-up mode. In this event, it ignores the abnormal sensor signal and assumes a pre-programmed value which will allow the engine to continue running (albeit at reduced efficiency). If the ECU enters this back-up mode, the relevant fault code will be stored in the ECU memory.

**11** If a fault is suspected, the vehicle should be taken to a BMW dealer at the earliest opportunity. A complete test of the engine management system can then be carried out, using a special electronic diagnostic test unit which is simply plugged into the system's diagnostic connector.

## 7 Fuel injection system - depressurisation and priming

### Depressurisation

**1** Remove the fuel pump fuse from the fusebox. The fuse is located in the engine compartment fusebox, and the exact location is given on the fusebox cover (see Chapter 12).

**2** Start the engine, and wait for it to stall. Switch off the ignition.

**3** Remove the fuel filler cap.

**4** The fuel system is now depressurised. **Note:** *Place a wad of rag around fuel lines before disconnecting, to prevent any residual fuel from spilling onto the engine.*

**5** Disconnect the battery negative lead before working on any part of the fuel system.

### Priming

**6** Refit the fuel pump fuse, then switch on the ignition and wait for a few seconds for the fuel pump to run, building up fuel pressure. Switch off the ignition unless the engine is to be started.

## 8 Fuel pump/fuel gauge sender unit - removal and refitting

Refer to Part B of this Chapter.

## 9 Fuel gauge sender unit - removal and refitting

Refer to Part B of this Chapter.

## 10 Fuel injection system - testing and adjustment

### Testing

**1** If a fault appears in the fuel injection system, first ensure that all the system wiring connectors are securely connected and free of corrosion. Ensure that the fault is not due to poor maintenance; ie, check that the air cleaner filter element is clean, the spark plugs are in good condition and correctly gapped, the cylinder compression pressures are correct, and that the engine breather hoses are clear and undamaged, referring to Chapters 1, 2 and 5 for further information.

**2** If these checks fail to reveal the cause of the problem, the vehicle should be taken to a BMW dealer for testing. A wiring block connector is incorporated in the engine management circuit, into which a special electronic diagnostic tester can be plugged. The connector is clipped to the right-hand suspension turret. The tester will locate the fault quickly and simply, alleviating the need to test all the system components individually, which is a time-consuming operation that also carries a risk of damaging the ECU.

### Adjustment

**3** Experienced home mechanics with a considerable amount of skill and equipment (including a tachometer and an accurately calibrated exhaust gas analyser) may be able to check the exhaust CO level and the idle speed. However, if these are found to be in need of adjustment, the car *must* be taken to a BMW dealer for further testing.

**4** To adjust the CO level or idle speed, special diagnostic equipment is required.

## 11 Throttle body - removal and refitting

### M40 engine

**Note:** *A new throttle body gasket and a new throttle body heater sealing ring will be required on refitting.*

#### Removal

**1** Disconnect the battery negative lead.

**2** Unscrew the securing screw, and fold back the throttle body cover to expose the remaining two cover securing screws.

**3** Remove the securing screws, and withdraw the cover from the throttle body.

**4** Disconnect the throttle cable(s) from the throttle body and the cable support bracket.

**5** Unscrew the securing bolts, and withdraw the throttle cable support bracket from the throttle body.

**6** Loosen the clamp screw, and disconnect the inlet air trunking from the throttle body.

**7** Disconnect the throttle position sensor wiring plug.

**8** Disconnect the vacuum hoses from the throttle body.

**9** Unscrew the bolts and withdraw the throttle body heater from the front of the throttle body. Recover the sealing ring. Leave the coolant hoses connected, and move the assembly to one side clear of the working area.

**10** Unscrew the four securing bolts and withdraw the throttle body from the inlet manifold. Recover the gasket.

#### Refitting

**11** Refitting is a reversal of removal, bearing in mind the following points.

a) *Use new throttle body gasket, and use a new throttle body heater sealing ring.*

b) *Reconnect and if necessary adjust the throttle cable as described in Section 4.*

### M42 and M43 engines

**Note:** *New throttle body heater gaskets will be required on refitting.*

#### Removal

**12** Disconnect the battery negative lead.

**13** Where applicable, remove the screw(s), and lift the cover from the throttle body.

**14** Disconnect the throttle cable(s) from the throttle body and the cable support bracket.

**15** Loosen the clamp screw securing the air inlet trunking to the throttle body.

**16** Remove the upper section of the air cleaner, complete with the airflow meter and the air inlet trunking as described in Section 12.

**17** Disconnect the throttle position sensor wiring plug.

**18** Disconnect the vacuum hoses from the throttle body.

**19** Disconnect the coolant hose(s) from the throttle body. Be prepared for coolant spillage, and clamp the open ends of the hoses to prevent further coolant loss.

**20** Unscrew the four securing nuts/bolts, and withdraw the throttle body from the inlet manifold **(see illustrations)**. Recover the throttle body heater which fits between the throttle body and the manifold, and recover the gaskets which fit either side of the heater.

#### Refitting

**21** Refitting is a reversal of removal, bearing in mind the following points.

a) *Use new gaskets either side of the throttle body heater.*

**11.20a Throttle body securing nuts and bolts (arrowed) - M42 engine**

*b) Reconnect and if necessary adjust the throttle cable with reference to Section 4.*

*c) On completion, check and if necessary top-up the coolant level as described in "Weekly Checks".*

## 12 Fuel injection system components - removal and refitting

### Electronic control unit (ECU)

**1** Proceed as described in Part B of this Chapter, but note that for access to the ECU, the battery must be removed, as described in Chapter 5A.

### Fuel rail and injectors - M40 engine

***Warning: Refer to the warning notes in Section 1 before proceeding.***

**Note:** *New fuel injector O-rings should be used on refitting.*

#### Removal

**2** Depressurise the fuel system as described in Section 7, then disconnect the battery negative lead.

**3** Where necessary, to allow sufficient clearance for the fuel rail to be removed, remove the heater/ventilation inlet air ducting from the rear of the engine compartment as follows.

*a) Lift the grille from the top of the ducting (on certain Coupe models, it will be necessary to remove the windscreen wiper arms, then remove the plastic securing screws and lift off the complete scuttle grille assembly).*

*b) Working through the top of the ducting, remove the screws securing the cable ducting to the air ducting and move the cable ducting clear.*

*c) Unscrew the nuts and/or screw(s) securing the air ducting to the bulkhead (where applicable, bend back the heat shielding for access).*

*d) Remove the air ducting by pulling upwards.*

*e) Move the previously removed cable ducting clear of the cylinder head cover.*

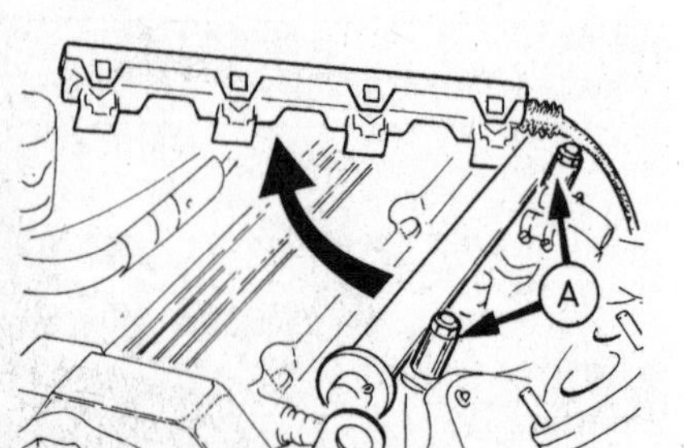


**12.8 Pull wiring ducting from the fuel rail**
*A Fuel rail securing bolts*

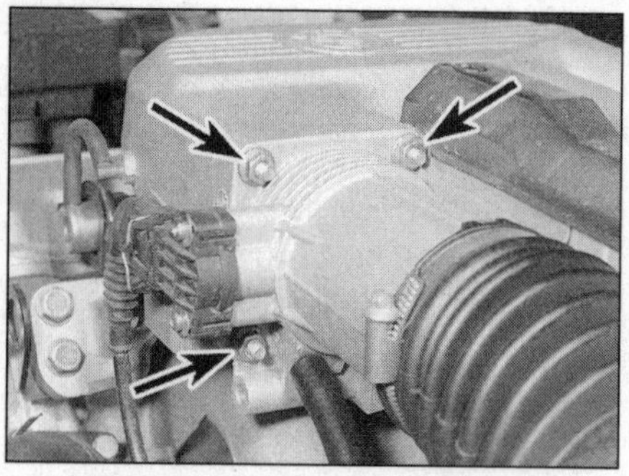

**11.20b Three of the throttle body securing nuts (arrowed) - M43 engine**

**4** Unscrew the securing screw, and fold back the throttle body cover to expose the remaining two cover securing screws.

**5** Remove the securing screws, and withdraw the cover from the throttle body.

**6** Loosen the clamp bolts, and remove the air inlet trunking from the throttle body and the airflow meter.

**7** Remove the upper section of the inlet manifold as described in Section 13.

**8** Pull up the wiring ducting to release the wiring plugs from the fuel injectors **(see illustration)**.

**9** Loosen the hose clips, and disconnect the fuel feed and return hoses from the fuel rail. Be prepared for fuel spillage, and take adequate fire precautions. Plug the open ends of the pipes and hoses to prevent dirt entry and further fuel spillage.

**10** Disconnect the vacuum hose from the fuel pressure regulator.

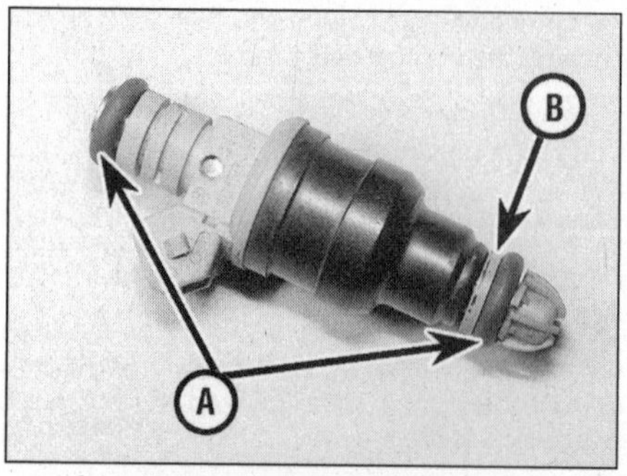


**12.15 Fuel injector O-rings (A) and plastic washer (B)**

**11** Unscrew the two bolts securing the fuel rail to the inlet manifold.

**12** Carefully pull the fuel rail upwards to release the fuel injectors from the cylinder head, then withdraw the complete fuel rail/fuel injector assembly.

**13** To remove a fuel injector from the fuel rail, proceed as follows.

*a) Prise off the metal securing clip, using a screwdriver.*

*b) Pull the fuel injector from the fuel rail.*

#### Refitting

**14** Before refitting, it is wise to renew all the fuel injector O-rings as a matter of course.

**15** Check that the plastic washer at the bottom of each injector is positioned above the lower O-ring **(see illustration)**.

**16** Lightly lubricate the fuel injector O-rings with a little petroleum jelly or SAE 90 gear oil.

**17** Where applicable, refit the fuel injectors to the fuel rail, ensuring that the securing clips are correctly fitted. Note that the injectors should be positioned so that the wiring sockets are uppermost when the assembly is refitted.

**18** Slide the fuel rail/fuel injector assembly into position, ensuring that the injectors engage with their bores in the inlet manifold.

**19** Further refitting is a reversal of removal, but refit the upper section of the inlet manifold as described in Section 13, and pressurise the fuel system (refit the fuel pump fuse and switch on the ignition) and check for leaks before starting the engine.

### Fuel rail and injectors - M42 engines, and M43 engines up to 1995 model year

***Warning: Refer to the warning notes in Section 1 before proceeding.***

**Note:** *New fuel injector O-rings should be used on refitting.*

#### Removal

**20** Depressurise the fuel system as described in Section 7, then disconnect the battery negative lead.

**21** Remove the upper section of the inlet manifold as described in Section 13.

**22** Proceed as described in paragraphs 8 to 13.

#### Refitting

**23** Proceed as described in paragraphs 14 to 19.

### Fuel rail and injectors - M43 engines from 1996 model year

**24** At the time of writing, no information was available on removal and refitting the fuel injectors on models from 1996 model year.

### Fuel pressure regulator - M40 engine

***Warning: Refer to the warning notes in Section 1 before proceeding.***

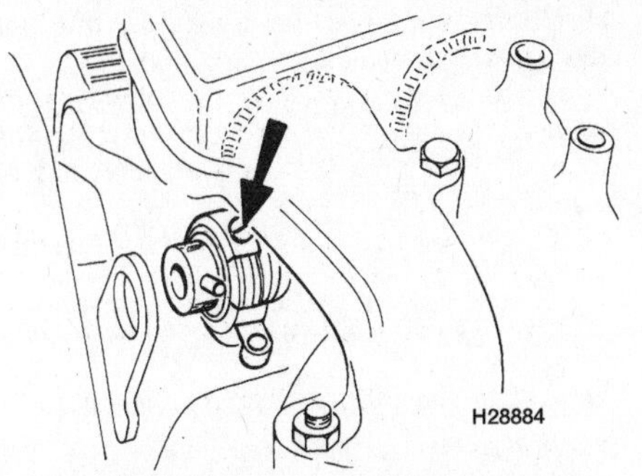


**12.28 Unscrew the clamp bolt (arrowed) and remove the pressure regulator clamping ring - M40 engine**

**Note:** *New O-rings may be required on refitting.*

**25** Depressurise the fuel system as described in Section 7, then disconnect the battery negative lead.

**26** Pull the vacuum hose from the pressure regulator.

**27** Disconnect the breather hose from the front of the cylinder head cover.

**28** Unscrew the clamp bolt and remove the pressure regulator clamping ring, then lift off the thrustwasher, and pull the pressure regulator from the fuel rail **(see illustration)**. Note that it will be difficult to pull the regulator from the fuel rail due to the tight-fitting O-rings.

### Refitting

**29** Before refitting, check the condition of the O-rings, and renew if necessary **(see illustration)**.

**30** Refitting is a reversal of removal, but ensure that the thrustwasher is correctly positioned.

**31** On completion, pressurise the fuel system (refit the fuel pump fuse and switch on the ignition) and check for leaks before starting the engine.

## *Fuel pressure regulator - M42 and M43 engines*

***Warning: Refer to the warning notes in Section 1 before proceeding.***

**Note:** *New O-rings may be required on refitting.*

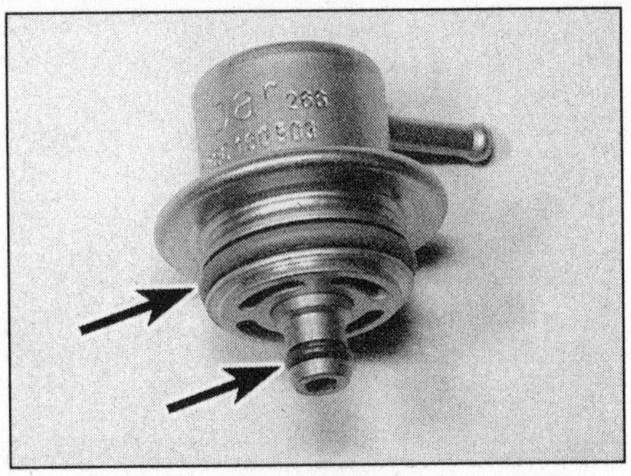

**12.29 Check the condition of the O-rings (arrowed)**

### Removal

**32** Depressurise the fuel system as described in Section 7, then disconnect the battery negative lead.

**33** Pull the vacuum hose from the pressure regulator.

**34** Where applicable, to improve access, disconnect the breather hose from the front of the cylinder head cover.

**35** Note the angle of the vacuum inlet on the pressure regulator, so that it can be refitted in the same position.

**36** Where applicable, to give sufficient clearance to remove the pressure regulator, unbolt the engine lifting bracket from the cylinder head.

**37** On models where the pressure regulator is secured by a clamping ring, unscrew the clamp bolt and remove the clamping ring and lift off the thrustwasher.

**38** On models where the regulator is secured by a clamping bracket retained by a nut, unscrew the securing nut and withdraw the clamping bracket **(see illustration)**.

**39** On models where the regulator is secured by a retaining ring retained by a locking clip, pull out the locking clip and remove the retaining ring **(see illustration)**.

**40** Twist and pull the regulator from the fuel rail. Note that it will be difficult to pull the regulator from the fuel rail due to the tight-fitting O-rings.

### Refitting

**41** Before refitting, check the O-rings, and renew if necessary **(see illustration 12.15)**.

**42** Refitting is a reversal of removal, bearing in mind the following points.

a) *Ensure that the regulator is pushed firmly into position in the end of the fuel rail.*
b) *Make sure that the regulator vacuum inlet is positioned as noted before removal.*
c) *Where applicable, ensure that the thrustwasher is correctly positioned.*
d) *On models where the regulator is retained by a ring and locking clip, make sure that the cut-out in the retaining ring is aligned with the regulator vacuum inlet (to avoid damage to the vacuum hose).*
e) *On completion, pressurise the fuel system (refit the fuel pump fuse and switch on the ignition) and check for leaks before starting the engine.*

## *Airflow meter*

**Note:** *A new airflow meter seal will be required on refitting.*

### Removal

**43** Disconnect the battery negative lead.

**44** Turn the locking collar, and disconnect the wiring plug from the airflow meter **(see illustration)**.

**45** Remove the screw securing the carbon canister hose to the airflow meter.

**46** Loosen the hose clip, and disconnect the air trunking from the airflow meter.

**47** Release the clips, and lift off the air cleaner cover, complete with the airflow meter.

**48** Disconnect the breather hose(s) from the air trunking, and the airflow meter (as applicable), and release any wires or hoses from the clips on the air trunking.

**49** Working inside the air cleaner cover, unscrew the four securing nuts, and withdraw the airflow meter from the air cleaner cover **(see illustration)**. Recover the seal.

### Refitting

**50** Refitting is a reversal of removal, but use a new seal between the airflow meter and the air cleaner cover, and ensure any wire/hoses are securely positioned in their clips.

## *Throttle position sensor - M40 engine*

### Removal

**51** Disconnect the battery negative lead.

**52** To improve access, slacken the clamp

4A

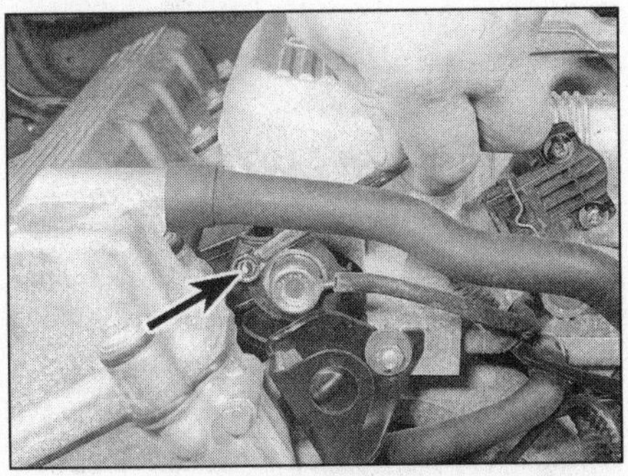

**12.38 Unscrewing pressure regulator clamp bracket nut (arrowed) - M42 engine**

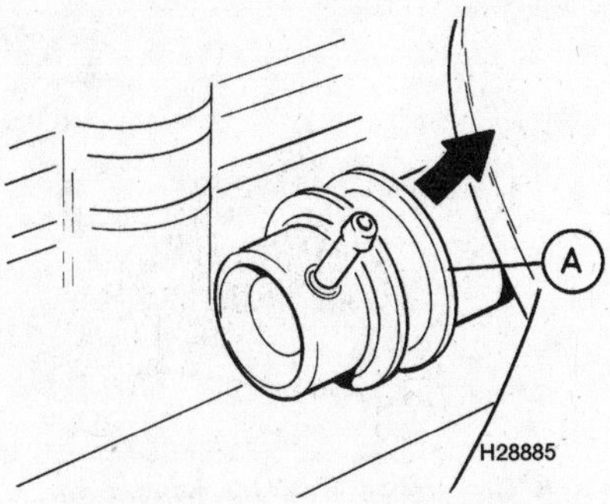


**12.39 Pull out the pressure regulator retaining ring locking clip (A)**

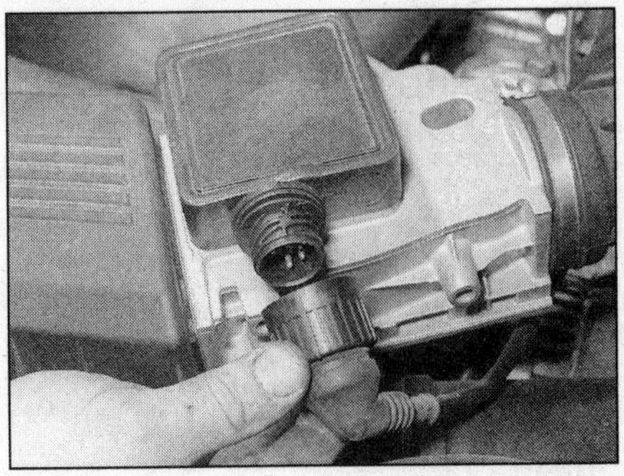

**12.44 Disconnecting the airflow meter wiring plug - M43 engine**

**12.49 Airflow meter securing nuts (arrowed) - M43 engine**

screws, and remove the air inlet trunking connecting the airflow meter to the throttle body. Note the locations of any breather hoses connected to the trunking.

**53** Disconnect the wiring plug from the sensor, located under the throttle body.

**54** Mark the position of the sensor on the throttle body, so that it can be refitted in exactly the same position.

**55** Remove the two securing screws, and withdraw the sensor.

### Refitting

**56** Refitting is a reversal of removal, but ensure that the sensor is refitted in its original position. If there is any doubt about the position of the sensor, have the adjustment checked by a BMW dealer.

## *Throttle position sensor - M42 and M43 engines*

**Note:** *A new O-ring may be required on refitting.*

### Removal

**57** Disconnect the battery negative lead.

**58** Disconnect the wiring plug from the sensor **(see illustration)**.

**59** Unscrew the two securing screws, and withdraw the sensor from the throttle body. Where applicable, recover the O-ring

### Refitting

**60** Refitting is a reversal of removal, but where applicable, check the condition of the O-ring and renew if necessary, and ensure that the O-ring is correctly positioned.

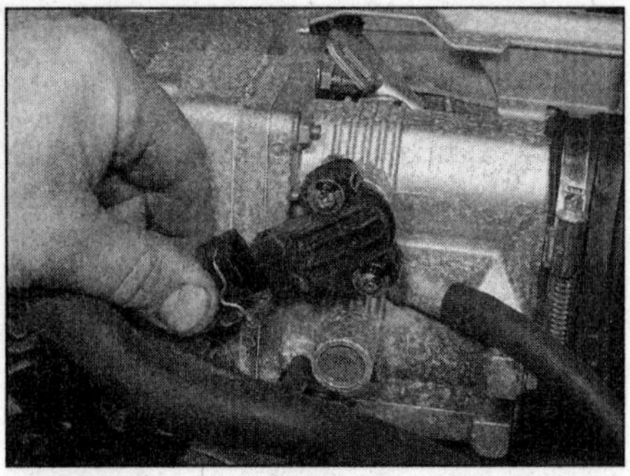

**12.58 Disconnecting the throttle position sensor wiring plug - M42 engine**

## *Coolant temperature sensor*

**61** The sensor is located in the left-hand side of the cylinder head. Refer to Chapter 3 for removal and refitting details.

## *Crankshaft position sensor - all except M43 engine models from 1996 model year*

**Note:** *At the time of writing, no information was available for the sensor which is fitted to M43 engine models from 1996 model year.*

### Removal

**62** To improve access, remove the viscous cooling fan and fan cowl assembly as described in Chapter 3.

**63** On M42 engine models from 1994 model year and M43 engine models, remove the upper section of the inlet manifold as described in Section 13, and release the wiring ducting from the manifold.

**64** Trace the wiring back from the sensor to the connector, located on a bracket behind the oil filter. Note that there are two wiring connectors, and the crankshaft position sensor is the lower connector - if both connectors are to be disconnected, mark them to avoid confusion on refitting **(see illustration)**.

**65** Release the wiring from any clips and brackets on the engine.

**66** Unscrew the sensor securing bolt, then withdraw the sensor from its mounting bracket **(see illustration)**.

### Refitting

**67** Refitting is a reversal of removal, bearing in mind the following points.

*a) Ensure that the sensor wiring is securely refitted to its securing clips to avoid the wiring from rubbing on the auxiliary drivebelt.*

*b) Ensure that the sensor wiring connector is correctly reconnected as noted before removal.*

*c) Where applicable, refit the upper section of the inlet manifold (see Section 13).*

*d) Refit the viscous cooling fan and fan cowl assembly as described in Chapter 3.*

## *Camshaft position sensor - M40 engine*

**Note:** *The HT lead will almost certainly be damaged during this procedure. Do not remove the sensor unless it is to be renewed.*

### Removal

**68** On M40 engines, the camshaft position sensor is attached to No 4 cylinder HT lead at the distributor cap **(see illustration)**.

**69** Disconnect the battery negative lead.

**70** Locate the sensor wiring connector on the bracket behind the oil filter. Note that there are two connectors, and the camshaft position sensor wiring plug is the lower one - if both connectors are to be disconnected, mark them to avoid confusion on refitting.

**71** Disconnect the wiring plug, then trace the wiring towards the sensor, and release the wiring from any clips.

**72** Release the wiring from the ducting on the front of the engine.

**73** Using a small flat-bladed screwdriver, release the securing clips at the top and bottom of the distributor cap cover, then pull off the cover.

**74** Disconnect No 4 cylinder HT lead from the distributor cap.

**75** Disconnect the shielded connector from the end of the HT lead. It may be necessary to cut the connector off the end of the lead.

**76** Pull the sensor from the lead.

### Refitting

**77** Refitting is a reversal of removal, but fit a new connector to the end of the HT lead, or

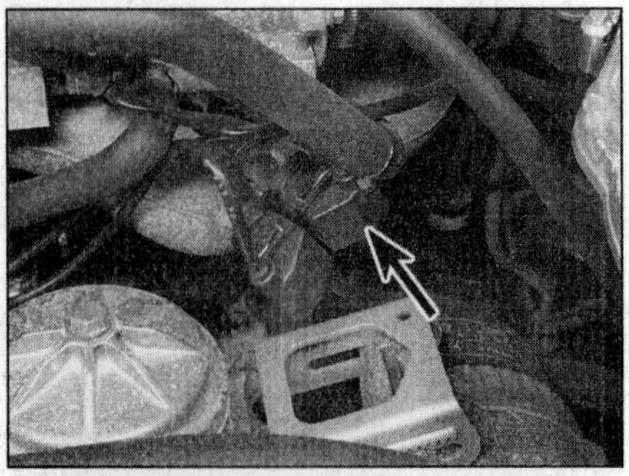

**12.64 Crankshaft position sensor wiring connector (arrowed) - pre-1994 model year M42 engine**

**12.66 Crankshaft position sensor securing bolt (arrowed) - M42 engine**

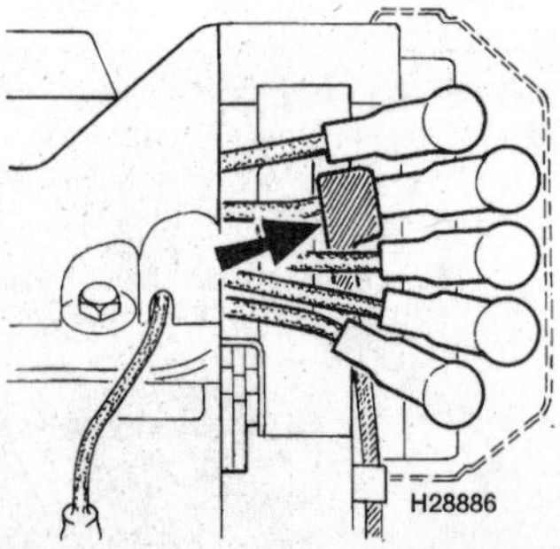


**12.68 Camshaft position sensor location (arrowed) - M40 engine**

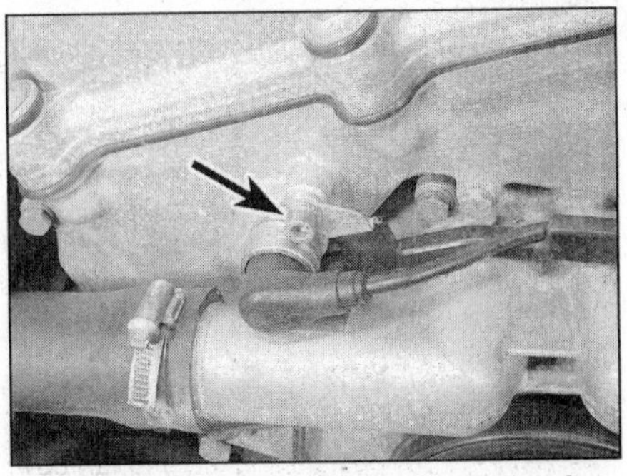

12.83 **Camshaft position sensor securing bolt (arrowed) - M42 engine**

renew the complete lead assembly. Ensure that the sensor wiring connector is correctly reconnected.

## *Camshaft position sensor - M42 and M43 engines*

### Removal

**78** The sensor is located in the front of the upper timing chain cover.

**79** Disconnect the battery negative lead.

**80** On M42 engine models from 1994 model year and M43 engine models, remove the upper section of the inlet manifold as described in Section 13, and release the wiring ducting from the manifold.

**81** Trace the wiring back from the sensor, and locate the wiring connector attached to the bracket behind the oil filter. Note that there are two connectors, and the camshaft position sensor connector is the top connector - if both connectors are to be disconnected, mark them to avoid confusion on refitting. Disconnect the wiring connector.

**82** Remove the screw, and/or release the clips securing the wiring ducting to the front of the engine, then release the sensor wiring from the ducting.

**83** Unscrew the sensor securing bolt, and withdraw the sensor **(see illustration)**. Recover the O-ring if it is loose.

### Refitting

**84** Refitting is a reversal of removal, bearing in mind the following points.

*a) Make sure that the sensor O-ring is correctly seated.*

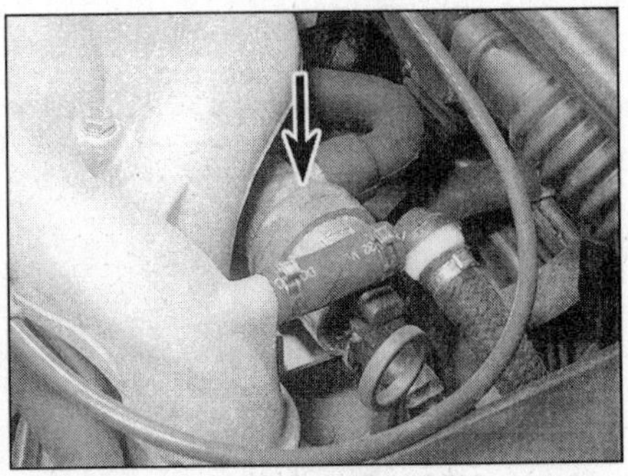

12.93 **Idle speed control valve location (arrowed) - M42 engine**

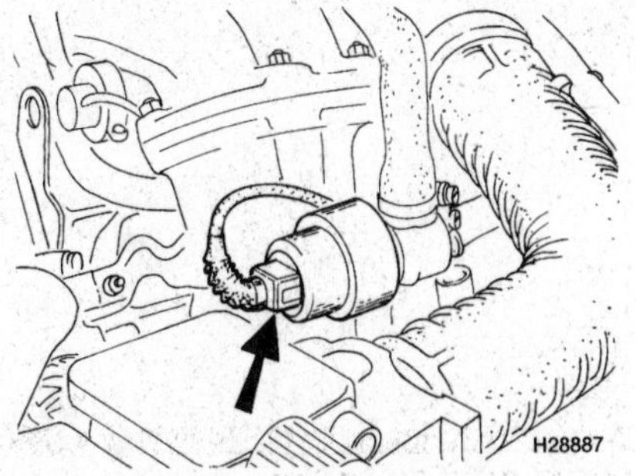


12.87 **Idle speed control valve wiring plug (arrowed) - M40 engine**

*b) Ensure that the wiring connector is correctly reconnected as noted before removal.*

*c) Where applicable, refit the upper section of the inlet manifold as described in Section 13.*

## *Oxygen sensor*

**85** Refer to Chapter 4C.

## *Idle speed control valve - M40 engine*

### Removal

**86** Disconnect the battery negative lead.

**87** Disconnect the wiring plug from the idle speed control valve **(see illustration)**.

**88** Loosen the hose clips, and disconnect the hoses from the valve. Note the hose locations to ensure correct refitting.

**89** Cut the cable-tie round the valve, then push the valve from its mounting collar.

### Refitting

**90** Refitting is reversal of removal, but use a new cable-tie, and ensure that the hoses are correctly reconnected.

## *Idle speed control valve - M42 engine, and M43 engine up to 1995 model year*

### Removal

**91** Disconnect the battery negative lead.

**92** Disconnect the wiring plug from the valve.

**93** Pull the valve, complete with its rubber mounting, from the retaining bracket **(see illustration)**.

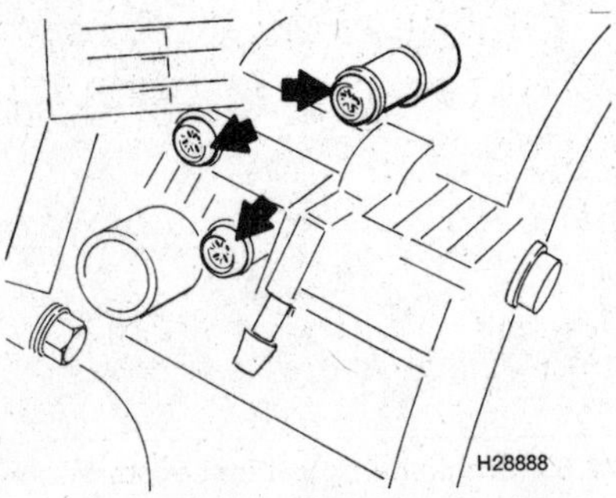


12.97 **Idle speed control valve screws (arrowed) - M43 engine, 1996 model year**

**94** Disconnect the hoses from the valve, noting their locations to ensure correct refitting.

**95** Withdraw the valve.

### Refitting

**96** Refitting is a reversal of removal, but make sure that the hoses are correctly reconnected.

## *Idle speed control valve - M43 engine from 1996 model year*

### Removal

**97** The valve is mounted on the side of the throttle body **(see illustration)**.

**98** Disconnect the battery negative lead.

**99** Disconnect the wiring plug from the valve.

**100** Disconnect the hose from the valve.

**101** Remove the two securing screws, and withdraw the valve from the throttle body. Recover the gasket.

### Refitting

**102** Refitting is a reversal of removal, but clean the sealing face of the valve, and check the condition of the gasket. Renew the gasket if necessary.

# 13 Manifolds - removal and refitting

## *Inlet manifold upper section - M40 engine*

**Note:** *New gaskets will be required on refitting.*

### Removal

**1** Disconnect the battery negative lead.

**2** Where necessary, to allow sufficient clearance for the manifold to be removed, remove the heater/ventilation inlet air ducting from the rear of the engine compartment as follows. **4A**

*a) Lift the grille from the top of the ducting (on certain Coupe models, it will be necessary to remove the windscreen wiper arms, then remove the plastic securing screws and lift off the complete scuttle grille assembly).*

*b) Working through the top of the ducting, remove the screws securing the cable ducting to the air ducting and move the cable ducting clear.*

*c) Unscrew the nuts and/or screw(s) securing the air ducting to the bulkhead (where applicable, bend back the heat shielding for access).*

*d) Remove the air ducting by pulling upwards.*

*e) Move the previously removed cable ducting clear of the cylinder head cover.*

**3** To improve access, slacken the clamp screws, and remove the air inlet trunking connecting the airflow meter to the throttle body. Note the locations of any breather hoses connected to the trunking.

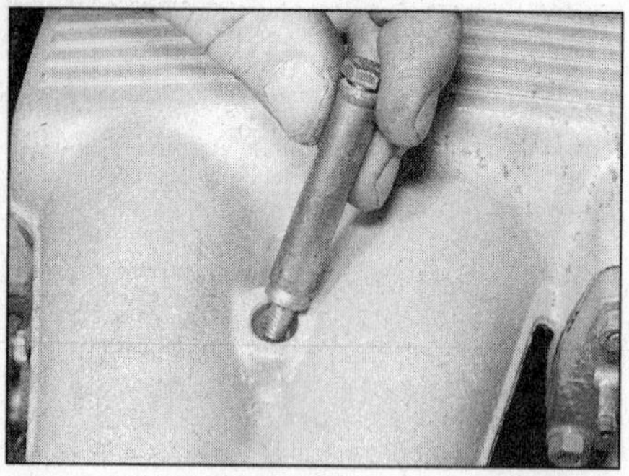

13.8a Removing an inlet manifold upper section securing bolt - M40 engine

13.8b Lifting off the upper section of the inlet manifold - M40 engine

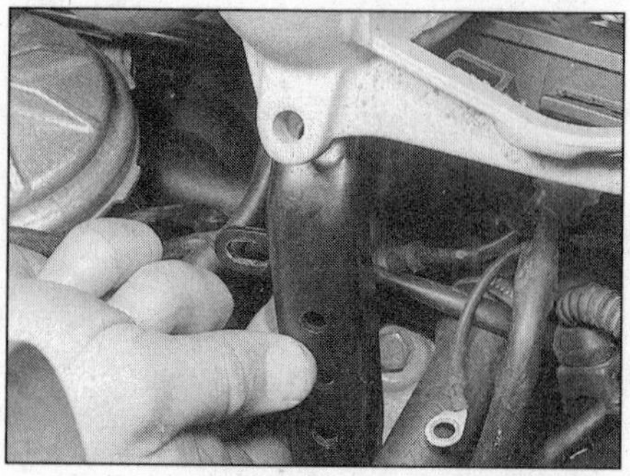

13.15 Removing the manifold support bracket - M40 engine

**4** Disconnect the throttle cable from the throttle linkage on the throttle body with reference to Section 4.

**5** Disconnect the wiring plug from the throttle position sensor.

**6** Where applicable, disconnect the coolant hoses from the throttle body. Be prepared for coolant spillage, and clamp or plug the hoses to prevent further coolant loss.

**7** Disconnect any vacuum and breather hoses from the throttle body and the upper section of the manifold, noting their locations to ensure correct refitting.

**8** Unscrew the securing nuts and bolts, and lift off the upper section of the manifold **(see illustrations)**. Recover the gaskets.

### Refitting

**9** Refitting is a reversal of removal, bearing in mind the following points.

*a) Use new gaskets.*
*b) Ensure that all hoses are connected to their correct locations as noted before removal.*
*c) Reconnect and if necessary adjust the throttle cable with reference to Section 4.*
*d) Where applicable, on completion check the coolant level as described in "Weekly Checks".*

## Inlet manifold lower section - M40 engine

**Note:** *A new gasket will be required on refitting.*

### Removal

**10** Depressurise the fuel system as described in Section 7, then disconnect the battery negative lead.

**11** Remove the upper section of the manifold as described previously in this Section.

**12** Pull up the wiring ducting to release the wiring plugs from the fuel injectors.

**13** Loosen the hose clips, and disconnect the fuel feed and return hoses from the fuel rail. Be prepared for fuel spillage, and take adequate fire precautions. Plug the open ends of the pipes and hoses to prevent dirt entry and further fuel spillage.

**14** Disconnect the vacuum hose from the fuel pressure regulator.

**15** Unscrew the securing bolts and remove the manifold support bracket **(see illustration)**. Note the locations of any wiring or hose brackets attached to the support bracket.

**16** Disconnect and release any remaining hoses and wiring looms from the manifold, noting their locations and routing to ensure correct refitting.

**17** Unscrew the securing nuts, and withdraw the manifold from the cylinder head **(see illustration)**. Recover the gasket.

### Refitting

**18** Refitting is a reversal of removal, bearing in mind the following points.

*a) Fit the manifold using a new gasket, and tighten the nuts to the specified torque.*
*b) Ensure that all wiring and hoses are correctly routed and reconnected as noted before removal.*
*c) Refit the upper section of the manifold as described previously in this Section.*
*d) On completion, pressurise the fuel system (refit the fuel pump fuse and switch on the ignition) and check for leaks before starting the engine.*

## Inlet manifold upper section - M42 engine

**Note:** *New gaskets will be required on refitting.*

### Removal

**19** Proceed as described in paragraphs 1 and 2.

**20** Where applicable, unscrew the bolt securing the charcoal canister hose to the airflow meter assembly.

**21** Loosen the clamp screw securing the air inlet trunking to the throttle body.

**22** Remove the upper section of the air cleaner, complete with the airflow meter and the air inlet trunking as described in Section 12.

**23** Unbolt the rear manifold support bracket **(see illustration)**.

**24** Disconnect the idle speed control valve hose from the rear of the manifold.

**25** Loosen the nut securing the manifold to the front support bracket **(see illustration)**.

**26** Disconnect the throttle cable from the throttle linkage at the throttle body with reference to Section 4.

**27** Disconnect the throttle position sensor wiring plug.

**28** Disconnect the vacuum hoses from the throttle body.

**29** Disconnect the vacuum hose from the fuel pressure regulator.

**30** Disconnect the coolant hoses from the

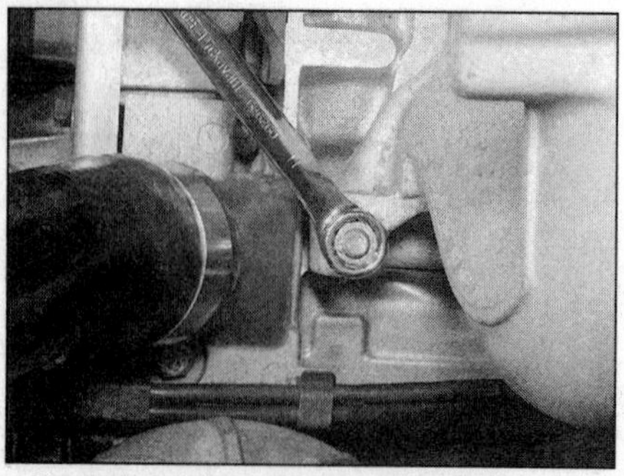

13.17 Unscrewing a manifold lower section securing nut - M40 engine

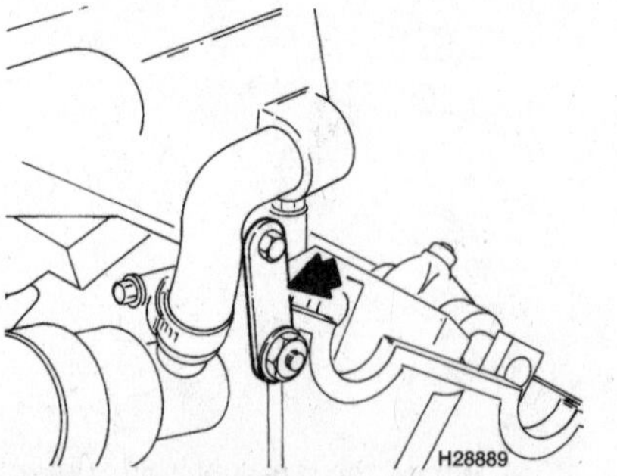


13.23 Inlet manifold upper section rear support bracket (arrowed) - M42 engine

13.25 Loosen the manifold-to-front support bracket nut (arrowed) - M42 engine

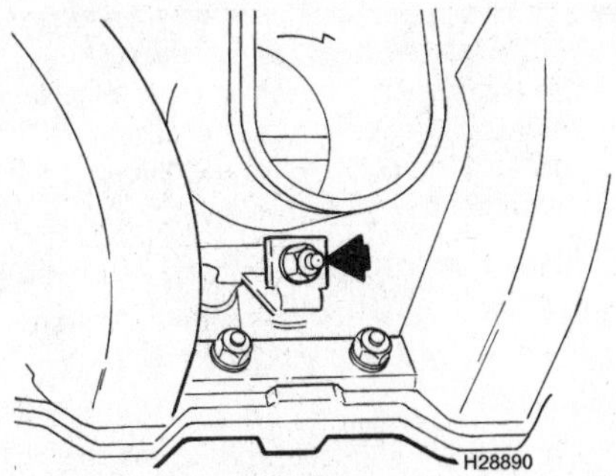


13.31 Throttle body heater securing nut (arrowed) - M42 engine

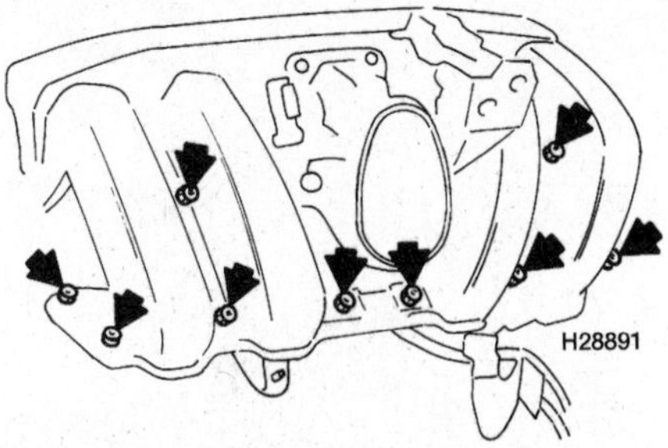


13.33 Inlet manifold upper section nuts and bolts (arrowed) - M42 engine

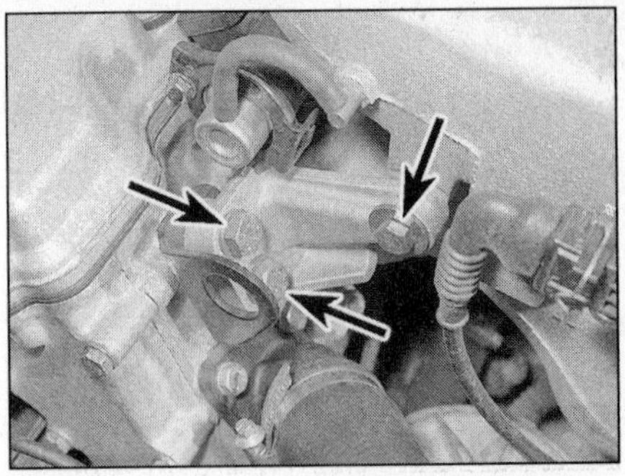

13.47 Inlet manifold upper section support bracket bolts (arrowed) - M43 engine

throttle body. Be prepared for coolant spillage, and clamp the open ends of the hoses to prevent further coolant loss.

**31** Where applicable, unscrew the nut securing the throttle body heater **(see illustration)**.

**32** Disconnect and release any remaining hoses and wiring looms from the manifold, noting their locations and routing to ensure correct refitting.

**33** Unscrew the securing nuts/bolts and lift off the upper section of the inlet manifold **(see illustration)**. Recover the gasket.

### Refitting

**34** Refitting is a reversal of removal, bearing in mind the following points.

a) *Use new gaskets.*
b) *Ensure that the upper section of the manifold engages securely on the dowels.*
c) *Ensure that all hoses are connected to their correct locations as noted before removal.*
d) *Reconnect and if necessary adjust the throttle cable with reference to Section 4.*
e) *Where applicable, on completion check the coolant level as described in "Weekly Checks".*

## Inlet manifold lower section - M42 engine

**Note:** *A new gasket will be required on refitting.*

### Removal

**35** Depressurise the fuel system as described in Section 7, then disconnect the battery negative lead.

**36** Remove the upper section of the manifold as described previously in this Section.

**37** Pull up the wiring ducting to release the wiring plugs from the fuel injectors. Move the wiring ducting to one side, clear of the working area.

**38** Loosen the hose clips, and disconnect the fuel feed and return hoses from the fuel rail. Be prepared for fuel spillage, and take adequate fire precautions. Plug the open ends of the pipes and hoses to prevent dirt entry and further fuel spillage.

**39** Where applicable, unscrew the clamp bolt securing the fuel pipes to the manifold bracket.

**40** Where applicable, unbolt the manifold support bracket.

**41** Disconnect and release any remaining hoses and wiring looms from the manifold, noting their locations and routing to ensure correct refitting.

**42** Unscrew the securing nuts and withdraw the manifold from the cylinder head. Recover the gasket.

### Refitting

**43** Refitting is a reversal of removal, bearing in mind the following points.

a) *Fit the manifold using a new gasket, and tighten the securing nuts to the specified torque. Ensure that the manifold engages correctly with the locating dowels.*
b) *Ensure that all wiring and hoses are correctly routed and reconnected as noted before removal.*
c) *Refit the upper section of the manifold as described previously in this Section.*
d) *On completion, pressurise the fuel system (refit the fuel pump fuse and switch on the ignition) and check for leaks before starting the engine.*

## Inlet manifold upper section - M43 engine

**Note:** *A new manifold gasket and new pressure control valve seals will be required on refitting.*

### Removal

**44** Proceed as described in paragraphs 1 and 2.

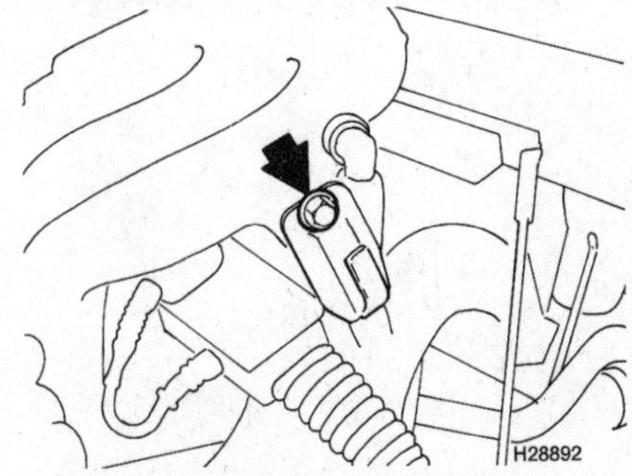


13.54 Unbolt the rear manifold support bracket (arrowed) - M43 engine

**45** Disconnect the throttle cable from the throttle linkage on the throttle body, with reference to Section 4.

**46** Drain the cooling system as described in Chapter 1.

**47** Unbolt the front manifold support bracket from the manifold and the cylinder head **(see illustration)**. Note that two of the bolts also secure the engine lifting bracket.

**48** Disconnect the vacuum hose from the front of the manifold.

**49** Slacken the clamp screw, and disconnect the inlet air trunking from the throttle body.

**50** Disconnect the throttle position sensor wiring plug.

**51** Disconnect the coolant hose(s) from the throttle body. Be prepared for coolant spillage, and clamp the open ends of the hoses to prevent further coolant loss.

**52** Disconnect the remaining hoses from the throttle body, noting their locations to ensure correct refitting.

**53** Unclip the bracket securing the cylinder head cover breather hose, and lift the hose clear of the manifold.

**54** Unbolt the rear manifold support bracket **(see illustration)**.

**55** Disconnect the idle speed control valve hose from the rear of the upper section of the manifold.

**56** Disconnect the vacuum hose from the brake servo.

**57** Disconnect the vacuum hose from the vacuum reservoir, and unclip the hose from the bracket on the upper section of the manifold **(see illustration)**.

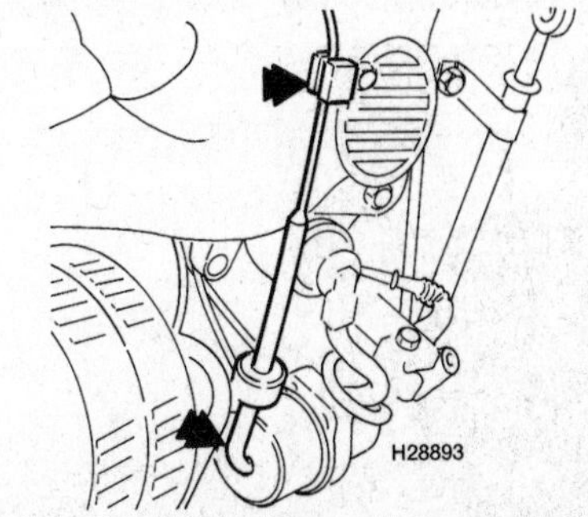


13.57 Disconnect the hose from the vacuum reservoir and unclip the hose from the bracket - M43 engine

4A

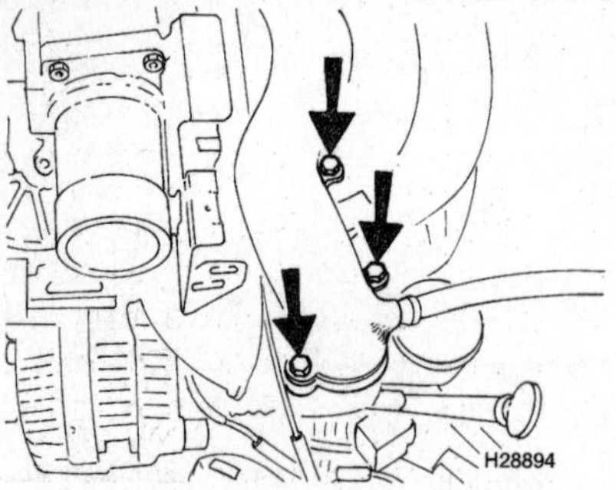


**13.58 Inlet manifold upper section securing nuts/bolts (arrowed) - M43 engine**

**58** Unscrew the securing nuts/bolts, and lift off the upper section of the manifold **(see illustration)**.

**59** Remove the flange for the DISA (variable length inlet tract system) pressure control valve. Recover the seals.

### Refitting

**60** Refitting is a reversal of removal, bearing in mind the following points.

a) *Use new seals when refitting the pressure control valve. Make sure that the valve and the seals locate over the studs in the lower section of the manifold.*
b) *Use a new gasket when refitting the upper section of the manifold.*
c) *Ensure that all wires and hoses are correctly routed and reconnected as noted before removal.*
d) *Reconnect and if necessary adjust the throttle cable with reference to Section 4.*
e) *On completion, refill the cooling system as described in Chapter 1.*

## Inlet manifold lower section - M43 engine

**Note:** *A new manifold gasket and new pressure control valve seals will be required on refitting.*

### Removal

**61** Depressurise the fuel system as described in Section 7, then disconnect the battery negative lead.

**62** Remove the upper section of the manifold as described previously in this Section.

**63** Release the engine wiring harness from the lower section of the manifold.

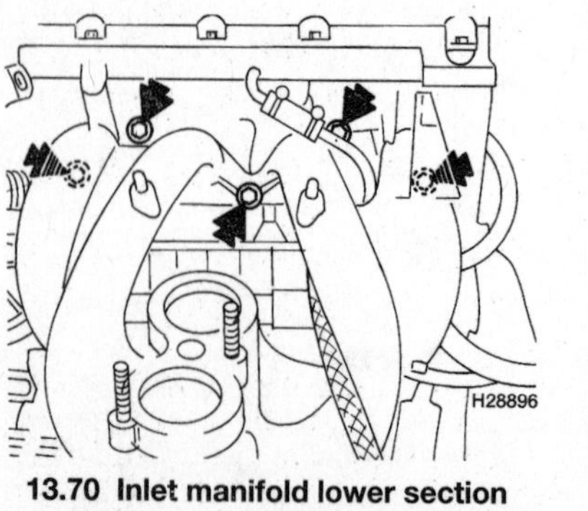


**13.70 Inlet manifold lower section securing nuts (arrowed) - M43 engine**

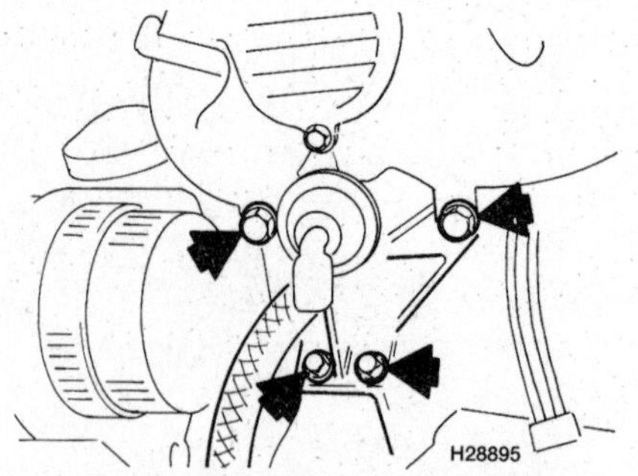


**13.67 Manifold support bracket securing bolts (arrowed) - M43 engine**

**64** Remove the fuel injectors as described in Section 12.

**65** Unscrew the bolt securing the dipstick tube support bracket to the manifold.

**66** Disconnect the vacuum hose from the DISA (variable length inlet tract system) actuator, then unscrew the bolt and withdraw the vacuum reservoir from the bracket under the manifold.

**67** Unbolt and remove the manifold support bracket **(see illustration)**.

**68** Disconnect and release any remaining hoses and wiring looms from the manifold, noting their locations and routing to ensure correct refitting.

**69** Disconnect the coolant hose from the flange for the DISA (variable length inlet tract system) pressure control valve.

**70** Unscrew the securing nuts, and lift the lower section of the manifold from the cylinder head **(see illustration)**. Recover the gasket.

### Refitting

**71** Refitting is a reversal of removal, bearing in mind the following points.

a) *Use a new gasket when refitting the lower section of the manifold, and tighten the manifold securing nuts to the specified torque.*
b) *Use new seals either side of the pressure control valve. Make sure that the valve and the seals locate over the studs in the lower section of the manifold.*
c) *Ensure that all wiring and hoses are correctly routed and reconnected as noted before removal.*
d) *Refit the fuel injectors (see Section 12).*

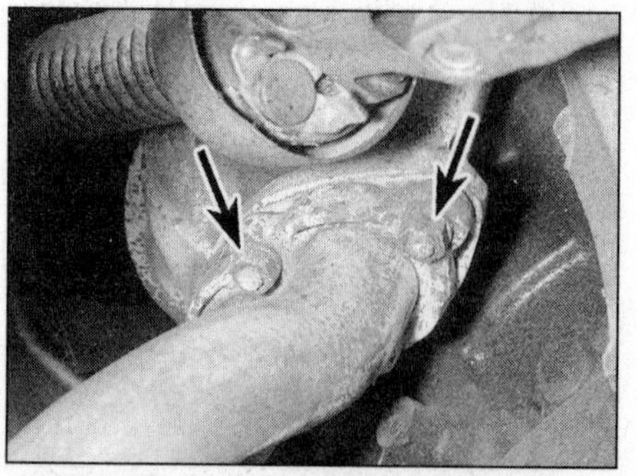

**13.73 Two of the exhaust front section nuts (arrowed) - M43 engine model**

e) *Refit the upper section of the manifold as described previously in this Section.*
f) *On completion, pressurise the fuel system (refit the fuel pump fuse and switch on the ignition) and check for leaks before starting the engine.*

## Exhaust manifold

**Note:** *New gaskets and new manifold securing nuts will be required on refitting.*

### Removal

**72** To improve access, jack up the front of the vehicle and support securely on axle stands (see *"Jacking and vehicle support"*).

**73** Working underneath the vehicle, unscrew the nuts securing the exhaust front section to the manifold **(see illustration)**.

**74** Working at the gearbox/transmission exhaust bracket, unscrew the bolt(s) securing the two exhaust mounting clamp halves together.

**75** Loosen the bolt securing the clamp halves to the bracket on the gearbox/transmission, then lower the exhaust downpipes down from the manifold studs. Recover the gasket(s).

**76** Working in the engine compartment, unscrew the manifold securing nuts.

**77** Withdraw the manifold from the studs and recover the gasket(s).

**78** It is possible that some of the manifold studs may be unscrewed from the cylinder head when the manifold securing nuts are unscrewed. In this event, the studs should be screwed back into the cylinder head once the manifolds have been removed, using two manifold nuts locked together.

### Refitting

**79** Refitting is a reversal of removal, but use new gaskets and new manifold securing nuts.

## 14 Exhaust system - general information, removal and refitting

## General information

**1** The original equipment exhaust system consists of two sections. The front section incorporates the catalytic converter and the oxygen sensor (where applicable) and the centre expansion box. The rear section incorporates the rear silencer box.

**2** The system is suspended throughout its length by rubber mountings and a metal bracket.

## Complete system

**Note:** *New exhaust front section-to-manifold gaskets and securing nuts will be required on refitting.*

### Removal

**3** Jack up the vehicle and support securely on axle stands (see *"Jacking and vehicle support"*).

**4** On models with a catalytic converter, turn

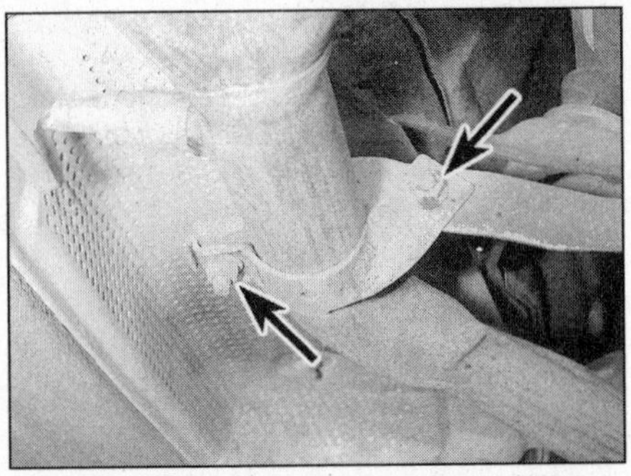

**14.6 Unscrew the exhaust clamp nuts and bolts (arrowed) - M43 engine model**

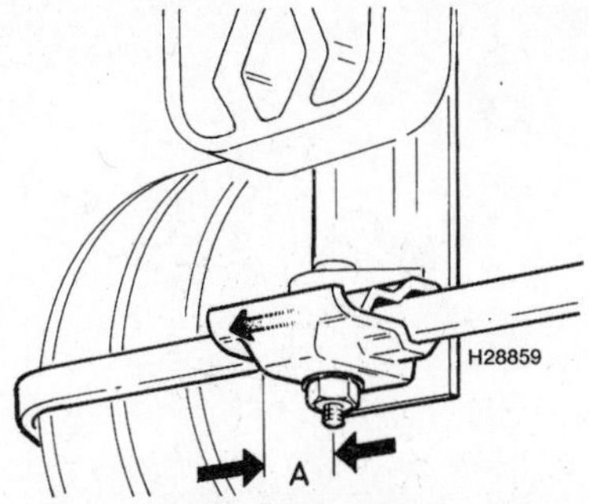


**14.10a Preload the system by sliding the clamps to the rear of the silencer box**
*A = 15.0 mm*

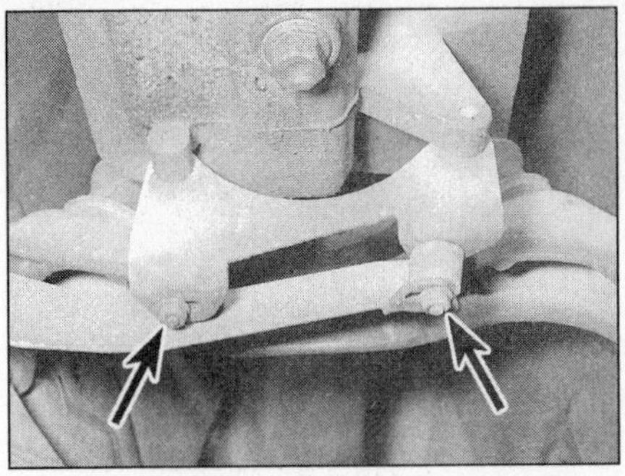

**14.10b Slacken the nuts (arrowed) and slide the bracket to release any tension on the exhaust system**

the securing ring, and disconnect the oxygen sensor wiring connector at the bracket under the vehicle.

**5** Unscrew the securing nuts, and disconnect the exhaust front sections from the manifold. Recover the gasket.

**6** Unscrew the clamp bolt securing the two halves of the gearbox/transmission exhaust mounting bracket together, then unscrew the clamp pivot bolt, and pivot the clamp halves away from the exhaust system **(see illustration)**.

**7** Slide the rear exhaust mounting rubbers from the brackets on the exhaust system.

**8** Working at the rear of the exhaust system, unscrew the nuts securing the rear silencer box mounting clamps.

**9** Withdraw the complete exhaust system from under the vehicle.

### Refitting

**10** Refitting is a reversal of removal, bearing in mind the following points **(see illustrations)**.

*a) Use new gaskets when reconnecting the exhaust front section to the manifold. Also use new nuts, and coat the threads of the new nuts with copper grease.*

*b) When refitting the rear silencer box clamps, slide the clamps onto the silencer box and allow the system to hang so that the mountings are free from tension, then slide the clamps towards the rear of the silencer by 15.0 mm to give a preload, forcing the system towards the front of the vehicle.*

*c) Check the position of the tailpipes in relation to the cut-out in the rear valence, and if necessary adjust the exhaust mountings to give sufficient clearance between the system and the valence.*

*d) Once the mountings have been reconnected and tightened, slacken the two nuts and bolts securing the exhaust mounting bracket to the gearbox/transmission bracket, and if necessary slide the bracket within the elongated holes to release any sideways tension on the system. Once the system is correctly positioned, tighten the nuts and bolts.*

## Front section

### Removal

**11** If desired, the exhaust front section can be removed leaving the rear section in place.

**12** Follow the procedure in paragraphs 3 to 7.

**13** Counterhold the bolts, and unscrew the clamp nuts securing the exhaust front section to the rear section, then slide the front section from the rear section and remove the front section from under the vehicle.

### Refitting

**14** Refer to paragraph 10.

## Rear section

### Removal

**15** Counterhold the bolts, and unscrew the clamp nuts securing the exhaust front section to the rear section.

**16** Working at the rear of the exhaust system, unscrew the nuts securing the rear silencer box mounting clamps, then slide the rear section from the front section and withdraw the rear section from under the vehicle.

### Refitting

**17** Refitting is a reversal of removal, but coat the threads of the clamp mounting nuts and bolts with a little copper grease before fitting, and preload the rear mounting as described in paragraph 10b.

# Chapter 4 Part B:
# 6-cylinder engine fuel and exhaust systems

## Contents



## Degrees of difficulty

| | | | | |
|---|---|---|---|---|
| **Easy,** suitable for novice with little experience | **Fairly easy,** suitable for beginner with some experience | **Fairly difficult,** suitable for competent DIY mechanic | **Difficult,** suitable for experienced DIY mechanic | **Very difficult,** suitable for expert DIY or professional |

## Specifications

### System type

| | |
|---|---|
| Models up to 1992 | Bosch Motronic M3.1 sequential injection |
| Models from 1993 | Bosch Motronic M3.3.1 sequential injection or Siemens MS40 engine management |

### Fuel system data

| | |
|---|---|
| Fuel pump type | Electric, immersed in tank |
| Fuel pressure regulator rating | 3.0 ± 0.06 bar |
| Specified idle speed | 700 ± 40 rpm (not adjustable - controlled by ECU) |
| Specified idle mixture CO content: | |
| Models without catalytic converter | 0.7 ± 0.5% |
| Models with catalytic converter | 0.5 to 1.5% (not adjustable - controlled by ECU) |

### Recommended fuel

| | |
|---|---|
| Models without catalytic converter | 95 RON unleaded (UK unleaded premium) or 98 RON leaded (UK 4-star) |
| Models with catalytic converter | 95 RON unleaded (UK unleaded premium). Leaded fuel **must not** be used |

### Torque wrench settings

| Torque wrench settings | Nm | lbf ft |
|---|---|---|
| Inlet manifold nuts: | | |
| M6 nuts | 10 | 7 |
| M7 nuts | 15 | 11 |
| M8 nuts | 22 | 16 |
| Exhaust manifold nuts: | | |
| M6 nuts | 10 | 7 |
| M7 nuts | 20 | 15 |
| M8 nuts | 22 | 16 |
| Crankshaft position sensor bolt | 7 | 5 |
| Camshaft position sensor bolt | 7 | 5 |
| Air temperature sensor to inlet manifold | 13 | 10 |
| Fuel rail-to-inlet manifold bolts | 10 | 7 |
| Fuel tank mounting bolts | 23 | 17 |
| Fuel tank retaining strap bolts | 8 | 6 |

## 1 General information and precautions

### General information

The fuel supply system consists of a fuel tank (which is mounted under the rear of the vehicle, with an electric fuel pump immersed in it), a fuel filter, fuel feed and return lines. The fuel pump supplies fuel to the fuel rail, which acts as a reservoir for the six fuel injectors which inject fuel into the inlet tracts. The fuel filter incorporated in the feed line from the pump to the fuel rail ensures that the fuel supplied to the injectors is clean.

Refer to Section 6 for further information on the operation of the fuel injection system, and to Section 14 for information on the exhaust system.

### Precautions

***Warning: Many of the procedures in this Chapter require the disconnection of fuel lines and connections, which may result in some fuel spillage. Before carrying out any operation on the fuel system, refer to the precautions given in "Safety first!", and follow then implicitly. Petrol is a highly dangerous and volatile liquid, and the precautions necessary when handling it cannot be overstressed.***

***Warning: Residual pressure will remain in the fuel lines long after the vehicle was last used. When disconnecting any fuel line, first depressurise the fuel system as described in Section 7.***

## 2 Air cleaner assembly - removal and refitting

### Removal

**1** Remove the air mass meter, as described in Section 12. Alternatively, disconnect the wiring plug from the air mass meter, slacken

**2.1a Disconnect the air mass meter wiring plug**

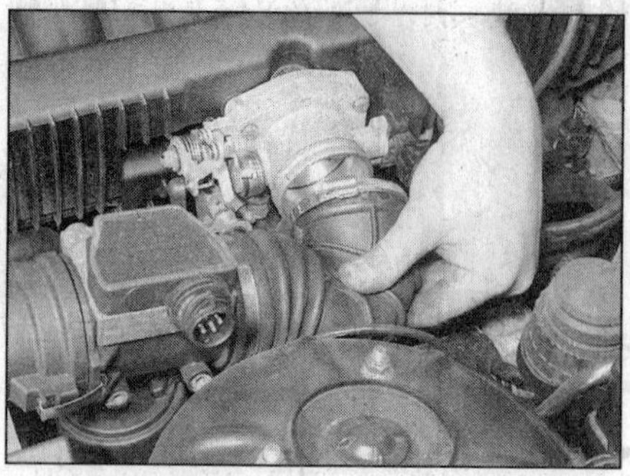

**2.1b Disconnect the air trunking from the throttle body**

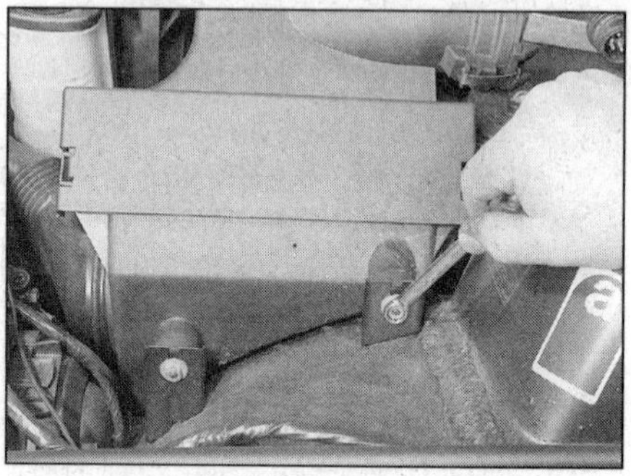

**2.2a Loosen the air cleaner securing nuts . . .**

**2.2b . . . then pull the casing upwards**

the clip securing the air trunking to the throttle body, and leave the air mass meter attached to the air cleaner casing **(see illustrations)**.

**2** Loosen the two nuts securing the air cleaner casing to the mounting bracket, then pull the casing upwards, and unclip the inlet duct from the front body panel **(see illustrations)**.

**Note:** *If the inlet duct cannot be released from the front body panel, unbolt the alternator air ducting from the top of the front body panel, and reach down behind the front grille panel to for access to the air inlet duct securing clip.*

**3** Where applicable, remove the securing bolt, and withdraw the coolant bypass valve from the air cleaner casing, leaving the coolant hoses connected **(see illustration)**.

**4** If the assembly is being removed complete with the air trunking and air mass meter, disconnect the breather hoses from the bottom of the air trunking, then withdraw the assembly from the engine compartment.

### Refitting

**5** Refitting is a reversal of removal, but ensure that the lower mounting engages with the plastic lug on the body, and where applicable refit the air mass meter with reference to Section 12 **(see illustration)**.

## 3 Fuel tank - removal and refitting

### Removal

**Note:** *New fuel hose clips will be required on refitting.*

**1** Disconnect the battery negative lead.

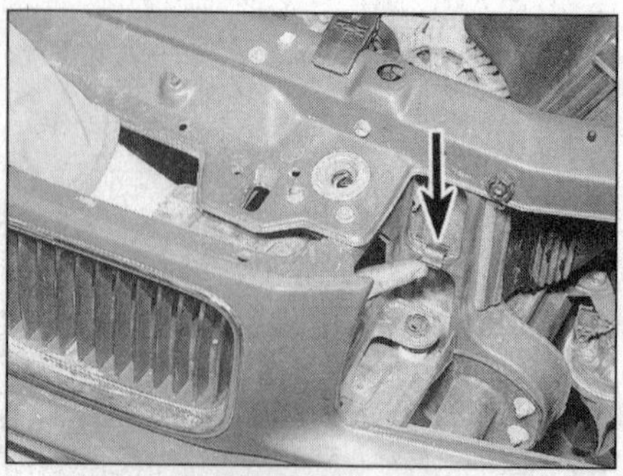

**2.2c Reach behind the grille to depress the air intake duct securing clip (arrowed) - viewed with headlight removed for clarity**

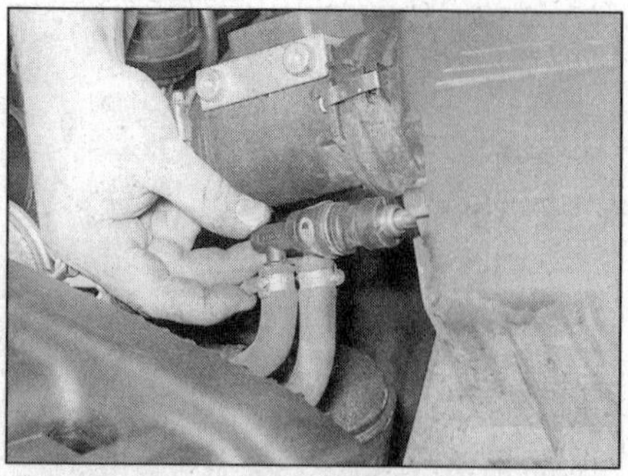

**2.3 Withdrawing the coolant bypass valve from the air cleaner casing**

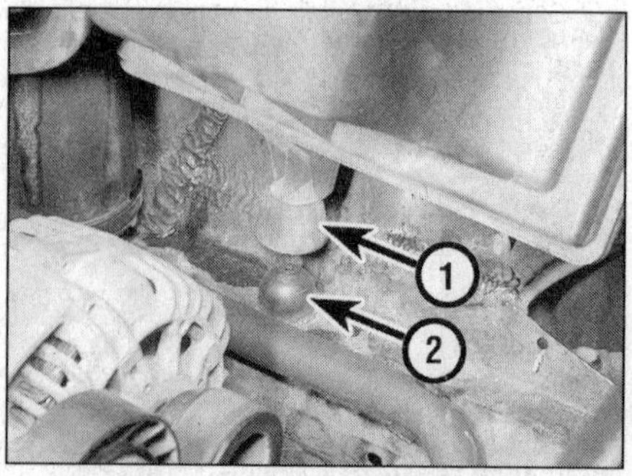


**2.5 Ensure that the air cleaner lower mounting (1) engages with the lug (2) on the body**

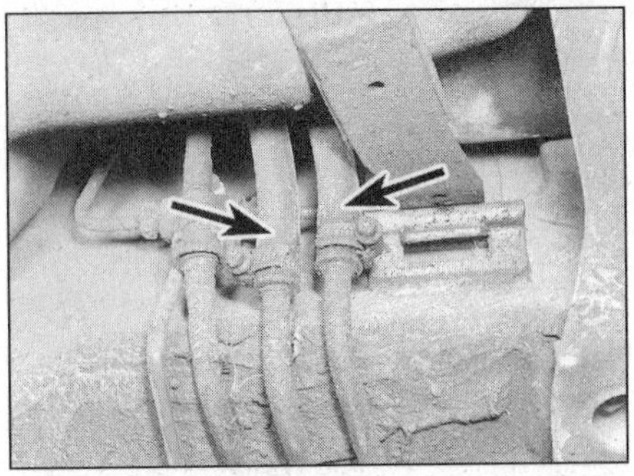

**3.5 Disconnect the fuel hoses (arrowed)**

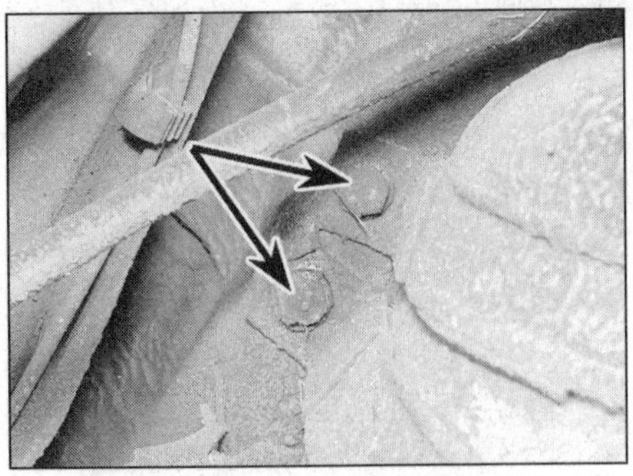

**3.11a Left-hand fuel tank strap securing bolts (arrowed)**

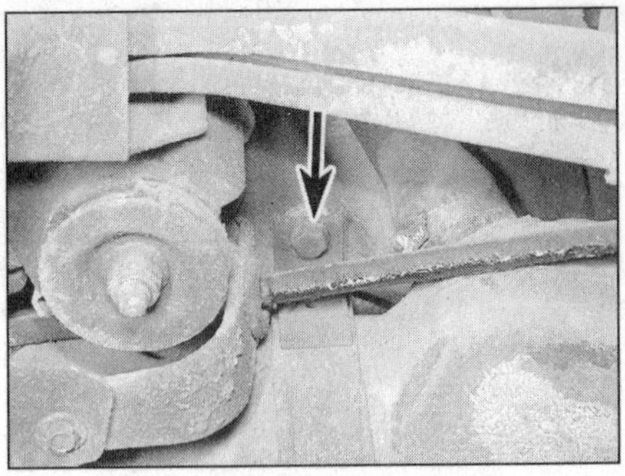

**3.11b Right-hand fuel tank strap securing bolt (arrowed)**

**2** Before removing the fuel pump/fuel gauge sender unit, all fuel should be drained from the fuel tank. Since a fuel tank drain plug is not provided, it is preferable to carry out the removal operation when the tank is nearly empty. Before proceeding, disconnect the battery negative lead and syphon or hand-pump the remaining fuel from the tank.

**3** Working under the rear seats, disconnect the wiring plugs and the fuel hoses from the fuel pump and fuel gauge senders, with reference to Sections 8 and 9.

**4** Jack up the rear of the vehicle and support securely on axle stands (see *"Jacking and vehicle support"*).

**5** Working under the rear of the vehicle, disconnect the two fuel hoses from the pipes in front of the fuel tank **(see illustration)**. Be prepared for fuel spillage, and clamp or plug the open ends of the hoses and pipes to prevent dirt entry and further fuel spillage.

**6** Remove the rear section of the exhaust system as described in Section 14.

**7** Remove the propeller shaft (see Chapter 8).

**8** Disconnect the handbrake cables from the handbrake lever as described in Chapter 9, then release the cables from the clips under the vehicle, and pull them through the retaining clips at the rear of the fuel tank.

**9** Loosen the hose clip, and disconnect the fuel filler hose from the right-hand side of the fuel tank.

**10** Support the fuel tank using a trolley jack and interposed block of wood.

**11** Unscrew the fuel tank strap securing bolts, noting the locations of any washers to ensure correct refitting, then pivot the strap down, and lower the tank sufficiently to disconnect the vent pipes from the top of the tank **(see illustrations)**.

**12** Disconnect the vent pipes, and withdraw the tank from under the rear of the vehicle.

### Refitting

**13** Refitting is a reversal of removal, bearing in mind the following points.

*a) Ensure that any washers are fitted to the fuel tank strap bolts as noted before removal.*

*b) Reconnect and adjust the handbrake cables as described in Chapter 9.*

*c) Refit the propeller shaft (see Chapter 8).*

*d) Use new hose clips when reconnecting the fuel hoses.*

*e) On completion, before starting the engine, check that the fuel tank is correctly earthed by measuring the electrical resistance between the tank filler pipe earth and the rear wheel hub - the reading should be approximately 0.6 ohms. Fill the tank with at least 5 litres of fuel before attempting to start the engine.*

## 4 Throttle cable - removal, refitting and adjustment

### Removal

**1** Working in the engine compartment, depress the retaining tangs, and release the cable end fitting from the bracket on the end of the throttle lever. Prise the end fitting from the end of the cable **(see illustrations)**.

**2** Prise the cable grommet from the bracket on the throttle body, and withdraw the cable through the bracket to free it from the throttle body.

**3** Working inside the vehicle, remove the two screws, and withdraw the driver's side lower facia panel for access to the pedals.

**4** Pull the end of the throttle cable from the grommet in the end of the throttle cable operating lever **(see illustration)**.

**5** Working on the interior side of the engine compartment bulkhead, depress the retaining clip and push the cable guide from the bulkhead into the engine compartment.

**6** Make a careful note of the routing of the cable, then release it from any clips and brackets, and withdraw the cable assembly from the engine compartment.

### Refitting

**7** Refitting is a reversal of removal, bearing in mind the following points.

*a) Ensure that the cable is correctly routed as noted before removal.*

*b) Check the condition of the grommet in the end of the throttle cable operating lever, and renew if necessary.*

*c) On completion check the cable adjustment as described in the following paragraphs.*

### Adjustment

#### Models with manual gearbox

**8** Check that the accelerator pedal is in the rest position, against the pedal idle stop.



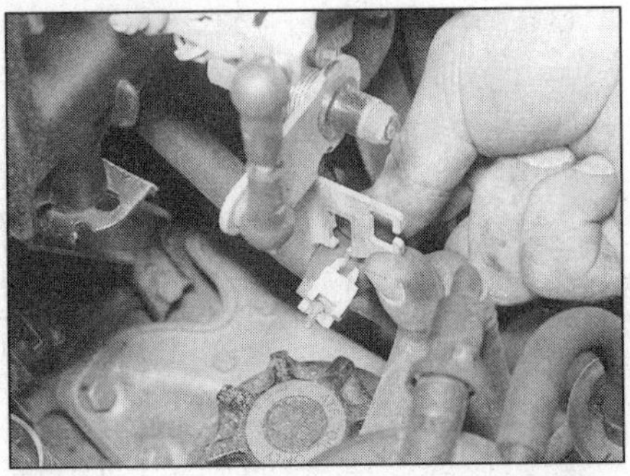

**4.1a Release the cable end fitting from the bracket . . .**

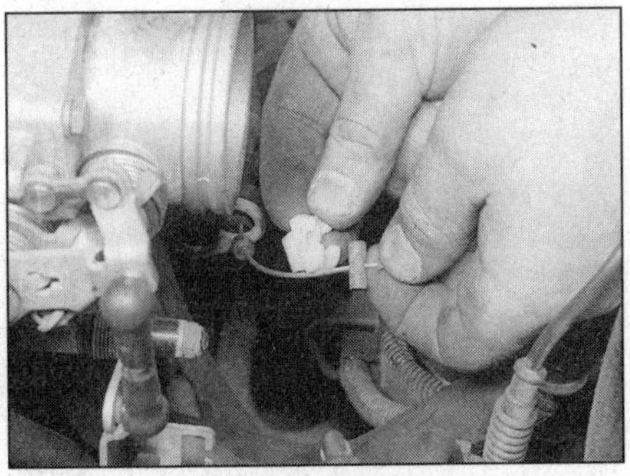

**4.1b . . . then prise the end fitting from the cable**

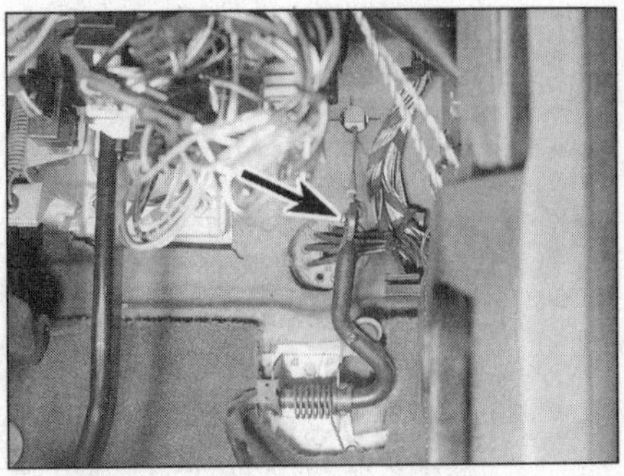

**4.4 Pull the end of the throttle cable from the grommet (arrowed)**

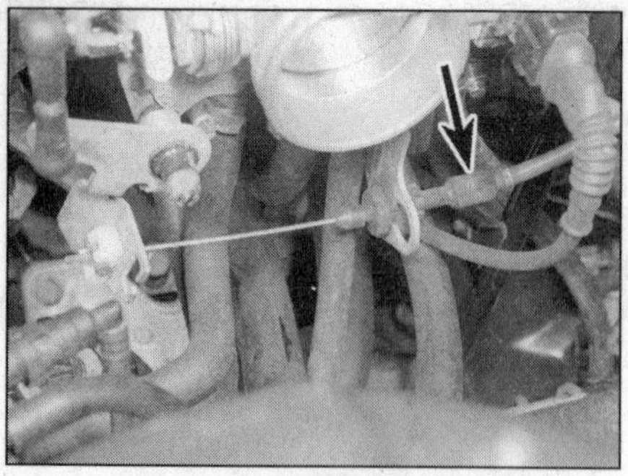

4.10 Throttle cable adjuster screw (arrowed)

9 Check that the throttle lever on the throttle body is in the rest (idle) position.

10 Turn the cable adjuster screw at the throttle body bracket to eliminate free-play in the cable **(see illustration)**.

11 Have an assistant fully depress the throttle pedal, and check that, with the pedal fully depressed, there is still 0.5 mm of free-play at the throttle valve in the throttle body.

12 If necessary, turn the pedal full-throttle stop (screwed into the floor) to give the specified free-play (see paragraph 11) at the throttle valve. On some models, it will be necessary to slacken a locknut before the full-throttle stop can be adjusted. Note that turning the full-throttle stop by 1.5 turns will adjust the throttle valve free-play by 0.5 mm.

13 Where applicable, tighten the full-throttle stop locknut on completion.

### Models with automatic transmission

14 At the time of writing, no information was available regarding throttle cable adjustment for models with automatic transmission. Consult a BMW dealer for advice.

## 5 Throttle pedal - removal and refitting

### *Pedal assembly*

***Warning: Once the throttle pedal has been removed, it <u>must</u> be renewed. Removal will damage the pedal retaining clips, and if the original pedal is refitted, it could work loose, causing an accident.***

#### Removal

1 Prise off the clip securing the top of the pedal to the throttle cable operating lever.

2 Press down on the carpet under the pedal, then bend back the lower pedal retaining clips, and lever the pedal upwards to release it from the floor **(see illustration)**. Discard the pedal - a new pedal must be used on refitting. Withdraw the pedal.

#### Refitting

3 Place the new pedal in position, engaging the top of the pedal with the throttle cable operating lever.

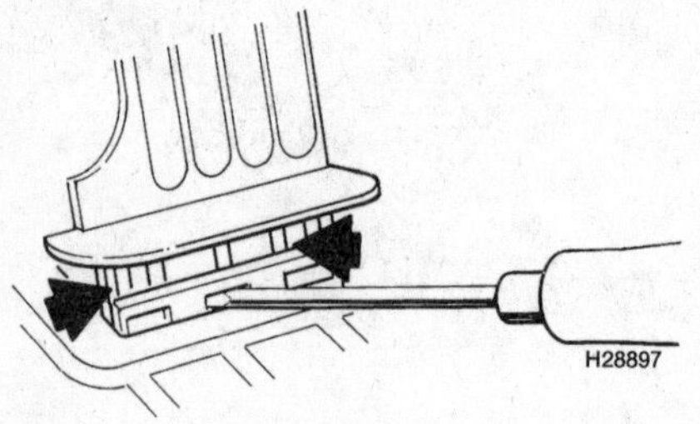


5.2 Releasing the throttle pedal from the floor

4 Push the pedal down to engage the lower retaining clips with the floor plate.

***Warning: Ensure that the retaining clips snap securely into place.***

5 Refit the clip to secure the pedal to the throttle cable operating lever.

6 Check the throttle cable adjustment as described in Section 4.

### *Throttle cable operating lever*

#### Removal

7 Working inside the vehicle, remove the two securing screws, and withdraw the driver's side lower facia panel for access to the pedals.

8 Pull the end of the throttle cable from the grommet in the end of the throttle cable operating lever.

9 Prise off the clip securing the top of the pedal assembly to the throttle cable operating lever.

10 Prise the locking clip from the end of the throttle cable operating lever pivot shaft, noting its orientation to ensure correct refitting.

11 Disconnect the return spring from the lever, then slide the lever to the left against the pressure of the return spring on the shaft, to free the right-hand end of the pivot shaft.

12 Withdraw the lever assembly.

#### Refitting

13 Refitting is a reversal of removal, bearing in mind the following points.

a) *Ensure that the return spring is correctly positioned on the lever.*
b) *Ensure that the locking clip is correctly fitted to the end of the lever pivot shaft, as noted before removal.*
c) *Ensure that the clip securing the pedal to the cable operating lever is correctly fitted.*
d) *Check the condition of the grommet in the end of the throttle cable operating lever, and renew if necessary.*
e) *On completion, check the cable adjustment as described in Section 4.*

## 6 Fuel injection system - general information

1 An integrated engine management system known as DME (Digital Motor Electronics) is fitted to all models, and the system controls all fuel injection and ignition system functions using a central ECU (Electronic Control Unit). A Bosch Motronic or Siemens engine management system may be used, depending on model, but in most respects the systems are similar (sensors and actuators are identical) - the only significant difference is in the ECU.

2 On most models, the system incorporates a closed-loop catalytic converter and an evaporative emission control system, and complies with the very latest emission control standards. Refer to Chapter 5B for information on the ignition side of the system; the fuel side of the system operates as follows.

3 The fuel pump (which is immersed in the fuel tank) supplies fuel from the tank to the fuel rail, via a filter. Fuel supply pressure is controlled by the pressure regulator in the fuel rail. When the optimum operating pressure of the fuel system is exceeded, the regulator allows excess fuel to return to the tank.

4 The electrical control system consists of the ECU, along with the following sensors:

a) *Air mass meter - informs the ECU of the mass of air entering the engine.*
b) *Throttle position sensor - informs the ECU of the throttle position, and the rate of throttle opening/closing.*
c) *Coolant temperature sensor - informs the ECU of engine temperature.*
d) *Inlet air temperature sensor - informs the ECU of the temperature of the air passing through the inlet manifold.*
e) *Crankshaft position sensor - informs the ECU of the crankshaft position and speed of rotation.*
f) *Camshaft position sensor - informs the ECU of the inlet camshaft position.*
g) *Oxygen sensor - informs the ECU of the oxygen content of the exhaust gases (explained in greater detail in Part C of this Chapter).*

5 All the above signals are analysed by the ECU which selects the fuelling response appropriate to those values. The ECU controls the fuel injectors (varying the pulse width - the length of time the injectors are held open - to provide a richer or weaker mixture, as appropriate). The mixture is constantly varied by the ECU, to provide the best setting for cranking, starting (with either a hot or cold engine), warm-up, idle, cruising and acceleration.

6 The ECU also has full control over the engine idle speed, via an auxiliary air valve which bypasses the throttle valve. When the throttle valve is closed, the ECU controls the

opening of the valve, which in turn regulates the amount of air entering the manifold, and so controls the idle speed.

**7** The ECU also controls the exhaust and evaporative emission control systems, which are described in detail in Part C of this Chapter.

**8** The throttle body is coolant heated, and on certain models, a thermostatic coolant bypass valve fitted in the air cleaner housing ensures that warm coolant reaches the throttle body quickly (before the thermostat opens) when the ambient air temperature is low.

**9** If there is an abnormality in any of the readings obtained from the sensors, the ECU enters its back-up mode. In this event, it ignores the abnormal sensor signal and assumes a pre-programmed value which will allow the engine to continue running (albeit at reduced efficiency). If the ECU enters this back-up mode, the relevant fault code will be stored in the ECU memory.

**10** If a fault is suspected, the vehicle should be taken to a BMW dealer at the earliest opportunity. A complete test of the engine management system can then be carried out, using a special electronic diagnostic test unit which is simply plugged into the system's diagnostic connector.

## 7 Fuel injection system - depressurisation and priming

### Depressurisation

**1** Remove the fuel pump fuse from the fusebox. The fuse is located in the engine compartment fusebox, and the exact location is given on the fusebox cover.

**2** Start the engine, and wait for it to stall. Switch off the ignition.

**3** Remove the fuel filler cap.

**4** The fuel system is now depressurised. **Note:** *Place a wad of rag around fuel lines before disconnecting, to prevent any residual fuel from spilling onto the engine.*

**5** Disconnect the battery negative lead before working on any part of the fuel system.

### Priming

**6** Refit the fuel pump fuse, then switch on the ignition and wait for a few seconds for the fuel pump to run, building up fuel pressure. Switch off the ignition unless the engine is to be started.

## 8 Fuel pump/fuel gauge sender unit - removal and refitting

***Warning: Refer to the warning notes in Section 1 before proceeding.***

**Note:** *A new sealing ring and a new locking ring must be used on refitting.*

**8.5 Withdraw the cover to expose the fuel pump/sender unit**

### Removal

**1** The fuel pump is integral with the right-hand fuel gauge sender, in the right-hand half of the fuel tank.

**2** Disconnect the battery negative lead.

**3** Before removing the fuel pump/fuel gauge sender unit, all fuel should be drained from the fuel tank. Since a fuel tank drain plug is not provided, it is preferable to carry out the removal operation when the tank is nearly empty. Before proceeding, disconnect the battery negative lead and syphon or hand-pump the remaining fuel from the tank.

**4** Remove the rear seat cushion with reference to Chapter 11.

**5** Lift up the floor insulation to expose the fuel pump/sender unit cover. Remove the securing screws and withdraw the cover from the floor **(see illustration)**.

**6** Disconnect the two wiring plugs from the fuel pump/sender unit.

**7** Loosen the hose clips, then disconnect the fuel hoses from the fuel pump/sender unit. Mark the hoses to ensure that they are correctly reconnected. Be prepared for fuel spillage.

**8** Unscrew the fuel/pump sender unit locking ring and remove it from the tank. This is best accomplished by using a large pair of grips to push on two opposite raised ribs on the locking ring. Alternatively, use two screwdrivers on the raised ribs, but take care not to damage the locking ring. Turn the ring anti-clockwise until it can be unscrewed by hand.

**9** Carefully lift the fuel pump/sender unit from

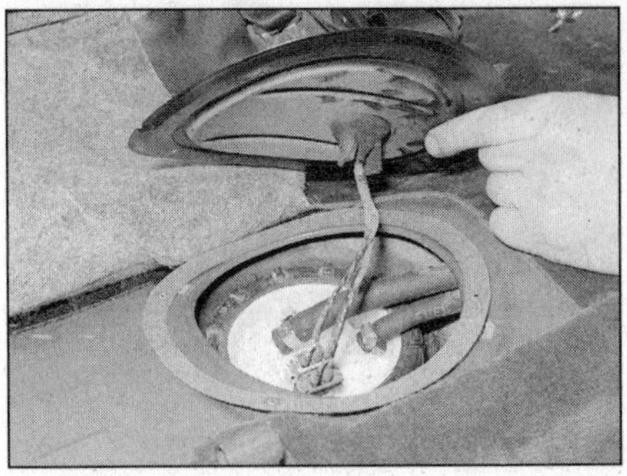

**8.9 Removing the fuel pump/sender unit**

the fuel tank, taking great care not to bend the sender unit float arm (gently push the float arm towards the unit if necessary). Recover the sealing ring **(see illustration)**.

### Refitting

**10** Before refitting, check the condition of the fuel pick-up strainer, and clean if necessary.

**11** Refitting is a reversal of removal, bearing in mind the following points.

*a) Use a new sealing ring and a new locking ring.*

*b) To allow the unit to pass through the aperture in the fuel tank, press the float arm against the fuel pick-up strainer.*

*c) When the unit is refitted, the raised ribs on the unit must align with the corresponding mark on the fuel tank.*

## 9 Fuel gauge sender unit - removal and refitting

4B

**1** Two fuel level sender units are fitted, one in each (left- and right-hand) half of the fuel tank.

**2** The right-hand sender unit is integral with the fuel pump, and removal and refitting are described in Section 8.

**3** Removal and refitting of the left-hand sender unit is also as described in Section 8, noting the following differences **(see illustrations)**.

*a) There is only one wiring plug.*

*b) The fuel return and pick-up pipes are pressed against the bottom of the fuel*

**9.3a Disconnecting the wiring plug from the left-hand fuel gauge sender unit**

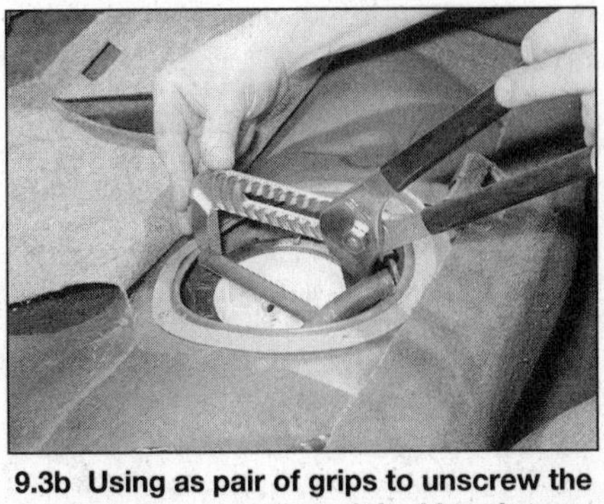

**9.3b Using as pair of grips to unscrew the fuel gauge sender unit locking ring**

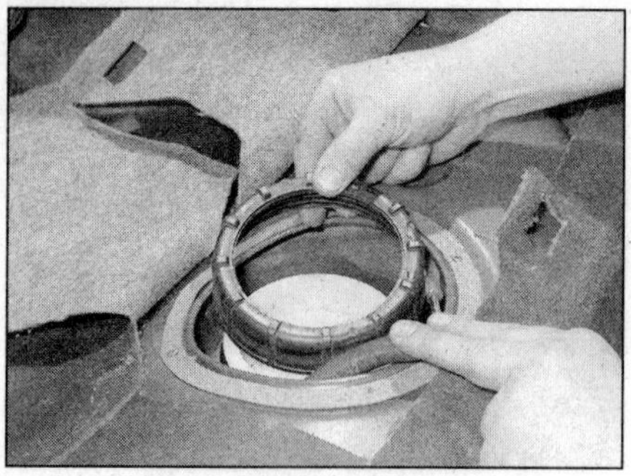

9.3c Remove the locking ring . . .

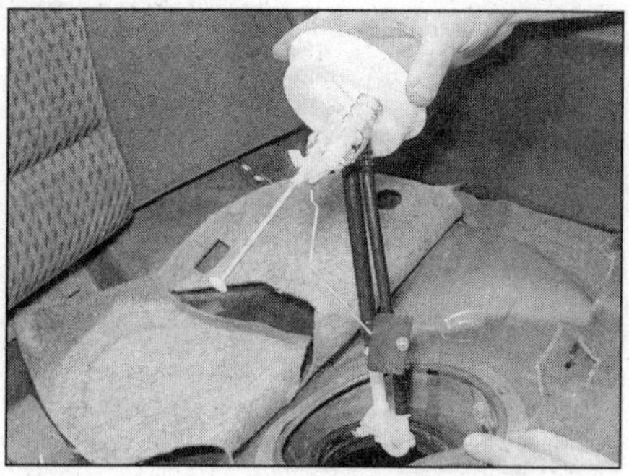

9.3d . . . then lift out the sender unit . . .

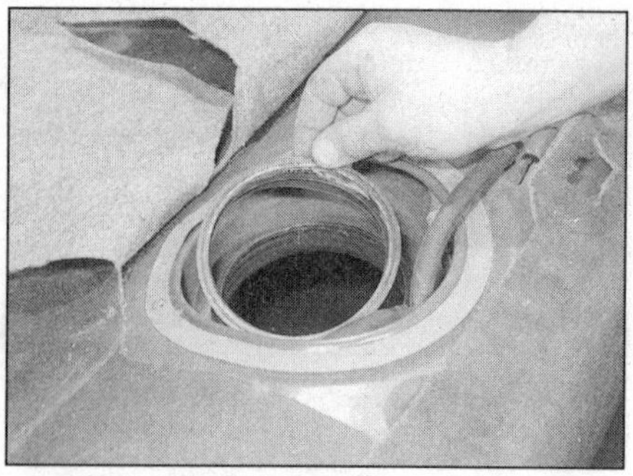

9.3e . . . and recover the sealing ring

*tank. When refitting the unit, check that the pipes are pressed firmly into position, and that the float arm is still free to move.*

## 10 Fuel injection system - testing and adjustment

### Testing

**1** If a fault appears in the fuel injection system, first ensure all the system wiring connectors are securely connected and free of corrosion. Ensure the fault is not due to poor maintenance; ie, check that the air cleaner filter element is clean, the spark plugs are in good condition and correctly gapped, the cylinder compression pressures are correct, and that the engine breather hoses are clear and undamaged, referring to Chapters 1, 2 and 5 for information.

**2** If these checks fail to reveal the cause of the problem, the vehicle should be taken to a BMW dealer for testing. A wiring block connector is incorporated in the engine management circuit, into which a special electronic diagnostic tester can be plugged. The connector is clipped to the right-hand suspension turret. The tester will locate the fault quickly and simply, alleviating the need to test all the system components individually, which is a time-consuming operation that also carries a risk of damaging the ECU.

### Adjustment

**3** Experienced home mechanics with a considerable amount of skill and equipment (including a tachometer and an accurately calibrated exhaust gas analyser) may be able to check the exhaust CO level and the idle speed. However, if these are found to be in need of adjustment, the car *must* be taken to a BMW dealer for further testing.

**4** To adjust the CO level or idle speed, special diagnostic equipment is required.

## 11 Throttle body - removal and refitting

**Note:** *A new sealing ring must be used on refitting.*

### Removal

**1** Remove the air mass meter as described in Section 12.

**2** Disconnect the throttle cable from the throttle linkage, and move the cable to one side, with reference to Section 4.

**3** Loosen the hose clips, and disconnect the coolant hoses from the bottom of the throttle body. Be prepared for coolant spillage, and plug or clamp the open ends of the hoses.

**4** Disconnect the wiring plug from the throttle position sensor.

**5** Unscrew the securing bolts, and remove the throttle body from the inlet manifold **(see illustration)**.

**6** Recover the sealing ring.

### Refitting

**7** Refitting is a reversal of removal, but use a new sealing ring, and refit the air mass meter with reference to Section 12 **(see illustration)**.

## 12 Fuel injection system components - removal and refitting

### Electronic control unit (ECU)

#### Removal

**1** Disconnect the battery negative lead.

**2** Where necessary, for improved access, unbolt the anti-theft alarm siren, and move it to one side, clear of the ECU housing.

**3** Similarly, for improved access, unclip the cover from the engine compartment fusebox, then remove the relay cover and withdraw the rearmost relay from its connector **(see illustrations)**.

**4** Unscrew the screws, and remove the ECU cover from the engine compartment bulkhead. Unclip the wiring harness from the cover as the cover is removed **(see illustrations)**.

11.5 Removing the throttle body

11.7 Use a new sealing ring when refitting the throttle body

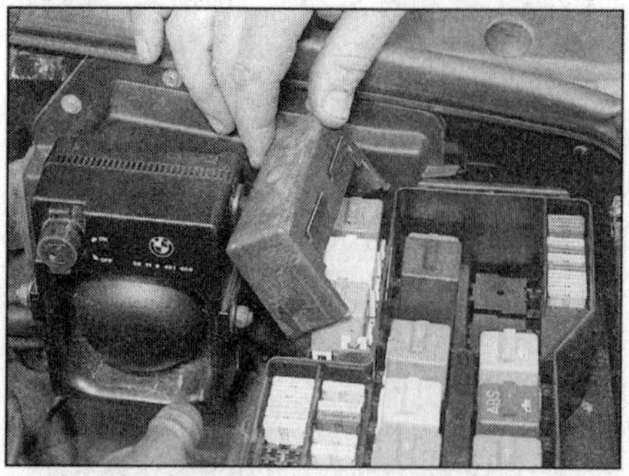

12.3a Remove the relay cover . . .

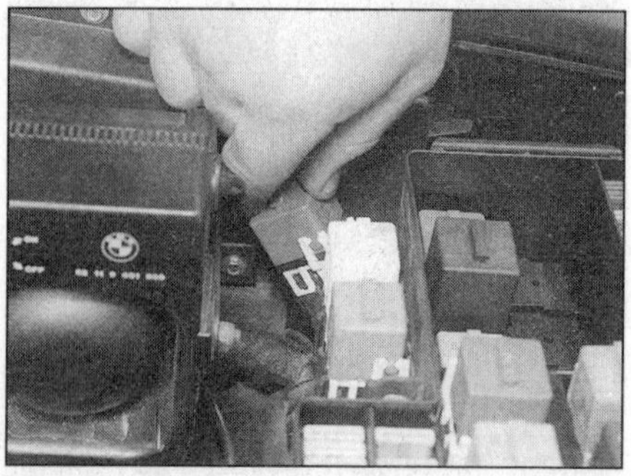

12.3b . . . and withdraw the rearmost relay

12.4a Unscrew the securing screws . . .

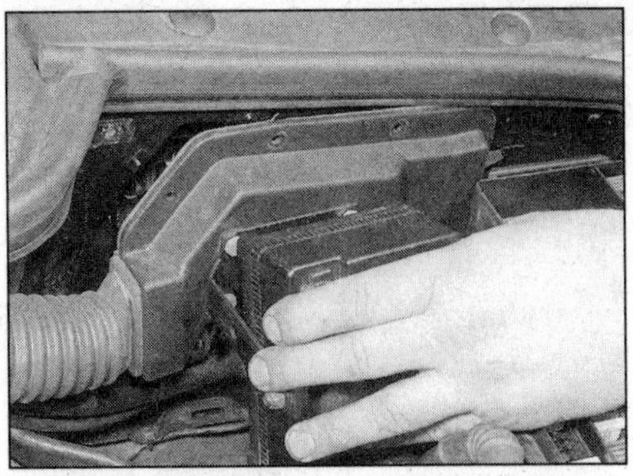

12.4b . . . then remove the ECU cover . . .

12.4c . . . and unclip the wiring harness

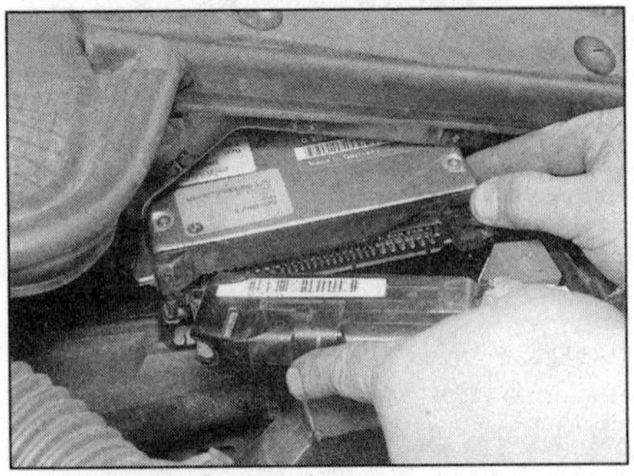

12.5 Disconnect the wiring plug . . .

12.6 . . . and remove the ECU

**5** Release the locking clip, and pull the wiring plug from the ECU. Take great care not to damage the pins on the ECU or the wiring connector **(see illustration)**.

**6** Pull the ECU forwards and manipulate it from its housing **(see illustration)**.

### Refitting

**7** Refitting is a reversal of removal.

## Fuel rail and injectors

***Warning: Refer to the warning notes in Section 1 before proceeding.***

**Note:** *New fuel injector O-rings should be used on refitting.*

### Removal

**8** Depressurise the fuel system as described in Section 7, then disconnect the battery negative lead.

**9** Where necessary, to allow sufficient clearance for the fuel rail to be removed, remove the heater/ventilation inlet air ducting from the rear of the engine compartment as follows.

*a) Lift the grille from the top of the ducting (on certain Coupe models, it will be necessary to remove the windscreen wiper arms, then remove the plastic securing screws and lift off the complete scuttle grille assembly).*

*b) Working through the top of the ducting, remove the screws securing the cable ducting to the air ducting and move the cable ducting clear.*

*c) Unscrew the nuts and/or screw(s) securing the air ducting to the bulkhead (where applicable, bend back the heat shielding for access).*

*d) Remove the air ducting by pulling upwards.*

*e) Move the previously removed cable ducting clear of the cylinder head cover.*

**10** Remove the engine oil filler cap.

**11** Remove the plastic cover from the top of the cylinder head cover. To remove the cover, prise out the cover plates and unscrew the two nuts, then lift and pull the cover forwards. Manipulate the cover over the oil filler neck.

**12** Prise out the cover plates, then unscrew the bolts and remove plastic cover from the top of the fuel injectors.

**13** Loosen the hose clip, and disconnect the fuel feed hose from the front of the fuel rail **(see illustration)**. Be prepared for fuel spillage, and take adequate fire precautions. Plug the open end of the fuel pipe and hose to prevent dirt entry and further fuel spillage.

**14** Similarly, disconnect the fuel return hose from the fuel pressure regulator at the rear of the fuel rail.

**15** Disconnect the vacuum hose from the fuel pressure regulator.

**16** Remove the two nuts securing the engine wiring ducting to the fuel rail, then pull the ducting up to release the wiring plugs from the fuel injectors **(see illustration)**.

**17** Unscrew the two bolts securing the fuel rail to the inlet manifold **(see illustration)**.

**18** Carefully pull the fuel rail upwards to release the fuel injectors from the cylinder head, then withdraw the complete fuel rail/fuel injector assembly **(see illustration)**.

**19** To remove a fuel injector from the fuel rail, proceed as follows.

*a) Prise off the metal securing clip, using a screwdriver.*

*b) Pull the fuel injector from the fuel rail* ***(see illustration)****.*

### Refitting

**20** Before refitting, it is wise to renew all the fuel injector O-rings as a matter of course.

12.13 Disconnect the fuel feed hose from the fuel rail

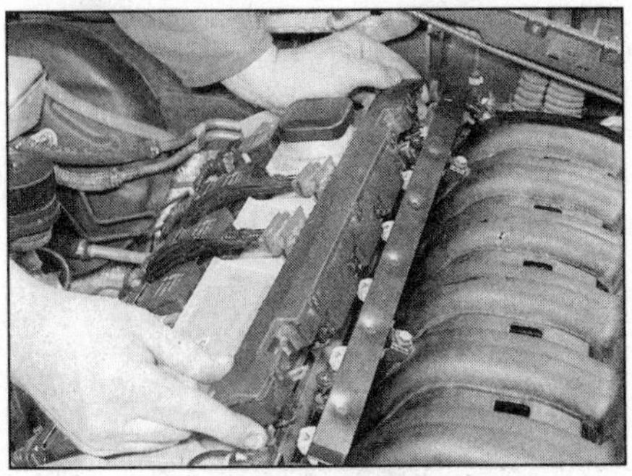

12.16 Pulling the wiring ducting from the fuel injectors

12.17 Unscrew the bolts securing the fuel rail

12.18 Withdraw the fuel rail/fuel injector assembly

12.19 Removing a fuel injector

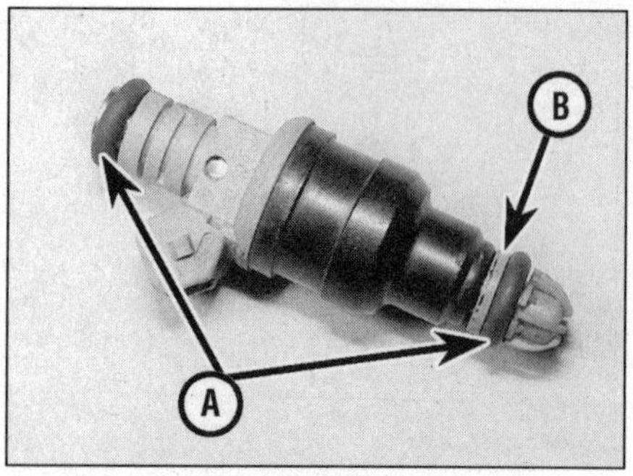


12.21 Fuel injector O-rings (A) and plastic washer (B)

**21** Check that the plastic washer at the bottom of each injector is positioned above the lower O-ring **(see illustration)**.

**22** Lightly lubricate the fuel injector O-rings with a little petroleum jelly or SAE 90 gear oil.

**23** Where applicable, refit the fuel injectors to the fuel rail, ensuring that the securing clips are correctly fitted. Note that the injectors should be positioned so that the wiring sockets are uppermost when the assembly is refitted.

**24** Slide the fuel rail/fuel injector assembly into position, ensuring that the injectors engage with their bores in the inlet manifold.

**25** Further refitting is a reversal of removal, but pressurise the fuel system (refit the fuel pump fuse and switch on the ignition) and check for leaks before starting the engine.

## Fuel pressure regulator

⚠ ***Warning: Refer to the warning notes in Section 1 before proceeding.***

**Note:** *New O-rings may be required on refitting.*

### Removal

**26** Remove the fuel rail/fuel injector assembly as described previously in this Section.

**27** Unscrew the clamp bolt and remove the pressure regulator clamping ring, then lift off the thrustwasher, and pull the pressure regulator from the fuel rail. Note that it will be difficult to pull the regulator from the fuel rail due to the tight-fitting O-rings **(see illustrations)**.

### Refitting

**28** Before refitting, check the condition of the O-rings, and renew if necessary **(see illustration)**.

**29** Refitting is a reversal of removal, but ensure that the thrustwasher is correctly positioned, and refit the fuel rail/fuel injector assembly as described previously in this Section.

## Air mass meter

**Note:** *New filter grilles and/or a new O-ring may be required on refitting.*

### Removal

**30** Disconnect the battery negative lead.

**31** Turn the locking collar, and disconnect the wiring plug from the air mass meter. Where applicable, release the wiring from any clips on the air trunking and air mass meter.

**32** Loosen the hose clip, and disconnect the air trunking from the throttle body **(see illustration)**.

**33** Unscrew the securing screws, or release the clips (as applicable) securing the air mass meter to the air cleaner casing. Pull the air mass meter from the air cleaner casing.

**34** Either release the two breather hoses from the air trunking and remove the air trunking complete with the air mass meter, or loosen the hose clip and disconnect the air trunking from the air mass meter, leaving the trunking in position.

**35** Withdraw the air mass meter assembly.

### Refitting

**36** Refitting is a reversal of removal, bearing in mind the following points.

*a) Check the condition of the filter grilles at the inlet and outlet of the air mass meter (the grilles are secured by large circlips). Renew the grilles if they are contaminated or damaged* ***(see illustrations)****.*

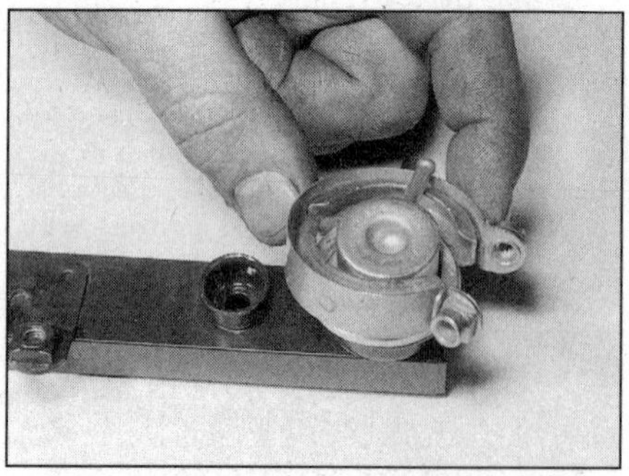

12.27a Remove the pressure regulator clamping ring . . .

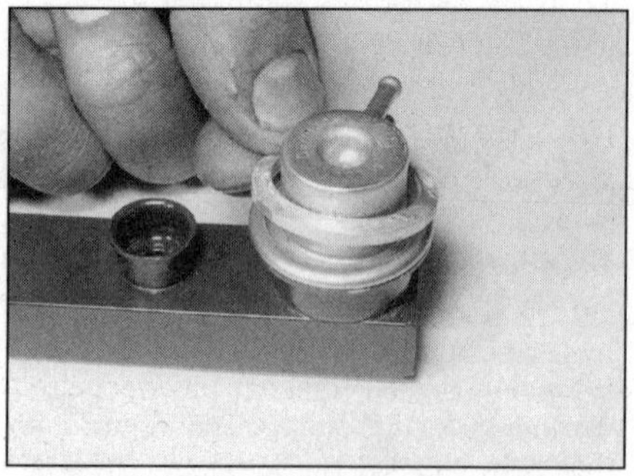

12.27b . . . lift off the thrust washer . . .

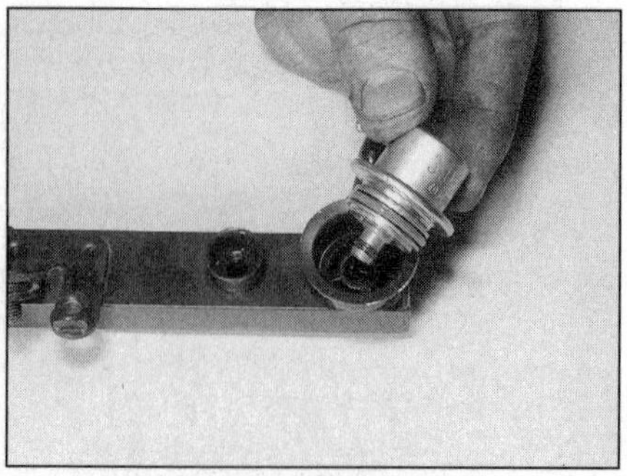

12.27c . . . and pull the regulator from the fuel rail

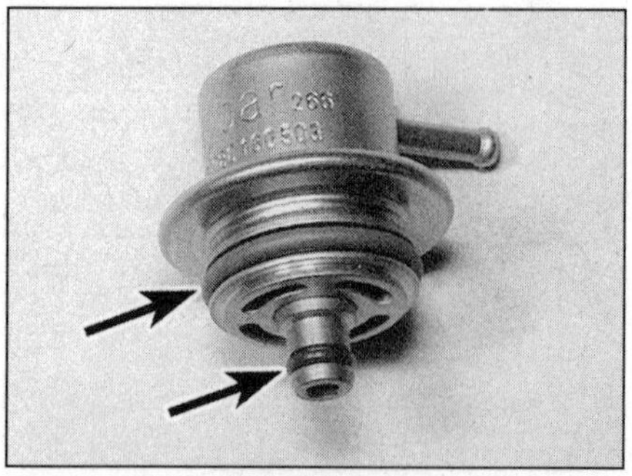

12.28 Check the condition of the O-rings (arrowed)

12.32 Disconnect the air trunking from the throttle body

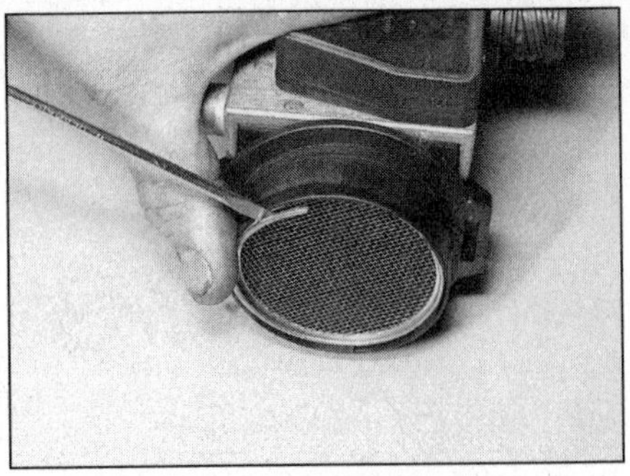

**12.36a Prise out the circlip . . .**

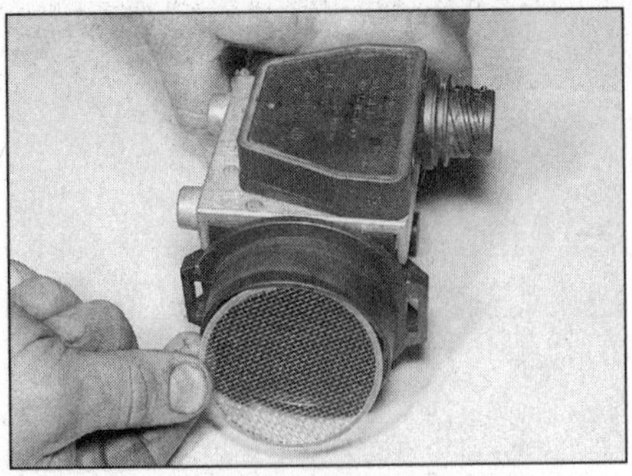

**12.36b . . . to release the filter grille from the air mass meter**

**12.38 Disconnecting the wiring plug from the throttle position sensor (air trunking removed for clarity)**

*b) Check the condition of the O-ring fitted to the air cleaner casing outlet, and renew if necessary.*

## Throttle position sensor

### Removal

**37** Disconnect the battery negative lead.

**38** Disconnect the wiring plug from the sensor **(see illustration)**.

**39** Where applicable, to improve access to the switch, disconnect the wiring plug from the air temperature sensor mounted in the inlet manifold.

**40** Unscrew the two securing screws, and withdraw the sensor from the throttle body.

### Refitting

**41** Refitting is a reversal of removal.

## Coolant temperature sensor

**42** The sensor is located in the left-hand side of the cylinder head. Refer to Chapter 3 for removal and refitting details.

## Inlet air temperature sensor

**Note:** *A new O-ring may be required on refitting.*

### Removal

**43** The sensor may be located in the side of the inlet manifold, next to the throttle position sensor (mounted on the throttle body), or in the bottom of the inlet manifold towards the rear of the engine.

**44** Disconnect the battery negative lead.

**45** On models where the sensor is mounted in the side of the manifold, proceed as follows.

*a) Remove the air mass meter as described previously in this Section.*

*b) Disconnect the wiring plug from the throttle position sensor, then disconnect the wiring plug from the air temperature sensor.*

*c) Unscrew the air temperature sensor from the inlet manifold.*

**46** On models where the sensor is mounted in the bottom of the manifold, proceed as follows **(see illustration)**.

*a) Reach down under the rear of the manifold to locate the sensor.*

*b) Depress the securing clip, and disconnect the wiring plug from the sensor.*

*c) Using a ring spanner or a long-reach socket, unscrew the sensor from the manifold. Note that it may be necessary to move certain wires and/or hoses to one side to improve access (note the locations of any wires and hoses to ensure correct routing on refitting).*

### Refitting

**47** Refitting is a reversal of removal but, where applicable, use a new sealing ring when refitting the sensor. Ensure all wires and hoses are routed as noted before removal.

## Crankshaft position sensor - engines without VANOS

**Note:** *A new sealing ring may be required on refitting.*

**12.46 Air temperature sensor (arrowed) mounted in bottom of inlet manifold - manifold removed for clarity**

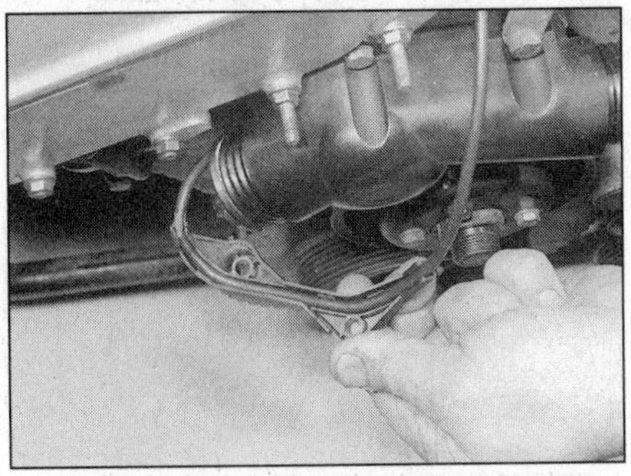

**12.49b . . . and withdraw the crankshaft position sensor wiring cover**

### Removal

**48** Locate the sensor, mounted beneath the thermostat housing.

**49** Prise off the securing clips, and withdraw the sensor wiring cover from the upper timing chain cover studs. Release the wiring from the cover **(see illustrations)**.

**50** Unscrew the bolt, and withdraw the sensor from its mounting bracket **(see illustration)**.

**51** Trace the sensor wiring back to the connector mounted on the bracket under the inlet manifold. Note that there are two connectors mounted on the bracket, and the crankshaft position sensor connector is the lower connector. Disconnect the wiring connector **(see illustration)**.

**52** Note the routing of the wiring, then withdraw the sensor from the engine. Where applicable, recover the sealing ring.

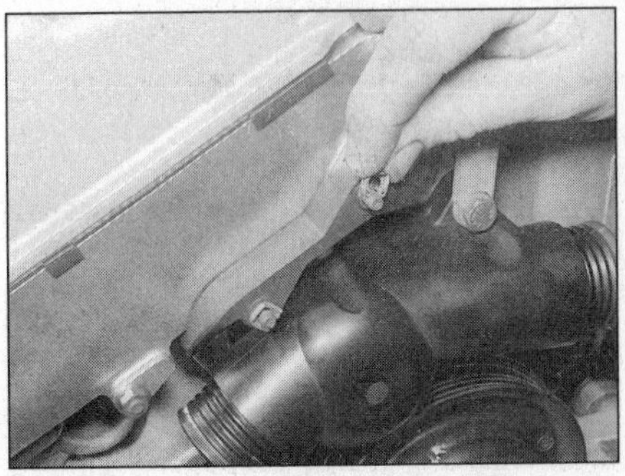

**12.49a Prise off the securing clips . . .**

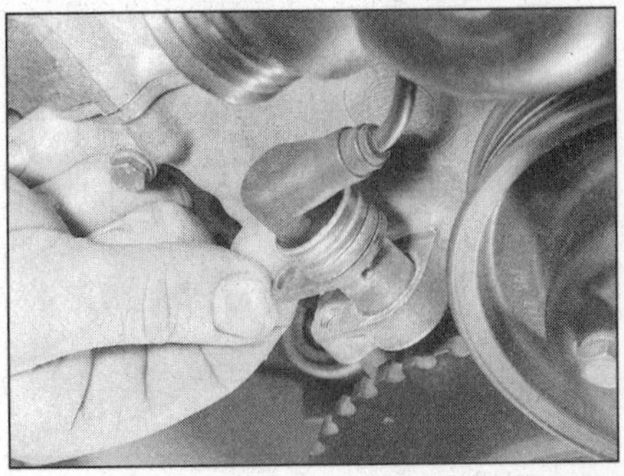

**12.50 Withdrawing the crankshaft position sensor from its mounting bracket**

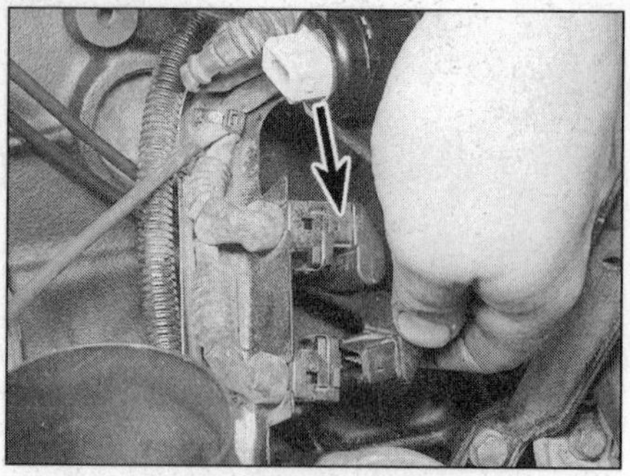

**12.51 Disconnecting the crankshaft position sensor wiring connector - camshaft position sensor wiring connector arrowed**

### Refitting

**53** Refitting is a reversal of removal, but ensure that the wiring is correctly routed as noted before removal. Where applicable, check the condition of the sealing ring and renew if necessary.

## Crankshaft position sensor - VANOS engines

**Note:** *New VANOS unit oil feed pipe sealing rings may be required on refitting.*

### Removal

**54** Locate the sensor, mounted beneath the thermostat housing.

**55** Unscrew the union bolt, and disconnect the oil feed pipe from the VANOS adjustment unit. Be prepared for oil spillage; plug or cover the open ends of the pipe and the VANOS adjustment unit. Recover the sealing rings.

**56** Unscrew the securing nut and bolt, and remove the engine lifting bracket from the front of the cylinder head. Note the location of the earth lead on the lower bracket mounting bolt.

**57** Prise off the securing clips, and withdraw the sensor wiring cover from the studs. Release the wiring from the cover.

**58** Proceed as described in paragraphs 50 to 52.

### Refitting

**59** Refitting is a reversal of removal, but ensure that the wiring is correctly routed a noted before removal. Before reconnecting

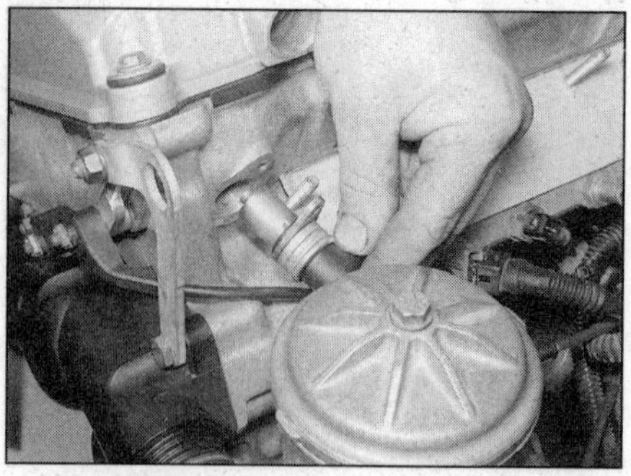

**12.61 Withdrawing the camshaft position sensor - seen with inlet manifold removed**

the oil feed pipe to the VANOS adjustment unit, check the condition of the sealing rings and renew if necessary.

## Camshaft position sensor - engines without VANOS

### Removal

**60** The sensor is located at the front left-hand corner of the cylinder head.

**61** Unscrew the securing bolt, and withdraw the sensor from its housing **(see illustration)**.

**62** Trace the sensor wiring back to the connector mounted on the bracket under the inlet manifold. Note that there are two connectors mounted on the bracket, and the camshaft position sensor connector is the upper connector **(see illustration 12.51)**.

**63** Note the routing of the wiring, then withdraw the sensor from the engine.

### Refitting

**64** Refitting is a reversal of removal, but ensure that the wiring is routed as noted before removal.

## Camshaft position sensor - VANOS engines

**Note:** *A new VANOS solenoid valve sealing ring will be required on refitting.*

### Removal

**65** The sensor is located at the front left-hand corner of the cylinder head.

**66** For access to the sensor, remove the VANOS solenoid valve (see Chapter 2B).

**12.70a Idle speed control valve location (arrowed)**

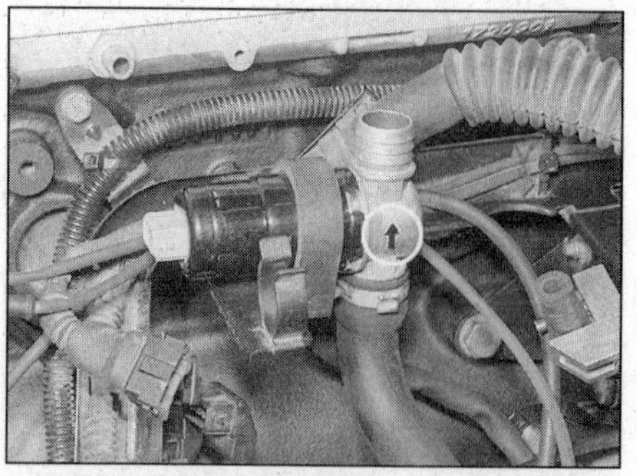

**12.70b Idle speed control valve location (inlet manifold removed). Note arrow on body must point vertically upwards**

**67** Proceed as described in paragraphs 61 to 63.

### Refitting

**68** Refitting is a reversal of removal, but ensure that the wiring is routed as noted before removal, and refit the VANOS solenoid valve using a new sealing ring.

## Oxygen sensor

**69** Refer to Chapter 4C.

## Idle speed control valve

### Removal

**70** The valve is mounted on a bracket under the inlet manifold **(see illustrations)**.

**71** Disconnect the battery negative lead.

**72** Reach under the inlet manifold, and disconnect the hoses from the valve. Alternatively, disconnect the hoses from the bottom of the inlet manifold (depress the clip to release the connector), the breather connector on the cylinder head cover, and the air trunking, and leave the hoses attached to the valve.

**73** Disconnect the wiring plug from the valve.

**74** Push the valve rearwards (towards the engine compartment bulkhead) to release it from its mounting clamp.

**75** Note the routing of the hoses, then manipulate the valve out from under the manifold.

### Refitting

**76** Refitting is a reversal of removal, but ensure that the arrow on the valve is pointing vertically upwards, and ensure the hoses are securely reconnected and correctly routed.

# 13 Manifolds - removal and refitting

## Inlet manifold

**Note:** *New sealing rings may be required on refitting.*

### Removal

**1** Depressurise the fuel system as described in Section 7, then disconnect the battery negative lead.

**2** Remove the air cleaner/air mass meter assembly as described in Section 2.

**3** To allow sufficient clearance for the manifold to be removed, raise the bonnet to its fully open position, referring to Chapter 11, then remove the heater/ventilation inlet air ducting from the rear of the engine compartment as follows **(see illustrations)**.

*a) Lift the grille from the top of the ducting (on certain Coupe models, it will be necessary to remove the windscreen wiper arms, then remove the plastic securing screws, peel back the weatherstrip, and lift off the complete scuttle grille assembly).*

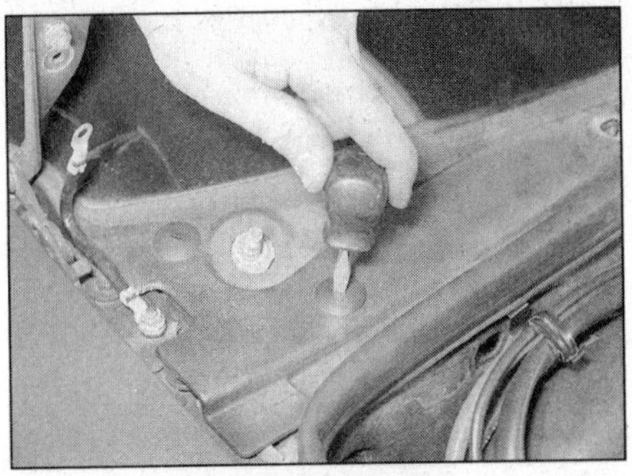

13.3a Remove the plastic securing screws . . .

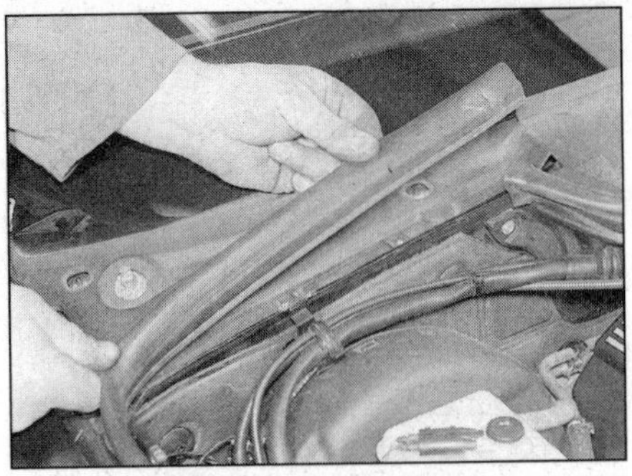

13.3b . . . then peel back the weatherstrip . . .

13.3c . . . and lift off the complete scuttle grille assembly

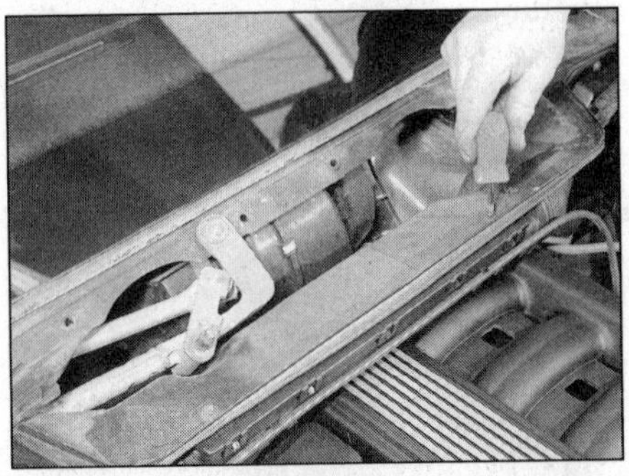

13.3d Remove the screws securing the cable ducting

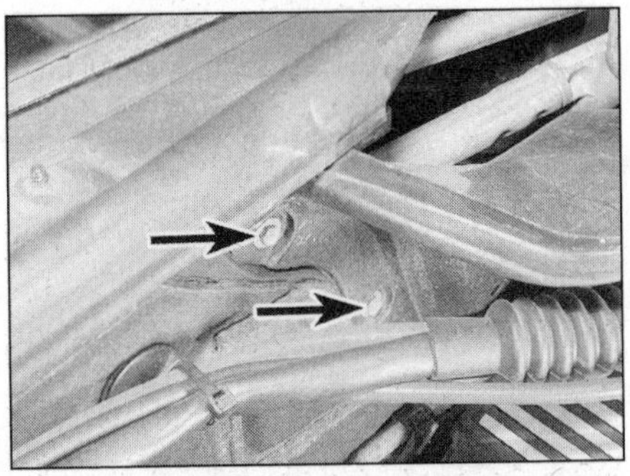

13.3e Right-hand air ducting securing screws (arrowed)

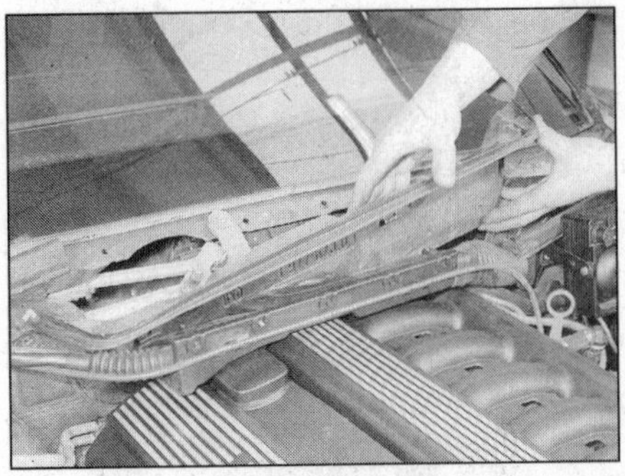

13.3f Removing the air ducting

13.5 Disconnecting the brake servo vacuum hose

13.7 Unscrew the bolts securing the manifold to the support brackets

13.8a Prise out the cover plates to reveal the securing bolts . . .

*b) Working through the top of the ducting, remove the screws securing the cable ducting to the air ducting and move the cable ducting clear.*

*c) Unscrew the nuts and/or screw(s) securing the air ducting to the bulkhead (where applicable, bend back the heat shielding for access).*

*d) Remove the air ducting by pulling upwards.*

*e) Move the previously removed cable ducting clear of the manifold.*

**4** Disconnect the throttle position sensor wiring plug.

**5** Disconnect the brake servo vacuum hose from the manifold **(see illustration)**.

**6** Disconnect the throttle cable from the manifold, with reference to Section 4.

**7** Working under the manifold, unscrew the bolts securing the manifold to the two support brackets **(see illustration)**.

13.8b . . . and remove the cover from the fuel injectors

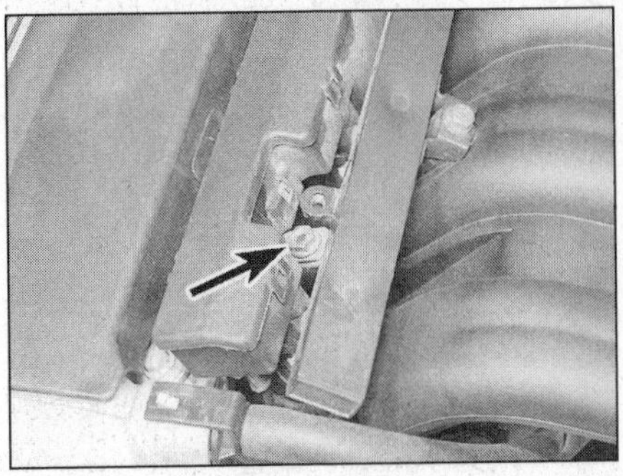

13.9 Engine wiring ducting securing nut (arrowed)

**8** Prise out the cover plates, then unscrew the bolts and remove plastic cover from the top of the fuel injectors **(see illustrations)**.

**9** Remove the two nuts securing the engine wiring ducting to the fuel rail, then pull the ducting up to release the wiring plugs from the fuel injectors **(see illustration)**.

**10** To improve access, loosen the securing clip, and remove the alternator cooling trunking **(see illustration)**.

13.10 Loosening the alternator cooling trunking securing clip

13.17 Where applicable, disconnect the air temperature wiring plug as the manifold is removed

**11** Disconnect the breather hose from the bottom of the manifold.

**12** If the cooling system is not going to be drained at a later stage, clamp the two throttle body coolant hoses to prevent spillage, then loosen the clips and disconnect the hoses.

**13** Disconnect the two fuel hoses from the pipes at the rear of the manifold **(see illustration)**. Be prepared for fuel spillage, and clamp or plug the hoses to prevent further fuel loss and dirt ingress.

**14** Disconnect the smaller breather hose from the cylinder head cover.

**15** Reach under the manifold, and carefully pull the air hose from the top of the idle speed control valve.

**16** Disconnect the wiring plug from the air temperature sensor. The sensor may be located in the side of the manifold, or underneath the manifold (in which case it may prove easier to disconnect the plug as the manifold is removed), depending on model.

**17** Lift the manifold off the cylinder head studs and withdraw it from the engine **(see illustration)**. Recover the sealing rings if loose.

### Refitting

**18** Refitting is a reversal of removal, bearing in mind the following points.

a) *Before refitting, examine the condition of the sealing rings, and renew if necessary* ***(see illustration)****.*

b) *Reconnect and if necessary adjust the throttle cable as described in Section 4.*

c) *On completion, prime the fuel system as described in Section 7.*

13.13 Disconnect the fuel hoses (arrowed)

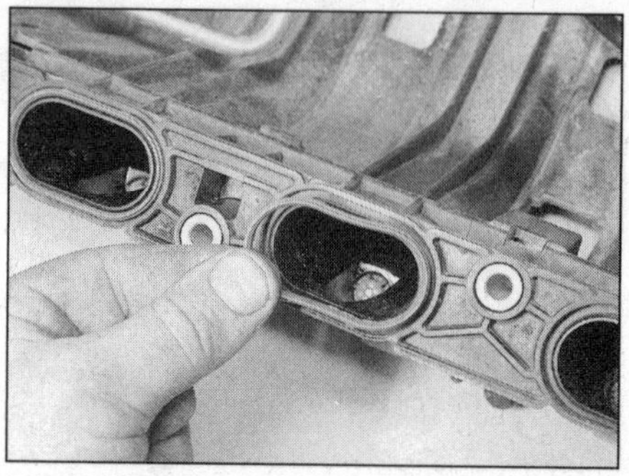

13.18 Fitting a new manifold sealing ring

## *Exhaust manifold*

**Note:** *New manifold-to-cylinder head and manifold-to-exhaust front section gaskets and new manifold nuts will be required on refitting.*

### Removal

**19** The engine has twin exhaust manifolds, each manifold serving three cylinders.

**20** Remove the washer fluid reservoir, as described in Chapter 12.

**21** To improve access, jack up the front of the vehicle and support securely on axle stands (see *"Jacking and vehicle support"*).

**22** Working underneath the vehicle, unscrew the nuts securing the exhaust downpipes to the manifolds.

**23** Working at the gearbox/transmission exhaust bracket, unscrew the two bolts securing the two exhaust mounting clamp halves together.

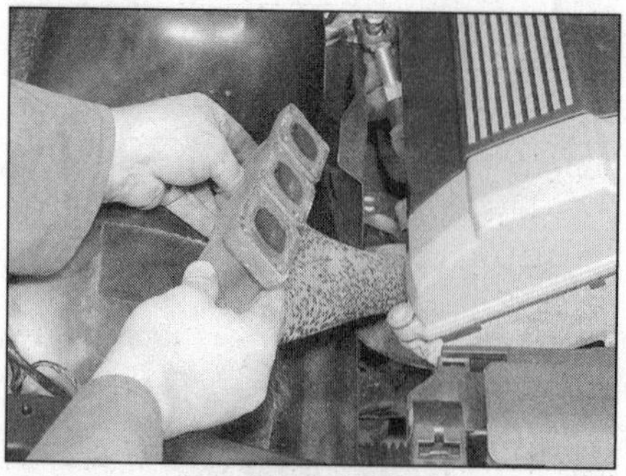

13.26 Withdrawing an exhaust manifold

**24** Loosen the bolt securing the clamp halves to the bracket on the gearbox/transmission, then lower the exhaust downpipes down from the manifold studs. Recover the gaskets.

**25** Working in the engine compartment, unscrew the manifold securing nuts.

**26** Withdraw the manifolds from the studs and recover the gaskets **(see illustration)**.

**27** It is possible that some of the manifold studs may be unscrewed from the cylinder head when the manifold securing nuts are unscrewed. In this event, the studs should be screwed back into the cylinder head once the manifolds have been removed, using two manifold nuts locked together.

### Refitting

**28** Refitting is a reversal of removal, but use new gaskets and new manifold securing nuts.

## 14 Exhaust system - general information, removal and refitting

## *General information*

**1** The original equipment exhaust system consists of two sections. The front section incorporates the catalytic converter and the oxygen sensor (where applicable) and the centre expansion box. The rear section incorporates the rear silencer box.

**2** The system is suspended throughout its length by rubber mountings and a metal bracket.

## *Complete system*

**Note:** *New exhaust front section-to-manifold gaskets and securing nuts will be required on refitting.*

### Removal

**3** Jack up the vehicle and support securely on axle stands (see *"Jacking and vehicle support"*).

**4** On models with a catalytic converter, turn the securing ring, and disconnect the oxygen sensor wiring connector at the bracket on the gearbox/transmission crossmember.

**5** Unscrew the securing nuts, and disconnect the exhaust front sections from the manifolds **(see illustration)**. Recover the gaskets.

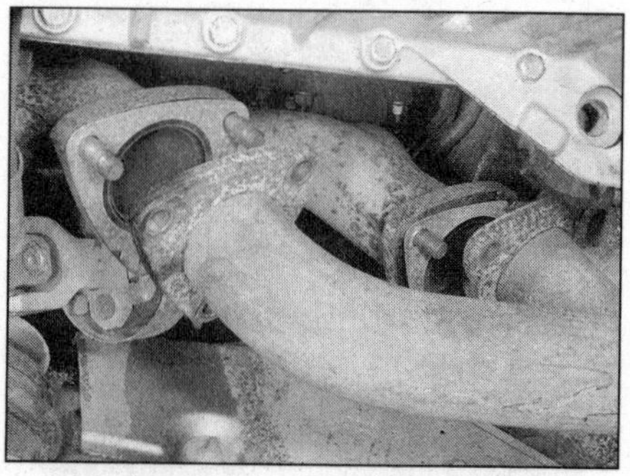

14.5 Disconnecting the exhaust front sections from the manifolds

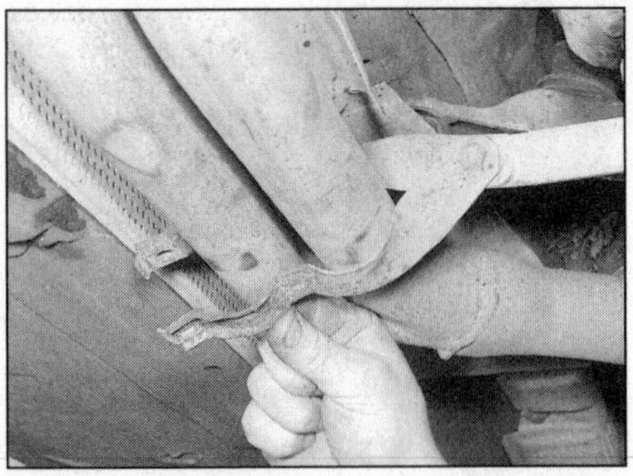

**14.7 Pivot the clamp halves away from the exhaust system**

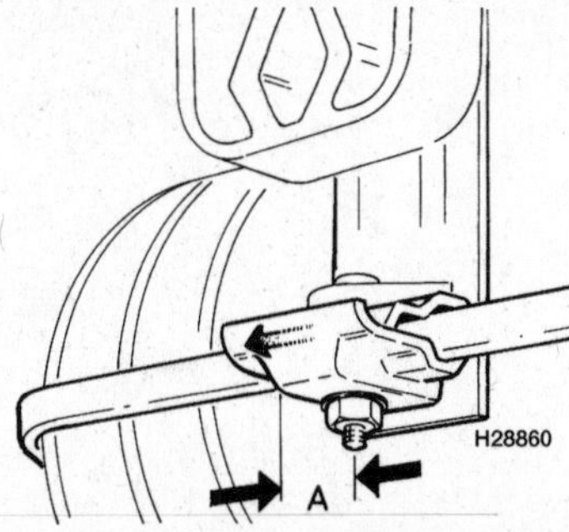


**14.11a Preload the system by sliding the clamps to the rear of the silencer box**
*A = 15.0 mm*

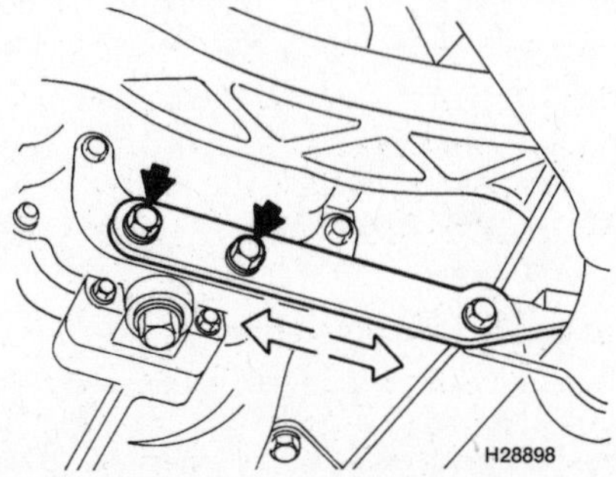


**14.11b Slacken the bolts (arrowed) and slide the bracket to release any tension on the exhaust system**

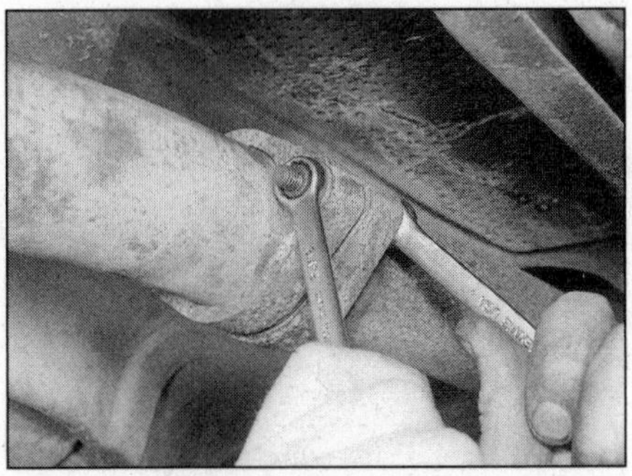

**14.14 Counterhold the bolts and unscrew the exhaust clamp nuts**

**6** On models with automatic transmission, unscrew the securing bolts, and remove the front transmission crossmember from under the vehicle.

**7** Unscrew the clamp bolts securing the two halves of the gearbox/transmission exhaust mounting bracket together, then unscrew the clamp pivot bolt, and pivot the clamp halves away from the exhaust system **(see illustration)**.

**8** Slide the rear exhaust mounting rubbers from the brackets on the exhaust system.

**9** Working at the rear of the exhaust system, unscrew the nuts securing the rear silencer box mounting clamps.

**10** Withdraw the complete exhaust system from under the vehicle.

### Refitting

**11** Refitting is a reversal of removal, bearing in mind the following points **(see illustrations)**.

*a) Use new gaskets when reconnecting the exhaust front section to the manifolds. Also use new nuts, and coat the threads of the new nuts with copper grease.*

*b) When refitting the rear silencer box clamps, slide the clamps onto the silencer box and allow the system to hang so that the mountings are free from tension, then slide the clamps towards the rear of the silencer by 15.0 mm to give a preload, forcing the system towards the front of the vehicle.*

*c) Check the position of the tailpipes in relation to the cut-out in the rear valence, and if necessary adjust the exhaust mountings to give sufficient clearance between the system and the valence.*

*d) Once the mountings have been reconnected and tightened, slacken the two nuts and bolts securing the exhaust mounting bracket to the gearbox/transmission bracket, and if necessary slide the bracket within the elongated holes to release any sideways tension on the system. Once the system is correctly positioned, tighten the nuts and bolts.*

## Front section

### Removal

**12** If desired, the exhaust front section can be removed leaving the rear section in place.

**13** Follow the procedure described previously in paragraphs 3 to 8.

**14** Counterhold the bolts, and unscrew the clamp nuts securing the exhaust front section to the rear section, then slide the front section from the rear section and remove the front section from under the vehicle **(see illustration)**.

### Refitting

**15** Refer to paragraph 11.

## Rear section

### Removal

**16** Counterhold the bolts, and unscrew the clamp nuts securing the exhaust front section to the rear section.

**17** Working at the rear of the exhaust system, unscrew the nuts securing the rear silencer box mounting clamps, then slide the rear section from the front section and withdraw the rear section from under the vehicle.

### Refitting

**18** Refitting is a reversal of removal, but coat the threads of the clamp mounting nuts and bolts with a little copper grease before fitting, and preload the rear mounting as described in paragraph 11b.

# Notes

# Chapter 4 Part C: Emission control systems

## Contents



## Degrees of difficulty

| | | | | |
|---|---|---|---|---|
| **Easy,** suitable for novice with little experience | **Fairly easy,** suitable for beginner with some experience | **Fairly difficult,** suitable for competent DIY mechanic | **Difficult,** suitable for experienced DIY mechanic | **Very difficult,** suitable for expert DIY or professional |

## Specifications

### Torque wrench setting

| | Nm | lbf ft |
|---|---|---|
| Oxygen sensor-to-exhaust system | 50 | 37 |

## 1 General information

**1** All models have various built-in fuel system features which help to minimise emissions, and all models have at least the crankcase emission-control system described in the following paragraphs. Models with a catalytic converter are also fitted with the exhaust and evaporative emission control systems.

**2** Refer to the "Specifications" in Chapter 4A or 4B, as applicable, for fuel recommendations. Note that leaded fuel **must not** be used in models equipped with a catalytic converter.

### *Crankcase emission control*

**3** To reduce the emission of unburned hydrocarbons from the crankcase into the atmosphere, the engine is sealed, and the blow-by gases and oil vapour are drawn from the crankcase and the cylinder head cover, through an oil separator, into the inlet tract, to be burned by the engine during normal combustion.

**4** Under conditions of high manifold depression (idling, deceleration) the gases will be sucked positively out of the crankcase. Under conditions of low manifold depression (acceleration, full-throttle running) the gases are forced out of the crankcase by the (relatively) higher crankcase pressure; if the engine is worn, the raised crankcase pressure (due to increased blow-by) will cause some of the flow to return under all manifold conditions.

### *Exhaust emission control*

**5** To minimise the amount of pollutants which escape into the atmosphere, some models are fitted with a catalytic converter in the exhaust system. On all models where a catalytic converter is fitted, the system is of the "closed-loop" type; an oxygen (lambda) sensor in the exhaust system provides the fuel injection/ignition system ECU with constant feedback, enabling the ECU to adjust the mixture to provide the best possible conditions for the converter to operate.

**6** The oxygen sensor has a built-in heating element, controlled by the ECU, to quickly bring the sensor's tip to an efficient operating temperature. The sensor's tip is sensitive to oxygen, and sends the ECU a varying voltage depending on the amount of oxygen in the exhaust gases. If the inlet air/fuel mixture is too rich, the exhaust gases are low in oxygen, so the sensor sends a low-voltage signal. The voltage rises as the mixture weakens and the amount of oxygen in the exhaust gases rises. Peak conversion efficiency of all major pollutants occurs if the inlet air/fuel mixture is maintained at the chemically-correct ratio for the complete combustion of petrol - 14.7 parts (by weight) of air to 1 part of fuel (the "stoichiometric" ratio). The sensor output voltage alters in a large step at this point, the ECU using the signal change as a reference point, and correcting the inlet air/fuel mixture accordingly by altering the fuel injector pulse width (the length of time that the injector is open).

### *Evaporative emission control*

**7** To minimise the escape into the atmosphere of unburned hydrocarbons, an evaporative emissions control system is fitted to later models. The fuel tank filler cap is sealed, and a charcoal canister, mounted in the engine compartment, collects the petrol vapours generated in the tank when the car is parked. The canister stores them until they can be cleared from the canister (under the control of the fuel injection/ignition system ECU) via the purge solenoid valve. When the valve is opened, the fuel vapours pass into the inlet tract, to be burned by the engine during normal combustion.

**8** To ensure that the engine runs correctly when it is cold and/or idling, the ECU does not open the purge control valve until the engine has warmed up and is under load; the valve solenoid is then modulated on and off, to allow the stored vapour to pass into the inlet tract.



## 2 Emission control systems - component renewal

### *Crankcase emission control*

**1** The components of this system require no routine attention, other than to check that the hoses are clear and undamaged at regular intervals.

### *Evaporative emission control*

#### Charcoal canister - renewal

**2** The canister may be located in the engine compartment, on a bracket attached to the left-hand suspension turret, or under the air inlet trunking **(see illustration)**.

**3** Move any surrounding pipes and hoses to one side to improve access to the canister.

**4** Disconnect the hoses from the canister. If the hose is secured by a plastic locking clip, squeeze the ends of the clip to release it from the connection on the canister. Note the hose locations to ensure correct refitting.

**5** Unscrew the securing screws, and withdraw the canister/bracket assembly from the engine compartment **(see illustration)**.

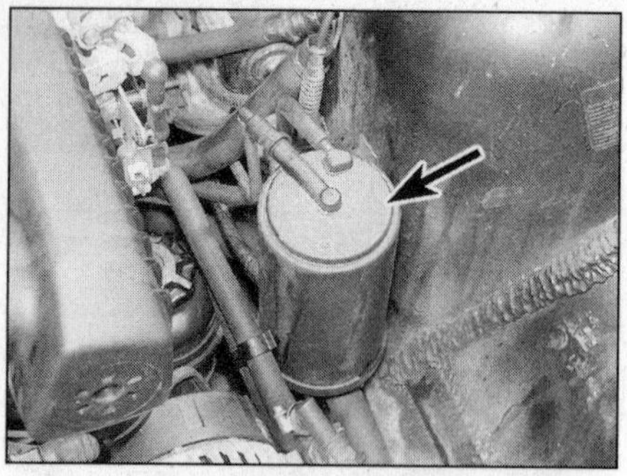
2.2 Carbon canister location (arrowed) - 6-cylinder engine model

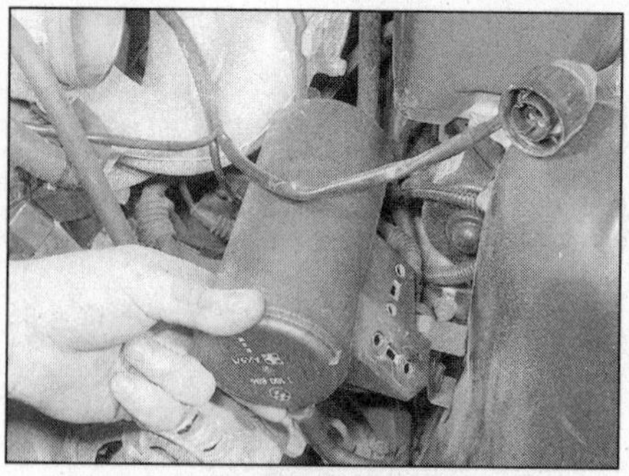
2.5 Removing the carbon canister - M42 4-cylinder engine model

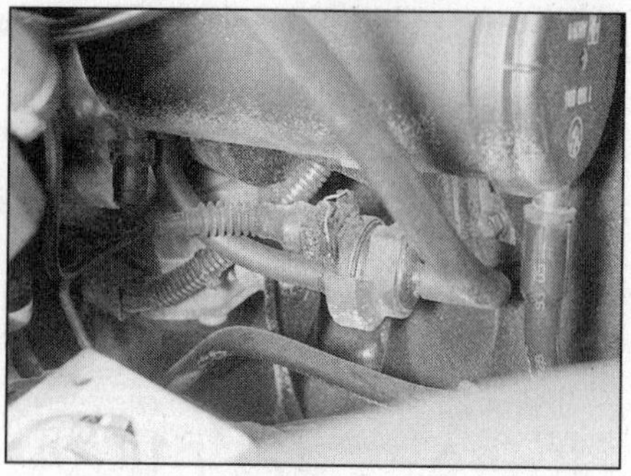
2.7 Purge valve location (arrowed) - M42 4-cylinder engine

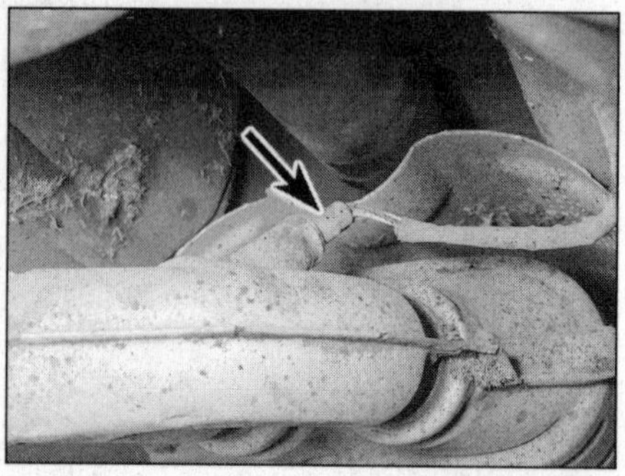
2.15 Oxygen sensor location (arrowed) in front section of exhaust system - 6-cylinder engine model

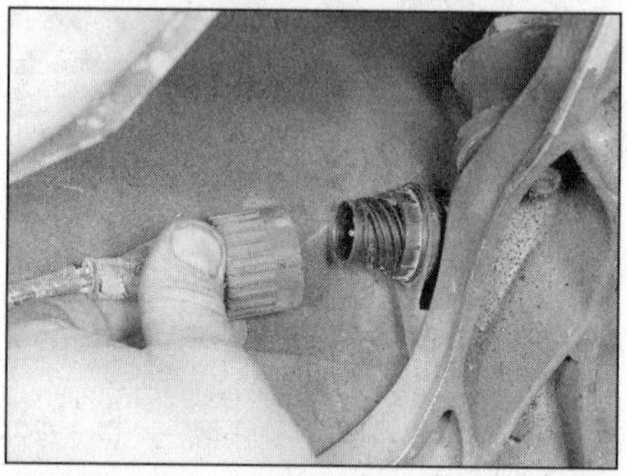
2.18 Disconnecting the oxygen sensor wiring plug - 6-cylinder engine model

**6** Refitting is a reversal of removal, but ensure that the hoses are correctly reconnected as noted before removal, and make sure that the hose securing clips are correctly engaged.

### Purge valve (solenoid valve) - renewal

**7** The valve is located on a bracket, next to the carbon canister, or under the air inlet trunking **(see illustration)**.

**8** Disconnect the battery negative lead.

**9** If necessary, to improve access, loosen the clips, and remove the air trunking. Note the locations of any breather hoses connected to the trunking.

**10** Disconnect the hoses from the valve, noting their locations to ensure correct refitting.

**11** Disconnect the wiring plug from the valve.

**12** Pull the valve from its rubber mounting.

**13** Refitting is a reversal of removal, but make sure that all hoses are correctly reconnected as noted before removal.

## *Exhaust emission control*

### Catalytic converter - renewal

**14** The catalytic converter is integral with the front section of the exhaust system. Refer to Part A or B of this Chapter (as applicable) for details of removal and refitting.

### Oxygen sensor - renewal

**Note:** *Ensure that the exhaust system is cold before attempting to remove the oxygen sensor.*

**15** The oxygen sensor is screwed into the front section of the exhaust system under the vehicle **(see illustration)**.

**16** Disconnect the battery negative lead.

**17** Apply the handbrake, then jack up the front of the vehicle and support securely on axle stands (see *"Jacking and vehicle support"*).

**18** Trace the wiring back from the sensor to the wiring connector under the vehicle, and disconnect the connector **(see illustration)**.

**19** Unscrew the sensor and remove it from the exhaust pipe.

**20** Refitting is a reverse of the removal procedure. Tighten the sensor to the specified torque. Check that the wiring is correctly routed, and in no danger of contacting the exhaust system.

## 3 Catalytic converter - general information and precautions

The catalytic converter is a reliable and simple device, which needs no maintenance in itself, but there are some facts of which an owner should be aware, if the converter is to function properly for its full service life.

*a) DO NOT use leaded petrol in a car equipped with a catalytic converter - the lead will coat the precious metals, reducing their converting efficiency, and will eventually destroy the converter.*

*b) Always keep the ignition and fuel systems well-maintained in accordance with the manufacturer's schedule.*

*c) If the engine develops a misfire, do not drive the car at all (or at least as little as possible) until the fault is cured.*

*d) DO NOT push- or tow-start the car - this will soak the catalytic converter in unburned fuel, causing it to overheat when the engine does start.*

*e) DO NOT switch off the ignition at high engine speeds.*

*f) DO NOT use fuel or engine oil additives - these may contain substances harmful to the catalytic converter.*

*g) DO NOT continue to use the car if the engine burns oil to the extent of leaving a visible trail of blue smoke.*

*h) Remember that the catalytic converter operates at very high temperatures. DO NOT, therefore, park the car in dry undergrowth, or over long grass or piles of dead leaves after a long run.*

*i) Remember that the catalytic converter is FRAGILE - do not strike it with tools during servicing work.*

*j) In some cases, a sulphurous smell (like that of rotten eggs) may be noticed from the exhaust. This is common to many catalytic converter-equipped cars, and once the car has covered a few thousand miles the problem should disappear.*

*k) The catalytic converter, used on a well-maintained and well-driven car, should last for between 50 000 and 100 000 miles - if the converter is no longer effective, it must be renewed.*

# Chapter 5 Part A:
# Starting and charging systems

## Contents



## Degrees of difficulty

| | | | | |
|---|---|---|---|---|
| **Easy,** suitable for novice with little experience | **Fairly easy,** suitable for beginner with some experience | **Fairly difficult,** suitable for competent DIY mechanic | **Difficult,** suitable for experienced DIY mechanic | **Very difficult,** suitable for expert DIY or professional |

## Specifications

### System type
12-volt negative earth

### Alternator

| | |
|---|---|
| Regulated voltage (at 1500 rpm engine speed with no electrical equipment switched on) | 13.5 to 14.2 volts |

### Starter motor

| | |
|---|---|
| Rated output | 1.7 kW |

### Torque wrench settings

| | Nm | lbf ft |
|---|---|---|
| Starter motor-to-gearbox/transmission nuts and bolts | 50 | 37 |
| Starter motor support bracket-to-starter motor nuts | 5 | 4 |
| Starter motor support bracket-to-engine bolts | 47 | 35 |
| Oil pressure warning light switch | 40 | 30 |



## 1 General information and precautions

### General information

The engine electrical system consists mainly of the charging and starting systems. Because of their engine-related functions, these components are covered separately from the body electrical devices such as the lights, instruments, etc (which are covered in Chapter 12). On 4-cylinder engine models refer to Part B for information on the ignition system, and on 6-cylinder models refer to Part C.

The electrical system is of the 12-volt negative earth type.

The battery is of the low maintenance or "maintenance-free" (sealed for life) type and is charged by the alternator, which is belt-driven from the crankshaft pulley.

The starter motor is of the pre-engaged type incorporating an integral solenoid. On starting, the solenoid moves the drive pinion into engagement with the flywheel ring gear before the starter motor is energised. Once the engine has started, a one-way clutch prevents the motor armature being driven by the engine until the pinion disengages from the flywheel.

### Precautions

Further details of the various systems are given in the relevant Sections of this Chapter. While some repair procedures are given, the usual course of action is to renew the component concerned. The owner whose interest extends beyond mere component renewal should obtain a copy of the *"Automobile Electrical & Electronic Systems Manual"*, available from the publishers of this manual.

***It is necessary to take extra care when working on the electrical system to avoid damage to semi-conductor devices (diodes and transistors), and to avoid the risk of personal injury. In addition to the precautions given in "Safety first!" at the beginning of this manual, observe the following when working on the system:***

***Always remove rings, watches, etc before working on the electrical system. Even with the battery disconnected, capacitive discharge could occur if a component's live terminal is earthed through a metal object. This could cause a shock or nasty burn.***

***Do not reverse the battery connections. Components such as the alternator, electronic control units, or any other components having semi-conductor circuitry could be irreparably damaged.***

***If the engine is being started using jump leads and a slave battery, connect the batteries positive-to-positive and negative-to-negative (see "Jump starting", at the beginning of this manual). This also applies when connecting a battery charger.***

***Never disconnect the battery terminals, the alternator, any electrical wiring or any test instruments when the engine is running.***

***Do not allow the engine to turn the alternator when the alternator is not connected.***

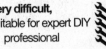

***Never "test" for alternator output by "flashing" the output lead to earth.***

***Never use an ohmmeter of the type incorporating a hand-cranked generator for circuit or continuity testing.***

***Always ensure that the battery negative lead is disconnected when working on the electrical system.***

***Before using electric-arc welding equipment on the car, disconnect the battery, alternator and components such as the fuel injection/ignition electronic control unit to protect them from the risk of damage.***

***If a radio/cassette unit with a built-in security code is fitted, note the following precautions. If the power source to the unit is cut, the anti-theft system will activate. Even if the power source is immediately reconnected, the radio/cassette unit will not function until the correct security code has been entered. Therefore, if you do not know the correct security code for the radio/cassette unit do not disconnect the battery negative terminal of the battery or remove the radio/cassette unit from the vehicle. Refer to "Radio/cassette unit anti-theft system - Precaution" Section for further information.***

## 2 Electrical fault finding - general information

Refer to Chapter 12.

## 3 Battery - testing and charging

**Note:** *The following is intended as a guide only. Always refer to the manufacturer's recommendations (often printed on a label attached to the battery) before charging a battery.*

**1** All models are fitted with a maintenance-free battery in production, which should require no maintenance under normal operating conditions.

**2** If the condition of the battery is suspect, remove the battery as described in Section 4, and check that the electrolyte level in each cell is up to the "MAX" mark on the outside of the battery case (about 5.0 mm above the tops of the plates in the cells). If necessary, the electrolyte level can be topped up by removing the cell plugs from the top of the battery and adding distilled water (**not** acid).

**3** An approximate check on battery condition can be made by checking the specific gravity of the electrolyte, using the following as a guide.

**4** Use a hydrometer to make the check and compare the results with the following table. The temperatures quoted are ambient (air) temperatures. Note that the specific gravity readings assume an electrolyte temperature of 15°C (60°F); for every 10°C (48°F) below 15°C (60°F) subtract 0.007. For every 10°C (48°F) above 15°C (60°F) add 0.007.

| | Above 25°C(77°F) | Below 25°C (77°F) |
|---|---|---|
| **Fully-charged** | *1.210 to 1.230* | *1.270 to 1.290* |
| **70% charged** | *1.170 to 1.190* | *1.230 to 1.250* |
| **Discharged** | *1.050 to 1.070* | *1.110 to 1.130* |

**5** If the battery condition is suspect, first check the specific gravity of electrolyte in each cell. A variation of 0.040 or more between any cells indicates loss of electrolyte or deterioration of the internal plates.

**6** If the specific gravity variation is 0.040 or more, the battery should be renewed. If the cell variation is satisfactory but the battery is discharged, it should be charged in accordance with the manufacturer's instructions.

**7** If testing the battery using a voltmeter, connect the voltmeter across the battery. A fully-charged battery should give a reading of 12.5 volts or higher. The test is only accurate if the battery has not been subjected to any kind of charge for the previous six hours. If this is not the case, switch on the headlights for 30 seconds, then wait four to five minutes before testing the battery after switching off the headlights. All other electrical circuits must be switched off, so check that the doors and tailgate are fully shut when making the test.

**8** Generally speaking, if the voltage reading is less than 12.2 volts, then the battery is discharged, whilst a reading of 12.2 to 12.4 volts indicates a partially discharged condition.

**9** If the battery is to be charged, remove it from the vehicle (Section 4) and charge it in accordance with its maker's instructions..

## 4 Battery - removal and refitting

**Note:** *When the battery is disconnected, any fault codes stored in the engine management ECU memory will be erased. If any faults are suspected, do not disconnect the battery until the fault codes have been read by a BMW dealer. If the vehicle is fitted with a code-protected radio, refer to "Radio/cassette unit anti-theft system - Precaution".*

### *4-cylinder engine models*

#### Removal

**1** On 4-cylinder engine models, the battery is located at the rear right-hand corner of the engine compartment.

**2** Where applicable, release the securing clips, and open the battery cover **(see illustration)**.

**3** Slacken the clamp bolt, and disconnect the clamp from the battery negative (earth) terminal.

**4** Remove the insulation cover (where fitted) and disconnect the positive terminal lead in the same way.

**5** Where applicable, side off the battery cover.

**6** Unscrew the bolt and remove the battery retaining clamp **(see illustration)**.

**7** Lift out the battery. Take care as the battery is heavy!

#### Refitting

**8** Refitting is a reversal of removal, but smear petroleum jelly on the terminals when reconnecting the leads, and always reconnect the positive lead first, and the negative lead last.

### *6-cylinder engine models*

#### Removal

**9** On 6-cylinder engine models, the battery is located beneath a cover on the right-hand side of the luggage compartment.

**10** Open the boot lid, and unclip the battery cover/first aid kit tray from the right-hand side of the luggage compartment **(see illustration)**.

**11** Slacken the clamp bolt, and disconnect the clamp from the battery negative (earth) terminal.

**12** Remove the insulation cover (where fitted) and disconnect the positive terminal lead in the same way.

**13** Unscrew the bolt, and remove the battery retaining clamp **(see illustration)**.

**14** Lift the battery from its housing. Take care as the battery is heavy!

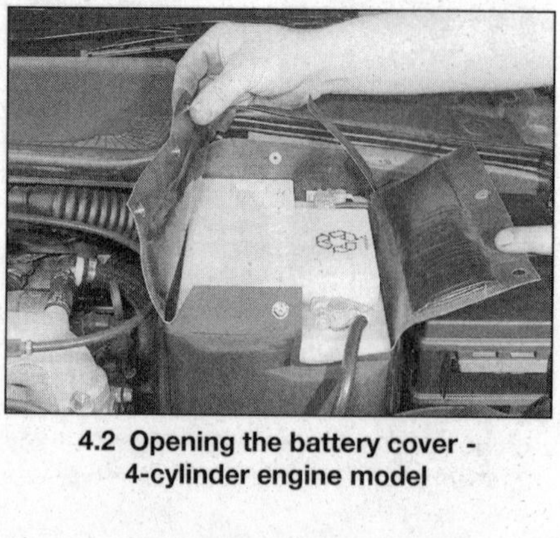

**4.2 Opening the battery cover - 4-cylinder engine model**

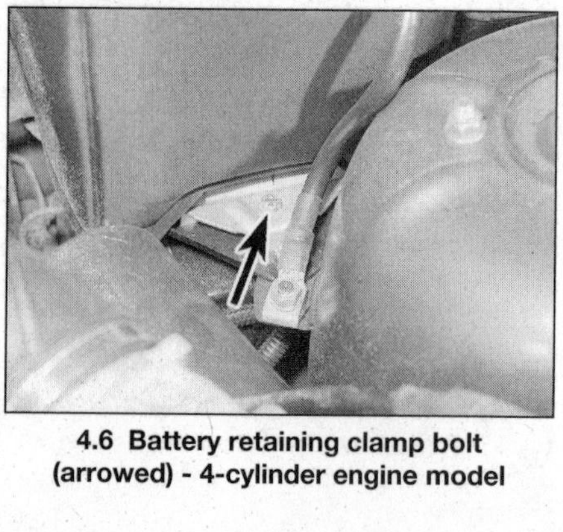

**4.6 Battery retaining clamp bolt (arrowed) - 4-cylinder engine model**

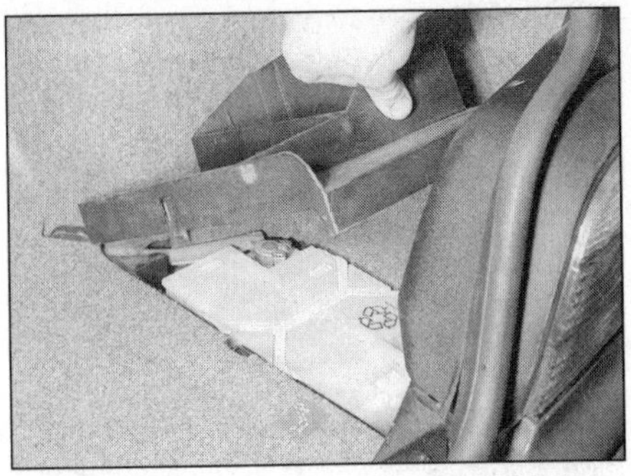

**4.10 Unclip battery cover/first aid kit tray to expose the battery - 6-cylinder model**

### Refitting

**15** Refitting is a reversal of removal, but smear petroleum jelly on the terminals when reconnecting the leads, and always reconnect the positive lead first, and the negative lead last.

## 5 Charging system - testing

**Note:** *Refer to the warnings given in "Safety first!" and in Section 1 of this Chapter before starting work.*

**1** If the ignition warning light fails to illuminate when the ignition is switched on, first check the alternator wiring connections for security. If satisfactory, check that the warning light bulb has not blown, and that the bulbholder is secure in its location in the instrument panel. If the light still fails to illuminate, check the continuity of the warning light feed wire from the alternator to the bulbholder. If all is satisfactory, the alternator is at fault and should be renewed or taken to an auto-electrician for testing and repair.

**2** If the ignition warning light illuminates when the engine is running, stop the engine and check that the drivebelt is correctly tensioned (see Chapter 1) and that the alternator connections are secure. If all is so far satisfactory, have the alternator checked by an auto-electrician for testing and repair.

**3** If the alternator output is suspect even though the warning light functions correctly,

**4.13 Battery clamp bolt (arrowed) - 6-cylinder model**

the regulated voltage may be checked as follows.

**4** Connect a voltmeter across the battery terminals and start the engine.

**5** Increase the engine speed until the voltmeter reading remains steady; the reading should be approximately 12 to 13 volts, and no more than 14.2 volts.

**6** Switch on as many electrical accessories (eg, the headlights, heated rear window and heater blower) as possible, and check that the alternator maintains the regulated voltage at around 13 to 14 volts.

**7** If the regulated voltage is not as stated, the fault may be due to worn alternator brushes, weak brush springs, a faulty voltage regulator, a faulty diode, a severed phase winding or worn or damaged slip rings. The alternator should be renewed or taken to an auto-electrician for testing and repair.

## 6 Alternator drivebelt - removal, refitting and tensioning

Refer to the procedure given for the auxiliary drivebelt(s) in Chapter 1.

## 7 Alternator - removal and refitting

### *4-cylinder engines*

#### Removal

**1** Disconnect the battery negative lead.

**2** Remove the air cleaner assembly and the air mass meter as described in Chapter 4A.

**3** Remove the auxiliary drivebelt as described in Chapter 1.

**4** Prise the cover(s) from the rear of the alternator, then unscrew the nuts and bolt, and disconnect the wiring **(see illustration)**.

**5** Where applicable, prise the cover from the centre of the drivebelt guide pulley, then unbolt the pulley for access to the upper alternator securing bolt. Note the location of the pulley to ensure correct refitting. Note that on some engines, the pulley bolt acts as the upper alternator securing through-bolt **(see illustration)**.

**6** Counterhold the nuts and unscrew the upper and lower alternator securing through-bolts **(see illustrations)**.

**7** Withdraw the alternator from the engine.

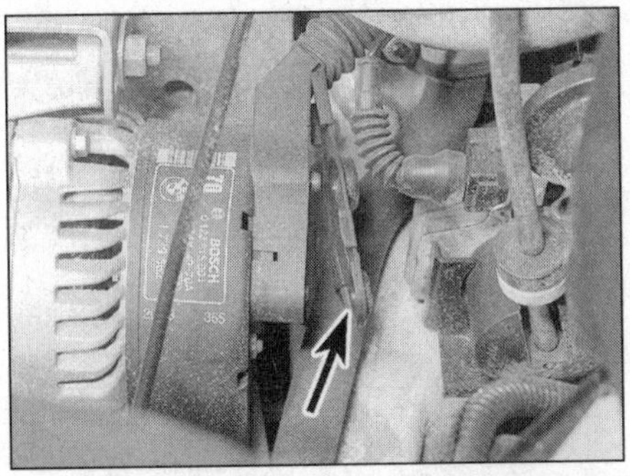

**7.4 Prise the cover (arrowed) from the rear of the alternator - M42 engine model**

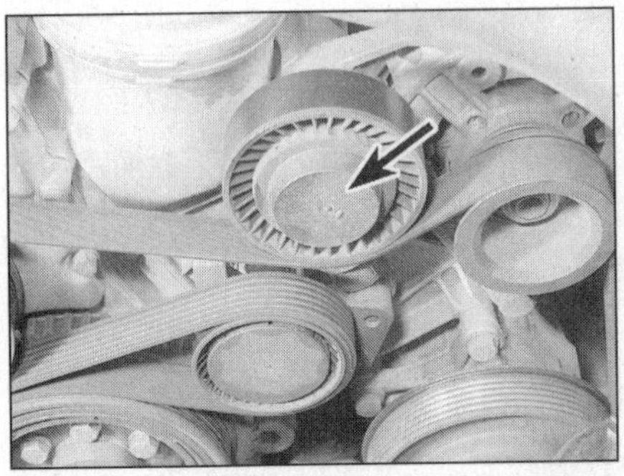

**7.5 Prise the cover from the guide pulley/ alternator upper bolt - M43 engine model**

5A

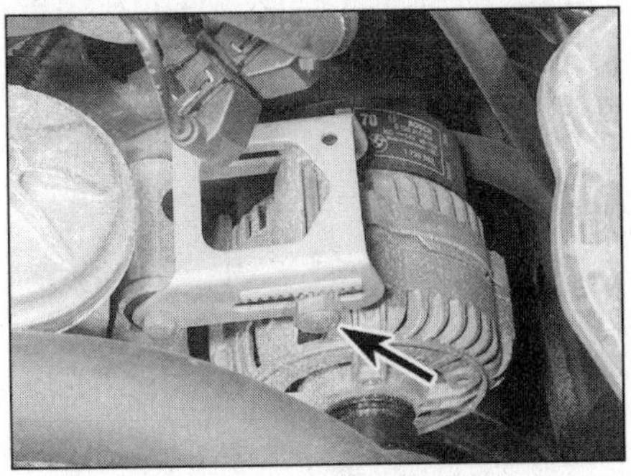

**7.6a Unscrew the upper . . .**

**7.6b . . . and lower alternator securing bolts (arrowed)- M42 engine model**

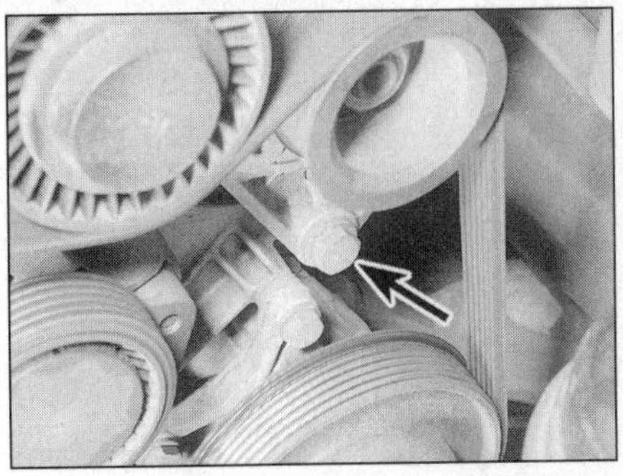

**7.6c Lower alternator securing bolt (arrowed) - M43 engine model**

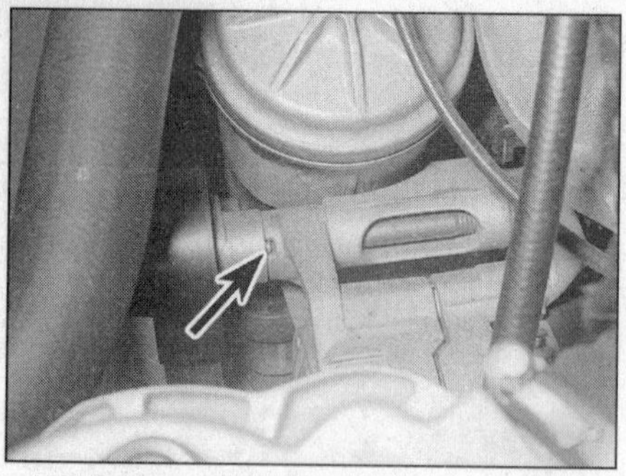

7.8 Ensure lug (arrowed) engages with cut-out in alternator - M43 engine model

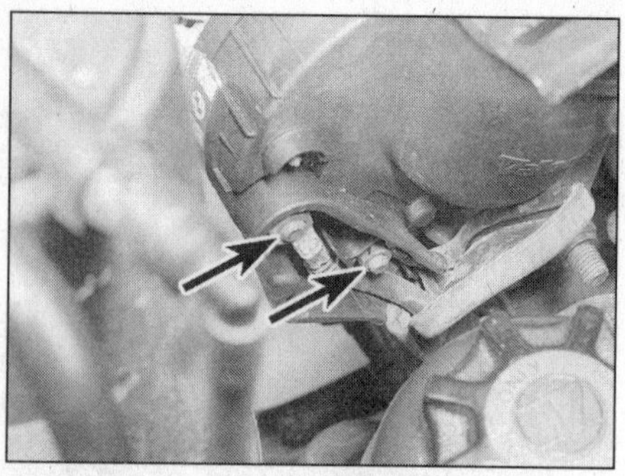

7.12 Disconnect wiring (arrowed) from the rear of the alternator - 6-cylinder engine

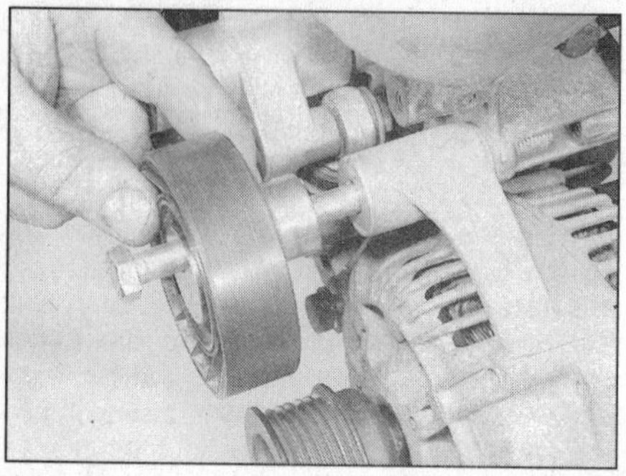

7.13 Unscrew upper through-bolt securing the idler pulley - 6-cylinder engine

7.15 Withdraw the alternator from the engine

### Refitting

**8** Refitting is a reversal of removal, but ensure that the drivebelt guide pulley is correctly fitted as noted before removal, and refit the auxiliary drivebelt as described in Chapter 1. Where applicable, make sure that the lug on the drivebelt guide pulley engages with the cut-out in the alternator **(see illustration)**.

## *6-cylinder engines*

### Removal

**9** Disconnect the battery negative lead.
**10** Remove the air cleaner assembly and the air mass meter as described in Chapter 4B.
**11** Remove the auxiliary drivebelt as described in Chapter 1.
**12** Pull off the cover(s), then unscrew the nuts and disconnect the wiring from the rear of the alternator **(see illustration)**.
**13** Prise the cover from the centre of the auxiliary drivebelt tensioner idler pulley, then unscrew the upper through-bolt securing the idler pulley and the alternator **(see illustration)**.
**14** Counterhold the nut and unscrew the lower alternator securing through-bolt.
**15** Withdraw the alternator from the engine **(see illustration)**.

### Refitting

**16** Refitting is a reversal of removal, bearing in mind the following points.

*a) When refitting the tensioner idler pulley, ensure that the lug on the rear of the pulley assembly engages with the corresponding cut-out in the mounting bracket.*
*b) Refit the auxiliary drivebelt (see Chapter 1).*

## 8 Alternator - testing and overhaul

If the alternator is thought to be suspect, it should be removed from the vehicle and taken to an auto-electrician for testing. Most auto-electricians will be able to supply and fit brushes at a reasonable cost. However, check on the cost of repairs before proceeding as it may prove more economical to obtain a new or exchange alternator.

## 9 Starting system - testing

**Note:** *Refer to the precautions given in "Safety first!" and in Section 1 of this Chapter before starting work.*

**1** If the starter motor fails to operate when the ignition key is turned to the appropriate position, the following possible causes may be to blame.

*a) The battery is faulty.*
*b) The electrical connections between the switch, solenoid, battery and starter motor are somewhere failing to pass the necessary current from the battery through the starter to earth.*
*c) The solenoid is faulty.*
*d) The starter motor is mechanically or electrically defective.*

**2** To check the battery, switch on the headlights. If they dim after a few seconds, this indicates that the battery is discharged - recharge (see Section 3) or renew the battery. If the headlights glow brightly, operate the ignition switch and observe the lights. If they dim, then this indicates that current is reaching the starter motor, therefore the fault must lie in the starter motor. If the lights continue to glow brightly (and no clicking sound can be heard from the starter motor solenoid), this indicates that there is a fault in the circuit or solenoid - see following paragraphs. If the starter motor turns slowly when operated, but the battery is in good condition, then this indicates that either the starter motor is faulty, or there is considerable resistance somewhere in the circuit.
**3** If a fault in the circuit is suspected, disconnect the battery leads (including the earth connection to the body), the starter/solenoid wiring and the engine/transmission earth strap. Thoroughly clean the connections, and reconnect the leads and wiring, then use a voltmeter or test lamp to check that full battery voltage is available at the battery positive lead connection to the solenoid, and that the earth is sound. Smear petroleum jelly around the battery terminals to prevent corrosion - corroded connections are amongst the most frequent causes of electrical system faults.
**4** If the battery and all connections are in good condition, check the circuit by disconnecting the wire from the solenoid blade terminal. Connect a voltmeter or test lamp between the wire end and a good earth (such as the battery negative terminal), and check that the wire is live when the ignition switch is turned to the "start" position. If it is, then the circuit is sound - if not the circuit wiring can be checked as described in Chapter 12.
**5** The solenoid contacts can be checked by connecting a voltmeter or test lamp between the battery positive feed connection on the starter side of the solenoid, and earth. When the ignition switch is turned to the "start" position, there should be a reading or lighted bulb, as applicable. If there is no reading or lighted bulb, the solenoid is faulty and should be renewed.
**6** If the circuit and solenoid are proved sound, the fault must lie in the starter motor. In this event, it may be possible to have the starter motor overhauled by a specialist, but check on the cost of spares before proceeding, as it may prove more economical to obtain a new or exchange motor.

## 10 Starter motor - removal and refitting

## *M40 4-cylinder engines*

### Removal

**1** Disconnect the battery negative lead.

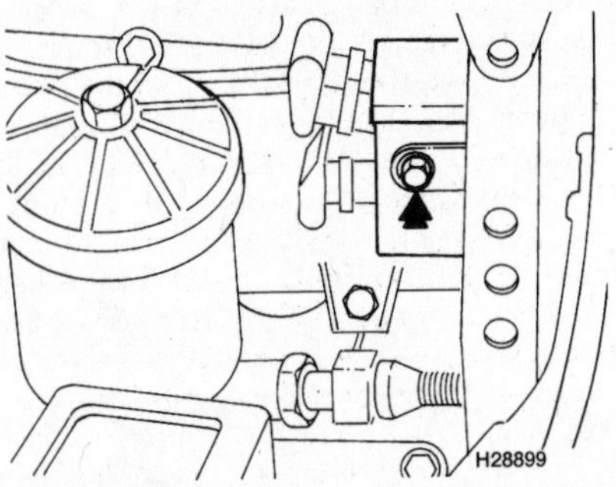


**10.6 Wiring ducting-to-manifold securing nut (arrowed) - M40 engine**

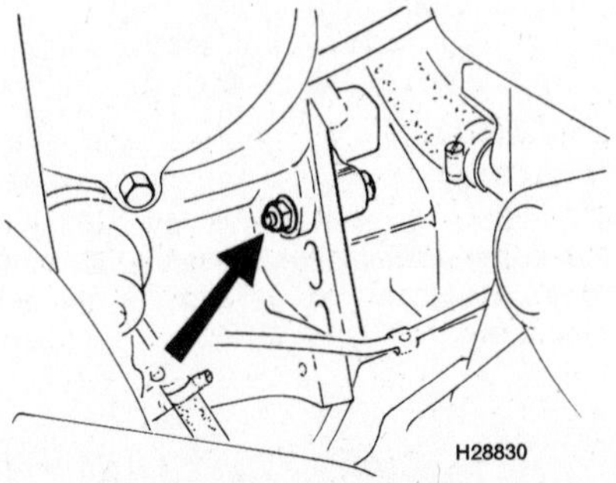


**10.15 Working under the vehicle, unscrew the lower starter motor securing nut and bolt (arrowed) - M42 and M43 engines**

**2** Remove the air cleaner and the air mass meter as described in Chapter 4A.

**3** Release the securing clips, and release the wiring from the dipstick tube.

**4** Release the idle speed control valve from its rubber mounting, and move it to one side, clear of the dipstick tube.

**5** Unscrew the upper dipstick mounting bracket from the engine, then pull the lower end of the dipstick/tube assembly from the cylinder block and withdraw the assembly.

**6** To improve access, unbolt the wiring ducting from the inlet manifold **(see illustration)**. On certain models, it may be necessary to unbolt other components (and unclip hoses and wiring) for access to the starter motor bolts. Where this is necessary, note the routing and location of all hoses and wiring to avoid confusion on refitting.

**7** Unscrew the securing nuts and disconnect the wiring from the rear of the starter motor **(see illustration)**.

**8** Counterhold the bolts, and unscrew the starter motor securing nuts. Note that it will be necessary to pull the coolant hose down for access to the top nut - take care not to damage the hose.

**9** Withdraw the mounting bolts, and manipulate the starter motor out through the engine compartment.

### Refitting

**10** Refitting is a reversal of removal, bearing in mind the following points.

*a) Ensure that all wires and hoses are routed as noted before removal.*

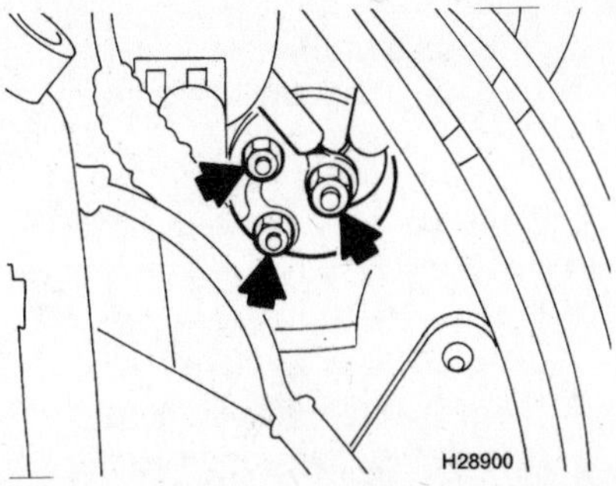


**10.7 Disconnect wiring (arrowed) from the rear of the starter motor - M40 engine**

**10.20 Disconnect the starter motor wiring (arrowed) - 6-cylinder engine**

*b) Before refitting the dipstick tube, check the condition of the O-ring at the bottom of the tube, and renew if necessary.*

*c) Refit the air cleaner and the air mass meter with reference to Chapter 4A.*

## M42 and M43 4-cylinder engines

### Removal

**11** Disconnect the battery negative lead.

**12** Unscrew the nuts and disconnect the wiring from the rear of the starter motor.

**13** Working from the engine compartment, reach down behind the engine, and unscrew the upper starter motor securing nut and bolt. For improved access to the bolt, unscrew the bolt securing the dipstick tube bracket to the engine, then pull the dipstick tube from the cylinder block.

**14** Apply the handbrake, then jack up the front of the vehicle and support securely on axle stands (see *"Jacking and vehicle support"*).

**15** Working underneath the vehicle, unscrew the lower starter motor securing nut and bolt **(see illustration)**.

**16** Still working underneath the vehicle, pull the starter motor back to release it from the gearbox/transmission bellhousing, then turn the motor so that the solenoid is at the top.

**17** Pivot the rear of the motor down, and manipulate it out from under the vehicle.

### Refitting

**18** Refitting is a reversal of removal, but check the condition of the O-ring at the bottom of the dipstick tube and renew if necessary.

## 6-cylinder engines

### Removal

**19** Remove the inlet manifold (Chapter 4B).

**20** Unscrew the nuts and disconnect the wiring from the starter motor terminals **(see illustration)**.

**21** Unscrew the bolt securing the starter motor front mounting bracket to the cylinder block, then unscrew the two nuts securing the bracket to the motor, and remove the bracket **(see illustration)**

**22** Unscrew the two rear motor nuts and bolts. A Torx spanner may be required to counterhold the bolts, as there is insufficient clearance to use a socket **(see illustration)**.

**23** Manipulate the motor out from the engine compartment **(see illustration)**.

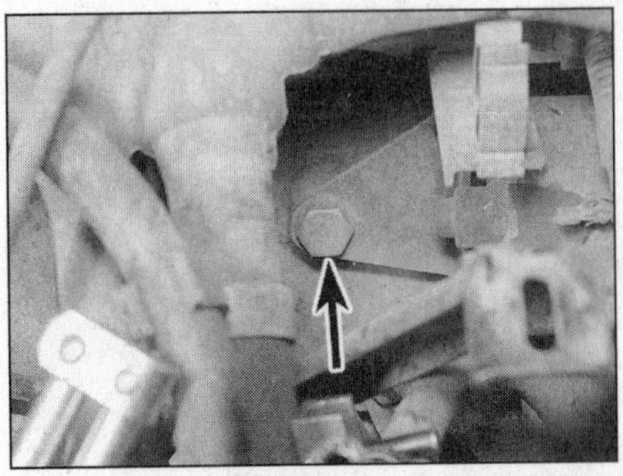

**10.21 Unscrew the bolt (arrowed) securing the starter motor bracket to the cylinder block - 6-cylinder engine**

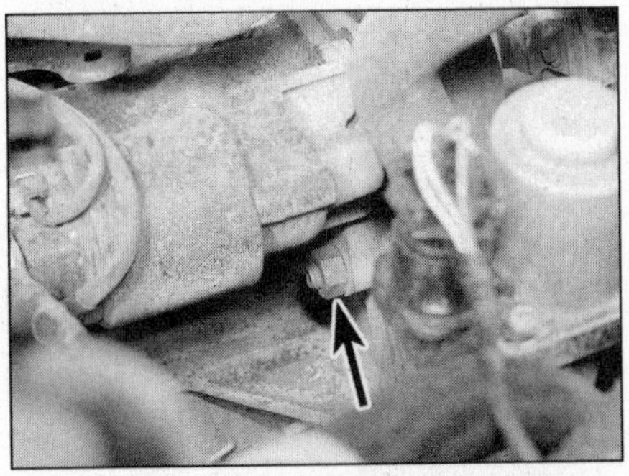

**10.22 Lower starter motor securing nut (arrowed) - 6-cylinder engine**

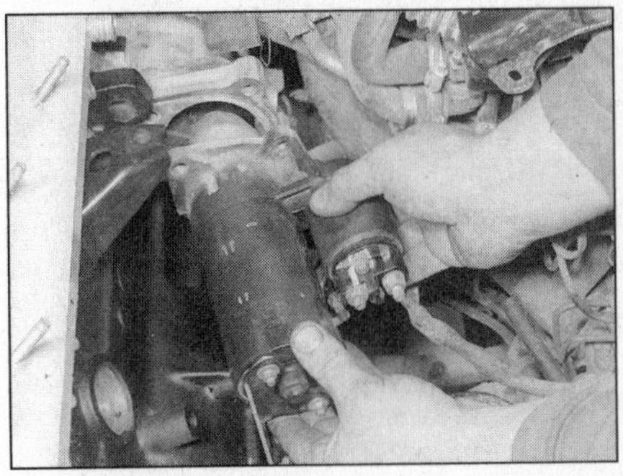

**10.23 Removing the starter motor - 6-cylinder engine**

### Refitting

**24** Refitting is a reversal of removal, but refit the inlet manifold as described in Chapter 4B.

## 11 Starter motor - testing and overhaul

If the starter motor is thought to be suspect, it should be removed from the vehicle and taken to an auto-electrician for testing. Most auto-electricians will be able to supply and fit brushes at a reasonable cost. However, check on the cost of repairs before proceeding as it may prove more economical to obtain a new or exchange motor.

## 12 Ignition switch - removal and refitting

The ignition switch is integral with the steering column lock, and can be removed as described in Chapter 10.

## 13 Oil pressure warning light switch - removal and refitting

### *Removal*

**1** The switch is screwed into the rear of the oil filter housing on the left-hand side of the engine.

**2** Disconnect the battery negative lead.

**3** Disconnect the switch wiring plug, then unscrew the switch from the housing **(see illustration)**. Be prepared for oil spillage, and if the switch is to be left removed from the engine for any length of time, plug the hole in the housing.

**13.3 Disconnecting the oil pressure warning light switch wiring plug - 6-cylinder engine**

### *Refitting*

**4** Refitting is a reversal of removal, but tighten the switch securely, and on completion check the engine oil level as described in Chapter 1.

# Chapter 5 Part B:
# Ignition systems

## Contents



## Degrees of difficulty

| | | | | |
|---|---|---|---|---|
| **Easy,** suitable for novice with little experience | **Fairly easy,** suitable for beginner with some experience | **Fairly difficult,** suitable for competent DIY mechanic | **Difficult,** suitable for experienced DIY mechanic | **Very difficult,** suitable for expert DIY or professional |

## Specifications

### Firing order

| | |
|---|---|
| 4-cylinder engines | 1-3-4-2 |
| 6-cylinder engines | 1-5-3-6-2-4 |

### Ignition timing

Electronically-controlled by DME - no adjustment possible

### Torque wrench settings

| | Nm | lbf ft |
|---|---|---|
| Rotor arm securing screws (M40 engine) | 3 | 2 |
| Distributor cap securing screws (M40 engine) | 4 | 3 |
| Spark plugs | 30 | 22 |
| Knock sensor securing bolt | 20 | 15 |

## 1 General information and precautions

### *General information*

The ignition system is controlled by the engine management system (see Chapter 4), known as DME (Digital Motor Electronics). The DME system controls all ignition and fuel injection functions using a central ECU (Electronic Control Unit).

The ignition timing is based on inputs provided to the ECU by various sensors supplying information on engine load, engine speed, coolant temperature sensor and inlet air temperature (see Chapter 4).

Some engines are fitted with knock sensors to detect "knocking" (also known as "pinking" or pre-ignition). The knock sensors are sensitive to vibration and detect the knocking which occurs when a cylinder starts to pre-ignite. The knock sensor provides a signal to the ECU which in turn retards the ignition advance setting until the knocking ceases.

On all engines except the M40 4-cylinder engine, a distributorless ignition system is used, with a separate HT coil for each cylinder. No distributor is used, and the coils provide the high voltage signal direct to each spark plug.

On M40 4-cylinder engines, the only function the distributor performs is the distribution of the high voltage signal to the individual spark plugs.

The ECU uses the inputs from the various sensors to calculate the required ignition advance and the coil charging time.

### *Precautions*

Refer to the precautions in Chapter 5A.

Testing of ignition system components should be entrusted to a BMW dealer. Improvised testing techniques are time-consuming and run the risk of damaging the engine management ECU.

## 2 Ignition systems - testing

**1** If a fault appears in the engine management (fuel/injection) system, first ensure that the fault is not due to a poor electrical connection, or to poor maintenance, ie check that the air cleaner filter element is clean, that the spark plugs are in good condition and correctly gapped, and that the engine breather hoses are clear and undamaged.

**2** On models with the M40 4-cylinder engine, check the condition of the distributor cap and rotor arm, as described in Section 4.

**3** On 4-cylinder engines, check the condition of the HT leads as follows.

*a) Make sure that the leads are numbered to ensure correct refitting, then pull the end of one of the leads from the spark plug.*

*b) Check inside the end fitting for corrosion, which looks like a white crusty powder.*

*c) Push the end fitting back onto the spark plug, ensuring that it is a tight fit on the plug. If not, remove the lead again, and use pliers to carefully crimp the metal connector inside the end fitting until it fits securely on the end of the spark plug.*

*d) Using a clean rag, wipe the entire length of the lead to remove any built up dirt and grease. Once the lead is clean, check for burns, cracks and other damage. Do not bend the lead excessively, nor pull the lead lengthways - the conductor inside might break.*

*e) Disconnect the other end of the lead from the distributor cap (release the clips and pull off the cover for access to the leads), or coil, as applicable, and check the end fitting in the same manner as the spark plug end. Again ensure that the lead is identified to ensure correct refitting.*

*f) Refit the lead securely on completion.*

*g) Check the remaining leads one at a time in the same manner.*

**4** Check that the throttle cable is correctly adjusted as described in Chapter 4.

**5** If the engine is running very roughly, check the compression pressures as described in Chapter 2.

**6** If these checks fail to reveal the cause of the problem, then the vehicle should be taken to a BMW dealer for testing using the appropriate specialist diagnostic equipment. The ECU incorporates a self-diagnostic function which stores fault codes in the system memory (note that stored fault codes are erased if the battery is disconnected). These fault codes can be read using the appropriate BMW diagnosis equipment. Improvised testing techniques are time-consuming and run the risk of damaging the engine management ECU.

## 3 Ignition HT coil - removal and refitting

### *M40 4-cylinder engines*

#### Removal

**1** The coil is located on a bracket attached to the right-hand suspension turret in the engine compartment.

**2** Disconnect the battery negative lead.

**3** Where applicable, pull the top cover from the coil, and disconnect the coil HT lead.

**4** Unscrew the nuts, and disconnect the LT wires from the coil, noting their locations.

**5** Unscrew the nut securing the bracket to the body panel, and withdraw the coil/bracket assembly.

#### Refitting

**6** Refitting is a reversal of removal, but ensure that all wiring is correctly reconnected.

### *M42 4-cylinder engines*

#### Removal

**7** Each spark plug is fed by its own coil, and coils are mounted together on the right-hand suspension turret in the engine compartment.

**8** Disconnect the battery negative lead.

**9** On early models, disconnect the HT leads from the coils, noting their locations to ensure correct refitting (mark the leads if necessary), then unclip the cover from the top of the coils.

**10** On later models, unclip the cover from the top of the coil assembly, and disconnect the HT lead from the coil **(see illustration)**. If all the coils are to be removed, ensure that the HT leads are marked to avoid confusion on refitting.

**11** Lift the securing clip and disconnect the wiring plug from the relevant coil **(see illustration)**. Again if all the coils are to be removed, ensure that the wiring is marked.

**12** Unscrew the coil securing nuts and/or bolts, noting the location of any earth wires or brackets secured by the bolts, then withdraw the coil(s) **(see illustration)**.

#### Refitting

**13** Refitting is a reversal of removal, ensuring that the HT leads and coil wiring plugs are correctly reconnected. Where applicable, ensure that any earth leads and/or brackets are in place on the coil securing bolts.

### *M43 4-cylinder engines*

#### Removal

**14** Each spark plug is fed by its own coil, and the coils are combined as one unit mounted on the right-hand suspension turret in the engine compartment **(see illustration)**.

**15** Disconnect the battery negative lead.

**16** Turn the locking collar and disconnect the coil wiring plug.

**17** Disconnect the HT leads from the bottom of the coil unit, noting their locations to ensure correct refitting. Note that the cylinder numbers for the respective leads are marked on the top of the coil unit. If necessary mark the leads.

**18** Unscrew the securing nuts and withdraw the coil unit from the body panel.

#### Refitting

**19** Refitting is a reversal of removal, but ensure that the HT leads are correctly reconnected.

### *6-cylinder engines*

#### Removal

**20** Each spark plug is fed by its own coil, and the coils are mounted directly on top of the spark plugs, in the cylinder head cover.

**21** Disconnect the battery negative lead.

**22** Remove the engine oil filler cap.

**23** Remove the plastic cover from the top of the cylinder head cover. To remove the cover, prise out the cover plates and unscrew the two securing nuts, then lift and pull the cover forwards. Manipulate the cover over the oil filler neck **(see illustrations)**.

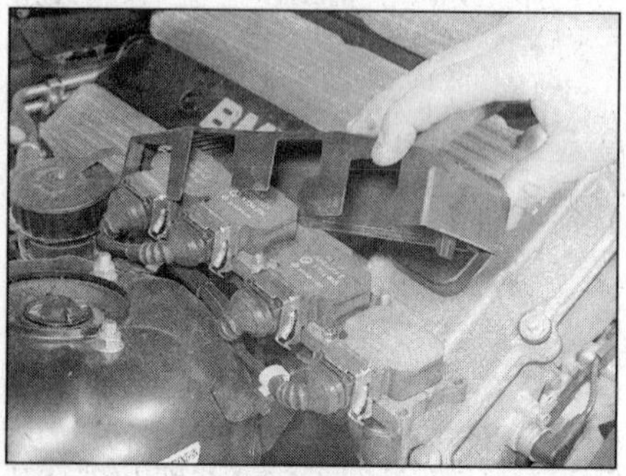

**3.10 Unclip the cover from the top of the coil assembly - M42 engine**

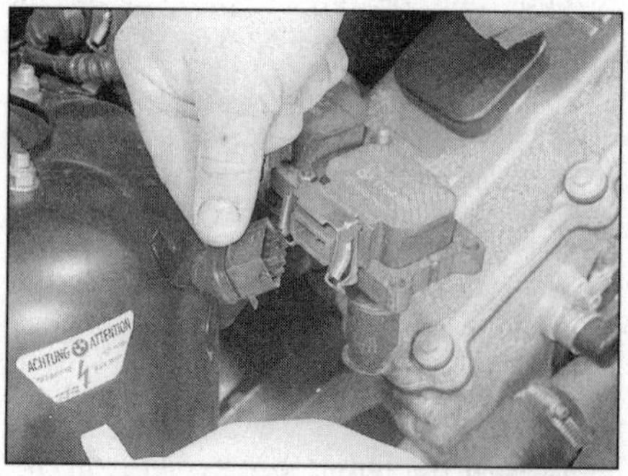

**3.11 Disconnecting a coil wiring plug - M42 engine**

**3.12 Unscrewing a coil securing nut - M42 engine**

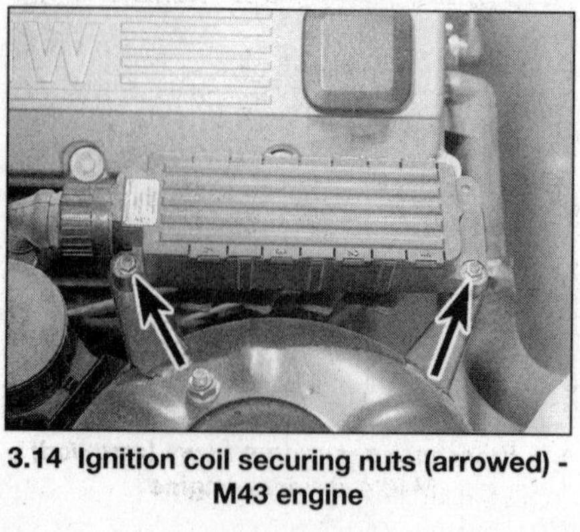

**3.14 Ignition coil securing nuts (arrowed) - M43 engine**

**3.23a Prise out the covers for access to the securing nuts . . .**

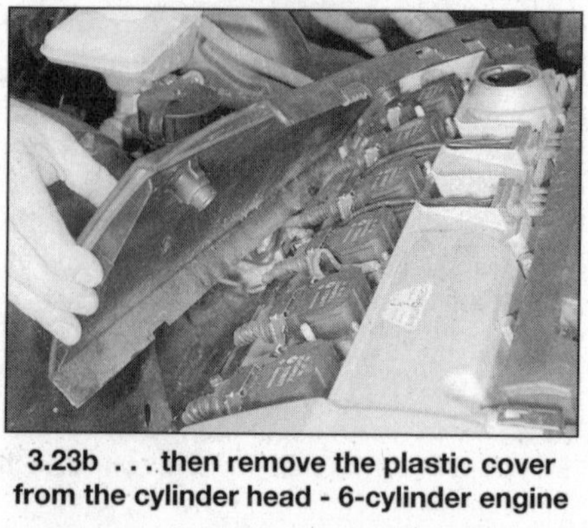

**3.23b . . . then remove the plastic cover from the cylinder head - 6-cylinder engine**

**3.24 Disconnecting a coil wiring plug - 6-cylinder engine**

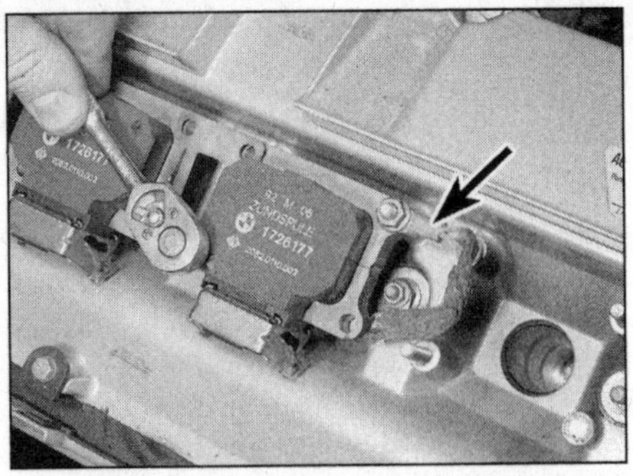

**3.25a Unscrewing a coil securing nut. Note the location of the earth lead (arrowed) - 6-cylinder engine**

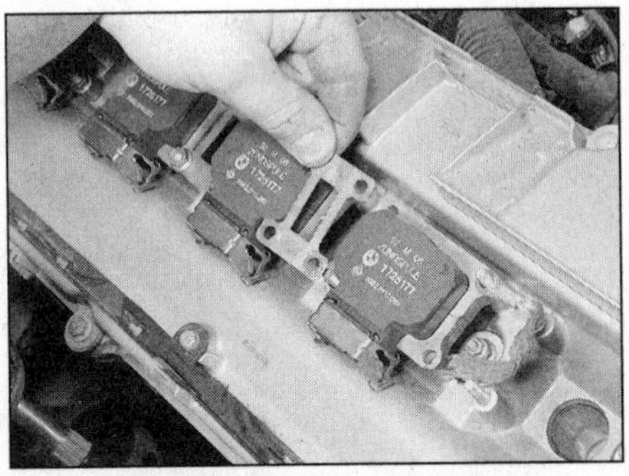

**3.25b Where applicable, remove the bracket . . .**

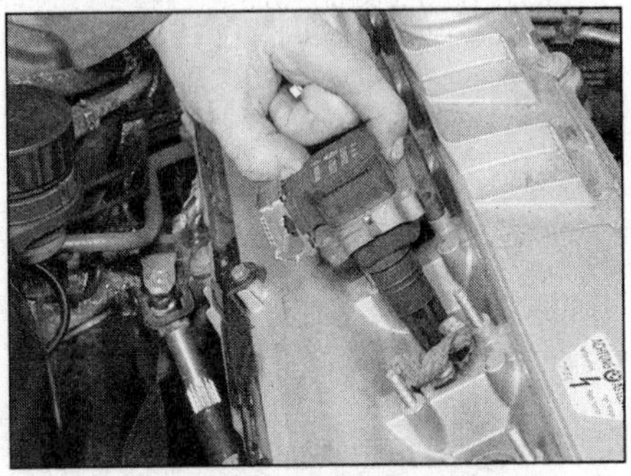

**3.26 . . . then withdraw the coil - 6-cylinder engine**

**24** Lift the securing clip, and disconnect the wiring plug from the relevant coil **(see illustration)**. If all the coils are to be removed, disconnect all the wiring connectors, then unscrew the nut securing the coil wiring earth lead to the stud on the front of the timing chain cover - the wiring harness can then be unclipped from the camshaft cover and moved to one side.

**25** Unscrew the two coil securing nuts, noting the locations of any earth leads and/or brackets secured by the nuts (note that where one of the nuts also secures a metal wiring bracket, it may be necessary to unscrew the bracket securing nut from the adjacent coil, allowing the bracket to be removed to enable coil removal) **(see illustrations)**. Note that the coil connectors are spring-loaded, so the top of the coil will lift as the nuts are unscrewed.

**26** Pull the coil from the camshaft cover and spark plug, and withdraw it from the engine **(see illustration)**.

### Refitting

**27** Refitting is a reversal of removal, but ensure that any earth leads and brackets are in position as noted before removal. The earth leads connect to the studs for Nos 3 and 6 cylinder coils.

## 4 Distributor components (M40 4-cylinder engines) - removal and refitting

### *Distributor cap*

### Removal

**1** Disconnect the battery negative lead.

**2** Using a small flat-bladed screwdriver, release the securing clips at the top and bottom of the cap cover, then pull off the cover.

**3** Check the HT leads for identification marks, and if necessary mark the leads to ensure correct refitting. Disconnect the HT leads from the cap.

**4** Unscrew the three securing screws and withdraw the distributor cap **(see illustration)**.

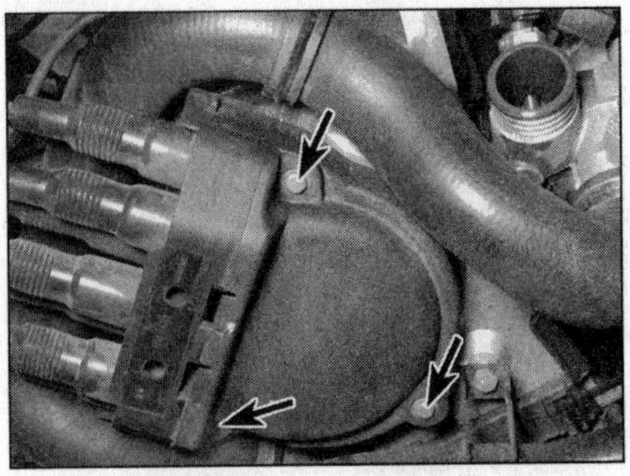

**4.4 Distributor cap securing screws (arrowed) - M40 4-cylinder engine**

### Inspection

**5** Wipe the cap clean, and carefully inspect it inside and out for signs of cracks, carbon tracks (tracking) and worn, burned or loose contacts. Check that the carbon brush in the cap is unworn, free to move against spring pressure and making good contact with the rotor arm.

**6** If the cap is to be renewed, it is advisable to renew the rotor arm at the same time.

### Refitting

**7** Refitting is a reversal of removal, but ensure that the HT leads are correctly reconnected.

### *Rotor arm*

### Removal

**8** Remove the distributor cap as described previously in this Section.

**9** Unscrew the three securing screws, and pull the rotor arm from the camshaft **(see illustration)**.

### Inspection

**10** Clean the rotor arm, and check for cracks and damage. Also check for wear and burning on the contact. Any minor corrosion and carbon deposits can be removed from the contact by careful scraping, or using fine emery paper.

### Refitting

**11** Refitting is a reversal of removal, but check that the HT leads are correctly reconnected when refitting the distributor cap.

## 5 Knock sensor - removal and refitting

### *M42 4-cylinder engine*

### Removal

**1** Two knock sensors are fitted, screwed into the left-hand side of the cylinder block. One sensor detects knocking in Nos 1 and 2 cylinders, and the other sensor detects knocking in Nos 3 and 4 cylinders.

**2** Disconnect the battery negative lead.

**3** Release the securing clips, and pull the wiring ducting from the fuel injectors.

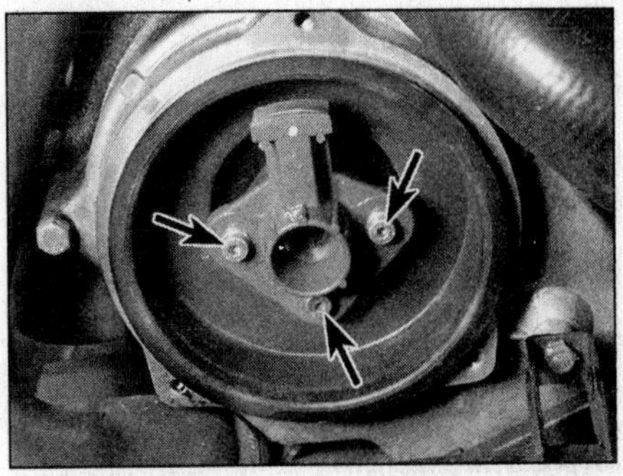

**4.9 Rotor arm securing screws (arrowed) - M40 4-cylinder engine**

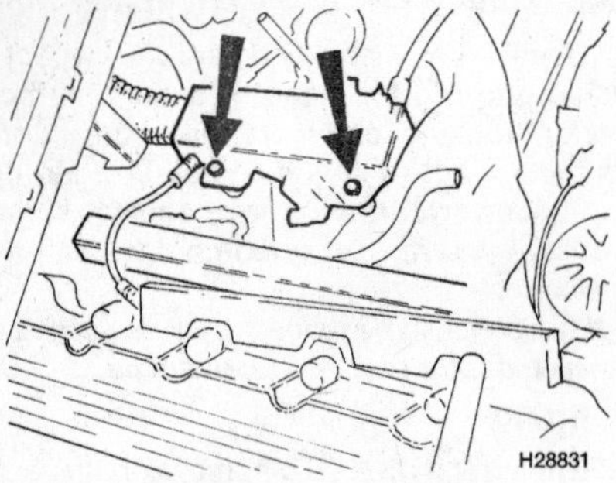


**5.5 Wiring ducting-to-manifold securing bolts (arrowed) - M42 4-cylinder engine**

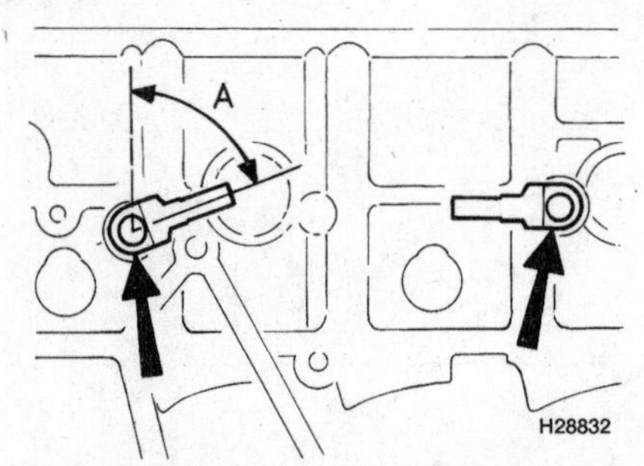


**5.13 Knock sensor locations (arrowed) - M42 4-cylinder engine**

*A Ensure that the wiring is positioned at an angle of 70° as shown*

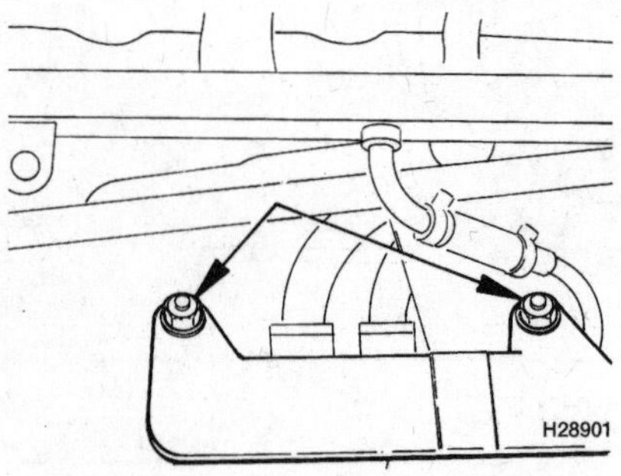


**5.22 Connector bracket securing bolts (arrowed) - M42 4-cylinder engine**

**4** Remove the upper section of the inlet manifold as described in Chapter 4A.

**5** Unscrew the bolts securing the wiring ducting to the lower section of the inlet manifold **(see illustration)**.

**6** Release the clips and pull the wiring ducting from the knock sensor wiring connectors. Move the wiring ducting to one side.

**7** Remove the idle speed control valve as described in Chapter 4A.

**8** Disconnect the wiring from the starter motor and the alternator.

**9** Trace the wiring back from the relevant sensor, and release the wiring plug from the clip.

***Warning: If both sensors are being removed, take note of the plug locations, as if the plugs are mixed up and incorrectly reconnected, engine damage could result.***

**10** Disconnect the coolant hose, and move it to one side for access to the sensors. Be prepared for coolant spillage, and plug the openings to prevent further coolant loss.

**11** Unscrew the securing bolt, and withdraw the sensor from the engine. Note that angle of the wiring in relation to the cylinder block.

### Refitting

**12** Commence refitting by thoroughly cleaning the mating faces of the sensor and the cylinder block.

**13** Refit the sensor to the cylinder block ensuring that the wiring is positioned as shown **(see illustration)**. Ensure that the wiring is routed so that it will not chafe on surrounding components.

**14** With the sensor correctly positioned, tighten the securing bolt to the specified torque.

**15** Refit the wiring connector to the clip, ensuring that it is correctly positioned as noted before removal.

***Warning: If the plugs for the two sensors are incorrectly connected (ie, mixed up), engine damage may result. Ensure that the plugs are reconnected as noted before removal. Normally the connectors are positioned so that they cannot be mixed up.***

**16** Further refitting is a reversal of removal, bearing in mind the following points.

*a) Refit the idle speed control valve with reference to Chapter 4A.*

*b) Refit the upper section of the inlet manifold with reference to Chapter 4A.*

*c) On completion, check and if necessary top-up the coolant level as described in Chapter 1.*

## M43 4-cylinder engine up to 1995 model year

**17** The procedure is as described previously for M40 engine models, noting that it is not necessary to disconnect the wiring ducting from the fuel injectors, or disconnect the coolant hose.

## M43 4-cylinder engine from 1996 model year

### Removal

**18** Two knock sensors are fitted, screwed into the left-hand side of the cylinder block. One sensor detects knocking in Nos 1 and 2 cylinders, and the other sensor detects knocking in Nos 3 and 4 cylinders.

**19** Depressurise the fuel system as described in Chapter 4A, then disconnect the battery negative lead.

**20** Remove the upper section of the inlet manifold as described in Chapter 4A.

**21** Disconnect the camshaft and crankshaft position sensor wiring connectors from the connector bracket, noting their locations to ensure correct refitting.

**22** Unscrew the two bolts securing the connector bracket to the lower section of the inlet manifold **(see illustration)**.

**23** Disconnect the knock sensor wiring plug, and release it from the connector bracket.

**24** The sensor for cylinders 1 and 2 is located between the oil filter and the inlet manifold, and can be removed as follows **(see illustrations)**.

*a) Access to the sensor can be gained from above, between the manifold inlet tracts for cylinders 2 and 3 after disconnecting the fuel line from the fuel rail. Be prepared for fuel spillage; plug the open ends of the fuel line and fuel rail to prevent dirt ingress.*

*b) To allow clearance for the sensor to be removed, it will be necessary to slacken the bolt securing the coolant pipe to the engine, and pull the coolant pipe slightly away from the engine.*

*c) Unscrew the securing bolt and remove the sensor.*

**25** Access to the sensor for cylinders 3 and 4 is more straightforward, and the sensor can simply be unbolted from the cylinder block **(see illustration)**.

### Refitting

**26** Commence refitting by thoroughly cleaning the mating faces of the sensor and the cylinder block.

**27** Refit the sensor and tighten the securing bolt to the specified torque.

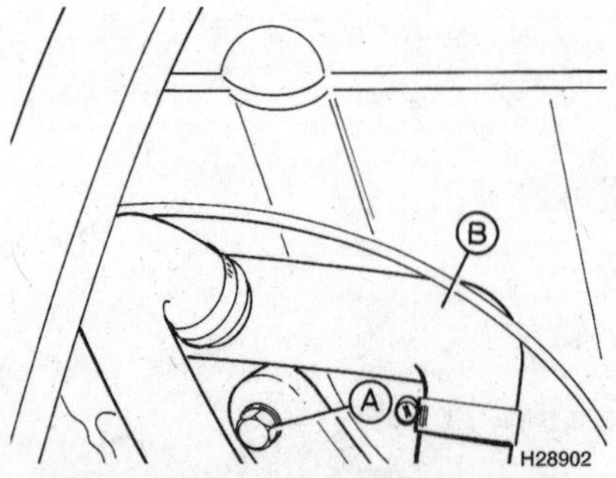


**5.24a Location of knock sensor for cylinders 1 and 2 - M43 4-cylinder engine**

*A Knock sensor bolt B Coolant pipe*

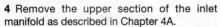

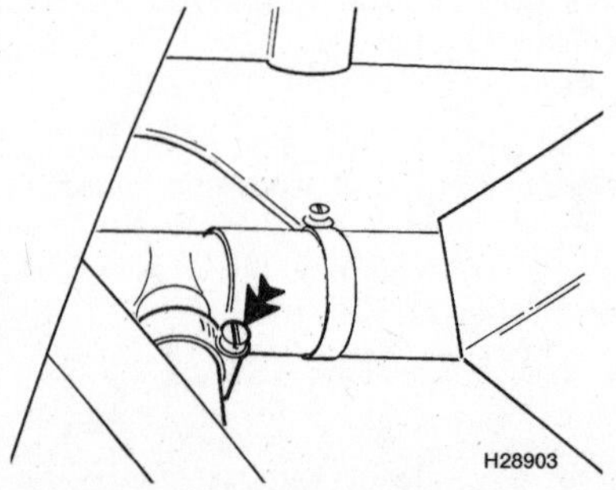


**5.24b Coolant pipe securing bolt (arrowed) - M43 4-cylinder engine**

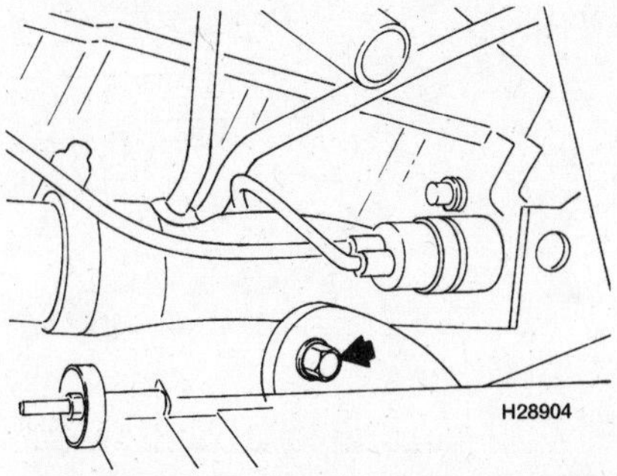


**5.25 Location of knock sensor (arrowed) for cylinders 3 & 4 - M43 4-cylinder engine**

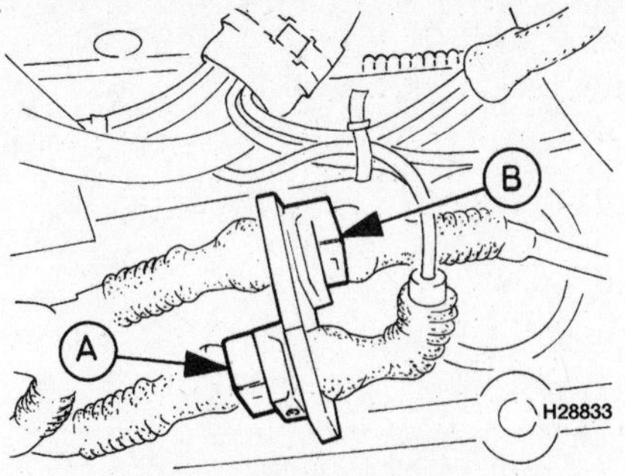


**5.32 Knock sensor wiring plug locations - M50 6-cylinder engine**

*A Plug for Nos 1 to 3 cylinders knock sensor*
*B Plug for Nos 4 to 6 cylinders knock sensor*

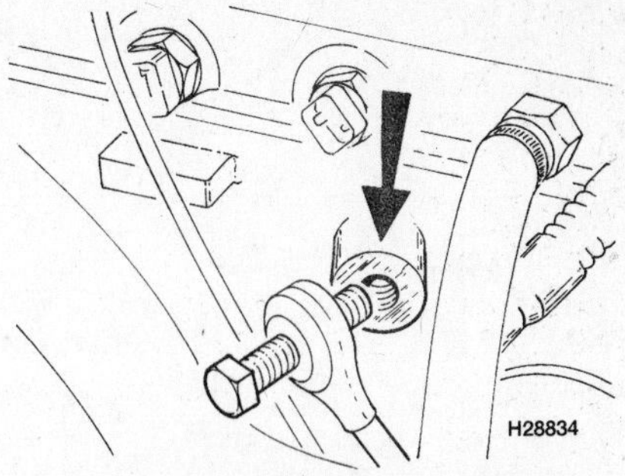


**5.34 Removing the knock sensor (arrowed) for cylinders 1 to 3 - M50 6-cylinder engine**

**28** Further refitting is a reversal of removal, bearing in mind the following points.

a) *Ensure that all wiring connectors are correctly reconnected as noted before removal.*
b) *Refit the upper section of the inlet manifold as described in Chapter 4A.*
c) *Where applicable, on completion prime the fuel system as described in Chapter 4A.*

## M50 6-cylinder engine

### Removal

**29** Two knock sensors are fitted, screwed into the left-hand side of the cylinder block. One sensor detects knocking in Nos 1 to 3 cylinders, and the other sensor detects knocking in Nos 4 to 6 cylinders.

**30** Disconnect the battery negative lead.

**31** Remove the inlet manifold as described in Chapter 4B.

**32** Locate the sensor connector bracket which is located beneath the idle speed control valve **(see illustration).**

***Warning: If both knock sensors are to be removed, mark the wiring connectors to ensure correct refitting. Incorrect reconnection may result in engine damage.***

**33** Disconnect the sensor wiring connector(s).

**34** Unscrew the securing bolt and remove the knock sensor, noting the routing of the wiring. The sensor for cylinders 1 to 3 is located beneath the temperature sensors in the cylinder head **(see illustration)**. The sensor for cylinders 4 to 6 is located to the rear of the sensor wiring connector bracket.

### Refitting

**35** Commence refitting by thoroughly cleaning the mating faces of the sensor and the cylinder block.

**36** Refit the sensor to the cylinder block, tightening the securing bolt to the specified torque.

**37** Route the wiring as noted before removal, then reconnect the connector(s) to the bracket, ensuring that the connectors are positioned as noted before removal.

***Warning: Ensure that the wiring connectors are correctly connected as noted before removal. If the connectors are incorrectly connected (ie, mixed up), engine damage may result.***

**38** Refit the inlet manifold as described in Chapter 4A.

# Notes

# Chapter 6
# Clutch

## Contents



## Degrees of difficulty

| | | | | |
|---|---|---|---|---|
| **Easy,** suitable for novice with little experience | **Fairly easy,** suitable for beginner with some experience | **Fairly difficult,** suitable for competent DIY mechanic | **Difficult,** suitable for experienced DIY mechanic | **Very difficult,** suitable for expert DIY or professional |

## Specifications

| | | |
|---|---|---|
| **Type** | Single dry plate with diaphragm spring, hydraulically-operated | |
| **Driveplate** | | |
| Minimum thickness | 7.5 mm | |
| **Torque wrench settings** | **Nm** | **lbf ft** |
| Clutch cover-to-flywheel bolts | 24 | 18 |
| Clutch slave cylinder nuts | 22 | 16 |
| Clutch master cylinder bolts | 22 | 16 |
| Hydraulic pipe unions | 16 | 12 |

### 1 General information

All models are fitted with a single dry plate clutch, which consists of five main components; friction disc, pressure plate, diaphragm spring, cover and release bearing.

The friction disc is free to slide along the splines of the gearbox input shaft, and is held in position between the flywheel and the pressure plate, by the pressure exerted on the pressure plate by the diaphragm spring. Friction lining material is riveted to both sides of the friction disc, and cushioning springs between the friction surfaces help to absorb transmission shocks and ensure a smooth take-up of power as the clutch is engaged. Two types of friction disc are fitted to models covered by this manual, depending on the type of flywheel. On engines with a conventional flywheel, the friction disc has integral damping springs (visible in the hub, between the centre of the hub and the friction material). On engines with a "dual-mass" flywheel (refer to the relevant Part of Chapter 2 for details), the damping springs are integrated into the flywheel itself. The damping springs serve a similar purpose to the cushioning springs described previously.

The diaphragm spring is mounted on pins, and is held in place in the cover by annular fulcrum rings.

The release bearing is located on a guide sleeve at the front of the gearbox, and the bearing is free to slide on the sleeve, under the action of the release arm which pivots inside the clutch bellhousing.

The release mechanism is operated by the clutch pedal, using hydraulic pressure. The pedal acts on the hydraulic master cylinder pushrod, and a slave cylinder, mounted on the gearbox bellhousing, operates the clutch release lever via a pushrod.

When the clutch pedal is depressed, the release arm pushes the release bearing forwards, to bear against the centre of the diaphragm spring, thus pushing the centre of the diaphragm spring inwards. The diaphragm spring acts against the fulcrum rings in the cover, and so as the centre of the spring is pushed in, the outside of the spring is pushed out, so allowing the pressure plate to move backwards away from the friction disc.

When the clutch pedal is released, the diaphragm spring forces the pressure plate into contact with the friction linings on the friction disc, and simultaneously pushes the friction disc forwards on its splines, forcing it against the flywheel. The friction disc is now firmly sandwiched between the pressure plate and the flywheel, and drive is taken up.

The clutch is self-adjusting. As wear takes place on the friction disc over a period of time, the pressure plate automatically moves closer to the friction plate to compensate.

6

### 2 Clutch assembly - removal, inspection and refitting

***Warning: Dust created by clutch wear and deposited on the clutch components may contain asbestos, which is a health hazard. DO NOT blow it out with compressed air, or inhale any of it. DO NOT use petrol (or petroleum-based solvents) to clean off the dust. Brake system cleaner or methylated spirit should be used to flush the dust into a suitable***

**2.4 Removing the clutch assembly**

**2.12 Offering the clutch friction disc into position**

**2.13 Ensure that the clutch cover locates over the dowels (arrowed) on the flywheel**

**2.15 Using a clutch alignment tool to centre the friction disc**

***receptacle. After the clutch components are wiped clean with rags, dispose of the contaminated rags and cleaner in a sealed, marked container.***

## Removal

**1** Remove the gearbox, as described in Chapter 7A.

**2** If the original clutch is to be refitted, make alignment marks between the clutch cover and the flywheel, so that the clutch can be refitted in its original position.

**3** Progressively unscrew the bolts securing the clutch cover to the flywheel, and where applicable recover the washers.

**4** Withdraw the clutch cover from the flywheel **(see illustration)**. Be prepared to catch the clutch friction disc, which may drop out of the cover as it is withdrawn, and note which way round the friction disc is fitted - the two sides of the disc are normally marked "Engine side" and "Transmission side". The greater projecting side of the hub faces away from the flywheel.

## Inspection

**5** With the clutch assembly removed, clean off all traces of dust using a dry cloth. Although most friction discs now have asbestos-free linings, some do not, and it is wise to take suitable precautions; *asbestos dust is harmful, and must not be inhaled.*

**6** Examine the linings of the friction disc for wear and loose rivets, and the disc for distortion, cracks, broken damping springs (where applicable) and worn splines. The surface of the friction linings may be highly glazed, but, as long as the friction material pattern can be clearly seen, this is satisfactory. If there is any sign of oil contamination, indicated by a continuous, or patchy, shiny black discolouration, the disc must be renewed. The source of the contamination must be traced and rectified before fitting new clutch components; typically, a leaking crankshaft rear oil seal or gearbox input shaft oil seal - or both - will be to blame (renewal procedures are given in the relevant Part of Chapter 2, and Chapter 7A respectively). The disc must also be renewed if the lining thickness has worn down to, or just above, the level of the rivet heads. Note that BMW specify a minimum friction material thickness (see Specifications) - on models with a conventional flywheel (and a friction disc with damping springs, see Section 1), the measurement should be made with the edge of the friction disc at the measurement point compressed in a vice.

**7** Check the machined faces of the flywheel and pressure plate. If either is grooved, or heavily scored, renewal is necessary. The pressure plate must also be renewed if any cracks are apparent, or if the diaphragm spring is damaged or its pressure suspect.

**8** With the clutch removed, it is advisable to check the condition of the release bearing, as described in Section 3.

**9** Check the spigot bearing in the end of the crankshaft. Make sure that it turns smoothly and quietly. If the gearbox input shaft contact face on the bearing is worn or damaged, fit a new bearing, as described in the relevant Part of Chapter 2.

## Refitting

**10** If new clutch components are to be fitted, where applicable, ensure that all anti-corrosion preservative is cleaned from the friction material on the disc, and the contact surfaces of the pressure plate.

**11** It is important to ensure that no oil or grease gets onto the friction disc linings, or the pressure plate and flywheel faces. It is advisable to refit the clutch assembly with clean hands, and to wipe down the pressure plate and flywheel faces with a clean rag before assembly begins.

**12** Apply a smear of molybdenum disulphide grease to the splines of the friction disc hub, then offer the disc to the flywheel, with the greater projecting side of the hub facing away from the flywheel (most friction discs will have an "Engine side" marking which should face the flywheel) **(see illustration)**. Hold the friction disc against the flywheel while the cover/pressure plate assembly is offered into position.

**13** Fit the clutch cover assembly, where applicable aligning the marks on the flywheel and clutch cover. Ensure that the clutch cover locates over the dowels on the flywheel **(see illustration)**. Insert the securing bolts and washers, and tighten them finger-tight, so that the friction disc is gripped, but can still be moved.

**14** The friction disc must now be centralised, so that when the engine and gearbox are mated, the gearbox input shaft splines will pass through the splines in the friction disc hub.

**15** Centralisation can be carried out by inserting a round bar or a long screwdriver through the hole in the centre of the friction disc, so that the end of the bar rests in the spigot bearing in the centre of the crankshaft. Where possible, use a blunt instrument, but if a screwdriver is used, wrap tape around the blade to prevent damage to the bearing surface. Moving the bar sideways or up and down as necessary, move the friction disc in whichever direction is necessary to achieve centralisation. With the bar removed, view the friction disc hub in relation to the hole in the centre of the crankshaft and the circle created by the ends of the diaphragm spring fingers. When the hub appears exactly in the centre, all is correct. Alternatively, if a suitable clutch alignment tool can be obtained, this will eliminate all the guesswork, and obviate the need for visual alignment **(see illustration)**.

**16** Tighten the cover retaining bolts gradually in a diagonal sequence, to the specified torque **(see illustration)**. Remove the alignment tool.

**17** Refit the gearbox as described in Chapter 7A.

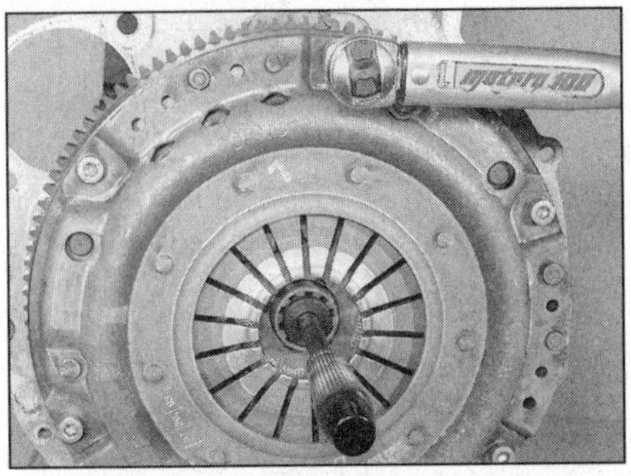

2.16 Tightening a clutch cover bolt

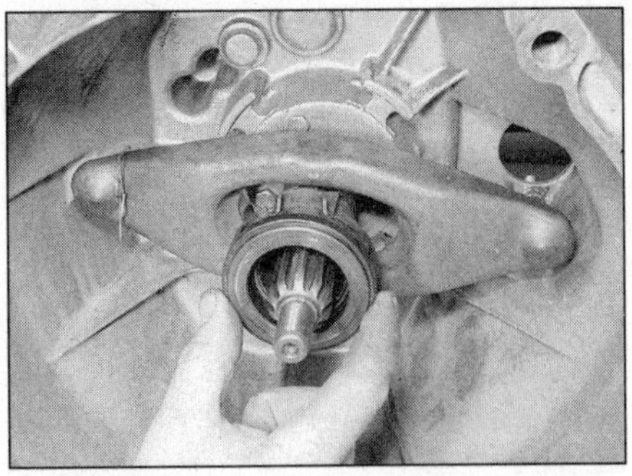

3.2 Removing the clutch release bearing

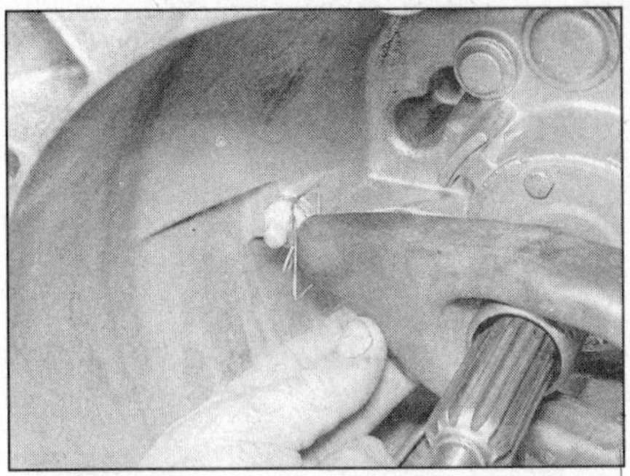

3.8a Slide the clutch release lever sideways to release the spring clip . . .

## 3 Clutch release bearing and lever - removal, inspection and refitting

***Warning: Dust created by clutch wear and deposited on the clutch components may contain asbestos, which is a health hazard. DO NOT blow it out with compressed air, or inhale any of it. DO NOT use petrol (or petroleum-based solvents) to clean off the dust. Brake system cleaner or methylated spirit should be used to flush the dust into a suitable receptacle. After the clutch components are wiped clean with rags, dispose of the contaminated rags and cleaner in a sealed, marked container.***

### *Release bearing*

#### Removal

**1** Remove the gearbox as described in Chapter 7A.

**2** Pull the bearing forwards, and slide it from the guide sleeve in the gearbox bellhousing **(see illustration)**.

#### Inspection

**3** Spin the release bearing, and check it for excessive roughness. Hold the outer race, and attempt to move it laterally against the inner race. If any excessive movement or roughness is evident, renew the bearing. If a new clutch has been fitted, it is wise to renew the release bearing as a matter of course.

#### Refitting

**4** Clean and then lightly grease the release bearing contact surfaces on the release lever. **Do not** apply grease to the guide sleeve.

**5** Slide the bearing into position on the guide sleeve, ensuring that the bearing engages correctly with the release lever.

**6** Refit the gearbox, referring to Chapter 7A.

### *Release lever*

#### Removal

**7** Remove the release bearing, as described previously in this Section.

**8** Slide the release lever sideways to release it from the retaining spring clip and pivot, then pull the lever forwards from the guide sleeve **(see illustrations)**.

3.8b . . . then slide the lever from the guide sleeve

#### Inspection

**9** Inspect the release bearing, pivot and slave cylinder pushrod contact faces on the release lever for wear. Renew the lever if excessive wear is evident.

**10** Check the release lever retaining spring clip, and renew if necessary. It is advisable to renew the clip as a matter of course.

#### Refitting

**11** Clean and then lightly grease the release bearing contact surfaces on the release lever. **Do not** apply grease to the guide sleeve.

**12** Slide the release lever into position over the guide sleeve, then push the end of the lever over the pivot, ensuring that the retaining spring clip engages correctly over the end of the release lever **(see illustration)**.

**13** Refit the release bearing as described previously in this Section.

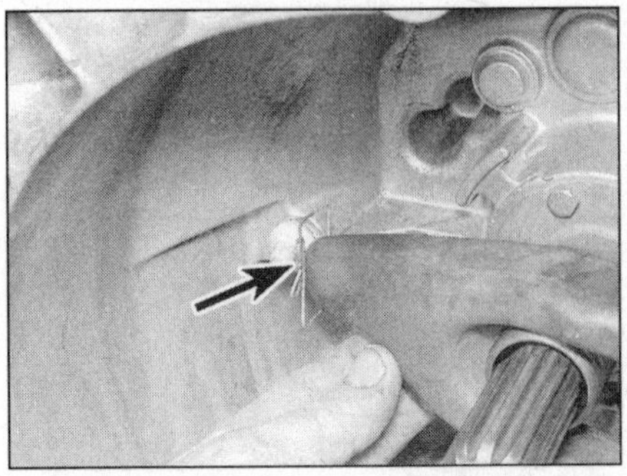

3.12 Ensure that the retaining spring clip (arrowed) engages correctly

## 4 Hydraulic slave cylinder - removal, inspection and refitting

***Warning: Hydraulic fluid is poisonous; wash off immediately and thoroughly in the case of skin contact, and seek immediate medical advice if any fluid is swallowed or gets into the eyes. Certain types of hydraulic fluid are inflammable, and may ignite when allowed into contact with hot components; when servicing any hydraulic system, it is safest to assume that the fluid is inflammable, and to take precautions against the risk of fire as though it is petrol that is being handled. Hydraulic fluid is also an effective paint stripper, and will attack plastics; if any is spilt, it should be washed off immediately, using copious quantities of fresh water. Finally, it is hygroscopic (it absorbs moisture from the air) - old fluid may be contaminated and unfit for further use. When topping-up or renewing the fluid, always use the recommended type, and ensure that it comes from a freshly-opened sealed container.***

### *Removal*

**1** Remove the brake fluid reservoir cap, and siphon out sufficient hydraulic fluid so that the fluid level is below the level of the reservoir fluid hose connection to the clutch master cylinder (the brake fluid reservoir feeds both the brake and clutch hydraulic systems). **Do not** empty the reservoir, as this will draw air into the brake hydraulic circuits.

**2** To improve access, jack up the vehicle, and support it securely on axle stands (see *"Jacking and vehicle support"*).

**3** Where applicable, remove the underbody shield for access to the gearbox bellhousing.

**4** Place a container beneath the hydraulic pipe connection on the clutch slave cylinder to catch escaping hydraulic fluid. Unscrew the union nut and disconnect the fluid pipe.

**5** Unscrew the two securing nuts, and withdraw the slave cylinder from the mounting studs on the bellhousing **(see illustrations)**.

4.5a Unscrew the securing nuts . . .

4.5b . . . and withdraw the clutch slave cylinder

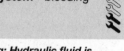

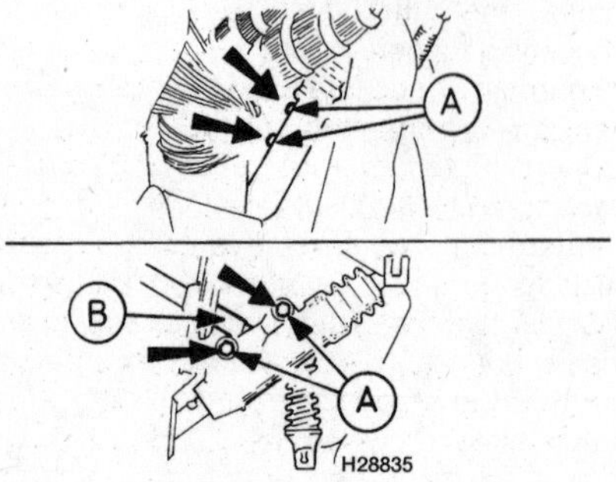


5.6 Clutch master cylinder securing bolts (A) and fluid hose (B)

### Inspection

**6** Inspect the slave cylinder for fluid leaks and damage, and renew if necessary. No spare parts are available for the slave cylinder, and if faulty, the complete unit must be renewed.

### Refitting

**7** Refitting is a reversal of removal, bearing in mind the following points.

*a) Before refitting, clean and then lightly grease the end of the slave cylinder pushrod.*

*b) Tighten the mounting nuts to the specified torque.*

*c) On completion, top-up the hydraulic fluid level and bleed the clutch hydraulic circuit as described in Section 6.*

## 5 Hydraulic master cylinder - removal, inspection and refitting

***Warning: Hydraulic fluid is poisonous; wash off immediately and thoroughly in the case of skin contact, and seek immediate medical advice if any fluid is swallowed or gets into the eyes. Certain types of hydraulic fluid are inflammable, and may ignite when allowed into contact with hot components; when servicing any hydraulic system, it is safest to assume that the fluid is inflammable, and to take precautions against the risk of fire as though it is petrol that is being handled. Hydraulic fluid is also an effective paint stripper, and will attack plastics; if any is spilt, it should be washed off immediately, using copious quantities of fresh water. Finally, it is hygroscopic (it absorbs moisture from the air) - old fluid may be contaminated and unfit for further use. When topping-up or renewing the fluid, always use the recommended type, and ensure that it comes from a freshly-opened sealed container.***

**Note:** *A new master cylinder self-locking securing nut should be used on refitting.*

### Removal

**1** Remove the brake fluid reservoir cap, and siphon out sufficient hydraulic fluid so that the fluid level is below the level of the reservoir fluid hose connection to the clutch master cylinder (the brake fluid reservoir feeds both the brake and clutch hydraulic systems). **Do not** empty the reservoir, as this will draw air into the brake hydraulic circuits.

**2** Disconnect the clutch master cylinder hose from the brake fluid reservoir. Be prepared for fluid spillage, and plug the open end of the hose to prevent dirt entry.

**3** Working inside the vehicle, remove the securing screws, and remove the driver's side lower facia trim panel.

**4** Where applicable, disconnect the clutch pedal return spring, using a suitable pair of pliers, to enable the clutch master cylinder pushrod-to-pedal clevis pin to be removed.

**5** Prise off the clip securing the master cylinder pushrod-to-pedal clevis pin, then withdraw the clevis pin.

**6** Unscrew the two bolts and nut securing the master cylinder to the pedal bracket in the footwell, noting that the bolts also secure the stop light mounting bracket **(see illustration)**. Release the master cylinder from the bracket, and ease the fluid hose through the bulkhead grommet, taking care not to strain the pipe.

### Inspection

**7** Inspect the master cylinder for fluid leaks and damage, and renew if necessary. No spare parts are available for the master cylinder, and if faulty, the complete unit must be renewed.

### Refitting

**8** Refitting is a reversal of removal, bearing in mind the following points.

*a) Take care not to strain the master cylinder fluid pipe during refitting.*

*b) Use a new master cylinder self-locking securing nut.*

*c) On completion, top-up the level in the brake fluid reservoir, then bleed the clutch hydraulic system (see Section 6).*

## 6 Hydraulic system - bleeding

***Warning: Hydraulic fluid is poisonous; wash off immediately and thoroughly in the case of skin contact, and seek immediate medical advice if any fluid is swallowed or gets into the eyes. Certain types of hydraulic fluid are inflammable, and may ignite when allowed into contact with hot components; when servicing any hydraulic system, it is safest to assume that the fluid is inflammable, and to take precautions against the risk of fire as though it is petrol that is being handled. Hydraulic fluid is also an effective paint stripper, and will attack plastics; if any is spilt, it should be washed off immediately, using copious quantities of fresh water. Finally, it is hygroscopic (it absorbs moisture from the air) - old fluid may be contaminated and unfit for further use. When topping-up or renewing the fluid, always use the recommended type, and ensure that it comes from a freshly-opened sealed container.***

**Note:** *BMW recommend that pressure-bleeding equipment is used to bleed the clutch hydraulic system.*

### General

**1** The correct operation of any hydraulic system is only possible after removing all air from the components and circuit; this is achieved by bleeding the system.

**2** During the bleeding procedure, add only clean, unused hydraulic fluid of the recommended type; never re-use fluid that has already been bled from the system. Ensure that sufficient fluid is available before starting work.

**3** If there is any possibility of incorrect fluid being already in the system, the brake and clutch components and circuit must be flushed completely with uncontaminated, correct fluid, and new seals should be fitted to the various components.

**4** If hydraulic fluid has been lost from the system, or air has entered because of a leak, ensure that the fault is cured before proceeding further.

**5** To improve access, apply the handbrake, then jack up the front of the vehicle, and support it securely on axle stands (see *"Jacking and vehicle support"*).

**6** Where applicable, remove the underbody shield for access to the gearbox bellhousing.

**7** Check that the clutch hydraulic pipe(s) and hose(s) are secure, that the unions are tight, and that the bleed screw on the rear of the clutch slave cylinder (mounted under the vehicle on the lower left-hand side of the gearbox bellhousing) is closed. Clean any dirt from around the bleed screw.

**8** Unscrew the brake fluid reservoir cap, and top the fluid up to the "MAX" level line; refit the cap loosely, and remember to maintain the fluid level at least above the "MIN" level line throughout the procedure, or there is a risk of further air entering the system. Note that the brake fluid reservoir feeds both the brake and clutch hydraulic systems.

**9** It is recommended that pressure-bleeding equipment is used to bleed the system. Alternatively, there are a number of one-man, do-it-yourself brake bleeding kits currently available from motor accessory shops. These kits greatly simplify the bleeding operation, and also reduce the risk of expelled air and fluid being drawn back into the system. If such a kit is not available, the basic (two-man) method must be used, which is described in detail below.

**10** If pressure-bleeding equipment or a one-man kit is to be used, prepare the vehicle as described previously, and follow the equipment/kit manufacturer's instructions, as the procedure may vary slightly according to the type being used; generally, they are as outlined below in the relevant sub-section.

**11** Whichever method is used, the same basic process must be followed to ensure that the removal of all air from the system.

### *Bleeding - basic (two-man) method*

**12** Collect a clean glass jar, a suitable length of plastic or rubber tubing which is a tight fit over the bleed screw, and a ring spanner to fit the screw. The help of an assistant will also be required.

**13** Where applicable, remove the dust cap from the bleed screw. Fit the spanner and tube to the screw, place the other end of the tube in the jar, and pour in sufficient fluid to cover the end of the tube.

**14** Ensure that the reservoir fluid level is maintained at least above the "MIN" level line throughout the procedure.

**15** Have the assistant fully depress the clutch pedal several times to build up pressure, then maintain it on the final downstroke.

**16** While pedal pressure is maintained, unscrew the bleed screw (approximately one turn) and allow the compressed fluid and air to flow into the jar. The assistant should maintain pedal pressure, following it down to the floor if necessary, and should not release it until instructed to do so. When the flow stops, tighten the bleed screw again, have the assistant release the pedal slowly, and recheck the reservoir fluid level.

**17** Repeat the steps given in paragraphs 15 and 16 until the fluid emerging from the bleed screw is free from air bubbles.

**18** When no more air bubbles appear, tighten the bleed screw securely. Do not overtighten the bleed screw.

**19** Temporarily disconnect the bleed tube from the bleed screw, and move the container of fluid to one side.

**20** Unscrew the two securing nuts, and withdraw the slave cylinder from the bellhousing, taking care not to strain the fluid hose.

**21** Reconnect the bleed tube to the bleed screw, and submerge the end of the tube in the container of fluid.

**22** With the bleed screw pointing vertically upwards, unscrew the bleed screw (approximately one turn), and slowly push the slave cylinder pushrod into the cylinder until no more air bubbles appear in the fluid.

**23** Hold the pushrod in position, then tighten the bleed screw.

**24** Slowly allow the pushrod to return to its rest position. **Do not** allow the pushrod to return quickly, as this will cause air to enter the slave cylinder.

**25** Remove the tube and spanner, and refit the dust cap to the bleed screw.

**26** Refit the slave cylinder to the bellhousing, and tighten the securing nuts to the specified torque.

### *Bleeding - using a one-way valve kit*

**27** As their name implies, these kits consist of a length of tubing with a one-way valve fitted, to prevent expelled air and fluid being drawn back into the system; some kits include a translucent container, which can be positioned so that the air bubbles can be more easily seen flowing from the end of the tube.

**28** The kit is connected to the bleed screw, which is then opened. The user returns to the driver's seat, depresses the clutch pedal with a smooth, steady stroke, and slowly releases it; this is repeated until the expelled fluid is clear of air bubbles.

**29** Note that these kits simplify work so much that it is easy to forget the reservoir fluid level; ensure that this is maintained at least above the "MIN" level line at all times.

### *Bleeding - using a pressure-bleeding kit*

**30** These kits are usually operated by the reservoir of pressurised air contained in the spare tyre. However, note that it will probably be necessary to reduce the pressure to a lower level than normal; refer to the instructions supplied with the kit.

**31** By connecting a pressurised, fluid-filled container to the fluid reservoir, bleeding can be carried out simply by opening the bleed screw, and allowing the fluid to flow out until no more air bubbles can be seen in the expelled fluid.

**32** This method has the advantage that the large reservoir of fluid provides an additional safeguard against air being drawn into the system during bleeding.

### *All methods*

**33** When bleeding is complete, and firm pedal feel is restored, wash off any spilt fluid, check that the bleed screw is tightened securely, and refit the dust cap.

**34** Check the hydraulic fluid level in the reservoir, and top-up if necessary (Chapter 1).

**35** Discard any hydraulic fluid that has been bled from the system; it will not be fit for re-use.

**36** Check the feel of the clutch pedal. If it feels at all spongy, air must still be present in the system, and further bleeding is required. Failure to bleed satisfactorily after a reasonable repetition of the bleeding procedure may be due to worn master or slave cylinder seals.

**37** On completion, where applicable refit the underbody shield and lower the vehicle to the ground.

## 7 Clutch pedal - removal and refitting

### *Removal*

**Note:** *A new self-locking nut should be used to secure the clutch master cylinder on refitting.*

**1** Working inside the vehicle, remove the securing screws, and withdraw the driver's side lower facia panel.

**2** Remove the stop light switch as described in Chapter 9.

**3** Where applicable, remove the clutch pedal switch.

**4** Remove the two screws and the nut securing the clutch master cylinder, noting that they also secure the stop light switch/clutch switch mounting bracket, and remove the switch bracket.

**5** On models fitted with a conventional clutch pedal return spring, carefully disconnect the return spring from the pedal using a pair of pliers. Prise off the clevis pin securing clip, and remove the clevis pin securing the clutch master cylinder pushrod to the pedal.

**6** On models where the clutch pedal is fitted with an over-centre helper spring, prise off the securing clip from the clutch master cylinder-to-pedal clevis pin. Hold the clutch pedal tightly, then push out the clevis pin. Pull the clutch pedal slowly upwards, then release the top of the helper spring from the pedal mounting bracket.

**7** Move the clutch master cylinder to one side, taking care not to strain the fluid pipe.
**8** Prise off the clip securing the pedal to the pivot shaft, then slide off the clutch pedal. Recover the pivot bushes if they are loose.

## Refitting

**9** Before refitting the pedal to the pivot shaft, check the condition of the pivot bushes, and renew if necessary.
**10** Refitting is a reversal of removal, bearing in mind the following points.

*a) Before refitting the pedal, lightly grease the pedal pivot pin.*

*b) Where applicable, ensure that the end of the over-centre helper spring is correctly located in the pedal bracket* ***(see illustration)****.*

*c) Use a new self-locking nut to secure the clutch master cylinder.*

*d) Take care not to strain the clutch master cylinder fluid pipe during refitting.*

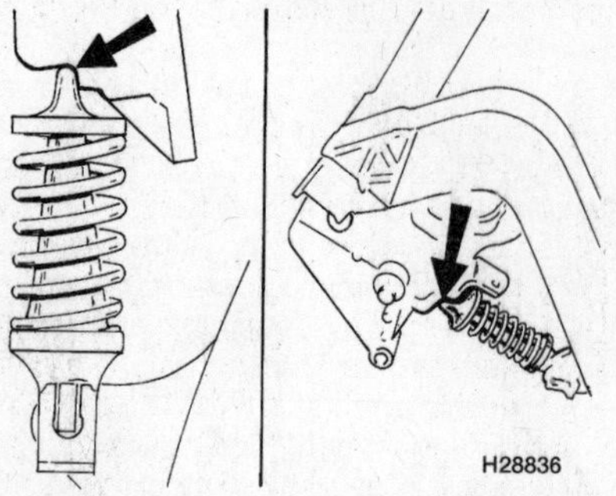


**7.10 Ensure the helper spring is correctly located when refitting the clutch pedal**

# Chapter 7 Part A: Manual gearbox

## Contents



## Degrees of difficulty

| | | | | |
|---|---|---|---|---|
| **Easy,** suitable for novice with little experience | **Fairly easy,** suitable for beginner with some experience | **Fairly difficult,** suitable for competent DIY mechanic | **Difficult,** suitable for experienced DIY mechanic | **Very difficult,** suitable for expert DIY or professional |

## Specifications

### Lubrication

| | |
|---|---|
| Recommended oil | Dexron II type automatic transmission fluid (ATF) |
| Capacity (from dry) | 1.0 litre |

### Torque wrench settings

| Torque wrench settings | Nm | lbf ft |
|---|---|---|
| Gearbox-to-engine bolts: | | |
| Hexagon head bolts: | | |
| M8 bolts | 25 | 18 |
| M10 bolts | 49 | 36 |
| M12 bolts | 74 | 55 |
| Torx head bolts: | | |
| M8 bolts | 22 | 16 |
| M10 bolts | 43 | 32 |
| M12 bolts | 72 | 53 |
| Oil drain plug | 50 | 37 |
| Oil filler/level plug | 50 | 37 |
| Output flange-to-output shaft nut*: | | |
| Stage 1 | 170 | 125 |
| Stage 2 | Fully loosen nut | |
| Stage 3 | 120 | 89 |
| Gearbox crossmember-to-body bolts | | |
| M8 bolts | 21 | 15 |
| M10 bolts | 42 | 31 |
| Gearbox mounting-to-gearbox nuts: | | |
| M8 nuts | 21 | 15 |
| M10 nuts | 42 | 31 |

**Note:** *Coat the threads of the nut with thread-locking compound.*



## 1 General information

The gearbox is a 5-speed unit, and is contained in a cast-alloy casing bolted to the rear of the engine.

Drive is transmitted from the crankshaft via the clutch to the input shaft, which has a splined extension to accept the clutch friction plate. The output shaft transmits the drive via the propeller shaft to the rear differential.

The input shaft runs in line with the output shaft. The input shaft and output shaft gears are in constant mesh with the layshaft gear cluster. Selection of gears is by sliding synchromesh hubs, which lock the appropriate output shaft gears to the output shaft.

Gear selection is via a floor-mounted lever and selector mechanism. The selector mechanism causes the appropriate selector fork to move its respective synchro-sleeve along the shaft, to lock the gear pinion to the synchro-hub. Since the synchro-hubs are splined to the output shaft, this locks the pinion to the shaft, so that drive can be transmitted. To ensure that gear-changing can be made quickly and quietly, a synchro-mesh system is fitted to all forward gears, consisting of baulk rings and spring-loaded fingers, as well as the gear pinions and synchro-hubs. The synchro-mesh cones are formed on the mating faces of the baulk rings and gear pinions.

## 2 Manual gearbox oil level check

**1** To improve access, jack up the vehicle and support on axle stands (see *"Jacking and vehicle support"*). Ensure that the car is level.

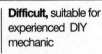

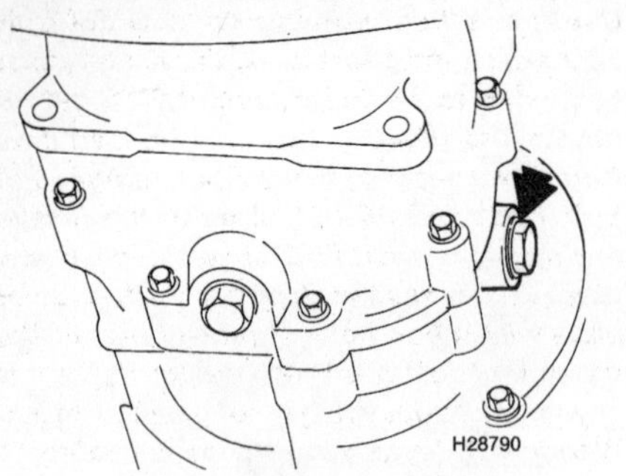


**2.2 Manual gearbox oil level/filler plug location (arrowed)**

**2** Unscrew the gearbox oil level/filler plug from the right-hand side of the gearbox casing **(see illustration)**.
**3** The oil level should be up to the bottom of the level/filler plug hole.
**4** If necessary, top-up the level, using the correct type of fluid (see "*Specifications*") until the oil overflows from the filler/level plug hole.
**5** Wipe away any spilt oil, then refit the filler/level plug, and tighten to the specified torque.
**6** Lower the vehicle to the ground.

## 3 Gearchange components - removal and refitting

### *Gear lever*

**Note:** *A new gear lever bearing will be required on refitting.*

#### Removal

**1** Jack up the car and support securely on axle stands (see *"Jacking and vehicle support"*).
**2** Remove the knob from the gear lever by pulling it sharply upwards.
**3** Unclip the gear lever gaiter from the centre console, and withdraw the gaiter over the gear lever. Where applicable, also remove the foam insulation.
**4** Working under the vehicle, prise the securing clip from the end of the gear selector rod pin. Withdraw the selector rod pin from eye on the end of the gear lever, and recover the washers **(see illustration)**.

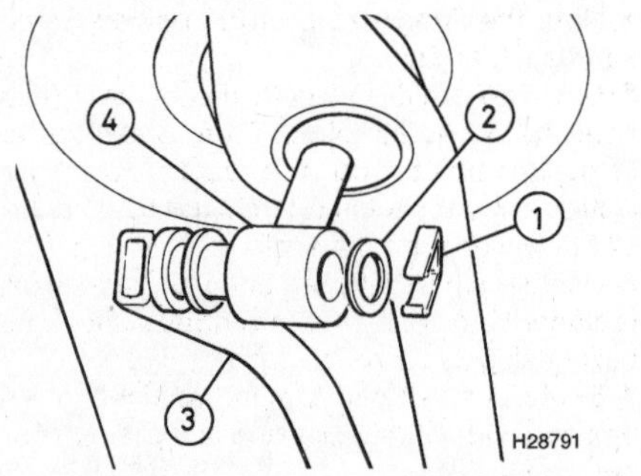


**3.4 Prise off the clip and disconnect the gear selector rod pin from the gear lever**

*1 Securing clip*
*2 Washer*
*3 Selector rod*
*4 Gear lever eye*

**5** It is now necessary to release the gear lever lower bearing retaining ring from the gear selector arm. A special tool is available for this purpose, but two screwdrivers, with the tips engaged in opposite slots in the bearing ring can be used instead. To unlock the bearing ring, turn it a quarter-turn anti-clockwise **(see illustration)**.
**6** The bearing can now be pushed up through the housing, and the gear lever can be withdrawn from inside the vehicle.
**7** If desired, the bearing can be removed from the gear lever ball by pressing it downwards. To withdraw the bearing over the lever eye, rotate the bearing until the eye passes through the slots provided in the bearing.
**8** Fit a new bearing using a reversal of the removal process. Ensure that the bearing is pressed securely into position on the gear lever ball.

#### Refitting

**9** Refit the lever using a reversal of the removal process, bearing in mind the following points.

- a) *Grease the contact faces of the bearing before refitting.*
- b) *Lower the gear lever into position, ensuring that the arrow on the gear lever grommet points towards the front of the vehicle.*
- c) *Make sure that the gear lever grommet is correctly engaged with the gear selector arm and with the opening in the vehicle floor **(see illustration)**.*
- d) *When engaging the bearing with the selector arm, make sure that the arrows or tabs (as applicable) on the top of the bearing point towards the rear of the vehicle.*
- e) *To lock the bearing in position in the selector arm, press down on the top of the bearing retaining tab locations until the tabs are heard to click into position.*
- f) *Grease the selector rod pin before engaging it with the gear lever eye.*

### *Gear selector shaft eye*

**Note:** *A new selector shaft eye securing roll-pin will be required on refitting.*

#### Removal

**10** Jack up the car and support securely on axle stands (see *"Jacking and vehicle support"*).
**11** Disconnect the propeller shaft from the gearbox flange, and support it clear of the gearbox using wire or string. Refer to Chapter 8 for details.
**12** Prise the retaining clip from the end of the gear selector rod pin. Withdraw the selector rod pin from the selector shaft eye, and recover the washers.
**13** Slide back the locking sleeve, then drive out the roll-pin securing the gear selector shaft eye to the end of the gear selector shaft **(see illustration)**.
**14** Pull the gear selector shaft eye off the end of the selector shaft.

#### Refitting

**15** Refitting is a reversal of removal, bearing in mind the following points.

- a) *Before refitting, check the condition of the rubber washer in the end of the selector shaft eye and renew if necessary.*
- b) *Use a new roll-pin to secure the eye to the selector shaft.*
- c) *Grease the selector rod pin.*
- d) *Reconnect the propeller shaft to the gearbox flange as described in Chapter 8.*

### *Gear selector arm rear mounting*

#### Removal

**16** Jack up the car and support securely on axle stands (see *"Jacking and vehicle support"*).
**17** Disconnect the propeller shaft from the

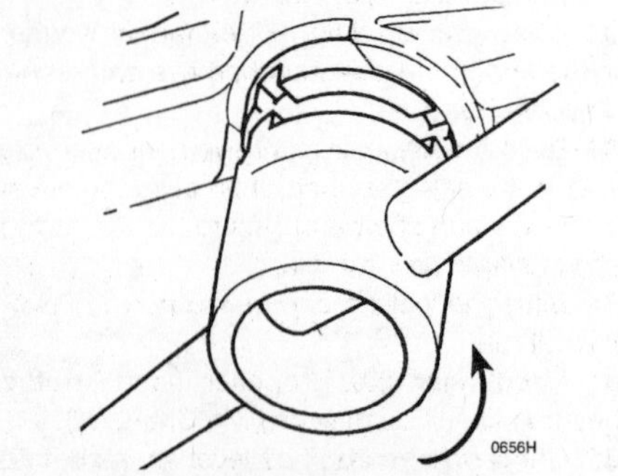


**3.5 Turn the bearing ring anti-clockwise - special tool shown**

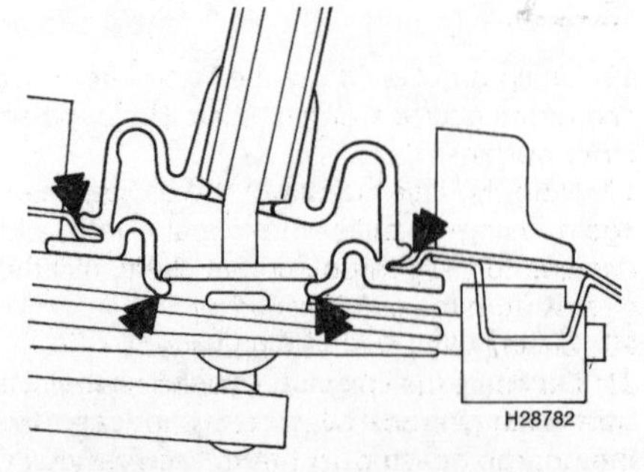


**3.9 Gear lever grommet correctly engaged with selector arm and vehicle floor**

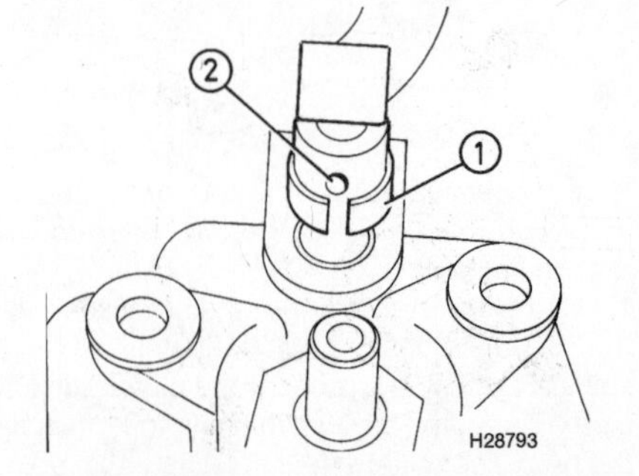


**3.13 Slide back sleeve (1), and drive out roll-pin (2) securing gear selector shaft eye**

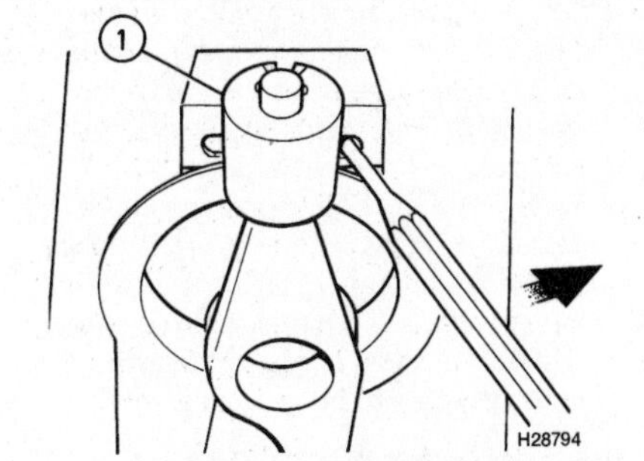


**3.19 Levering the gear selector arm rear mounting sleeve (1) from the body bracket**

gearbox flange, and support it clear of the gearbox using wire or string. See Chapter 8 for details.

**18** Remove the gear lever as described previously in this Section.

**19** Using a screwdriver or a small pin-punch, lever the mounting sleeve from the bracket on the body **(see illustration)**.

**20** Pull the mounting from the selector arm.

### Refitting

**21** Grease the mounting, then push the mounting onto the selector arm, with the cut-out facing the rear of the vehicle, and the arrow pointing vertically upwards.

**22** Clip the mounting into position in the bracket, making sure that the mounting is securely located.

**23** Reconnect the propeller shaft to the gearbox flange as described in Chapter 8, then lower the vehicle to the ground.

## 4 Oil seals - renewal

### *Input shaft oil seal*

**1** With the gearbox removed as described in Section 6, proceed as follows.

**2** Remove the clutch release bearing and lever as described in Chapter 6.

**3** Unscrew the securing bolts and withdraw the clutch release bearing guide sleeve from the gearbox bellhousing **(see illustration)**.

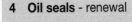

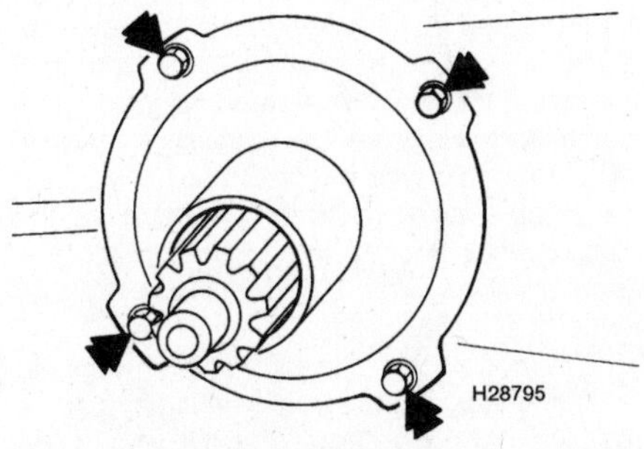


**4.3 Clutch release bearing guide sleeve securing bolts (arrowed)**

**4** Note the fitted depth of the now-exposed input shaft oil seal.

**5** Drill two small holes in the oil seal (two small pilot holes should be provided at opposite points on the seal - a sharp instrument can be used to extend these holes all the way though the seal).

**6** Using a small drift, tap one side of the seal (adjacent to one of the holes) into the bellhousing as far as the stop.

**7** Screw a small self-tapping screw into the opposite side of the seal, and use pliers to pull out the seal.

**8** Clean the oil seal seating surface.

**9** Wind a length of tape over the splines on the input shaft to prevent damage to the new seal as it is slid over the shaft.

**10** Lubricate the lips of the new oil seal with a little clean gearbox oil, then carefully slide the seal over the input shaft into position in the bellhousing.

**11** Remove the tape from the input shaft then, using a tube of the correct diameter, tap the oil seal into the bellhousing to the previously noted depth.

**12** Refit the clutch release lever and bearing as described in Chapter 6.

**13** Refit the gearbox as described in Section 6, then check the gearbox oil level as described in Section 2.

### *Output flange oil seal*

**Note:** *Thread-locking compound will be required for the gearbox flange nut on refitting.*

**14** Jack up the vehicle and support securely on axle stands (see *"Jacking and vehicle support"*).

**15** Disconnect the propeller shaft from the gearbox flange, and support it clear of the gearbox using wire or string. See Chapter 8 for details.

**16** Where applicable, prise the gearbox flange nut cover plate from the flange using a screwdriver. Discard the cover plate - it is not required on refitting.

**17** Counterhold the gearbox flange by bolting a forked or two-legged tool to two of the flange bolt holes, then unscrew the flange securing nut using a socket and extension bar.

***Warning: The nut is very tight.***

**18** Using a puller, draw the flange from the end of the gearbox output shaft. Be prepared for oil spillage.

**19** Note the fitted depth of the oil seal then, again using a puller (take care to avoid damage to the gearbox output shaft), pull the oil seal from the gearbox casing.

**20** Clean the oil seal seating surface.

**21** Lubricate the lips of the new oil seal with a little clean gearbox oil, then tap the seal into the gearbox casing to the to the previously noted depth.

**22** Refit the flange to the output shaft.

***Caution: When working on S5D 260Z or S5D 310Z-type gearboxes, the flange must be heated to a temperature of 80°C before fitting. The gearbox type can be identified from the shape of the output flange - on S5D 260Z and S5D 310Z units the flange has three arms with a bolt hole in each - on other gearboxes the flange has a triangular plate with a bolt hole at each corner of the triangle. Consult a BMW dealer if there is any doubt about the type of gearbox fitted.***

***Warning: If the gearbox flange is heated, take precautions against burns - the metal will stay hot for some time.***

**23** Coat the threads of the flange nut with thread-locking compound, then tighten the nut to the specified torque in the three stages given in the Specifications. Counterhold the flange as during removal.

**24** If a flange nut cover plate was originally fitted, discard it. There is no need to fit a cover plate on refitting.

**25** Reconnect the propeller shaft to the gearbox flange as described in Chapter 8, then check the gearbox oil level as described in Section 2, and lower the vehicle to the ground.

### *Gear selector shaft oil seal*

**Note:** *A new selector shaft eye securing roll-pin will be required on refitting.*

**26** Jack up the vehicle and support securely on axle stands (see *"Jacking and vehicle support"*).

**27** Disconnect the propeller shaft from the gearbox flange, and support it clear of the gearbox using wire or string. Refer to Chapter 8 for details.

**28** Slide back the locking sleeve, then drive out the roll-pin securing the gear selector shaft eye to the end of the gear selector shaft.

**29** Pull the gear selector shaft eye (complete with gear linkage) off the end of the selector shaft, and move the linkage clear of the selector shaft.

**30** Using a small flat-bladed screwdriver, prise the selector shaft oil seal from the gearbox casing.

**31** Clean the oil seal seating surface, then tap the new seal into position using a small socket or tube of the correct diameter.

**32** Check the condition of the rubber washer in the end of the selector shaft eye and renew if necessary.

**33** Push the selector shaft eye back onto the end of the selector shaft, then align the holes in the eye and shaft and secure the eye to the shaft using a new roll-pin.

**34** Slide the locking sleeve into position over the roll-pin.

**35** Reconnect the propeller shaft to the gearbox flange as described in Chapter 8.

**36** Check the gearbox oil level as described in Section 2, then lower the vehicle to the ground.

## 5 Reversing light switch - testing, removal and refitting

### Testing

**1** The reversing light circuit is controlled by a plunger-type switch screwed into the left-hand side of the gearbox casing. If a fault develops in the circuit, first ensure that the circuit fuse has not blown.

**2** To test the switch, disconnect the wiring connector, and use a multimeter (set to the resistance function) or a battery-and-bulb test circuit to check that there is continuity between the switch terminals only when reverse gear is selected. If this is not the case, and there are no obvious breaks or other damage to the wires, the switch is faulty, and must be renewed.

### Removal

**3** Disconnect the wiring connector, then unscrew the switch from the gearbox casing **(see illustration)**.

### Refitting

**4** Screw the switch back into position in the gearbox housing and tighten it securely. Reconnect the wiring connector, and test the operation of the circuit.

## 6 Manual gearbox - removal and refitting

### Removal

**Note:** *This is an involved operation. Read through the procedure thoroughly before starting work, and ensure that adequate lifting tackle and/or jacking/support equipment is available.*

**1** Open the bonnet, then raise the bonnet to its fully open position, referring to Chapter 11.

**2** Disconnect the battery negative lead.

**3** Jack up the car and support securely on axle stands (see *"Jacking and vehicle support"*). Note that the car must be raised sufficiently to allow clearance for the gearbox to be removed from under the car.

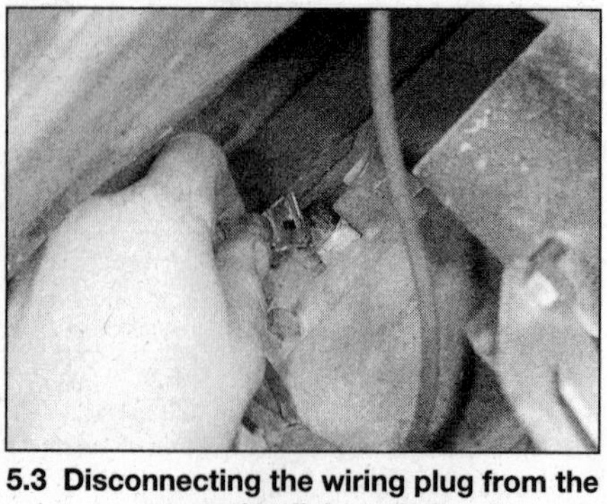

**5.3 Disconnecting the wiring plug from the reversing light switch**

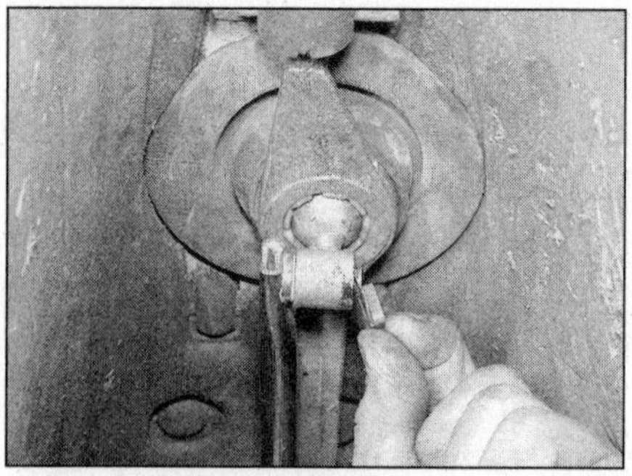

**6.6a Remove the retaining clips from the gear selector rod pins . . .**

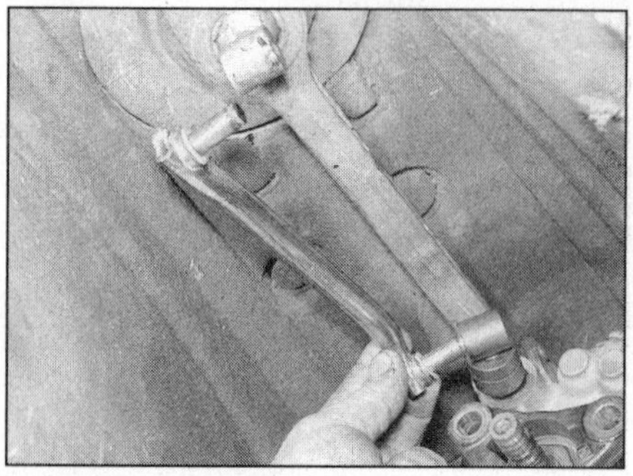

**6.6b . . . then withdraw the selector rod**

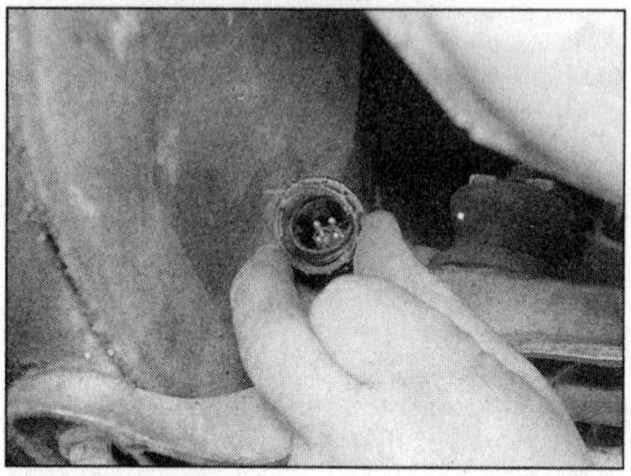

**6.9 Releasing the oxygen sensor wiring connector from bracket on the gearbox**

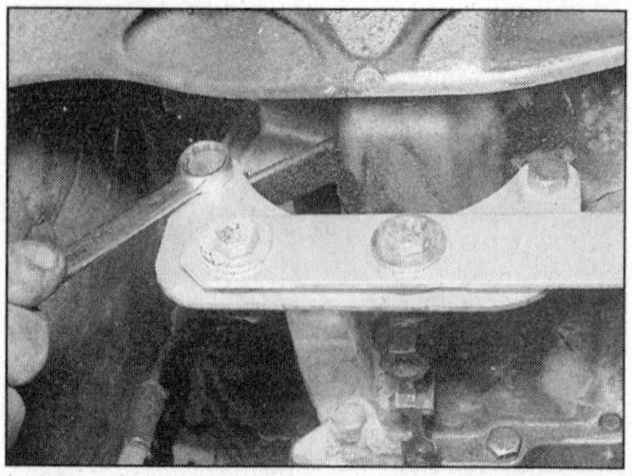

**6.10 Unbolt the exhaust mounting bracket from the rear of the gearbox**

**4** Remove the starter motor as described in Chapter 5A.

**5** Remove the propeller shaft as described in Chapter 8.

**6** Working under the car, prise the retaining clip from the end of the gear selector rod pin. Withdraw the selector rod pin from the eye on the end of the gearbox selector shaft, and recover the washers. Similarly, disconnect the selector rod pin from the end of the gear lever, and withdraw the selector rod **(see illustrations)**.

**7** Working at the gearbox bellhousing, unscrew the nuts, and withdraw the clutch slave cylinder from the studs on the bellhousing. Support the slave cylinder clear of the working area, but do not strain the hose.

**8** Disconnect the wiring from the reversing light switch, located in the left-hand side of the gearbox casing, and release the switch wiring from the clips on the gearbox.

**9** Separate the two halves of the oxygen sensor wiring connector, then withdraw the clamping ring to release the connector from the bracket, and unbolt the connector bracket from the gearbox **(see illustration)**.

**10** Where applicable, unbolt the exhaust mounting bracket from the rear of the gearbox and move the bracket clear **(see illustration)**. If necessary, loosen the clamp on the exhaust to allow the bracket to be pivoted clear of the working area.

**11** If necessary, to provide extra clearance, unbolt the bracing tube from the floor of the car.

**12** On models with M40 or M50 engines, if not already done, remove the heater/ventilation inlet air ducting from the rear of the engine compartment as follows.

*a) Lift the grille from the top of the ducting (on certain Coupe models, it will be necessary to remove the securing screws and lift off the complete scuttle grille assembly).*

*b) Working through the top of the ducting, remove the screws securing the cable ducting to the air ducting and move the cable ducting clear.*

*c) Unscrew the nuts and/or screw(s) securing the air ducting to the bulkhead (where applicable, bend back the heat shielding for access).*

*d) Remove the air ducting by pulling upwards.*

*e) Move the previously removed cable ducting clear of the cylinder head cover.*

**13** On models with the M40 and M42 engines, unbolt the wiring ducting from the rear of the engine, then connect an engine hoist and lifting tackle to the engine lifting eye (incorporated in the rear flange of the cylinder block casting) at the rear left-hand corner of the cylinder block. Raise the lifting tackle to just take the weight of the engine.

**14** On models with the M43 engine, support the engine using a trolley jack under the sump, with a block of wood between the jack and sump to spread the load. Raise the jack to just touch the sump.

**15** On models with the M50 engine, connect the lifting tackle to the engine lifting eye at the rear left-hand corner of the cylinder block (incorporated in the rear flange of the cylinder block casting).

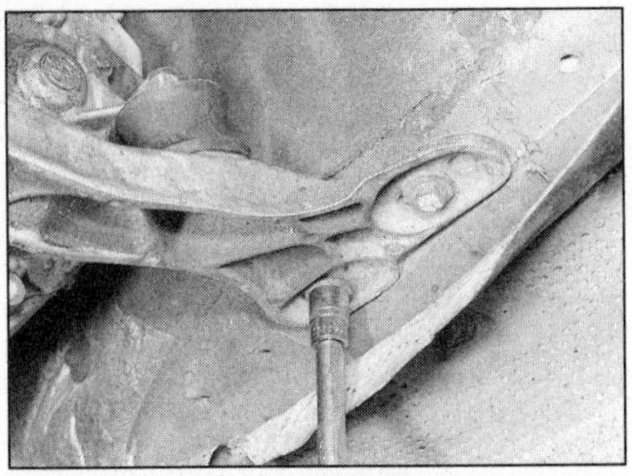

**6.18 Unscrewing a gearbox crossmember securing bolt**

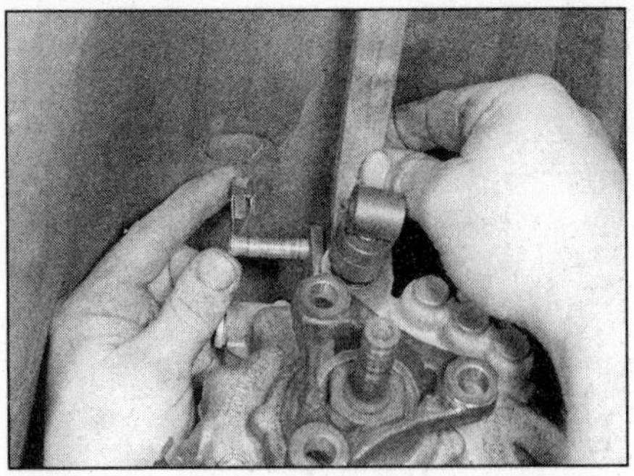

**6.20 Releasing the gear selector arm from the gearbox**

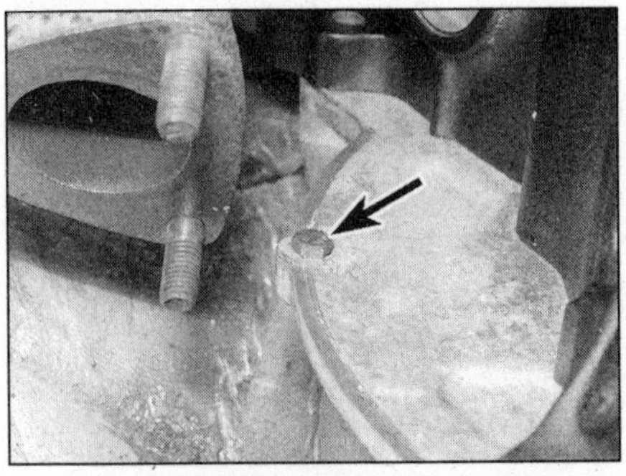

**6.21 Engine/gearbox adapter plate (arrowed)**

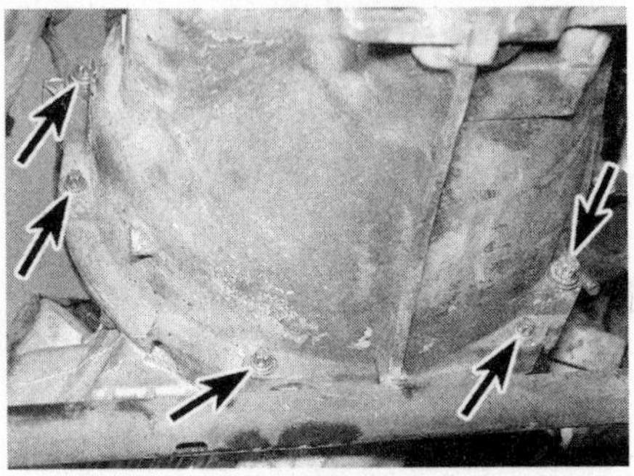

**6.22 Lower engine-to-gearbox bolts (arrowed)**

**16** Place a trolley jack under the gearbox casing, just forward of the bellhousing. Use a block of wood to spread the load, then raise the jack to just take the weight of the gearbox.

**17** Check to ensure that the engine and gearbox are adequately supported then, working under the car, unscrew the nuts securing the gearbox rubber mountings to the lugs on the gearbox casing.

**18** Remove the bolts securing the gearbox crossmember to the body, then withdraw the crossmember from under the car **(see illustration)**. If necessary, bend back or unbolt the exhaust heat shield for access to the crossmember bolts.

**19** Using the jack(s) and engine hoist (where applicable), lower the engine and gearbox until the rear of the engine cylinder head/manifold assembly is almost touching the engine compartment bulkhead. Check that the assembly is not resting against the heater hose connections on the bulkhead.

**20** Working at the top of the gearbox, prise up the clip securing the gear selector arm pivot pin to the gearbox casing, then pull out the pivot pin to release the selector arm from the gearbox **(see illustration)**.

**21** Where applicable, unscrew the bolt securing the engine/gearbox adapter plate to the right-hand side of the gearbox bellhousing **(see illustration)**.

**22** Unscrew the engine-to-gearbox bolts, and recover the washers, then slide the gearbox rearwards to disengage the input shaft from the clutch **(see illustration)**. Take care during this operation to ensure that the weight of the gearbox is not allowed to hang on the input shaft. As the gearbox is released from the engine, check to make sure that the engine is not forced against the heater hose connections or the bulkhead.

**23** Lower the gearbox and carefully withdraw it from under the car. If the gearbox is to be removed for some time, ensure that the engine is adequately supported in the engine compartment.

### Refitting

**24** Commence refitting by checking that the clutch friction disc is centralised as described in Chapter 6 (*"Clutch assembly - removal, inspection and refitting"*).

**25** Before refitting the gearbox, it is advisable to inspect and grease the clutch release bearing and lever as described in Chapter 6.

**26** The remainder of the refitting procedure is a reversal of removal, bearing in mind the following points.

*a) Check that the gearbox positioning dowels are securely in place at the rear of the engine.*

*b) Make sure that the washers are in place on the engine-to-gearbox bolts.*

*c) Tighten all fixings to the specified torque.*

*d) Lightly grease the gear selector arm pivot pin and the gear selector rod pin before refitting.*

*e) Reconnect the propeller shaft to the gearbox flange as described in Chapter 8.*

*f) Refit the starter motor as described in Chapter 5A.*

## 7 Manual gearbox overhaul - general information

Overhauling a manual gearbox is a difficult and involved job for the DIY home mechanic. In addition to dismantling and reassembling many small parts, clearances must be precisely measured and, if necessary, changed by selecting shims and spacers. Internal gearbox components are also often difficult to obtain, and in many instances, extremely expensive. Because of this, if the gearbox develops a fault or becomes noisy, the best course of action is to have the unit overhauled by a specialist repairer, or to obtain an exchange reconditioned unit. Be aware that some gearbox repairs can be carried out with the gearbox in the car.

Nevertheless, it is not impossible for the more experienced mechanic to overhaul the gearbox, provided the special tools are available, and the job is done in a deliberate step-by-step manner, so that nothing is overlooked.

The tools necessary for an overhaul include internal and external circlip pliers, bearing pullers, a slide hammer, a set of pin punches, a dial test indicator, and possibly a hydraulic press. In addition, a large, sturdy workbench and a vice will be required.

During dismantling of the gearbox, make careful notes of how each component is fitted, to make reassembly easier and more accurate.

Before dismantling the gearbox, it will help if you have some idea what area is malfunctioning. Certain problems can be closely related to specific areas in the gearbox, which can make component examination and replacement easier. Refer to the *"Fault finding"* Section at the end of this manual for more information.

# Chapter 7 Part B:
# Automatic transmission

## Contents



## Degrees of difficulty

| | | | | |
|---|---|---|---|---|
| **Easy,** suitable for novice with little experience | **Fairly easy,** suitable for beginner with some experience | **Fairly difficult,** suitable for competent DIY mechanic | **Difficult,** suitable for experienced DIY mechanic | **Very difficult,** suitable for expert DIY or professional |

## Specifications

| Torque wrench settings | Nm | lbf ft |
|---|---|---|
| Engine-to-transmission bolts: | | |
| Hexagon bolts: | | |
| M8 bolts | 24 | 18 |
| M10 bolts | 45 | 33 |
| M12 bolts | 82 | 61 |
| Torx bolts: | | |
| M8 bolts | 21 | 15 |
| M10 bolts | 42 | 31 |
| M12 bolts | 63 | 46 |
| Engine/transmission adapter plate bolt | 23 | 17 |
| Transmission crossmember-to-body bolts | | |
| M8 bolts | 21 | 15 |
| M10 bolts | 42 | 31 |
| Transmission mounting-to-gearbox nuts: | | |
| M8 nuts | 21 | 15 |
| M10 nuts | 42 | 31 |
| Torque-converter-to-driveplate bolts: | | |
| All except A4S 310R, A5S 310Z and A5S 300J transmissions: | | |
| M8 bolts | 26 | 19 |
| M10 bolts | 49 | 36 |
| A4S 310R, A5S 310Z and A5S 300J transmissions | 45 | 33 |

### 1 General information

Certain models covered in this manual have a four-speed(1.6 and 1.8 litre engine models) or five-speed (2.0 litre and 2.5 litre engine models) fully-automatic transmission, consisting of a torque converter, an epicyclic geartrain and hydraulically-operated clutches and brakes.

The torque converter provides a fluid coupling between engine and transmission, which acts as a clutch, and also provides a degree of torque multiplication when accelerating.

The epicyclic geartrain provides either of the five forward or one reverse gear ratio, according to which of its component parts are held stationary or allowed to turn. The components of the geartrain are held or released by brakes and clutches which are activated by a hydraulic control unit. A fluid pump within the transmission provides the necessary hydraulic pressure to operate the brakes and clutches.

Driver control of the transmission is by a seven-position selector lever, and a four-position switch. The transmission has a "drive" position, and a "hold" facility on the first three gear ratios (four-speed transmission) or gear ratios 2 to 4 (five-speed transmissions). The "drive" position ("D") provides automatic changing throughout the range of all forward gear ratios, and is the position selected for normal driving. An automatic kickdown facility shifts the transmission down a gear if the accelerator pedal is fully depressed. The "hold" facility is very similar, but limits the number of gear ratios available - ie, when the selector lever is in the "3" position, only the first three ratios can be selected; in the "2" position, only the first two can be selected, and so on. The lower ratio "hold" is useful when travelling down steep gradients, or for preventing unwanted selection of top gear on twisty roads. Three driving programs are provided for selection by the switch; "economy", "sport", and "manual" (four-speed transmission) or "winter" (five-speed transmission).

Due to the complexity of the automatic transmission, any repair or overhaul work must be left to a BMW dealer with the necessary special equipment for fault diagnosis and repair. The contents of the following Sections are therefore confined to supplying general information, and any service information and instructions that can be used by the owner.

## 2 Gear selector lever - removal and refitting

### Selector lever - models without "interlock" system

#### Removal

**1** Disconnect the battery negative lead.

**2** Unscrew the securing screw from the front of the selector lever handle, then pull off the handle **(see illustration)**.

**3** Remove the cigarette lighter and housing, as described in Chapter 12.

**4** Unclip the selector lever cover, and disconnect the wiring from the switch and the light mounted in the cover.

**5** Disconnect the wiring plug from the lever assembly.

**6** Prise off the clip securing the selector cable to the lever, then unscrew the cable sleeve securing nut, and pull the cable forwards. Unhook the cable end from the lever **(see illustrations)**.

**7** Unscrew the three mounting bolts, then tilt the lever assembly, and withdraw upwards **(see illustration)**. Recover the seal between the lever assembly and the floor panel.

#### Refitting

**8** Refitting is a reversal of removal, bearing in mind the following points.

a) *Ensure the seal is correctly fitted between the lever assembly and the floor panel.*

b) *When reconnecting the selector cable, ensure the lug on the lever assembly engages the hole in the cable sleeve plate.*

c) *When refitting the lever handle, ensure that the pin on the button under the handle engages with the hole in the top of the lever. Fit the handle with the button released* ***(see illustration)****.*

d) *On completion, adjust the selector cable as described in Section 3.*

### Selector lever - models with "interlock" system

#### Removal

**9** Proceed as described in paragraphs 1 to 6.

**10** Unscrew the interlock cable clamp bolt, and remove the clamp **(see illustration)**.

**11** Disconnect the end of the interlock cable from the pin on the lever.

**12** Disconnect the interlock cable from the steering lock as described in Chapter 10.

**13** Working at the linkage, separate the two halves of the interlock wiring connector.

**14** Unscrew the three mounting bolts, then tilt the lever assembly, and withdraw upwards. Recover the seal between the lever assembly and the floor.

#### Refitting

**15** Reconnect the cable to the steering lock as described in Chapter 10.

**16** Manipulate the lever assembly into position, then refit and tighten the bolts. Ensure the seal is correctly fitted between the lever assembly and the floor panel.

**17** Reconnect the selector cable to the lever, ensuring that the lug on the lever assembly engages with the hole in the cable sleeve plate. Tighten the securing nut.

**18** Reconnect the wiring plug to the lever assembly.

**19** Move the selector lever into position "P" (the forward position).

**20** Reconnect the end of the interlock cable to the pin on the lever.

**21** Lay the cable sleeve in position, then refit the clamp and tighten the clamp bolt by hand only. It should be possible for the cable to slide easily through the clamp.

**22** Turn the ignition key to the "zero" position, and remove the key.

**23** Check that the interlock mechanism operates correctly as follows.

a) *Turn the ignition key to the centre (radio/cassette player) position.*

b) *It should be possible to move the selector lever in and out of all positions.*

c) *It should only be possible to turn the ignition key back to the "zero" position and remove the key with the selector in position "P".*

d) *It must not be possible to move the selector lever our of position "P" with the ignition key in the "zero" position or removed.*

**24** Press the locking lever down and tighten the cable clamp bolt **(see illustration)**.

**25** Again, check the operation of the interlock mechanism (see paragraph 23).

**26** Further refitting is a reversal of removal,

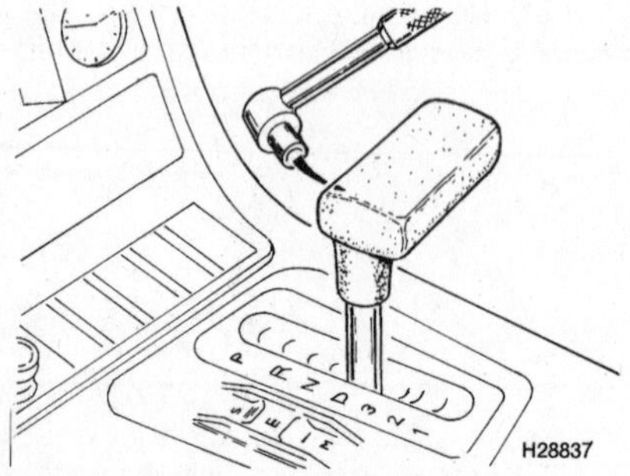


**2.2 Unscrewing the selector lever handle securing screw**

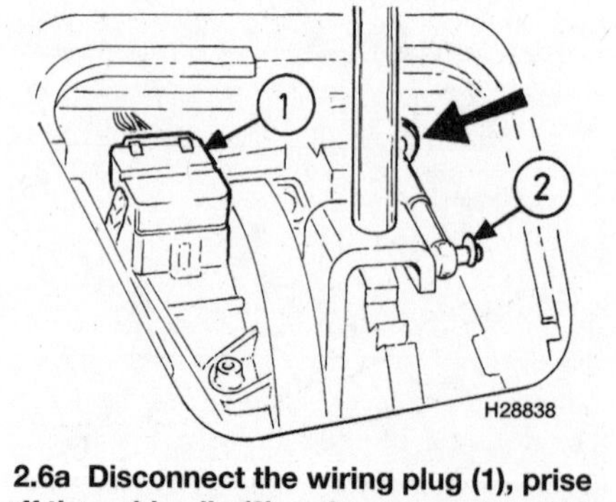


**2.6a Disconnect the wiring plug (1), prise off the cable clip (2) and unscrew the cable sleeve securing nut (arrowed) . . .**

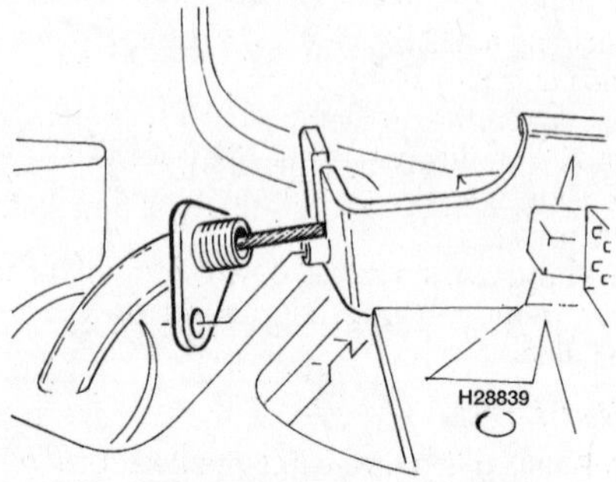


**2.6b . . . then pull the cable forwards**

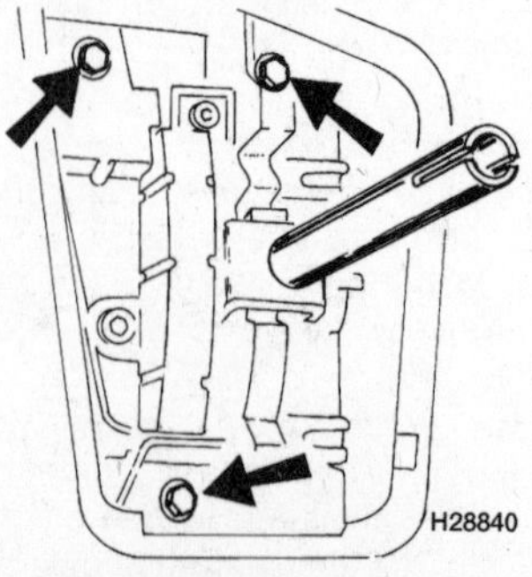


**2.7 Selector lever assembly mounting bolts (arrowed)**

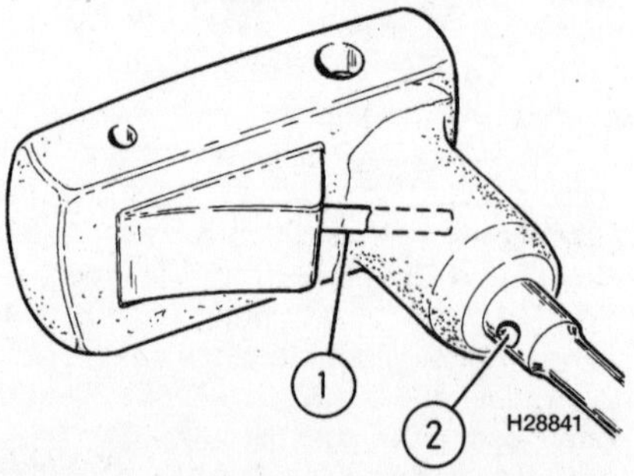


**2.8 Ensure that the pin (1) engages with the hole (2) in the lever**

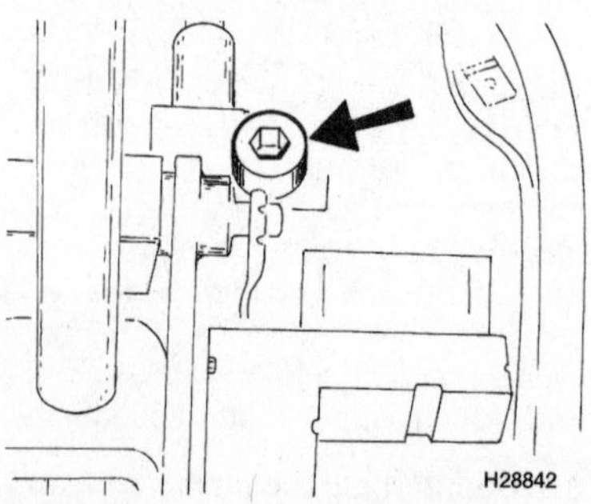


**2.10 Unscrew the interlock cable clamp bolt (arrowed)**

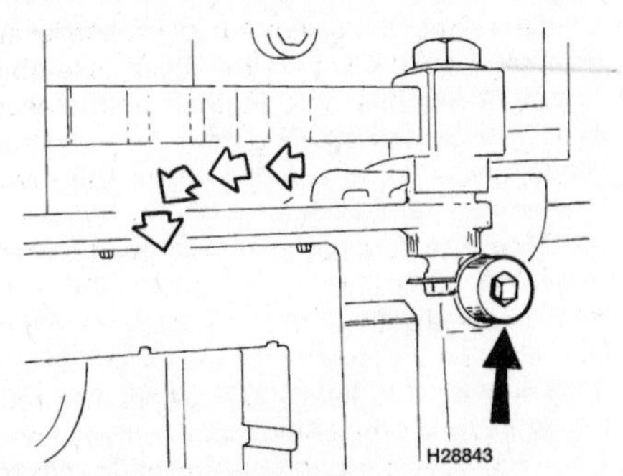


**2.24 Press the locking lever down and tighten the clamp bolt (arrowed)**

but when refitting the lever handle, ensure that the pin on the button under the handle engages with the hole in the top of the lever. Fit the handle with the button released.

**27** On completion, adjust the selector cable as described in Section 3.

## 3 Gear selector cable - removal, refitting and adjustment

### Removal

**1** Disconnect the cable from the selector lever assembly as described in Section 2.

**2** To improve access, apply the handbrake, then jack up the front of the car and support securely on axle stands (see *"Jacking and vehicle support"*).

**3** Working at the end of the cable, counterhold the clamp bolt, and loosen the securing nut. Take care not to bend the end of the cable **(see illustration)**.

**4** Loosen the securing nut, and release the cable from the bracket on the transmission.

**5** Slide the end of the cable from the end fitting.

**6** Withdraw the cable down from under the car, noting its routing to ensure correct refitting.

### Refitting

**7** Refitting is a reversal of removal, bearing in mind the following points.

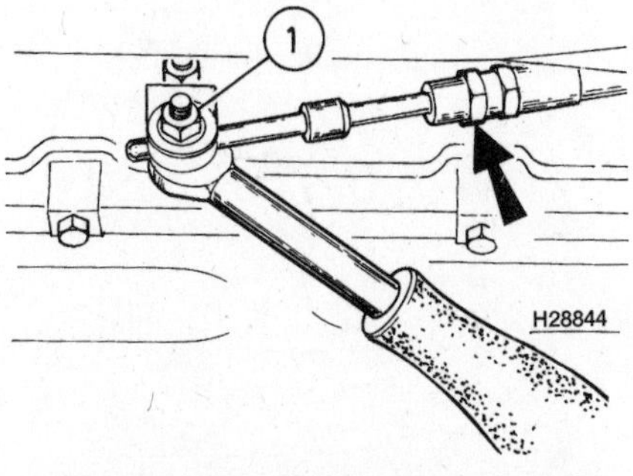


**3.3 Counterhold the clamp bolt, and loosen the selector cable securing nut (1)**
*Cable-to-bracket securing nut arrowed*

*a) Do not tighten the cable end securing nut and bolts until the cable has been adjusted.*
*b) Reconnect the cable to the selector lever assembly with reference to Section 2.*
*c) On completion, adjust the cable as described in the following paragraphs.*

### Adjustment

**8** Move the selector lever to position "P".

**9** If not already done, counterhold clamp bolt and loosen the clamp nut securing the cable to the end fitting (the car should be raised for access).

**10** Push the operating lever on the transmission away from the cable bracket on the transmission (towards the "Park" position).

**11** Press the end of the cable in the opposite direction (ie, towards the cable bracket), then release the cable and tighten the clamp nut (again, counterhold the bolt) **(see illustration)**.

**12** Check that the cable is correctly adjusted by starting the engine, applying the brakes firmly, and moving the selector lever through all the selector positions.

## 4 Fluid seals - renewal

### Torque converter seal

**1** Remove the transmission and the torque converter as described in Section 5.

**2** Using a hooked tool, prise the old oil seal from the transmission bellhousing. Alternatively, drill a small hole, then screw a self-tapping screw into the seal and use pliers to pull out the seal.

**3** Lubricate the lip of the new seal with clean fluid, then carefully drive it into place using a large socket or tube.

**4** Refit the torque converter and transmission as described in Section 5.

### Output flange oil seal

**5** Renewal of the oil seal involves partial dismantling of the transmission, which is a complex operation - see Section 6. Oil seal renewal should be entrusted to a BMW dealer.

## 5 Automatic transmission - removal and refitting

### Removal

**Note:** *This is an involved operation. Read through the procedure thoroughly before starting work, and ensure that adequate lifting tackle and/or jacking/support equipment is available. A suitable tool will be required to align the torque converter when refitting the transmission, and new fluid pipe O-rings may be required.*

**1** Open the bonnet, then raise the bonnet to its fully open position, referring to Chapter 11.

**2** Disconnect the battery negative lead.

**3** Jack up the car and support securely on axle stands (see *"Jacking and vehicle support"*). Note that the car must be raised sufficiently to allow clearance for the gearbox to be removed from under the car.

**4** Remove the starter motor as described in Chapter 5A.

**5** Where applicable, unbolt the exhaust mounting crossmember from under the car.

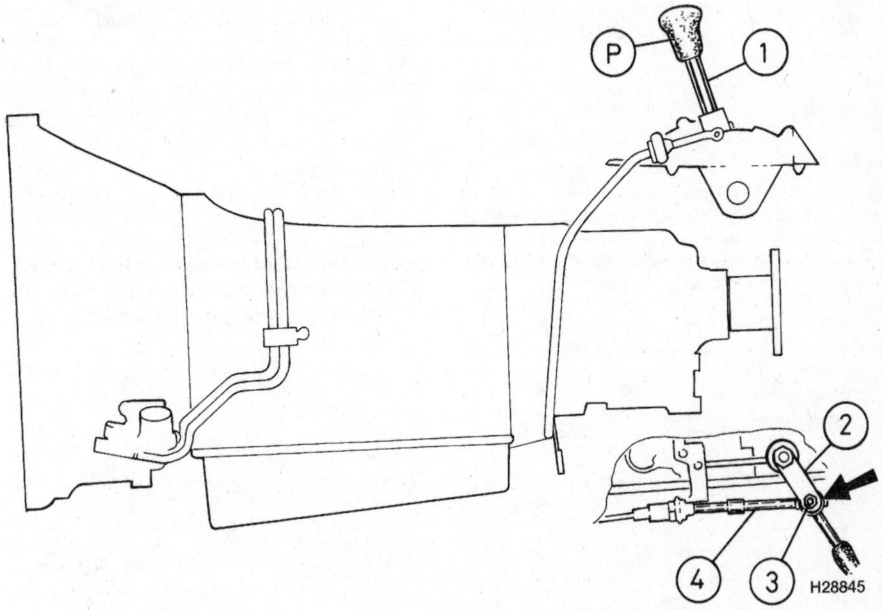


**3.11 Adjusting the selector cable**

*P Park position*
*1 Selector lever*
*2 Operating lever*
*3 Clamp nut*
*4 Selector cable*

7B

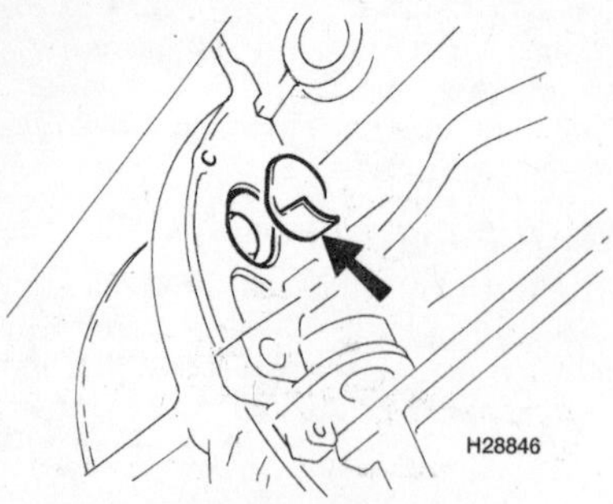


**5.13a Prise the plug (arrowed) from the engine/transmission adapter plate . . .**

6 Remove the propeller shaft as described in Chapter 8.
7 Drain the automatic transmission fluid as described in Chapter 1.
8 Where applicable, unscrew the union nut, and remove the fluid filler pipe from the transmission fluid pan.
9 Disconnect the selector cable from the transmission with reference to Section 3.
10 Disconnect the transmission wiring harness plug(s). Release the wiring harness from the brackets and clips on the transmission.
11 Where applicable, release the oxygen sensor from the bracket on the transmission.
12 Unbolt the fluid cooler pipe brackets and clamps, then pull the fluid cooler pipes from the transmission fluid pan.
13 Prise the plug from the aperture in the engine/transmission adapter plate, above the sump, or from the aperture in the crankcase, depending on model, for access to the torque converter securing bolts **(see illustrations)**.
14 Unscrew the three torque converter bolts, turning the crankshaft using a spanner or socket on the pulley hub bolt, for access to each bolt in turn.
15 Support the transmission using a trolley jack and interposed block of wood. ***Caution: The transmission is heavy, so ensure that it is adequately supported.***
16 On models with M40 or M50 engines, if not already done, remove the heater/ventilation inlet air ducting from the rear of the engine compartment as follows.

a) *Lift the grille from the top of the ducting (on certain Coupe models, it will be necessary to remove the securing screws and lift off the complete scuttle grille assembly).*
b) *Working through the top of the ducting, remove the screws securing the cable ducting to the air ducting and move the cable ducting clear.*
c) *Unscrew the nuts and/or screw(s) securing the air ducting to the bulkhead (where applicable, bend back the heat shielding for access).*
d) *Remove the air ducting by pulling upwards.*
e) *Move the previously removed cable ducting clear of the cylinder head cover.*

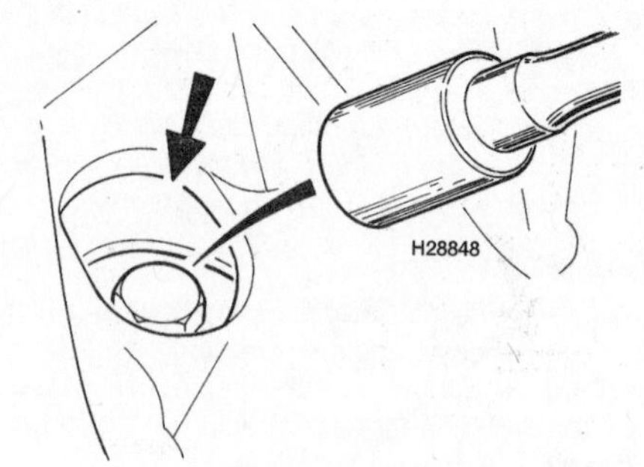


**5.13b . . . or from the aperture in the crankcase**

17 On models with the M40 and M42 engines, unbolt the wiring ducting from the rear of the engine, then connect an engine hoist and lifting tackle to the engine lifting eye (incorporated in the rear flange of the cylinder block casting) at the rear left-hand corner of the cylinder block. Raise the lifting tackle to just take the weight of the engine.
18 On models with the M43 engine, support the engine using a trolley jack under the sump, with a block of wood between the jack and sump to spread the load. Raise the jack to just touch the sump.
19 On models with the M50 engine, connect the lifting tackle to the engine lifting eye at the rear left-hand corner of the cylinder block (incorporated in the rear flange of the cylinder block casting).
20 Unbolt the crosstube from the car floor, under the transmission bellhousing.
21 Where applicable, unbolt the gearbox front mounting assembly **(see illustration)**.
22 Check to ensure that the engine and transmission are adequately supported then, working under the car, unscrew the nuts securing the transmission rubber mountings to the lugs on the transmission casing.
23 Remove the bolts securing the transmission crossmember to the body, then withdraw the crossmember from under the car. If necessary, bend back or unbolt the exhaust heat shield for access to the crossmember bolts.
24 Using the jack(s) and engine hoist (where applicable), lower the engine and gearbox until the rear of the engine cylinder head/manifold assembly is almost touching the engine compartment bulkhead. Check that the assembly is not resting against the heater hose connections on the bulkhead.
25 Where applicable, unscrew the bolt securing the engine/transmission adapter plate to the right-hand side of the transmission bellhousing.
26 Unscrew the engine-to-transmission bolts, and recover the washers, then slide the transmission rearwards.
27 Insert a suitable metal or wooden lever through the slot in the bottom of the bellhousing to retain the torque converter. As the transmission is released from the engine, check to make sure that the engine is not forced against the heater hose connections or the bulkhead.
28 Lower the transmission and carefully withdraw it from under the car, making sure that the torque converter is held in position. If the transmission is to be removed for some time, ensure that the engine is adequately supported in the engine compartment.
29 To remove the torque converter, first remove the retaining lever.
30 Fit two long bolts to two of the torque converter securing bolt holes, and use the bolts to pull the torque converter from the transmission **(see illustration)**. Pull evenly on both bolts. Be prepared for fluid spillage.

### *Refitting*

31 Where applicable, refit the torque converter, using the two bolts to manipulate the converter into position.
32 Ensure that the transmission locating dowels are in position on the engine.
33 Before mating the transmission with the engine, it is essential that the torque converter is perfectly aligned with the driveplate. Once the engine and transmission have been mated, it is no longer possible to turn the torque converter to allow re-alignment.
34 To align the driveplate with the torque converter, BMW use a special tapered tool which screws into the driveplate. It may be possible to improvise a suitable tool using an old torque converter-to-driveplate bolt with the head cut off, or a length of threaded

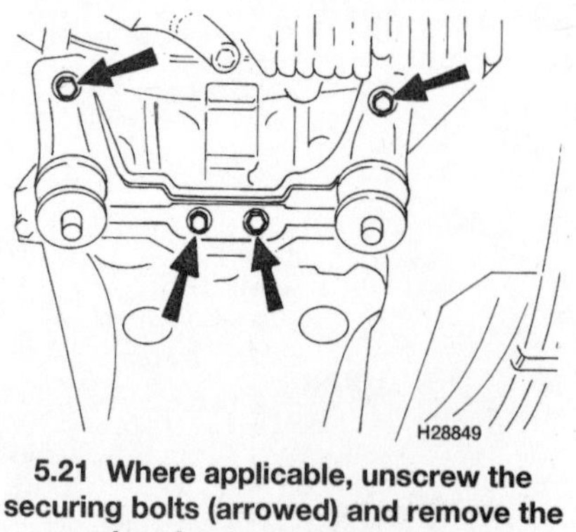


**5.21 Where applicable, unscrew the securing bolts (arrowed) and remove the gearbox front mounting assembly**

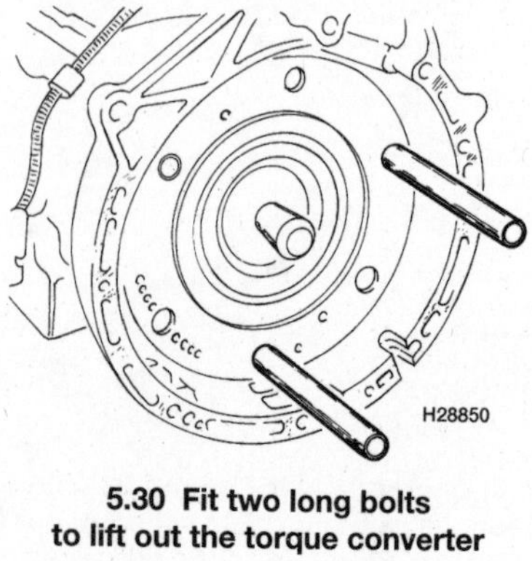


**5.30 Fit two long bolts to lift out the torque converter**

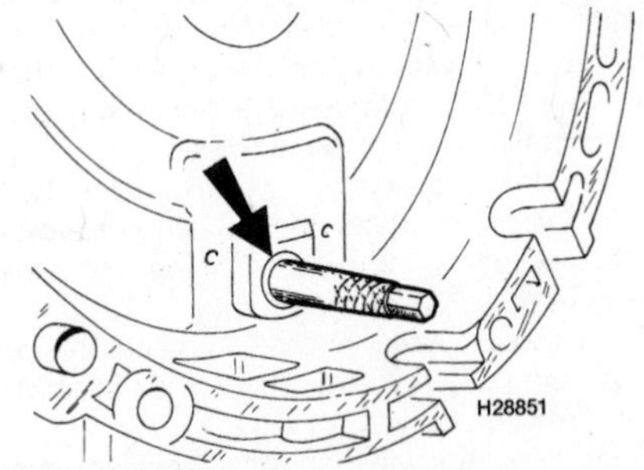


**5.36a Alignment tool (arrowed) screwed into driveplate, aligned with aperture in bottom of sump/bellhousing**

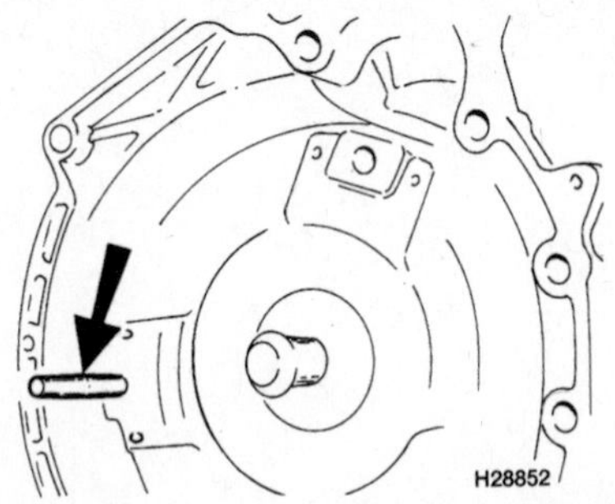


**5.36b Alignment tool screwed into driveplate, aligned with aperture in engine/ transmission adapter plate - A5S 310Z transmission**

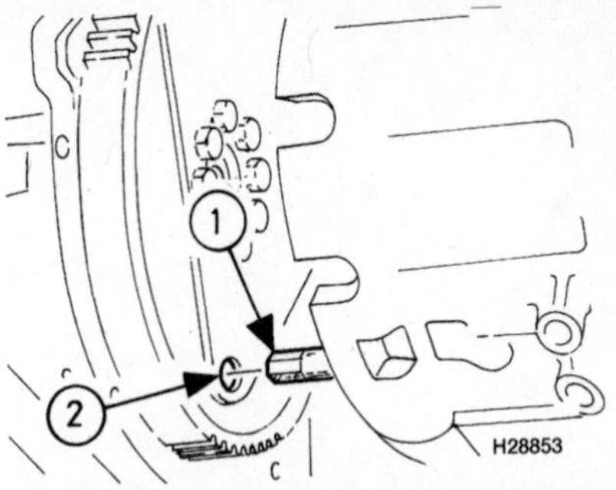


**5.40 Ensure that the alignment tool (1) passes through the hole (2) in the torque converter**

bar - note that the end of the bolt or bar must either have a slot cut in the end, or flats machined on it to allow it to be unscrewed once the engine and transmission have been mated.

**35** Turn the flywheel to align one of the torque converter-to-driveplate bolt holes with the aperture in the bottom of the sump/bellhousing (for access to the sump securing bolt), or on models with the A5S 310Z 5-speed transmission, with the aperture in the engine/transmission adapter plate. This is essential to enable the alignment stud to be removed after the engine and transmission have been mated.

**36** Screw the alignment tool into the relevant hole in the driveplate **(see illustrations)**.

**37** Where applicable, remove the retaining lever from the torque converter.

**38** Ensure that the transmission is adequately supported, and manoeuvre it into position under the car.

**39** Turn the torque converter to align one of the torque converter-to-driveplate bolt holes with the alignment tool fitted to the driveplate, then offer the transmission into position.

**40** Ensure that the alignment tool passes through the hole in the torque converter, then refit and tighten the engine-to-transmission bolts, ensuring that the washers are in place **(see illustration)**.

**41** Unscrew the alignment tool from the driveplate, then refit the torque converter-to-driveplate bolt. Tighten the bolt to the specified torque.

**42** Turn the crankshaft as during removal for access to the remaining two torque converter-to-driveplate bolt locations. Refit and tighten the bolts.

**43** Further refitting is a reversal of removal, bearing in mind the following points.

*a) Tighten all fixings to the specified torques, where applicable.*

*b) Check the condition of the transmission fluid pipe O-rings and renew if necessary.*

*c) Refit the propeller shaft (see Chapter 8).*

*d) Refit the starter motor (see Chapter 5A).*

*e) Reconnect and adjust the selector cable as described in Section 3.*

*f) On completion, refill the transmission with fluid as described in Chapter 1.*

## 6 Automatic transmission overhaul - general information

In the event of a fault occurring with the transmission, it is first necessary to determine whether it is of an electrical, mechanical or hydraulic nature, and to do this special test equipment is required. It is therefore essential to have the work carried out by a BMW dealer if a transmission fault is suspected.

Do not remove the transmission from the car for possible repair before professional fault diagnosis has been carried out, since most tests require the transmission to be in the car.

# Notes

# Chapter 8
# Final drive, driveshafts and propeller shaft

## Contents



## Degrees of difficulty

| | | | | |
|---|---|---|---|---|
| **Easy,** suitable for novice with little experience | **Fairly easy,** suitable for beginner with some experience | **Fairly difficult,** suitable for competent DIY mechanic | **Difficult,** suitable for experienced DIY mechanic | **Very difficult,** suitable for expert DIY or professional |

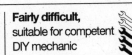

## Specifications

### Final drive
Type ........................... Unsprung, attached to rear suspension crossmember

### Driveshaft
Type ........................... Steel shafts with ball-and-cage type constant velocity joints at each end

### Propeller shaft
Type ........................... Two-piece tubular shaft with centre bearing, centre and rear universal joint. Front joint is either rubber coupling or universal joint (depending on model)

### Torque wrench settings
**Note**: *On some fixings different grades of bolt can be used; the grade of each bolt is stamped on the bolt head. Ensure that each bolt is tightened to the correct torque for its specific grade.*

| **Final drive unit** | **Nm** | **lbf ft** |
|---|---|---|
| Mounting bolts: | | |
| Front bolt | 95 | 70 |
| Rear bolts | 77 | 59 |
| Propeller shaft flange retaining nut (approximate - see text): | | |
| M20 nut | 175 | 131 |
| M22 nut | 185 | 138 |
| **Driveshaft** | | |
| Shaft to final drive flange bolts: | | |
| Allen bolts: | | |
| M10 bolts: | | |
| Bolts with locking teeth | 96 | 71 |
| Bolts without locking teeth | 83 | 61 |
| M12 bolts | 110 | 81 |
| Torx bolts: | | |
| M10 bolts: | | |
| Bolts with locking teeth | 100 | 74 |
| Bolts without locking teeth | 83 | 61 |
| M8 bolts | 64 | 48 |
| Driveshaft retaining nut | 250 | 186 |

## Torque wrench settings (continued)

| | Nm | lbf ft |
|---|---|---|
| **Propeller shaft** | | |
| Front universal joint to transmission | 64 | 48 |
| Rubber coupling to transmission/propeller shaft: | | |
| M10 (Grade 8.8) bolts | 48 | 35 |
| M10 (Grade 10.9) bolts | 64 | 48 |
| M12 (Grade 8.8) bolts | 81 | 60 |
| M12 (Grade 10.9) bolts | 100 | 74 |
| Support bearing bracket nuts | 21 | 15 |
| Rear universal joint to final drive unit: | | |
| Nyloc nut ("squeeze nut") | 64 | 48 |
| Ribbed nut | 90 | 67 |
| Threaded sleeve | 10 | 7 |
| **Roadwheels** | | |
| Wheel bolts | 100 | 74 |

## 1 General information

Power is transmitted from the transmission to the rear axle by a two-piece propeller shaft, joined behind the centre bearing by a "slip joint," a sliding, splined coupling. The slip joint allows slight fore-and-aft movement of the propeller shaft. The forward end of the propeller shaft is attached to the output flange of the transmission either by a flexible rubber coupling or a universal flange joint. On some models, a vibration damper is mounted between the front of the propeller shaft and coupling. The middle of the propeller shaft is supported by the centre bearing which is bolted to the vehicle body. Universal joints are located at the centre bearing and at the rear end of the propeller shaft, to compensate for movement of the transmission and differential on their mountings and for any flexing of the chassis.

The final drive assembly includes the drive pinion, the ring gear, the differential and the output flanges. The drive pinion, which drives the ring gear, is also known as the differential input shaft and is connected to the propeller shaft via an input flange. The differential is bolted to the ring gear and drives the rear wheels through a pair of output flanges bolted to driveshafts with constant velocity (CV) joints at either end. The differential allows the wheels to turn at different speeds when cornering.

The driveshafts deliver power from the final drive unit output flanges to the rear wheels. The driveshafts are equipped with Constant Velocity (CV) joints at each end. The inner CV joints are bolted to the differential flanges. and the outer CV joints engage the splines of the wheel hubs, and are secured by a large nut.

Major repair work on the differential assembly components (drive pinion, ring-and-pinion, and differential) requires many special tools and a high degree of expertise, and therefore should not be attempted by the home mechanic. If major repairs become necessary, we recommend that they be performed by a BMW service department or other suitably equipped automotive engineer.

## 2 Final drive unit - removal and refitting

**Note:** *New propeller shaft rear coupling nuts and driveshaft retaining bolts will be required on refitting.*

### Removal

**1** Chock the front wheels. Jack up the rear of the vehicle and support it on axle stands (see "*Jacking and vehicle support*"). Remove both rear wheels. If necessary, drain the final drive unit as described in Chapter 1.

**2** Using paint or a suitable marker pen, make alignment marks between the propeller shaft and final drive unit flange. Unscrew the nuts securing the propeller shaft to the final drive unit and discard them; new ones must be used on refitting.

**3** Slacken and remove the retaining bolts and plates securing the right-hand driveshaft to the final drive unit flange and support the driveshaft by tying it to the vehicle underbody using a piece of wire. **Note:** *Do not allow the driveshaft to hang under its own weight as the CV joint may be damaged.* Discard the bolts, new ones should be used on refitting.

**4** Disconnect the left-hand driveshaft from the final drive as described in paragraph 3.

**5** Disconnect the wiring connector from the speedometer drive on the rear of the final drive unit.

**6** Slacken and remove the left- and right-hand anti-roll bar mountings (see Chapter 10).

**7** Move a jack and interposed block of wood into position and raise it so that it is supporting the weight of the final drive unit.

**8** Making sure the final drive unit is safely supported, slacken and remove the two bolts securing the rear of the unit in position and the single bolt securing the front of the unit in position **(see illustrations)**.

**9** Carefully lower the final drive unit out of position and remove it from underneath the vehicle. Examine the final drive unit mounting rubbers for signs of wear or damage and renew if necessary.

### Refitting

**10** Refitting is a reversal of removal noting the following.

*a) Raise the final drive unit into position and engage it with the propeller shaft rear joint, making sure the marks made prior to removal are correctly aligned.*

*b) Tighten the final drive unit mounting bolts to the specified torque setting.*

*c) Fit the new propeller shaft joint nuts and tighten them to the specified torque.*

*d) Refit the anti-roll bar mountings (see Chapter 10).*

*e) Fit the new driveshaft joint retaining bolts and plates and tighten them to the specified torque.*

*f) On completion, refill/top-up the final drive unit with oil as described in Chapter 1.*

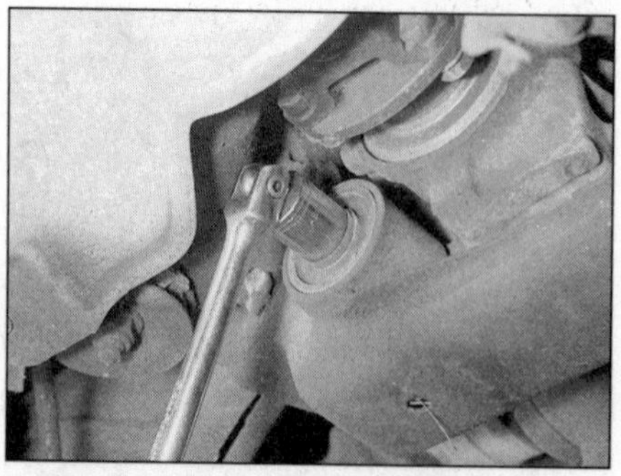

**2.8a Slacken and remove the front . . .**

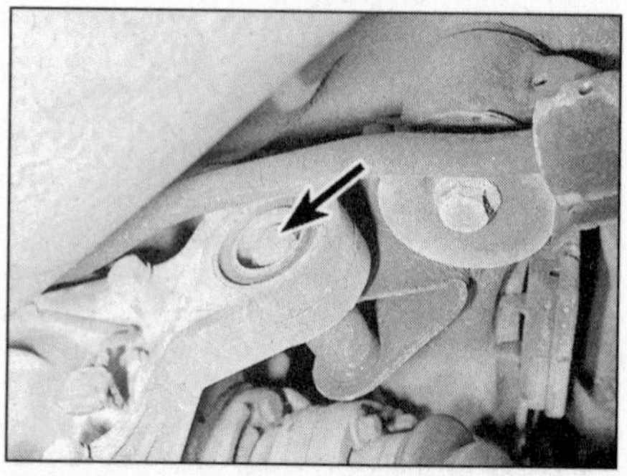

**2.8b . . . and rear final drive unit mounting bolts (arrowed)**

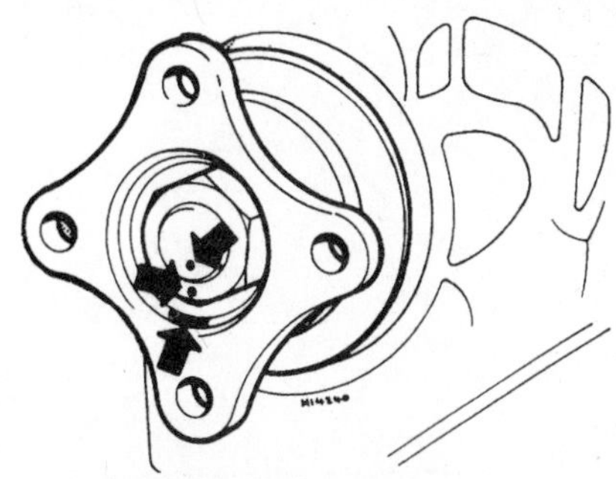

**3.3 Scribe or paint alignment marks (arrowed) on the flange, the pinion shaft and nut to ensure proper reassembly**

## 3 Final drive unit oil seals - renewal

### Propeller shaft flange oil seal

**Note:** *A new flange nut retaining plate will be required.*

**1** Drain the final drive unit as described in Chapter 1.

**2** Remove the final drive unit as described in Section 2 and secure the unit in a vice.

**3** Remove the retaining plate and make alignment marks between the propeller flange nut, the drive flange and pinion **(see illustration)**. Discard the retaining plate a new one must be used on refitting.

**4** Hold the drive flange stationary by bolting a length of metal bar to it, then unscrew the nut noting the exact number of turns necessary to remove it.

**5** Using a suitable puller, draw the drive flange from the pinion and remove the dust cover. If the dust cover shows signs of wear, renew it.

**6** Lever the oil seal from the final drive casing with a screwdriver. Wipe clean the oil seal seating.

**7** Smear a little oil on the sealing lip of the new oil seal, then press it squarely into the casing until flush with the outer face. If necessary the seal can be tapped into position using a metal tube which bears only on its hard outer edge.

**8** Fit the dust cover and locate the drive flange on the pinion aligning the marks made on removal. Refit the flange nut, screwing it on by the exact number of turns counted on removal, so that the alignment marks align.

***Warning: Do not overtighten the flange nut. If the nut is overtightened, the collapsible spacer behind the flange will be deformed necessitating its renewal. This is a complex operation requiring the final drive unit to be dismantled (see Section 1).***

**9** Secure the nut in position with the new retaining plate, tapping it squarely into position.

**10** Refit the final drive unit as described in Section 2 and refill it with oil as described in Chapter 1.

### Driveshaft flange oil seal

**Note:** *New driveshaft joint retaining bolts and a driveshaft flange circlip will be required.*

**11** Drain the final drive unit oil as described in Chapter 1.

**12** Slacken and remove the bolts securing the driveshaft constant velocity joint to the final drive unit and recover the retaining plates. Position the driveshaft clear of the flange and tie it to the vehicle underbody using a piece of wire. **Note:** *Do not allow the driveshaft to hang under its own weight as the CV joint may be damaged.*

**13** Using a suitable lever, carefully prise the driveshaft flange out from the final drive unit taking care not to damage the dust seal or casing **(see illustration)**. Remove the flange and recover dust seal. If the dust seal shows signs of damage, renew it.

**14** Carefully lever the oil seal out from the final drive unit. Wipe clean the oil seal seating.

**15** With the seal removed, prise out the circlip from the centre of the final drive unit gear **(see illustration)**.

**16** Fit a new circlip, making sure its is correctly located in the final drive unit groove.

**17** Smear a little oil on the sealing lip of the new oil seal, then press it squarely into the casing until it reaches its stop. If necessary the seal can be tapped into position using a metal tube which bears only on its hard outer edge **(see illustration)**.

**18** Fit the dust cover and insert the drive flange. Push the drive flange fully into position and check that it is securely retained by the circlip.

**19** Align the driveshaft with the flange and refit the new retaining bolts and plates, tightening them to the specified torque.

**20** Refill the final drive unit with oil as described in Chapter 1.

## 4 Driveshaft - removal and refitting

**Note:** *A new driveshaft retaining nut and bolts will be required on refitting.*

### Removal

**1** Remove the wheel trim/hub cap (as applicable) and slacken the driveshaft retaining nut with the vehicle resting on its wheels. Also slacken the wheel bolts.

**2** Chock the front wheels, then jack up the rear of the vehicle and support it on axle stands (see "*Jacking and vehicle support*").

**3** Remove the relevant rear roadwheel.

**4** If the left-hand driveshaft is to be removed, remove the exhaust system tailpipe to improve access (see relevant Part of Chapter 4).

**5** Slacken and remove the left- and right-hand anti-roll bar mountings and pivot the bar downwards (see Chapter 10).

**6** Unscrew and remove the driveshaft nut.

**7** Slacken and remove the bolts securing the driveshaft constant velocity joint to the final drive unit and recover the retaining plates. Position the driveshaft clear of the flange and tie it to the vehicle underbody using a piece of wire. **Note:** *Do not allow the driveshaft to hang under its own weight as the CV joint may be damaged.*

**8** Withdraw the driveshaft outer constant velocity joint from the hub assembly. The outer joint will be very tight, tap the joint out of the hub using a soft-faced mallet. If this fails to free it from the hub, the joint will have to be pressed out using a suitable tool which is bolted to the hub.

**9** Remove the driveshaft from underneath the vehicle.



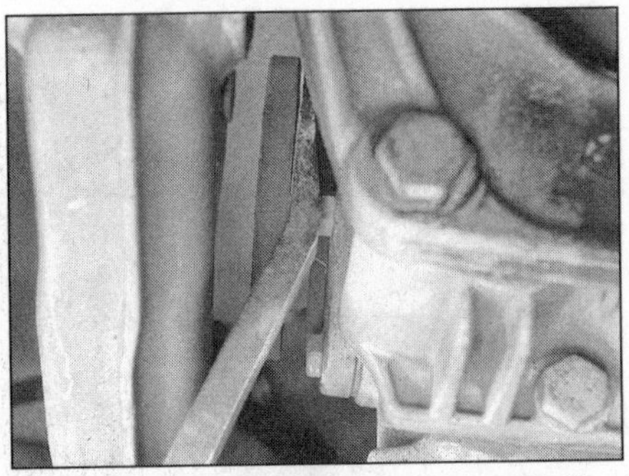

**3.13 Using a suitable lever to remove the driveshaft flange from the final drive unit**

**3.15 Remove the flange retaining circlip from the centre of the final drive unit gear**

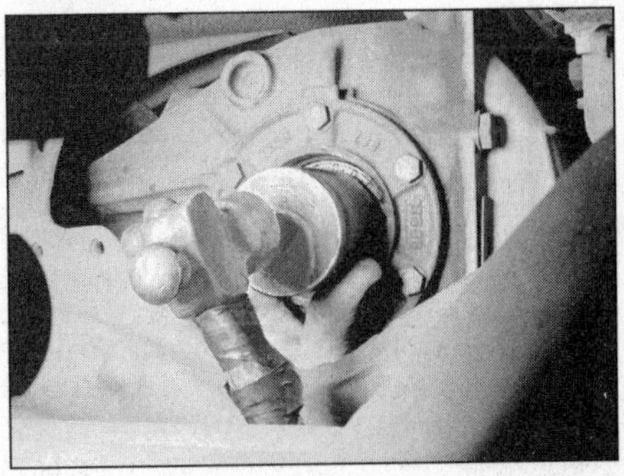

**3.17 Tap the new seal into position with a hammer and socket which bears only on the outer edge of the seal**

5.3 Carefully tap the sealing cover off from the inner end of the joint

5.4 Release the gaiter retaining clips and slide the gaiter down the shaft

5.5 Removing the inner joint circlip from the driveshaft

### Refitting

**10** Refitting is the reverse of removal noting the following points.

*a) Lubricate the threads of the new driveshaft nut with clean engine oil prior to fitting and tighten it to the specified torque. If necessary, wait until the vehicle is lower to the ground and then tighten the nut to the specified torque.*

*b) Fit new inner joint retaining bolts and plates and tighten to the specified torque.*

## 5 Driveshaft gaiters - renewal

**1** Remove the driveshaft (see Section 4).

**2** Clean the driveshaft and mount it in a vice.

**3** Lever off the sealing cover from the end of the inner constant velocity (CV) joint **(see illustration)**.

**4** Release the two inner joint gaiter retaining clips and free the gaiter and dust cover from the joint **(see illustration)**.

**5** Scoop out excess grease and remove the inner joint circlip from the end of the driveshaft **(see illustration)**.

**6** Securely support the joint inner member and tap the driveshaft out of position using a hammer and suitable drift **(see illustration)**. If the joint is a tight fit, a suitable puller will be required to draw off the joint. Do not dismantle the inner joint.

**7** With the joint removed, slide the inner gaiter and dust cover off from the end of the driveshaft **(see illustration)**.

**8** Release the outer joint gaiter retaining clips then slide the gaiter along the shaft and remove it.

**9** Thoroughly clean the constant velocity joints using paraffin, or a suitable solvent, and dry thoroughly. Carry out a visual inspection as follows.

**10** Move the inner splined driving member from side to side to expose each ball in turn at the top of its track. Examine the balls for cracks, flat spots or signs of surface pitting.

**11** Inspect the ball tracks on the inner and outer members. If the tracks have widened, the balls will no longer be a tight fit. At the same time check the ball cage windows for wear or cracking between the windows.

5.6 Support the inner joint inner member then tap the driveshaft out of position . . .

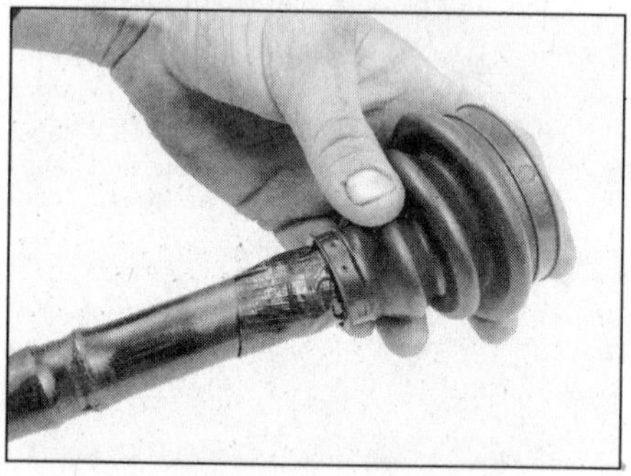
5.7 . . . and slide off the gaiter

**12** If on inspection any of the constant velocity joint components are found to be worn or damaged, it must be renewed. The inner joint is available separately but if the outer joint is worn it will be necessary to renew the complete joint and driveshaft assembly. If the joints are in satisfactory condition, obtain new gaiter repair kits which contain gaiters, retaining clips, an inner constant velocity joint circlip and the correct type and quantity of grease required.

**13** Tape over the splines on the end of the driveshaft.

**14** Slide the new outer gaiter onto the end of the driveshaft.

**15** Pack the outer joint with the specified type of grease. Work the grease well into the bearing tracks whilst twisting the joint, and fill the rubber gaiter with any excess.

**16** Ease the gaiter over the joint and ensure that the gaiter lips are correctly located on both the driveshaft and constant velocity joint. Lift the outer sealing lip of the gaiter to equalise air pressure within the gaiter.

**17** Fit the large metal retaining clip to the gaiter. Pull the retaining clip tight then bend it back to secure it in position and cut off any excess clip. Secure the small retaining clip using the same procedure.

**18** Engage the new inner gaiter with its dust cover and slide the assembly onto the driveshaft.

**19** Remove the tape from the driveshaft splines and fit the inner constant velocity joint. Press the joint fully onto the shaft and secure it in position with a new circlip.

**20** Work the grease supplied fully into the inner joint and fill the gaiter with any excess **(see illustrations)**.

**21** Slide the inner gaiter into position and

5.20a Fill the inner joint with the grease supplied . . .

5.20b . . . and work it into the bearing tracks

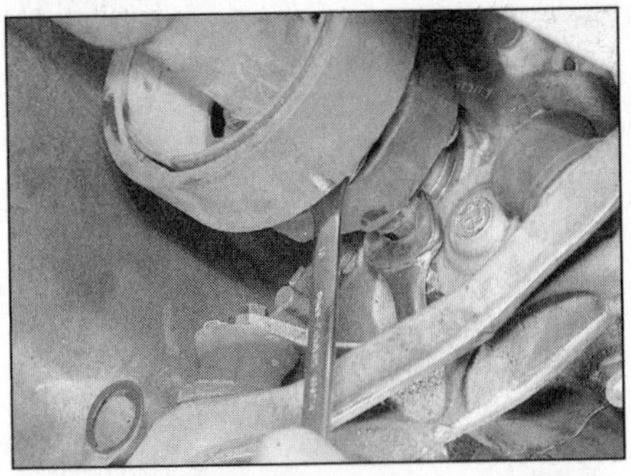

**6.4 On models with a rubber coupling, slacken and remove the bolts securing the coupling to the transmission flange**

**6.5 Unscrew the large threaded sleeve nut by a couple of turns**

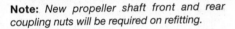

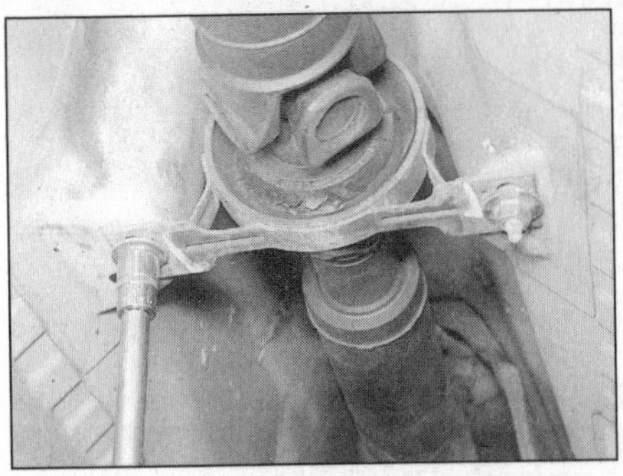

**6.7 Unscrew the centre bearing bracket retaining nuts and remove the propeller shaft from underneath the vehicle**

press the dust cover onto the joint, making sure the retaining bolt holes are correctly aligned. Lift the outer sealing lip of the gaiter, to equalise air pressure within the gaiter, and secure it in position with the retaining clips (see paragraph 17).

**22** Apply a smear of suitable sealant (BMW recommend BMW sealing gel) and press the new sealing cover fully onto the end of the inner joint.

**23** Check that both constant velocity joints are free to move easily then refit the driveshaft as described in Section 4.

## 6 Propeller shaft - removal and refitting

**Note:** *New propeller shaft front and rear coupling nuts will be required on refitting.*

### Removal

**1** Chock the front wheels. Jack up the rear of the vehicle and support it on axle stands (see "*Jacking and vehicle support*").

**2** Remove the exhaust system and heatshield as described in the relevant Part of Chapter 4. Where necessary, unbolt the exhaust system mounting bracket(s) in order to gain the necessary clearance required to remove the propeller shaft.

**3** On models where the front of the propeller shaft is bolted straight onto the transmission output flange, make alignment marks between the shaft and transmission then slacken and remove the retaining nuts. Discard the nuts, new ones should be used on refitting.

**4** On models where a rubber coupling is fitted between the front end of the propeller shaft and transmission output flange, make alignment marks between the shaft, transmission and (where necessary) vibration damper. Slacken and remove the nuts and bolts securing the coupling to the transmission **(see illustration)**. Discard the nuts, new ones should be used on refitting.

**5** Using a large open-ended spanner, loosen the threaded sleeve nut, which is situated near the support bearing, through a couple of turns **(see illustration)**.

**6** Using paint or a suitable marker pen, make alignment marks between the propeller shaft and final drive unit flange. Unscrew the nuts securing the propeller shaft to the final drive unit and discard them; new ones must be used on refitting.

**7** With the aid of an assistant, support the propeller shaft then unscrew the centre support bearing bracket retaining nuts **(see illustration)**. Slide the two halves of the shaft towards each other then lower the centre of the shaft and disengage it from the transmission and final drive unit. Remove the shaft from underneath the vehicle. **Note:** *Do not separate the two halves of the shaft without first making alignment marks. If the shafts are incorrectly joined, the propeller shaft assembly may become imbalanced, leading to noise and vibration during operation.*

**8** Inspect the rubber coupling (where fitted), the support bearing and shaft universal joints as described in Sections 7, 8 and 9. Inspect the transmission flange locating pin and propeller shaft bush for signs of wear or damage and renew as necessary.

### Refitting

**9** Apply a smear of molybdenum disulphide grease (BMW recommend Molykote Longterm 2) to the transmission pin and shaft bush and manoeuvre the shaft into position.

**10** Align the marks made prior to removal and engage the shaft with the transmission and final drive unit flanges. With the marks correctly aligned, refit the support bracket retaining nuts, tightening them lightly only at this stage.

**11** Fit new retaining nuts to the rear coupling of the propeller shaft and tighten them to the specified torque.

**12** On models where the propeller shaft is bolted straight onto the transmission flange, fit the new retaining nuts and tighten them to the specified torque.

**13** On models with a rubber coupling, insert the bolts and fit the new retaining nuts. Tighten them to the specified torque, noting that the nut/bolt should only be rotated on the flange side to avoid stressing the rubber coupling.

**14** Tighten the propeller shaft threaded sleeve to the specified torque.

**15** Loosen the centre bearing bracket nuts. Slide the bracket forwards to remove all freeplay, then preload the bearing by moving the bracket forwards a further 4 to 6 mm. Hold the bracket in this position and tighten its retaining nuts to the specified torque.

**16** Refit the exhaust system and associated components as described in Chapter 4.

## 7 Propeller shaft rubber coupling - check and renewal

**Note:** *A rubber coupling is not fitted to all models. On some models, a universal joint is fitted to the front of the propeller shaft instead (see Section 9).*

### Check

**1** Firmly apply the handbrake, then jack up the front of the vehicle and support it on axle stands (see "*Jacking and vehicle support*").

**2** Closely examine the rubber coupling, links the propeller shaft to the transmission, looking for signs of damage such as cracking or splitting or for signs of general deterioration. If necessary, renew the coupling as follows.

### Renewal

**Note:** *New propeller shaft coupling nuts will be required.*

**3** Carry out the operations described in paragraphs 1, 2, 4 and 5 of Section 6.

**4** Slide the front half of the propeller shaft to the rear then disengage it from the transmission locating pin and pivot it downwards.

**5** Slacken and remove the nuts securing the coupling to the shaft and remove it **(see illustration)**. If necessary, also remove the vibration damper; the damper should also be renewed if it shows signs of wear or damage.

**6** Aligning the marks made on removal, fit the vibration damper (where fitted) to the propeller shaft.

**7** Fit the new rubber coupling noting that the arrows on the side of the coupling must point towards the propeller shaft/transmission

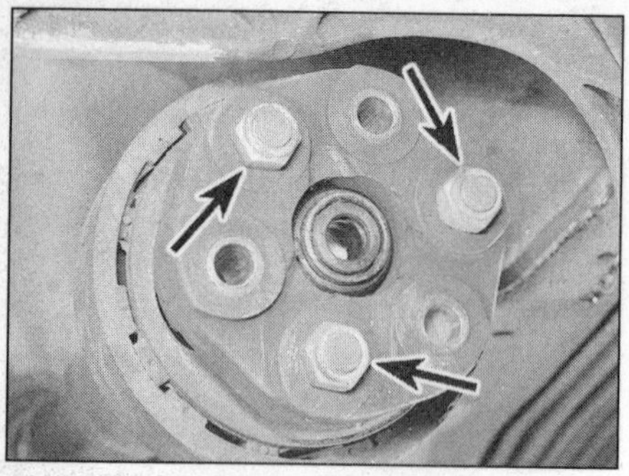

**7.5 Coupling to propeller shaft retaining bolts (arrowed)**

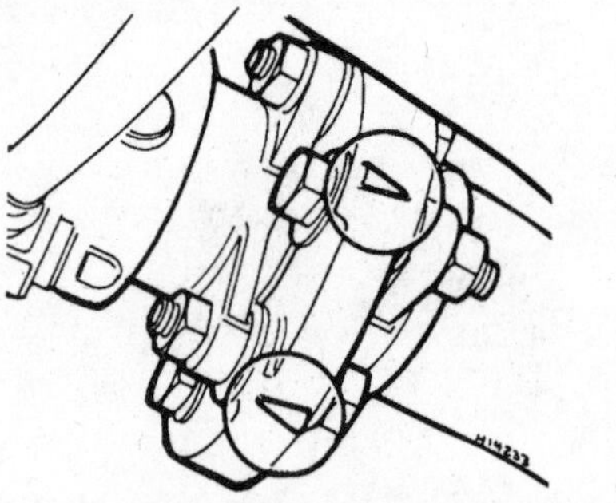

**7.7 If the coupling has directional arrows, make sure the arrows are pointing towards the propeller shaft/transmission flanges and not the bolt heads**

flanges **(see illustration)**. Fit the new retaining nuts and tighten them to the specified torque.

**8** Apply a smear of molybdenum disulphide grease (BMW recommend Molykote Longterm 2) to the transmission pin and shaft bush and manoeuvre the shaft into position.

**9** Align the marks made prior to removal and engage the shaft with the transmission flange. With the marks correctly aligned, insert the bolts and fit the new retaining nuts. Tighten them to the specified torque, noting that the nut/bolt should only be rotated on the flange side to avoid stressing the rubber coupling.

**10** Tighten the propeller shaft threaded sleeve to the specified torque.

**11** Refit the exhaust system and associated components as described in Chapter 4.

## 8 Propeller shaft support bearing - check and renewal

### *Check*

**1** Wear in the support bearing will lead to noise and vibration when the vehicle is driven. The bearing is best checked with the propeller shaft removed (see Section 7). To gain access to the bearing with the shaft in position, remove the exhaust system and heatshields as described in the relevant Part of Chapter 4.

**2** Rotate the bearing and check that it turns smoothly with no sign of freeplay; if it's difficult to turn, or if it has a gritty feeling, renew it. Also inspect the rubber portion. If it's cracked or deteriorated, renew it.

### *Renewal*

**3** Remove the propeller shaft as described in Section 7.

**4** Make alignment marks between the front and rear sections of the propeller shaft then unscrew the threaded sleeve nut and separate the two halves. Recover the sleeve nut, washer and bush noting their correct fitted locations.

**5** Remove the circlip and slide off the support bearing rear dust cover.

**6** Draw the support bearing off from the propeller shaft using a suitable puller then remove the front dust cover in the same way.

**7** Firmly support the support bearing bracket and press out the bearing with a suitable tubular spacer.

**8** Fit the new bearing to the bracket and press it into position using a tubular spacer which bears only on the bearing outer race.

**9** Thoroughly clean the shaft splines and carefully press the new front dust seal onto the propeller shaft, making sure it is fitted the correct way around.

**10** Press the support bearing fully onto the propeller shaft using a tubular spacer which bears only on the bearing inner race.

**11** Check that the bearing is free to rotate smoothly, then fit the new rear dust seal.

**12** Apply a smear of molybdenum disulphide grease (BMW recommend Molykote Longterm 2) to the splines and fit the threaded sleeve, washer and bush to the front section of the propeller shaft.

**13** Align the marks made prior to separation and joint the front and rear sections of the propeller shaft.

**14** Refit the propeller shaft as described in Section 6.

## 9 Propeller shaft universal joints - check and renewal

**Note:** *On some models a rubber coupling is fitted between the propeller shaft and transmission instead of a universal joint (see Section 7).*

### *Check*

**1** Wear in the universal joints is characterised by vibration in the transmission, noise during acceleration, and metallic squeaking and grating sounds as the bearings disintegrate. The joints can be checked with the propeller shaft still fitted noting that it will be necessary to remove the exhaust system and heatshields (see Chapter 4) to gain access.

**2** If the propeller shaft is in position on the vehicle, try to turn the propeller shaft while holding the transmission/final drive flange. Free play between the propeller shaft and the front or rear flanges indicates excessive wear.

**3** If the propeller shaft is already removed, you can check the universal joints by holding the shaft in one hand and turning the yoke or flange with the other. If the axial movement is excessive, renew the propeller shaft.

### *Renewal*

**4** At the time of writing, no spare parts were available to enable renewal of the universal joints to be carried out. Therefore, if any joint shows signs of damage or wear the complete propeller shaft assembly must be renewed. Consult your BMW dealer for latest information on parts availability.

**5** If renewal of the propeller shaft is necessary, it may be worthwhile seeking the advice of an automotive engineering specialist. They may be able to repair the original shaft assembly or supply a reconditioned shaft on an exchange basis.

# Chapter 9
# Braking system

## Contents



## Degrees of difficulty

| | | | | |
|---|---|---|---|---|
| **Easy,** suitable for novice with little experience | **Fairly easy,** suitable for beginner with some experience | **Fairly difficult,** suitable for competent DIY mechanic | **Difficult,** suitable for experienced DIY mechanic | **Very difficult,** suitable for expert DIY or professional |

## Specifications

### Front brakes

| | |
|---|---|
| Disc diameter | 286 mm |
| Disc thickness: | |
| New: | |
| Solid disc | 12.0 mm |
| Ventilated disc | 22.0 mm |
| Minimum (stamped on disc): | |
| Solid disc | 10.4 mm |
| Ventilated disc | 20.4 mm |
| Maximum disc runout | 0.2 mm |
| Brake pad friction material minimum thickness | 2 mm |

### Rear drum brakes

| | |
|---|---|
| Drum diameter: | |
| New | 228.5 mm |
| Maximum diameter | 229.5 mm |
| Maximum drum out-of-round | 0.05 mm |
| Brake shoe friction material minimum thickness | 1.5 mm |

### Rear disc brakes

| | |
|---|---|
| Disc diameter | 280 mm |
| Disc thickness: | |
| New | 10.0 mm |
| Minimum (stamped on disc) | 8.4 mm |
| Maximum disc runout | 0.2 mm |
| Brake pad friction material minimum thickness | 2 mm |
| Handbrake drum diameter | 160 mm |

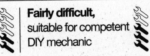

## Torque wrench settings

| | Nm | lbf ft |
|---|---|---|
| ABS wheel sensor retaining bolts | 10 | 7 |
| Brake disc retaining screw | 16 | 12 |
| Brake drum retaining screw | 16 | 12 |
| Brake hose unions: | | |
| M10 thread | 17 | 11 |
| M12 thread | 19 | 12 |
| Front brake caliper: | | |
| Guide pin bolts | 35 | 26 |
| Mounting bracket bolts | 110 | 81 |
| Master cylinder mounting nuts | 26 | 19 |
| Rear brake caliper: | | |
| Guide pin bolts | 35 | 26 |
| Mounting bracket bolts | 67 | 49 |
| Rear brake backplate bolts | 65 | 48 |
| Rear brake wheel cylinder bolts | 10 | 7 |
| Roadwheel bolts | 100 | 74 |
| Servo unit mounting nuts | 22 | 16 |

## 1 General information

The braking system is of the servo-assisted, dual-circuit hydraulic type. Under normal circumstances, both circuits operate in unison. However, if there is hydraulic failure in one circuit, full braking force will still be available at two wheels.

Most 1.6 and 1.8 litre models are fitted with front disc brakes and rear drum brakes. All 2.0 litre and larger models have disc brakes all round as standard, as do some 1.8 litre models. ABS is fitted as standard to some models, and was offered as an option on most other models (refer to Section 22 for further information on ABS operation). **Note:** *On models also equipped with Automatic Stability Control plus Traction (ASC+T), the ABS system also operates the traction control side of the system.*

The front disc brakes are actuated by single-piston sliding type calipers, which ensure that equal pressure is applied to each disc pad.

On models with rear drum brakes, the rear brakes incorporate leading and trailing shoes, which are actuated by twin-piston wheel cylinders. A self-adjust mechanism is incorporated, to automatically compensate for brake shoe wear.

On models with rear disc brakes, the brakes are actuated by single-piston sliding calipers.

The handbrake provides an independent mechanical means of rear brake application. On rear drum brake models, the handbrake actuates the brake shoes. On rear disc brake models, a separate drum brake arrangement is fitted in the centre of the brake disc.

**Note:** *When servicing any part of the system, work carefully and methodically; also observe scrupulous cleanliness when overhauling any part of the hydraulic system. Always renew components (in axle sets, where applicable) if in doubt about their condition, and use only genuine BMW replacement parts, or at least those of known good quality. Note the warnings given in "Safety first" and at relevant points in this Chapter concerning the dangers of asbestos dust and hydraulic fluid.*

## 2 Hydraulic system - bleeding

***Warning: Hydraulic fluid is poisonous; wash off immediately and thoroughly in the case of skin contact, and seek immediate medical advice if any fluid is swallowed or gets into the eyes. Certain types of hydraulic fluid are flammable, and may ignite when allowed into contact with hot components; when servicing any hydraulic system, it is safest to assume that the fluid IS flammable, and to take precautions against the risk of fire as though it is petrol that is being handled. Hydraulic fluid is also an effective paint stripper, and will attack plastics; if any is spilt, it should be washed off immediately, using copious quantities of fresh water. Finally, it is hygroscopic (it absorbs moisture from the air) - old fluid may be contaminated and unfit for further use. When topping-up or renewing the fluid, always use the recommended type, and ensure that it comes from a freshly-opened sealed container.***

***Warning: On models with ABS (with or without ASC+T), if the high-pressure hydraulic system linking the master cylinder, hydraulic unit and (where fitted) accumulator has been disturbed, then bleeding of the brakes should be entrusted to a BMW dealer. They will have access to the special service tester which is needed to bleed the high-pressure hydraulic system safely.***

### General

**1** The correct operation of any hydraulic system is only possible after removing all air from the components and circuit; this is achieved by bleeding the system.

**2** During the bleeding procedure, add only clean, unused hydraulic fluid of the recommended type; never re-use fluid that has already been bled from the system. Ensure that sufficient fluid is available before starting work.

**3** If there is any possibility of incorrect fluid being already in the system, the brake components and circuit must be flushed completely with uncontaminated, correct fluid, and new seals should be fitted to the various components.

**4** If hydraulic fluid has been lost from the system, or air has entered because of a leak, ensure that the fault is cured before continuing further.

**5** Park the vehicle on level ground, switch off the engine and select first or reverse gear, then chock the wheels and release the handbrake.

**6** Check that all pipes and hoses are secure, unions tight and bleed screws closed. Clean any dirt from around the bleed screws.

**7** Unscrew the master cylinder reservoir cap, and top the master cylinder reservoir up to the "MAX" level line; refit the cap loosely, and remember to maintain the fluid level at least above the "MIN" level line throughout the procedure, or there is a risk of further air entering the system.

**8** There are a number of one-man, do-it-yourself brake bleeding kits currently available from motor accessory shops. It is recommended that one of these kits is used whenever possible, as they greatly simplify the bleeding operation, and reduce the risk of expelled air and fluid being drawn back into the system. If such a kit is not available, the basic (two-man) method must be used, which is described in detail below.

**9** If a kit is to be used, prepare the vehicle as described previously, and follow the kit manufacturer's instructions, as the procedure may vary slightly according to the type being used; generally, they are as outlined below in the relevant sub-section.

**10** Whichever method is used, the same sequence must be followed (paragraphs 11 and 12) to ensure the removal of all air from the system.

### Bleeding sequence

**11** If the system has been only partially disconnected, and suitable precautions were taken to minimise fluid loss, it should be necessary only to bleed that part of the system.

**12** If the complete system is to be bled, then it should be done working in the following sequence:

*a) Right-hand rear brake.*
*b) Left-hand rear brake.*
*c) Right-hand front brake.*
*d) Left-hand front brake.*

⚠ ***Warning: On models with ABS (with or without ASC+T), after bleeding, the operation of the braking system should be checked at the earliest possible opportunity by a BMW dealer.***

### Bleeding - basic (two-man) method

**13** Collect a clean glass jar, a suitable length of plastic or rubber tubing which is a tight fit over the bleed screw, and a ring spanner to fit the screw. The help of an assistant will also be required.

**14** Remove the dust cap from the first screw in the sequence. Fit the spanner and tube to the screw, place the other end of the tube in the jar, and pour in sufficient fluid to cover the end of the tube.

**15** Ensure that the master cylinder reservoir fluid level is maintained at least above the "MIN" level line throughout the procedure.

**16** Have the assistant fully depress the brake pedal several times to build up pressure, then maintain it on the final downstroke.

**17** While pedal pressure is maintained, unscrew the bleed screw (approximately one turn) and allow the compressed fluid and air to flow into the jar. The assistant should maintain pedal pressure, following it down to the floor if necessary, and should not release it until instructed to do so. When the flow stops, tighten the bleed screw again, have the assistant release the pedal slowly, and recheck the reservoir fluid level.

**18** Repeat the steps in paragraphs 16 and 17 until the fluid emerging from the bleed screw is free from air bubbles. If the master cylinder has been drained and refilled, and air is being bled from the first screw in the sequence, allow about 5 seconds between cycles for the master cylinder passages to refill.

**19** When no more air bubbles appear, tighten the bleed screw securely, remove the tube and spanner, and refit the dust cap. Do not overtighten the bleed screw.

**20** Repeat the procedure on the remaining screws in the sequence, until all air is removed from the system and the brake pedal feels firm again.

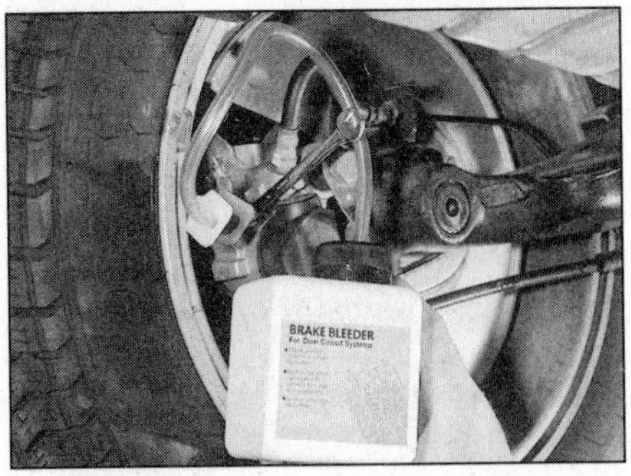


**2.21 Bleeding a rear brake caliper using a one-way valve kit**

### Bleeding - using a one-way valve kit

**21** As their name implies, these kits consist of a length of tubing with a one-way valve fitted, to prevent expelled air and fluid being drawn back into the system; some kits include a translucent container, which can be positioned so that the air bubbles can be more easily seen flowing from the end of the tube **(see illustration)**.

**22** The kit is connected to the bleed screw, which is then opened. The user returns to the driver's seat, depresses the brake pedal with a smooth, steady stroke, and slowly releases it; this is repeated until the expelled fluid is clear of air bubbles.

**23** Note that these kits simplify work so much that it is easy to forget the master cylinder reservoir fluid level; ensure that this is maintained at least above the "MIN" level line at all times.

### Bleeding - using a pressure-bleeding kit

**24** These kits are usually operated by the reservoir of pressurised air contained in the spare tyre. However, note that it will probably be necessary to reduce the pressure to a lower level than normal; refer to the instructions supplied with the kit. **Note:** *BMW specify that a pressure of 2 bar (29 psi) should not be exceeded.*

**25** By connecting a pressurised, fluid-filled container to the master cylinder reservoir, bleeding can be carried out simply by opening each screw in turn (in the specified sequence), and allowing the fluid to flow out until no more air bubbles can be seen in the expelled fluid.

**26** This method has the advantage that the large reservoir of fluid provides an additional safeguard against air being drawn into the system during bleeding.

**27** Pressure-bleeding is particularly effective when bleeding "difficult" systems, or when bleeding the complete system at the time of routine fluid renewal.

### All methods

**28** When bleeding is complete, and firm pedal feel is restored, wash off any spilt fluid, tighten the bleed screws securely, and refit their dust caps.

**29** Check the hydraulic fluid level in the master cylinder reservoir, and top-up if necessary (Chapter 1).

**30** Discard any hydraulic fluid that has been bled from the system; it will not be fit for re-use.

**31** Check the feel of the brake pedal. If it feels at all spongy, air must still be present in the system, and further bleeding is required. Failure to bleed satisfactorily after a reasonable repetition of the bleeding procedure may be due to worn master cylinder seals.

## 3 Hydraulic pipes and hoses - renewal

⚠ ***Warning: On models with ABS (with or without ASC+T), under no circumstances should the hydraulic pipes/hoses linking the master cylinder, hydraulic unit and (where fitted) the accumulator be disturbed. If these unions are disturbed and air enters the high-pressure hydraulic system, bleeding of the system can only be safely carried out by a BMW dealer using the special service tester.***

**Note:** *Before starting work, refer to the warnings at the beginning of Section 2.*

**1** If any pipe or hose is to be renewed, minimise fluid loss by first removing the master cylinder reservoir cap, then tightening it down onto a piece of polythene to obtain an airtight seal. Alternatively, flexible hoses can be sealed, if required, using a proprietary brake hose clamp; metal brake pipe unions can be plugged (if care is taken not to allow dirt into the system) or capped immediately they are disconnected. Place a wad of rag under any union that is to be disconnected, to catch any spilt fluid.

**2** If a flexible hose is to be disconnected, unscrew the brake pipe union nut before removing the spring clip which secures the hose to its mounting bracket.

**3** To unscrew the union nuts, it is preferable to obtain a brake pipe spanner of the correct size; these are available from most large motor accessory shops. Failing this, a close-fitting open-ended spanner will be required, though if the nuts are tight or corroded, their flats may be rounded-off if the spanner slips. In such a case, using self-locking pliers is often the only way to unscrew a stubborn union, but it follows that the pipe and the damaged nuts must be renewed on reassembly. Always clean a union and surrounding area before disconnecting it. If disconnecting a component with more than one union, make a careful note of the connections before disturbing any of them.

**4** If a brake pipe is to be renewed, it can be obtained, cut to length and with the union nuts and end flares in place, from BMW dealers. All that is then necessary is to bend it to shape, following the line of the original, before fitting it to the car. Alternatively, most motor accessory shops can make up brake pipes from kits, but this requires very careful measurement of the original, to ensure that the replacement is of the correct length. The safest answer is usually to take the original to the shop as a pattern.

**5** On refitting, do not overtighten the union nuts. It is **not** necessary to exercise brute force to obtain a sound joint.

**6** Ensure that the pipes and hoses are correctly routed, with no kinks, and that they are secured in the clips or brackets provided. After fitting, remove the polythene from the reservoir, and bleed the hydraulic system as described in Section 2. Wash off any spilt fluid, and check carefully for fluid leaks.

## 4 Front brake pads - renewal

***Warning: Renew both sets of front brake pads at the same time - NEVER renew the pads on only one wheel, as uneven braking may result. Note that the dust created by wear of the pads may contain asbestos, which is a health hazard. Never blow it out with compressed air, and do not inhale any of it. An approved filtering mask should be worn when working on the brakes. DO NOT use petrol or petroleum-based solvents to clean brake parts; use brake cleaner or methylated spirit only.***

**1** Apply the handbrake, then jack up the front of the vehicle and support it on axle stands. Remove the front roadwheels.

**2** Unclip the anti-rattle spring from the side of the brake caliper, noting its correct fitted position **(see illustration)**.

**3** Unclip the brake pad wear sensor (where fitted) and remove it from the caliper aperture.

**4** Remove the plastic plugs from the caliper guide bushes to gain access to the guide pin bolts **(see illustration)**.

**5** Slacken and remove the guide pin bolts, noting that a suitable Allen socket may be needed. Lift the caliper away from the caliper mounting bracket, and tie it to the suspension strut using a suitable piece of wire **(see illustrations)**. Do not allow the caliper to hang unsupported on the flexible brake hose.

**6** Unclip the inner brake pad from the caliper piston, and withdraw the outer pad from the caliper mounting bracket **(see illustrations)**.

**7** First measure the thickness of each brake pad's friction material. If either pad is worn at any point to the specified minimum thickness or less, all four pads must be renewed. Also, the pads should be renewed if any are fouled with oil or grease; there is no satisfactory way of degreasing friction material, once contaminated. If any of the brake pads are worn unevenly, or are fouled with oil or grease, trace and rectify the cause before reassembly. New brake pad kits are available from BMW dealers.

**8** If the brake pads are still serviceable, carefully clean them using a clean, fine wire brush or similar, paying particular attention to the sides and back of the metal backing. Clean out the grooves in the friction material (where applicable), and pick out any large embedded particles of dirt or debris. Carefully clean the pad locations in the caliper body/mounting bracket.

**9** Prior to fitting the pads, check that the guide pin bolts are a light, sliding fit in the caliper body bushes, with little sign of freeplay. Brush the dust and dirt from the caliper and piston, but *do not* inhale it, as it is a health hazard. Inspect the dust seal around the piston for damage, and the piston for evidence of fluid leaks, corrosion or damage. If attention to any of these components is necessary, refer to Section 10.

**10** If new brake pads are to be fitted, the caliper piston must be pushed back into the cylinder to make room for them. Either use a G-clamp or similar tool, or use suitable pieces of wood as levers. Provided that the master cylinder reservoir has not been overfilled with hydraulic fluid, there should be no spillage, but keep a careful watch on the fluid level while retracting the piston. If the fluid level rises above the "MAX" level line at any time, the surplus should be syphoned off or ejected through a plastic tube connected to the bleed screw (see Section 2). **Note:** *Do not syphon the fluid by mouth, as it is poisonous; use a syringe or an old poultry baster.*

**11** Apply a smear of brake grease (BMW recommend Plastilube lubricant) to the backing plate of each pad; do not apply excess grease, nor allow the grease to contact the friction material.

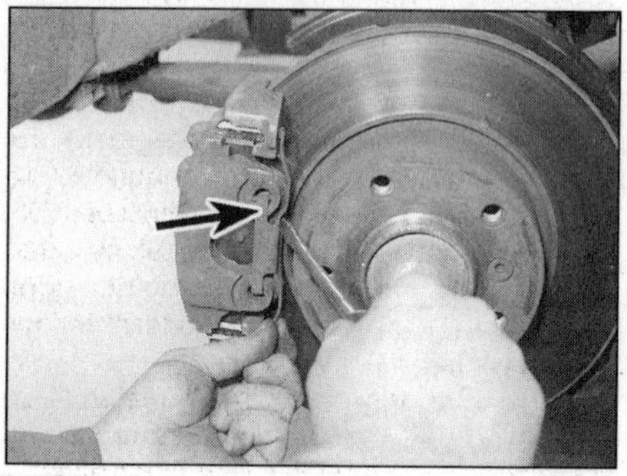

**4.2 Using a large screwdriver, carefully unclip the anti-rattle spring from the caliper**

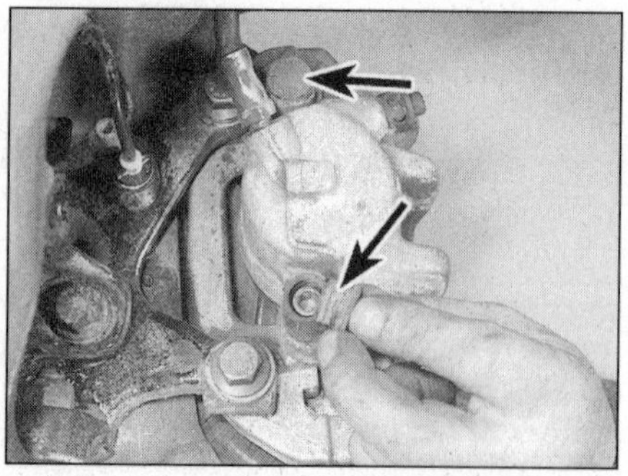

**4.4 Remove the plastic plugs (arrowed) to gain access to the guide pin bolts**

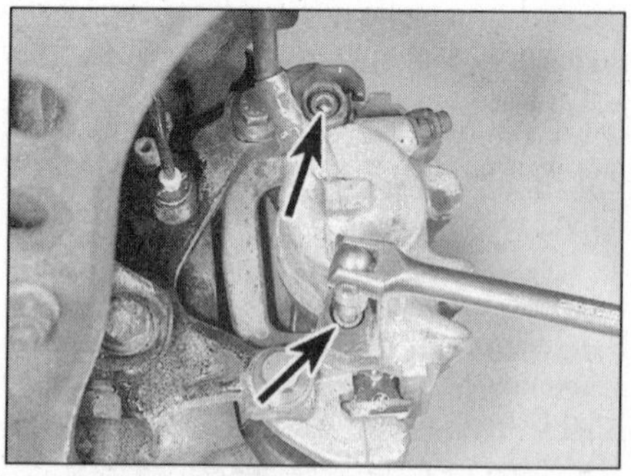

**4.5a Unscrew the guide pin bolts (arrowed) . . .**

**4.5b . . . and lift the caliper away from the disc**

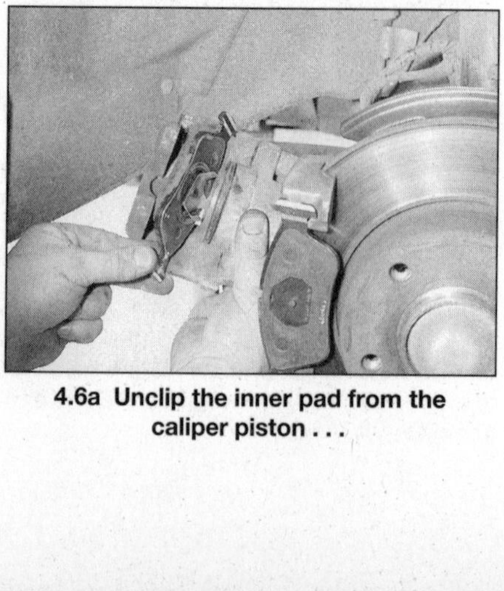

**4.6a Unclip the inner pad from the caliper piston . . .**

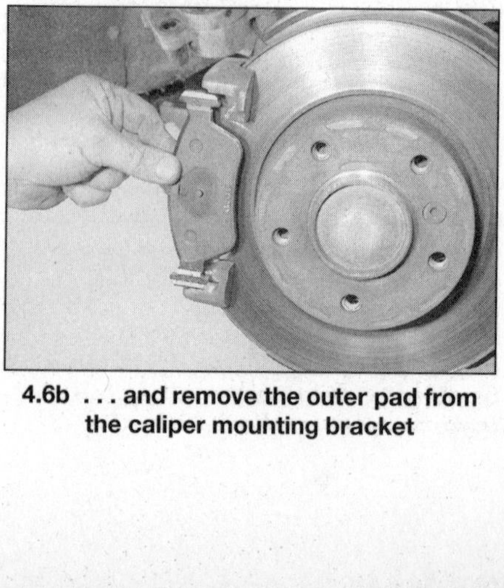

**4.6b . . . and remove the outer pad from the caliper mounting bracket**

**6.11 While the shoes are removed, wrap a strong elastic band around the wheel cylinder to retain the pistons**

**6.14 Apply high-temperature brake grease to the areas (arrowed) where the shoes contact the backplate**

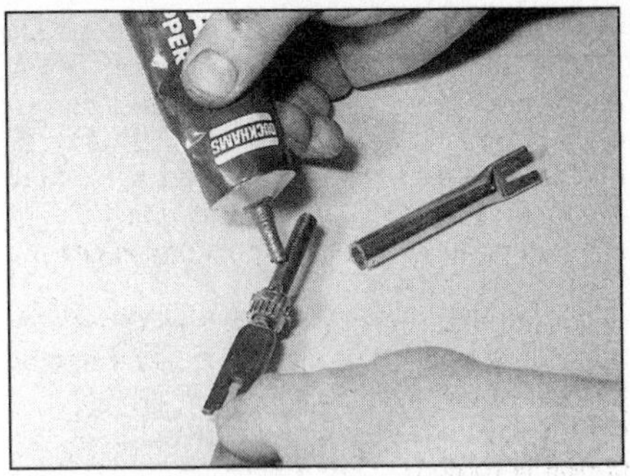

**6.15 Clean the adjuster strut threads and apply brake grease to them**

**12** Fit the outer pad to the caliper mounting bracket, ensuring that its friction material is against the brake disc.

**13** Clip the inner pad into the caliper piston, and manoeuvre the caliper assembly into position.

**14** Install the caliper guide pin bolts, and tighten them to the specified torque setting. Refit the plugs to the ends of the caliper guide bushes.

**15** Clip the pad wear sensor back into position in the outer pad, making sure its wiring is correctly routed.

**16** Clip the anti-rattle spring into position in the caliper. Depress the brake pedal repeatedly, until the pads are pressed into firm contact with the brake disc, and normal (non-assisted) pedal pressure is restored.

**17** Repeat the above procedure on the remaining front brake caliper.

**18** Refit the roadwheels, then lower the vehicle to the ground and tighten the roadwheel bolts to the specified torque setting.

> **HAYNES HiNT** ***New pads will not give full braking efficiency until they have bedded in. Be prepared for this, and avoid hard braking as far as possible for the first hundred miles or so after pad renewal.***

## 5 Rear brake pads - renewal

> ***Warning: Renew both sets of rear brake pads at the same time - NEVER renew the pads on only one wheel, as uneven braking may result. Note that the dust created by wear of the pads may contain asbestos, which is a health hazard. Never blow it out with compressed air, and do not inhale any of it. An approved filtering mask should be worn when working on the brakes. DO NOT use petrol or petroleum-based solvents to clean brake parts; use brake cleaner or methylated spirit only.***

The rear brake calipers are very similar to those fitted at the front. Refer to Section 4 for pad inspection and renewal details.

## 6 Rear brake shoes - renewal

> ***Warning: Brake shoes must be renewed on both rear wheels at the same time - NEVER renew the shoes on only one wheel, as uneven braking may result. Also, the dust created by wear of the shoes may contain asbestos, which is a health hazard. Never blow it out with compressed air, and do not inhale any of it. An approved filtering mask should be worn when working on the brakes. DO NOT use petrol or petroleum-based solvents to clean brake parts; use brake cleaner or methylated spirit only.***

**1** Remove the brake drum (see Section 9.

**2** Working carefully, and taking the necessary precautions, remove all traces of brake dust from the brake drum, backplate and shoes.

**3** Measure the thickness of the friction material of each brake shoe at several points; if either shoe is worn at any point to the specified minimum thickness or less, all four shoes must be renewed as a set. The shoes should also be renewed if any are fouled with oil or grease; there is no satisfactory way of degreasing friction material, once contaminated.

**4** If any of the brake shoes are worn unevenly, or fouled with oil or grease, trace and rectify the cause before reassembly.

**5** To renew the brake shoes, continue as follows. If all is well, refit the brake drum as described in Section 9.

**6** Note the position of the brake shoes and springs, and mark the webs of the shoes, if necessary, to aid refitting.

**7** Remove the upper return spring retaining clip then, using a pair of pliers, carefully unhook the upper and lower return springs, and remove them from the brake shoes.

**8** Remove the shoe retainer spring cups by depressing and turning them through 90°. With the cups removed, lift off the springs and withdraw the retainer pins.

**9** Unhook the trailing shoe from the adjuster strut, and remove it from the backplate. Unhook the spring from the trailing shoe adjuster lever, and lift off the adjuster lever.

**10** Remove the adjuster strut assembly, noting which way round it is fitted.

**11** Detach the leading shoe from the handbrake cable, and remove it from the backplate. Do not depress the brake pedal until the brakes are reassembled; wrap a strong elastic band around the wheel cylinder pistons to retain them **(see illustration)**.

**12** Examine all components for signs of wear or damage, and renew as necessary. All return springs should be renewed, regardless of their apparent condition. Brake shoe and return spring kits are available from BMW dealers.

**13** Peel back the rubber protective caps, and check the wheel cylinder for fluid leaks or other damage; check that both cylinder pistons are free to move easily. Refer to Section 12, if necessary, for information on wheel cylinder overhaul.

**14** Prior to installation, clean the backplate, and apply a thin smear of high-temperature brake grease or anti-seize compound to all those surfaces of the backplate which bear on the shoes, particularly the wheel cylinder pistons and upper pivot point **(see illustration)**. Do not allow the lubricant to foul the friction material.

**15** Dismantle and clean the adjuster strut assembly. Apply a smear of brake grease to its threads and reassemble **(see illustration)**.

**16** Manoeuvre the leading shoe into position, attaching it to the handbrake cable. Refit the retainer pin and spring, and secure the shoe in position with the spring cup **(see illustrations)**.

**17** Fit the adjuster strut assembly, making sure it is correctly engaged with the leading shoe **(see illustration)**.

**18** Ensure that the adjuster lever pivot pin is correctly fitted to the trailing shoe, and secured in position with the retaining clip. Engage the trailing shoe with the adjuster strut, then refit the retainer pin and spring. Secure the shoe in position with the spring cup **(see illustrations)**.

**19** Fit the adjuster lever to its pivot on the trailing shoe. Make sure the lever is correctly

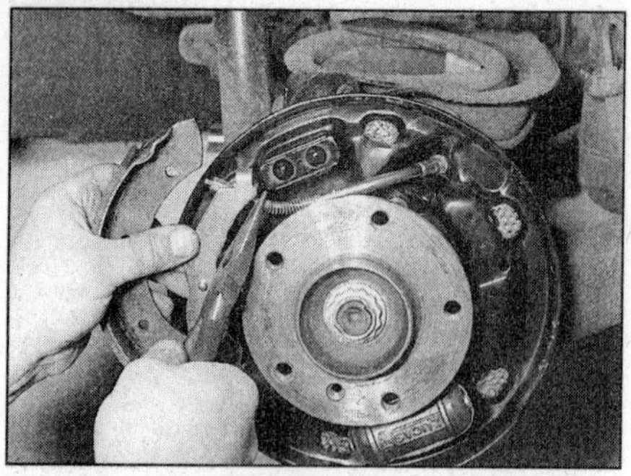

6.16a Attach the leading shoe to the handbrake cable . . .

6.16b . . . then refit the retainer pin and spring . . .

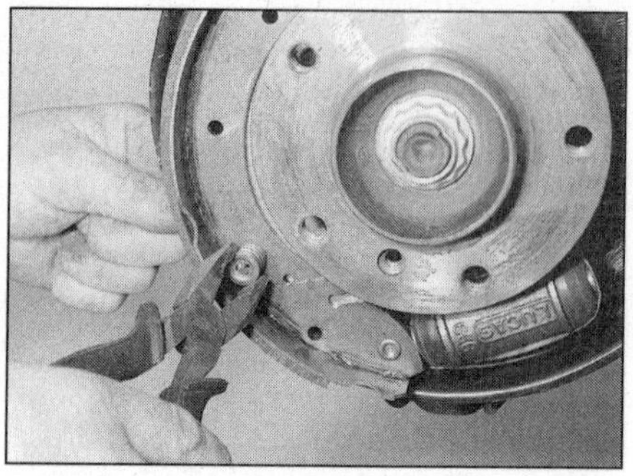

6.16c . . . and secure it in position with the spring cup

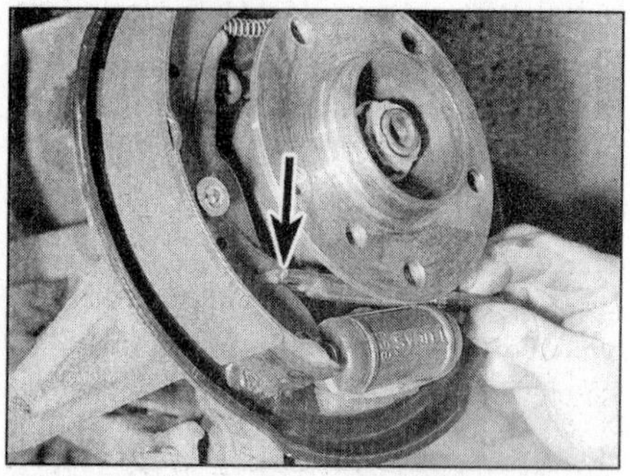

6.17 Fit the adjuster strut, making sure it is correctly engaged with the leading shoe (arrowed)

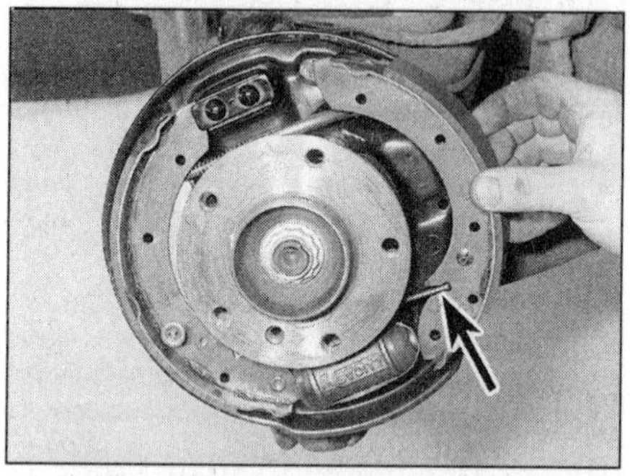

6.18a Engage the trailing shoe with the opposite end of the adjuster strut (arrowed) . . .

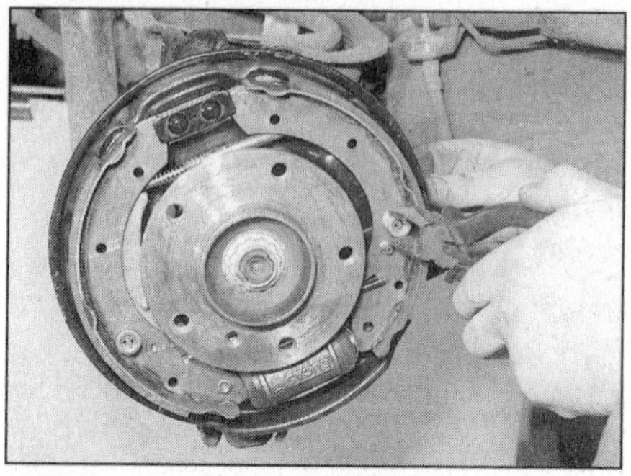

6.18b . . . and secure the shoe in position with the retainer pin, spring and spring cup

engaged with the strut knurled wheel, then fit the new return spring which connects the adjuster lever to the trailing shoe **(see illustration)**.

**20** Remove the elastic band from the wheel cylinder, then centralise the brake shoes on the wheel cylinder and upper pivot. Fit the brake shoe upper and lower return springs, and secure the upper spring in position with the retaining clip **(see illustrations)**.

**21** Refit the brake drum as described in Section 9.

**22** Repeat the above procedure on the remaining rear brake.

**23** Once both sets of rear shoes have been renewed, fully release the handbrake then adjust the lining-to-drum clearance by repeatedly depressing the brake pedal until normal (non-assisted) pedal pressure returns.

**24** Check and, if necessary, adjust the handbrake as described in Section 17.

**25** On completion, check the hydraulic fluid level as described in *"Weekly Checks"*.

**HAYNES HiNT** ***New shoes will not give full braking efficiency until they have bedded in. Be prepared for this, and avoid hard braking as far as possible for the first hundred miles or so after shoe renewal.***

6.19 Locate the adjuster lever on the trailing shoe pivot (arrowed) and hook the return spring onto the shoe

6.20a Hook the lower return spring into the leading and trailing shoe holes (arrowed) . . .

6.20b . . . then fit the upper return spring . . .

6.20c . . . and secure it in position with the retaining clip

7.3 Measuring the brake disc thickness with a micrometer

7.7a Undo the retaining screw . . .

7.7b . . . and remove the brake disc from the hub

## 7 Front brake disc - inspection, removal and refitting

**Note:** *Before starting work, refer to the note at the beginning of Section 4 concerning the dangers of asbestos dust.*

### Inspection

**Note:** *If either disc requires renewal, BOTH should be renewed at the same time, to ensure even and consistent braking. New brake pads should also be fitted.*

**1** Apply the handbrake, then jack up the front of the car and support it on axle stands. Remove the appropriate front roadwheel.

**2** Slowly rotate the brake disc so that the full area of both sides can be checked; remove the brake pads if better access is required to the inboard surface. Light scoring is normal in the area swept by the brake pads, but if heavy scoring or cracks are found, the disc must be renewed.

**3** It is normal to find a lip of rust and brake dust around the disc's perimeter; this can be scraped off if required. If, however, a lip has formed due to excessive wear of the brake pad swept area, then the disc's thickness must be measured using a micrometer **(see illustration)**. Take measurements at several places around the disc, at the inside and outside of the pad swept area; if the disc has worn at any point to the specified minimum thickness or less, the disc must be renewed.

**4** If the disc is thought to be warped, it can be checked for run-out. Either use a dial gauge mounted on any convenient fixed point, while the disc is slowly rotated, or use feeler blades to measure (at several points all around the disc) the clearance between the disc and a fixed point, such as the caliper mounting bracket. If the measurements obtained are at the specified maximum or beyond, the disc is excessively warped, and must be renewed; however, it is worth checking first that the hub bearing is in good condition (Chapters 1 and/or 10). If the run-out is excessive, the disc must be renewed.

**5** Check the disc for cracks, especially around the wheel bolt holes, and any other wear or damage, and renew if necessary.

### Removal

**6** Unscrew the two bolts securing the brake caliper mounting bracket to the swivel hub, then slide the caliper assembly off the disc. Using a piece of wire or string, tie the caliper to the front suspension coil spring, to avoid placing any strain on the hydraulic brake hose.

**7** Use chalk or paint to mark the relationship of the disc to the hub, then remove the screw securing the brake disc to the hub, and remove the disc **(see illustrations)**. If it is tight, lightly tap its rear face with a hide or plastic mallet.

### Refitting

**8** Refitting is the reverse of the removal procedure, noting the following points:

- *a) Ensure that the mating surfaces of the disc and hub are clean and flat.*
- *b) Align (if applicable) the marks made on removal, and tighten the disc retaining screw to the specified torque.*
- *c) If a new disc has been fitted, use a suitable solvent to wipe any preservative coating from the disc, before refitting the caliper.*
- *d) Slide the caliper into position over the disc, making sure the pads pass either side of the disc. Lightly oil the threads of the caliper bracket mounting bolts prior to installation, and tighten them to the specified torque setting.*
- *e) Refit the roadwheel, then lower the vehicle to the ground and tighten the roadwheel bolts to the specified torque. On completion, repeatedly depress the brake pedal until normal (non-assisted) pedal pressure returns.*

## 8 Rear brake disc - inspection, removal and refitting

**Note:** *Before starting work, refer to the note at the beginning of Section 5 concerning the dangers of asbestos dust.*

### Inspection

**Note:** *If either disc requires renewal, BOTH should be renewed at the same time, to ensure even and consistent braking. New brake pads should also be fitted.*

**1** Firmly chock the front wheels, then jack up the rear of the car and support it on axle stands. Remove the appropriate rear roadwheel.

**2** Inspect the disc as described in Section 7.

### Removal

**3** Unscrew the two bolts securing the brake caliper mounting bracket in position, then slide the caliper assembly off the disc. Using a piece of wire or string, tie the caliper to the rear suspension coil spring, to avoid placing any strain on the hydraulic brake hose **(see illustration)**.

**4** Slacken and remove the brake disc retaining screw and release the handbrake **(see illustration)**.

8.3 Slide the rear caliper assembly off the disc

8.4 Undo the retaining screw and remove the rear disc

5 It should now be possible to withdraw the brake disc from the stub axle by hand. If it is tight, lightly tap its rear face with a hide or plastic mallet. If the handbrake shoes are binding, first check that the handbrake is fully released, then continue as follows.
6 Referring to Section 17 for further details, fully slacken the handbrake adjustment, to obtain maximum free play in the cable.
7 Insert a screwdriver through one of the wheel bolt holes in the brake disc, and rotate the adjuster knurled wheel on the upper pivot to retract the shoes **(see illustrations 17.9a and 17.9b)**. The brake disc can then be withdrawn.

### Refitting

8 If a new disc is been fitted, use a suitable solvent to wipe any preservative coating from the disc.
9 Align (if applicable) the marks made on removal, then fit the disc and tighten the retaining screw to the specified torque.
10 Slide the caliper into position over the disc, making sure the pads pass either side of the disc. Tighten the caliper bracket mounting bolts to the specified torque setting.
11 Adjust the handbrake shoes and cable as described in Section 17.
12 Refit the roadwheel, then lower the car to the ground, and tighten the roadwheel bolts to the specified torque. On completion, repeatedly depress the brake pedal until normal (non-assisted) pedal pressure returns. Recheck the handbrake adjustment.

## 9 Rear brake drum - removal, inspection and refitting

**Note:** *Before starting work, refer to the note at the beginning of Section 6 concerning the dangers of asbestos dust.*

### Removal

1 Chock the front wheels, then jack up the rear of the vehicle and support it on axle stands. Remove the appropriate rear wheel.
2 Slacken and remove the drum retaining screw and fully release the handbrake **(see illustration)**.
3 It should now be possible to withdraw the brake drum assembly from the stub axle by hand. It may be difficult to remove the drum, due to corrosion, or due to the brake shoes binding on the inner circumference of the drum. If the drum is corroded onto the hub, tap the periphery of the drum using a hide or plastic mallet; alternatively, use a universal puller, secured to the drum with the wheel bolts, to pull it off. If the brake shoes are binding, first check that the handbrake is fully released, then continue as follows.
4 Referring to Section 17 for further information, fully slacken the handbrake adjustment, to obtain maximum free play in the cable.

**9.2 Slacken and remove the brake drum retaining screw**

5 Insert a screwdriver through one of the wheel bolt holes in the brake drum, and push the handbrake lever back to retract the brake shoes. It should then be possible to withdraw the brake drum. If the drum is still tight, position the drum as shown, and insert a hooked piece of wire and a small flat-bladed screwdriver through the bolt hole. Hold the adjuster lever away from the strut with the wire, and rotate the adjuster strut knurled wheel with the screwdriver to fully retract the shoes **(see illustration)**.

### Inspection

**Note:** *If either drum requires renewal, BOTH should be renewed at the same time, to ensure even and consistent braking. New brake shoes should also be fitted.*
6 Working carefully, remove all traces of brake dust from the drum, but *avoid inhaling the dust, as it is a health hazard.*
7 Clean the outside of the drum, and check it for obvious signs of wear or damage, such as cracks around the roadwheel bolt holes; renew the drum if necessary.
8 Examine the inside of the drum carefully. Light scoring of the friction surface is normal, but if heavy scoring is found, the drum must be renewed. It is usual to find a lip on the drum's inboard edge which consists of a mixture of rust and brake dust; this should be scraped away, to leave a smooth surface which can be polished with fine (120- to 150-grade) emery paper. If, however, the lip is due to the friction surface being recessed by excessive wear, then the drum must be renewed.

**9.5 If necessary, release the brake shoes by rotating the adjuster strut knurled wheel whilst holding the adjuster lever (arrowed) away from the strut - shown with drum removed**

9 If the drum is thought to be excessively worn, or oval, its internal diameter must be measured at several points using an internal micrometer. Take measurements in pairs, the second at right-angles to the first, and compare the two, to check for signs of ovality. Provided that it does not enlarge the drum to beyond the specified maximum diameter, it may be possible to have the drum refinished by skimming or grinding; if this is not possible, the drums on both sides must be renewed. Note that if the drum is to be skimmed, BOTH drums must be refinished, to maintain a consistent internal diameter on both sides.

### Refitting

10 If a new brake drum is to be installed, use a suitable solvent to remove any preservative coating that may have been applied to its interior.
11 Prior to refitting, fully retract the brakes shoes by rotating the adjuster strut knurled wheel. Ensure that the handbrake lever is correctly positioned with its stop against the edge of the shoe.
12 Fit the drum and tighten its retaining screw to the specified torque setting.
13 With the handbrake released, adjust the lining-to-drum clearance by repeatedly depressing the brake pedal until normal (non-assisted) pedal pressure returns.
14 Repeat the above procedure on the remaining rear brake assembly (where necessary), then check and, if necessary, adjust the handbrake cable as described in Section 17.
15 On completion, refit the roadwheel(s), then lower the vehicle to the ground and tighten the wheel bolts to the specified torque.

## 10 Front brake caliper - removal, overhaul and refitting

**Note:** *Before starting work, refer to the note at the beginning of Section 2 concerning the dangers of hydraulic fluid, and to the warning at the beginning of Section 4 concerning the dangers of asbestos dust.*

### Removal

1 Apply the handbrake, then jack up the front of the vehicle and support it on axle stands. Remove the appropriate roadwheel.
2 Minimise fluid loss by first removing the master cylinder reservoir cap, and then tightening it down onto a piece of polythene, to obtain an airtight seal. Alternatively, use a brake hose clamp, a G-clamp or a similar tool to clamp the flexible hose.
3 Clean the area around the union, then loosen the brake hose union nut.
4 Remove the brake pads (see Section 4).

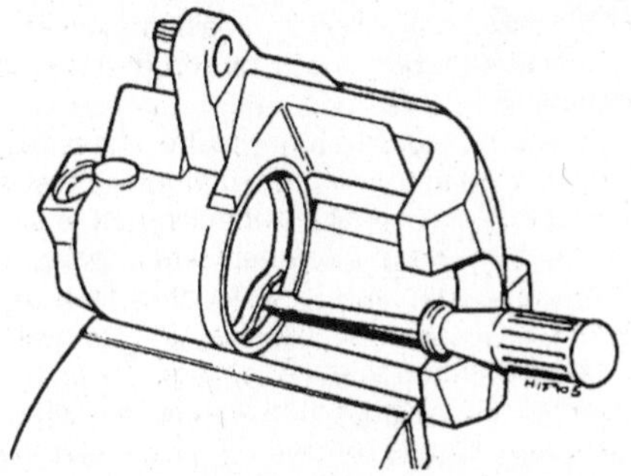

10.8 **Extracting the piston seal - take care not to scratch the surface of the bore**

**5** Unscrew the caliper from the end of the brake hose and remove it from the vehicle.

### Overhaul

**6** With the caliper on the bench, wipe away all traces of dust and dirt, but *avoid inhaling the dust, as it is a health hazard.*

**7** Withdraw the partially-ejected piston from the caliper body, and remove the dust seal.

> **HAYNES HiNT** ***If the piston cannot be withdrawn by hand, it can be pushed out by applying compressed air to the brake hose union hole. Only low pressure should be required, such as is generated by a foot pump. As the piston is expelled, take great care not to trap your fingers between the piston and caliper.***

**8** Using a small screwdriver, extract the piston hydraulic seal, taking great care not to damage the caliper bore **(see illustration)**.

**9** Thoroughly clean all components, using only methylated spirit, isopropyl alcohol or clean hydraulic fluid as a cleaning medium. Never use mineral-based solvents such as petrol or paraffin, as they will attack the hydraulic system's rubber components. Dry the components immediately, using compressed air or a clean, lint-free cloth. Use compressed air to blow clear the fluid passages.

**10** Check all components, and renew any that are worn or damaged. Check particularly the cylinder bore and piston; these should be renewed (note that this means the renewal of the complete body assembly) if they are scratched, worn or corroded in any way. Similarly check the condition of the guide pins and their bushes; both pins should be undamaged and (when cleaned) a reasonably tight sliding fit in the bushes. If there is any doubt about the condition of any component, renew it.

**11** If the assembly is fit for further use, obtain the appropriate repair kit; the components are available from BMW dealers in various combinations. All rubber seals should be renewed as a matter of course; these should never be re-used.

**12** On reassembly, ensure that all components are clean and dry.

**13** Soak the piston and the new piston (fluid) seal in clean hydraulic fluid. Smear clean fluid on the cylinder bore surface.

**14** Fit the new piston (fluid) seal, using only your fingers (no tools) to manipulate it into the cylinder bore groove.

**15** Fit the new dust seal to the piston. Locate the rear of the seal in the recess in the caliper body, and refit the piston to the cylinder bore using a twisting motion. Ensure that the piston enters squarely into the bore, and press it fully into the bore.

### Refitting

**16** Screw the caliper fully onto the flexible hose union.

**17** Refit the brake pads (see Section 4).

**18** Securely tighten the brake pipe union nut.

**19** Remove the brake hose clamp or polythene, as applicable, and bleed the hydraulic system as described in Section 2. Note that, providing the precautions described were taken to minimise brake fluid loss, it should only be necessary to bleed the relevant front brake.

**20** Refit the roadwheel, then lower the vehicle to the ground and tighten the roadwheel bolts to the specified torque. On completion, check the hydraulic fluid level as described in *"Weekly Checks"*.

## 11 Rear brake caliper - removal, overhaul and refitting

**Note:** *Before starting work, refer to the note at the beginning of Section 2 concerning the dangers of hydraulic fluid, and to the warning at the beginning of Section 5 concerning the dangers of asbestos dust.*

### Removal

**1** Chock the front wheels, then jack up the rear of the vehicle and support on axle stands. Remove the relevant rear wheel.

**2** Minimise fluid loss by first removing the master cylinder reservoir cap, and then tightening it down onto a piece of polythene, to obtain an airtight seal. Alternatively, use a brake hose clamp, a G-clamp or a similar tool to clamp the flexible hose.

**3** Clean the area around the union, then loosen the brake hose union nut.

**4** Remove the brake pads as described in Section 5.

**5** Unscrew the caliper from the end of the flexible hose, and remove it from the vehicle.

### Overhaul

**6** Refer to Section 10, noting that the piston dust seal is secured in position with a circlip.

### Refitting

**7** Screw the caliper fully onto the flexible hose union.

**8** Refit the brake pads (refer to Section 5).

**9** Securely tighten the brake pipe union nut.

**10** Remove the brake hose clamp or polythene, as applicable, and bleed the hydraulic system as described in Section 2. Note that, providing the precautions described were taken to minimise brake fluid loss, it should only be necessary to bleed the relevant rear brake.

**11** Refit the roadwheel, then lower the vehicle to the ground and tighten the roadwheel bolts to the specified torque. On completion, check the hydraulic fluid level as described in *"Weekly Checks"*.

## 12 Rear wheel cylinder - removal, overhaul and refitting

**Note:** *Before starting work, refer to the note at the beginning of Section 2 concerning the dangers of hydraulic fluid, and to the warning at the beginning of Section 6 concerning the dangers of asbestos dust.*

### Removal

**1** Remove the brake drum (see Section 9).

**2** Using pliers, carefully unhook the brake shoe lower return spring, and remove it from both brake shoes. Pull the lower ends of the shoes away from the wheel cylinder to disengage them from the pistons.

**3** Minimise fluid loss by first removing the master cylinder reservoir cap, and then tightening it down onto a piece of polythene, to obtain an airtight seal. Alternatively, use a brake hose clamp, a G-clamp or a similar tool to clamp the flexible hose at the nearest convenient point to the wheel cylinder.

**4** Wipe away all traces of dirt around the brake pipe union at the rear of the wheel cylinder, and unscrew the union nut **(see illustration)**. Carefully ease the pipe out of the wheel cylinder, and plug or tape over its end to prevent dirt entry. Wipe off any spilt immediately.

**5** Unscrew the two wheel cylinder retaining bolts from the rear of the backplate, and remove the cylinder, taking great care not to allow surplus hydraulic fluid to contaminate the brake shoe linings.

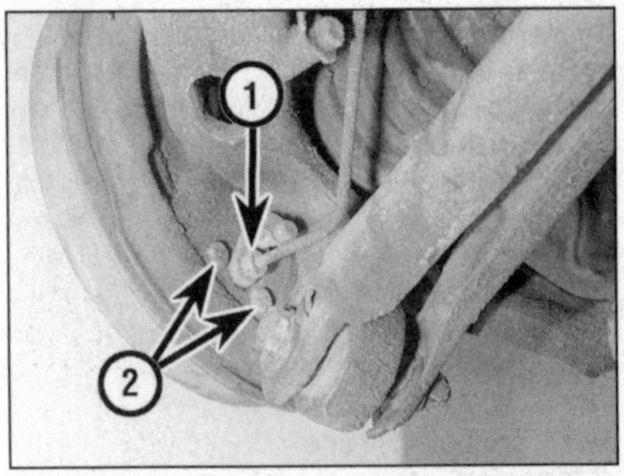


**12.4 Rear wheel cylinder brake pipe union (1) and retaining bolts (2)**

### Overhaul

**6** Brush the dirt and dust from the wheel cylinder, but take care not to inhale it.
**7** Pull the rubber dust seals from the ends of the cylinder body.
**8** The pistons will normally be ejected by the pressure of the coil spring, but if they are not, tap the end of the cylinder body on a piece of wood, or apply low air pressure - eg, from a foot pump - to the hydraulic fluid union hole to eject the pistons from their bores.
**9** Inspect the surfaces of the pistons and their bores in the cylinder body for scoring, or evidence of metal-to-metal contact. If evident, renew the complete wheel cylinder assembly.
**10** If the pistons and bores are in good condition, discard the seals and obtain a repair kit, which will contain all the necessary renewable items.
**11** Remove the seals from the pistons, noting their correct fitted orientation. Lubricate the new piston seals with clean brake fluid, and fit them onto the pistons with their larger diameters innermost.
**12** Dip the pistons in clean brake fluid, then fit the spring to the cylinder.
**13** Insert the pistons into the cylinder bores using a twisting motion.
**14** Fit the dust seals, and check that the pistons can move freely in their bores.

### Refitting

**15** Ensure that the backplate and wheel cylinder mating surfaces are clean, then spread the brake shoes and manoeuvre the wheel cylinder into position.
**16** Engage the brake pipe, and screw in the union nut two or three turns to ensure that the thread has started.
**17** Insert the two wheel cylinder retaining bolts, and tighten them to the specified torque setting. Now fully tighten the brake pipe union nut.
**18** Remove the clamp from the flexible brake hose, or the polythene from the master cylinder reservoir (as applicable).
**19** Ensure that the brake shoes are correctly located in the cylinder pistons, then carefully refit the brake shoe lower return spring, using a screwdriver to stretch the spring into position.
**20** Refit the brake drum as described in Section 9.
**21** Bleed the brake hydraulic system as described in Section 2. Providing suitable precautions were taken to minimise loss of fluid, it should only be necessary to bleed the relevant rear brake.

## 13 Master cylinder - removal, overhaul and refitting

### Models with ABS (with or without ASC+T)

**1** On models fitted with ABS, it is not possible for the home mechanic to remove the master cylinder. If the hydraulic unions are disconnected from the master cylinder, air will enter the high-pressure hydraulic system linking the master cylinder and hydraulic unit. Bleeding of the high-pressure system can only be safely carried out by a BMW dealer who has access to the service tester (see Section 2). Master cylinder removal and refitting should therefore be entrusted to a BMW dealer.

### Models without ABS

#### Removal

**Note:** *Before starting work, refer to the warning at the beginning of Section 2 concerning the dangers of hydraulic fluid.*
**Note:** *New master cylinder retaining nuts will be required on refitting.*
**2** Disconnect the battery negative terminal. To improve access to the master cylinder, disconnect the engine wiring harness connectors.
**3** Remove the master cylinder reservoir cap, and syphon the hydraulic fluid from the reservoir. **Note:** *Do not syphon the fluid by mouth, as it is poisonous; use a syringe or an old poultry baster.* Alternatively, open any convenient bleed screw in the system, and gently pump the brake pedal to expel the fluid through a plastic tube connected to the screw (see Section 2). Disconnect the wiring connector from the brake fluid level sender unit.
**4** Where necessary, disconnect the fluid hose(s) from the side of the reservoir, and plug the hose end(s) to minimise fluid loss.
**5** Carefully ease the fluid reservoir out from the top of the master cylinder. Recover the reservoir seals, and plug the cylinder ports to prevent dirt entry.
**6** Wipe clean the area around the brake pipe unions on the side of the master cylinder, and place absorbent rags beneath the pipe unions to catch any surplus fluid. Make a note of the correct fitted positions of the unions, then unscrew the union nuts and carefully withdraw the pipes. Plug or tape over the pipe ends and master cylinder orifices, to minimise the loss of brake fluid, and to prevent the entry of dirt into the system. Wash off any spilt fluid immediately with cold water.
**7** Slacken and remove the two nuts and washers securing the master cylinder to the vacuum servo unit, then withdraw the unit from the engine compartment. Remove the O-ring from the rear of the master cylinder. Discard the retaining nuts, new ones should be used on refitting.

#### Overhaul

**8** If the master cylinder is faulty, it must be renewed. Repair kits are not available from BMW dealers so the cylinder must be treated as a sealed unit. Renew the master cylinder O-ring seal and reservoir seals regardless of their apparent condition.

#### Refitting

**9** Remove all traces of dirt from the master cylinder and servo unit mating surfaces, and fit a new O-ring to the groove on the master cylinder body.
**10** Fit the master cylinder to the servo unit, ensuring that the servo unit pushrod enters the master cylinder bore centrally. Fit the new master cylinder retaining nuts and washers, and tighten them to the specified torque.
**11** Wipe clean the brake pipe unions, then refit them to the master cylinder ports and tighten them securely.
**12** Press the new reservoir seals firmly into the master cylinder ports, then ease the reservoir into position. Where necessary, reconnect the fluid hose(s) to the reservoir.
**13** Refill the master cylinder reservoir with new fluid, and bleed the complete hydraulic system as described in Section 2.

## 14 Brake pedal - removal and refitting

### Removal

**1** Disconnect the battery negative terminal.
**2** Remove the stop-light switch as described in Section 21.
**3** Using a pair of pliers, carefully unhook the return spring from the brake pedal.
**4** Slide off the retaining clip and remove the clevis pin securing the brake pedal to the servo unit pushrod.
**5** Slide off the pedal pivot pin retaining clip and remove the pedal from the pivot.
**6** Carefully clean and inspect all components, renewing any that are worn or damaged

### Refitting

**7** Refitting is the reverse of removal. Apply a smear of multi-purpose grease to the pedal pivot and clevis pin.

## 15 Vacuum servo unit - testing, removal and refitting

### Models with ABS (with or without ASC+T)

**1** On models fitted with ABS, it is not possible for the home mechanic to remove the vacuum servo unit. If the hydraulic unions are disconnected from the master cylinder, air will enter the high-pressure hydraulic system linking the master cylinder, hydraulic unit. Bleeding of the high-pressure system can only be safely carried out by a BMW dealer who has access to the service tester (see Section 2). The servo unit can be tested as described in paragraphs 2 to 4 below, but removal and refitting should be entrusted to a BMW dealer.

### Models without ABS

#### Testing

**2** To test the operation of the servo unit, depress the footbrake several times to exhaust the vacuum, then start the engine whilst keeping the pedal firmly depressed. As the engine starts, there should be a noticeable "give" in the brake pedal as the vacuum builds up. Allow the engine to run for at least two minutes, then switch it off. If the brake pedal is now depressed it should feel normal, but further applications should result in the pedal feeling firmer, with the pedal stroke decreasing with each application.

**3** If the servo does not operate as described, first inspect the servo unit check valve as described in Section 16.

**4** If the servo unit still fails to operate satisfactorily, the fault lies within the unit itself. Repairs to the unit are not possible - if faulty, the servo unit must be renewed.

#### Removal

**Note:** *New retaining nuts will be required on refitting*

**5** Remove the master cylinder as described in Section 13.

**6** Disconnect the vacuum hose from the servo unit check valve.

**7** Slacken and remove the retaining screws securing the driver's side lower facia panel. Unclip the panel and remove it from the vehicle.

**8** Referring to Section 14, unhook the brake pedal return spring, then slide off the retaining clip and remove the clevis pin securing the pedal to the servo unit pushrod.

**9** Slacken and remove the four servo unit retaining nuts, then return to the engine compartment and remove the servo unit from the vehicle.

### Refitting

**10** Refitting is the reverse of removal, noting the following points.

*a) Check the servo unit check valve sealing grommet for signs of damage or deterioration, and renew if necessary.*

*b) If a new servo unit is being installed, remove the sound insulation material from the original, and transfer it to the new one.*

*c) Ensure that the servo unit pushrod is correctly engaged with the brake pedal, then fit the new retaining nuts and tighten them to the specified torque.*

*d) Apply a smear of grease to the servo pushrod clevis pin, and secure it in position with the retaining clip.*

*e) Refit the master cylinder as described in Section 13 of this Chapter.*

*f) Refit the stop-light switch as described in Section 21.*

*g) On completion, start the engine and check for air leaks at the vacuum hose-to-servo unit connection; check the operation of the braking system.*

## 16 Vacuum servo unit check valve - removal, testing and refitting

### Removal

**1** Disconnect the vacuum hose from the servo unit check valve.

**2** Carefully ease the check valve out of the servo unit, taking care not to displace the grommet.

### Testing

**3** Examine the check valve for signs of damage, and renew if necessary.

**4** The valve may be tested by blowing through it in both directions; air should flow through the valve in one direction only - when blown through from the servo unit end of the valve. Renew the valve if this is not the case.

**5** Examine the servo unit rubber sealing grommet for signs of damage or deterioration, and renew as necessary.

### Refitting

**6** Ensure that the sealing grommet is correctly fitted to the servo unit.

**7** Ease the valve into position in the servo, taking great care not to displace or damage the grommet.

**8** Reconnect the vacuum hose securely to the valve.

**9** On completion, start the engine and ensure there are no air leaks at the check valve-to-servo unit connection.

## 17 Handbrake - adjustment

**1** On drum brake models, with the handbrake released, apply the footbrake firmly several times to establish correct shoe-to-drum clearance, then apply and release the handbrake several times.

**2** On all models, applying normal moderate pressure, pull the handbrake lever to the fully applied position, counting the number of clicks emitted from the handbrake ratchet mechanism. If adjustment is correct, there should be approximately 7 or 8 clicks before the handbrake is fully applied. If there are more than 10 clicks, adjust as follows.

### Rear drum brake models

**3** Apply the footbrake several times to ensure that the brake shoe self-adjust mechanism is fully adjusted, then apply and release the handbrake several times.

**4** Chock the front wheels, then jack up the rear of the vehicle and support it on axle stands.

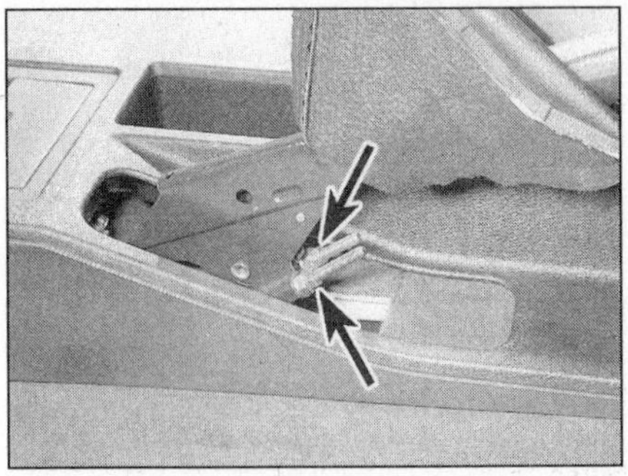

**17.5 Unclip the handbrake gaiter from the centre console to gain access to the handbrake cable adjustment nuts (arrowed)**

**5** Access to the handbrake cable adjusting nuts can be gained by removing the handbrake lever gaiter from the centre console **(see illustration)**. If greater access is required, the rear section of the centre console will have to be removed (Chapter 11).

**6** With the handbrake set on the sixth notch of the ratchet mechanism, slacken the locknuts and rotate the adjusting nuts equally until it is difficult to turn both rear wheels/drums. Once this is so, fully release the handbrake lever, and check that the wheels/hubs rotate freely. Slowly apply the handbrake, and check that the brake shoes start to contact the drums when the handbrake is set to the second notch of the ratchet mechanism. Check the adjustment by applying the handbrake fully, counting the clicks emitted from the handbrake ratchet and, if necessary, re-adjust.

**7** Once adjustment is correct, hold the adjusting nuts and securely tighten the locknuts. Check the operation of the handbrake warning light switch, then refit the centre console section/handbrake lever gaiter (as applicable). Refit the roadwheels, then lower the vehicle to the ground and tighten the wheel bolts to the specified torque.

### Rear disc brake models

**8** Slacken and remove one wheel bolt from each rear wheel then chock the front wheels, jack up the rear of the vehicle and support it on axle stands.

**9** Starting on the left-hand rear wheel, fully release the handbrake and position the wheel/disc so the exposed bolt hole is positioned 65° clockwise from the vertical position. Make sure the handbrake lever is fully released, then insert a screwdriver in through the bolt hole and fully expand the handbrake shoes by rotating the adjuster knurled ring. When the wheel/disc can no longer be turned, back the knurled ring off by 18 teeth (catches) so that the wheel is free to rotate easily **(see illustrations)**.

**10** Repeat paragraph 9 on the right-hand wheel.

**11** Adjust the handbrake cables as described in paragraphs 5 to 7.

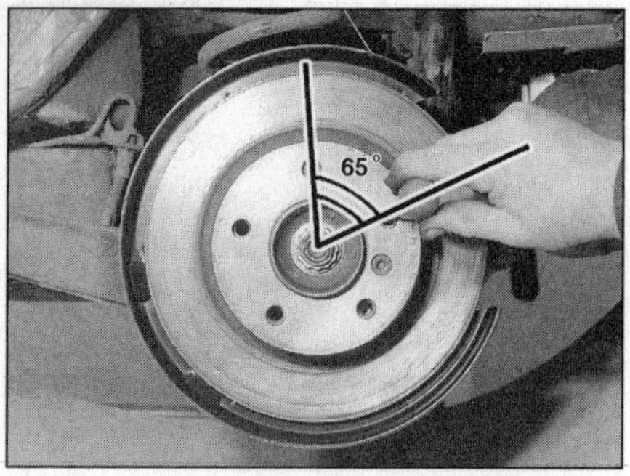


17.9a Position one of the wheel bolt holes as shown, then insert a screwdriver through the hole . . .

17.9b . . . and rotate the handbrake shoe adjuster knurled ring (shown with disc removed)

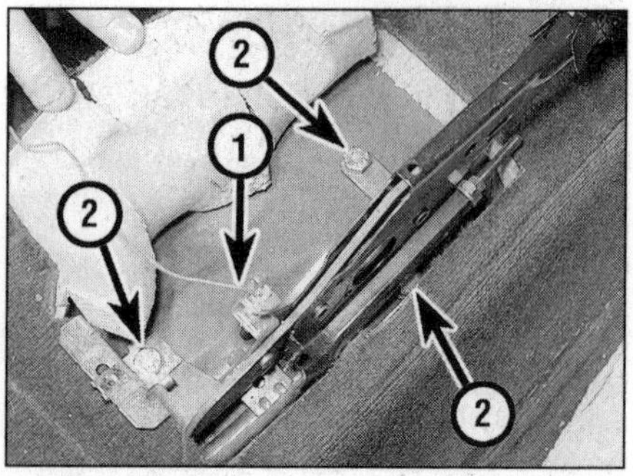


18.3 Handbrake lever switch wire (1) and lever retaining bolts (2)

## 18 Handbrake lever - removal and refitting

### Removal

**1** Remove the rear section of the centre console as described in Chapter 11 to gain access to the handbrake lever.

**2** Slacken and remove both the handbrake cable locknuts and adjusting nuts, and detach the cables from the compensator plate.

**3** Disconnect the wiring connector from the warning light switch then undo the retaining nuts/bolts, and remove the lever from the vehicle **(see illustration)**.

### Refitting

**4** Refitting is a reversal of the removal. Prior to refitting the centre console, adjust the handbrake as described in Section 17.

## 19 Handbrake cables - removal and refitting

### Removal

**1** Remove the rear section of the centre console as described in Chapter 11 to gain access to the handbrake lever. The handbrake cable consists of two sections, a right- and a left-hand section, which are linked to the lever by a compensator plate. Each section can be removed individually.

**2** Slacken and remove the relevant handbrake cable locknut and adjusting nut, and disengage the inner cable from the handbrake compensator plate.

**3** Firmly chock the front wheels, then jack up the rear of the car and support it on axle stands.

**4** Referring to the relevant Part of Chapter 4, remove the exhaust system heatshield to gain access to the handbrake cables. Note that on some models, it may also be necessary to remove part of the exhaust system.

**5** Free the front end of the outer cable from the body, and withdraw the cable from its support guide.

**6** Working back along the length of the cable, noting its correct routing, and free it from all the relevant retaining clips.

**7** On models with rear drum brakes, remove the relevant rear brake drum as described in Section 9. Detach the cable from the leading shoe handbrake lever, and remove it from underneath the vehicle.

**8** On models with rear disc brakes, remove the handbrake shoes as described in Section 20. Unfold the expander, then withdraw the cable pivot pin and detach the handbrake shoe expander from the cable end. Release the cable from the backplate, and remove it from the vehicle **(see illustrations)**.

### Refitting

**9** Refitting is a reversal of the removal procedure; on disc brake models, apply a smear of grease to the cable pivot pin prior to refitting the handbrake shoes. Prior to refitting the centre console, adjust the handbrake as described in Section 17.

## 20 Handbrake shoes (rear disc brake models) - removal and refitting

### Removal

**1** Remove the rear brake disc as described in Section 8, and make a note of the correct fitted position of all components.

**2** Using a pair of pliers, carefully unhook and remove the handbrake shoe return springs **(see illustrations)**.

**3** Release the shoe retaining pins using pliers by depressing them and rotating them

19.8a On rear disc brake models, unfold expander, then withdraw pin (arrowed) . . .

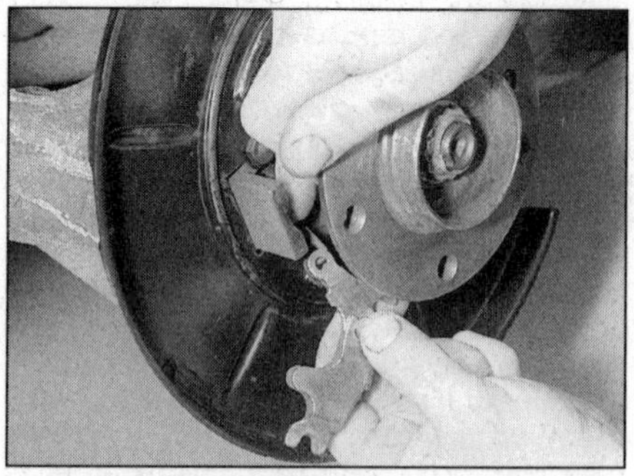

19.8b . . . and detach the expander from the end of the handbrake cable

20.2a Using pliers, unhook and remove the handbrake shoe front . . .

20.2b . . . and rear return springs

**20.3a Using a suitable Allen key, rotate the retainer pins through 90° . . .**

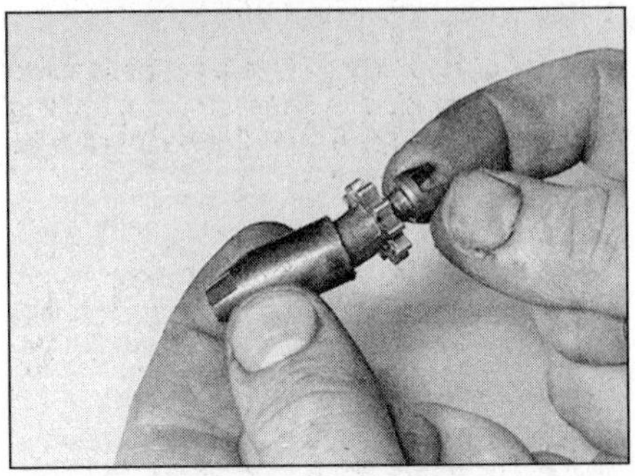

**20.6 Clean the adjuster assembly and coat it with fresh brake grease**

through 90°, then remove the pins and springs **(see illustrations)**.

**4** Remove both handbrake shoes, and recover the shoe adjuster mechanism, noting which way around it is fitted **(see illustration)**.

**5** Inspect the handbrake shoes for wear or contamination, and renew if necessary. It is recommended that the return springs are renewed as a matter of course. BMW do not state any wear limit for shoe friction material thickness, but any less than 1.5 mm is not ideal.

**6** While the shoes are removed, clean and inspect the condition of the shoe adjuster and expander mechanisms, renew them if they show signs of wear or damage. If all is well, apply a fresh coat of brake grease (BMW recommend Molykote Paste G) to the threads of the adjuster and sliding surfaces of the expander mechanism **(see illustration)**. Do not allow the grease to contact the shoe friction material.

### *Refitting*

**7** Prior to installation, clean the backplate, and apply a thin smear of high-temperature brake grease or anti-seize compound to all those surfaces of the backplate which bear on the shoes. Do not allow the lubricant to foul the friction material.

**8** Offer up the handbrake shoes, and secure them in position with the retaining pins and springs.

**9** Make sure the lower ends of the shoes are correctly engaged with the expander, then slide the adjuster mechanism into position between the upper ends of the shoes **(see illustration)**.

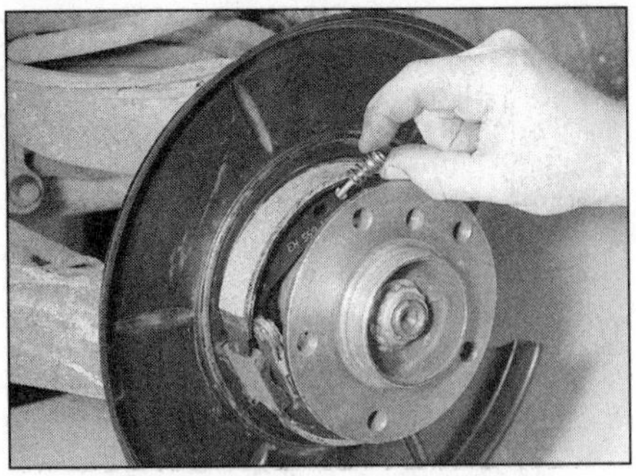

**20.3b . . . then remove the pins and springs . . .**

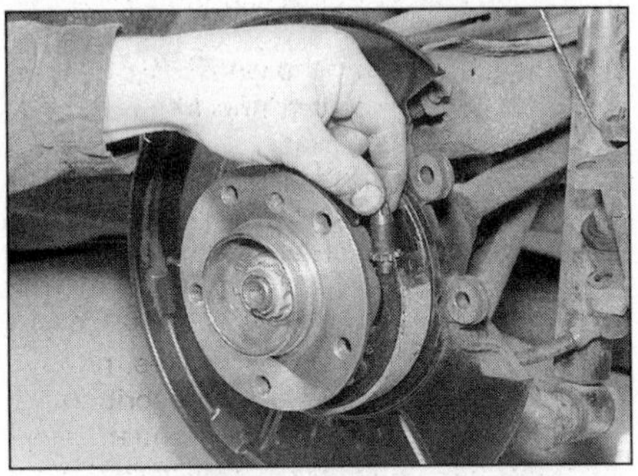

**20.9 Refit the adjuster assembly, making sure it is correctly engaged with both handbrake shoes**

**10** Check all components are correctly fitted, and fit the upper and lower return springs using a pair of pliers.

**11** Centralise the handbrake shoes, and refit the brake disc as described in Section 8.

**12** Prior to refitting the roadwheel, adjust the handbrake as described in Section 17.

## 21 Stop-light switch - removal and refitting

### *Removal*

**1** The stop-light switch is located on the pedal bracket behind the facia. **Note:** *On models equipped with a check control system, the switch also operates the check control system stop-light function (refer to Chapter 12 for further information).*

**2** Slacken and remove the retaining screws securing the driver's side lower facia panel. Unclip the panel and remove it from the vehicle.

**3** Reach up behind the facia and disconnect the wiring connector from the switch

**4** Depress the brake pedal fully, then withdraw the plunger sleeve from the front of the switch to gain access to the switch retaining clips. Depress the clips and withdraw the switch from the pedal bracket **(see illustrations)**.

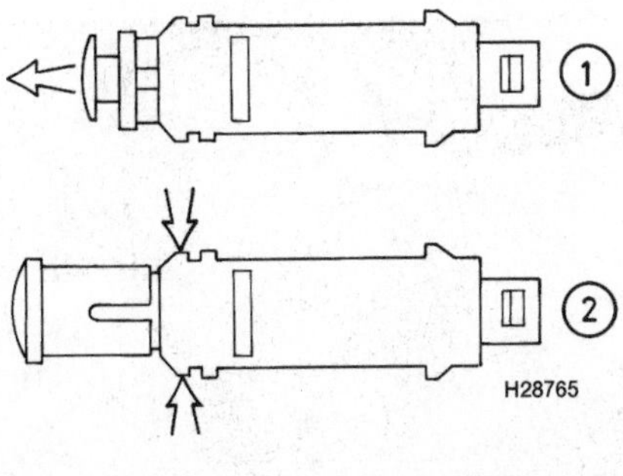


**21.4a Depress the pedal and withdraw the plunger sleeve from the switch body (1) then depress the retaining clips (2) . . .**

**20.4 . . . and handbrake shoes from the backplate**

### *Refitting*

**5** Ensure that the stop-light switch plunger and sleeve are fully withdrawn from the switch body.

**6** Fully depress the brake pedal and hold it down, then manoeuvre the switch into position. Hold the switch fully in position, then **slowly** release the brake pedal and allow it to return to its stop. This will automatically adjust the stop-light switch. **Note:** *If the pedal is released too quickly, the switch will be incorrectly adjusted.*

**7** Reconnect the wiring connector, and check the operation of the stop-lights. The stop-lights should illuminate after the brake pedal has travelled approximately 5 mm. If the switch is not functioning correctly, it is faulty and must be renewed; no other adjustment is possible.

**8** On completion, refit the driver's side lower facia panel.

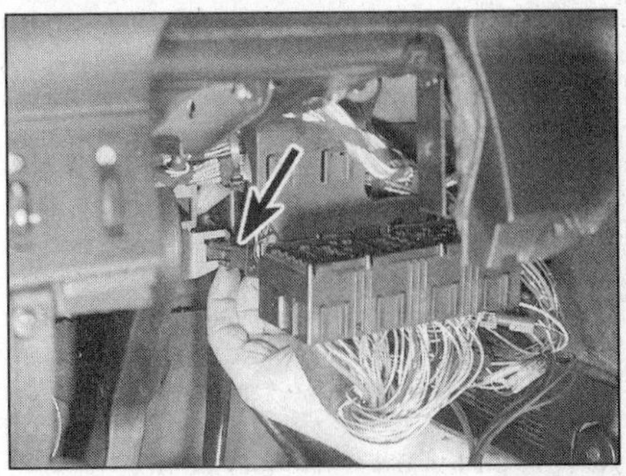

**21.4b . . . and remove the switch from its mounting bracket**

## 22 Anti-lock braking system (ABS) - general information

**Note:** *On models equipped with traction control, the ABS unit is a dual function unit, and works both the anti-lock braking system (ABS) and traction control function of the Automatic Stability Control plus Traction (ASC+T) system.*

1 ABS is fitted to most models as standard, and was available as an option on all others. The system comprises a hydraulic block which contains the hydraulic solenoid valves and the electrically-driven return pump, the four roadwheel sensors (one fitted to each wheel), the electronic control unit (ECU) and the brake pedal position sensor. The purpose of the system is to prevent the wheel(s) locking during heavy braking. This is achieved by automatic release of the brake on the relevant wheel, followed by re-application of the brake.

2 The solenoids are controlled by the ECU, which itself receives signals from the four wheel sensors (one fitted on each hub), which monitor the speed of rotation of each wheel. By comparing these signals, the ECU can determine the speed at which the vehicle is travelling. It can then use this speed to determine when a wheel is decelerating at an abnormal rate, compared to the speed of the vehicle, and therefore predicts when a wheel is about to lock. During normal operation, the system functions in the same way as a non-ABS braking system. In addition to this, the brake pedal position sensor (which is fitted to the vacuum servo unit) also informs the ECU of how hard the brake pedal is being depressed.

3 If the ECU senses that a wheel is about to lock, it operates the relevant solenoid valve in the hydraulic unit, which then isolates the brake caliper on the wheel which is about to lock from the master cylinder, effectively sealing-in the hydraulic pressure.

4 If the speed of rotation of the wheel continues to decrease at an abnormal rate, the ECU switches on the electrically-driven return pump operates, and pumps the hydraulic fluid back into the master cylinder, releasing pressure on the brake caliper so that the brake is released. Once the speed of rotation of the wheel returns to an acceptable rate, the pump stops; the solenoid valve opens, allowing the hydraulic master cylinder pressure to return to the caliper, which then re-applies the brake. This cycle can be carried out at up to 10 times a second.

5 The action of the solenoid valves and return pump creates pulses in the hydraulic circuit. When the ABS system is functioning, these pulses can be felt through the brake pedal.

6 The operation of the ABS system is entirely dependent on electrical signals. To prevent the system responding to any inaccurate signals, a built-in safety circuit monitors all signals received by the ECU. If an inaccurate signal or low battery voltage is detected, the ABS system is automatically shut down, and the warning light on the instrument panel is illuminated, to inform the driver that the ABS system is not operational. Normal braking should still be available, however.

7 If a fault does develop in the ABS system, the vehicle must be taken to a BMW dealer for fault diagnosis and repair.

8 On models equipped with ASC+T, an accumulator is also incorporated into the hydraulic system. As well as performing the ABS function as described above, the hydraulic unit also works the traction control side of the ASC+T system. If the ECU senses that the wheels are about to lose traction under acceleration, the hydraulic unit momentarily applies the rear brakes to prevent the wheel(s) spinning. In the same way as the ABS, the vehicle must be taken to a BMW dealer for testing if a fault develops in the ASC+T system.

## 23 Anti-lock braking system (ABS) components - removal and refitting

### *Hydraulic unit*

1 It is not possible for the home mechanic to remove the hydraulic unit. If the hydraulic unions are disconnected from the unit, air will enter the high-pressure hydraulic system linking the master cylinder and hydraulic unit. Bleeding of the high-pressure system can only be safely carried out by a BMW dealer who has access to the service tester (see Section 2). Hydraulic unit removal and refitting should therefore be entrusted to a BMW dealer.

### *Accumulator - models with Automatic Stability Control plus Traction (ASC+T)*

2 It is not possible for the home mechanic to remove the accumulator unit. If the hydraulic unions are disconnected from the unit, air will enter the high-pressure hydraulic system linking the accumulator and hydraulic unit. Bleeding of the high-pressure system can only be safely carried out by a BMW dealer who has access to the service tester (see Section 2). Accumulator removal and refitting should therefore be entrusted to a BMW dealer.

### *Electronic control unit (ECU)*

**Note:** *On vehicles equipped with Automatic Stability Control plus Traction (ASC+T), if the ECU is disconnected, on reconnection it must be initialised using BMW diagnostic equipment. Note that the traction control system will be disabled until the ECU has been initialised.*

#### Removal

3 Disconnect the battery negative terminal and remove the glovebox as described in Chapter 11, Section 27. Unclip the facia undercover and remove it.

4 Lift the ECU wiring connector locking clip, and carefully disconnect the wiring connector **(see illustration)**.

5 Slacken and remove the nuts/bolts securing the ECU mounting bracket, and remove it from the car **(see illustration)**.

#### Refitting

6 Refitting is a reversal of the removal procedure, ensuring the ECU wiring connector is correctly and securely reconnected.

### *Front wheel sensor*

#### Removal

7 Chock the rear wheels, then firmly apply the handbrake, jack up the front of the vehicle and support on axle stands. Remove the appropriate front roadwheel. Trace the wiring back from the sensor to the connector which is situated in a protective plastic box. Unclip the lid, then free the wiring connector and disconnect it from the main harness **(see illustration)**.

8 Slacken and remove the bolt securing the sensor to the steering knuckle, and remove the sensor and lead assembly from the vehicle **(see illustration)**.

#### Refitting

9 Prior to refitting, apply a thin coat of multi-purpose grease to the sensor tip (BMW recommend the use of Staborax NBU 12/k).

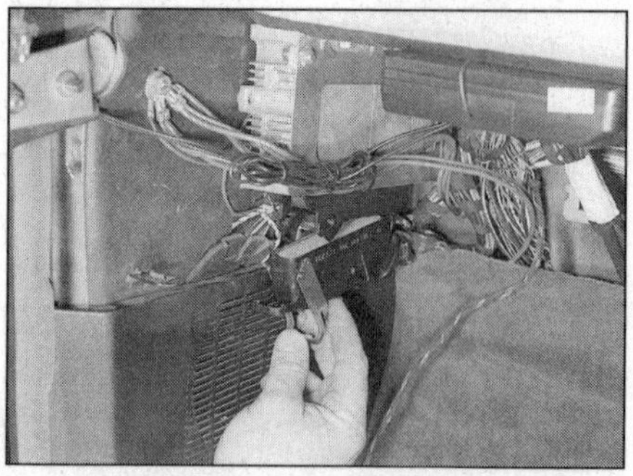

**23.4 Release the retaining clip and disconnect the wiring connector from the ABS ECU**

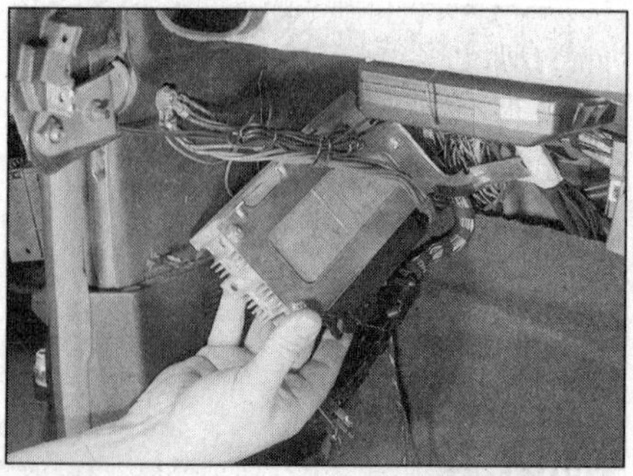

**23.5 Undo the retaining bolts and remove the ABS ECU and mounting bracket from the underneath the facia**

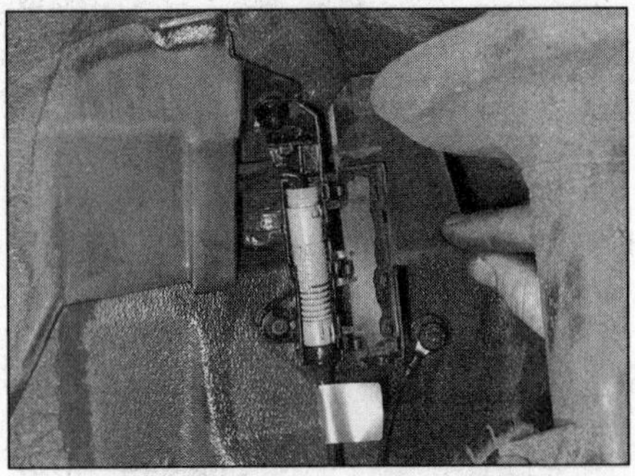

23.7 Unclip the cover then free the wheel sensor from its protective box and disconnect it

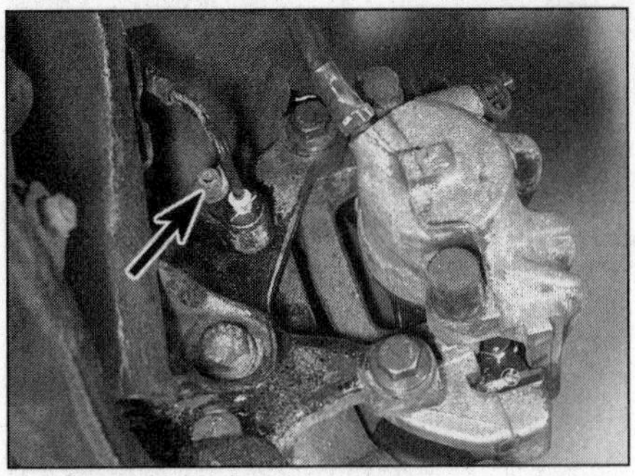

23.8 Undo the retaining bolt (arrowed) and withdraw the front wheel sensor from the steering knuckle

**10** Ensure that the sensor and steering knuckle sealing faces are clean, then fit the sensor to the hub. Refit the retaining bolt and tighten it to the specified torque.
**11** Ensure that the sensor wiring is correctly routed and retained by all the necessary clips, and reconnect it to its wiring connector. Refit the sensor into the box and securely clip the lid in position.
**12** Refit the roadwheel, then lower the vehicle to the ground and tighten the roadwheel bolts to the specified torque.

## Rear wheel sensor

### Removal

**13** Chock the front wheels, then jack up the rear of the vehicle and support it on axle stands. Remove the appropriate roadwheel.
**14** Remove the sensor as described in paragraphs 7 and 8.

### Refitting

**15** Refit the sensor as described above in paragraphs 9 to 12.

## Front reluctor rings

**16** The front reluctor rings are fixed onto the rear of wheel hubs. Examine the rings for damage such as chipped or missing teeth. If renewal is necessary, the complete hub assembly must be dismantled and the bearings renewed, with reference to Chapter 10.

## Rear reluctor rings

**17** The rear reluctor rings are pressed onto the driveshaft outer joints. Examine the rings for signs of damage such as chipped or missing teeth, and renew as necessary. If renewal is necessary, the driveshaft assembly must be renewed (see Chapter 8).

## Brake pedal position sensor

**18** Release the vacuum from inside the servo unit by depressing the brake pedal several times. Although not absolutely necessary, to improve access to the sensor, remove the master cylinder fluid reservoir as described in Section 13.
**19** Disconnect the battery negative terminal, then disconnect the wiring connector from the pedal position sensor.
**20** Using a small screwdriver, carefully lever off the sensor retaining clip, then withdraw the sensor from the front of the vacuum servo unit. Recover the sealing ring and circlip.

### Refitting

**21** If a new sensor is being fitted, note the colour of the spacer fitted to the original sensor, and fit the relevant colour spacer to the new sensor. This is vital to ensure that the correct operation of the anti-lock braking system.
**22** Fit the new circlip to the groove on the front of the vacuum servo unit, positioning its end gap over the servo unit sensor locating slot.
**23** Fit the new sealing ring to the sensor, lubricating it with a smear of oil to aid installation.
**24** Fit the sensor to the vacuum servo, aligning its locating notch with the servo unit upper groove. Push the sensor until it clicks into position, and check that it is securely retained by the circlip.
**25** Reconnect the sensor wiring, and connect the battery negative terminal.

# Chapter 10
# Suspension and steering

## Contents



## Degrees of difficulty

| | | | | |
|---|---|---|---|---|
| **Easy,** suitable for novice with little experience | **Fairly easy,** suitable for beginner with some experience | **Fairly difficult,** suitable for competent DIY mechanic | **Difficult,** suitable for experienced DIY mechanic | **Very difficult,** suitable for expert DIY or professional |

## Specifications

### Front suspension

| | |
|---|---|
| Type | Independent, with MacPherson struts incorporating coil springs and telescopic shock absorbers. Anti-roll bar fitted to most models |

### Rear suspension

| | |
|---|---|
| Type | Independent, trailing arms located by upper and lower control arms with coil springs and shock absorbers. Anti-roll bar fitted to most models |

### Steering

| | |
|---|---|
| Type | Rack and pinion. Power assistance standard on most models, optional on others |

### Wheel alignment and steering angles

| | |
|---|---|
| Front wheel: | |
| Camber angle: | |
| Standard | -40' ± 30' |
| Models with Sports suspension | -58' ± 30' |
| Maximum difference between sides | 30' |
| Castor angle: | |
| Standard | 3° 44' ± 30' |
| Models with Sports suspension | 3° 50' ± 30' |
| Maximum difference between sides | 30' |
| Toe setting (total) | 0° ± 10' |
| Rear wheel: | |
| Camber angle: | |
| Standard: | |
| Early (pre 1992) models | -1° 30' ± 15' |
| Later (1992 on) models | -1° 40' ± 15' |
| Models with Sports suspension | -2° 00' ± 15' |
| Maximum difference between sides | 15' |
| Toe setting (total) | 24' ± 6' |

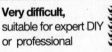

## Roadwheels

| | |
|---|---|
| Type | Pressed steel or aluminium alloy (depending on model) |
| Size | 6J x 15, 6.5J x 15, 7J x 15 or 7J x 16 |

## Tyres

| | |
|---|---|
| Size:* | |
| Roadwheels: | |
| 6J x 15 wheels | 185/65 R 15 |
| 6.5J x 15 and 7J x 15 wheels | 205/60 R 15 or 225/55 R 15 |
| 7J x 16 wheels | 225/50 R 16 |
| Pressures | See end of *"Weekly Checks"* |

**Consult your handbook, a BMW dealer or a suitable tyre dealer for the correct size for your vehicle*

## Torque wrench settings

| | Nm | lbf ft |
|---|---|---|
| **Front suspension** | | |
| Anti-roll bar connecting link nuts: | | |
| Models with connecting link mounted on the strut | 59 | 43 |
| Models with connecting link mounted on lower arm | 47 | 34 |
| Anti-roll bar mounting clamp nuts | 22 | 16 |
| Hub nut | 290 | 215 |
| Lower arm balljoint nut | 62 | 45 |
| Lower arm rear mounting bracket bolts | 47 | 34 |
| Lower arm-to-crossmember nut | 85 | 63 |
| Strut mounting plate nut: | | |
| M12 thread: | | |
| Piston with an external hexagon end (retain with socket) | 64 | 47 |
| Piston with an internal hexagon end (retain with Allen key) | 44 | 32 |
| M14 thread | 64 | 47 |
| Strut-to-steering knuckle bolt nut | 107 | 79 |
| Strut upper mounting nuts | 22 | 16 |
| **Rear suspension** | | |
| Control arm-to-subframe pivot bolt | 77 | 57 |
| Shock absorber lower mounting bolt | 100 | 74 |
| Shock absorber upper mounting nuts | 22 | 16 |
| Trailing arm-to-control arm pivot bolts | 110 | 81 |
| Trailing arm mounting bracket-to-body bolts | 77 | 57 |
| Trailing arm-to-mounting bracket pivot bolt | 110 | 81 |
| **Steering** | | |
| Intermediate shaft clamp bolts | 19 | 13 |
| Power steering pipe union bolts: | | |
| M14 union bolt | 35 | 26 |
| M16 union bolt | 40 | 30 |
| Power steering pump bolts | 22 | 16 |
| Steering gear mounting nuts | 42 | 31 |
| Steering wheel bolt | 63 | 46 |
| Track rod | 71 | 53 |
| Track rod balljoint: | | |
| Retaining nut | 45 | 33 |
| Locknut | 14 | 11 |
| **Roadwheels** | | |
| Roadwheel bolts | 100 | 74 |

## 1 General information

The independent front suspension is of the MacPherson strut type, incorporating coil springs and integral telescopic shock absorbers. The MacPherson struts are located by transverse lower suspension arms, which use rubber inner mounting bushes, and incorporate a balljoint at the outer ends. The front steering knuckles, which carry the brake calipers and the hub/disc assemblies, are bolted to the MacPherson struts, and connected to the lower arms through balljoints. A front anti-roll bar is fitted to most models. The anti-roll bar is rubber-mounted and is connected to both suspension struts/lower arms (as applicable) by connecting links.

The rear suspension is of the fully independent type consisting of trailing arms, which are linked to the rear axle carrier by upper and lower control arms. Coil springs are fitted between the upper control arms and vehicle body, and shock absorbers are connected to the vehicle body and trailing arms. A rear anti-roll bar is fitted on most models. The anti-roll bar is rubber-mounted, and is connected to the upper control arms by connecting links.

The steering column is connected to the steering gear by an intermediate shaft, which incorporates a universal joint.

The steering gear is mounted onto the front subframe, and is connected by two track rods, with balljoints at their outer ends, to the steering arms projecting forwards from the steering knuckles. The track rod ends are threaded, to facilitate adjustment.

Power-assisted steering is fitted as standard to most models, and is available as an option on all others. The hydraulic steering system is powered by a belt-driven pump, which is driven off the crankshaft pulley.

**Note:** *The information contained in this Chapter is applicable to the standard suspension set-up. On models with M-Technic sports suspension, slight differences will be found. Refer to your BMW dealer for details.*

## 2 Front hub assembly - removal and refitting

**Note:** *The hub assembly should not be removed unless it is to be renewed. The hub bearing inner race is a press-fit on the steering knuckle, and removal of the hub will almost certainly damaged the bearings; BMW state that the hub assembly must be renewed whenever it is removed. A new hub nut and grease cap will also be required on refitting.*

### Removal

**1** Remove the front brake disc (Chapter 9). On models with ABS, also remove the front wheel sensor.

**2** Tap the grease cap out from the centre of the hub **(see illustration)**.

**3** Using a hammer and suitable pointed-nosed chisel, tap up the staking securing the hub retaining nut in position, then slacken and remove the nut **(see illustration)**.

**4** Attach a suitable puller to the hub assembly and draw the assembly off the steering knuckle. If the bearing inner race remains on the steering knuckle, a knife-edge type puller will be required to remove it **(see illustration)**. Note that the hub bearings are not available separately - the hub must be renewed as a complete assembly.

**5** Inspect the steering knuckle shaft for damage, and renew if necessary (Section 3). If required, undo the retaining screws and remove the disc guard from the steering knuckle.

### Refitting

**6** Where removed, refit the disc guard to the steering knuckle, and securely tighten its retaining screws.

**7** Ensure the dust cover is correctly fitted to the rear of the hub assembly, and locate the hub on the steering knuckle. Tap or press the hub assembly fully onto the steering knuckle shaft using a tubular spacer which bears only on the bearing inner race **(see illustration)**.

**8** Screw the new hub nut onto the steering knuckle. Tighten the nut to the specified torque setting, and secure it in position by staking it firmly into the knuckle groove using a hammer and punch.

**9** Check that the hub rotates freely, and press the new grease cap into the hub centre.

**2.2 Tap out the grease cap from the centre of the hub**

**2.3 Using a hammer and pointed-nosed chisel, tap out the hub nut staking**

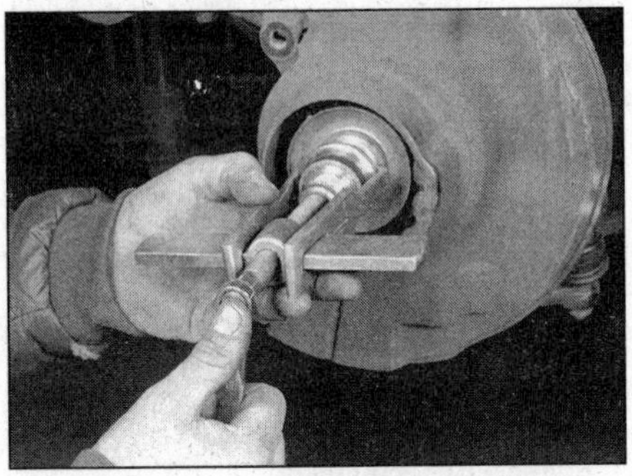

**2.4 If the hub bearing inner race remains on the steering knuckle, use a puller to get it off**

**2.7 Tap the hub assembly into position using a socket which bears only on the inner race of the new bearing**

**10** Refit the brake disc as described in Chapter 9. Where necessary, also refit the ABS wheel sensor.

## 3 Front steering knuckle - removal and refitting

**Note:** *New suspension strut-to-steering knuckle lower bolts, and track rod balljoint, lower arm balljoint, and strut-to-knuckle upper bolt nuts, will be required on refitting.*

### Removal

**1** Firmly apply the handbrake, then jack up the front of the car and support it on axle stands. Remove the relevant front roadwheel.

**2** If the steering knuckle is to be renewed, remove the hub assembly (see Section 2).

**3** If the steering knuckle assembly is to be refitted, slacken and remove the two bolts securing the brake caliper mounting bracket to the knuckle then slide the caliper assembly off the disc. Using a piece of wire or string, tie the caliper to the front suspension coil spring, to avoid placing any strain on the hydraulic brake hose. On models with ABS, also remove the wheel sensor (see Chapter 9).

**4** Slacken and remove the nut securing the steering gear track rod balljoint to the steering knuckle, and release the balljoint tapered shank using a universal balljoint separator.

**5** Slacken and remove the two lower bolts securing the suspension strut to the steering knuckle, and the upper nut and bolt.

**6** Unscrew the lower arm balljoint and remove the steering knuckle from the car. If necessary, release the steering knuckle from the lower arm using the balljoint separator.

**7** Examine the knuckle for signs of wear or damage, and renew if necessary.

### Refitting

**8** Prior to refitting, clean the threads of the strut-to-steering knuckle lower bolt holes by running a tap of the correct thread size and pitch down them.

> **HAYNES HiNT** *If a suitable tap is not available, clean out the holes using one of the old bolts with slots cut in its threads.*

**9** Engage the knuckle with the lower arm bush stud, and fit the new retaining nut.

**10** Locate the knuckle correctly with the suspension strut, and insert the upper retaining bolt and new nut. Fit the two new lower bolts securing the strut to the knuckle, and tighten both the lower and upper bolt to the specified torque.

**11** Tighten the lower arm balljoint nut to the specified torque

**12** Engage the track rod balljoint in the steering knuckle, then fit a new retaining nut and tighten it to the specified torque.

**13** Fit the new hub assembly (see Section 2).

**14** On models where the hub was not disturbed, slide the caliper into position over the disc, making sure the pads pass either side of the disc. Lightly oil the threads of the caliper bracket mounting bolts prior to installation, and tighten them to the specified torque setting (see Chapter 9).

**15** Refit the roadwheel, then lower the car to the ground and tighten the wheel bolts to the specified torque.

## 4 Front suspension strut - removal, overhaul and refitting

**Note:** *New suspension strut upper mounting nuts, a strut-to-knuckle upper bolt nut and lower retaining bolts will be required on refitting. On models where the anti-roll bar is mounted onto the strut, a connecting link retaining nut will also be required.*

### Removal

**1** Chock the rear wheels, apply the handbrake, then jack up the front of the car and support on axle stands. Remove the appropriate roadwheel.

**2** To prevent the lower arm assembly hanging down whilst the strut is removed, screw a wheel bolt into the hub, then wrap a piece of wire around the bolt and tie it to the car body. This will support the weight of the hub assembly. Alternatively, support the hub assembly with a jack.

**3** Unclip the brake hose and wiring harness from its clips on the base of the strut **(see illustration)**.

**4** On models where the anti-roll bar connecting link is mounted onto the suspension strut, slacken and remove the retaining nut and washer, and position the connecting link clear of the strut.

**5** On all models, slacken and remove the two lower bolts securing the suspension strut to the steering knuckle, and also the upper nut and bolt.

**6** From within the engine compartment, unscrew the strut upper mounting nuts, then carefully lower the strut assembly out from underneath the wing **(see illustration)**.

### Overhaul

***Warning: Before attempting to dismantle the front suspension strut, a suitable tool to hold the coil spring in compression must be obtained. Adjustable coil spring compressors are readily available, and are recommended for this operation. Any attempt to dismantle the strut without such a tool is likely to result in damage or personal injury.***

**Note:** *A new mounting plate nut will be required.*

**7** With the strut removed from the car, clean away all external dirt, then mount it upright in a vice.

**8** Fit the spring compressor, and compress the coil spring until all tension is relieved from the upper spring seat **(see illustration)**.

**9** Remove the cap from the top of the strut to gain access to the strut upper mounting retaining nut. Slacken the nut whilst retaining the strut piston with a suitable Allen key **(see illustrations)**.

**10** On all 4-cylinder engine models and later (June 1992-on) 6-cylinder models, remove the mounting nut and washer, and lift off the rubber mounting plate. Remove the gasket and dished washer followed by the upper spring plate and upper spring seat.

**11** On early (pre-June 1992) 6-cylinder engine models, remove the mounting nut and lift off the special washer. Remove the mounting assembly and lift off the upper spring seat.

**12** On all models, lift off the coil spring and remove the lower spring seat.

**13** Slide the rubber seat (where fitted), rubber damper stop and piston dust cover off the strut

**14** With the strut assembly now completely dismantled, examine all the components for wear, damage or deformation, and check the upper mounting bearing for smoothness of operation. Renew any of the components as necessary.

**15** Examine the strut for signs of fluid leakage. Check the strut piston for signs of pitting along its entire length, and check the strut body for signs of damage. While holding it in an upright position, test the operation of the strut by moving the piston through a full stroke, and then through short strokes of 50 to 100 mm. In both cases, the resistance felt should be smooth and continuous. If the resistance is jerky, or uneven, or if there is any visible sign of wear or damage to the strut, renewal is necessary.

**16** If any doubt exists about the condition of the coil spring, carefully remove the spring compressors, and check the spring for distortion and signs of cracking. Renew the spring if it is damaged or distorted, or if there is any doubt as to its condition.

**17** Inspect all other components for damage or deterioration, and renew any that are suspect.

**18** Slide the rubber damper and piston gaiter onto the strut piston and (where necessary) refit the rubber seat.

**19** Fit the spring seat and coil spring onto the strut, making sure the seat ridge and spring end are correctly located against the strut stop.

**20** Fit the upper spring seat so that the spring end is against the seat stop.

**21** On all 4-cylinder engine models and later (June 1992-on) 6-cylinder models, fit the upper spring plate, aligning its stop with that of the seat, and fit the dished washer and

**4.3 Unclip the brake hose and wiring harness from the base of the strut**

**4.6 Removing a front suspension strut**

**4.8 Compress the suspension strut coil spring with a suitable spring compressor**

**4.9a Remove the cap from the top of the strut mounting . . .**

**4.9b . . . then slacken and remove the upper mounting retaining nut**

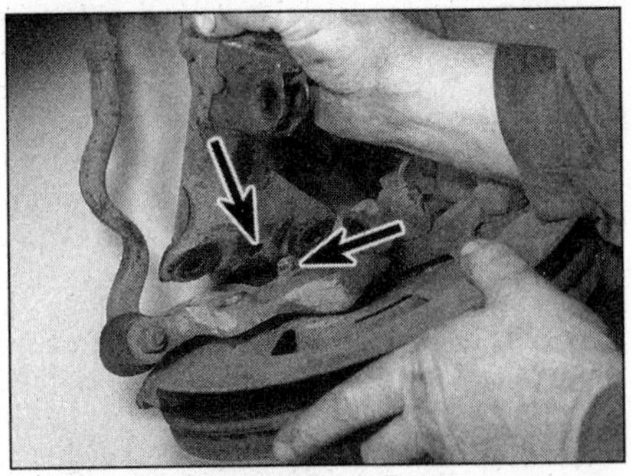

**4.26a Ensure strut is correctly engaged with steering knuckle peg (arrows) . . .**

gasket followed by the upper mounting plate. Locate the washer on the strut piston, then fit the new mounting plate nut and tighten it to the specified torque.

**22** On early (pre-June 1992) 6-cylinder engine models, locate the mounting assembly on the spring seat, aligning it with the spring seat. Fit the special washer, then screw on the new mounting nut and tighten it to the specified torque.

**23** Ensure the spring ends and seats are correctly located, then carefully release the compressor and remove it from the strut. Refit the cap to the top of the strut.

### Refitting

**24** Prior to refitting, clean the threads of the strut-to-steering knuckle lower bolt holes by running a tap of the correct thread size and pitch down them **(see Haynes Hint)**.

**25** Manoeuvre the strut assembly into position, and fit the new upper mounting nuts.

**26** Locate the knuckle correctly with the suspension strut, and insert the upper retaining bolt and new nut. Fit the two new lower bolts securing the strut to the knuckle, and tighten both the lower and upper bolts to the specified torque **(see illustrations)**.

**27** Tighten the strut upper mounting nuts to the specified torque.

**28** Where necessary, engage the anti-roll bar connecting link with the strut. Make sure the flat on the balljoint shank is correctly located against the lug on the strut, then fit the washer and new retaining nut and tighten to the specified torque.

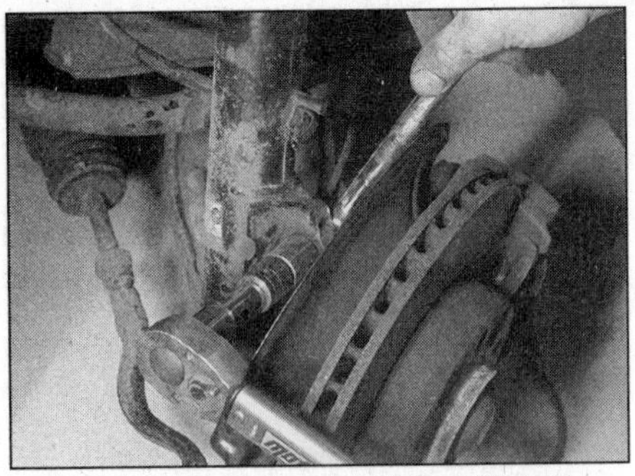

**4.26b . . . then fit the strut-to-knuckle bolts, and tighten to the specified torque**

**29** Clip the hose/wiring back onto the strut, then refit the roadwheel. Lower the car to the ground and tighten the wheel bolts to the specified torque.

## 5 Front suspension lower arm - removal, overhaul and refitting

**Note:** *New lower arm front mounting and balljoint nuts, a strut-to-knuckle upper bolt nut and lower retaining bolts, will be required on refitting. On models where the anti-roll bar is connected to the lower arm, a connecting link retaining nut will also be required.*

### Removal

**1** Chock the rear wheels, firmly apply the handbrake, then jack up the front of the car and support on axle stands. Remove the appropriate front roadwheel.

**2** To prevent the hub assembly hanging down whilst the lower arm is removed, screw a wheel bolt into the hub, then wrap a piece of wire around the bolt and tie it to the car body. This will support the weight of the hub assembly.

**3** On models where the anti-roll bar is connected to the lower arm, slacken and remove the nut and washer securing the connecting link to the arm **(see illustration)**.

**4** Slacken and remove the two lower bolts securing the suspension strut to the steering knuckle, and also the upper nut and bolt.

**5** Unscrew the lower arm balljoint nut, and release the arm from the steering knuckle. If necessary release the steering knuckle from the arm using the balljoint separator.

**6** Slacken and remove the two bolts securing the lower arm rear mounting to the car body **(see illustration)**.

**7** Unscrew the nut from the lower arm front mounting stud, and remove the lower arm assembly from underneath the car **(see illustration)**. Note that the stud may be a tight fit in the crossmember, and may need to be tapped out of position.

### Overhaul

**8** Thoroughly clean the lower arm and the area around the arm mountings, removing all traces of dirt and underseal if necessary, then check carefully for cracks, distortion or any other signs of wear or damage, paying particular attention to the mounting bushes and balljoint. If either bush or the balljoint requires renewal, the lower arm should be taken to a BMW dealer or suitably-equipped garage. A hydraulic press and suitable spacers are required to press the bushes out of position and install the new ones.

### Refitting

**9** Prior to refitting, clean the threads of the strut-to-steering knuckle lower bolt holes by running a tap of the correct thread size and pitch down them.

**HAYNES HiNT** ***If a suitable tap is not available, clean out the holes using one of the old bolts with slots cut in its threads***

**10** Ensure the mounting studs are clean and dry, then offer up the lower arm.

**11** Locate the front mounting stud in the crossmember, and engage the balljoint stud with the steering knuckle. Where necessary, also align the anti-roll bar connecting link with the arm hole. If necessary, press the front mounting bush stud into position using a jack position beneath the arm

**12** Fit a new nut to the front mounting stud and tighten it to the specified torque.

**13** Fit a new nut to the balljoint shank, and tighten it to the specified torque setting.

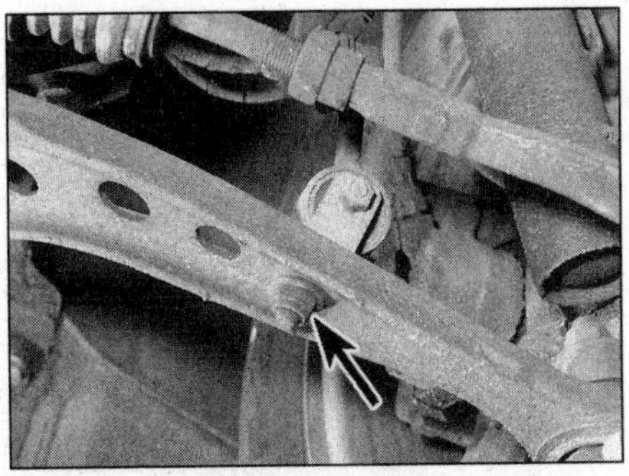

**5.3 Slacken and remove the nut and washer (arrowed) securing the connecting link to the lower arm**

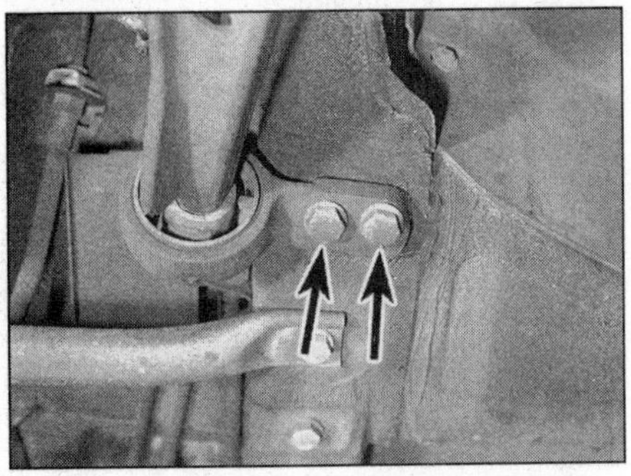

**5.6 Lower arm rear mounting bracket retaining bolts (arrowed)**

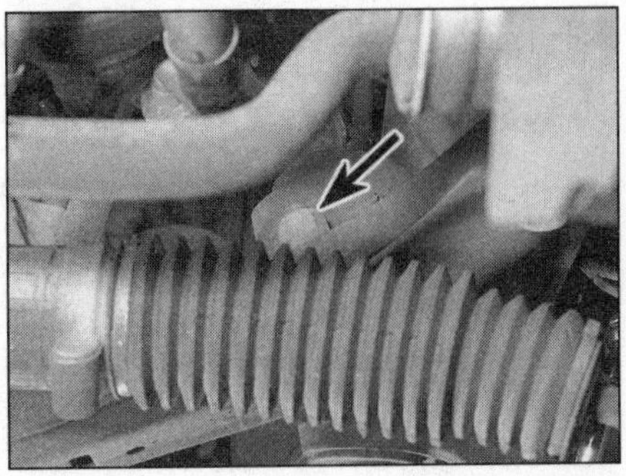

**5.7 Lower arm front mounting stud nut (arrowed)**

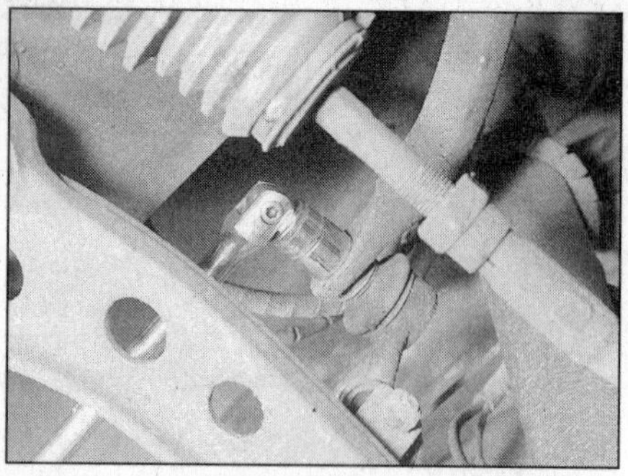

**7.2 Unscrew the retaining nuts and free the connecting links from the anti-roll bar**

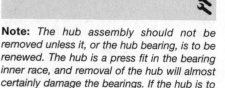

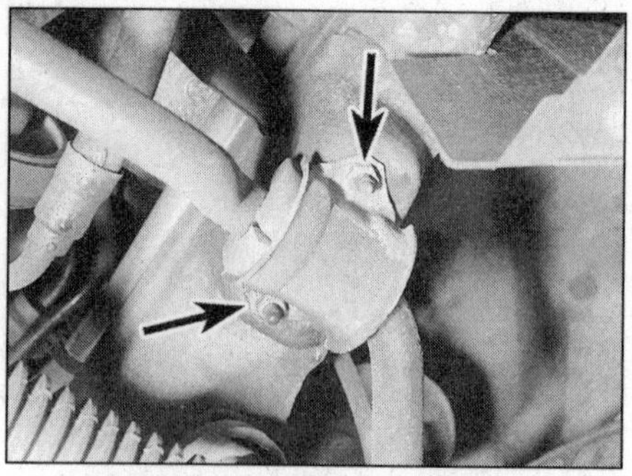

**7.3 Anti-roll bar mounting clamp retaining nuts (arrowed)**

**14** Refit the lower arm rear mounting bracket bolts, and tighten them to the specified torque setting.

**15** Locate the knuckle correctly with the suspension strut, and insert the upper retaining bolt and new nut. Fit the two new lower bolts securing the strut to the knuckle, and tighten both the lower and upper bolt to the specified torque.

**16** Where necessary, fit the washer and new retaining nut to the anti-roll bar connecting link, and tighten it to the specified torque.

**17** Refit the roadwheel, then lower the car to the ground and tighten the wheel bolts to the specified torque.

## 6 Front suspension lower arm balljoint - renewal

Front suspension lower arm balljoint renewal requires the use of a hydraulic press and several suitable spacers if it is to be carried out safely and successfully. If renewal is necessary, then the arm should be removed (Section 5) and taken to a BMW dealer or suitably-equipped workshop. **Note:** *BMW dealers with the necessary tools can renew the balljoint without removing the lower suspension arm from the car.*

## 7 Front suspension anti-roll bar - removal and refitting

**Note:** *New mounting clamp nuts and connecting link nuts will be required on refitting.*

### Removal

**1** Chock the rear wheels, firmly apply the handbrake, then jack up the front of the car and support on axle stands. Remove both front roadwheels.

**2** Unscrew the retaining nuts, and free the connecting link from each end of the anti-roll bar **(see illustration)**.

**3** Make alignment marks between the mounting bushes and anti-roll bar, then slacken the two anti-roll bar mounting clamp retaining nuts **(see illustration)**.

**4** Remove both clamps from the subframe, and manoeuvre the anti-roll bar out from underneath the car. Remove the mounting bushes from the bar.

**5** Carefully examine the anti-roll bar components for signs of wear, damage or deterioration, paying particular attention to the mounting bushes. Renew worn components as necessary.

### Refitting

**6** Fit the rubber mounting bushes to the anti-roll bar, aligning them with the marks made prior to removal. Rotate each bush so that its flat surface is uppermost.

**7** Offer up the anti-roll bar, and manoeuvre it into position. Refit the mounting clamps, ensuring that their ends are correctly located in the hooks on the subframe, and fit the new retaining nuts. Ensure that the bush markings are still aligned with the marks on the bars, then tighten the mounting clamp retaining nuts to the specified torque.

**8** Engage the anti-roll bar connecting links with the bar. Make sure the flats on the balljoint shank are correctly located against the lugs on the bar then fit the new retaining nuts and tighten to the specified torque.

**9** Refit the roadwheels then lower the car to the ground and tighten the wheel bolts to the specified torque.

## 8 Front suspension anti-roll bar connecting link - removal and refitting

**Note:** *New connecting link nuts will be required on refitting.*

### Removal

#### Models where the anti-roll bar is connected to the lower arms

**1** Firmly apply the handbrake, then jack up the front of the car and support it on axle stands.

**2** Unscrew the retaining nut, and free the connecting link from the anti-roll bar.

**3** Slacken and remove the nut and bolt securing the link to its lower arm mounting bracket, and remove the link. If necessary, unscrew the nut and washer, and remove the connecting link bracket from the lower arm.

**4** Inspect the connecting link balljoint and bush for signs of wear or damage. Check that the balljoint is free to move easily, and that its rubber gaiter is undamaged. Renew the link/mounting bracket if they are damaged, noting that all self-locking nuts should be renewed as a matter of course.

#### Models where the anti-roll bar is connected to the suspension struts

**5** Carry out the operations described in paragraphs 1 and 2.

**6** Unscrew the retaining nut and washer securing the link to the strut, and remove the link from the car.

**7** Check the connecting link balljoints for signs of wear. Check that each balljoint is free to move easily, and that the rubber gaiters are undamaged. If necessary renew the connecting link.

### Refitting

#### Models where the anti-roll bar is connected to the lower arms

**8** Refitting is a reverse of the removal sequence, using new nuts and tightening them to the specified torque setting.

#### Models where the anti-roll bar is connected to the suspension struts

**9** Refitting is the reverse of removal, ensuring the balljoint shank flats are correctly engaged with the strut/anti-roll bar lugs. Fit the new retaining nuts and tighten them to the specified torque.

## 9 Rear hub assembly - removal and refitting

**Note:** *The hub assembly should not be removed unless it, or the hub bearing, is to be renewed. The hub is a press fit in the bearing inner race, and removal of the hub will almost certainly damage the bearings. If the hub is to be removed, be prepared to renew the hub bearing at the same time.*

**Note:** *A long bolt/length of threaded bar and suitable washers will be required on refitting.*

### Removal

**1** Remove the relevant driveshaft as described in Chapter 8.

**2** Remove the brake drum/brake disc (as applicable) as described in Chapter 9.

**3** Bolt a slide hammer to the hub surface, and use the hammer to draw the hub out from the bearing. If the bearing inner race stays attached to the hub, a puller will be required to draw it off.

**4** With the hub removed, closely examine the hub bearing for signs of damage. Check that the bearing rotates freely and easily, without any sign of roughness. If the inner race remains attached to the hub, or there is any doubt about its condition, renew the bearing as described in Section 10.

### Refitting

**5** Apply a smear of oil to the hub surface, and locate it in the bearing inner race.

**6** Draw the hub into position using a long bolt or threaded length of bar and two nuts. Fit a large washer to either end of the bolt/bar, so the inner one bears against the bearing inner race, and the outer one against the hub. Slowly tighten the nut(s) until the hub is pulled fully into position. **Note:** *Do not be tempted to knock the hub into position with a hammer and drift, as this will almost certainly damage the bearing.*

**7** Remove the bolt/threaded bar and washers (as applicable), and check that the hub bearing rotates smoothly and easily.

**8** Refit the brake disc/drum (as applicable) as described in Chapter 9.

**9** Refit the driveshaft, referring to Chapter 8.

## 10 Rear hub bearings - renewal

**1** Remove the rear hub as described in Section 9.

**2** Remove the hub bearing retaining circlip from the trailing arm.

**3** Tap the hub bearing out from the trailing arm using a hammer and suitable punch.

**4** Thoroughly clean the trailing arm bore, removing all traces of dirt and grease, and polish away any burrs or raised edges which might hinder reassembly. Renew the circlip if there is any doubt about its condition.

**5** On reassembly, apply a light film of clean engine oil to the bearing outer race to aid installation.

**6** Locate the bearing in the trailing arm and tap it fully into position, ensuring that it enters the arm squarely, using a suitable tubular spacer which bears only on the bearing outer race.

**7** Secure the bearing in position with the circlip, making sure it is correctly located in the trailing arm groove.

**8** Fit the rear hub as described in Section 9.

## 11 Rear suspension shock absorber - removal, overhaul and refitting

**Note:** *New shock absorber upper mounting nuts and a new mounting gasket will be required on refitting.*

### Removal

**1** Check the front wheels, then jack up the rear of the car and support it on axle stands. To improve access, remove the rear roadwheel.

**2** Remove the rear loudspeaker as described in Chapter 12. Release the rear light access cover fastener by rotating it through 90° and remove the cover. Prise out the retaining clips securing the luggage compartment side trim cover in position, and remove the trim and insulation panel to gain access to the shock absorber upper mounting **(see illustrations)**.

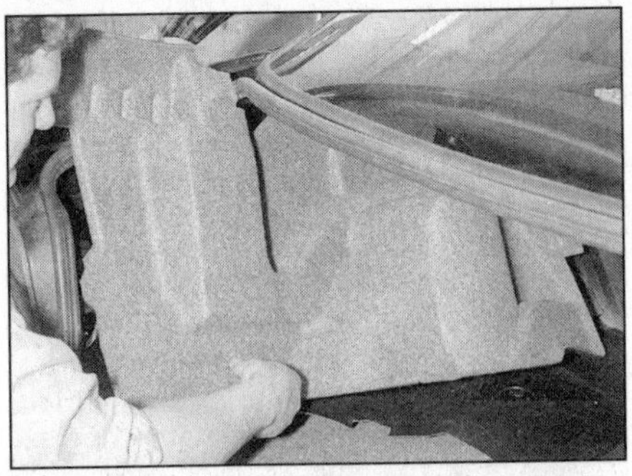

**11.2a To gain access to the rear shock absorber upper mounting, remove the luggage compartment side trim panel . . .**

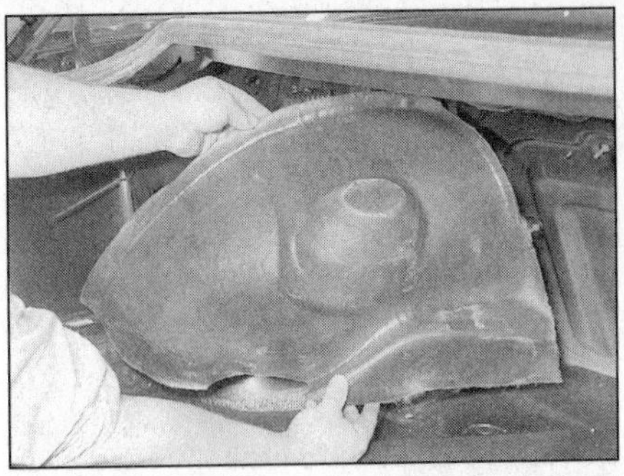

**11.2b . . . and lift out the insulation panel**

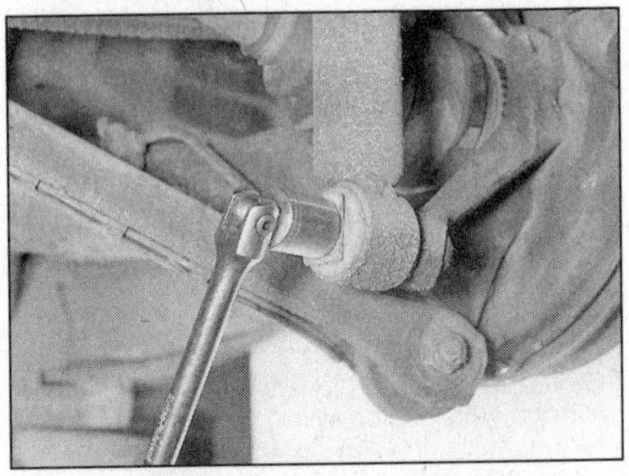

**11.4 Slacken and remove the shock absorber lower mounting bolt . . .**

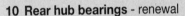

**11.5 . . . then unscrew the upper mounting nuts (arrowed)**

**3** Position a jack underneath the trailing arm, and raise the jack so that it is supporting the weight of the arm. This will prevent the arm dropping when the shock absorber is unbolted.

**4** Slacken and remove the bolt securing the shock absorber to the trailing arm **(see illustration)**.

**5** From within the luggage compartment, unscrew the upper mounting nuts **(see illustration)**. Lower the shock absorber out from underneath the car, and recover the gasket which is fitted between the upper mounting and body.

### Overhaul

**Note:** *A new piston nut will be required.*

**6** Remove the trim cap from the top of the shock absorber, then remove all traces of dirt. Slacken and remove the piston nut and dished washer, noting which way around it is fitted.

**7** Lift off the upper mounting plate and remove the dust cover.

**8** Slide the spacer and rubber stop off from the shock absorber piston.

**9** Examine the shock absorber for signs of fluid leakage. Check the piston for signs of pitting along its entire length, and check the body for signs of damage. While holding it in an upright position, test the operation of the shock absorber by moving the piston through a full stroke, and then through short strokes of 50 to 100 mm. In both cases, the resistance felt should be smooth and continuous. If the resistance is jerky, or uneven, or if there is any visible sign of wear or damage, renewal is necessary.

**10** Inspect all other components for signs of damage or deterioration, and renew any that are suspect.

**11** Slide the rubber stop and spacer onto the strut piston, and fit the dust cover.

**12** Fit the upper mounting plate and dished washer, and screw on the new piston nut and tighten it securely. Refit the trim cap.

### Refitting

**13** Ensure the upper mounting plate and body contact surfaces are clean and dry, and fit a new gasket to the upper mounting plate.

**14** Manoeuvre the shock absorber into position, and fit the new upper mounting nuts.

**15** Ensure the lower end of the shock absorber is positioned with the mounting bush spacer thrustwasher facing towards the bolt. Screw in the lower mounting bolt, tightening it by hand only at this stage.

**16** Tighten the upper mounting nuts to the specified torque setting then refit the insulation panel, luggage compartment trim panel, rear light access cover and loudspeaker (as applicable).

**17** Refit the roadwheel and lower the car to the ground. With the car resting on its wheels, tighten the shock absorber lower mounting bolt and roadwheel bolts to the specified torque.

## 12 Rear suspension coil spring - removal and refitting

### Removal

**1** Chock the front wheels, then jack up the rear of the car and support it on axle stands. Remove the relevant roadwheel.
**2** Referring to Chapter 8, slacken and remove the bolts and plates securing the right-hand driveshaft to the final drive unit flange. Free the driveshaft and support it by tying it to the car underbody using a piece of wire. **Note:** *Do not allow the driveshaft to hang under its own weight as the CV joint may be damaged.*
**3** Remove the rear suspension anti-roll-bar (where fitted) as described in Section 16.
**4** Position a jack underneath the rear of the trailing arm, and support the weight of the arm.
**5** Slacken and remove the shock absorber lower mounting bolt.
**6** Slowly lower the trailing arm, keeping watch on the brake pipe/hose to ensure no excess strain is placed on them, until it is possible to withdraw the coil spring.
**7** Recover the spring seats from the car body and control arm. If the car is to be left for some time, raise the trailing back up and refit the shock absorber lower mounting bolt.
**8** Inspect the spring closely for signs of damage, such as cracking, and check the spring seats for signs of wear. renew worn components as necessary.

### Refitting

**9** Fit the upper and lower spring seats, making sure they are correctly located on the pegs.
**10** Apply a little grease to the spring ends and engage the spring with its upper seat.
**11** Hold the spring in position and carefully raise the trailing arm whilst aligning the coil spring with its lower seat.
**12** Raise the arm fully and refit the shock absorber lower mounting bolt, tightening it by hand only at this stage.
**13** Refit the anti-roll bar (see Section 16).
**14** Referring to Chapter 8, connect the driveshaft to the final drive unit, then refit the retaining plates and bolts and tighten them to the specified torque.
**15** Refit the roadwheel then lower the car to the ground. Tighten the wheel bolts and shock absorber lower bolt to the specified torque.

## 13 Rear suspension trailing arm - removal, overhaul and refitting

### Removal

**1** Chock the front wheels, then jack up the rear of the car and support it on axle stands. Remove the relevant roadwheel.
**2** Remove the relevant driveshaft (see Chapter 8) and continue as described under the relevant sub-heading.

#### Models with rear drum brakes

**3** Referring to Chapter 9, remove the brake drum and disconnect the handbrake cable from the brake shoes. Free the cable from the rear of the backplate, and position it clear of the trailing arm.
**4** Minimise fluid loss by first removing the master cylinder reservoir cap, and then tightening it down onto a piece of polythene, to obtain an airtight seal. Alternatively, use a brake hose clamp, a G-clamp or a similar tool to clamp the flexible hose at the nearest convenient point to the wheel cylinder. Wipe away all traces of dirt around the brake pipe union at the rear of the wheel cylinder, and unscrew the union nut. Carefully ease the pipe out of the wheel cylinder, and plug or tape over its end to prevent dirt entry. Wipe off any spilt immediately.
**5** Undo the retaining bolts and release the brake pipe bracket from the trailing arm.
**6** Position a jack underneath the rear of the trailing arm, and support the weight of the arm.
**7** Slacken and remove the shock absorber lower mounting bolt.
**8** Using paint or a suitable marker pen, make alignment marks between the lower control arm pivot bolt eccentric washer and the trailing arm. Also make alignment marks between the trailing arm front mounting bracket and the vehicle underbody **(see illustration)**. This is necessary to ensure that the rear wheel alignment and camber are correct on refitting.
**9** Slacken and remove the nut and washer from the lower control arm pivot bolt. Withdraw the pivot bolt, then slowly lower the arm and remove the jack.
**10** Slacken and remove the nut and pivot bolt securing the upper control arm to the trailing arm.
**11** Unscrew the three bolts securing the trailing arm mounting bracket to the vehicle body and remove the trailing arm. **Note:** *Do not slacken the trailing arm pivot bush bolt unless renewal of the bush/mounting bracket is necessary.*

#### Models with rear disc brakes

**12** Unscrew the two bolts securing the brake caliper mounting bracket in position, then slide the caliper assembly off the disc. Using a piece of wire or string, tie the caliper to the rear suspension coil spring, to avoid placing any strain on the hydraulic brake hose.
**13** Referring to Chapter 9, disconnect the handbrake cable from the rear of the backplate. On models with ABS, also remove the rear wheel sensor.
**14** Remove the trailing arm as described in paragraphs 5 to 11.

### Overhaul

**15** Slacken and remove the nut and pivot bolt and separate the front mounting bracket and trailing arm.
**16** Thoroughly clean the trailing arm and the area around the arm mountings, removing all traces of dirt and underseal if necessary. Check carefully for cracks, distortion or any other signs of wear or damage, paying particular attention to the mounting bushes. If either bush requires renewal, the lower arm should be taken to a BMW dealer or suitably-equipped garage. A hydraulic press and suitable spacers are required to press the bushes out of position and install the new ones. Inspect the pivot bolts for signs of wear or damage and renew as necessary.

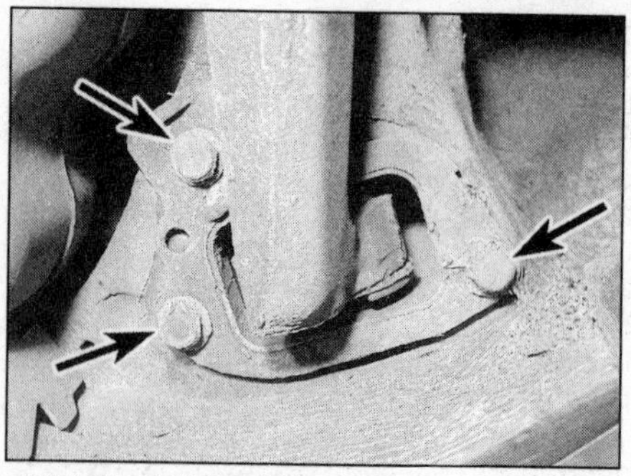

**13.8 Mark the position of the trailing arm bracket on the body prior to slackening the mounting bolts (arrowed)**

**17** Fit the mounting bracket to trailing arm, and install the pivot bolt and nut. Position the bracket as shown, using an 8 mm rod, and tighten the pivot bolt to the specified torque **(see illustration)**.

### Refitting

#### Models with rear drum brakes

**18** Offer up the trailing arm assembly, and refit the mounting bracket retaining bolts. Align the marks made prior to removal, then tighten the mounting bracket bolts to the specified torque.
**19** Engage the upper control arm with the trailing arm and fit the pivot bolt and nut. Tighten the bolt by hand only at this stage.
**20** Raise the trailing arm with the jack, making sure the coil spring is correctly aligned with its spring seats, and fit the lower arm

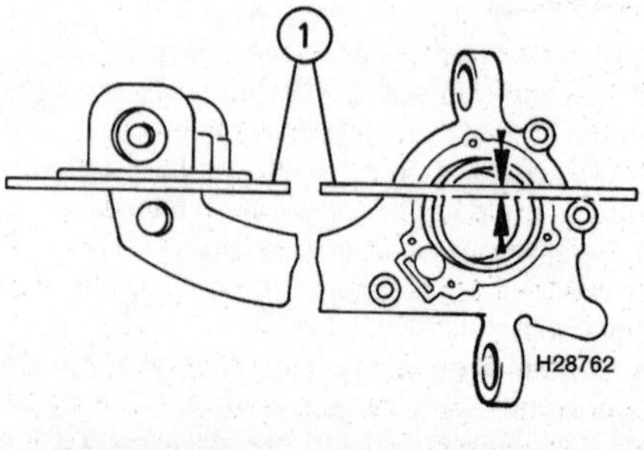


**13.17 To position the mounting bracket correctly in relation to the trailing arm, place an 8 mm rod (1) against the mounting bracket and rest it on the trailing arm as shown. The mounting bracket pivot bolt can then be tightened to the specified torque**

pivot bolt, eccentric washer and nut. Align the washer with the mark made prior to removal, then refit the shock absorber lower mounting bolt. Tighten both the pivot bolt and mounting bolt by hand only.

**21** Refit the brake pipe retaining bracket to the trailing arm, and fully tighten the bolts.

**22** Referring to Chapter 9, reconnect the brake pipe to the wheel cylinder, securely tighten the union nut and remove the polythene/clamp. Connect the handbrake cable to the brake shoe, then refit the brake drum. Bleed the braking system, noting that providing suitable precautions were taken to minimise loss of fluid, it should only be necessary to bleed the relevant rear brake.

**23** Refit the driveshaft as described in Chapter 8 and lower the car to the ground.

**24** With the car on its wheels, rock the car to settle the disturbed components in position, then tighten the shock absorber lower mounting bolt and the upper control arm pivot bolts to the specified torque. Check that the lower arm eccentric washer is still correctly aligned with the mark, then tighten it to the specified torque. **Note:** *On completion, it is advisable to have the camber angle and wheel alignment checked and, if necessary, adjusted.*

### Models with rear disc brakes

**25** Carry out the operations described in paragraphs 18 to 21.

**26** Referring to Chapter 9, reconnect the handbrake cable to the expander lever and (where necessary) refit the ABS wheel sensor. Slide the caliper into position over the disc, making sure the pads pass either side of the disc, and tighten the caliper bracket mounting bolts to the specified torque setting.

**27** Carry out the operations described in paragraphs 23 and 24.

## 14 Rear suspension upper control arm - removal, overhaul and refitting

**Note:** *A new control arm-to-rear subframe pivot bolt and nut will be required on refitting.*

### *Removal*

**1** Remove the coil spring (see Section 12).

**2** Release the wiring from its retaining clips on the side of the upper control arm.

**3** Slacken and remove the control arm-to-trailing arm pivot bolt **(see illustration)**.

**4** Referring to Chapter 8, support the weight of the unit with a jack, and remove the final drive unit mounting bolts.

**5** Slacken and remove the nut from the control arm to the rear subframe pivot bolt. Withdraw the bolt, moving the final drive unit slightly to the rear, and remove the control arm from underneath the car **(see illustration)**. Note that on some models it may be necessary to detach the propeller shaft from the final drive unit in order to gain the clearance required to remove the pivot bolt. **Note:** *If the car is to be left for*

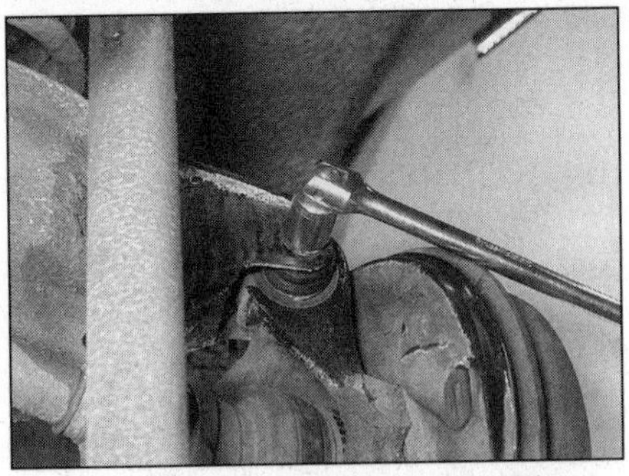

**14.3 Slacken and remove the upper control arm-to-trailing arm pivot bolt . . .**

*some time, refit the final drive unit mounting bolts and tighten securely.*

### *Overhaul*

**6** Thoroughly clean the control arm and the area around the arm mountings, removing all traces of dirt and underseal if necessary. Check for cracks, distortion or any other wear or damage, paying particular attention to the mounting bush. If the bush requires renewal, the arm should be taken to a BMW dealer or suitably-equipped garage. A hydraulic press and suitable spacers are required to press the bushes out of position and fit the new ones.

**7** Inspect the pivot bolts for signs of wear or damage, and renew as necessary. The control arm-to-subframe bolt and nut should be renewed as a matter of course.

### *Refitting*

**8** Manoeuvre the control arm into position, and fit the new arm to subframe pivot bolt and nut. Tighten the nut lightly only at this stage.

**9** Referring to Chapter 8, manoeuvre the final drive unit into position, and tighten its mounting bolts to the specified torque. Where necessary, reconnect the propeller shaft to the final drive unit.

**10** Refit the pivot bolt and nut securing the control arm to the trailing arm, tightening it lightly only at this stage.

**11** Clip the wiring back into position on the upper control arm.

**12** Refit the coil spring (see Section 12).

**13** On completion, lower the car to the ground and rock the car to settle all disturbed components. With the car resting on its

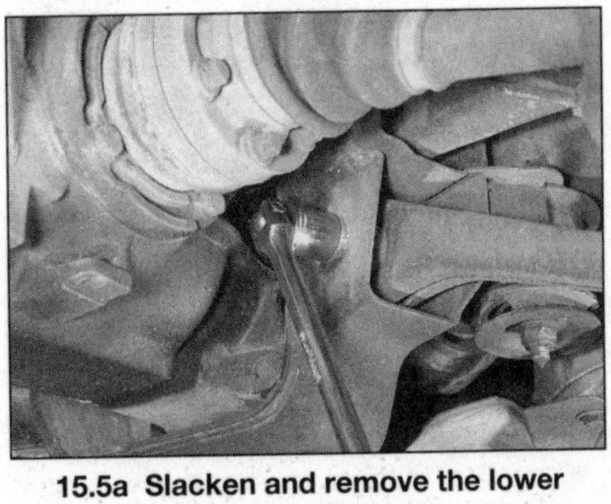

**15.5a Slacken and remove the lower control arm pivot bolt . . .**

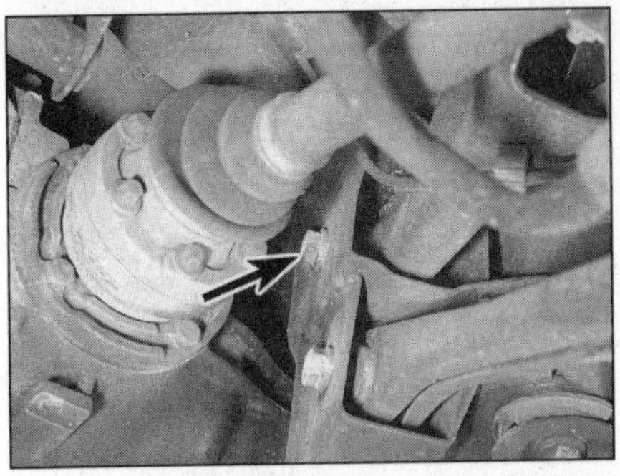

**14.5 . . . and the control arm-to-subframe pivot bolt (arrowed)**

wheels tighten the wheel bolts, shock absorber lower mounting bolt and the control arm pivot bolts to their specified torque settings. **Note:** *On completion, it is advisable to have the camber angle and wheel alignment checked and, if necessary, adjusted.*

## 15 Rear suspension lower control arm - removal, overhaul and refitting

**Note:** *A new control arm-to-rear subframe pivot bolt and nut will be required on refitting.*

### *Removal*

**1** Chock the front wheels, then jack up the rear of the car and support it on axle stands. To improve access, remove the rear wheel.

**2** Using paint or a suitable marker pen, make alignment marks between the lower control arm pivot bolt eccentric washer and the trailing arm. This is necessary to ensure that the rear wheel alignment and camber are correct on refitting.

**3** Support the trailing arm with a jack, then remove the nut and washer from the lower control arm pivot bolt. Withdraw the pivot bolt.

**4** Referring to Chapter 8, support the weight of the final drive unit with a jack, and remove the unit mounting bolts.

**5** Slacken and remove the pivot bolt securing the control arm to the rear subframe. Withdraw the bolt, moving the final drive unit slightly to the rear, and remove the control arm from underneath the car. Recover the special nut from the subframe **(see illustrations)**. **Note:** *On*

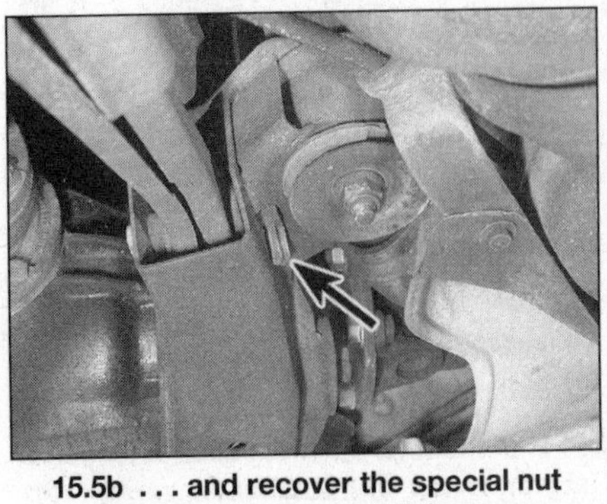

**15.5b . . . and recover the special nut (arrowed) from the subframe**

*some models it may be necessary to detach the propeller shaft from the final drive unit in order to gain the clearance required to remove the pivot bolt. If the car is to be left for some time, refit the final drive unit mounting bolts and tighten securely.*

### Overhaul

**6** Refer to paragraphs 6 and 7 of Section 14.

### Refitting

**7** Locate the special nut in the subframe cut-out, and manoeuvre the control arm into position. Fit the new pivot bolt, tightening it lightly only at this stage.
**8** Referring to Chapter 8, manoeuvre the final drive unit into position and tighten its mounting bolts to the specified torque. Where necessary, reconnect the propeller shaft to the final drive unit.
**9** Fit the lower arm-to-trailing arm pivot bolt, eccentric washer and nut. Align the washer with the mark made prior to removal and lightly tighten it.
**10** Refit the roadwheel and lower the car to the ground.
**11** With the car on its wheels, rock the car to settle the disturbed components in position. Check that the lower arm eccentric washer is still correctly aligned with the mark, then tighten both the control arm pivot bolts to the specified torque wrench setting. Where necessary also tighten the wheel bolts to the specified torque. **Note:** *On completion, it is advisable to have the camber angle and wheel alignment checked and, if necessary, adjusted.*

## 16 Rear suspension anti-roll bar - removal and refitting

**Note:** *New mounting clamp nuts and connecting link nuts will be required on refitting.*

### Removal

**1** Chock the front wheels, then jack up the rear of the car and support it on axle stands. To improve access, remove the rear roadwheels.
**2** Slacken and remove the nut securing each connecting link to the upper control arms **(see illustration)**.
**3** Make alignment marks between the mounting bushes and anti-roll bar, then slacken the two anti-roll bar mounting clamp retaining nuts and bolts **(see illustration)**.
**4** Remove both clamps from the subframe, and manoeuvre the anti-roll bar and connecting link assembly out from underneath the car. Remove the mounting bushes and connecting links from the bar.
**5** Carefully examine the anti-roll bar components for signs of wear, damage or deterioration, paying particular attention to the mounting bushes. Renew any worn components as necessary.

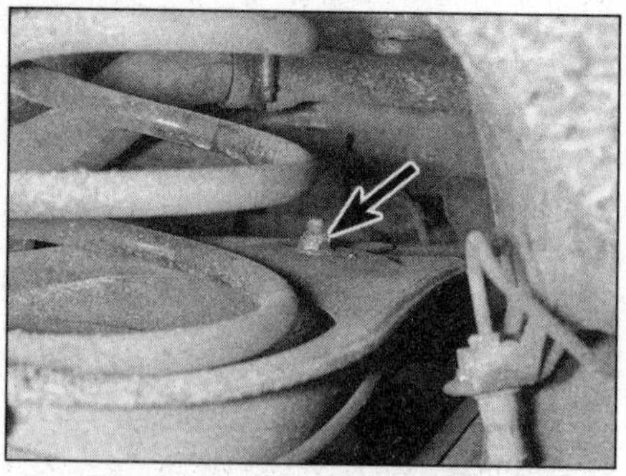

**16.2 Rear anti-roll bar connecting link-to-control arm nut (arrowed)**

### Refitting

**6** Fit the rubber mounting bushes to the anti-roll bar, aligning them with the marks made prior to removal. Rotate each bush so that its flat surface is facing forwards.
**7** Offer up the anti-roll bar, and manoeuvre it into position. Locate the connecting links in the upper control arms, and fit the new retaining nuts and tighten securely.
**8** Refit the mounting clamps, ensuring that their ends are correctly located in the hooks on the subframe, and fit the bolts and new retaining nuts. Ensure that the bush markings are still aligned with the marks on the bars, then securely tighten the mounting clamp retaining nuts.
**9** Refit the roadwheels then lower the car to the ground and tighten the wheel bolts to the specified torque.

## 17 Steering wheel - removal and refitting

### Removal

**1** Set the front wheels in the straight-ahead position, and release the steering lock by inserting the ignition key.

#### Models not fitted with an airbag

**2** Prise the BMW emblem/horn pad out from the centre of the wheel **(see illustration)**.
**3** Slacken and remove the steering wheel retaining bolt.

**17.4a Slacken and remove the retaining bolt, then lift off the steering wheel . . .**

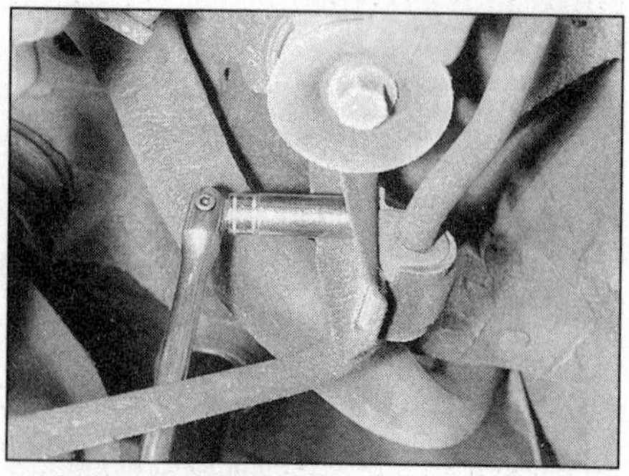

**16.3 Slacken and remove the rear anti-roll bar clamp retaining nuts and bolts**

**4** Mark the steering wheel and steering column shaft in relation to each other, then lift the steering wheel off the column splines. If it is tight, tap it up near the centre, using the palm of your hand, or twist it from side to side, whilst pulling upwards to release it from the shaft splines. Remove the spacer from the top of the steering column **(see illustrations)**.
**5** Inspect the horn contact ring/indicator cancelling cam for signs of wear or damage, and renew as necessary.

#### Models with an airbag

**6** Remove the airbag unit from the centre of the steering wheel, referring to Chapter 12.
**7** Remove the steering wheel as described above in paragraphs 3 and 4. The airbag contact unit will automatically be locked in position as the wheel is removed; do not attempt to rotate whilst the wheel is removed.

**17.2 Removing the horn pad from the steering wheel (sports wheel shown)**

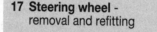

**17.4b . . . and remove the spacer from the top of the column**

## Refitting

### Models not fitted with an airbag

**8** Refitting is a reversal of removal, noting the following.

*a) Prior to refitting, ensure the indicator switch stalk is in the central (OFF) position. Failure to do so could lead to the steering wheel lug breaking the switch tab.*

*b) Coat the steering wheel horn contact ring with a smear of petroleum jelly and engage the wheel with the column splines, aligning the marks made on removal.*

*c) Tighten the steering wheel retaining bolt to the specified torque setting.*

### Models with an airbag

**9** Refitting is the reverse of removal, noting the following points.

*a) If the contact unit has been rotated with the wheel removed, centralise it by pressing down on the contact unit and rotating its centre fully anti-clockwise. From this position, rotate the centre back through three complete rotations in a clockwise direction.*

*b) Prior to refitting, ensure the indicator switch stalk is in the central (OFF) position. Failure to do so could lead to the steering wheel lug breaking the switch tab.*

*c) Coat the steering wheel horn contact ring with a smear of petroleum jelly and refit the wheel, making sure the contact unit wiring is correctly routed.*

*d) On early models, ensure that the locating peg on the top of the column engages correctly with the contact unit hole as the steering wheel is refitted.*

*e) Engage the wheel with the column splines, aligning the marks made on removal, and tighten the steering wheel retaining bolt to the specified torque.*

*f) Refit the airbag unit (see Chapter 12).*

## 18 Steering column - removal, inspection and refitting

**Note:** *New steering column shear-bolts, and an intermediate shaft clamp bolt nut, will be required on refitting.*

## Removal

**1** Disconnect the battery negative terminal.

**2** Remove the steering wheel as described in Section 17.

**3** Remove the steering column combination switches (refer to Chapter 12, Section 4).

**4** Working in the engine compartment, using paint or a suitable marker pen, make alignment marks between the lower end of the steering column and the intermediate shaft upper joint.

**5** Slacken and remove the nut and clamp bolt, and disengage the shaft from the column.

**6** Disconnect the wiring connectors from the ignition switch and free the harness from its retaining clips on the column **(see illustration)**.

**7** Release the steering column lower fixing ring by rotating it anti-clockwise.

**8** Where necessary, slacken and remove the nut and bolt securing the column support bracket to the bulkhead and withdraw the spacer from the column. Also unscrew the interlock cable (where fitted) from steering lock.

**9** The steering column is secured in position with shear-bolts. The shear-bolts can be extracted using a hammer and suitable chisel to tap the bolt heads around until they can be unscrewed by hand. Alternatively, drill a hole in the centre of each bolt head and extract them using a bolt/stud extractor (sometimes called an "easy-out").

**10** Pull the column upwards and away from the bulkhead, and slide off the rubber mounting, mounting seat, washer and fixing ring off from the column lower end. Remove the collars and rubber mountings from the column mountings **(see illustration)**.

## Inspection

**11** The steering column incorporates a telescopic safety feature. In the event of a front-end crash, the shaft collapses and prevents the steering wheel injuring the driver. Before refitting the steering column, examine the column and mountings for damage and deformation, and renew as necessary.

**12** Check the steering shaft for signs of free play in the column bushes. If any damage or wear is found on the steering column bushes, the column should be overhauled. Overhaul of the column is a complex task requiring several special tools, and should be entrusted to a BMW dealer.

## Refitting

**13** Ensure the mounting rubbers are in position, and fit the collars to the rear of the mounting rubbers.

**14** Slide the fixing ring, washer, mounting seat and rubber mounting onto the base of the steering column **(see illustration)**.

**15** Manoeuvre the column into position and engage it with the intermediate shaft splines, aligning the marks made prior to removal **(see illustration)**.

**16** Locate the lower end of the column in its seat and screw in the new shear-bolts; tighten them lightly only at this stage **(see illustration)**.

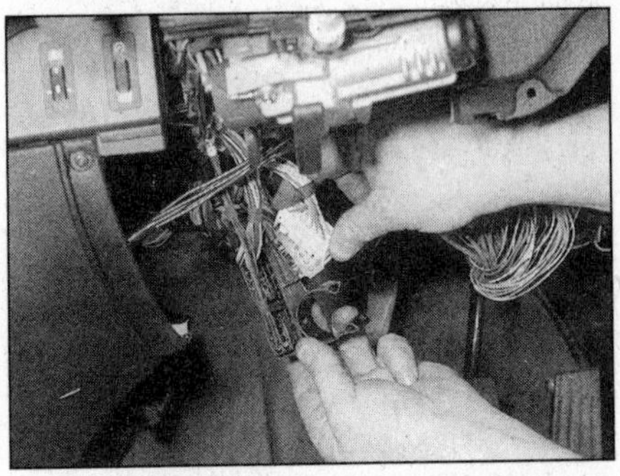

**18.6 Unclip the wiring connectors from the column and disconnect the ignition switch connector**

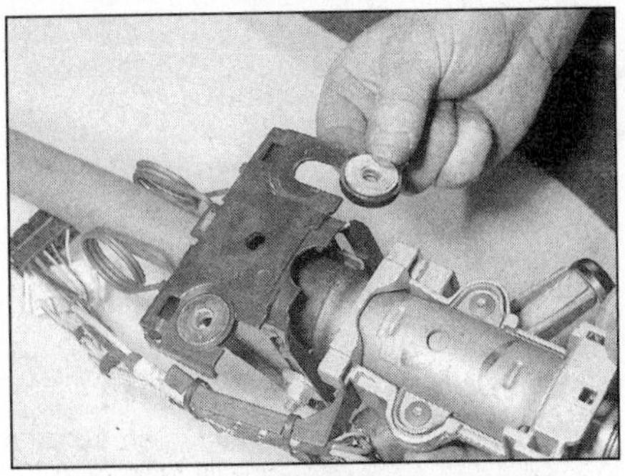

**18.10 Remove the steering column and recover the rubber mountings and collars**

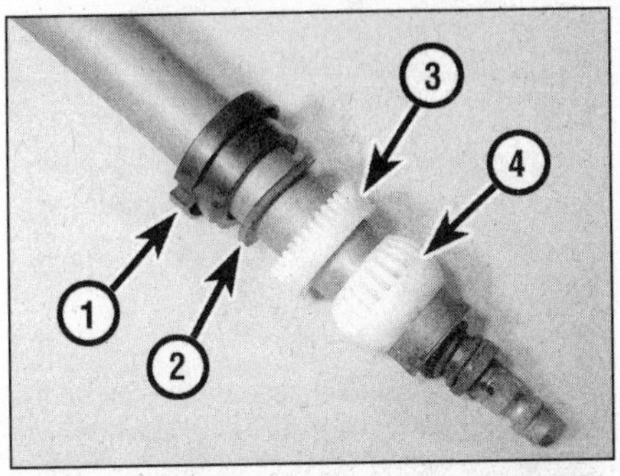


**18.14 Slide the fixing ring (1), washer (2), mounting seat (3) and rubber mounting (4) onto the base of the steering column . . .**

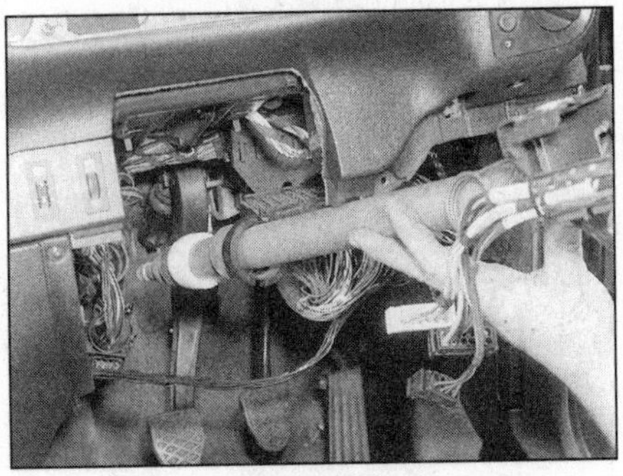

**18.15 . . . and refit the column to the vehicle**

**18.16 Seat the column in its lower mounting, and fit the new shear-bolts**

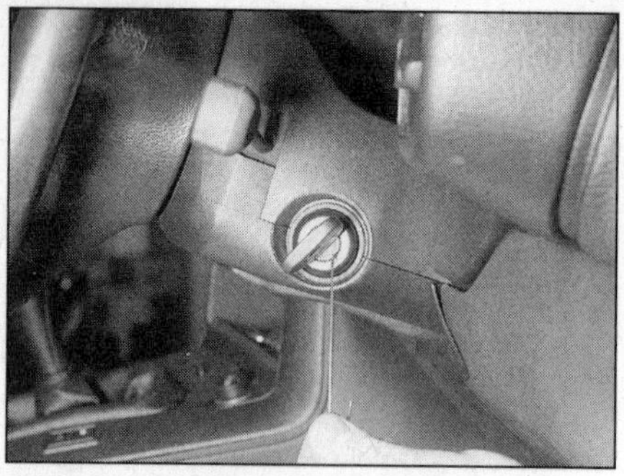

19.3a Position the lock cylinder as shown, and insert the rod into the hole . . .

19.3b . . . depress the detent and withdraw the lock cylinder

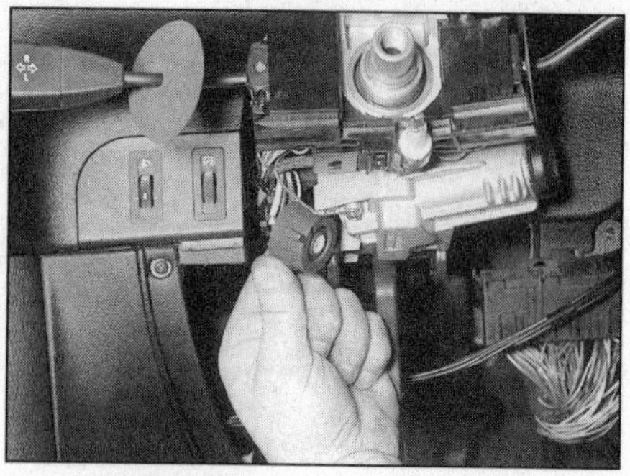

19.8 Removing the ignition switch wiring block

**17** Where necessary, refit the spacer, washer and bolt securing the column support bracket to the bulkhead and fit its retaining nut.
**18** Secure the lower end of the column in position by rotating the fixing ring clockwise until it clicks into position.
**19** Tighten the column shear-bolts evenly until both their heads break off. Where necessary, also securely tighten the support bracket bolt.
**20** Reconnect the wiring connectors to the ignition switch, and secure the wiring to the column, ensuring it is correctly routed.
**21** Ensure the intermediate shaft and column marks are correctly aligned, and insert the clamp bolt. Fit the new clamp bolt nut and tighten it to the specified torque.
**22** Where necessary, reconnect the interlock cable to the switch and secure it in position.
**23** Fit the combination switches as described in Chapter 12.
**24** Refit the steering wheel as described in Section 17.

## 19 Ignition switch/steering column lock - removal and refitting

### *Lock assembly*

**1** Renewal of the lock assembly requires the steering column to be dismantled. This task requires the use of several special tools, and for this reason should be entrusted to a BMW dealer.

### *Lock cylinder*

#### Removal

**2** Disconnect the battery negative terminal. Insert the key into the lock and release the steering lock.
**3** Position the lock cylinder as shown, then insert a 1.2 mm diameter rod into the hole in the cylinder. Depress the lock cylinder detent, and slide the lock cylinder out of position **(see illustrations)**.

#### Refitting

**4** Position the lock cylinder as shown in paragraph 3 and insert the cylinder into the housing until it clicks in to position.

### *Ignition switch block*

#### Removal

**5** Disconnect the battery negative terminal.
**6** Slacken and remove the retaining screws securing the driver's side lower facia panel. Unclip the panel and remove it from the car.
**7** Unscrew the steering column shroud lower fastener screw and pull out the fastener. Unclip the lower half of the shroud and remove it from the column.
**8** Disconnect the wiring connector from the switch, then undo the two grub screws and remove the switch block from the lock assembly **(see illustration)**.

#### Refitting

**9** Refitting is the reverse of removal, noting the following points:

*a) Apply varnish to the switch grub screws prior to refitting, to lock them in position.*
*b) Reconnect the battery and check the operation of the switch prior to refitting the steering column shroud.*

## 20 Steering column intermediate shaft - removal and refitting

**Note:** *New intermediate shaft clamp bolt nuts will be required on refitting.*

### *Removal*

**1** Chock the rear wheels, firmly apply the handbrake, then jack up the front of the car and support on axle stands. Set the front wheels in the straight-ahead position.

#### Models with a one-piece intermediate shaft

**2** Using paint or a suitable marker pen, make alignment marks between the intermediate shaft universal joint and the steering column, the shaft and flexible coupling and the flexible coupling and the steering gear pinion.
**3** Slacken and remove the nuts and clamp bolts, then slide the two halves of the shaft together and remove the shaft assembly from the car **(see illustration)**.
**4** Inspect the intermediate shaft universal joint for signs of roughness in its bearings and ease of movement. Also examine the shaft rubber coupling for signs of damage or deterioration, and check that the rubber is securely bonded to the flanges. If the universal joint or rubber coupling are suspect, the complete intermediate shaft should be renewed.

#### Models with a two-piece intermediate shaft

**5** Using paint or a suitable marker pen, make alignment marks between the intermediate shaft universal joint and the steering column, and the flexible coupling and steering gear pinion.
**6** Slacken and remove all three intermediate shaft clamp bolts and nuts.
**7** Slide the shaft downwards and disengage its upper end from the steering column. Release its lower end from the rubber coupling.
**8** Remove the rubber coupling from the steering gear.
**9** Inspect the intermediate shaft universal joint for signs of roughness in its bearings and ease of movement. If the universal joint is worn, renew the intermediate shaft. Examine the rubber coupling for signs of damage or deterioration, and check that the rubber securely bonded to the flanges. If the rubber coupling is suspect, it should be renewed.

### *Refitting*

#### Models with a one-piece intermediate shaft

**10** Check that the front wheels are still in the straight-ahead position, and that the steering wheel is correctly positioned.

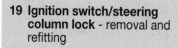

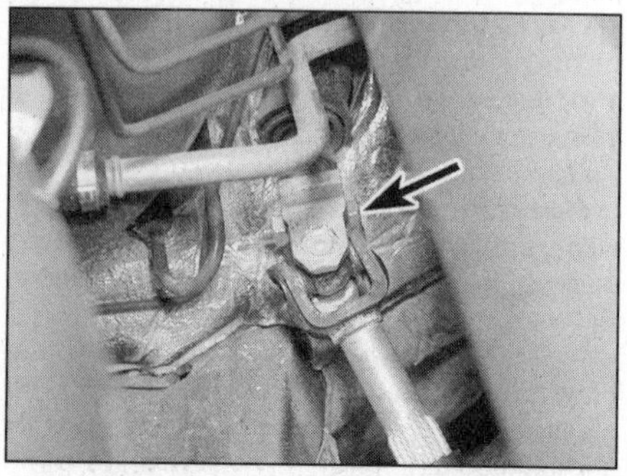

20.3 Steering column-to-intermediate shaft clamp bolt (arrowed)

**11** Align the marks made on removal, and engage the intermediate shaft joint with the steering column and the coupling with the steering gear.

**12** Insert the clamp bolts, then fit the new nuts and tighten them to the specified torque setting. Lower the car to the ground.

### Models with a two-piece intermediate shaft

**13** Check that the front wheels are still in the straight-ahead position and the steering wheel is correctly positioned.

**14** Align the marks made prior to removal and engage the rubber coupling with the steering gear pinion.

**15** Insert the intermediate shaft into the coupling, then engage the shaft joint with the steering gear, aligning the marks made on removal.

**16** Ensure all the alignment marks are correctly positioned, then insert the clamp bolts.

**17** Fit a new nut to each clamp bolt, tightening them to the specified torque setting, and lower the car to the ground.

## 21 Steering gear assembly - removal, overhaul and refitting

**Note:** *New track rod balljoint nuts, steering gear mounting nuts, and an intermediate shaft clamp bolt nut, will be required on refitting. On power-assisted steering models, new fluid pipe union bolt sealing washers will also be needed.*

### Removal

**1** Chock the rear wheels, firmly apply the handbrake, then jack up the front of the car and support on axle stands. Remove both front roadwheels.

**2** Slacken and remove the nuts securing the steering gear track rod balljoints to the steering knuckles, and release the balljoint tapered shanks using a universal balljoint separator.

**3** Using paint or a suitable marker pen, make alignment marks between the intermediate shaft flexible coupling and the steering gear pinion.

**4** On models with power-assisted steering, using brake hose clamps, clamp both the supply and return hoses near the power steering fluid reservoir. This will minimise fluid loss. Mark the unions to ensure they are correctly positioned on reassembly, then slacken and remove the feed and return pipe union bolts and recover the sealing washers. Be prepared for fluid spillage, and position a suitable container beneath the pipes whilst unscrewing the bolts. Plug the pipe ends and steering gear orifices, to prevent fluid leakage and to keep dirt out of the hydraulic system.

**5** Slacken and remove the steering gear mounting bolts and nuts, and remove the steering gear from underneath the car **(see illustration)**.

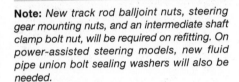

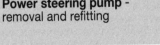

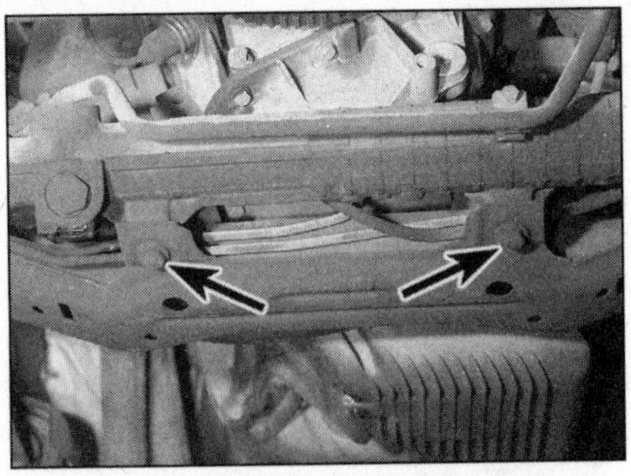

**21.5 Steering gear mounting bolts (arrowed)**

### Overhaul

**6** Examine the steering gear assembly for signs of wear or damage, and check that the rack moves freely throughout the full length of its travel, with no signs of roughness or excessive free play between the steering gear pinion and rack. It is not possible to overhaul the steering gear assembly housing components; if it is faulty, the assembly must be renewed. The only components which can be renewed individually are the steering gear gaiters, the track rod balljoints and the track rods. These procedures are covered later in this Chapter.

### Refitting

**7** Offer up the steering gear, and insert the mounting bolts. Fit new nuts to the bolts, and tighten them to the specified torque setting.

**8** On power-assisted steering models, position a new sealing washer on each side of the pipe hose unions and refit the union bolts. Tighten the union bolts to the specified torque.

**9** Align the marks made on removal, and connect the intermediate shaft coupling to the steering gear. Insert the clamp bolt then fit the new nut and tighten it to the specified torque.

**10** Locate the track rod balljoints in the steering knuckles, then fit the new nuts and tighten them to the specified torque.

**11** Refit the roadwheels, then lower the car to the ground and tighten the wheel bolts to the specified torque.

**12** On models with power steering, bleed the hydraulic system as described in Section 23.

## 22 Power steering pump - removal and refitting

**Note:** *New feed pipe union bolt sealing washers will be required on refitting*

### Removal

**1** Chock the front wheels, then jack up the rear of the car and support it on axle stands.

**2** Working as described in Chapter 1, release the drivebelt tension and unhook the drivebelt from the pump pulley, noting that the pulley retaining bolts should be slackened prior to releasing the tension.

**3** Unscrew the retaining bolts and remove the pulley from the power steering pump, noting which way around it is fitted.

**4** Using brake hose clamps, clamp both the supply and return hoses near the power steering fluid reservoir. This will minimise fluid loss during subsequent operations.

**5** Mark the unions to ensure they are correctly positioned on reassembly, then slacken and remove the feed and return pipe union bolts and recover the sealing washers. Be prepared for fluid spillage, and position a suitable container beneath the pipes whilst unscrewing the bolts. Plug the pipe ends and steering pump orifices, to prevent fluid leakage and to keep dirt out of the hydraulic system.

**6** On 4-cylinder engines, slacken and remove the bolt securing the pump to the adjuster strap and the pump pivot bolt, then remove the pump from the engine unit.

**7** On 6-cylinder engines, slacken and remove the bolts securing the power steering pump front and rear mounting brackets in position, and remove the pump from the engine.

**8** If the power steering pump is faulty, seek the advice of your BMW dealer as to the availability of spare parts. If spares are available, it may be possible to have the pump overhauled by a suitable specialist, or alternatively obtain an exchange unit. If not, the pump must be renewed.

### Refitting

**9** Where necessary, transfer the rear mounting bracket to the new pump, and securely tighten its mounting bolts.

**10** Prior to fitting, ensure that the pump is primed by injecting the specified type of fluid in through the supply hose union and rotating the pump shaft.

**11** On 4-cylinder engines, manoeuvre the pump into position and refit the pivot bolt and adjuster strap bolt, tightening them lightly only at this stage.

**12** On 6-cylinder engines, manoeuvre the pump into position and refit its mounting bolts, tightening them to the specified torque.

**13** Position a new sealing washer on each side of the pipe hose unions and refit the union bolts. Tighten the union bolts to the specified torque.

**14** Remove the hose clamps and refit the pump pulley. Ensure the pulley is the right way around, and securely tighten its retaining bolts.

**15** Refit the auxiliary drivebelt and tension it as described in Chapter 1.

**16** On completion, lower the car to the ground and bleed the hydraulic system as described in Section 23.

## 23 Power steering system - bleeding

**1** With the engine stopped, fill the fluid reservoir right up to the top with the specified type of fluid.
**2** With the engine stopped, slowly move the steering from lock-to-lock several times to purge out the trapped air, then top-up the level in the fluid reservoir. Repeat this procedure until the fluid level in the reservoir does not drop any further.
**3** Have an assistant start the engine, whilst you keep watch on the fluid level. Be prepared to add more fluid as the engine starts as the fluid level is likely to drop quickly. The fluid level must be kept above the "MIN" mark at all times.
**4** With the engine running at idle speed, turn the steering wheel slowly two or three times approximately 45° to the left and right of the centre, then turn the wheel twice from lock to lock. Do not hold the wheel on either lock, as this imposes strain on the hydraulic system. Repeat this procedure until bubbles cease to appear in fluid reservoir.
**5** If, when turning the steering, an abnormal noise is heard from the fluid lines, it indicates that there is still air in the system. Check this by turning the wheels to the straight-ahead position and switching off the engine. If the fluid level in the reservoir rises, then air is present in the system and further bleeding is necessary.
**6** Once all traces of air have been removed from the power steering hydraulic system, turn the engine off and allow the system to cool. Once cool, check that fluid level is up to the maximum mark on the power steering fluid reservoir, topping-up if necessary (see *"Weekly Checks"*)

## 24 Steering gear rubber gaiters - renewal

### *Models with power-assisted steering*

**1** Remove the track rod balljoint as described in Section 25.
**2** Note the correct fitted position of the gaiter on the track rod, then release the retaining clip(s) and slide the gaiter off the steering gear housing and track rod end.
**3** Thoroughly clean the track rod and the steering gear housing, using fine abrasive paper to polish off any corrosion, burrs or sharp edges, which might damage the new gaiter's sealing lips on installation. Scrape off all the grease from the old gaiter, and apply it to the track rod inner balljoint. (This assumes that grease has not been lost or contaminated as a result of damage to the old gaiter. Use fresh grease if in doubt).
**4** Carefully slide the new gaiter onto the track rod end, and locate it on the steering gear housing. Position the outer edge of the gaiter on the track rod, as was noted prior to removal.
**5** Make sure the gaiter is not twisted, then lift the outer sealing lip of the gaiter to equalise air pressure within the gaiter. Secure the gaiter in position with the new retaining clip(s).
**6** Refit the track rod balljoint as described in Section 25.

### *Models with manual steering*

#### Passenger side gaiter on models with steering damper

**7** Note the correct fitted positions of the gaiter ends, and release the retaining clips.
**8** Remove the track rod as described in Section 26.
**9** Unscrew the nut from the end of the steering damper, and remove the washer, collar and spacer from the damper piston. Slide off the steering damper bracket, and remove the gaiter from the end of the steering gear.
**10** Thoroughly clean the track rod and the steering gear housing, using fine abrasive paper to polish off any corrosion, burrs or sharp edges, which might damage the new gaiter's sealing lips on installation. Scrape off all the grease from the old gaiter, and apply it to the track rod inner balljoint. (This assumes that grease has not been lost or contaminated as a result of damage to the old gaiter. Use fresh grease if in doubt).
**11** Fit the new gaiter to the steering gear and secure it in position with the retaining clip.
**12** Fit the steering damper bracket, spacer and collar to the damper piston and securely tighten its retaining nut.
**13** Refit the track rod as described in Section 26, and secure the gaiter in position as described in paragraph 5.

#### All other gaiters

**14** Refer to paragraphs 1 to 6.

## 25 Track rod balljoint - removal and refitting

**Note:** *A new balljoint retaining nut will be required on refitting.*

### *Removal*

**1** Apply the handbrake, then jack up the front of the car and support it on axle stands. Remove the appropriate front roadwheel.
**2** Make a mark on the track rod and measure the distance from the mark to the centre of the balljoint. Note this measurement down, as it will be needed to ensure the wheel alignment remains correctly set when the balljoint is installed.
**3** Hold the track rod, and unscrew the balljoint locknut.
**4** Slacken and remove the nut securing the track rod balljoint to the steering knuckle, and release the balljoint tapered shank using a universal balljoint separator.
**5** Counting the **exact** number of turns necessary to do so, unscrew the balljoint from the track rod end.
**6** Carefully clean the balljoint and the threads. Renew the balljoint if its movement is sloppy or too stiff, if excessively worn, or if damaged in any way; carefully check the stud taper and threads. If the balljoint gaiter is damaged, the complete balljoint assembly must be renewed; it is not possible to obtain the gaiter separately.

### *Refitting*

**7** If necessary, transfer the locknut and collar to the new track rod balljoint.
**8** Screw the balljoint onto the track rod by the number of turns noted on removal. This should position the balljoint at the relevant distance from the track rod mark that was noted prior to removal.
**9** Refit the balljoint shank to the steering knuckle, then fit a new retaining nut and tighten it to the specified torque.
**10** Refit the roadwheel, then lower the car to the ground and tighten the roadwheel bolts to the specified torque.
**11** Check and, if necessary, adjust the front wheel toe setting as described in Section 27, then tighten the balljoint locknut to the specified torque setting.

## 26 Track rod - renewal

**Note:** *A new track rod locking plate and steering gaiter retaining clip(s)will be required.*

### *Models with power-assisted steering*

**1** Remove the steering gear gaiter as described in Section 24.
**2** Using a pair of pliers, bend back the track rod locking plate. **Note:** *Do not use a hammer and chisel, as this could damage the steering gear.*
**3** Unscrew the track rod from the end of the steering rack.
**4** Fit the new locking plate to the steering rack, making sure it is locating tabs are correctly seated in the steering rack grooves.
**5** Screw in the track rod and tighten it to the specified torque. Secure the track rod in position by bending down the locking plate with a pair of pliers.
**6** Refit the steering gaiter as described in Section 24.

### *Models with manual steering*

#### Passenger side track rod on models with a steering damper

**7** Remove the track rod balljoint as described in Section 25.
**8** Renew the track rod as described in

paragraphs 2 to 5, ensuring the locking plate is correctly engaged with the steering damper bracket.

**9** Refit the track rod balljoint as described in Section 25.

### All other track rods

**10** Refer to paragraphs 1 to 6.

## 27 Wheel alignment and steering angles - general information

### *Definitions*

**1** A car's steering and suspension geometry is defined in four basic settings - all angles are expressed in degrees (toe settings are also expressed as a measurement); the steering axis is defined as an imaginary line drawn through the axis of the suspension strut, extended where necessary to contact the ground.

**2 Camber** is the angle between each roadwheel and a vertical line drawn through its centre and tyre contact patch, when viewed from the front or rear of the car. Positive camber is when the roadwheels are tilted outwards from the vertical at the top; negative camber is when they are tilted inwards.

**3** The front camber angle is not adjustable, and is given for reference only (see paragraph 5). The rear camber angle is adjustable and can be adjusted using a camber angle gauge.

**4 Castor** is the angle between the steering axis and a vertical line drawn through each roadwheel's centre and tyre contact patch, when viewed from the side of the car. Positive castor is when the steering axis is tilted so that it contacts the ground ahead of the vertical; negative castor is when it contacts the ground behind the vertical.

**5** Castor is not adjustable, and is given for reference only; while it can be checked using a castor checking gauge, if the figure obtained is significantly different from that specified, the car must be taken for careful checking by a professional, as the fault can only be caused by wear or damage to the body or suspension components.

**6 Toe** is the difference, viewed from above, between lines drawn through the roadwheel centres and the car's centre-line. "Toe-in" is when the roadwheels point inwards, towards each other at the front, while "toe-out" is when they splay outwards from each other at the front.

**7** The front wheel toe setting is adjusted by screwing the right-hand track rod in or out of its balljoint, to alter the effective length of the track rod assembly.

**8** Rear wheel toe setting is also adjustable. The toe setting is adjusted by slackening the trailing arm mounting bracket bolts and repositioning the bracket.

### *Checking and adjustment*

### Front wheel toe setting

**9** Due to the special measuring equipment necessary to check the wheel alignment, and the skill required to use it properly, the checking and adjustment of these settings is best left to a BMW dealer or similar expert. Note that most tyre-fitting shops now possess sophisticated checking equipment.

**10** To check the toe setting, a tracking gauge must first be obtained. Two types of gauge are available, and can be obtained from motor accessory shops. The first type measures the distance between the front and rear inside edges of the roadwheels, as previously described, with the car stationary. The second type, known as a "scuff plate", measures the actual position of the contact surface of the tyre, in relation to the road surface, with the car in motion. This is achieved by pushing or driving the front tyre over a plate, which then moves slightly according to the scuff of the tyre, and shows this movement on a scale. Both types have their advantages and disadvantages, but either can give satisfactory results if used correctly and carefully.

**11** Make sure that the steering is in the straight-ahead position when making measurements.

**12** If adjustment is necessary, apply the handbrake then jack up the front of the car and support it securely on axle stands.

**13** First clean the track rod threads; if they are corroded, apply penetrating fluid before starting adjustment. Release the rubber gaiter outer clips, peel back the gaiters and apply a smear of grease so that both are free and will not be twisted or strained as their respective track rods are rotated.

**14** Retain the track rod with a suitable spanner and slacken the balljoint locknut. Alter the length of the track rod, by screwing them into or out of the balljoints by rotating the track rod using an open-ended spanner fitted to the track rod flats provided; shortening the track rods (screwing them onto their balljoints) will reduce toe-in/increase toe-out.

**15** When the setting is correct, hold the track rod and tighten the balljoint locknut to the specified torque setting. If after adjustment, the steering wheel spokes are no longer horizontal when the wheels are in the straight-ahead position, remove the steering wheel and reposition it (see Section 17).

**16** Check that the toe setting has been correctly adjusted by lowering the car to the ground and re-checking the toe setting; re-adjust if necessary. Ensure that the rubber gaiters are seated correctly and are not twisted or strained, and secure them in position with the retaining clips; where necessary fit a new retaining clip (see Section 24).

### Rear wheel toe setting

**Note:** *Prior adjusting the toe setting, the camber angle should first be checked.*

**17** The procedure for checking the rear toe setting is same as described for the front in paragraph 10.

**18** To adjust the setting, slacken the trailing arm mounting bracket bolts slightly and reposition the bracket as required. Once the toe setting is correct, tighten the mounting bracket bolts to the specified torque.

### Rear wheel camber angle

**19** Checking and adjusting of the camber angle should be entrusted to a BMW dealer or other suitably-equipped specialist. Note that most tyre-fitting shops now possess sophisticated checking equipment. For reference, adjustments are made by slackening the lower control arm-to-trailing arm pivot bolts, and rotating the eccentric washer. Once adjustment is correct, tighten the bolt to the specified torque.

# Chapter 11
# Bodywork and fittings

## Contents



## Degrees of difficulty

| | | | | |
|---|---|---|---|---|
| **Easy,** suitable for novice with little experience | **Fairly easy,** suitable for beginner with some experience | **Fairly difficult,** suitable for competent DIY mechanic | **Difficult,** suitable for experienced DIY mechanic | **Very difficult,** suitable for expert DIY or professional |

## Specifications

| **Torque wrench settings** | **Nm** | **lbf ft** |
|---|---|---|
| Door exterior handle nut/bolt | 10 | 7 |
| Door lock retaining bolts | 9 | 6 |
| Door window glass and regulator fixings - Saloon models: | | |
| Regulator stop bolt | 9 | 6 |
| Regulator mounting bolts | 6 | 4 |
| Window guide bolts | 10 | 7 |
| Exterior mirror bolts | 6 | 4 |
| Front seat belt height adjustment mechanism bolts | 24 | 18 |
| Front seat mounting nuts\bolts | 55 | 41 |
| Rear vent window hinge bolts/screw - Coupe models | 6 | 4 |
| Seat belt mounting bolts | 48 | 35 |

### 1 General information

The bodyshell is made of pressed-steel sections. Most components are welded together, but some use is made of structural adhesives.

The bonnet, door and some other vulnerable panels are made of zinc-coated metal, and are further protected by being coated with an anti-chip primer before being sprayed.

Extensive use is made of plastic materials, mainly in the interior, but also in exterior components. The front and rear bumpers and front grille are injection-moulded from a synthetic material that is very strong and yet light. Plastic components such as wheel arch liners are fitted to the underside of the vehicle, to improve the body's resistance to corrosion.

### 2 Maintenance - bodywork and underframe

**1** The condition of a vehicle's bodywork is the one thing that significantly affects its value. Maintenance is easy, but needs to be regular. Neglect, particularly after minor damage, can lead quickly to further deterioration and costly repair bills. It is important also to keep watch on those parts of the vehicle not immediately visible, for instance the underside, inside all the wheel arches, and the lower part of the engine compartment.

**2** The basic maintenance routine for the bodywork is washing - preferably with a lot of water, from a hose. This will remove all the loose solids which may have stuck to the vehicle. It is important to flush these off in such a way as to prevent grit from scratching the finish. The wheel arches and underframe need washing in the same way, to remove any accumulated mud which will retain moisture and tend to encourage rust. Oddly enough, the best time to clean the underframe and wheel arches is in wet weather, when the mud is thoroughly wet and soft. In very wet weather, the underframe is usually cleaned of large accumulations automatically, and this is a good time for inspection.

**3** Periodically, except on vehicles with a wax-based underbody protective coating, it is a good idea to have the whole of the underframe of the vehicle steam-cleaned, engine compartment included, so that a thorough inspection can be carried out to see what minor repairs and renovations are necessary. Steam cleaning is available at many garages, and is necessary for the removal of the accumulation of oily grime, which sometimes is allowed to become thick in certain areas. If steam-cleaning facilities are not available, there are some excellent grease solvents available which can be brush-applied; the dirt can then be simply hosed off. Note that these methods should not be used on vehicles with wax-based underbody protective coating, or the coating will be removed. Such vehicles should be inspected annually, preferably just before Winter, when the underbody should be washed down, and repair any damage to the wax coating. Ideally, a completely fresh coat should be applied. It would also be worth considering the use of such wax-based protection for injection into door panels, sills, box sections, etc, as an additional safeguard against rust damage, where such protection is not provided by the vehicle manufacturer.

**4** After washing paintwork, wipe off with a chamois leather to give an unspotted clear finish. A coat of clear protective wax polish will give added protection against chemical pollutants in the air. If the paintwork sheen has dulled or oxidised, use a cleaner/polisher combination to restore the brilliance of the shine. This requires a little effort, but such dulling is usually caused because regular washing has been neglected. Care needs to be taken with metallic paintwork, as special non-abrasive cleaner/polisher is required to avoid damage to the finish. Always check that the door and ventilator opening drain holes and pipes are completely clear, so that water can be drained out. Brightwork should be treated in the same way as paintwork. Windscreens and windows can be kept clear of the smeary film which often appears, by proprietary glass cleaner. Never use any form of wax or other body or chromium polish on glass.

## 3 Maintenance - upholstery and carpets

Mats and carpets should be brushed or vacuum-cleaned regularly, to keep them free of grit. If they are badly stained, remove them from the vehicle for scrubbing or sponging, and make quite sure they are dry before refitting. Seats and interior trim panels can be kept clean by wiping with a damp cloth and a proprietary brand of cleaner. If they do become stained (which can be more apparent on light-coloured upholstery), use a little liquid detergent and a soft nail brush to scour the grime out of the grain of the material. Do not forget to keep the headlining clean in the same way as the upholstery. When using liquid cleaners inside the vehicle, do not over-wet the surfaces being cleaned. Excessive damp could get into the seams and padded interior, causing stains, offensive odours or even rot. If the inside of the vehicle gets wet accidentally, it is worthwhile taking some trouble to dry it out properly, particularly where carpets are involved. *Do not leave oil or electric heaters inside the vehicle for this purpose.*

## 4 Minor body damage - repair

### Repairs of minor scratches in bodywork

**1** If the scratch is very superficial, and does not penetrate to the metal of the bodywork, repair is very simple. Lightly rub the area of the scratch with a paintwork renovator or a very fine cutting paste to remove loose paint from the scratch, and to clear the surrounding bodywork of wax polish. Rinse the area with clean water.

**2** Apply touch-up paint to the scratch using a fine paint brush; continue to apply fine layers of paint until the surface of the paint in the scratch is level with the surrounding paintwork. Allow the new paint at least two weeks to harden, then blend it into the surrounding paintwork by rubbing the scratch area with a paintwork renovator or a very fine cutting paste. Finally, apply wax polish.

**3** Where the scratch has penetrated right through to the metal of the bodywork, causing the metal to rust, a different repair technique is required. Remove any loose rust from the bottom of the scratch with a penknife, then apply rust-inhibiting paint to prevent the formation of rust in the future. Using a rubber or nylon applicator, fill the scratch with bodystopper paste. If required, this paste can be mixed with cellulose thinners to provide a very thin paste which is ideal for filling narrow scratches. Before the stopper-paste in the scratch hardens, wrap a piece of smooth cotton rag around the top of a finger. Dip the finger in cellulose thinners, and quickly sweep it across the surface of the stopper-paste in the scratch; this will ensure that the surface of the stopper-paste is slightly hollowed. The scratch can now be painted over as described earlier in this Section.

### Repairs of dents in bodywork

**4** When deep denting of the vehicle's bodywork has taken place, the first task is to pull the dent out, until the affected bodywork almost attains its original shape. There is little point in trying to restore the original shape completely, as the metal in the damaged area will have stretched on impact, and cannot be reshaped fully to its original contour. It is better to bring the level of the dent up to a point which is about 3 mm below the level of the surrounding bodywork. In cases where the dent is very shallow anyway, it is not worth trying to pull it out at all. If the underside of the dent is accessible, it can be hammered out gently from behind, using a mallet with a wooden or plastic head. Whilst doing this, hold a suitable block of wood firmly against the outside of the panel, to absorb the impact from the hammer blows and thus prevent a large area of the bodywork from being "belled-out".

**5** Should the dent be in a section of the bodywork which has a double skin, or some other factor making it inaccessible from behind, a different technique is called for. Drill several small holes through the metal inside the area - particularly in the deeper section. Then screw long self-tapping screws into the holes, just sufficiently for them to gain a good purchase in the metal. Now the dent can be pulled out by pulling on the protruding heads of the screws with a pair of pliers.

**6** The next stage of the repair is the removal of the paint from the damaged area, and from an inch or so of the surrounding "sound" bodywork. This is accomplished most easily by using a wire brush or abrasive pad on a power drill, although it can be done just as effectively by hand, using sheets of abrasive paper. To complete the preparation for filling, score the surface of the bare metal with a screwdriver or the tang of a file, or alternatively, drill small holes in the affected area. This will provide a good "key" for the filler paste.

**7** To complete the repair, see the Section on filling and respraying.

### Repairs of rust holes or gashes in bodywork

**8** Remove all paint from the affected area, and from an inch or so of the surrounding "sound" bodywork, using an abrasive pad or a wire brush on a power drill. If these are not available, a few sheets of abrasive paper will do the job most effectively. With the paint removed, you will be able to judge the severity of the corrosion, and therefore decide whether to renew the whole panel (if this is possible) or to repair the affected area. New body panels are not as expensive as most people think, and it is often quicker and more satisfactory to fit a new panel than to attempt to repair large areas of corrosion.

**9** Remove all fittings from the affected area, except those which will act as a guide to the original shape of the damaged bodywork (eg headlamp shells etc). Then, using tin snips or a hacksaw blade, remove all loose metal and any other metal badly affected by corrosion. Hammer the edges of the hole inwards, to create a slight depression for the filler paste.

**10** Wire-brush the affected area to remove the powdery rust from the surface of the remaining metal. Paint the affected area with rust-inhibiting paint; if the back of the rusted area is accessible, treat this also.

**11** Before filling can take place, it will be necessary to block the hole in some way. This can be achieved with aluminium or plastic mesh, or aluminium tape.

**12** Aluminium or plastic mesh, or glass-fibre

matting, is probably the best material to use for a large hole. Cut a piece to the approximate size and shape of the hole to be filled, then position it in the hole so that its edges are below the level of the surrounding bodywork. It can be retained in position by several blobs of filler paste around its periphery.

**13** Aluminium tape should be used for small or very narrow holes. Pull a piece off the roll, trim it to the approximate size and shape required, then pull off the backing paper (if used) and stick the tape over the hole; it can be overlapped if the thickness of one piece is insufficient. Burnish down the edges of the tape with the handle of a screwdriver or similar, to ensure that the tape is securely attached to the metal underneath.

## Bodywork repairs - filling and respraying

**14** Before using this Section, see the Sections on dent, deep scratch, rust holes and gash repairs.

**15** Many types of bodyfiller are available, but generally speaking, those proprietary kits which contain a tin of filler paste and a tube of resin hardener are best for this type of repair which can be used directly from the tube. A wide, flexible plastic or nylon applicator will be found invaluable for imparting a smooth and well-contoured finish to the surface of the filler.

**16** Mix up a little filler on a clean piece of card or board - measure the hardener carefully (follow the maker's instructions on the pack), otherwise the filler will set too rapidly or too slowly. Using the applicator, apply the filler paste to the prepared area; draw the applicator across the surface of the filler to achieve the correct contour and to level the surface. When a contour that approximates to the correct one is achieved, stop working the paste - if you carry on too long, the paste will become sticky and begin to "pick-up" on the applicator. Continue to add thin layers of filler paste at 20-minute intervals, until the level of the filler is just proud of the surrounding bodywork.

**17** Once the filler has hardened, the excess can be removed using a metal plane or file. From then on, progressively-finer grades of abrasive paper should be used, starting with a 40-grade production paper, and finishing with a 400-grade wet-and-dry paper. Always wrap the abrasive paper around a flat rubber, cork, or wooden block - otherwise the surface of the filler will not be completely flat. During the smoothing of the filler surface, the wet-and-dry paper should be periodically rinsed in water. This will ensure that a very smooth finish is imparted to the filler at the final stage.

**18** At this stage, the "dent" should be surrounded by a ring of bare metal, which in turn should be encircled by the finely "feathered" edge of the good paintwork. Rinse the repair area with clean water, until all the dust produced by the rubbing-down operation has gone.

**19** Spray the whole area with a light coat of primer - this will show up any imperfections in the surface of the filler. Repair these imperfections with fresh filler paste or bodystopper, and again smooth the surface with abrasive paper. If bodystopper is used, it can be mixed with cellulose thinners, to form a thin paste which is ideal for filling small holes. Repeat this spray-and-repair procedure until you are satisfied that the surface of the filler, and the feathered edge of the paintwork, are perfect. Clean the repair area with clean water, and allow to dry fully.

**20** The repair area is now ready for final spraying. Paint spraying must be carried out in a warm, dry, windless and dust-free atmosphere. This condition can be created artificially if you have access to a large indoor working area, but if you are forced to work in the open, you will have to pick your day very carefully. If you are working indoors, dousing the floor in the work area with water will help to settle the dust which would otherwise be in the atmosphere. If the repair area is confined to one body panel, mask off the surrounding panels; this will help to minimise the effects of a slight mis-match in paint colours. Bodywork fittings (eg chrome strips, door handles etc) will also need to be masked off. Use genuine masking tape, and several thickness of newspaper, for the masking operations.

**21** Before starting to spray, agitate the aerosol can thoroughly, then spray a test area (an old tin, or similar) until the technique is mastered. Cover the repair area with a thick coat of primer; the thickness should be built up using several thin layers of paint, rather than one thick one. Using 400 grade wet-and-dry paper, rub down the surface of the primer until it is smooth. While doing this, the work area should be thoroughly doused with water, and the wet-and-dry paper periodically rinsed in water. Allow to dry before spraying on more paint.

**22** Spray on the top coat, again building up the thickness by using several thin layers of paint. Start spraying in the centre of the repair area, and then, using a circular motion, work outwards until the whole repair area and about 2 inches of the surrounding original paintwork is covered. Remove all masking material 10 to 15 minutes after spraying on the final coat of paint.

**23** Allow the new paint at least two weeks to harden, then, using a paintwork renovator or a very fine cutting paste, blend the edges of the paint into the existing paintwork. Finally, apply wax polish.

## Plastic components

**24** With the use of more and more plastic body components by the vehicle manufacturers (eg bumpers. spoilers, and in some cases major body panels), rectification of more serious damage to such items has become a matter of either entrusting repair work to a specialist in this field, or renewing complete components. Repair of such damage by the DIY owner is not feasible, owing to the cost of the equipment and materials required for effecting such repairs. The basic technique involves making a groove along the line of the crack in the plastic, using a rotary burr in a power drill. The damaged part is then welded back together, using a hot air gun to heat up and fuse a plastic filler rod into the groove. Any excess plastic is then removed, and the area rubbed down to a smooth finish. It is important that a filler rod of the correct plastic is used, as body components can be made of different types (eg polycarbonate, ABS, polypropylene).

**25** Damage of a less serious nature (abrasions, minor cracks etc) can be repaired by the DIY owner using a two-part epoxy filler repair material which can be used directly from the tube. Once mixed in equal proportions, this is used in similar fashion to the bodywork filler used on metal panels. The filler is usually cured in twenty to thirty minutes, ready for sanding and painting.

**26** If the owner is renewing a complete component himself, or if he has repaired it with epoxy filler, he will be left with the problem of finding a suitable paint for finishing which is compatible with the type of plastic used. At one time, the use of a universal paint was not possible, owing to the complex range of plastics met with in body component applications. Standard paints, generally speaking, will not bond to plastic or rubber satisfactorily, but professional matched paints, to match any plastic or rubber finish, can be obtained from some dealers. However, it is now possible to obtain a plastic body parts finishing kit which consists of a pre-primer treatment, a primer and coloured top coat. Full instructions are normally supplied with a kit, but basically the method of use is to first apply the pre-primer to the component concerned, and allow it to dry for up to 30 minutes. Then the primer is applied, and left to dry for about an hour before finally applying the special-coloured top coat. The result is a correctly coloured component, where the paint will flex with the plastic or rubber, a property that standard paint does not normally posses.

## 5 Major body damage - repair

Where serious damage has occurred, or large areas need renewal due to neglect, it means that complete new panels will need welding-in, and this is best left to professionals. If the damage is due to impact, it will also be necessary to check completely the alignment of the bodyshell, and this can only be carried out accurately by a BMW dealer using special jigs. If the body is left misaligned, it is primarily dangerous, as the car will not handle properly, and secondly, uneven stresses will be imposed on the steering, suspension and possibly transmission, causing abnormal wear, or complete failure, particularly to such items as the tyres.

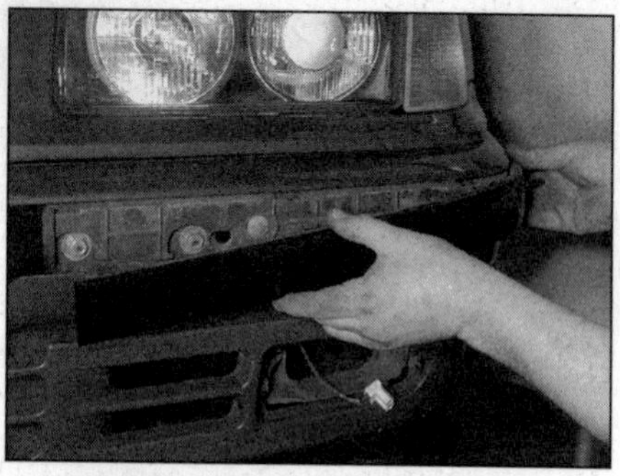

6.2a Unclip the trim strip from the left-hand end of the bumper . . .

6.2b . . . and remove the towing eye hole cover

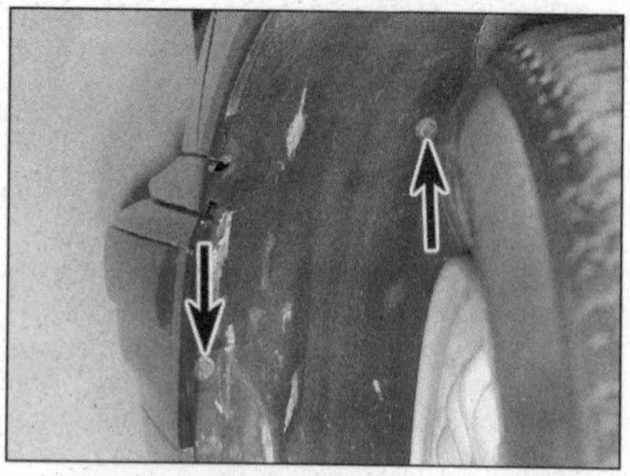

6.5 Undo the screws securing the wheelarch liner in position (arrowed)

## 6 Front bumper - removal and refitting

### *Removal*

**1** Apply the handbrake, then jack up the front of the vehicle and support it on axle stands (see "*Jacking and vehicle support*").

**2** To gain access to the bumper mounting nuts, using a flat-bladed screwdriver, carefully unclip the rubber trim strip from the left-hand end of the bumper and the towing eye cover **(see illustrations)**. Take great care not to the damage the painted finish of the bumper.

**3** On models with front foglights, remove the access covers from the base of the bumper and disconnect the wiring connectors from the foglights.

**4** Where necessary, disconnect the wiring connector(s) from the temperature sensor/thermostatic switch which is/are clipped into the brake cooling duct(s).

**5** Slacken and remove the bumper end retaining screws which are accessed from underneath the left and right-hand wheelarches **(see illustration)**.

**6** Unscrew the bumper mounting nuts and remove the bumper forwards and away from the vehicle **(see illustrations)**.

**7** Inspect the bumper mountings for signs of damage and renew if necessary.

### *Refitting*

**8** Refitting is a reverse of the removal procedure, ensuring that the bumper mounting nuts and screws are securely tightened.

## 7 Rear bumper - removal and refitting

### *Removal*

**1** To improve access, chock the front wheels, then jack up the rear of the vehicle and support it on axle stands (see "*Jacking and vehicle support*").

**2** Remove the fasteners and carefully unclip the panel from the base of the rear bumper.

6.6a Slacken and remove the mounting nuts (arrowed) . . .

6.6b . . . and remove the bumper from the vehicle

The fasteners are released by pulling out their centre pins **(see illustrations)**.

**3** Undo the screws securing the wheelarch liners to the bumper ends. Prise out the retaining clip centre pins and remove the clips securing the liner to the bumper.

**4** Slacken and remove the bumper lower mounting bolts and remove the bumper from the rear of the vehicle. Where necessary, disconnect the wiring connectors from the bumper distance sensors **(see illustrations)**.

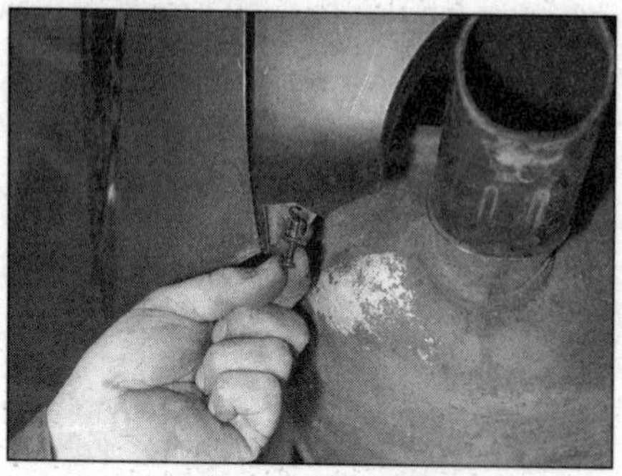

7.2a Remove the fastener from each end . . .

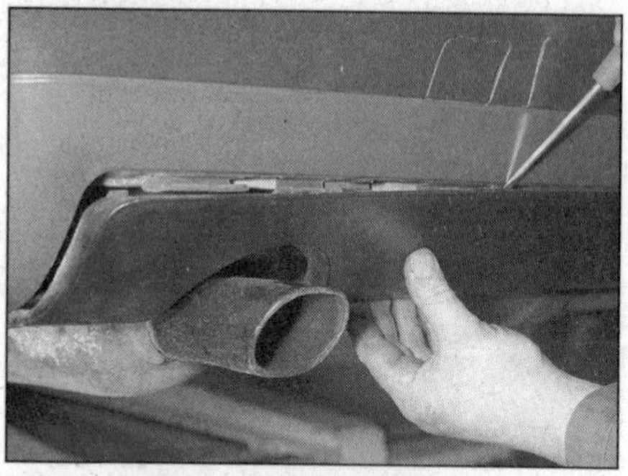

7.2b . . . and unclip the trim panel from the base of the rear bumper

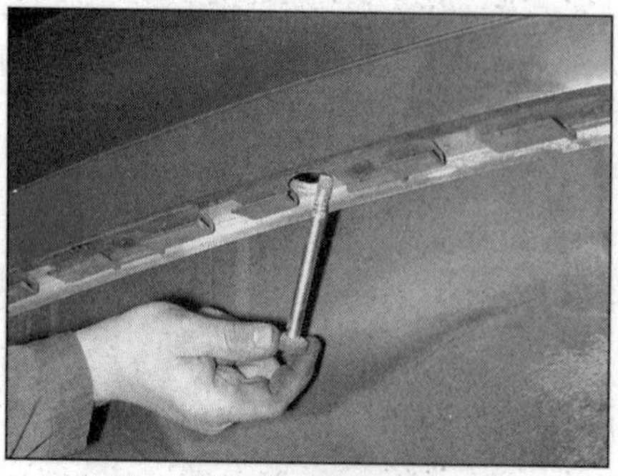

7.4a Unscrew the mounting bolts . . .

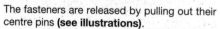

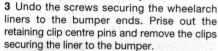

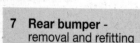

7.4b . . . and remove the bumper from the vehicle

### Refitting

**5** Refitting is a reverse of the removal procedure ensuring that the bumper ends are correctly engaged with their slides. Apply locking compound to the bumper mounting bolts and tighten them securely.

## 8 Bonnet - removal, refitting and adjustment

### Removal

**Note:** *The bonnet can be raised to the near-vertical position to enable improved access when carrying out work in the engine compartment. To fully raise the bonnet, proceed as follows.* ***Caution: Do not operate the windscreen wipers with the bonnet in the fully open position, as the wiper blades will foul the bonnet.***

*a) On Saloon models, either release the safety catch(es), or remove the safety bolt(s) (as applicable) from the bonnet strut upper mounting brackets. Lift the bonnet, and pivot the mounting bracket hinges down over the dead-centre point to lock the bonnet in the fully open (near vertical) position. Check that the bonnet is locked securely in position.*

*b) On Coupe models, have an assistant hold the bonnet in the open position, then release the securing catches and remove the bonnet struts (see Section 16). Unbolt the bonnet hinge earth strap(s), then remove the safety bolts from the bonnet hinges. Lift the bonnet and pull the hinge levers forwards to raise the bonnet to the fully open (near vertical) position. Support the bonnet in this position using two strong metal rods shaped to engage in the slots provided in the bonnet and body panels.*

**1** Open the bonnet and have an assistant support it. Using a pencil or felt tip pen, mark the outline of each bonnet hinge relative to the bonnet, to use as a guide on refitting.

**2** Disconnect the hose from the washer jets. On models with heated jets also disconnect the wiring connectors and free the wiring from the bonnet.

**3** With the aid of an assistant, support the bonnet in the open position then remove the retaining clips and detach the support struts from the bonnet.

**4** Slacken and remove the left and right-hand hinge to bonnet rear bolts and loosen the front bolts. Slide the bonnet forwards to disengage it from the hinges and remove it from the vehicle. Recover any shims which are fitted between the hinge and bonnet.

**5** Inspect the bonnet hinges for signs of wear and free play at the pivots, and if necessary renew. Each hinge is secured to the body by two bolts. Mark the position of the hinge on the body then undo the retaining bolts and remove it from the vehicle. On refitting, align the new hinge with the marks and securely tighten the retaining bolts.

### Refitting and adjustment

**6** Fit the shims (where fitted) to the hinge and, with the aid of an assistant, engage the bonnet with the hinges. Refit the rear bolts and tighten them by hand only. Align the hinges with the marks made on removal, then tighten the retaining bolts securely.

**7** Close the bonnet, and check for alignment with the adjacent panels. If necessary, slacken the hinge bolts and re-align the bonnet to suit. Once the bonnet is correctly aligned, securely tighten the hinge bolts. Once the bonnet is correctly aligned, check that the bonnet fastens and releases satisfactorily.

## 9 Bonnet release cable - removal and refitting

### Removal

**1** The bonnet release cable is in two sections, the main cable linking the release lever to the first lock assembly and the joining cable which links both lock assemblies.

**2** Remove the driver's side bonnet lock as described in Section 10.

**3** To remove the main cable, work back along the length of the cable, noting its correct routing, and free it from the retaining clips and ties. Tie a length of string to the end of the cable. From inside the vehicle, undo the two retaining screws then unclip and remove the driver's side lower facia panel. Undo the retaining screw and remove the bonnet release lever. Peel the door sealing strip away from the footwell side panel then release the trim panel fastener by rotating it through 90°. Unclip the panel. Undo the two retaining bolts and withdraw the cable assembly from the bulkhead **(see illustrations)**. Once the cable is free, untie the string and leave it in position in the vehicle; the string can then be used to draw the new cable back into position.

**4** To remove the joining cable, remove the second lock assembly (see Section 10) then release the cable from its retaining clips and remove it from the vehicle.

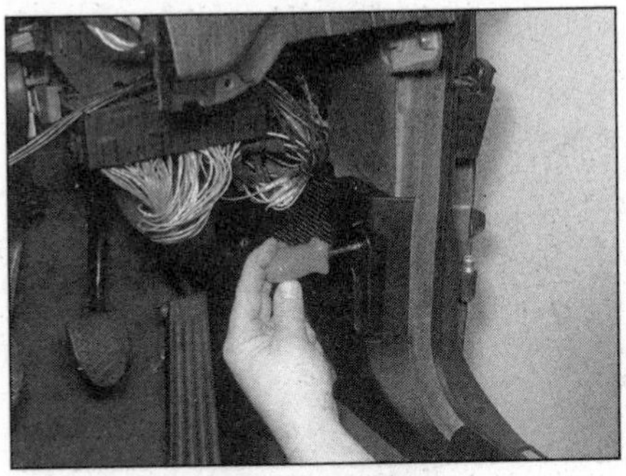

**9.3a Undo the retaining screw . . .**

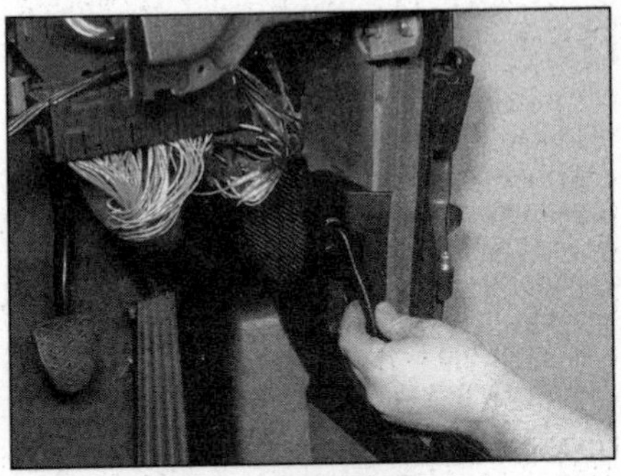

**9.3b . . . and remove the bonnet release lever**

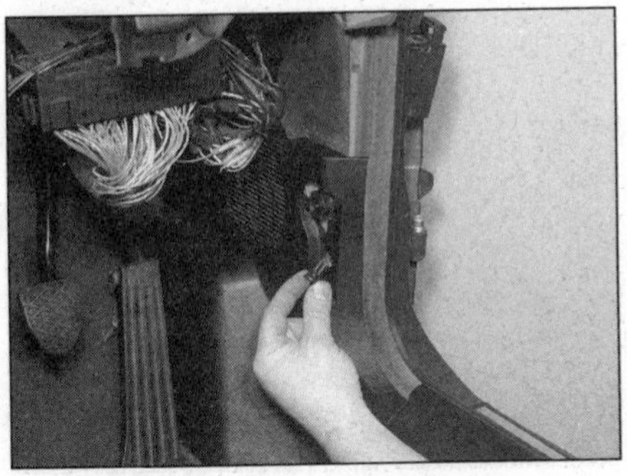

**9.3c Remove the panel fastener . . .**

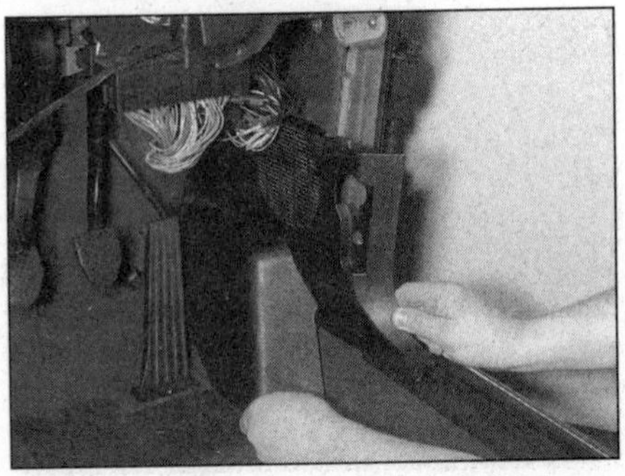

**9.3d . . . then unclip the panel and remove it from the driver's side footwell**

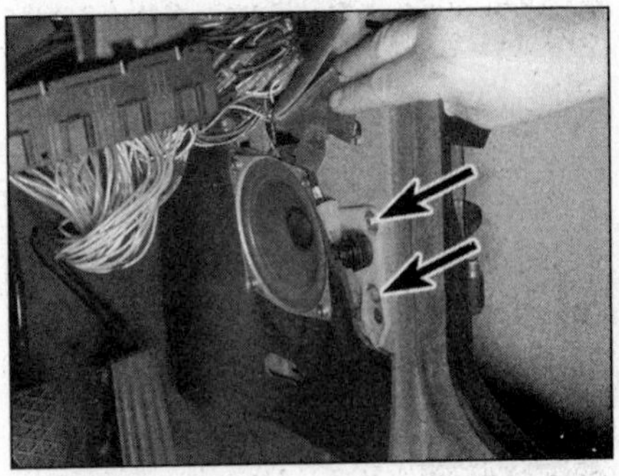

**9.3e Undo two bolts (arrowed) and withdraw the release cable from bulkhead**

### Refitting

**5** Refitting is the reverse of removal ensuring that the cable is correctly routed, and secured to all the relevant retaining clips. Refit the bonnet lock and adjust the cable as described in Section 10.

## 10 Bonnet lock(s) - removal and refitting

### Removal

**1** Open up the bonnet then undo the retaining screws and remove the plastic cover from the centre of the bonnet lock crossmember.

**2** To gain access to the rear of the lock(s), remove the radiator described in Chapter 3. Undo the retaining screws then release the clips and withdraw the radiator cooling duct.

**3** Using a suitable marker pen, mark the outline of the relevant bonnet lock retaining screws on the crossmember.

**4** Slacken and remove the lock retaining screws then free the release outer cable(s) from the lock lever then detach the inner cable(s) from the lock bracket and remove the lock from the vehicle.

### Refitting

**5** Locate the bonnet release inner cable(s) in the lock bracket and reconnect the outer cable(s) to the lever. Seat the lock on the crossmember.

**6** Align the lock with the marks made prior to removal then refit the bolts and tighten them securely.

**7** Check that the locks operate smoothly when the release lever is moved, without any sign of undue resistance. Check that the bonnet fastens and releases satisfactorily. If necessary, adjust the cable using the threaded adjuster which is located in the centre of the joining cable.

**8** Once the locks are operating correctly, refit the cooling duct and panel and install the radiator as described in Chapter 3.

## 11 Door - removal, refitting and adjustment

### Removal

**1** Disconnect the battery negative terminal.

**2** Open up the door and slacken and remove the bolts securing the wiring connector block to the pillar. Withdraw the connector, then release the securing clip by pulling it upwards and disconnect the wiring **(see illustrations)**.

**3** Slide off the retaining clip and withdraw the pivot pin securing the check link to the pillar. Where the check link is secured in position with a roll pin, tap the pin out of position with a hammer and punch. Recover the rubber from the door pillar **(see illustration)**.

**4** Unscrew the hinge pivot bolts from both the upper and lower door hinges **(see illustration)**.

**5** With the aid of an assistant, lift the door upwards and away from the vehicle.

**6** Examine the hinges for signs of wear or damage. If renewal is necessary, mark the position of the hinge(s) then undo the retaining bolts and remove them from the vehicle. Recover any shims which are fitted between the hinge and door/pillar (where fitted). Fit the new hinge(s), complete with shims (where fitted), align with the marks made before removal and lightly tighten the retaining bolts.

### Refitting

**7** Ensure the hinge pins are clean and apply a smear of fresh multi-purpose to them.

**8** Manoeuvre the door into position and engage it with the hinges.

**9** Slide the rubber onto the check link then align the link with its bracket and refit the pivot pin and retaining clip/roll pin (as applicable). Seat the rubber on the door pillar **(see illustration)**.

**10** Reconnect the door wiring connector, and fasten the securing clip. Seat the connector block in the pillar and securely tighten its retaining bolts.

**11** Check the door alignment and if necessary adjust, then reconnect the battery negative terminal. If the paintwork around the hinges has been damaged, paint the affected area with a suitable touch-in brush to prevent corrosion.

### Adjustment

**12** Close the door and check the door alignment with surrounding body panels. If necessary, slight adjustment of the door position can be made by slackening the hinge retaining bolts and repositioning the hinge/ door as necessary. Once the door is correctly positioned, securely tighten the hinge bolts. If the paint work around the hinges has been damaged, paint the affected area with a suitable touch-in brush to prevent corrosion.

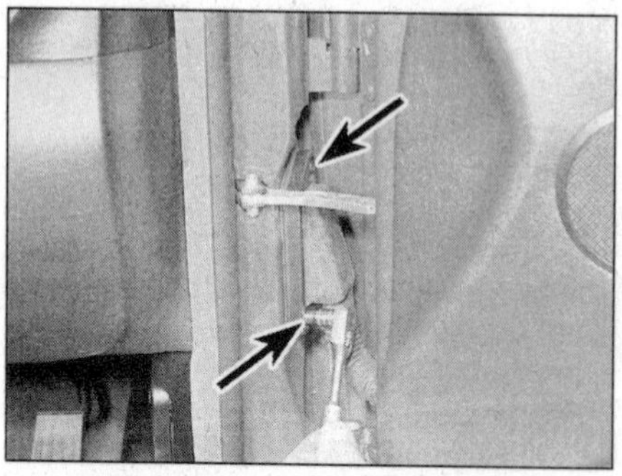

**11.2a Undo the retaining screws (arrowed) . . .**

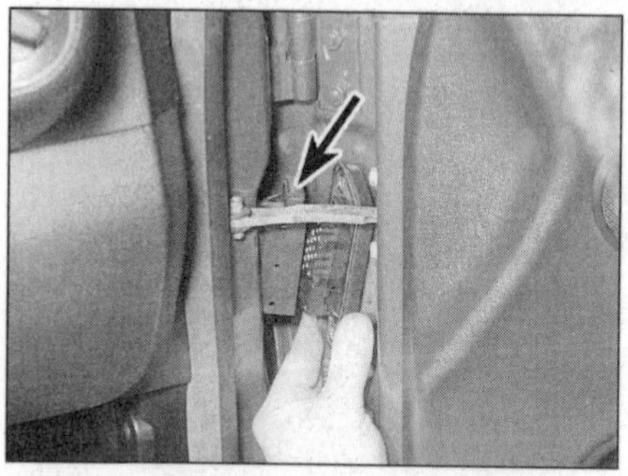

**11.2b . . . then lift up the clip (arrowed) and disconnect the door wiring connector**

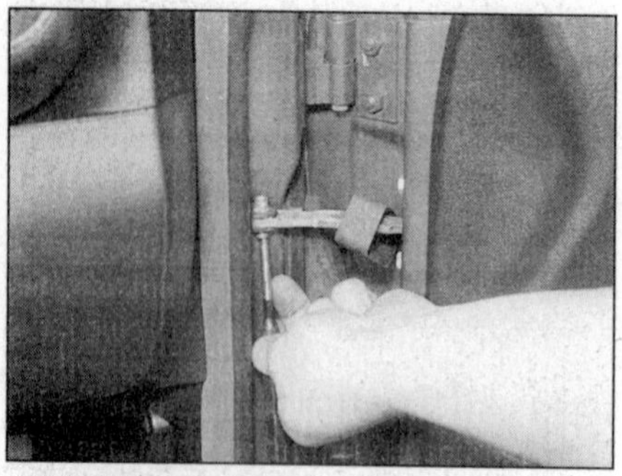

**11.3 Where the check link is held in with a roll pin, tap it out with a hammer and punch**

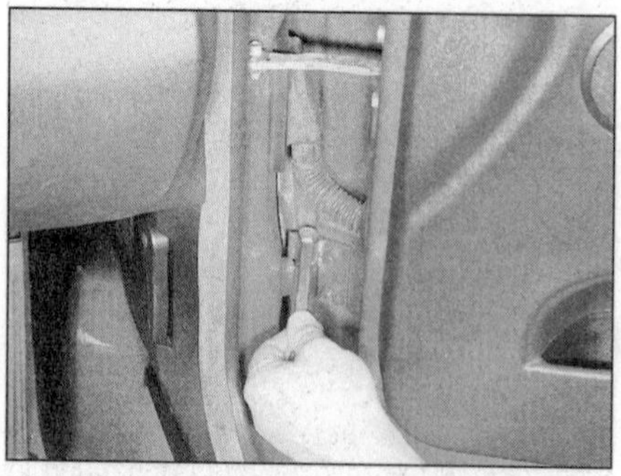

**11.4 Unscrew the hinge pivot bolts then lift the door upwards and away from the car**

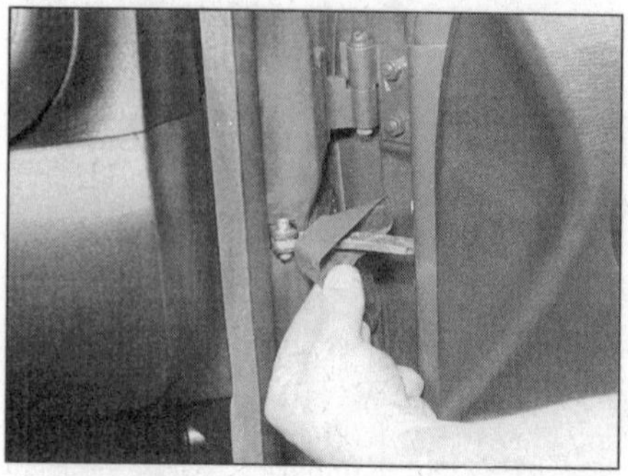

**11.9 Secure the check link in position and seat the rubber on the door pillar**

12.3a On models with manual windows, prise off the trim cover . . .

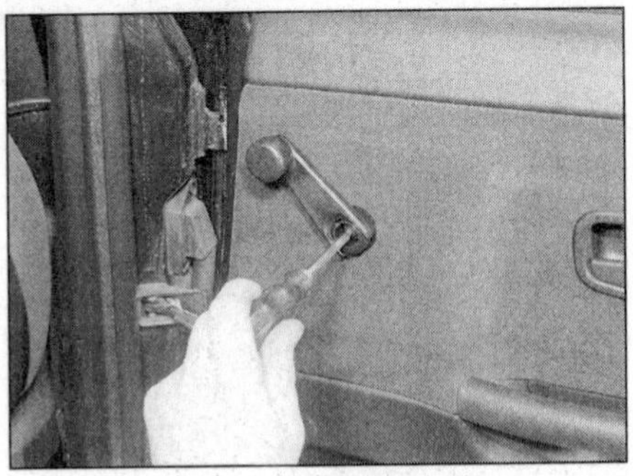

12.3b . . . then undo the retaining screw . . .

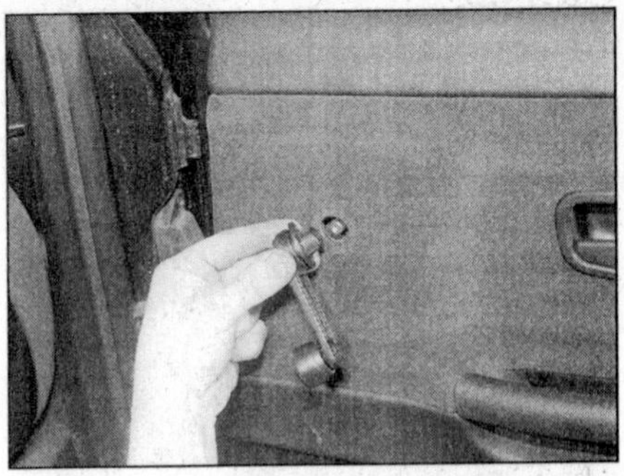

12.3c . . . and remove the regulator handle and spacer from the door

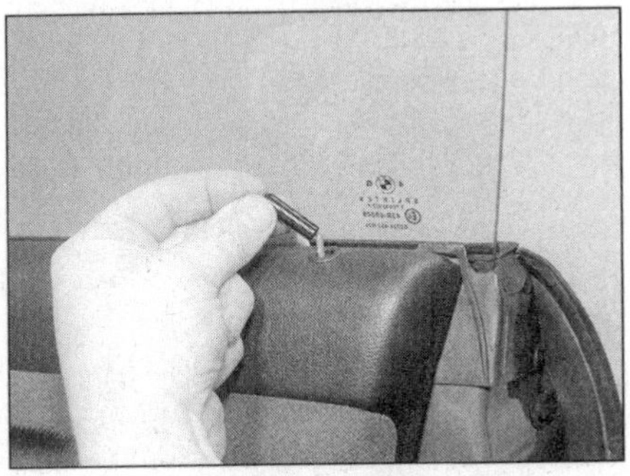

12.4 Removing the lock inner operating knob

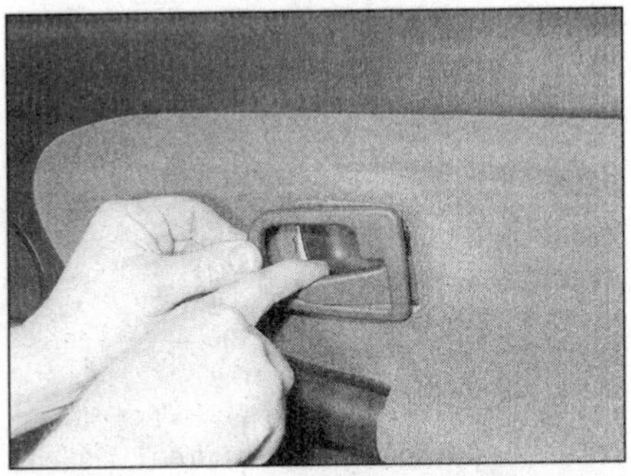

12.5 Removing the inner handle trim cover

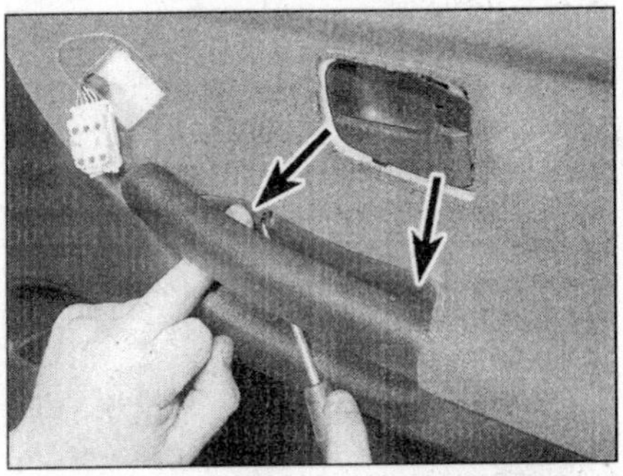

12.6a Prise out the trim caps (arrowed) . . .

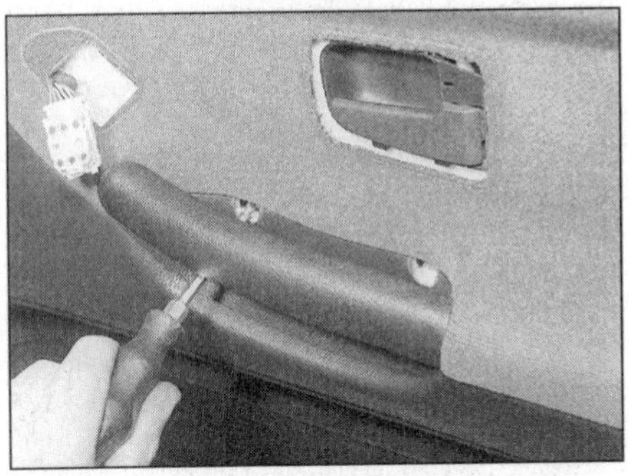

12.6b . . . then undo the retaining screws

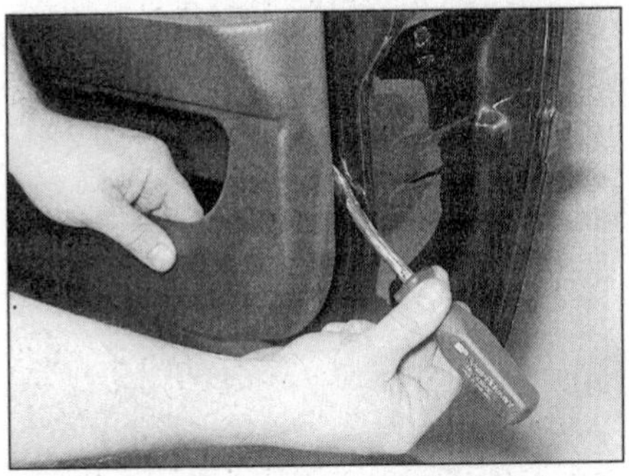

12.7a Carefully unclip the trim panel and remove it from the door . . .

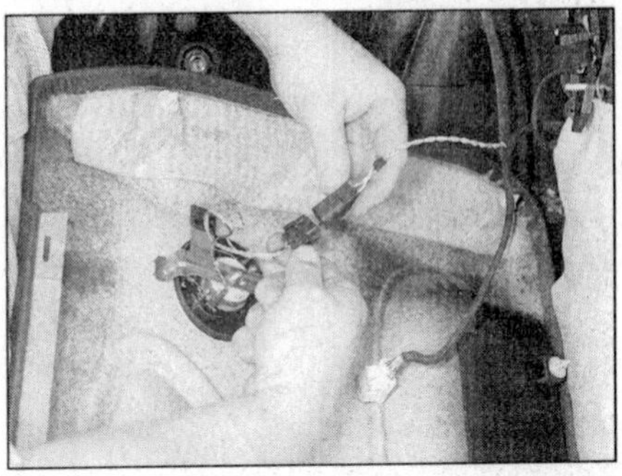

12.7b . . . disconnecting the wiring from the speakers

## 12 Door inner trim panel - removal and refitting

### *Removal*

#### Front door

**1** Disconnect the battery negative terminal then open the door.

**2** On models with electrical mirrors remove the mirror switch (driver's door only) as described in Chapter 12, Section 4.

**3** On models with manual windows, unclip the trim cover from the regulator handle then undo the screw and remove the handle and spacer **(see illustrations)**.

**4** Unscrew and pull off the door lock inner operating knob from its rod **(see illustration)**.

**5** Lift the door lock inner handle and unclip the trim cover from around the handle by sliding it forwards **(see illustration)**.

**6** Unclip the trim caps from the door handle and slacken and remove the handle screws **(see illustrations)**.

**7** Release the door trim panel clips, carefully levering between the panel and door with a flat-bladed screwdriver. Work around the outside of the panel, and when all the studs are released, ease the panel away from the door, disconnecting the wiring connector the speaker as it becomes accessible **(see illustrations)**.

#### Rear door

**8** Disconnect the battery negative terminal then remove the trim panel as described in paragraphs 3 to 7, unclipping the panel from the top first.

### *Refitting*

**9** Refitting of the trim panel is the reverse of removal. Before refitting, check whether any of the trim panel retaining clips were broken on removal, and renew them as necessary.

## 13 Door handle and lock components - removal and refitting

### *Removal*

**1** Remove the door inner trim panel as described in Section 12. Carefully peel the plastic weathershield off from the door to gain access to the lock components and continue as described under the relevant sub-heading **(see illustration)**. If the weathershield is damaged on removal it must be renewed.

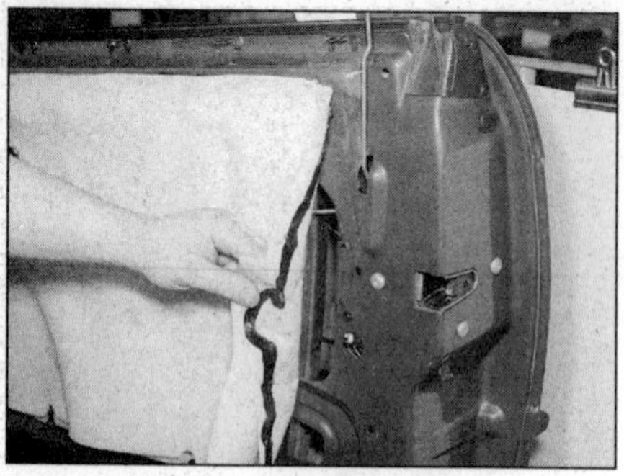

13.1 Carefully peel the weathershield away from the door

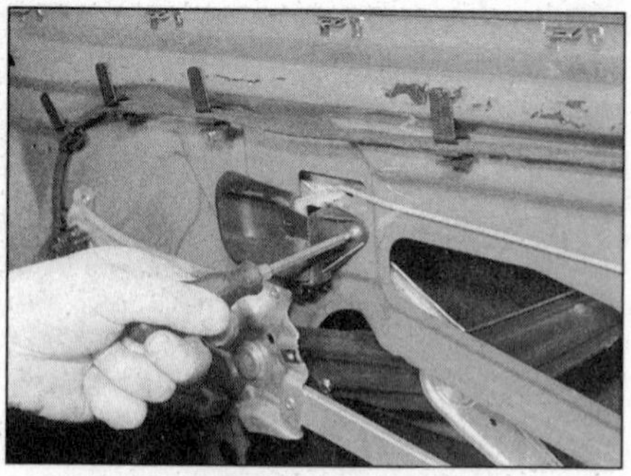

13.2a Undo the retaining screw . . .

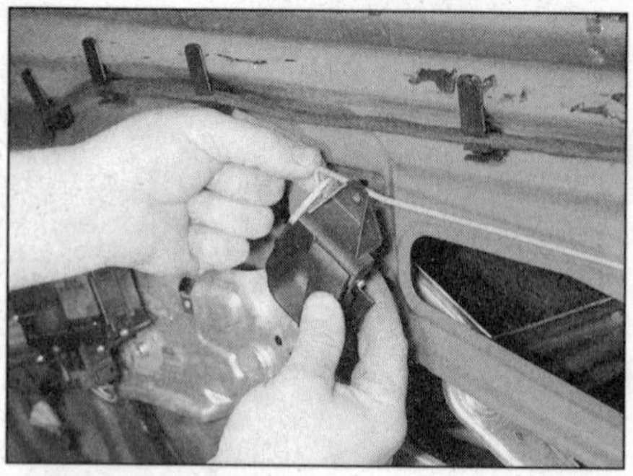

13.2b . . . then detach the interior handle from the link rod and remove it

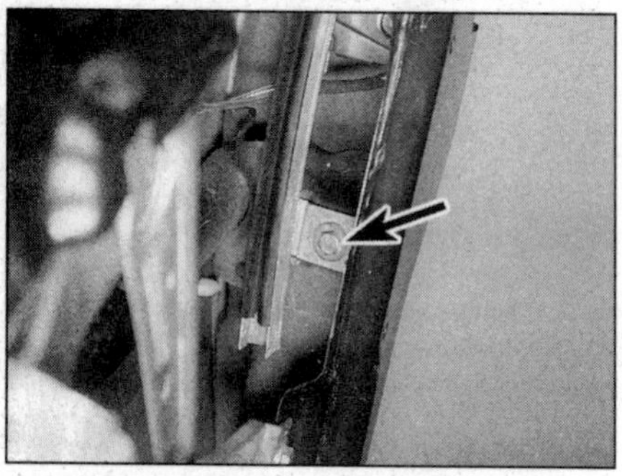

13.4a On Saloon models, undo the retaining bolt (arrowed) . . .

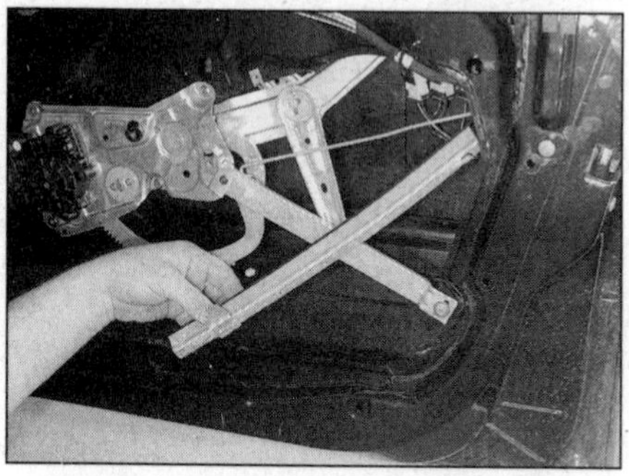

13.4b . . . and remove the window rear guide rail from the door

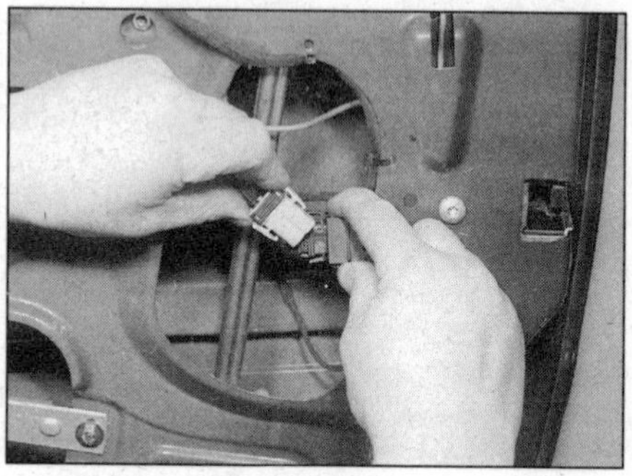

13.5 Disconnect the wiring connectors from the door lock

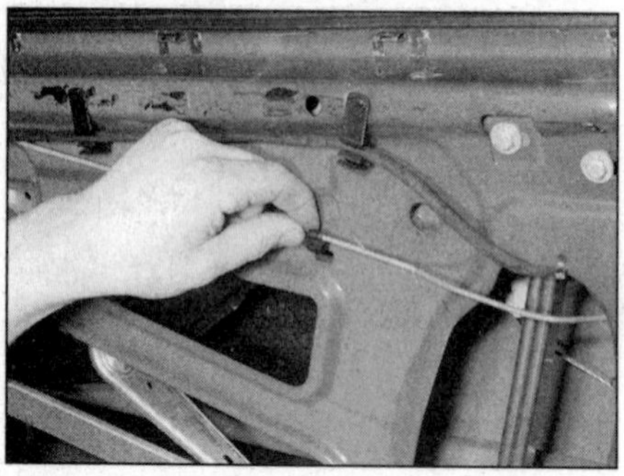

13.6 Release the link rod guide from the door . . .

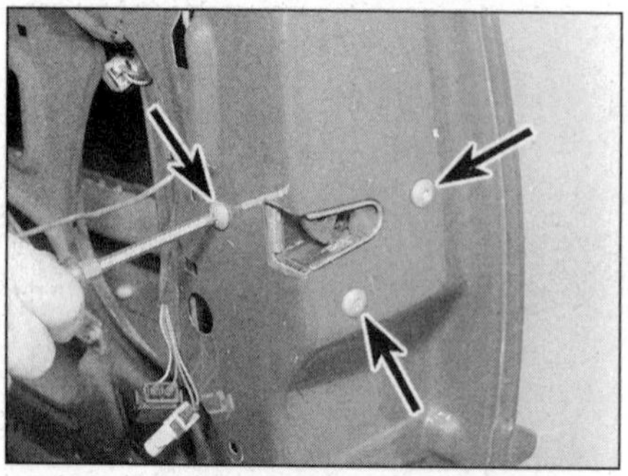

13.7a . . . then undo the retaining screws (arrowed) . . .

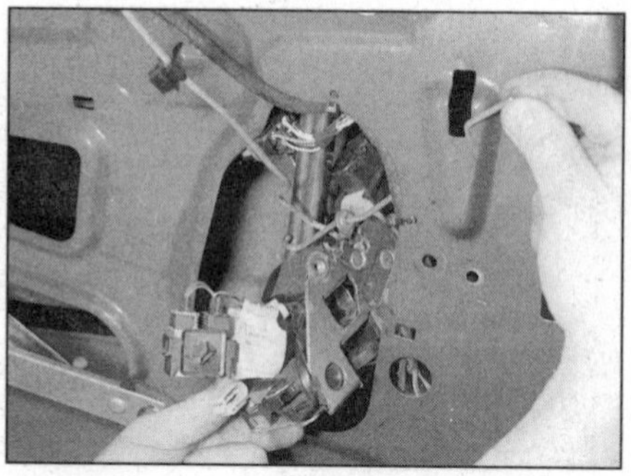

13.7b . . . and manoeuvre the lock assembly out of position (Coupe shown)

## Interior door handle

**2** Undo the retaining screw then free the handle from the link rod and remove it from the door **(see illustrations)**.

## Front door lock assembly

**3** Undo the retaining screw and remove the interior door handle from the door.

**4** On Saloon models, slacken and remove the window rear guide rail retaining bolt then unhook the rail and remove it from the door **(see illustrations)**.

**5** Release the lock assembly wiring retaining clips and disconnect the wiring connector(s) **(see illustration)**.

**6** Unhook the lock cylinder link rod from the rear of the lock. Unclip the interior handle link rod guide from the door so the rod is free to be removed with the lock assembly **(see illustration)**.

**7** Slacken and remove the lock assembly retaining screws then detach the lock assembly from the exterior handle linkage and manoeuvre it out from the door **(see illustrations)**.

## Front door exterior handle

**Note:** *Since the exterior handle cannot be removed without first removing the window glass. On Coupe models this task should be entrusted to a BMW dealer (see Section 15). With the glass removed the lock is removed and refitted as described below.*

**8** Remove the window glass as described in Section 14.

**9** Remove the lock assembly as described in paragraphs 3 to 7.

**10** Prise out the rubber plug from the rear edge of the door to gain access to the door handle cover retaining clip **(see illustration)**.

**11** Insert a screwdriver or piece of wire in through the door access hole then release the handle trim cover clip by pushing it into the door. Remove the handle trim cover and seal from the outside of the door **(see illustrations)**.

13.10 Remove the rubber plug from the rear edge of the door . . .

13.11a . . . then release the retaining clip with a piece of wire/screwdriver . . .

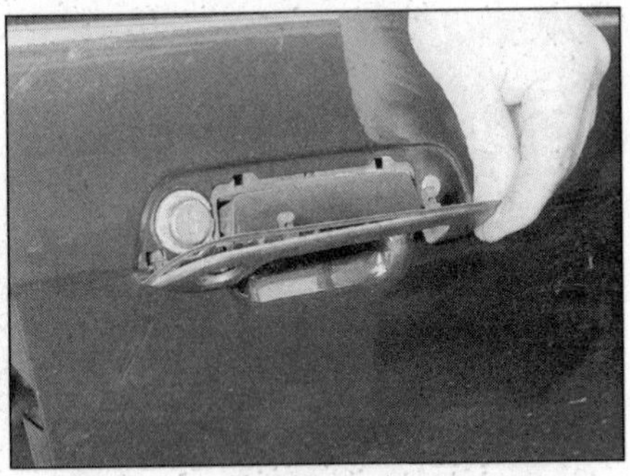

13.11b . . . and remove the handle trim cover and seal

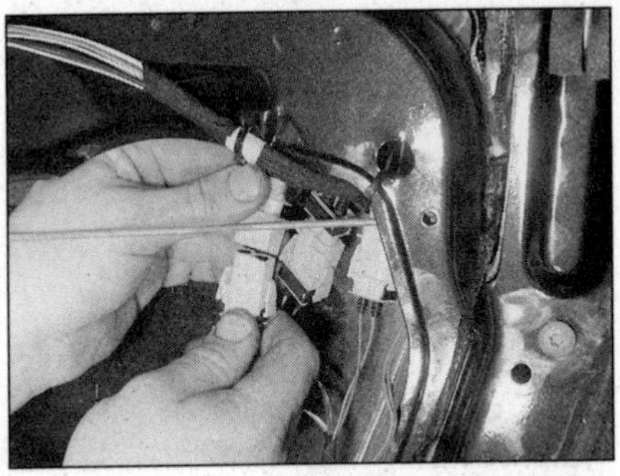

13.12 Disconnect the wiring connectors from the handle

13.13a Slide off the retaining clip (arrowed) . . .

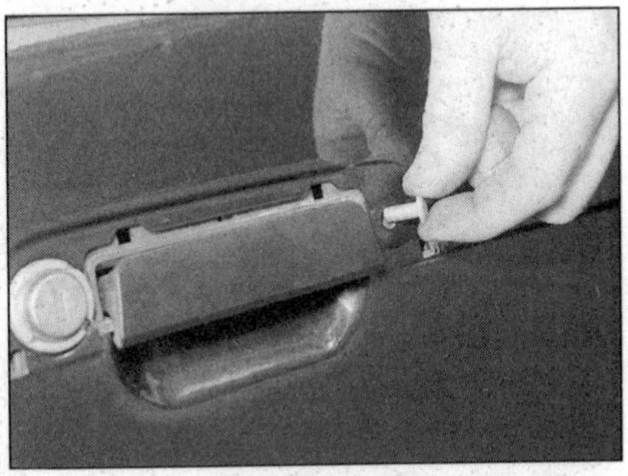

13.13b . . . and withdraw the handle retaining pin

13.14 Unscrew the handle ring nut using a suitable pair of circlip pliers

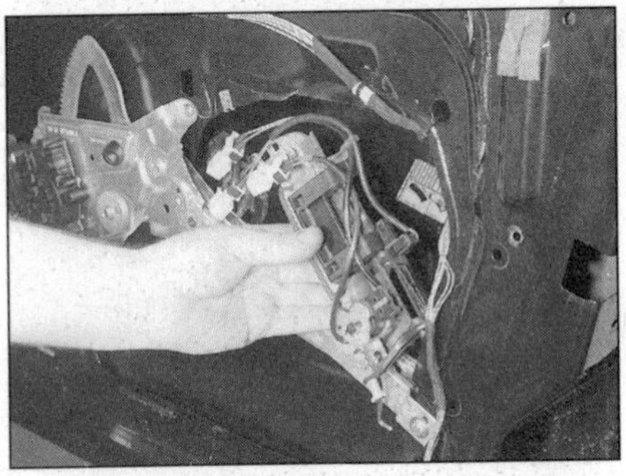

13.15 Removing the exterior handle from the door

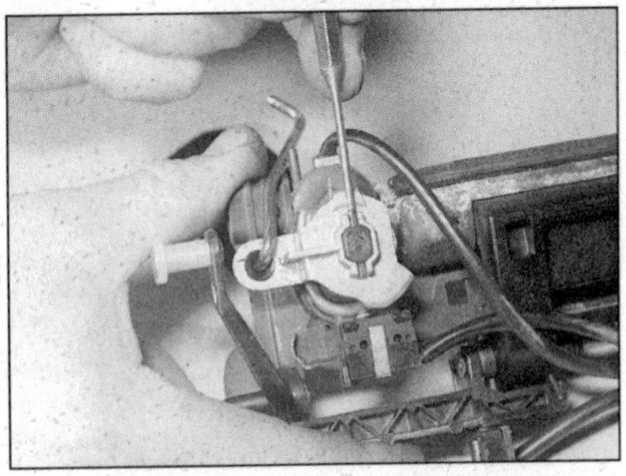

13.17a Tap out the roll pin . . .

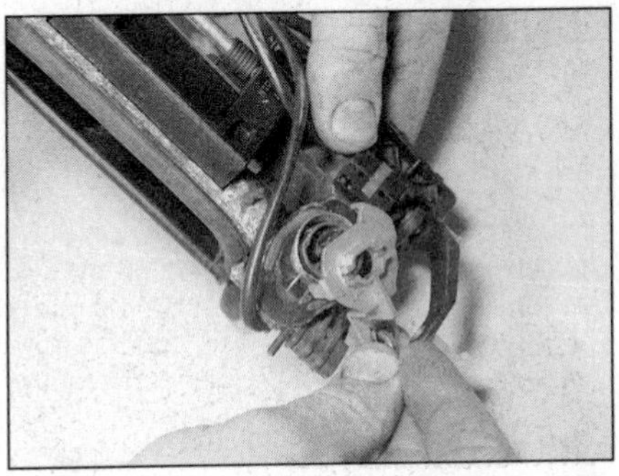

13.17b . . . then remove the retaining plate from the rear of the handle . . .

**12** Where necessary, disconnect the wiring connector(s) from the handle assembly **(see illustration)**.

**13** Slide off the retaining clip and withdraw the handle retaining pin **(see illustrations)**.

**14** Using a pair of circlip pliers, unscrew the ring nut from the outside of the lock cylinder and recover the rubber seal **(see illustration)**.

**15** Manoeuvre the handle assembly out from inside the door **(see illustration)**.

## Front door lock cylinder

**16** Remove the exterior handle as described in paragraphs 8 to 15.

**17** With the key in the lock, tap out the roll pin and remove the retaining plate and link rod plate from the rear of the lock cylinder, noting their correct fitted locations **(see illustrations)**.

**18** Withdraw the lock cylinder from the lock assembly **(see illustration)**. Recover the sealing ring from the cylinder and renew it if it is damaged.

## Rear door lock

**19** Remove the window glass as described in Section 14.

**20** Remove the sealing strip (if not already done so) then slacken and remove the window guide rail retaining screw and bolts and reposition the guide clear of the lock.

**21** Slacken and remove the retaining screw and remove the interior door handle from the link rod.

**22** Undo the screw securing the link rod pivot to the door and unhook it from the link rod. Release the link rod guide from the door so the rod is free to be removed with the lock **(see illustrations)**.

**23** Where necessary, release the retaining clip and disconnect the wiring connector from the lock.

**24** Slacken and remove the retaining screws then detach the lock assembly from the handle and remove it from the door **(see illustrations)**.

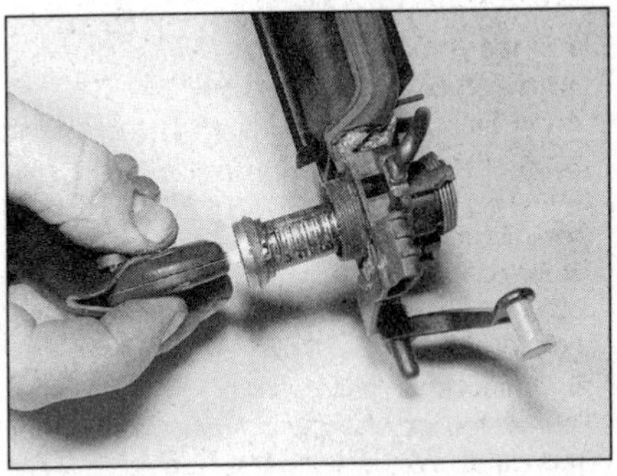

13.18 . . . and withdraw the lock cylinder

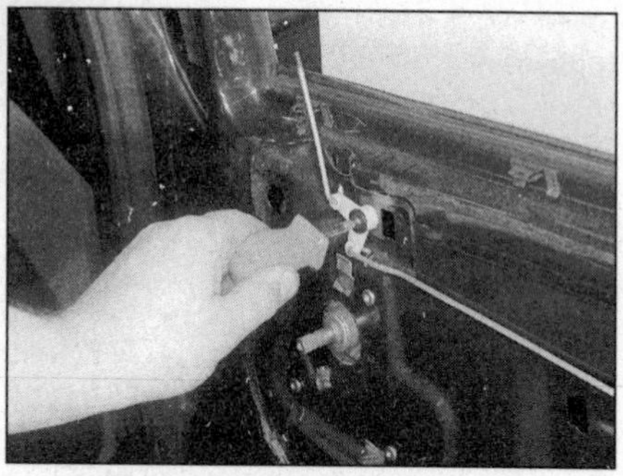

13.22a Undo the retaining screw . . .

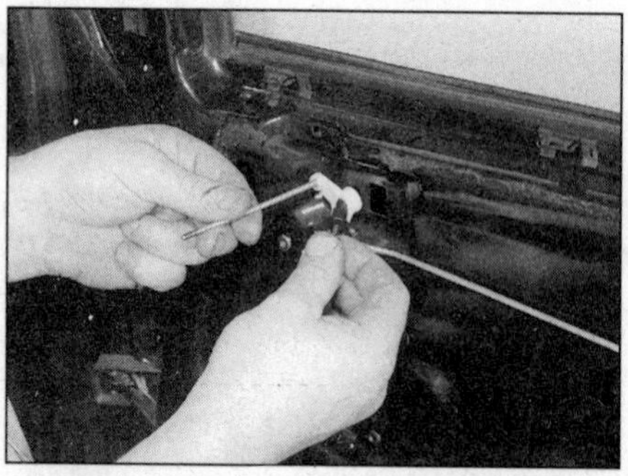

13.22b . . . then detach the link rod pivot and remove it from the door

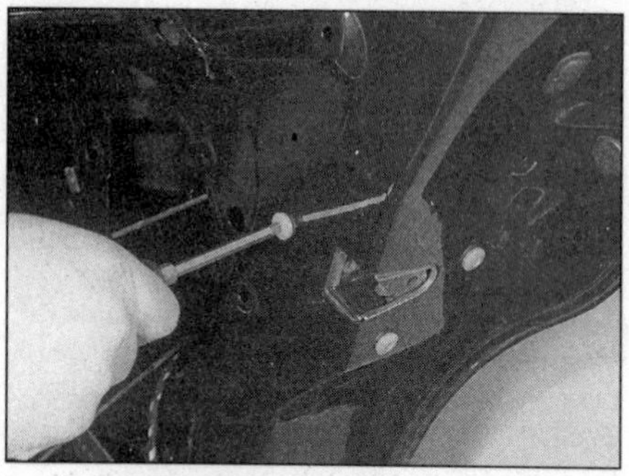

13.24a Slacken and remove the three retaining screws . . .

13.24b . . . and manoeuvre the lock assembly out from the door

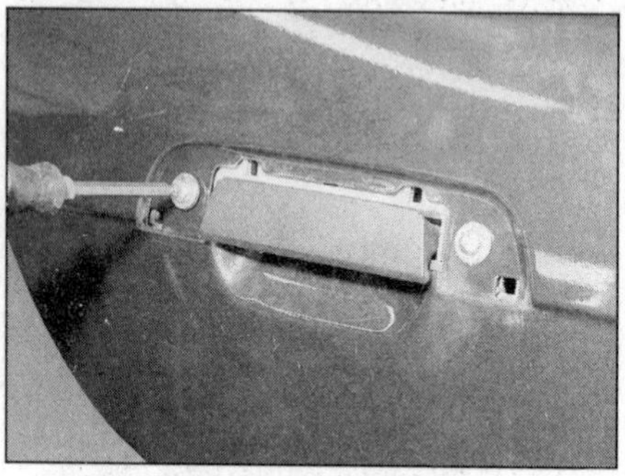

13.28a Slacken and remove the two retaining screws and seals . . .

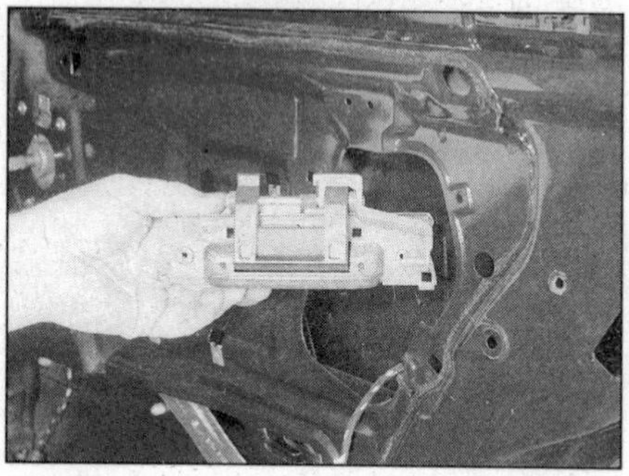

13.28b . . . and remove handle assembly from the rear door - Saloon models

## Rear door exterior handle

25 Remove the lock assembly as described above in paragraphs 19 to 24.
26 Prise out the rubber plug from the rear edge of the door to gain access to the door handle cover retaining clip.
27 Insert a screwdriver in through the door aperture and release the handle trim cover retaining clip by pushing it into the door. Remove the handle trim cover and seal from the outside of the door.
28 Slacken and remove the retaining screws and seals and remove the handle assembly from the door **(see illustrations)**.

## *Refitting*

### Interior door handle

29 Engage the handle with the link rod and securely tighten its retaining screw. Make sure the handle operates correctly then stick the weathershield to the door and refit the trim panel as described in Section 12.

### Front door lock assembly

30 Prior to refitting, remove all traces of old locking compound from the lock retaining screws.
31 Manoeuvre the lock assembly into position making sure all the link rods are correctly positioned. Hook the lock onto the exterior handle linkage and reconnect the link rod(s).
32 Apply fresh locking compound to the lock screws (BMW recommend Loctite 270) then refit them and tighten them to the specified torque.
33 Reconnect the wiring connector(s) and secure the wiring in position with the relevant clips.
34 On Saloon models, hook the top of the guide rail into the door and secure it in position with the retaining bolt.
35 Clip the link rod guide into the door then refit the interior handle and securely tighten the retaining screw.
36 Check the operation of the lock assembly then stick the plastic weathershield to the door. Refit the trim panel as described in Section 12.

### Front door exterior handle

37 Manoeuvre the handle assembly into position. Fit the rubber seal and ring nut to the lock cylinder and tighten it securely.
38 Fit the handle pin and secure it in position with the retaining clip.
39 Reconnect the handle wiring connectors (where necessary) and clip the trim cover into position.
40 Fit the handle trim cover and seal to the door and secure it in position by pulling the retaining clip back using a hooked piece of wire. Make sure the trim cover is securely held and refit the rubber plug to the door.
41 Refit the lock assembly as described in paragraphs 30 to 36.

### Front door lock cylinder

42 Lubricate the outside of the lock cylinder with a suitable grease.
43 Fit a new sealing ring to the lock cylinder and insert the cylinder into the handle **(see illustration)**.
44 Refit the link rod plate and retaining plate to the rear of the lock cylinder. Make sure all components are correctly fitted and secure them in position with the roll pin.
45 Refit the exterior handle as described in paragraphs 37 to 41.

### Rear door lock

46 Prior to refitting, remove all traces of old locking compound from the lock retaining screws.
47 Manoeuvre the lock assembly into position, making sure the link rods are correctly positioned, and hook it onto the exterior handle linkage.
48 Where necessary, reconnect the wiring connector(s) and secure the wiring in position with the relevant clips.
49 Apply fresh locking compound to the lock screws (BMW recommend Loctite 270) then refit them and tighten to the specified torque.

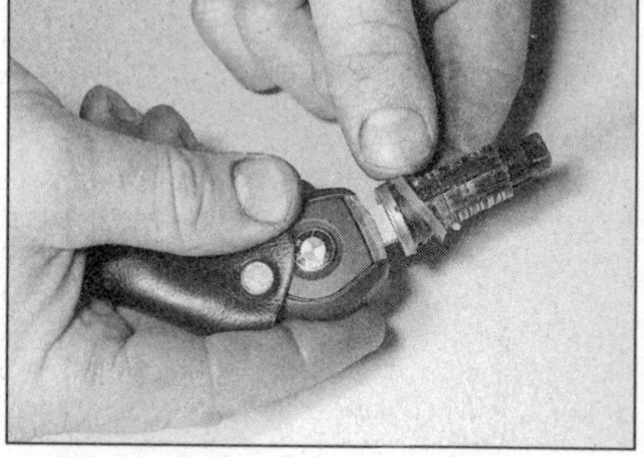

13.43 On refitting do not forget to fit the seal to the lock cylinder

**50** Clip the link rod guide into the door then refit the link rod pivot and securely tighten its retaining screw.

**51** Connect the interior handle to the link rod and securely tighten the handle retaining screw.

**52** Seat the window guide rail in position and securely tighten its retaining screw and bolts. Refit the sealing strip.

**53** Check the operation of the lock assembly then refit the window glass as described in Section 14.

### Rear door exterior handle

**54** Refit the handle assembly and tighten its retaining screws to the specified torque.

**55** Fit the handle trim cover and seal to the door and secure it in position by pulling the retaining clip back using a hooked piece of wire. Make sure the trim cover is securely held and refit the rubber plug to the door.

**56** Refit the lock assembly as described in paragraphs 46 to 53.

## 14 Door window glass and regulator (Saloon models) - removal and refitting

### *Removal*

### Front door window

**1** Fully close the window then lower it approximately 30 cm.

**2** Remove the inner trim panel (Section 12).

**3** Carefully peel the plastic weathershield away from the door panel to gain access to the window components. If the shield is damaged on removal it must be renewed.

**4** Slacken and remove the window rear guide rail retaining bolt then unhook the rail and remove it from the door **(see illustration)**.

**5** Carefully unclip the window inner sealing strip and remove it from the top of the door **(see illustration)**.

**6** On models fitted with electric windows disconnect the wiring connector from the window motor, to immobilise the motor **(see illustration)**.

**7** With the aid of an assistant, hold the window in position then slide out the retaining clips and detach the regulator arms from the glass **(see illustrations)**.

**8** Carefully manoeuvre the window glass upwards and out of the door and recover the slide from the glass guide rails **(see illustration)**.

### Front door window regulator

**9** Remove the window glass as described earlier in this Section.

**10** Undo the retaining screw securing the interior handle to the regulator then detach the handle from the link rod and remove.

**11** Slacken and remove the regulator lower retaining screw **(see illustration)**.

**12** Using a drill and 6 mm drill bit, carefully drill the heads off the regulator retaining rivets **(see illustration)**. On refitting replace the rivets with 6 mm bolts, approximately 10 mm in length, washers and nuts.

**13** Manoeuvre the regulator assembly out from the door.

### Rear door window glass

**14** Remove the door inner trim panel as described in Section 12.

**15** Peel back the window sealing strip from the front edge of the door to gain access to

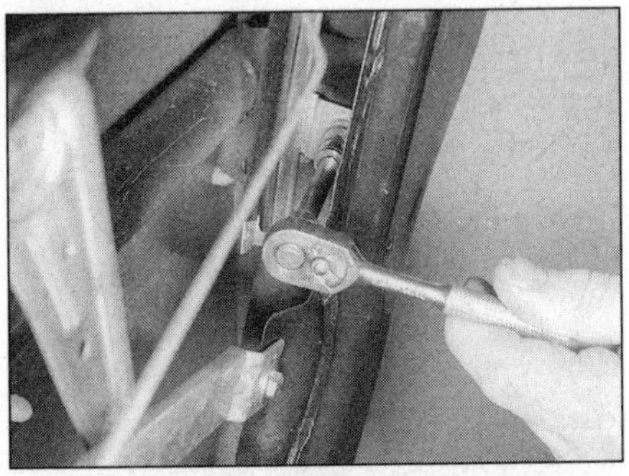

**14.4 Undo the retaining bolt and remove the window rear guide from the door**

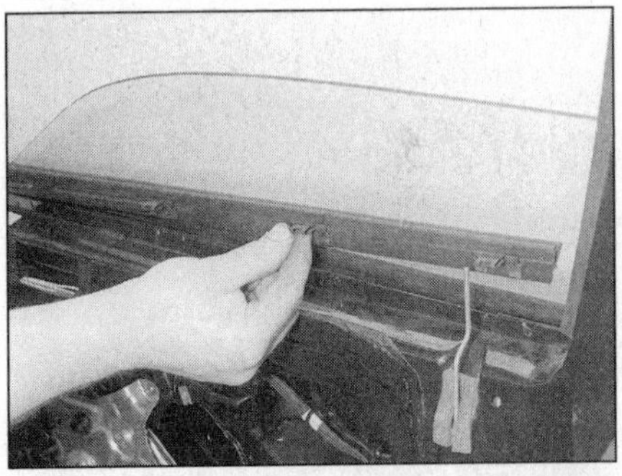

**14.5 Unclip the window inner sealing strip from the top of the door**

**14.6 On models with electric windows disconnect the motor wiring connector**

**14.7a Slide out the retaining clip . . .**

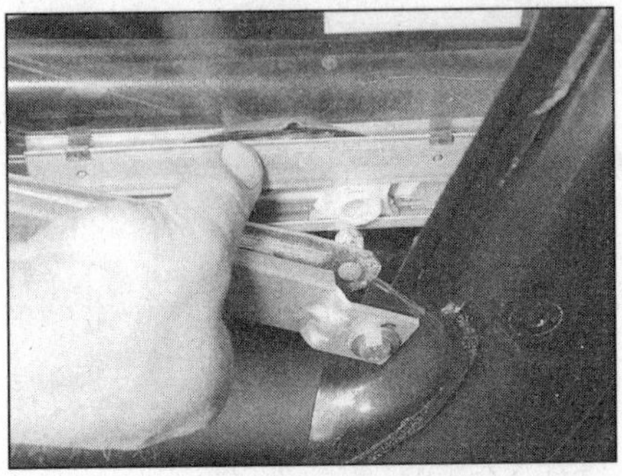

**14.7b . . . and unclip the regulator arms from window glass slides**

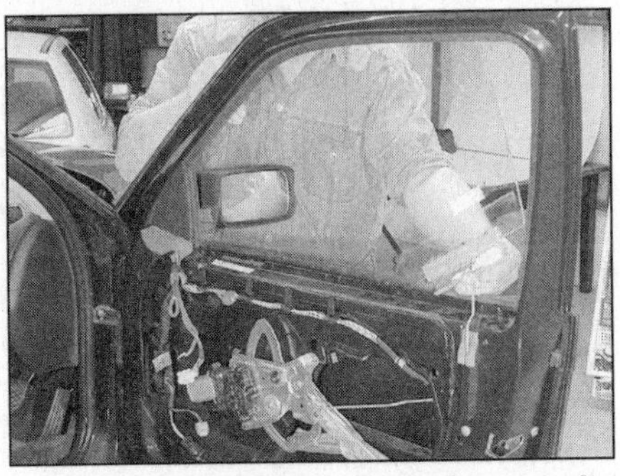

**14.8 Tilt the window glass and remove it from the front door**

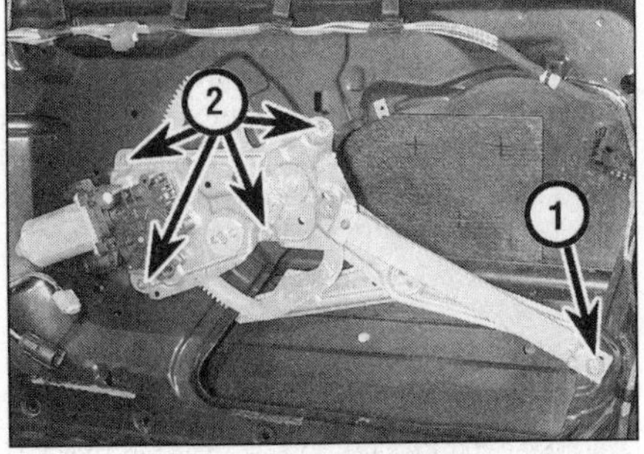


**14.11 Front window regulator retaining bolt (1) and rivets (2)**

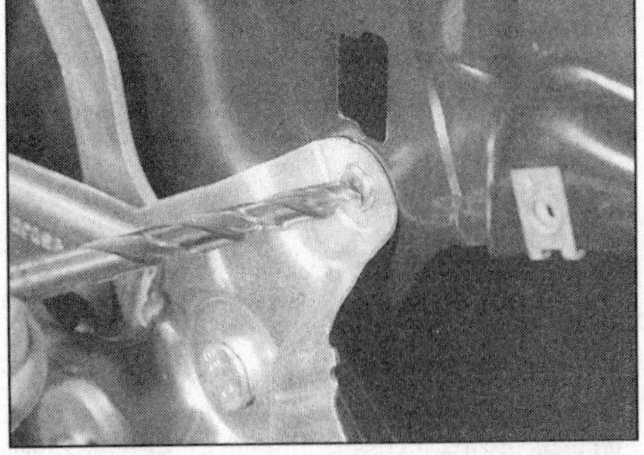

**14.12 Drill out the regulator rivets - replace with 6 mm bolts and nuts on refitting**

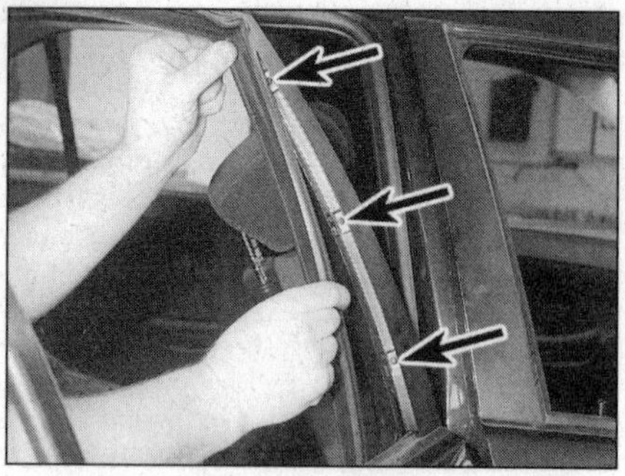

14.15a Peel the sealing strip away from the front edge of the door then undo the three retaining screws (arrowed) . . .

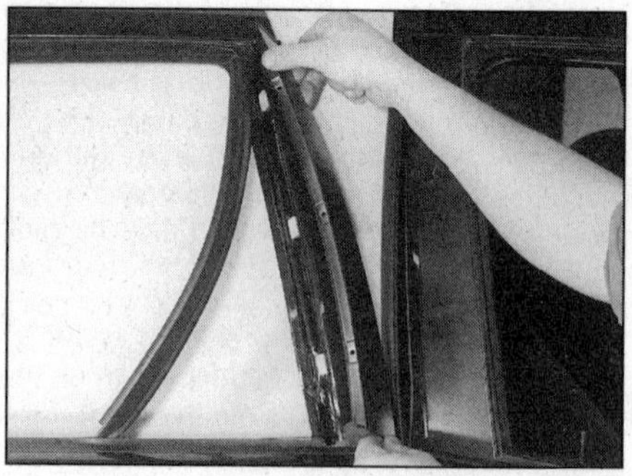

14.15b . . . and remove the window trim panels from the rear door

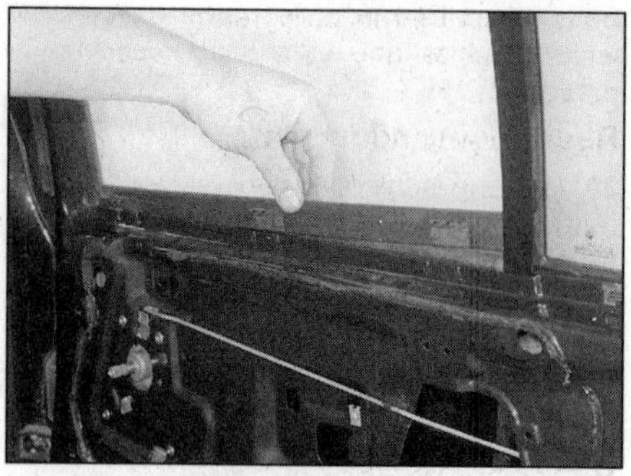

14.17 Unclip the inner sealing strip from the top of the door

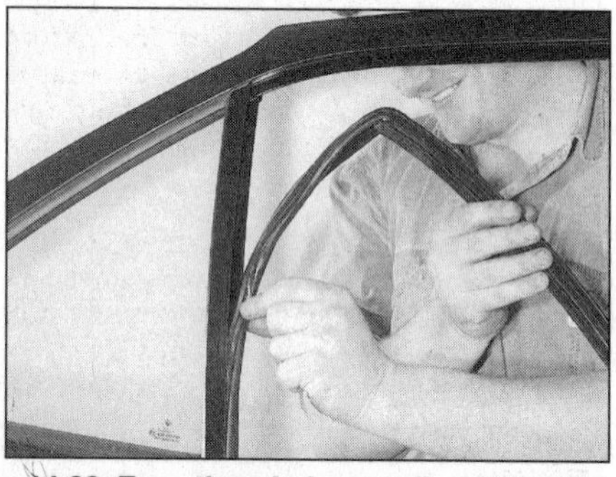

14.20 Ease the window sealing strip out from the door frame

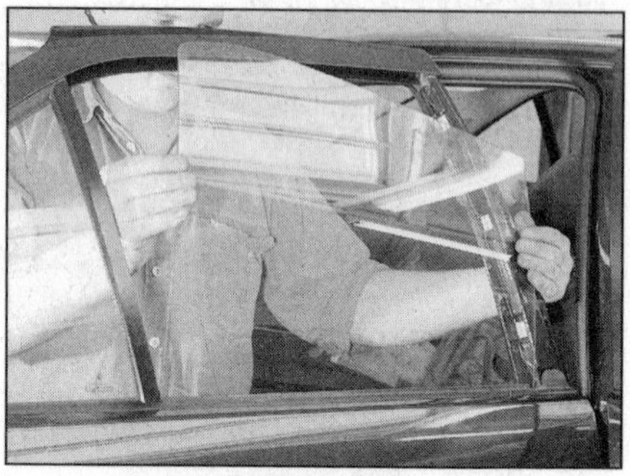

14.22 Removing the rear door window glass

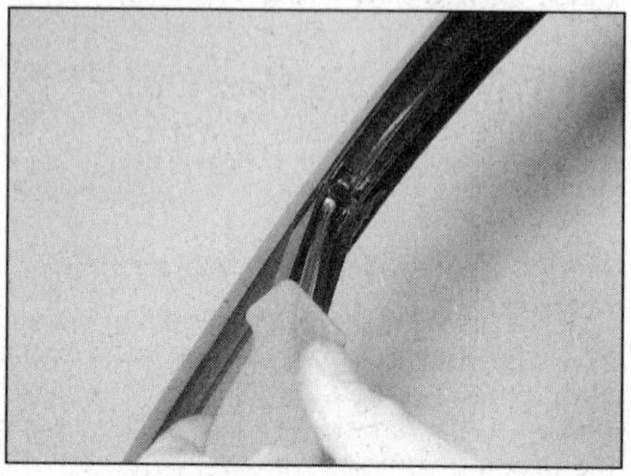

14.24a Slacken and remove the upper retaining screw . . .

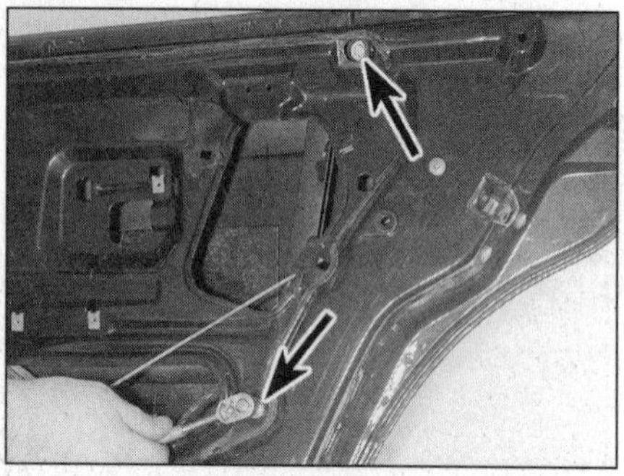

14.24b . . . and the lower retaining bolts (arrowed) . . .

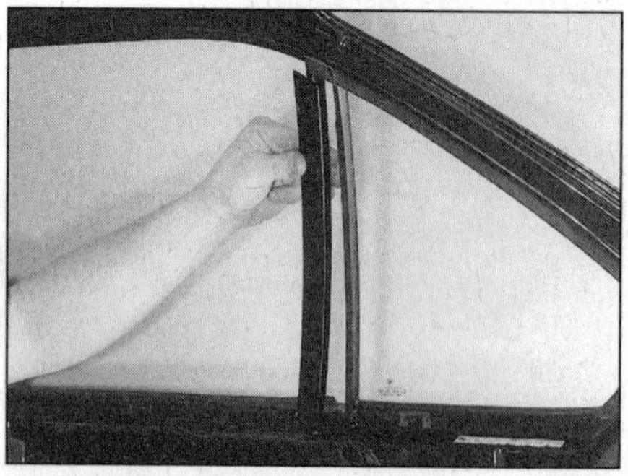

14.24c . . . and position the window guide rail clear of the fixed window

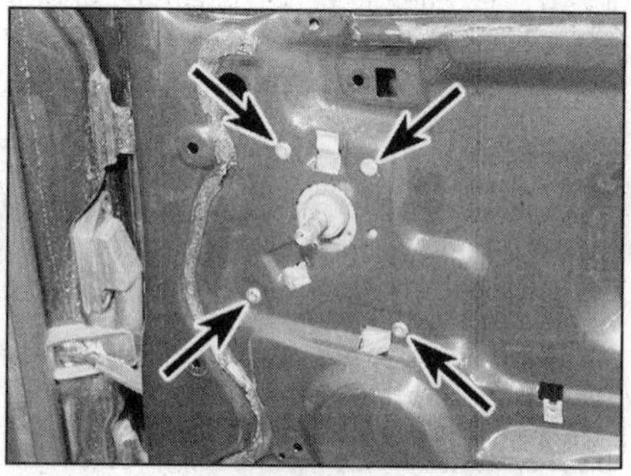

14.27 Rear window regulator retaining rivets (arrowed)

the window trim panel screws. Undo the retaining screws and remove the panel from the door **(see illustrations)**.

**16** Carefully peel the plastic weathershield away from the door panel to gain access to the window components. If the shield is damaged on removal it must be renewed.

**17** Carefully remove the window inner sealing strip from the top of the door **(see illustration)**.

**18** Lower the window so that access to the window guide clip can be gained.

**19** On models with electric windows, disconnect the wiring connector from the window motor.

**20** Carefully ease the window sealing strip out from the door frame **(see illustration)**.

**21** Slide out the retaining clip and free the regulator arm from the window guide clip **(see illustrations 14.7a and 14.7b)**.

**22** Lift the window out through the top of the door and recover the slide from the window guide.**(see illustration)**

### Rear door fixed window glass

**23** Remove the window glass as described in paragraphs 14 to 22.

**24** Remove the sealing strip (if not already done so) then slacken and remove the window guide rail retaining screw and bolts and reposition the guide clear of the fixed window **(see illustrations)**.

**25** Release the fixed window sealing strip from the door and remove the window.

### Rear door window regulator

**26** Remove the window as described in paragraphs 14 to 22.

**27** Remove the regulator as described in paragraphs 12 and 13 **(see illustration)**.

## *Refitting*

**Note:** *On models with electric windows, initialise the windows on completion (see Section 19).*

### Front door window

**28** Refitting is the reverse of removal. Make sure the regulator arms are securely clipped in position. Prior to fitting the weathershield, operate the window and check that it moves easily and squarely in the door frame. If necessary, adjustments can be made by slackening the stop bolt on the regulator mechanism and moving the position of the bolt in its slot. Once the window is correctly adjusted tighten the stop bolt to the specified torque.

### Front door window regulator

**29** Refitting is the reverse of removal, replacing the regulator rivets with the 6 mm bolts described in paragraph 10. Refit the window glass and adjust as described in paragraph 26.

### Rear door window glass

**30** Refitting is the reverse of removal. Prior to refitting the weathershield, check that the window operates smoothly and easily.

### Rear door fixed window glass

**31** Refitting is the reverse of removal making sure the window seal is correctly located in the door.

### Rear door window regulator

**32** Refitting is the reverse of removal. Prior to refitting the weathershield, check that the window operates smoothly and easily.

## 15 Door glass/regulator and rear vent window (Coupe models) - removal and refitting

### *Front door window glass and regulator*

**1** Removal of the front door window glass and regulator should be entrusted to a BMW dealer. If the window glass or regulator are disturbed a complex adjustment procedure must be performed on refitting. Failure to adjust the window properly will lead to the glass contacting the body when the door is shut, resulting in breakage of the glass.

### *Rear vent window*

#### Removal

**2** Open up the rear vent window and carefully unclip the trim panel from the rear pillar. Disconnect the wiring connector from the interior light and remove the panel.

**3** Support the glass then slacken and remove the screw and spacer securing the hinge to the glass and recover the trim cap and seal from outside the glass.

**4** Disengage the glass from its front pivot and remove it from the vehicle complete with its sealing strip. Renew the sealing strip if it shows signs of damage or deterioration.

**5** If necessary, slacken and remove the retaining bolts and nuts and remove the window hinge from the rear pillar.

**6** If the window front locating rail needs replacing, referring to Section 26, remove the remove the rear seat side trim panel, detach the seat belt from its upper mounting and remove the door pillar trim panel. Undo the two bolts and remove the seat belt height adjustment mechanism from the door pillar. Slacken and remove the two retaining screws and remove the rail from the pillar.

### *Refitting*

**7** If the window locating rail has been removed, ensure that the retaining screw sealing washers are in good condition. Fit the washers to the screws and tighten them lightly. Position the locating rail so that the gap between it and the front door window glass is approximately 5 mm along its entire length then tighten the screws to the specified torque. Refit the disturbed seat belt and trim components as described in Section 26.

**8** Ensure the sealing strip is correctly located on the glass and engage the glass with the locating strip.

**9** If the hinge was removed, fit the hinge to the pillar and lightly tighten its nuts and bolts.

**10** Insert the trim cap and seal from the outside of the glass and fit the spacer and retaining screw to the inside.

**11** Close the window and check that it is correctly aligned with the surrounding body panels. Adjust if necessary then tighten the hinge bolts and screw to the specified torque.

**12** Check the operation of the window then refit the trim panel to the rear pillar making sure it is retained by all the relevant clips.

## 16 Boot lid and support struts - removal and refitting

### *Removal*

#### Boot lid

**1** Open up the boot lid then disconnect the battery negative terminal.

**2** Remove the trim caps then undo the retaining screws securing the tool kit to the boot lid. Remove the tool kit then unclip the trim panel from the boot lid **(see illustrations)**.

**3** Support the boot lid in the open position and unclip the support struts (refer to paragraph 7).

**4** Disconnect the wiring connectors from the number plate lights, luggage compartment light switch and central locking servo (as applicable) and tie a piece of string to the end of the wiring. Noting the correct routing of the wiring harness, release the harness rubber grommets from the boot lid and withdraw the wiring. When the end of the wiring appears, untie the string and leave it in position in the boot lid; it can then be used on refitting to draw the wiring into position.

**5** Draw around the outline of each hinge with a suitable marker pen then slacken and remove the hinge retaining bolts and remove the boot lid from the vehicle **(see illustration)**.

**6** Inspect the hinges for signs of wear or damage and renew if necessary; the hinges are secured to the vehicle by bolts.

#### Support struts

**7** Support the boot lid in the open position. Using a small flat-bladed screwdriver raise the spring clip, and pull the support strut off its upper mounting **(see illustration)**. Repeat the procedure on the lower strut mounting and remove the strut from the vehicle.

### *Refitting*

#### Boot lid

**8** Refitting is the reverse of removal, aligning the hinges with the marks made before removal.

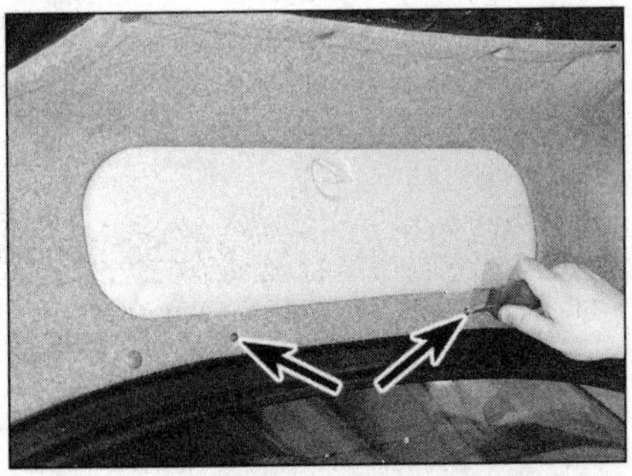

**16.2a Undo the retaining screws (arrowed) and remove the tool kit**

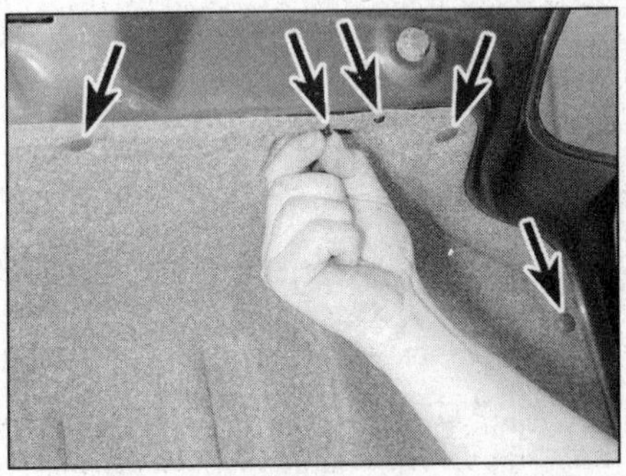

**16.2b Remove the retaining clips (arrowed) . . .**

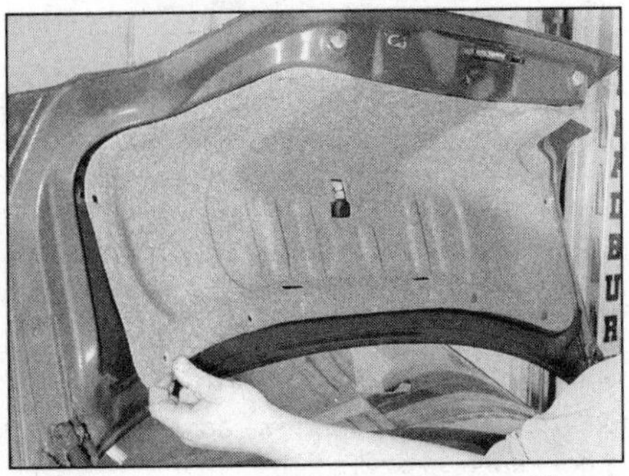

**16.2c . . . and remove the trim panel from the boot lid**

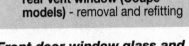

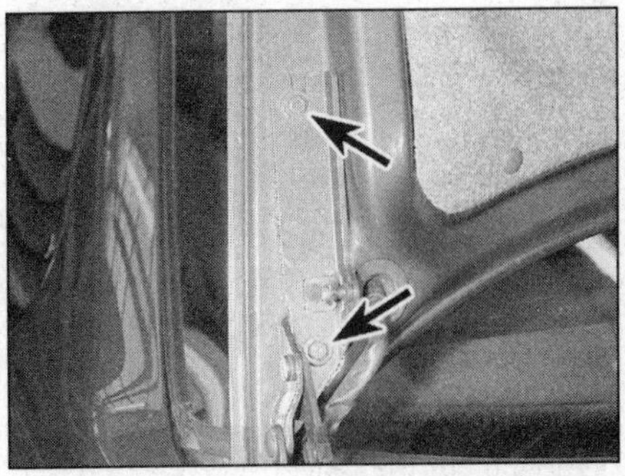

**16.5 Boot lid hinge retaining bolts (arrowed)**

11

16.7 Lift the retaining clip and unclip the support strut from the hinge

9 On completion, close the boot lid and check its alignment with the surrounding panels. If necessary slight adjustment can be made by slackening the retaining bolts and repositioning the boot lid on its hinges. If the paint work around the hinges has been damaged, paint the affected area with a suitable touch-in brush to prevent corrosion.

### Support struts

10 Refitting is a reverse of the removal procedure, ensuring that the strut is securely retained by its retaining clips.

## 17 Boot lid lock components - removal and refitting

### *Removal*

#### Boot lid lock

1 Open up the boot lid then disconnect the battery negative terminal.
2 Remove the trim caps then undo the retaining screws securing the tool kit to the boot lid. Remove the tool kit and unclip the trim panel from the boot lid.
3 Unclip the link rod from the boot lock cylinder **(see illustration)**.
4 Slacken and remove the lock retaining screws and withdraw the lock and link rod from the boot lid **(see illustrations)**.

#### Boot lid lock cylinder

5 Carry out the operations described in paragraphs 1 and 2.
6 Unclip the link rods from the lock cylinder, then undo the retaining bolts and remove the lock cylinder from the boot lid **(see illustrations)**.

### *Refitting*

#### Boot lid lock

7 Refit the lock and link rod to the boot and securely tighten its retaining screws.
8 Align the link rod with the lock cylinder and check that it is the correct length so that it clips into the lock without any tension in the rod. If necessary, adjust the rod length prior to refitting by screwing it into/out off the threaded adjustment piece.
9 Check the operation of the lock, then clip the trim panel back onto the boot lid. Refit the tool kit and securely tighten its retaining screws.
10 Reconnect the battery then close the boot lid and check the operation of the lock. If necessary, adjustments can be made by either slackening the retaining bolts and reposition the lock catch or by adjusting the boot lid rubber buffers.

#### Boot lid lock cylinder

11 Refit the lock cylinder and securely tighten its retaining screws.
12 Clip the central locking solenoid link rod onto the lock cylinder.
13 Carry out the operations described in paragraphs 8 to 10.

## 18 Central locking components - removal and refitting

### *Removal*

#### Electronic control unit (ECU) - right-hand drive models

**Note:** *On some models the central locking system is controlled by the central body electronics (ZKE IV) control unit (depending on model and specification) which is located behind the glovebox. Refer to Chapter 12, Section 27 for removal and refitting details.*
1 Slacken and remove the two retaining screws then unclip the driver's side lower facia panel and remove it from the vehicle. Unclip and remove the undercover to gain access to the ECU which is clipped in position above the pedals.
2 Release the retaining clips and lower the ECU out of position.
3 Release the retaining clip then disconnect the wiring connector(s) and remove the ECU from the vehicle.

#### Electronic control unit (ECU) - left-hand drive models

**Note:** *On some models the central locking system is controlled by the central body electronics (ZKE IV) control unit (depending on model and specification). Refer to Chapter 12, Section 27 for removal and refitting details.*
4 Remove the glovebox as described in Section 27. Release the retaining clips and

17.3 Unclip the lock link rod from the lock cylinder . . .

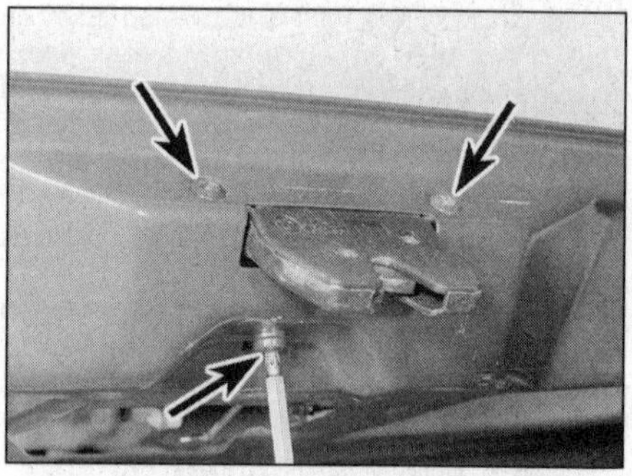

17.4a . . . then undo the retaining screws (arrowed) . . .

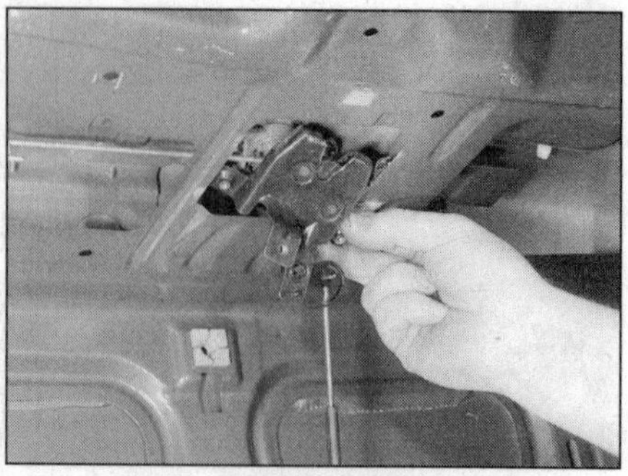

17.4b . . . and remove the lock from the boot

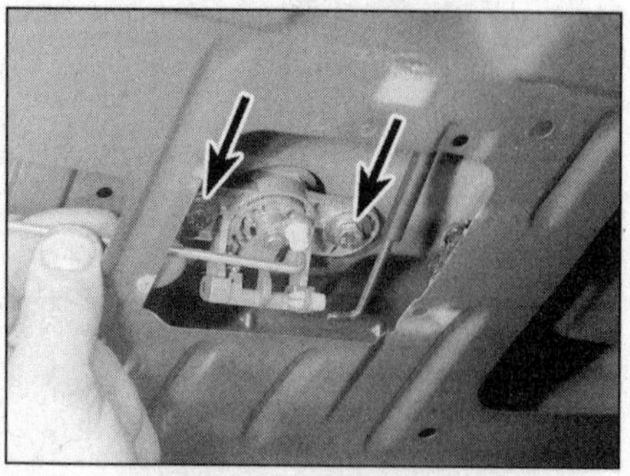

17.6a Unclip the link rods then undo the retaining bolts (arrowed) . . .

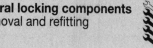

17.6b . . . and remove the lock cylinder from the boot lid

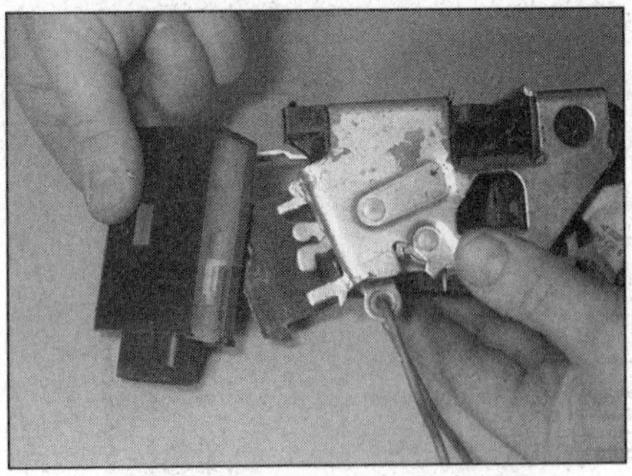

**18.7 Removing a door lock central locking solenoid**

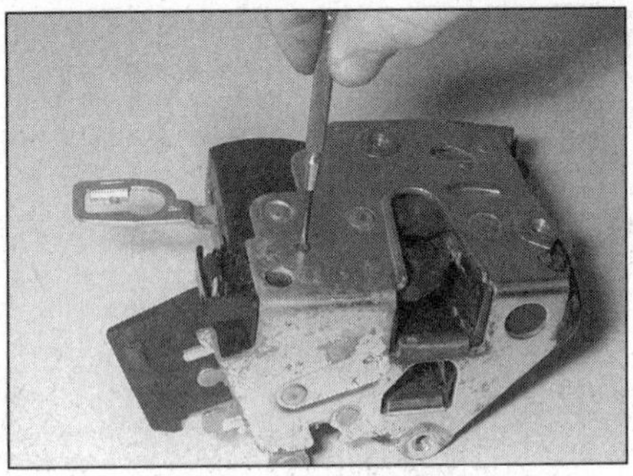

**18.9a On Coupe models, undo the retaining screw . . .**

**18.9b . . . and withdraw the central locking microswitch from the front door lock**

remove the facia panel from underneath the glovebox aperture to gain access to the ECU.

**5** Disconnect the wiring connector from the control unit then unclip it and remove it from the vehicle. On models with anti-lock brakes (ABS) it will be necessary to remove the ABS ECU (see Chapter 9) to gain access to the central locking control unit.

## Door lock solenoid

**6** Remove the door lock as described in Section 13.

**7** Release the retaining clip and detach the solenoid from the door lock, noting how it is connected **(see illustration)**.

## Door lock microswitch - Coupe models

**8** Remove the door lock as described in Section 13.

**9** Free the wiring from its retaining clips then slacken and remove the retaining screw and remove the switch from the lock **(see illustrations)**.

## Door handle microswitch - Saloon models

**10** Remove the door exterior handle as described in Section 13.

**11** Remove the retaining clip and detach the switch from the handle **(see illustration)**.

## Boot lock solenoid

**12** Open up the boot lid then disconnect the battery negative terminal.

**13** Remove the trim caps then undo the retaining screws securing the tool kit to the boot lid. Remove the tool kit and unclip the trim panel from the boot lid.

**14** Disconnect the wiring connector then unclip the solenoid link rod from the boot lock cylinder then undo the retaining screws and remove the solenoid and link rod **(see illustration)**.

## Fuel filler flap solenoid

**15** Rotate the retaining clip through 90° and remove the access cover from the right-hand rear light unit.

**16** Lift out the first aid box plate and peel back the luggage compartment trim to reveal the solenoid **(see illustration)**.

**17** Disconnect the wiring connector then slacken the retaining screws and manoeuvre the solenoid out from the luggage compartment **(see illustrations)**.

## Glovebox lock solenoid

**18** Remove the glovebox (see Section 27).

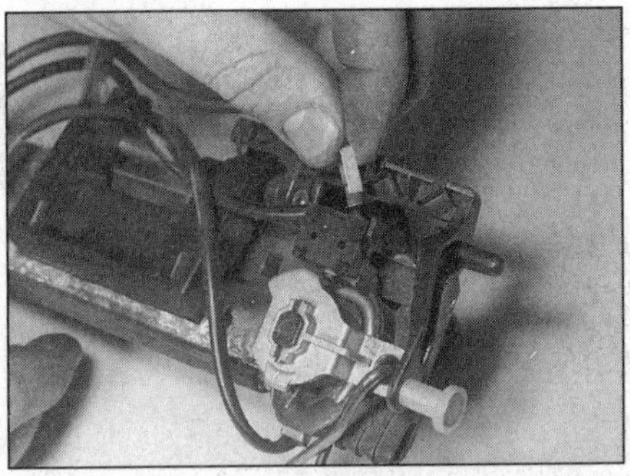

**18.11 On Saloon models release the retaining clip and remove the central locking microswitch from the handle**

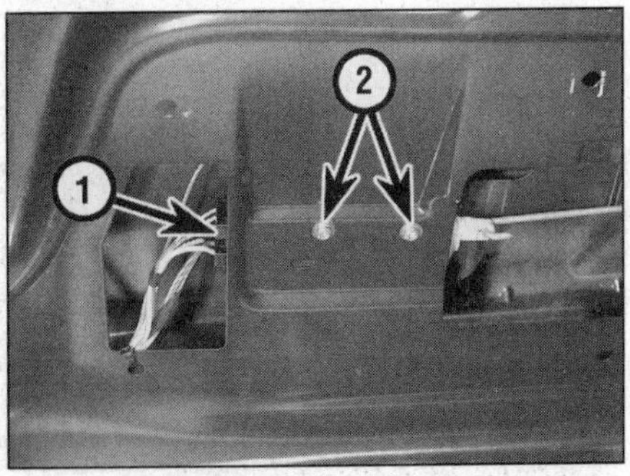


**18.14 Boot locking solenoid wiring connector (1) and retaining screws (2)**

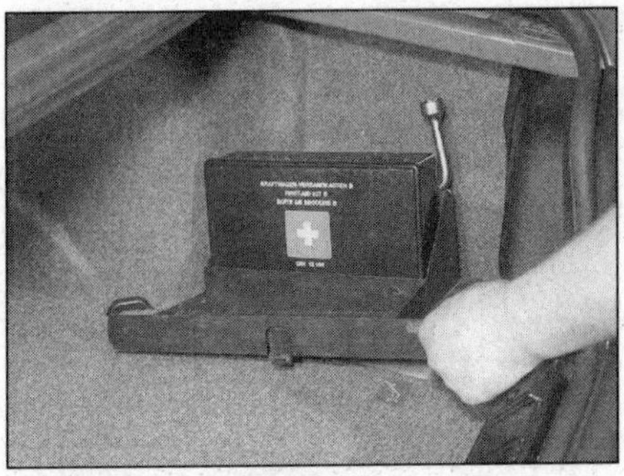

**18.16 Lift out the first aid box plate and peel back the luggage compartment trim to access the fuel filler flap solenoid**

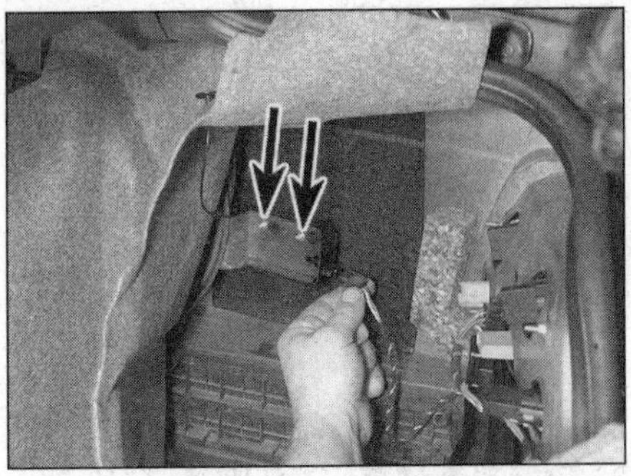

**18.17a Disconnect the wiring connector then slacken the screws (arrowed) . . .**

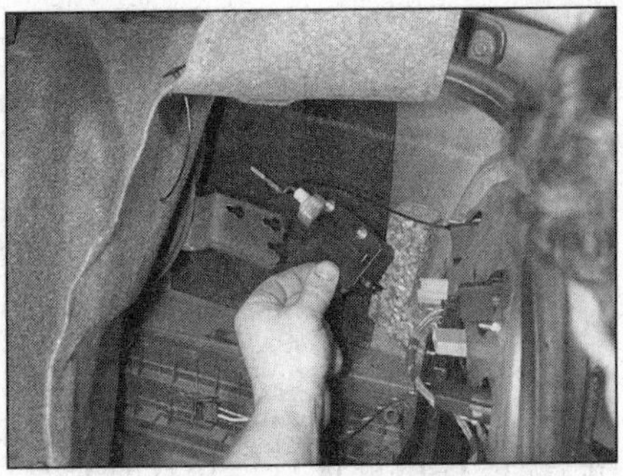

**18.17b . . . and remove the solenoid from its mounting bracket**

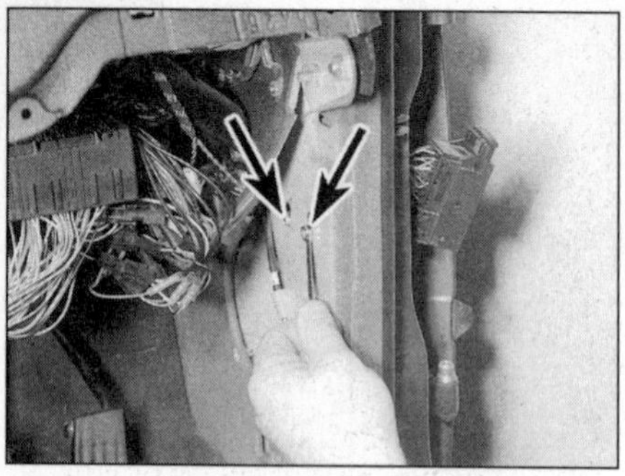

18.21a Slacken the two screws (arrowed) . . .

18.21b . . . and remove the central locking impact sensor from behind the pillar

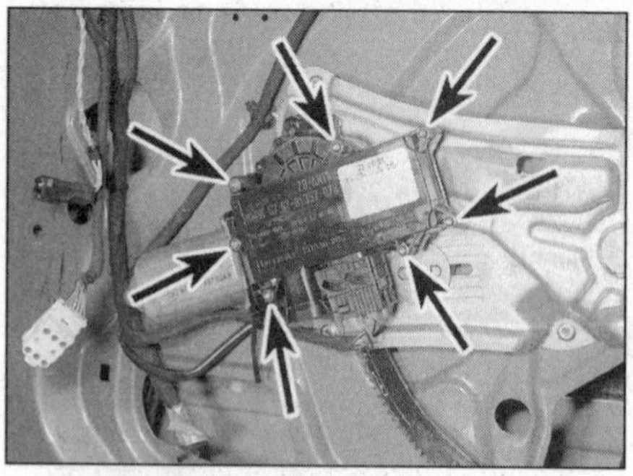

19.13 Electric window ECU retaining screws (arrowed) - Coupe models

19 Unclip the solenoid rod from the lock and guide then undo the retaining bolts and remove the solenoid.

### Central locking system impact sensor

20 Working as described in Chapter 12, on right-hand drive models remove the driver's side front loudspeaker and on left-hand drive models remove the passenger side front loudspeaker. Release the insulation panel from the body and remove it from the vehicle.

21 Loosen the two retaining screws securing the sensor to the body then manoeuvre it out through the speaker aperture and disconnect it from the wiring connector **(see illustrations)**.

### *Refitting*

22 Refitting is the reverse of removal. Prior to refitting any trim panels removed for access thoroughly check the operation of the central locking system.

## 19 Electric window components - removal and refitting

**Note:** *Whenever any component of the electric window electrical system is disconnected, the electronic control unit must be initialised once the battery is reconnected. To do this, close the doors then raise each windows to the fully closed position and hold down the switch for approximately 5 seconds. This will enable the one-touch switch facility and the anti-jam window system.*

### *Window switches*

1 Refer to Chapter 12.

### *Window winder motors - Saloon models*

2 Remove the window regulator as described in Section 14.

3 Slacken and remove the retaining screws and remove the motor from the regulator.

4 On refitting, fit the motor to the regulator and securely tighten its retaining screws.

5 Refit the regulator assembly as described in Section 14 and initialise the windows (see **Note** above).

### *Window winder motors - Coupe models*

6 Removal and refitting of the motors requires the regulator to the removed from the door. This task should be entrusted to a BMW dealer (see Section 15).

### *Electronic control unit (ECU) - Saloon models*

**Note:** *On some models the windows are controlled by the central body electronics (ZKE IV) control unit (depending on model and specification). Refer to Chapter 12, Section 27 for removal and refitting details.*

7 Disconnect the battery and remove the glovebox as described in Section 27.

8 Release the retaining clips and remove the lower facia panel from beneath the glovebox aperture.

9 Disconnect the wiring connector then release the clip and withdraw the ECU.

10 Refitting is a reverse of removal. On completion initialise the windows (see **Note** at the start of Section).

### *Electronic control unit (ECU) - Coupe models*

11 On Coupe models there are two ECUs, one for each window. Each unit is bolted onto its respective window motor. Prior to removal, lower the window slightly then disconnect the battery negative terminal.

12 Remove the door inner trim panel as described in Section 12 and carefully peel the plastic weathershield away from the door to reveal the ECU.

13 Disconnect the wiring connector(s) then undo the retaining screws and remove the ECU squarely from the motor **(see illustration)**. Recover the sealing ring from the motor groove; if the seal shows signs of damage it must be renewed.

14 Prior to refitting, ensure that the motor and ECU connecting terminals are free from dirt and corrosion.

15 Fit the sealing ring to the groove in the motor. Align the ECU with the motor terminals and squarely locate it in the motor recess.

16 Refit the ECU retaining screws and tighten them securely.

17 Reconnect the battery then initialise the windows (see **Note** at the start of Section) and check the window operation.

18 If all is well, stick the weathershield to the door and refit the trim panel as described in Section 12.

## 20 Exterior mirrors and associated components - removal and refitting

### *Mirror assembly*

1 Carefully unclip the mirror interior trim panel from the inside of the door, then disconnect the wiring connector **(see illustrations)**.

2 Undo the retaining bolts and remove the mirror from the door. Recover the rubber seal which is fitted between the door and mirror; if the seal is damaged it must be renewed **(see illustration)**.

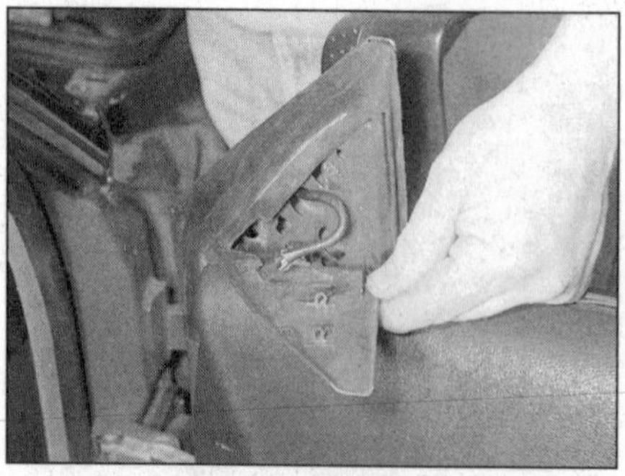

20.1 Unclip the inner trim panel from the door . . .

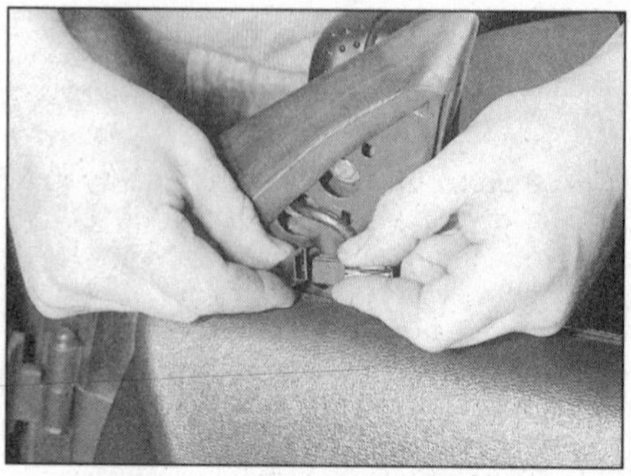

20.1b . . . and disconnect the mirror wiring connector

20.2 Undo the three retaining bolts and remove the mirror assembly from the door

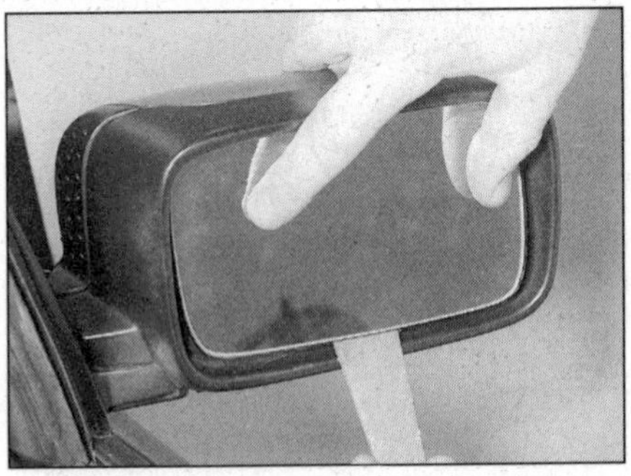

20.5 Take great care not to break the glass when removing it from the mirror

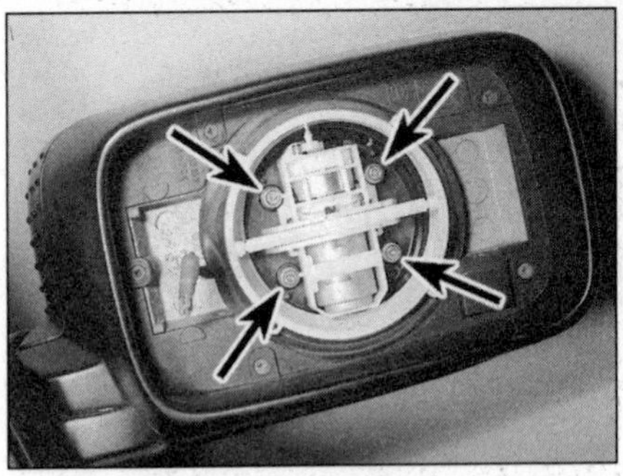

20.10 Exterior mirror motor retaining screws (arrowed)

**3** Refitting is the reverse of removal, tightening the mirror bolts to the specified torque.

### Mirror glass

**Note:** *If the mirror glass is removed when the mirror is cold the glass retaining clips are likely to break.*

**4** Tilt the mirror glass fully upwards.

**5** Insert a wide plastic or wooden wedge in between the base of the mirror glass and mirror housing and carefully prise the glass from the motor **(see illustration)**. Take great care when removing the glass; do not use excessive force as the glass is easily broken.

**6** Remove the glass from the mirror and, where necessary, disconnect the wiring connectors from the mirror heating element.

**7** On refitting, reconnect the wiring to the glass and clip the glass onto the motor, taking great care not to break it.

### Mirror switch

**8** Refer to Chapter 12.

### Mirror motor

**9** Remove the mirror glass as described above.

**10** Undo the retaining screws and remove the motor, disconnecting its wiring connector as it becomes accessible **(see illustration)**.

**11** On refitting reconnect the wiring connector and securely tighten the motor screws. Check the operation of the motor then refit the glass as described above.

## 21 Windscreen and rear screen glass - general information

These areas of glass are secured by the tight fit of the weatherstrip in the body aperture, and are bonded in position with a special adhesive. Renewal of such fixed glass is a difficult, messy and time-consuming task, which is beyond the scope of the home mechanic. It is difficult, unless one has plenty of practice, to obtain a secure, waterproof fit. Furthermore, the task carries a high risk of breakage; this applies especially to the laminated glass windscreen. In view of this, owners are strongly advised to have this sort of work carried out by one of the many specialist windscreen fitters.

## 22 Sunroof - general information

Due to the complexity of the sunroof mechanism, considerable expertise is needed to repair, replace or adjust the sunroof components successfully. Removal of the roof first requires the headlining to be removed, which is a complex and tedious operation, and not a task to be undertaken lightly. Therefore, any problems with the sunroof should be referred to a BMW dealer.

On models with an electric sunroof, if the sunroof motor fails to operate, first check the relevant fuse. If the fault cannot be traced and rectified, the sunroof can be opened and closed manually using an Allen key to turn the motor spindle (a suitable key is supplied with the vehicle tool kit). To gain access to the motor, unclip the cover from the headlining. Remove the Allen key from the tool kit and insert it into the motor spindle. Disconnect the motor wiring connector and rotate the key to move the sunroof to the required position **(see illustration)**.

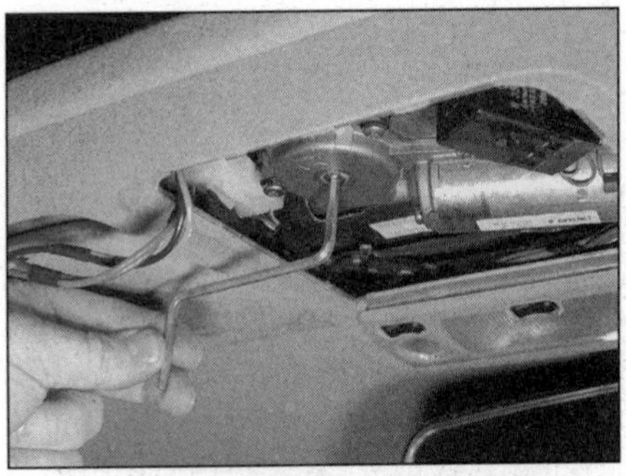

22.2 If the electric sunroof fails, the sunroof can be moved using the Allen key supplied with the vehicle tool kit

## 23 Body exterior fittings - removal and refitting

### Wheel arch liners and body under-panels

**1** The various plastic covers fitted to the underside of the vehicle are secured in position by a mixture of screws, nuts and retaining clips and removal will be fairly obvious on inspection. Work methodically around the removing its retaining screws and releasing its retaining clips until the panel is free and can be removed from the underside of the vehicle. Most clips used on the vehicle are simply prised out of position. Other clips can be released by unscrewing/prising out the centre pins and then removing the clip.

**2** On refitting, renew any retaining clips that may have been broken on removal, and ensure that the panel is securely retained by all the relevant clips and screws.

### Body trim strips and badges

**3** The various body trim strips and badges are held in position with a special adhesive tape. Removal requires the trim/badge to be heated, to soften the adhesive, and then cut away from the surface. Due to the high risk of damage to the vehicle's paintwork during this operation, it is recommended that this task should be entrusted to a BMW dealer.

## 24 Seats - removal and refitting

### Removal

#### Front seat

**1** Slide the seat fully forwards and raise the seat cushion fully.

**2** Slacken and remove the bolts and washers securing the rear of the seat rails to the floor **(see illustration)**.

**3** Slide the seat fully backwards and disable the seat belt tensioner, referring to Section 25.

**24.2 Front seat rear mounting bolt (arrowed)**

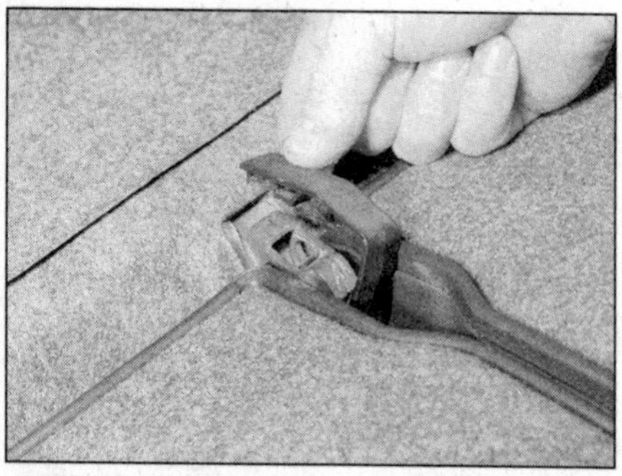

**24.12 On models with a folding rear seat, unclip the cover from the seat back pivot . . .**

**4** On all models, remove the trim caps from the seat front mounting nuts/bolts then slacken and remove the nuts/bolts and washers **(see illustration)**.

**5** On Saloon models, undo the mounting bolt and free the seat belt lower mounting from the base of the seat.

**6** Lift the seat out from the vehicle, where necessary, disconnecting its wiring connectors as they become accessible.

### Rear seat assembly - models with fixed rear seat

**7** Pull down the rear seat armrest (where fitted) and unclip it from the seat back.

**8** Pull up on the cushion to release the left- and right-hand retaining clips and remove it from the vehicle.

**9** Unclip the top of the seat back then slide it upwards to release its lower retaining pins and remove it from the vehicle.

### Rear seat assembly - models with folding rear seat

**10** Pull up on the cushion to release the left and right-hand retaining clips and remove it from the vehicle **(see illustration)**.

**11** Slacken and remove the bolts securing the seat belt lower mountings to the body.

**12** Fold the seat backs forward and unclip the cover from the seat pivot **(see illustration)**.

**13** Release the pivot locking clip by levering it backwards with a screwdriver and remove the seat backs from the vehicle **(see illustration)**.

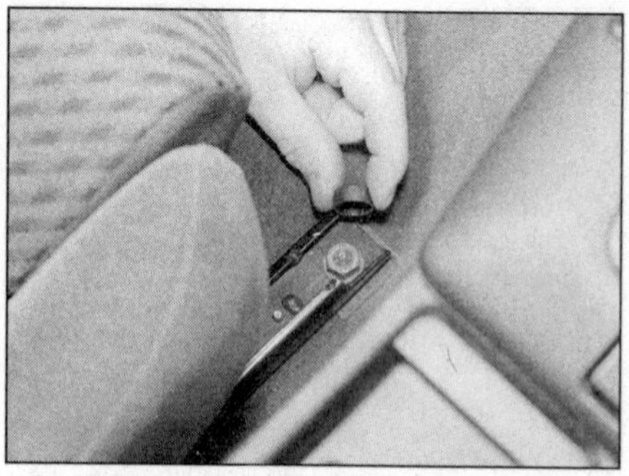

**24.4 Remove the rim cap to gain access to the front seat front mountings**

**24.13 . . . then release the retaining clip and unhook the seat pivot**

## *Refitting*

### Front seats

**14** Refitting is the reverse of removal, noting the following points.

*a) On manually adjusted seats, fit the seat retaining bolts and tighten them by hand only. Slide the seat fully forwards and then slide it back by two stops of the seat locking mechanism. Rock the seat to ensure that the seat locking mechanism is correctly engaged then tighten the mounting bolts to the specified torque.*

*b) On electrically adjusted seats, ensure that the wiring is connected and correctly routed then tighten the seat mounting bolts to the specified torque.*

*c) Enable the seat belt tensioner mechanism as described in Section 25.*

*d) On Saloon models tighten the seat belt mounting bolt to the specified torque.*

### Rear seat assembly - models with fixed rear seat

**15** Refitting is the reverse of removal making sure the seat back lower locating pegs are correctly engaged with the body.

### Rear seat assembly - models with folding rear seats

**16** Refitting is the reverse of removal ensuring that the seat pivot is clipped securely in position. Tighten the seat belt lower mounting bolts to the specified torque setting.

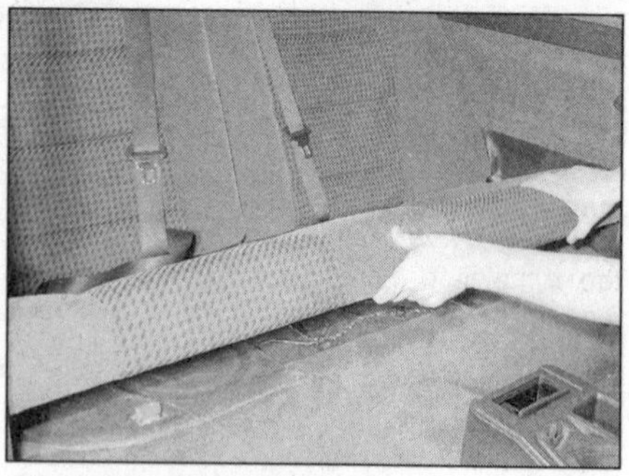

**24.10 Unclip and remove the rear seat cushion**

## 25 Front seat belt tensioning mechanism - general information

**1** Most models are fitted with a front seat belt tensioner system. The system is designed to instantaneously take up any slack in the seat belt in the case of a sudden frontal impact, therefore reducing the possibility of injury to the front seat occupants. Each front seat is fitted with its system, the tensioner being situated behind the sill trim panel.

**2** The seat belt tensioner is triggered by a frontal impact above a pre-determined force. Lesser impacts, including impacts from behind, will not trigger the system.

**3** When the system is triggered, a large spring in the tensioner mechanism retracts and locks the seat belt through a cable which acts on the inertia reel. This prevents the seat belt moving and keeps the occupant in position in the seat. Once the tensioner has been triggered, the seat belt will be permanently locked and the assembly must be renewed.

**4** There is a risk of injury if the system is triggered inadvertently when working on the vehicle. If any work is to be carried out on the seat/seat belt disable the tensioner as follows.

**5** On models with manually adjusted seats, free the seat belt tensioner cable from the front of the seat base by rotating the outer cable retaining clip through 90° and pulling it upwards **(see illustration)**. On completion of work, enable the tensioner by clipping the

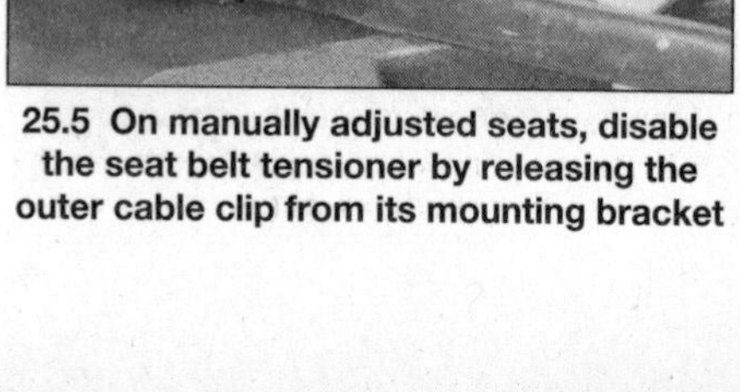

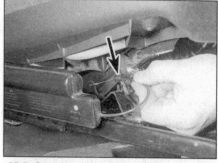

**25.5 On manually adjusted seats, disable the seat belt tensioner by releasing the outer cable clip from its mounting bracket**

outer cable back into its bracket, ensuring the inner cable is correctly hooked onto the base.

6 On models with electrically adjusted seats, the seat belt tensioner mechanism is disabled by rotating the screw situated in the front outer edge of the seat base. The position of the screw is indicated by the sight glass in the top of the base. When the sight glass is green the tensioner is enabled and when it is red the tensioner is disabled. Rotate screw to disable the tensioner before carrying out the work and, on completion, enable the tensioner by rotating the screw back again.

7 Also note the following warnings before contemplating any work on the front seat.

***Warning: If the tensioner mechanism is dropped, it must be renewed, even it has suffered no apparent damage.***

***Do not allow any solvents to come into contact with the tensioner mechanism.***

***Do not subject the seat to any form of shock as this could accidentally trigger the seat belt tensioner.***

## 26 Seat belt components - removal and refitting

### *Removal*

#### Front seat belt - Saloon models

***Warning: On models equipped with seat belt tensioners refer to Section 25 before proceeding.***

1 Remove the front seat as described in Section 24 and free the seat belt from the seat.

2 Unclip the rear seat cushion and remove it from the body.

3 Carefully unclip the trim panel from the rear door sill panel **(see illustration)**.

4 Carefully unclip the front sill trim panel and remove it from the vehicle **(see illustration)**.

5 Unclip the trim cover from the seat belt upper mounting. Slacken and remove the seat belt mounting nut and detach the belt from its height adjustment mechanism **(see illustrations)**.

6 Release the retaining lug on the bottom of the height adjustment lever and remove the lever **(see illustration)**.

7 Peel the front and rear door sealing strips away from the door pillar trim panel **(see illustration)**.

8 Carefully unclip the trim panel from the door pillar and remove it from the vehicle.

9 Undo the screw(s) and remove the seat belt guide from the pillar **(see illustration)**.

10 Unscrew the inertia reel retaining bolt and remove the seat belt from the door pillar **(see illustration)**.

11 If necessary, undo the retaining bolts and remove the height adjustment mechanism from the door pillar.

#### Front seat belt - Coupe models

12 Disable the seat belt tensioner as described in Section 25.

13 Remove the rear seat as described in Section 24.

14 On models with folding rear seats, remove the seat back pivot bush from the mounting bracket then unclip the top of the seat side section and remove it from the vehicle body **(see illustrations)**.

15 On all models, open the door and rear window and free the sealing strips from the

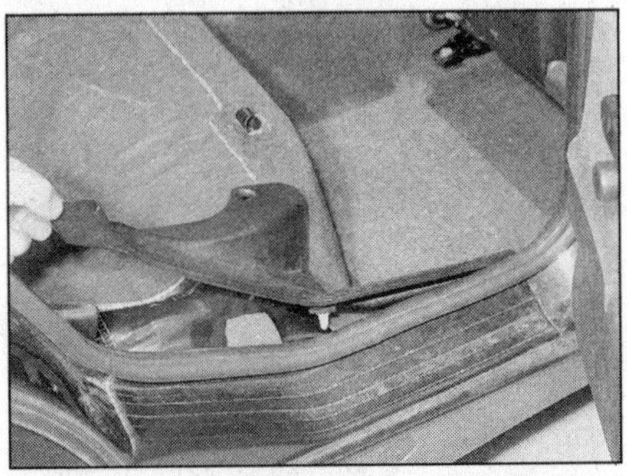

**26.3 Unclip the trim panel from the rear door sill . . .**

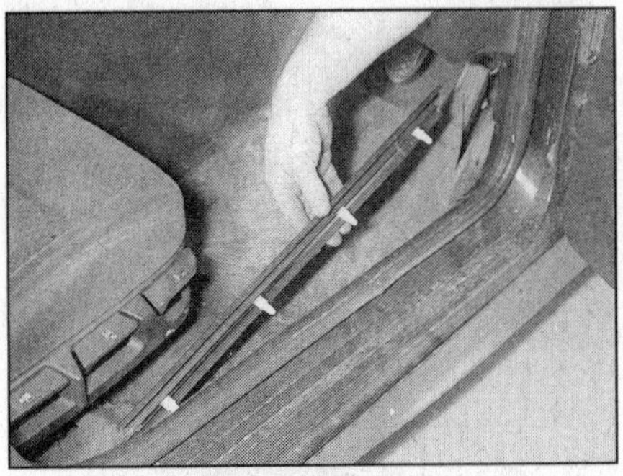

**26.4 . . . and the panel from the front door sill**

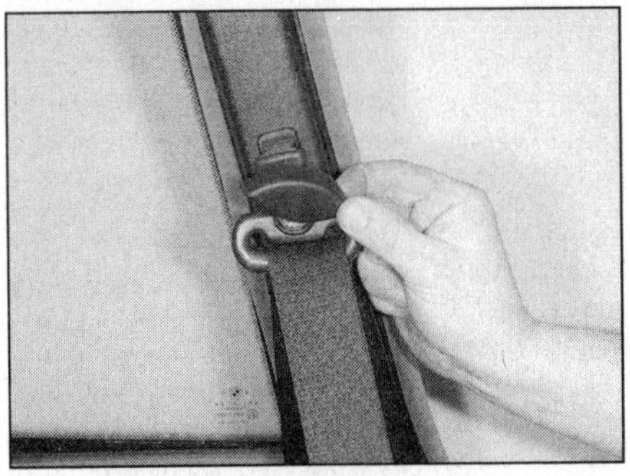

**26.5a Remove the trim cover . . .**

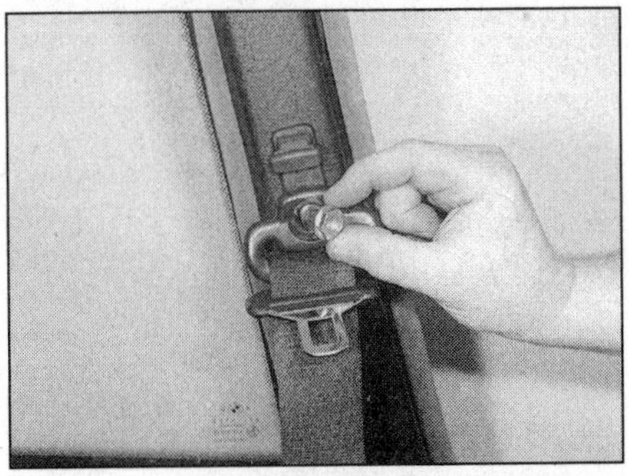

**26.5b . . . then unscrew the nut and free the front seat belt from its upper mounting**

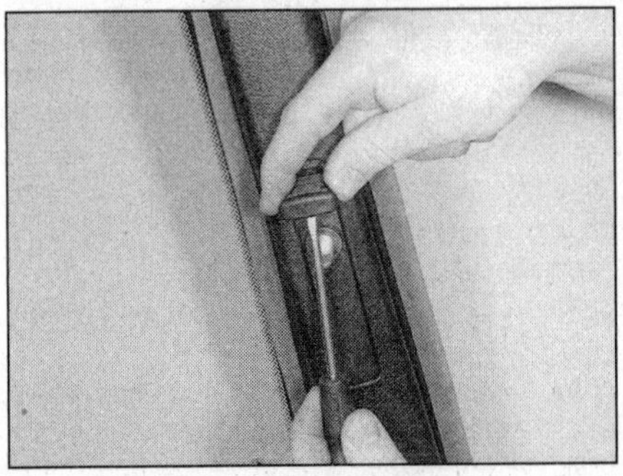

**26.6 Release the retaining clip and pull off the height adjustment lever**

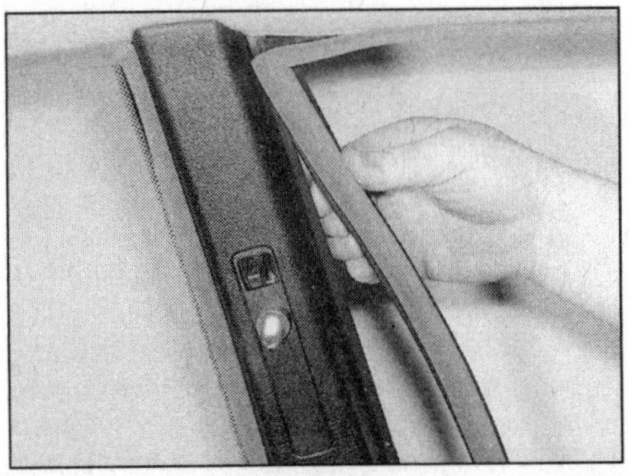

**26.7 Release the trim strips and unclip the pillar trim panel**

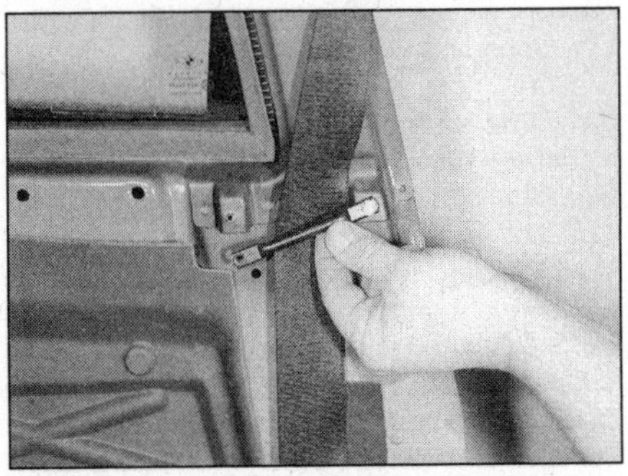

**26.9 Undo the screws and remove seat belt guide from the pillar (Coupe shown)**

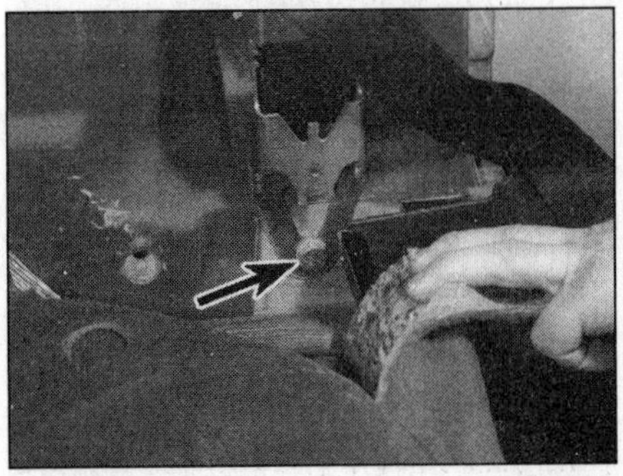

**26.10 Undo the inertia reel bolt (arrowed) and remove the seat belt (Coupe shown)**

11

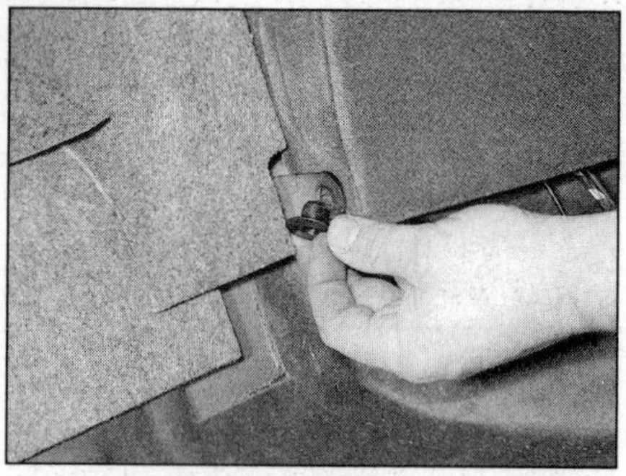
26.14a On Coupe models, remove the seat back pivot bush . . .

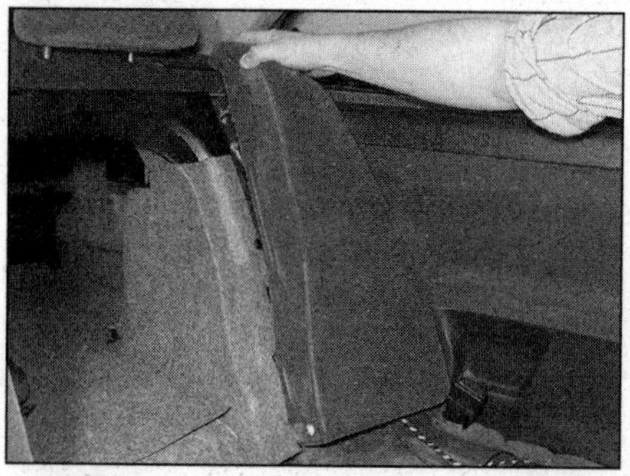
26.14b . . . then unclip the seat side section and remove it from the vehicle

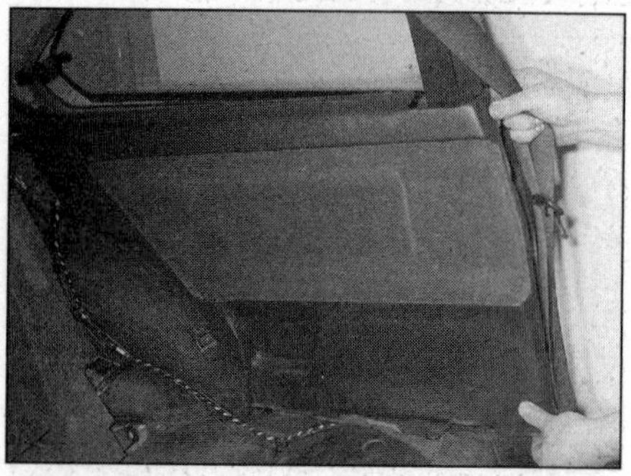
26.15 Unclip the rear seat side trim panel and remove it from the vehicle

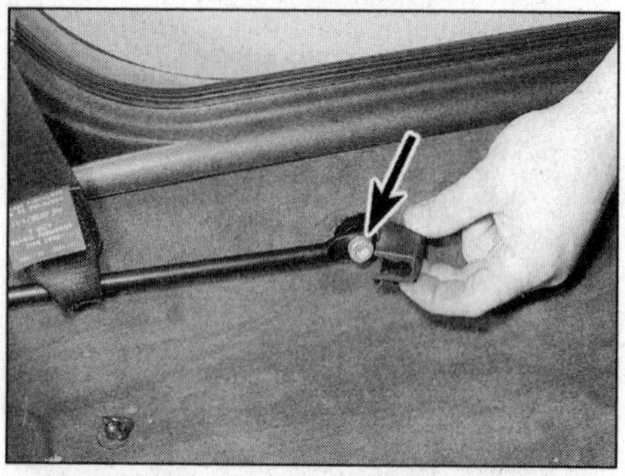
26.16a Remove trim cap, then remove seat belt lower fixing rail bolt (arrowed) . . .

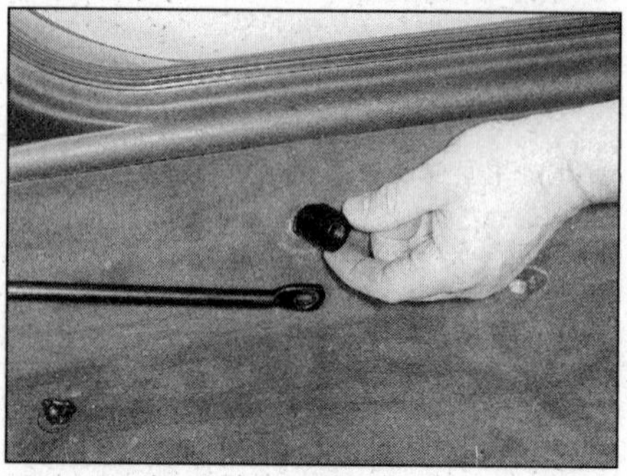
26.16b . . . and recover the spacer fitted between the rail and body

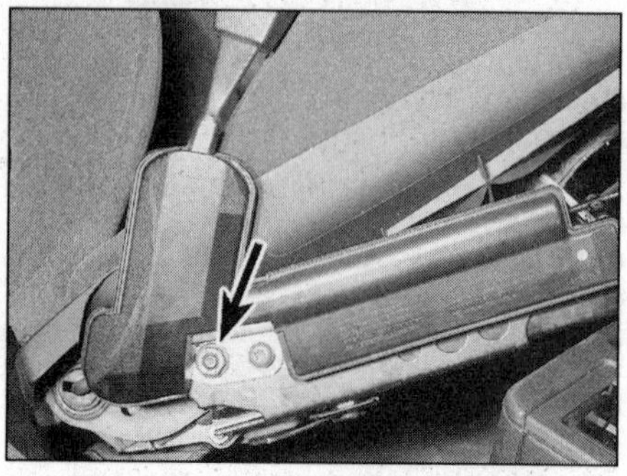
26.19 Front seat belt stalk assembly retaining nut (arrowed)

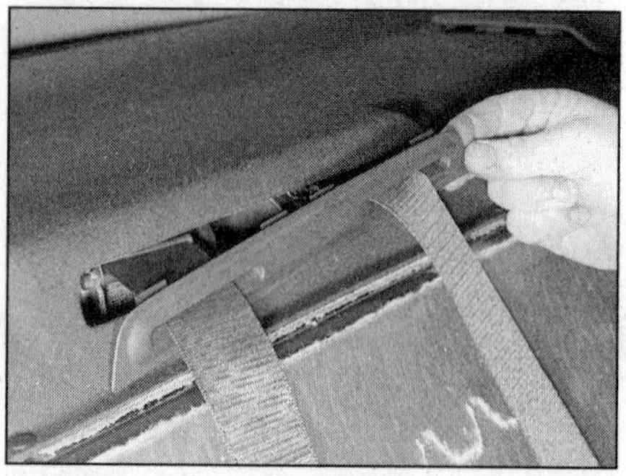
26.22 On models with fixed rear seats, unclip trim cover from front of parcel shelf

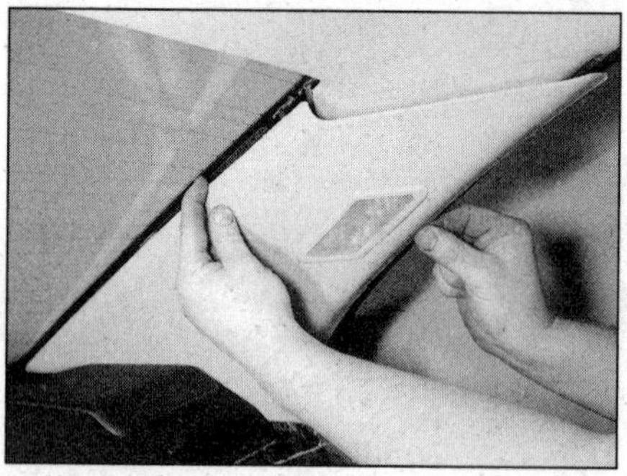
26.23 Unclip the rear pillar trim panels and remove them from the vehicle

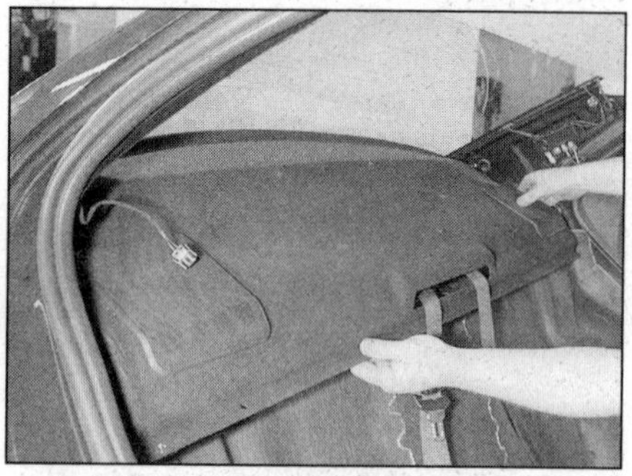
26.24 Remove the retaining clips and remove the parcel shelf

edge of the rear seat side trim panel. Unclip the trim panel and remove it from the vehicle **(see illustration)**.

**16** Remove the trim cap from the front mounting bolt of the seat belt lower fixing rail. Slacken and remove the retaining bolt then recover the spacer which is fitted between the rail and body and slide the belt off from the rail **(see illustrations)**.

**17** Remove the seat belt as described in paragraphs 5 to 11.

## Front seat belt stalk (incorporating seat belt tensioner mechanism)

**18** Remove the seat as described in Section 24.

**19** Ensuring the tensioner mechanism is disabled, slacken and remove the stalk assembly retaining nut and remove the assembly from the side of the seat **(see illustration)**.

## Rear seat side belts - models with fixed rear seat

**20** Remove the rear seat as described in Section 24.

**21** Slacken and remove the bolts and washers securing the rear seat belts to the vehicle body and remove the centre belt and buckle.

**22** Unclip the trim cover from the front of the parcel shelf and detach it from the seat belts **(see illustration)**.

**23** Carefully unclip the left and right-hand trim panels from the rear pillars, disconnecting the wiring from the interior lights as the panels are removed **(see illustration)**.

**24** Remove the retaining clips from the front edge of the parcel shelf and slide the shelf forwards and out of position **(see illustration)**. As the shelf is removed, disconnect the wiring connectors from the high-level stop-light (where fitted).

**25** Unscrew the inertia reel retaining nut and remove the seat belt(s) **(see illustration)**.

26.25 Inertia reel retaining nuts (arrowed)

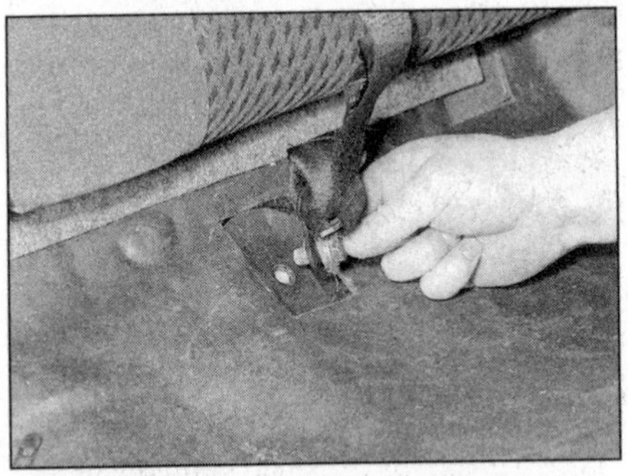

26.27 On models with folding rear seats, slacken and remove the seat belt lower mounting bolt . . .

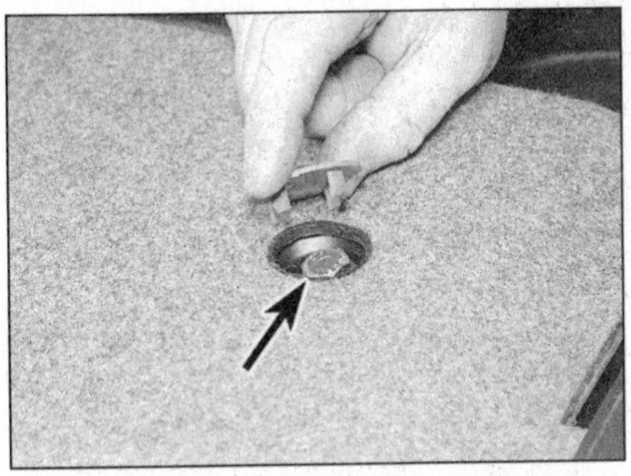

26.28 . . . then remove the trim cap from seat back and undo the inertia reel retaining bolt (arrowed)

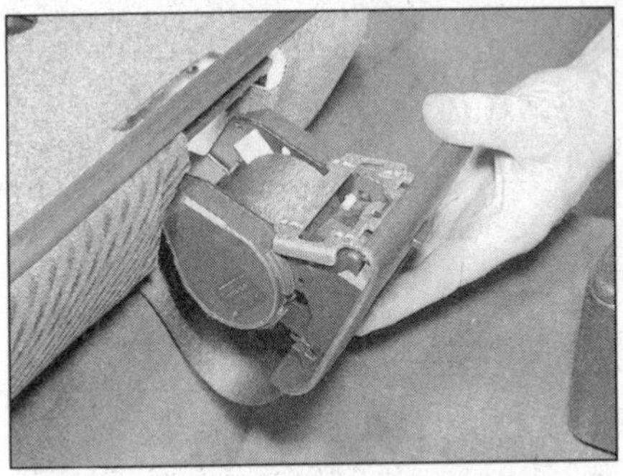

26.29 Unclip the inertia reel from the seat back and remove the seat belt

### Rear seat side belts - models with folding rear seats

**26** Unclip the rear seat cushion and remove it from the vehicle.

**27** Slacken and remove the bolt securing the lower end of the belt to the body **(see illustration)**.

**28** Fold the seat forwards and prise out the circular trim cap from the rear of the seat to gain access to the inertia reel bolt **(see illustration)**. Slacken and remove the retaining bolt and washer.

**29** Unclip the seat belt trim cover from the top of the seat and withdraw the inertia reel assembly from the seat back **(see illustration)**.

### Rear seat side belt stalk

**30** Unclip the rear seat cushion and remove it from the body.

**31** On Saloon models, carefully unclip the trim panel from the rear door sill.

**32** Slacken and remove the bolt and washer and remove the stalk from the vehicle.

### Rear seat centre belt and buckle

**33** Unclip the rear seat cushion and remove it from the vehicle.

**34** Slacken and remove the bolt securing the centre belt/buckle to the body and remove it from the vehicle.

## *Refitting*

### Front seat belt - all models

**35** Refitting is a reversal of the removal procedure, ensuring that all the seat belt mounting bolts are securely tightened, and all disturbed trim panels are securely retained by all the relevant retaining clips.

### Front seat belt stalk (incorporating seat belt tensioner mechanism)

**36** Ensure the tensioner mechanism is correctly engaged with the seat and tighten its retaining nut to the specified torque. Refit the seat as described in Section 24 and enable the tensioner mechanism.

### Rear seat side belts - models with fixed rear seat

**37** Refitting is the reverse of removal ensuring that all seat belt mountings are tighten to the specified torque and all trim panels are clipped securely in position.

### Rear seat side belts - models with folding rear seat

**38** Refitting is the reverse of removal making sure the inertia reel is clipped securely in position and all seat belt mounting bolts are tightened to the torque.

### Rear seat belt stalk

**39** Refitting is the reverse of removal, tightening the mounting bolt to the specified torque.

### Rear seat centre belt and buckle

**40** Refitting is the reverse of removal tighten the mounting bolts to the specified torque.

## 27 Interior trim - removal and refitting

## *Interior trim panels*

**1** The interior trim panels are secured using either screws or various types of trim fasteners, usually studs or clips.

**2** Check that there are no other panels overlapping the one to be removed; usually there is a sequence that has to be followed that will become obvious on close inspection.

**3** Remove all obvious fasteners, such as screws. If the panel will not come free, it is held by hidden clips or fasteners. These are usually situated around the edge of the panel and can be prised up to release them; note, however that they can break quite easily so replacements should be available. The best way of releasing such clips without the correct type of tool, is to use a large flat-bladed screwdriver. Note in many cases that the adjacent sealing strip must be prised back to release a panel.

**4** When removing a panel, **never** use excessive force or the panel may be damaged; always check carefully that all fasteners have been removed or released before attempting to withdraw a panel.

**5** Refitting is the reverse of the removal procedure; secure the fasteners by pressing them firmly into place and ensure that all disturbed components are correctly secured to prevent rattles.

## *Glovebox*

**6** Where the glovebox heater vents are not moulded into the glovebox, unclip and remove them **(see illustration)**.

**7** Open up the glovebox lid and prise off the trim caps from the two centre retaining screws. Slacken and remove the retaining screws securing the glovebox to the facia. Where the heater vents are part of the glovebox, access to the upper screws is gained through the vents **(see illustration)**.

**8** Close the lid and undo the two screws from the base of the glovebox.

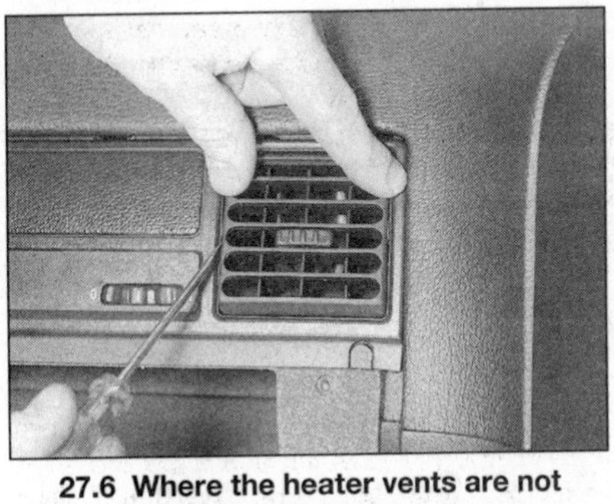

27.6 Where the heater vents are not moulded into the glovebox, carefully unclip and remove them

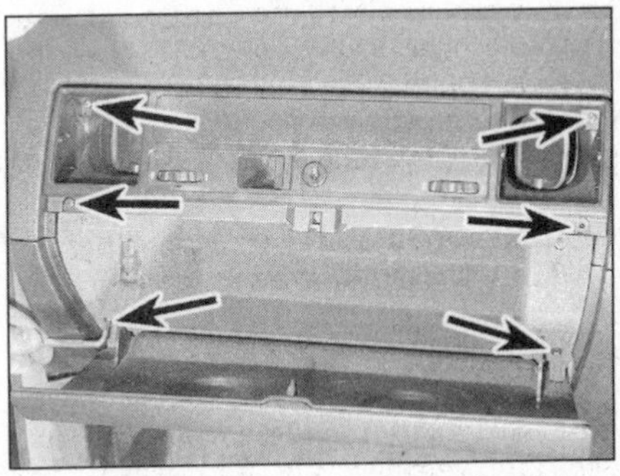

27.7 Slacken and remove the glovebox retaining screws (arrowed)

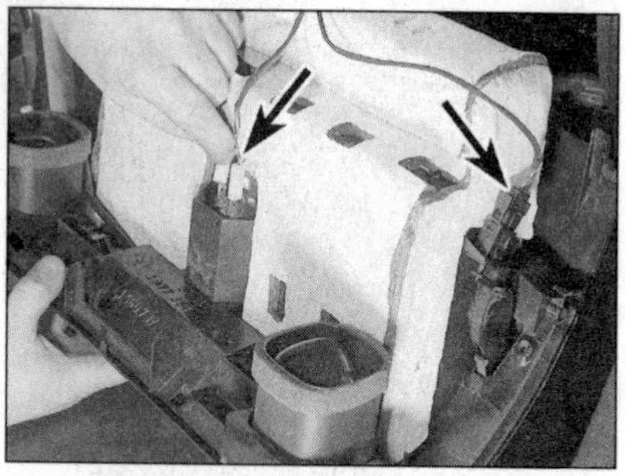

**27.9 Slide out the glovebox and disconnect its wiring connectors (arrowed)**

**9** Slide the glovebox out of position disconnecting the wiring connector(s) as they become accessible **(see illustration)**.

**10** Refitting is the reverse of removal.

### Carpets

**11** The passenger compartment floor carpet is in one piece, secured at its edges by screws or clips, usually the same fasteners used to secure the various adjoining trim panels.

**12** Carpet removal and refitting is reasonably straightforward but very time-consuming because all adjoining trim panels must be removed first, as must components such as the seats, the centre console and seat belt lower anchorages.

### Headlining

**13** The headlining is clipped to the roof and can be withdrawn only once all fittings such as the grab handles, sun visors, sunroof (if fitted), windscreen and rear quarter windows and related trim panels have been removed and the door, tailgate and sunroof aperture sealing strips have been prised clear.

**14** Note that headlining removal requires considerable skill and experience if it is to be carried out without damage and is therefore best entrusted to an expert.

## 28 Centre console - removal and refitting

### Removal

**1** Disconnect the battery negative terminal.

**2** Remove the hazard warning light switch as described in Chapter 12.

**3** Where ashtrays are fitted, unclip the ashtrays and remove them from the centre console. Undo the retaining screws and remove the ashtray surrounds, freeing the illumination bulbholders from them **(see illustration)**.

**4** Where no ashtrays are fitted, unclip the storage compartment(s) and remove them from the centre console.

**5** On all models unclip the handbrake lever gaiter from the console.

**6** Slacken and remove the retaining screws and remove the rear section of the console **(see illustrations)**.

**7** If the front section is also to be removed, remove the clock/multi-information display unit (as applicable) as described in Chapter 12.

**8** Remove the glovebox (see Section 27).

**9** Slacken and remove the retaining screws securing the driver's side lower facia panel. Unclip the panel and remove it from the vehicle **(see illustration)**.

**10** Unclip the storage compartment from the front of the centre console and disconnect the wiring from the cigarette lighter.

**11** Slacken and remove the retaining screws and nut then manoeuvre the front section of the centre console upwards over the gearchange/selector lever and out of the vehicle, disconnecting the various wiring connectors as they become accessible **(see illustrations)**.

### Refitting

**12** Refitting is the reverse of removal making sure all fasteners are securely tightened.

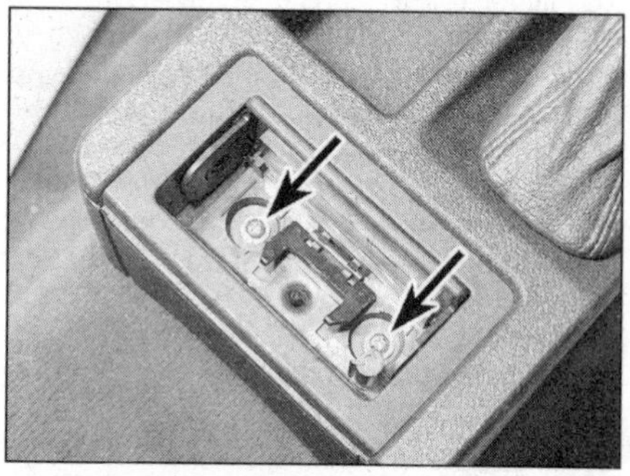

**28.3 Lift out the rear ashtray, then undo two retaining screws (arrowed) and remove the ashtray surround**

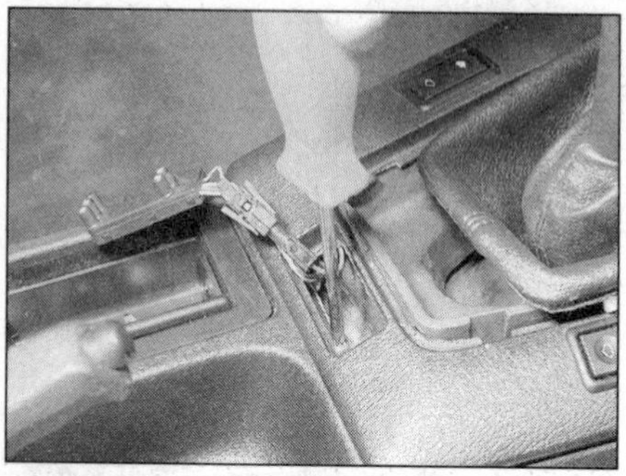

**28.6a Slacken and remove the front . . .**

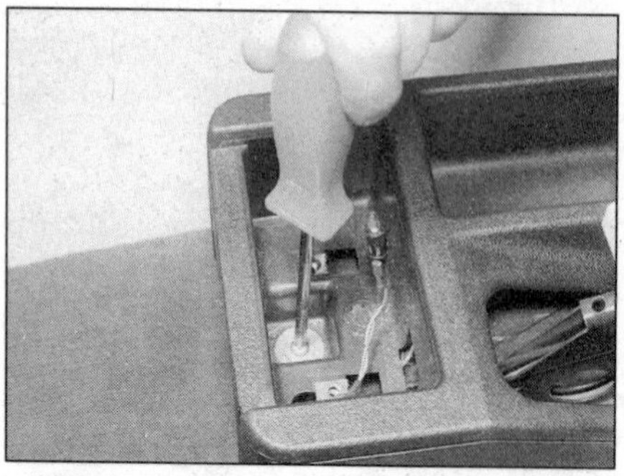

**28.6b . . . and rear retaining screws . . .**

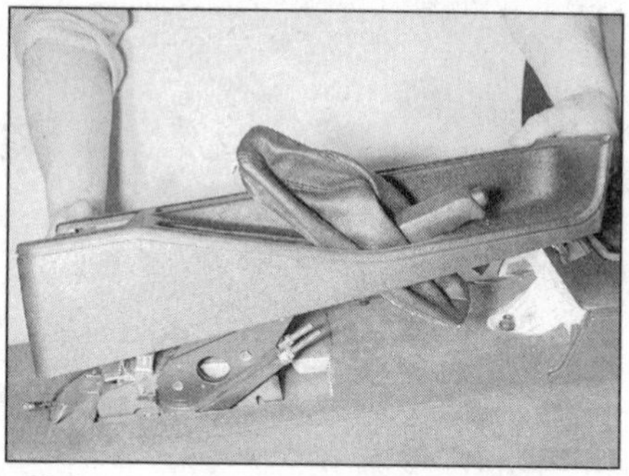

**28.6c . . . and remove the rear section of the centre console**

**28.9 Undo the retaining screws (arrowed) and remove the driver's side lower facia panel (Coupe shown)**

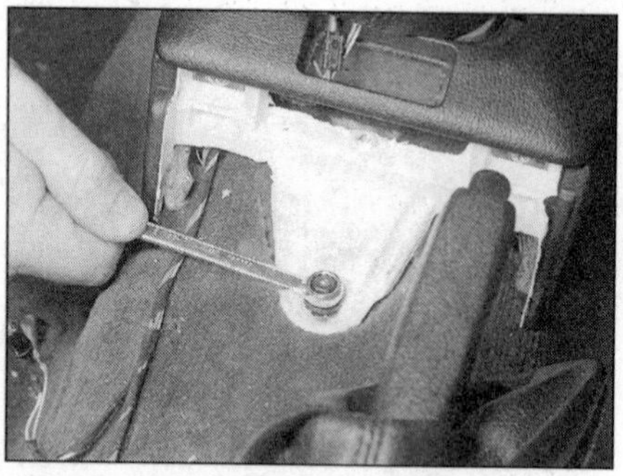

**28.11a Unscrew the rear retaining nut . . .**

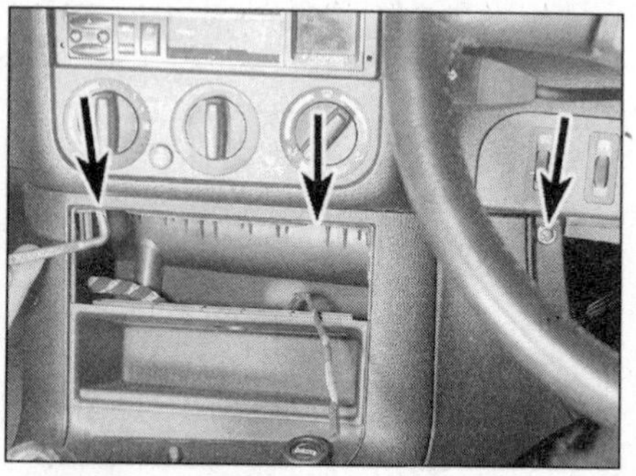

**28.11b . . . and the four upper retaining screws (three arrowed) and remove the centre console front section**

## 29 Facia panel assembly - removal and refitting

**HAYNES HiNT** ***Label each wiring connector as it is disconnected from its relevant component. The labels will prove useful on refitting, when routing the wiring and feeding the wiring through the facia apertures.***

### *Removal*

**1** Disconnect the battery negative terminal.

**2** Remove the centre console as described in Section 28.

**3** Remove the steering column as described in Chapter 10.

**4** Remove the instrument panel assembly, cigarette lighter and radio/cassette unit as described in Chapter 12.

**5** On models equipped with a passenger side airbag, remove the airbag unit as described in Chapter 12. Undo the airbag mounting frame retaining bolts and remove the frame from the facia.

**6** Carefully unclip the left and right-hand windscreen pillar trim panels and remove them **(see illustration)**.

**7** Slacken and remove the retaining screws and remove the small section of trim from the passenger end of the facia **(see illustration)**.

**8** Unclip the trim covers from around the left and right-hand windscreen vents and undo the screws securing the vents to the facia **(see illustration)**.

**9** Slacken and remove the retaining bolts from the left and right-hand ends of the facia and recover the spacers **(see illustration)**.

**10** Carefully ease the facia assembly away from the bulkhead. As it is withdrawn, release the wiring harness from its retaining clips on the rear of the facia, whilst noting its correct routing (see ***Hint*** at the start of this Section). Remove the facia assembly from the vehicle.

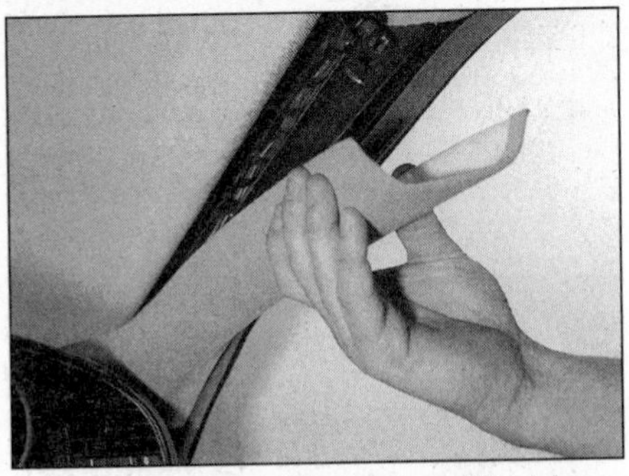

**29.6 Unclip the windscreen pillar trim panels and remove them from the vehicle**

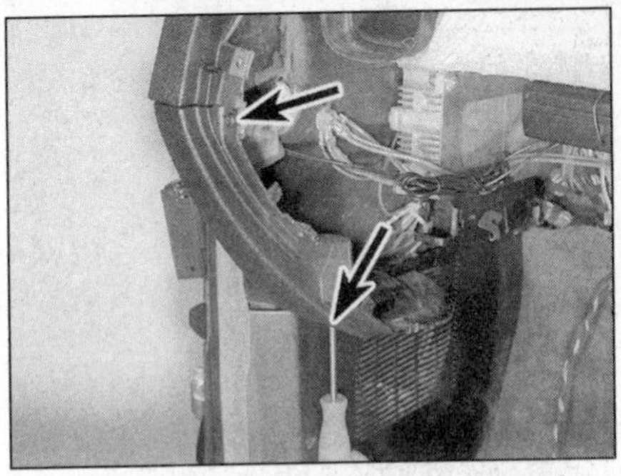

**29.7 Undo the retaining screws and remove the trim panel from the passenger end of the facia**

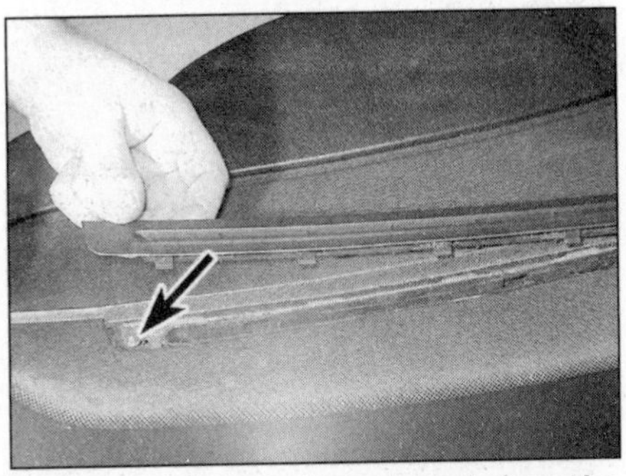

**29.8 Unclip the windscreen vents from the top of the facia to gain access to the vent screws (arrowed)**

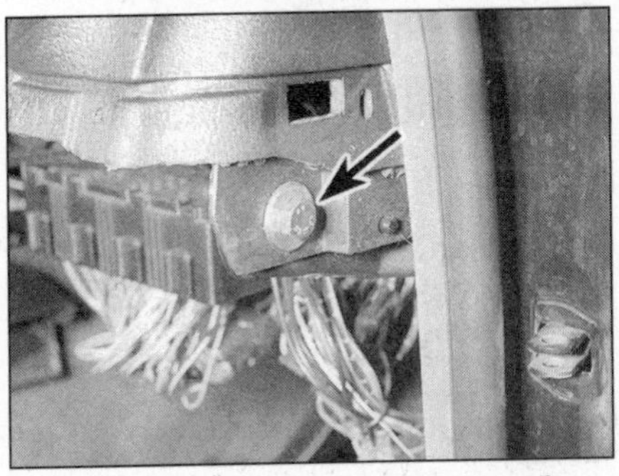

**29.9 Facia retaining bolt (arrowed)**

### *Refitting*

**11** Refitting is a reversal of the removal procedure, noting the following points:

*a) Manoeuvre the facia into position and, using the labels stuck on during removal, ensure that the wiring is correctly routed and securely retained by its facia clips.*

*b) Clip the facia back into position, making sure all the wiring connectors are feed through their respective apertures, then refit all the facia fasteners, and tighten them securely.*

*c) On completion, reconnect the battery and check that all the electrical components and switches function correctly.*

# Chapter 12
# Body electrical system

## Contents



## Degrees of difficulty

| | | | | |
|---|---|---|---|---|
| **Easy,** suitable for novice with little experience | **Fairly easy,** suitable for beginner with some experience | **Fairly difficult,** suitable for competent DIY mechanic | **Difficult,** suitable for experienced DIY mechanic | **Very difficult,** suitable for expert DIY or professional |

## Specifications

| | |
|---|---|
| **System type** | 12-volt negative earth |
| **Fuses** | See inside fusebox lid |
| **Bulbs** | **Wattage** |
| **Exterior lights** | |
| Headlight (dipped and main beam) | 55 (H7 type) |
| Front foglight | 55 (H1 type) |
| Front sidelight | 5 |
| Direction indicator | 21 |
| Direction indicator side repeater | 5 |
| Stoplight | 21 |
| Taillight | 5 |
| Reversing light | 21 |
| Rear foglight | 21/4 |
| Number plate light | 5 |
| **Interior light** | |
| Front courtesy lights | 10 |
| Rear courtesy lights | 5 |
| Luggage compartment light | 10 |
| Glovebox light | 5 |
| Instrument panel: | |
| Illumination bulbs | 3 |
| Warning light bulbs | 1.5 |

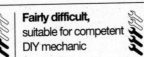

## Torque wrench settings

| | Nm | lbf ft |
|---|---|---|
| Wiper arm to wiper spindle nut | 25 | 18 |
| Wiper motor and linkage fixings: | | |
| Motor to linkage bolts | 10 | 7 |
| Crank to motor nut | 27 | 19 |
| Wiper spindle nuts | 12 | 9 |
| Support bracket bolts | 10 | 7 |
| Airbag system fixings: | | |
| Driver's side airbag retaining screws | 8 | 6 |
| Impact sensor mounting bolts | 10 | 7 |

## 1 General information and precautions

***Warning: Before carrying out any work on the electrical system, read through the precautions given in Safety First! at the beginning of this manual and Chapter 5.***

The electrical system is of the 12 volt negative earth type. Power for the lights and all electrical accessories is supplied by a lead/acid type battery which is charged by the alternator.

This Chapter covers repair and service procedures for the various electrical components not associated with engine. Information on the battery, alternator and starter motor can be found in Chapter 5.

It should be noted that prior to working on any component in the electrical system, the battery negative terminal should first be disconnected to prevent the possibility of electrical short circuits and/or fires.

## 2 Electrical fault finding - general information

**Note:** *Refer to the precautions given in `Safety first!' and in Section 1 of this Chapter before starting work. The following tests relate to testing of the main electrical circuits, and should not be used to test delicate electronic circuits (such as anti-lock braking systems), particularly where an electronic control module (ECU) is used.*

### General

**1** A typical electrical circuit consists of an electrical component, any switches, relays, motors, fuses, fusible links or circuit breakers related to that component, and the wiring and connectors which link the component to both the battery and the chassis. To help to pinpoint a problem in an electrical circuit, wiring diagrams are included at the end of this Manual.

**2** Before attempting to diagnose an electrical fault, first study the appropriate wiring diagram to obtain a complete understanding of the components included in the particular circuit concerned. The possible sources of a fault can be narrowed down by noting if other components related to the circuit are operating properly. If several components or circuits fail at one time, the problem is likely to be related to a shared fuse or earth connection.

**3** Electrical problems usually stem from simple causes, such as loose or corroded connections, a faulty earth connection, a blown fuse, a melted fusible link, or a faulty relay (refer to Section 3 for details of testing relays). Visually inspect the condition of all fuses, wires and connections in a problem circuit before testing the components. Use the wiring diagrams to determine which terminal connections will need to be checked in order to pinpoint the trouble spot.

**4** The basic tools required for electrical fault-finding include a circuit tester or voltmeter (a 12-volt bulb with a set of test leads can also be used for certain tests); a self-powered test light (sometimes known as a continuity tester); an ohmmeter (to measure resistance); a battery and set of test leads; and a jumper wire, preferably with a circuit breaker or fuse incorporated, which can be used to bypass suspect wires or electrical components. Before attempting to locate a problem with test instruments, use the wiring diagram to determine where to make the connections.

**5** To find the source of an intermittent wiring fault (usually due to a poor or dirty connection, or damaged wiring insulation), a `wiggle' test can be performed on the wiring. This involves wiggling the wiring by hand to see if the fault occurs as the wiring is moved. It should be possible to narrow down the source of the fault to a particular section of wiring. This method of testing can be used in conjunction with any of the tests described in the following sub-Sections.

**6** Apart from problems due to poor connections, two basic types of fault can occur in an electrical circuit - open circuit, or short circuit.

**7** Open circuit faults are caused by a break somewhere in the circuit, which prevents current from flowing. An open circuit fault will prevent a component from working, but will not cause the relevant circuit fuse to blow.

**8** Short circuit faults are caused by a `short' somewhere in the circuit, which allows the current flowing in the circuit to `escape' along an alternative route, usually to earth. Short circuit faults are normally caused by a breakdown in wiring insulation, which allows a feed wire to touch either another wire, or an earthed component such as the bodyshell. A short circuit fault will normally cause the relevant circuit fuse to blow.

### Finding an open circuit

**9** To check for an open circuit, connect one lead of a circuit tester or voltmeter to either the negative battery terminal or a known good earth.

**10** Connect the other lead to a connector in the circuit being tested, preferably nearest to the battery or fuse.

**11** Switch on the circuit, bearing in mind that some circuits are live only when the ignition switch is moved to a particular position.

**12** If voltage is present (indicated either by the tester bulb lighting or a voltmeter reading, as applicable), this means that the section of the circuit between the relevant connector and the battery is problem-free.

**13** Continue to check the remainder of the circuit in the same fashion.

**14** When a point is reached at which no voltage is present, the problem must lie between that point and the previous test point with voltage. Most problems can be traced to a broken, corroded or loose connection.

### Finding a short circuit

**15** To check for a short circuit, first disconnect the load(s) from the circuit (loads are the components which draw current from a circuit, such as bulbs, motors, heating elements, etc).

**16** Remove the relevant fuse from the circuit, and connect a circuit tester or voltmeter to the fuse connections.

**17** Switch on the circuit, bearing in mind that some circuits are live only when the ignition switch is moved to a particular position.

**18** If voltage is present (indicated either by the tester bulb lighting or a voltmeter reading, as applicable), this means that there is a short circuit.

**19** If no voltage is present, but the fuse still blows with the load(s) connected, this indicates an internal fault in the load(s).

### Finding an earth fault

**20** The battery negative terminal is connected to `earth'- the metal of the engine/transmission and the car body - and most systems are wired so that they only receive a positive feed, the current returning through the metal of the car body. This means that the component mounting and the body form part of that circuit. Loose or corroded mountings can therefore cause a range of electrical faults, ranging from total failure of a circuit, to a puzzling partial fault. In particular, lights may shine dimly (especially when another circuit sharing the same earth point is in operation), motors (eg. wiper motors or the radiator cooling fan motor) may run slowly, and the operation of one circuit may have an apparently unrelated effect on another. Note that on many vehicles, earth straps are used between certain components, such as the engine/transmission and the body, usually where there is no metal-to-metal contact between components due to flexible rubber mountings, etc.

**21** To check whether a component is properly earthed, disconnect the battery and connect one lead of an ohmmeter to a known good earth point. Connect the other lead to the wire or earth connection being tested. The resistance reading should be zero; if not, check the connection as follows.

**22** If an earth connection is thought to be faulty, dismantle the connection and clean back to bare metal both the bodyshell and the wire terminal or the component earth connection mating surface. Be careful to remove all traces of dirt and corrosion, then use a knife to trim away any paint, so that a clean metal-to-metal joint is made. On reassembly, tighten the joint fasteners securely; if a wire terminal is being refitted, use serrated washers between the terminal and the bodyshell to ensure a clean and secure connection. When the connection is remade, prevent the onset of corrosion in the future by applying a coat of petroleum jelly or silicone-based grease or by spraying on (at regular intervals) a proprietary ignition sealer or a water dispersant lubricant.

## 3 Fuses and relays - general information

### Main fuses

**1** The fuses are located behind the fusebox in the left-hand rear corner of the engine compartment.

**2** To remove the fusebox cover, release its front retaining clip then unclip the cover.

**3** A list of the circuits each fuse protects is given on the label attached to the inside of the fusebox cover. A pair of tweezers for removing the fuses is also clipped to the lid **(see illustration)**.

**4** To remove a fuse, first switch off the circuit concerned (or the ignition), then pull the fuse out of its terminals using the tweezers which are clipped to the inside of the fusebox cover. The wire within the fuse should be visible; if the fuse is blown it will be broken or melted.

**5** Always renew a fuse with one of an identical rating; never use a fuse with a different rating from the original or substitute anything else. Never renew a fuse more than once without tracing the source of the trouble. The fuse rating is stamped on top of the fuse; note that the fuses are also colour-coded for easy recognition.

**6** If a new fuse blows immediately, find the cause before renewing it again; a short to earth as a result of faulty insulation is most likely. Where a fuse protects more than one circuit, try to isolate the defect by switching on each circuit in turn (if possible) until the fuse blows again. Always carry a supply of spare fuses of each relevant rating on the vehicle, a spare of each rating should be clipped into the base of the fusebox.

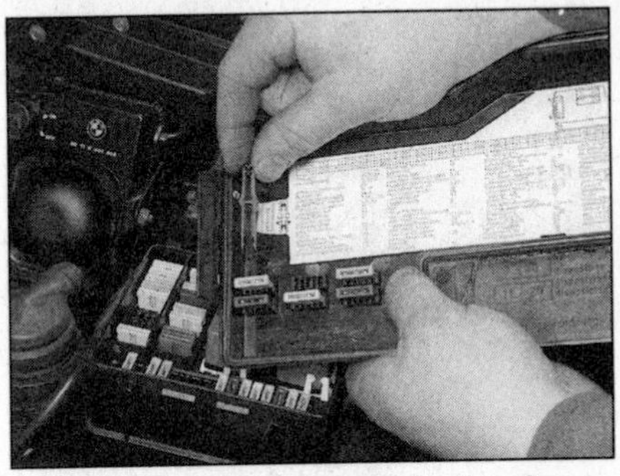

**3.3 Fuse can be removed using the tweezers which are clipped to the fusebox lid. Fuse locations are given on the sticker attached to the lid**

### Relays

**7** The majority of relays are located in the fusebox in the left-hand rear corner of the engine compartment. Additional relays can be found in the relay carrier under the left-hand side of the facia or attached to the connector strips under the left and right-hand sides of the facia **(see illustrations)**.

**8** If a circuit or system controlled by a relay develops a fault and the relay is suspect, operate the system; if the relay is functioning it should be possible to hear it click as it is energised. If this is the case the fault lies with the components or wiring of the system. If the relay is not being energised then either the relay is not receiving a main supply or a switching voltage or the relay itself is faulty. Testing is by the substitution of a known good unit but be careful; while some relays are identical in appearance and in operation, others look similar but perform different functions.

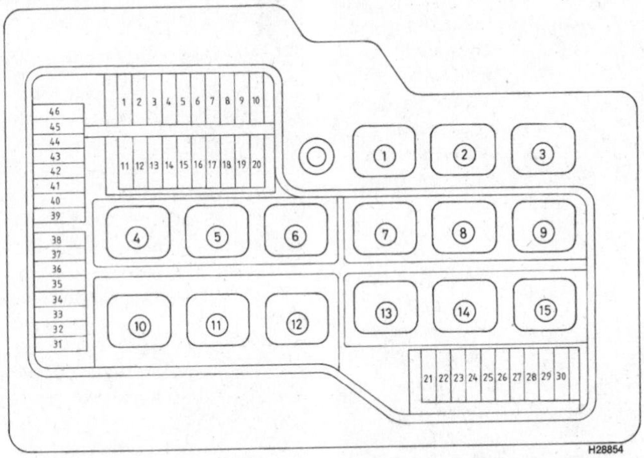


**3.7a Fusebox relay locations (fuse locations also numbered)**

*1 Fuel pump relay*
*2 DME relay*
*3 Oxygen sensor relay*
*4 Horn relay*
*5 Foglight relay*
*6 Headlight relay*
*7 Main beam relay*
*8 Hazard warning light relay*
*9 Blower motor relay*
*10 Heated rear screen relay*
*11 ABS overvoltage protection relay*
*12 ABS pump motor relay*
*13 Auxiliary cooling fan stage 2 relay*
*14 Air conditioning compressor relay*
*15 Auxiliary cooling fan stage 1 relay*
**Not all relays fitted to all models*

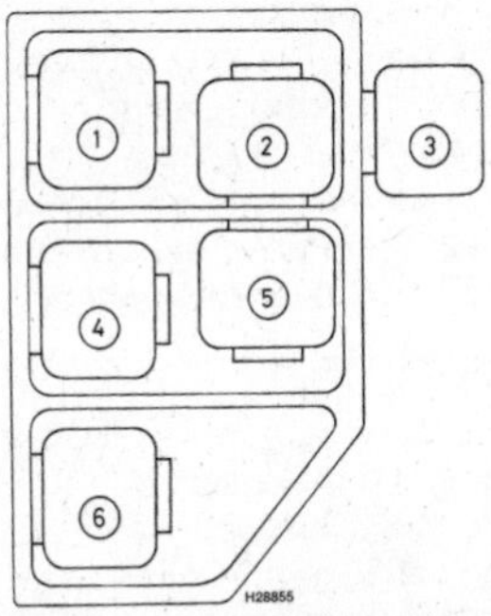


**3.7b Relay carrier under behind left-hand side of facia**

*1 Independent ventilation relay*
*2 Double relay module*
*3 Rear window opening relay - Coupe models*
*4 Crash alarm sensor relay*
*5 Headlight washer module relay*
*6 Comfort relay*
**Not all relays fitted to all models*

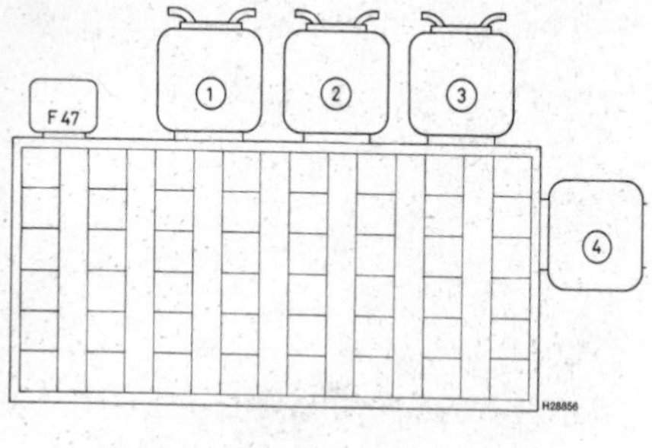


**3.7c Connector strip behind left-hand side of the facia**

*1 Unloader relay or starter interlock relay (depending on model)*
*2 Wiper relay*
*3 Wiper motor relay*
*4 Unloader relay or starter interlock relay (depending on model)*
**Not all relays fitted to all models*

**9** To renew a relay first ensure that the ignition switch is off. The relay can then simply be pulled out from the socket and the new relay pressed in **(see illustration)**.

## 4 Switches - removal and refitting

**Note:** *Disconnect the battery negative lead before removing any switch, and reconnect the lead after refitting the switch.*

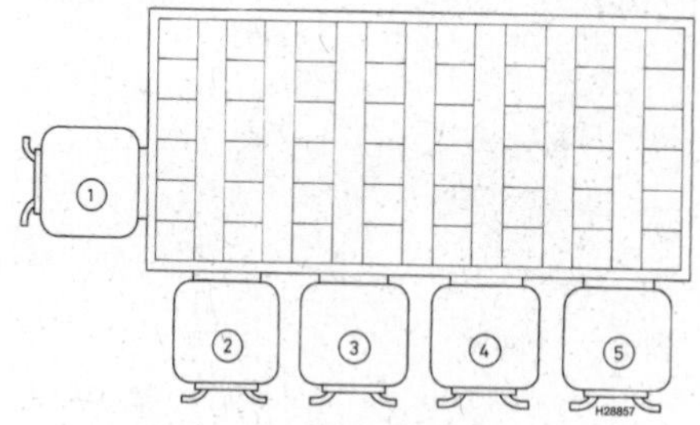


**3.7d Connector strip behind right-hand side off facia**

*1 Alarm horn relay*
*2 Right-hand parking light/ number plate light relay*
*3 Left-hand parking light relay*
*4 Central locking relay*
*5 Rear window blower motor relay*
**Not all relays fitted to all models*

### Ignition switch/ steering column lock

**1** Refer to Chapter 10.

### Steering column combination switches

**2** Remove the steering wheel as described in Chapter 10.

**3** Undo the driver's side lower facia panel retaining screws then unclip the panel and remove it from the vehicle **(see illustration)**.

**4** Unscrew the steering column upper and lower fastener screws and pull out the fasteners. Unclip the two halves of the shroud and remove them from the column **(see illustrations)**.

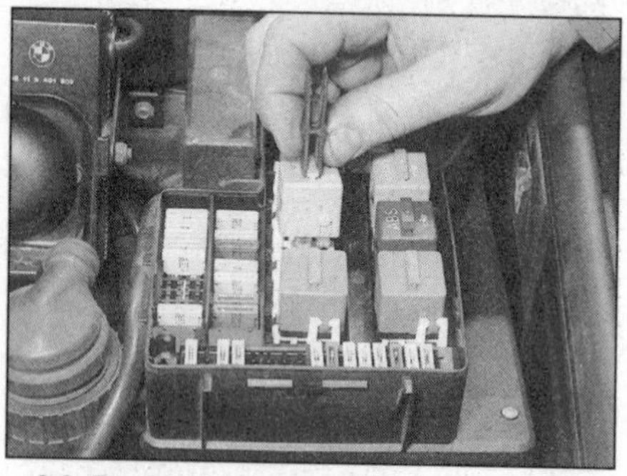

**3.9 Removing a relay from the fusebox**

**5** Trace the wiring back from the switch, freeing it from the steering column, and disconnect it at the wiring connector **(see illustration)**.

**6** Loosen the switch holder fastener screw and pull out the fastener **(see illustration)**.

**7** Release the switch holder from the column then depress the retaining tangs and slide the switch(es) out from the holder **(see illustration)**.

**8** Refitting is a reversal of the removal procedure, ensuring that the wiring is correctly routed.

### Lighting switch

**9** Undo the driver's side lower facia panel retaining screws then unclip the panel and remove it from the vehicle.

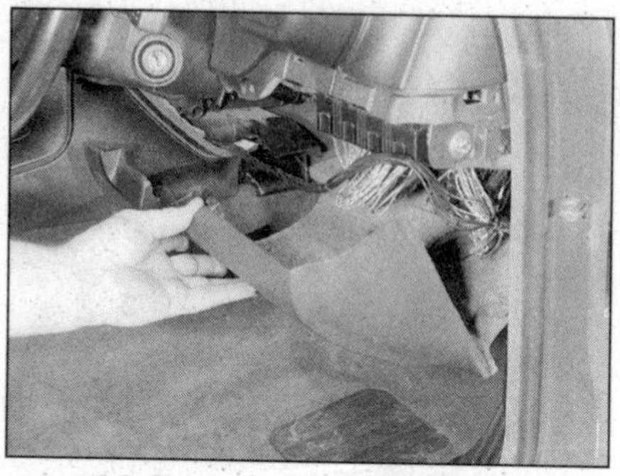

**4.3 Removing the driver's side lower facia panel**

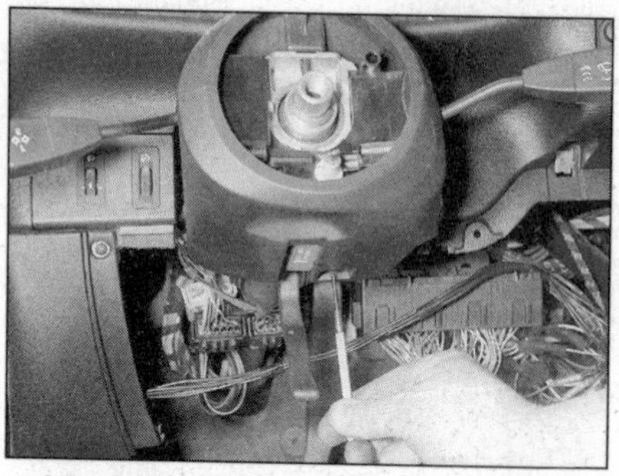

**4.4a Undo the screws and remove the fasteners . . .**

**4.4b . . . then unclip and remove the steering column shrouds**

**4.5 Disconnect the combination switch connector and free the wiring**

**4.6 Unscrew and unclip the fastener . . .**

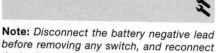

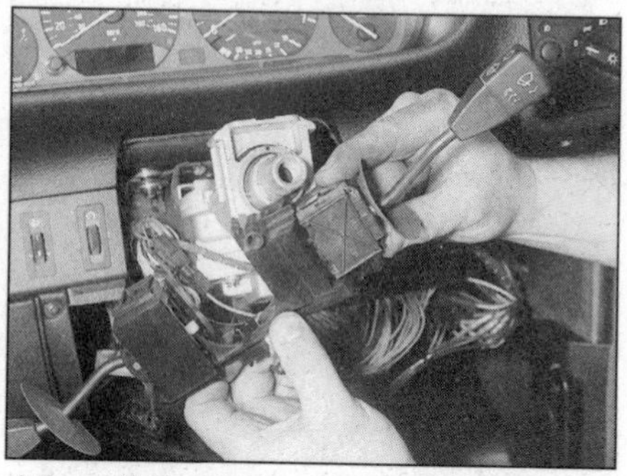

**4.7 . . . then release the holder from top of column and slide out the relevant switch**

4.10 Pull off the control knob from the lighting switch . . .

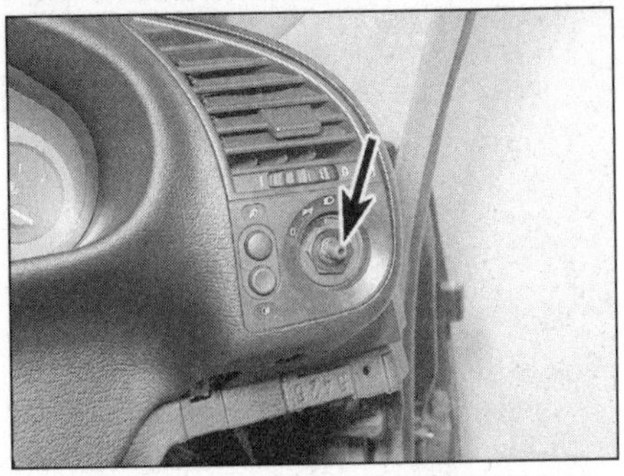

4.11 . . . and unscrew the retaining nut

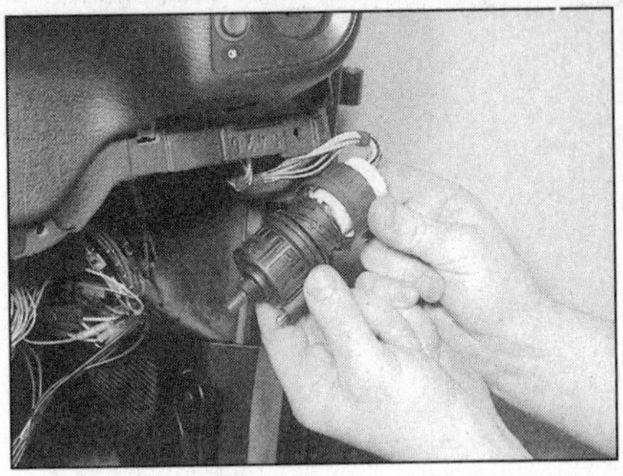

4.12 Lower the lighting switch and disconnect its wiring connector

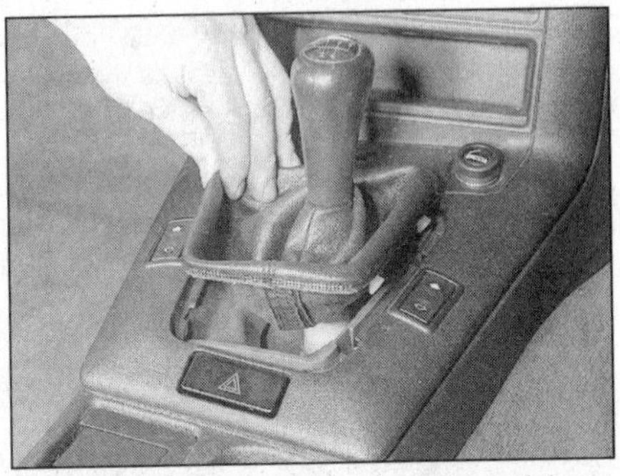

4.14 On manual transmission models, unclip the gaiter from the centre console and fold it back over the lever

4.16 Unclip the hazard warning light switch and disconnect its wiring connector

**10** Pull off the light switch knob to access the switch retaining nut **(see illustration)**.

**11** Unscrew the retaining nut then free the switch from the rear of the panel and lower it out of position **(see illustration)**.

**12** Disconnect the wiring connector and remove the switch **(see illustration)**.

**13** Refitting is the reverse of removal making sure the switch groove is correctly engaged with the panel lug.

### Hazard warning light and electric window switches

**14** On manual transmission models, carefully unclip the gearchange lever gaiter from the centre console and fold it back over the lever. Where necessary slide the rubber insert up the gearchange lever **(see illustration)**.

**15** On models with automatic transmission undo the retaining screw then depress the detent button and slide the handle off from the top of the selector lever. Unclip the selector lever position display panel from the top of the centre console and slide off the selector lever. If the position display panel is a tight fit in the console, remove the storage compartment (see Section 12) and push the panel out from behind.

**16** Reach in behind the centre console and push the switch out of position and disconnect its wiring connector **(see illustration)**.

**17** Refitting is the reverse of removal. On automatic transmission models make sure the selector lever handle detent button is correctly engaged with the lever rod before fitting the retaining screw.

### Foglight, instrument panel dimmer and headlight levelling switches

**18** Undo the driver's side lower facia panel retaining screws then carefully unclip the panel and remove it from the vehicle.

**19** Reach up behind the facia and disconnect the wiring connector from the switch.

**20** Depress the retaining tabs and slide the switch out of position **(see illustration)**.

**21** Refitting is the reverse of removal.

### Exterior mirror adjustment switch

**22** Carefully lever the switch out from the door panel **(see illustration)**.

**23** Disconnect the wiring connector and remove the switch **(see illustration)**.

**24** Refitting is the reverse of removal.

### Cruise control system switch

**25** Undo the driver's side lower facia panel retaining screws then unclip the panel and remove it from the vehicle.

**26** Unscrew the steering column lower shroud fastener screw and pull out the fastener. Unclip the lower shroud and remove it from the column.

**27** Trace the wiring back from the switch, freeing it from the steering column, and disconnect it at the wiring connector.

**28** Depress the retaining clips and slide the switch out of position.

**29** Refitting is the reverse of removal.

### Heated rear window switch

#### Models with automatic air conditioning system

**30** On these models the switch is an integral

4.20 Removing the foglight switch

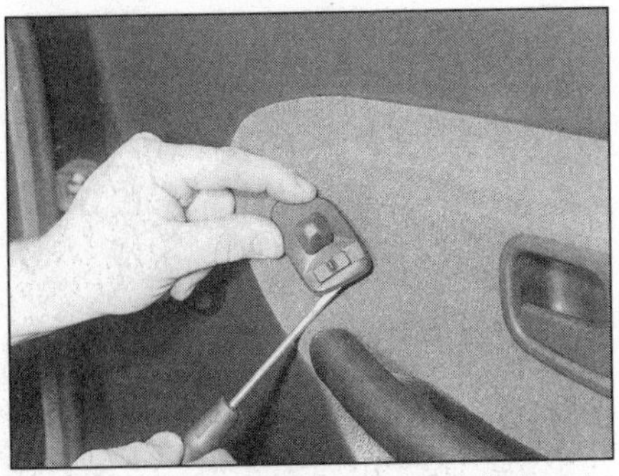

4.22 Prise the electric mirror switch out from the door trim panel . . .

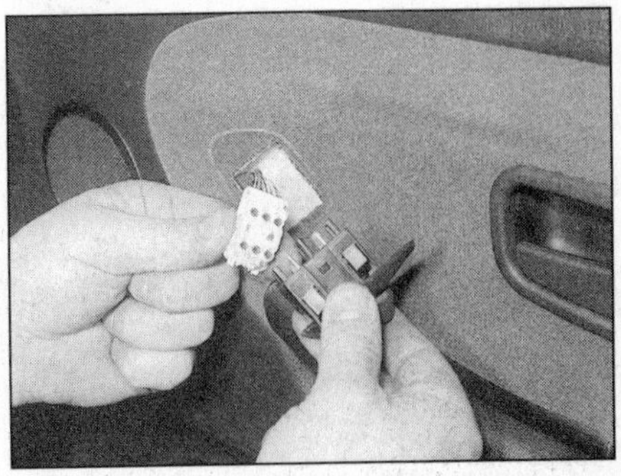

4.23 . . . and disconnect its wiring connector

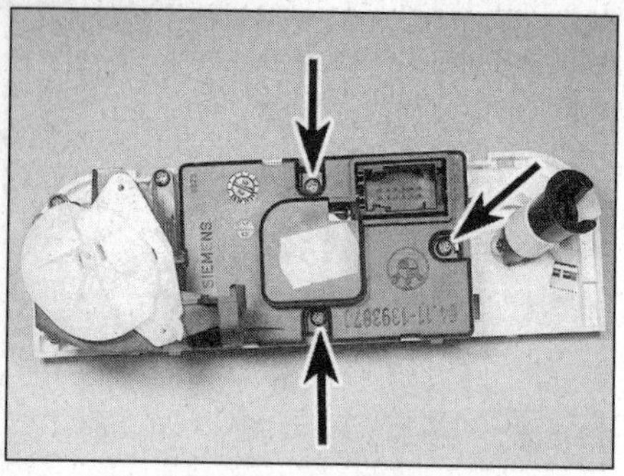

4.33a Undo the retaining screws (arrowed) . . .

part of the control unit and cannot be renewed. If the switch is faulty seek the advice of a BMW dealer.

### Models with a manually adjusted air conditioning system, and models without air conditioning

**31** On these models the switch is an integral part of the heater control panel printed circuit.

**32** Remove the heater control panel as described in Chapter 3.

**33** Undo the retaining screws then release the retaining clips and detach the printed circuit cover from the rear of the control unit. Lift out the printed circuit board **(see illustrations)**.

**34** Refitting is the reverse of removal. Check the operation of the switch before refitting the control panel to the facia.

## Heater blower motor switch

### Models with automatic air conditioning system

**35** On these models the switch is an integral part of the control unit and cannot be renewed. If the switch is faulty seek the advice of a BMW dealer.

### Models with a manually adjusted air conditioning system, and models without air conditioning

**36** Remove the heater control panel as described in Chapter 3.

**37** Undo the retaining screws then unclip the switch from the rear of the control panel and remove it **(see illustrations)**.

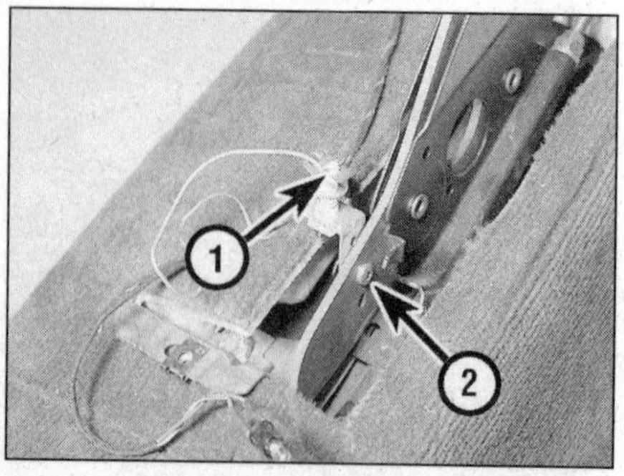


4.44 Handbrake warning light switch wiring connector (1) and retaining screw (2)

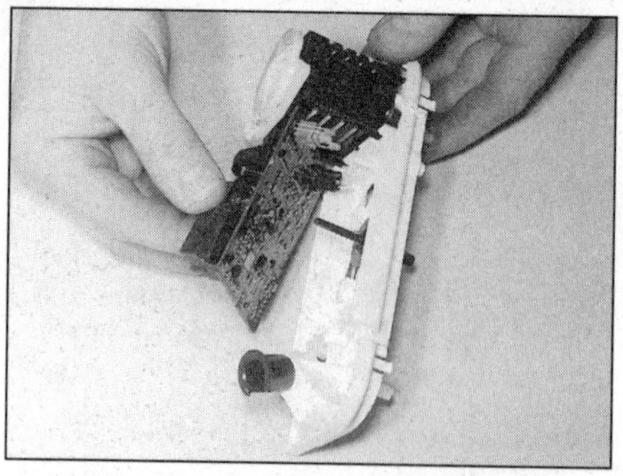

4.33b . . . then unclip the cover and remove the printed circuit board from the heater control panel

**38** Refitting is the reverse of removal. Check the operation of the switch before refitting the control panel to the facia.

## Air conditioning system switches

**39** Refer to paragraphs 35 to 38.

## Heated seat, electric rear sun blind and traction control (ASC+T) switches

**40** Remove the storage compartment from the centre console as described in Section 12.

**41** Disconnect the wiring connector then depress the retaining clips and slide the switch out from the panel.

**42** Refitting is the reverse of removal.

## Handbrake warning light switch

**43** Remove the rear section of the centre console as described in Chapter 11 to gain access to the handbrake lever.

**44** Disconnect the wiring connector from the warning light switch then undo the screw and remove the switch **(see illustration)**.

**45** Refitting is the reverse of removal. Check the operation of the switch before refitting the centre console, the warning light should illuminate between the first and second clicks of the ratchet mechanism.

## Stop-light switch

**46** Refer to Chapter 9.

## Front door courtesy light switch - Saloon models

**47** Open the door. The courtesy light switch is an integral part of the lock catch.

**48** Using a suitable marker pen, mark the outline of the catch on the door pillar.

**49** Slacken and remove the catch retaining screws then disconnect the wiring connector and remove the catch from the pillar. Take great care not to allow the caged nut plate or wiring connector to fall down inside the door pillar **(see illustrations)**. If either component falls down inside the pillar the trim panel will have to be removed (see Chapter 11).

**50** Refitting is the reverse of removal, aligning the catch with the marks made prior to removal. Shut the door and check that it locks securely; if necessary adjust by slackening the screws and repositioning the catch.

## Front door courtesy light switch - Coupe models

**51** Remove the door lock (see Chapter 11).

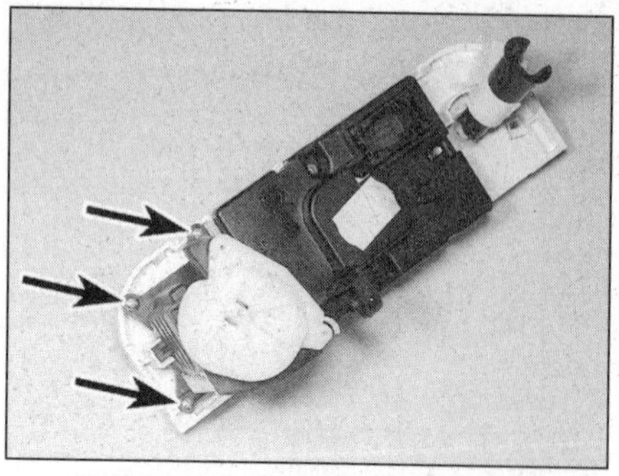

4.37a Undo the retaining screws (arrowed) . . .

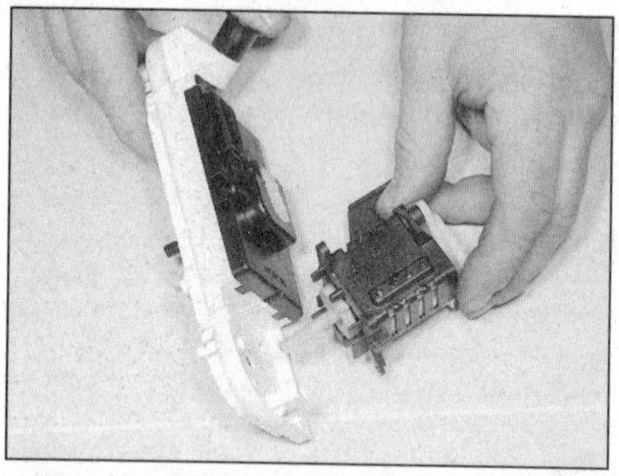

4.37b . . . and remove blower motor switch from the rear of the heater control panel

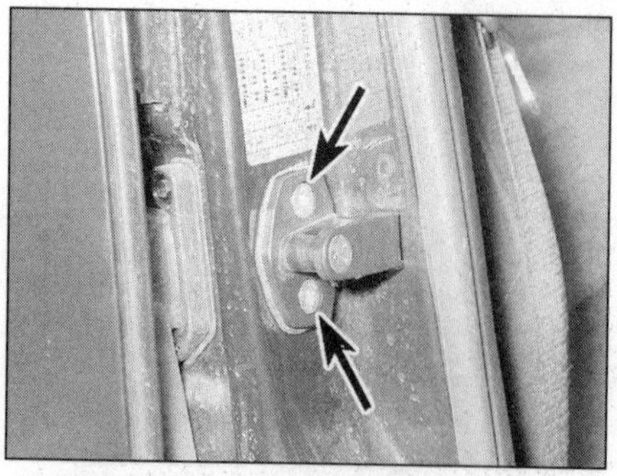

4.49a On Saloon models, undo the two retaining screws (arrowed) . . .

4.49b . . . then remove the catch and disconnect the wiring connector

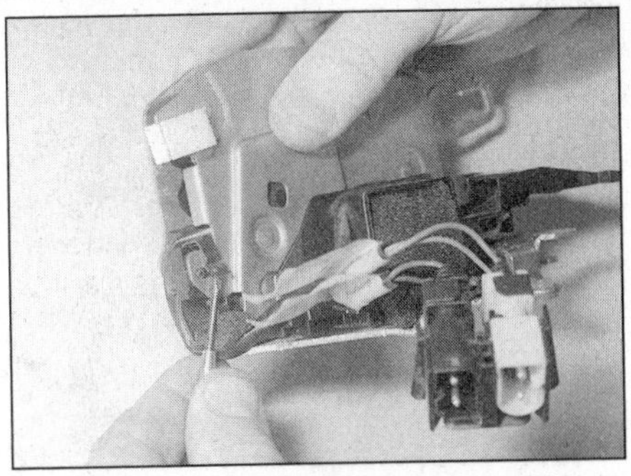

4.52a On Coupe models, release the retaining clip . . .

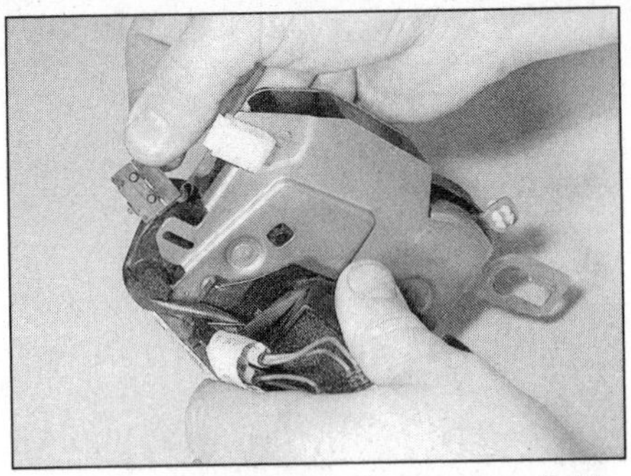

4.52b . . . and remove the courtesy light switch from the door lock

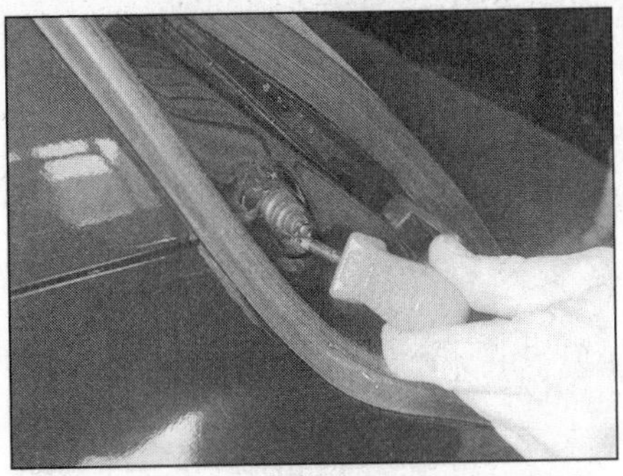

4.55 On the rear door on Saloon models, undo the retaining screw . . .

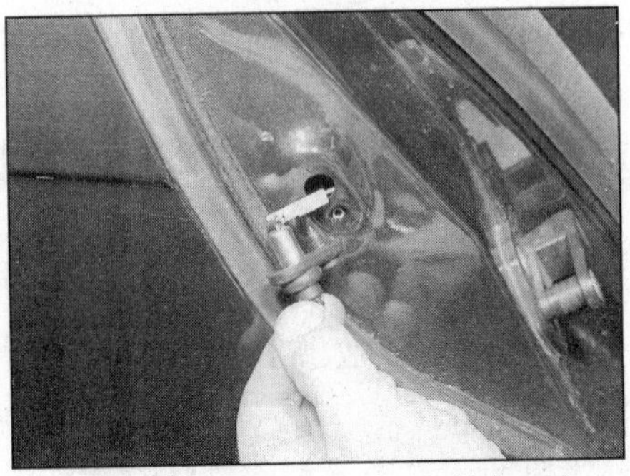

4.56 . . . the remove the switch and disconnect the wiring connector

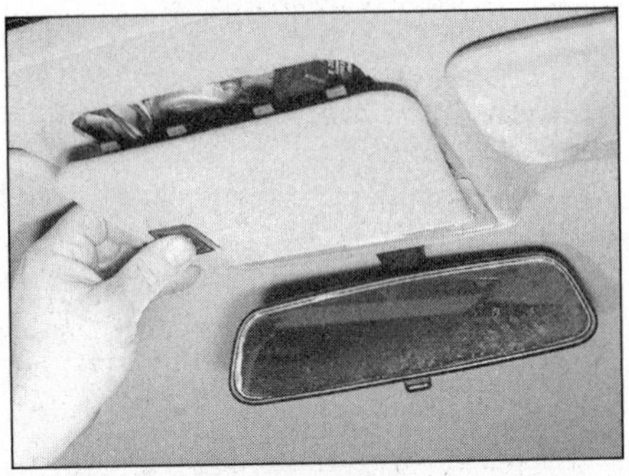

4.61 Unclip the switch panel from the headlining . . .

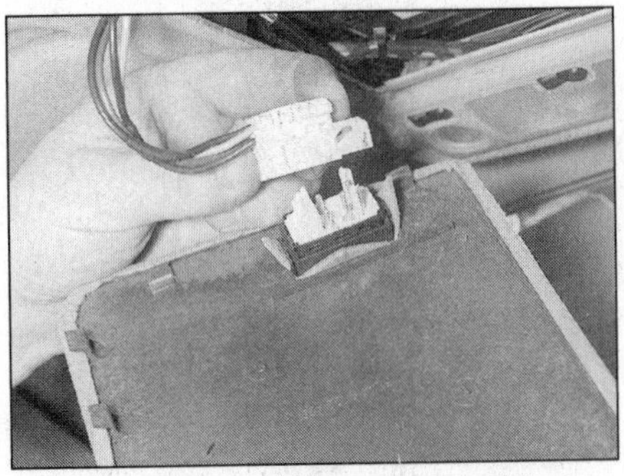

4.62 . . . then disconnect the wiring connector and separate the sunroof switch and panel

**52** Release the retaining clip and detach the microswitch from the lock **(see illustrations)**.

**53** Fit the new switch making sure it is securely retained by the clip.

**54** Refit the lock as described in Chapter 11.

### Rear door courtesy light switch - Saloon models

**55** Open up the door and slacken the switch retaining screw **(see illustration)**.

**56** Withdraw the switch, disconnecting its wiring connector as it becomes accessible. Tie a piece of string to the wiring to prevent it falling back into the door pillar **(see illustration)**.

**57** Refitting is a reverse of the removal procedure.

### Luggage compartment light switch

**58** Open up the boot lid then slacken and remove the screw securing the switch to the base of the lid.

**59** Disconnect the wiring connector and remove the switch.

**60** Refitting is the reverse of removal.

### Electric sunroof switch

**61** Carefully unclip the switch panel from the headlining **(see illustration)**.

**62** Disconnect the switch wiring connector then depress the retaining clips and slide the switch out of position **(see illustration)**.

**63** Refitting is the reverse of removal.

## 5 Bulbs (exterior lights) - renewal

### General

**1** Whenever a bulb is renewed, note the following points.

a) *Disconnect the battery negative lead before starting work.*
b) *Remember that if the light has just been in use the bulb may be extremely hot.*
c) *Always check the bulb contacts and holder, ensuring that there is clean metal-to-metal contact between the bulb and its live(s) and earth. Clean off any corrosion or dirt before fitting a new bulb.*
d) *Wherever bayonet-type bulbs are fitted (see Specifications) ensure that the live contact(s) bear firmly against the bulb contact.*
e) *Always ensure that the new bulb is of the correct rating and that it is completely clean before fitting it; this applies particularly to headlight/foglight bulbs (see below).*

### Headlight

**2** Release the retaining clip and remove the relevant access cover from the rear of the headlight unit **(see illustration)**. To improve access to the left-hand headlight, remove the air cleaner housing as described in Chapter 4.

**3** Disconnect the wiring connector from the rear of the bulb **(see illustration)**.

5.2 Release the retaining clips and remove the access cover from the rear of the headlight

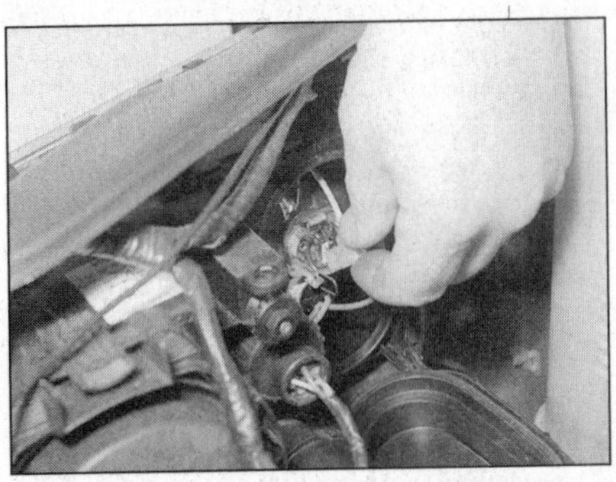

5.3 Disconnect the wiring connector . . .

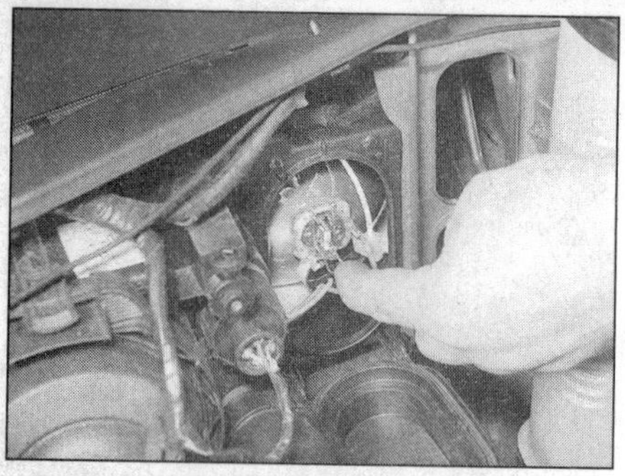

5.4a ... then release the spring clip ...

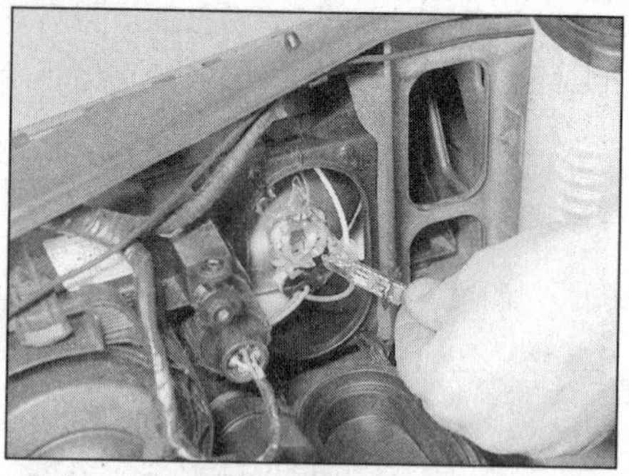

5.4b ... and withdraw the bulb from the headlight

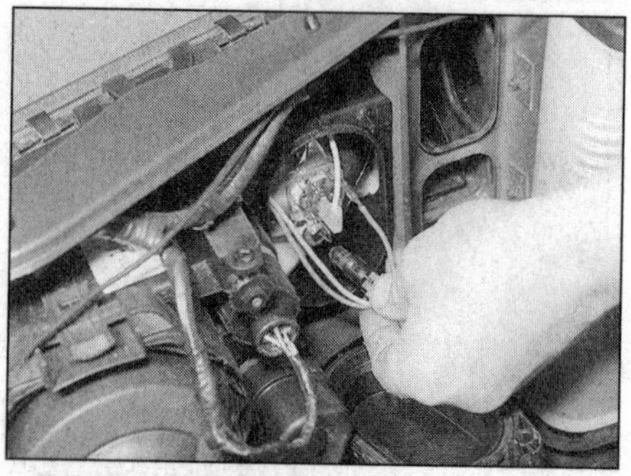

5.9 Removing the sidelight bulb holder from the headlight

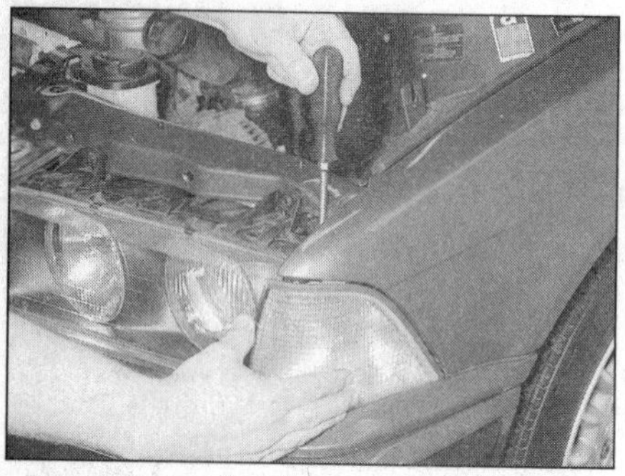

5.11 Release the direction indicator light retaining clip with a screwdriver ...

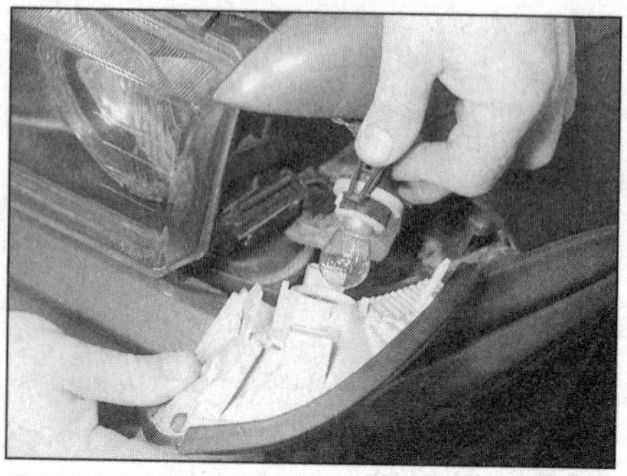

5.12 ... then slide the light out of position and unclip the bulbholder

5.14 Undo the retaining screw ...

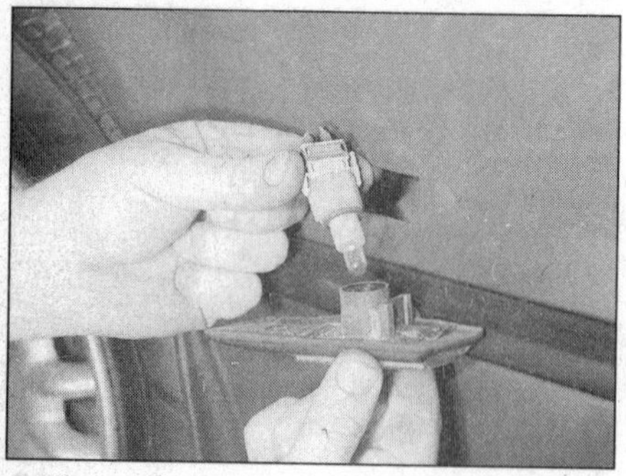

5.15a ... then release the bulbholder from the rear of the lens ...

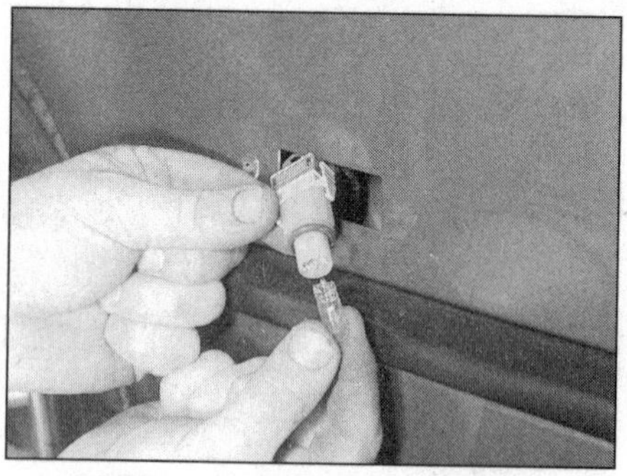

5.15b ... and pull out the bulb

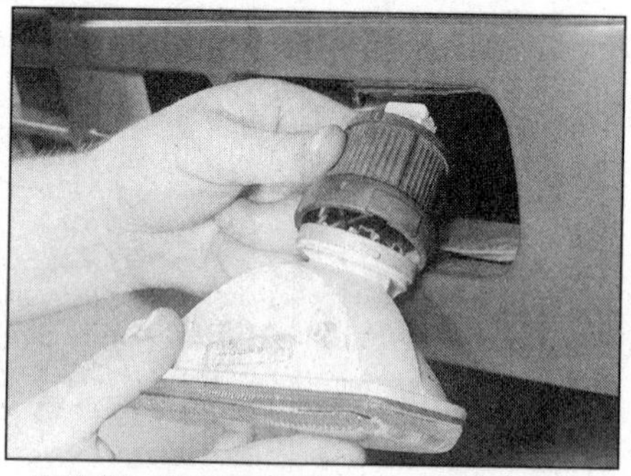

5.18 Unclip the foglight and release the bulb cover by twisting it anti-clockwise

**4** Unhook and release the ends of the bulb retaining clip and release it from the rear of the light unit. Withdraw the bulb **(see illustrations)**.

**5** When handling the new bulb, use a tissue or clean cloth to avoid touching the glass with the fingers; moisture and grease from the skin can cause blackening and rapid failure of this type of bulb. If the glass is accidentally touched, wipe it clean using methylated spirit.

**6** Install the new bulb, ensuring that its locating tabs are correctly located in the light cutouts, and secure it in position with the retaining clip

**7** Reconnect the wiring connector and refit the access cover, making sure it is securely refitted.

## Front sidelight

**8** Depress the retaining clip and remove the access cover from the rear of the headlight.

**9** Withdraw the sidelight bulbholder from the headlight unit **(see illustration)**. The bulb is of the capless type and is a push fit in the holder.

**10** Refitting is the reverse of the removal procedure making sure the access cover is securely refitted.

## Front direction indicator

**11** Using a screwdriver, release the retaining clip and withdraw the direction indicator light from the wing **(see illustration)**.

**12** Unclip the bulbholder and remove it from the rear of the light unit **(see illustration)**. The bulb is a bayonet fit in the holder and can be removed by pressing it and twisting in an anti-clockwise direction.

**13** Refitting is a reverse of the removal procedure making sure the light unit is securely retained by its spring.

## Front direction indicator side repeater

**14** Undo the retaining screw and withdraw the light unit from the wing **(see illustration)**.

**15** Twist the bulbholder anti-clockwise and remove it from the light. The bulb is of the capless (push-fit) type and is simply pulled out of the bulbholder **(see illustrations)**.

**16** Refitting is a reverse of the removal procedure. Do not overtighten the retaining screws as the lens is easily cracked.

## Front foglight

**17** Insert a flat-bladed screwdriver through the front bumper grille and release the foglight retaining clip.

**18** Withdraw the foglight from the bumper and rotate the foglight cover anti-clockwise and release it from the rear of the light unit **(see illustration)**.

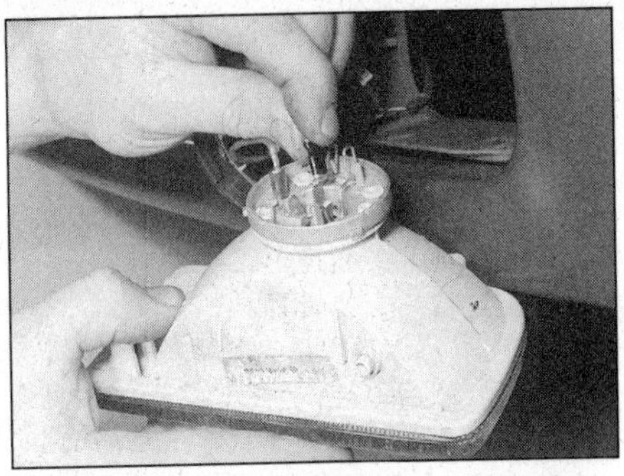

**5.19a Disconnect the wiring connector then release the retaining clip . . .**

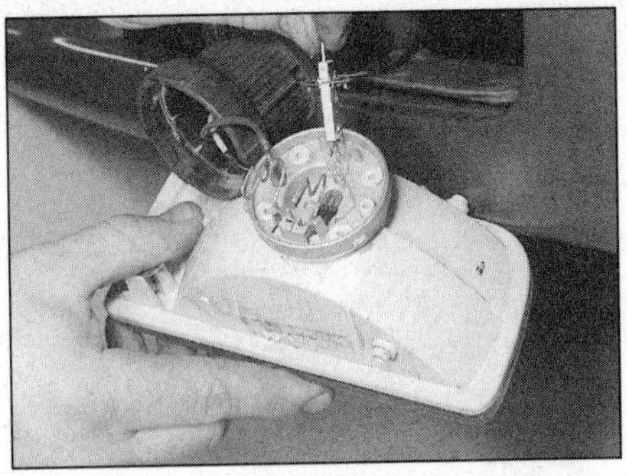

**5.19b . . . and withdraw the bulb**

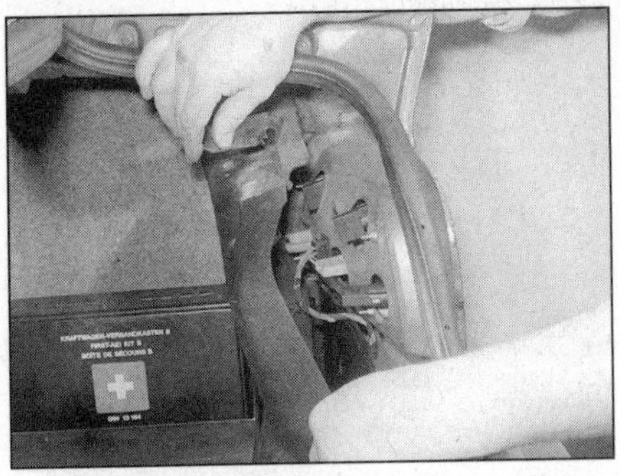

**5.24 Release the clip and remove the cover to gain access to the rear light bulbs**

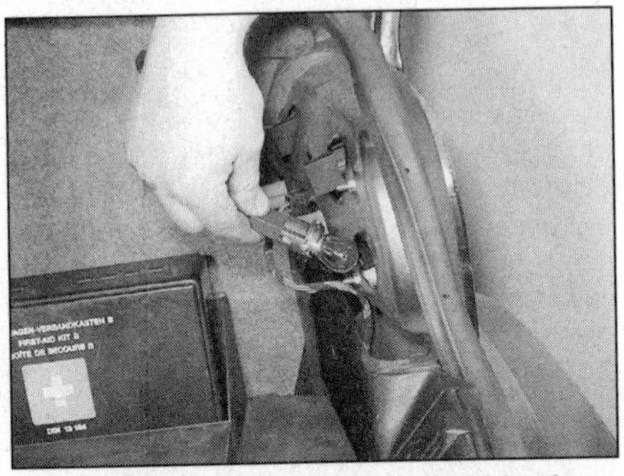

**5.25 Remove the relevant bulbholder from the light unit by twisting it anti-clockwise**

**5.29 Removing the trim cover from around the number plate lights**

**5.31 Unclip the number plate light from the boot lid and remove the bulb**

**19** Disconnect the bulb wiring then release the spring clip and withdraw the foglight bulb **(see illustrations)**.

**20** When handling the new bulb, use a tissue or clean cloth to avoid touching the glass with the fingers; moisture and grease from the skin can cause blackening and rapid failure of this type of bulb. If the glass is accidentally touched, wipe it clean using methylated spirit.

**21** Insert the new bulb, making sure it is correctly located, and secure it in position with the spring clip.

**22** Connect the wiring to the bulb then refit the cover to the rear of the unit.

**23** Refit the foglight to the bumper, making sure it is clipped securely in position.

### *Rear light cluster*

**24** From inside the vehicle luggage compartment, rotate the clip through 90° and remove the plastic access cover from the rear of the light cluster **(see illustration)**.

**25** Rotate the relevant bulbholder anti-clockwise and remove it from the light unit **(see illustration)**. The bulbs have bayonet fittings and are removed, by pressing in and rotating anti-clockwise.

**26** Refitting is a reversal of removal.

### *High-level stop light*

**27** From within the luggage compartment, rotate the bulbholder anti-clockwise and release it from the light unit. The bulb is a bayonet fit in the holder and can be removed by pressing it and twisting in an anti-clockwise direction.

**28** Refit by reversing the removal procedure.

### *Number plate light*

**29** Undo the retaining screws and remove the trim cover from around the lights **(see illustration)**.

**30** Press the light unit towards the left and unclip it from the boot lid.

**31** Release the bulb from the contacts and remove it from the light unit **(see illustration)**.

**32** Refitting is the reverse of removal, making sure the bulb is securely held in position by the contacts.

## 6 Bulbs (interior lights) - renewal

### *General*

**1** Refer to Section 5, paragraph 1.

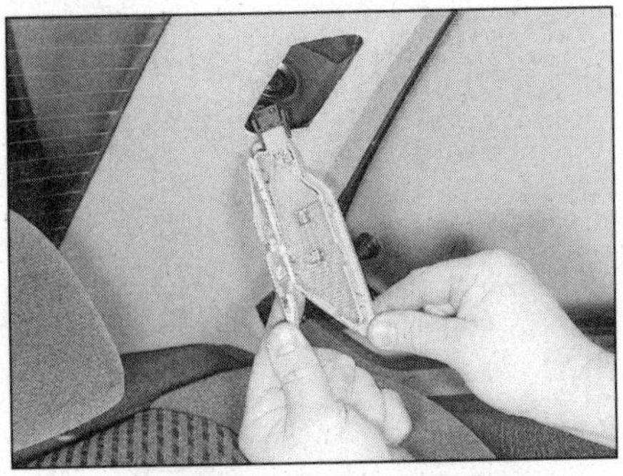

**6.2 Renewing the rear pillar courtesy light bulb**

### *Courtesy light*

**2** Using a small, flat-bladed screwdriver, carefully prise light unit out of position and release the bulb from the light unit contacts. On some lights it is necessary to unclip the reflector to access the bulb **(see illustration)**.

**3** Install the new bulb, ensuring it is securely held in position by the contacts, and clip the lens back into position.

### *Front seat reading light*

**4** Carefully lever the courtesy light lens out from the headlining.

**5** Rotate the reading light bulb anti-clockwise and remove it from the light unit **(see illustration)**.

**6** Fit the new bulb into position and refit the lens to the light unit.

### *Luggage compartment light*

**7** Refer to paragraphs 2 and 3.

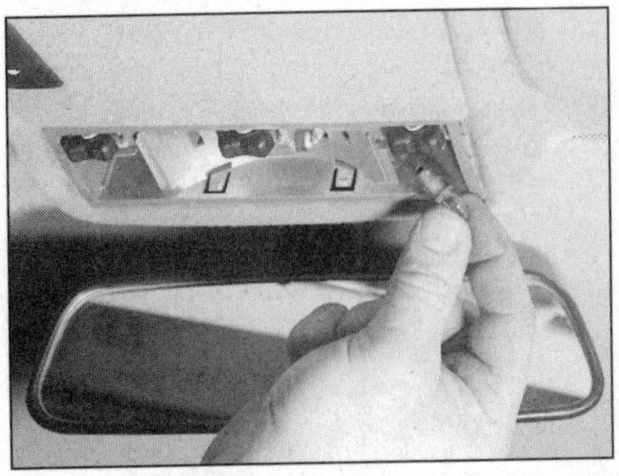

**6.5 Renewing the front seat reading light bulb**

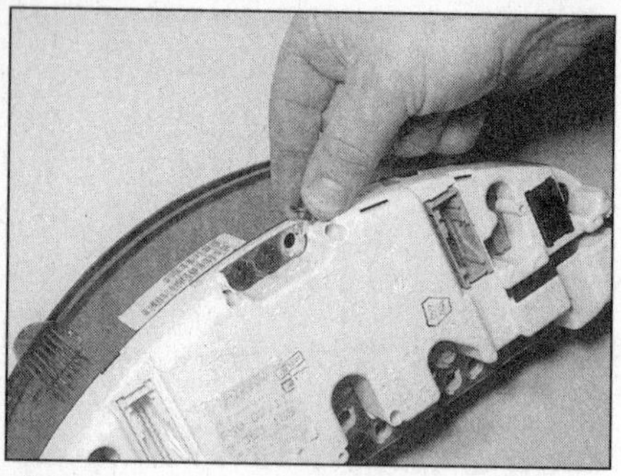
6.9 Instrument panel bulbholders can be removed by twisting them anti-clockwise

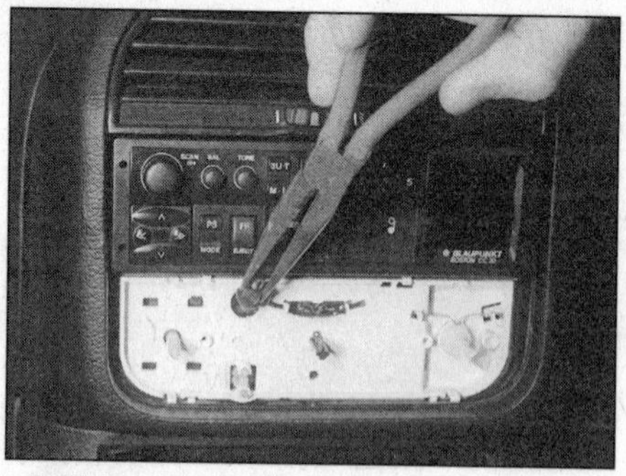
6.17 Removing the heater control panel illumination bulb

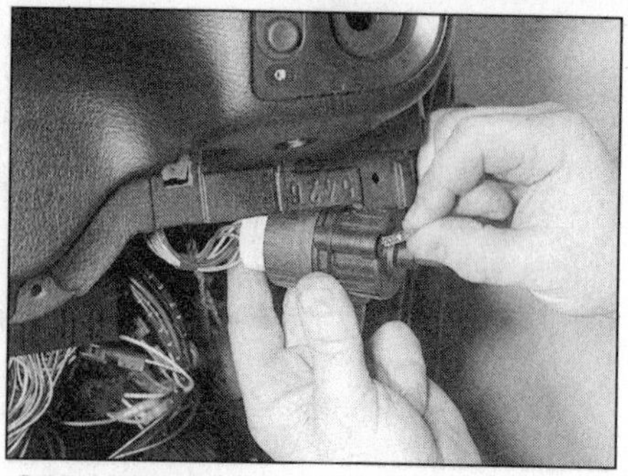
6.19 Lighting switch illumination bulb is a push-fit in the switch

### Instrument panel illumination/warning lights

8 Remove the instrument panel as described in Section 9.

9 Twist the relevant bulbholder anti-clockwise and withdraw it from the rear of the panel **(see illustration)**.

10 All bulbs are integral with their holders. Be very careful to ensure that the new bulbs are of the correct rating, the same as those removed; this is especially important in the case of the ignition/battery charging warning light.

11 Refit the bulbholder to the rear of the instrument panel then refit the instrument panel as described in Section 9.

### Glovebox illumination light bulb

12 Open up the glovebox. Using a small flat-bladed screwdriver carefully prise the top of the light assembly and withdraw it. Release the bulb from its contacts.

13 Install the new bulb, ensuring it is securely held in position by the contacts, and clip the light unit back into position.

### Heater control panel illumination bulb

#### Models with an automatic air conditioning system

14 Remove the heater control panel from the facia as described in Chapter 3 and remove the bulbholder from the rear of the control unit.

15 Refitting is the reverse of removal.

#### Models with a manually adjusted air conditioning, and models without air conditioning

16 Pull off the heater control panel knobs then undo the retaining screws and unclip the faceplate from the front of the control unit.

17 Using a pair of pointed-nose pliers, rotate the bulbholder anti-clockwise and remove it from the vehicle **(see illustration)**.

18 Refitting is the reverse of removal.

### Switch illumination bulbs

19 All of the switches are fitted with illuminating bulbs; some are also fitted with a bulb to show when the circuit concerned is operating. On most switches, these bulbs are an integral part of the switch assembly and cannot be obtained separately. Bulb replacement will therefore require the renewal of the complete switch assembly. The exception to this is the lighting switch illumination bulb which can be removed once the switch has been removed (see Section 4); the bulb is a push-fit in its holder **(see illustration)**.

## 7 Exterior light units - removal and refitting

**Note:** *Disconnect the battery negative lead before removing any light unit, and reconnect the lead after refitting the light*

### Headlight

1 To improve access to the left-hand headlight, remove the air cleaner housing as described in Chapter 4.

2 Rotate the retaining ring anti-clockwise and detach the main wiring connector from the headlight **(see illustration)**. Where necessary, release the retaining clip and disconnect the other wiring connector.

3 Remove the turn signal light as described in paragraph 8.

4 Undo the retaining screws and remove the plastic cover from above the radiator **(see illustration)**.

5 Slacken and remove the headlight retaining screws **(see illustration)**. **Note:** *As the screws are removed, do not allow the plastic retaining clips to rotate. If necessary retain the clips with a suitable open-ended spanner.*

6 Remove the headlight unit from the vehicle. On models equipped with a headlight levelling system, if necessary, remove the motor from the rear of the light unit by rotating it ant-clockwise and unclipping its balljoint **(see illustrations)**. **Note:** *The motor can be removed with the headlight unit in position on the vehicle.*

7 Refitting is a direct reversal of the removal procedure. Lightly tighten the retaining screws and check the alignment of the headlight with the bumper and bonnet. If necessary adjust the position of the headlight by screwing the plastic retaining clips in or out of the body (as applicable). Once the light unit is correctly positioned, securely tighten the

7.2 Turn the locking ring and disconnect the main wiring connector from the headlight

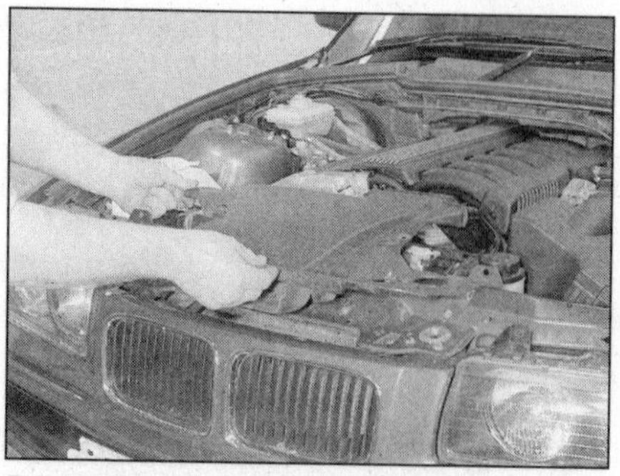
7.4 Undo the retaining screws and remove the plastic cover from above the radiator

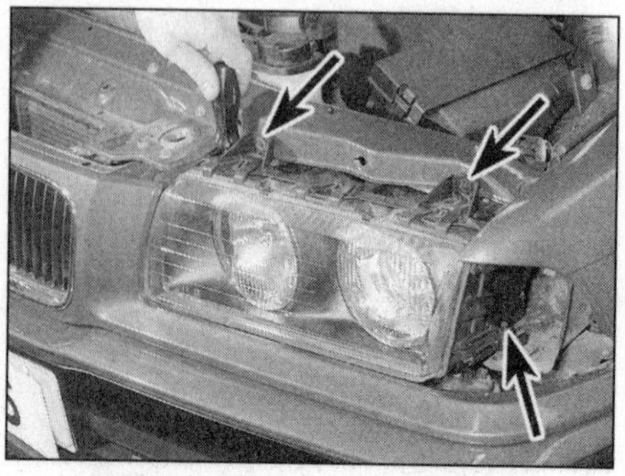
7.5 Undo the retaining screws (arrowed) . . .

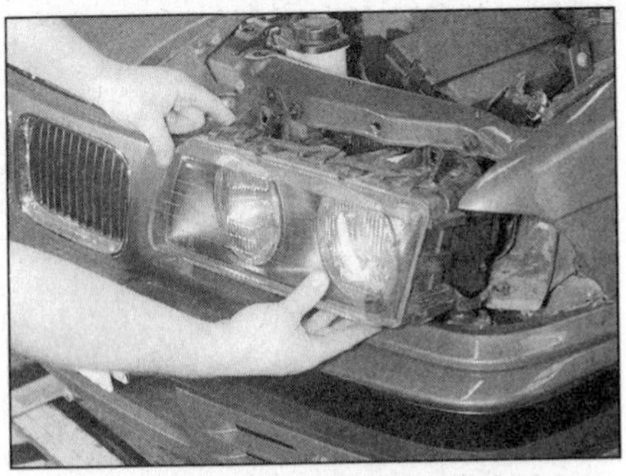

7.6a . . . and remove the headlight from the vehicle

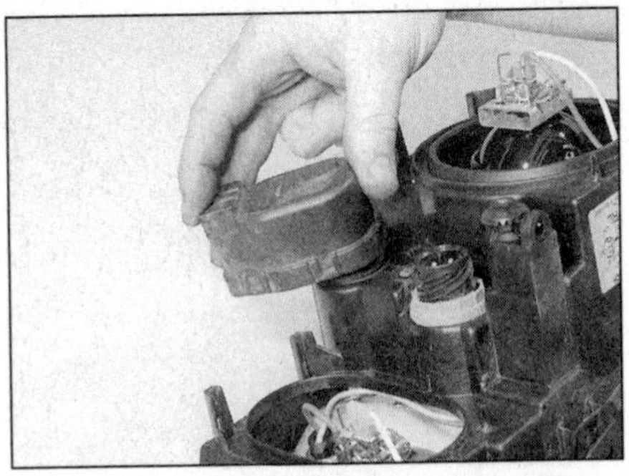

7.6b Rotate the levelling motor anti-clockwise . . .

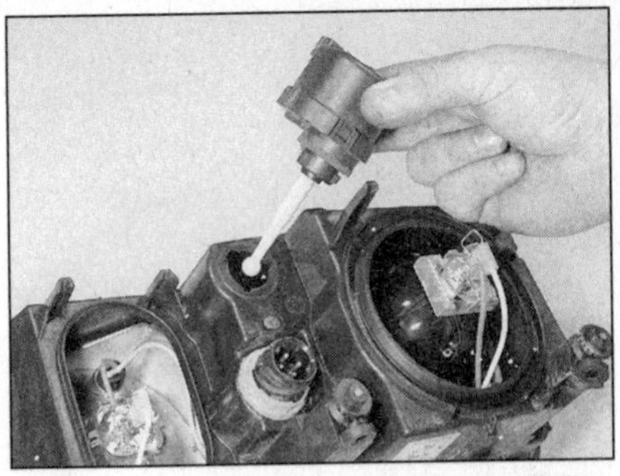

7.6c . . . and unclip it from the headlight

retaining screws and check the headlight beam alignment using the information given in Section 8.

### Front direction indicator light

**8** Using a screwdriver, unhook the retaining spring and withdraw the direction indicator light from the wing. Disconnect the wiring connector from the light unit and remove it from the vehicle.

**9** Refitting is a reverse of the removal procedure making sure the light unit is securely retained by its spring.

### Front direction indicator side repeater

**10** Undo the retaining screw and withdraw the light unit from the wing. Free the bulbholder by rotating it anti-clockwise and remove the light unit from the vehicle

**11** Refitting is a reverse of the removal procedure. Do not overtighten the retaining screw as the lens is easily cracked.

### Front foglight

**12** Insert a flat-bladed screwdriver, in through the front bumper grille and release the foglight retaining clip.

**13** Withdraw the foglight from the bumper and disconnect its wiring connector **(see illustration)**.

**14** Refitting is the reverse of removal, making sure the foglight is clipped securely in position. If necessary adjust the foglight aim using the adjusting screw which is accessed through the lower bumper grille.

### Rear light cluster

**15** From inside the vehicle luggage compartment, rotate the retaining clip through 90° and remove the plastic access cover from the rear of the light cluster.

**16** Disconnect the wiring connector then unscrew the retaining nuts and remove the light unit from the vehicle **(see illustrations)**.

**17** Recover the seal which is fitted between the light unit and body and renew it if it shows signs of damage or deterioration.

**18** Refitting is the reverse of the removal sequence making sure the seal is correctly positioned.

### Number plate light

**19** Undo the retaining screws and remove the trim cover from around the lights.

**20** Press the light unit towards the left and unclip it from the boot lid **(see illustration)**.

**21** Disconnect the wiring connector and remove the light unit.

**22** Refitting is the reverse of removal.

## 8 Headlight beam alignment - general information

Accurate adjustment of the headlight beam is only possible using optical beam setting equipment and this work should therefore be carried out by a BMW dealer or suitably equipped workshop.

For reference, the headlights can be adjusted by rotating the adjuster screws on the top of the headlight unit **(see illustration)**. The outer adjuster alters the horizontal position of the beam whilst the centre adjuster alters the vertical aim of the beam.

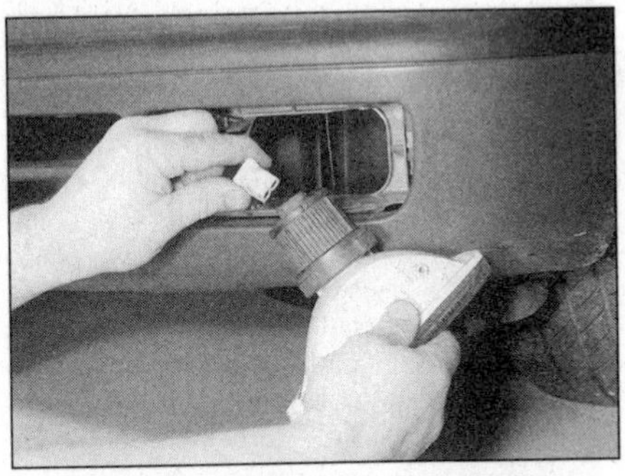

7.13 Unclip foglight from front bumper, then disconnect its wiring connector

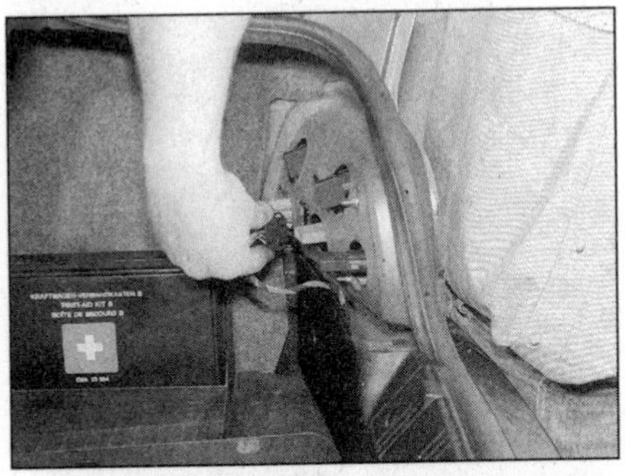

7.16a Disconnect the wiring connector, then undo the retaining nuts . . .

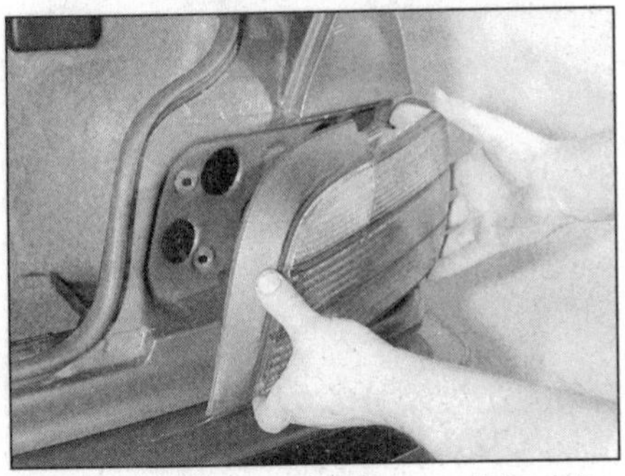

7.16b . . . and remove the rear light unit from the vehicle

7.20 Removing a number plate light

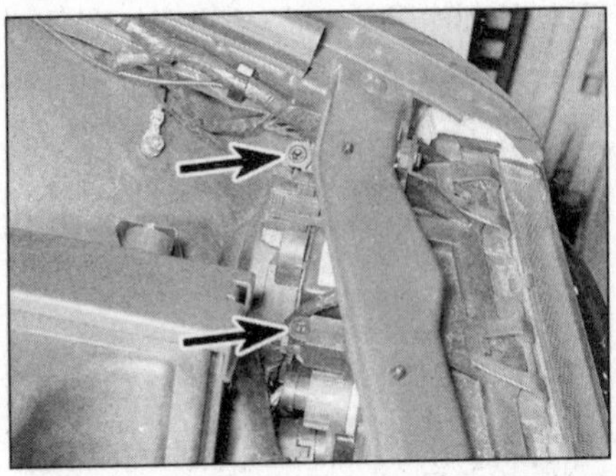

8.2 Headlight unit adjustment screws (arrowed)

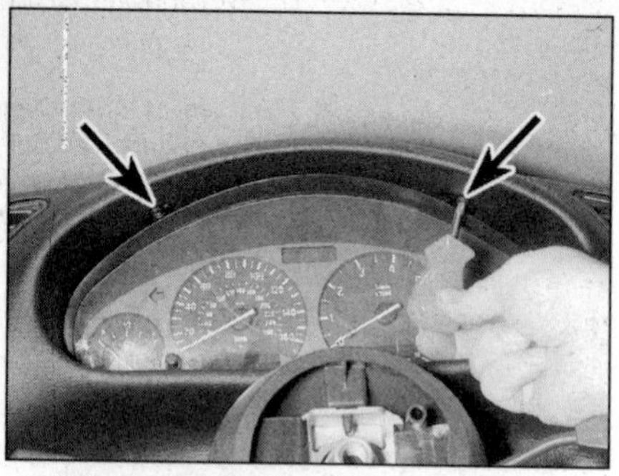

9.3a Undo the two retaining screws (arrowed) . . .

Some models have an electrically operated headlight beam adjustment system which is controlled through the switch in the facia. On these models ensure that the switch is set to the off position before adjusting the headlight aim.

## 9 Instrument panel - removal and refitting

### Removal

**1** Disconnect the battery negative terminal.

**2** Remove the steering wheel as described in Chapter 10.

**3** Slacken and remove the retaining screws from the top of the instrument panel and carefully withdraw the panel from the facia **(see illustrations)**.

**4** Lift up the retaining clips then disconnect the wiring connectors and remove the instrument panel from the vehicle.

### Refitting

**5** Refitting is the reverse of removal making sure the instrument panel wiring is correctly reconnected and securely held in position by the retaining clips. On completion reconnect the battery and check the operation of the panel warning lights to ensure that they are functioning correctly.

9.3b . . . then remove the instrument panel from the facia

## 10 Instrument panel components - removal and refitting

At the time of writing, no individual components are available for the instrument panel and therefore the panel must be treated as a sealed unit. If there is a fault with one of the instruments, remove the panel as described in Section 9 and take it to your BMW dealer for testing. They have access to a special diagnostic tester which will be able to locate the fault and will then be able to advise you on the best course of action.

## 11 Speedometer drive sender unit - removal and refitting

### Removal

**1** Chock the front wheels then jack up the rear of the vehicle and support it on axle stands (see "*Jacking and vehicle support*").

**2** Disconnect the wiring from the speedometer drive sender unit screwed into the rear of the final drive unit **(see illustration)**.

**3** Slacken and remove the retaining bolts and withdraw the sender unit. Recover the sender unit sealing ring and discard it; a new one should be used on refitting.

### Refitting

**4** Apply a smear of oil to the new sealing ring to aid installation and slide the ring up to tapered face of the sender unit **(see illustration)**. Do not push the seal right up to the sender unit mating surface.

**5** Fit the sender to the final drive unit and evenly and progressively tighten its retaining bolts.

**6** Reconnect the wiring connector, ensuring that a clean connection is made, and lower the vehicle to the ground.

## 12 Cigarette lighter - removal and refitting

### Removal

**1** Disconnect the battery negative terminal.

**2** Remove the clock/multi-information display unit as described in Section 13. On models with a clock, insert a feeler blade in between the clock mounting frame and storage compartment then release the retaining clip and slide the mounting frame out of position **(see illustration)**.

**3** On all models with no clock, carefully prise the upper storage compartment out from the facia centre panel.

**4** On all models, carefully unclip the storage compartment (which contains the cigarette lighter) and withdraw it from the centre facia panel. Disconnect the wiring connectors from cigarette lighter and (where fitted) switches and remove the storage compartment **(see illustrations)**.

**5** Unclip the bulbholder from the lighter then depress the retaining tangs and push the lighter out of the panel.

### Refitting

**6** Refitting is a reversal of the removal procedure, ensuring all the wiring connectors are securely reconnected.

11.2 The speedometer drive sender unit is mounted in the final drive unit rear cover (arrowed)

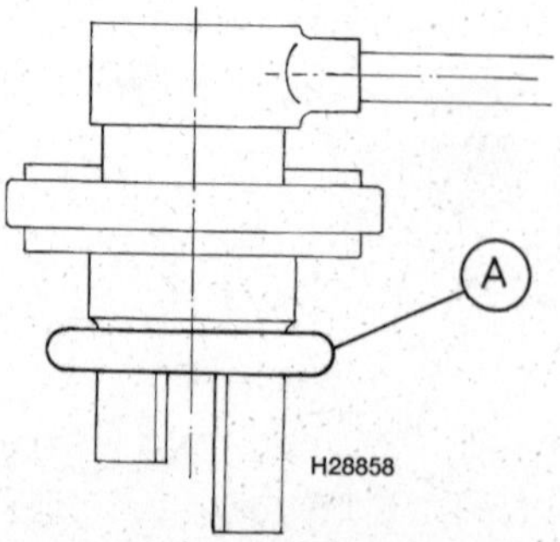


11.4 Fit the new sealing ring (A) to the speedometer drive sender and position it as shown. DO NOT slide it right up to the sender unit face

12.2 On models with a clock, unclip and remove the clock mounting frame/storage compartment from the centre console

12.4a Unclip the storage compartment from the console . . .

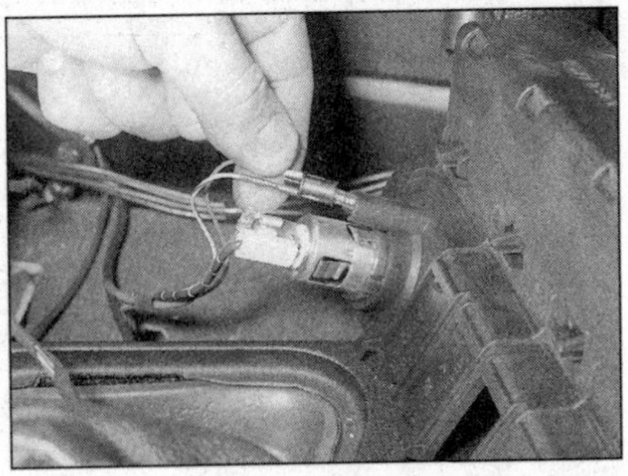

12.4b . . . and disconnect the wiring from the cigarette lighter

## 13 Clock/multi-information display unit - removal and refitting

### Removal

1 Disconnect the battery negative terminal.
2 Insert a feeler blade (approximately 1 mm thick) in between the base of clock/multi-information display and mounting.
3 Carefully release the retaining clip then slide the clock/multi-information display unit out from the facia centre panel and remove it, disconnecting its wiring connectors as they become accessible **(see illustrations)**.

### Refitting

4 Refitting is the reverse of removal.

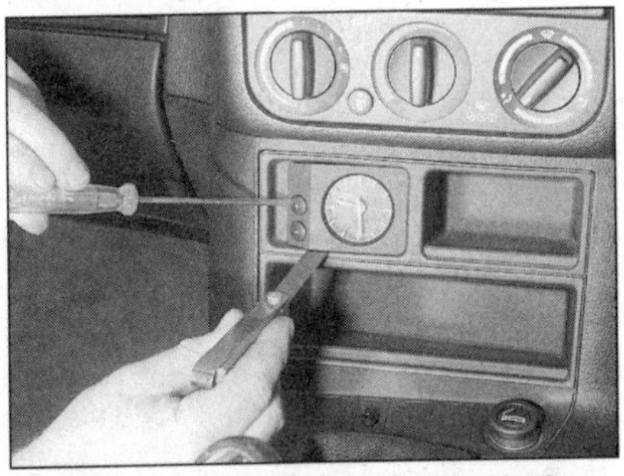

13.3a Unclip and remove the clock as shown . . .

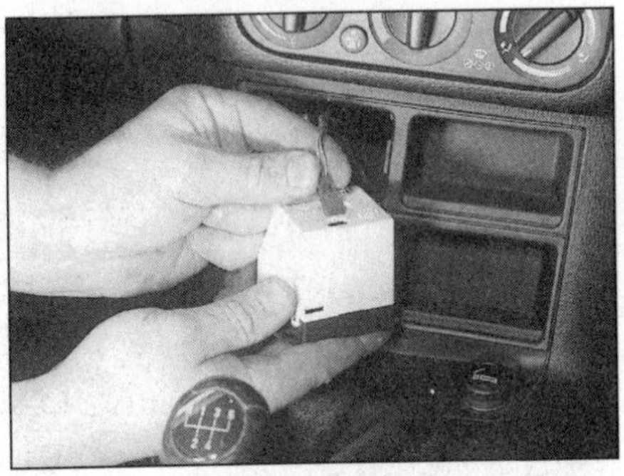

13.3b . . . and disconnect it from the wiring connector

## 14 Horn(s) - removal and refitting

### Removal

1 The horn(s) is/are located behind the left-hand end of the front bumper.
2 To gain access to the horn(s) from below, apply the handbrake then jack up the front of the vehicle and support it on axle stands (see "*Jacking and vehicle support*"). Undo the retaining screws and remove the access cover from the left-hand underside of the bumper. Unclip and remove the brake disc cooling duct.
3 To gain access to the horns from above, remove the left-hand headlight as described in Section 7 **(see illustration)**.
4 Undo the retaining nut/bolt and remove the horn, disconnecting its wiring connectors as they become accessible.

### Refitting

5 Refitting is the reverse of removal.

## 15 Wiper arm - removal and refitting

### Removal

1 Operate the wiper motor then switch it off so that the wiper arm returns to the at rest position.
2 Stick a piece of masking tape along the edge of the wiper blade to use as an alignment aid on refitting.
3 Prise off the wiper arm spindle nut cover then slacken and remove the spindle nut. Lift the blade off the glass and pull the wiper arm off its spindle. If necessary the arm can be levered off the spindle using a suitable flat-bladed screwdriver.
**Note:** *If both windscreen wiper arms are to be removed at the same time mark them for identification; the arms are not interchangeable.*

### Refitting

4 Ensure that the wiper arm and spindle splines are clean and dry then refit the arm to the spindle, aligning the wiper blade with the tape fitted on removal. Refit the spindle nut, tightening it to the specified torque setting, and clip the nut cover back in position. **Note:** *BMW recommend that the spindle nut torque should be checked again after 15 minutes.*

14.3 Horns viewed from above with the left-hand headlight unit removed

## 16 Windscreen wiper motor and linkage - removal and refitting

### Removal

1 Disconnect the battery negative terminal.
2 Remove the wiper arms as described in the previous Section.
3 Raise the bonnet to the vertical position as described in Chapter 11, Section 8.
4 Remove the rubber seal from the top of the heating/ventilation system inlet.
5 Remove the retaining clips securing the wiper motor cover panel in position.
6 Remove the release the grille from the top of the inlet and remove the cover panel(s) (as applicable) from the vehicle.
7 Undo the retaining screws and free the wiring harness duct from the inlet duct.
8 Slacken and remove the retaining screws and retaining plate and remove the inlet from the bulkhead. **Note:** *On 6-cylinder engines it may be necessary to remove the injector and spark plug covers from the engine to enable the inlet to be removed.*
9 Unscrew the large nut(s) from the wiper spindle(s) and remove the washer(s) (as applicable) **(see illustration)**.

16.9 Unscrew the nut (arrowed) from the wiper motor spindle and lift off the washer

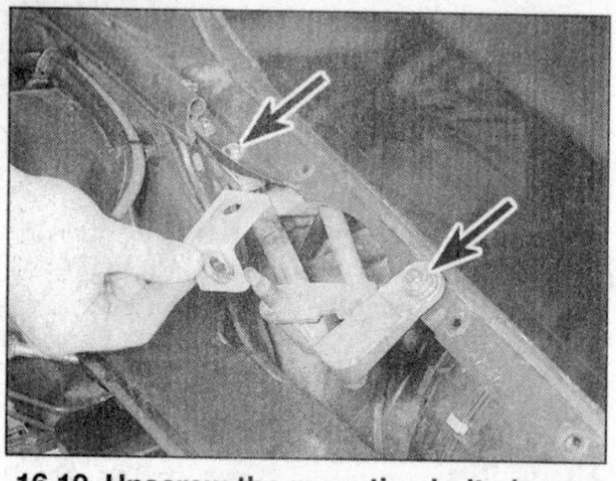

**16.10 Unscrew the mounting bolts (upper two arrowed) and remove the wiper motor support bracket**

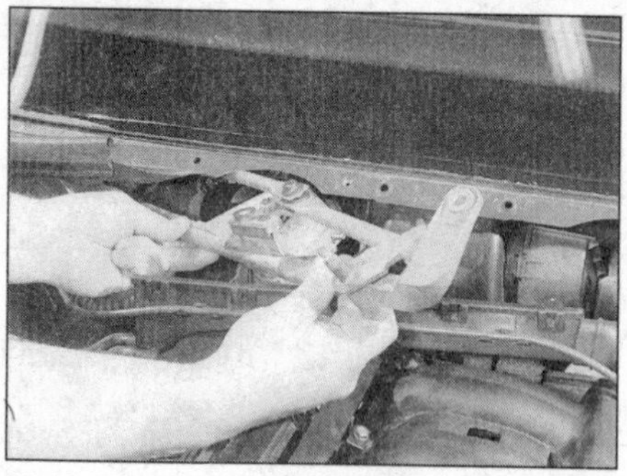

**16.12 Removing the wiper motor assembly from the vehicle**

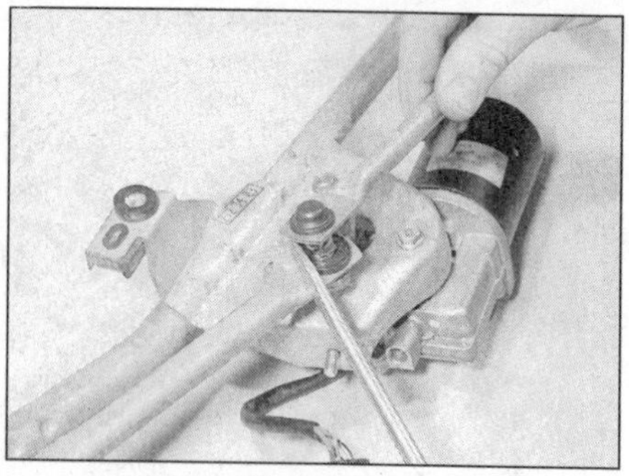

**16.13a Unclip the wiper linkage from the balljoint . . .**

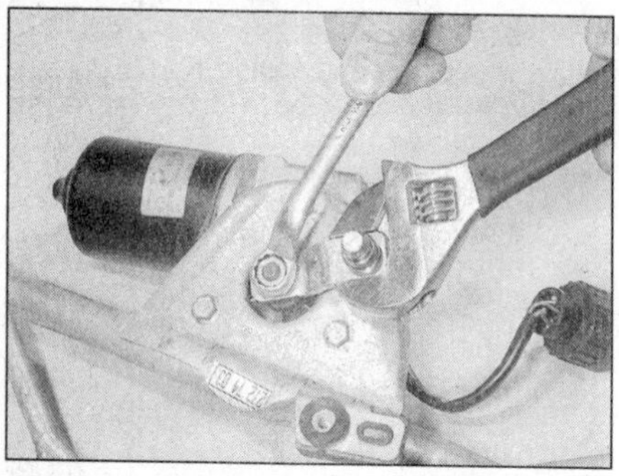

**16.13b . . . then undo the retaining nut and remove the crank from the motor spindle**

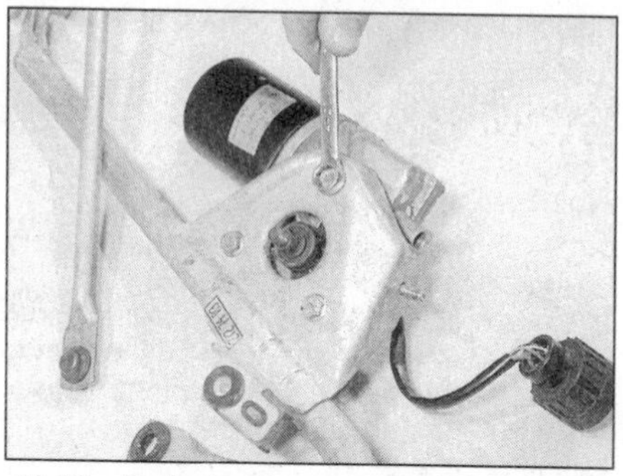

**16.13c Undo the three retaining bolts and separate the motor and wiper linkage**

**10** Slacken and remove the retaining bolts and remove the wiper motor support bracket **(see illustration)**. Recover the spacer and mounting rubbers from the motor.

**11** Release the retaining clip and disconnect the wiring connector from the motor.

**12** Manoeuvre the motor and linkage assembly out of position **(see illustration)**. Recover the rubber grommets from the spindles, inspect them for signs of damage or deterioration, and renew if necessary.

**13** If necessary, mark the relative positions of the motor shaft and crank then release the wiper linkage from the motor balljoint. Unscrew the retaining nut and free the crank from the motor spindle. Unscrew the motor retaining bolts and separate the motor and linkage **(see illustrations)**.

### Refitting

**14** Refitting is the reverse of removal, noting the following points.

a) *If removed, tighten the motor retaining bolts and crank arm nut to the specified torque.*

b) *Ensure that the spindle grommets are correctly fitted and manoeuvre the motor into position. Refit the support bracket and tighten both the bracket bolts and spindle nuts to the specified torque.*

c) *On completion refit the wiper arms as described in Section 15.*

## 17 Windscreen/headlight washer system components - removal and refitting

**1** The windscreen washer reservoir is situated in the engine compartment. On models equipped with headlight washers the reservoir also supplies the headlight washer jets via an additional pump. **Note:** *On some models a second smaller reservoir is also incorporated into the washer system. This reservoir is designed to be filled with concentrated washer fluid for intensive cleaning (refer to your BMW dealer for details).*

### Washer system reservoir

**2** Empty the contents of the reservoir or be prepared for fluid spillage.

**3** Disconnect the wiring connector(s) from the washer pump(s). Carefully ease the pump(s) out from the reservoir and position them clear. Inspect the pump sealing grommet(s) for signs of damage or deterioration and renew if necessary.

**4** Disconnect the wiring connector from the reservoir level switch.

**5** Slacken and remove the reservoir fastener and lift the reservoir upwards and out of position. Wash off any spilt fluid with cold water.

**6** Refitting is a reversal of removal. Ensure the pump(s) are correctly clipped into the reservoir. Refill the reservoir and check for leakage.

### Washer pump

**7** Disconnect the wiring connector and washer hose from the pump.

**8** Carefully ease the pump out from the reservoir and recover its sealing grommet. Wash off any spilt fluid with cold water.

**9** Refitting is the reverse of removal, using a new sealing grommet if the original one shows signs of damage or deterioration. Refill the reservoir and check the pump grommet for leaks.

### Washer reservoir level switch

**10** Empty the contents of the reservoir or be prepared for fluid spillage as the pump is removed.

**11** Disconnect the wiring connector from the level switch and carefully ease the switch out from the reservoir. Recover the sealing grommet and wash off any spilt fluid with cold water.

**12** Refitting is the reverse of removal, using a new sealing grommet if the original one shows signs of damage or deterioration. Refill the reservoir and check for leaks.

### Windscreen washer jets

**13** Open up the bonnet then remove the retaining clips and free the insulation panel from the area around the base of the washer jet.

**14** Disconnect the washer hose(s) from the base of the jet. Where necessary, also disconnect the wiring connector from the jet.

**15** Release the retaining clip and carefully ease the jet out from the bonnet, taking great care not to damage the paintwork.

**16** On refitting, securely connect the jet to the hose and clip it into position in the bonnet; where necessary also reconnect the wiring connector. Check the operation of the jet. If necessary adjust the nozzles using a pin, aiming one nozzle to a point slightly above the centre of the swept area and the other to slightly below the centre point to ensure complete coverage.

### Headlight washer jets

**17** To improve access, apply the handbrake then jack up the front of the vehicle and support it on axle stands (see "*Jacking and vehicle support*").

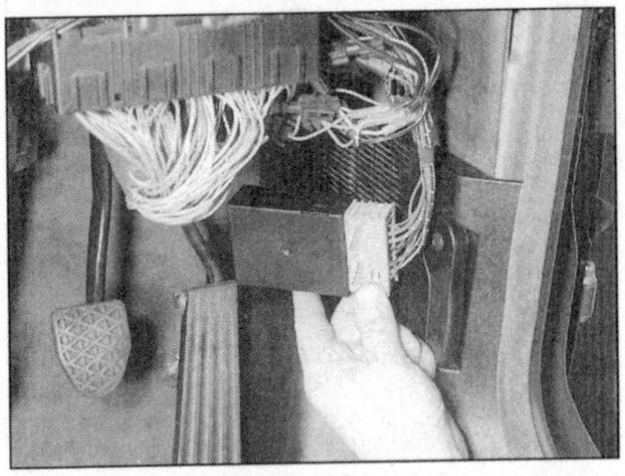

17.26 Removing the wash/wipe system control module

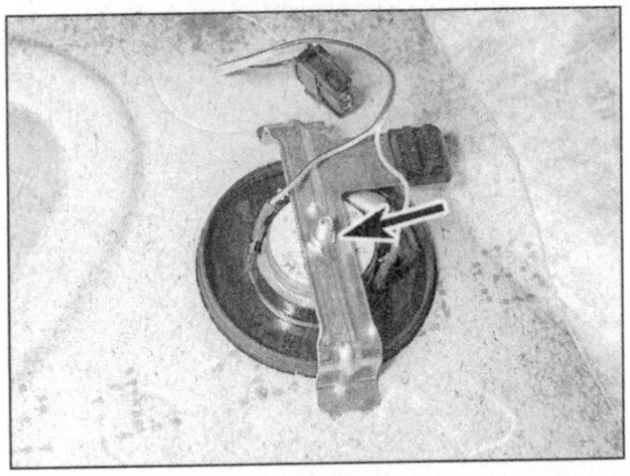

19.2 Undo the nut (arrowed) then remove the mounting bracket and withdraw the speaker from the door trim panel

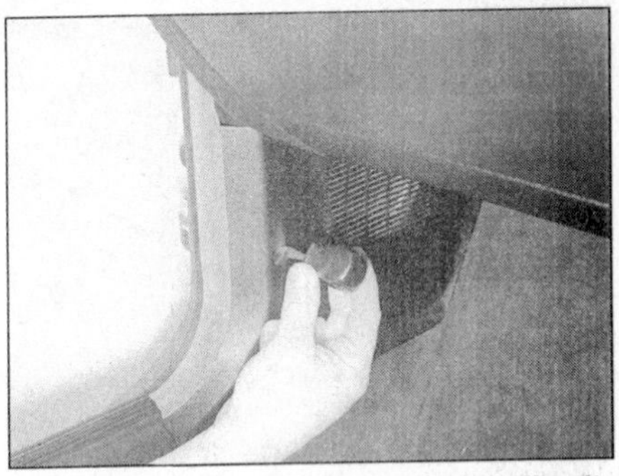

19.10a Release the fastener by rotating it through 90° . . .

18 Undo the retaining screws and remove the small access cover from the bottom of the bumper.

19 Release the retaining clip and remove the brake duct from the bumper.

20 Pull the washer jet assembly off from the supply tube and recover the bush from the supply tube.

21 Undo the retaining screws and release the washer jet supply tube from the body.

22 Slacken the retaining clip then disconnect the hose and remove the supply tube.

23 On refitting, refit the bush and push the jet assembly firmly onto the supply tube. Position the supply tube so the jet is flush with the body panel and securely tighten its retaining screws.

### Wash/wipe system control module

24 Undo the two retaining screws then unclip and remove the driver's side lower facia panel.

25 Unclip and remove the undercover to gain access to the module which is clipped in position above the pedals.

26 Release the retaining clips and lower the module out of position **(see illustration)**.

27 Release the retaining clip then disconnect the wiring connector(s) and remove the module from the vehicle.

28 Refitting is the reverse of removal.

### Heated washer jet thermostatic switch

29 The heated washer jet thermostatic switch is clipped into the right-hand front brake cooling duct. If necessary, to improve access, apply the handbrake then jack up the front of the vehicle and support it on axle stands (see "*Jacking and vehicle support*").

30 Disconnect the wiring connector then unclip the sensor and remove it from the brake duct.

31 Refitting is the reverse of removal ensuring that the switch is clipped securely into position.

## 18 Audio unit - removal and refitting

**Note:** *The following removal and refitting procedure is for the range of radio/cassette units which BMW fit as standard equipment. Removal and refitting procedures of non-standard will differ slightly.*

### Removal

1 The audio unit fitted as standard have DIN standard fixings. Two special tools, obtainable from most car accessory shops, are required for removal. Alternatively suitable tools can be fabricated from 3 mm diameter wire, such as welding rod.

2 Disconnect the battery negative lead.

3 Carefully unclip the access covers from each side of the unit to reveal the removal holes.

4 Insert the tools into the holes on each side of the unit and push them until they snap into place. The audio unit can then be slid out of the facia and the wiring connectors and aerial disconnected.

### Refitting

5 Reconnect the wiring connector and aerial lead then push the unit into the facia until the retaining lugs snap into place.

## 19 Loudspeakers - removal and refitting

### Door panel speaker(s)

1 Remove the door inner trim panel as described in Chapter 11.

2 Unscrew the retaining nut and remove the retaining bracket (where fitted) then unclip the speaker from the trim panel **(see illustration)**.

3 Refitting is the reverse of removal.

### Driver's side front loudspeaker (situated behind footwell side panel)

4 Undo the two retaining screws then unclip and remove the driver's side lower facia panel. Release the undercover and remove it from the facia.

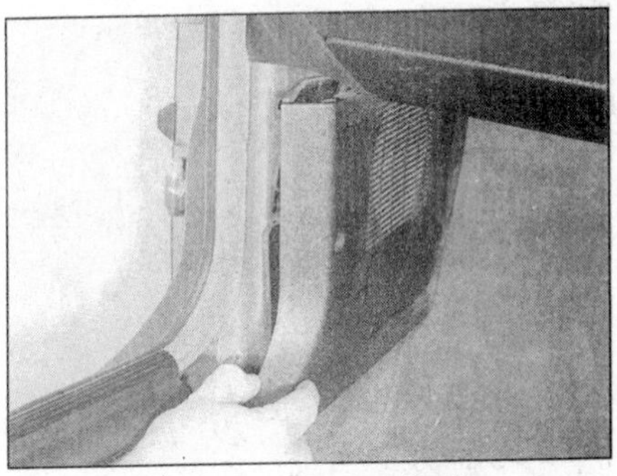

19.10b . . . then unclip the footwell side trim panel

5 Undo the retaining screw and remove the bonnet release lever.

6 Release the trim panel fastener by rotating it through 90° then unclip the footwell side trim panel and remove it from the vehicle.

7 Undo the retaining screws and remove the speaker, disconnect its wiring connectors as they become accessible.

8 Refitting is the reverse of removal making sure the speaker is correctly located.

### Passenger side front loudspeaker (situated behind footwell side panel)

9 Undo the two retaining screws and remove the undercover from beneath the facia.

10 Release the trim panel fastener by rotating it through 90° then unclip the footwell side trim panel and remove it from the vehicle **(see illustrations)**.

11 Undo the retaining screws and remove the speaker, disconnect its wiring connectors as they become accessible **(see illustrations)**.

12 Refitting is the reverse of removal making sure the speaker is correctly located.

### Rear loudspeaker

13 Carefully prise the speaker grille out from the rear parcel shelf **(see illustration)**.

14 Disconnect the wiring connector then slacken and remove the speaker retaining screws. Depress the retaining clips and lower

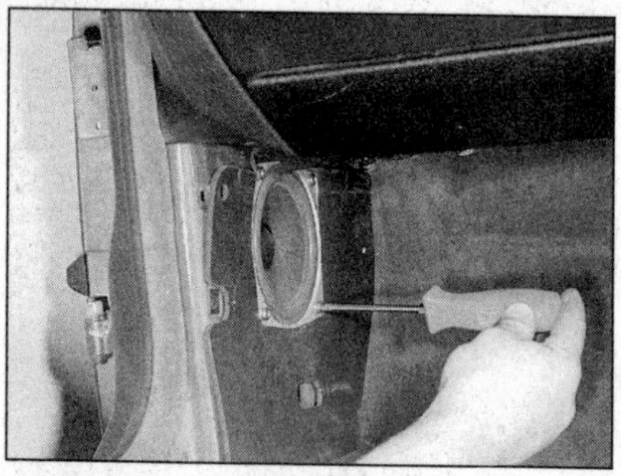

**19.11a Undo the four retaining screws . . .**

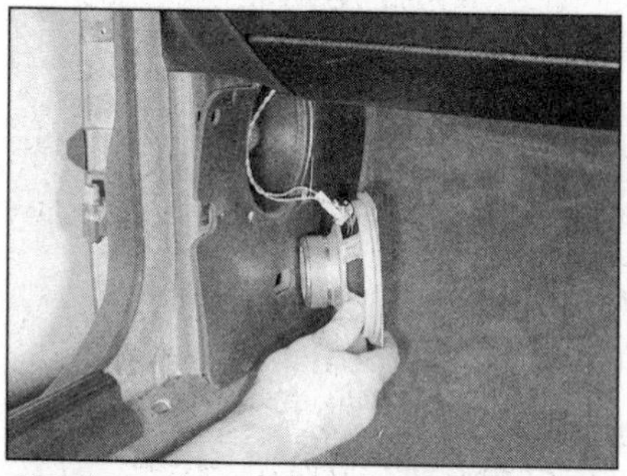

**19.11b . . . then withdraw the speaker and disconnect its wiring connector**

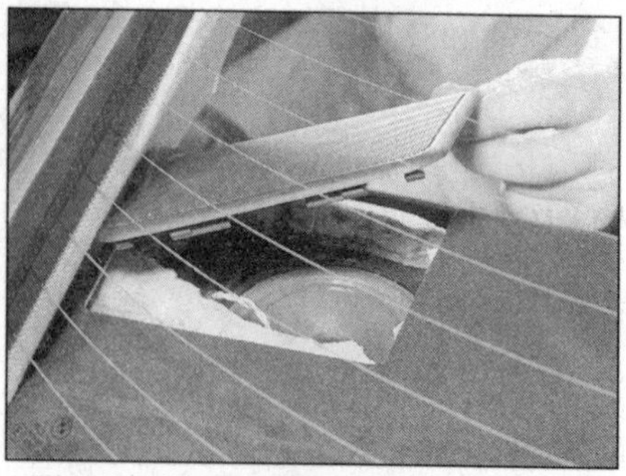

**19.13 Unclip the rear speaker grille from the parcel shelf . . .**

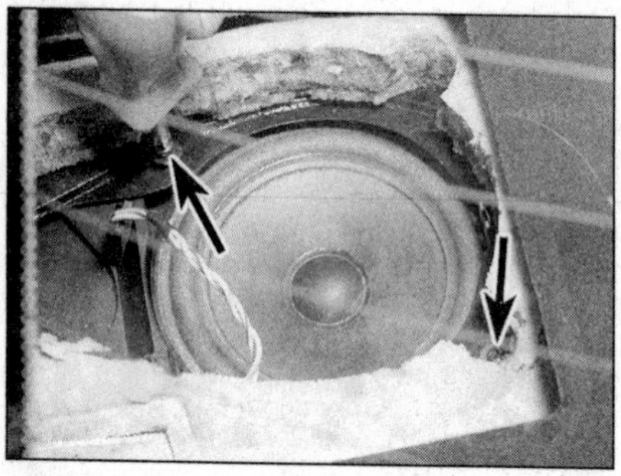

**19.14a . . . and undo the retaining screws (arrowed) . . .**

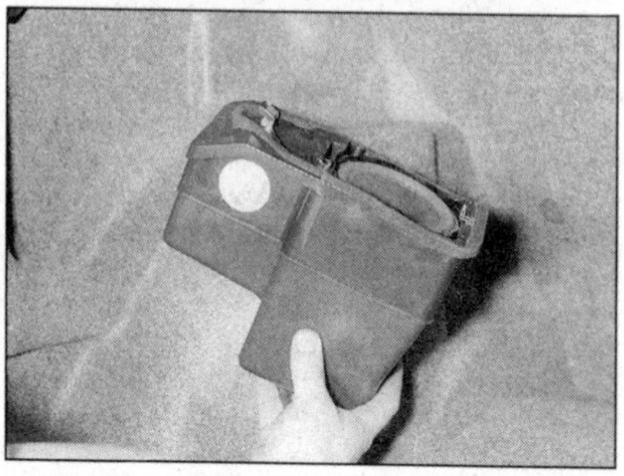

**19.14b . . . then disconnect the wiring connector and lower the speaker out of position**

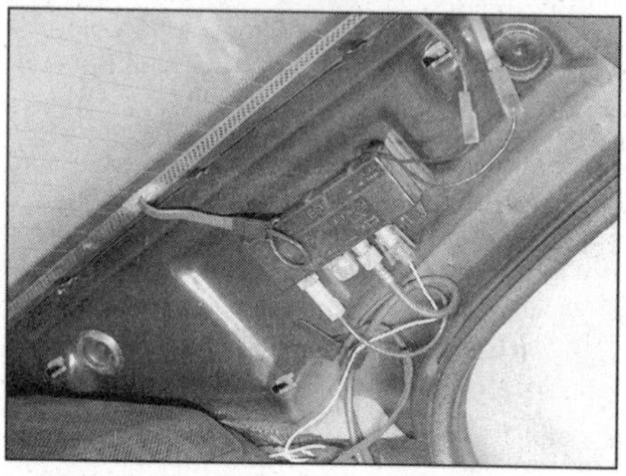

**20.2 Radio aerial amplifier is mounted onto the left-hand rear pillar**

the speaker assembly downwards and out through the luggage compartment **(see illustrations)**. If necessary, undo the screws and separate the speaker and mounting box.

**15** Refitting is the reverse of removal.

## 20 Radio aerial - general information

The radio aerial is built into the rear screen. In order to improve reception an amplifier is fitted to boost the signal to the radio/cassette unit. The amplifier unit is located behind the left hand rear pillar trim panel.

To gain access to the aerial amplifier unit, carefully unclip the left hand trim panel from the rear pillar, disconnecting the wiring from the interior light as the panel is removed. Disconnect the aerial lead and wiring then undo the retaining screws and remove the amplifier **(see illustration)**. Refitting is the reverse of removal

## 21 Cruise control system components - removal and refitting

### Electronic control unit (ECU)

**1** Remove the glovebox (see Chapter 11).

**2** Unclip the lower facia panel and remove it from underneath the glovebox aperture.

**3** Release the retaining clip, withdraw the ECU then release the retaining clip and disconnect wiring connector.

**4** Refitting is the reverse of removal.

### Cruise control actuator

**5** The cruise control actuator is located in the engine compartment.

**6** Disconnect the wiring connector from the actuator.

**7** Remove the outer cable retaining clip, then release the cable from the bracket and detach the inner cable from the actuator.

**8** Undo the retaining nuts and remove the actuator from the engine compartment.

**9** Refitting is the reverse of removal.

### System operating switch

**10** Refer to Section 4.

### Brake and clutch pedal switches

**11** Refer to Chapter 9, Section 21, and to Chapter 6, Section 7, respectively.

## 22 Anti-theft alarm system - general information

**Note:** *This information is applicable only to the anti-theft alarm system fitted by BMW as standard equipment.*

**1** Some models in the range are fitted with an anti-theft alarm system as standard equipment. The alarm has switches on all the doors (including the boot lid), the bonnet, the glovebox and the ignition switch and also a tilt switch which is sensitive to shocks. If the boot lid, bonnet, glovebox or either of the doors are opened or the ignition switch is switched on whilst the alarm is set, or if the tilt switch senses the vehicle is being tampered with, the alarm horn will sound and the hazard warning lights/headlights will flash. The alarm also has an immobiliser function which makes the ignition system inoperable whilst the alarm is triggered.

**2** The alarm is set using the key in the driver's or passenger front door lock or when the doors are locked using the remote central locking device. The LED in the facia will flash to indicate that the alarm system is operational. If a door or window or the glovebox are not fully closed when the alarm is set, the LED will flash quicker than normal. After a short period the alarm will then operate as normal but with the switch for the open door/window or glovebox switched off.

**3** If necessary, the tilt switch sensing function of the alarm can be disabled. To do this turn the alarm on as normal, then turn the alarm on again for a second time (either using the door lock or remote locking device). This will disable the tilt switch but leave all the other switches turned on.

**4** Should the alarm system become faulty the vehicle should be taken to a BMW dealer for examination. They will have access to a special diagnostic tester which will quickly trace any fault present in the system.

## 23 Heated front seat components - removal and refitting

### Heater mats

On models equipped with heated front seats, a heater pad is fitted to the both the seat back and seat cushion. Renewal of either heater mat involves peeling back the upholstery, removing the old mat, sticking the new mat in position and then refitting the upholstery. Note that upholstery removal and refitting requires considerable skill and experience if it is to be carried out successfully and is therefore best entrusted to your BMW dealer. In practice, it will be very difficult for the home mechanic to carry out the job without ruining the upholstery.

### Heated seat switches

Refer to Section 4.

## 24 Airbag system - general information and precautions

Both a driver's and passenger airbag were fitted as standard to some models in the range; on other models they were available as an optional extra. Models fitted with a driver's side airbag have the word AIRBAG or SRS stamped on the airbag unit, which is fitted to the centre of the steering wheel. Models also equipped with a passenger side airbag also have the word AIRBAG or SRS stamped on the passenger airbag unit which is fitted to the top of the facia. The airbag system comprises of the airbag unit(s) (complete with gas generators), an impact sensor, the control unit and a warning light in the instrument panel.

The airbag system is triggered in the event of a heavy frontal impact above a predetermined force; depending on the point of impact. The airbag is inflated within milliseconds and forms a safety cushion between the driver and steering wheel and (where fitted) the passenger and facia. This prevents contact between the upper body and wheel/facia and therefore greatly reduces the risk of injury. The airbag then deflates almost immediately.

Every time the ignition is switched on, the airbag control unit performs a self-test. The self-test takes approximately 2 to 6 seconds and during this time the airbag warning light on the facia is illuminated. After the self-test has been completed the warning light should go out. If the warning light fails to come on, remains illuminated after the initial period or comes on at any time when the vehicle is being driven, there is a fault in the airbag system. The vehicle be taken to a BMW dealer for examination at the earliest possible opportunity.

***Warning: Before carrying out any operations on the airbag system, disconnect the battery negative terminal, and wait for 10 minutes. This will allow the capacitors in the system to discharge. When operations are complete, make sure no one is inside the vehicle when the battery is reconnected.***

***Note that the airbag(s) must not be subjected to temperatures in excess of 90°C (194°F). When the airbag is removed, ensure that it is stored the correct way up to prevent possible inflation.***

***Do not allow any solvents or cleaning agents to contact the airbag assemblies. They must be cleaned using only a damp cloth.***

***The airbags and control unit are both sensitive to impact. If either is dropped or damaged they should be renewed.***

***Disconnect the airbag control unit wiring plug prior to using arc-welding equipment on the vehicle.***

## 25 Airbag system components - removal and refitting

**Note:** *Refer to the warnings in Section 24 before carrying out the following operations.*

**1** There are possible types of airbag system fitted, Airbag system I and Airbag system II. The earlier (Airbag I) system using a control unit and two separate impact sensors, one fitted to each front suspension strut turret. On the later (Airbag II) system a control unit with an integral impact sensor is used, the control unit being mounted underneath the rear seat cushion.

**2** Disconnect the battery negative terminal. Undo the driver's side lower facia panel retaining screws then unclip the panel and remove it from the vehicle. Unscrew the steering column lower shroud fastener screw and pull out the fastener. Unclip the lower shroud and remove it from the column.

**3** Release the airbag unit wiring connector from the column and disconnect it then continue as described under the relevant heading.

### Driver's side airbag

**4** Slacken and remove the two airbag retaining screws from the rear of the steering wheel, rotating the wheel as necessary to gain access to the screws.

**5** Return the steering wheel to the straight-ahead position then carefully lift the airbag assembly away from the steering wheel and disconnect the wiring connector from the rear of the unit. Note that the airbag must not be knocked or dropped and should be stored the correct way up with its padded surface uppermost.

**6** On refitting reconnect the wiring connector and seat the airbag unit in the steering wheel, making sure the wire does not become trapped. Fit the retaining screws and tighten them to the specified torque setting, noting the right-hand retaining screw should be tightened first. Reconnect the wiring connector and clip it onto the column then refit the column shroud and connect the battery.

### Passenger side airbag

**7** Remove the glovebox as described in Chapter 11.

**8** Carefully unclip the access cover from the airbag then undo the retaining bolts situated along the lower edge of the airbag.

**9** Move the airbag assembly out from the facia, disconnecting the wiring connector as it becomes accessible.

**10** On refitting, securely reconnect the wiring connector and seat the airbag in position.

**11** Refit the retaining screws, tightening them securely and clip on the cover (where fitted).

**12** Refit the glovebox as described in Chapter 11.

**13** Reconnect the wiring connector, clip it onto the steering column then refit the column shroud and reconnect the battery.

### Airbag control unit

#### Early models (Airbag system I)

**15** Remove the glovebox as described in Chapter 11.

**16** Release the unit from its mounting bracket and disconnect the wiring connector(s).

**17** Refitting is the reverse of removal.

#### Later models (Airbag system II)

**18** Unclip the rear seat cushion and remove it from the vehicle.

**19** Disconnect the wiring connector then undo the retaining bolts and remove the unit from the vehicle **(see illustration)**.

**20** Refitting is the reverse of removal. Note that the control unit must be installed with the arrow pointing towards the front of the vehicle.

### Airbag wiring contact unit

**21** Remove the steering wheel as described in Chapter 10.

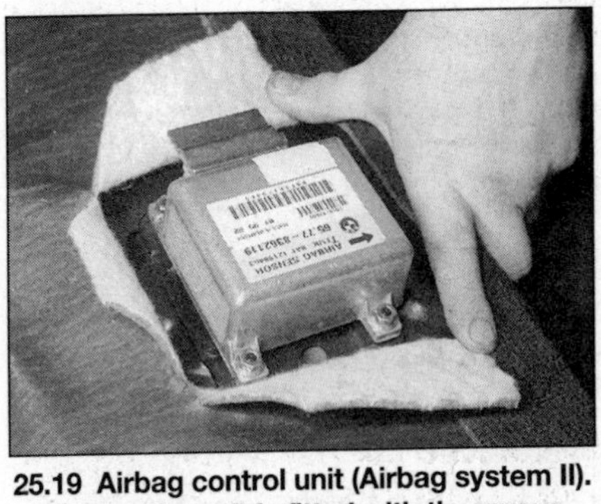

**25.19 Airbag control unit (Airbag system II). Ensure the unit is fitted with the arrow pointing towards the front of the vehicle**

### Early models (Airbag system I)

**22** Remove the locking tab from the contact unit and lift out the spring.
**23** Unscrew the retaining nuts and remove the contact unit from the steering wheel.
**24** Fit the contact ring to the steering wheel, ensuring that the wiring is correctly routed. Refit the retaining nuts, tightening them securely, and lock them in position by applying a dab of varnish/paint to their ends. If a new contact unit is being fitted, unscrew the locking screw from the unit.
**25** Fit the spring to the contact unit and clip the locking tab back into position. Refit the steering wheel as described in Chapter 10.
**26** Reconnect the wiring connector and clip it onto the column then refit the column shroud and connect the battery.

### Later models (Airbag system II)

**27** Unclip the trim cover and undo the screw securing the earth lead to the steering wheel.
**28** Undo the retaining screws and remove the contact unit from the wheel.
**29** Fit the new contact unit to the steering wheel, ensuring that the wiring is correctly routed, and securely tighten the retaining screws. If a new contact unit is being fitted, depress the retaining tangs and remove the locking peg.
**30** Connect the earth lead to the steering wheel, tightening its retaining screw securely, and refit the cover.
**31** Refit the steering wheel (see Chapter 10).
**32** Reconnect the wiring connector and clip it onto the column then refit the column shroud and connect the battery.

## *Impact sensor*

### Early models (Airbag system I)

**33** There are two impact sensors, one on each side of the engine compartment.
**34** Disconnect the wiring connector then undo the retaining bolts and remove the sensor from the side of the suspension strut mounting turret.
**35** Refitting is the reverse of removal ensuring that the sensor is positioned with its arrow pointing towards the front of the vehicle. Tighten the sensor mounting bolts to the specified torque.

### Later models (Airbag system II)

**36** The impact sensor is an integral part of the control unit.

# 26 Multi-information system - information and component removal and refitting

## *General information*

**1** On some models a multi-information system was fitted as standard, and on most other models it is available as an optional extra. There are various types of system all of which are similar in appearance but vary in the amount of functions they carry out. All control units contain a clock along with the following functions:

a) *Outside temperature display - displays the ambient air temperature.*
b) *Check control system - monitors the rear lights, number plate lights and informs the driver of a fault. Also informs the driver if the engine coolant or windscreen washer fluid reservoir levels are low. May also display the outside air temperature.*
c) *On-board computer - monitors vehicle speed, distance travelled, fuel consumption etc. as well as air temperature.*

**2** Refer to your BMW handbook for details on how to use the various functions of each unit. Any problems should be referred to a BMW dealer.

## *Component removal and refitting*

### Multi-information display unit

**3** Refer to Section 13.

### Check control system electronic control unit (ECU)

**4** Remove the glovebox as described in Chapter 11. Unclip the undercover and remove it from beneath the facia.
**5** Release the ECU from its mounting then release the retaining clips and disconnect the wiring connectors and remove the ECU from the vehicle.
**6** Refitting is the reverse of removal.

### Ambient air temperature sensor

**7** The air temperature sensor is clipped into the left-hand front brake cooling duct. If necessary, to improve access, apply the handbrake then jack up the front of the vehicle and support it on axle stands (see "*Jacking and vehicle support*").
**8** Disconnect the wiring connector then unclip the sensor and remove it from the brake duct.
**9** Refitting is the reverse of removal.

# 27 Door lock heating system - information and component removal and refitting

## *General information*

**1** Some models are fitted with a door lock heating system. The heating element is also built into the handle assembly and is wrapped around the lock housing. The system is switched on by lifting the door handle, a microswitch on the handle switches on the heating element. On later models the system is controlled either by the central locking control unit (ECU) or by the central body electronics (ZKE IV) control unit (depending on model and specification).

## *Component removal and refitting*

### Central locking system control unit (ECU)

**2** Refer to Chapter 11.

### Central body electronics (ZKE IV) control unit

**3** Disconnect the battery negative terminal, then remove the glovebox (see Chapter 11).
**4** Release the retaining clips and slide the control unit out from its retaining bracket. Disconnect the wiring connectors and remove the control unit.
**5** Refitting is the reverse of removal ensuring that the wiring connectors are securely reconnected.

### Door lock heating microswitch

**6** Remove the door exterior handle as described in Chapter 11.
**7** Release the retaining clip and detach the microswitch from the handle **(see illustration)**.
**8** Refitting is the reverse of removal ensuring that the switch is clipped securely in position.

### Door lock heating element

**9** At the time of writing it appears the heating element is an integral part of the handle assembly and is not available separately. Consult your BMW dealer for the latest information on parts availability.

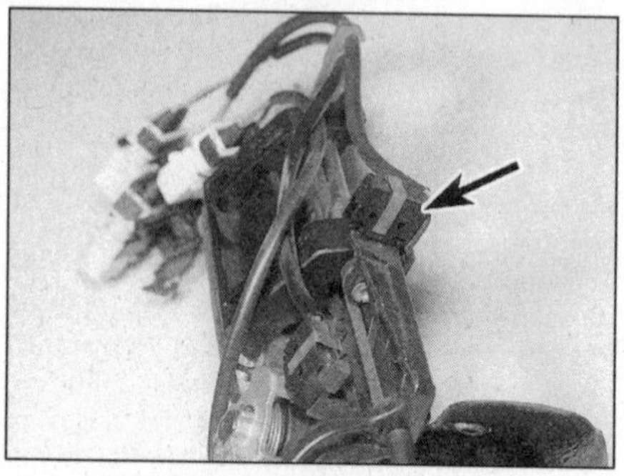

**27.7 Door lock heating system microswitch (arrowed)**

## Notes

1. Wires may interconnect between diagrams and are located by using a grid reference e.g. 2/A1 denotes a position on diagram 2 grid location A1.
2. Brackets show how circuits may be wired in more than one way.
3. Not all items are fitted to all models.

### Key to symbols

| | |
|---|---|
| Bulb | Connecting wires |
| Switch | Connection to other circuits (e.g. diagram 3/grid location B2). Direction of arrow denotes current flow. (3/B2) |
| Fuse (F13) | |
| Item no. (7) | Solenoid actuator |
| Pump/motor (M) | Wire - battery positive potential (double line) |
| Earth | Wire - battery negative potential (thick line) |
| Variable resistor | Wire - interconnecting (thin line) |
| Resistor | Wire colour and cross sectional area (in mm2) — 0.5 GN — |
| Diode | |

### Earth locations

- E1 LH front engine compartment
- E2 Under LH side of dash
- E3 Centre console near gear lever
- E4 Behind RH footwell trim
- E5 Centre console near gear lever
- E6 Under LH side of dash
- E7 Behind RH footwell trim
- E8 Under RH rear seat
- E9 Rear RH side of engine compartment
- E10 Rear RH side of engine compartment behind RH strut
- E11 RH front of engine
- E12 Behind RH footwell trim
- E13 Behind RH footwell trim
- E14 In top of RH rear backrest
- E15 In top of LH rear backrest
- E16 Behind RH footwell trim
- E17 Under LH side of dash
- E18 Behind RH footwell trim
- E19 Under LH side of dash

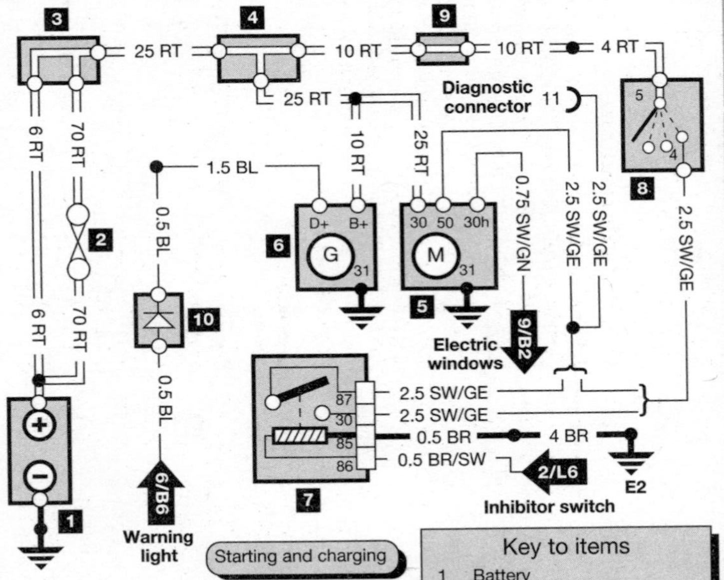


### Key to items

1. Battery
2. Fusible link
3. B+ External start terminal
4. Distributor B+
5. Starter motor
6. Alternator
7. Starter relay (auto. trans.)
8. Ignition switch
9. Front power distribution box
10. Decoupling diode
11. Headlight relay
12. Main beam relay
13. Light switch
14. Indicator/dip switch
15. LH headlight assembly
16. RH headlight assembly

### Wire colours

| | | | |
|---|---|---|---|
| BL | Blue | RS | Pink |
| BR | Brown | RT | Red |
| GE | Yellow | SW | Black |
| GN | Green | VI | Violet |
| GR | Grey | WS | White |
| OR | Orange | TR | Transparent |

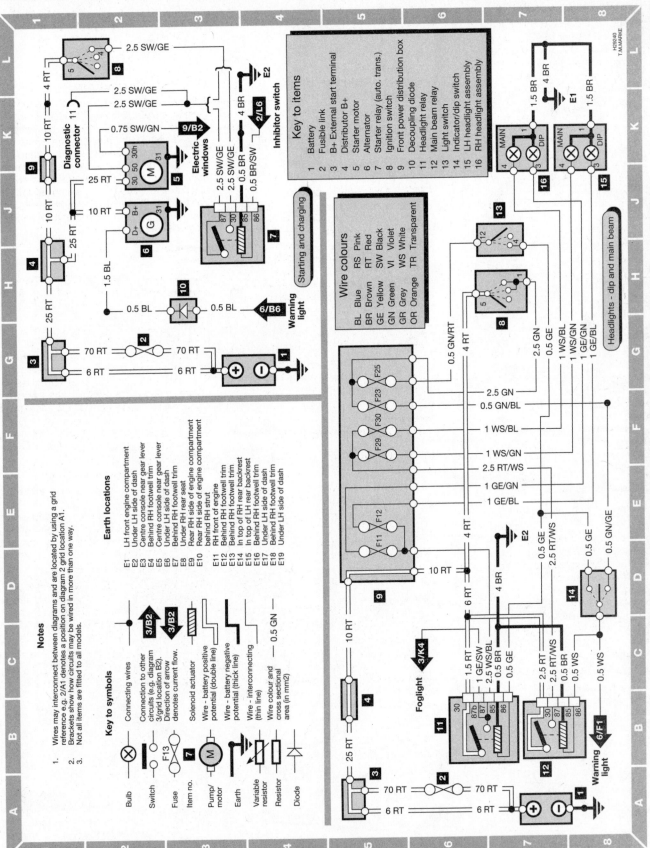

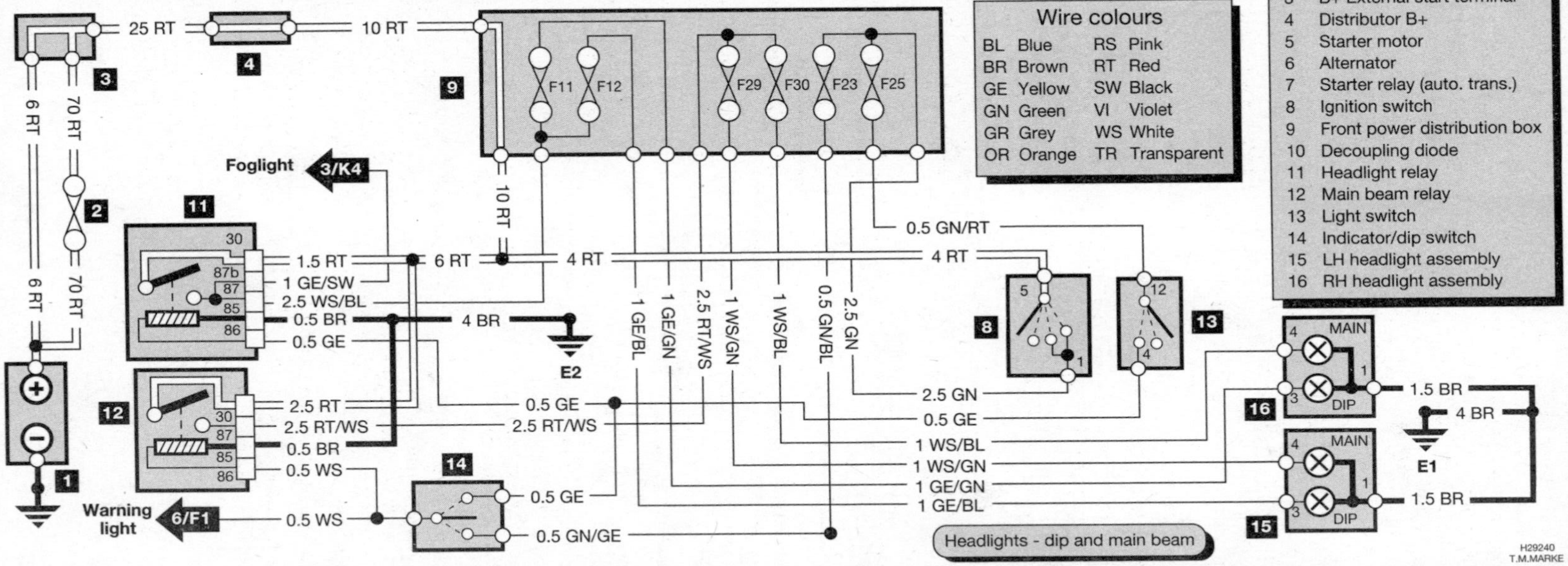


Diagram 1 : Notes, key to symbols, earth locations, typical starting, charging and headlights

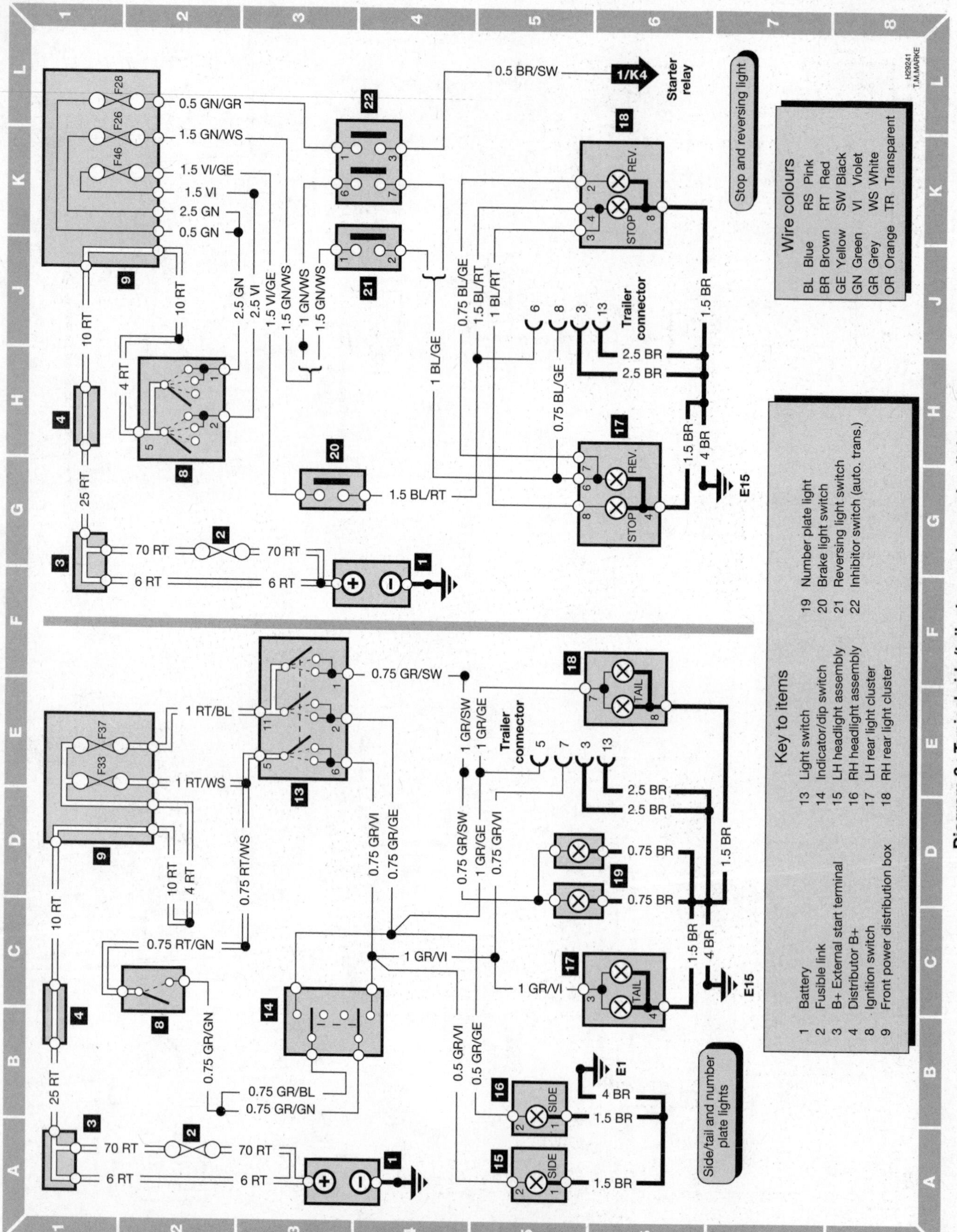


**Diagram 2 : Typical side/tail, stop and reversing lights**

### Key to items

1 Battery
2 Fusible link
3 B+ External start terminal
4 Distributor B+
8 Ignition switch
9 Front power distribution box
13 Light switch
14 Indicator/dip switch
15 LH headlight assembly
16 RH headlight assembly
17 LH rear light cluster
18 RH rear light cluster
19 Number plate light
20 Brake light switch
21 Reversing light switch
22 Inhibitor switch (auto. trans.)

### Wire colours

| | | | |
|---|---|---|---|
| BL | Blue | RS | Pink |
| BR | Brown | RT | Red |
| GE | Yellow | SW | Black |
| GN | Green | VI | Violet |
| GR | Grey | WS | White |
| OR | Orange | TR | Transparent |

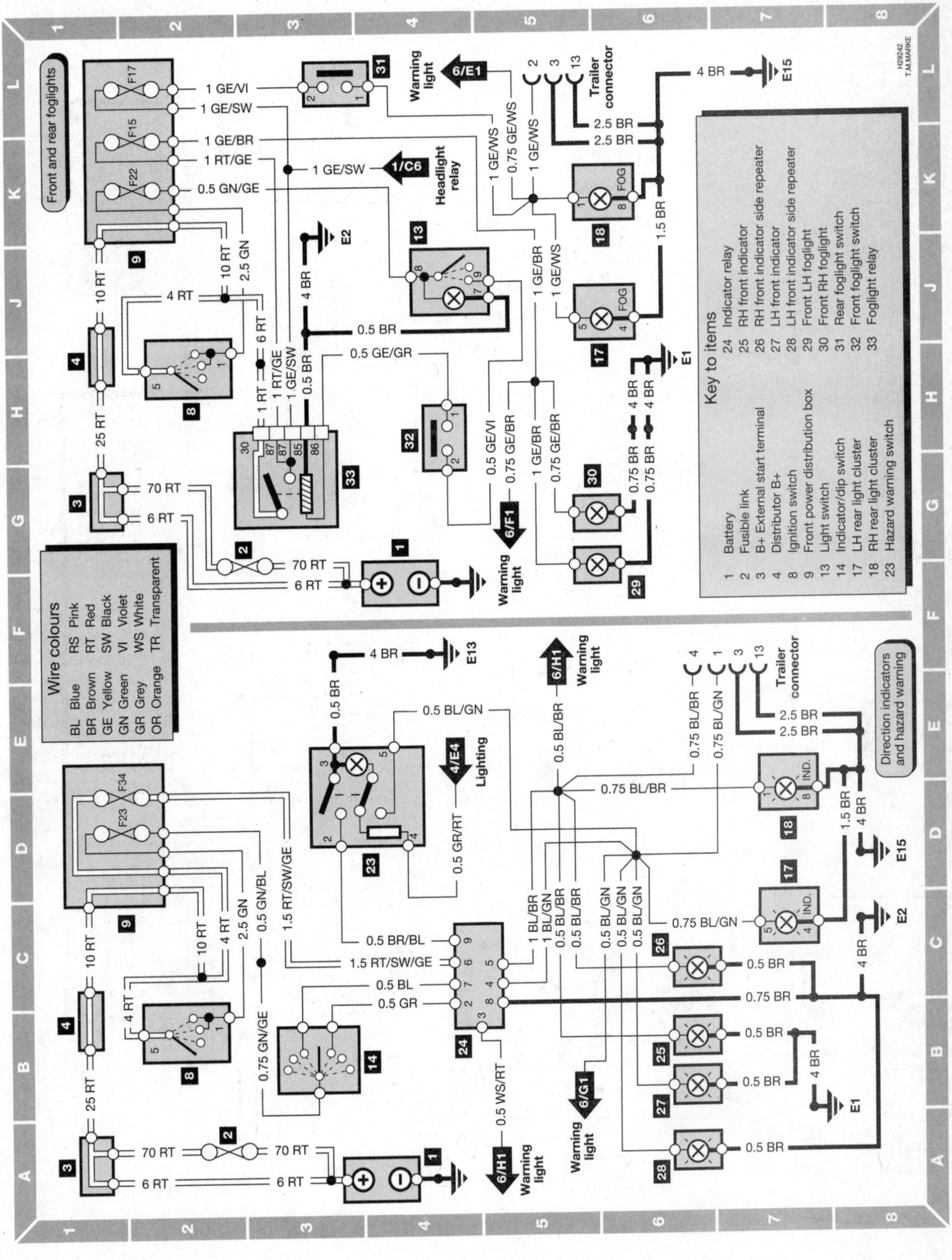
Front and rear foglights
Wire colours
BL Blue
BR Brown
GE Yellow
GN Green
GR Grey
OR Orange
RS Pink
RT Red
SW Black
VI Violet
WS White
TR Transparent
Key to items
1 Battery
2 Fusible link
3 B+ External start terminal
4 Distributor B+
8 Ignition switch
9 Front power distribution box
13 Light switch
14 Indicator/dip switch
17 LH rear light cluster
18 RH rear light cluster
23 Hazard warning switch
24 Indicator relay
25 RH front indicator
26 RH front indicator side repeater
27 LH front indicator
28 LH front indicator side repeater
29 Front LH foglight
30 Front RH foglight
31 Rear foglight switch
32 Front foglight switch
33 Foglight relay
Warning light
Headlight relay
Lighting
Trailer connector
Direction indicators and hazard warning
H29242 T.M.MARKE

Diagram 3 : Typical hazard/direction indicators and foglights

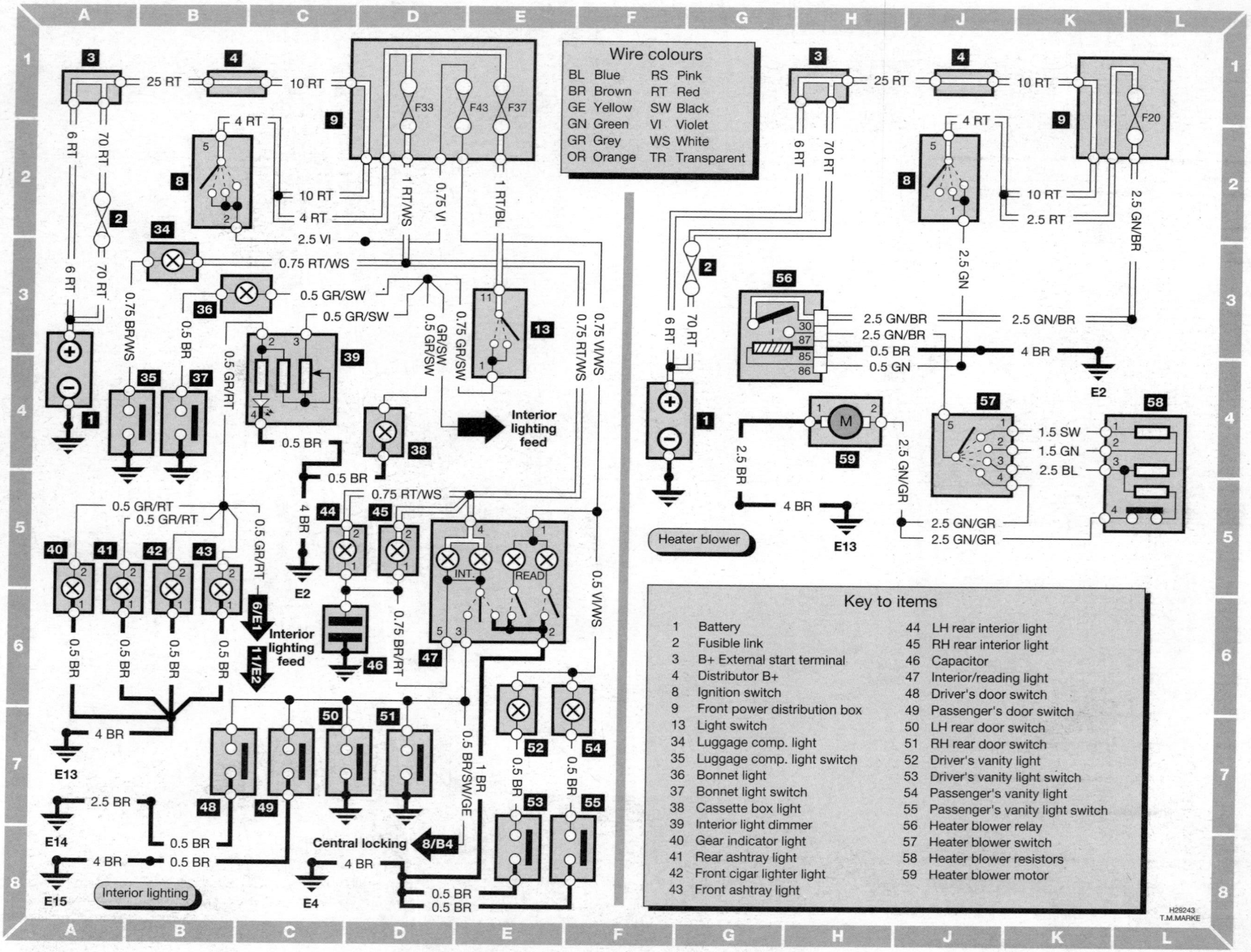


## Wire colours

| | | | |
|---|---|---|---|
| BL | Blue | RS | Pink |
| BR | Brown | RT | Red |
| GE | Yellow | SW | Black |
| GN | Green | VI | Violet |
| GR | Grey | WS | White |
| OR | Orange | TR | Transparent |

## Key to items

| | | | |
|---|---|---|---|
| 1 | Battery | 44 | LH rear interior light |
| 2 | Fusible link | 45 | RH rear interior light |
| 3 | B+ External start terminal | 46 | Capacitor |
| 4 | Distributor B+ | 47 | Interior/reading light |
| 8 | Ignition switch | 48 | Driver's door switch |
| 9 | Front power distribution box | 49 | Passenger's door switch |
| 13 | Light switch | 50 | LH rear door switch |
| 34 | Luggage comp. light | 51 | RH rear door switch |
| 35 | Luggage comp. light switch | 52 | Driver's vanity light |
| 36 | Bonnet light | 53 | Driver's vanity light switch |
| 37 | Bonnet light switch | 54 | Passenger's vanity light |
| 38 | Cassette box light | 55 | Passenger's vanity light switch |
| 39 | Interior light dimmer | 56 | Heater blower relay |
| 40 | Gear indicator light | 57 | Heater blower switch |
| 41 | Rear ashtray light | 58 | Heater blower resistors |
| 42 | Front cigar lighter light | 59 | Heater blower motor |
| 43 | Front ashtray light | | |

**Diagram 4 : Typical interior lighting and heater blower**

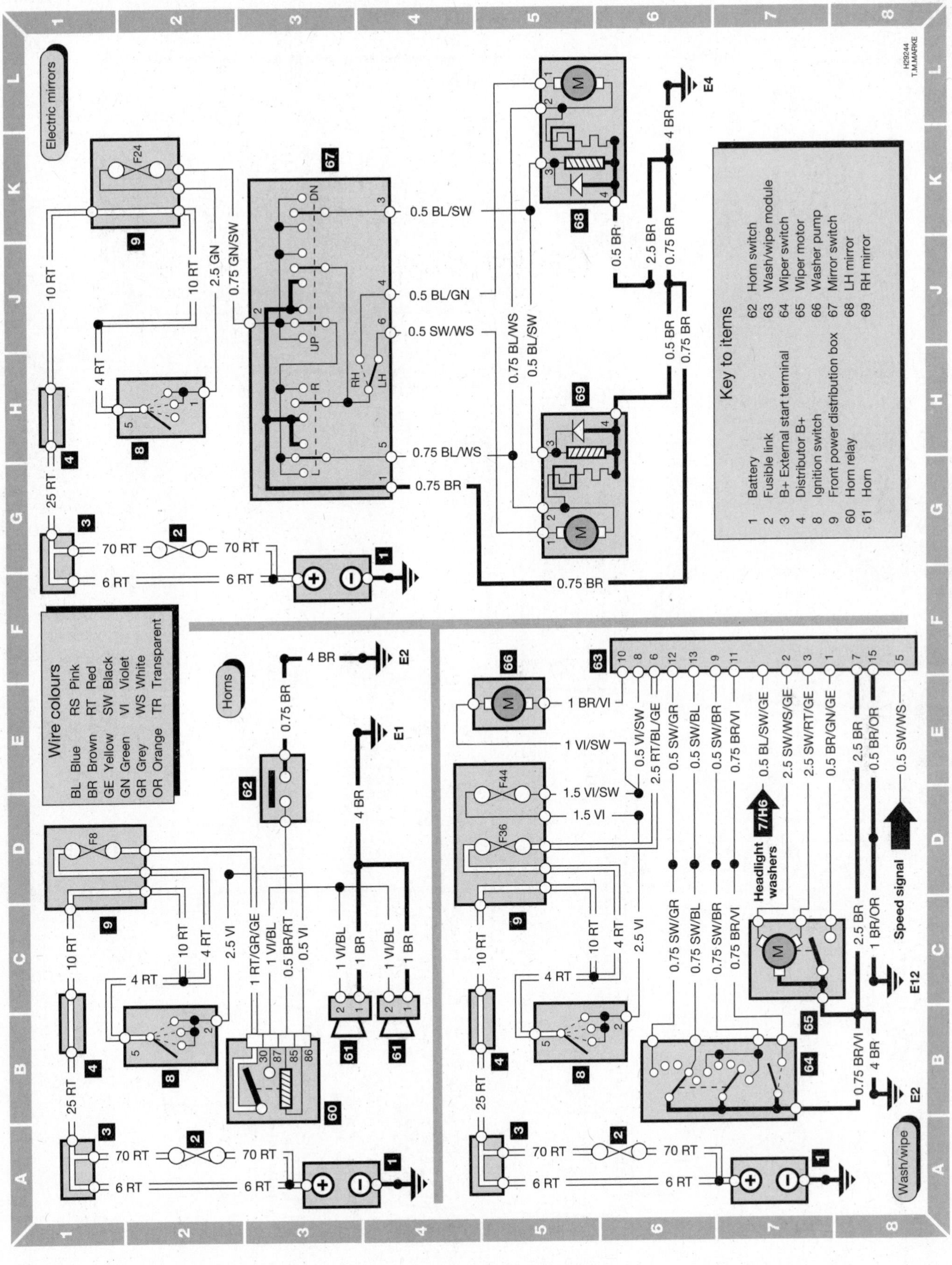

Electric mirrors
Horns
Wash/wipe
Wire colours
BL Blue
BR Brown
GE Yellow
GN Green
GR Grey
OR Orange
RS Pink
RT Red
SW Black
VI Violet
WS White
TR Transparent
Key to items
1 Battery
2 Fusible link
3 B+ External start terminal
4 Distributor B+
8 Ignition switch
9 Front power distribution box
60 Horn relay
61 Horn
62 Horn switch
63 Wash/wipe module
64 Wiper switch
65 Wiper motor
66 Washer pump
67 Mirror switch
68 LH mirror
69 RH mirror
Headlight washers
Speed signal
H29244
T.M.MARKE


Diagram 5 : Typical horn, wash/wipe and electric mirrors

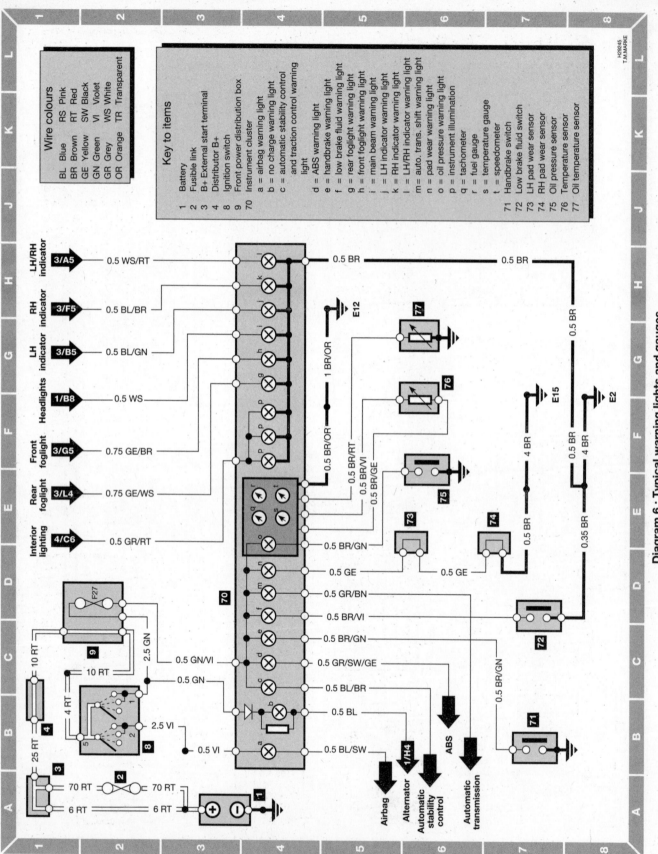

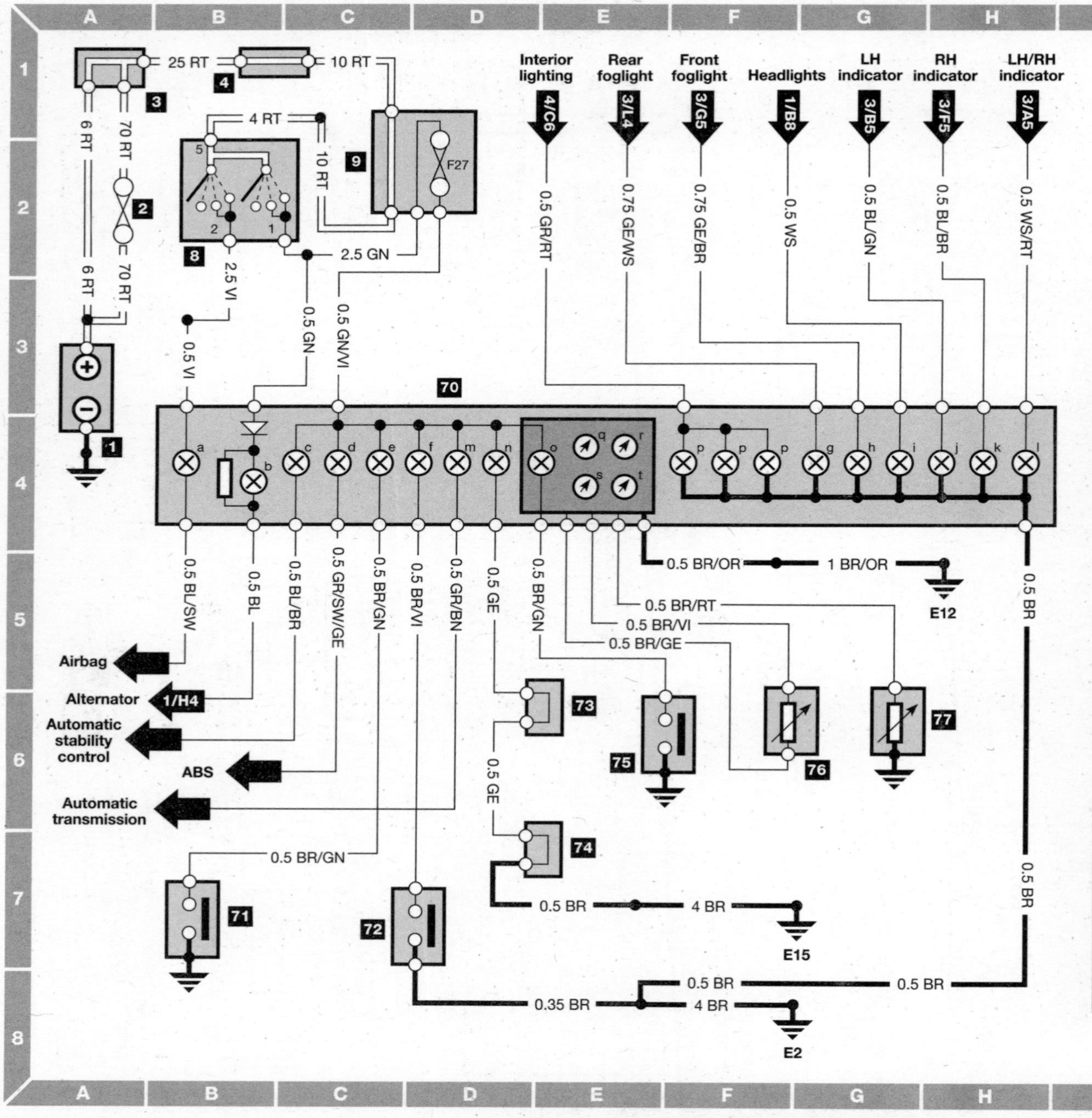


Wire colours

| | | | |
|---|---|---|---|
| BL | Blue | RS | Pink |
| BR | Brown | RT | Red |
| GE | Yellow | SW | Black |
| GN | Green | VI | Violet |
| GR | Grey | WS | White |
| OR | Orange | TR | Transparent |

Key to items

1 Battery
2 Fusible link
3 B+ External start terminal
4 Distributor B+
8 Ignition switch
9 Front power distribution box
70 Instrument cluster
- a = airbag warning light
- b = no charge warning light
- c = automatic stability control and traction control warning light
- d = ABS warning light
- e = handbrake warning light
- f = low brake fluid warning light
- g = rear foglight warning light
- h = front foglight warning light
- i = main beam warning light
- j = LH indicator warning light
- k = RH indicator warning light
- l = LH/RH indicator warning light
- m = auto. trans. shift warning light
- n = pad wear warning light
- o = oil pressure warning light
- p = instrument illumination
- q = tachometer
- r = fuel gauge
- s = temperature gauge
- t = speedometer

71 Handbrake switch
72 Low brake fluid switch
73 LH pad wear sensor
74 RH pad wear sensor
75 Oil pressure sensor
76 Temperature sensor
77 Oil temperature sensor

Diagram 6 : Typical warning lights and gauges

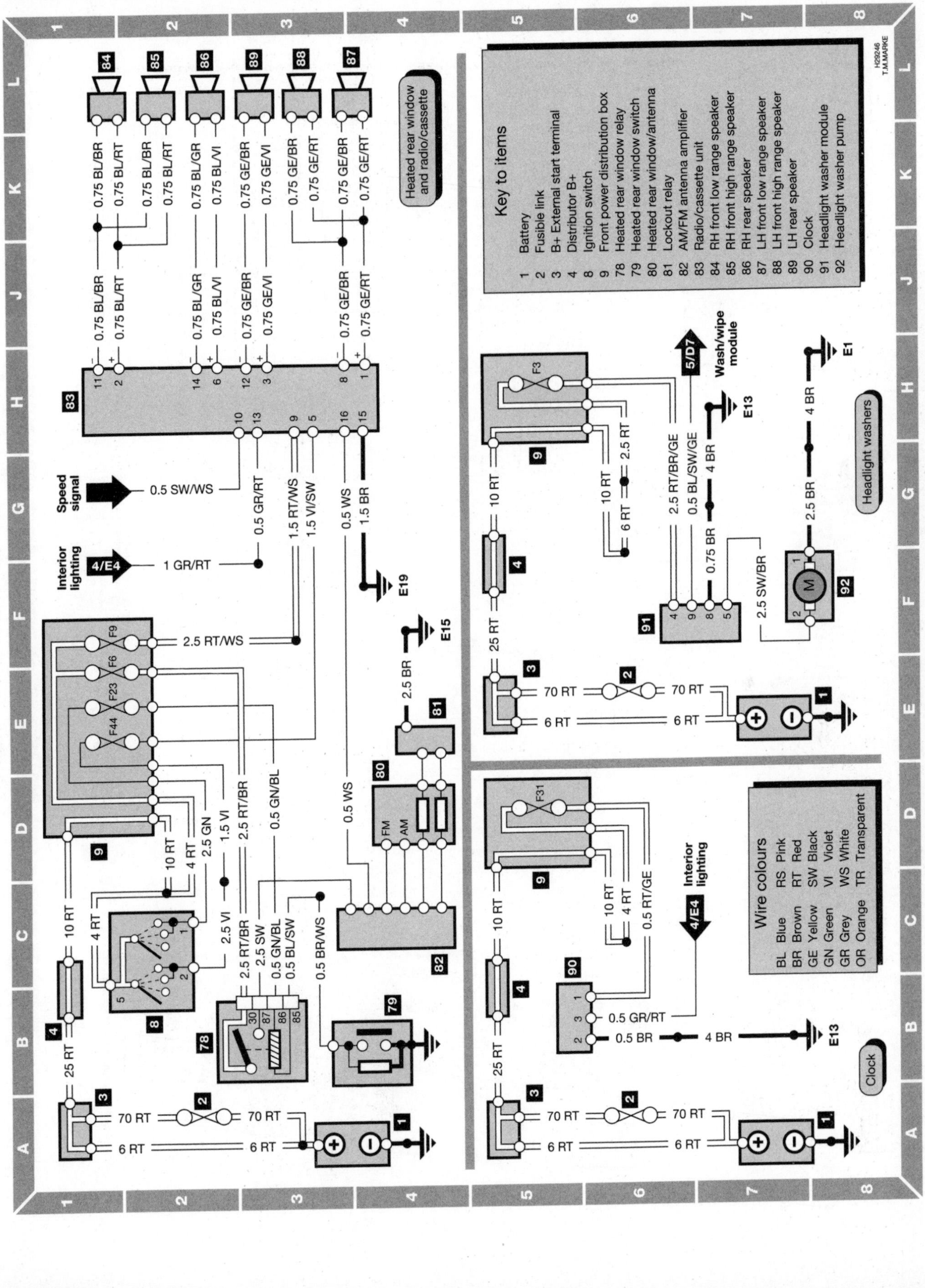

Key to items
1 Battery
2 Fusible link
3 B+ External start terminal
4 Distributor B+
8 Ignition switch
9 Front power distribution box
78 Heated rear window relay
79 Heated rear window switch
80 Heated rear window/antenna
81 Lockout relay
82 AM/FM antenna amplifier
83 Radio/cassette unit
84 RH front low range speaker
85 RH front high range speaker
86 RH rear speaker
87 LH front low range speaker
88 LH front high range speaker
89 LH rear speaker
90 Clock
91 Headlight washer module
92 Headlight washer pump
Wire colours
BL Blue
BR Brown
GE Yellow
GN Green
GR Grey
OR Orange
RS Pink
RT Red
SW Black
VI Violet
WS White
TR Transparent
Heated rear window and radio/cassette
Headlight washers
Clock
Speed signal
Interior lighting
4/E4
Wash/wipe module
5/D7
H29246
T.M.MARKE


Diagram 7 : Typical heated rear window, clock, radio/cassette and headlight washers

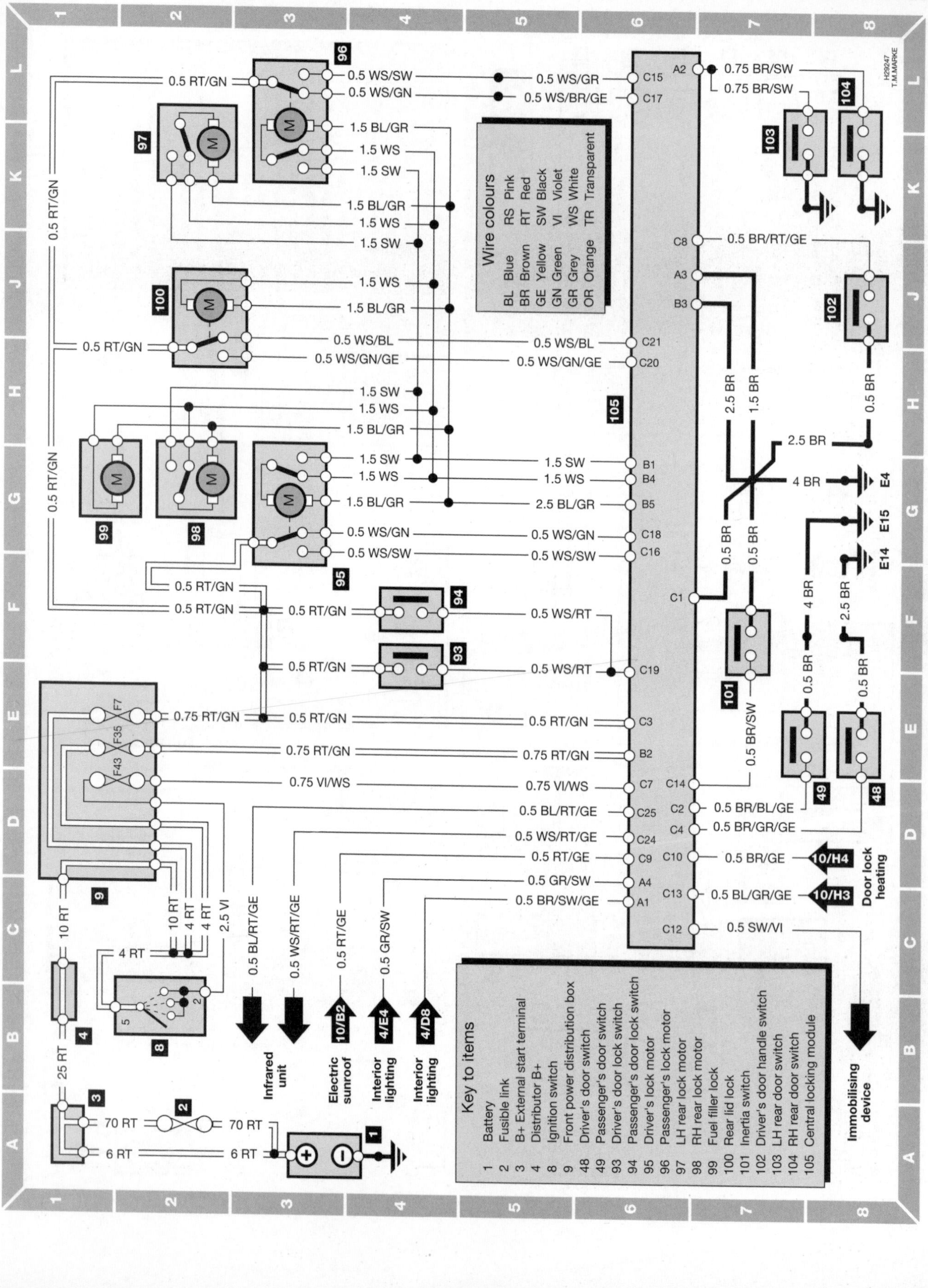
Wire colours
BL Blue
BR Brown
GE Yellow
GN Green
GR Grey
OR Orange
RS Pink
RT Red
SW Black
VI Violet
WS White
TR Transparent
Key to items
1 Battery
2 Fusible link
3 B+ External start terminal
4 Distributor B+
8 Ignition switch
9 Front power distribution box
48 Driver's door switch
49 Passenger's door switch
93 Driver's door lock switch
94 Passenger's door lock switch
95 Driver's lock motor
96 Passenger's lock motor
97 LH rear lock motor
98 RH rear lock motor
99 Fuel filler lock
100 Rear lid lock
101 Inertia switch
102 Driver's door handle switch
103 LH rear door switch
104 RH rear door switch
105 Central locking module
Infrared unit
Electric sunroof
Interior lighting
Interior lighting
Immobilising device
Door lock heating
H29247
T.M.MARKE

Diagram 8 : Typical central locking

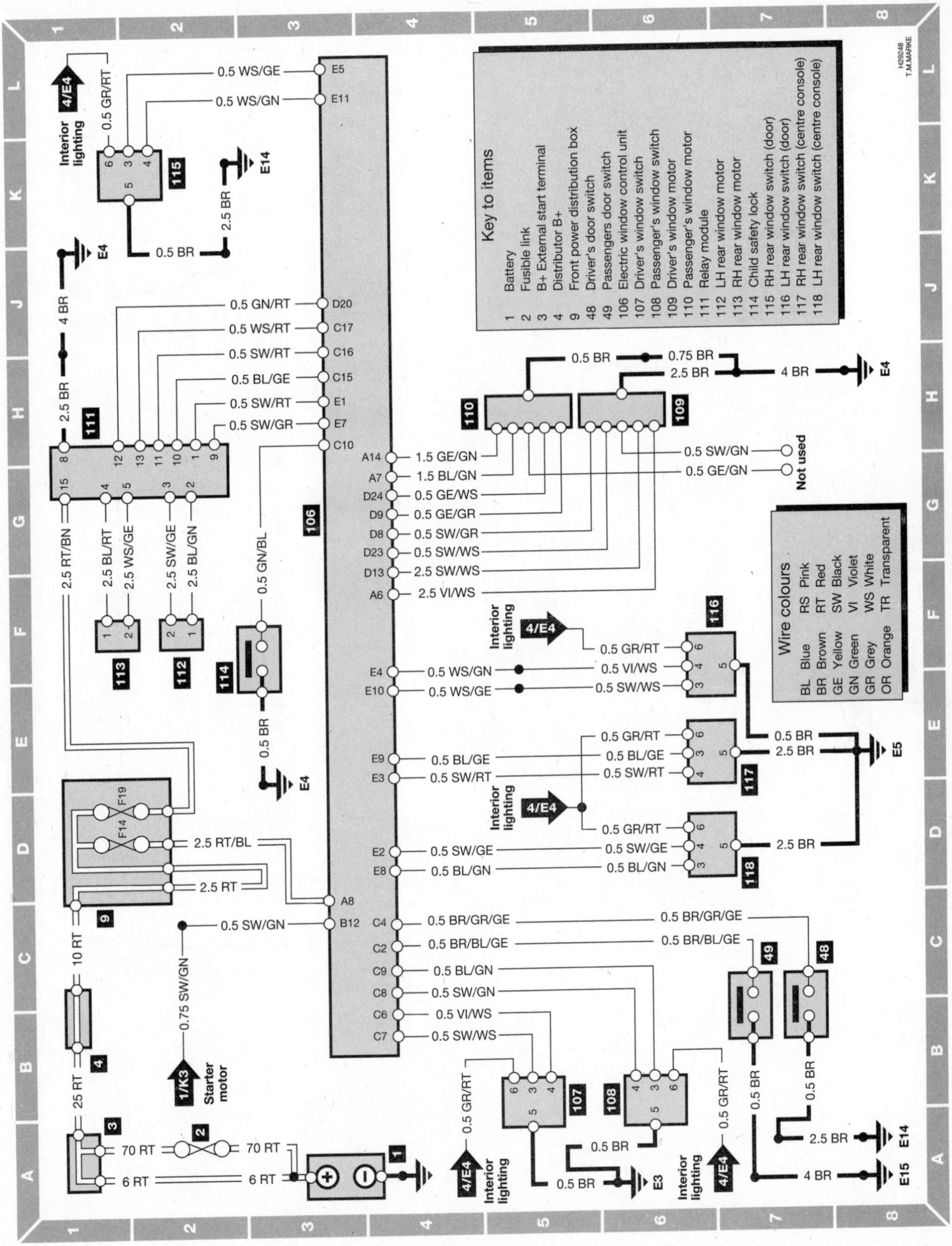


**Key to items**

1 Battery
2 Fusible link
3 B+ External start terminal
4 Distributor B+
9 Front power distribution box
48 Driver's door switch
49 Passengers door switch
106 Electric window control unit
107 Driver's window switch
108 Passenger's window switch
109 Driver's window motor
110 Passenger's window motor
111 Relay module
112 LH rear window motor
113 RH rear window motor
114 Child safety lock
115 RH rear window switch (door)
116 LH rear window switch (door)
117 RH rear window switch (centre console)
118 LH rear window switch (centre console)

**Wire colours**

BL Blue  RS Pink
BR Brown  RT Red
GE Yellow  SW Black
GN Green  VI Violet
GR Grey  WS White
OR Orange  TR Transparent

**Diagram 9 : Typical electric windows**

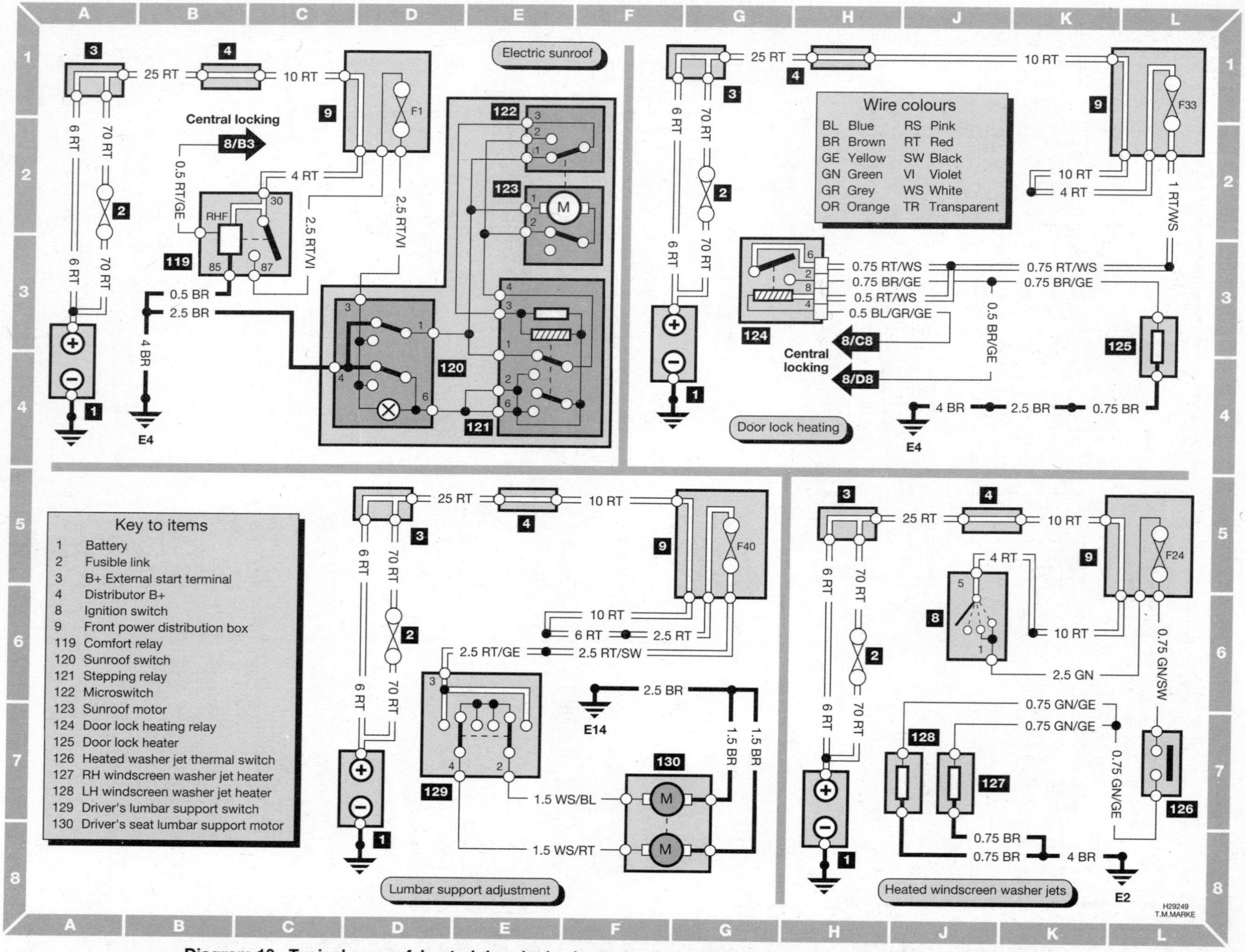


Diagram 10 : Typical sunroof, heated door locks, heated washer jets and driver's lumbar support adjustment

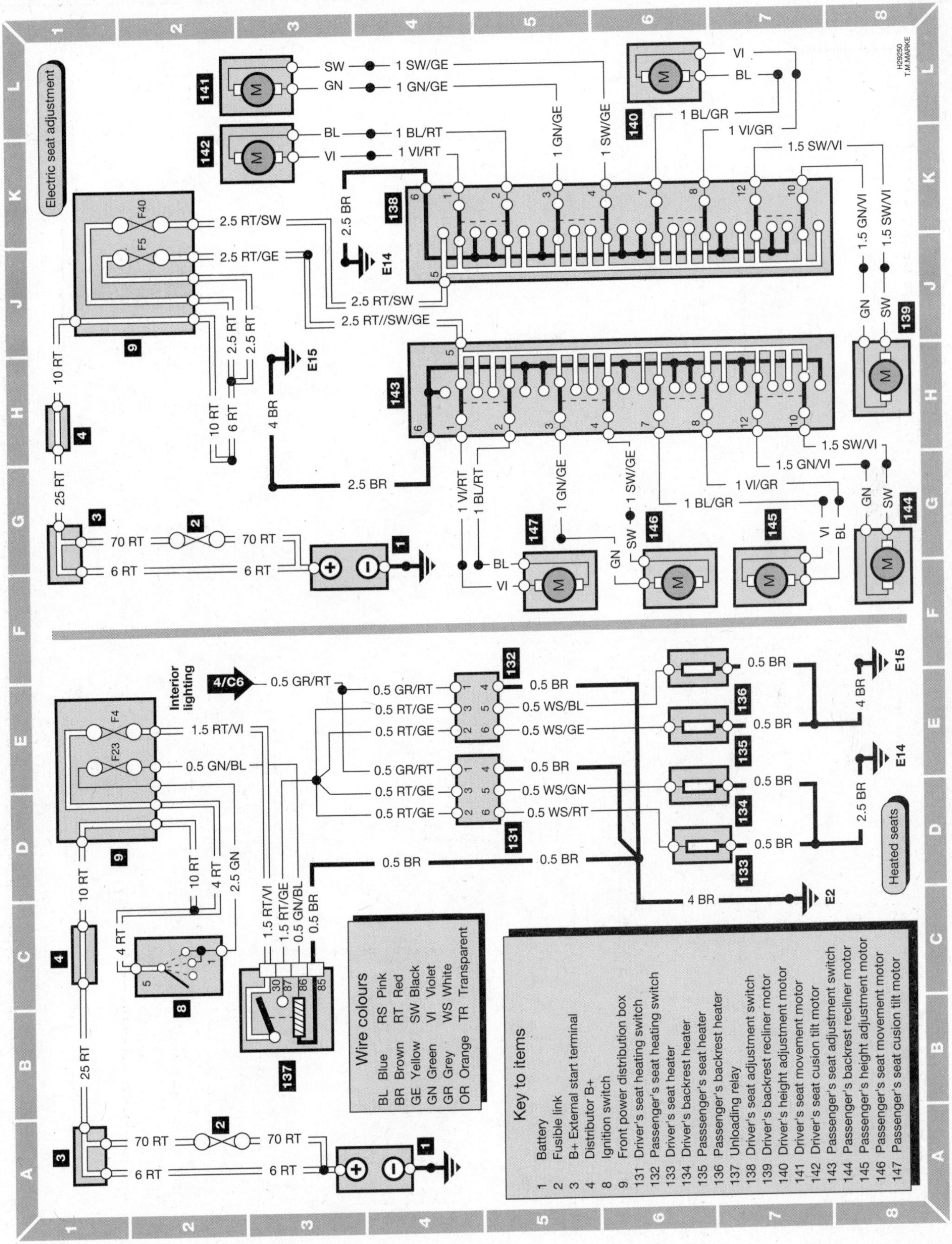


Diagram 11 : Typical heated seats and electric seats

# Dimensions and Weights

**Note:** *All figures are approximate, and may vary according to model. Refer to manufacturer's data for exact figures.*

## Dimensions

| | |
|---|---|
| Overall length | 4433 mm |
| Overall width | 1710 mm |
| Overall height (unladen) | 1393 mm |
| Wheelbase | 2700 mm |

## Weights

| | |
|---|---|
| Kerb weight*: | |
| 1.6 litre models | 1190 to 1230 kg |
| 1.8 litre models | 1205 to 1245 kg |
| 2.0 litre models | 1285 to 1320 kg |
| 2.5 litre models | 1330 to 1365 kg |
| Maximum gross vehicle weight*: | |
| 1.6 litre models | 1650 to 1690 kg |
| 1.8 litre models | 1665 to 1705 kg |
| 2.0 litre models | 1745 to 1780 kg |
| 2.5 litre models | 1790 to 1825 kg |
| Maximum roof rack load | 75 kg |
| Maximum towing weight**: | |
| Unbraked trailer | 630 to 670 kg |
| Braked trailer | 1250 to 1600 kg |

**Depending on model and specification*
**Refer to BMW dealer for exact recommendation*

# Conversion Factors

## Length (distance)

| | | | | | | | |
|---|---|---|---|---|---|---|---|
| Inches (in) | x 25.4 | = | Millimetres (mm) | x 0.0394 | = | Inches (in) |
| Feet (ft) | x 0.305 | = | Metres (m) | x 3.281 | = | Feet (ft) |
| Miles | x 1.609 | = | Kilometres (km) | x 0.621 | = | Miles |

## Volume (capacity)

| | | | | | | |
|---|---|---|---|---|---|---|
| Cubic inches (cu in; in³) | x 16.387 | = | Cubic centimetres (cc; cm³) | x 0.061 | = | Cubic inches (cu in; in³) |
| Imperial pints (Imp pt) | x 0.568 | = | Litres (l) | x 1.76 | = | Imperial pints (Imp pt) |
| Imperial quarts (Imp qt) | x 1.137 | = | Litres (l) | x 0.88 | = | Imperial quarts (Imp qt) |
| Imperial quarts (Imp qt) | x 1.201 | = | US quarts (US qt) | x 0.833 | = | Imperial quarts (Imp qt) |
| US quarts (US qt) | x 0.946 | = | Litres (l) | x 1.057 | = | US quarts (US qt) |
| Imperial gallons (Imp gal) | x 4.546 | = | Litres (l) | x 0.22 | = | Imperial gallons (Imp gal) |
| Imperial gallons (Imp gal) | x 1.201 | = | US gallons (US gal) | x 0.833 | = | Imperial gallons (Imp gal) |
| US gallons (US gal) | x 3.785 | = | Litres (l) | x 0.264 | = | US gallons (US gal) |

## Mass (weight)

| | | | | | | |
|---|---|---|---|---|---|---|
| Ounces (oz) | x 28.35 | = | Grams (g) | x 0.035 | = | Ounces (oz) |
| Pounds (lb) | x 0.454 | = | Kilograms (kg) | x 2.205 | = | Pounds (lb) |

## Force

| | | | | | | |
|---|---|---|---|---|---|---|
| Ounces-force (ozf; oz) | x 0.278 | = | Newtons (N) | x 3.6 | = | Ounces-force (ozf; oz) |
| Pounds-force (lbf; lb) | x 4.448 | = | Newtons (N) | x 0.225 | = | Pounds-force (lbf; lb) |
| Newtons (N) | x 0.1 | = | Kilograms-force (kgf; kg) | x 9.81 | = | Newtons (N) |

## Pressure

| | | | | | | |
|---|---|---|---|---|---|---|
| Pounds-force per square inch (psi; lbf/in²; lb/in²) | x 0.070 | = | Kilograms-force per square centimetre (kgf/cm²; kg/cm²) | x 14.223 | = | Pounds-force per square inch (psi; lbf/in²; lb/in²) |
| Pounds-force per square inch (psi; lbf/in²; lb/in²) | x 0.068 | = | Atmospheres (atm) | x 14.696 | = | Pounds-force per square inch (psi; lbf/in²; lb/in²) |
| Pounds-force per square inch (psi; lbf/in²; lb/in²) | x 0.069 | = | Bars | x 14.5 | = | Pounds-force per square inch (psi; lbf/in²; lb/in²) |
| Pounds-force per square inch (psi; lbf/in²; lb/in²) | x 6.895 | = | Kilopascals (kPa) | x 0.145 | = | Pounds-force per square inch (psi; lbf/in²; lb/in²) |
| Kilopascals (kPa) | x 0.01 | = | Kilograms-force per square centimetre (kgf/cm²; kg/cm²) | x 98.1 | = | Kilopascals (kPa) |
| Millibar (mbar) | x 100 | = | Pascals (Pa) | x 0.01 | = | Millibar (mbar) |
| Millibar (mbar) | x 0.0145 | = | Pounds-force per square inch (psi; lbf/in²; lb/in²) | x 68.947 | = | Millibar (mbar) |
| Millibar (mbar) | x 0.75 | = | Millimetres of mercury (mmHg) | x 1.333 | = | Millibar (mbar) |
| Millibar (mbar) | x 0.401 | = | Inches of water (inH$_2$O) | x 2.491 | = | Millibar (mbar) |
| Millimetres of mercury (mmHg) | x 0.535 | = | Inches of water (inH$_2$O) | x 1.868 | = | Millimetres of mercury (mmHg) |
| Inches of water (inH$_2$O) | x 0.036 | = | Pounds-force per square inch (psi; lbf/in²; lb/in²) | x 27.68 | = | Inches of water (inH$_2$O) |

## Torque (moment of force)

| | | | | | | |
|---|---|---|---|---|---|---|
| Pounds-force inches (lbf in; lb in) | x 1.152 | = | Kilograms-force centimetre (kgf cm; kg cm) | x 0.868 | = | Pounds-force inches (lbf in; lb in) |
| Pounds-force inches (lbf in; lb in) | x 0.113 | = | Newton metres (Nm) | x 8.85 | = | Pounds-force inches (lbf in; lb in) |
| Pounds-force inches (lbf in; lb in) | x 0.083 | = | Pounds-force feet (lbf ft; lb ft) | x 12 | = | Pounds-force inches (lbf in; lb in) |
| Pounds-force feet (lbf ft; lb ft) | x 0.138 | = | Kilograms-force metres (kgf m; kg m) | x 7.233 | = | Pounds-force feet (lbf ft; lb ft) |
| Pounds-force feet (lbf ft; lb ft) | x 1.356 | = | Newton metres (Nm) | x 0.738 | = | Pounds-force feet (lbf ft; lb ft) |
| Newton metres (Nm) | x 0.102 | = | Kilograms-force metres (kgf m; kg m) | x 9.804 | = | Newton metres (Nm) |

## Power

| | | | | | | |
|---|---|---|---|---|---|---|
| Horsepower (hp) | x 745.7 | = | Watts (W) | x 0.0013 | = | Horsepower (hp) |

## Velocity (speed)

| | | | | | | |
|---|---|---|---|---|---|---|
| Miles per hour (miles/hr; mph) | x 1.609 | = | Kilometres per hour (km/hr; kph) | x 0.621 | = | Miles per hour (miles/hr; mph) |

## Fuel consumption*

| | | | | | | |
|---|---|---|---|---|---|---|
| Miles per gallon (mpg) | x 0.354 | = | Kilometres per litre (km/l) | x 2.825 | = | Miles per gallon (mpg) |

## Temperature

Degrees Fahrenheit = (°C x 1.8) + 32

Degrees Celsius (Degrees Centigrade; °C) = (°F - 32) x 0.56

** It is common practice to convert from miles per gallon (mpg) to litres/100 kilometres (l/100km), where mpg x l/100 km = 282*

Spare parts are available from many sources, including maker's appointed garages, accessory shops, and motor factors. To be sure of obtaining the correct parts, it will sometimes be necessary to quote the vehicle identification number. If possible, it can also be useful to take the old parts along for positive identification. Items such as starter motors and alternators may be available under a service exchange scheme - any parts returned should be clean.

Our advice regarding spare parts is as follows.

### Officially appointed garages

This is the best source of parts which are peculiar to your car, and which are not otherwise generally available (eg, badges, interior trim, certain body panels, etc). It is also the only place at which you should buy parts if the vehicle is still under warranty.

### Accessory shops

These are very good places to buy materials and components needed for the maintenance of your car (oil, air and fuel filters, light bulbs, drivebelts, greases, brake pads, touch-up paint, etc). Components of this nature sold by a reputable shop are usually of the same standard as those used by the car manufacturer.

Besides components, these shops also sell tools and general accessories, usually have convenient opening hours, charge lower prices, and can often be found close to home. Some accessory shops have parts counters where components needed for almost any repair job can be purchased or ordered.

### Motor factors

Good factors will stock all the more important components which wear out comparatively quickly, and can sometimes supply individual components needed for the overhaul of a larger assembly (eg, brake seals and hydraulic parts, bearing shells, pistons, valves). They may also handle work such as cylinder block reboring, crankshaft regrinding, etc.

### Tyre and exhaust specialists

These outlets may be independent, or members of a local or national chain. They frequently offer competitive prices when compared with a main dealer or local garage, but it will pay to obtain several quotes before making a decision. When researching prices, also ask what "extras" may be added - for instance fitting a new valve and balancing the wheel are both commonly charged on top of the price of a new tyre.

### Other sources

Beware of parts or materials obtained from market stalls, car boot sales or similar outlets. Such items are not invariably sub-standard, but there is little chance of compensation if they do prove unsatisfactory. in the case of safety-critical components such as brake pads, there is the risk not only of financial loss, but also of an accident causing injury or death.

Second-hand components or assemblies obtained from a car breaker can be a good buy in some circumstances, but this sort of purchase is best made by the experienced DIY mechanic.

# Vehicle Identification

Modifications are a continuing and unpublicised process in vehicle manufacture, quite apart from major model changes. Spare parts manuals and lists are compiled upon a numerical basis, the individual vehicle identification numbers being essential to correct identification of the component concerned.

When ordering spare parts, always give as much information as possible. Quote the car model, year of manufacture and registration, chassis and engine numbers as appropriate.

The *Vehicle Identification Number (VIN)* plate is riveted to the right-hand side body panel in the engine compartment. The vehicle identification number is also stamped onto the top of the engine compartment bulkhead.

The *engine number* is stamped on the left hand face of the cylinder block near the base of the oil level dipstick.

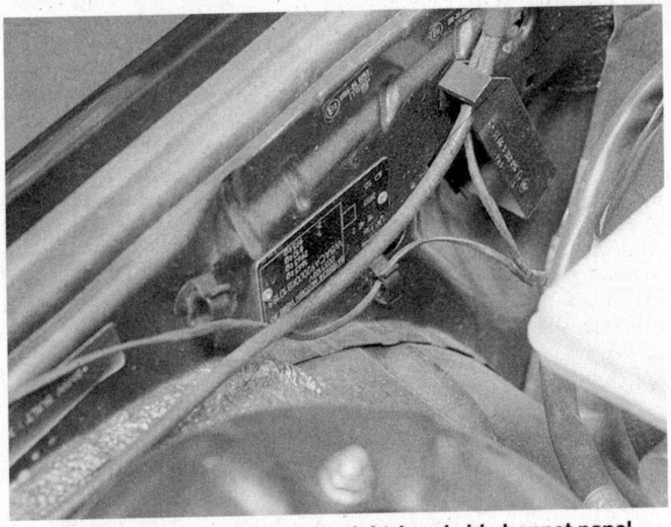

**The VIN plate is riveted to the right-hand side bonnet panel in the engine compartment**

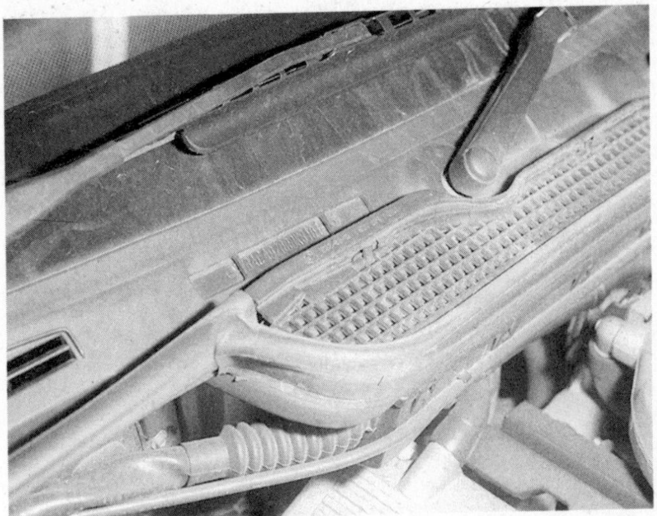

**The chassis number is stamped onto the top of the engine compartment bulkhead**

Whenever servicing, repair or overhaul work is carried out on the car or its components, it is necessary to observe the following procedures and instructions. This will assist in carrying out the operation efficiently and to a professional standard of workmanship.

## Joint mating faces and gaskets

When separating components at their mating faces, never insert screwdrivers or similar implements into the joint between the faces in order to prise them apart. This can cause severe damage which results in oil leaks, coolant leaks, etc upon reassembly. Separation is usually achieved by tapping along the joint with a soft-faced hammer in order to break the seal. However, note that this method may not be suitable where dowels are used for component location.

Where a gasket is used between the mating faces of two components, ensure that it is renewed on reassembly, and fit it dry unless otherwise stated in the repair procedure. Make sure that the mating faces are clean and dry, with all traces of old gasket removed. When cleaning a joint face, use a tool which is not likely to score or damage the face, and remove any burrs or nicks with an oilstone or fine file.

Make sure that tapped holes are cleaned with a pipe cleaner, and keep them free of jointing compound, if this is being used, unless specifically instructed otherwise.

Ensure that all orifices, channels or pipes are clear, and blow through them, preferably using compressed air.

## Oil seals

Oil seals can be removed by levering them out with a wide flat-bladed screwdriver or similar tool. Alternatively, a number of self-tapping screws may be screwed into the seal, and these used as a purchase for pliers or similar in order to pull the seal free.

Whenever an oil seal is removed from its working location, either individually or as part of an assembly, it should be renewed.

The very fine sealing lip of the seal is easily damaged, and will not seal if the surface it contacts is not completely clean and free from scratches, nicks or grooves. If the original sealing surface of the component cannot be restored, and the manufacturer has not made provision for slight relocation of the seal relative to the sealing surface, the component should be renewed.

Protect the lips of the seal from any surface which may damage them in the course of fitting. Use tape or a conical sleeve where possible. Lubricate the seal lips with oil before fitting and, on dual-lipped seals, fill the space between the lips with grease.

Unless otherwise stated, oil seals must be fitted with their sealing lips toward the lubricant to be sealed.

Use a tubular drift or block of wood of the appropriate size to install the seal and, if the seal housing is shouldered, drive the seal down to the shoulder. If the seal housing is unshouldered, the seal should be fitted with its face flush with the housing top face (unless otherwise instructed).

## Screw threads and fastenings

Seized nuts, bolts and screws are quite a common occurrence where corrosion has set in, and the use of penetrating oil or releasing fluid will often overcome this problem if the offending item is soaked for a while before attempting to release it. The use of an impact driver may also provide a means of releasing such stubborn fastening devices, when used in conjunction with the appropriate screwdriver bit or socket. If none of these methods works, it may be necessary to resort to the careful application of heat, or the use of a hacksaw or nut splitter device.

Studs are usually removed by locking two nuts together on the threaded part, and then using a spanner on the lower nut to unscrew the stud. Studs or bolts which have broken off below the surface of the component in which they are mounted can sometimes be removed using a stud extractor. Always ensure that a blind tapped hole is completely free from oil, grease, water or other fluid before installing the bolt or stud. Failure to do this could cause the housing to crack due to the hydraulic action of the bolt or stud as it is screwed in.

When tightening a castellated nut to accept a split pin, tighten the nut to the specified torque, where applicable, and then tighten further to the next split pin hole. Never slacken the nut to align the split pin hole, unless stated in the repair procedure.

When checking or retightening a nut or bolt to a specified torque setting, slacken the nut or bolt by a quarter of a turn, and then retighten to the specified setting. However, this should not be attempted where angular tightening has been used.

For some screw fastenings, notably cylinder head bolts or nuts, torque wrench settings are no longer specified for the latter stages of tightening, "angle-tightening" being called up instead. Typically, a fairly low torque wrench setting will be applied to the bolts/nuts in the correct sequence, followed by one or more stages of tightening through specified angles.

## Locknuts, locktabs and washers

Any fastening which will rotate against a component or housing during tightening should always have a washer between it and the relevant component or housing.

Spring or split washers should always be renewed when they are used to lock a critical component such as a big-end bearing retaining bolt or nut. Locktabs which are folded over to retain a nut or bolt should always be renewed.

Self-locking nuts can be re-used in non-critical areas, providing resistance can be felt when the locking portion passes over the bolt or stud thread. However, it should be noted that self-locking stiffnuts tend to lose their effectiveness after long periods of use, and should be renewed as a matter of course.

Split pins must always be replaced with new ones of the correct size for the hole.

When thread-locking compound is found on the threads of a fastener which is to be re-used, it should be cleaned off with a wire brush and solvent, and fresh compound applied on reassembly.

## Special tools

Some repair procedures in this manual entail the use of special tools such as a press, two or three-legged pullers, spring compressors, etc. Wherever possible, suitable readily-available alternatives to the manufacturer's special tools are described, and are shown in use. In some instances, where no alternative is possible, it has been necessary to resort to the use of a manufacturer's tool, and this has been done for reasons of safety as well as the efficient completion of the repair operation. Unless you are highly-skilled and have a thorough understanding of the procedures described, never attempt to bypass the use of any special tool when the procedure described specifies its use. Not only is there a very great risk of personal injury, but expensive damage could be caused to the components involved.

## Environmental considerations

When disposing of used engine oil, brake fluid, antifreeze, etc, give due consideration to any detrimental environmental effects. Do not, for instance, pour any of the above liquids down drains into the general sewage system, or onto the ground to soak away. Many local council refuse tips provide a facility for waste oil disposal, as do some garages. If none of these facilities are available, consult your local Environmental Health Department, or the National Rivers Authority, for further advice.

With the universal tightening-up of legislation regarding the emission of environmentally-harmful substances from motor vehicles, most current vehicles have tamperproof devices fitted to the main adjustment points of the fuel system. These devices are primarily designed to prevent unqualified persons from adjusting the fuel/air mixture, with the chance of a consequent increase in toxic emissions. If such devices are encountered during servicing or overhaul, they should, wherever possible, be renewed or refitted in accordance with the vehicle manufacturer's requirements or current legislation.

OIL CARE
FOLLOW THE CODE
OIL BANK LINE
0800 66 33 66

***Note: It is antisocial and illegal to dump oil down the drain. To find the location of your local oil recycling bank, call this number free.***

The jack supplied with the vehicle tool kit should only be used for changing the roadwheels - see *"Wheel changing"* at the front of this manual. When carrying out any other kind of work, raise the vehicle using a hydraulic (or "trolley") jack, and always supplement the jack with axle stands positioned under the vehicle jacking points.

When using a hydraulic jack or axle stands, always position the jack head or axle stand head under the relevant rubber lifting blocks. These are situated directly underneath the vehicle jack location holes in the sill **(see illustration)**.

The jack supplied with the vehicle locates in the holes provided in the sill. Unscrew the access plug and insert the jack fully into the hole in the sill. Ensure that the jack head is correctly engaged before attempting to raise the vehicle.

**Never** work under, around, or near a raised vehicle, unless it is adequately supported in at least two places.

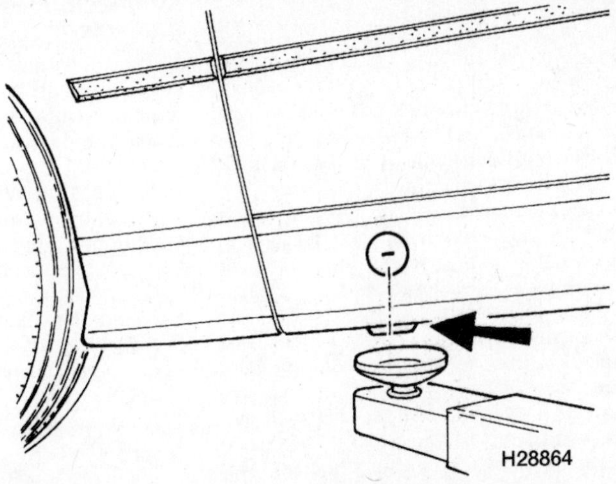


**When raising the front of the vehicle, locate the jack underneath the rubber lifting block (arrowed) located directly under the vehicle jack location holes in the sill**

# Radio/cassette unit Anti-Theft System - Precaution

The radio/cassette/CD player/autochanger unit fitted as standard equipment by BMW is equipped with a built-in security code, to deter thieves. If the power source to the unit is cut, the anti-theft system will activate. Even if the power source is immediately reconnected, the radio/cassette unit will not function until the correct security code has been entered. Therefore if you do not know the correct security code for the unit, **do not** disconnect the battery negative lead, or remove the radio/cassette unit from the vehicle.

The procedure for reprogramming a unit that has been disconnected from its power supply varies from model to model - consult the handbook supplied with the unit for specific details or refer to your BMW dealer.

## Introduction

A selection of good tools is a fundamental requirement for anyone contemplating the maintenance and repair of a motor vehicle. For the owner who does not possess any, their purchase will prove a considerable expense, offsetting some of the savings made by doing-it-yourself. However, provided that the tools purchased meet the relevant national safety standards and are of good quality, they will last for many years and prove an extremely worthwhile investment.

To help the average owner to decide which tools are needed to carry out the various tasks detailed in this manual, we have compiled three lists of tools under the following headings: *Maintenance and minor repair, Repair and overhaul*, and *Special*. Newcomers to practical mechanics should start off with the *Maintenance and minor repair* tool kit, and confine themselves to the simpler jobs around the vehicle. Then, as confidence and experience grow, more difficult tasks can be undertaken, with extra tools being purchased as, and when, they are needed. In this way, a *Maintenance and minor repair* tool kit can be built up into a *Repair and overhaul* tool kit over a considerable period of time, without any major cash outlays. The experienced do-it-yourselfer will have a tool kit good enough for most repair and overhaul procedures, and will add tools from the *Special* category when it is felt that the expense is justified by the amount of use to which these tools will be put.

## Maintenance and minor repair tool kit

The tools given in this list should be considered as a minimum requirement if routine maintenance, servicing and minor repair operations are to be undertaken. We recommend the purchase of combination spanners (ring one end, open-ended the other); although more expensive than open-ended ones, they do give the advantages of both types of spanner.

- ☐ *Combination spanners:*
  *Metric - 8 to 19 mm inclusive*
- ☐ *Adjustable spanner - 35 mm jaw (approx.)*
- ☐ *Spark plug spanner (with rubber insert) - petrol models*
- ☐ *Spark plug gap adjustment tool - petrol models*
- ☐ *Set of feeler gauges*
- ☐ *Brake bleed nipple spanner*
- ☐ *Screwdrivers:*
  *Flat blade - 100 mm long x 6 mm dia*
  *Cross blade - 100 mm long x 6 mm dia*
- ☐ *Combination pliers*
- ☐ *Hacksaw (junior)*
- ☐ *Tyre pump*
- ☐ *Tyre pressure gauge*
- ☐ *Oil can*
- ☐ *Oil filter removal tool*
- ☐ *Fine emery cloth*
- ☐ *Wire brush (small)*
- ☐ *Funnel (medium size)*

## Repair and overhaul tool kit

These tools are virtually essential for anyone undertaking any major repairs to a motor vehicle, and are additional to those given in the *Maintenance and minor repair* list. Included in this list is a comprehensive set of sockets. Although these are expensive, they will be found invaluable as they are so versatile - particularly if various drives are included in the set. We recommend the half-inch square-drive type, as this can be used with most proprietary torque wrenches.

The tools in this list will sometimes need to be supplemented by tools from the *Special* list:

- ☐ *Sockets (or box spanners) to cover range in previous list (including Torx sockets)*
- ☐ *Reversible ratchet drive (for use with sockets)*
- ☐ *Extension piece, 250 mm (for use with sockets)*
- ☐ *Universal joint (for use with sockets)*
- ☐ *Torque wrench (for use with sockets)*
- ☐ *Self-locking grips*
- ☐ *Ball pein hammer*
- ☐ *Soft-faced mallet (plastic/aluminium or rubber)*
- ☐ *Screwdrivers:*
  *Flat blade - long & sturdy, short (chubby), and narrow (electrician's) types*
  *Cross blade – Long & sturdy, and short (chubby) types*
- ☐ *Pliers:*
  *Long-nosed*
  *Side cutters (electrician's)*
  *Circlip (internal and external)*
- ☐ *Cold chisel - 25 mm*
- ☐ *Scriber*
- ☐ *Scraper*
- ☐ *Centre-punch*
- ☐ *Pin punch*
- ☐ *Hacksaw*
- ☐ *Brake hose clamp*
- ☐ *Brake/clutch bleeding kit*
- ☐ *Selection of twist drills*
- ☐ *Steel rule/straight-edge*
- ☐ *Allen keys (inc. splined/Torx type)*
- ☐ *Selection of files*
- ☐ *Wire brush*
- ☐ *Axle stands*
- ☐ *Jack (strong trolley or hydraulic type)*
- ☐ *Light with extension lead*

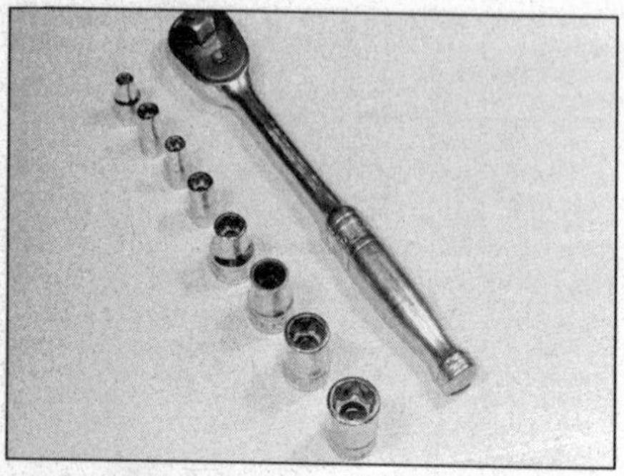

**Sockets and reversible ratchet drive**

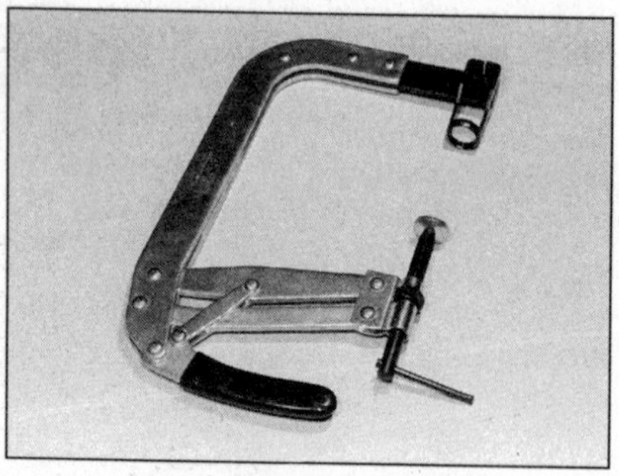

**Valve spring compressor**

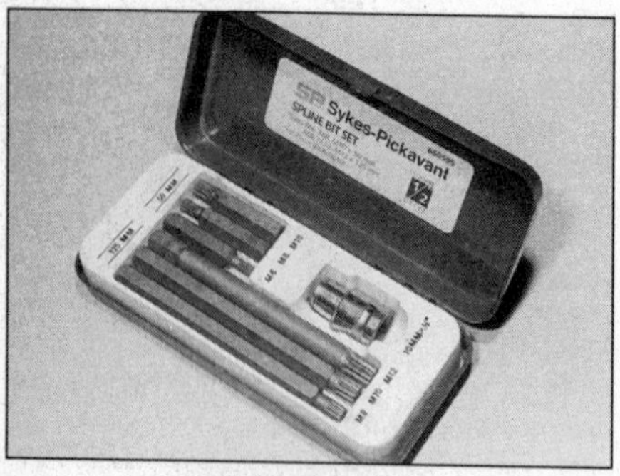


**Spline bit set**

**Piston ring compressor**

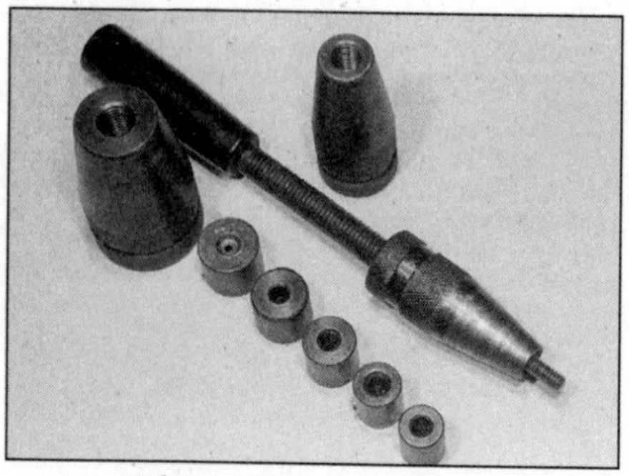

**Clutch plate alignment set**

## Special tools

The tools in this list are those which are not used regularly, are expensive to buy, or which need to be used in accordance with their manufacturers' instructions. Unless relatively difficult mechanical jobs are undertaken frequently, it will not be economic to buy many of these tools. Where this is the case, you could consider clubbing together with friends (or joining a motorists' club) to make a joint purchase, or borrowing the tools against a deposit from a local garage or tool hire specialist. It is worth noting that many of the larger DIY superstores now carry a large range of special tools for hire at modest rates.

The following list contains only those tools and instruments freely available to the public, and not those special tools produced by the vehicle manufacturer specifically for its dealer network. You will find occasional references to these manufacturers' special tools in the text of this manual. Generally, an alternative method of doing the job without the vehicle manufacturers' special tool is given. However, sometimes there is no alternative to using them. Where this is the case and the relevant tool cannot be bought or borrowed, you will have to entrust the work to a dealer.

- ☐ *Valve spring compressor*
- ☐ *Valve grinding tool*
- ☐ *Piston ring compressor*
- ☐ *Piston ring removal/installation tool*
- ☐ *Cylinder bore hone*
- ☐ *Balljoint separator*
- ☐ *Coil spring compressors (where applicable)*
- ☐ *Two/three-legged hub and bearing puller*
- ☐ *Impact screwdriver*
- ☐ *Micrometer and/or vernier calipers*
- ☐ *Dial gauge*
- ☐ *Stroboscopic timing light*
- ☐ *Dwell angle meter/tachometer*
- ☐ *Universal electrical multi-meter*
- ☐ *Cylinder compression gauge*
- ☐ *Hand-operated vacuum pump and gauge*
- ☐ *Clutch plate alignment set*
- ☐ *Brake shoe steady spring cup removal tool*
- ☐ *Bush and bearing removal/installation set*
- ☐ *Stud extractors*
- ☐ *Tap and die set*
- ☐ *Lifting tackle*
- ☐ *Trolley jack*

## Buying tools

Reputable motor accessory shops and superstores often offer excellent quality tools at discount prices, so it pays to shop around.

Remember, you don't have to buy the most expensive items on the shelf, but it is always advisable to steer clear of the very cheap tools. Beware of 'bargains' offered on market stalls or at car boot sales. There are plenty of good tools around at reasonable prices, but always aim to purchase items which meet the relevant national safety standards. If in doubt, ask the proprietor or manager of the shop for advice before making a purchase.

## Care and maintenance of tools

Having purchased a reasonable tool kit, it is necessary to keep the tools in a clean and serviceable condition. After use, always wipe off any dirt, grease and metal particles using a clean, dry cloth, before putting the tools away. Never leave them lying around after they have been used. A simple tool rack on the garage or workshop wall for items such as screwdrivers and pliers is a good idea. Store all normal spanners and sockets in a metal box. Any measuring instruments, gauges, meters, etc, must be carefully stored where they cannot be damaged or become rusty.

Take a little care when tools are used. Hammer heads inevitably become marked, and screwdrivers lose the keen edge on their blades from time to time. A little timely attention with emery cloth or a file will soon restore items like this to a good finish.

## Working facilities

Not to be forgotten when discussing tools is the workshop itself. If anything more than routine maintenance is to be carried out, a suitable working area becomes essential.

It is appreciated that many an owner-mechanic is forced by circumstances to remove an engine or similar item without the benefit of a garage or workshop. Having done this, any repairs should always be done under the cover of a roof.

Wherever possible, any dismantling should be done on a clean, flat workbench or table at a suitable working height.

Any workbench needs a vice; one with a jaw opening of 100 mm is suitable for most jobs. As mentioned previously, some clean dry storage space is also required for tools, as well as for any lubricants, cleaning fluids, touch-up paints etc, which become necessary.

Another item which may be required, and which has a much more general usage, is an electric drill with a chuck capacity of at least 8 mm. This, together with a good range of twist drills, is virtually essential for fitting accessories.

Last, but not least, always keep a supply of old newspapers and clean, lint-free rags available, and try to keep any working area as clean as possible.

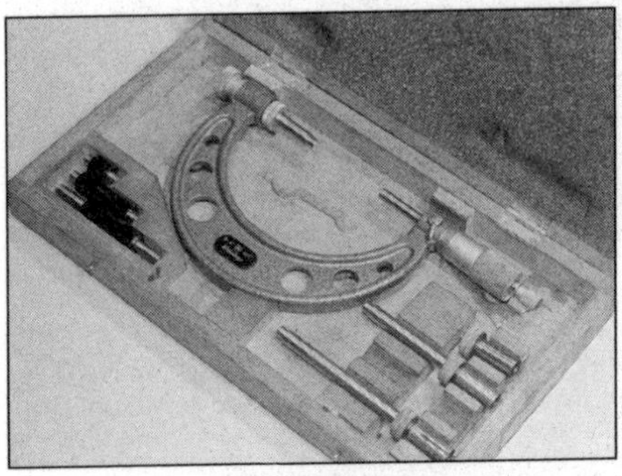

**Micrometer set**

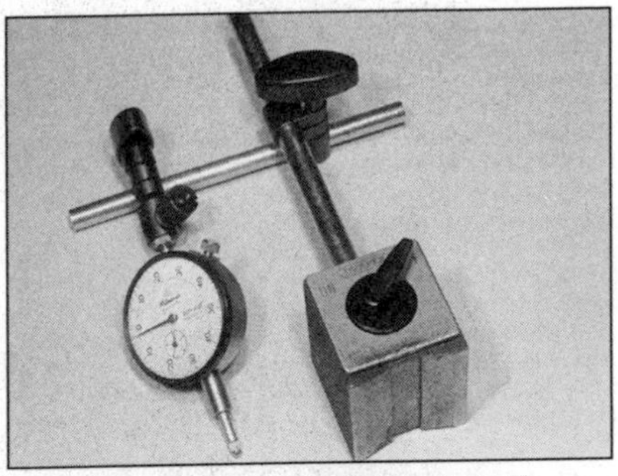

**Dial test indicator ("dial gauge")**

**Stroboscopic timing light**

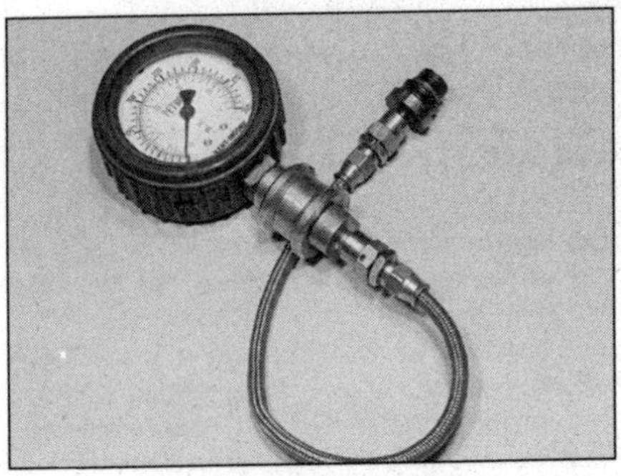

**Compression tester**

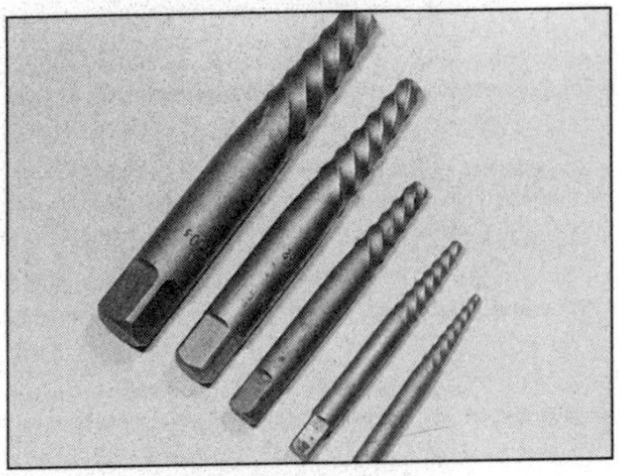

**Stud extractor set**

This is a guide to getting your vehicle through the MOT test. Obviously it will not be possible to examine the vehicle to the same standard as the professional MOT tester. However, working through the following checks will enable you to identify any problem areas before submitting the vehicle for the test.

Where a testable component is in borderline condition, the tester has discretion in deciding whether to pass or fail it. The basis of such discretion is whether the tester would be happy for a close relative or friend to use the vehicle with the component in that condition. If the vehicle presented is clean and evidently well cared for, the tester may be more inclined to pass a borderline component than if the vehicle is scruffy and apparently neglected.

It has only been possible to summarise the test requirements here, based on the regulations in force at the time of printing. Test standards are becoming increasingly stringent, although there are some exemptions for older vehicles. For full details obtain a copy of the Haynes publication Pass the MOT! (available from stockists of Haynes manuals).

An assistant will be needed to help carry out some of these checks.

*The checks have been sub-divided into four categories, as follows:*

**1** Checks carried out **FROM THE DRIVER'S SEAT**

**2** Checks carried out **WITH THE VEHICLE ON THE GROUND**

**3** Checks carried out **WITH THE VEHICLE RAISED AND THE WHEELS FREE TO TURN**

**4** Checks carried out on **YOUR VEHICLE'S EXHAUST EMISSION SYSTEM**

## 1 Checks carried out FROM THE DRIVER'S SEAT

### Handbrake

☐ Test the operation of the handbrake. Excessive travel (too many clicks) indicates incorrect brake or cable adjustment.

☐ Check that the handbrake cannot be released by tapping the lever sideways. Check the security of the lever mountings.

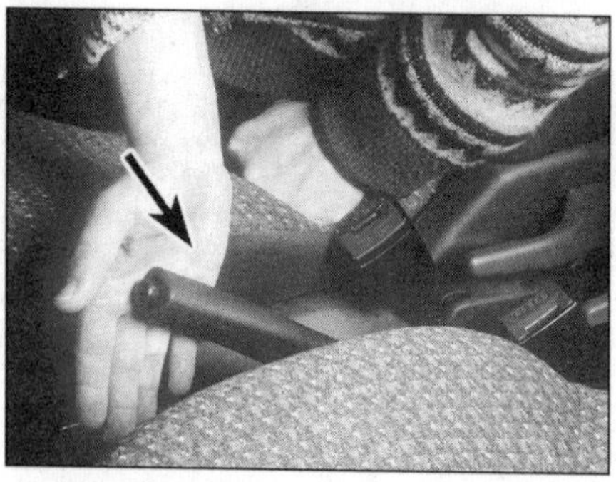

### Footbrake

☐ Depress the brake pedal and check that it does not creep down to the floor, indicating a master cylinder fault. Release the pedal, wait a few seconds, then depress it again. If the pedal travels nearly to the floor before firm resistance is felt, brake adjustment or repair is necessary. If the pedal feels spongy, there is air in the hydraulic system which must be removed by bleeding.

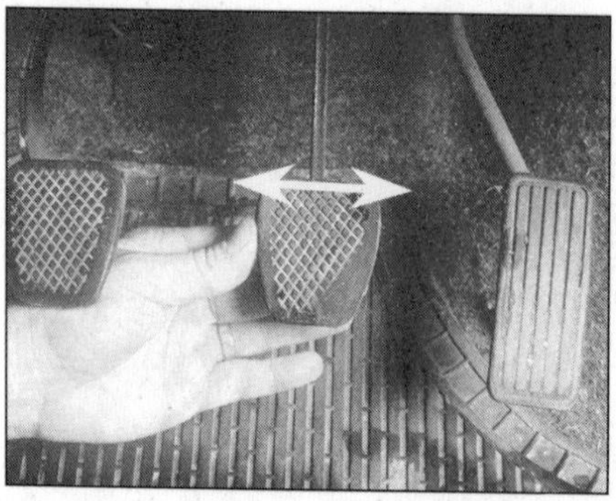

☐ Check that the brake pedal is secure and in good condition. Check also for signs of fluid leaks on the pedal, floor or carpets, which would indicate failed seals in the brake master cylinder.

☐ Check the servo unit (when applicable) by operating the brake pedal several times, then keeping the pedal depressed and starting the engine. As the engine starts, the pedal will move down slightly. If not, the vacuum hose or the servo itself may be faulty.

### Steering wheel and column

☐ Examine the steering wheel for fractures or looseness of the hub, spokes or rim.

☐ Move the steering wheel from side to side and then up and down. Check that the steering wheel is not loose on the column, indicating wear or a loose retaining nut. Continue moving the steering wheel as before, but also turn it slightly from left to right.

☐ Check that the steering wheel is not loose on the column, and that there is no abnormal movement of the steering wheel, indicating wear in the column support bearings or couplings.

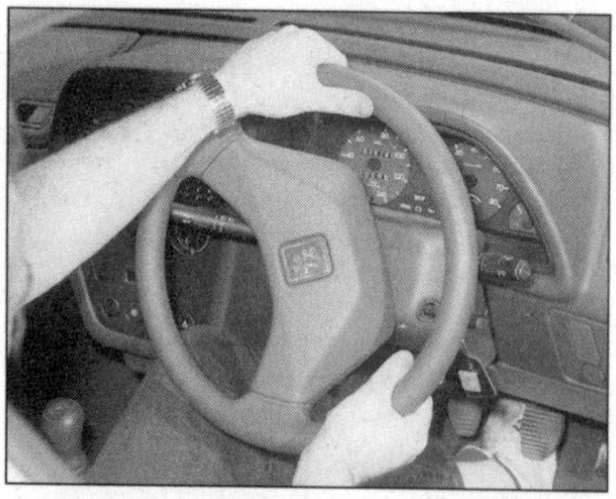

### Windscreen and mirrors

☐ The windscreen must be free of cracks or other significant damage within the driver's field of view. (Small stone chips are acceptable.) Rear view mirrors must be secure, intact, and capable of being adjusted.

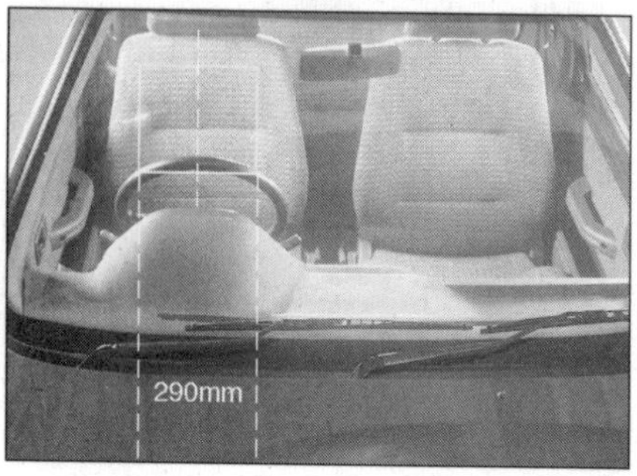

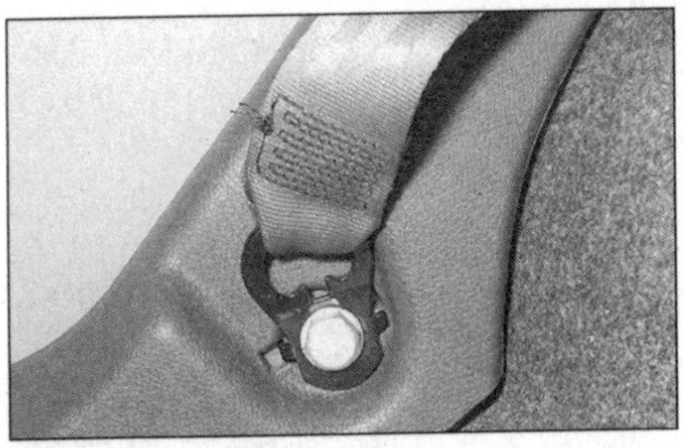

### Seat belts and seats

**Note:** *The following checks are applicable to all seat belts, front and rear.*

☐ Examine the webbing of all the belts (including rear belts if fitted) for cuts, serious fraying or deterioration. Fasten and unfasten each belt to check the buckles. If applicable, check the retracting mechanism. Check the security of all seat belt mountings accessible from inside the vehicle.

☐ The front seats themselves must be securely attached and the backrests must lock in the upright position.

### Doors

☐ Both front doors must be able to be opened and closed from outside and inside, and must latch securely when closed.

## 2 Checks carried out **WITH THE VEHICLE ON THE GROUND**

### Vehicle identification

☐ Number plates must be in good condition, secure and legible, with letters and numbers correctly spaced – spacing at (A) should be twice that at (B).

☐ The VIN plate and/or homologation plate must be legible.

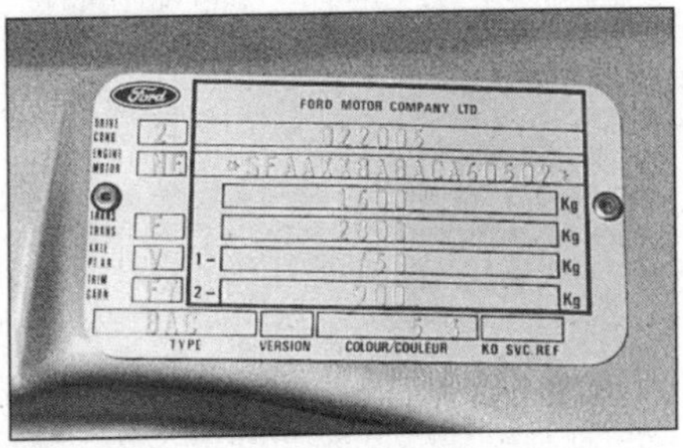


### Electrical equipment

☐ Switch on the ignition and check the operation of the horn.

☐ Check the windscreen washers and wipers, examining the wiper blades; renew damaged or perished blades. Also check the operation of the stop-lights.

☐ Check the operation of the sidelights and number plate lights. The lenses and reflectors must be secure, clean and undamaged.

☐ Check the operation and alignment of the headlights. The headlight reflectors must not be tarnished and the lenses must be undamaged.

☐ Switch on the ignition and check the operation of the direction indicators (including the instrument panel tell-tale) and the hazard warning lights. Operation of the sidelights and stop-lights must not affect the indicators - if it does, the cause is usually a bad earth at the rear light cluster.

☐ Check the operation of the rear foglight(s), including the warning light on the instrument panel or in the switch.

### Footbrake

☐ Examine the master cylinder, brake pipes and servo unit for leaks, loose mountings, corrosion or other damage.

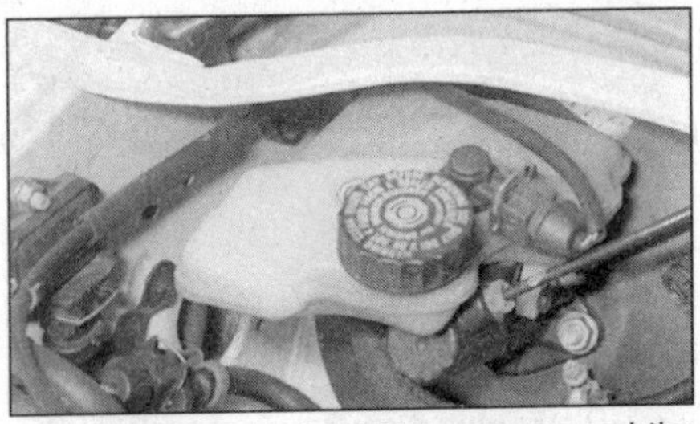

☐ The fluid reservoir must be secure and the fluid level must be between the upper (**A**) and lower (**B**) markings.

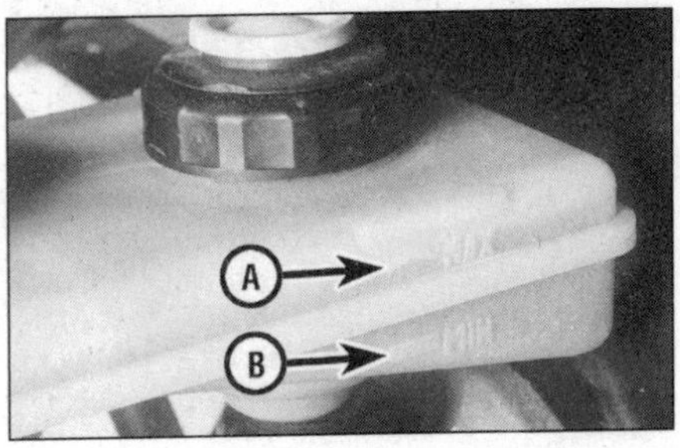


☐ Inspect both front brake flexible hoses for cracks or deterioration of the rubber. Turn the steering from lock to lock, and ensure that the hoses do not contact the wheel, tyre, or any part of the steering or suspension mechanism. With the brake pedal firmly depressed, check the hoses for bulges or leaks under pressure.

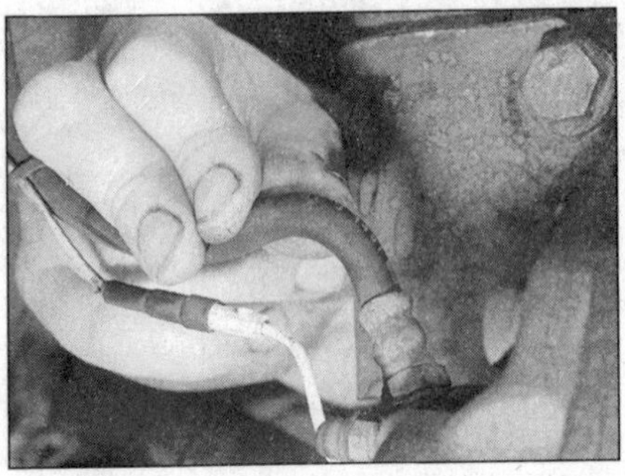

### Steering and suspension

☐ Have your assistant turn the steering wheel from side to side slightly, up to the point where the steering gear just begins to transmit this movement to the roadwheels. Check for excessive free play between the steering wheel and the steering gear, indicating wear or insecurity of the steering column joints, the column-to-steering gear coupling, or the steering gear itself.

☐ Have your assistant turn the steering wheel more vigorously in each direction, so that the roadwheels just begin to turn. As this is done, examine all the steering joints, linkages, fittings and attachments. Renew any component that shows signs of wear or damage. On vehicles with power steering, check the security and condition of the steering pump, drivebelt and hoses.

☐ Check that the vehicle is standing level, and at approximately the correct ride height.

### Shock absorbers

☐ Depress each corner of the vehicle in turn, then release it. The vehicle should rise and then settle in its normal position. If the vehicle continues to rise and fall, the shock absorber is defective. A shock absorber which has seized will also cause the vehicle to fail.

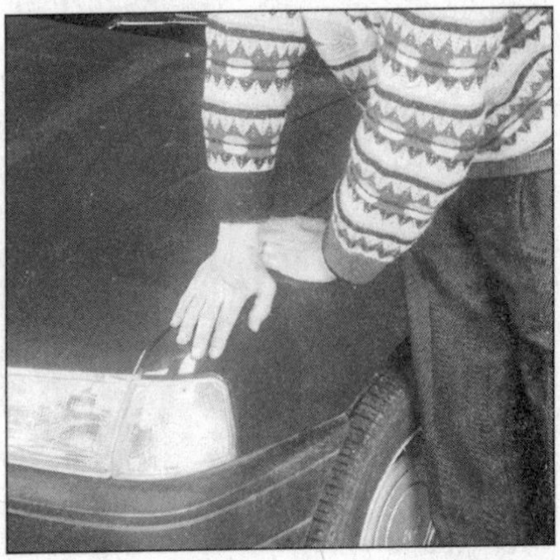

### Exhaust system

☐ Start the engine. With your assistant holding a rag over the tailpipe, check the entire system for leaks. Repair or renew leaking sections.

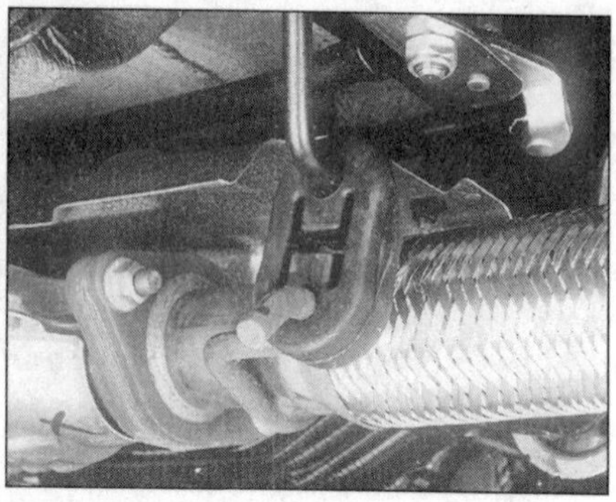

**3** Checks carried out
**WITH THE VEHICLE RAISED AND THE WHEELS FREE TO TURN**

***Jack up the front and rear of the vehicle, and securely support it on axle stands. Position the stands clear of the suspension assemblies. Ensure that the wheels are clear of the ground and that the steering can be turned from lock to lock.***

### Steering mechanism

☐ Have your assistant turn the steering from lock to lock. Check that the steering turns smoothly, and that no part of the steering mechanism, including a wheel or tyre, fouls any brake hose or pipe or any part of the body structure.
☐ Examine the steering rack rubber gaiters for damage or insecurity of the retaining clips. If power steering is fitted, check for signs of damage or leakage of the fluid hoses, pipes or connections. Also check for excessive stiffness or binding of the steering, a missing split pin or locking device, or severe corrosion of the body structure within 30 cm of any steering component attachment point.

### Front and rear suspension and wheel bearings

☐ Starting at the front right-hand side, grasp the roadwheel at the 3 o'clock and 9 o'clock positions and shake it vigorously. Check for free play or insecurity at the wheel bearings, suspension balljoints, or suspension mountings, pivots and attachments.
☐ Now grasp the wheel at the 12 o'clock and 6 o'clock positions and repeat the previous inspection. Spin the wheel, and check for roughness or tightness of the front wheel bearing.

☐ If excess free play is suspected at a component pivot point, this can be confirmed by using a large screwdriver or similar tool and levering between the mounting and the component attachment. This will confirm whether the wear is in the pivot bush, its retaining bolt, or in the mounting itself (the bolt holes can often become elongated).

☐ Carry out all the above checks at the other front wheel, and then at both rear wheels.

### Springs and shock absorbers

☐ Examine the suspension struts (when applicable) for serious fluid leakage, corrosion, or damage to the casing. Also check the security of the mounting points.
☐ If coil springs are fitted, check that the spring ends locate in their seats, and that the spring is not corroded, cracked or broken.
☐ If leaf springs are fitted, check that all leaves are intact, that the axle is securely attached to each spring, and that there is no deterioration of the spring eye mountings, bushes, and shackles.
☐ The same general checks apply to vehicles fitted with other suspension types, such as torsion bars, hydraulic displacer units, etc. Ensure that all mountings and attachments are secure, that there are no signs of excessive wear, corrosion or damage, and (on hydraulic types) that there are no fluid leaks or damaged pipes.
☐ Inspect the shock absorbers for signs of serious fluid leakage. Check for wear of the mounting bushes or attachments, or damage to the body of the unit.

### Driveshafts (fwd vehicles only)

☐ Rotate each front wheel in turn and inspect the constant velocity joint gaiters for splits or damage. Also check that each driveshaft is straight and undamaged.

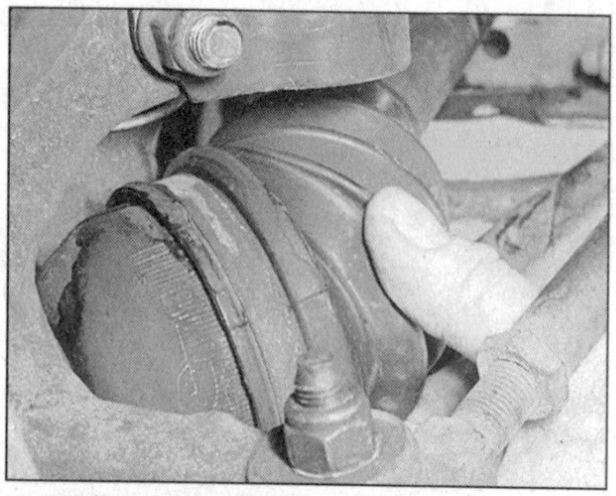

### Braking system

☐ If possible without dismantling, check brake pad wear and disc condition. Ensure that the friction lining material has not worn excessively, (A) and that the discs are not fractured, pitted, scored or badly worn (B).

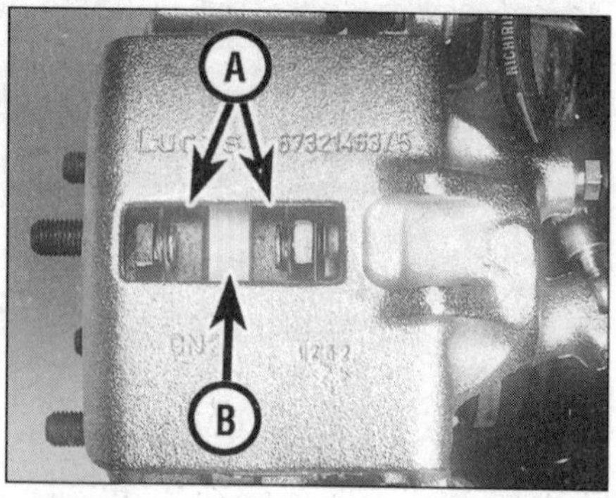


☐ Examine all the rigid brake pipes underneath the vehicle, and the flexible hose(s) at the rear. Look for corrosion, chafing or insecurity of the pipes, and for signs of bulging under pressure, chafing, splits or deterioration of the flexible hoses.
☐ Look for signs of fluid leaks at the brake calipers or on the brake backplates. Repair or renew leaking components.
☐ Slowly spin each wheel, while your assistant depresses and releases the footbrake. Ensure that each brake is operating and does not bind when the pedal is released.

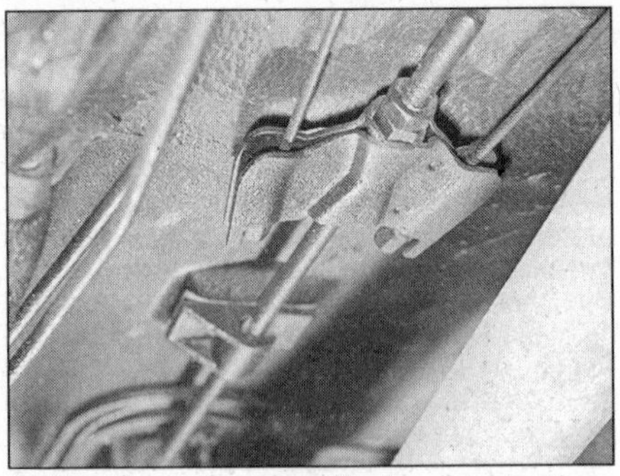

☐ Examine the handbrake mechanism, checking for frayed or broken cables, excessive corrosion, or wear or insecurity of the linkage. Check that the mechanism works on each relevant wheel, and releases fully, without binding.

☐ It is not possible to test brake efficiency without special equipment, but a road test can be carried out later to check that the vehicle pulls up in a straight line.

### Fuel and exhaust systems

☐ Inspect the fuel tank (including the filler cap), fuel pipes, hoses and unions. All components must be secure and free from leaks.

☐ Examine the exhaust system over its entire length, checking for any damaged, broken or missing mountings, security of the retaining clamps and rust or corrosion.

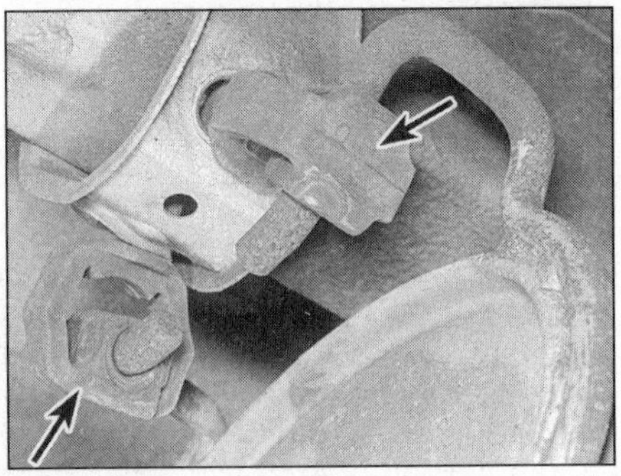

### Wheels and tyres

☐ Examine the sidewalls and tread area of each tyre in turn. Check for cuts, tears, lumps, bulges, separation of the tread, and exposure of the ply or cord due to wear or damage. Check that the tyre bead is correctly seated on the wheel rim, that the valve is sound and

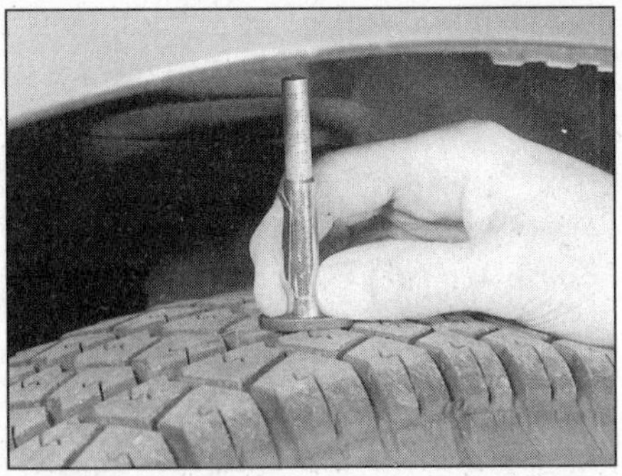

properly seated, and that the wheel is not distorted or damaged.

☐ Check that the tyres are of the correct size for the vehicle, that they are of the same size and type on each axle, and that the pressures are correct.

☐ Check the tyre tread depth. The legal minimum at the time of writing is 1.6 mm over at least three-quarters of the tread width. Abnormal tread wear may indicate incorrect front wheel alignment.

### Body corrosion

☐ Check the condition of the entire vehicle structure for signs of corrosion in load-bearing areas. (These include chassis box sections, side sills, cross-members, pillars, and all suspension, steering, braking system and seat belt mountings and anchorages.) Any corrosion which has seriously reduced the thickness of a load-bearing area is likely to cause the vehicle to fail. In this case professional repairs are likely to be needed.

☐ Damage or corrosion which causes sharp or otherwise dangerous edges to be exposed will also cause the vehicle to fail.

## 4 Checks carried out on YOUR VEHICLE'S EXHAUST EMISSION SYSTEM

### Petrol models

☐ Have the engine at normal operating temperature, and make sure that it is in good tune (ignition system in good order, air filter element clean, etc).

☐ Before any measurements are carried out, raise the engine speed to around 2500 rpm, and hold it at this speed for 20 seconds. Allow the engine speed to return to idle, and watch for smoke emissions from the exhaust tailpipe. If the idle speed is obviously much too high, or if dense blue or clearly-visible black smoke comes from the tailpipe for more than 5 seconds, the vehicle will fail. As a rule of thumb, blue smoke signifies oil being burnt (engine wear) while black smoke signifies unburnt fuel (dirty air cleaner element, or other carburettor or fuel system fault).

☐ An exhaust gas analyser capable of measuring carbon monoxide (CO) and hydrocarbons (HC) is now needed. If such an instrument cannot be hired or borrowed, a local garage may agree to perform the check for a small fee.

### CO emissions (mixture)

☐ At the time of writing, the maximum CO level at idle is 3.5% for vehicles first used after August 1986 and 4.5% for older vehicles. From January 1996 a much tighter limit (around 0.5%) applies to catalyst-equipped vehicles first used from August 1992. If the CO level cannot be reduced far enough to pass the test (and the fuel and ignition systems are otherwise in good condition) then the carburettor is badly worn, or there is some problem in the fuel injection system or catalytic converter (as applicable).

### HC emissions

☐ With the CO emissions within limits, HC emissions must be no more than 1200 ppm (parts per million). If the vehicle fails this test at idle, it can be re-tested at around 2000 rpm; if the HC level is then 1200 ppm or less, this counts as a pass.

☐ Excessive HC emissions can be caused by oil being burnt, but they are more likely to be due to unburnt fuel.

### Diesel models

☐ The only emission test applicable to Diesel engines is the measuring of exhaust smoke density. The test involves accelerating the engine several times to its maximum unloaded speed.

**Note:** *It is of the utmost importance that the engine timing belt is in good condition before the test is carried out.*

☐ Excessive smoke can be caused by a dirty air cleaner element. Otherwise, professional advice may be needed to find the cause.

# Introduction

The vehicle owner who does his or her own maintenance according to the recommended service schedules should not have to use this section of the manual very often. Modern component reliability is such that, provided those items subject to wear or deterioration are inspected or renewed at the specified intervals, sudden failure is comparatively rare. Faults do not usually just happen as a result of sudden failure, but develop over a period of time. Major mechanical failures in particular are usually preceded by characteristic symptoms over hundreds or even thousands of miles. Those components which do occasionally fail without warning are often small and easily carried in the vehicle.

With any fault-finding, the first step is to decide where to begin investigations. Sometimes this is obvious, but on other occasions, a little detective work will be necessary. The owner who makes half a dozen haphazard adjustments or replacements may be successful in curing a fault (or its symptoms), but will be none the wiser if the fault recurs, and ultimately may have spent more time and money than was necessary. A calm and logical approach will be found to be more satisfactory in the long run. Always take into account any warning signs or abnormalities that may have been noticed in the period preceding the fault - power loss, high or low gauge readings, unusual smells, etc - and remember that failure of components such as fuses or spark plugs may only be pointers to some underlying fault.

The pages which follow provide an easy-reference guide to the more common problems which may occur during the operation of the vehicle. These problems and their possible causes are grouped under headings denoting various components or systems, such as Engine, Cooling system, etc. The Chapter and/or Section which deals with the problem is also shown in brackets. Whatever the fault, certain basic principles apply. These are as follows:

*Verify the fault*. This is simply a matter of being sure that you know what the symptoms are before starting work. This is particularly important if you are investigating a fault for someone else, who may not have described it very accurately.

*Don't overlook the obvious*. For example, if the vehicle won't start, is there fuel in the tank? (Don't take anyone else's word on this particular point, and don't trust the fuel gauge either!) If an electrical fault is indicated, look for loose or broken wires before using the test gear.

*Cure the disease, not the symptom*. Substituting a flat battery with a fully-charged one will get you off the hard shoulder, but if the underlying cause is not attended to, the new battery will go the same way. Similarly, changing oil-fouled spark plugs for a new set will get you moving again, but remember that the reason for the fouling (if it wasn't simply an incorrect grade of plug) will have to be established and corrected.

*Don't take anything for granted*. Particularly, don't forget that a "new" component may itself be defective (especially if it's been rattling around in the boot for months), and don't leave components out of a fault diagnosis sequence just because they are new or recently-fitted. When you do finally diagnose a difficult fault, you'll probably realise that all the evidence was there from the start.

# 1 Engine

### Engine fails to rotate when attempting to start

- ☐ Battery terminal connections loose or corroded (*"Weekly Checks"*)
- ☐ Battery discharged or faulty (Chapter 5)
- ☐ Broken, loose or disconnected wiring in the starting circuit (Chapter 5)
- ☐ Defective starter solenoid or switch (Chapter 5)
- ☐ Defective starter motor (Chapter 5)
- ☐ Starter pinion or flywheel ring gear teeth loose or broken (Chapters 2 or 5)
- ☐ Engine earth strap broken or disconnected (Chapter 5)

### Engine rotates, but will not start

- ☐ Fuel tank empty
- ☐ Battery discharged (engine rotates slowly) (Chapter 5)
- ☐ Battery terminal connections loose or corroded (*"Weekly Checks"*)
- ☐ Air filter element dirty or clogged (Chapter 1)
- ☐ Low cylinder compressions (Chapter 2)
- ☐ Major mechanical failure (eg broken timing belt) (Chapter 2)
- ☐ Ignition components damp or damaged (Chapter 5)
- ☐ Fuel injection system fault (Chapter 4)
- ☐ Worn, faulty or incorrectly-gapped spark plugs (Chapter 1)
- ☐ Broken, loose or disconnected wiring in ignition circuit (Chapter 5)

### Engine difficult to start when cold

- ☐ Battery discharged (Chapter 5)
- ☐ Battery terminal connections loose or corroded (*"Weekly Checks"*)
- ☐ Air filter element dirty or clogged (Chapter 1)
- ☐ Worn, faulty or incorrectly-gapped spark plugs (Chapter 1)
- ☐ Low cylinder compressions (Chapter 2)
- ☐ Fuel injection system fault (Chapter 4)
- ☐ Ignition system fault (Chapter 5)

### Engine difficult to start when hot

- ☐ Battery discharged (Chapter 5)
- ☐ Battery terminal connections loose or corroded (*"Weekly Checks"*)
- ☐ Air filter element dirty or clogged (Chapter 1)
- ☐ Fuel injection system fault (Chapter 4)

### Starter motor noisy or excessively-rough in engagement

- ☐ Starter pinion or flywheel ring gear teeth loose or broken (Chapter 2 or 5)
- ☐ Starter motor mounting bolts loose or missing (Chapter 5)
- ☐ Starter motor internal components worn or damaged (Chapter 5)

### Starter motor turns engine slowly

- ☐ Battery discharged (Chapter 5)
- ☐ Battery terminal connections loose or corroded (*"Weekly Checks"*)
- ☐ Earth strap broken or disconnected (Chapter 5)
- ☐ Starter motor wiring loose (Chapter 5)
- ☐ Starter motor internal fault (Chapter 5)

### Engine starts, but stops immediately

- ☐ Loose ignition system wiring (Chapter 5)
- ☐ Dirt in fuel system (Chapter 4)
- ☐ Fuel injector fault (Chapter 4)
- ☐ Fuel pump or pressure regulator fault (Chapter 4)
- ☐ Vacuum leak at throttle body, inlet manifold or hoses (Chapters 2 and 4)

### Engine idles erratically

- ☐ Air filter element clogged (Chapter 1)
- ☐ Air in fuel system (Chapter 4)
- ☐ Worn, faulty or incorrectly-gapped spark plugs (Chapter 1)
- ☐ Vacuum leak at throttle body, inlet manifold or hoses (Chapters 2 and 4)
- ☐ Uneven or low cylinder compressions (Chapter 2)
- ☐ Timing belt/chain incorrectly fitted or tensioned (Chapter 2)
- ☐ Camshaft lobes worn (Chapter 2)
- ☐ Faulty fuel injector(s) (Chapter 4)

### Engine misfires at idle speed

- ☐ Distributor cap cracked or tracking internally (Chapter 5)
- ☐ Faulty fuel injector(s) (Chapter 4)
- ☐ Uneven or low cylinder compressions (Chapter 2)
- ☐ Disconnected, leaking, or perished crankcase ventilation hoses (Chapter 4)
- ☐ Vacuum leak at the throttle body, inlet manifold or associated hoses (Chapter 4)

### Engine misfires throughout the driving speed range

- ☐ Fuel filter choked (Chapter 1)
- ☐ Fuel pump faulty, or delivery pressure low (Chapter 4)
- ☐ Fuel tank vent blocked, or fuel pipes restricted (Chapter 4)
- ☐ Uneven or low cylinder compressions (Chapter 2)
- ☐ Worn, faulty or incorrectly-gapped spark plugs (Chapter 1)
- ☐ Faulty spark plug HT leads (Chapter 1)

# 1 Engine (continued)

### Engine stalls

- ☐ Fuel filter choked (Chapter 1)
- ☐ Blocked injector/fuel injection system fault (Chapter 4)
- ☐ Fuel pump faulty, or delivery pressure low (Chapter 4)
- ☐ Vacuum leak at the throttle body, inlet manifold or associated hoses (Chapter 4)
- ☐ Fuel tank vent blocked, or fuel pipes restricted (Chapter 4)

### Engine lacks power

- ☐ Fuel filter choked (Chapter 1)
- ☐ Timing belt/chain incorrectly fitted or tensioned (Chapter 2)
- ☐ Fuel pump faulty, or delivery pressure low (Chapter 4)
- ☐ Worn, faulty or incorrectly-gapped spark plugs (Chapter 1)
- ☐ Vacuum leak at the throttle body, inlet manifold or associated hoses (Chapter 4)
- ☐ Uneven or low cylinder compressions (Chapter 2)
- ☐ Brakes binding (Chapters 1 and 9)
- ☐ Clutch slipping (Chapter 6)
- ☐ Blocked injector/fuel injection system fault (Chapter 4)

### Engine backfires

- ☐ Timing belt/chain incorrectly fitted (Chapter 2)
- ☐ Faulty injector/fuel injection system fault (Chapter 4).

### Oil pressure warning light illuminated with engine running

- ☐ Low oil level, or incorrect oil grade (*"Weekly Checks"*)
- ☐ Faulty oil pressure sensor (Chapter 5)
- ☐ Worn engine bearings and/or oil pump (Chapter 2)
- ☐ Excessively high engine operating temperature (Chapter 3)
- ☐ Oil pressure relief valve defective (Chapter 2)
- ☐ Oil pick-up strainer clogged (Chapter 2)

**Note:** *Low oil pressure in a high-mileage engine at tickover is not necessarily a cause for concern. Sudden pressure loss at speed is far more significant. In any event, check the gauge or warning light sender before condemning the engine.*

### Engine runs-on after switching off

- ☐ Excessive carbon build-up in engine (Chapter 2)
- ☐ Excessively high engine operating temperature (Chapter 3)

### Engine noises

#### Pre-ignition (pinking) or knocking during acceleration or under load

- ☐ Excessive carbon build-up in engine (Chapter 2)
- ☐ Faulty fuel injector(s) (Chapter 4)
- ☐ Ignition system fault (Chapter 5)

#### Whistling or wheezing noises

- ☐ Leaking exhaust manifold gasket (Chapter 4)
- ☐ Leaking vacuum hose (Chapter 4 or 9)
- ☐ Blowing cylinder head gasket (Chapter 2)

#### Tapping or rattling noises

- ☐ Worn valve gear or camshaft (Chapter 2)
- ☐ Ancillary component fault (coolant pump, alternator, etc) (Chapters 3, 5, etc)

#### Knocking or thumping noises

- ☐ Worn big-end bearings (regular heavy knocking, perhaps less under load) (Chapter 2)
- ☐ Worn main bearings (rumbling and knocking, perhaps worsening under load) (Chapter 2)
- ☐ Piston slap (most noticeable when cold) (Chapter 2)
- ☐ Ancillary component fault (coolant pump, alternator, etc) (Chapters 3, 5, etc)

# 2 Cooling system

### Overheating

- ☐ Insufficient coolant in system (*"Weekly Checks"*)
- ☐ Thermostat faulty (Chapter 3)
- ☐ Radiator core blocked, or grille restricted (Chapter 3)
- ☐ Cooling fan or viscous coupling faulty (Chapter 3)
- ☐ Inaccurate temperature gauge sender unit (Chapter 3)
- ☐ Airlock in cooling system (Chapter 3)
- ☐ Expansion tank pressure cap faulty (Chapter 3)

### Overcooling

- ☐ Thermostat faulty (Chapter 3)
- ☐ Inaccurate temperature gauge sender unit (Chapter 3)
- ☐ Viscous coupling faulty (Chapter 3)

### External coolant leakage

- ☐ Deteriorated or damaged hoses or hose clips (Chapter 1)
- ☐ Radiator core or heater matrix leaking (Chapter 3)
- ☐ Pressure cap faulty (Chapter 3)
- ☐ Coolant pump internal seal leaking (Chapter 3)
- ☐ Coolant pump-to-block seal leaking (Chapter 3)
- ☐ Boiling due to overheating (Chapter 3)
- ☐ Core plug leaking (Chapter 2)

### Internal coolant leakage

- ☐ Leaking cylinder head gasket (Chapter 2)
- ☐ Cracked cylinder head or cylinder block (Chapter 2)

### Corrosion

- ☐ Infrequent draining and flushing (Chapter 1)
- ☐ Incorrect coolant mixture or inappropriate coolant type (Chapter 1)

# 3 Fuel and exhaust systems

### Excessive fuel consumption

- ☐ Air filter element dirty or clogged (Chapter 1)
- ☐ Fuel injection system fault (Chapter 4)
- ☐ Ignition timing incorrect/ignition system fault (Chapters 1 and 5)
- ☐ Tyres under-inflated ("Weekly checks")

### Fuel leakage and/or fuel odour

- ☐ Damaged or corroded fuel tank, pipes or connections (Chapter 4)

### Excessive noise or fumes from exhaust system

- ☐ Leaking exhaust system or manifold joints (Chapters 1 and 4)
- ☐ Leaking, corroded or damaged silencers or pipe (Chapters 1 and 4)
- ☐ Broken mountings causing body or suspension contact (Chapter 1)

# 4 Clutch

### Pedal travels to floor - no pressure or very little resistance

- ☐ Hydraulic fluid level low/air in the hydraulic system (Chapter 6)
- ☐ Broken clutch release bearing or fork (Chapter 6)
- ☐ Broken diaphragm spring in clutch pressure plate (Chapter 6)

### Clutch fails to disengage (unable to select gears)

- ☐ Hydraulic fluid level too high
- ☐ Clutch disc sticking on gearbox input shaft splines (Chapter 6)
- ☐ Clutch disc sticking to flywheel or pressure plate (Chapter 6)
- ☐ Faulty pressure plate assembly (Chapter 6)
- ☐ Clutch release mechanism worn or poorly assembled (Chapter 6)

### Clutch slips (engine speed increases, with no increase in vehicle speed)

- ☐ Hydraulic fluid level too high
- ☐ Clutch disc linings excessively worn (Chapter 6)
- ☐ Clutch disc linings contaminated with oil or grease (Chapter 6)
- ☐ Faulty pressure plate or weak diaphragm spring (Chapter 6)

### Judder as clutch is engaged

- ☐ Clutch disc linings contaminated with oil or grease (Chapter 6)
- ☐ Clutch disc linings excessively worn (Chapter 6)
- ☐ Faulty or distorted pressure plate or diaphragm spring (Chapter 6)
- ☐ Worn or loose engine or gearbox mountings (Chapter 2A or 2B)
- ☐ Clutch disc hub or gearbox input shaft splines worn (Chapter 6)

### Noise when depressing or releasing clutch pedal

- ☐ Worn clutch release bearing (Chapter 6)
- ☐ Worn or dry clutch pedal bushes (Chapter 6)
- ☐ Faulty pressure plate assembly (Chapter 6)
- ☐ Pressure plate diaphragm spring broken (Chapter 6)
- ☐ Broken clutch disc cushioning springs (Chapter 6)

# 5 Manual transmission

### Noisy in neutral with engine running

- ☐ Input shaft bearings worn (noise apparent with clutch pedal released, but not when depressed) (Chapter 7A)*
- ☐ Clutch release bearing worn (noise apparent with clutch pedal depressed, possibly less when released) (Chapter 6)

### Noisy in one particular gear

- ☐ Worn, damaged or chipped gear teeth (Chapter 7A)*

### Difficulty engaging gears

- ☐ Clutch fault (Chapter 6)
- ☐ Worn or damaged gearchange linkage/cable (Chapter 7A)
- ☐ Incorrectly-adjusted gearchange linkage/cable (Chapter 7A)
- ☐ Worn synchroniser units (Chapter 7A)*

### Jumps out of gear

- ☐ Worn or damaged gearchange linkage/cable (Chapter 7A)
- ☐ Incorrectly-adjusted gearchange linkage/cable (Chapter 7A)
- ☐ Worn synchroniser units (Chapter 7A)*
- ☐ Worn selector forks (Chapter 7A)*

### Vibration

- ☐ Lack of oil (Chapter 1)
- ☐ Worn bearings (Chapter 7A)*

### Lubricant leaks

- ☐ Leaking differential output oil seal (Chapter 7A)
- ☐ Leaking housing joint (Chapter 7A)*
- ☐ Leaking input shaft oil seal (Chapter 7A)*

**Although the corrective action necessary to remedy the symptoms described is beyond the scope of the home mechanic, the above information should be helpful in isolating the cause of the condition, so that the owner can communicate clearly with a professional mechanic.*

# 6 Automatic transmission

**Note:** *Due to the complexity of the automatic transmission, it is difficult for the home mechanic to properly diagnose and service this unit. For problems other than the following, the vehicle should be taken to a dealer service department or automatic transmission specialist. Do not be too hasty in removing the transmission if a fault is suspected, as most of the testing is carried out with the unit still fitted.*

### Fluid leakage

☐ Automatic transmission fluid is usually dark in colour. Fluid leaks should not be confused with engine oil, which can easily be blown onto the transmission by airflow

☐ To determine the source of a leak, first remove all built-up dirt and grime from the transmission housing and surrounding areas using a degreasing agent, or by steam-cleaning. Drive the vehicle at low speed, so airflow will not blow the leak far from its source. Raise and support the vehicle, and determine where the leak is coming from. The following are common areas of leakage:

*a) Oil pan (Chapter 1 and 7B).*
*b) Dipstick tube (Chapter 1 and 7B)*
*c) Transmission-to-fluid cooler pipes/unions (Chapter 7B)*

### Transmission fluid brown, or has burned smell

☐ Transmission fluid level low, or fluid in need of renewal (Chapter 1)

### General gear selection problems

☐ Chapter 7B deals with checking and adjusting the selector cable on automatic transmissions. The following are common problems which may be caused by a poorly-adjusted cable:

*a) Engine starting in gears other than Park or Neutral*
*b) Indicator panel indicating a gear other than the one actually being used*
*c) Vehicle moves when in Park or Neutral*
*d) Poor gear shift quality or erratic gear changes*

☐ Refer to Chapter 7B for the selector cable adjustment procedure

### Transmission will not downshift (kickdown) with accelerator pedal fully depressed

☐ Low transmission fluid level (Chapter 1)
☐ Incorrect selector cable adjustment (Chapter 7B).

### Engine will not start in any gear, or starts in gears other than Park or Neutral

☐ Incorrect starter/inhibitor switch adjustment (Chapter 7B)
☐ Incorrect selector cable adjustment (Chapter 7B)

### Transmission slips, shifts roughly, is noisy, or has no drive in forward or reverse gears

☐ There are many probable causes for the above problems, but the home mechanic should be concerned with only one possibility - fluid level. Before taking the vehicle to a dealer or transmission specialist, check the fluid level and condition of the fluid as described in Chapter 1. Correct the fluid level as necessary, or change the fluid and filter if needed. If the problem persists, professional help will be necessary

# 7 Differential and propshaft

### Vibration when accelerating or decelerating

☐ Worn universal joint (Chapter 8)
☐ Bent or distorted propeller shaft (Chapter 8)

### Low-pitched whining; increasing with road speed

☐ Worn differential (Chapter 8)

# 8 Braking system

**Note:** *Before assuming that a brake problem exists, make sure that the tyres are in good condition and correctly inflated, that the front wheel alignment is correct, and that the vehicle is not loaded with weight in an unequal manner. Apart from checking the condition of all pipe and hose connections, any faults occurring on the anti-lock braking system should be referred to a BMW dealer for diagnosis.*

### Vehicle pulls to one side under braking

☐ Worn, defective, damaged or contaminated brake pads/shoes on one side (Chapters 1 and 9)
☐ Seized or partially-seized front brake caliper/wheel cylinder piston (Chapters 1 and 9)
☐ A mixture of brake pad/shoe lining materials fitted between sides (Chapters 1 and 9)
☐ Brake caliper or backplate mounting bolts loose (Chapter 9)
☐ Worn or damaged steering or suspension components (Chapters 1 and 10)

### Noise (grinding or high-pitched squeal) when brakes applied

☐ Brake pad or shoe friction lining material worn down to metal backing (Chapters 1 and 9)
☐ Excessive corrosion of brake disc or drum. (May be apparent after the vehicle has been standing for some time (Chapters 1 and 9)
☐ Foreign object (stone chipping, etc) trapped between brake disc and shield (Chapters 1 and 9)

### Excessive brake pedal travel

☐ Inoperative rear brake self-adjust mechanism - drum brakes (Chapters 1 and 9)
☐ Faulty master cylinder (Chapter 9)
☐ Air in hydraulic system (Chapters 1 and 9)
☐ Faulty vacuum servo unit (Chapter 9)

### Brake pedal feels spongy when depressed

☐ Air in hydraulic system (Chapters 1 and 9)
☐ Deteriorated flexible rubber brake hoses (Chapters 1 and 9)
☐ Master cylinder mounting nuts loose (Chapter 9)
☐ Faulty master cylinder (Chapter 9)

## 8 Braking system (continued)

### *Excessive brake pedal effort required to stop vehicle*

☐ Faulty vacuum servo unit (Chapter 9)
☐ Disconnected, damaged or insecure brake servo vacuum hose (Chapter 9)
☐ Primary or secondary hydraulic circuit failure (Chapter 9)
☐ Seized brake caliper or wheel cylinder piston(s) (Chapter 9)
☐ Brake pads or brake shoes incorrectly fitted (Chapters 1 and 9)
☐ Incorrect grade of brake pads or brake shoes fitted (Chapters 1 and 9)
☐ Brake pads or brake shoe linings contaminated (Chapters 1 and 9)

### *Judder felt through brake pedal or steering wheel when braking*

☐ Excessive run-out or distortion of discs/drums (Chapters 1 and 9)
☐ Brake pad or brake shoe linings worn (Chapters 1 and 9)
☐ Brake caliper or brake backplate mounting bolts loose (Chapter 9)
☐ Wear in suspension or steering components or mountings (Chapters 1 and 10)

### *Brakes binding*

☐ Seized brake caliper or wheel cylinder piston(s) (Chapter 9)
☐ Incorrectly-adjusted handbrake mechanism (Chapter 9)
☐ Faulty master cylinder (Chapter 9)

### *Rear wheels locking under normal braking*

☐ Rear brake shoe linings contaminated (Chapters 1 and 9)
☐ Faulty brake pressure regulator (Chapter 9)

## 9 Suspension and steering

**Note:** *Before diagnosing suspension or steering faults, be sure that the trouble is not due to incorrect tyre pressures, mixtures of tyre types, or binding brakes.*

### *Vehicle pulls to one side*

☐ Defective tyre (*"Weekly checks"*)
☐ Excessive wear in suspension or steering components (Chapters 1 and 10)
☐ Incorrect front wheel alignment (Chapter 10)
☐ Accident damage to steering or suspension components (Chapter 1)

### *Wheel wobble and vibration*

☐ Front roadwheels out of balance (vibration felt mainly through the steering wheel) (Chapters 1 and 10)
☐ Rear roadwheels out of balance (vibration felt throughout the vehicle) (Chapters 1 and 10)
☐ Roadwheels damaged or distorted (Chapters 1 and 10)
☐ Faulty or damaged tyre (*"Weekly checks"*)
☐ Worn steering or suspension joints, bushes or components (Chapters 1 and 10)
☐ Wheel bolts loose (Chapters 1 and 10)

### *Excessive pitching and/or rolling around corners, or during braking*

☐ Defective shock absorbers (Chapters 1 and 10)
☐ Broken or weak spring and/or suspension component (Chapters 1 and 10)
☐ Worn or damaged anti-roll bar or mountings (Chapter 10)

### *Wandering or general instability*

☐ Incorrect front wheel alignment (Chapter 10)
☐ Worn steering or suspension joints, bushes or components (Chapters 1 and 10)
☐ Roadwheels out of balance (Chapters 1 and 10)
☐ Faulty or damaged tyre (*"Weekly checks"*)
☐ Wheel bolts loose (Chapters 1 and 10)
☐ Defective shock absorbers (Chapters 1 and 10)

### *Excessively-stiff steering*

☐ Lack of steering gear lubricant (Chapter 10)
☐ Seized track rod end balljoint or suspension balljoint (Chapters 1 and 10)
☐ Broken or incorrectly-adjusted drivebelt - power steering (Chapter 1)
☐ Incorrect front wheel alignment (Chapter 10)
☐ Steering rack or column bent or damaged (Chapter 10)

### *Excessive play in steering*

☐ Worn steering column intermediate shaft universal joint (Chapter 10)
☐ Worn steering track rod end balljoints (Chapters 1 and 10)
☐ Worn rack-and-pinion steering gear (Chapter 10)
☐ Worn steering or suspension joints, bushes or components (Chapters 1 and 10)

### *Lack of power assistance*

☐ Broken or incorrectly-adjusted auxiliary drivebelt (Chapter 1)
☐ Incorrect power steering fluid level (*"Weekly checks"*)
☐ Restriction in power steering fluid hoses (Chapter 1)
☐ Faulty power steering pump (Chapter 10)
☐ Faulty rack-and-pinion steering gear (Chapter 10)

### *Tyre wear excessive*

#### Tyres worn on inside or outside edges

☐ Tyres under-inflated (wear on both edges) (*"Weekly checks"*)
☐ Incorrect camber or castor angles (wear on one edge only) (Chapter 10)
☐ Worn steering or suspension joints, bushes or components (Chapters 1 and 10)
☐ Excessively-hard cornering.
☐ Accident damage.

#### Tyre treads exhibit feathered edges

☐ Incorrect toe setting (Chapter 10)

#### Tyres worn in centre of tread

☐ Tyres over-inflated (*"Weekly checks"*)

#### Tyres worn on inside and outside edges

☐ Tyres under-inflated (*"Weekly checks"*)

#### Tyres worn unevenly

☐ Tyres/wheels out of balance (Chapter 1)
☐ Excessive wheel or tyre run-out (Chapter 1)
☐ Worn shock absorbers (Chapters 1 and 10)
☐ Faulty tyre (*"Weekly checks"*)

# 10 Electrical system

**Note:** *For problems associated with the starting system, refer to the faults listed under "Engine" earlier in this Section.*

## *Battery will only hold a charge for a few days*

- ☐ Battery defective internally (Chapter 5)
- ☐ Battery terminal connections loose or corroded (*"Weekly checks"*)
- ☐ Auxiliary drivebelt worn or incorrectly adjusted (Chapter 1)
- ☐ Alternator not charging at correct output (Chapter 5)
- ☐ Alternator or voltage regulator faulty (Chapter 5)
- ☐ Short-circuit causing continual battery drain (Chapters 5 and 12)

## *Ignition/no-charge warning light remains illuminated with engine running*

- ☐ Auxiliary drivebelt broken, worn, or incorrectly adjusted (Chapter 1)
- ☐ Alternator brushes worn, sticking, or dirty (Chapter 5)
- ☐ Alternator brush springs weak or broken (Chapter 5)
- ☐ Internal fault in alternator or voltage regulator (Chapter 5)
- ☐ Broken, disconnected, or loose wiring in charging circuit (Chapter 5)

## *Ignition/no-charge warning light fails to come on*

- ☐ Warning light bulb blown (Chapter 12)
- ☐ Broken, disconnected, or loose wiring in warning light circuit (Chapter 12)
- ☐ Alternator faulty (Chapter 5)

## *Lights inoperative*

- ☐ Bulb blown (Chapter 12)
- ☐ Corrosion of bulb or bulbholder contacts (Chapter 12)
- ☐ Blown fuse (Chapter 12)
- ☐ Faulty relay (Chapter 12)
- ☐ Broken, loose, or disconnected wiring (Chapter 12)
- ☐ Faulty switch (Chapter 12)

## *Instrument readings inaccurate or erratic*

### Instrument readings increase with engine speed

- ☐ Faulty voltage regulator (Chapter 12)

### Fuel or temperature gauges give no reading

- ☐ Faulty gauge sender unit (Chapters 3 and 4)
- ☐ Wiring open-circuit (Chapter 12)
- ☐ Faulty gauge (Chapter 12)

### Fuel or temperature gauges give continuous maximum reading

- ☐ Faulty gauge sender unit (Chapters 3 and 4)
- ☐ Wiring short-circuit (Chapter 12)
- ☐ Faulty gauge (Chapter 12)

## *Horn inoperative, or unsatisfactory in operation*

### Horn operates all the time

- ☐ Horn push either earthed or stuck down (Chapter 12)
- ☐ Horn cable-to-horn push earthed (Chapter 12)

### Horn fails to operate

- ☐ Blown fuse (Chapter 12)
- ☐ Cable or cable connections loose, broken or disconnected (Chapter 12)
- ☐ Faulty horn (Chapter 12)

### Horn emits intermittent or unsatisfactory sound

- ☐ Cable connections loose (Chapter 12)
- ☐ Horn mountings loose (Chapter 12)
- ☐ Faulty horn (Chapter 12)

## *Windscreen wipers inoperative, or unsatisfactory in operation*

### Wipers fail to operate, or operate very slowly

- ☐ Wiper blades stuck to screen, or linkage seized or binding (Chapters 1 and 12)
- ☐ Blown fuse (Chapter 12)
- ☐ Cable or cable connections loose, broken or disconnected (Chapter 12)
- ☐ Faulty relay (Chapter 12)
- ☐ Faulty wiper motor (Chapter 12)

### Wiper blades sweep over too large or too small an area of the glass

- ☐ Wiper arms incorrectly positioned on spindles (Chapter 1)
- ☐ Excessive wear of wiper linkage (Chapter 12)
- ☐ Wiper motor or linkage mountings loose or insecure (Chapter 12)

### Wiper blades fail to clean the glass effectively

- ☐ Wiper blade rubbers worn or perished (*"Weekly checks"*)
- ☐ Wiper arm tension springs broken, or arm pivots seized (Chapter 12)
- ☐ Insufficient windscreen washer additive to adequately remove road film (*"Weekly checks"*)

## *Windscreen washers inoperative, or unsatisfactory in operation*

### One or more washer jets inoperative

- ☐ Blocked washer jet (Chapter 1)
- ☐ Disconnected, kinked or restricted fluid hose (Chapter 12)
- ☐ Insufficient fluid in washer reservoir (*"Weekly checks"*)

### Washer pump fails to operate

- ☐ Broken or disconnected wiring or connections (Chapter 12)
- ☐ Blown fuse (Chapter 12)
- ☐ Faulty washer switch (Chapter 12)
- ☐ Faulty washer pump (Chapter 12)

### Washer pump runs for some time before fluid is emitted from jets

- ☐ Faulty one-way valve in fluid supply hose (Chapter 12)

## *Electric windows inoperative, or unsatisfactory in operation*

### Window glass will only move in one direction

- ☐ Faulty switch (Chapter 12)

### Window glass slow to move

- ☐ Regulator seized or damaged, or in need of lubrication (Chapter 11)
- ☐ Door internal components or trim fouling regulator (Chapter 11)
- ☐ Faulty motor (Chapter 11)

## *Window glass fails to move*

- ☐ Blown fuse (Chapter 12)
- ☐ Faulty relay (Chapter 12)
- ☐ Broken or disconnected wiring or connections (Chapter 12)
- ☐ Faulty motor (Chapter 11)

### *Central locking system inoperative, or unsatisfactory in operation*

#### Complete system failure

- ☐ Blown fuse (Chapter 12)
- ☐ Faulty relay (Chapter 12)
- ☐ Broken or disconnected wiring or connections (Chapter 12)
- ☐ Faulty motor (Chapter 11)

#### Latch locks but will not unlock, or unlocks but will not lock

- ☐ Faulty master switch (Chapter 12)
- ☐ Broken or disconnected latch operating rods or levers (Chapter 11)
- ☐ Faulty relay (Chapter 12)
- ☐ Faulty motor (Chapter 11)

#### One solenoid/motor fails to operate

- ☐ Broken or disconnected wiring or connections (Chapter 12)
- ☐ Faulty operating assembly (Chapter 11)
- ☐ Broken, binding or disconnected latch operating rods or levers (Chapter 11)
- ☐ Fault in door latch (Chapter 11)

# A

**ABS (Anti-lock brake system)** A system, usually electronically controlled, that senses incipient wheel lockup during braking and relieves hydraulic pressure at wheels that are about to skid.

**Air bag** An inflatable bag hidden in the steering wheel (driver's side) or the dash or glovebox (passenger side). In a head-on collision, the bags inflate, preventing the driver and front passenger from being thrown forward into the steering wheel or windscreen.

**Air cleaner** A metal or plastic housing, containing a filter element, which removes dust and dirt from the air being drawn into the engine.

**Air filter element** The actual filter in an air cleaner system, usually manufactured from pleated paper and requiring renewal at regular intervals.

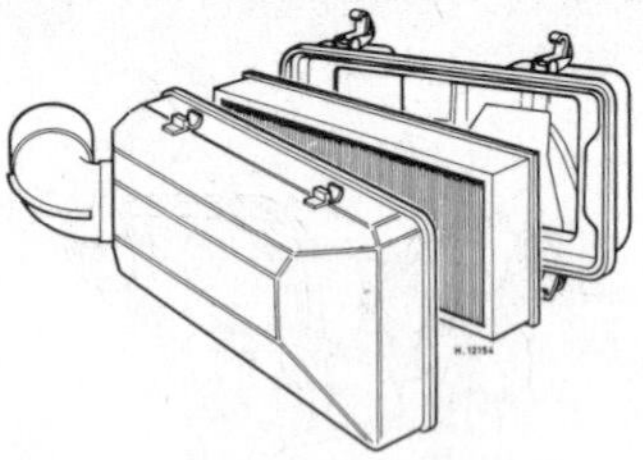

*Air filter*

**Allen key** A hexagonal wrench which fits into a recessed hexagonal hole.

**Alligator clip** A long-nosed spring-loaded metal clip with meshing teeth. Used to make temporary electrical connections.

**Alternator** A component in the electrical system which converts mechanical energy from a drivebelt into electrical energy to charge the battery and to operate the starting system, ignition system and electrical accessories.

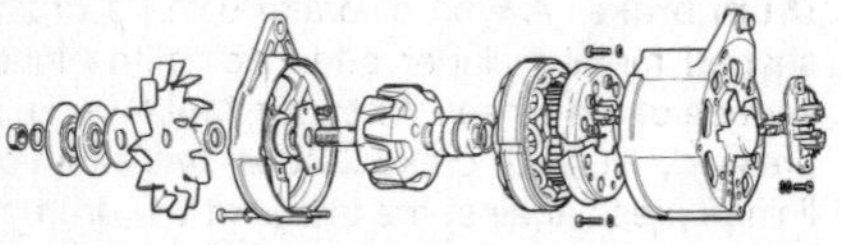

*Alternator (exploded view)*

**Ampere (amp)** A unit of measurement for the flow of electric current. One amp is the amount of current produced by one volt acting through a resistance of one ohm.

**Anaerobic sealer** A substance used to prevent bolts and screws from loosening. Anaerobic means that it does not require oxygen for activation. The Loctite brand is widely used.

**Antifreeze** A substance (usually ethylene glycol) mixed with water, and added to a vehicle's cooling system, to prevent freezing of the coolant in winter. Antifreeze also contains chemicals to inhibit corrosion and the formation of rust and other deposits that would tend to clog the radiator and coolant passages and reduce cooling efficiency.

**Anti-seize compound** A coating that reduces the risk of seizing on fasteners that are subjected to high temperatures, such as exhaust manifold bolts and nuts.

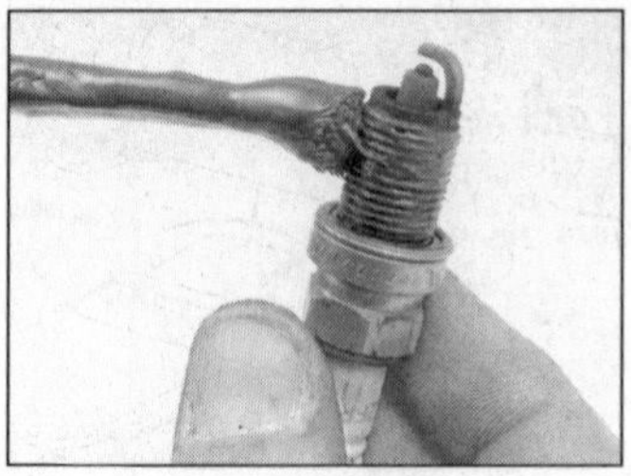

*Anti-seize compound*

**Asbestos** A natural fibrous mineral with great heat resistance, commonly used in the composition of brake friction materials. Asbestos is a health hazard and the dust created by brake systems should never be inhaled or ingested.

**Axle** A shaft on which a wheel revolves, or which revolves with a wheel. Also, a solid beam that connects the two wheels at one end of the vehicle. An axle which also transmits power to the wheels is known as a live axle.

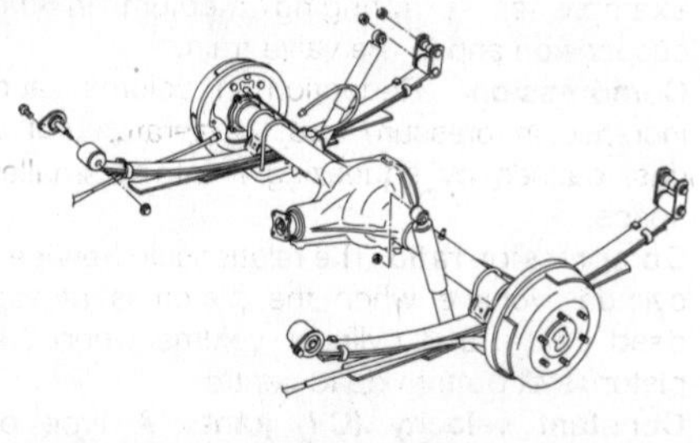

*Axle assembly*

**Axleshaft** A single rotating shaft, on either side of the differential, which delivers power from the final drive assembly to the drive wheels. Also called a driveshaft or a halfshaft.

# B

**Ball bearing** An anti-friction bearing consisting of a hardened inner and outer race with hardened steel balls between two races.

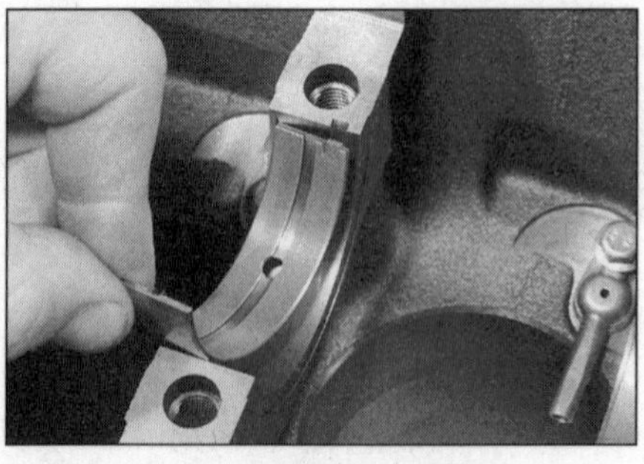

*Bearing*

**Bearing** The curved surface on a shaft or in a bore, or the part assembled into either, that permits relative motion between them with minimum wear and friction.

**Big-end bearing** The bearing in the end of the connecting rod that's attached to the crankshaft.

**Bleed nipple** A valve on a brake wheel cylinder, caliper or other hydraulic component that is opened to purge the hydraulic system of air. Also called a bleed screw.

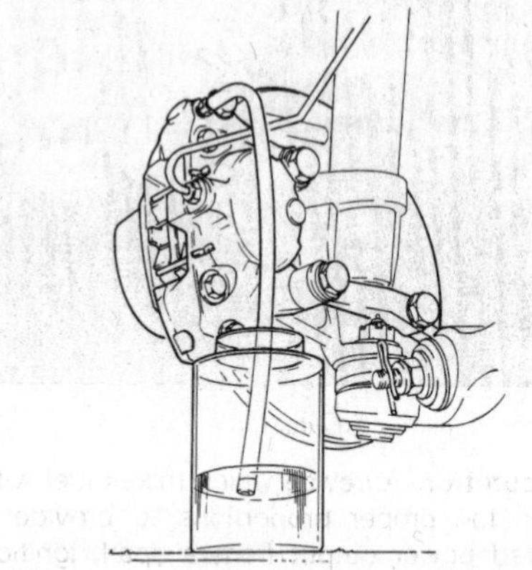

*Brake bleeding*

**Brake bleeding** Procedure for removing air from lines of a hydraulic brake system.

**Brake disc** The component of a disc brake that rotates with the wheels.

**Brake drum** The component of a drum brake that rotates with the wheels.

**Brake linings** The friction material which contacts the brake disc or drum to retard the vehicle's speed. The linings are bonded or riveted to the brake pads or shoes.

**Brake pads** The replaceable friction pads that pinch the brake disc when the brakes are applied. Brake pads consist of a friction material bonded or riveted to a rigid backing plate.

**Brake shoe** The crescent-shaped carrier to which the brake linings are mounted and which forces the lining against the rotating drum during braking.

**Braking systems** For more information on braking systems, consult the *Haynes Automotive Brake Manual*.

**Breaker bar** A long socket wrench handle providing greater leverage.

**Bulkhead** The insulated partition between the engine and the passenger compartment.

# C

**Caliper** The non-rotating part of a disc-brake assembly that straddles the disc and carries the brake pads. The caliper also contains the hydraulic components that cause the pads to pinch the disc when the brakes are applied. A caliper is also a measuring tool that can be set to measure inside or outside dimensions of an object.

**Camshaft** A rotating shaft on which a series of cam lobes operate the valve mechanisms. The camshaft may be driven by gears, by sprockets and chain or by sprockets and a belt.

**Canister** A container in an evaporative emission control system; contains activated charcoal granules to trap vapours from the fuel system.

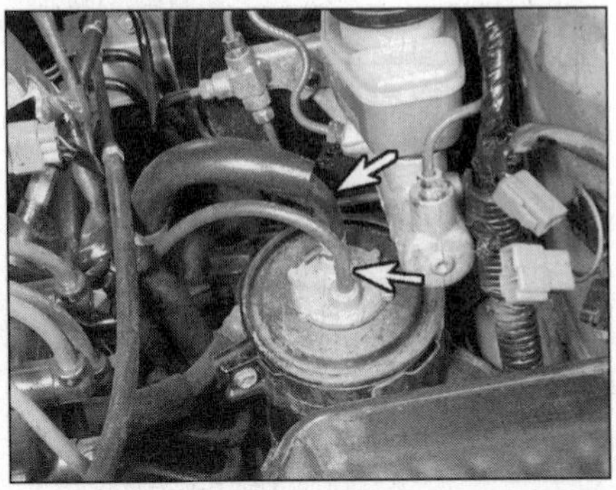

*Canister*

**Carburettor** A device which mixes fuel with air in the proper proportions to provide a desired power output from a spark ignition internal combustion engine.

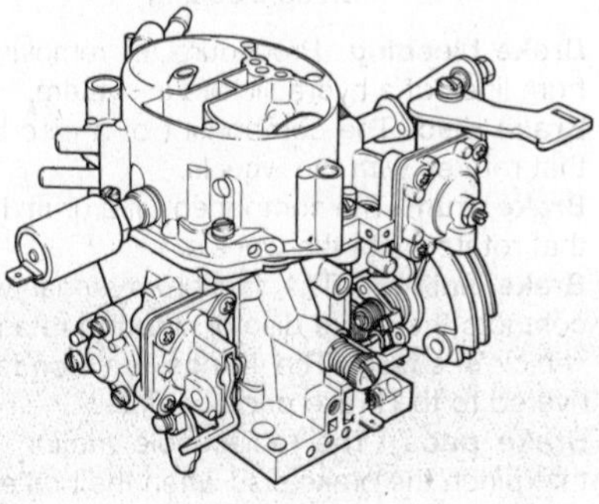

*Carburettor*

**Castellated** Resembling the parapets along the top of a castle wall. For example, a castellated balljoint stud nut.

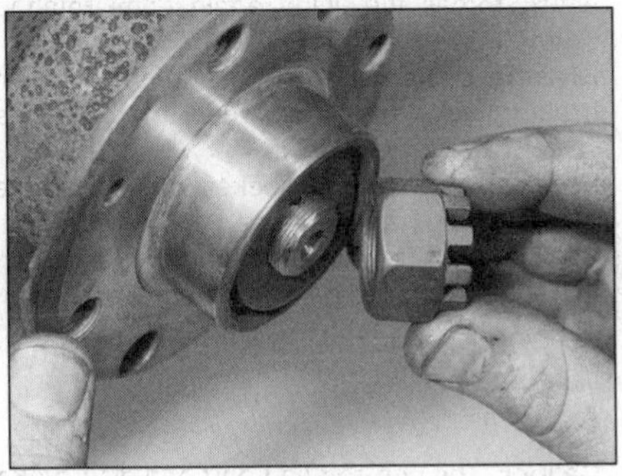

*Castellated nut*

**Castor** In wheel alignment, the backward or forward tilt of the steering axis. Castor is positive when the steering axis is inclined rearward at the top.

**Catalytic converter** A silencer-like device in the exhaust system which converts certain pollutants in the exhaust gases into less harmful substances.

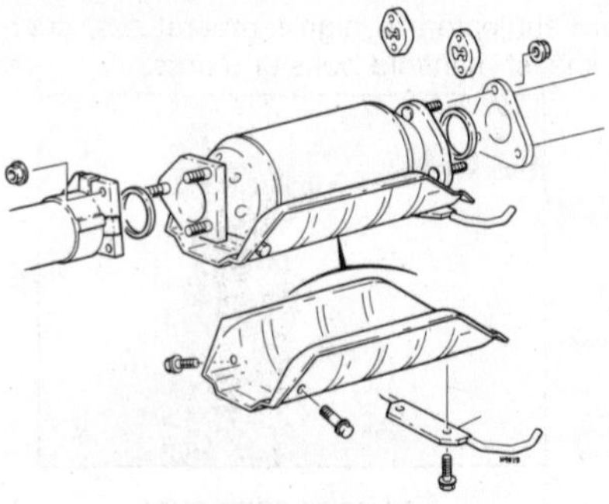

*Catalytic converter*

**Circlip** A ring-shaped clip used to prevent endwise movement of cylindrical parts and shafts. An internal circlip is installed in a groove in a housing; an external circlip fits into a groove on the outside of a cylindrical piece such as a shaft.

**Clearance** The amount of space between two parts. For example, between a piston and a cylinder, between a bearing and a journal, etc.

**Coil spring** A spiral of elastic steel found in various sizes throughout a vehicle, for example as a springing medium in the suspension and in the valve train.

**Compression** Reduction in volume, and increase in pressure and temperature, of a gas, caused by squeezing it into a smaller space.

**Compression ratio** The relationship between cylinder volume when the piston is at top dead centre and cylinder volume when the piston is at bottom dead centre.

**Constant velocity (CV) joint** A type of universal joint that cancels out vibrations caused by driving power being transmitted through an angle.

**Core plug** A disc or cup-shaped metal device inserted in a hole in a casting through which core was removed when the casting was formed. Also known as a freeze plug or expansion plug.

**Crankcase** The lower part of the engine block in which the crankshaft rotates.

**Crankshaft** The main rotating member, or shaft, running the length of the crankcase, with offset "throws" to which the connecting rods are attached.

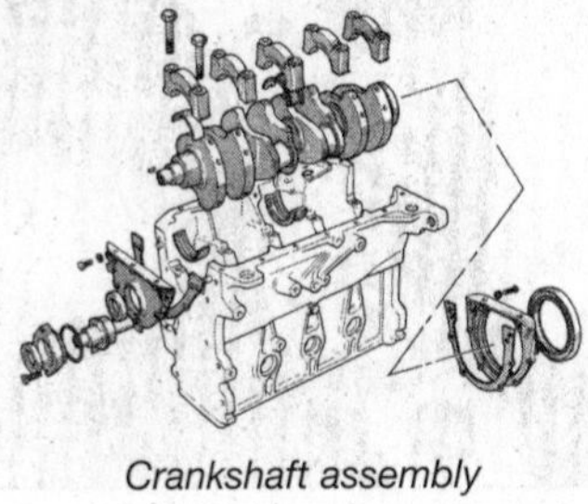

*Crankshaft assembly*

**Crocodile clip** See Alligator clip

# D

**Diagnostic code** Code numbers obtained by accessing the diagnostic mode of an engine management computer. This code can be used to determine the area in the system where a malfunction may be located.

**Disc brake** A brake design incorporating a rotating disc onto which brake pads are squeezed. The resulting friction converts the energy of a moving vehicle into heat.

**Double-overhead cam (DOHC)** An engine that uses two overhead camshafts, usually one for the intake valves and one for the exhaust valves.

**Drivebelt(s)** The belt(s) used to drive accessories such as the alternator, water pump, power steering pump, air conditioning compressor, etc. off the crankshaft pulley.

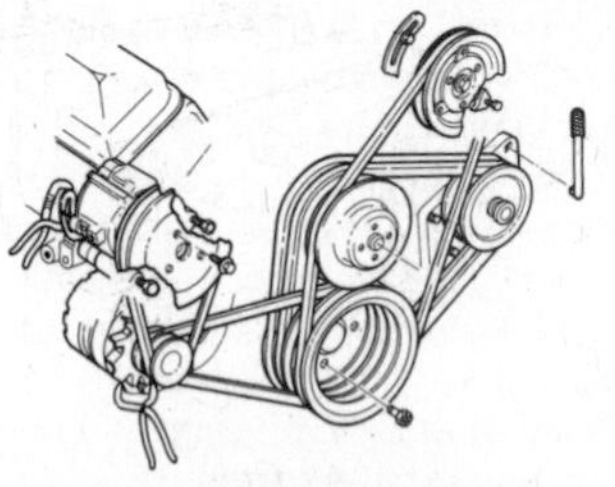

*Accessory drivebelts*

**Driveshaft** Any shaft used to transmit motion. Commonly used when referring to the axleshafts on a front wheel drive vehicle.

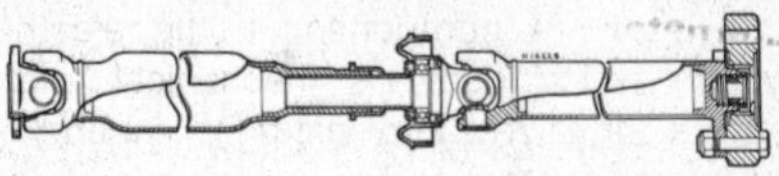

*Driveshaft*

**Drum brake** A type of brake using a drum-shaped metal cylinder attached to the inner surface of the wheel. When the brake pedal is pressed, curved brake shoes with friction linings press against the inside of the drum to slow or stop the vehicle.

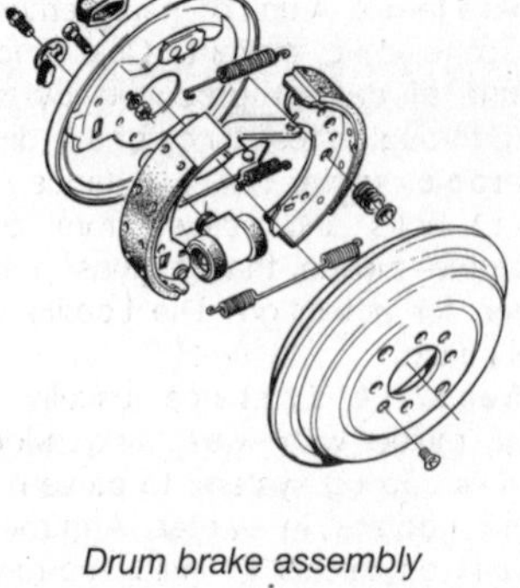

*Drum brake assembly*

## E

**EGR valve** A valve used to introduce exhaust gases into the intake air stream.

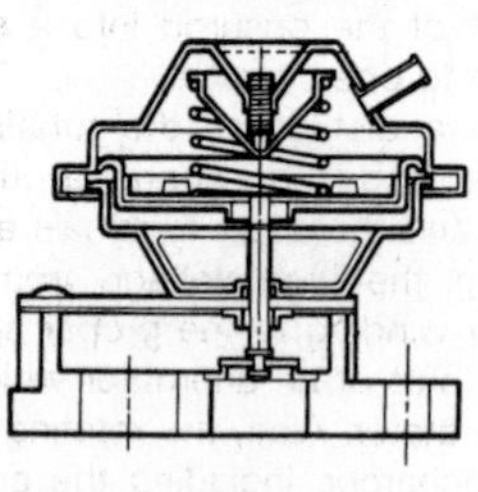

*EGR valve*

**Electronic control unit (ECU)** A computer which controls (for instance) ignition and fuel injection systems, or an anti-lock braking system. For more information refer to the *Haynes Automotive Electrical and Electronic Systems Manual.*

**Electronic Fuel Injection (EFI)** A computer controlled fuel system that distributes fuel through an injector located in each intake port of the engine.

**Emergency brake** A braking system, independent of the main hydraulic system, that can be used to slow or stop the vehicle if the primary brakes fail, or to hold the vehicle stationary even though the brake pedal isn't depressed. It usually consists of a hand lever that actuates either front or rear brakes mechanically through a series of cables and linkages. Also known as a handbrake or parking brake.

**Endfloat** The amount of lengthwise movement between two parts. As applied to a crankshaft, the distance that the crankshaft can move forward and back in the cylinder block.

**Engine management system (EMS)** A computer controlled system which manages the fuel injection and the ignition systems in an integrated fashion.

**Exhaust manifold** A part with several passages through which exhaust gases leave the engine combustion chambers and enter the exhaust pipe.

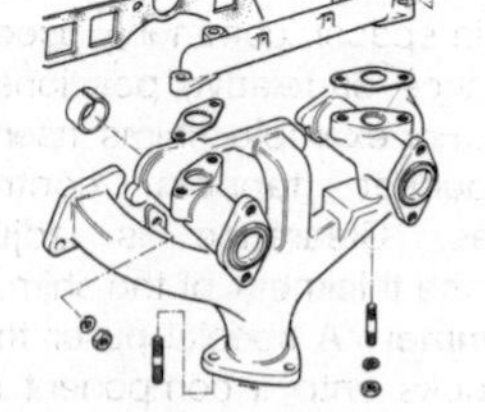

*Exhaust manifold*

## F

**Fan clutch** A viscous (fluid) drive coupling device which permits variable engine fan speeds in relation to engine speeds.

**Feeler blade** A thin strip or blade of hardened steel, ground to an exact thickness, used to check or measure clearances between parts.

*Feeler blade*

**Firing order** The order in which the engine cylinders fire, or deliver their power strokes, beginning with the number one cylinder.

**Flywheel** A heavy spinning wheel in which energy is absorbed and stored by means of momentum. On cars, the flywheel is attached to the crankshaft to smooth out firing impulses.

**Free play** The amount of travel before any action takes place. The "looseness" in a linkage, or an assembly of parts, between the initial application of force and actual movement. For example, the distance the brake pedal moves before the pistons in the master cylinder are actuated.

**Fuse** An electrical device which protects a circuit against accidental overload. The typical fuse contains a soft piece of metal which is calibrated to melt at a predetermined current flow (expressed as amps) and break the circuit.

**Fusible link** A circuit protection device consisting of a conductor surrounded by heat-resistant insulation. The conductor is smaller than the wire it protects, so it acts as the weakest link in the circuit. Unlike a blown fuse, a failed fusible link must frequently be cut from the wire for replacement.

## G

**Gap** The distance the spark must travel in jumping from the centre electrode to the side electrode in a spark plug. Also refers to the spacing between the points in a contact breaker assembly in a conventional points-type ignition, or to the distance between the reluctor or rotor and the pickup coil in an electronic ignition.

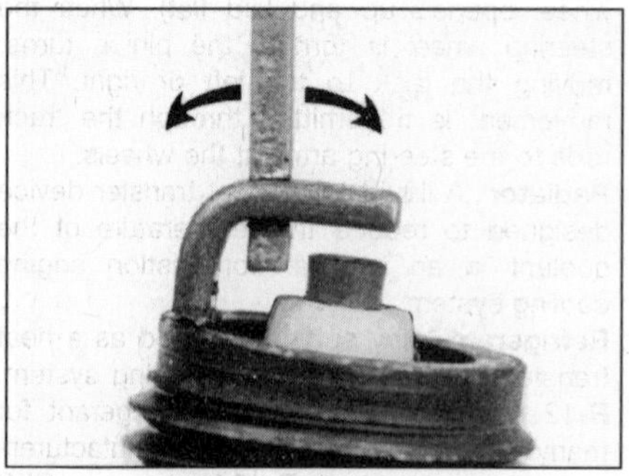

*Adjusting spark plug gap*

**Gasket** Any thin, soft material - usually cork, cardboard, asbestos or soft metal - installed between two metal surfaces to ensure a good seal. For instance, the cylinder head gasket seals the joint between the block and the cylinder head.

*Gasket*

**Gauge** An instrument panel display used to monitor engine conditions. A gauge with a movable pointer on a dial or a fixed scale is an analogue gauge. A gauge with a numerical readout is called a digital gauge.

## H

**Halfshaft** A rotating shaft that transmits power from the final drive unit to a drive wheel, usually when referring to a live rear axle.

**Harmonic balancer** A device designed to reduce torsion or twisting vibration in the crankshaft. May be incorporated in the crankshaft pulley. Also known as a vibration damper.

**Hone** An abrasive tool for correcting small irregularities or differences in diameter in an engine cylinder, brake cylinder, etc.

**Hydraulic tappet** A tappet that utilises hydraulic pressure from the engine's lubrication system to maintain zero clearance (constant contact with both camshaft and valve stem). Automatically adjusts to variation in valve stem length. Hydraulic tappets also reduce valve noise.

## I

**Ignition timing** The moment at which the spark plug fires, usually expressed in the number of crankshaft degrees before the piston reaches the top of its stroke.

**Inlet manifold** A tube or housing with passages through which flows the air-fuel mixture (carburettor vehicles and vehicles with throttle body injection) or air only (port fuel-injected vehicles) to the port openings in the cylinder head.

## J

**Jump start** Starting the engine of a vehicle with a discharged or weak battery by attaching jump leads from the weak battery to a charged or helper battery.

## L

**Load Sensing Proportioning Valve (LSPV)** A brake hydraulic system control valve that works like a proportioning valve, but also takes into consideration the amount of weight carried by the rear axle.

**Locknut** A nut used to lock an adjustment nut, or other threaded component, in place. For example, a locknut is employed to keep the adjusting nut on the rocker arm in position.

**Lockwasher** A form of washer designed to prevent an attaching nut from working loose.

## M

**MacPherson strut** A type of front suspension system devised by Earle MacPherson at Ford of England. In its original form, a simple lateral link with the anti-roll bar creates the lower control arm. A long strut - an integral coil spring and shock absorber - is mounted between the body and the steering knuckle. Many modern so-called MacPherson strut systems use a conventional lower A-arm and don't rely on the anti-roll bar for location.

**Multimeter** An electrical test instrument with the capability to measure voltage, current and resistance.

## N

**NOx** Oxides of Nitrogen. A common toxic pollutant emitted by petrol and diesel engines at higher temperatures.

## O

**Ohm** The unit of electrical resistance. One volt applied to a resistance of one ohm will produce a current of one amp.

**Ohmmeter** An instrument for measuring electrical resistance.

**O-ring** A type of sealing ring made of a special rubber-like material; in use, the O-ring is compressed into a groove to provide the sealing action.

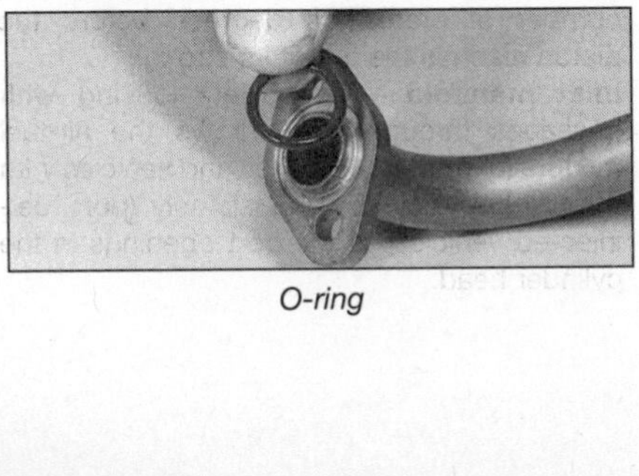

*O-ring*

**Overhead cam (ohc) engine** An engine with the camshaft(s) located on top of the cylinder head(s).

**Overhead valve (ohv) engine** An engine with the valves located in the cylinder head, but with the camshaft located in the engine block.

**Oxygen sensor** A device installed in the engine exhaust manifold, which senses the oxygen content in the exhaust and converts this information into an electric current. Also called a Lambda sensor.

## P

**Phillips screw** A type of screw head having a cross instead of a slot for a corresponding type of screwdriver.

**Plastigage** A thin strip of plastic thread, available in different sizes, used for measuring clearances. For example, a strip of Plastigage is laid across a bearing journal. The parts are assembled and dismantled; the width of the crushed strip indicates the clearance between journal and bearing.

*Plastigage*

**Propeller shaft** The long hollow tube with universal joints at both ends that carries power from the transmission to the differential on front-engined rear wheel drive vehicles.

**Proportioning valve** A hydraulic control valve which limits the amount of pressure to the rear brakes during panic stops to prevent wheel lock-up.

## R

**Rack-and-pinion steering** A steering system with a pinion gear on the end of the steering shaft that mates with a rack (think of a geared wheel opened up and laid flat). When the steering wheel is turned, the pinion turns, moving the rack to the left or right. This movement is transmitted through the track rods to the steering arms at the wheels.

**Radiator** A liquid-to-air heat transfer device designed to reduce the temperature of the coolant in an internal combustion engine cooling system.

**Refrigerant** Any substance used as a heat transfer agent in an air-conditioning system. R-12 has been the principle refrigerant for many years; recently, however, manufacturers have begun using R-134a, a non-CFC substance that is considered less harmful to the ozone in the upper atmosphere.

**Rocker arm** A lever arm that rocks on a shaft or pivots on a stud. In an overhead valve engine, the rocker arm converts the upward movement of the pushrod into a downward movement to open a valve.

**Rotor** In a distributor, the rotating device inside the cap that connects the centre electrode and the outer terminals as it turns, distributing the high voltage from the coil secondary winding to the proper spark plug. Also, that part of an alternator which rotates inside the stator. Also, the rotating assembly of a turbocharger, including the compressor wheel, shaft and turbine wheel.

**Runout** The amount of wobble (in-and-out movement) of a gear or wheel as it's rotated. The amount a shaft rotates "out-of-true." The out-of-round condition of a rotating part.

## S

**Sealant** A liquid or paste used to prevent leakage at a joint. Sometimes used in conjunction with a gasket.

**Sealed beam lamp** An older headlight design which integrates the reflector, lens and filaments into a hermetically-sealed one-piece unit. When a filament burns out or the lens cracks, the entire unit is simply replaced.

**Serpentine drivebelt** A single, long, wide accessory drivebelt that's used on some newer vehicles to drive all the accessories, instead of a series of smaller, shorter belts. Serpentine drivebelts are usually tensioned by an automatic tensioner.

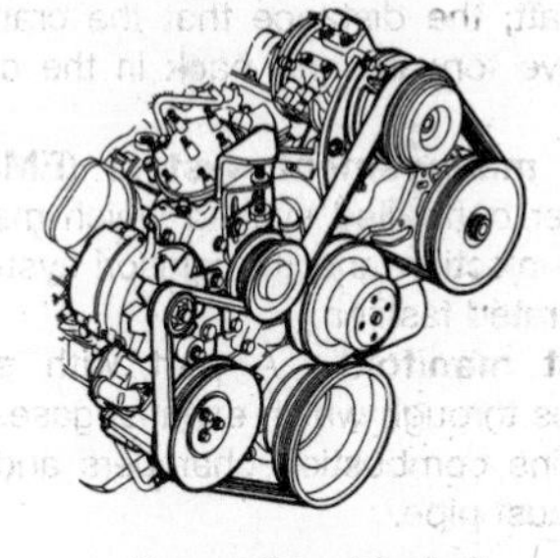

*Serpentine drivebelt*

**Shim** Thin spacer, commonly used to adjust the clearance or relative positions between two parts. For example, shims inserted into or under bucket tappets control valve clearances. Clearance is adjusted by changing the thickness of the shim.

**Slide hammer** A special puller that screws into or hooks onto a component such as a shaft or bearing; a heavy sliding handle on the shaft bottoms against the end of the shaft to knock the component free.

**Sprocket** A tooth or projection on the periphery of a wheel, shaped to engage with a chain or drivebelt. Commonly used to refer to the sprocket wheel itself.

**Starter inhibitor switch** On vehicles with an

automatic transmission, a switch that prevents starting if the vehicle is not in Neutral or Park.

**Strut** See MacPherson strut.

# T

**Tappet** A cylindrical component which transmits motion from the cam to the valve stem, either directly or via a pushrod and rocker arm. Also called a cam follower.

**Thermostat** A heat-controlled valve that regulates the flow of coolant between the cylinder block and the radiator, so maintaining optimum engine operating temperature. A thermostat is also used in some air cleaners in which the temperature is regulated.

**Thrust bearing** The bearing in the clutch assembly that is moved in to the release levers by clutch pedal action to disengage the clutch. Also referred to as a release bearing.

**Timing belt** A toothed belt which drives the camshaft. Serious engine damage may result if it breaks in service.

**Timing chain** A chain which drives the camshaft.

**Toe-in** The amount the front wheels are closer together at the front than at the rear. On rear wheel drive vehicles, a slight amount of toe-in is usually specified to keep the front wheels running parallel on the road by offsetting other forces that tend to spread the wheels apart.

**Toe-out** The amount the front wheels are closer together at the rear than at the front. On front wheel drive vehicles, a slight amount of toe-out is usually specified.

**Tools** For full information on choosing and using tools, refer to the *Haynes Automotive Tools Manual.*

**Tracer** A stripe of a second colour applied to a wire insulator to distinguish that wire from another one with the same colour insulator.

**Tune-up** A process of accurate and careful adjustments and parts replacement to obtain the best possible engine performance.

**Turbocharger** A centrifugal device, driven by exhaust gases, that pressurises the intake air. Normally used to increase the power output from a given engine displacement, but can also be used primarily to reduce exhaust emissions (as on VW's "Umwelt" Diesel engine).

# U

**Universal joint or U-joint** A double-pivoted connection for transmitting power from a driving to a driven shaft through an angle. A U-joint consists of two Y-shaped yokes and a cross-shaped member called the spider.

# V

**Valve** A device through which the flow of liquid, gas, vacuum, or loose material in bulk may be started, stopped, or regulated by a movable part that opens, shuts, or partially obstructs one or more ports or passageways. A valve is also the movable part of such a device.

**Valve clearance** The clearance between the valve tip (the end of the valve stem) and the rocker arm or tappet. The valve clearance is measured when the valve is closed.

**Vernier caliper** A precision measuring instrument that measures inside and outside dimensions. Not quite as accurate as a micrometer, but more convenient.

**Viscosity** The thickness of a liquid or its resistance to flow.

**Volt** A unit for expressing electrical "pressure" in a circuit. One volt that will produce a current of one ampere through a resistance of one ohm.

# W

**Welding** Various processes used to join metal items by heating the areas to be joined to a molten state and fusing them together. For more information refer to the *Haynes Automotive Welding Manual.*

**Wiring diagram** A drawing portraying the components and wires in a vehicle's electrical system, using standardised symbols. For more information refer to the *Haynes Automotive Electrical and Electronic Systems Manual.*

**Note:** *References throughout this index are in the form - "Chapter number" • "page number"*

## J



## K



## L



## M



## N



## O



## P



## R



## S

# Haynes Manuals – The Complete List

| Title | Book No. |
|---|---|
| **ALFA ROMEO** | |
| Alfa Romeo Alfasud/Sprint (74 - 88) up to F | 0292 |
| Alfa Romeo Alfetta (73 - 87) up to E | 0531 |
| **ALFA ROMEO** | |
| Audi 80 (72 - Feb 79) up to T | 0207 |
| Audi 80, 90 (79 - Oct 86) up to D & Coupe (81 - Nov 88) up to F | 0605 |
| Audi 80, 90 (Oct 86 - 90) D to H & Coupe (Nov 88 - 90) F to H | 1491 |
| Audi 100 (Oct 82 - 90) up to H & 200 (Feb 84 - Oct 89) A to G | 0907 |
| Audi 100 & A6 Petrol & Diesel (May 91 - May 97) H to P | 3504 |
| Audi A4 (95 - Feb 00) M to V | 3575 |
| **AUSTIN** | |
| Austin/MG/Rover Maestro 1.3 & 1.6 (83 - 95) up to M | 0922 |
| Austin/MG Metro (80 - May 90) up to G | 0718 |
| Austin/Rover Montego 1.3 & 1.6 (84 - 94) A to L | 1066 |
| Austin/MG/Rover Montego 2.0 (84 - 95) A to M | 1067 |
| Mini (59 - 69) up to H | 0527 |
| Mini (69 - Oct 96) up to P | 0646 |
| Austin/Rover 2.0 litre Diesel Engine (86 - 93) C to L | 1857 |
| **BEDFORD** | |
| Bedford CF (69 - 87) up to E | 0163 |
| Bedford/Vauxhall Rascal & Suzuki Supercarry (86 - Oct 94) C to M | 3015 |
| **BMW** | |
| BMW 316, 320 & 320i (4-cyl) (75 - Feb 83) up to Y | 0276 |
| BMW 320, 320i, 323i & 325i (6-cyl) (Oct 77 - Sept 87) up to E | 0815 |
| BMW 3-Series (Apr 91 - 96) H to N | 3210 |
| BMW 3- & 5-Series (sohc) (81 - 91) up to J | 1948 |
| BMW 520i & 525e (Oct 81 - June 88) up to E | 1560 |
| BMW 525, 528 & 528i (73 - Sept 81) up to X | 0632 |
| **CITROEN** | |
| Citroën 2CV, Ami & Dyane (67 - 90) up to H | 0196 |
| Citroën AX Petrol & Diesel (87 - 97) D to P | 3014 |
| Citroën BX (83 - 94) A to L | 0908 |
| Citroën C15 Van Petrol & Diesel (89 - Oct 98) F to S | 3509 |
| Citroën CX (75 - 88) up to F | 0528 |
| Citroën Saxo Petrol & Diesel (96 - 98) N to S | 3506 |
| Citroën Visa (79 - 88) up to F | 0620 |
| Citroën Xantia Petrol & Diesel (93 - 98) K to S | 3082 |
| Citroën XM Petrol & Diesel (89 - 98) G to R | 3451 |
| Citroën ZX Diesel (91 - 93) J to L | 1922 |
| Citroën ZX Petrol (91 - 94) H to M | 1881 |
| Citroën 1.7 & 1.9 litre Diesel Engine (84 - 96) A to N | 1379 |
| **COLT** | |
| Colt/Mitsubishi 1200, 1250 & 1400 (79 - May 84) up to A | 0600 |
| **FIAT** | |
| Fiat 500 (57 - 73) up to M | 0090 |
| Fiat Cinquecento (93 - 98) K to R | 3501 |
| Fiat Panda (81 - 95) up to M | 0793 |
| Fiat Punto Petrol & Diesel (94 - Oct 99) L to V | 3251 |
| Fiat Regata (84 - 88) A to F | 1167 |

| Title | Book No. |
|---|---|
| Fiat Tipo (88 - 91) E to J | 1625 |
| Fiat Uno (83 - 95) up to M | 0923 |
| Fiat X1/9 (74 - 89) up to G | 0273 |
| **FORD** | |
| Ford Capri II (& III) 1.6 & 2.0 (74 - 87) up to E | 0283 |
| Ford Capri II (& III) 2.8 & 3.0 (74 - 87) up to E | 1309 |
| Ford Cortina Mk IV (& V) 1.6 & 2.0 (76 - 83) up to A | 0343 |
| Ford Escort (75 - Aug 80) up to V | 0280 |
| Ford Escort (Sept 80 - Sept 90) up to H | 0686 |
| Ford Escort & Orion (Sept 90 - 97) H to P | 1737 |
| Ford Escort Mk II Mexico, RS 1600 & RS 2000 (75 - 80) up to W | 0735 |
| Ford Fiesta (76 - Aug 83) up to Y | 0334 |
| Ford Fiesta (Aug 83 - Feb 89) A to F | 1030 |
| Ford Fiesta (Feb 89 - Oct 95) F to N | 1595 |
| Ford Fiesta Petrol & Diesel (Oct 95 - 97) N to R | 3397 |
| Ford Granada (Sept 77 - Feb 85) up to B | 0481 |
| Ford Granada & Scorpio (Mar 85 - 94) B to M | 1245 |
| Ford Ka (96 - 99) P to T | 3570 |
| Ford Mondeo Petrol (93 - 99) K to T | 1923 |
| Ford Mondeo Diesel (93 - 96) L to N | 3465 |
| Ford Orion (83 - Sept 90) up to H | 1009 |
| Ford Sierra 4 cyl. (82 - 93) up to K | 0903 |
| Ford Sierra V6 (82 - 91) up to J | 0904 |
| Ford Transit Petrol (Mk 2) (78 - Jan 86) up to C | 0719 |
| Ford Transit Petrol (Mk 3) (Feb 86 - 89) C to G | 1468 |
| Ford Transit Diesel (Feb 86 - 99) C to T | 3019 |
| Ford 1.6 & 1.8 litre Diesel Engine (84 - 96) A to N | 1172 |
| Ford 2.1, 2.3 & 2.5 litre Diesel Engine (77 - 90) up to H | 1606 |
| **FREIGHT ROVER** | |
| Freight Rover Sherpa (74 - 87) up to E | 0463 |
| **HILLMAN** | |
| Hillman Avenger (70 - 82) up to Y | 0037 |
| **HONDA** | |
| Honda Accord (76 - Feb 84) up to A | 0351 |
| Honda Civic (Feb 84 - Oct 87) A to E | 1226 |
| Honda Civic (Nov 91 - 96) J to N | 3199 |
| **HYUNDAI** | |
| Hyundai Pony (85 - 94) C to M | 3398 |
| **JAGUAR** | |
| Jaguar E Type (61 - 72) up to L | 0140 |
| Jaguar MkI & II, 240 & 340 (55 - 69) up to H | 0098 |
| Jaguar XJ6, XJ & Sovereign; Daimler Sovereign (68 - Oct 86) up to D | 0242 |
| Jaguar XJ6 & Sovereign (Oct 86 - Sept 94) D to M | 3261 |
| Jaguar XJ12, XJS & Sovereign; Daimler Double Six (72 - 88) up to F | 0478 |
| **JEEP** | |
| Jeep Cherokee Petrol (93 - 96) K to N | 1943 |
| **LADA** | |
| Lada 1200, 1300, 1500 & 1600 (74 - 91) up to J | 0413 |
| Lada Samara (87 - 91) D to J | 1610 |
| **LAND ROVER** | |
| Land Rover 90, 110 & Defender Diesel (83 - 95) up to N | 3017 |
| Land Rover Discovery Diesel (89 - 95) G to N | 3016 |
| Land Rover Series IIA & III Diesel (58 - 85) up to C | 0529 |

| Title | Book No. |
|---|---|
| Land Rover Series II, IIA & III Petrol (58 - 85) up to C | 0314 |
| **MAZDA** | |
| Mazda 323 (Mar 81 - Oct 89) up to G | 1608 |
| Mazda 323 (Oct 89 - 98) G to R | 3455 |
| Mazda 626 (May 83 - Sept 87) up to E | 0929 |
| Mazda B-1600, B-1800 & B-2000 Pick-up (72 - 88) up to F | 0267 |
| **MERCEDES BENZ** | |
| Mercedes-Benz 190, 190E & 190D Petrol & Diesel (83 - 93) A to L | 3450 |
| Mercedes-Benz 200, 240, 300 Diesel (Oct 76 - 85) up to C | 1114 |
| Mercedes-Benz 250 & 280 (68 - 72) up to L | 0346 |
| Mercedes-Benz 250 & 280 (123 Series) (Oct 76 - 84) up to B | 0677 |
| Mercedes-Benz 124 Series (85 - Aug 93) C to K | 3253 |
| **MG** | |
| MGB (62 - 80) up to W | 0111 |
| MG Midget & AH Sprite (58 - 80) up to W | 0265 |
| **MITSUBISHI** | |
| Mitsubishi Shogun & L200 Pick-Ups (83 - 94) up to M | 1944 |
| **MORRIS** | |
| Morris Ital 1.3 (80 - 84) up to B | 0705 |
| Morris Minor 1000 (56 - 71) up to K | 0024 |
| **NISSAN** | |
| Nissan Bluebird (May 84 - Mar 86) A to C | 1223 |
| Nissan Bluebird (Mar 86 - 90) C to H | 1473 |
| Nissan Cherry (Sept 82 - 86) up to D | 1031 |
| Nissan Micra (83 - Jan 93) up to K | 0931 |
| Nissan Micra (93 - 99) K to T | 3254 |
| Nissan Primera (90 - Aug 99) H to T | 1851 |
| Nissan Stanza (82 - 86) up to D | 0824 |
| Nissan Sunny (May 82 - Oct 86) up to D | 0895 |
| Nissan Sunny (Oct 86 - Mar 91) D to H | 1378 |
| Nissan Sunny (Apr 91 - 95) H to N | 3219 |
| **OPEL** | |
| Opel Ascona & Manta (B Series) (Sept 75 - 88) up to F | 0316 |
| Opel Ascona (81 - 88) *(Not available in UK see Vauxhall Cavalier 0812)* | 3215 |
| Opel Astra (Oct 91 - Feb 98) *(Not available in UK see Vauxhall Astra 1832)* | 3156 |
| Opel Calibra (90 - 98) *(See Vauxhall/Opel Calibra Book No. 3502)* | |
| Opel Corsa (83 - Mar 93) *(Not available in UK see Vauxhall Nova 0909)* | 3160 |
| Opel Corsa (Mar 93 - 97) *(Not available in UK see Vauxhall Corsa 1985)* | 3159 |
| Opel Frontera Petrol & Diesel (91 - 98) *(See Vauxhall/Opel Frontera Book No. 3454)* | |
| Opel Kadett (Nov 79 - Oct 84) | 0634 |
| Opel Kadett (Oct 84 - Oct 91) *(Not available in UK see Vauxhall Astra & Belmont 1136)* | 3196 |
| Opel Omega & Senator (86 - 94) *(Not available in UK see Vauxhall Carlton & Senator 1469)* | 3157 |
| Opel Omega (94 - 99) *(See Vauxhall/Opel Omega Book No. 3510)* | |
| Opel Rekord (Feb 78 - Oct 86) up to D | 0543 |

| Title | Book No |
|---|---|
| Opel Vectra (Oct 88 - Oct 95) *(Not available in UK see Vauxhall Cavalier 1570)* | 3158 |
| Opel Vectra Petrol & Diesel (95 - 98) (Not available in UK see Vauxhall Vectra 3396) | 3523 |

## PEUGEOT

| Title | Book No |
|---|---|
| Peugeot 106 Petrol & Diesel (91 - 98) J to S | 1882 |
| Peugeot 205 (83 - 95) A to N | 0932 |
| Peugeot 305 (78 - 89) up to G | 0538 |
| Peugeot 306 Petrol & Diesel (93 - 99) K to T | 3073 |
| Peugeot 309 (86 - 93) C to K | 1266 |
| Peugeot 405 Petrol (88 - 96) E to N | 1559 |
| Peugeot 405 Diesel (88 - 96) E to N | 3198 |
| Peugeot 406 Petrol & Diesel (96 - 97) N to R | 3394 |
| Peugeot 505 (79 - 89) up to G | 0762 |
| Peugeot 1.7/1.8 & 1.9 litre Diesel Engine (82 - 96) up to N | 0950 |
| Peugeot 2.0, 2.1, 2.3 & 2.5 litre Diesel Engines (74 - 90) up to H | 1607 |

## PORSCHE

| Title | Book No |
|---|---|
| Porsche 911 (65 - 85) up to C | 0264 |
| Porsche 924 & 924 Turbo (76 - 85) up to C | 0397 |

## PROTON

| Title | Book No |
|---|---|
| Proton (89 - 97) F to P | 3255 |

## RANGE ROVER

| Title | Book No |
|---|---|
| Range Rover V8 (70 - Oct 92) up to K | 0606 |

## RELIANT

| Title | Book No |
|---|---|
| Reliant Robin & Kitten (73 - 83) up to A | 0436 |

## RENAULT

| Title | Book No |
|---|---|
| Renault 5 (Feb 85 - 96) B to N | 1219 |
| Renault 9 & 11 (82 - 89) up to F | 0822 |
| Renault 18 (79 - 86) up to D | 0598 |
| Renault 19 Petrol (89 - 94) F to M | 1646 |
| Renault 19 Diesel (89 - 95) F to N | 1946 |
| Renault 21 (86 - 94) C to M | 1397 |
| Renault 25 (84 - 92) B to K | 1228 |
| Renault Clio Petrol (91 - May 98) H to R | 1853 |
| Renault Clio Diesel (91 - June 96) H to N | 3031 |
| Renault Espace Petrol & Diesel (85 - 96) C to N | 3197 |
| Renault Fuego (80 - 86) up to C | 0764 |
| Renault Laguna Petrol & Diesel (94 - 96) L to P | 3252 |
| Renault Mégane & Scénic Petrol & Diesel (96 - 98) N to R | 3395 |

## ROVER

| Title | Book No |
|---|---|
| Rover 213 & 216 (84 - 89) A to G | 1116 |
| Rover 214 & 414 (89 - 96) G to N | 1689 |
| Rover 216 & 416 (89 - 96) G to N | 1830 |
| Rover 211, 214, 216, 218 & 220 Petrol & Diesel (Dec 95 - 98) N to R | 3399 |
| Rover 414, 416 & 420 Petrol & Diesel (May 95 - 98) M to R | 3453 |
| Rover 618, 620 & 623 (93 - 97) K to P | 3257 |
| Rover 820, 825 & 827 (86 - 95) D to N | 1380 |
| Rover 3500 (76 - 87) up to E | 0365 |
| Rover Metro, 111 & 114 (May 90 - 96) G to N | 1711 |

## SAAB

| Title | Book No |
|---|---|
| Saab 90, 99 & 900 (79 - Oct 93) up to L | 0765 |
| Saab 900 (Oct 93 - 98) L to R | 3512 |
| Saab 9000 (4-cyl) (85 - 95) C to N | 1686 |

## SEAT

| Title | Book No |
|---|---|
| Seat Ibiza & Cordoba Petrol & Diesel (Oct 93 - Oct 99) L to V | 3571 |
| Seat Ibiza & Malaga (85 - 92) B to K | 1609 |

## SKODA

| Title | Book No |
|---|---|
| Skoda Estelle (77 - 89) up to G | 0604 |
| Skoda Favorit (89 - 96) F to N | 1801 |
| Skoda Felicia Petrol & Diesel (95 - 99) M to T | 3505 |

## SUBARU

| Title | Book No |
|---|---|
| Subaru 1600 & 1800 (Nov 79 - 90) up to H | 0995 |

## SUZUKI

| Title | Book No |
|---|---|
| Suzuki SJ Series, Samurai & Vitara (4-cyl) (82 - 97) up to P | 1942 |
| Suzuki Supercarry (86 - Oct 94) C to M | 3015 |

## TALBOT

| Title | Book No |
|---|---|
| Talbot Alpine, Solara, Minx & Rapier (75 - 86) up to D | 0337 |
| Talbot Horizon (78 - 86) up to D | 0473 |
| Talbot Samba (82 - 86) up to D | 0823 |

## TOYOTA

| Title | Book No |
|---|---|
| Toyota Carina E (May 92 - 97) J to P | 3256 |
| Toyota Corolla (Sept 83 - Sept 87) A to E | 1024 |
| Toyota Corolla (80 - 85) up to C | 0683 |
| Toyota Corolla (Sept 87 - Aug 92) E to K | 1683 |
| Toyota Corolla (Aug 92 - 97) K to P | 3259 |
| Toyota Hi-Ace & Hi-Lux (69 - Oct 83) up to A | 0304 |

## TRIUMPH

| Title | Book No |
|---|---|
| Triumph Acclaim (81 - 84) up to B | 0792 |
| Triumph GT6 & Vitesse (62 - 74) up to N | 0112 |
| Triumph Spitfire (62 - 81) up to X | 0113 |
| Triumph Stag (70 - 78) up to T | 0441 |
| Triumph TR7 (75 - 82) up to Y | 0322 |

## VAUXHALL

| Title | Book No |
|---|---|
| Vauxhall Astra (80 - Oct 84) up to B | 0635 |
| Vauxhall Astra & Belmont (Oct 84 - Oct 91) B to J | 1136 |
| Vauxhall Astra (Oct 91 - Feb 98) J to R | 1832 |
| Vauxhall/Opel Calibra (90 - 98) G to S | 3502 |
| Vauxhall Carlton (Oct 78 - Oct 86) up to D | 0480 |
| Vauxhall Carlton & Senator (Nov 86 - 94) D to L | 1469 |
| Vauxhall Cavalier 1600, 1900 & 2000 (75 - July 81) up to W | 0315 |
| Vauxhall Cavalier (81 - Oct 88) up to F | 0812 |
| Vauxhall Cavalier (Oct 88 - 95) F to N | 1570 |
| Vauxhall Chevette (75 - 84) up to B | 0285 |
| Vauxhall Corsa (Mar 93 - 97) K to R | 1985 |
| Vauxhall/Opel Frontera Petrol & Diesel (91 - Sept 98) J to S | 3454 |
| Vauxhall Nova (83 - 93) up to K | 0909 |
| Vauxhall/Opel Omega (94 - 99) L to T | 3510 |
| Vauxhall Vectra Petrol & Diesel (95 - 98) N to R | 3396 |
| Vauxhall/Opel 1.5, 1.6 & 1.7 litre Diesel Engine (82 - 96) up to N | 1222 |

## VOLKSWAGEN

| Title | Book No. |
|---|---|
| Volkswagen Beetle 1200 (54 - 77) up to S | 0036 |
| Volkswagen Beetle 1300 & 1500 (65 - 75) up to P | 0039 |
| Volkswagen Beetle 1302 & 1302S (70 - 72) up to L | 0110 |
| Volkswagen Beetle 1303, 1303S & GT (72 - 75) up to P | 0159 |
| Volkswagen Golf & Jetta Mk 1 1.1 & 1.3 (74 - 84) up to A | 0716 |
| Volkswagen Golf, Jetta & Scirocco Mk 1 1.5,1.6 & 1.8 (74 - 84) up to A | 0726 |
| Volkswagen Golf & Jetta Mk 1 Diesel (78 - 84) up to A | 0451 |
| Volkswagen Golf & Jetta Mk 2 (Mar 84 - Feb 92) A to J | 1081 |
| Volkswagen Golf & Vento Petrol & Diesel (Feb 92 - 96) J to N | 3097 |
| Volkswagen LT vans & light trucks (76 - 87) up to E | 0637 |
| Volkswagen Passat & Santana (Sept 81 - May 88) up to E | 0814 |
| Volkswagen Passat Petrol & Diesel (May 88 - 96) E to P | 3498 |
| Volkswagen Polo & Derby (76 - Jan 82) up to X | 0335 |
| Volkswagen Polo (82 - Oct 90) up to H | 0813 |
| Volkswagen Polo (Nov 90 - Aug 94) H to L | 3245 |
| Volkswagen Polo Hatchback Petrol & Diesel (94 - 99) M to S | 3500 |
| Volkswagen Scirocco (82 - 90) up to H | 1224 |
| Volkswagen Transporter 1600 (68 - 79) up to V | 0082 |
| Volkswagen Transporter 1700, 1800 & 2000 (72 - 79) up to V | 0226 |
| Volkswagen Transporter (air-cooled) (79 - 82) up to Y | 0638 |
| Volkswagen Transporter (water-cooled) (82 - 90) up to H | 3452 |

## VOLVO

| Title | Book No. |
|---|---|
| Volvo 142, 144 & 145 (66 - 74) up to N | 0129 |
| Volvo 240 Series (74 - 93) up to K | 0270 |
| Volvo 262, 264 & 260/265 (75 - 85) up to C | 0400 |
| Volvo 340, 343, 345 & 360 (76 - 91) up to J | 0715 |
| Volvo 440, 460 & 480 (87 - 97) D to P | 1691 |
| Volvo 740 & 760 (82 - 91) up to J | 1258 |
| Volvo 850 (92 - 96) J to P | 3260 |
| Volvo 940 (90 - 96) H to N | 3249 |
| Volvo S40 & V40 (96 - 99) N to V | 3569 |
| Volvo S70, V70 & C70 (96 - 99) P to V | 3573 |

## YUGO/ZASTAVA

| Title | Book No. |
|---|---|
| Yugo/Zastava (81 - 90) up to H | 1453 |

## AUTOMOTIVE TECHBOOKS

| Title | Book No. |
|---|---|
| Automotive Brake Manual | 3050 |
| Automotive Carburettor Manual | 3288 |
| Automotive Diagnostic Fault Codes Manual | 3472 |
| Automotive Diesel Engine Service Guide | 3286 |
| Automotive Disc Brake Manual | 3542 |
| Automotive Electrical and Electronic Systems Manual | 3049 |
| Automotive Engine Management and Fuel Injection Systems Manual | 3344 |
| Automotive Gearbox Overhaul Manual | 3473 |
| Automotive Service Summaries Manual | 3475 |
| Automotive Timing Belts Manual – Austin/Rover | 3549 |
| Automotive Timing Belts Manual - Ford | 3474 |
| Automotive Timing Belts Manual – Peugeot/Citroën | 3568 |
| Automotive Timing Belts Manual – Vauxhall/Opel | 3577 |
| Automotive Welding Manual | 3053 |
| In-Car Entertainment Manual (3rd Edition) | 3363 |

## OTHER TITLES

| Title | Book No. |
|---|---|
| Haynes Diesel Engine Systems & Data Book (91 -00) | 3548 |
| Haynes Petrol Models Data Book (94 - 00) | 3718 |

CL09.04/00